A HENRY JAMES
Encyclopedia

A HENRY JAMES
Encyclopedia

Robert L. Gale

Greenwood Press
NEW YORK
WESTPORT, CONNECTICUT
LONDON

Library of Congress Cataloging-in-Publication Data

Gale, Robert L.
  A Henry James encyclopedia / Robert L. Gale.
     p. cm.
  Bibliography: p.
  ISBN 0–313–25846–5 (lib. bdg. : alk. paper)
  1. James, Henry, 1843–1916—Dictionaries, indexes, etc.
I. Title.
PS2122.G35   1989
813'.4—dc19   88–21338

British Library Cataloguing in Publication Data is available.

Library of Congress Catalog Card Number: 88–21338
ISBN: 0–313–25846–5

First published in 1989

Greenwood Press, Inc.
88 Post Road West, Westport, Connecticut 06881

Printed in the United States of America

The paper used in this book complies with the
Permanent Paper Standard issued by the National
Information Standards Organization (Z39.48–1984).

10 9 8 7 6 5 4 3 2 1

This book is gratefully dedicated to those Ph.D.s of mine at the University of Pittsburgh, of whom I am justly proud, whether they liked Henry James or not:

Sandra C. Alexander, Robert W. Bell, Richard L. Blevins
Harry S. Craig, Warren E. DeArment, Linda D. DeLowry-Fryman
Constance Ayres Denne, Ronald R. Emerick, Bernhard Frank
Edward S. Grejda, Raj Kumar Gupta, James B. Haines
William Hickman, James K. Hoeveler, Evelyn Hovanec
Mabel Jackson, Granville H. Jones, Dorothy Kish
Frederick J. Koloc, Gay Lavi, Anna Lomando
Janet Lacey McCann, Daniel Marder, Gabriel Menkin
Letitia Ramirez Molter, Robert E. Mossman, Joseph C. Nucci
Arlene Prendergast, John E. Pyron, Jr., Irving N. Rothman
Kenneth Seib, Donald A. Short, Mary Therese Strauss
Robert H. Sykes, Barbara W. Tedford, Ronald E. Tranquilla
James G. Watson, Elizabeth Wiley, Ellie Buntag Wymard

CONTENTS

Foreword *by Daniel Mark Fogel*   xi

Preface   xv

Chronology   xix

The Encyclopedia   1

APPENDIX A: Fiction   749

APPENDIX B: Critical Essays, Critical Books, Theater Essays
and Notes, and Autobiographical Volumes   753

APPENDIX C: Travel Books and Essays   755

APPENDIX D: Plays   757

APPENDIX E: Art Essays, Reviews, and Notices   759

APPENDIX F: Nonliterary Essays and Notes   761

APPENDIX G: Writers Whom James Reviewed, Commented on,
Mentioned, or Was Influenced By   763

APPENDIX H: Artists, Sculptors, Architects, and Photographers
Mentioned by James   769

APPENDIX I: Actors, Actresses, Theater Managers,
Composers, and Singers Mentioned by James   771

APPENDIX J: Miscellaneous Names of Persons and Other
                Items Mentioned by or Associated with James   773

APPENDIX K: Items Relating to James Personally   775

APPENDIX L: Friends of James   777

Bibliography   783

FOREWORD

The present volume, Robert L. Gale's *Henry James Encyclopedia*, is the greatest single compilation of knowledge about Henry James and about James's world since the completion of Leon Edel's *Life of Henry James* nearly twenty years ago. To gauge the magnitude of Professor Gale's undertaking, we have only to consider for a moment the life and contacts of Henry James: the nearly 80 books and 600 periodical contributions he published, the 15,000 odd extant letters, the wide and changing networks of acquaintances, colleagues, and friends in America, England, France, and Italy. Dauntlessly rising to the challenge presented by the myriad data of James's life, the encyclopedist has provided us here with a compendium of information on James's publications (his travel writing and journalism and his literary and art criticism as well as his fiction), his plots and characters, his correspondents, his residences, friendships, professional associations, his judgments of his contemporaries and predecessors in literary art, his publishers, even his domestic servants.

This should have been, one thinks at first, a task for many hands. The sheer vastness of the Jamesian imperium would, one thinks, defeat the encyclopedic labors of any single scholar. But Professor Gale's achievement annihilates such initial misgivings. We ourselves might be defeated by such an undertaking. But he has succeeded magnificently. From A to Z, from Edwin Austin Abbey to Émile Zola, here is everything we have ever wanted to have in the way of a ready-reference volume on Henry James, well over 3,000 entries by my rough count, in one alphabetical, cross-referenced sequence, plus a dozen helpful appendices that group entry terms under convenient headings (for example, "Artists, Sculptors, Architects, and Photographers Mentioned by James" and "Friends of James").

The *Henry James Encyclopedia* is a handy reference work, but the words ready reference cannot adequately convey the generosity with which Robert Gale annotates important items in this volume. Many of the entries are substantial articles. The remarkable entry on *The American Scene* is over 4,000 words; there are 3,000 words on George Eliot; some 2,000 on Zola. Even comparatively minor entries are richly informative. In the 500 or so words on Abbey, for instance, we get a summary of the painter's career, of his friendship with James, of James's published comments on him (three different items—one a newspaper column—with enough bibliographical information on each to lead us to James's original remarks should we wish to consult them), along with the information that "it is believed that James helped Abbey's wife write a catalogue for some of the panels of *The Quest of the Holy Grail* by her husband, designed for the Boston public library and exhibited in London in 1895. And, for a further, brief example, in the entry on Thomas Sargeant Perry, Gale tells us where we can find Henry James's letters to his boyhood friend (in the appendix to Virginia Harlow's 1950 biography of Perry).

To prepare this encyclopedia, Professor Gale has read "all of James"—the self-deprecating quotation marks are his own, in his preface to the volume. But more has been required than a reading through of all of Henry James, though that in itself is no mean achievement (one that I would guess has been matched by no more than half a dozen persons since Henry James himself). The *Henry James Encyclopedia* is the fruit of Robert Gale's lifetime saturation in Henry James. He began by reading James as an undergraduate in the 1930s, wrote on James for his master's and his doctorate, published a fine critical study of James *(The Caught Image: Figurative Language in the Fiction of Henry James)*, also published a Henry James reference work of narrower scope than the present volume *(Plots and Characters in the Fiction of Henry James)*, wrote the James chapters in the Duke University annual *American Literary Scholarship* for a decade, and continues to serve on the editorial board of the *Henry James Review* (offering me, as *HJR* editor, some of the liveliest, most acute, and most constructive reader's reports it has ever been my pleasure to read and to pass on to those who have submitted work to the journal). Professor Gale's continuing immersion in James studies is a warrant that the information in the *Henry James Encyclopedia* is abreast of current scholarship. For example, in his entry on Baron Lyon Playfair (1818–1898), Gale notes that James's "*Pocket Diaries* indicate that James continued to socialize with Lady Playfair into the 1910s." For this information, Gale has drawn on the recently published *Complete Notebooks of Henry James* (1987), where the editors (Leon Edel and Lyall H. Powers) first made James's pocket diaries available.

As an editor who has relied on Robert Gale's advice throughout the decade during which I have known him, I have been very much in his debt. As a student of Henry James, I find that I am now inestimably more so because of the *Henry James Encyclopedia*, as will be everyone who admires the work of this great author and who wishes to know more about that work, about its creator, and

about the world in which he lived. I consider it an act of enormous generosity that in preparing this volume—a labor that required enviable energy as well as great knowledge—Robert Gale has allowed us to share in his deep Jamesian saturation. I have found myself reading sequentially through the manuscript of the encyclopedia, discovering instruction and illumination on every page. Coming to the entry on Christian Bernhard Tauchnitz, for example, I remembered the few James titles I have examined in Tauchnitz editions and the Tauchnitz volumes that figure in his fiction (in *The Reverberator*, for instance, and in *The Wings of the Dove*), but I did not know, until I read the entry, the name of the series in which these books appeared (the Tauchnitz *Collection of British and American Authors*), the starting date of the series (1841), the fact that the volumes were not sold in England (to protect copyright there), and that between 1878 and 1912 Tauchnitz republished sixteen books by Henry James. Nor had I remembered that, as Gale observes, "In 'The Third Person' James has Amy Frush smuggle an illegal Tauchnitz into England to appease the ghost of an ancestor hanged for more serious smuggling." The encyclopedist says in his Preface that he almost never "offers any critical insights, since this is a reference book." Happily, this determination does not entail the suspension of judgment or the eradication of the author's distinctive character. Besides delighting in innumerable tidbits of knowledge such as the facts on Tauchnitz, I have found considerable pleasure in the personal savor of such Gale judgments as the pungent dismissal of James's play "The Album" as "this wretched drama" and the just as tenable praise of "The Pupil" as "one of the finest short stories ever written."
In sum, if I may presume to say so on behalf of Jamesians everywhere, present and to come, thank you, Bob, for having created this essential resource, the *Henry James Encyclopedia*, a monumental job, superbly done.

DANIEL MARK FOGEL
LOUISIANA STATE UNIVERSITY

PREFACE

My *Henry James Encyclopedia* has been a labor of love for more than three years. It is the result of my reading every published work by Henry James except five unavailable items. Since James was prolific and versatile, this reading has been extensive and certainly illuminating as well. In his lifetime (1843–1916), James published 576 items in periodicals, from 1864 through 1915, and 76 books (many containing reprints of previously issued material, to be sure), from 1875 to 1916. In addition, he contributed items to three dozen books by others, beginning in 1884 and continuing to 1916. Several posthumous items have appeared, notably two fragmentary novels and a fragmentary short story. In addition, hundreds and hundreds of his 15,000 or so extant letters, as well as his *Notebooks* and *Pocket Diaries*, have now been published. I estimate that well over ten million words penned and dictated by James are now in print.

The average interested reader or even committed scholar cannot master such literary fecundity. In the face of today's information explosion, we need all the help we can get. Hence the usefulness of my *Henry James Encyclopedia*. I have read and revered James since my undergraduate days, beginning in the late 1930s. After World War II, I wrote my master's thesis on James at Columbia University under Vernon Loggins, and then my doctoral dissertation, also on James and also at Columbia under Lionel Trilling. I began to publish on James in the 1950s, and for this *Encyclopedia* I have drawn heavily on my 1965 *Plots and Characters in the Fiction of Henry James* (with the kind permission of James Thorpe III, editor of Archon Books, Hamden, CT). In the process of writing the James chapter for *Eight American Authors* (rev. ed., New York: Norton, 1971) and ten James chapters for the ongoing *American Literary Scholarship: An Annual* (Duke University Press), as well as serving on the editorial board of the *Henry James Review*, I have tried to keep abreast of the best Jamesian scholarship. But nothing prepared me adequately for the surprises in store for me in connection with preparing this *Encyclopedia*. Reading ''all of James'' has convinced me that he is peerless among his contemporaries. Maintaining a consistent high quality, he wrote novels, short stories, plays, travel books and essays, critical essays and prefaces, reviews, art and dramatic notices, biography and autobiography, directions to himself in his *Notebooks*, and matchless letters to an incredible array of relatives, friends, and professional colleagues and opponents. He was amazingly well read, in French, German, and Italian, as well as English and American literature. (In addition to his unique brand of English, he spoke French, German, and Italian, and he wrote letters, as well as notes to himself, in French and Italian.) His eclectic reading is reflected in much that he wrote. The cosmopolitan nature of his friendships is probably unique in nineteenth-century literary annals. In this *Encyclopedia*, I offer somewhat detailed information about his friends to show his network of personal associates and to indicate his ''participation,'' to use his word. Further, I detail aspects of the lives of the authors whom he knew in person and through his reading to show his bookish activities and his world of ideas.

This *Encyclopedia* is obviously not a substitute for reading and rereading James or reading about him in depth. Nothing can be. But I hope that it may serve as an overture, an extended preface, an introduction to this genius, and also as a source of casual information about his personality, his work, his intellectual milieu, his society. A little preliminary riffling through the *Encyclopedia* will show the reader that I summarize each of James's works, identify every fictional and dramatic character in them, identify writers and artists James reviewed, discuss each important man and woman he associated with or wrote about, and define the members of his extended family. Everything is in one alphabetized sequence. Asterisks indicate cross-referencing. (I do not cross-reference James's works, characters, or family members, since all of them can be assumed to be included.) A work is usually entered under its revised title. Other titles are indicated for clarity. I do not compare and contrast first publications to revisions; James simply revised too much. Instead I usually consider the latest text of a given work. I do not say whether a work was signed or unsigned. I treat the many untitled notes under their contents. I almost never offer any critical insights, since this is a reference book. My chronology might easily have been longer, but I hope that it is generally sufficient. The dozen appendices are probably self-explanatory; although there is some overlapping in them, I do not include all of my nearly three thousand alphabetized entries in these appendix subdivisions. By the classifying of so many of the entries within these twelve major categories, the appendices in large part serve to index the encyclopedia.

In spite of operating largely on my own, I have benefited from much previously published material on James. It is obvious that for reasons of space, and therefore of cost, I could not use textual footnotes to identify sources for my informational entries; therefore, I have listed in one bibliography all of the sources I consulted for this work. I hereby thank all persons responsible for the monumental work behind those titles. I would like to extend special words of gratitude to a few scholars and friends whose efforts have been of unusual benefit to me. First, to Leon Edel. Without his biography of James, and his editions of James's plays, letters, and notebooks, I would never have undertaken this project. Edel's extensive annotations have proved essential. Any experienced reader of my work can see that I have profited enormously from them, and I hereby thank and commend Professor Edel, as all Jamesians must do. Further, the James bibliography by Edel, Dan H. Laurence, and James Rambeau was a necessity. I am grateful to Lyall H. Powers for his part in annotating the *Notebooks*. Also exceptionally welcome has been the biographical, editorial, and critical work— some old, some new—of Michael Anesko (for information on James's income), Oscar Cargill (on James's novels), William G. Coleman and Liam Kelly (history of Bailieborough, County Cavan, Ireland), Frederick W. Dupee (James's life), Roger Gard (James's sales figures), H. Montgomery Hyde (James's home life), R. W. B. Lewis (James's friend Edith Wharton), Percy Lubbock (James's letters), Jane Maher (James's younger brothers), F. O. Matthiessen and Kenneth B. Murdock (James's *Notebooks*), Rayburn S. Moore (James's friend Edmund Gosse), Robert E. Mossman (index of James's works), Simon Nowell-Smith (anecdotes about James), Norman Page (anecdotes about James), William T. Stafford (index of James's works), John L. Sweeney (James's art essays), Adeline R. Tintner (James's sources and his use of other art forms), Allan Wade (James's dramatic essays), and Edward Wagenknecht (James's fiction, and British and American fiction). Some of these individuals, a few of them now deceased, have been among my best professional friends. I must add that the ongoing Library of America volumes by James have made my reading more efficient.

I considered including entries in the *Encyclopedia* concerning the major Jamesian scholars, past and present, but such a task would have been difficult and the result perhaps unbalanced. Further, with the forthcoming publication of *A Companion to Henry James Studies* edited by Daniel Mark Fogel, such entries were deemed unnecessary, since Professor Fogel has enlisted several of the best contemporary scholars to write critical essays, and they will surely pay proper respect to their predecessors and contemporary colleagues.

Next, I wish to extend my sincere thanks to Susan C. Metzger and Harvard University Press, Allison Crane and Oxford University Press, and Alexander R. James of Glandore, County Cork, Ireland, grandson of William James and hence great-nephew of Henry James, for graciously granting permission to quote from James's published letters and *Notebooks*. (Most of the letters that I quote are from the Harvard Volumes. In the absence of prohibitively expensive footnotes, the interested reader will have to combine the context, my bibliography, and ingenuity to find sources for a few others.) I wish to express appreciation for the professional help and personal encouragement given me by H. David Brumble III, Bruce Dobler, Daniel Mark Fogel, Tanya Kotys, Rayburn S. Moore, Ernest

J. Parent, Herbert Ruhm, Philip E. Smith, William L. Smith, and the librarians at the University of Pittsburgh (especially Laurie Cohen, Anne W. Gordon, Dennis Hennessey, and Amy E. Knapp), Carnegie-Mellon University, and Duquesne University. I also wish to thank my editor, Marilyn Brownstein of Greenwood Press, for her expert and practical advice, unwavering cooperation, and patience, and Lynn E. Wheeler and Teresa R. Metz, for their superb copyediting and production work. Once again, I express my undiminished gratitude to my wife Maureen for her love, understanding, tolerance, and humor. Let me add that this work would never have evolved into its present form without a generous and much-appreciated Christmas gift in 1984 from our son James Gale of a computer, word processor, and printer.

Finally, I shall be grateful if readers of this *Henry James Encyclopedia* will send me notices of any errors I have made in it, or any suggestions of how to improve it, to be rectified and included, as the case may be, in a later edition.

CHRONOLOGY

1843   Henry James, Jr., born on 15 April, at 21 Washington Place, New York City, the second of five children (the others being William James [1842–1910], Garth Wilkinson James [1845–1883], Robertson James [1846–1910], and Alice James [1848–1892]) of Henry James, Sr. (1811–1882) and Mary Robertson Walsh James (1810–1882).

1843–1845   Lives in England and France with family.

1845–1855   Lives with family in the United States, mostly in New York, attending various schools and being privately tutored.

1855–1858   Attends schools in Geneva, London, and France.

1858–1859   Returns with family to Newport, Rhode Island.

1859–1860   Attends schools in Geneva and Bonn.

1860–1863   Returns with family to Newport, takes art classes (1860), injures back (1861), enters Harvard Law School (1862–1863).

1864   Moves with family to Boston, publishes first short story and first book review.

1865–1868   Publishes extensively (fifty-three reviews and critical notes, eleven short stories). Moves with family to Cambridge, Massachusetts (1866), takes vacations, meets important men and women of letters.

1869–1870   Travels alone to England (meeting important writers) and on the Continent.

1870–1872   Returns to Cambridge (1870), writes numerous travel sketches (1870–1872), serializes *Watch and Ward* (1871), writes several art reviews (early 1872).

1872–1874   Travels to England and the Continent (partly with aunt and with sister Alice, until October 1872), stays on (self-supporting now) in Italy, welcomes brother William there (October 1873–March 1874), returns to the United States (September 1874).

1875   Lives in New York, then Cambridge. Serializes *Roderick Hudson*, writes
       reviews and essays, publishes first two books (*A Passionate Pilgrim,
       and other Tales* and *Transatlantic Sketches*). Moves to Paris (Novem-
       ber), begins to meet numerous Continental men and women of letters.

1876   Is Paris correspondent for New York *Tribune* (briefly). Moves to London
       (December, 3 Bolton Street, Piccadilly—until 1886). *Roderick Hudson*
       is published in book form. Begins a pattern of steady writing and pub-
       lishing (in magazines and in book form), meeting significant writers and
       other persons, relentless socializing, theater-going, and occasional
       travel.

1877   *The American.*

1878   *French Poets and Novelists* and *The Europeans*, "Daisy Miller: A Study."

1879   *Confidence* and *Hawthorne.*

1880   Resides in Florence, Italy (March–May). Serializes *The Portrait of a Lady*
       (autumn 1880–autumn 1881) for high fees (published in book form
       1881). *Washington Square.*

1881–1882   Returns to the United States (Boston, October 1881, New York and Wash-
       ington, December 1881–January 1882), mourns death of mother in Bos-
       ton (January), returns to London (May), tours France (autumn), returns
       to Boston, mourns death of father there (December).

1883   Acts as executor of father's estate, then returns to London (August). *The
       Siege of London* and *Portraits of Places.*

1884   Welcomes sister Alice to England (November). "The Art of Fiction," *A
       Little Tour in France*, and *Tales of Three Cities.*

1885   *The Author of Beltraffio* and *Stories Revived* (3 vols.).

1886   Moves to 34 De Vere Gardens, Kensington (March—until 1896). *The Bos-
       tonians* and *The Princess Casamassima* (both selling badly). Goes to
       Italy (December).

1887   Stays in Florence and Venice (until July).

1888   Vacations in Geneva, Italy, and Paris (October–December). *Partial Por-
       traits, The Reverberator*, and *The Aspern Papers.*

1889   *A London Life.*

1890   Begins to write plays. Visits Italy (summer). *The Tragic Muse.*

1891   Visits Ireland (July). *The American* produced.

1892   Mourns death of sister Alice in London (March). Meets brother William
       James and family in Switzerland (summer; again summer 1893). *The
       Lesson of the Master.*

1893   *The Real Thing and Other Tales, Picture and Text, The Private Life, Essays
       in London and Elsewhere*, and *The Wheel of Time.*

1894   Visits Italy (March–May). *Theatricals* (2 vols.).

1895   *Guy Domville* produced unsuccessfully. *Terminations.*

1896   *Embarrassments* and *The Other House.*

1897   Begins habit of dictating (February). *The Spoils of Poynton* and *What Maisie Knew*.

1898   Moves into Lamb House (June). *In the Cage* and *The Two Magics* (containing "The Turn of the Screw").

1899   Vacations in France and Italy (March–July). *The Awkward Age*.

1900   Shaves beard (June). *The Soft Side*.

1901   *The Sacred Fount*.

1902   In poor health. *The Wings of the Dove*.

1903   *The Better Sort, The Ambassadors*, and *William Wetmore Story and His Friends*.

1904–1905   Tours the United States (August 1904–July 1905) to sightsee and lecture. Begins revising his selected fiction (1905–1908). *The Golden Bowl* (1904) and *English Hours* (1905).

1907   Tours France by automobile (summer). *The American Scene* and *The Novels and Tales of Henry James* (1907–1909).

1908   *The High Bid* produced. *Views and Reviews*.

1909   Sick. *Italian Hours*.

1910   Sick. Returns to the United States (August, remaining until August 1911) with fatally ill brother William. *The Finer Grain*.

1911   *The Saloon* produced. *The Outcry*.

1912   Rents rooms at 21 Carlyle Mansions, Chelsea (for winter quarters). Sick.

1913   Sits for portrait by John Singer Sargent (April). *A Small Boy and Others*.

1914   *Notes of a Son and Brother* and *Notes on Novelists*.

1915   Does war-relief work (to 1916). Becomes British citizen (July). Suffers two strokes (December).

1916   Receives British Order of Merit (January). Dies 28 February, 21 Carlyle Mansions.

1917   *The Ivory Tower, The Sense of the Past* and *The Middle Years*.

1919   *Within the Rim and Other Essays*.

A HENRY JAMES
ENCYCLOPEDIA

A

"The Abasement of the Northmores." Short story (7,100 words), published in *The Soft Side*, 1900; revised and reprinted in *The Novels and Tales of Henry James*, Volume XVI, 1909. (Characters: Warren Hope, Mrs. Warren Hope, Johnson, Lord John Northmore, Lady Northmore, Thompson.) Though sick, Warren Hope goes to Lord Northmore's funeral, where he catches cold and soon dies. His loving widow Mrs. Hope believes that Northmore used Warren, who left nothing publishable to justify her high opinion of his mind. She furnishes Lady Northmore with letters from Lord Northmore for a collected edition—all the letters, that is, save the love letters that Northmore sent to Mrs. Hope before her marriage. She decides to issue a collection of Warren's letters, only to find that none were preserved. Northmore's published letters, though courteously reviewed, seem inane to Mrs. Hope. She is tempted to publish Lord Northmore's old love letters to her; but, on going to his widow for permission, she senses a Northmore family abasement; so she prepares her Warren's lovely letters to her and has one copy printed—for posterity. This story contrasts hollow fame and intrinsic worth and also dramatizes revenge abandoned. Is it possible that Mrs. Hope is an unreliable, almost demented narrator, and that her late husband was in truth unexceptional? In a Notebook entry (12 Nov 1899), James sketches what became the plot of the story but closed with this: *"Or is there anything* ELSE *in it?—in connection with the letters she eventually publishes????"* In the preface to Volume XVI of *The Novels and Tales of Henry James*, James says that this "developmental" story is really a *nouvelle* pretending to be an anecdote.

Abbey, Edwin Austin (1852–1911). Philadelphia-born painter, mural painter, watercolorist, etcher, and illustrator. He drew illustrations for *Harper's Weekly*, then moved to London (1878), where he became a great success. His big break

came in 1890 when he was commissioned to do murals for the Boston Public
Library. He also executed panels and murals in Harrisburg, Pennsylvania. James
dined with Abbey before a Royal Academy function in December 1883, came
to know both Abbey and his wife Gertrude well, and occasionally visited him
at work in London and in the Costwolds (Abbey shared a studio there with
Francis Davis Millet* and John Singer Sargent*), Gloucestershire. In a letter to
his brother William (1 Oct 1887), James called Abbey "genial and gifted" and
"a pure genius." In his "Edwin A. Abbey" (*Harper's Weekly*, 4 Dec 1886;
reprinted in part in *A Catalogue of the Drawings of Mr. Edward A. Abbey for
"She Stoops to Conquer . . . ,"* New York, 1886; reprinted in *Picture and Text*,
1893), James explains that Abbey learned to sketch by observing American
scenes and by having to work efficiently for *Harper's Weekly* (beginning in
1872), where he proved himself to be "irremediably native." But then, soon
after, he went to England (first in 1878) and found himself at home in its
eighteenth century. Proof is contained in his uniquely fine illustrations for a new
edition of *She Stoops to Conquer* by Oliver Goldsmith.* In "Our Artists in
Europe" (1889; reprinted as "Black and White" in *Picture and Text*), James
calls Abbey "a mixture of confidence and excitement" for his public, says that
his skill is "ripe" but not "mechanical," adds that he likes Abbey so much
that he cannot be "judicial" about him, extols his illustrations for *Judith Shakespeare* by William Black* and (again) for *She Stoops to Conquer* by Oliver
Goldsmith, and opines that he combines "truth . . . with poetry." It is believed
that James helped Abbey's wife write an exhibition catalogue entitled *"The
Quest of the Holy Grail." The First Portion of a Series of Paintings to Be Done
for the Decoration of the Public Library of Boston, U.S.A. by Edwin A. Abbey.*
It was published in London, in 1895, and in New York (with a slightly revised
subtitle and text) by R. H. Russell and Son, in 1895. Exhibitions were held in
London, in 1895 and 1901, and in New York, in 1901. The writing does not
sound much like James's, and his help was probably negligible. In "London"
(5 Jun 1897) James generalizes that Abbey has grown from an able black-and-
white illustrator to a painter of works "noble in color and strongly composed,"
which "show . . . him as one of the first dramatic painters."

"Abbeys and Castles." Travel essay, published in *Lippincott's Magazine* (Oct
1877); reprinted in *Portraits of Places*, 1883, and in *English Hours*, 1905. Much
that is beautiful in England, except hedgerows and churches, is private property.
Should private beauty be publicly written about? Visiting the resident of a certain
private place, James agreed with him that it was "the loveliest corner of the
world" (edged hills, modulated slopes, woodlands, castles, abbeys, farmhouses,
parks with big old oaks, full streams). James describes his friend's home as "a
ci-devant priory" (Norman doorway, two-storied, thirteenth-century gallery,
narrow-windowed rooms) with adjoining ruins. One soon gets used to living in
a house 600 years old: "The new life and the old have melted together; there
is no dividing-line." An American persuaded James to see Stokesay (moat, gate

house, defenseless little castle, medieval court, long hall, irregular staircase, tower—all redolent of Edward IV and Elizabeth) and also Ludlow ("charming ... provincial town," fine castle, "goodly Severn" River, old houses—all smacking of "pre-Victorian ... narrowness of custom" and "insular propriety").

About, Edmond (1828–1885). A powerful, liberal French journalist and exuberant, romantic novelist, now considered best as a writer when farcical. He was elected to the French Academy but died before he could be seated. About's works include sprightly farces such as *Le Roi des montagnes* (1856) and *Le Nez d'un notaire* (1862), and the once-popular *Roman d'un brave homme* (1880). James remembered with pleasure his early reading of About's first novel, *Tolla* (1855), but was aware that the popular French novelist though clever was of only minor importance. James wrote to his mother from Rome (26 Jan 1873) that he had seen About, who "has a capital, clever face," in the Villa Medici gardens. In his essay "The Minor French Novelists" (*Galaxy* Feb 1876), James calls About a "brilliant talent ... but less clever than George Sand[*] and even Victor Cherbuliez[*]." About's *Germaine* (1858) contains a plot situation that James adapted in *The Portrait of a Lady*. James's library contained one book by About.

Acton, Lizzie. In *The Europeans*, Robert Acton's sister, and the cousin of Gertrude, Charlotte, and Clifford Wentworth.

Acton, Mrs. In *The Europeans*, Robert and Lizzie Acton's gentle mother.

Acton, Robert. In *The Europeans*, Lizzie Acton's brother, and the cousin of Gertrude, Charlotte, and Clifford Wentworth. He is attracted to Baroness Eugenia Münster but decides not to propose to her.

Adair, Sir Robin. In *A Monologue by Henry James*, Cora Tuff's British friend, who comes for tea.

Adams, Henry (1838–1918). Boston-born great-grandson and grandson of American presidents. Adams was educated at Harvard and in Germany, and then he served as his ambassador father's secretary in the American embassy in London during the Civil War. He professed in his incomparable autobiography, *The Education of Henry Adams*, to be prepared inadequately for the intellectual life of the later nineteenth century and the beginning of the twentieth. Starting in 1868, he launched a career that featured much writing and some teaching (at Harvard), and he concerned himself with a variety of subjects in many forms: Reconstruction-era politics, European medieval history and arts, early nineteenth-century American history, American social and religious life, Oriental mores and Polynesian history, modern physics (including the possible relationship between thermodynamics and the acceleration of historical events), and contemporary chaos—all cast in journalistic essays, lectures, books in single or multiple volumes, biographies, editorial essays, poems, novels, an autobiography, and letters. Adams's major works are *Chapters of Erie* (1871, with his brother Charles Francis Adams), *The Life of Albert Gallatin* (1879), *Democracy* (1880), *John Randolph* (1882), *Esther* (1884), *History of the United States during the Administrations of Jefferson and Madison* (1889–1891), *Memoirs of Marau Taaroa, Last Queen of Tahiti* (1893), *Mont-Saint-Michel and Chartres* (1904), *The Education of Henry Adams* (1907, 1918), *A Letter to American Teachers of History* (1910), and several collections of letters. James and Adams met in about 1870. James wrote somewhat superciliously to Grace Norton* (26 Sep [1870]) that Adams "is I believe a youth of genius and enthusiasm—or at least of talent and energy." Thereafter, James and Adams intermittently socialized, both in the United States and—more often—in Italy, France, and England. Because of the social contacts Adams had developed during the Civil War, he was able, early in their relationship, to help James meet important persons in England. The two men, both being important culturally and socially, had many illustrious or merely charming friends in common, including Ruth Draper,* Walter Gay* and his wife Matilda, Edwin Lawrence Godkin,* Ephraim Whitman Gurney* (Adams's brother-in-law), John Milton Hay,* Isabella Stewart Gardner,* Lord Houghton,* William Dean Howells,* Clarence King,* John La Farge,* Henry Cabot Lodge (of the famous Lodge family*), Charles Eliot Norton,* Thomas Sergeant Perry,* Augustus Saint-Gaudens,* John Singer Sargent,* Robert Louis Stevenson,* Whitelaw Reid,* and Edith Newbold Jones Wharton.* As their middle years began, James seemed to feel that Adams and his wife Marian Adams* (married since 1872) were idle, unstable, and negative. He wrote to Elizabeth Boott* from London (28 Jun [1879]) that "[t]he Henry Adamses are here—very pleasant, friendly, conversational, critical, ironical. They are to be here all summer and to go in the autumn to Spain; then to return here for the winter. Clover [Mrs. Adams] chatters rather less . . . " To his father, James wrote (11 Oct [1879]) that "Henry is very sensible, though a trifle dry." And to Grace Norton he wrote (20 Sep 1880) that the Adamses in England "are rather too critical and invidious." By contrast, James earlier wrote to Adams (5 May 1877) of his life in London: "I didn't come here on a lark but to lead my usual quiet workaday life." James appreciated Adams's anonymously published novel *Democracy*, wondered at first whether a man or a woman had written it, and pronounced it so good that he wished it were a bit better. He soon knew that the author was Adams, to whose wife James reported (28 Feb [1883]) that, according to Mary Morton Sands,* *Democracy* "forms the favourite reading of Mr. [Prime Minister William Ewart] Gladstone[*]." James used his pleasant 1882 visit to the Adamses in Washington, D.C., as the basis of his 1884 story "Pandora." After the 1885 suicide of Mrs. Adams, which permanently blackened her husband's life, James wrote to Godkin thus: "I am more sorry for poor Henry than I can say—too sorry, almost, to think of him." In an effort to recover, Adams traveled around the world (1890–1891), stopping in Tahiti and Samoa, with a visit to Stevenson. Adams's illustrious traveling companion was La Farge, who wrote about their experiences in *Reminiscences of the South Seas* (1901). On his way home, Adams called on James in London, in October 1891, and regaled him with travel talk. But James soon thereafter wrote to John Clark (13 Dec [1891]) first to decry Adams's "monotonous disappointed pessimism" and then to go on, perhaps jealously, to the effect that Adams is "a man of wealth and leisure . . . while I am a penniless toiler." During his 1904–1905 tour of the United States, James was a week-long guest of Adams, who with Hay took James to dinner in 1905 at the White House, then presided over by Theodore Roosevelt.* James resisted the temptation to go on a Nile River trip with an Adams and Hay party in 1898; but he was entertained by their extended social group at Surrenden Dering, near Rye, later in 1898, where he was able to observe Adams and Elizabeth Cameron*, the lovely wife of old Senator James Donald Cameron* and the long-standing object of Adams's adoration. James later wrote to Henrietta Reubell* (27 Feb 1901) that Mrs. Cameron, twenty-three years younger than her husband, "sucked the lifeblood of poor Henry Adams." Adams held James in sufficiently high regard to send him a privately printed copy of *The Education of Henry Adams* in 1908. James acknowledged receipt of it in a gushy letter (8 May 1908) without commenting on its contents. Much later, James replied to epistolary bitterness from Adams occasioned by his reading of a gift copy of James's *Notes of a Son and Brother* with one of his most famous letters (21 Mar 1814). In it he reveals that, although they are "lone survivors," life remains endlessly interesting to him, because he is an artist of "inexhaustible sensibility." Finally, later that year, James saw Adams in London and wrote to Wharton (20 Oct 1814) that he was "more changed and gone than he had been reported." James's library contained one book by Adams.

Adams, Marian (née Hooper) (Clover) (1843–1885). Daughter of Boston physician Robert William Hooper and his wife Ellen Sturgis Hooper. Marian married Henry Adams* in 1872. Marian's sister Ellen Hooper married Ephraim Whitman Gurney.* Marian Adams was a brilliant conversationalist, hostess, and letter-writer, and a fine amateur photographer. James met her in Newport, Rhode Island, in the late 1860s, and associated her in his mind with Mary Temple.* In a letter to his brother William (8 Mar 1870), he said that Clover Hooper had "intellectual grace" and, later, in a letter to Grace Norton* (20 Sep 1880) called her "a perfect Voltaire in petticoats." He also thought that she was a rather idle socialite in Washington, D.C.; from there, he wrote to Isabella Stewart Gardner* (23 Jan [1882]) that Mrs. Adams, his hostess, has "a very pretty little life here. Mrs. A. has perennial afternoon tea—two or three times a day—and frequent dinners at a little round table." In her turn, she admired James greatly, but she regarded him as frivolous for expatriating himself in England and urged him to return to the United States. She is reputed to have made the often-quoted comment on James that "he chaws more than he bites off." When she committed suicide by drinking potassium cyanide, which was used in developing photographs, James theorized in a letter to Elizabeth Boott* (7 Jan [1886]) that she had "succumbed to hereditary melancholy" and also wrote poignantly to Edwin Lawrence Godkin* (6 Feb [1886]) that suicide was her "solution to the knottiness of existence." In addition to her part in his story "Pandora," Marian Adams figures in James's characterization of Isabel Archer in *The Portrait of a Lady* as a woman who experiences loss of freedom through marriage. Further, soon after Marian Adams's suicide, James wrote two stories, "The Modern Warning" and "The Patagonia," each of which ends in the suicide of a fine woman. It is possible that the excessively close relationship of Adam Verver and his daughter Maggie in *The Golden Bowl* owes something to James's notion of Marian's relationship to her father both before and after her marriage.

Addard, C. P. In "Fordham Castle," pseudonym of Abel F. Taker.

"Adina." Short story (16,100 words), published in *Scribner's Monthly* (May–Jun 1874). (Characters: Angelo Beati, Castillani, Prince Doria, Esther, Padre Girolamo, Ninetta, Sam Scrope, Adina Waddington, Mrs. Waddington.) Sam Scrope tricks a callow Italian named Angelo Beati out of a priceless old intaglio. In revenge, Angelo woos and wins Scrope's fiancée Adina Waddington, whereupon Scrope throws the topaz into the Tiber. This slight story, which offers the dark Italian past as backdrop, contrasts a vicious modern scholar and a simple shepherd, whose revenge might have taken a more violent turn.

Adney, Blanche. In "The Private Life," the fine actress who admires Clarence Vawdrey and sees through Lord Mellifont.

Adney, Vincent. In "The Private Life," Blanche's violinist husband.

Adolph of Silberstadt-Schreckenstein, Prince. In *The Europeans*, Eugenia Münster's husband.

"The Afghan Difficulty." Political letter, published in the *Nation* (14 Nov 1878). After reporting some trivial social items, James notes that war in Afghanistan, ruled by Shir Ali, the Amir, seems imminent. A British "military embassy" sent there from India was insulted; and Russia, despite promises in 1875 to the contrary, is extending its sphere of influence to "Cabul." If Russia either invades or tries to colonize Afghanistan, the annoyed British public will wonder how to protect India and, further, at what frontier.

"The After-Season at Rome." The 1873 title of "The After-Season in Rome."

"The After-Season in Rome." (1873 title, "The After-Season at Rome"). Travel essay, published in the *Nation* (12 Jun 1873); reprinted in *Transatlantic Sketches*, 1875, and in *Italian Hours*, 1909. In it, James reports that Rome is best seen when foreign tourists leave, at the end of May. Then the city becomes herself again. Her rich colors come out again. Landeaus, dandies, and guidebooks are few. James likes both to monopolize deserted museums and to publicize them. The Roman spring is sweet and frank, and one can watch its progress from many villas. From the "good" Borghese or the "charming" Medici, for example, each view is a picture. Even reports of a papal illness or political unrest are mild.

"After the Play." Drama essay in dialogue form, published in the *New Review* (Jun 1889); reprinted in *Picture and Text*, 1893. (Characters: Amicia, Auberon, Dorriforth, Florentia.) After a matinee performance by a Parisian company in London's Soho district, Florentia invites fellow playgoers Amicia, Auberon, and Dorriforth home to tea. They chat about the contemporary British stage. Amicia, Auberon, and Florentia make minor comments. Dorriforth does most of the critical talking. Amicia liked the play as a French experiment in realism: she is a socialite and an agreeable person. Auberon likes "symmetrical . . . form," praises Richard Wagner for using all possible stage effects, notes that ticket sales are up in London, and praises British acting. Florentia goes to plays to escape from life to "fable and romance"; she numbers herself among the "dense and vulgar" public, and she enjoyed a recent production of *The Merry Wives of Windsor* by William Shakespeare.* Dorriforth says that we should attend a play as we read a novel, to seek and find, to be led into the writer's mind; stage "appointments" should suggest, to inspire fine acting; elaborate sets corrupt acting, make the audience (which is "huge and good-natured and common") prefer pictorial to dramatic effects, and will soon dominate the theater with "big, unmistakable, knock-down effects"; the best "conceptions" are "the most actable"; good new plays are rare; we lack authoritative criticism; stage adaptations should be as good as the novels adapted; the British should have plays, including satirical ones, "to represent our own life"; plays should be published; ticket sales indicate only popularity, not quality; the competent British actors need good material; and Londoners are too rushed to attend inconveniently located theaters. Florentia wants to break for dinner.

Agnesina. In *The Awkward Age*, Duchess Jane's sheltered niece.

Aïdé, Charles Hamilton (1826–1906). Paris-born aesthete, the son of an Armenian father and an English mother. Hamilton Aïdé was educated in England and Bonn, Germany; then he served in the British army until 1853. He traveled widely, and he was a prolific, voguish poet, musical composer, artist, playwright, and fiction writer. His publications include poetry (*Eleanore* [1856]), novels (*Rita* [1859], *Introduced to Society* [1884], and *Passages in the Life of a Lady* [1887]), and short stories (*Morals and Mysteries* [1872]). He is probably best known now for being an ageless London host. James was often his grateful dinner guest, meeting through him, for example, George Du Maurier* and Anne

Benson Skepper Proctor,* both in 1877. James and Aïdé also both knew William
Morton Fullerton.* James described Aïdé in a letter to Grace Norton* (4 Jan
[1879]) as "my friend . . . an amiable—very amiable—literary bachelor, who
has charming rooms, innumerable friends and hospitable habits." He and James
occasionally met while traveling on the Continent, and on at least one occasion
(summer 1901) he was James's guest at Lamb House.* In a letter to Henrietta
Reubell* (15 Dec 1901), James calls Aïdé "fabulous," noting that he is "75,
still singing, and now starting for Egypt." After attending his funeral, James
described him in a letter to Lady Anne Isabella Ritchie* (21 Dec 1906) as "the
soul of . . . *mondanité* . . . benignant and blessed."

Aikin, Lucy (1781–1864). Versatile English authoress of books on various
British monarchs, and, under the pen name Mary Godolphin, books for shorthand
students and children. She rewrote certain classics in words of one syllable. She
met and greatly admired William Ellery Channing.* The Channing-Aikin correspondence was published in 1874.

Akers, Elizabeth (real name, Mrs. Elizabeth Ann Akers Allen [née Chase]; pen
name, Florence Percy) (1832–1911). American poetess whose 1866 *Poems* James
reviewed (*North American Review*, Apr 1867). He praises her "unassuming
good taste" and says that she is tender, pensive, and in sympathy with nature.

The Album. Three-act play, published in *Theatricals: Second Series: The Album*
[and] *The Reprobate*, 1894. (Characters: Teddy Ashdown, Lady Basset, Bedford,
Mark Moorsom Bernal, Sir Ralph Damant, Grace Jesmond, Lamb, Maud Van-
neck.) Confusion reigns in the country house of Courtland outside London.
Bedford, its owner, is dying upstairs, and the disposition of his estate is uncertain.
Sir Ralph Damant rushes in: As the closest heir, he feels entitled to it. Artist
Mark Moorsom Bernal, another relative (missing and thought dead), wanders
in (with an album of his sketches, signed and dated "September '91") indifferent
to inheritance since he has neglected Bedford. Three women are on the scene:
Lady Basset, Bedford's friend who now sets her cap for Sir Ralph; Maud Vanneck, another friend, loved by Teddy Ashdown but aiming higher; and Grace
Jesmond, Bedford's amaneunsis for the past five years, now criticized by Lady
Basset and Maud, and admiring Mark when she meets him. Teddy shows Grace
the album inscribed by Mark. Mark gives it to Grace. Sir Ralph will sit for his
portrait if Mark can lure the females away. Sir Ralph tries to keep knowledge
of Mark's presence from Bedford, who, however, sees Mark and then Sir Ralph,
and then whose death the latter then announces. A short while later Mark, low
on funds, gives art lessons in London to Lady Basset and Maud, with Teddy
hanging about as his studio servant. Bringing the album, Grace enters and seeks
employment as a model. Sir Ralph enters and will sit for his portrait if the ladies
leave. Grace wants a word with him first: When she accuses him of deceiving
Bedford about Mark (adding that Teddy can prove it because of the album), he

tries to bribe her and, when she declines, assumes she wants to marry him. He tells Mark she proposed; Mark asks her to leave. Finally all enter and leave Sir Ralph's Portland Place drawing room at various times: Grace sees Sir Ralph to seek money for Mark. Teddy comes with Mark's painting materials. He will encourage Mark for Grace if she will recommend Teddy to Maud. Mark comes, thinking Grace wants Sir Ralph. Lady Basset comes, knowing she wants Sir Ralph and therefore hoping Mark will get Grace away. Mark tells Grace he urged her to leave his studio to free her from Sir Ralph. She says she is here now to induce Sir Ralph to relieve Mark's poverty. When Sir Ralph enters and, alone with Grace, accepts her imagined proposal of marriage, she wants him instead to divide his inheritance with Mark and adds that Teddy will support her evidence that Sir Ralph misled Bedford. Sir Ralph proposes to her but is rejected. Grace praises Maud, who praises Teddy, and he her. Sir Ralph returns, dressed to sit for his portrait. Mark admits that he cannot lure Lady Basset from Sir Ralph and therefore withdraws his requirement that Sir Ralph buy a portrait. The two men decide to help each other. Sir Ralph exits with Lady Basset; Mark tells Grace he loves her, and the two prepare to forget Sir Ralph. Teddy and Maud decide to wed. Returning, Sir Ralph not only says Lady Basset accepts him but also promises Mark the Bedford inheritance. This causes Lady Basset to reject Sir Ralph and decamp, which thrills him. James wrote this wretched drama, undoubtedly in 1891, for Edward Compton* and his British theatrical company. It was never produced.

Alcibiade. In "Four Meetings," waiter at the Le Havre inn seen by Caroline Spencer.

Alcott, Louisa May (1832–1888). The daughter of Bronson Alcott, who along with Ralph Waldo Emerson* and Henry David Thoreau taught her. She published poems and short stories early, was a nurse briefly during the Civil War, and then issued her first novel, *Moods* (1865). After her best selling, partly auto-biographical *Little Women* (1869), she wrote several other novels, including *Little Men* (1871) and *Eight Cousins: or, the Aunt-Hill* (1875). James snobbishly reviewed *(North American Review*, Jul 1865) her *Moods*, saying that Miss Alcott again offers a stale old triangle plot, which should now be used only if it can be made unusually "entertaining or . . . instructive." (James used similar plots himself later.) He notes that the heroine is yet another "precocious little girl . . . " pursued by yet another "unprofitable middle-aged lover." James ridicules the "inconceivable" plot—friendly villain so meddles in lives of young couple as to cause high-minded separation and worse. The last half of the novel is prettily told, but Alcott is ignorant and cocky. Still, she has considerable potential. Soon after this review appeared, Alcott dined with James's parents and the future novelist at their Boston home and was not particularly amused. Ten years later, James reviewed *(Nation*, 14 Oct 1875) *Eight Cousins*. He begins by wondering why foreigners label American boys "aggressive and knowing" and American girls "pert and shrill." Perhaps it is because of such works as *Eight Cousins*, in which the heroine and her "seven boisterous boy-cousins" are so sympathetically treated that they seem to be teaching their elders instead of learning from them. The book has "no glow and no fairies"; instead, it is "vulgar prose."

Alden, Bessie. In "An International Episode," Kitty Alden Westgate's unmarried sister. She is attracted to Lord Lambeth, but international pride and prejudice separate the pair.

Aldershaw, Lord and Lady. In *The Wings of the Dove*, the couple who live at Matcham, where Milly Theale sees a Bronzino portrait.

Aldis, Margaret. In "De Grey: A Romance," an orphan girl adopted by the De Greys, whose scion Paul De Grey loves her.

Aldrich, Thomas Bailey (1836–1907). New Hampshire–born author and editor. He spent ten childhood years in New Orleans. His father's death in 1852 prevented his going to college. Aldrich became successively a clerk, a reporter, a literary critic, and an editor in New York (where he knew James Bayard Taylor* and Walt Whitman*) and then in Boston; he published many books of poetry (from 1855) and fiction (from 1870), and he is now best remembered for his autobiographical novel *The Story of a Bad Boy* (1870) and his short story "Marjorie Daw" (1873). He succeeded William Dean Howells* as editor of the *Atlantic Monthly* (1881–1890), and this position put him in contact with most of the New England writers of his time. James is prescient when, in a letter to Howells (9 Jan 1874), he writes that in Aldrich's 1874 novel *Prudence Palfrey*, just starting as a serial in the *Atlantic*, "we shall get a great deal of prettiness." James is again cognizant of Aldrich's limitations when, in a letter to his sister Alice (19 May [1879]), describing a visit from Aldrich to him in London, he says that after vacationing in Spain the man had "nothing very appreciative or discriminating to relate." In 1887 James urged Aldrich, but to no avail, to print "The Aspern Papers" in the *Atlantic* in two installments, not three. In a letter to Charles Eliot Norton* (15 Nov 1893), James complained that his edition of the letters of James Russell Lowell* features Aldrich and Richard Watson Gilder* too much. In the preface to Volume VII of *The Novels and Tales of Henry James*, James recalls Aldrich as "the gentle editor of the 'Atlantic Monthly' " when *The Tragic Muse* was published in it.

Alexander, Sir George (1858–1918). English actor, born in Reading and first appeared as an amateur in London in 1875. Sir Henry Irving* hired him (1881) and took him on tour to the United States (1884). Alexander became a successful theater manager (from 1890). In "A Poor Play Well Acted" James comments that Alexander "acts with abundant zeal and care" but "neglects the realities of the part" he takes; in "The Acting in Mr. Irving's *Faust*" (*Century Magazine*, Dec 1887), James dismisses Alexander as "insignificant." James attended the first performance of *Lady Windermere's Fan* (1892), by Oscar Wilde,* with Alexander playing Lord Windermere. In July 1893, James sent Alexander his *Guy Domville* and ideas for two more plays. The actor-manager quickly accepted the first play and responded satisfactorily to James's quibbles about terms. In the ensuing year and a half, James became enthusiastic but then apprehensive, as *Guy Domville* went into rehearsal. Alexander produced and starred in the title role of the drama, beginning on 5 January 1895, with disastrous results. James wrote to his brother William (4 Feb [1895]) that "Alexander . . . *is* atrocious. His whole treatment of, and attitude to, the *material* of the part was, from the first, fatal—portentous to me in its gross want of perception of the intentions delicacies and atmosphere, of the character generally." Still, some years later, James permitted passages from *Guy Domville* to be published in *The George Alexander Birthday Book* (London: Lane, 1903).

Alger, William Rounseville (1822–1905). Popular New England Unitarian theologian, biographer, essayist, and literary critic. In 1865 two of his children died, and Alger traveled extensively in Europe for solace, during which time he met and was helpful to William Dean Howells* in Venice. In 1871 a mental collapse debilitated Alger to a degree for the remainder of his life. His 1868 book *The Friendship of Women* James promptly reviewed (*Nation*, 26 Dec 1867), calling the author sentimental, optimistic, and uncritical, but with a "generous interest in the idiosyncrasies and pursuits of women." James criticizes Alger's comments on "Mesdames de Staël, Récamier, [Anne Sophie] Swetchine[*], etc." for lacking any satirical thrust, but he calls the book courageous, given our "cynical . . . days." In 1881 James, while visiting his parents in Cambridge, Massachusetts, declined an invitation extended to him by Alger's daughter Abby Langdon Alger to speak at her club. In 1915 James wrote an essay on Benoît Constant Coquelin* as an introduction to Coquelin's *Papers on Acting: Art and the Actor*, translated by Abby Alger. James's characterizations of both the Rev. Mr. Benjamin Babcock of *The American* and the Rev. Mr. Brand of *The Europeans* may owe something to William Rounseville Alger.

"Allen D. Loney—In Memoriam." Tribute James wrote for the New York *Times* (12 Sep 1915) in memory of Allen D. Loney.*

Allen, Elizabeth Ann Akers (née Chase). Woman who wrote under the name of Elizabeth Akers.*

Allen, Mrs. In "The Patagonia," the Mavises' neighbor in Boston.

Almond, Elizabeth. In *Washington Square*, Dr. Austin Sloper's sister and Jefferson Almond's wife.

Almond, Jefferson. In *Washington Square*, prosperous New York merchant and Dr. Austin Sloper's brother-in-law.

Almond, Marian. In *Washington Square*, daughter of Jefferson and Elizabeth Almond.

Alsager. In "Nona Vincent," husband of Mrs. Alsager.

Alsager, Mrs. In "Nona Vincent," Allen Wayworth's adviser and financial support. Her gentle nature owes something to the personality of James's friend Lady Florence Eveleen Eleanore Bell.*

"The Altar of the Dead." Short story (13,100 words), published in *Terminations*, 1895; revised and reprinted in *The Novels and Tales of Henry James*, Volume XVII, 1909. (Characters: Mary Antrim, Kate Creston, Paul Creston, Mrs. Paul Creston, Acton Hague, George Stransom.) Aging George Stransom loved Mary Antrim, whose death has inspired him to make a religion of remembering his dead at a spiritual altar. He reads of the death of the brilliant, evil Acton Hague, a whilom friend who once hurt him grievously. One gray London day, Stransom walks to a Catholic chapel and lights candles for all his dead except Hague. Later he meets and talks with a mourning woman never named at "his" chapel. When he calls on her, he sees Hague's picture. She explains that, although Hague wronged her, she can forgive him. Since Stransom cannot, Hague splits the two survivors. After a time, Stransom, now dying, goes to his altar again and senses that Mary's spirit infuses him with a desire to forgive. Dying, he turns and sees the other woman, who has come for his sake. One added candle Stransom feels is Hague's, but the woman regards it as his. This requiem-like story concerning Jamesian reverence for the dead suggests James's awareness of the superior sensitivity of women, poetizes on the necessity to forgive, and posits the interpenetration of religion and art in the beautiful realm of silence. In a letter to Annie Adams Fields* (26 Jan 1892), James laments the fact that his essay on James Russell Lowell,* recently dead, did little to make others remember the man; then he generalizes: "In London, at least, the waves sweep dreadfully over the dead—they drop out and their names are unuttered." Two years later, his friend Constance Fenimore Woolson* died. He may have been partly motivated to write "The Altar of the Dead" as an allegorical little memorial to both of these people. Notebook entries (29 Sep; 2, 24 Oct 1894) leading to the story show that James progressed from the idea of a mental altar, to a physical altar, to a Catholic altar. But he grew displeased with what he called his " 'conceit,' after all," his "little fancy which doesn't hold a great deal," and "put it by" for a time. By the time he wrote the preface to Volume XVII of *The Novels and Tales of Henry James*, he says of "The Altar of the Dead," perhaps uncandidly, that he cannot remember "the influences attending its birth"; goes on to say that its subject is the "cultivated habit . . .

of regularly taking thought'' of ''the lost Dead''; and records his anguish when on two occasions acquaintances were not thought worth talking or writing about, because they were dead. Incredibly, James could not place this glorious fable in any magazine for serial publication.

Altemura, Contessa. In ''The Aspern Papers,'' a supposedly high-society former friend of the Bordereaus.

Altsheler, Joseph Alexander (1862–1919). Journalist, in Kentucky and then in New York, and popular historical novelist. James briefly comments in ''American Letter'' (28 May 1898) on Altsheler's *A Soldier of Manhattan* (1897), regarding it as dangerously cast in the past. He goes on to complain that historical fiction is ''drench[ing]'' us now. It is difficult for historical novels to remake the reader's ''consciousness.''

Amanda. In ''Georgina's Reasons,'' the maid of Georgina Gressie's parents, Mr. and Mrs. Gressie.

The Ambassadors. Novel (147,600 words), published in the *North American Review* (Jan–Dec 1903); revised and reprinted in London by Methuen, 1903, and in New York by Harper, 1903; revised and reprinted in *The Novels and Tales of Henry James*, Volumes XXI, XXII, 1909. (Characters: Baptiste, Miss Barrace, John Little Bilham, François, Gloriani and Mme. Gloriani, Maria Gostrey, M. de Montbron, Mr. and Mrs. Munster, Mrs. Abel Newsome, Chadwick Newsome, Jim Pocock, Sarah Newsome Pocock, Mamie Pocock, Lewis Lambert Strether, Mrs. Lewis Lambert Strether, Strether, Jeanne de Vionnet, Comtesse Marie de Vionnet, Comte de Vionnet, Waymarsh, Mrs. Waymarsh.) In England, on his way to Paris to rescue Chad, the son of his widowed fiancée, Mrs. Newsome, from some woman or other, Lambert Strether first meets Maria Gostrey, another American, long a resident in Paris. Once across the English Channel, Strether sees Chad again and notes much improvement in the brash young ''pagan,'' whose friend Little Bilham assures Strether that Chad's attachment is virtuous. At sculptor Gloriani's garden party, Strether meets lovely Madame Marie de Vionnet, who is estranged from her reportedly brutal husband and is the mother of sweet young Jeanne. Wondering whether Chad loves Marie or Jeanne, Strether begins to delight in lolling about in vernal Paris. He delays so much that Chad's impatient mother dispatches as new ambassadors her daughter Sarah Pocock, Sarah's common husband Jim, and his gentle sister Mamie Pocock, whom almost everyone wishes Chad to marry once he returns home to the thriving family business. Strether learns that Jeanne is to wed an eligible young Frenchman, urges Chad to remain in sophisticated France, and tries to get Bilham to marry Mamie, who rather likes the young man. When Sarah reports for duty, she viciously criticizes Marie, denies seeing any improvement in Chad, and begins to tour about in Paris and beyond. Feeling self-sacrificial,

Strether one lonely Sunday takes a train into rural France and by mere chance sees Chad and Marie weekending together. Strether later tries to mitigate Marie's continuing embarrassment and her fear of losing Chad, beseeches that cool young man never to desert his generous beloved, and confides a final time in Maria Gostrey (in Paris all this while) that despite her manifest interest in him he must return from his foreign mission without personal gain. *The Ambassadors* is generally regarded as a triumph of the Jamesian restricted point of view, since we learn pretty much only as stimuli impinge on Strether, register in his consciousness, and are relayed to the reader. Further, Maria Gostrey is an outstanding example of James's employment of the *ficelle* technique. Another brilliant touch is James's characterization of Mrs. Abel Newsome, who is intelligent, influential, massive—but is never encountered directly by the reader. Ambiguity pervades the novel because of various permissible definitions of what Little Bilham calls "a virtuous attachment," that is, Chad's relationship with Marie de Vionnet. Chiasmus is featured: In subtle ways, Strether experiences the process of becoming sophisticated like Chad, whereas our opinion of that young man retrogresses to something resembling our notion of initially inept Strether. In some ways, Marie de Vionnet is James's most wondrous heroine. To many critics, the centerpiece of the novel is jewel-like Paris—"what seemed all surface one moment seemed all depth the next." Unanswered questions concern Chad's future conduct and Strether's reasons for not accepting what amounts to a proposal from Miss Gostrey. James used language from his 1872 travel essay "Chester" in describing Strether's visit to that charming city in the first chapter of the novel. James places Marie de Vionnet's Parisian residence on the Rue de Bellechasse, which he knew well, because his friend Alphonse Daudet,* the French novelist, lived and entertained James there. Further, when James sent the young photographer Alvin Langdon Coburn* to Paris to shoot a street scene, he recommended the Rue de Bellechasse as a possible locale. According to James's Notebook entry (31 Oct 1895), the inspiration for this novel came when Jonathan Sturges* told him that William Dean Howells,* lamenting in the Parisian garden of James Abbott McNeill Whistler,* had urged him to live all he could, since it was a mistake not to. Strether passionately adjures Little Bilham to do so, in almost identical words, in Gloriani's Parisian garden. James wrote a 20,000-word "Project of Novel (1 September 1900)" for what became *The Ambassadors*, showed it to his agent James Brand Pinker,* and then sent it to Harper, the New York publisher of this work. Not closely following his scenario, James made Strether more imaginative and also more conscience-stricken, wrong in judging the nature of Chad's intimacy with Marie, and subsequently betrayed. In the preface to Volume XXI of *The Novels and Tales of Henry James*, James calls *The Ambassadors*, "frankly, quite the best, 'all round,' of my productions." He touches on its source—"a thing or two said . . . by a man of distinction . . . in Paris . . . in a charming old garden attached to a house of art." James's task was to find a big subject to wrap around what was said about living all one can, then to lead his hero to his outburst. James must send his provincial American to Paris, that "most interesting of great cities," in which "people's moral scheme *does* break down." He mentions several theoretical considerations: making Mrs. Newsome present while absent, not allowing Strether to be the first-person "historian" (through James's chronic dislike of "the terrible *fluidity* of self-revelation"), the creation of "a confidant or two" for him, Maria Gostrey as *ficelle* ("the reader's friend" and source of information), the danger of and "deviation" from one's original plan, the introduction of Chad, Mamie's "suspense," and the counterpointing of the "representational" and the "scenic" to augment "intensity." In a letter to Fanny Prothero, the wife of Sir George Walter Prothero* (14 Sep 1913), James offered two lists of five of his novels he would recommend to a new reader; interestingly, *The Ambassadors* was on only "the more 'advanced' " list.

Amber, Blanche. In *The Reprobate*, Bonsor's niece, who likes his ward Paul Doubleday more than she does her uncle's pompous friend Pitt Brunt.

Amber, Mrs. In "The Patagonia," the Mavises' neighbor in Boston.

Ambient, Beatrice. In "The Author of Beltraffio," the unsympathetic wife of Mark Ambient. She withholds medicine from their dying son so that the boy will not grow up and read Mark's allegedly decadent novels.

Ambient, Dolcino. In "The Author of Beltraffio," the delicate little son of Mark and Beatrice Ambient, and the victim of their animosity.

Ambient, Gwendolyn. In "The Author of Beltraffio," Mark Ambient's sister, who is pre-Raphaelitesque in appearance.

Ambient, Mark. In "The Author of Beltraffio," a gifted novelist whose wife dislikes his writings. The characters of the Ambients are based partly on John Addington Symonds* and his wife.

The American. Novel (136,700 words), published in the *Atlantic Monthly* (Jun 1876–May 1877); revised and reprinted in Boston by Osgood, 1877, and in London by Ward, Locke, 1877; revised and reprinted in *The Novels and Tales of Henry James*, Volume II, 1907. (Characters: Rev. Mr. Benjamin Babcock, Blanche de Bellegarde, Mme. Emmeline Atheling de Bellegarde, Marquis Henri-Urbain de Bellegarde, Marquis Urbain de Bellegarde, Mme. Urbain de Bellegarde, Comte Valentin de Bellegarde, Princess Borealska, Catherine Bread, Comtesse Claire de Bellegarde de Cintré, M. and Mme. Dandelard, Lord Deepmere, Dora Finch, M. de Grosjoyeux, C. P. Hatch, Stanislas Kapp, Ledoux, Duchesse de Lusignan, Christopher Newman, Noémie Nioche, Nioche, Mme. d'Outreville, General Packard, Mme. Robineau, Count and Countess de la Rochefidèle, Lord Earl of Saint Dunstans, Lizzie and Tom Tristram, Kitty Upjohn.)

Christopher Newman, a rich, retired Civil War veteran, comes to Paris in 1868, first meets an unscrupulous copyist, Noémie Nioche, who is busy daubing canvas at the Louvre, and then allows Lizzie Tristram, the wife of an old friend now living in Paris, to find him a suitable wife—the best that money can buy. Lizzie introduces him to Claire de Cintré, a lovely, young French widow. Her mother Madame de Bellegarde and her older brother Urbain de Bellegarde reluctantly let Newman court Claire, but, when Claire later agrees to marry the rich Yankee, the family orders her not to do so, because he is too commercial after all. Urbain's dashing younger brother Valentin de Bellegarde likes Newman and tries to help, but Valentin, who has met Noémie, is mortally wounded in a duel with Stanislas Kapp over her affections. While he is dying, Valentin voices his shame concerning his family's perfidy and tells his envied American friend that if he can learn about an old family secret (known by a servant named Mrs. Bread) he may be able by threat of exposure to pressure Madame de Bellegarde to relent. Newman learns from Mrs. Bread that Madame de Bellegarde murdered her husband; however, confronting her (and Urbain) with the incriminating evidence proves to be unavailing. Meanwhile, Claire has taken strict Catholic convent vows; Newman, sickened by everything but the warm memory of lost love, burns the evidence. This novel shows James at his early best in adapting for his own fictive needs a variety of literary inspirations, in this case, from Guillaume Victor Emile Augier,* Alexandre Dumas *fils*,* George Sand,* and Ivan Sergeyevich Turgenev.* Perhaps the most immediate influence was the 1876 play *L'Étrangère* by Dumas, in which Americans intruding into French society are caricatured. (The first name of the heroine in Dumas's play is Noémie.) James's hero Christopher Newman is likably naive and idealistic, but also gauche, cocksure, and opinionated—rather like a Mark Twain* "innocent abroad." James was right when he concluded in a letter to William Dean Howells* (30 Mar [1877]) that his hero and heroine would have been "an impossible couple, with an impossible problem before them." James was outraged when a German translation of *The American* appeared in Stuttgart in 1877, complete with a happy ending. He wrote to his brother William (28 Jun [1877]): "If those are your Germans I give them up." (Yet when James converted *The American* into a play, he gave it a happy ending.) *The American* is perhaps the earliest international novel on record, that is, an extended fictional study of the impingement of a representative national type on the culture of another nation, with a concomitant dramatizing of pride, prejudice, intrusion, adaptation, and exclusion. When in 1905 James began the task of revising many of his novels and short stories for what became *The Novels and Tales of Henry James*, he correctly saw that *The American* would be subjected to the most rewriting. He wrote to Chicago novelist Robert Herrick (7 Aug 1905), who had tactfully argued against any revising of works for a selected edition, to explain inaccurately that "[t]he retouching with any insistence will . . . bear but on one book (*The American* . . .)." In the preface to Volume II of *The Novels and Tales of Henry James*, he says that he planned from the start for Newman to turn away from revenge, with his bitterness yielding to aversion. James came to deplore the blatant romanticism of *The American* (the cable holding "[t]he balloon of experience . . . to the earth" must not be too obviously cut), felt that he had not presented Paris well, thought that the evil Bellegardes "would positively have jumped" to seize his rich American's money, and regretted not sufficiently showing Newman and Claire alone together.

The American: A Comedy in Four Acts. Dramatized version (originally to be called *The Californian*) of the 1877 novel *The American*, privately printed by William Heinemann,* 1891; and published in Philadelphia and New York by Lippincott, 1949, in *The Complete Plays of Henry James*, ed. Leon Edel. (Characters: Marquise Emmeline de Bellegarde, Marquis Urbain de Bellegarde, Comte Valentin de Bellegarde, Catherine Bread, Comtesse Claire de Bellegarde de Cintré, Comte de Cintré, Lord Deepmere, Gaston de Marignac, Christopher Newman, Noémie Nioche, Nioche.) In the Parisian home of Nioche and his daughter Noémie, three men come and go: Lord Deepmere, Valentin de Bellegarde (whom Noémie met earlier), and Christopher Newman (introduced by Nioche to Noémie at the Louvre). Newman now meets Valentin; liking each other, the two men agree to be sociable. When Newman learns about Valentin's widowed sister Claire de Cintré, he is doubly eager to visit the Bellegardes' fashionable residence. Several months later, Newman, a guest at a huge party given there by the Bellegardes, is accepted as Claire's suitor until Deepmere, just returned from England, reports on his extensive land holdings. Claire's ambitious mother now prefers Deepmere, who accordingly has a quarrel (partly over Noémie) with Valentin, after which they plan a duel. Next, Madame de Bellegarde and her older son Urbain call at Newman's newly purchased house in Paris, find Noémie hanging her copies of paintings there, and tell Newman that Claire will not wed him. Meanwhile, Valentin and Deepmere have dueled in Newman's garden. Wounded, Valentin tells Newman that Mrs. Bread knows a usable family secret, says farewell to Claire, who has been summoned, and dies. At the Bellegarde château in Fleurières, Claire, though in mourning and secretly planning to enter a convent, agrees to see Newman. From Mrs. Bread and with Marignac's help, he obtains a deathbed letter written by Madame de Bellegarde's husband: Emmeline withheld his medicine to cause his death and thus permit Claire's marriage to Emmeline's blackmailing lover Cintré. Claire agrees to see Newman, who shows her the sealed letter, hinting at its contents, which are unknown to her. She persuades him to give it to Urbain. When he does so, she agrees to marry him. To improve the somewhat somber play, James in 1892 wrote a new fourth act (some pages of which are now missing), which now takes place (as does the third act) in Newman's house rather than at Fleurières (as the original fourth act does). In the new fourth act, Newman tells Noémie that he wants Mrs. Bread to give him the letter. Noémie arranges through Deepmere for Claire to return from her convent (before she takes vows) so that she and Newman will meet again. Claire enters to see Valentin, now recovering after surgery. Mrs. Bread obeys Newman's request to appear. Feeling that Claire is lost to him, Newman wants revenge, tells Mrs. Bread that he has learned Madame de Bellegarde (not appearing here) caused the death ten years earlier not only of her husband but also of her lover/son-in-law Cintré, thus torturing Claire's conscience. Claire accepts Newman; Noémie, Deepmere. Edward Compton,* who first had the idea in 1889 of converting the novel into a play, opened with it in Southport, near Liverpool, on 3 January 1891, and then took it on tour. He opened in London on 26 September 1891; Compton, his sister-in-law Kate Bateman, and Elizabeth Robins* starred as Newman, Madame de Bellegarde, and Claire, respectively. The opening night was attended by the following, among others: William Archer,* Rhoda Broughton,* John Augustin Daly,* George du Maurier,* William James, Robert Todd Lincoln,* George Meredith,* Sir Arthur Wing Pinero,* John Singer Sargent,* George Frederick Watts,* and Constance Fenimore Woolson.* A few weeks later, the Prince of Wales (later to become King Edward VII*) also saw the play, which closed early in December. From the start, James was lukewarm about the project, and he seems to have proceeded with it only to make money. In a Notebook entry (12 May 1889), he says that "there is a play in it [the novel]. I must extract the simplest, strongest, baldest, most rudimentary, at once most humorous and most touching one, in a form whose main *souci* shall be pure situation and pure point combined with pure brevity. Oh, how it must not be too good and how very bad it must be!" James permitted a passage from *The American* to be published in *The Drama Birthday Book* (London: MacQueen, 1895), prepared by Percy S. Phillips.

"An American Art-Scholar: Charles Eliot Norton." Critical essay on Charles Eliot Norton,* published in *Burlington Magazine* (Jan 1909); reprinted in *Notes on Novelists*, 1914.

"American Letter." Any of a series of eleven "letters," usually brief, published in *Literature*, the precursor of the *Times Literary Supplement* (26 Mar–9 July 1898), in which James discusses (for $200 per month) critical problems and reviews current American publications, usually in groups. Letter of 26 March 1898: James laments the large sales figures of popular books in vast America, compared to the small number of real classics. He says that the English language homogenizes our varied populace and hence is in danger. Will the supply of books demanded by a "billion" readers ever include real literature? Perhaps authors will have to specialize and write for "individual publics." Writers for Puritan New England are giving way to Western authors. One day the American businessman will become a valid literary subject, not least because of his relations to women, who are his "link with civilization." Sadly, it is hard for one person not only to understand the world but then to depict it. American taste, writers, and readers are predominantly feminine. Letter of 9 April 1898: There are now so many American books that readers must be selective. James likes American fiction best when it is "most confined and most local"; note Hamlin Garland* and Mary Eleanor Wilkins (Freeman*). James deplores *American Wives and English Husbands* by Gertrude Franklin Atherton.* Letter of 16 April 1898: James reviews letters by Ulysses Simpson Grant,* the *Calamus* letters of Walt Whitman,* and *A Year from a Correspondent's Notebook* by Richard Harding Davis.* Letter of 23 April 1898: James reviews *American Ideals and Other Essays Social and Political* by Theodore Roosevelt,* *Essays on the Civil War and Reconstruction* by William Archibald Dunning,* and *The Workers* by Walter Augustus Wyckoff.* Letter of 30 April 1898: James wonders whether American fiction can be divided into schools having certain inclinations. In England, books are said to succeed, whereas in France authors are said to do so. What about the United States? One type of American novel is the satirical; recent examples are *The Celebrity* by Winston Churchill* and *His Fortunate Grace* by Gertrude Atherton. And then we have Bret Harte,* "the chief . . . " of "a 'school' " of "wild West" fiction. Letter of 7 May 1898: The advent of war makes James turn to recently published Civil War literature, including 1862–1864 letters by Walt Whitman to his mother and *Southern Soldier Stories* by George Cary Eggleston.* Then James adversely discusses *The Honorable Peter Sterling* by Paul Leicester Ford.* Letter of 21 May 1898: James turns to books concerned with "local history": *Story of the Palatines* by Sanford H. Cobb* and *The Coming People* by Charles F. Dole.* Then James briefly discusses *Literary Statesman and Others* by Norman Hapgood.* Letter of 28 May 1898: James treats three war novels. We are critically concerned only with how their subjects are treated. He mainly dislikes *Lorraine, a Romance* by Robert William Chambers,* *A Soldier of Manhattan* by Joseph Alexander Altsheler,* and *The General's Double* by Charles King,* especially the first two. Letter of 11 June 1898: Magazines, often too copiously illustrated, reflect more than newspapers do the American mind on the subject of literature. James gives many examples past and present. Too often, pictures overshadow the text. Then James comments on *Across the Everglades* by Hugh Laussat Willoughby,* *Cheerful Yesterdays* by Thomas Wentworth Storrow Higginson,* and *Emerson and Other Essays* by John Jay Chapman.* Letter of 25 June 1898: James devotes much time to *Unforeseen Tendencies of Democracy* by his friend, Edwin Lawrence Godkin,* more briefly considers *The Meaning of Education* by Nicholas Murray Butler,* then touches on three articles in the June *Atlantic Monthly* concerning education. Letter of 9 July 1898: The flood of recent American fiction includes two books, *The Juggler* by Charles Egbert Craddock,* and *The Durkett Sperret* by Sarah Barnwell Elliott,* which are written in dialect, a fact which gives James the opportunity both to praise and to criticize that technique. The last part of the essay is devoted to *Story of a Play* by William Dean Howells* and *Silence* by Mary Wilkins (Freeman).

The American Scene. A book of travel essays, some of which were published intermittently (with separate titles) in the *North American Review*, *Harper's Magazine*, and the *Fortnightly Review* (Apr 1905–Nov 1906); reprinted as parts of a book of fourteen chapters, including four new ones ("The Bowery and Thereabouts," "Concord and Salem," "Charleston," and "Florida"), in London by Chapman and Hall, 1907, and in New York by Harper, 1907. When James toured the United States from August 1904 to July 1905, he did so partly to write *The American Scene*. In it, he calls himself, variously, the "reinstated absentee," "repatriated absentee," "restored absentee," "brooding analyst," "fond critic," "incurable eccentric," "recent immigrant," "musing moralist," "initiated native," "earnest observer," "expatriated observer," "lone observer," "mooning observer," "painter of life," "intelligent pilgrim," "palpitating pilgrim," "pious pilgrim," "shuddering pilgrim," "excited sensibility," "revisiting spirit," "inquiring stranger," "student of manners," "brooding visitor," "earnest . . . visitor," and (dozens of times) "restless analyst." James's purpose is to rediscover, describe, and interpret his America after an absence of twenty-one years. (1) "New England: An Autumn Impression": The waterfront of New York which is repeatedly called "the terrible town," is squalid and barbarous but picturesque; James "surrender[s] to impressions." After Washington Square, which is a trap for memories, comes a trip by boat to "New York in *villeggiatura*" (i.e., New Jersey), with "featureless" roads, new houses, "German Jewry," barracks-like hotels, and "ample villas" speaking of crude new money. Then the "Arcadian" landscape of Chocorua, New Hampshire, with trees and water, and nature, as in Italy, "feminine": She asks to be lived with, not farmed. James comments on "the summer people," loose appearances, and the "abolition of *forms*." On to North Conway, by automobile, the "rural" Valley of the Saco ("brownness . . . as of liquid agate") and a Swiss-looking village; next morning, mountains, with unromantic names like "the smudge of a great vulgar thumb," a "brawling river," and a summering trio of young people too immodest to be anything but innocent. Cape Cod: an unforgettable "triumph of 'impressionism,' " with "evergreen boskage" and "brave wash of cobalt," but also with secretive "manners . . . most queer." James names many towns, then generalizes on the New England village—"verdurous" in summer, best in October, "fierce" in winter—with fine houses, steepled churches, trains, and "Umbrian" hills beyond. The people seem to lack "social and sensual margin, overflow and by-play," while beneath the surface are "crudity and levity," even the "darkness of Cenci-drama." In the "Alpine" Berkshires is New England's heart, happy and sad. A Shaker village has an "air of active, operative death." James wonders if New York state has any heart. By the Hudson River and near the Catskills are pleasant Dutch houses; then James thinks of Albany. Fresh perceptions tend to make him repudiate the stale past. Back to his "Boston neighbourhood": Cambridge and "the rustle of the trees," "expansive Harvard" now surrounded by a passion for money but still evoking tender memories. In the Law library he sees an unnamed old friend [John Chipman Gray*], but he does not walk over to speak to him. James goes to the Union, pauses before the incomparable John Singer Sargent* portrait of Henry Lee Higginson, then visits ship-like Alumni Hall (with Civil War tablets) and the Yard. Will the "ingenuous youths" swarming there help or hinder America's racial melting-pot process? American men seem more businesslike now; woman, "of . . . finer texture," perhaps helped by their men by indirection. James closes by remembering not Harvard football games, but "old Cambridge ghosts"—"robust" James Russell Lowell,* Henry Wadsworth Longfellow* (and his "tourist-haunted" home), and sympathetic, patient William Dean Howells.* (2) "New York Revisited": On approaching "extravagant" New York by the light-colored bay, James senses its prosaic, "dauntless power." Then the pin cushion and bouquet of "impudently" tall, traditionless, "money-making" buildings, eclipsing and "crushing" bits of beauty (such as Trinity Church, almost extinguished) in "felt" old New York. Observing the "poignant and unforgettable" Ellis Island drama "overhaul[s]" one's sense of national traditions and gives one a "sense of dispossession." James can escape from "the ubiquitous alien" only by a "backward reach" to his boyhood Washington Square and Fifth Avenue neighborhood. But its old walls have given way to new skyscrapers. He can visit the Church of the Ascension, with its John La Farge* mural (rare because New York prefers commercial light to aesthetic color), and even City Hall, an "elegant" building of "perfect taste and finish," which has been spared and in which he sees "florid ghosts," that is, portraits of former political leaders. James samples the "pandemonium" of the [old] Waldorf-Astoria (a "gilded and storied labyrinth," "a playhouse of the richest rococo"), its "frontal majesty" typical of cramped Manhattan so "meanly intersected" that it lacks squares and gardens, nooks and corners. The typical big American hotel is the "social, . . . aesthetic ideal" of gregarious promiscuity welcoming all but the poor and the disreputable. The forceful manager of such a hotel is like an orchestra leader, like a puppeteer. Outside on quiet streets again, James senses not only some beauty in "the terrible town," full of "blight"—it is a "compromised charmer"—but also much loyalty to it in himself, even as the derisively noisy traffic resembles rats and whirlwinds. Attempts here at urban renewal, unlike those in London, Paris, and Rome, sweep away the past (including "full sections of streets"), "gild the [new] temporary," and hence defeat history. James concludes by noting that the newly rich in New York are proud of themselves and vaguely amiable toward others. (3) "New York and the Hudson: A Spring Impression": New York seems unified (like a chain, a stew, a keyboard, a feast, a machine). Yet aliens are singular, not brotherly, although their children may be. James worries over the "*abracadabrant*" infusion of races here. Many aliens in warm New York corners form an "obstinate, . . . unconverted residuum." If various types of aliens make themselves so "at home" here, who is indeed the alien? In the streetcars, James feels like one even while breathing his "natal air." The American "white-wash" (later the image is the hot tub) takes away fine manners from some aliens (James specifies Italians, blacks, and Chinese here). Will the manners appear again? James muses on the "swarming . . . of Israel," of all ages, "burst[ing] all bounds" along the East Side. Though revering the intellect of Jews, he deplores "the Hebrew conquest of New York"; hates the fire escapes disfiguring "New Jerusalem" tenements; notes the "overtowering School"; fears that "the smaller fry" will be sacrificed to profiteering "[t]rusts and . . . monopolies"; and senses—judging from East Side café talk—that future American literature will not be written in his English. He turns for relief to the Hudson River and Riverside Drive, despite the "extemporized" tall buildings resembling the "jagged" teeth of a "broken hair-comb turned up" and the "enthroned" railway, alongside. He notes Columbia University, " 'moved up' " and "ampler" now, comments on the countryside retreating to the north, and inspects with pleasure Ulysses S. Grant's "naked" and "august" tomb one wintry morning. James takes a train later from the Far West through Buffalo ("character . . . sacrificed") and "antique" Albany, along the "luminous" Hudson, and indirectly to West Point. It is distinguished, stern to some, but shy too. Its position has "classical elegance." Its "type and tone" are painterly. Next he savors "the old-time charm and the general legendary fusion" of Sunnyside, the home of Washington Irving,* appreciated because it shows that "the man of letters of the unimproved age, the age of processes still comparatively slow, could have wanted no deeper, softer dell for mulling material over." We now have too much arrangement, too little leisure. Do we envy writers of those old times? They whisper "of a felicity forever gone." (4) "New York: Social Notes": James compares American houses bulldozed in the name of progress to "bewildered and stainless" young victims guillotined during the French Revolution. New York growth is especially wasteful because it does not "know . . . what to grow *on.*" Example: a glittering dinner party James attended, given for no occasion and followed by nothing. American women in tiaras see nothing in their men to curtsey to. Clubs, though hospitable, lack tradition, are too "empirical." James analyzes the "merciless" openness of American house and club interiors, lacking as they do privacy-ensuring walls and doors. New York society people are like children: unaware of the past, demanding, inattentive, unwilling to be criticized, destructive. Next James analyzes the statue by Augustus Saint-Gaudens* of William Tecumseh Sherman: It symbolizes not only desolation but also, ambiguously and wrongly here, a hope for peace. It stands at the Fifth Avenue entrance to Central Park, which James gratefully likens to a busy hostess, a unique actress, a small polyglot globe. He especially notes good shoes, healthy teeth, and ugly hats here, then walks away, thinking that the whole region is too new, "modern," and auction-like to have any history yet. Next he praises that Fifth-Avenue "Palladian pile" called the Tiffany Building and then that "inestimable . . . project," the new Public Library, properly seated rather than standing, and hence needing fewer elevators, those "packed and hoisted basket[s]." On to the "great exemplary" Presbyterian Hospital, with its "cool corridors" and "delicacy." Then to the new Metropolitan Museum, "a palace of art, . . . rearing itself with a radiance, yet offering you expanses to tread," with costly possessions teaching you "the sense of beauty." (5) "The Bowery and Thereabouts": James goes by elevated train "through . . . sinister over-roofed clangorous darkness" to the Bowery Theatre, full—as in the old days—of dust, tobacco juice, peanuts, orange peels, and other evidence of the Irish. Why is so much money spent on candy? The play was American, that is, "convention[al]" and hence did not teach its audience of foreigners anything about real America. James visits a Bowery beer cellar and then a soft-drink café, populated by people with ugly and fine faces, respectively. He also samples "a Yiddish comedy of manners" in "a small crammed convivial theatre," then an uptown, East Side Slavic restaurant with its arrogant "exotic boss," and finally a "nocturnal . . . bacchanal" with "booming orchestra" and flowers, at an address never to be disclosed. (6) "The Sense of Newport": Newport is still charming, also still impossible to describe or define. It is a place of sky, sea, and sunsets. It lies like the back of a delicate open hand waiting to be kissed, not turned over to see what is in it. It has been sadly filled with ugly, expensive things. It resembles the foreground of an engraving now superimposed on, or an "ancient surface" painted over, by cottages growing into palaces. One tries to recall "the valid . . . past"; the Old Town's streets, like timid, frugal old ladies; the jutting little promontory with verandahs and piers, boats in the sunset, the "Dutch dignity" of public buildings around the "sleepy" Parade. Entering a house he once knew, James senses "special ghosts on the staircase"; he takes a familiar cliff walk and recalls innocent, good-faith activities on "old lawns" and "old shining sands." That was during the time of "the ivory idol . . . leisure" and before the time of macadamized drives, "*blasé* . . . absent proprietors," and "the great black ebony god of business." Newport's old society has left no seed; it would, anyway, have been "trampled by the white elephants," that is, the big, ugly, present-day mansions which have "taken . . . over" Newport. (7) "Boston": James offers his impressions of Boston, despite having too many. Combining to give him a "pang of loss" are many changes, including some around Ashburton Place, his former home. The State House remains beautiful, but atop Beacon Hill he is disturbed by "a continuous passage of men and women," all "gross little aliens" not speaking English. He goes on to the Athenaeum, an "exquisite institution" overshadowed now by an ugly new building next to it. Park Street used to be "*honnête*" but now has loud little shops selling high-priced articles of low quality. Making conscience-salving money "is . . . the main American formula." If you do not make money, "America is no place for you." James admires the Park Street Church, a "happy landmark" with its thin spire, for continuing to hold the right note (despite its plain name) and asking only to be loved. He misses the old Museum Theatre, an item "of the 'great' period," but Mount Vernon Street is still "wandering up the hill . . . to . . . the State House," rather like "some good . . . lady . . . a little spent." Down on Charles Street, James recalls a certain drawing room [of James Thomas Fields* and his wife Annie Adams Fields*] which offered hospitality to many great writers, American and foreign. He deplores the monotonous residential expansion along Marlborough Street. The new Public Library says more about money and business than about "the old intellectual . . . or . . . moral sensibility." After glancing at the Augustus

Saint-Gaudens* monument to Robert Gould Shaw, James returns to his criticism of the library: It may have "tawny marble" like a palace in Florence, but it lacks "*penetralia*" and hence resembles a huge railway station. He rushes across Copley Square to "the rapidly-expanding Art Museum," the centerpiece of which is an Aphrodite head. He ends by praising "the wonderfully-gathered and splendidly-lodged [Isabella Stewart] Gardner[*] Collection," as an instance of traditional private Boston energy triumphant. (8) "Concord and Salem": The "identity" of Concord, "the biggest little place in America," is incomparably "palpable," with its history and " 'transcendental' company." The town is like an intelligent old woman, remembering everything as though it were still in the present. James notes the site of the battle of Concord, that "hinge . . . on which the large revolving future was to turn," and lingers by the "melancholy" river, "so irresistibly touching." The fallen heroes offer us more than they could have known. James is struck again by the small size of "historic site[s] in general." He compares "the 'Concord school' " of writers to that of Weimar. He likens Johann Wolfgang von Goethe* and Ralph Waldo Emerson* to gold, Johann Christoph Friedrich von Schiller and Henry David Thoreau to silver. Then he suggests that Emerson drew much inspiration from Concord's seasons and manners. On to Salem, where an Italian-born resident cannot direct James to the House of the Seven Gables; however, "a civil Englishman" helps out. The better houses are more "ample and charming" in "their preserved and unsophisticated state" than James remembers them from an earlier visit. But are they like "expensive toy[s], . . . too good to be used"? The Salem Witch House is old, and seeing old things in America makes us wonder when they will collapse. Hurrying past the wooden (hence "provisional") structure, James encounters a bright, shrill little boy who shows him the birthplace of Nathaniel Hawthorne* and a lane leading to a seven-gabled house. (9) "Philadelphia": The critic, analyst, "painter of life" must believe that places have "a mystic meaning" which he can "*make* a sense" of. Making sense as "*méridional*," flat, unbristling (unlike New York and Chicago), is Philadelphia, to which the "beguiling" Pennsylvania Railroad has carried James. "Philadelphia . . . was . . . a *society*," with "serenity," "consanguinity," "animated intimacy" (again, unlike certain other cities). It reaches directly back some centuries and thus has historical "consistency." There is a homogeneity of housing on slow-paced streets flattened down like "tough parchment." James suddenly hears of "political corruption," "organized . . . plunder and rapine," and he ponders the fact that it is all accepted with grand indifference, like "a skeleton at the banquet of life . . . gracefully veiled." James touches on the Quakers, their original gray "flush[ed]" a little by material success. They seem to be detachedly "dancing . . . on the thin crust of a volcano," like members of "an *ancien régime*." James likes and plays with this comparison. The city has his own "free vernacular." Our "historic past," a "lucky legacy," is in Philadelphia "in visible form." Independence Hall, a "symmetry of pink and drab," is totally "charming" and widely reflects its distinction. If the hall had been in New York, it would have been torn down to clear the land for skyscrapers. Its best feature is its "fine interior." James imagines the Declaration signing itself there. He reveres half-hidden Carpenters' Hall, too, and is then often reminded of crumple-faced, wittily smiling, all-presiding Benjamin Franklin. James discusses the implications of a winter soirée at the Pennsylvania Academy of Fine Arts. America combines "loud statistical shout[s]" and shyness. One "excrescence . . . on the general scene" is the "modern" state penitentiary (with "massive majesty," resembling "a sunny Club"), full of individually sequestered prisoners, with one of whom, "a charming reprieved murderer," James talks. Finally, he is a winter houseguest in the country. (10) "Baltimore": The winter is lingering, and James is happy to retrograde to the pagan South. He arrives in "amiable" Baltimore on a "lovely" day. All is peaceful, frictionless. A recollection of Maryland and the Civil War "brush[es]" past. He notes leafy rows of brick houses with door steps: All resembles "ladies seated, with their toes tucked-up on uniform foot-stools, under the shaded candlesticks of old-fashioned tea parties." All vice seems absent. The "ingenuous" is forceful in America; "propriety" is too. James feels like a guest in a house without a host. The Washington Monument thus resembles an "old-fashioned clock, a decorative 'piece,' an heirloom"; and time in the tepid South, near "the citronic belt," is slow. James is invited to see a "burnt district" in a commercial region, now being restored. The absence of tall buildings pleases his sense of manners. He trusts that a spirit of commerce is not hurting the love of culture at Johns Hopkins University, the hospital of which—even with its "chambers of woe"—weaves a poetic spell. James praises "the high beauty of applied science" in concerned America thus evidenced. Next he raves about "blest" country clubs as "a clear American felicity," as familially minimizing European-style "differences." He extols "the sweet old Carroll house," full of an "intimation of [family] 'annals,' " where "the past and the present were in friendliest fusion." (11) "Washington": May in Washington is a "lovely leafy moment." Nature repaints the whole scene. Mount Vernon is "exquisite," on its "sublime" site, suffused by George Washington's presence, and with "architectural interest and architectural nullity become one and the same." Here "the slight, pale, bleeding Past stands . . . taking the thanks of the bloated Present." The city, "bourgeois," flat, and perspective conscious, has two faces for James. One is "[i]mperial" ("public and official," even "monumental" and majestic, forceful, "in possession," but with few politicians permeating society); the other, "provisional" (painted, rather queer, with a sameness). The social city is conversational but talks only of itself. James finds diplomats "bland and . . . blank" here. There are, uniquely, no businessmen. American businessmen elsewhere are nothing but commercial, hence surrender other responsibilities to their women, who treat the "windfall . . . as perfectly normal." They constitute all of the social life. Men in Washington are beginning to see that life is not all business; "the particular male presence [Theodore Roosevelt*] supremely presiding there" now has "the interests of civilization" in his "masculine hands." But can men, beginning to return, ever "catch up" to their women? A newly struck balance between the sexes might make Washington "as good as 'Europe.' " Among the "salient . . . landmarks" are the White House, the Capitol, and especially the Library of Congress. It "glitters in . . . almost frivolous irrelevance of form"; "though money alone can gather in on such a scale the treasures of knowledge, these treasures, in the form of books and documents, themselves organize and furnish their world." The White House "appeal[s] to that musing and mooning visitor whose perceptions alone . . . I hold worthy of account." James notes the equestrian statue of Andrew Jackson, "as archaic as a Ninevite king, prancing and rocking through the ages." The new statues to the Marquis de Lafayette and the Comte de Rochambeau are tributes to "our old friendship with France." The whole federal city should make American voters proud, but to what end and to what expression? The Capitol is "a vast and many-voiced creation," "the hugest . . . of all the homes of debate," "a builded record of half the collective vibrations of a people." It also offers amusement, like St. Peter's in Rome. It has spittoons and "unassorted marble mannikins." It resembles "a motherly . . . Columbia" who chats about all her offspring. Also it is positioned "for 'raking' " the entire national scene and future. (12) "Richmond": James says that, as Europe became real for him, America, especially its South, turned romantic and mysterious for him. He remembers Richmond's part in the "holocaust" of the Civil War, but the city now looks "blank and void," a consequence of absurdly establishing a slave state (such "vanity and fatuity") in this world. Resultant sorrow should have created beauty here, just as California soil benefits from rain. But Richmond is merely "*weak*—'adorably' weak: that was the word into which the whole impression flowered." Slavery required the South to rewrite history and bowlderize books. James adverts to the South's "legacy of . . . ragged and rudimentary" blacks now "in possession of . . . rights." Back to the sights: the locale of "vanished" Libby prison, many hills, the Virginia State Capitol ("strange intellectual centre of the general [Confederate] enterprise"), the equestrian *Washington* by Thomas Crawford,* the Square ("shapeless"), Jefferson Davis's wartime residence, an odd absence of churches (as well as of legends). James does find "sanctified" but "ugly" mementos ("sorry objects," all) of the bloody past in the Confederate Museum, presided over by "a little old lady" with "thoroughly 'sectional' good manners." The place should have been bigger, given the collapse of such a cause. He chats with an unreconstructed son of a Confederate combat veteran. James, who admires public libraries (their riches compare favorably to all things material in America), finds Richmond's "disprovincializing" city library "flushing with colour and resource, with confidence and temperament." Finally, he finds the statue of Robert E. Lee masterly in style (it was executed by Marius Jean Antonin Mercié in France), its subject handsome, even noble, but presiding indifferently over desolation, and all suggestive of "a lost cause . . . that could never have been gained." (13) "Charleston": After spending "a week in a castle of enchantment" [the Biltmore House of George Washington Vanderbilt* near Asheville, North Carolina], which is proof that someone cared to improve "the dreary land," James takes a long, unsociable train ride through "bland air" to Charleston and engages a "saloon-like apartment" in a hotel. Outside, in the "warm and radiant" day, the South smiles at him, but lifelessly, like a pretty corpse. James's anticipated friend [Owen Wister*] arrives and soon holds up Charleston's charms as out of a not very full "grab-bag." They visit the Battery (with its guns, live oaks, moss, and palmettos), note the distant forts, muse on the Civil War "folly" registered there, and sense "softness" (even femininity) now all about, also "social shrinkage and . . . economic blight." James images Charleston as a toothless, clawless lioness. He comments on luncheon rooms, antebellum homes, and the marshy old Charleston cemetery. Does the South have "to be tragic . . . in order to beguile"? He closes by admiring "the bright south wall of St. Michael's Church," part of a fine canvas for spring to embroider. (14) "Florida" is James's last, slowly achieved stop. The topics along the way are black servants' inefficiency, traveling salesmen's talkativeness, big breakfasts, and immodestly ill-mannered young people (especially "uncorrected" girls in Savannah's railroad station). James samples Jacksonville on "a Southern night . . . I had dreamed of" but in a "public garden" which is "new and scant and crude." From Jacksonville by tiresome train to Palm Beach, all was one "dense cypress swamp," and James recalls *The War Trail*, the Florida adventure novel (1857) by Mayne Reid, to pass the time. A "famous" Palm Beach hotel closes its "shining crystal walls" about him with an indescribably pleasant effect. James expatiates on "the hotel-spirit" evinced here in "the great, glittering caravansery." Do guests here, "partaking" of "things . . . too good for their context," become supercilious? James says that the Royal Poinciana Hotel is "the biggest thing of its sort in the world," that "nothing but the processional outline of Windsor Castle . . . could appear to march with it," that it boasts an "insolence of flame-coloured flower and golden fruit," and that it imposes "the standard, . . . teaching the affluent . . . how to 'garden,' how, in fact, to tidy up its 'yard.' " America would have "the space and the freedom" to dictate "the future of beauty" itself but for taste, which they desire but lack. Palm Beach is "Vanity Fair in full blast—and Vanity Fair not scattered, not discriminated and parcelled out, as among the comparative privacies and ancientries of Newport, but compressed under one vast cover, enclosed in a single huge *vitrine* . . . " Adjacent is a fruity jungle into which James can briefly bicycle. He also visits an ambrosial ranch on nearby fresh-water Lake Worth. Back at the region of hotels (including the old Breakers), he analyzes the moneyed ambience of the unromantic, indistinguishable boarders. "Was it they who had invented it, or had it inscrutably invented them?" James pursues them to spectacular shops, watches them drink "strange, sweet iced liquidities," and concludes that they are too uniform a type to be "a discussable quantity." A near exception might be the successful businessmen. The women fail to tease his imagination. The young, especially the girls, are on exhibition, like "goldfish in a crystal jar." On up to St. Augustine, where he concludes that the "pictorial 'hankey-pankey' " of black-and-white illustrations of Florida's Spanish past are phony. The moral is that "when you haven't what you like you must . . . misrepresent . . . what you have." Further, "novelists improvise, with the aid of the historians, a romantic local past." The Ponce de Leon Hotel is remarkable, Moorish in style, and fun. James meditates in the empty old Spanish fort, by the shore, and on the thinness of the Spanish legend thereabouts. But Florida still pleases him. In retrospect, he sees it (and later California) as older than the Nile region because of a lack of history. In a final section of *The American Scene* (omitted from the American edition but appearing in the English one), James asks America why its "hugeness . . . [is] a ground for complacency" and what America is making of that hugeness. Is there "charm . . . in the solitude you have ravaged"? America plants ugliness in "the great lonely land" and then brags with unique cynicism. The damage can never be undone, the lost beauty never retrieved. America has become a vast floor for a devil's dance. In his preface to *The American Scene*, James says that he would "go to the stake" for the impressions recorded in his book, further, that he had returned to America in 1904–1905 only to gather them. James chose the title he did after first deciding against *The Return of the Native,* because Thomas Hardy* had used it, and then abandoning *The Return of the Novelist* as a title. Late in 1905 he was planning a second volume, on his travels to the Far West, but he never composed it. James wrote to his literary agent James Brand Pinker* (5 May 1907) to complain of his American publisher's "real *mutilation* of my volume": The final section and the right-page headlines, all carefully provided, had been silently omitted.

"The American Volunteer Motor-Ambulance Corps in France." War essay, published in pamphlet form in London by Macmillan, 1914, and shortened and reprinted as "Famous Novelist Describes Deeds of U.S. Motor Corps," New York *World* (4 Jan 1915); reprinted in *Within the Rim and Other Essays: 1914–1915,* 1919. James praises Richard Norton, the son of his friend Charles Eliot Norton,* for organizing the American ambulance corps in France and describes how the drivers transport the wounded and sick, and sometimes civilian refugees, to hospitals and railroad stations for attention. He also praises the bravery of the French women who aid them. He mentions the specific evacuation of 400 wounded, he appeals to doctors to volunteer, he discusses the means of identifying the dead, he criticizes the Germans for committing atrocities, and he closes by asking for donations in the name of "pride and pity."

"Americans Abroad." Travel essay, published in the *Nation* (3 Oct 1878). James says that only Americans would think of discussing their behavior abroad. Other national groups would be either unaware of or indifferent to any impressions they might collectively make away from home. Plenty of Americans are in Europe now, as vacationers or residents, and they are regarded as alien, innocent, vulgar, and rough. Our motives for traveling are misunderstood. We combine self-consciousness and "unsuspectingness." We are patronized by Europeans, who are usually ignorant of the vastness of America.

Amerigo, Prince. In *The Golden Bowl*, Princess Maggie Verver's husband, Adam Verver's son-in-law, and Charlotte Stant's lover. Ultimately he returns to his wife.

Amicia. In "After the Play," the fellow playgoer in London with Auberon, Dorriforth, and Florentia. Amicia, who liked the play they saw in Soho, is a rather agreeable socialite.

Ampère, André-Marie (1775–1836). French mathematician, scientist, linguist, professor (of physics and chemistry, at Bourg), and inventor; born near Lyons. His father was guillotined during the French Revolution. The ampere was named after André-Marie. Jean-Jacques Ampère (1800–1864), his son, was a philologist, essayist, poet, literary historian, travel writer, and professor (of French literary history). Born in Lyons, he traveled in northern Europe, Scandinavia, Africa, Greece, Italy, and North America (retracing in 1851 some of the steps of his close friend Alexis de Tocqueville). Under the title of "The Two Ampères," James reviewed (*Galaxy*, Nov 1875; reprinted in *French Poets and Novelists*, 1878) *Journal et Correspondance de André-Marie Ampère*, 1875, and *André-Marie Ampère et Jean-Jacques Ampère: souvenirs et correspondance*, 1875. James notes Jean-Jacques's friendship with de Tocqueville and adds that Jean-Jacques was so versatile that he "sacrificed erudition to observation" and vice versa, but that his letters were wonderfully self-revealing and also depict a society that "has pretty well passed away." He never married but he knew Madame Récamier (from 1820) and then Madame L— (from 1853). Then the review turns to Jean-Jacques's "profoundly simple" genius of a father, André-Marie, whose courtship of, and marriage to, Julie Carron, James lovingly dwells on as "redolent of youthful freshness." He quotes from family papers, including letters of Julie's peppy sister Elise; her words "make . . . the dead things of the past live again." Separated by his work, André-Marie and Julie correspond touchingly, until her death in 1803. James soon turns to their son Jean-Jacques: He was reared "in an atmosphere of learning and morality," associated with that "social sovereign" Madame Récamier in France and Italy, wrote inept tragedies, sent his sweetly sagacious beloved letters of no "salient points," naively aspired to " 'universal knowledge,' " traveled to Germany (where he met Barthold Georg Niebuhr and Johann Wolfgang von Goethe*) and then to Scandinavia. James, seeming to tire, slights the third volume and abruptly ends his review. James's library contained one book by Jean Ampère.

Amy. In *Watch and Ward*, Rev. Mr. Hubert Lawrence's fiancée.

Anatole, M. and Mme. In "Rose-Agathe," Rose-Agathe's barber-owner and his wife.

Andersen, Hendrik Christian (1872–1940). Norwegian-American sculptor, distantly related to Hans Christian Andersen. Born in Bergen, he was taken to America in 1873 and grew up in Newport, Rhode Island. Andersen studied art and architecture in Boston, Paris, Naples, and Rome. He specialized in idealistic, biblical, and athletic statuary. He was working in Rome when James met him there in 1899, in the studio of American sculptor John Elliott. (Elliott was the husband of Maud Howe Elliott,* daughter of Julia Ward Howe* and cousin of Francis Marion Crawford.*) James bought a small bust of an Italian boy by Andersen for $250 and had it shipped to Lamb House. In a tender, flattering letter to the sculptor (19 Jul 1899), he called the work "admirable and exquisite." Andersen visited James for a few days later in the summer of 1899. When he left, James wrote to offer him studio room in his Rye property. In many later letters, James touchingly sought affection: "my dear boy, . . . I hold out to you . . . a pair of tightly-grasping, closely-drawing hands" (4 May 1901); "I shall, at the station take very personal possession of you" (13 Sep 1901); "I return to Rye . . . to *have* you there and do for you [after the death of Andersen's brother], to put my arm around you and *make* you lean on me as on a brother and a lover . . . " (9 Feb 1902); "please feel now . . . that I lay my hands on you and draw you close to me" (30 Apr 1903); and "I want . . . to catch you in my arms" (10 Aug 1904). The two men were together again in Newport during James's 1904–1905 tour of the United States. James met members of Andersen's family. He occasionally criticized Andersen's statues, often after merely examining photographs of them, as in "I sometimes finds your sexes . . . not quite intensely enough differentiated" (20 Jul 1906); he called Andersen's ridiculous plans for a world city "this culmination of your madness" (14 Apr 1912). But more often he wrote in this vein of the mediocre artist: "I wonder at you and am proud of you, and send up hosannas and hymns of praise to the skies" (31 May 1906). In Rome in 1907, James sat to Andersen for a bust. Later, James wrote sadly, "I so hold out my arms to you. Somehow it may still come—but it seems far off. Well, may life still be workable for you" (16 Aug 1911); then "[i]f you can come to Paris can't you come on to London?" (2 Jan 1912). Toward the end, James properly dismissed Andersen's pretentious world-city statuary: "you appear to have forgotten the impression I tried . . . to give you . . . ; for you urge me again as if I . . . had uttered no warning. . . . Reality, . . . the seeing of things as they *are* . . . come back to that with me, and then, even now, we can talk!" (4 Sep 1913). The two men drifted apart. It may be that Andersen, hoping vainly for more professional aid from James, became a frustrated opportunist and turned considerably indifferent.

Anderson, Mary Antoinette (1859–1940). California-born actress, whose father was a Confederate Army officer in the Civil War who died in 1863. Anderson was educated as a Roman Catholic and first appeared professionally, as a notable young beauty, in a theater in Louisville, Kentucky, at the age of sixteen. Her roles, partly in London (from 1883), included Shakespearean parts. Anderson retired from the stage in 1889, and a year later in England she married Antonio Fernando de Navarro,* a friend of James. The couple resided in Broadway, Worcestershire. She returned to the stage briefly during World War I to participate in fund drives. She published *A Few Memories* (1896) and *A Few More Memories* (1936, as Mary Anderson de Navarro); in the latter, she commented on James with great affection. Her professional success in London was the inspiration for *Miss Bretherton* (1884) by Mrs. Mary Augusta Ward* and therefore indirectly contributed to James's portrayal of Miriam Rooth in *The Tragic Muse*. James knew and admired both Mary and Antonio de Navarro, and their little boy. In letters to "dear Tony," he called Mary "your matchless mate" ([27 Feb 1899]) and "radiant mother" (1 Nov 1905).

"An Animated Conversation." Critical essay or sketch, with dialogue, published in *Scribner's Magazine* (Mar 1889); reprinted in *Essays in London and Elsewhere*, 1893. (Characters: Belinda, Belwood, Camilla, Clifford, Darcy, Oswald.) This is a tedious, confusing sketch by James in dialogue form, with six characters, in London one November, discussing literature, the reading public, cosmopolitanism, and copyright laws. Belinda, the brilliant, feisty American hostess, feels that men and women need not be hostile to each other, but she is occasionally bothersome herself. Belwood, who is British, likes easygoing women and blames the newspapers for fomenting national antagonisms. Camilla is "artless"; she lives in Paris with her husband Oswald, and she wants someone to recommend a "nice" novel for her to read. Clifford is British, unanalytical, and prejudiced. Darcy is an observant American critic; he is optimistic about the congeniality of the sexes, figures that America and England should minimize their differences to "make life larger and the arts finer," and explains as inevitable the distinctions between American and British English—given America's vastness and democratic institutions. Oswald (Camilla's husband) is an American painter in Paris, which he praises as a locus of ideas, and says that British novels are all right for little girls.

Antrim, Mary. In "The Altar of the Dead," altar-tending George Stransom's deceased but unforgotten love.

Antrobus, Charlotte. In "The Point of View," the daughter of Edward and Susan Antrobus.

Antrobus, Edward, M.P. In "The Point of View," a British politician traveling in America and writing home adversely about almost everything he sees.

Antrobus, Gwendolyn. In "The Point of View," the daughter of Edward and Susan Antrobus.

Antrobus, Susan. In "The Point of View," Edward Antrobus's wife and the recipient of his letters from America.

Anvoy. In "The Coxon Fund," Ruth Anvoy's father. He suffers financial reverses and soon dies.

Anvoy, Ruth. In "The Coxon Fund," Lady Coxon's American niece, whose scrupulous management of the Coxon Fund prevents her from marrying George Gravener.

April, Rev. Mr. and Mrs. In "The Siege of London," the clergyman at the Desmesne family estate at Longlands and his wife.

Archdean, Captain and Mrs. In "Hugh Merrow," the attractive husband and wife who ask Hugh Merrow to paint them a portrait of a child they never had and can never have. Hesitant at first, he agrees.

Archer, Isabel. In *The Portrait of a Lady*, the attractive, lithe heroine who when orphaned is sponsored from America to England by her Aunt Lydia Touchett and is then bequeathed a fortune by her Uncle Daniel Tracy Touchett. She and her cousin Ralph Touchett grow very fond of one another, but his chronic and eventually fatal sickness disqualifies him from marriage. Isabel rejects proposals of marriage by Caspar Goodwood, a rich American, and Lord Warburton, a handsome Britisher. She unfortunately marries Gilbert Osmond instead and is stifled. She befriends Gilbert's daughter Pansy.

Archer. In *The Portrait of a Lady*, the convivial, liberal, traveling father of Isabel Archer; he is now deceased.

Archer, Lilian. In *The Portrait of a Lady*, the maiden name of Lilian Archer Ludlow.

Archer, William (1856–1924). British drama critic, translator of works by Henrik Johan Ibsen,* and author—among other plays—of the popular melodrama *The Green Goddess* (1923). Archer summered with Norwegian relatives, learned their language, gave up law in 1875 for journalism, and spent a year in Australia. When he returned to London in 1878, he became a drama critic, wrote a book antagonistic toward the acting style of Sir Henry Irving* (1883), began to promote the cause of Ibsen (whom he met in Rome in 1881), and started making excellent translations (published by William Heinemann*) of his work in 1888. In his 1888 essay on Robert Louis Stevenson,* James calls Archer's essay on Stevenson

(*Time*, Nov 1885) "gracefully and ingeniously turned" even as it wrongly deprecates its subject. James and his sister Alice were both upset by Archer's comments on *The American*, James's play, when it opened in Southport, near Liverpool, on 3 January 1891. Archer also attended its London opening, on 26 September 1891, but was then more complimentary. James was distressed when Archer turned critical of some 1891 work by James's friend Sir Edmund Wilson Gosse* on the subject of Scandinavian literature. (A year later, however, Archer and Gosse collaborated on a translation of Ibsen's *The Master Builder*.) Archer praised James's essay on Ibsen (*New Review*, Jun 1891) but cautioned the novelist to see symbolism rather than realism in Ibsen. James was puzzled by Archer's approval of certain plays by Oscar Wilde.* Archer was favorably disposed toward James's disastrously received play *Guy Domville*, of which he attended the first performance, in London, on 5 January 1895. James did not know that Archer was a secret lover of his actress friend Elizabeth Robins.* In "London" (6 Feb 1897), James mentions Archer's 1897 translation of Ibsen's *John Gabriel Borkman*; in "London" (24 Apr 1897), he takes as his "capital text" Archer's essay "The Blight on the Drama" (*Fortnightly Review*, 1 Jan 1897). In 1903 Archer and Harley Granville Granville-Barker,* whom James knew, sought to found a national theater.

Armiger, Rose. In *The Other House*, the novel, the stern object of Dennis Vidal's affections. Loving Anthony Bream instead, she drowns his baby daughter Effie Bream to free him from a curious vow. After the cover-up of the murder, she goes away after all with Vidal. In *The Other House*, the play, her age at the start is twenty-five. Her aunt, Mrs. Griffin, was Julia Bream's stepmother. Rose kills Effie, tries to blame Jean Martle, and is taken away by Vidal (but not into matrimony).

Arnold, Matthew (1822–1888). Distinguished British poet, critic, lecturer, professor, and inspector of schools. He was the son of Thomas Arnold, influential headmaster of Rugby, and the uncle of Mary Augusta Ward.* Matthew Arnold graduated from Balliol College, Oxford (1844), was a prize-winning poet there, and became a school inspector (1851–1883) and then a professor of poetry at Oxford (1857–1867). He published two early volumes of poetry (1849, 1852), both of which he repudiated and withdrew. More volumes followed in 1853, 1855, and 1867. By 1850, however, he was beginning to turn to criticism, both general (for example, *Essays in Criticism* [1865, 1888], *Culture and Anarchy* [1869], *Friendship's Garland* [1871], and *Mixed Essays* [1879]), and also specific, academic, and theological (for example, published lectures on Homer [1861, 1862] and Celtic literature [1867], *St. Paul and Protestantism* [1870], *Literature and Dogma* [1873], and *God and the Bible* [1875]). He twice visited the United States to lecture, confer with eminent writers, and travel (1883–1884, 1886). James reviewed (*North American Review*, Jul 1865) Arnold's first *Essays in Criticism*, praising the author for style and feeling, but adding that the work

showed "questionable reasoning." Such a British book on literary topics compares well with similar French and German books, which are usually better.
James indicates Arnold's range, praises certain essays, calls the whole work
"fascinating" though lacking in force, says that "healthy" and amiable Arnold
evokes our "affection," likes his attempts to Frenchify England and thus make
it less "provincial," and relishes his "critical feeling and observation." Although some readers label Arnold too poetic and sentimental, James admires his
"delicate perceptions." He was right to praise his alma mater as a leader of
idealistic Romanticism and the enemy of the commonplace, which allies itself
to Philistinism, which holds civilization back. James lauds Arnold for defining
the critic's duties: to get at the best current thought, to see rightly, and "to be
disinterested." James discusses Philistinism at some length, lamenting that it
has vulgarized the English mind and "reaches us [in America] too." The British
are too narrowly practical, which trait they equate with the useful and the ornamental; criticism should "make truth . . . accessible" but "not . . . apply it."
Arnold may have faults, but he should be praised for having an important theme,
for taking the "high ground" in a memorable and serious manner, and for being
"profoundly conscious of his time," which is melancholy because it has lost
its innocence. Arnold read and praised this anonymously published essay by
James. In February 1865, James saw Arnold in a Roman café with his family
and met him the next day in the residence of William Wetmore Story* in Rome,
but he pronounced the British poet and critic superficial conversationally. James
met Arnold again at Story's and also at another dinner party in Rome later, and
he wrote to his sister Alice (25 Apr [1873]) that the poet's monocle was off-
putting. In an untitled note (*Nation*, 22 Mar 1877), James says that Arnold in
a few pages in *Nineteenth Century*, a new monthly journal, "illuminates a
secondary historical figure with the light of his beautiful style"; the reference
is to Arnold's essay on Viscount Falkland, a Moderate Royalist who died in the
Civil War in 1643. A year later, James wrote to his father (25 Mar [1878]) that
he was pleased that Arnold "writes just as he does; even his limitations have a
practical excellence." A year later James wrote to his sister Alice (26 Mar
[1879]) that, at the home of a mutual friend, he had met Arnold's whole family,
including his daughter, who was "as pretty as an American girl" and as talkative.
Late in 1879 Arnold wrote to James to commend him for his *Roderick Hudson*.
From England, James closely followed Arnold's first American lecture tour,
writing many friends about details; for example, to Thomas Sargeant Perry* he
wrote (25 Nov [1883]), "I am very sorry you didn't like poor dear old Mat. I
like him—love him rather— . . . with an affection that is proof against anything
he may say or do today, and proof also against taking him too seriously." James
wrote to Charles Eliot Norton* (6 Dec [1886]) to convey Arnold's happy memories of visiting him in Massachusetts. James wrote a general essay on Arnold
(*English Illustrated Magazine*, Jan 1884) on the occasion of that man's first
"visit to the great country of the Philistines." Arnold can delicately explain
"English life to . . . the alien," even though he "has a kind of European accent."

Arnold resembles Charles Augustin Sainte-Beuve*: Both may seem "unscientific" and "tiresome," but they know their subjects. Americans regret Arnold's fuss over "the differences . . . between Dissenters and Anglicans," but we must remember that this critic regards "the religious life . . . [as] the most important thing in the spectacle humanity offers us" since religion lights up morality. Further, like Joseph Ernest Renan,* he relates religion to art. Arnold is "saturated with the Bible." James notes that Arnold "has a real genius for quotation" to elucidate his points. James explains that he first came to admire Arnold because of his "singular," chance-taking poetry, which may possibly be a bit "sterilized" by William Wordsworth. Arnold has been what James calls "the *general* critic" since 1864 and thereby has much "quickened and coloured" the English mind, adding "to the interest of life, to the charm of knowledge." He has hung pretty lanterns in the gray "region [of] Philistinism." *Culture and Anarchy* is "perhaps his most ingenious and suggestive production." He throws "light darts" effectively, but in disputes he plays fair and is so good-humored that some might call him light and impractical. James chooses, however, to regard him instead as a supremely fine, cultured prose-writer and an "inveterate satirist." To Americans, Arnold is "the cultivated man" who can tactfully explain culture, but he should have said neither that "Philistinism was predominant" in America nor that "poetry . . . is a criticism of life." Lately Arnold has been pushing an eccentric, wordy style, but he remains a standard-bearing example for persons in both England and America who "care for literature." James concludes thus: *Friendship's Garland* is humorous and witty; *Culture and Anarchy*, luminous; *Mixed Essays*, dazzling. Arnold is distinguished and inspires our sensibilities. James's library contained thirteen books by Arnold.

"Art." Art review, published in the *Atlantic Monthly* (Jan 1872). James briefly discusses works by Constant Troyon, Alexandre-Gabriel Decamps,* Théodore Rousseau, Ferdinand Victor Eugène Delacroix,* John La Farge,* and a few others, being exhibited in Boston. The show reveals not only schools but also the French mind. Troyon's forest scene is "diffuse," half realism and half "rough generalization." A small Decamps reveals "cunning *morbidezza*"; a larger one, "factitious art." The latter is a delicately picturesque New Testament scene with admirable pagan Capernaum architecture. Delacroix combines charming strength and irritating weakness. The most important of several American works is a La Farge seascape.

"Art." Art review, published in the *Atlantic Monthly* (Feb 1872). James begins by discussing a Boston exhibit of art school work done in France (the best), England (improving rapidly), and Germany (too few drawings for any conclusion). He recommends the British system for Massachusetts elementary schools. Then he criticizes a Boston exhibition of works by William Morris Hunt* as unrepresentative. James highly praises *The Cock-Fight* by Jean Léon Gérôme,* also in the exhibition. Théodore Rousseau displays "dogged soberness"; a small picture expresses "condensed light and fresh air," while a larger landscape presents "as true a sunset as ever was painted," the "death-song in a muffled key" of "a serious old-world day."

"Art." Art review, published in the *Atlantic Monthly* (Nov 1874). James reviews an exhibit at the Boston Athenaeum of thirty pictures, mostly Spanish, on loan from the Duke of Montpensier. The best are a tender Bartolomé Esteban Murillo* and a fine sketch by Diego de Silva y Velasquez.* James touches on works by other artists, notably Francisco Zurburan ("not a colourist, though . . . a clever master of light and shade"), Jusepe de Ribera, Salvator Rosa, and others more minor. He closes by suggesting that American spectators may be "simple as yet" in judging art but should still define most items in the present exhibit as inferior.

"Art." Art review, published in the *Atlantic Monthly* (Jan 1875). James lightly touches on works shown in a Boston gallery by Hamilton Wilde (amateurish but likable, frankly colorful and nothing more, neither imaginative nor realistic, but fine for Nile River scenes); George Henry Boughton*; J. Appleton Brown ("a large, vigorous landscape," with an "excellent" sky, but too Frenchified in its now "conventional" realism); Mrs. W. J. Stillman (a watercolor self-portrait, unvaried but showing "good faith"); and Rogelio de Egusquiza (an ugly-faced female portrait, with cloth fashionably painted à la Japanese, a "piece of artistic depravity").

"Art and Letters in Paris." Paris letter, published in the New York *Tribune* (22 Apr 1876); reprinted in *Parisian Sketches*, 1957. James discusses the Paris art market, then, specifically, the works of the admirable Jean-Louis-Ernest Meissonier,* the "superlative" Alexandre-Gabriel Decamps,* the Orientalist Prosper-Georges-Antoine Marilhat, the animal painter Jacques Raymond Brascassat, the rural painter Ernest Baillet, and the "skillful" Jean Boldini. James touches on the recent Seine flood and *Souvenirs d'enfance* by Joseph Ernest Renan.*

"Art: Boston." Art review, published in the *Atlantic Monthly* (Mar 1872). James comments on a Boston gallery showing of landscapes by Foxcroft Cole (French in style but not weakly "imitative," instead honest and sensible, though perhaps stressing greens and grays too much); a superb Karl Daubigny autumnal landscape ("simple to baldness," "low-voiced," but with "truth and beauty" wrung from it); and J. Appleton Brown's *Grindelwald Valley* (simple in composition, "rough" and sketch-like, meagre even, but superficially effective).

"Art in France." Paris letter, published in the New York *Tribune* (27 May 1876); reprinted in *Parisian Sketches*, 1957. Having gone three times to the new Salon art exhibition, James discusses in detail the work of ten painters shown there. He especially comments on Gustave Doré ("nothing [here] but an immense mechanical facility"), Joseph Blanc ("brilliant and elegant"), Joseph Noel Sylvestre ("accomplished and picturesque"), Jean Baptiste Edouard Detaille ("admirable military painter"), and Michel Munkacsy ("solid and superb").

"Art in Paris." Paris letter, published in the New York *Tribune* (5 Jun 1876); reprinted in *Parisian Sketches*, 1957. James succinctly comments on Salon works by more than twenty artists, mostly painters but also several sculptors. He lauds paintings by Jules Bastien-Lepage ("the best portrait in the exhibition"), Charles Chaplin ("distilled rose leaves and dewdrops"), Antoine Vollon ("magnificent"), Jean Léon Gérôme* ("conspicuous for his cleverness"), and Joseph Chelmonski ("admirable . . . winter scenes in Russia"). Then James offers limited praise of Gustave Moreau* ("an original and interesting, if not a satisfactory colorist") and Jehan Georges Vibert (concerning "the carnal infirmities, humorously viewed, of monks and priests"). James calls paintings by Americans shown here "agreeable and entertaining."

The Art of Authorship: Literary Reminiscences, Methods of Work, and Advice to Young Beginners: Personally Contributed by Leading Authors of the Day, compiled and edited by George Bainton (London: Clarke, 1890; New York: Appleton, 1890). A book of advice for young writers. James contributed a paragraph (on literary form), of which he did not authorize publication. He says that he is fond of literary form, has never cultivated it, tries (despite journalistic and other vulgar traps) for clarity, concision, and grace, and has evolved his style through taste and patience.

"The Art of Fiction," critical essay, published in *Longman's Magazine* (Sep 1884); reprinted as a book and including the essay by Walter Besant* to which James's essay replied, in Boston by Cupples, Upham, 1884; revised and reprinted in *Partial Portraits*, 1888. One of James's most significant, short critical pieces, written as a refutation of an essay by Sir Walter Besant entitled "Fiction as One of the Fine Arts," in which, among other things, Besant said that the art of fiction writing could be taught, that novels should have a conscious moral purpose, and that fiction writers should not stray from their own class. James argues that fiction should compete with reality, should depict as painting does, and should record as history does. He feels that fiction should end as unhappily as life does, should be bold to experiment in forms, should proceed from the writer's ability to guess the unseen from the seen. Be one on whom nothing is lost, urges James, who further dismisses such distinctions as the romance vs. the novel, and the novel of character vs. that of incident. He contends that a novel is an inextricably intertwined combination of scene, action, and character. Allow the writer his donnée, he pleads, and criticize him or her only for what is made of it. Let the novel move to the irregular rhythm of life itself. Declining to discuss morality in fiction, James posits that a profound work will never proceed from a superficial mind, and that is all the morality with which one needs to be concerned. James closes by praising the novel as the most open of the art forms. This important essay has been called the manifesto of fictional realism. James's friend Robert Louis Stevenson* undertook to reply to it in "A Humble Remonstrance," arguing that the best fiction is neither popular hack work (as Besant implies) nor a re-creation of reality (as James wishes), but a "make-believe" concoction not properly in competition with life.

"Art: The Dutch and Flemish Pictures in New York." Art review, published in the *Atlantic Monthly* (Jun 1872). James reviews a New York exhibition of 175 mostly Dutch and Flemish paintings purchased in Paris and Brussels in 1870. The collection is not brilliant and has no gems, but it is important for American students. He comments (with wit and feeling, sometimes harshly) on item after item, by more than thirty major and minor painters, including Francesco Goya y Lucientes ("cunning hand"), Jean-Baptiste Greuze ("indubitably French"), Francesco Guardi ("cold, colourless, sceptical"), Franz Hals ("inelegant vigour"), Meindert Hobbema ("pleasing but not brilliant"), Sir Joshua Reynolds* (one example, "indifferent"), Peter Paul Rubens* (one picture, "lack[ing] the Rubens lustre"), Solomon Ruysdael ("frank . . . and . . . wholesome veracity"), Sassoferrato ("velegance"), Jan Steen ("vigour and . . . crudity"), David Teniers ("almost . . . the gem of the museum"), Sir Anthony Van Dyck ("two imperfect, but interesting works"), and Diego de Silva y Velasquez* ("rugged breadth of touch"). James likes landscapes, touches on minor works lovingly, and praises two paintings by women for "exhibit[ing] a magnificent elaboration of detail, an almost masculine grasp of the resources of high finish."

Artemisia. In "The Real Thing," a fictional character in Philip Vincent's *Rutland Ramsey*.

Arthur, Chester A. (1830–1886). Twenty-first president of the United States (1881–1885). While James was visiting Henry Adams* and his wife Marian Adams* in Washington, D.C., he met President Arthur at a big dinner given by Senator James G. Blaine. Through his work as a New York lawyer in the 1850s and 1860s, Arthur knew Albany well. He and James discussed Albany Jameses and the Van Buren family.* In a letter to his mother (22 Jan [1882]), James says that President Arthur "pleased, if he didn't fascinate me," had "aspirations to culture," and amused him by thinking that James's father was William James, Henry James, Sr.'s half-brother. President Arthur is in the background of James's 1884 short story "Pandora."

Ash, Bob. In "A Round of Visits," the husband of Florence Ash, who plans to obtain a divorce.

Ash, Florence. In "A Round of Visits," a slight friend of Mark P. Monteith, who visits her in New York.

Ash, Susan. In *What Maisie Knew*, a housemaid for Beale Farange.

Ashburner family. James family neighbors in Cambridge, Massachusetts. Anne, Grace, and Sarah Ashburner were sisters. Sarah, who married Theodore Sedgwick, was the mother of Arthur George Sedgwick* and Susan Sedgwick Norton, wife of Charles Eliot Norton,* all of whom James knew. Anne and Grace Ashburner had cared for Arthur, Susan, and their two sisters upon the death of their mother in 1860. The Ashburner family also knew other persons whom James knew. The Ashburners lived for a while in Notting Hill, outside London. Shortly after James moved to London permanently in 1876, they invited him to call. In a snobbish letter to his mother (31 Jan [1877]), James writes that "[t]hey live in a remote, depressing quarter. . . . They were very friendly, and seemed to cling to me for society. I got an impression . . . that my coming was really a social event for them." In several later letters home, James gossips about the following Ashburners: Anne (deaf); George, Grace, and Sam (angry); and Walter (pampered). According to a Notebook entry (22 Aug 1901), George Ashburner gave James the idea for "Mora Montravers." In *Notes of a Son and Brother*, James quotes a letter from his father in which the Ashburners are mentioned.

Ashbury, Maud. In "Lord Beaupré," a friend of Guy Firminger.

Ashbury, Mrs. In "Lord Beaupré," Maud Ashbury's mother.

Ashdown, Teddy. In *The Album*, a young man who can confirm for Grace Jesmond that Sir Ralph Damant lied about Mark Moorsom Bernal. He helps Mark in his art studio. He loves and finally wins Maud Vanneck, partly because Grace praises Teddy to Maud.

Ashmore, Mr. and Mrs. Arthur. In "The Liar," Sir David Ashmore's brusque son and vapid daughter-in-law.

Ashmore, Sir David. In "The Liar," the genial ninety-year-old subject of a portrait which Oliver Lyon paints while he is visiting at Stayes.

Aspern, Jeffrey. In "The Aspern Papers," the long-deceased American poet whose papers Juliana Bordereau, his now aged former mistress, has treasured for many decades. Could Jeffrey Aspern and Juliana Bordereau be Tina Bordereau's parents?

"The Aspern Papers." Long short story (35,300 words), published in the *Atlantic Monthly* (Mar–May 1888); reprinted in *The Aspern Papers*, 1888; revised and reprinted in *The Novels and Tales of Henry James*, Volume XII, 1908. (Characters: Contessa Altemura, Jeffrey Aspern, Cavaliere Bombici, Juliana Bordereau, Tina Bordereau, John Cumnor, Mr. and Mrs. Churton, Mr. and Mrs.

Goldie, Olimpia, Pasquale, Pochintesta, Mrs. Prest, Mrs. Stock-Stock.) The unnamed narrator, an American literary scholar, comes to Venice to try to lay hands on papers of deceased American poet Jeffrey Aspern, whose former mistress, the aged Juliana Bordereau, has reputedly held them for decades. At the suggestion of his friend Mrs. Prest, the narrator rents rooms from her and tells her timid niece Tina Bordereau about his hopes. The greedy old aunt callously throws the two younger people together and offers to sell the man a portrait of Aspern for an inflated price. When Juliana gets sick, the narrator sneaks into her room and is caught rifling her desk. She shames him terribly, brands him a "publishing scoundrel," and then collapses. After some days away, the narrator returns to find Juliana now dead and buried and Tina hinting that she could let him have the papers only if he were a member of the family. Aghast, the narrator rushes off. When he returns virtually prepared to propose marriage, Tina tells him that she has burned all the papers, one by one. The narrator never sees the papers, but he does send Tina money for Aspern's portrait. James skillfully characterizes the narrator as a combination of professional ruthlessness and personal obtuseness, and yet also an object of reader sympathy. It has been wondered whether Tina Bordereau is the granddaughter of Juliana Bordereau, or perhaps her daughter by Jeffrey Aspern. James reveals in a Notebook entry (12 Jan 1887) that the source of this splendid story was an incident mentioned to him in Florence, Italy, by Eugene Jacob Lee-Hamilton*: A Captain [Edward] Silsbee, from Boston, discovered that Clare Clairmont,* the sister-in-law of Percy Bysshe Shelley* and the mistress of George Gordon, Lord Byron,* was still living with her niece in Florence; Silsbee subsequently tried without success to obtain the Byron and Percy Bysshe Shelley* letters in her possession. James changed the scene from Florence to Venice, which he evokes marvelously, and changed the two British writers of the papers into one American poet. The Bordereaus' rare Venetian garden, which is essential in the story, may have been suggested to James by a similar one that was part of the Palazzo Barbaro in Venice rented by Daniel Sargent and Ariana Randolph Curtis,* which James had enjoyed in the early 1880s. By letter, James informed his photographer Alvin Langdon Coburn* (6 Dec 1906) that the Venetian residence of Julia Constance Fletcher* was "the old house I had more or less in mind for the Aspern Papers." In the preface to Volume XII of *The Novels and Tales of Henry James*, James explains his love of "the inexhaustible charm" of Italy, his surprise upon learning years ago that "Jane Clairmont . . . should have been living on in Florence . . . up to our own day," his half-wish not to see her in person but instead to let "the minimum of valid suggestion" challenge his imagination more and his seeming obligation to alter the "the Florentine legend" considerably. Critics disagree on the degree of culpability in the narrator and also on poor Tina's qualities and mixed motives.

The Aspern Papers. Collection of three short stories, published in London by Macmillan, 1888: "The Aspern Papers," "Louisa Pallant," and "The Modern Warning."

Asquith, Herbert Henry, Earl of Oxford and Asquith (1852–1928). A classical scholar (Balliol College, Oxford), barrister, and Liberal member of Parliament (from 1886). After being Home Secretary and then Chancellor of the Exchequer, Asquith served as prime minister of England (1908–1916), until he was ousted by Lloyd George during World War I. James knew Asquith from the 1890s, and he had long been happily acquainted with Asquith's second wife, the former Margaret "Margot" Tennant, a gifted and stimulating woman, and a lively London hostess. (The first wife of Asquith had died in 1891, and he remarried three years later.) A mutual fried of Asquith and James was Sir Edmund Wilson Gosse.* In 1913, 1914, and early 1915, James occasionally had luncheon and dinner at 10 Downing Street, London, with the Asquiths, through whom he was able to meet Winston Churchill.* On 28 June 1915, James wrote to Asquith to ask him to sponsor James in becoming a British subject. Asquith happily agreed; James became British exactly one month later and was Asquith's dinner guest that evening. Through Sir Edward Howard Marsh,* Asquith was persuaded to recommend James for the Order of Merit, which was granted by King George V on 1 January 1916. Early in 1915, Asquith's wife loaned James her voluminous and gossipy diaries, which led him extravagantly to call the authoress, in a letter to her (9 Apr 1915), "the [Honoré de] Balzac[*] of diarists."

Assingham, Colonel Robert (Bob). In *The Golden Bowl*, Fanny's patient, long-listening husband, who is close to the Ververs, Prince Amerigo, and Charlotte Stant. He is wiser than he pretends.

Assingham, Fanny. In *The Golden Bowl*, the well-intentioned but windy friend of the Ververs, Prince Amerigo, and Charlotte Stant. She tries to explain to her husband Bob all of the Verver activities. Fanny later breaks the seemingly accursed golden bowl.

Assunta. In *Roderick Hudson* and *The Princess Casamassima*, the maid of Christina Light, who becomes the Princess Casamassima.

Atherton, Gertrude Franklin (née Horn) (1857–1948). Prolific, California-born novelist, essayist, feminist, and autobiographer, widowed in 1888 and thereafter living much abroad (including in London, 1895 and later, and in France). In "American Letter" (9 Apr 1898), James says that Mrs. Atherton's 1898 novel *American Wives and English Husbands* (later retitled *Transplanted*) is "looking for a situation rather than . . . finding one." In it, the authoress neither sees in her subject what we would see nor shows us what she did see. James implies that Mrs. Atherton should not have strayed from her native locale. James comments on her 1897 novel *His Fortunate Grace* in "American Letter" (30 Apr 1898), calling it "sharply satiric," with fresh details in an "antique" situation, but puzzling as to intention.

"At Isella." Short story (12,100 words), published in the *Galaxy* (Aug 1871). (Characters: Mrs. B., Miss B., Madeleine Brohan, Ernesto, Giuseppino.) Walking from Switzerland to Isella, in Italy, the simple narrator meets and helps a beautiful woman, who is much too confiding, to escape from her husband and join her lover over the border. This is one of James's thinnest stories, valuable, if at all, for its scenic backdrop. James wrote to his sister Alice (31 Aug [1869]) the details of his journey (with its "delightful flavor of romance") over the Swiss border to "the little frontier Village of Isella where I spent the night," and where Italy "lay before me warm and living and palpable."

Auberon. In "After the Play," the fellow playgoer in London with Amicia, Dorriforth, and Florentia. Auberon likes well-formed plays, praises big stage effects and British acting, and measures success by ticket sales.

Aubert, Abbé. In *The American*, Lizzie Tristram's friend; he tells her that Claire de Cintré has become a nun.

Augier, Guillaume Victor Émile (1820–1889). Valence-born French writer, grandson of a novelist. Augier was well educated and at first planned to be a lawyer. He began his writing career as a poet and then turned to verse comedies, notably *La Ciguë* (1844). He sometimes wrote with collaborators, such as Jules Sandeau.* The best of his twenty-five plays are comedies of manners, mostly *drames bourgeois*, and include *L'Aventurière* (1848), *Gabrielle* (1849), *Philiberte* (1853), *Le Gendre de Monsieur Poirier* (1854, highly successful), *Le Mariage d'Olympe* (1855, about a real, not a romantic, courtesan), *Les Lionnes pauvres* (1858), *Les Effrontés* (1861), *Le Fils de Giboyer* (1862), *Maître Guérin* (1864), *Lions et renards* (1869), *Madame Caverlet* (1876, favoring legalized divorce), and *Les Fourchamboult* (1878, his last play). Augier definitively expresses the French bourgeois temperament of his epoch, during which he, Alexandre Dumas *fils*,* and Victorien Sardou* dominated the French stage. James saw at least nine plays by Augier, many in the 1870s at the Théâtre Français in Paris. In 1878 he wrote to his brother William (1 May [1878]), "I have thoroughly mastered Dumas, Augier and Sardou." In an untitled note (*Nation*, 27 Jun 1878), James calls Augier an "author of . . . masterly dramas" and especially praises *L'Aventurière*, *Le Mariage d'Olympe*, *Les Lionnes pauvres*, and *Maître Guérin* as strong and *Philiberte* as charming. James first notes that in his plays Augier seeks "to keep the family well together," then he comments on how this is managed specifically in *Les Fourchamboult*. The English may not only deplore all the fuss in such plays to protect families not in serious danger, but also miss the beautiful shapeliness of such plays. James's *The American* owes much to Augier's frequently used intrusion plots, in which an intruder tries—and usually fails—to gain acceptance by a tightly knit social unit. The clever dialogue in *Confidence* may be James's dismal attempt to imitate Augier. James's library contained three books by Augier.

Augustine. In *The Europeans*, Eugenia Münster's maid.

Austen, Jane (1775–1817). British novelist. She was the daughter of a Hampshire rector. When he died, she lived uneventfully with her mother and sisters at Bath, Southampton, and Chawton. Austen completed the following novels: *Sense and Sensibility* (1811), *Pride and Prejudice* (1813), *Mansfield Park* (1814), *Emma* (1815), and the posthumous *Northanger Abbey* (1818) and *Persuasion* (1818). Her fiction, which has a narrow range, concerns social, domestic, and family relationships; it is marked by common sense, humor, subtlety, and irony. Although James never devoted an essay to Austen, he often mentioned her, usually in comments about other women novelists. In his 1865 review of *Aurora Floyd* by Mary Elizabeth Braddon,* he notes by the way that "Miss Austen . . . [initiated] the novel of domestic tranquillity." In his 1875 review of *Mr. Smith* by Lucy Bethia Walford,* he mentions his decided preference for Jane Austen, who, he notes, "in her best novels, is interesting to the last page; the tissue of her narrative is always close and firm, and though she is minute and analytical, she is never prolix or redundant." In a letter to a young Austen scholar named George Pellew (23 Jun [1883]), James writes of "delightful Jane" and "of the extraordinary vividness with which she saw what she did see, and of her narrow unconscious perfection of form." James closes his 1901 essay on Matilde Serao,* whom he admires but also regards as vulgar, by stating his preference for "dear old Jane Austen," who is more discreet. In his 1905 lecture "The Lesson of Balzac," he returns to the idea of her unconsciousness: "The key to Jane Austen's fortune with posterity has been in part the extraordinary grace . . . of her unconsciousness: as if . . . she sometimes, over her work-basket, her tapestry flowers, . . . fell a-musing, lapsed . . . into wool-gathering, and her dropped stitches . . . were afterwards picked up as little touches of human truth, little glimpses of steady vision, little master-strokes of imagination." James's library contained one book by Austen.

Austin, Maximus (Max). In "A Light Man," Theodore Lisle's worthless, "light" friend whose journal tells the story.

Austin, Mrs. In "A Light Man," Maximus Austin's deceased mother. She once knew Frederick Sloane.

"The Author of Beltraffio." Short story (17,400 words), published in the *English Illustrated Magazine* (Jun–Jul 1884); reprinted in *The Author of Beltraffio* and in *Stories Revived*, 1885; revised and reprinted in *The Novels and Tales of Henry James*, Volume XVI, 1909. (Characters: Dolcino Ambient, Beatrice Ambient, Gwendolyn Ambient, Mark Ambient, Dr. Mackintosh.) Admiring the works of British novelist Mark Ambient, whose novel *Beltraffio* seems especially fine, the initially naive American narrator visits him at his country estate, where he also meets Ambient's coldly beautiful wife Beatrice, their sickly son Dolcino, age seven, and the novelist's strange sister Gwendolyn Ambient. Through Gwendolyn, the narrator learns that Mark is worried about his son's worsening health and his wife's lack of concern. That woman rudely dismisses a physician who suspects diphtheria; further, she so dislikes her husband's writing and so fears its possible corrupting influence upon Dolcino in later life that she withholds his medicine and the boy dies. The author's latest book, which the mother, now dead herself, read in proofs while their son was sick, is finally published. This morbid story was suggested to James, according to a Notebook entry (26 Mar 1884), by his friend Sir Edmund Wilson Gosse,* who told him that the wife of John Addington Symonds* regarded her husband's writing as immoral and overly aesthetic. James misleadingly wrote to his brother William (15 Feb [1885]) from London thus: "I am told, on all sides, here, that my *Author of Beltraffio* is a living and scandalous portrait of J. A. Symonds and his wife, whom I have never seen." (James had, in fact, met Symonds in 1877.) James wrote to Gosse (9 Jun [1884]) that "The Author of Beltraffio" was "tragic—almost repulsively so." Its poignancy centers in the helplessness of Dolcino, the innocent little victim of his parents' cruelly disparate creeds. The novelist is an uneasy amalgam of many fin-de-siècle writers whom James knew and varyingly disliked, while Ambient's sister is vaporously pre-Raphaelitesque.

The Author of Beltraffio. Collection of five short stories, published in Boston by Osgood, 1885: "The Author of Beltraffio," "Pandora," "Georgina's Reasons," "The Path of Duty," and "Four Meetings."

Autobiography. The so-called *Autobiography* of Henry James is really two volumes and a fragment of a third: *A Small Boy and Others* (1913), *Notes of a Son and Brother* (1914), and *The Middle Years* (incomplete, 1917). James had planned to write five such volumes.

"An Autumn Journey." The 1874 title of the travel sketch retitled "The St. Gothard" in 1875 and "The Old Saint-Gothard" in 1909.

"The Autumn in Florence." Travel essay, published in the *Nation* (1 Jan 1874); reprinted in *Transatlantic Sketches*, 1875, and in *Italian Hours*, 1909. James begins by discussing the summer weather lingering into October but now giving way to moist melancholy. Oldtimers lament social and architectural changes; still, new forms reflect old Florentine grace. Old streets and buildings offer a message from the past. Old houses by the yellow Arno seem coated with ancient mud and yet they "create their own standard of felicity." The general sanity here may be due to Florentine art and "the tenderness of time." James mentions Dante ("greatest of literary artists"), Filippo Lippi, Fra Angelico, Luca della Robbia, and the unique Giotto bell tower ("the graceful, indestructible soul of the place made visible"). The cathedral has "fine Tuscan geniality." Pitti Palace and Uffizi holdings are a "central treasure-chamber." James comments that a certain Botticelli, neglected and badly framed in the Academy, would be a wonder in America, and notes the inventive Botticelli's influence on certain pre-Raphaelites. Then he comprehensively praises early Florentine painters even over Raphael, and he commends an anonymous Frenchman's copy of a Ghirlandaio Adoration as patient and miraculous.

Awdry, Frances (fl. 1875–1906). British authoress whose *The Story of a Fellow-Soldier*, an 1875 abridgement of the two-volume *Life of John Coleridge Patteson, Missionary Bishop to the Melanesian Islands*, by Charlotte Mary Yonge,* James reviewed (*Nation*, 8 Apr 1875), together with the longer work. He merely calls Awdry's work "a happy idea" because "even infant minds may perceive the beauty and impressiveness" of the martyred bishop's work. Yonge provided a preface for the 1883 edition of Awdry's abridgement.

The Awkward Age. Novel (130,400 words), published in *Harper's Weekly* (1 Oct 1898–7 Jan 1899); revised and reprinted in London by Heinemann, 1899, and in New York by Harper, 1899; revised and reprinted in *The Novels and Tales of Henry James*, Volume IX, 1908. (Characters: Agnesina, Mr. and Mrs. Bagger, Dr. Beltram, Edward Brookenham, Mrs. Edward Brookenham, Fernanda Brookenham, Harold Brookenham, Lady Fanny and Lord Cashmore, Susan Curd, Sir Digby Dence, Captain Dent-Douglas, Beach Donner, Carrie Donner, Garlick, Gelsomina, Harry and Tishy Grendon, Duchess Jane, Lady Julia, Longdon, Algie Manger, Booby Manger, Mr. and Mrs. Manger, Miss Merriman, Mitchett, Lord Petherton, Mary Pinthorpe, Randage, Baron Schack, Tatton, Nancy Toovey, Gustavus Vanderbank, Mary and Miles Vanderbank.) Long ago Longdon, now in his late fifties, loved Lady Julia, but she married someone else and had a daughter, now Mrs. Brookenham. That lady is the center of an effete social circle and is the mother of wastrel Harold and sweet Nanda (age eighteen). Vanderbank, pleasant but not very well-to-do, admires both mother and daughter. Mrs. Brook welcomes Duchess Jane, her husband's cousin and the mother of Agnesina, long sheltered and hence a contrast to Nanda. The two women begin to discuss marriage prospects for their daughters. Rich, ugly Mitchett might do for Nanda, except for Van's interest in her. Longdon dislikes the tangled gossip he is now hearing: Nanda should visit loose Tishy Grendon, the sister of Carrie Donner, who is intimate with Cashmore, whose wife Fanny's brother Lord Petherton sponges off Mitchy. Mrs. Brook hopes to capitalize on the fact that Longdon sees dead Lady Julia in her granddaughter Nanda. He urges the girl to marry Mitchy and thus avoid loneliness of the sort he has suffered. But Jane wants Mitchy to wed Aggie, although Mrs. Brook would prefer to have Van, whom she likes very much, hang around Nanda in prolonged uncertainty. When Van tells Longdon that he loves Nanda, the older man promises a dowry, which offer Van reveals to Mrs. Brook, who says that she is instead backing Mitchy for the girl. When Mrs. Brook tells this to Mitchy, he sees that Van wants him to marry Aggie and leave the field. Van visits Longdon's country estate and finds Nanda and some others there. She is critical of her heartless family. She urges Mitchy to marry Aggie. At a party at Tishy's (after Mitchy and Aggie have wed), Mrs. Brook shows her anger: Mitchy is lost to Nanda, and Van may have reservations about the girl. Much meddling gossip unnerves Longdon, with whom Nanda has by now been staying for some months. Petherton chases Aggie for a questionable book Nanda has borrowed. Mrs. Brook's social circle seems to be breaking apart. Cashmore visits tea-giving Nanda, while generally disgusted Van hesitates to come calling. Mitchy hints at marital unhappiness; further, at Mrs. Brook's prompting, he praises unselfish, sad Nanda to Longdon, whose proffered sum to her he even promises to augment. At tea, Nanda asks both Van and Mitchy to remain kind to her bright mother; the girl also praises Aggie to doubting Mitchy. Later Nanda tells Longdon that she does not love Van but then starts to weep. Longdon seems to regret the fact that Van did not accept his offer of money and marry Nanda, but he also feels that Van might have married Aggie instead and thus left Nanda for Mitchy. Nanda rejects this version of imagined happiness, admits to a concern for Mitchy, and plans to go soon with Longdon to his estate. In a long Notebook entry (4 Mar 1895) James jotted down an idea for "a short tale" (which became this novel): London girl listens to free-talking mother; young man likes girl but thinks she knows too much; contrasting mother has married off her daughter unhappily to get her away from adult talk. In this entry, James fretted further with the topics of desperate mothers, manners, and adolescents hearing bold talk. Once completed, *The Awkward Age* pleased James but not the public. In a letter to Paul Bourget* (23 Dec 1898), he describes it as "the production of about 135,000 words arranged as a fable of superior quality." He wrote to Henrietta Reubell* a defensive letter ([12 Nov 1899]) about the thickness of readers who were bewildered by *The Awkward Age* and therefore denounced it; then he added, "I think Mrs. Brook the best thing I've ever done—and Nanda also much *done*." The photograph by Alvin Langdon Coburn* of James's Lamb House entrance became the frontispiece for *The Awkward Age* as reprinted in *The Novels and Tales of Henry James* and may thereby attest to the author's fondness for the novel. In the preface to Volume IX of *The Novels and Tales of Henry James*, James rather smugly overvalues *The Awkward Age* because in it he has responded with technical success to the challenge of composing it as a drama in novelistic form (with acts and scenes, entrances and exits, and much conversation). In this regard, his work resembles the admired dialogue novels of Gyp* (Countess de Martel de Janville). The result, says James, has symmetry, like a fine dance or an attractive building. There was the difficulty that, as in a play, though not most novels, he had to avoid "going behind" his characters to explain them and to amplify. James likes his theme too: how adults should conduct fashionable drawing room conversation in the presence of maturing but unmarried daughters. When in the summer of 1914 James dictated notes for what he hoped would become *The Ivory Tower*, he toyed with the idea of developing some of its scenes according to the drama technique used in *The Awkward Age*.

Azarina. In *The Europeans*, a taciturn, old, black maid for the Wentworths.

B _____

B., Miss. In "At Isella," the Philadelphia woman who is to marry the narrator.

B., Mrs. In "At Isella," a Philadelphia woman who is to be the narrator's mother-in-law.

B—, Monsignor. In *Roderick Hudson*, a church office and the uncle of Prince Gennaro Casamassima.

B—. In "Travelling Companions," Signora B—'s child.
meets.

Babcock, Rev. Mr. Benjamin. In *The American*, a Dorchester, Massachusetts, Unitarian minister. He travels briefly with Christopher Newman and experiences disquieting moral reactions to European art. Babcock's attitudes may owe something to those of Rev. Mr. William Rounseville Alger.*

Babe, The. In "A London Life," a member of the Rifles. Lady Davenant introduces him to Laura Wing. Perhaps James is having fun with the nickname of William Haynes Smith, who was known as "The Babe" and who was the boyfriend of Howard Overing Sturgis.*

Bagger, Mr. and Mrs. In *The Awkward Age*, casual friends named by the Brookenhams.

Bagley, Sir Bruce. In "Mora Montravers," the man whom Mora Montravers loves.

Bagshaw, Mrs. In "The Siege of London," a woman who is to help Nancy Grenville Beck Headway enter British society.

Baker, Sir Samuel White (1821–1893). London-born explorer who lived in early maturity on Indian Ocean islands (1843–1855), then traveled in the Middle East (1856–1860), and helped find the Nile River sources (1861–1864), for which he was knighted at home (1866). Ismail Pasha, viceroy of Egypt, persuaded Baker to lead a military expedition far to the south, where he reduced the slave trade, augmented the pasha's land holdings, and became military governor of the region (1869–1873). Baker's several books about travel, exploration, and hunting include *Ismailia: A Narrative of the Expeditions to Central Africa for the Suppression of the Slave Trade, Organized by Ismail, Khedive of Egypt* (1874), which James reviewed (*Nation*, 4 Feb 1875), beginning with a sketch of Baker's mission under the pasha. James says the expedition was lavishly equipped but "ill-seconded by . . . officials and local functionaries" and compares it to a "squadron out of Spenser or Ariosto." The expedition, which Lady Baker bravely accompanied, had trouble getting up the Nile and stamped out a good deal of slavery thereafter, but they were attacked by hordes of savage and treacherous Baris. Baker's force shrank from 2,000 to less than 500. Baker built a military station in Unyoro. When the young leader there proved to be a dramatic villain, Baker burned him out, packed up, and hastily retreated, first to Victoria Nyanza and then back to Khartum. Apologizing for the few details given in his review, James concludes that regardless of his pasha's future sincerity, Baker is an example of magnificent British qualities.

Bald (or Bold). In "A London Life," Lionel Berrington's former governess.

Baldi, Mme. In *Roderick Hudson*, Christina Light's chic bonnet maker.

Baldwin, William Wilberforce (1850–1910). Distinguished American physician, professional writer, and genial friend of literati. He was born in Walton, New York, studied medicine at the Long Island College Hospital and in Vienna, and expatriated himself with his wife to Italy, practicing first in Florence and later in Rome for a quarter of a century. Dr. Baldwin treated royalty and peasants alike, and also William Dean Howells,* Mark Twain,* Edith Newbold Jones Wharton,* Constance Fenimore Woolson,* Alice James, William James, and, beginning in 1887, Henry James as well. James and Dr. Baldwin exchanged several letters, which concerned sickness, travel, the Baldwins' hospitality, mutual friends (including Woolson), and Dr. Baldwin's charity work in Italy. It was Dr. Baldwin who, in Italy in 1890, told James the anecdote which he developed into the short story "The Pupil." Dr. Baldwin was in London in July

1891, and Woolson (in James's brief absence) recommended that he see Alice James, whose malady he diagnosed after four visits as breast cancer. She liked and admired him. In a letter to Sir Edmund Wilson Gosse* (30 May [1894]), James called Dr. Baldwin a "genius." Sir Luke Strett, Milly Theale's physician in *The Wings of the Dove*, may be partly patterned after Dr. Baldwin.

Balestier, Charles Wolcott (1861–1891). Versatile young man—actor, traveler, businessman, administrator, editor, publisher, literary agent, and writer—born in Rochester, New York, into a wealthy Huguenot family. In London (starting in 1888) as a representative of the energetic American publisher Samuel Sidney McClure* and then as a successful agent of writers, he went into partnership with William Heinemann* to publish an inexpensive "English Library" (of books by British and America authors) in competition on the Continent with Christian Bernhard Tauchnitz.* Balestier obtained the American rights to the works of Rudyard Kipling.* He coauthored *The Naulahka* (1892) with Kipling, who married Balestier's sister Caroline a year after Balestier died of typhoid fever in Dresden, Germany. James met Balestier in London in December 1888, admired and socialized with him there, and engaged the young man as his agent briefly (1890–1891 or so), after Alexander Pollack Watt* and before James Brand Pinker.* In a letter to his sister Alice (6 Jun [1890]), James commends the young man's "capital intelligence and competence. . . . He . . . strikes me . . . as the perfection of an 'agent.' " James went with Heinemann to Balestier's funeral in Germany. James never especially liked Caroline Balestier Kipling. He published an essay on Wolcott Balestier (*Cosmopolitan*, May 1892; reprinted as the preface to Balestier's book of four stories called *The Average Woman . . .*, 1892), in which he begins by saying that when our friends die young they cannot disappoint or fail us. James, however, deplores the loss of Balestier's "talent . . . at the very moment it had begun to expand." He defines Balestier as "a man of business of altogether peculiar genius," unselfish and concerned with money only so far as it granted him freedom. He notes that Balestier revered the works of William Dean Howells,* favored "the novel of observation, the undiscourageable study of the actual," knew well "the far West . . . [and] mining camps and infant cities" there, and appreciated American humor. James is happy to remember that he saw Balestier often just before his death, recalling that the young man had attended the first performance of James's play *The American* in Southport, on 3 January 1891, and that the two had vacationed together that August on the Isle of Wight. Sir Edmund Wilson Gosse* memorialized Balestier in *Portraits and Sketches*. James's library contained one book by Balestier, in addition to the one coauthored with Kipling.

"Baltimore." Travel essay, published in the *North American Review* (August 1906); reprinted in *The American Scene*, 1907.

Balzac, Honoré de (1799–1850). Prolific and influential French novelist. Born Honoré Balzac in Tours to an aging father whose real family name was Balssa, and a domineering mother, he added the "de" to his name after 1830. Balzac had a varied education (including law school), survived a half-starved garret life (1820–1822) of scribbling, combined more writing with disastrous dabblings in the printing and publishing business (1825–1828), and wrote his first good works in 1829. Thereafter, he failed at more commercial ventures, formed a variety of friendships (including those with Victor-Marie Hugo,* Alexandre Dumas,* and Théophile Gautier*) and amours (with Laure de Berny [1820–1831] and then Madame Evelina Hanska [1833–1850], who finally married him [1850]), and wrote with incredible zeal, often sixteen hours a day, during which he consumed quarts of coffee. His canon is enormous. In his *Comédie Humaine* (ultimately consisting of more than ninety novels, plus about fifty that were left in draft form), Balzac undertook the impossibly ambitious task of representing in novels all of early nineteenth-century French life and manners—private, provincial, Parisian, military, political, and rural. James, who regarded Balzac as the world's greatest novelist, devoted to him a long essay, two reviews, a lecture (subsequently published), and an introduction to a translation of one of his novels. Even before any of these items appeared, however, James had praised Balzac in an 1867 review of historical novelist Anne E. Manning* for accurately rather than fancifully reporting historical realities of French society. James begins his long essay entitled "Honoré de Balzac" (*Galaxy*, Dec 1875; reprinted in *French Poets and Novelists*, 1878) by dismissing earlier critics: Even Hippolyte Taine,* though "worthy," is "incomplete"; Charles Augustin Sainte-Beuve* reveals "inexplicable inadequacy." James calls Balzac's apprentice work "unreadable," but then names *Les Parents pauvres* and *Les Père Goriot* as Balzac's best, identifies money (with concomitant greed) as the main ingredient in his *Comédie*, and adds that his knowledge of Paris became "the vast mosaic pavement" of his canon. James notes that Balzac has intensity but not reach and that his "hungry and predatory" garret years made him observant; James then calls Balzac's *Peau de chagrin* (1830) the earliest reputable novel of the "dense" web he weaves. (By contrast, Alexandre Dumas *fils*, George Sand,* and Anthony Trollope* all weave "loose[ly]".) Balzac's great years were from 1830 to 1840. James wonders when Balzac conceived his master plan, in which every novel became a "block in a single immense edifice," as explained in that "remarkable manifesto," Balzac's 1842 preface. James admires the attempt more than the execution and adds that only a French writer would have dared to shape a gallery of characters into "an organic whole." Balzac creates reappearing characters more often than William Makepeace Thackeray* or Trollope. With a variety of opinions on all subjects, Balzac is grounded in conservative faith in the French monarchy and the Catholic Church, which provide him with "picturesque" and hierarchical "*chiaroscuro*." He presents all feelings—high, low, and unclean—and can write both spontaneously and reflectively. James advises critics to handle brutal Balzac brutally. Compared with Thackeray, George Eliot,* Sand, and

Ivan Sergeyevich Turgenev,* who have "great consciences and great minds," Balzac has "a great temperament" rather than any "natural sense of morality." We find misers (showing vehemence, astuteness, eagerness, and patience) everywhere in his fiction, since Balzac, too, is this-worldly, with a "passion for *things.*" He especially likes patience because it permits "duplicity," which is "more picturesque than honesty." In the second part of the essay, James explains that Balzac has an "overmastering sense of the present world" and can describe its physical elements—towns, houses, rooms, and so on—in a "definite and masterly" way. Balzac's "strongest gift" is his ability to create and portray characters, nearly 2,000 in all, many of whom recur in successive fictions. James provides pages of carefully chosen and analyzed examples; then he turns to his subject's "meager . . . philosophy," which results from his hatred of the bourgeoisie from which he sprang and which despised him. James contends that Balzac writes weak dialogue; depicts all passions, even those "deemed unmentionable"; avoids dramatizing flirtations but stresses "ardent love in a thousand forms"; cites *Le Père Goriot* as "among the few greatest novels we possess"; wonders about its relationship to *King Lear* by William Shakespeare*; briefly discusses dozens of Balzac's characters to show that, although his portraiture is "unerring," his narrative "often goes woefully astray"; and regards his female characters as his "greatest triumphs." Balzac, taking "the old-fashioned view" and hence risking "hisses at any convention for giving women the suffrage . . . ," sees women as endlessly capable, devoted, and cruel. Again, James offers dozens of examples—rich, poor, Parisian, rural, and sensual. He finds "snobbish" Balzac's "grandes dames" (and fops) failures compared to his plebeian creatures. In sum, Balzac has an "all devouring love of reality," wrongly sought to force reality to prevail over the imagination, was a fine but also a coarse artist with a "swaggering" style, employed instinct well but theory ill, regarded himself as almost divine in creativity, and can bear comparison with Shakespeare since each is "a final authority upon human nature." Balzac lacked "charm" but possessed "incomparable power." Next, James reviewed the two-volume, 1876 edition of Balzac's letters (*Galaxy*, Feb 1877; reprinted in *French Poets and Novelists*, 1914). James begins by deploring the issuance of such private correspondence at all, concerned as this set is with Balzac's "money-hunger" and "painful processes." Balzac often wrote his beloved older sister Laure de Surville about his oppressive work habits, their demanding mother, and his desire for a rich widow. There are no letters between 1822 and 1827, during which time he tried debt-producing commercial ventures. In 1829 he wrote friendly letters to Napoleon's "rough marshal" Junot's widow. The year 1830 was pivotal: Fame was beginning to come. Balzac wrote to Mme. Zulma Carraud, whom he had met through Laure and who proved to be "one of the brightest and most salutary influences of his life." James writes much about Balzac's curious *Louis Lambert* (1832), which its author thought erudite but which James calls "unreadable" in toto, much preferring the "marvelous" *Contes drolatiques* (1832 . . .). Mme.

de Castries, of Aix-les-Bains, instructed Balzac in high-society ladies' manners. In 1833 he vowed to write fourteen hours a day for the next three years. (James points out that the debt-plagued genius did so for the next fifteen.) In 1836 Balzac wrote of Mme. de Berny's imminent death and called the woman a divinity and the inspiration of Mme. de Mortsauf, in his *Le Lys de la vallée* (1835). James devotes much space to Balzac's love for Mme. Hanska but with it his increasingly "somber and bitter" tone and "lugubrious egotism." Indeed, his letters show no history of ideas, but rather the nature of a writer both debased and rejuvenated by work. In later years he traveled—to Italy, Germany (which he "detested"), Russia, and Poland (he luxuriated in Countess Hanska's "tranquil, opulent family life" there)—and bought "things," that is, pottery, pictures, houses (notably his villa "Les Jardies" at Sèvres, near Paris), and furniture to fit out the villa for his marriage to Mme. Haska. Debts paid off at last, he spent the winter of 1848–1849 at her Polish estate but could follow ease only with death. "One cannot do what Balzac did and live," James concludes and then awesomely adds this: "His terrible industry had blasted the soil it passed over; he had sacrificed to his work the very things he worked for." James compares Balzac with Charles Dickens*: Both had vigor, character, self-confidence, variety, commercial ambition, and power to depict the imagined; and each overworked his talent "as a gold-mine, violently and brutally." (Only Shakespeare rivals them.) Balzac was energetic, coarse, tender, corrupt, natural, voracious. "Certainly no solider intellectual work has ever been achieved by man." His *Comédie humaine* has faults, but it is a monument. James wrote a letter to his friend Katherine Prescott Wormeley* (8 Feb 1900) to praise her for her painstaking work on Balzac. Next, repeating some previous insights, James provided a lengthy introduction to an English translation, entitled *The Two Young Brides*, of Balzac's *Deux jeunes mariées* (London: Heinemann, 1902; reprinted in *Notes on Novelists*, 1914), in which he calls the great Frenchman "Gulliver among the pygmies," repeats his fixed idea that Balzac is not charming but serious, and images him not only as plowing all of France like a "great garden" but also as holding up a mirror to the most rounded, organized society ever seen on earth. Balzac is twin brothers, since he is both scientist and reporter, both artist and historian—with data, ideas, observations, facts, and details. James cites *Le Curé de village* as particularly illustrative of this point, with its "fatal break of 'tone.' " Citing more fiction, James images Balzac as a "seated mass . . . in our path," one which we cannot avoid. When he decided "to 'do' France," Fate punished him by letting him try. James repeats his notion that Balzac presents the female character, will, and personality uniquely well, especially old families' great ladies, amid whom he sits like a pasha in his seraglio. But Balzac was also a prisoner in a cage he built around himself, "condemned to hard labour for life." His *Comédie humaine* became his Frankenstein's monster. He saw his subject so harmoniously that critics (James cites several) ought to keep quiet. How could Balzac have had time to write and yet have any time for observing and living? His dry, "starved" letters read like a galley slave's "wail . . . at the oar." James then compares him to Émile Zola,* who, however, was lucky enough to have Balzac's artistic example, then survive his work and enjoy life. Was "swagger[ing]" Balzac "audacious" or "innocent" to plan and then write his incomparable *Comédie humaine*? He cared mainly for the passionate play and revelation of characters— "the natural food of novelists." At last, James briefly adverts to *Deux jeunes mariées*, details of which illustrate the "penetrating power" of Balzac, who may be historic or romantic and may have escaped his cage by "smash[ing] . . . the window-pane of the real." Perhaps James's most helpful work on Balzac came next. It is his lecture "The Lesson of Balzac," delivered frequently in the United States in 1905 and then published (*Atlantic Monthly*, Aug 1905; reprinted in *The Question of Our Speech. The Lesson of Balzac. Two Lectures*, 1905). James begins by saying that literary criticism increases appreciation, which augments enjoyment. Balzac, "the father of us [novelists] all," fills our attention, educates the critical reader, is more complex than George Sand or Jane Austen,* for example, or the Brontë* sisters, who are liked partly for sentimental reasons. No one of his novels sums him up; we must take him "in the mass." James has learned more from him than from any other novelist. Poets are lyrical—they laugh, cry, and "express . . . life," whereas the novelist presents an image of life. Balzac's *Comédie humaine*, which rode the man to death in twenty years, is "a rank tropical forest of detail and specification"—later James calls it Balzac's "garden of France" with attached picture galleries—created as the author multiplied experience by intellectual vibration. It is a mystery how he could quarry so much material and then use it all. Fellow novelists envy him his "[q]uantity and intensity." Each novelist unconsciously colors the air of his picture by the light of his unique temperament. James describes the individual fictive air of several novelists but concludes that Balzac offers a mixture "richer and thicker" and, in addition, packs his corridors in it with "figures representing . . . ideas" derived from experience within himself. He worked like a monk illuminating manuscripts of legends about "strugglers and sinners." James compares Balzac to Zola, who is less complete, less fine, more mechanical. Balzac represents, whereas Zola imitates representations. Balzac may have faults, but he saturated himself with his ideas and (as Taine so nicely puts it) loved his creations, whom he penetrated and from whose "point of vision" he saw. He risks his readers' well-being, whereas British novelists want to make sure of their readers' moral judgment. The modern novel, too easily manufactured " 'on the cheap,' " is now bankrupt. Novelists should seek completeness but must compromise; Balzac fuses his elements into a mass. See, for example, *Le Père Goriot, Eugénie Grandet*, and *Le Curé de village*, all of which "compose," though not necessarily with any great sense of proportion. Balzac foreshortens brilliantly and shows us the lapse of time. He kept dialogue strictly in its place. At its best, the novel is a tapestry, not a "capacious tepid tank" filled with talk. Yes, Balzac is "the master of us all," and James images him as "our towering idol," heavy and gilded, in the forest of fiction. James's weakest comments on Balzac are in his review of *Balzac* (1913) by Émile Faguet* (*Times Literary Supplement*, 19 Jun

1913; reprinted in *Living Age*, 9 Aug 1913, and in *Notes on Novelists*, 1914). In it, James agrees with Faguet that Balzac was vulgar, but he praises him anyway for using vulgarity to present his "immensely human" gallery of characters. James extols Balzac for pouring his mould exactly full and painting every picture to its frame edge. He used himself as material for twenty frenzied years because he had "a pre-experiential inspiration." He was "an historian unprecedented" of his identified France. While Sand is now waning in the public eye, Balzac is waxing. Whereas she treats love as the "most representable thing," he puts it in its place. James names as Balzac's best critics Taine, Ferdinand Brunetière, and Faguet; all prefer the realistic to the romantic Balzac, whose "geniality" inspires reader "loyalty." Once again, James praises his handling of money, homes, and clothes—as a way to show class differences. James agrees with Faguet that their subject displays more quantity than quality, but then he discriminates by suggesting that Balzac's individualized middle-class characters are best of all, and better than those of Zola, who is best at "muster[ing] . . . groups and crowds," which, however, lack well-drawn women. Balzac's "fertile vulgarity, his peccant taste," were necessary in a novelist who saw mankind as "deformedly conditioned" and tragically doomed. James's letters are filled with references to Balzac; for one example among dozens, in a letter to Grace Norton* (3 Nov 1884) James says of Balzac "I have a great affection, a kind of reverence for him, as for the founder and father of our modern effort, and on the whole the greatest genius in his line. He is an immense comfort to me . . . " James's library contained four books by Balzac.

Bamborough, Lord. In "A London Life," Selina Wing Berrington's former lover.

Banker, Miss. In "The Two Faces," a gossip who talks with Shirley Sutton about Lady Valda Gwyther.

Banks. In *The Outcry*, the novel, and *The Outcry*, the play, Lord Theign's butler at Dedborough.

Bannister. In "A Landscape Painter," the man whom Miriam Quarterman decides not to marry.

Bantling, Bob. In *The Portrait of a Lady*, the Britisher who escorts Henrietta Stackpole and whom she will eventually marry.

Baptiste. In *The Ambassadors*, one of Chadwick Newsome's servants.

Barbara, Lady. In *The American*, a relative of Lord Deepmere.

Barbey d'Aurevilly, Jules-Amédée (1808–89). Weirdly orthodox, reactionary, and romantic novelist, biographer, and literary critic. James dined with Barbey once in Paris and later wrote to Sir Edmund Wilson Gosse* (16 Jun [1896]), who had just published some critical comments on Barbey, that the man "scared & depressed" him for being "grotesquely self-conscious & invraisemblablement figged out." James added that Barbey "was a *pen* & praeteria nihil." James's library contained one book by Barbey d'Aurevilly.

Bardi. In *The Outcry*, the novel, the Milan art scholar who overrules the opinion of Pappendick and says that Lord Theign's supposed Moretto painting is really by Mantovano.* In *The Outcry*, the play, this scholar from Milan is named Caselli. Bardi may be modeled partly on art scholar Bernard Berenson.*

Barker family. Relatives of James, whose father's sister Jeannette (Janet) James married William H. Barker of New York City. The couple's children, who were James's cousins, included Robert (Bob) Barker, Elizabeth Barker, and Augustus (Gus, Gussy) Barker, who was killed in action in 1863, during the Civil War. James mentions them in *A Small Boy and Others* and *Notes of a Son and Brother*. He also identifies members of the Barker family in a letter to Howard Overing Sturgis* (12 or 13 May 1913).

Barker, Harley Granville. British man of the theater, more commonly known as Harley Granville Granville-Barker.*

Baron, Peter. In "Sir Dominick Ferrand," the writer who finds and destroys the Ferrand papers and then marries Mrs. Ryves, who is Sir Dominick Ferrand's illegitimate, widowed daughter.

Barrace, Miss. In *The Ambassadors*, a friend of Chad Newsome, Little Bilham, and their group. She rather likes Waymarsh later. The character is probably based on James's friend Henrietta Reubell.*

Barrès, Auguste Maurice (1862–1923). Pro-Lorraine French novelist, politician, journalist, traveler, and author of essays concerning World War I. In the early 1890s, through mutual friends Paul Bourget* and Alphonse Daudet,* James met and socialized briefly with Barrès in Florence and Paris. In letters to friends, James expresses his dislike for both the writer and his works. Barrès's 1888 *Huit jours chez M. Renan* is "dreary," and the author is "*sick* with affection hiding real poverty" (to Theodore E. Child* [23 Mar (1888)]); his 1894 novel *Du Sang* is "exquisite in its fearfully intelligent impertinence & its diabolical [Ernest]

Renanisation'' (to Sir Edmund Wilson Gosse* [9 Nov 1894]); and his novel *Les Déracinés* (1897) is "very curious and serious, but a gruesome picture of young France" (to Grace Norton* [Christmas Day 1897]). For *The Book of France* (London: Macmillan, 1915; and Paris: Champion, 1915), James translated Barrès's "Les Saints de la France." James's library contained two books by Barrès.

Barrett, Lawrence (1838–1891). New Jersey-born actor whose parents were Irish. He served as a Union Army captain during the Civil War, managed a San Francisco theatrical company, acted in Shakespearean and other roles, and performed on occasion in London (mostly in the early 1880s). James knew Barrett slightly and wrote him (18 Jul [1884]) to veto the idea of dramatizing *The Portrait of a Lady*, which he called "a study of character" with action not "vivid enough to keep a play on its legs."

Barrie, Sir James Matthew (1860–1937). British dramatist and novelist, born to a humble family in Scotland and educated at Edinburgh University. He achieved success first as a writer of sketches, essays, and loosely constructed novels. Then he turned to the theater, alternated plays and more fiction, and achieved his greatest stage triumphs with *The Admirable Crichton* (1903), *Peter Pan* (1904), *The Twelve-Pound Look* (1910), and *Dear Brutus* (1917). His nondramatic works include *Auld Licht Idylls* (1888, village sketches), *A Window in Thrums* (1889, connected sketches), *My Lady Nicotine* (1891, essays), *The Little Minister* (1891, sentimental novel, dramatized 1897), *Margaret Ogilvy* (1894, biography of his mother), *Sentimental Tommy* (1896, novel), and *Tommy and Grizel* (1900, novel). James met Barrie because of their common interest in the theater. While James unsuccessfully prepared *The Outcry* for the Duke of York's Theatre 1910 repertory season at Barrie's urging, Barrie contributed a success with *The Twelve-Pound Note*. Barrie bequeathed the copyright on *Peter Pan* to London's Great Ormond Street Hospital for Sick Children, which received unspecified but enormous royalties through 1987. James's library contained two books by Barrie.

Bartram, May. In "The Beast in the Jungle," the woman who selflessly loves John Marcher. She identifies the beast in the sterile jungle of his life long before he does.

Baskerville. In *The Princess Casamassima*, an actor whom Hyacinth Robinson and Millicent Henning see when they go to the theater.

Basset, Lady. In *The Album*, a guest, evidently widowed, in Bedford's country house. After the owner's death, she sets her cap for Sir Ralph Damant, Bedford's heir. When, partly to avoid her, woman-hating Sir Ralph gives the inheritance to Mark Moorsom Bernal, she decamps.

Bates. In "The Two Faces," May Grantham's butler.

Battledown, Lady. In "A Bundle of Letters," a friend of Evelyn Vane.

Baudelaire, Charles (1821–1867). Controversial French poet and also translator of tales by Edgar Allan Poe.* Baudelaire is most famous for his decadent poems, collected as *Les Fleurs du mal* (1857). He led a group of nineteenth-century French sophisticates who stressed the neurotic and abnormal. Adversely reviewing *Les Fleurs du mal* (*Nation* 27, Apr 1876; reprinted in *French Poets and Novelists*, 1878), James said that Baudelaire was only gropingly aware of life's "moral complexities" and called his "evil" merely external (preferring the depiction of inner evil by Nathaniel Hawthorne*), but he admitted that the poet had a fine technique. He regarded Baudelaire as weakened by a fondness for that "greater charlatan" and "greater genius," Poe. James's library contained one book by Baudelaire.

Baxley, Henry Willis (1803–1876). Professor of anatomy and physiology at the University of Maryland. He published his medical lectures and also books on politics and travel. James reviewed (*Nation*, 20 May 1875) Baxley's 1876 *Spain: Art Remains and Art Realities . . .*, describing it "in form and manner . . . simply barbarous" with too much material on theology, but admittedly having something of value concerning architecture. James calls the author "fanatical" regarding Bartolomé Esteban Murillo,* weak on Diego de Silva y Velasquez,* and foolish to tilt with John Ruskin.* James recommends abridging the work if it is to be useful to any traveler.

Baxter, Stephen. In "The Story of a Masterpiece," the painter whose portrait of Marian Everett distresses her fiancé John Lennox.

Bayswater, Duke and Duchess of. In "An International Episode," Lord Lambert's parents. The Duchess's heavy-handed prejudice helps to ruin her son's relationship with Bessie Alden.

Beaconsfield, Lord. Title of Benjamin Disraeli.*

Beadel-Muffet, Lady. In "The Papers," Sir A. B. C. Beadel-Muffet's recently deceased wife.

Beadel-Muffet, Miranda. In "The Papers," Sir Beadel-Muffet's daughter, who is reported to be not marrying Guy Devereux.

Beadel-Muffet, Sir. A. B. C., K.C.B., M.P. In "The Papers," the publicity seeker the report of whose disappearance causes the sensation he desires. He has three daughters. His wife has recently died.

Beadel-Muffet, The Misses. In "The Papers," either of Sir A. B. C. Beadel-Muffet's two daughters not named Miranda.

Beadle, Dr. In "Crawford's Consistency," a physician who once attended Elizabeth Ingram.

Beardsley, Aubrey Vincent (1872–1898). Brighton-born artist, art editor, and poet. He first worked in an architect's office and then as an insurance company clerk. While still in his teens, he started his short career as a decadent but skillful illustrator of books (including *The Pierrot of the Minute*, by Ernest Dowson, *Mademoiselle de Maupin* by Théophile Gautier,* *Volpone*, by Ben Jonson, *Le Morte D'Arthur*, by Thomas Malory, "The Rape of the Lock" by Alexander Pope, and *Salomé* by Oscar Wilde*). Beardsley became the art editor of the *Yellow Book* in 1894. He was then associated with the *Savoy*, in which he published a few poems. He converted to Roman Catholicism shortly before his death from tuberculosis in Menton, France. His works are best in black and white; notable for deviations from normal perspective and proportion, they include startling posters. James published three short stories and an essay on George Sand* in the *Yellow Book*, through his friendship with Henry Harland,* its editor. According to Marc André Raffalovich,* James once visited Beardsley and his sister, and he was a bit shocked by a Japanese print she showed him. When Raffalovich sent him a copy of *Last Letters of Aubrey Beardsley* (1904), James wrote a thank-you letter (7 Nov 1913) in which he comments on Beardsley: "I knew him a little, and he was . . . touching, and extremely individual; but I hated his productions and thought them extraordinarily base—and couldn't find . . . the formula that reconciled this baseness, aesthetically, with his being so perfect a case of the artistic spirit. . . . The poor boy remains quite one of the few distinguished images on the roll of young English genius brutally clipped . . . I am glad to have three or four very definite . . . recollections of him." Other friends whom James and Beardsley had in common include Sir Max Beerbohm,* Jacques-Émile Blanche,* and Hubert Montague Crackanthorpe.*

"The Beast in the Jungle." Short story (16,700 words), published in *The Better Sort*, 1903; revised and reprinted in *The Novels and Tales of Henry James*, Volume XVII, 1909. (Characters: May Bartram, Mr. and Mrs. Boyer, John Marcher, Mr. and Mrs. Pemble.) When John Marcher meets May Bartram again, she reminds him that he told her almost ten years earlier at Sorrento that life was going to spring something highly unusual on him—something like a beast out of the jungle of life. She wonders if it might be love. He hints at a previous affair, which was not, he adds, momentous. She agrees to watch and wait with him, in London, for the event. Years pass, and Marcher calls on her regularly and takes her to the opera frequently. Later she implies that she has identified the beast, but will not tell him what it is, and she says that he will never know. More time passes, and she develops a fatal illness, which makes Marcher feel unfairly deprived. She says that she would live on for him if she could, but she dies, and he is only a casual mourner. After uneventful travel, he returns to her cemetery; at a fresh grave near May's, Marcher is shocked to see a man so ravaged by grief that his face looks burned and hacked. This, then, is profound feeling? Marcher concludes that May loved him for himself and the good she might do for him, whereas he was ruinously egotistical. Sick though she was that late April day, he still might have saved her by genuinely unselfish love. He knows that he was destined to be the one man in all the world to whom nothing was to happen. Too late, he feels the spring of the beast and falls on her grave. A Notebook entry (5 Feb 1895) sketches out an idea which resulted in "The Way It Came" (later entitled "The Friends of the Friends") but which also seems to point to "The Beast in the Jungle," since the note ends thus: "the wasting of life is the implication of death." A later Notebook entry (27 Aug 1901) details the situation in "The Beast in the Jungle": a protective woman's early identification of her egocentric friend's obsession, her death, and his tardy realization that love "was what might have happened, and what *has* happened is that it didn't." Almost all critics agree that this is one of James's finest stories. Whether it was based on personal experience is more questionable. Did James regard himself as a person who did not sufficiently live? It is much to be doubted. Yet it is likely that May Bartram's passive devotion to her lover manqué may be James's reflection of the unrequited love Constance Fenimore Woolson* felt for her too-cerebral novelist friend. Incredibly, James seems to have dictated this haunting work in three sessions (1 July, and 12 and 16 October, 1902), to his secretary Mary Weld,* at Lamb House.* In the preface to Volume XVII of *The Novels and Tales of Henry James*, he apologizes for his "attested predilection for poor sensitive gentleman." Marcher resembles a character out of Nathaniel Hawthorne* in his monstrous egotism; yet, again like Hawthornean sinners, he is sympathetically limned. The story is ultramodern, connecting as it does to morals in T. S. Eliot's *Waste Land*, to Ernest Hemingway's celebrated *Nada*, and to absurdist literature, featuring a search which turns from outward to inward.

Beati, Angelo. In "Adina," the Italian who found and lost the itaglio but, in the process, won Sam Scrope's fiancée Adina Waddington.

Beatrice. In "A New England Winter," Susan Daintry's maid.

Beauchemin, Lady Lucretia. In "Lady Barbarina," the lady who introduces Dr. Jackson Lemon to her sister Lady Barbarina Clement.

Beauchemin, Lord. In "A London Life," Lucretia's husband and hence Lord Philip and Lady Canterville's son-in-law.

Beaumont, Beatrice. In "The Papers," an actress mentioned for a part in Mortimer Marshal's play.

Beaumont, Mr. and Mrs. In "Nona Vincent," the actor-manager of the Legitimate Theater and his wife.

Beaumont, Percy. In "An International Episode," Lord Lambeth's friend, who fears that Lambeth is falling in love with Bessie Alden.

Beaupré. In "Lord Beaupré," Guy Firminger's cousin, the son of the elder Lord Beaupré; he dies.

Beaupré, Lord. In "Lord Beaupré," the father of Guy Firminger's cousin. The lord dies, as does his son thereafter.

Beaupré, Lord. In "Lord Beaupré," the lord's son who also dies.

Beaupré, Lord. In "Lord Beaupré," Guy Firminger, whom deaths in his family turn into a titled lord. Matrimonially inclined women then seek him out.

Beaurepas, Mlle. In "The Pension Beaurepas," Mme. Beaurepas's niece.

Beaurepas, Mme. In "The Pension Beaurepas," the keeper of the pension.

Beck, Clara. In "Guest's Confession," Laura Guest's widowed duenna and the object of Crawford's affections.

Beck, Philadelphus. In "The Siege of London," Nancy Grenville Beck Headway's previous husband.

Becky. In "A Day of Days," Herbert and Adela Moore's maid.

Bedford. In *The Album*, the dying owner of Courtlands, a lovely estate. When his relative Sir Ralph Damant lies about Mark Moorsom Bernal, another potential heir, Bedford wills the place to Sir Ralph, who ultimately gives it to Mark.

Beerbohm, Sir Max (1872–1956). London-born, Oxford-educated essayist, drama critic, caricaturist, and wit. He was the half-brother of the actor and theater manager Sir Herbert Beerbohm Tree,* whom James also knew. Max Beerbohm's prolific sketches pleasantly skewer the absurd pretensions of his friends and contemporaries. He published essays in the *Yellow Book* while he was still a student. He published some early essays and caricatures in book form in 1896. In 1910 he married actress Florence Kahn and established a long residence in Rapallo, Italy. He published the satirical *Zuleika Dobson*, his only novel, in 1911. His collection of parodies called *The Christmas Garland* (1911) includes "The Mote in the Middle Distance," which mimics the excesses of James's major-phase prose. (James relished it.) Beerbohm's most celebrated caricature of James was inspired by a remark the novelist made in his 1904 essay on Gabriele D'Annunzio,* in which he says that the Italian writer's shutting sexual activity "out from the rest of life" is like "double pairs" of shoes placed outside shut doors "in the corridors of promiscuous hotels." Beerbohm also drew a cartoon of James and Joseph Conrad* in conversation. One artist whom both Beerbohm and James knew in the 1890s was the ill-starred Aubrey Vincent Beardsley.* When Beerbohm wrote to James to praise his short story "The Jolly Corner," James replied ornately (19 Dec 1908) to register his delight that his "ambitious Muse does work upon you." Beerbohm unsuccessfully proposed to William James's widow Alice that Sir Edmund Wilson Gosse* be named the editor of James's letters. James's library contained one book by Beerbohm.

Beever, Kate. In *The Other House*, the novel, banker Paul Beever's widow and the head of the house (called Eastmead) near Anthony Bream's house (called Bounds). The nearby town is Wilverley. Her son is also named Paul. In *The Other House*, the play, she is forty-five years old at the outset and is called Cousin Kate by Jean Martle, whom she wants her son Paul to marry. Her more daring friends call Mrs. Beever the Queen-Mother.

Beever, Paul. In *The Other House*, the novel, Kate Beever's deceased husband. Their son is also named Paul. The older man was a banker at Wilverley and the former partner of Paul Bream.

Beever, Paul. In *The Other House*, the novel, the son of Kate Beever, who wants him to marry Jean Martle. In *The Other House*, the play, Paul is a nineteen-year-old Oxford student at the outset. Later, he is in love with Rose Armiger, and he offers to aid the murderess in any way he can.

"The Beldonald Holbein." Short story (7,700 words), published in *Harper's New Monthly Magazine* (Oct 1901); reprinted in *The Better Sort*, 1903; revised and reprinted in *The Novels and Tales of Henry James*, Volume XVIII, 1909. (Characters: Lady Nina Beldonald, Louisa Brash, Miss Dadd, Mrs. Munden, Paul Outreau.) The painter-narrator learns that Lady Nina Beldonald has hired as a foil for her hard beauty an ugly, widowed cousin named Louisa Brash from America. But at a reception given by the narrator, a French colleague, Paul Outreau, declares Mrs. Brash a perfect Hans Holbein the younger* and as such must be painted. Lady Beldonald is soon so jealous of Mrs. Brash's fame among the artists that she sends the old woman back to America and replaces her with a new foil—this time a vapidly pretty, blank-faced creature. James begins with a plastic beauty, for characteristic symmetry uses poor old Mrs. Brash as her foil, and creates an ironic fable on human vanity. According to a Notebook entry (16 May 1899), the idea of artists becoming ecstatic over the paintability of a wrinkled old woman came to James when Maud Howe Elliott* told him that her aged mother Julia Ward Howe* was so seen by Roman art folk in 1899.

The same Notebook entry says that Mrs. Howe might be regarded as "being thought *the* most picturesque, striking, lovely old (wrinkled and *marked*) 'Holbein,' etc., that ever was." Specific details concerning Mrs. Brash may owe something to *Lady Butts* by Holbein, purchased in 1899 by James's friend Isabella Stewart Gardner.*

Beldonald, Lady Nina. In "The Beldonald Holbein," a hard beauty who wants a plain foil but is satisfied with Louisa Brash for only a short time.

Belfield, Diana. In "Longstaff's Marriage," a selfish beauty who refuses the hand of supposedly dying Reginald Longstaff. Then, when she is really dying, she wants him.

Belfield, Mrs. In "Longstaff's Marriage," Diana Belfield's mother, whose death unites Diana and her companion Agatha Josling.

Belinda. In "The Ghostly Rental," Captain Diamond's black maid.

Belinda. In "An Animated Conversation," a bright and spirited American hostess in London.

Bell, Lady Florence Eveleen Eleanore (née Olliffe) (1851–1930). Woman of letters, wife of rich Yorkshireman Sir Hugh Bell (1844–1931), and mother of Gertrude Margaret Lowthian Bell and Mary Katharine Bell. Mary Bell married Charles Philips Trevelyan, of the distinguished Trevelyan family.* Lady Bell wrote one-act comediettas, dramatic versions of nursery rhymes and fairy tales for children, drawing-room monologues, elementary French and German language books, adult fiction, and essays on conduct. Her most significant work is *At the Works: A Study of a Manufacturing Town* (1907), about Yorkshire iron-workers. Her letters were published in 1928. Hugh Bell wrote about the iron industry, finance, and free trade. James and Mrs. Bell shared good conversation, a love of the theater, and knowledge of France, and came especially to admire Elizabeth Robins.* Some of James's sweetest letters are addressed to Lady Bell, who provided moral support when James was trying so hard and so unsuccessfully to conquer the London Stage. The character of Mrs. Alsager in "Nona Vincent" is based on Mrs. Bell. James is surely punning for his loyal friends the Hugh Bells when he writes toward the end of the short story "The Middle Years," that "Doctor Hugh . . . put . . . into his young voice the ring of a marriage-bell."

Bellamy, D. F. In "Pandora," the fiancé of Pandora Day, who obtains a consular assignment for him in Holland.

Bellegarde, Blanche de. In *The American*, Urbain de Bellegarde's daughter.

Bellegarde, Comte Valentin de. In *The American*, Claire de Cintré's younger brother and Christopher Newman's ebullient, would-be helpful friend. He is killed by Stanislas Kapp in a duel over Noémie Nioche. In *The American: A Comedy in Four Acts*, he has met Noémie a year before the action commences, first meets Newman at her home, quarrels with Lord Deepmere over family etiquette (and to a degree over Noémie), and in a duel (seconded by Gaston de Marignac) is killed by Deepmere. In the rewritten fourth act, Valentin recovers after surgery and is reconciled with Deepmere.

Bellegarde, Marquis Henri-Urbain de. In *The American*, he is mentioned as the murdered husband of Mme. Emmeline Atheling de Bellegarde. Catherine Bread gives Christoper Newman evidence concerning the murder.

Bellegarde, Marquis Urbain (Henri-Urbain) de. In *The American*, the nominal head of the Bellegarde family. He is the son of Mme. Emmeline Atheling de Bellegarde and the brother of Valentin de Bellegarde and Claire de Bellegarde de Cintré. Urbain is married and has a little daughter, named Blanche. He constantly defers to his domineering mother. He and Christopher Newman despise each other. In *The American: A Comedy in Four Acts*, he opposes Newman but ultimately sees his sister Claire accept the American.

Bellegarde, Mme. Emmeline Atheling de. In *The American*, the widowed mother of Marquis Urbain de Bellegarde, Claire de Cintré, and Valentin de Bellegarde. She is Christopher Newman's pluckily implacable foe. In *The American: A Comedy in Four Acts*, she prefers Lord Deepmere as a second husband for Claire but ultimately sees her daughter accept Newman. In the rewritten fourth act, Madame de Bellegarde is revealed as the cause of the death of both her husband and her lover/son-in-law Comte de Cintré ten years earlier; furthermore, she is not present to see Claire accept Newman.

Bellegarde, Mme. Urbain de. In *The American*, Urbain's wife and little Blanche's mother. She loathes her husband, calls him wooden, feels socially frustrated, and likes Christopher Newman.

Bellevue, Lady Beatrice. In "An International Episode," a fashionable lady seen in Hyde Park.

Bellhouse, Lady. In "Mrs. Medwin," a fashionable lady who evidently approves of Mrs. Medwin.

Beltram, Dr. In *The Awkward Age*, Agnesina's physician.

Belwood. In "An Animated Conversation," an easygoing Britisher in London, who criticizes jingoistic journalism.

"The Bench of Desolation." Short story (18,200 words), published in *Putnam's Magazine* (Oct 1909–Jan 1910); reprinted in *The Finer Grain*, 1910. (Characters: Kate Cookham, Charley Coote, Dean, Herbert Dodd, Nan Drury Dodd, the Misses Dodd, Drury, Bill Frankle, David Geddes, Captain Roper.) Long ago, Kate Cookham told Herbert Dodd, her fiancé, that she would jolly well sue him if he did not marry her right away. In annoyance he paid her off (£270 of a demanded £400), mortgaged his secondhand book business and lost it, married poor Nan Drury, and had two daughters by her. Time and poverty have killed off all of his family, and Dodd is now a gas-company clerk near the southern English seacoast, where he often sits on a desolate bench. Suddenly Kate returns, no longer—in fact, never—vicious and now a transmogrified lady. She offers him his money back with substantial accrued interest (i.e., £1,260). She explains that she had hoped by her ruse to force him into marriage, since he was slow and she deeply loved him. They discuss matters over tea at her hotel. They meet next Sunday at the bench of desolation. She is active; he, fatefully passive still. A Notebook entry (26 Dec 1908) sketches the details of this sad story's plot, which is simply not credible save as a parable. The action is a nightmare, ringing changes on *The Winter's Tale* by William Shakespeare* to dramatize anemic forgiveness and sad reconciliation.

Bender, Breckenridge. In *The Outcry*, the novel, and *The Outcry*, the play, the rich American (age fifty-six) whose purchase of art treasures causes an "outcry" in England. He buys Lady Lappington's Longhi and tries unsuccessfully to buy Lord Theign's Mantovano* and Lady Amy Sandgate's Sir Thomas Lawrence. Bender may owe something both to Alexander Turney Stewart,* a wealthy American buyer of art objects, and also to art-scholar Bernard Berenson,* who bought paintings for Isabella Stewart Gardner.*

Benedict, Clara Woolson (?–1923). The younger sister of James's close friend Constance Fenimore Woolson.* Mrs. Benedict was the mother of writer Clare Benedict (died c. 1961). Mrs. Benedict was widowed in 1871 when her husband was killed in a railroad accident. Her mother died in 1879, and later that same year she, her daughter, and "Connie" went abroad. Constance Woolson never returned to the United States. When she died in 1894, James wrote elaborately considerate letters to both Mrs. Benedict and her daughter, who were flattered and appreciative. He met the two women in Italy and helped them prepare some twenty-seven boxes of Woolson's effects to be shipped home. Later, Clara and her daughter Clare adopted a pattern of leaving America in March or April, traveling in Europe for about eighteen months, returning home, and the next spring doing it all over again. Clara appears to have been cultured, conceited, spoiled, and prissy. A name-dropper in her letters and autobiographical notes, she mentioned the following persons familiar to James: William Wilberforce Baldwin,* Ariane Randolph Curtis and Daniel Sargent Curtis,* Sir Henry Irving,* John Milton Hay,* George Meredith,* and Edmund Clarence Stedman.* James came to know both women well and he wrote one or both of them twenty-eight letters in all (1894–1912). He often met them in London during their tours abroad. He called Clara "Eagle,"; Clare, "Dove" and "Clarima." The best letters concern Woolson, Queen Victoria, and Edward VII.* In a letter to Francis Boott* (11 Oct [1895]), he called Clara and her daughter "very futile and foolish, poor things," adding that Clara was "very considerably mad." She once wrote that James and her daughter shared "a strong telephathic sympathy" lasting from "the earliest times until their last meeting in 1913." James's library contained one book by Clare Benedict.

Benedict, Frank Lee (1834–1910). Prolific American novelist, short-story writer, and translator, who often published anonymously. James reviewed (*Nation*, 13 Jan 1876) Benedict's *St. Simon's Niece: A Novel* (1875), which James says is about American Helen Devereux's high-society "round of visits" in Windsor and, especially, in the American "Colony" in Paris. She is nominally chaperoned by her uncle St. Simon and his wife Fanny. James sarcastically concludes that the vulgar, unwholesome novel is probably by a woman in spite of the name of the author on the title page.

Benson, Arthur Christopher (1862–1925). Son of Edward White Benson* and the older brother of Edward Frederic Benson.* A. C. Benson was educated at Eton College and then at King's College, Cambridge. He was an influential master at Eton (1885–1903) but in time found that his duties interfered with his writing; so he moved to Cambridge, where he wrote and also coedited selections from Queen Victoria's voluminous correspondence (3 vols., 1907). He became a fellow at Magdalene College, Cambridge (1904), suffered nervous breakdowns (1908, 1917) and was named president of Magdalene (1912) and master there (1915). He helped Magdalene gain greater prominence. Benson's literary activity was prodigious, amounting to more than a hundred volumes, including books on William Morris,* Walter Horatio Pater,* Dante Gabriel Rossetti,* John Ruskin,* and Alfred, Lord Tennyson*; numerous short biographies; some novels and poetry; studies of Eton; autobiographical fantasy; and reflective essays. Some of his most important titles are *The Upton Letters* (1905), *From a College Window* (1906), *Beside Still Waters* (1907), and *The Leaves of the Tree* (1911). He also wrote a biography of his father. A. C. Benson's 180-volume diary (one volume is now missing) totals more than 24,500 pages (well over 4,000,000 words). It was edited and published in small part by his friend Percy Lubbock* (1926) and more fully by David Newsome (1980). Benson met James at the home of Frederic William Henry Myers,* in July 1884; the two became great friends and often visited each other and wrote to each other. On the day James signed the lease papers for Lamb House* he wrote to Benson (25 Sept 1897) that the place "has a beautiful room for *you*"; in the same letter, he happily agrees to let Benson send his diary for James to read. Less than a week later (1 Oct 1897), James wrote to Benson again, to praise his diary, especially his account of the death at prayer of his father. James wrote to Benson (5 Jun 1909) to thank him fulsomely for making James acquainted with Sir Hugh Seymour Walpole.* Benson later reminisced charmingly about James at Lamb House. He admired James enormously but regarded his prose as unnecessarily dense. They had many friends in common, including Sir Edmund Wilson Gosse* (to whom James probably introduced Benson), Gaillard Thomas Lapsley,* Lubbock, Howard Overing Sturgis,* and Walpole (whose intimate friendship with James eventually caused Benson some envy). Benson deplored James's pontifical adulation of the poetry of Rupert Brooke.* Benson's father gave James the idea for "The Turn of the Screw." Benson's brother E. F. Benson had a tenancy at Lamb House for part of the year, which tenancy A. C. Benson later shared for vacations. After A. C. Benson's death, E. F. Benson published, in London (Elkin Mathews & Marrot, 1930) and New York (Scribner, 1930), fifty-one letters, mostly innocuous and unrevealing, which James had written to A. C. Benson (1892–1915). James's library contained two books by A. C. Benson.

Benson, Edward Frederic (1867–1940). Son of Edward White Benson* and younger brother of Arthur Christopher Benson.* E. F. Benson was educated at Marlborough College and then at King's College, Cambridge. He did archaeological work in Greece and also worked for the Hellenic Society in Egypt. He wrote voluminously, publishing more than ninety books, including fiction, plays, biographies, reminiscences, and works on sports and politics. His fiction includes social satire, stories of school life, and tales of supernaturalism and horror. His *Dodo* series (1893, 1914, 1921) and his *Spook* books (1928, 1934) were once very popular. His most valuable nonfictional books are *Account Rendered* (1911), *Our Family Affairs, 1867–1897* (1920), *As We Were: A Victorian Peep-Show* (1930), *As We Are* (1932), and *Final Edition: Informal Autobiography* (1940). E. F. Benson was the mayor of Rye (1934–1937), and he lived for a time in Lamb House.* His so-called *Lucia* novels (beginning with *Queen Lucia* [1920] and *Lucia in London* [1927]) take place in Rye. James knew E. F. Benson, though not so well as he knew Benson's brother A. C. Benson. In a letter to Jonathan Sturges* ([10 Jul 1900]), James calls E. F. Benson " 'Dodo' Benson."

Benson, Edward White (1829–1896). Anglican priest, educator, and father of Arthur Christopher Benson,* Edward Frederic Benson,* Robert Hugh Benson, and other children. E. W. Benson received a B.A. from Cambridge and became the first headmaster of Wellington College, the bishop of Truro, and then the Archbishop of Canterbury (1883–1896). He sponsored legislative reform. He died while kneeling at prayer. His publications include books of sermons and prayers, *Cyprian* (1897) and *The Apocalypse* (1900). His son R. H. Benson, whom James knew, was an Anglican clergyman, became a Roman Catholic priest, and wrote mystical, historical, and modern fiction. James records in his Notebook (12 Jan 1895) details of a ghost story which the archbishop told him when James was his guest at Addington, some thirteen miles from Cambridge. The anecdote was the start of "The Turn of the Screw." Not long after James had published this celebrated story, he wrote to Sir Edmund Wilson Gosse* ([12 Oct 1898]) to express his hope that the Bensons did not object to his basing a "foully ugly" story upon an anecdote their late, "good old" father had "ineffectually tried to tell me."

Benson, Eugene (1839–1908). American painter long resident in Italy. He knew James's father; therefore, early in 1873 James called on him at his studio in Rome, examined a few of his landscapes, and described them in a letter home (4 Mar [1873]) as "careful and conscientious but very uninspired." James later knew Benson in Venice, where he was the stepfather of James's friend the novelist and playwright Julia Constance Fletcher.* Benson may be the model for Sam Singleton, the diminutive painter in *Roderick Hudson.*

Benton, Laura. In "A Day of Days," a friend of Adela Moore.

Benvolio. In "Benvolio," a poetic personality torn between love of the Countess and of Scholastica.

"Benvolio." Short story (16,600 words), published in the *Galaxy* (Aug 1875); reprinted in *The Madonna of the Future,* 1879. (Characters: Benvolio, Scholastica.) Split-personality Benvolio loves Scholastica and enjoys talking with her blind philosopher father. He also likes the Countess, who is worldly and gets a traveling family to hire Scholastica as a governess. Benvolio denounces the haughty Countess and returns to seek out Scholastica. Her father has died; Benvolio soon finds and comforts the girl. This story is James's only allegorical fiction: Scholastica represents the humble intellectual life; the Countess, haughty materialism. Written during his lonely time in New York in 1875, James surely seems here to be weighing the full, happy life against the lonely life of the articulate artist.

Benyon. In "Georgina's Reasons," the son of Raymond Benyon and his wife Georgina, who abandoned the boy in Italy. He is now unlocatable.

Benyon, Captain Raymond. In "Georgina's Reasons," an honorable American naval officer and the first husband of the bigamous Georgina Gressie Benyon Roy. He later falls in love with Kate Theory, although it is hopeless, because he cannot get out of his marriage.

Benyon, Georgina. In "Georgina's Reasons," the woman who becomes Georgina Gressie Benyon Roy.

Berenson, Bernard (1865–1959). Distinguished art scholar, critic, connoisseur, and author of Jewish extraction, born in Lithuania. He migrated with his parents to Boston (about 1872), studied under Charles Eliot Norton* (art history) and William James at Harvard University, graduated (1887), and married (1900) Mary Logan Whitall Smith Costello, the sister of Logan Pearsall Smith.* The Berensons settled permanently at Settignano, just northeast of Florence, Italy, where they bought (1900), restored, and decorated a forty-room, eighteenth-century Italian villa, called Villa I Tatti, in which he amassed his art collection, library (40,000 books), and numerous photographs. Berenson became the world's leading authority on Italian Renaissance paintings. He "discovered" the identities of two Renaissance painters. He was sequestered in Tuscany during World War II. His extensive publications include *Venetian Painters of the Renaissance* (1894), *The Study and Criticism of Italian Art* (1901, 1902, 1915), *The Drawings of Florentine Painters* (1903, rev. 1938), *Three Essays in Method* (1927), *Essays in Mediaeval Art* (1930), *Italian Pictures of the Renaissance* (1932), *Aesthetics and History in the Visual Arts* (1948), *Rumor and Reflection, 1941–1944* (1952), *Italian Painters in the Renaissance* (1952), *The Passionate Sightseer* (1960), and *One Year's Reading for Fun—1942* (1960). I Tatti was a Mecca for art lovers and scholars who knew Berenson, and it is now the Harvard Center for the Study of Renaissance Art. Beginning in 1894, Berenson helped his early sponsor and later his close friend Isabella Stewart Gardner* amass her $3,000,000 art collection at Fenway Court, Boston. Berenson became a major influence on Edith Newbold Jones Wharton* from the time of their first effective meeting in Paris (1909); he advised her about Italy and art and occasionally traveled with her. James evidently met Berenson only once, in the late 1900s; but the two had many mutual friends. Berenson later alleged anti-Semitism in James. It is possible that Bardi, the art expert in *The Outcry*, and Breckenridge Bender, the rich American art buyer in the same work, owe something to Berenson.

Bergerac, Baron de. In "Gabrielle de Bergerac," the narrator's grandfather.

Bergerac, Baron de. In "Gabrielle de Bergerac," Gabrielle's offensive brother whose conduct precipitates her elopement.

Bergerac, Baroness de. In "Gabrielle de Bergerac," the baron's wife and the narrator's mother.

Bergerac, Chevalier de. In "Gabrielle de Bergerac," the narrator; he is Gabrielle's nephew and Pierre's pupil.

Bergerac, Gabrielle de. In "Gabrielle de Bergerac," the narrator's aunt who elopes with and marries his boyhood tutor Pierre Coquelin and later dies with him during the French Revolution.

Bernal, Mark Moorsom. In *The Album*, an artist, now age thirty-three and long thought dead in America. (He was in a fracas in Portland, Oregon.) He returns to London, hears that his distant relative Bedford is dying, does not seek an inheritance, is deprived of it by his dishonest distant cousin Sir Ralph Damant, but gains it back through the intervention of Bedford's amanuensis Grace Jesmond. Mark and Grace then marry.

Bernard, Charles de (1804–1850). French novelist, who was born in Besançon, was educated for law, practiced journalism, and then was encouraged by Honoré de Balzac to write novels in Paris. His best novel is *Gerfaut* (1838). James in "The Minor French Novelists" (*Galaxy*, Feb 1876) praises Bernard for being "enjoyable" though "a trifle primitive and meagre." James says that he provided the last "fresh and free" fictional depictions of "antediluvian Parisians" before the Second Empire. He died without having time to become corrupted by " 'decadence.' " James likes the forcefully sketched characters in Bernard's *Les Ailes d'Icare* (1839), *Un Homme sérieux* (1843), *Le Gentilhomme Campagnard* (1846–1847), and especially *Gerfaut*. Admitting that Bernard lacks any "moral imagination" beyond the traditional, James still remembers him tenderly. James's library contained one book by Bernard.

Bernard, Clara. In "A Bundle of Letters," a friend of Miranda Hope.

Bernardstone, General. In "The Path of Duty," Lady Emily's husband and Joscelind's father.

Bernardstone, Joscelind. In "The Path of Duty," the fiancée and then wife of Ambrose Tester, who all along has loved Lady Margaret Vandeleur.

Bernardstone, Lady Emily. In "The Path of Duty," General Bernardstone's wife and Joscelind's mother.

Bernhardt, Sarah (1844–1923). Phenomenal Paris-born actress, of French, Dutch, and Jewish extraction. She was also a stage manager, playwright, sculptor, poet, and novelist. She debuted at the Comédie Française in a Jean Racine play at the age of eighteen. She helped convert the Odéon theater into a military hospital during the Franco-Prussian War. She acted in London (1879), New York (1880, subsequently touring in the United States nine more times in the next forty years), and around the world. She converted an old Parisian theater into the Théâtre Sarah Bernhardt. Her marvelous career included starring roles in plays by Gabriele D'Annunzio,* François Coppée,* Francis Marion Crawford,*

Alexandre Dumas *pére* and Alexandre Dumas *fils*,* Victor-Marie Hugo,* Maurice Maeterlinck,* Racine, Edmond Rostand,* Victorien Sardou,* Augustin Eugene Scribe,* William Shakespeare,* and Voltaire. In many cases, the plays were written specifically with Bernhardt in mind. Her beauty, her grace, and especially her voice earned her the name "the Divine Sarah." She is often considered the greatest French actress. In her day, her only stage rival was Eleanora Duse, whom George Bernard Shaw* preferred. Bernhardt, born Sarah Henriette Rosine Bernard, was illegitimate, was educated in a convent, had an illegitimate son, and was later married (then separated after a year). Some years after an injurious stage fall, Bernhardt's right knee became gangrenous and her leg was amputated (1915). She published her autobiography (1907), a novel (1920), and a treatise on acting (1923). James often saw her on stage, but neither unreservedly liked her style nor could conclude definitively about her as a person. In a letter to Grace Norton* (28 Dec 1880), he called Bernhardt "The great humbug of the age." Reviewing *L'Etrangère* by Dumas *fils* in "Parisian Affairs" (1876), James merely calls her "that very interesting actress." In "Art in Paris" (1876), he defines her statue of a peasant holding a drowned grandson "extremely amateurish." But in an untitled review of *Rome Vaincue* by Dominique Alexandre Parodi* (*Nation*, 16 Nov 1876), he says that Bernhardt, acting as the blind grandmother, displays "extraordinary intelligence and versatility." In "The Théâtre Français" (1877), he criticizes her stage tirades as "rather weak" but concludes that she is "one of the great figures of the day" and an incomparable "embodiment of feminine success." In "The Comédie Française in London" (1879), he demeans her terribly: He calls her a self-advertising opportunist ("the muse of the newspaper"), compares her unfavorably with other actresses, says that her "repertory is . . . narrow" and that "she forces her note beyond all reason" in scenes of violence, images her in one play as a weeping willow, but predicts that she will triumph on tour in America. James waxes sarcastic again in "Coquelin" (1887), noting that Bernhardt has succeeded because "wonderful dresses and draperies" augment "her extraordinary cleverness . . . [and] singular beauty."

Bernier, Charles. In "A Tragedy of Error," Hortense's crippled husband, whose murder she tries unsuccessfully to arrange.

Bernier, Hortense. In "A Tragedy of Error," Charles's wife and Vicomte Louis de Meyrau's mistress. She hires a murderer to kill her husband; but, through a mix-up, Louis is drowned instead.

Bernier, Mme. In "A Tragedy of Error," Charles Bernier's mother and Hortense's mother-in-law.

Berridge, John. In "The Velvet Glove," a splendid novelist who refuses to succumb to gorgeous Amy Evans and write a puff for her trashy novel.

Berrington, Ferdy (Parson). In "A London Life," the son of Lionel and Selina Berrington.

Berrington, Geordie (Scratch). In "A London Life," the other son of Lionel and Selina Berrington.

Berrington, Lionel. In "A London Life," loose Selina's outraged husband and Laura Wing's brother-in-law.

Berrington, Mrs. In "A London Life," Lionel's expropriated mother.

Berrington, Selina Wing (Lina). In "A London Life," Lionel's adulterous American wife and Laura Wing's sister. She tries to drag Laura down.

Berry, Walter Van Rensselaer (1859–1927). Brilliant, versatile lawyer and diplomat, born in Paris of rich New York State stock. He attended Harvard, then Columbia Law School. He practiced law in New York, Washington, D.C., and Paris. A lifelong bachelor, he became an officer of the International Tribunal in Egypt (1909–1912), then the president of the American Chamber of Commerce in Paris (1916–1923). He was pro-French and anti-German during and after World War I, and he was interested in painting, architecture, and literature. He knew, among dozens of other important friends and acquaintances, James, Marcel Proust,* Harry Crosby (a cousin) and his wife Caresse Crosby, Jacques-Émile Blanche,* and Edith Newbold Jones Wharton.* As for Wharton, he helped shape some of her writings; she became his admiring, trusting lover and traveling companion in Europe; and she handled his funeral arrangements. Berry was brilliant, dry, egocentric, snobbish, dictatorial, and unimaginative. James evidently knew Berry by 1904, since James's letters to Wharton from that year are dotted with references to him. For example, while James was in the United States on his 1904–1905 tour, he wrote to her from Washington, D.C. (16 Jan 1905) that "I miss, intensely, Walter Berry—and fear I shall continue to do so." Still, James crossed the Atlantic with him in July 1905. Then, a few months later, James again wrote to Wharton (8 Nov 1905), "news of Walter Berry I greatly want too, who, after having greatly endeared himself to me, in the summer, . . . vanished from my sight." Some time later, James wrote to Wharton (13 Oct 1908) to comment vaguely but sympathetically on her personal problems and to hope she could sail to Europe with Berry. Then James wrote from Lamb House* (3 Aug 1909) to suggest that Wharton and Berry "both come *here* to me for two or three days." In a letter to Howard Overing Sturgis* from a New York hotel (18 Oct 1910), James, home in the United States because of the fatal illness of his brother William, describes what must have been an unusual event: "last night she [Wharton] and Walter Berry and [William] Morton Fullerton[*] dined with me here." After World War I started, James wrote to Wharton (20 Oct 1914) vaguely about diplomatic work which brought Berry from France to

London and how "[h]e is evidently . . . interestingly occupied here for these next days." James often wrote Berry rococo letters from the United States (1905, 1910), from Lamb House (1905, 1907, 1908, 1909, 1911, 1912, 1914), and from London (1912), concerning many subjects: travel plans, aging, James's hopes for seeing him, Berry's letter-writing ability (his "extraordinary grace and wit" [18 Aug 1909]), Berry's being in Egypt, mutual friends, English weather, James family members, Edith Wharton ("I bless you both and envy you well" [27 Sep 1911]), their plans for meeting, James's sickness, a lavish gift from Berry ("Ah, Walter, Walter, why do you do these things?" [14 Feb 1912]), and high government officials (including Herbert Henry Asquith* and Winston Churchill*).

Besant, Sir Walter (1836–1901). English novelist and critic. Educated at Cambridge, he first published on French literature and then about the Holy Land. He wrote too much fiction, some of it in collaboration and virtually all of it facile and conservative. He left unfinished a work surveying aspects of London. He and James's casual friend James Payn* worked to improve authors' rights. Besant's 1884 "Fiction as One of the Arts" provoked James's "The Art of Fiction" as a sharp rejoinder. James's essay, in turn, evoked "A Humble Remonstrace" by Robert Louis Stevenson.* James's library contained thirteen books by Besant.

Bessie. In *Roderick Hudson*, Cecilia's little daughter.

Beston. In "John Delavoy," a conservative, opinionated publisher whose crassness costs him the affection of Miss Delavoy.

Bestwick, Raymond. In "Mrs. Temperly," the patient, unsuccessful suitor of his cousin Maria Temperly's daughter Dora.

"The Bethnal Green Museum." Art review, published in the *Atlantic Monthly* (Jan 1873). James describes journeying through a "labyrinth of . . . alleys and slums" to the Bethnal Green Museum to see its loaned exhibit of Sir Richard Wallace art treasures. He finds the group eclectic. He likes a Thomas Gainsborough* and a pair by Sir Joshua Reynolds,* but he finds the other English works "moderate," except for a few watercolors by Joseph Mallord William Turner* and many by Richard Parkes Bonington.* James then discusses works by some French painters, notably Alexandre-Gabriel Decamps,* Paul Delaroche,* Jean-Louis-Ernest Meissonier,* and Antoine Watteau ("surely the sweetest French genius who ever handled a brush"). Finally, James mentions several Dutch masters represented, but he says he lacks space to go into detail, beyond noting that Rembrandt* "abuse[s] . . . chiaroscuro."

The Better Sort. Collection of eleven short stories, published in London by Methuen, 1903, and in New York by Scribner, 1903: "Broken Wings," "The Beldonald Holbein," "The Two Faces," "The Tone of Time," "The Special Type," "Mrs. Medwin," "Flickerbridge," "The Story in It," "The Beast in the Jungle," "The Birthplace," and "The Papers."

Betterman, Frank B. In *The Ivory Tower*, Graham Fielder's uncle and Abel Gaw's former business associate. Betterman's death enriches Graham but causes problems.

Betterman, Mrs. In *The Golden Bowl*, a London hostess of Charlotte Stant.

Betty. In "Glasses," Mrs. Medrum's niece, who refused Geoffrey Dawling.

Bight, Howard. In "The Papers," Maud Blandy's close friend and a journalist who caters to publicity seekers.

Bilham, John Little. In *The Ambassadors*, Chad Newsome's American dilettante painter friend in Paris. Little Bilham misleadingly tells Lewis Lambert Strether that Chad's liaison is "a virtuous attachment." Strether would like to see Bilham marry Mamie Pocock. Bilham may owe something to James's friend Jonathan Sturges,* who in 1895 gave James the idea for *The Ambassadors*. To James, both men were witty, passive, and attractive to the ladies. (Unlike Bilham, however, Sturges was crippled by polio.) James called Sturges "Little Brother Jonathan" in a letter to Sir Edmund Wilson Gosse* (30 Oct [1890]), and, in several letters to friends, called him "little demon."

Billinghurst, Mrs. In *The Tragic Muse*, a friend of Julia Sherringham Dallow. The two are to see each other at Versailles.

Bingham, George. In "My Friend Bingham," the man who accidentally kills the son of widowed Lucy Hicks and later marries her.

Birdseye, Miss. In *The Bostonians*, a sweet little old Boston feminist who is totally ineffectual. James unpersuasively denied that her character was based in part on that of Elizabeth Palmer Peabody,* the Boston reformeress and sister-in-law of Nathaniel Hawthorne.*

"The Birthplace." Short story (20,200 words), published in *The Better Sort*, 1903; revised and reprinted in *The Novels and Tales of Henry James*, Volume XVII, 1909. (Characters: Morris Gedge, Isabel Gedge, Grant-Jackson, Mr. and Mrs. B. D. Hayes, Miss Putchin.) Morris Gedge and his wife Isabel are happy when Grant-Jackson, remembering a past favor, hires librarian Morris away from Blackport-on-Dwindle—"all granite, fog and female fiction"—to become caretaker of The Birthplace, near Oxford, of a renowned British poet. Gedge replaces the retiring Miss Putchin but soon objects to the commercialism rampant about the place. Isabel grows fearful that Grant-Jackson will hear reports of Morris's grumbling and will discharge the man. In fact, Grant-Jackson issues such a severe warning that Morris turns into a prevaricating barker at The Birthplace. Grant-Jackson descends upon Morris again—but this time to give him a "rise" in pay because gate receipts are up. According to a Notebook entry (12 Jun 1901), Lady Caroline Trevelyan, wife of George Otto Trevelyan of the distinguished Trevelyan family,* gave James the idea for this story while he was their guest at Welcombe, their country mansion near Stratford-on-Avon. The original Notebook sketch calls for the couple who became the Gedges to "end by denying Shakespeare . . . in the presence of a big, gaping, admiring batch. *Then* they must go." In the preface to Volume XVII of *The Novels and Tales of Henry James*, James explains that the idea for "The Birthplace" came to him when he heard that an intelligent caretaker of an English literary shrine had quit his job because he was expected to talk nonsense about the place; further, that Gedge illustrates one of James's favorite types, the "poor gentleman . . . too fine for his rough fate." William Shakespeare,* for whom James had the greatest respect all his life, is named twice in the Notebook entry but never in the story; it is clear enough, however, that he is the genius hallowing "the birthplace." Surely James's main purpose here is to urge his audience to read literary works, not literary biographies. Details of Shakespeare's life, if known, cannot explain either his genius or his production. Gedge is saved from being a tragic figure by James's tone of high comedy.

Black, William (1841–1898). Scottish journalist, novelist, short-story writer, and biographer who worked mostly in London. He was a war correspondent during the Seven Weeks' War (1866), after, which, between 1869 and the year of his death, he published upward of thirty books, mostly romantic novels. His best books include *A Princess of Thule* (1874), *Madcap Violet* (1876), *Macleod of Dare* (1878), and *Judith Shakespeare* (1884, illustrated by Edwin Austin Abbey*). James reviewed (*Nation*, 22 Mar 1877) the 1 March 1877 issue of a then-new journal called *The Portrait: A Weekly Photograph and Memoir*, which featured a picture of Black and his brief autobiography. Black summarizes his career to date, calls *Madcap Violet* his best work, and promises to write more seriously in the future. James also reviewed (*Nation*, 19 Dec 1878) *Macleod of Dare*, commenting at the outset that the truth concerning its value lies between the many extreme comments by critics. James, who compares it to five other works by Black, regards it as a zestful, romantic story with a Sir Walter Scott-like "fatality" in the affair in it of a "love-crazed Caledonian" and a faithless London actress. James calls Black's "method of narrative . . . lax and soft." The man missed an opportunity to contrast hero and heroine, as certain French novelists would have done well, but he does describe "coast scenery and . . . boating" with "color and brilliancy." Privately, in a letter to his brother William

(10 Jul [1877]), James defined Black, whom he met at a Lord Houghton* luncheon, as "a little red-faced cad of a Scotchman."

Black. In *The Other House*, the play, Anthony Bream's butler.

"Black and White." Art essay, published as "Our Artists in Europe" in *Harper's New Monthly Magazine* (Jun 1889); reprinted in *Picture and Text*, 1893. James begins by praising the editors of *Harper's Magazine* in general for encouraging black-and-white illustrations; then he launches into specific praise of black-and-white Edwin Austin Abbey,* Alfred Parsons,* Francis Davis Millet,* George Henry Boughton,* George Du Maurier,* and Charles Stanley Reinhart.* Beautiful old Broadway (in the English Midlands) is an inspiration for some of the above artists.

Blackborough, Marquis. In "A International Episode," a Hyde Park dandy.

Blanchard, Augusta. In *Roderick Hudson*, an American flower painter who seems to like Rowland Mallet in Rome but in frustration takes up with rich Leavenworth.

Blanche. In "Paste," Charlotte Prime's pupil.

Blanche, Jacques-Émile (1861–1942). Passy-born French portrait painter and writer. His portrait of James was done at the request of Edith Newbold Jones Wharton,* in Paris in May 1908; she called it the best likeness of the novelist. Oddly, although Blanche painted James almost full face while the noveliest sat for him, the finished portrait is in profile. Blanche wrote *Mes Modèles* (1928), in which he discusses how he painted portraits of Auguste Maurice Barrès,* Aubrey Vincent Beardsley,* André Gide, Thomas Hardy,* George Moore, and Marcel Proust.* In his *Portraits of a Lifetime: 1870–1914* (1937), Blanche reminisces about James: his friends, painting him, admiring his conversation and hospitality, visiting him once at Lamb House,* sharing criticism of him with Walter Van Rensselaer Berry* (Blanche told Berry that James lacked the mind to handle abstruse problems and that his art was static), and his attitude toward certain French writers (James admired Alphonse Daudet* too much and Émile Zola* too little). Blanche disliked the John Singer Sargent* portrait of James, feeling that it made the novelist look like "a business man from the provinces." Blanche's *Aymeris* (1922) is a roman à clef about the rich, talented, decadent circle surrounding Guy de Maupassant,* including Maupassant's mistress Blanche Roosevelt,* whom James knew slightly. In a letter to a member of the Temple family*—his cousin Ellen Temple Emmet's daughter, the portrait painter Ellen Emmet Rand (2 Nov 1908)—James described Blanche as "rather a queer 'mondain' do-you-any-way-you-like sort of painter . . . but . . . agreeable to sit to . . . by reason of his extraordinary conversational powers." James wrote

Wharton (13 Dec 1909) that Blanche struck him as "very genial and intelligent and gentil," but that he had a "genius for pushing his fortune par toutes les voies."

Bland, Rev. Mr. In "My Friend Bingham," the minister at the funeral of Lucy Hicks's son.

Bland, Sir Cantopher. In *The Sense of the Past*, a Midmore family friend suspicious of Ralph Pendrel. Bland may be patterned in part after James's friend Sir Hugh Seymour Walpole.*

Blandy, Maud. In "The Papers," a sensitive newspaperwoman who likes Howard Bight, is liked by Mortimer Marshal, and becomes disgusted with sensational journalistic tactics.

Blankenberg, Miss. In "A Landscape Painter," a friend of Miriam Quarterman.

Blessingbourne, Maud. In "The Story in It," the charming young widow whose quietly exciting love for Colonel Voyt he learns about only when Mrs. Dyot tells him.

Blint. In *The Golden Bowl*, Lady Castledean's sleek little lover.

Blocqueville, Louise Adélaïde d'Eckmühl, Marquise de (1815–1892). French writer whose main claim to fame now is that she wrote the biography (1879–1880) of her father, Marshal Louis-Nicholas Davout, one of Napoleon's most distinguished field commanders. She also edited his correspondence (1887). James was a guest at the Marquise de Blocqueville's Paris salon in 1876; through her, he associated with several important members of the French literati, including her pensioner Émile Montégut.* James describes her graphically in a letter to his brother William (14 Mar [1876]) as a "very gracious and caressing woman . . . a great invalid, very corpulent . . . has her head swathed in long veils and laces *à la sultane*–but with the remains of beauty."

Bloodgood, Phil. In "A Round of Visits," Mark P. Monteith's trusted friend who absconds with some of Mark's money.

Blumenthal. In "Eugene Pickering," Anastasia's unpleasant Jewish husband, now deceased.

Blumenthal, Anastasia. In "Eugene Pickering," a complex widow who is briefly the object of Eugene Pickering's infatuation. Her puzzling, ruthless nature may owe much to James's opinion of George Sand.* Madame Blumenthal has written a novel on marriage "in the George Sand manner."

Blyth, Reggie. In "Hugh Merrow," the peppy six-year-old whose portrait by Hugh Merrow inspires Captain and Mrs. Archdean to ask the painter to create a picture for them of the child they never had and never can have.

Bobby, Lady. In "Paste," a woman who becomes sick at a party. Her doing so necessitates the substitution for her by Mrs. Guy, who then meets Charlotte Prime.

Bogle, Miss. In *The Golden Bowl*, the nurse of the son of Prince Amerigo and his wife Princess Maggie Verver.

Boit, Edward Darley (Ned) (1840–1915). Boston-born artist. After graduating from Harvard (1863) and marrying (1864), he studied art in Boston and Paris, then established studios in Rome and Paris. He and his wife Mary Louisa (Iza) Boit (née Cushing) later settled in Florence. Boit became a close associate of John Singer Sargent* and exhibited with him in Boston and New York. Sargent notably painted both Mrs. Boit and the four Boit daughters. James met the Boits in Rome in 1873, admired flirtatious Mrs. Boit's horsemanship, saw the Boits in Normandy in 1876 and in London and Paris in the 1880s, and visited their striking villa near Valombrosa, outside Florence, at least in 1894 and 1907. When Boit died, James wrote to their mutual friend Howard Overing Sturgis* (27 Apr 1915) that he was "a very beautiful and benignant person, a natural *grand seigneur* of purely private life." James curiously added that Boit had a "papier-mâché quality, out of which the passions and troubles of men didn't ring and in which they didn't reverberate." James also felt it necessary to call Mrs. Boit a *"petite comtesse . . . with a kind of toy-shop rattling."* James and the Boits had many friends in common, including Henrietta Reubell* and Edith Newbold Jones Wharton.* James first saw Wharton at the Boits' apartment in Paris.

Bolitho, Lady. In "The Modern Warning," Sir Rufus Chasemore's sister.

Bolitho, Lord. In "The Solution," Blanche Goldie's deceased father.

Bolton-Brown. In "Lord Beaupré," the New Yorker who loves and wins Mary Gosselin, his friend Hugh Gosselin's sister.

Bolton-Brown, Mrs. In "Lord Beaupré," Bolton-Brown's mother.

Bolton-Brown, The Misses. In "Lord Beaupré," Bolton-Brown's sisters.

Bolton Street. At 3 Bolton Street, Piccadilly, in London, James rented spacious rooms (1876–1886). On the site at present are office buildings.

Bombici, Cavaliere. In "The Aspern Papers," a supposedly high-society former friend of the Bordereaus.

Bonifazio. In "At Isella," the host at the Isella inn visited by the narrator.

Bonington, Richard Parkes (1801?–1828). Promising English genre and landscape painter, who spent much of his short life in France, was associated with Ferdinand Victor Eugène Delacroix* in helping to evolve historical painting, and was instrumental in introducing British watercoloring methods to the Barbizon school. In "The Bethnal Green Museum" (1873), James contrasts Bonington's gaiety with the gravity of Joseph Mallord William Turner,* and he praises the former's rich and surprisingly packed watercolors, which are lovingly picturesque and shadowy with "romantic suggestion."

Bonnycastle, Alfred. In "Pandora," the Washington, D.C., host at one of whose parties Pandora Day meets the president. Bonnycastle is partly based on Henry Adams.*

Bonnycastle, Mrs. Alfred. In "Pandora," Alfred's wife, partly modeled on Marian Adams.*

Bonsor. In *The Reprobate*, the bachelor friend of deceased Doubleday, father of Paul Doubleday. Bonsor is coguardian of Paul with the second Mrs. Doubleday, Paul's stepmother. Bonsor wants his niece Blanche Amber to like his friend Pitt Brunt, but she prefers Paul. The play takes place at Bonsor's villa at Hampton Court.

Bonus, Alfred. In "Collaboration," an American friend of Herman Heidenmauer and Félix Vendemer.

Booker. In "A London Life," Wendover's casual friend from Baltimore.

Boott, Elizabeth (Lizzie) (1846–1888). One of James's closest friends. James knew her in his youth in Cambridge, Massachusetts, and then in Newport, Rhode Island. She and her father Francis Boott* (widowed since 1847) had a permanent residence in Italy, where James often visited them. For example, in the spring of 1872, he and his sister Alice and his Aunt Kate (Catherine Walsh*) rendezvoused with the Bootts briefly in Geneva, Switzerland; later that year, James saw them for Christmas in Rome, where Lizzie was taking art lessons. James was a frequent visitor (from 1874) at the apartment of the Bootts in a villa on glorious Bellosguardo, outside Florence. He also wrote many letters to both Bootts, full of friendship and gossip, when the pair were in Italy and when they were visiting back in Massachusetts. James even sent his "cara Lisa" (8 Mar [1875]) a letter from New York "scritta nella vera lingua di Dante." After introducing her to a foreign friend, he happily reported to his brother William (22 Jun [1876]), that "Lizzie, among her unsuspected accomplishments, reveals a complete mastery of the French tongue." James closely observed father and daughter as they aged. He had great platonic affection for Lizzie but little respect for her ability or her progress as a painter. He wrote to his father (30 Mar [1880]) that she "seems to spend her life in learning, or rather in studying without learning, and commencing afresh, to paint in someone's manner." He knew well the gruff American expatriate painter Frank Duveneck,* who gave Lizzie art lessons, first in Munich and later in Florence, married her in 1886, and had a son by her. In a letter to Grace Norton* (25 Jan [1887]), James calls the marriage "most interest-quenching." He intensely grieved when Lizzie died of pneumonia, in Paris in 1888. Duveneck created a bronze monument for her grave in Florence. James and the Bootts had innumerable friends in common, from William Wetmore Story* and his old circle forward to Edward Darley Boit* and his wife Mary, and on to Constance Fenimore Woolson.* James wrote indiscreetly about the Bootts to many friends, for example, to Ariana Randolph Curtis,* Grace Norton, and Henrietta Reubell,* in addition to members of his family. James exploited his observation of Lizzie and her father: In *The Portrait of a Lady*, Pansy Osmond is as sheltered in Italy by her American father Gilbert Osmond (who, however, is unlike Francis Boott) as poor Lizzie ever was by hers; and in *The Golden Bowl*, the father-daughter relationship of Adam and Maggie Verver is almost as smothery as was that of Francis and Lizzie Boott. In *Notes of a Son and Brother*, James mentions that his cousin Mary Temple* knew and extolled Lizzie Boott, whom he described lovingly as "[t]his delightful girl, educated, cultivated, accomplished, toned above all, as from steeping in a rich old medium, to a degree of the rarest among her coevals."

Boott, Francis (Frank) (1813–1904). Long-time friend of the James family. They knew each other in Boston. Boott was a brother-in-law of Henry Greenough, a member of the international Greenough family.* When his wife died in 1847, Boott moved to Italy with their baby daughter Elizabeth Boott* and lived for decades in a villa on Bellosguardo, outside Florence. He composed music, played the piano, and sang. He and his daughter occasionally met James in Paris and called on him in London. Boott became obsessively devoted to Lizzie's upbringing and welfare. In a letter to his parents (23 Dec [1886]), James calls Boott's attempts to adjust to the bohemian ways of his son-in-law Frank Duveneck* "pathetic and heroic" and adds that the pair "might have been made the subject of a little tale by Turgénieff [Ivan Sergeyevich Turgenev*]." Soon after his daughter's death in 1888, Boott returned to America with his grandson Frank Duveneck, Jr. James much preferred Lizzie to her father. In letters to his sister Alice, James punned that someone was "as dry as Mr. Boott" (24 Mar [1876]) and later that "[t]he simplicity of Bootts' [sic] mental constitution only increases with age" (25 Apr [1880]). Even more harshly, James wrote to his mother (16 Mar 1881) that Boott "is . . . as simple as a milkmaid." Boott called upon

James's sick father in Boston just before he died in 1882. After Lizzie's death, James in a letter to their mutual friend Henrietta Reubell* (1 Apr 1888) gloomily described Boott and Duveneck as "those two poor uncongenial men tied together by that helpless baby." Late in life, Boott prepared *Recollections of Francis Boott* (privately printed, 1912), for his grandson's information.

Boquet, Mlle. In "An International Episode," Lord Lambeth's former governess.

Bordereau, Juliana. In "The Aspern Papers," the extremely old former mistress of Jeffrey Aspern, the long-deceased American poet. She is living in Venice with her niece Tina Bordereau. The scholar narrator tries to obtain her Aspern documents. She teases him and thwarts his efforts, and then dies. It has been wondered whether Juliana Bordereau is the grandmother of Tina Bordereau, or perhaps her mother (by Aspern). Juliana Bordereau is based partly on Clare Clairmont,* one of the mistresses of George Gordon, Lord Byron.*

Bordereau, Tina. In "The Aspern Papers," the unmarried niece of Juliana Bordereau. The scholar narrator wants the Aspern papers, which her dying old aunt leaves with Tina, but he is most reluctant to marry the middle-aged woman to obtain them. It has been theorized that Tina is Juliana Bordereau's granddaughter or perhaps her daughter (by Jeffrey Apsern). In the 1888 version of "The Aspern Papers," Tina is named Tita.

Borealska, Princess. In *The American*, a Polish princess whose invitation Christopher Newman declines.

Bornier, Vicomte Henri de (1825–1901). French poet and historical dramatist who was also a librarian for fifty years. His dramas concern Martin Luther, Roland's "daughter," Attila, and Mahomet. James reviewed (*Galaxy*, Aug 1875) Bornier's 1875 *La Fille de Roland*. James notes that the play stresses the French virtues of patriotism, heroism, self-sacrifice, and love of family. Summarizing its melodramatic renunciation plot, he calls the verse play "a finished literary work."

Bosanquet, Theodora (1880–1961). James's third and last secretary, educated in Cheltenham and at University College, London. She learned to type so that she could take dictation from and otherwise work for James, which she did from October 1907, after the departure of his former secretary Mary Weld* (who had replaced William MacAlpine*) until his death, shortly before which his dictating to her in delirium had a certain therapeutic value. Thereafter Bosanquet did secretarial work for the British government (1916–1920) and for the International Federation of University Women (1920–1935); then she performed editorial work for *Time and Tide* (1935–1958). Her book *Henry James at Work* (based in part on her careful diary and published by the Hogarth Press of Virginia Woolf* and her husband, 1924) discusses their working arrangements at Rye and in London, James's dictating habits, what dictating did for his literary style, problems with his revisions, his friendships, and his attitude toward England. Bosanquet later wrote *Harriet Martineau: An Essay in Comprehension* (1927) and *Paul Valéry* (1933). From the start, James was delighted with her: He wrote to his brother William (17 Oct 1907) that "young boyish Miss Bosanquet . . . is worth all the other (females) that I have had put together and . . . confirms me in the perception . . . that for certain . . . kinds of diligence and production, the intervention of the agent is . . . an intense aid and a true economy!" His Pocket Diaries for 1909, 1911, 1912, 1913, and 1914 are dotted with entries concerning Bosanquet, her work for him, her being away, and their going to the theater together. In 1911 he wrote to Bosanquet (27 Oct 1911), calling her his "Remington priestess," to ask her to find him some rooms in London in which to dictate to her at her typewriter; she found space for him near her Lawrence Street flat in Chelsea. In the last letter James dictated (to his niece Margaret James, 1 Dec 1915), he called Bosanquet "wonderfully helpful." A few days later, he muttered to her the last of his December 1915 ramblings, including the famous "Napoleonic" message.

Bosio, Mme. In "A Passionate Pilgrim," a Covent Garden opera singer.

"Boston." Travel essay, published in the *North American Review* (Mar 1906), and the *Fortnightly Review* (Mar 1906); reprinted in *The American Scene*, 1907.

The Bostonians. Novel (150,500 words), published in the *Century Magazine* (Feb 1885–Feb 1886); revised and reprinted in London and in New York by Macmillan, 1886. (Characters: Miss Birdseye, Henry Burrage, Jr., Mrs. Henry Burrage, Sr., Miss Catching, Olive Chancellor, Charlie, Mrs. Croucher, Mr. and Mrs. Amariah Farrinder, Filer, Ada T. P. Foat, Professor Gougenheim, Gracie, Mr. and Mrs. Abraham Greenstreet, Adelina Chancellor Luna, Newton Luna, Mirandola, Eliza P. Moseley, Matthias Pardon, Dr. Mary J. Prance, Basil Ransom, Marie Verneuil, Miss Winkworth, Dr. and Mrs. Selah Tarrant, Verena Tarrant.) Mississippi Civil War veteran and lawyer Basil Ransom takes a trip in 187—[1877] from New York, his present location, to Boston to visit his cousins Adelina Luna (widowed and rich) and her unmarried sister Olive Chancellor (politically radical [and perhaps lesbian]). At a feminist-movement meeting, Olive introduces Ransom to Mrs. Farrinder (militant), Miss Birdseye (impractical and aged), Dr. Mary J. Prance (down-to-earth), and others. He also sees speaker Verena Tarrant, beautiful and thrilling, and the daughter of phony mesmerist "Dr." Selah Tarrant and his passive wife. Annoyed with Ransom, who dislikes Verena's talk but is smitten by her beauty, jealous and possessive Olive invites the girl to come and study German and the history of women's suffering with her. Verena prefers Olive to the exploitative Matthias Pardon (a

young journalist) and Henry Burrage (a dilatory Harvard law school student and
the son of a rich, domineering New York widow). Olive buys off Dr. Tarrant
and thus gets Verena to move in with her. Doing badly in law in New York,
Ransom occasionally calls on eager Mrs. Luna there. On business up in Boston,
he and Verena walk pleasantly through the Harvard College grounds, pausing
at its impressive Civil War memorial. At Mrs. Burrage's New York soirée,
Verena lectures while Ransom attends; so does Olive, who suspects the two of
drifting amorously closer. The two women agree to stay in New York together
for a time, Olive hoping that Verena will attract Henry Burrage, that is, until
Ransom is discouraged. But the girl, liking Ransom upsettingly, returns to
Boston. Late in the summer, old Miss Birdseye is dying in Marmion, Dr. Prance
attends her, and Ransom proposes to Verena. She resists and asks Olive's assistance, but she loves her suitor. After some weeks, Ransom learns that Verena
is to speak at the Boston Music Hall, and he goes there, confronts her with a
choice, and takes her away in tears—not likely to be her last—to the discomfiture
of Olive and other feminists. As early as 1863, James was aware of the oratory
of New York and Bostonian feminists. In a letter to Thomas Sergeant Perry*
from New York ([1 Nov 1863]), he reports that he and Bob Temple, one of his
Temple family* relatives, "went to listen to the preaching of Mrs. Cora V. L.
Hatch." James ridicules the "underground" place of meeting, its circus and
séance aspects, and the speaker's "arrant platitudes"; he dubs Cora's husband
"Chorus"; and he reports that he and Temple "fled" early. *The Bostonians* is
James's most ambitious American novel. It sprang from his desire to "do"
America in a big Balzacian way (to "write an American story" as he commented
in his Notebook, 8 Apr 1883), to criticize American reformers (Boston feminism
of James's 1870s here has roots in earlier abolition and temperance movements),
and to respond artistically to *The Blithedale Romance* by Nathaniel Hawthorne,*
Dr. Breen's Practice by William Dean Howells,* and *L'Évangéliste* by Alphonse
Daudet.* In addition, James wanted to present in fictional form a morality play,
in which reactionary, hot Ransom vies with progressive, chilly Miss Chancellor
for pliant Verena's very soul. This struggle has sexual, social, and political
overtones. In a sense, it fights again the Civil War, only recently concluded at
the time of the novel's action. Thus, Miss Chancellor would purport to be
progressively Northern, whereas unreconstructed Ransom would still represent
lost causes. The first serial installment of *The Bostonians* started a controversy:
James was accused of satirically patterning Miss Birdseye on Elizabeth Palmer
Peabody,* the reformeress and Hawthorne's sister-in-law. James's disclaimers,
especially in a long letter to his brother William (14 Feb [1885]), do not ring
true; in it, he judges Miss Birdseye to be "the best figure in the book." In a
second letter to William, written the next day, James adds that Miss Birdseye's
"death . . . is the prettiest thing in the book." As successive installments of the
novel appeared, it gained no accolades; in fact, *Century* editor Richard Watson
Gilder* wrote to James that nothing he had ever published interested his readers
so little, and the novelist became depressed, bitter, and critical. To add to his

misery, his American publisher James Ripley Osgood,* who had contracted to pay James $5,000 for book rights to *The Bostonians* for a period of five years, went bankrupt before paying; the novelist had to scramble to recoup part of his losses. Shortly after Howells published *The Rise of Silas Lapham* (1885), James complained in a letter from London to Grace Norton* (9 Dec [1885]) that "Everyone here admires extremely the truth and power of 'Silas Lapham,' including myself. But what hideousness of life! They don't revile Howells when he does America, and such an America as that, and why do they revile me? The 'Bostonians' is sugar-cake, compared with it." But James was able to write to his brother William soon thereafter (9 Mar [1886]) that *The Bostonians* in book form "appears to be having a goodish success" in England. Later that year, he wrote to William again (13 Jun 1886) suggesting that he might write *The Other Bostonians* since he "hadn't a dream of generalizing" in *The Bostonians*. He was right to comment in a letter to Howells (2 Jan 1888) that reaction to *The Bostonians* had caused him to "hold . . . the 'critical world' at large in a singular contempt." Shortly before his death, James wrote to Sir Edmund Wilson Gosse* (25 Aug 1915) that he had for a long while planned to include *The Bostonians* in his New York edition, but he delayed because "revision of it loomed particularly formidable & time-consuming"; he added that he "never was very thoroughly happy about it [the novel]," even though he would have liked to revise it into "a much truer and more curious thing," complete with a preface. It is now regarded as one of his most provocative works, not least because of the current interest in the women's liberation movement and because of James's finely balanced gallery of females in the novel. Mark Twain,* who disliked James, wrote to their mutual friend Howells (21 Jul 1885) the celebrated comment that he "would rather be damned to John Bunyan's heaven than read" *The Bostonians*.

Bostwick, Captain Teddy. In "Sir Edmund Orme," a minor friend of the narrator.

Bottomley, Lord. In "The Point of View," one of Edward Antrobus's friends in England.

Bottomley, Lord. In *The Tragic Muse*, a friend of Charles Carteret.

Bouche, Adolfe. In "The Point of View," the recipient of Gustave Lejaune's letter.

Boughton, George Henry (1833–1905). British-born painter reared in Albany, New York. He then usually resided in London (from 1861). His subjects were frequently American colonial scenes. He illustrated Washington Irving's *Knickerbocker History* and "Rip Van Winkle." In "Art" (Jan 1875), James describes an American winter scene by Boughton as "exquisite" but then goes on to say it has a "tearful, invalidish sort of grace." In "On Some Pictures Lately Exhibited" (Jul 1875), he ridicules a Boughton effort ("In calling it a composition we speak perhaps with culpable laxity") for its "fatally meagre execution"; he then praises parts of a Boughton landscape only to laugh at the people therein as "little figures . . . of the cut-paper school." Two years later, James met Boughton in London and described him to his brother William (28 Feb [1877]) as "an American—Londonized" and "a good plain man." Thereafter James praised him. In "The Grosvenor Gallery and the Royal Academy" (31 May 1877), he says that two works by Boughton are "touched with ingenious fancy, interesting in sentiment, and peculiarly refined in color." In an untitled note (*Nation*, 23 Jul 1878), he opines of Boughton that "[m]ore exactly than any one else he preserves the balance between landscape and figures." But later, on the occasion of Boughton's kindly taking James to a Royal Academy prize-giving ceremony, he wrote to William again (11 Dec [1883]); this time Boughton "is a very good fellow, if a weak painter." In "Our Artists in Europe" (1889; reprinted as "Black and White" in *Picture and Text*, 1893), James comments favorably on "the charming, amusing text" of Boughton's 1884 *Sketching Rambles in Holland* and calls the accompanying pictures "the delightful, irresponsible, visual, sensual, pictorial, capricious impressions of a painter in a strange land." James likes Boughton's pictorial combinations elsewhere of old English, old American, and old and new Dutch local color, and landscape detail. He finds it odd that Boughton lives in a pretty and hospitable London house but strikes melancholy, autumnal, wintry notes in his work. In still later art reviews, James accords Boughton only vague, general praise.

Bounder. In "The Death of the Lion," a man involved in a divorce scandal.

Bourde, Mlle. In "Mrs. Temperly," the Temperly children's governess in Paris.

Bourget, Paul (1852–1935). Amiens-born and Paris-educated novelist, short-story writer, literary critic, travel writer, playwright, and poet. He began a habit of travel in 1874 when he went to Italy and Greece. He became a drama critic in 1879. Long influenced by Hippolyte Taine,* he published several essays (from 1883) showing that his current pessimism came from the writings of Charles Baudelaire,* Gustave Flaubert,* Joseph Ernest Renan,* and Stendhal.* Many of Bourget's early novels—*Cruelle enigme* (1885, dedicated to James), *Un Crime d'amour* (1886), and *André Cornélis* (1887) among them—are psychological and naturalistic studies that often feature leisure-class living and high-society passions. By the time of *Le Disciple* (1889), which was a sensational moralistic success, and *Cosmopolis* (1893), Bourget was more convservative. He was elected to the French Academy in 1894. In 1901 he formally returned to Roman Catholicism, after which his *L'Étape* (1902), *Un Divorce* (1904), and *Le Démon de Midi* (1914), as well as other works, show reactionary didacticism. James met

Bourget in 1884. Soon Paul became a kind of disciple to Henry, as Paul Overt does to Henry St. George in James's 1888 allegorical short story "The Lesson of the Master." James always preferred cosmopolitan, well-traveled Bourget's charm and talk to his writings. In a letter to Charles Eliot Norton* (4 Jul [1892]), he calls Bourget "the first . . . of all the talkers I have ever encountered." Equally sure was James of his dislike for Bourget's naturalistic, superficial fiction, the monetary success of which, however, he envied. He wrote thus to Bourget (15 May 1900): "I am always conscious of . . . a deviation from you on the ground of method. . . . You tend often to make me take your *nouvelle* rather for an essay . . . on the subject, than as a direct exhibition . . . of that subject, and this not at all from your famous excess of analysis . . . but from a way you have of going . . . in front of your story or action like an epiloguist. . . ." He wrote to his brother William and his wife (9 Aug [1899]) of "the bitterness of humiliation" when he compared "the splendour of . . . my confrères"—and he named Bourget among others—to his own "poor little $10,000 shelter," that is, Lamb House,* at Rye. James put his opinion of Bourget as a person best in a letter to William (29 Dec 1893): "He has . . . a . . . charming and affectionate side, but it loses itself in an abyss of *corruption* and in a sort of avidity, a habit of inconsiderate manners. . . . Hélas, with all his brilliancy, all his literary *mondanité*, etc., he isn't a gentleman"; but James goes on to blame Bourget's "race" and "abominable *milieu*" for his faults. Each of the two men introduced friends to the other: James saw to it that Bourget met Ariane Randolph Curtis* and Daniel Sargent Curtis* in Venice; Bourget arranged for Urbain Mengin* to meet James in London. James and Bourget also had many friends in common, notably Edith Newbold Jones Wharton.* When Bourget married Minnie David in 1890, James disapproved on both professional and personal grounds, but he soon came to like his robust friend's fragile, attentive wife. The three spent happy weeks together in Siena, Italy, in 1892; James admired Bourget's *Sensations d'Italie* (1891), which reflects the Bourgets' residence in James's favorite country. James occasionally entertained and went out with the Bourgets in London and Rye, and he was also a guest at their French Riviera home, at Hyères, in the 1890s. Although he doubted Bourget's ability to understand America, James, in a letter to Sir Edmund Wilson Gosse* (22 Aug [1894]), describes *Outre-mer: Notes sur L'Amérique* (1895), the book which came of Bourget's 1893–1894 visit to the United States, as "singularly agreeable & lively." When Bourget lectured on Flaubert at Oxford University in June 1897, James felt it his duty to attend an academic ceremony in which mere novelists were honored; so he inconveniently got himself there and wrote up his impressions in "London" (21 Aug 1897; reprinted in *Notes on Novelists*, 1914). Finally, James offers the barest and most routine praise of Bourget in his 1899 essay "The Present Literary Situation in France." He deplored Bourget's anti-Semitic attitude during the Alfred Dreyfus* affair, siding instead with the pro-Dreyfusard position of their friend Mengin. According to Notebook entries (20 Jun 1887, 22 Sep 1895, 7 May 1898, 11 Sep 1900), the Bourgets gave James ideas for several stories: "A London Life" was suggested to James by a conversation between the two men in Venice in June 1887; in Torquay, Cornwall, in September 1895, James recorded an idea from Minnie Bourget which resulted in "The Tone of Time"; in May 1898, James seems to have been inspired to write "The Two Faces" by something that had happened at the Bourgets' Riviera villa a month earlier; and both "Maud-Evelyn" and the unfinished "Hugh Merrow" owe something to Bourget talk, according to a note by James in September 1900. James's library contained thirty-two books by Bourget.

Bousefield. In "The Next Time," the owner of a magazine which Ralph Limbert edited briefly.

Boutroux, Étienne Émile (1845–1921). French philosopher, teacher, and author of *William James* (1911). Henry James attended a lecture by Boutroux at the British Academy in London, and a day later in a letter to Walter Van Rensselaer Berry* (11 Dec 1914) called the philosopher "really charming."

Bowerbank, Mrs. In *The Princess Casamassima*, a prison official who informs Amanda Pynsent that Hyacinth Robinson's mother Florentine Vivier is dying.

Bowles, William. In "A Most Extraordinary Case," the servant to whom Ferdinand Mason leaves some money.

Boyer, Mr. and Mrs. In "The Beast in the Jungle," casual friends of May Bartram and John Marcher.

Braby, Miss. In "The Death of the Lion," the subject of a sensational article in Pinhorn's magazine.

Bracken, Mrs. In "Flickerbridge," the subject of one of Frank Granger's portraits.

Braddle, Bertram. In "The Great Condition," the man who loves Mrs. Damerel but is so suspicious of her that he loses out to Henry Chilver.

Braddon, Mary Elizabeth (1837–1915). The sister of Sir Edward Braddon, an official in India, premier in Tasmania, and member of the Australian Commonwealth Parliament. Mary Braddon started her career as a Brighton newspaper contributor (1855). When she was encouraged by publisher John Maxwell, whom she subsequently married, to try a novel, she wrote the triple-decker *Lady Audley's Secret* (1862), one of her most lurid novels and certainly one of her most successful financially. Ultimately she became an editor and a prolific writer of many plays and of about eighty meritorious if sensational novels, the best of which excite the Victorian reader (without unduly provoking the Victorian censor) through melodrama, social satire, and evocation of atmosphere. Two of her sons were also novelists. James reviewed (*Nation*, 9 Nov 1865) Braddon's *Aurora Floyd* (1865), beginning with comments on *Lady Audley's Secret* as a lucky hit by an audacious writer more popular than meritorious. James then notes her similarities to and differences from Ann Radcliffe and Wilkie Collins: The latter has degothicized the former's effects by rightly connecting the ghostly with the real and also has incidentally anticipated Braddon's "domestic mysteries." Still, Braddon is "the founder of the sensation novel." Lady Audley was a "diabolically wicked" character, whereas Aurora Floyd is merely "foolish, . . . indiscreet, . . . indelicate." Braddon's recent novels are "fundamentally a repetition of 'Aurora Floyd.' " James defines the reading public as really many small publics, one of which reads Braddon, rather than good novelists, and insistently demands "something new" of her. So she skillfully combines old "[b]igamy, murder, and arson" into new works, all of which "from a literary point of view . . . are contemptible." She "interprets the illegitimate world to the legitimate," all the while "overload[ing] . . . her canvas with detail," romanticizing "the incidents of vice," and paying lip service to morality "with a woman's *finesse.*" James closes his review (*Nation*, 1 Mar 1866) of *A Noble Life* by Dinah Maria Mulock Craik* with an expression of his preference for her honest sentimentality to the hard brilliance of Braddon, whom he would "never dream of calling . . . *honnête.*" According to a Notebook entry (4 Jun 1895), James had what he too harshly regarded as Braddon's tawdry slickness in mind when he was beginning satirically to portray popular novelist Jane Highmore in "The Next Time." However, late in his life, James wrote a correspondent addressed as Miss Frith (15 Aug 1911), perhaps disingenuously, to the effect that Braddon had cast a "spell . . . on my younger time," even though he read her warily.

Bradeen, Lady. In "In the Cage," the gorgeous woman, recently widowed, who is to wed Captain Count Philip Everard. She receives a telegram from him which is processed by the girl "in the cage."

Bradeen, Lord. In "In the Cage," Lady Bradeen's recently deceased husband.

Bradham, Davey. In *The Ivory Tower*, Gussy's middle-aged husband and a friend of Graham Fielder and Rosanna Gaw.

Bradham, Gussy. In *The Ivory Tower*, Davey's wife, and a friend of Rosanna Gaw and Graham Fielder.

Bradshaw. In *The Golden Bowl*, presumably Prince Amerigo's servant.

Bradshaw, Miss. In "Paste," the actress who becomes Mrs. Prine.

Bradshaw, Mrs. In "A Most Extraordinary Case," the hostess at a dance attended by Caroline Hofmann and Dr. Horace Knight. Their attending the dance bothers Ferdinand Mason.

Brady, Dr. In *The Golden Bowl*, the physician of the son of Prince Amerigo and his wife Princess Maggie Verver.

Brand, Rev. Mr. In *The Europeans*, the New England Unitarian minister who will marry Charlotte Wentworth. His prejudices may owe something to those of Rev. Mr. William Rounseville Alger.*

Brandes, Georg Morris (née Cohen) (1842–1927). Pro-materialism professor, literary critic, biographer, historian, and journalist, born in Copenhagen, Denmark. When they first met in England, James praised Brandes in a letter to their friend Sir Edmund Wilson Gosse* (9 Nov 1895), calling him "a fine free foreign mind." In his introduction to a 1907 edition of *The Tempest* by William Shakespeare,* James rejects Brandes's theory that the play is the playwright's farewell to the theater. James's library contained one book by Brandes.

Brandon, Jack. In "The Visits," the bewildered object of Louisa Chantry's sudden and fatally embarrassing passion.

Bransby, Adam P. In "Miss Gunton of Poughkeepsie," the fiancé of Lily Gunton after she drops the Roman prince.

Bransby, The Misses. In "Miss Gunton of Poughkeepsie," Adam P. Bransby's sisters.

Bransby, Mrs. In "Miss Gunton of Poughkeepsie," Adam P. Bransby's mother.

Brash, Louisa. In "The Beldonald Holbein," the lovably ugly foil to hard, beautiful Lady Nina Beldonald. Miss Brash resembles a portrait by Hans Holbein the younger.* Her appearance may be patterned in part after that of Julia Ward Howe* in her old age.

Brasier. In *Guy Domville*, Maria Brasier Domville's deceased first husband. He was Lieutenant George Porter Round's uncle and the supposed father of Mary Brasier.

Brasier, Mary. In *Guy Domville*, the pure, young Catholic girl pushed by her parents Maria Brasier Domville and Lord Devenish to marry Guy Domville. When Guy learns that Mary loves Lieutenant George Porter Round, he helps the two of them to elope.

Bray, Mrs. In "The Chaperon," Lady Maresfield's rich sister, who unsuccessfully tries to invite Rose Tramore to a ball without including Rose's mother.

Bread, Catherine. In *The American*, Madame Emmeline Atheling de Belle-garde's English-born servant who, for a reward of lifetime employment, gives Christopher Newman evidence of the Bellegarde family secret, which is that Madame de Bellegarde killed her husband. In *The American: A Comedy in Four Acts*, the incriminating letter adds that Claire de Cintré's deceased husband the Comte de Cintré had been the unprincipled lover of Claire's mother. Valentin de Bellegarde affectionately calls Mrs. Bread, Catty. In the rewritten fourth act, Claire also calls her Catty.

Bream, Anthony (Tony). In *The Other House*, the novel, the owner of the other house, Bounds. The son of the deceased banker Paul Bream, Tony is the husband of Julia until her death. He is the father of little Effie and the object of the violent passion of Rose Armiger (who murders Effie), even though he loves Jean Martle. In *The Other House*, the play, his age at the outset if thirty-five; he is handsome, genial, and shallow. He attracts Rose, but he loves—and will probably wed— Jean after Rose murders Effie.

Bream, Effie. In *The Other House*, the novel, Tony and Julia Bream's little daughter, whom Rose Armiger drowns to nullify his promise to dying Julia that he will not remarry so long as the child lives. In *The Other House*, the play, Effie is age four.

Bream, Julia Grantham. In *The Other House*, Tony's dying wife. Tony promises not to remarry so long as their daughter Effie lives. Julia had a bad stepmother and does not want her daughter to suffer the same fate. In *The Other House*, the play, Julia dies at the age of twenty-two; her stepmother, Mrs. Griffin, is Rose Armiger's aunt.

Bream, Paul. In *The Other House*, Anthony's deceased father, who was a banker and the partner of the elder Paul Beever, in Wilverley.

Brécourt, Alphonse de. In *The Reverberator*, Suzanne's husband.

Brécourt, Suzanne de (Susan). In *The Reverberator*, Gaston Probert's sister.

Brench, Peter. In "The Tree of Knowledge," Morgan Mallow's friend who is harmlessly in love with Morgan's wife.

Bride, Julia. In "Julia Bride," the often-engaged New York beauty who, by unselfishly aiding her innocent stepfather Pitman, loses Murray Brush.

Bride, Mrs. In "Julia Bride," now Mrs. Connery.

Bridgenorth, Mrs. In "The Tone of Time," the woman who commissions Mary Juliana Tredick to paint a supposedly imaginary person's portrait, which turns out to be the likeness of a mutual friend.

Bridget, Lady. In *The American*, Lord Deepmere's mother.

Brigstock, Mona. In *The Spoils of Poynton*, Owen Gereth's large, unpleasant fiancée and then demanding wife.

Brigstock Mrs. In *The Spoils of Poynton*, Mona's unyielding mother.

Brinder, Sir John. In *The Golden Bowl*, an ambassador's London aide.

Brindes, Marie de. In "Collaboration," Paule's anti-German mother, whose husband was killed during the Franco-Prussian War.

Brindes, Paule de. In "Collaboration," the young woman who is too anti-German to continue her relationship with Félix Vendemer when he begins to associate professionally with Herman Heidenmauer.

Brine. In "Miss Gunton of Poughkeepsie," Mrs. Brine's husband, an American.

Brine, Mrs. In "Miss Gunton of Poughkeepsie," Lily Gunton's American traveling companion.

Briseux, Pierre. In "The Sweetheart of M. Briseux," a talented French painter. At the outset of his career, the female narrator gives up Harold Staines to let Briseux use her as a model while he improves Staines's mediocre portrait of her by painting over it.

Brisket, Lady Amy. In *Disengaged*, Sir Montagu Brisket's wife, who, thinking her husband is indifferent, responds to Percy Trafford until Mrs. Jasper helps her realize the truth.

Brisket, Sir Montagu. In *Disengaged*, Lady Amy Brisket's inept but faithful husband, Flora Wigmore's brother, and hence Blandina Wigmore's uncle. He thinks that his wife is uncaring until Mrs. Jasper, whom he likes, explains matters.

Brissenden, Grace (Mrs. Briss). In *The Sacred Fount*, aging Guy's apparently younger-growing wife. She later denies the narrator's "sacred fount" theory.

Brissenden, Guy (Briss). In *The Sacred Fount*, Grace's fast-aging husband and hence perhaps her "sacred fount."

Brives, Marquise de. In "Mrs. Temperly," a supposedly high-society Parisian friend of Mrs. Temperly.

Brives, Mme. de. In *The Reverberator*, Suzanne de Brécourt's friend.

Brivet, Frank. In "The Special Type," Rose Cavenham's lover. He incites his wife to divorce him by appearing in public compromisingly with Alice Dundene.

Brivet, Mrs. Frank. In "The Special Type," the woman who divorces her husband and then marries Remson Sturch.

Broderip. In *The Europeans*, William Wentworth's former Harvard Law School friend.

Brohan, Madeleine. In "At Isella," an actress whom the narractor sees at the Théâtre Français.

"Broken Wings." Short story (6,500 words), published in the *Century Magazine* (Dec 1900); revised and reprinted in *The Novels and Tales of Henry James*, Volume XVI, 1909. (Characters: Lady Claude, Mrs. Harvey, Stuart Straith.) Painter Stuart Straith and playwright Mrs. Harvey see each other again, after a long time apart, at a big house party, but they are not able to speak. She tells a friend that her career has gone badly and that she would long ago have married Straith but for his ambition. Some time later she meets Straith at a play, and he says he designed the costumes for it. She says she would like to do a story on him for her art column. They meet more times and exchange humble confidences; their pride gone, they embrace, decide to avoid unrewarding high society, and work together for art. A brief Notebook entry (16 Feb 1899) concerns the idea of two artists concealing from each other their absence of success until a "tragic" breakdown of their pride occurs, with "at least the effect of bringing them, for some consolatory purpose, together." This slight tale is unusual for being shot through with pathos; it also is sunken autobiography, for James, like his passed-by central "artists" here, suffered toward the end of the nineteenth century from a sense of unwantedness by his public.

Bronson, Katherine De Kay (?–1901). Wife of Arthur Bronson, and distinguished socialite and hostess, from New York and Newport, Rhode Island; she owned a home in Venice, called Casa Alvisi ("Ca'Alvisi"), the hospitality of which was legendary. Americans whom James knew and who were also welcomed by Mrs. Bronson in Venice (and at her summer home in nearby Asolo) included Ariana Randolph Curtis and Daniel Sargent Curtis,* Isabella Stewart

Gardner,* William Wetmore Story* and his family, and Constance Fenimore Woolson.* James may have first seen Mrs. Bronson (and her sister Helena De Kay Gilder, wife of Richard Watson Gilder*) at Newport in the 1860s. Mrs. Bronson was aboard the ship that in October 1875 took James back to Europe rather permanently. She played cards during that voyage with another fellow passenger, Anthony Trollope.* James frequently called upon Mrs. Bronson later in Venice, and she became his confidante "Katrina." She saw him in London on occasion as well. He wrote to her from Florence in 1887, in connection with the indiscretion of Mary McClellan, the daughter of George Brinton McClellan,* which gaffe James used as the basis for his novel *The Reverberator*. In December 1893 James wrote to Mrs. Bronson to request that she continue befriending their mutual friend Constance Fenimore Woolson, but within a few weeks (and later as well) they were communicating about Woolson's death from a fall in Venice and its consequences. James wrote a charming prefatory note to Mrs. Bronson's 1902 essay on their mutual friend Robert Browning,* entitled "Browning in Venice: Being Recollections by the Late Mrs. Katherine De Kay Bronson" (*Cornhill Magazine*, Feb 1902). James's preface became "Casa Alvisi" in *Italian Hours*, 1909. In his biography of Story, James rhapsodizes on Mrs. Bronson's hospitality. James never had occasion to alter his early definition of Mrs. Bronson, which was expressed in a letter to Grace Norton* (27 Feb [1887]): "Mrs. Bronson is a most benevolent, injudiciously (even) generous woman." When she died, James wrote to her daughter Edith Rucellai (15 Feb 1901) that her passing "is the end of so many things—so many delightful memories, histories, associations—some of the happiest elements of one's own past. . . . From years . . . back she was delightfully kind to me and I had for her the most sincere affection. Those long Venetian years will be for all her friends . . . a sort of legend and boast." There are some general likenesses between Mrs. Bronson and Mrs. Prest in "The Aspern Papers." Further, according to a Notebook entry (27 Feb 1895), James patterned the heroine of "Miss Gunton of Poughkeepsie" partly after Mrs. Bronson's daughter Edith, who married Count Cosimo Rucellai of Florence. In a gossipy letter to Ariana Curtis (1 Mar 1895), James registers annoyance that Mrs. Bronson should " 'wait on' the Rucellais in Florence. . . . A person here [in London] who has been . . . much in Florence, tells me the Rucellais have no title *at all*. . . . They are of the oldest *un*titled Florentine stock . . . " Late in his career (1909–1910), James sketched preliminary plans for a novel, which he tentatively called "The 'K.B.' Case," with "K.B." clearly standing for Katherine Bronson. The work was then retitled *The Ivory Tower*, but the advent of World War I and then death prevented his ever completing it.

Brontë sisters. Three novelist sisters who resided mostly in Yorkshire and had generally melancholy lives. Their father, Patrick Brontë, was Irish, and was educated in England and ordained in the Anglican church. His wife was Cornish. He became a curate at Haworth. Their children included Charlotte Brontë (1816–1855), Branwell Brontë (1817–1848), Emily Brontë (1818–1848), and Anne

Brontë (1820–1849), as well as two other daughters, who died at an early age. Their mother died in 1821. The children had a grim, controlled upbringing thereafter, with some harsh schooling at Cowan Bridge. Charlotte and Emily returned home and began to write secretly. Anne became a governess in 1839. Charlotte and Emily went to Brussels in 1842 for a while to study languages to teach back at Haworth. Branwell was unstable and became addicted to drugs. The three sisters published a book of poems pseudonymously together (1846). Then Charlotte published *Jane Eyre* (1847); Emily, *Wuthering Heights* (1847); and Anne, *Agnes Grey* (1847) and *The Tenant of Wildfell Hall* (1848). After Branwell, Emily, and Anne had died, Charlotte cared for their father, published *Shirley* (1849), and met William Makepeace Thackeray* in London and Elizabeth Cleghorn Gaskell* (who later wrote her first biography) in northern England. Charlotte published *Villette* (1853), married (1854), and died a year later; her posthumous novels are *The Professor* (1857) and the fragmentary *Emma* (1860). Brontë novels, especially *Jane Eyre* and *Wuthering Heights*, are notable for gothic and wild, romantic elements and for critically challenging techniques. In his 1866 essay on the novels of George Eliot,* James "suggest[s] a comparison" between *Jane Eyre* and *Adam Bede*. In an 1867 review of *Waiting for the Verdict* by Rebecca Harding Davis,* he notes an influence from *Jane Eyre* and *Wuthering Heights*, which he calls "great authorities." In an 1875 review of *Poets and Novelists* by George Barnett Smith,* James calls *Wuthering Heights* a "crude and morbid story." James wrote to Thomas Sergeant Perry* (22 Feb [1880]) that he had dined with Weemys Reid, a Leeds editor, who wrote a monograph on Charlotte Brontë, told him much about the Brontë family, and offered to show him 750 intimate letters by Charlotte to her school friend Ellen Nussey. James suggests that Perry "come over . . . to help me read 'em." In "London" (6 Feb 1897), James briefly notes *Charlotte Brontë and Her Circle* (1896) by Clement King Shorter,* calling it "very interesting" but not yet the final word on the subject. In a letter to Sir Edmund Wilson Gosse* (12 Jun 1903) praising his 1903 lecture on the Brontës, James adds that "[i]t was time the Fatal Sisters *should* have a smile play over them—sullen as I yet figure their 'psychic' response." In his 1916 essay on Rupert Brooke,* James listed Emily Brontë among writers whose "genius" was evoked by adverse circumstances. The possible influence of *Jane Eyre* on James's "The Turn of the Screw" has often been noted. James's library contained two books by Charlotte Brontë.

Brooke, Margaret Alice Lili (née de Windt), Ranee of Sarawak (1849–1936). Rich, extravagant, and talented international socialite of English, Dutch, and French descent. Her brother was the explorer Harry de Windt. Margaret, respecting though not loving him, married Charles Anthoni Johnson-Brooke (twenty years her senior) in 1869, a year after he had succeeded as rajah his uncle Sir James Brooke, the first white rajah of Sarawak. Sir Charles Brooke ruled almost fifty years. The couple had six children, three of whom died in 1873 aboard ship in the Red Sea, evidently from cholera and heat stroke. The other children were Charles Vyner De Windt Brooke (later a rajah), Bertram Brooke (the parents' favorite), and Harry Brooke. Lady Brooke loved Sarawak and was popular with the natives, but she spent fully half her married life in England and on the Continent, although she enjoyed occasional trips back to Sarawak (for example, in 1887 and 1895). She maintained permanent residences in London and Surrey, where she developed innumerable friendships, for example, with Sir James Matthew Barrie,* Paul Bourget,* Philip Burne-Jones (son of Sir Edward Burne-Jones*), Edward Elgar, Isabella Stewart Gardner,* W. H. Hudson, Violet Paget,* George Bernard Shaw,* Howard Overing Sturgis,* Algernon Charles Swinburne,* Herbert George Wells,* Edith Newbold Jones Wharton,* and Oscar Wilde* (whose family she aided in Italy). She especially liked William Morton Fullerton* and became one of his several lovers in the early 1890s. She was described by intimates as kind, charming, and courageous. A Notebook entry (5 Feb 1892) reveals that by 1892 James had met her socially. His Pocket Diaries indicate that they were still close friends in the 1910s. James also knew her sons when they were of an age to attend Cambridge. When a blackmailer threatened to expose Fullerton (along with Lady Brooke), James sent a message containing sensible advice to the foolish philanderer (14 Nov 1907): "sit tight and . . . *do* nothing." In one of the hundred letters he addressed to Lady Brooke (16 Aug 1902), James calls her "dearest old friend." Her husband Sir Charles, described as autocratic, tough, plain, cantankerous, and prophetic, was blinded in one eye in a 1912 hunting accident and died in 1917 at the age of eighty-seven. Margaret Brooke wrote *My Life in Sarawak* (1913), *Impromptus* (1923), and *Good Morning & Good Night* (1934). James's library contained one book by Brooke.

Brooke, Rupert (1887–1915). Handsome Rugby-born Rugby School student and athlete who went on to distinguish himself as a fellow at King's College, Cambridge, and as a Fabian socialist, and then to wander as a well-to-do scholar poet in Germany, Italy, and again in England. He published *Poems* (1911), then pushed still farther afield to the United States, Canada, and the far Pacific (1913–1914). Early in World War I, young Brooke joined the British Navy, participated in an abortive raid on Antwerp, died of blood poisoning on his way to the Dardanelles, and was buried on the Greek Island of Skyros. Brooke's war verses, entitled *1914 and Other Poems* (1915), thus take on added poignancy as do his *Letters from America* (1916), for which James provided a verbose, four-part preface. James, while visiting and being royally entertained at Cambridge in June 1909 by three undergraduates, Theodore Bartholomew, Charles Sayle, and Sir Geoffrey Langdon Keynes,* met Brooke and was impressed by his striking physical beauty. James's thank-you letter to Sayle (16 Jun 1909) waxes poetic concerning Brooke. Subsequent letters reveal that James followed Brooke's naval career anxiously. On learning of his death, James wrote to Sir Edmund Wilson Gosse* (25 Apr 1915): "It wrings the heart & makes the time still more hideous." He also sent a poignant letter to Sir Edward Howard Marsh,* who became

Brooke's literary executor and persuaded James, though chronically sick at the time, to write the preface to his *Letters from America*. James starts off by expressing his desire to see how a sincere poet "come[s] into his [artistic] estate" despite vicissitudes. Unlike other poets, Brooke did so by being notably modern and then by meeting death as a youth in wartime. Brooke is now seen as representing the "civility" and "social instincts" of his race during his epoch (better than quarrelsome George Gordon, Lord Byron* did his, for example), since young Brooke retained "the bloom" "of the inbred 'public school' character." He was almost universally "liked." He cast a spell. He displayed the "generic spontaneity" of the poet. James recalls details of his meeting Brooke at Cambridge and thanks Marsh for his work in assembling the young man's " 'literary baggage,' " all of which helped James write his preface. Brooke was "the heir of all the ages" poetically and socially and was always active. Should he have lived inwardly a little more? traveled a little less? Surely his poetic reactions to various places, especially Germany, were lively and fine. And self-conscious. Brooke's writings show "the young lyrist" to be connected to his times. He and most of his friends "were . . . young together." Then "the War came smashing down," just before which, however, Brooke fortunately traveled widely, in search of "unprejudiced culture, the true poetic, the vision of the life of man." In an aside, James expresses the wish that he could have shown young Brooke some New York sights he overlooked. It was characteristic of Brooke to like more than he disliked. His travel writing is direct and free of "[t]he ironies and paradoxes of his verse." His comments on Canada are those of "an impressionist." As for the Pacific Islands, he presents them simply to our jaded eyes and thus explains them better than Robert Louis Stevenson* and Pierre Loti* do. To Brooke, the islands were simply "a picture of the youth of the world at its blandest" and a place of "amphibious felicity." Then he returned to "so-called civilisation" with his "free poetic sense" incorruptibly sincere. Brooke's death in war symbolizes "desolating and heart-breaking waste," and James as "hovering spectator" must ask "the sickening . . . [but] strangely sustaining . . . why." James recalls his last sight of Brooke, soldier and friend, who did not then "let his intelligence interfere with his modesty." Given his death, his "New Numbers" sonnets now take on a deeper meaning, apart from their mere beauty, authority, and purity. Generous and joyful, he is now a monument to historic nobility. (This preface to Brooke's *Letters* was the last piece of writing James ever completed.)

Brooke, Stopford Augustus (1832–1916). Clergyman and writer, born in Donegal, Ireland. He attended Trinity College, Dublin, as a divinity student; he also wrote prize-winning verse there. He was ordained in the Church of England, but after twenty-four years of varied service in London and briefly in Berlin he seceded (1880). He became a Unitarian minister in Bloomsbury (1876–1895). He published rather widely on theological subjects but also on English literature. He also published some of his own poetry. James reviewed (*Nation*, 21 Jan

1875) Brooke's *Theology in the English Poets—Cowper, Coleridge, Words-worth, Burns* (1874). James says that Brooke "readily forgives a poor verse on the plea of a fine thought," since his aim is "to construct the religious belief of the poets from their works." But James avers that only William Cowper possessed any "theology"; William Wordsworth is "so vast and suggestive" that we can find vague hints as to all kinds of theology. Further, Brooke regards Robert Burns as a "subject for redemption and salvation"! James is happy to note that Brooke sees a movement in late eighteenth-century British verse toward the concrete, the real, the individual, and Nature, but he laments that he writes "diffusely" on "diffuse" Wordsworth. James quotes some fine lines by that poet but says that he later stiffened into conservatism, and yet he then evidently agrees with Brooke that Wordsworth is the best British poet since John Milton. James gleefully wrote to his father (29 May [1878]) that he had just been elected to the Reform Club and had recently sat at dinner there next to Brooke, "a capital un-clerical creature." A few years later, James wrote to his brother William (2 Jan 1885) that he planned to give Brooke a copy of their father's theological works, since that cleric would "have some attention and care for them." According to James's Notebooks (17 Feb 1894), when the two were fellow-dinner guests, Brooke gave the novelist an idea that eventuated as *The Sacred Fount*. Brooke provided an elegiac poem for *Last Studies* (1897) by Hubert Montague Crackanthorpe,* for which James wrote a prefatory appreci-ation. Brooke wrote to Crackanthorpe's mother that he could hardly understand the convoluted style in James's preface. James's library contained one book by Brooke.

Brooke. In "Travelling Companions," the narrator, a young American who seems to compromise Charlotte Evans in Padua by traveling unchaperoned with her. They later marry each other.

Brookenham, Edward. In *The Awkward Age*, Mrs. Brookenham's husband, the father of Fernanda and Harold, and the cousin of Duchess Jane.

Brookenham, Fernanda (Nanda). In *The Awkward Age*, the Brookenhams' daughter. She is Longdon's god-daughter and loves Gustavus Vanderbank.

Brookenham, Harold. In *The Awkward Age*, the Brookenhams' sponging son.

Brookenham, Mrs. Edward (Mrs. Brook). In *The Awkward Age*, the center of an effete social circle observed with distaste by Longdon.

Brooks. In "A Light Man," Frederick Sloane's lawyer.

Brooksmith. In "Brooksmith," Oliver Offord's impeccable butler. After the master's death, he and the narrator ultimately lose touch with one another.

Brooksmith, Mrs. In "Brooksmith," the butler's mother, who dies.

"Brooksmith." Short story (6,300 words), published in *Harper's Weekly* (2 May 1891) and in *Black and White* (2 May 1891); revised and reprinted in *The Novels and Tales of Henry James*, Volume XVIII, 1909. (Characters: Brooksmith, Mrs. Brooksmith, Lady Kenyon, Oliver Offord.) The narrator's charming London friend Oliver Offord dies. His salon was presided over by an impeccable servant named Brooksmith, who in his late thirties can find no other work that challenges his culture and loyalty. He and the narrator then lose touch with one another. According to a Notebook entry (19 Jun 1884), the idea for "Brooksmith" came to James when Christina Stewart Rogerson* told him about the fate of the intelligent, articulate maid (whose name, curiously, was Past) of her recently deceased mother, Mrs. Duncan Stewart.* James changed the sex of the maid because a male servant would be closer to the brilliant table talk. Just as "In the Cage" and "The Turn of the Screw" do, this story centers on a main character whom James's social milieu normally considered beneath notice. By touching a lowly servant into poignant life, James shows again his far-reaching humanity. Did Brooksmith commit suicide? He simply disappears. James originally planned to call this story "The Servant."

Broughton, Rhoda (1840–1920). Audacious, rebellious Victorian novelist, born in North Wales. She occasionally used as a fictional setting her happy family residence, called Broughton Hall, in Staffordshire. Her clergyman father educated her at home (in languages and literature, including the plays of William Shakespeare*). Losing both parents when she was in her early twenties, she quickly serialized two novels, *Not Wisely but Too Well* and *Cometh up as a Flower*, both in the *Dublin University Magazine* (owned by her novelist uncle Sheridan Le Fanu). Both works were reprinted in book form in 1867. They caused a sensation, as did their then-shocking successors, *Red as a Rose Is She* (1870) and *Goodbye, Sweetheart!* (1872). These first four novels she published anonymously. She never married, but she lived for a while with relatives in Wales and then Oxford. When she moved to London, she widened her circle of admirers and well-wishers, which ultimately included Matthew Arnold,* George Bentley, Augustus John Cuthbert Hare,* the Earl of Lytton, Mark Pattison, Lady Anne Isabella Ritchie,* Field-Marshal Viscount Garnet Joseph Wolseley,* and James. She remained a usually popular, always prolific novelist, whose best later works are *Joan* (1876), *Second Thoughts* (1880), *Belinda* (1883), *Alas!* (1890), *A Beginner* (1894), *Dear Faustina* (1897), *Foes in Law* (1899), *A Waif's Progress* (1905), and *A Fool in Her Folly* (1920). Her early works, which deal with thwarted love, are possibly autobiographical. Her later novels are more satirical. She is witty, pessimistic, indecorous, and sensual. Broughton revealingly said of herself once, "I began my life as [Émile] Zola[*]. I finish it as Miss [Charlotte Mary] Yonge[*]." James wrote to his brother William (10 Jul [1877]) that he had lunched with Broughton at the home of Lord Houghton* some time ago; their friendship went way back. She visited James and Constance Fenimore Woolson* in 1887, when the two happened to be together at Villa Brichieri, outside Florence. James wrote to Frances Anne Kemble* at that time (20 May [1887]) that he liked Broughton "in spite of her roughness." She attended the opening performance of his play *The American*, in London on 26 September 1891. In some agitation, James wrote to Broughton twice early in 1894 about Woolson's death. In a letter to Charles Eliot Norton* (26 Dec 1898), James called Broughton "that very mature child of nature." James wrote to Broughton one of his most eloquent letters (10 Aug 1914) to express his inconsolable anguish at the outbreak of World War I. James often took walks in Richmond Park with her; once they argued about William Shakespeare* and his background. James reviewed only one of Rhoda Broughton's books (*Nation* 21 Dec 1876). That was *Joan*, which James, who had not yet met Broughton, defines as "a farrago of puerility and nastiness, inanity and vulgarity." He dislikes the "strapping young Guardsmen" in it, also the "talk about legs and shoulders, . . . and the 'longevity' of first kisses." He deplores what he calls the indecency and "school-girl's" style of the book. He compares her "insidiousness" to "the gambols of an elephant" and imperceptively calls the ironic work immature, crude, coarse, and vacuous. In the same review, he contrasts *Joan* with the morally elevated but dull 1876 novel *Mercy Philbrick's Choice* by Helen Maria Hunt Jackson.*

Brown, Ford Madox (1821–1893). English painter influenced by the Pre-Raphaelites and the Nazarenes. Brown was born in France; having studied there and in Belgium, he began in 1846 to teach painting in London. His subjects are often romantic, historical, and literary; his style, dramatic, colorful, and detailed. In "London" (20 Feb 1897), James says that Brown was ignored during his lifetime and yet that his sincerity "lights up not only the vulgarity of his age, but too many of his own perversities and pedantries." James criticizes several of his paintings and concludes that he displays "an air . . . of *invraisemblable* innocence." But in "London" (5 Jun 1897), James praises Brown's famous *Farewell to England* for its "queer, hard, ugly, but rich and full sincerity." In the summer of 1896 Brown's grandson, Ford Madox Hueffer* (who later changed his name to Ford Madox Ford) called on James at Rye.

Brown, Lucinda. In *Watch and Ward*, Roger Lawrence's devoted housekeeper.

Brown. In "The Great Good Place," George Dane's servant.

Browning, Elizabeth Barrett (1806–1861). Distinguished English poetess, who could read Greek at the age of eight (and published a translation of *Prometheus Bound* at twenty-seven). After injuring her spine as a teenager, she was long an invalid, wrote much poetry, and established friendships with critic Richard Henry Horne, poet William Wordsworth, and benefactor John Kenyon. She recovered her health only slightly. She began to correspond with Robert Browning* in

1845, married him (without her outraged father's knowledge) the next year, and moved with him to Italy in 1847). In Florence, where the couple made their home (notably at Casa Guidi) until her death, Mrs. Browning first showed her husband her *Sonnets from the Portuguese* (1847), written earlier and expressing her profound love for him. The Brownings had one child, Robert Wiedemann Barrett (Pen) Browning, who was born 1849. After considerable political writing, as well as more poetry and a little travel (England, Paris, and Rome), Mrs. Browning died. She was buried in Florence; her tomb was designed by Lord Frederic Leighton.* Beginning with his earliest years in Italy, James heard much about the Brownings from his American friends William Wetmore Story,* Francis Boott,* and his daughter Elizabeth Boott* (later the wife of Frank Duveneck*), who knew the Brownings well. In an 1875 review of *Poets and Novelists* by George Barnett Smith,* James said that Elizabeth Barrett Browning's poetry unites "merits and defects," that her "laxity and impurity of style is [*sic*] constantly vitiating her felicity of thought." He reviewed (*Nation*, 15 Feb 1877) *Letters from Elizabeth Barrett Browning, Addressed to R. H. Horne* (1877), sketching the background of the two-volume work and calling the letters (dated 1839–1846) both "entertaining" and of "biographical value." In them, Miss Barrett writes about "her ideas, her fancies, and her literary impressions," all in a "natural and spontaneous" tone. She details her extremely wide reading and offers among other comments many, of which James approves, concerning recent French fiction. James notes that, as editor of these letters, Horne reminisces about Miss Barrett's friend Mary Russell Mitford and also about a guild for writers planned by Charles Dickens* more than thirty years before.

Browning, Robert (1812–1889). Profound and innovative Victorian poet whose father was a book-loving Bank of England clerk and whose mother adored music. They indulged their healthy son and had him privately tutored. He visited Russia in 1833, Italy the following spring. His early poetry (especially *Paracelsus* [1835], which shows the influence of Percy Bysshe Shelley,* and *Sordello* [1840]) attracted favorable critical attention. He then turned to some intermittent (and poor) playwriting (1837–1846). His *Bells and Pomegranates* (1841–1846) and poetic contributions to *Hood's Magazine* (1844) added to his renown. In 1846 Elizabeth Barrett became Elizabeth Barrett Browning,* and the devoted couple moved to Italy the next year. Their most notable residence was at Casa Guidi, in Florence. They had one child, Robert Wiedemann Barrett (Pen) Browning, who was born in 1849. Among the many friends of the Brownings in Italy were the expatriate Americans Francis Boott,* his daughter Elizabeth Boott* (later the wife of Frank Duveneck*), Nathaniel Hawthorne,* and William Wetmore Story.* During his years in Italy, Browning wrote somewhat less than usual (*Christmas Eve and Easter Day* [1850] and *Men and Women* [1855]); but upon his wife's death in 1861 he moved back to England and soon issued *Dramatis Personae* (1864). His masterpiece *The Ring and the Book* appeared in 1868–1869. Many of his later works, including *The Inn Album* (1875), betray an occasional falling off of poetic intensity. The correspondence of the Brownings was edited by their son in 1899. James by 1864 or so had begun to read Browning, who became a major influence on him, as well as a source of psychological confusion. Browning combined intense, sensitive, jealously guarded, private artistic activity with a forcefully masculine, public social presence. James negatively reviewed (*Nation*, 20 Jan 1876) *The Inn Album*, calling it "irritating and displeasing" and adding that it is getting harder to defend its author, who has become wanton, willful, and crude. James says that *The Inn Album* reads like "rough notes for a poem" and is neither narrative nor lyrical, but merely dramatic to a point. Only a reviewer would ever reread it. James summarizes the "barely comprehensible" work, right down to the final climactic death, which is so surprising that the poet must have started with it in mind and "worked backwards." Browning mixes his ingredients like a chemist, and the results bubble and smell. From his earliest Italian years, James had heard about the Brownings from Americans there, especially Story, whose biography by James, entitled *William Wetmore Story and His Friends*, is dotted with Browning data. In about January 1877, James met Browning at a fashionable dinner party held by George Washburn Smalley,* the European correspondent in London for the *New York Tribune*. (James and Browning often were fellow dinner guests later.) In a letter to his mother (31 Jan [1877]), James first touched on his eventually fixed opinion that Browning was a split personality. He wrote, "I forgot to say that after Smalley's dinner I had a long talk with Browning, who, personally, is no more like to *Paracelsus* than I to Hercules, but is a great gossip and a very 'sympathetic' easy creature." To William Dean Howells* later (30 Mar [1877]), he reported that Browning "is a great chatterer but no *Sordello*." Next, James theorized to his sister Alice (8 Apr 1877) that Browning had two personalities, one hidden, the other public. To Grace Norton* (26 Jul 1880) he even complained that Browning, when reading his poems aloud, seemed not to understand or like them. By 1883 James knew Browning's social habits well enough to write to Emma Lazarus* (9 May [1883]) telling her how to manage to see the great poet socially. By the late 1880s, James was closely acquainted with Pen Browning and his well-to-do American wife, and he gossiped in letters about him. In 1887 Browning rented an apartment at 22 De Vere Gardens, across the street from where James was then living. The following March the two went by carriage to the London funeral of a mutual friend. Shortly after visiting James's friend Katherine De Kay Bronson* at Asolo, Italy, Browning died in nearby Venice. James attended Browning's obsequies at Westminster Abbey, where the poet was laid to rest, and soon thereafter published "Browning in Westminster Abbey" (*The Speaker*, 4 Jan 1890); reprinted in *Essays in London and Elsewhere*, 1893; and in *English Hours*, 1905. In this essay, James remarks that it would have taken Browning himself to do justice to the event: This honor would have evoked his whimsical humor. The public during a conferral of a great national honor at Westminster, James avers, maintains a silence which becomes articulate. The company of lesser historic figures, now under their arches and in their chapels, eye the new arrival, who brings an unwonted "contemporary individualism" to the place. Westminster Abbey surely has both greatness and oddity, but—James neatly adds—"none of the odd ones have been so great and none of the great ones so odd" as Robert Browning. James says that Browning seems to have been an unconscious genius whose apparent "weaknesses" are, rather, rich, humorous "boldnesses." For his last twenty years, Browning had become a familiar figure—"with all his Italianisms and cosmopolitanisms"—back in London, that "great Valhalla by the Thames." He wrote of faith, life, mysteries, will, character, action, and passion; and he beautifully expressed "the special relation between man and woman." James was displeased with his *Speaker* essay, and wrote to the editor Thomas Wemyss Reid (30 Dec [1889]) that it had been hard to compose, that he had not wanted to do it, and that it must be published anonymously. In 1892 James published "The Private Life," in which playwright Clare Vawdrey socializes innocuously even as his alter ego is busy writing in a darkened upstairs room. James had Browning in mind when he developed Vawdrey's dual nature. Proof of this fact is contained not only in a Notebook entry (27 Jul 1891) which reads that "the little tale [is to be] founded on the idea of [Lord] F[rederic]. L[eighton].* and R.B.," but also in his later analysis of Browning in *William Wetmore Story and his Friends** as having "mastered the secret of dividing the personal consciousness into a pair of independent compartments." James wrote a preface for *Browning in Venice* (1902), by Katherine De Kay Bronson.* He reprinted this preface as "The Late Mrs. Arthur Bronson," in the *Critic* (Feb 1902), and as "Casa Alvisi" in *Italian Hours*, 1909. Finally, at the invitation of his friend Sir Edmund Wilson Gosse,* James composed an elaborate lecture called "The Novel in *The Ring and the Book*." It was published in *Transactions of the Royal Society of Literature* (1912); and revised and reprinted in the *Quarterly Review*, edited by Sir George Walter Prothero* (Jul 1912), and in *Notes on Novelists*, 1914. Describing his speech far too modestly in a letter to Gosse (1 May 1912) as "a . . . recreational performance . . . wholly," he delivered it before the Royal Society of Literature, in Caxton Hall, in London, on 7 May 1912, during a celebration of the hundredth anniversary of Browning's birth. So moving was James's performance that the huge audience was spellbound. Reporters even dropped their pencils to listen enraptured. Its conclusion was greeted with thunderous applause. James begins by calling *The Ring and the Book* a "vast and . . . essentially gothic . . . structure," adds that its creator remains " 'difficult,' " then notes that its theme could be well treated in prose. On first reading, the poem seems "loose and uncontrolled," like a historical novel, evolving, again like such a novel, from documents "of facts pitiful and terrible" concerning real people begging the poet to " 'express us, immortalise us as we'll immortalise *you*!' " Browning characteristically chose several points of view. We can imagine him scouting all around his subject, then producing his story, not anyone else's. James then grippingly summarizes the action of the historical events which inspired *The Ring and the Book*. Now, how would Browning, a "genius," take this "cumulative weight," this "mere crude evidence," and cast it into art? We work Browning over even as he works his material over, James warns, adding that the poem seems "flaw[ed]" by not concentrating on Pompilia (the central female character) for unity. We may regard a novel as "a picture of life," or "even a 'bloody' chunk . . . of life"; but it should have unity. James then tries to contend that we find "in the centre of our field . . . the embracing consciousness of [Canon Giuseppe] Caponsacchi" (the heroine's "splendid" would-be rescuer), with Pope Innocent XII deliberating "too high above" the events to be really in the drama at all. James now remarks that Browning magnifies his characters by the force of his poetic personality, whereas novelists may be "more mixed with" their characters. Still, Browning's poem is an "action . . . picture," with the "atmosphere" of Italy uniquely bathing us. To compare: "[Percy Bysshe] Shelley . . . is a light and [Algernon Charles] Swinburne[*] . . . a sound; Browning . . . is a temperature." The hand of Italy is "at once a caress and a menace" here, and a vivid story and a sharp impression "come off" as a result, whether "a great poem" does or not. James sees in it "the idea of . . . latent prose fiction." Browning throws "coloured light" over "three characters of the first importance," each "built up at us," whereas only one or two might have sufficed for novelist James, who now returns to his belief that "the enveloping consciousness . . . of Caponsacchi" could be the center of a novel avoiding the anecdotal. Such concentration would convert not only the disparate parts of the poem into unified prose but Caponsacchi into "comparatively a modern man." Browning places this hero, "a great round smooth, though as yet but little worn gold-piece," in James's hand. Further, another character (this a minor canon) is simply "handed over to us . . . as inapt for poetic illustration." But James is willing to conclude that what Browning the poet does supremely well is to "exhibit . . . the great constringent relation between man and woman at once at its maximum and as the relation most worth while in life for either party." This is "quite the main substance of our author's message"; and many details, for example those concerning the escape of Caponsacchi and Pompilia, cry out for "our perfect prose transcript," whereas the gory climax of the poem is a comparative "lapse to passivity." James even suggests that a better final scene would be Caponsacchi's going to the Vatican and seeing the Pope privately: "*There* is a scene if we will." James concludes by saying first that his respectful attempt at rewriting *The Ring and the Book* is harder than merely finding a literary source and second that Browning may even now be blessing the group here, generously. James's library contained ten books by Browning.

Brownrigg, Miss. In "Collaboration," a writer admired by Alfred Bonus but not by Herman Heidenmauer.

Bruce, Jane. In "The Story of a Year," Robert Bruce's sister.

Bruce, Robert. In "The Story of a Year," a young Leatherborough man who does not join the Union Army during the Civil War. Elizabeth Crowe falls in love with him after her fiancé Lieutenant John Ford enters the army.

Brunt, Pitt, M.P. In *The Reprobate*, the pompous House of Commons man from Blackport, friend of Bonsor, and admirer of his niece Blanche Amber, who prefers Paul Doubleday.

Brush, Murray. In "Julia Bride," a young man loved by Julia Bride. Stories about her, however, lead him away and into an engagement with Mary Lindeck.

Bryce, Viscount James (1838–1922). Belfast-born English historian, professor, politician, and diplomat. He was educated at Trinity College, Oxford, published *The Holy Roman Empire* early in his scholarly career (1864), taught civil law at Oxford (1870–1893), cofounded the *English Historical Review* (1885), served as a Liberal member of the House of Commons (1880–1907), and opposed the government policy resulting in the Boer War. Bryce often visited the United States and wrote a classic study called *The American Commonwealth* (3 vols., 1888; later revised). He was distinguished ambassador to the United States (1907–1913). Back in England, he did significant work during World War I and later favored the establishment of the League of Nations. Bryce steadily promoted better U.S.–British relations. Early in 1877 James was a dinner guest for the first time at Bryce's home, where he met Albert Venn Dicey* and his wife. In June 1877 James was Bryce's guest at an Oxford academic ceremony, which James described in his 1877 essay "Three Excursions." In a letter to his father (25 Mar [1878]), James praises Bryce: "[H]e always talks well." But to his brother William a year later (4 Mar [1879]) he offers the following decidedly incorrect judgment of Bryce: "He is a distinctly able fellow, but he gives me the impression of being on the whole a failure. He has three conflicting dispositions—to literature (History)—to the law—and to politics—and he has not made a complete thing of any of them." According to a Notebook entry (12 Nov 1892), during a dinner party at the Bryces, James Bryce's sister-in-law told James about a child of divorced and remarrying parents, all caught in a tangle of the sort he developed into *What Maisie Knew*. Both James and his brother William came to know and respect the Bryces well. James followed Bryce's work during World War I with interest and approval. In January 1915 Bryce visited the mortally stricken James on the occasion of his receiving the British Order of Merit.

Brydon, Spencer. In "The Jolly Corner," an expatriate who late in life returns to New York and confronts his ravaged American alter ego in his old family home on "the jolly corner." He is comforted by Alice Staverton.

Bubb, Mrs. In "In the Cage," a customer of Mrs. Jordan.

Buchan, John (1875–1940). British statesman, man of letters, educator, and publisher, born in Scotland, and educated at Glasgow University and Brasenose College, Oxford. He performed important governmental work in South Africa,

London, and Canada. His most famous literary work is *The Thirty-Nine Steps* (1915). In his autobiographical *Memory Hold-the-Door* (1940), Buchan explains that his wife's aunt, who was the widow of a grandson of George Gordon, Lord Byron,* asked Buchan and James in 1909 to review some unsavory Byron family papers. Buchan said that James found them disgusting but important, whereupon the two wrote and signed a joint opinion in April 1910.

Buckton. In "In the Cage," a man who works in the store where the telegraphist's "cage" is located.

Buddle. In *Summersoft,* the young man whom Cora Prodmore wishes to marry. He is her grandmother's godson, also the son of a rich businessman. Mrs. Gracedew helps Cora to make her desires come true.

Buffery, Dr. In *The Princess Casamassima*, Amanda Pynsent's loyal little physician.

Bunbury, Mr. and Mrs. In *The Princess Casamassima*, neighbors of the Princess Casamassima from Broome.

Bunchie. In *The Portrait of a Lady*, Ralph Touchett's yapping little terrier.

"A Bundle of Letters." Short story (12,800 words), published in the *Parisian* (18 Dec 1879); reprinted in *The Diary of a Man of Fifty*, 1880; revised and reprinted in *The Novels and Tales of Henry James*, Volume XIV, 1908. (Characters: Clara Bernard, Lady Battledown, Clementine, Mr. and Mrs. Desmond, Lady Augusta Fleming, Prosper Gobain, Dr. Julius Hirsch, Mrs. Abraham C. Hope, Miranda Hope, Johnson, Louis Leverett, Mme. de Maisonrouge, William Platt, Violet Ray, Mr. and Mrs. Ray, Agnes Rich, Dr. Rudolph Staub, Harvard Tremont, Miss Turnover, Adelaide Vane, Evelyn Vane, Fred Vane, Georgina Vane, Gus Vane, Harold Vane, Mary Vane, Mr. and Mrs. Vane, Léon Verdier.) From the Parisian pension of Madame de Maisonrouge, various guests write letters. Miranda Hope writes gushily home to Maine. New Yorker Violet Ray writes of Miranda's provinciality. Louis Leverett writes to a Boston friend about conceited Violet, angular Miranda, and British Evelyn Vane's prettiness. Miranda praises Leverett, mentions Violet's aloofness and Evelyn's timidity, and brings up Dr. Rudolph Staub's brilliance and the fluency of Madame de Maisonrouge's cousin Léon Verdier. In her turn, Evelyn describes Violet as nice, Miranda as vulgar, Leverett as too precious, Verdier as low, and Staub as boring. Verdier writes a friend to contrast the three young women. Staub by letter home castigates decadent Americans, Englishmen, and Frenchmen, and he predicts future German supremacy. Miranda writes a final letter reporting that she is leaving France to visit another interesting European country. In Paris in the fall of 1879, Theodore E. Child,* editor of the *Parisian*, asked James for a story.

He obliged by sending him "A Bundle of Letters," which was published quickly. James thus lost the American copyright, and the popular little story was promptly pirated in Boston (24 January 1880—at 25¢ a copy). The pirate was Frank Loring, whom James had used as a model for dour William Wentworth in *The Europeans*, published a year or so earlier. In the preface to Volume XIV of *The Novels and Tales of Henry James*, James reports details concerning his friend Child; he adds that he wrote "A Bundle of Letters" at one sitting—"an unusual straightness of labour"—while he was stuck in a Paris hotel during a long snowstorm. The story is a rare example of James's use of the epistolary form. He resurrected Louis Leverett and Harvard Tremont when he wrote "The Point of View," another epistolary story.

Bundy, Mrs. In "Sir Dominick Ferrand," Peter Baron's landlady.

Burfield. In "In the Cage," a name mentioned in a Captain Count Philip Everard telegram.

Burnaby, Frederick Gustavus (1842–1885). Incredibly strong British soldier-adventurer, balloonist, and amateur linguist, who was an army officer while still in his teens but exercised so violently that he had to travel to recover. So he visited Central and South America, Spain, North Africa, Russia, Italy, and France. To test the Russian blockade of Central Asia, he traveled light and fast to Khiva (winter 1875–1876). His account of the adventure, *A Ride to Khiva: Travels and Adventures in Central Asia* (1876), was popular and often reprinted. Next he went through Asia Minor, Armenia, and Turkey (1876–1877) in defiance of Russian authorities. *On Horseback through Asia Minor* (1877) was the popular and financially successful result. He turned to politics, and then resumed his military career as a volunteer in Egypt (1884), commanded a convoy to relieve Khartoum, and was speared to death through the throat. James reviewed (*Nation*, 19 Mar 1877) *A Ride to Khiva*, defining Burnaby as a "jovial and enterprising officer" who was meanly anti-Russian. His book illustrates an "English type," that is, "aristocratic soldier, opaque in intellect but indomitable in muscle." While in Khartoum visiting Colonel Charles George Gordon, successor of Sir Samuel White Baker,* Burnaby learned of Russia's plans and hoped to frustrate them. His month-long trek "over the frozen steppes, by sleigh, on horseback and on camel-back, herding with filthy Tartars and Kirghiz, passing nights in the open air, snow-bound and frost-bound, with the thermometer at 40° below zero," is all recorded with good-humored irony, James reports, adding that Burnaby unearthed no Russian atrocities.

Burne-Jones, Sir Edward (1833–1898). Birmingham-born painter and influential decorative designer. At Exeter College, Oxford (which he left prematurely in 1856), he met William Morris,* but he was then more interested in the works of Dante Gabriel Rossetti,* under whom Burne-Jones studied in London. He visited Italy in 1859 and again in 1862, the second time with his wife and also John Ruskin.* Thereafter Burne-Jones worked steadily in watercolors and oils— his subjects were mostly religious and literary—exhibiting with success and receiving commissions and honors. From 1861 on, he made numerous cartoons for stained glass manufactured by Morris's company and others, as well as illustrations and designs for books produced by Morris. Through Charles Eliot Norton,* James met Burne-Jones in England in 1869; the two became close friends. In a letter to John La Farge* (20 Jun [1869]), James expresses his early opinion of the artist's work: "They are very literary &c; but they have great merit." James twice reviewed exhibitions of Burne-Jones's works in 1877. In "The Grosvenor Gallery and the Royal Academy" (31 May 1877) he uniquely calls eight paintings by Burne-Jones at the Grosvenor "the most brilliant work offered at present by any painter to the London public" and "among the most eminent artistic productions of our day." Then in "The Picture Season in London" (Aug 1877), while criticizing remnants of pre-Raphaelitism in him, he places Burne-Jones "at the head of the English painters of our day." In an untitled note the following year (*Nation*, 23 May 1878), he dilutes his praise of Burne-Jones's "elegant" figures by calling them "flat" and not "manly." He amusingly reports (*Nation*, 19 Dec 1878), Burne-Jones's reluctant testimony in the libel suit brought by James Abbott McNeill Whistler* against Ruskin. In 1879 James introduced Burne-Jones to Isabella Stewart Gardner.* Three years later James noted ("London Pictures and London Plays") that an art exhibition "without Mr. Burne-Jones is a *Hamlet* with Hamlet left out," and he went on to defend his good friend from the charge that his subjects "look . . . sick" by saying that his paintings depict "[a] whole range of feeling about life." To Elizabeth Boott* he wrote (14 Oct 1883) that Burne-Jones "is a wonderfully nice creature, and . . . his art . . . has a great deal of beauty. His talent, weak in some ways, is one of the most individual there is today." James introduced John Singer Sargent* to Burne-Jones in 1884. From about this time, James valued forward-looking painters' efforts above those of Burne-Jones, whose "production," as he wrote to Norton (6 Dec [1886]), emanates from a "*studio* . . . with doors and windows closed, and no search for impressions outside." Still, he added, Burne-Jones has escaped "vulgarization and . . . claptrap." But then James later wrote to Norton (25 Mar [1889]) to praise Burne-Jones's recent "large allegorical designs" for their "abundance and beauty of imagination." Burne-Jones attended the first performance of James's *Guy Domville*, in London, on 5 January 1895. Finally, to Norton (24 Nov 1899) James lamented that Burne-Jones's work betrayed too much "painful, niggling embroidery—the stitch-by-stitch process that . . . beg[s] the *painter* question altogether." James attended Burne-Jones's funeral with William Holman Hunt* and his wife. James's library contained one book by Edward Burne-Jones.

Burnett, Frances Eliza (née Hodgson) (1849–1924). Anglo-American writer, born in Manchester, England, moved to Tennessee (1865), married (1873), divorced (1898), and remarried (1900). She was a prolific writer of fiction for children and adults, and of plays, sometimes in collaboration. She is now best remembered for her *Little Lord Fauntleroy* (1886). In "A Poor Play Well Acted" (*Pall Mall Gazette* 24 Oct 1883, and *Pall Mall Budget* 26 Oct 1883), James reviewed her coauthored play *Young Folks' Ways* (1881, based on her story "Esmeralda'") and the actors and actresses who put it on in London. He regards the play as "primitive" and shapeless, summarizes its "mawkish and unreal" plot, and criticizes the characterization as simple, but praises the acting as "delicate," "brilliant," zealous, "robust," and so on. James concludes that the whole effort shows "how an inanimate production may be . . . vivified." Nine years later James saw another play by Burnett and described it to Lady Florence Eveleen Eleanore Bell* (7 Jan 1892) as "primitive and provincial" and the authoress, whom he spoke to afterward, as "a fatally deluded little woman."

Burrage, Henry, Jr. In *The Bostonians*, a dilatory Harvard law school student, pleasant host, accomplished pianist, and unsuccessful admirer of Verena Tarrant. It is later said that he became engaged to Miss Winkworth.

Burrage, Mrs. Henry, Sr. In *The Bostonians*, Henry, Jr.'s rather domineering New York mother, a rich widow. She fails to persuade Olive Chancellor to help her son woo and win Verena Tarrant.

Burroughs, John (1837–1921). Famous American naturalist. After some years as a teacher and then as a government clerk in Washington, D.C. (where he met Walt Whitman*), Burroughs (from 1873) farmed in upstate New York. He published essays in the *Atlantic Monthly* beginning in 1865, and he wrote many books, among them *Notes on Walt Whitman as Poet and Person* (1867), *Wake Robin* (1871), *Winter Sunshine* (1875), *Birds and Poets* (1877), *Squirrels and Other Fur-Bearers* (1900), *Camping and Tramping with* [Theodore] *Roosevelt* [*] (1907), and *The Breath of Life* (1915). *The Heart of John Burroughs's Journals* appeared posthumously (1928). James reviewed (*Nation*, 27 Jan 1876) Burroughs's *Winter Sunshine*, calling it charming, pleasant, and savory, of a felicitous if unfinished style. He labels Burroughs "a sort of reduced, but also . . . more sociable Thoreau." He likes Burroughs' comments on birds and apples, but even more those of his "appreciative" and much-relished visit to England.

Busch, Moritz (1821–1899). German writer, journalist, confidant and press agent of Prince Otto von Bismarck, and author of *Graf Bismarck und seine Leute während des Krieges mit Frankreich* (1878). In 1876 Busch published in book form his translation of six James short stories; in the same year, his two-volume translation of *Roderick Hudson*; and a year later, his two-volume translation of *The American*. In an anonymous review (*Nation*, 19 Dec 1878) of *Graf Bismarck und seine Leute*, James calls Busch the Boswell of hypocritically anti-French, "brutally frank" Bismarck, and amusingly notes that Busch translated some tales of "H. James," among those of other American writers. James adds that "many of Dr. Busch's notes are autobiographic and relate to the Prince's personal idiosyncrasies and physical exploits," and he proves it by quotation and paraphrase. James's library contained one book by Busch.

Butler, Elizabeth Southerden. Married name of Elizabeth Thompson.*

Butler, Nicholas Murray (1862–1947). American professor, author, lecturer, liberal educator, and president of Columbia University (1902–1945). In "American Letter" (25 Jun 1898), James calls Butler's *The Meaning of Education* (1898) "deeply interesting," for its offering almost limitless hope while it constructively discusses the future of American education and the "complex relations" of its several levels.

Butterworth. In "Madame de Mauves," Madame de Mauves's New York uncle.

Butterworth, Mr. and Mrs. In "An International Episode," two of the Duke of Green-Erin's American hosts.

Buttons, Mr. and Mrs. In "In the Cage," a couple from Thrupp's apartment.

Butterick, Dr. In *The Wings of the Dove*, Milly Theale's Boston physician.

Buzzard, Dr. In "In the Cage," perhaps a code name for Lady Bradeen in Captain Count Philip Everard's telegrams.

Byng, Norman. In *Tenants*, Sir Frederick's son, who loves (and wins) Mildred Stanmore. She summons Norman home from his post as a civil sevant in India to counter Captain Lurcher's machinations. Norman is the older half-brother of Claude Vibert.

Byng, Sir Frederick. In *Tenants*, the fifty-seven-year-old widowed father of Norman Byng and illegitimate Claude Vibert, by Eleanor Vibert. Sir Frederick, now retired from the Indian civil service, is Mildred Stanmore's guardian.

Byron, George Gordon, Lord (1788–1824). Controversial British poet, traveler, lover, and freedom fighter. Born in London to a profligate father and his vile-tempered Scottish heiress wife and educated at Trinity College, Cambridge, Byron published juvenile verse, then traveled widely (1809–1811), returned to the House of Lords, and began to publish *Childe Harold* (1812, 1816, 1818). After more writing, he married Anne Isabella Milbanke in 1815, but they separated in 1816. Byron then left England forever, first going briefly to Switzerland to stay with Percy Bysshe Shelley,* Mary Godwin, Clare Clairmont,* and others.

Next, Byron established his passionate Italian residence (1816–1823). While there, he wrote voluminously—*Don Juan* (1819–1824) was one of his most notable works. In 1823 Byron went to Greece to aid the insurgents under Prince Mavrokordatos, but he soon died there from malaria. James reviewed (*North American Review*, Apr 1879) *Memoir of the Rev. Francis Hodgson, B.D., with Numerous Letters from Lord Byron and Others*, by Hodgson's son T. P. Hodgson (1879). James identifies Francis Hodgson as "an early and much-trusted intimate of Lord Byron" and also defines Hodgson as a scholar, a man of the world, and a poet, but "not a brilliant writer." James finds these newly published letters by Byron, his estranged wife, and his half-sister Augusta Leigh "extremely interesting," although they do not enlighten us much as to his marital and sibling problems. Hodgson, whose life James summarizes here, enjoyed Byron's friendship and received many letters from the poet "full of youthful wit and spontaneity" and also "cynicism . . . half natural and half affected." James is happy to find in the correspondence between Hodgson and Mrs. Leigh "the most striking intrinsic evidence of the purely phantasmal character of the famous accusation [of incest between Byron and Augusta Leigh]." But then James, after much quoting, adds that "it would be very profitless to inquire further as regards Byron's unforgivable sin." According to Sir Edward Walter Hamilton,* James told him, in the summer of 1886, that the person from the 1760–1830 period whom he would most like to have seen was Lord Byron. In a Notebook entry written in Florence (12 Jan 1887), James mentions Byron's letters and the burning of one of them, in the course of sketching his plot for "The Aspern Papers," which was suggested to him by the report that Miss Clairmont in her old age retained Byron and Shelley papers. Going into more detail in a letter from Venice to Grace Norton* (27 Feb [1887]), James mentioned conversing in Florence with a niece (by marriage) of Byron's inamorata Countess Teresa Guiccioli who claimed to have some "shocking and unprintable" Byron letters, one of which she had burned. In a much later Noteook entry (5 Feb 1895), James records seeing "some" papers concerning Byron and "bearing on the absolutely indubitable history of his relation to Mrs. Leigh, the sole *real* love, as he emphatically declares, of his life." In November 1909 he and John Buchan* studied the papers more thoroughly, and the following April they wrote and signed an opinion thereon. James's library contained the works of Lord Byron, together with the biography of Byron by Thomas Moore.

C

Calderoni. In *The Golden Bowl*, Prince Amerigo's lawyer.

The Californian. Original title of *The American: A Comedy in Four Acts.*

Caliph. In "The Impressions of a Cousin," Adrian Frank's half-brother and the unscrupulous handler of Eunice's financial affairs.

Calvert, George Henry (1803–1889). American poet, literary historian, biographer, dramatist, orator, and travel writer. James reviewed (*Nation*, 3 Jun 1875) Calvert's *Essays—Aesthetical* (1875), beginning with the statement that his prose is better than his poetry, but adding that his essays often are "ethereal" and "vague." Still, James likes his chapter on Charles Augustin Sainte-Beuve,* who also was pleased and wrote Calvert a gracious letter to say so. James finds amusingly reactionary Calvert's chapter on current "grammatical errors and literary vulgarisms."

Camerino, Count. In "The Diary of a Man of Fifty," the man who privately killed the husband of Countess Bianca Salvi in a duel and then married her.

Cameron, Elizabeth (née Sherman) (1857–1944). Socialite wife of Senator James Donald Cameron.* She was the daughter of a judge and the niece of soldier William Tecumseh Sherman and politician John Sherman. Her Washington, D.C., salon was famous. She was a close friend in the United States, England, and Paris of many people whom James knew, including Henry Adams,* John Milton Hay,* and Edith Newbold Jones Wharton.* Late in his life, Cameron and his wife were estranged.

Cameron, James Donald (1833–1918). Successful, ruthless, rich Pennsylvanian Republican-machine politician, secretary of war (1876–1877), and senator (1877–1897). Through Henry Adams,* James knew Cameron and his wife Elizabeth Cameron.* Late in his life, Cameron and his wife were estranged.

Cameron, Verney Lovett (1844–1894). English navy man and explorer. He commanded an expedition sponsored by the Royal Geographical Society starting in 1872 to map equatorial Africa, to try to find David Livingstone* (whose death was reported to him on his way inland to Lake Tanganyika), and to suppress the slave trade. Cameron's *Across Africa* (1877), an account of his two-year trek, was quickly translated into French, Italian, and Portuguese. Among his other books, *Our Future Highway to India* (1880) was especially popular. James reviewed (*Nation*, 5 Apr 1877) Cameron's *Across Africa*, calling it a "record of . . . heroic achievement." Cameron was the first white man to cross tropical Africa from the east. He offers a plain account of his march past filthy villages through beautiful scenery in a "baleful" climate. Hunger and ruined clothing, disloyal hired natives, and the sight of "foul and revolting" cannibals, as well as hideous burial rites in Urua, compounded the misery of his death-dogged group, remnants of which finally arrived at Benguela, a Portuguese trading port on the west coast. James closes with praise for the author's "simple manliness and veracity."

Camilla. In "An Animated Conversation," an ingenuous woman who lives with her husband Oswald in Paris and says once when in London that she would like to read some "nice" novels.

Campbell, Mrs. Patrick (née Beatrice Stella Tanner) (1865–1940). Famous Liverpool-born actress, who first appeared on stage in 1888 and was notable (with Sir George Alexander*) in *The Second Mrs. Tanqueray* (1893) by Sir Arthur Wing Pinero* and in plays by Henrik Johan Ibsen,* William Shakespeare,* and George Bernard Shaw.* Shaw wrote her many rather anemic love letters. In his youth, Harley Granville Granville-Barker* was a supporting actor under her. James attended plays in which she starred and occasionally commented on her performance.

Cannan, Gilbert (1884–1955). Versatile British novelist, critic, playwright, poet, and translator (from French and Russian). He wrote many books, including *Peter Homunculus, a Novel* (1909), *Little Brother* (1912), *Round the Corner: Being the Life and Death of Francis Christopher Folyat, Bachelor of Divinity, and Father of a Large Family* (1913), and *Old Mole* (1914). In a letter to Sir Hugh Seymour Walpole* (21 Aug 1913), James explains that he is resisting new novelists but that Cannan "did worm a little into the fortress." In "The New Novel" (1914), James says that Cannan's *Round the Corner* records an "enormous inauspicious amount" of material about the domestic life of "an amiable clergyman's family" in an ugly, Liverpool-like city.

Canterville, Lord Philip and Lady. In "Lady Barbarina," Lady Barbarina Clement's parents.

Capadose, Amy. In "The Liar," the young daughter of Colonel Clement and Everina Brant Capadose.

Capadose, Colonel Clement. In "The Liar," the liar. Oliver Lyon paints his character-revealing portrait, the fate of which the colonel lies about. A man whose name was Anton Capadose wrote to James to ask him how he happened to choose the name Capadose for his congenital fibber; James replied (13 Oct 1896) to explain that perhaps it came from the London *Times* and to "congratulate" his correspondent "on bearing a name that is at once particularly individual and not ungraceful."

Capadose, Dean. In "The Liar," the Dean of Rockingham and the brother of Colonel Capadose.

Capadose, Everina Brant. In "The Liar," the former object of Oliver Lyon's affections but now the liar's wife. Lyon tests her loyalty and "honor."

Capadose, General. In "The Liar," Colonel Clement Capadose's father.

Cardew, Mary. In "Crapy Cornelia," a woman whose photograph, which Cornelia Rasch shows White-Mason, evokes precious memories.

Carlyle, Thomas (1795–1881). Scottish essayist, philosopher, historian, biographer, and translator. He studied at Edinburgh University, taught briefly, associated with numerous men of letters in London, began publishing in the 1820s, married Jane Welsh in 1826, settled with her in remote Craigenputtock in 1828, then lived in Chelsea, London from 1834. Carlyle corresponded with Robert Browning,* Ralph Waldo Emerson,* Johann Wolfgang von Goethe,* and Charles Eliot Norton,* among others. Carlyle's main books are *Sartor Resartus* (1835), *The French Revolution* (1837), *Heroes and Hero Worship* (1841), *Past and Present* (1843), *Oliver Cromwell* (1845), *The History of Frederick the Great* (1858–1865), and *Reminiscences* (posthumous, 1881). His long-suffering wife, who was an invalid from 1858 until her death in 1866, was a superb letter-writer and kept a revealing diary. James Abbott McNeill Whistler* painted a memorable portrait of Carlyle. James Anthony Froude,* his first biographer, badly edited Carlyle's unauthorized *Reminiscences*. Using a letter of introduction from Emerson, James's father met Carlyle in England in late 1843, was much influenced by his writings, pungently wrote in an 1856 letter to Emerson from London that "Carlyle is the same old sausage, fizzing and sputtering in his own grease, only infinitely more unreconciled to the blessed Providence which guides human affairs"; upon Carlyle's death, he published negative comments in "Some Personal Recollections of Carlyle" (1881). William James admired Carlyle for trying to come to grips with the concept of evil, for advising one to use free will, and for praising practical work, although he deplored Carlyle's opposition to democracy. Henry James was less favorably disposed. In an 1866 review of *Hereward, the Last of the English* by Charles Kingsley,* James mentions Carlyle's "aggressively *earnest* tone." In a tiny 1877 review of *Note of an English Republican on the Muscovite Crusade* by Algernon Charles Swinburne,* James takes a swipe at Carlyle for his antidemocratic tendencies. More revealing is James's lengthy review of *The Correspondence of Thomas Carlyle and Ralph Waldo Emerson* (*Century Magazine*, Jun 1883), edited by Norton, who had met Carlyle in London in 1869. In it, James places Carlyle "among the very first of all letter-writers," mentions his praise of "The American Scholar" and *English Traits* by Emerson, notes Carlyle's disapproval of some aspects of transcendentalism, deplores his pessimism and crudity, and labels his style an "avalanche," his humor "tragic," and his imagination "haunted." Carlyle "invented a manner," which then "swallowed him up"; he thought that he "look[ed] at realities" but really looked "straight into this abysmal manner." All the same, he had "a great deal of tenderness even in . . . grimness" and "cleaved to his relations, to his brothers." In a few other reviews, James labels the florid style "Carlylese." In a letter to Violet Paget* (21 Oct [1884]), James curiously comments that "Carlyle . . . appears to me to have been no more of a *thinker* than my blotting paper, but absorbent (like that), to a tremendous degree, of life; a prodigious *feeler* and painter; as a painter indeed, one of the very first of all." To Grace Norton* (3 Nov 1884) he adds that Carlyle's "contempt . . . [for] all human things . . . seem[s] to me perfectly barren and verbose." A couple of years later, in a letter to Norton (6 Dec [1886]), James labels as "unspeakable" the handling of details about Carlyle's life by Froude, whom Norton soon exposed as unreliable. James's library contained ten books by Thomas Carlyle and three by Jane Carlyle.

Carlyle Mansions. At 21 Carlyle Mansions, Cheyne Walk, in the Chelsea section of London, James had a five-bedroom flat, at £125 a year, from January 1913 until his death. Amusingly, before being given a lease he had to obtain character references to satisfy his landlords, so he asked for one from his friend Sir Edmund Wilson Gosse,* who knew the prime minister and dined with the king. James could walk the relatively short distance from Carlyle Mansions to Westminster. He used the flat mainly during the London winter seasons. The building, then quite new, looks out onto the Thames immediately south, and James worked well in the more western front room. The structure now has about two dozen flats accessible by two entrances. James died on 28 February 1916 at his Carlyle Mansions flat. A few doors west is Chelsea Old Church, with a statue of Sir

Thomas More in its front. At this church, James's funeral service was held on 3 March 1916. A memorial tablet in the church reads: "In Memory of / Henry James: O.M. / Born in New York 1843: Died in Chelsea 1916; Lover & Interpreter of the Fine Amenities of Brave Decisions & Generous Loyalties: A Resident of This Parish Who Renounced a Cherished Citizenship to Give His Allegiance to England in the 1st. Year of the Great War."

Carolus. In *The Reverberator*, a friend of Charles Waterlow.

Carpenter, Mrs. In "Osborne's Revenge," a hostess who invites Philip Osborne to a picnic on one occasion.

Carr, Joseph William Comyns (1849–1916). Versatile British critic, editor, dramatist, and (briefly) play producer, educated at the University of London. He was an art critic on the *Pall Mall Gazette*, the English editor of *L'Art*, the founder and an editor of the *English Illustrated Magazine*, and the cofounder and a director of the New Gallery. Carr published numerous books in the fields of art (English, French, and Italian), literary criticism, biography, church architecture, and landscaping. His plays were adaptations from *Faust* by Johann Wolfgang von Goethe,* *Oliver Twist* by Charles Dickens,* and the King Arthur and Tristram legends. His books include *Essays on Art* (1879), *Art in Provincial France . . .* (1883), *Some Eminent Victorians: Personal Recollections in the World of Art and Letters* (1907), and *The Ideals of Painting* (1917). Carr was regarded as one of the best raconteurs of his time. In a letter to his mother (2 Feb [1880]), James reports "a few of my dinners" and names "Comyns Carr" among several other fellow guests. In a Notebook entry (11 Mar 1888), James frets over having to compress his short story "The Patagonia" to suit Comyns, editor of the *English Illustrated Magazine*, in which this story and six other pieces were published (1884–1892). In the early 1890s, it may be that James entertained the vain hope that Carr would produce a play of his.

Carré, Mme. Honorine. In *The Tragic Muse*, Miriam Rooth's acting coach in Paris.

Carteret, Charles. In *The Tragic Muse*, a rich old man who tries to bribe Nicholas Dormer to stay in politics.

"Casa Alvisi." Travel sketch, published in the *Cornhill Magazine* (Feb 1902, and in the *Critic*, Feb 1902); reprinted in *Italian Hours*, 1909. In it, James reviews *Browning in Venice* by Katherine De Kay Bronson,* simply by recalling the late American-born Venetian hostess Mrs. Bronson. She was charming, hospitable, and generous in her small but commanding Ca' Alvisi, opposite the S. Maria della Salute. She collected tiny Venetian art objects and offered cigarettes and gilded glasses to guests, while gondolas bobbed at her door. She was beneficent to Robert Browning* during his regular autumnal returns, and she was communicative with other visitors provided they loved Venice as she did. She admired the Venetian people, especially for their anecdotal humor, listened to them, and did them favors. She cast Venetian urchins in dialect plays she wrote for them. Toward the end, she repaired to Asolo occasionally, among other towns nearby, because of Browning associations. We remember her best for being unselfish in Venice.

Casamassima, Prince Gennaro. In *Roderick Hudson*, a rich Neapolitan who marries Christina Light. In *The Princess Casamassima*, he spies on his thrill-seeking wife in London.

Casamassima, Princess (Christina Light). In *Roderick Hudson*, the beauty in Rome who intrigues sculptor Roderick Hudson and whose marriage to the prince ends his artistic career. In *The Princess Casamassima*, she associates while in London with international anarchists and becomes the friend of Hyacinth Robinson, Paul Muniment, and others. Her mysterious character may have been inspired by James's brief encounter with Elena Lowe.*

Caselli. In *The Outcry*, the play, the Milan art scholar who overrules the opinion of Pappendick and says that Lord Theign's supposed Moretto is really a Mantovano.* In *The Outcry*, the novel, this scholar from Milan is named Bardi.

Cashmore, Lady Fanny and Lord. In *The Awkward Age*, members of Mrs. Brookenham's social circle. She is Lord Petherton's sister. He gives Harold Brookenham money.

Castillani. In "Adina," a Roman expert on antiquities.

Castledean, Lord and Lady. In *The Golden Bowl*, guests at Matcham. He leaves the estate before his wife; she stays on with sleek Blint. These lovers embolden Charlotte Stant and Prince Amerigo to stay on as well.

Catching, Miss. In *The Bostonians*, a Harvard College librarian.

Catching, Mrs. In "Poor Richard," the nurse at Richard Maule's home.

Cather, Willa (1873–1947). American fiction writer, born in Virginia and raised in Nebraska. After work as a journalist and a high-school teacher in the East, Cather published *April Twilights* (poetry, 1903) and *The Troll Garden* (short stories, 1905), then joined the staff of Samuel Sidney McClure* (1906–1912). After that, she published many novels, including *O Pioneers!* (1913), *My Ántonia* (1918), *One of Ours* (1922), *A Lost Lady* (clearly showing James's influence, 1923), *The Professor's House* (1925), *Death Comes for the Archbishop* (1926), and *Shadows on the Rock* (1931). Among her influential literary friends may be noted Annie Adams Fields* and Sarah Orne Jewett.* In 1906 James wrote to the poet Witter Bynner (1 Feb 1906) to acknowledge the receipt of a gift copy of *The Troll Garden*, but then to add that he now finds it difficult to read new work "from the innocent hands of young females, young American females perhaps above all." Cather actually wrote for McClure a book he called *My Autobiography* (1914).

Catherine, Sister. In *The Portrait of a Lady*, one of Pansy Osmond's teachers at the convent.

Cavenham, Rose. In "The Special Type," Frank Brivet's lover. To encourage his wife to divorce him, Frank compromises Alice Dundene and then marries Rose. To make up for her loss, Alice, who loves Frank, is allowed to keep a portrait of Frank commissioned by Rose.

Cecilia. In *Roderick Hudson*, Rowland Mallet's cousin and confidante. She lives with her daughter Bessie in Northampton, Massachusetts.

Célestine. In "The Pension Beaurepas," the pension cook.

Certain Impressions. The tentative title for a collection of essays which James planned and about which he wrote to Sir Frederick Orridge Macmillan* (8 May [1883]). It was never published, but some of its contents were included in *Partial Portraits*.

Chafer. In "The Private Life," a reviewer gossiped about by Clarence Vawdrey.

"A Chain of Cities" (1874 title, "A Chain of Italian Cities"). Travel sketch, published in the *Atlantic Monthly* (Feb 1874); reprinted as "A Chain of Cities" in *Transatlantic Sketches*, 1875, and in *Italian Hours*, 1909. The cities are Narni, Assisi, Perugia, Cortona, and Arezzo. One winter day years ago, James paused on his way from Rome to Florence at Narni, and he loved the picture made there by road, town wall, and walking monk. Later he saw Assisi, "a vignette out of some brown old missal," details of which he describes: the daringly built "two-fold temple of St. Francis" with "an air . . . heavy with holiness," the Giotto paintings, the streets and "small mouldy houses," a Jewish pedlar of religious objects, a hill castle outside town, and rugged scenery beyond. James hopes that they will stop straightening Perugian streets. What views! James liked the Etruscan Gate, the statue of Pope Julius II, and Perugino's brave Sala del Cambio frescoes. Beyond "the large weedy water of Lake Thrasymene" loom the "grey ramparts . . . of Cortona." The inn was "rough" but its landlord "all smoothness." The museum was closed, and festa crowds blocked all the churches, but James was privileged to see the mountain-top church of Saint Margaret on St.

Margaret's day: colorful contadini, "bedizened procession," piety—in short, "the after-taste of everything the still open maw of time had consumed." Finally Arezzo, where James was content to seek general Tuscan impressions only—castle, hills, cypresses, and a "tangle" of grains and gardens.

"A Chain of Italian Cities." The 1874 title of "A Chain of Cities."

Chalais, Marie de. In "Gabrielle de Bergerac," Gabrielle's gracious young friend.

Chalais, Marquis de. In "Gabrielle de Bergerac," Marie's grandfather.

Chalumeau. In "Madame de Mauves," an old roué whom Mme. Marie de Mauves Clairin likes.

Chambers, Robert William (1865–1933). Versatile, prolific American artist and illustrator, romantic novelist, musical librettist, and outdoorsman. In "American Letter" (28 May 1898), James used Chambers's *Lorraine, a Romance* (1897) as an example of recent "military novels," finding it full of energy but "little artistic sincerity," knowledgeable as to details, but with an "operetta" plot and a puppet for a heroine.

Chamousset, Mme. In "The Pension Beaurepas," a rival of pension-keeper Mme. Beaurepas.

Champer, Lady. In "Miss Gunton of Poughkeepsie," a woman sympathetic to the Roman prince, whom Lily Gunton seems to be insincerely leading on.

Chancellor, Olive. In *The Bostonians*, a well-to-do, morbid, unmarried feminist (perhaps inclined toward lesbianism) who is Mrs. Adelina Chancellor Luna's younger sister. She sponsors Verena Tarrant, seeks too much intimacy with her, is friendly with old Miss Birdseye, and bitterly opposes reactionary Basil Ransom. It has been suggested that Katharine Peabody Loring,* Alice James's friend and companion, was a model for Olive Chancellor.

A Change of Heart. One-act (fifteen-scene) play, published in the *Atlantic Monthly* (Jan 1872). (Characters: Hamilton, Jessop, the Misses Jessop, Jones, Mrs. Lewis, Martha Noel, Charles Pepperel, Mrs. Seymour, the Misses Seymour, Robert Staveley, Jane Thorne, Margaret Thorne, Wigmore.) The principal characters appear and reappear in the drawing room of sick Jane Thorne's country house. Robert Staveley, her nephew, decides against incontrovertibly proving to her haughty daughter Margaret Thorne, who is twenty-one today and hence an heiress, and whom he tries ineffectually to warn, that Charles Pepperel is a villain who stole from Martha Noel, now Jane's paid companion, and who is presently after Margaret's fortune. So Staveley asks Martha not to tell Margaret, to let the two worthless people have each other after all, and to accept him instead. Martha agrees.

Channing, William Ellery (1780–1842). Famous American religious leader, born in Newport, Rhode Island, and educated at Harvard. Breaking with Calvinism in 1819, he became the chief exponent of American Unitarianism; ultimately, he espoused pacificism, temperance, abolition of slavery, and labor and educational reforms. James reviewed (*Atlantic Monthly* Mar 1875) *Correspondence of William Ellery Channing, D.D., and Lucy Aikin, from 1826 to 1842* (1874), beginning with general praise of fine, old-fashioned letters as a combination of "conversation and . . . literature." He concludes that Channing's letters neither add to nor subtract from his reputation. Channing "writes like a disembodied spirit"—he is optimistic, sentimental, even ascetic—whereas Lucy Aikin,* herself a "vigorous" writer on Charles I and on Joseph Addison, is "sturdy and downright." Her pro-Italian tendencies clash with Channing's pro-French ones. They also differ as to the relative merits of American and British handsomeness and manners.

Chanter, Captain. In *The Reprobate*, the hypocritical former lover of Mrs. Freshville, who now prefers and will have well-to-do Mrs. Doubleday for a wife. Her stepson Paul Doubleday befriends Chanter.

Chantry, Christopher. In "The Visits," Helen's husband and Louisa's father.

Chantry, Helen. In "The Visits," Louisa's mother and the woman narrator's friend.

Chantry, Louisa. In "The Visits," the young woman whose uncontrollable passion for Jack Brandon ultimately sickens and kills her.

"The Chaperon." Short story (15,800 words), published in the *Atlantic Monthly* (Nov–Dec 1891); reprinted in *The Real Thing and Other Tales*, 1893; revised and reprinted in *The Novels and Tales of Henry James*, Volume X, 1908. (Characters: Mrs. Bray, Mrs. Donovan, Mrs. Hack, Captain Bertram Jay, Bessie, Fanny, Guy, and Maggie Mangler, Lady Maresfield, Mr. and Mrs. Charles Tramore, Edith Tramore, Eric Tramore, Julia Tramore, Rose Tramore, Mrs. Tramore, Bob and Charlotte Vaughan-Vesey, Lord Whiteroy.) When her father dies, Rose Tramore braves family opposition and goes to her mother, who years earlier had left her husband for a lover who died before they could marry. Bertram Jay has proposed to Rose, but he temporarily sides against her. Lady Maresfield tries to advance her son Guy Mangler's interest in Rose, but the young woman declines an invitation because it excludes her mother. The two Tramores remain ostracized through the London winter season. Next summer they vacation on the Continent and bump into vacationing Jay in Italy. The three quietly travel nonjudgmentally together. In Venice Lady Maresfield and her married daughter Charlotte Vaughan-Vesey meet Rose and her group and now fear that Rose, who has become a social sensation as her mother's chaperon, will prefer Jay to Guy. The lady first invites the Tramores to a luncheon, then her daughter senses their value and supports them both in society—so much so that Mrs. Tramore soon begins to go out alone, and Rose and Jay feel neglected. A Notebook entry (13 Jul 1891) explains that Maria Theresa Earle* suggested the idea for what became "The Chaperon." The note goes on to provide a detailed plot outline; James followed his plan until the end, which does not include a final little grievance he planned for Mrs. Tramore. In the preface to Volume X of *The Novels and Tales of Henry James*, James calls "The Chaperon" a "small fiction" concerning a subject "comparatively free from sharp under-tastes," and he describes the work as a "picture" rather than "an anecdote." The story is of interest mostly because James reverses the normal roles of mother as chaperon and daughter as protected one, and he presents the narrative through the daughter's consciousness. In May 1893 Sir Arthur Wing Pinero* wrote James that "The Chaperon" would make an excellent stage comedy. James wrote a note to himself (May?, 6 Jun 1893) and later the start of a long, rough scenario (Nov 1907) for such a venture, but nothing came of it. A tentative title for the play was *Monte-Carlo*. In his scenario, James changes the Manglers' name to Manger, provides Lady Maresfield a first name (Maud), and gives Rose Tramore's mother a first name (Flora, by a slip, May as well).

Chapman, John Jay (1862–1933). New York–born Harvard University graduate who became a lawyer (1888) and was also involved in politics (to 1898), but then began a literary career. He wrote essays, biographies, poetry, plays, and translations. His works include *Emerson and Other Essays* (1898), *Causes and Consequences* (1898), *Benedict Arnold: A Play for a Greek Theatre* (1909), *Learning and Other Essays* (1910), *William Lloyd Garrison* (1913, rev. 1921), *Memories and Milestones* (1915), *Greek Genius and Other Essays* (1915), *Songs and Poems* (1919), *A Glance toward Shakespeare* (1922), *Notes on Religion* (1922), *Dante* (1927), and *New Horizons in American Life* (1932). James wrote to Frances Anne Kemble* from Italy (24 Mar 1881) asking her to aid young Chapman and his family when they arrived in London. A few years later, James wrote to Sarah Butler Wister,* again from Italy (27 Feb [1887]), to advert to "this unspeakable *sinister* horror of Jack Chapman," who had impulsively slugged a man and had then burned off his own hand through guilt. In "American Letter" (26 Mar 1898), James calls Chapman's chapter on Emerson, in *Emerson and Other Essays* (1898), "the most penetrating study . . . of which that subject has been made the occasion." In "American Letter" (11 Jun 1898), James repeats his compliments, praising Chapman for his "detachment," "discriminations," and profundity, but he goes on to downgrade most of the other essays in the volume.

Charles, Elizabeth Rundle (1828–1896). English novelist and biographer. She published *Tales and Sketches of Christian Life in Different Lands and Ages* anonymously (1850), then *The Voice of Christian Life in Song* (1858), and much else, generally of a religious nature. She was the wife of Andrew Charles, a Wapping candlemaker, from 1851 until his death in 1868. She later lived at Swiss Cottage, Hampstead, where she died. James reviewed (*Nation*, 13 Sep 1865) her *Hearthstone Series: Chronicles of the Schönberg-Cotta Family . . .* (3 vols., 1864) and her *Mary, the Handmaid of the Lord* (1865), labeling them "Sunday reading," that is, juvenile literature combining history, fiction, and religion. Although Charles is sincere and pleasant, she wrongly gives her characters, living in the time of Martin Luther, nineteenth-century consciences and consciousnesses. James reviewed (*Nation*, 1 Feb 1866) Charles's *Winifred Bertram and the World She Lived In* (1866), which he calls "uncommonly well written" and fine of its class, but which he adds features a ridiculously sentimental young girl who is unnaturally charitable. Finally, James reviewed (*North American Review*, Apr 1867) Charles's *The Women of the Gospels: The Three Wakings, and Other Poems* (1867), calling the effort colorless, common, and destitute of both fervor and grace.

Charles. In "My Friend Bingham," the narrator and George Bingham's friend.

Charlie. In *The Bostonians*, any unimportant young man who successfully competed with Olive Chancellor for the attention of the pale shopgirls she tried to educate about the wrongs done to women.

Chart, Adela. In "The Marriages," the young woman who besmirches her dead mother's name to try to keep her father from remarrying. Adela's siblings are Basil, Beatrice, Godfrey, and Muriel.

Chart, Basil. In "The Marriages," Adela's brother, in the army in India.

Chart, Beatrice. In "The Marriages," Adela's young sister.

Chart, Colonel. In "The Marriages," the widowed father of Adela, Beatrice, Basil, Godfrey, and Muriel. Adela tries to keep him from marrying Mrs. Churchley.

Chart, Godfrey. In "The Marriages," Adela's brother, whose studies for admittance to the diplomatic service are hurt by his marriage to a floozy who is later paid off by his father to stay away.

Chart, Mrs. Godfrey. In "The Marriages," Godfrey's floozy of a wife, paid by her father-in-law to stay away.

Chart, Muriel. In "The Marriages," Adela's young sister.

"Chartres." Paris letter (1876 title, "Chartres Portrayed"), published in the New York *Tribune* (29 Apr 1876); reprinted in *Portraits of Places*, 1883. James honors the "ethereal mildness" of the Parisian spring by visiting "the ancient town of Chartres"; open carriage to railway station, breakfast with wine, two hours to the "rather shabby little *ville de province*." He observes the cathedral, from twenty points of view, in sunlight and by moonlight. He is "fascinated by [its] superpositions and vertical effects" and by the "inexpressible harmony in the facade." He describes portals, windows, sculpture, towers, and wintry interior ("the perfection of gothic in its prime"). Then nearby Saint-Aignan church, innumerable shops, "flinty lanes," and crumbling ramparts.

"Chartres Portrayed." Original title (1876) of "Chartres," travel essay, reprinted in *Portraits of Places*, 1883.

Chasemore, Lady Agatha. In "The Modern Warning," the married name of Agatha Grice.

Chasemore, Sir Rufus, K.C.B., M.P. In "The Modern Warning," Agatha Grice's anti-American, British husband.

Chataway, Mr. and Mrs. Ronald. In "The Married Son," a man and his New York healer-medium wife. (She is a friend of Elizabeth Talbert, introduced earlier in *The Whole Family*.)

Chatrian, Alexandre (1826–1890). French coauthor, as Erckmann-Chatrian,* with Émile Erckmann.*

Chatterton, Mrs. In *Watch and Ward*, Isabel Morton Keith's chatty New York friend.

Chayter. In *The Tragic Muse*, Charles Carteret's splendidly reserved butler.

Cherbuliez, Victor (1829–1899). French novelist, critic, and historian, born in Geneva, Switzerland, where his father was a professor of classics. Victor Cherbuliez wrote several novels (some of which show the influence of George Sand*), became a French citizen (1880), and was elected to the French Academy (1881). His novels include *Le Comte Kostia* (1863), *Paule Méré* (1864), *Le Roman d'une honnête femme* (1864), *Prosper Randoce* (1868), *L'Aventure de Ladislas Bolski* (1869), *La Revanche de Joseph Noirel* (1872), *Meta Holdenis* (1873), *Miss Rovel* (1875), *Le Fiancé de Mlle. St. Maur* (1876), and *Jacquine Vanesse* (1898). His nonfictional books include *L'Allemagne politique* (1870), *Études de littérature et d'art* (1873), *Profils étrangers* (1889), and *L'Art et la nature* (1892).

James published a review (*North American Review*, Oct 1873) of Cherbuliez's *Meta Holdenis* and another (*Nation*, 3 Jun 1875) of his *Miss Rovel*. James begins the former review by remembering *Le Comte Kostia* as promising (classic, polished, sensitive, stylish) but calls *Meta Holdenis* less charming. The latter betrays a Parisian "falsetto," shows better imagination than wit, has improbable action albeit an effective denouement, features a hateful heroine ("a clever failure" who betrays her creator's "anti-Teutonic" bias), and has a poorly manipulated point of view. James sarcastically summarizes the plot and compares the heroine unfavorably to Becky Sharpe, the heroine of *Vanity Fair* by William Makepeace Thackeray.* In his review of *Miss Rovel*, James says that Cherbuliez, who combines passionate observation with imagination, has slipped into an excess of cleverness, and that his latest novel is unpleasant to read. The heroine is both impossible and detestable. James then met Cherbuliez in Paris at the apartment of Gustave Flaubert* late in 1875 or early in 1876; thereafter, he wrote to Thomas Sergeant Perry* (2 Feb [1876]) that members of Flaubert's circle held both Cherbuliez and Gustave Droz* in contempt. In an untitled note (*Nation*, 29 Jun 1876), James comments negatively on Cherbuliez's "smart" remarks about the 1876 Salon but adds that he prefers them to his new novel *Le Fiancé de Mlle. St. Maur*, with its artificial style and unnatural dialogue. Soon James would appear to have no use at all for Cherbuliez and even called him "that pitiful prostitute" in a letter to William Ernest Henley* (28 Aug [1878]). However, James's "Daisy Miller" owes much to *Paule Méré*: Both works have Swiss and Italian settings, free-and-easy heroines hurt by slander, and weak "heroes." In *Notes of a Son and Brother*, James mentions that his cousin Anne King was Cherbuliez's student in Geneva and saw nothing remarkable about the young man.

"Chester." Travel essay, published in the *Nation* (4 Jul 1872, as Part I of "A European Summer"); reprinted in *Transatlantic Sketches*, 1875, and in *English Hours*, 1905. A traveler fresh from America finds Chester ("probably the most romantic city in the world"), with its "brave little walls," an essentially ancient place: "Roman substructure," towers, gables, "hoary humility," and blue Welsh hills beyond. James loves Chester's close houses, old and crooked streets, jumbled rows ("a sort of gothic edition of the blessed arcades and porticos of Italy"), overflowing population, and cathedral. Its darkened red sandstone mocks even intelligent renovators' efforts. Its interior only seems "pale and naked": In truth it is dizzily columned and softly lighted; its musty air, "sweet, cool"; its music, resonant and melodic. James did not like the service conducted there by Charles Kingsley.* James incorporated passages from his essay "Chester" in his description of Lambert Strether's visit to the city in the first chapter of *The Ambassadors*.

Chew, Mrs. In "Lady Barbarina," a guest at Lady Barbarina Clement Lemon's New York salon.

Child, Francis James (1825–1896). English professor at Harvard and editor of English and Scottish ballads. He was a close friend of the James family and was kind to James's father during his final illness. Both James and his brother William came to know Child well while they attended Harvard. James mentions him a few times in his *Notes of a Son and Brother*, describing him as a "delightful man" and an "admirable talker" and calling his ballad collection "a recognised monument." Alice James willed $1,000 to Child's daughter Henrietta in 1892.

Child, Theodore E. (1846–1892). Liverpool-born graduate of Merton College, Oxford. He then went to Paris as correspondent for the London *Telegraph*. He also wrote for the London *World* and *Illustrated News*. He became a correspondent for the New York *Sun*. He was editor of the *Parisian*. During his last ten years, he was a Paris agent for Harper and Brothers. For *Harper's Magazine*, of which he was chief agent in Europe, he wrote essays on Spanish-American republics, which were later published in book form. The *Figaro* translated and published his essays when they concerned Paris. He knew and was admired by most contemporary French, British, and American artists and writers in Paris. He was on his way to India, on an assignment for Harper, when he contracted cholera in Tabriz and died of typhoid near Tehran. (His would-be illustrator, Edwin Lord Weeks, also died on the trip with him.) Of Child's written and editorial work, which ranges from art criticism to the art of dining well, and from fashion and hairstyling to travel and politics, his best include *Summer Holidays, Traveling in Europe* (1889), *Spanish-American Republics* (1891), five chapters (on Russian cities and art) in *The Tsar and His People: or, Social Life in Russia* (1891, to which his friend Viscount Eugène Melchior de Vogüé* contributed two chapters), *The Praise of Paris* (1893), and *The Comédie Française* (1893, which includes an essay by Benoît Constant Coquelin* on acting and actors). James met Child in 1876 and described him thus in a letter to his mother (24 Dec [1876]): "[A] very pleasant young Englishman. . . . He is . . . a Jew and has a nose, but is handsome." James responded to Child's request for a short story by sending him his "A Bundle of Letters," first published in the *Parisian*. He also sent Child a review of *Nana* by Émile Zola* for publication in the *Parisian*. James often wrote to Child, many times to thank him for kindnesses, including gifts of French books and essays. In February 1884 Child introduced James to Edmond de Goncourt* and also escorted James to the Rue de Bellechasse home of Alphonse Daudet* and his wife Julie in Paris, for a memorable literary evening. Child then wrote up the splendid conversational results, à la Boswell, for the *Atlantic Monthly* (May 1884). In his preface to Volume XIV of *The Novels and Tales of Henry James*, 1908, James comments that Child "die[d], prematurely and lamentedly, during a gallant professional tour of exploration in Persia."

Childe, Edward Lee (1836–1911). Robert E. Lee's nephew, who lived much of his life in France. Childe's wife, Blanche de Triqueti Childe, inherited a French château at Varennes, near Montargis, and with her husband offered James much hospitality over the years, beginning in the summer of 1876, according to a Notebook entry by James (25 Nov 1881). He wrote to his father (24 Feb 1881) of his "pleasant . . . relations . . . with the Childes, who are intelligent and in many ways superior, and whose windows open only upon *l'ancienne* France." James also knew Sir (Henry) Paul Harvey,* Blanche Childe's talented nephew. James may have had both Childe and Daniel Sargent Curtis* in mind when he depicted old Probert in *The Reverberator*.

Chilver, Henry. In "The Great Condition," the trustful man who wins Mrs. Damerel. Suspicious Bertram Braddle fails to do so.

Chipperfield, Mr. and Mrs. In *The Princess Casamassima*, Mrs. Bowerbank's brother-in-law and sister. They live near Amanda Pynsent. He is an undertaker who is sick.

Chivers. In "Covering End," Captain Marmaduke Clement Yule's sad and gentle butler at Covering End. In *Summersoft*, Captain Yule's butler at Summersoft. In *The High Bid*, Yule's butler at Covering.

Chocarne, Bernard (1826–1895). Roman Catholic priest, best known for his *Vie du Père Lacordaire* (1866). James snidely reviewed (*Nation*, 16 Jan 1868) the 1867 translation of this work. He begins by describing the dual nature of Jean Baptiste Henri Lacordaire: a "medieval monk" and "political liberal," who displayed both "intensity of will" and "tenderness of feeling." James summarizes his varied life: law student, priest, traveler (including visits to the United States and England), editor, sacred orator at Notre Dame in Paris, Dominican monk, elected politician, founder of two French colleges, and teacher. James dismisses Father Lacordaire's writings as "of no great value" and his life as an escape from "the sounds and movements of our age."

Cholmondeley, Mary (1859–1925). English novelist and short-story writer, born into a Shropshire clergyman's large family. Tall, thin, and angular, she became a fine hostess; she lived in London and later in Suffolk. She valued the friendship of Percy Lubbock* and Howard Overing Sturgis.* She published eleven books, the most successful of which were *The Danvers Jewels* (1887), *Sir Charles Danvers* (1889), *Diana Tempest* (1893), *Red Pottage* (1899, a best-seller), and *Moth and Rust, and Other Stories* (1902). According to his Pocket Diaries, James socialized with her in the early 1910s.

Chorner, Mrs. In "The Papers," Sir A. B. C. Beadel-Muffet's publicity-seeking fiancée. It is ultimately revealed that she too likes publicity.

Chumleigh. In "The Wheel of Time," Lord Greyswood.

Church, Aurora. In "The Pension Beaurepas," a frugal American girl who is traveling with her mother through Europe. She is attracted to Pigeonneau at the pension. In "The Point of View," while returning with her mother to America, she meets Louis Leverett aboard ship.

Church, Francis Pharcellus (1839–1906). American journalist and cofounder in 1866, with his brother William Conant Church, of the *Galaxy*. The two sold it to the *Atlantic Monthly* in 1878. Francis Church published the world-famous "Is There a Santa Claus?" in the New York *Sun* (21 Sep 1897) in answer to Virginia O'Hanlon Douglas's query. James wrote several letters to Church in connection with work sent to the *Galaxy* for publication in the 1860s and 1870s.

Church, Mrs. In "The Pension Beaurepas," a woman who travels with her daughter Aurora in Europe. In "The Point of View," after docking in New York, she lets Aurora enjoy some independence before requiring the girl to accompany her to the West.

"The Churches in Florence." Travel sketch, published in the *Independent* (9 Jul 1874); reprinted as one part of the eight-part "Florentine Notes" in *Transatlantic Sketches*, 1875, and in *Italian Hours*, 1909.

Churchill, Sir Winston Spencer (1874–1965). Statesman, soldier, and writer; indomitable leader of England during World War II. At dinner in December 1914, James through Herbert Henry Asquith* met First Lord of the Admiralty Churchill, and he immediately judged him to be realistic and confident. James was happy to write to Walter Van Rensselaer Berry* (11 Dec 1914) of "the chance of my having lately, with rather a rush, dined and lunched successively with several high in authority—the Prime Minister, Lord Chancellor, Winston Churchill, Ian Hamilton, people I don't, in my sequestered way, often see." James and Churchill were fellow guests again in January 1915, at a castle overlooking the English Channel, and this time James regarded Churchill, nonplussed by the novelist's conversational powers, as a genius but with limitations. James knew Clara Frewen, who was Churchill's aunt and the wife of Moreton Frewen,* landlord of Stephen Crane* when he rented Brede Place. James's library contained one book by Churchill.

Churchill, Winston (1871–1947). United States Naval Academy graduate (1891), athlete, editor, and best-selling novelist, whose first work, *The Celebrity, an Episode* (1897), James cites in "American Letter" (30 Apr 1898) as an example of the satirical novel. But he adds that the satire has more intention than subject, and that the joke in it is unclear.

Churchley, Mrs. In "The Marriages," the widow who does not marry widower Colonel Chart because of his daughter Adela's lies.

Churm, Miss. In "The Real Thing," the talented Cockney model of the painter narrator. She dislikes and wrongly fears Major and Mrs. Monarch.

Churton, Mr. and Mrs. In "The Aspern Papers," former friends of the Bordereaus. They are supposedly in high society.

Cintré, Comte de. In *The American*, the deceased husband of Claire de Bellegarde de Cintré. In *The American: A Comedy in Four Acts*, it is revealed that he was the lover of Mme. Emmeline de Bellegarde, paid her, blackmailed her into allowing him to marry her seventeen-year-old daughter Claire, wasted his money, and died after three or four years of marriage. In the rewritten fourth act, it is inconsistently revealed that Claire's mother caused his death ten years earlier.

Cintré, Comtesse Claire de Bellegarde de. In *The American*, the attractive young Parisian widow to whom Christopher Newman proposes. In time she comes to love him and accepts him, but she is then pressured by her socially ambitious mother Mme. Emmeline de Bellegarde and her older brother Marquis Urbain de Bellegarde to reject him, whereupon she enters a Carmelite convent. In *The American: A Comedy in Four Acts*, Claire's mother wants Lord Deepmere as a son-in-law, but after Newman obeys Claire and gives Urbain the letter which reveals that their mother killed their father (although Claire is unwitting of its contents), Claire accepts Newman. In the play Claire is twenty-seven years old. In the rewritten fourth act, it is inconsistently revealed that Claire's mother caused the death not only of her husband but also of her lover/son-in-law Comte de Cintré ten years earlier. In the stage performances, Virginia Bateman, the wife of Edward Compton,* and then Elizabeth Robins* were cast as Claire.

Cissy. In "In the Cage," the recipient of one of Philip Everard's telegrams.

Clairin. In "Madame de Mauves," Marie's druggist husband.

Clairin, Mme. Marie de Mauves. In "Madame de Mauves," Richard de Mauves's sister and Mme. de Mauves's sister-in-law.

Clairmont, Clare (1798–1879). British philosopher-novelist William Godwin's stepdaughter. She was thus the stepsister of Mary Wollstonecraft Godwin Shelley, wife of Percy Bysshe Shelley.* Miss Clairmont was the mother of Allegra, the daughter of George Gordon, Lord Byron.* James's knowledge that Miss Clairmont, while living on in Florence, Italy, had retained possession of old letters by both Byron and Shelley inspired his "The Aspern Papers."

Clancy, Mrs. In "The Pupil," Mr. Moreen's sister.

Clanduffy, Lord. In "The Path of Duty," General Bernardstone's father-in-law.

Clarisse, Mamselle. In *The American*, a former maid of Mme. Emmeline de Bellegarde.

Clark, Sir John Forbes (1821–1910). Son of Queen Victoria's loyal, admired, sometimes tactless, and conservative physician, Sir James Clark. By the late 1870s, Henry James had met Sir John, a diplomat and landowner, and his wife, and he was the grateful recipient of their many kindnesses. James wrote to his sister Alice from Tillypronie, Aberdeen (15 Sep [1878]): "Behold me in Scotland and very well pleased to be here. I am staying with the Clarks, of whom you have heard me speak and than whom there could not be a more tenderly hospitable couple. Sir John caresses me like a brother, and her ladyship supervises me like a mother. It is a beautiful part of the country . . . the region of Balmoral and Braemar. This supremely comfortable house . . . has the honor . . . of being the highest placed laird's house in Scotland." A year or so later James visited the Clarks in Cornwall and described them in a letter to his mother (10 Jan [1881]) as "most kindly, talkative and harmlessly fussy." Mutual friends of James and the Clarks included Henry Adams,* his wife Marian Adams,* and Grace Norton.*

Clark, Rev. Mr. In "A Problem," Emma's helpful clergyman.

Claude, Lady. In "Broken Wings," Mrs. Harvey's would-be writer friend.

Claude, Sir. In *What Maisie Knew*, the second husband of Maisie's mother Ida Farange. He is genuinely friendly with little Maisie, but he becomes the lover of Miss Overmore after she marries Maisie's father Beale Farange.

Claudia, Donna. In "Miss Gunton of Poughkeepsie," the Roman prince's sister.

Claudine. In "Madame de Mauves," the painter's wife or—more likely—girl friend. Longmore sees and envies the young couple.

Clemens, Samuel Langhorne. Real name of Mark Twain.*

Clement, Lady Agnes. In "Lady Barbarina," Lady Barbarina Clement Lemon's younger sister, wooed and won by Herman Longstraw.

Clement, Lady Barbarina. In "Lady Barbarina," the maiden name of Barbarina Lemon.

Clementine. In "A Bundle of Letters," a dressmaker whom Violet Ray names.

Clementine, Mlle. In "Rose-Agathe," the name given to the hairdresser's second dummy.

Cleve, Euphemia. In "Madame de Mauves," the maiden name of Countess Euphemia Cleve de Mauves.

Cleve, Mrs. In "Madame de Mauves," Mme. de Mauves's mother.

Cleveland, Grover (1837–1909). Twenty-second and twenty-fourth president of the United States (1885–1889, 1893–1897). His Democratic reform policies and his 1885–1886 criticism of the British in the British Guiana–Venezuela boundary dispute caused James to make critical remarks in letters to friends. He was also saddened by Cleveland's 1885 recall of James Russell Lowell* from his position as ambassador to England. The Venezuela matter caused James to comment superficially in a letter to William Edward Norris* (4 Feb [1896]) on Cleveland's "explosion of jingoism," which he opined was caused by "domestic and internal conditions."

Cliché, Marguerite de (Margaret, Maggie, Margot). In *The Reverberator*, the Marquis's wife and one of Gaston Probert's sisters.

Cliché, Marquis Maxime de. In *The Reverberator*, the husband of Gaston Probert's sister Marguerite.

Clifford, Mrs. W. K. (Lucy Lane) (?–1929). Barbados-born wife of the distinguished British mathematician and philosopher William Kingdon Clifford, whose early death in 1879 left two young daughters and resulted in his widow's beginning a career as a popular novelist and playwright. Her best works include *Mrs. Keith's Crime* (1885) and *Aunt Anne* (1893). James mentions an essay by Professor Clifford in an 1877 letter to his brother William (29 Mar [1877]). James knew and admired Lucy Clifford for decades. Early in 1896 she intermediated with Clement King Shorter* and James for the serial publication of *The Other House*; later that same year, she sent Ford Madox Hueffer* to meet James in Rye. Later, having settled into Lamb House,* James wrote to Lucy that he missed her companionship in London. In 1901 she helped him replace his alcoholic servants Mr. and Mrs. Smith, who were finally not tolerated at Lamb House. Late in life James wrote to Sir Hugh Seymour Walpole* (19 May 1912) that she "gallantly flourishes—on all fine human and personal lines." James's Notebooks are filled with social notes concerning Mrs. Clifford. His library contained eight books by her.

Clifford. In "An Animated Conversation," a prejudiced, unanalytical Britisher in London.

Climber, Annie. In *The Portrait of a Lady*, a Wilmington social climber traveling in Europe with her sister.

Climber, Miss. In *The Portrait of a Lady*, Annie Climber's fellow traveling sister.

Cobb, Sanford H. (1838–1910). American writer on immigration, religious, and prohibition questions, whose *The Story of the Palatines: An Episode in Colonial History* (1897) James in "American Letter" (21 May 1898) mentions as an example of interesting "local history" works. This book by Cobb, whom James calls "unsophisticated," is a "melancholy epic" of injustice to the Germans moving into Pennsylvania early in the eighteenth century. He is fascinated by Cobb's evidence of "the Americanization" of many "ugly [German] names."

Coburn, Alvin Langdon (1882–1966). Born in Boston, this superb, innovative photographer was studying photographic techniques before he was ten, worked and traveled in England and on the Continent in 1899 and 1900, and even mounted a small exhibition in London during 1900. He joined the antiacademic Photo-Secession Group (working with Edward Steichen and Alfred Stieglitz) and the Salon of the Linked Ring (its British predecessor) a year later, held successful shows in Buffalo, again in London, and elsewhere, on into the period of World War I, and also experimented with controversial abstract vortographs. In the 1920s Coburn moved to Wales, put on a retrospective exhibit, donated his large professional library to the Royal Photographic Society, and then became relatively inactive. He made it his personal professional challenge to seek out and immortalize significant people on his plates. They include G. K. Chesterton, Harley Granville Granville-Barker,* Frank Harris, Wyndham Lewis, George Meredith,* Ezra Pound, George Bernard Shaw,* Mark Twain,* William Butler Yeats, and especially James. In 1905 Coburn wrote to James, who was then touring America, to ask for an interview and a sitting, which was granted in New York on 26 April. James later invited the young photographer to visit him at Lamb House,* and Coburn did so. He photographed James (12 June 1906) and his residence (3 July 1906) for *The Novels and Tales of Henry James*, volumes I and IX. James dispatched Coburn to Paris (October 1906), then to Rome and Venice (December 1906) with detailed instructions (for example, he was to report to James's friend Julia Constance Fletcher* in Venice), and even accompanied him through certain London suburbs—all in search of other locales to convert into other photographic frontispieces of *The Novels and Tales*. James wrote fifty letters to Coburn, and the two were in touch until the novelist's death. Critics and readers have noted a kind of Jamesian (as well as, obviously, French) impressionism in Coburn's art work for *The Novels and Tales*; later the photographer became post-impressionistic and even cubistic. Coburn tells in his *Men of Mark* (1913) how he and James found the original locale for "The Curiosity Shop," the frontispiece for *The Golden Bowl* (Volume XXIII), but will not reveal its whereabouts. In *Alvin Langdon Coburn Photographer: An Autobiography* (1966), Coburn also discusses his friend, most affectionately, in a chapter entitled "Illustrating Henry James."

Cocker. In "In the Cage," the owner of the store that houses the telegraphist's cage.

Cockerel, Marcellus C. In "The Point of View," Louis Leverett's pro-American friend.

"Collaboration." Short story (7,800 words), published in the *English Illustrated Magazine* (Sep 1892); republished in *The Private Life*, 1893, and *The Wheel of Time*, 1893. (Characters: Albert Bonus, Marie de Brindes, Paule de Brindes, Miss Brownrigg, Herman Heidenmauer, Félix Vendemer.) French poet Félix Vendemer meets German composer Herman Heidenmauer at the American narrator's Paris salon. When the two decide to collaborate on an opera, Vendemer's fiancée Paule de Brindes and her mother became ruinously critical because Paule's father was killed by the Germans at Sedan, in 1870. This may be a slight story, but it has relevant commentary in these days of international tension. The story has a rare holy-grail metaphor, in which "the religion of art" is equated with "the search for the holy grail."

Collective Edition of 1883. The first collected edition of selected fiction by James to its date. It was published in London by Macmillan, 1883, in fourteen volumes. The first ten volumes reprint the following novels: *The Portrait of a Lady, Roderick Hudson, The American, Washington Square, The Europeans*, and *Confidence*. The last four volumes reprint the following short stories: "The Siege of London," "Madame de Mauves," "An International Episode," "The Pension Beaurepas," "The Point of View," "Daisy Miller: A Study," "Four Meetings," "Longstaff's Marriage," "Benvolio," "The Madonna of the Future," "A Bundle of Letters," "The Diary of a Man of Fifty," and "Eugene Pickering."

Collingwood, Mr. and Mrs. In "A London Life," minor friends of Selina Wing Berrington.

Collop, Miss. In "The Death of the Lion," the real name of popular authoress Guy Walsingham.

Colvin, Sir Sidney (1845–1927). British critic of art and literature, graduated from Trinity College, Cambridge (1867), wrote in London for various journals, and joined several clubs. He was professor of fine arts in Cambridge (1873–1885), became director of the Fitzwilliam Museum (1876–1884), then was a keeper at the British Museum (1884–1912). His principal field was Italian art through the sixteenth century. He published in the English Men of Letters series, and he was an editor and biographer of John Keats. He edited the works (1894–1897) and the letters (1895, 1899, 1911) of his friend Robert Louis Stevenson.* He also knew and admired Joseph Conrad.* He married the long-estranged Mrs. Frances Sitwell late in life, in 1903, when she was sixty-four, and the two established an informal salon. In 1873 Charles Eliot Norton* thrilled James by reporting that John Ruskin* said that he would have preferred James over Colvin as fine-arts professor at Cambridge. James's friendship with Stevenson catalyzed his friendship with Colvin, whom James probably first met in 1885, to whom he wrote many letters (often about Stevenson), and whom he regularly mentions in letters to Stevenson. In one letter (18 Feb 1891) he reports that Colvin, who had been sick, "is really better . . . if any one can be better who is so absolutely good." In another (30 Oct 1891) he says, "Colvin has read me your letters when he discreetly could." In his 1900 review of Stevenson's letters, James praises Colvin for being Stevenson's "literary chargé d'affaires at home, the ideal friend and *alter ego* on whom he could unlimitedly rest." James also knew Colvin's wife. He gratefully attended their very private Marylebone Church wedding and subsequent luncheon, at which he first met Dudley Jocelyn Persse.* The Colvins attended James's funeral. In a 1924 *Empire Review* essay, Colvin analyzed and contrasted James and Stevenson at great length.

"The Comédie Française in London." Theater essay, published in *Nation* (31 Jul 1879). (This was James's last effort for years at journalistic writing, a form he deplored.) James applauds the completely successful six-weeks' "visit to London of the children of Molière." Some think that the Comédie Française performed here only for money. James was "only too delighted" to attend the offerings "in the Strand" but does agree that perhaps the company was thus "vulgarized." It was *the* topic of conversation, especially the "vogue" of Sarah Bernhardt,* whom James proceeds to demean, preferring actresses Sophie Croizette and Marie Favart. The actors were best of all, especially François Jules Edmond Got* and Benoît Constant Coquelin.*

Compton, Edward (1854–1918). British actor and manager of the Compton Comedy Company, at first a provincial group. His wife was Virginia Bateman Compton, an American actress. Their son was the novelist Sir Edward Montague Compton Mackenzie,* whom James later knew and reviewed. In December 1888 Compton asked James to dramatize his novel *The American*. He did so in 1889–1890, even providing the play with a happy ending, at Compton's suggestion. Compton produced it, opening in Southport, outside Liverpool, on 3 January

1891. Compton starred as Christopher Newman; his wife Virginia was cast as Claire de Cintré. In letters to friends during the time the play was first performed, James indicates his delight with the acting. Compton took the play on tour and offered it in London, in September 1891, with some cast changes: Elizabeth Robins* replaced the pregnant Virginia, and Virginia's sister Kate Bateman played old Madame de Bellegarde. At Compton's suggestion, James tinkered further with the last act; nevertheless, the play closed in December 1891. James evidently wrote *The Album* in 1891 with Compton and his company in mind, at least initially. While working on *Guy Domville* in the spring of 1893, James disputed with Compton, who wanted a happy ending; when he could not persuade James, Compton declined to consider the play. Later that spring, James wrote himself notes with the idea of reworking his short story "The Chaperon" for the stage, again with Compton in mind. In 1894 or 1895 James showed Compton a three-act scenario for *The Other House*, but it evidently failed to interest him. The two men remained friendly, however; a Pocket Diary entry indicates that James called on Compton at his home in London in January 1914.

Condit, Catherine. In "The Impressions of a Cousin," the painter narrator, who has just returned from Europe to New York, where Adrian Frank, her cousin Eunice's fiancé, falls in love with Catherine.

Condrip, Bertie, Guy, Kitty, and Maudie. In *The Wings of the Dove*, the small children of Marian Croy Condrip.

Condrip, Marian Croy. In *The Wings of the Dove*, Kate Croy's sister, the death of whose minister husband left her impoverished with four small children—Bertie, Guy, Kitty, and Maudie.

Condrip, Rev. Mr. In *The Wings of the Dove*, the fatuous husband of Marian Croy Condrip. He is now deceased.

Condrip, The Misses. In *The Wings of the Dove*, the sisters-in-law of the widowed Marian Croy Condrip.

Confidence. Short novel (74,200 words), published in *Scribner's Monthly* (Aug 1879–Jan 1880); revised and reprinted in London by Chatto & Windus, in 1879, and in Boston by Houghton, Osgood, in 1880. (Characters: Blanche Evers, Ella Maclane, Mr. and Mrs. Maclane, Bernard Longueville, Captain Augustus Lovelock, Angela Vivian, Mrs. Vivian, Waterworth, Gordon Wright.) Sketching in Siena, Bernard Longueville meets Angela Vivian and her mother. His friend Gordon Wright calls him to Baden-Baden to pass judgment on Blanche Evers (whom he wrongly concludes Wright loves), her follower Augustus Lovelock, and—again—the Vivians. Wright rather uncertainly loves Angela, who seems cynical. Wright goes to England, leaving the others to spy on her. When Wright returns, Longueville blurts out that Angela might marry Wright for his money. Two years pass. Wright has married Blanche. In New York, Longueville observes her flirting with Lovelock. On a beach in France, Longueville sees the Vivians again, feels that he wronged Angela, and realizes he is in love with her. They soon come to an understanding in Paris: Angela explains that she resented Wright's asking Longueville to judge her and therefore misbehaved on purpose. The Wrights and Lovelock come to Paris. News of Longueville's impending marriage to Angela puzzles Wright. Angela tells Longueville that she refused Wright when he proposed after the former's denunciation of her, hoping to evoke remorse and then love in Longueville. She also says that Wright probably hoped for that second refusal from her. Wright says that Blanche wants Lovelock and asks Angela to wait until he is free. She agrees to give him another chance at happiness and orders Longueville to London, where he sees Lovelock, who is annoyed. Angela then persuades Wright that he loves his wife. The happy couple, in Egypt, send a letter to the Longuevilles, who are honeymooning in Paris. It is possible that the differences James dramatized between artist Longueville and scientist Wright may owe something to James's recollection of temperamental clashes he and his brother William had experienced six years earlier, when they were together uneasily in Italy. In a long plot sketch in his *Notebooks* (7 Nov 1878), James has Blanche "cruelly unfaithful" to Gordon, who then is "supposed" to be "the means of his wife's death." Although James preferred *Confidence* to *The Europeans*, written a couple of years earlier, most critics agree that *Confidence* is his weakest novel. Even the title is unsatisfactory. *Confidence* proved popular, however, with contemporary readers and earned James good royalties.

Congreve, Henrietta. In "Osborne's Revenge," the decent girl unfairly accused of jilting Robert Graham, who committed suicide.

Conkling, Roscoe (1829–1888). New York lawyer, congressman, and senator. He had presidential aspirations, opposed the policies of both presidents Rutherford B. Hayes and James A. Garfield,* and resigned from the Senate in 1881. James met Conkling during a London party given by George Washburn Smalley,* and in a letter to his brother William (10 Jul [1877]) pronounced him "a most extraordinary specimen!" who was " 'orating' softly and longwindedly the whole dinner-time, with a kind of baleful fascination."

Connery. In "Julia Bride," a stepfather of Julia Bride.

Connery, Mrs. Bride Pitman. In "Julia Bride," Julia Bride's mother. Julia tells the truth about this often married and probably promiscuous woman to help Pitman, one of her mother's ex-husbands, in his marital ambitions.

Conrad, Joseph (1857–1924). Novelist and short-story writer born (as Josef Teodor Konrad Nalecz Korzeniowski) in Berdyczew, Poland, of Polish parents. His educated father's anti-Russian activities caused the family to be exiled to northern Russia. Orphaned in 1869, young Conrad attended school in Cracow, learned French, read William Shakespeare* and Charles Dickens* in Polish, and also read much sea fiction. Conrad became a sailor, first aboard French vessels out of lively Marseilles (1874–1877), and then mostly English merchant ships (1878–1894). By 1880 he had developed fluency in the English language. In 1886 he was certified as a master in the British merchant service and became a British subject. In 1890 he made a distressing voyage up the Congo. In 1894 he left the sea and turned to writing. Conrad had memories of a wild youth and a sailor's broad experiences to draw upon. While recovering from Congo fever, he started his first novel in 1889, *Almayer's Folly* (1895), which was immediately followed by *An Outcast of the Islands* (1896), *The Nigger of the "Narcissus"* (1897, Conrad's personal favorite), *Lord Jim* (1900), *Nostromo* (1904), and several short stories, including "Youth" (1902, one of his best), "Heart of Darkness" (1902, perhaps his best), and "Typhoon" (1903). By this time, Conrad had married an English woman (1896), had two sons, and began to see life and art somewhat differently. He continued to write, steadily but with painful slowness. The public was not aware of his greatness (though critics and confreres quickly were, including George Gissing,* Herbert George Wells,* Stephen Crane,* John Galsworthy,* and James). Next Conrad published *The Secret Agent* (1907, anti-Russian), *Under Western Eyes* (1911, also anti-Russian), *Chance* (1914, his first book to achieve real financial success), *Victory* (1915), *The Rescue* (1920), and *Suspense* (1925, fragmentary). In between came less significant novels and several collections of short stories (including *'Twixt Land and Sea*, 1912, with "The Secret Sharer"). Conrad collaborated with his friend Ford Madox Hueffer* on three novels (1901, 1903, 1924). Conrad also wrote four volumes of autobiography (including *The Mirror of the Sea*, 1906) and personal essays. He had read and admired James for some years before sending him an inscribed copy of *An Outcast of the Islands* in October 1896. James reciprocated with a copy of *The Spoils of Poynton* the next February and invited Conrad to luncheon at De Vere Gardens* later that month. The following year both men changed residences; James went to Rye and the Conrads moved to Aldington (until 1907), fourteen miles northeast of Rye. Their continuing friendship was assured. Conrad was able to know or know better several other friends of James's in that region, including Hueffer, Wells, and especially Crane. James enthusiastically praised *Lord Jim* in 1900. In a letter to Sir Edmund Wilson Gosse* (26 Jun 1902), he wrote that Conrad "has been to me, the last few years, one of the most interesting & striking of the novelists of the new generation. His production . . . has all been fine & valid." James went on to compare Conrad to Pierre Loti* and to call *The Nigger of the Narcissus* "the very finest & strongest picture of the sea and sea-life that our language possesses." All of this was in support of Gosse's successful effort to obtain a Royal Literary Fund grant for

Conrad. James permitted Conrad to read his prospectus for *The Wings of the Dove*. When Conrad sent *The Mirror of the Sea* to James, he replied beautifully (1 Nov 1906): "I read you as I listen to rare music. . . . No one has *known*—for intellectual use—the things you know, and you have, as the artist of the whole matter, an authority that no one has approached. I find you in it all, *writing* wonderfully, whatever you may say of your difficult medium and your *plume rebelle*. You knock about in the wide waters of expression like the raciest and boldest of privateers." Conrad sent James *The Secret Agent* in the fall of 1907. James did not say so directly, but his dislike of that novel, and of *Nostromo* and *Under Western Eyes* as well, is evident from his letter much later to Edith Newbold Jones Wharton* (27 Feb 1914) describing them as "wastes of desolation." But in a letter (5 Feb 1914) to James Brand Pinker,* who was not only James's literary agent but also Conrad's, James calls *Chance* "very remarkable." (In the same February 1914 letter to Wharton, James calls *Chance* "really rather *yieldingly* difficult and charming.") Only in "The Younger Generation" (retitled "The New Novel," 1914) does James comment publicly about Conrad's work. There James mutes his general praise of the "refinement of design" in *Chance*. From the first, this novel was "to be 'art' exclusively or to be nothing," with "invoked" difficulties overcome, especially with respect to the unnecessarily complex point of view selected. James does wish that the fictive "predicament" had been "invoked" too, instead of "imposed." Conrad reveals "a beautiful and generous mind at play" (but "in conditions comparatively thankless"); and "the common reader" surprisingly likes the results. James could not fully appreciate Conrad, who agonized over the act of writing, created baffled characters, and pessimistically exposed civilization's conflicts, squalor, rot, and inhumanity. James's library contained two books by Conrad.

Considine, Lord. In "Mrs. Medwin," Mamie Cutter's dinner partner on one occasion.

Considine, Lord and Lady. In "Glasses," the parents of Lord Iffield, whom Flora Saunt wishes to marry but does not.

Constantius. In "Daniel Deronda: A Conversation," the reviewer novelist whose critical position is closest to that of James himself. He mediates between Pulcheria and Theodora.

Cook, Dutton (1829–1883). English theater and art historian, who wrote several books and also frequently published in the *Gentleman's Magazine*. James reviewed (*Nation*, 8 Feb 1877) Cook's *A Book of the Play: Studies and Illustrations of Histrionic Story, Life, and Character* (1876), defining the work as a "readable" example of an inexhaustible genre, namely, the "compilation of theatrical anecdote and gossip." He wonders why readers are more tolerant if the actors and actresses discussed are from times gone by. After all, the stage of forty or more years ago was "a tolerably inelegant and dingy institution." Cook is not critical enough, and he contents himself with facts about mere playbills, newspaper accounts, tickets, seats, makeup, and so on, but James admits that everything is "agreeably presented."

Cookham, Kate. In "The Bench of Desolation," Herbert Dodd's well-intentioned victimizer. She invested his payment to her for breach of promise and years later offers the capital and interest to Dodd.

Cooler, Mrs. In "The Point of View," Marcellus Cockerel's sister.

Cooper. In "In the Cage," a name mentioned in a Lady Bradeen telegram.

Cooper, Dr. James. In "The Story of a Year," Lieutenant John Ford's physician at Glenham.

Cooper, Miss. In "The Story of a Year," Dr. Cooper's daughter. She is a friend of Lizzie Crowe.

Coote, Charley. In "The Bench of Desolation," a friend whom Herbert Dodd sees near Kate Cookham's hotel.

Cope. In "Master Eustace," a businessman back from an extended time in India. He marries Mrs. Garnyer. Eustace Garnyer is their illegitimate son.

Cope, Mrs. In "Master Eustice," the former Mrs. Henry Garnyer.

Copley, John Singleton (1738–1815). American historical and portrait painter, born in Boston of Irish parents. He established a studio there (about 1757), then went to Rome (1774) and on to London (1775). He was made a member of the Royal Academy (1783) following the exhibition of his *Death of Chatham*. In an untitled note (*Nation*, 9 Sep 1875), James describes Copley's portrait of Mrs. Skinner and praises it as "unsurpassable by the artist himself," whom he ranks with "almost . . . the very first." Being "a trifle hard and rigid," Copley is inferior to Hans Holbein the younger.*

Coppée, François (1842–1908). Paris-born French poet, dramatist in verse, fiction writer, writer of prose sketches, and archivist. James wrote to Sir Edmund Wilson Gosse* (18 Nov [1889]) that he was rushing off to have breakfast with Coppée. When in Paris early in 1891, James sought out but missed Coppée, who was then in Algiers. James's library contained four books by Coppée.

Coquelin, Benoît Constant (1841–1909). French actor and theater manager, born in Boulogne, studied for the theater, and made his debut at the Comédie Française in 1860. He became a phenomenal success in Paris (creating leading roles in more than forty new dramas), and later he toured in Europe and the United States (1887–1889 and 1900, at times with Sarah Bernhardt*). When he had disputes with the Comédie Française, he performed elsewhere. He wrote books and essays on the subject of dramatic art. James attended classes with Coquelin at the Collège Municipale, Boulogne (1857–1858), and in the 1870s and 1880s he observed and praised his fine performances at the Théâtre Français. In "The Théâtre Français" (1877) James compared Coquelin's "talent and . . . art" to those of the master actor François Jules Edmond Got* and defined the younger man as "wonderfully brillliant, elastic." In "The Comédie Française in London" (1879) James uniquely praises Coquelin, as "the rich, the rare, the admirable and inimitable," for his performance on tour in London. James begins his essay "Coquelin" (*Century*, Jan 1887; revised to become the introduction to Coquelin's *Papers on Acting: Art and the Actor*, translated by Abby Langdon Alger, daughter of William Rounseville Alger* [1915]), by calling the Théâtre Français a unique "school of taste" and his first lesson therein a performance by Coquelin in *Lions et renards* (1869) by Guillaume Victor Émile Augier.* James contrasts Coquelin with other foreign performers in America, noting that he relies on talent not physical attributes, and then places him with fine French players, many now gone. He praises Coquelin's play of features and range of voice ("astounding organ"), variety of successful roles (especially in Molière), presentation on stage of "the passion of impudence," "delivery of verse," and handling of "long . . . continuous aggregation of lines." Deploring the current overuse of stage properties, James recalls Coquelin in Charles Lomon's *Jean Dacier* (1877) as "the most memorable [evening] ever spent by him [James] in a theatre." He theorizes that a playgoer's ear is more impressionable than his eye, and he cites Aimée Desclée's success as proof, as well as that of Coquelin's "nerve-stirring voice." He discusses the actor's nonimpudent role in *L'Ami Fritz* (1876) by Erckmann-Chatrian,* finds that he lacks space to say much about the actor's role ("a closer realism") in *L'Étrangère* by Alexandre Dumas *fils* (1876), and labels Coquelin "the [Honoré de] Balzac[*] of actors" whom he hopes contact with the American public will not hurt. James entertained Coquelin at lunch in 1888 (at his home at De Vere Gardens*), and he discovered that, although the man was a brilliant actor, he was also an impossibly conceited human being. At the Théâtre Porte Saint Martin in 1897, Coquelin created the role of Cyrano in *Cyrano de Bergerac* by Edmond Rostand.* An amazing coincidence is the fact that James in 1869 named the hero of his short story "Gabrielle de Bergerac" Pierre Coquelin. Coquelin published an article on acting and actors in *The Comédie Française*, which was edited by Theodore E. Child* (1893).

Coquelin, Pierre. In "Gabrielle de Bergerac," Chevalier de Bergerac's tutor. He loves, elopes with, and marries Gabrielle de Bergerac; later they die together during the French Revolution. This character is surely named Coquelin because James recalled his Boulogne school chum Benoît Constant Coquelin,* then a lad of sixteen who later became the first actor to play the title role in *Cyrano de Bergerac* (1897) by Edmond Rostand.*

Coquelin, Mme. In "Gabrielle de Bergerac," Pierre's mother, who remarried after her first husband's death.

Corvick, George. In "The Figure in the Carpet," the critic narrator's critic friend. After claiming to have traced "the figure" in Hugh Vereker's literary works, Corvick marries Gwendolyn Erme and dies before he can publish his discovery.

Corvick, Gwendolyn Erme. In "The Figure in the Carpet," the former Gwendolyn Erme.

Costello, Mrs. Louisa. In "Daisy Miller," Frederick Forsyth Winterbourne's widowed, Europeanized aunt. She has two married sons in New York and a third in Europe. She superciliously disapproves of Daisy Miller's conduct. In *Daisy Miller: A Comedy in Three Acts*, Mrs. Costello is called Cousin Louisa by Alice Durant, who with Charles Reverdy accompanies the older woman to Europe. In the play she is ultimately less critical of Daisy Miller.

Courageau, M. de. In *The Reverberator*, an elderly friend of Suzanne de Brécourt.

"Cousin Maria." 1887 title of "Mrs. Temperly."

Coventry, Mrs. In "The Madonna of the Future," the American woman in Florence who rebukes Theobald for not being a productive painter.

"Covering End." Long short story (34,200 words), published in *The Two Magics*, 1898. (Characters: Chivers, Mrs. Gracedew, Hall Pegg, Cora Prodmore, Prodmore, Dame Dorothy Yule, John Anthony Yule, Captain Marmaduke Clement Yule.) To Clement Yule's mortgaged estate, called Covering End, Prodmore the taunting mortgage holder comes with his daughter Cora. He hopes that Yule will turn conservative and that the two young people will wed. An attractive and delightful young American widow, Mrs. Gracedew, enters as an antique-loving tourist to look over Covering End. She encourages Yule to keep the place at any cost. Cora explains that she prefers Hall Pegg, a rich London scion, to Yule. Mrs. Gracedew buys the mortgage at a high fee, forces Prodmore to support his daughter's marriage to Pegg, and will wed Yule herself. Osterley, a beautiful country house, in which James was a guest with James Russell Lowell* in June 1886, was the inspiration for the mansion in "Covering End." James originally used its plot in 1895 in a one-act play entitled *Summersoft*, written for his actress friend Dame Ellen Terry* at her request. She paid him

£100 against future royalties, but it remained unproduced; James reclaimed it and converted it into "Covering End" in 1898. In 1907 he reconverted it, back to the rather successful three-act play *The High Bid*.

Coverley, Charles. In *Disengaged*, Percy Trafford's friend and an admirer of Mrs. Jasper. To please her, he helps persuade Captain Llewellyn Prime to propose to Blandina Wigmore; then, again to please her, he helps undo the damage only to reel aghast at the news that Mrs. Jasper will marry Prime.

Coxon, Lady. In "The Coxon Fund," Lord Gregory Coxon's widow and the founder of the Coxon Fund. In her youth a "thin transcendental" Bostonian, she is Ruth Anvoy's aunt.

"The Coxon Fund." Short story (21,300 words), published in the *Yellow Book* (Jul 1894); reprinted in *Terminations*, 1895; revised and reprinted in *The Novels and Tales of Henry James*, Volume XV, 1909. (Characters: Ruth Anvoy, Anvoy, Lord Gregory and Lady Coxon, George Gravener, Lord and Lady Maddock, Adelaide and Kent Mulville, Mr. and Mrs. Pudney, Mr. and Mrs. Frank Saltram, Saltram.) While visiting the Mulvilles at Wimbleton, the narrator is impressed by their guest Frank Saltram's conversational powers. But George Gravener is critical of the slovenly Saltram's imposition. When Saltram fails to appear as a guest lecturer, the narrator is saddened by having to apologize to the audience but is happy thereafter to meet Ruth Anvoy. This well-to-do, pretty American, niece of Lord Gregory Coxon's widow, wants to meet Saltram. At Lady Coxon's estate, Gravener meets Ruth and soon becomes engaged to her. After some delays, she meets unreliable but impressive Saltram. Her father goes bankrupt in New York. Lady Coxon sets up a £13,000 fund to be administered by Ruth, to be paid to any brilliant, poor philosopher but to be kept by Ruth if she cannot find a worthy recipient. Then both Lady Coxon and Ruth's father die. Gravener urges the girl not to give money to Saltram. The narrator both resists the temptation to tell her that Saltram is an alcoholic and is distressed by Gravener's selfishness. Estranged Mrs. Saltram conscientiously delivers to the narrator some damaging evidence about her husband, which the narrator declines to show Ruth. Gravener wants the girl to know, so that she can then keep the money. When the narrator asks whether Gravener will wed her without the money, he will not reply. The narrator tells Ruth about the evidence in general terms, and she idealistically urges him to destroy it. She gives the funds to the genius, who proceeds to drink himself into inarticulateness and then death. The narrator loyally burns the evidence. Neither he nor Ruth marries, whereas Gravener marries money and eventually becomes a lord. In a Notebook entry (17 Apr 1894), James makes it clear that brilliant, unbalanced Samuel Taylor Coleridge was the inspiration for James's character Frank Saltram. Additional Notebook entries a few days later (25, 29 Apr 1894) show how fast James clarified his initial idea. In the preface to Volume XV of *The Novels and Tales of Henry*

James, James explains that he was less interested in Coleridge, although "[t]he wondrous figure of that genius had long haunted me," than in how his *"type"* could challenge James's imagination to "re-embody . . . it" into something fresh. The moral of James's prolix fable may well be that we should allow irresponsible geniuses their freedom but also be prepared to see that any help we give them may eventuate in inarticulateness and failure.

Coyle, Mr. and Mrs. Spencer. In "Owen Wingrave," a coach for Owen Wingrave and others aspiring to military careers, and his wife, who is sympathetic toward Owen Wingrave. The Coyles are guests at Paramore, the Wingrave estate. In *The Saloon*, the army coach (age forty-eight) and his gentle wife (age thirty-five), who finds the Wingrave home creepy. Coyle tells Owen Wingrave that his grandfather is disinheriting him.

Coyne. In *The Sense of the Past*, Aurora Coyne's elderly Wall Street father-in-law.

Coyne, Aurora. In *The Sense of the Past*, a wealthy, anti-European widow. She merely admires Ralph Pendrel, who genuinely loves her. She urges him to test his love of Europe by living there for a while.

Coyne, Townsend (Stent). In *The Sense of the Past*, Aurora Coyne's deceased husband.

Crackanthorpe, Hubert Montague (1870–1896). Talented but unstable London-born editor, short-story writer, and contributor to the *Yellow Book*. He came from a fine family, was tutored by George Gissing,* quit Cambridge University within a year, married, and began to publish with some success, but he became hopelessly depressed when his wife ran off with another man. His association with the *Yellow Book* brought him into contact with James's admiring friend Henry Harland.* Among Crackanthorpe's few published works are *Wreckage* (1893, well reviewed as a new-realism success), *Sentimental Studies and a Set of Village Tales* (1895, dedicated to Harland), *Vignettes: A Miniature Journal of Whim and Sentiment* (1896), and *Last Studies* (1897); the last work contains three tales, including "Trevor Perkins: A Platonic Episode." Crackanthorpe drowned, perhaps by suicidal intention, in the Seine, near Quai Voltaire in Paris. Posthumously published was a farce entitled *The Light Sovereign: A Farcical Comedy in Three Acts* (1917), which he wrote with Harland. In 1897 James provided a weirdly verbose preface for Crackanthorpe's *Last Studies* (published by their friend William Heinemann*), in which he praises the generosity of the young author to an older writer, suggests that his early death "give[s] him more meaning" (even refocusing for us "his own young vision of fate"), and discusses his particular import. Crackanthorpe is "a . . . touching case of . . . reaction against an experience of puerilities judged . . . inane, and a proportionate search

... for some artistic way of marking the force of the reaction." He seemed boyish, but he sensibly omitted immature romantic ingredients from his writing, avoided "the grossly obvious," and developed a distinct point of view. He liked a situation calling for a new form, foreshortening, and "objective intensity." Like French story writers, especially Guy de Maupassant,* Crackanthorpe preferred to present "a portrait of conditions" rather than a "chain of items." He found subjects in "deep, dark London" previously "untouched" by "the smug and superficial." He shows that England's Bohemia can be "uglier and more brutal" than Paris. Surely better are Crackanthorpe's sweet, sad tales of rural France. Naming several titles, James voices his preference for "Trevor Perkins" and *Vignettes*. Crackanthorpe combines joy with an awareness of "the cruelty of life" and "the deep insecurity of things." Stopford Augustus Brooke* pronounced James's essay on Crackanthorpe hard to comprehend.

Craddock, Charles Egbert. The pen name of Mary Noailles Murfree.*

Craik, Dinah Maria Mulock (1826–1887). Prolific English novelist of Irish extraction, whose *John Halifax, Gentleman* (1857) was once immensely popular, as was her later children's classic, *The Little Lame Prince* (1875). She also wrote in opposition to capital punishment and in favor of liberalizing marriage laws. In 1864 Mulock married publisher George Lillie Craik. James wrote a review (*Nation*, 1 Mar 1866) of Mulock's *A Noble Life* (1866), which he began with an extended discussion of *John Halifax*. Its perfectly virtuous hero he saw as oddly popular in an age usually sympathetic to "picturesque turpitude." We now accept depictions of goodness only when we are provided realistic proof of it. Mulock sees people "through a curtain of rose-colored gauze," and her consequent "excessive sentimentality . . . falsifies every fact and every truth it touches." In *A Noble Life* she presents a physically crippled hero who is also "sensitive, imaginative, manly-souled." He has a good nurse nearby but is threatened by an "insidious kinsman." James states that "a wise man" could have written the novel better than "a woman something less than wise," although in this case Mulock while lacking philosophy and style does display better "feeling and taste" than, say, Mary Elizabeth Braddon.* Mulock is at least *honnête*.

Crane, Anne Moncure. Maiden name of Anne Moncure Crane Seemüller.*

Crane, Stephen (1871–1900). Brilliant, eccentric American naturalistic fiction writer and poet. He was born in Newark, New Jersey, the last in a family of fourteen children, several of whom died young. His father was an itinerant Methodist minister; his mother, a religious journalist. The family moved about in New Jersey and New York, both before and after the father's death in 1880. Crane attended various schools, Lafayette College (1890), and Syracuse University (1891); boxing and baseball were his most important studies. After his mother died (1891), Crane went to New York City, became a New York *Tribune* stringer, lived in the Bowery, and drafted his first novel, *Maggie: A Girl of the Streets*. Failing to sell it to Richard Watson Gilder* of the *Century Magazine*, he published it pseudonymously at his own expense (1893; reissued as by Crane in 1896). It attracted the critical attention of Hamlin Garland,* whom Crane had met earlier (1891) and who told William Dean Howells* about it. Crane turned his longtime fascination for the Civil War into *The Red Badge of Courage* (short version 1894, full version 1895). Now immensely popular, he began to wander, as a notorious journalist and as an impression-gathering creative writer, to the American West, Mexico, and Florida. In Jacksonville, Florida, he met the hostess or proprietress of a house of assignation who called herself Cora Taylor. (She was born in Boston, in 1865, Cora Ethel Eaton Howorth. She married, in New York, then soon divorced Thomas Vinton Murphy; then married, in London, Donald William Stewart, and soon asked him for a divorce, which he never gave her.) Crane made himself unpopular with the New York police by testifying about the harassment of a chorus girl. He returned to Florida, was shipwrecked (1897) on his way to Cuba to supply guns to rebels, and published "The Open Boat" (1897) his most famous short story, as a direct result. Later in 1897 Crane and soon thereafter Cora, now calling herself Imogen Carter, went as war correspondents to cover the Greco-Turkish War. In summer 1897 the two, as Stephen and Cora Crane, common-law husband and wife, rented a house in Oxted, Surrey, outside London. Crane briefly covered the Spanish-American War in Cuba and Puerto Rico (1898), returned to England (1899), and then with Cora rented Brede Place (owned by Moreton Frewen* and his wife), in Sussex, where the two (who never paid the rent) were near and became friendly with Joseph Conrad,* Herbert George Wells,* Ford Madox Hueffer,* and other writers, including James. In England Crane also met Harold Frederic,* Edward Garnett and his wife the translator Constance Garnett, Sir Edmund Wilson Gosse,* Algernon Charles Swinburne,* and William Butler Yeats. William Heinemann* became the British publisher for Crane, who continued to write well but also did hack work for money, and suffered from tuberculosis. Other works of his include novels (*George's Mother* [1896], *The Third Violet* [1897], and *Active Service* [1899]), poetry (*The Black Riders* [1895] and *War Is Kind* [1899]), history (*Great Battles of the World* [1901]), and several collections of short stories. Soon after moving into Brede Place, eight miles from Rye, Crane, who (with Cora) had already met James in London (probably in 1898), began to see the older novelist often. James gave Crane several of his books. He was a photographed tea-party guest at Brede Place, where he also participated in a Christmas Eve party, complete with a multiple-authored ghost play. When Frederic died in 1898, Cora informally adopted his illegitimate children, appealed to various people for money, and accepted some from James. In 1900 when Cora took Crane to rest in Germany, where he died, James wrote "Dear Mrs. Crane" and sent her a check for £50 (5 Jun 1900): "I enclose . . . a convenience. Please view it as such and dedicate it to whatever service it may best render my stricken young friend. It meagrely represents my tender benediction to him." But James later felt obliged to write his agent James Brand Pinker* (29 Aug 1900) to complain that Cora, who had never paid Crane's devoted Rye doctor, "is . . . an unprofitable person, and I judge her . . . very sternly and unforgivingly." As for Cora, she buried Crane's body in New Jersey, returned to England (1900), tried free-lancing, never paid Crane's debts of $5,000, went back home (1901), built a Jacksonville brothel on borrowed funds (1902), married a Georgian named Hammond McNeil (arrested in 1907 for killing her alleged lover), and fled to England to avoid having to testify. Cora tried to visit James, but he wrote to her telling her not to call at Lamb House.* When McNeil was acquitted, Cora returned to Jacksonville, was shunned by all, and soon died (1910). James personally liked Stephen Crane, but regarded his naturalism as too Zolaesque, and could professionally admire only his potential. James's library contained one book by Crane.

"Crapy Cornelia." Short story (10,700 words), published in *Harper's Magazine* (Oct 1909); reprinted in *The Finer Grain*, 1910. (Characters: Mary Cardew, Cornelia Rasch, White-Mason, Mrs. Worthingham.) Musing in a New York park in April, middle-aged White-Mason thinks that he will soon go propose to flashily rich Mrs. Worthington. At her gaudy new residence, however, he meets Cornelia Rasch, an old friend, of whom Mrs. Worthington speaks critically. White-Mason resists popping the question and goes to the park again, where he recalls the charms of old New York as symbolized by Cornelia. When he calls upon the crapy old creature, they renew fond memories even as he delights in the polish of time on her old furnishings. When Cornelia mentions the rich woman, who she says loves White-Mason, he indicates his preference for the mellow past. The autobiographical impulse for this sweet story is James's own return to New York in 1904, with his consequent horror at Manhattan's sprawl and roar. The two central women stand for two ways of life, and White-Mason—and James—clearly enough opt for the old.

Crawford, Francis Marion (1854–1909). Popular, prolific, and versatile American novelist, born in Bagni di Lucca, Italy, the son of Thomas Crawford* and Louisa Ward Howe Crawford (sister of politician-lobbyist Samuel Ward and of Julia Ward Howe* and later the wife of the painter Luther Terry*). F. Marion Crawford lived mostly in Rome until 1879, but he also was a student in New Hampshire, Essex, Trinity College, Cambridge, and Karlsruhe and Heidelberg, Germany. He edited a newspaper in India (1879–1880), returned to Rome, then went to Boston (1881) to seek work as a writer. While there he met Isabella Stewart Gardner,* who ultimately became an intimate friend. In Boston Crawford wrote two popular novels, *Mr. Isaacs: A Tale of Modern India* (1882) and *Dr. Claudius: A True Story* (1882). From this point on, his life was a romantic legend. Using Sorrento and Rome as his main bases, Crawford quickly penned dozens of novels, married Elizabeth Berdan (daughter of General Hiram Berdan) in Constantinople (1884), purchased a Sorrentine villa (1887), traveled widely, enjoyed annual visits to the United States (1892–1907), bought a big yacht (1896), wrote a play (*Francesca da Rimini*, 1902) for Sarah Bernhardt,* and started a series of historical books on Rome, Naples, and Venice (1904). In all, Crawford published more than fifty book-length works (several in two and three volumes each). The titles of some of his most popular novels are *To Leeward* (1883), *Saracinesca* (1887), *Marzio's Crucifix* (1887), *Paul Patoff* (1887), *Sant' Ilario* (1889), *Khaled: A Tale of Arabia* (1891), *Don Orsino* (1892), *Katharine Lauderdale* (1894), *The Ralstons* (1895), *Casa Braccio* (1895), *Corleone: A Tale of Sicily* (1897), *In the Palace of the King: A Love Story of Old Madrid* (1900), *Fair Margaret: A Portrait* (1905), *A Lady of Rome* (1906), and *The White Sister* (1909). James met Sam Ward through Charles Eliot Norton,* in London, in March 1869. (The two met again in Rome in November or December 1873.) James evidently met Crawford in Rome late in 1869, but, in the 1870s, he was more interested in Crawford's sister Annie Crawford than in young Crawford. James called her in a letter to his father (4 Mar [1873]) "the most remarkable person I have seen in Rome," sympathized with her stepfather Luther Terry, judged her to be "hard as flint," and said that any "adorer" of hers would have to be "a real Lion-tamer." James was right: Annie soon married a Prussian, Count Erich von Rabé, a tall, stiff, wounded veteran of the Franco-Prussian War. James wrote to Sarah Butler Wister* an enigmatic comment (10 May [1874]) after Annie's marriage: "I never wanted to marry her, surely, but I don't care for her so much now that another man has done so." James also knew other members of the Crawford family: Crawford's sister Mimoli Crawford (who married Hugh Fraser); Crawford's half-sister Margaret Terry (later Mrs. Winthrop Chanler); Crawford's wife Bessie and her mother; Crawford's aunt, Julia Ward Howe, and her daughter, Maud Howe Elliott* (Crawford's cousin). There is explosive rancor in a letter by James to William Dean Howells* (21 Feb 1884), in which he alludes to Crawford's best-selling *To Leeward*: "What you tell me of the success of Crawford's last novel sickens and almost paralyses me. It seems to me so contemptibly bad and ignoble that the idea of people reading it in such numbers makes one . . . ask what is the use of trying to write anything decent or serious for a public so absolutely idiotic. . . . Work so shamelessly bad seems to me to dishonour the novelist's art . . . just as its success dishonours the people for whom one supposes one's self to write. Excuse my ferocity . . . and don't mention it, . . . as it will be set down to green-eyed jealousy." Yet, on at least two later occasions, James could write to Crawford politely. First (28 Oct [1892]), James congratulates him for something, perhaps the start of an American lecture tour, and adds: "Happy you to have such various gifts. You are like the mu[l]tiform Italians—your own people—of the renaissance." Second (19 Nov 1903), James thanks Crawford for compliments on his biography of William Wetmore Story,* then adds that "[t]he book . . . seems to be giving me in a small way the taste of the (to me,) rare sweet fruit of 'success' . . ." In between those letters, James visited Villa Crawford in Sorrento, immediately before being entertained by Axel Martin Fredrik Munthe* on Capri

(June 1899). James wrote to Story's daughter-in-law Mrs. Thomas Waldo Story ([17 Jun 1899]), from Crawford's "prodigious" home, about his host's "magnificence . . . and . . . complications of hospitality." Crawford attended the first performance of James's *Guy Domville*, in London, on 5 January 1895. In *Notes of a Son and Brother* (1914), James calls Crawford "[t]he most endowed and accomplished of men, . . . so that I have scarcely known another who had more aboundingly lived and wrought." (Crawford spoke more than a dozen languages, was a skillful public lecturer and reader, held master seaman's papers, was an amateur engineer and architect, and tried his hand as a silversmith and an artist.) James also reports that his cousin Mary Temple* knew Crawford's sister Annie in the United States in the old days. James and Crawford were opposed in their attitudes toward fiction. In his influential little book entitled *The Novel: What It Is* (1893), Crawford asserts that a novel is a luxury to provide the author money and the reader amusement; it should have no didactic purpose, should not merely picture and transcribe reality, should be idealistic, and may be called a "pocket theatre." James's library contained two books by Crawford.

Crawford, Thomas (1813?–1857). Neoclassical American sculptor, who was born in New York, trained and worked in Rome, and died of eye and brain cancer in London. He became very popular with traveling Americans, who placed ever-increasing numbers of orders for his often enormous works, usually in marble and bronze. His most famous pieces are the bronze doors of the Senate and the House of Representatives at the U.S. Capitol, *Freedom* (the bronze dome of the U.S. Capitol), *Progress of Civilization* (the Senate marble pediment at the U.S. Capitol), and the bronze *Washington Equestrian Monument* (Richmond, Virginia). In New York, in 1844, Crawford married Louisa Ward, the sister of Julia Ward Howe,* whom James knew. The couple lived in Rome. Crawford's widow married Luther Terry,* an expatriate American painter; James met them both in Rome, and also knew Crawford's son Francis Marion Crawford,* the popular and prolific novelist. The titular hero of James's *Roderick Hudson* may be patterned in part on Thomas Crawford. In *The American Scene*, James says that Crawford's *Washington* is of "high elegance . . . and yet . . . [is] indescribably archaic."

Crawford. In "Guest's Confession," a silver millionaire. He likes Clara Beck, Larua Guest's companion.

Crawford. In "Crawford's Consistency," a man who marries a lowbrow when Elizabeth Ingram jilts him. When he loses his fortune and becomes a druggist, his wife browbeats him and even cripples him by pushing him down the stairs.

Crawford, Mrs. In "Crawford's Consistency," Crawford's lowlife wife, who, after he loses his money, browbeats and cripples him. She later dies from overdrinking.

"Crawford's Consistency." Short story (11,700 words), published in *Scribner's Monthly* (Aug 1876). (Characters: Dr. Beadle, Mr. and Mrs. Crawford, Elizabeth Ingram, Peter and Sabrina Ingram, Niblett.) Rich and studious, young Crawford, a friend of the physician narrator, has been abruptly renounced by his socially ambitious, vapid fiancée, Elizabeth Ingram. He marries instead a common lowbrow and parades her before New York society. Elizabeth's second engagement is blasted when she contracts disfiguring smallpox. Crawford loses his money and becomes a druggist, and he is then crippled by his horrible wife when she pushes him down the stairs. The man never complains, since he has failed to provide her with money as promised. His wife later dies of drink. This story is weak and thinly melodramatic. James wrote to his father (11 Apr [1876]) that the "pretensions" of this story and "The Ghostly Rental" "are small." Proud Miss Ingram's loss of beauty echoes the fate of the haughty heroine in "Lady Eleanore's Mantle" by Nathaniel Hawthorne.*

Crawfurd, Oswald John Frederick (1834–1909). London-born, Eton-educated British consul at Oporto, Portugal (1866–1891). In his spare time there and strictly for recreation, he became a poet, essayist, editor, anthologist, playwright, and novelist. His travel books are *Travels in Portugal* (1875, under the pen name John Latouche), *Portugal Old and New* (1880), and *Round the Calendar in Portugal* (1890). His best novel is *Sylvia Arden* (1877). His first wife wrote a handbook on Spain. Crawfurd followed literary pursuits during his retirement in England and also in Switzerland, where he died. James reviewed (*Nation*, 21 Oct 1875) *Travels in Portugal* by John Latouche, beginning with this generalization: It is more important for a travel book to be about a little-known place than for the place discussed to be "worth knowing." He includes the snide remark that Portugal, which he never saw, is shown here to be "a good country to visit after one has been everywhere else." He praises the author for being "observant, humorous," sympathetic, and informative; but then he criticizes him for lacking "pictorial" skills, for narrative discontinuity, and for digressions (notably on the history of Portuguese Jews). James then details the traveler's route: Braganza, Oporto, Cintra, Lisbon, Elvas, and Guadiana, among other named places. Spain emerges in the book as a comparative winner, except for the fact that Portuguese bullfights are more "mild and tame." James later met Crawfurd; in 1896 he sent him his short story "The Way It Came" (later retitled "The Friends of the Friends") for *Chapman's Magazine of Fiction* (which Crawfurd edited). In 1907 he was embarrassed by comments from Violet Hunt* to the effect that she loved Crawfurd.

Creston, Kate. In "The Altar of the Dead," Paul Creston's deceased first wife.

Creston, Mrs. Paul. In "The Altar of the Dead," Paul Creston's present wife.

Creston, Paul. In "The Altar of the Dead," a man who displeased George Stransom by remarrying when his wife Kate, George's friend, died.

Crichton. In *The Golden Bowl*, Adam Verver's museum curator friend through whom Maggie Verver checks into her husband's Italian lineage.

Crick. In *The Ivory Tower*, Frank B. Betterman's estate lawyer who advises Betterman's heir, Graham Fielder.

Crimble, Hugh. In *The Outcry*, the novel, and *The Outcry*, the play, a young art scholar and Lady Grace's friend (age twenty-nine). He thinks Lord Theign's supposed Moretto is really a Mantovano.* At the end he is persuasive, and the two young people leave Theign's presence together. Crimble resembles James's close friend Sir Hugh Seymour Walpole* in physical appearance.

Crisford, Mr. and Mrs. In "The Wheel of Time," a minor host and hostess. He paints.

Crispin, Captain Charley. In "A London Life," one of Selina Berrington's lovers.

Crookenden, Mr. (Old Crook) and Mrs. In *The Princess Casamassima*, Hyacinth Robinson's London bookbinder employer and his wife. Hyacinth visits their home for Sunday tea. They hope that Hyacinth will propose to one of their six daughters.

Crookenden, The Misses. In *The Princess Casamassima*, the six Crookenden daughters.

Cross, John Walter (1840–1924). New York businessman and minor author. Two years after the death in 1878 of George Henry Lewes,* common-law husband of George Eliot,* Cross married Eliot but was widowed within months. James met Cross in London in 1877, was his dinner guest at the Devonshire Club in 1878, entertained Cross (together with others) at the Reform Club thereafter, and wrote a beautiful letter to Cross from Florence, Italy (14 May 1880) on the occasion of Cross's marriage to Eliot. Soon after she died, James paid Cross a visit of sympathy, which he described in a letter to Alice James (30 Jan 1881), relating that Cross had called himself "a cart-horse yoked to a racer." Cross narrated Eliot's life through an arrangement of her letters and journals (3 vols., 1885–1887) and also prepared an edition of her works (1908). In addition, he wrote about American railroads, bimetalism, Dante, farm labor, and New York society. James's library contained one book by Cross.

Crotty. In *The Princess Casamassima*, Susan Crotty's husband, who is a paroled convict.

Crotty, Susan. In *The Princess Casamassima*, a woman whom the princess gossips about, in imitation of Lady Aurora Langrish.

Croucher, Mrs. In *The Bostonians*, a New York feminist movement hostess.

Crouchley, Lord. In "The Death of the Lion," the subject of a publicity interview by the journalist narrator.

Crowe, Elizabeth (Lizzie, Liz). In "The Story of a Year," the light-headed Glenham girl who forgets her fiancé Lieutenant John Ford and falls in love with Robert Bruce.

Croy, Kate. In *The Wings of the Dove*, Lionel Croy's daughter, Marian Croy Condrip's sister, and Maude Manningham Lowder's niece. She loves Merton Densher and plots with him to have him obtain a fortune by marrying sick Milly Theale before she dies. Later, Milly's legacy to Densher spoils Kate's relationship with him.

Croy, Lionel. In *The Wings of the Dove*, the conniving father of Kate Croy and Marian Croy Condrip. His deceased wife was Maud Manningham Lowder's sister. One of their sons died of typhoid, another by drowning. Lionel disappears from the story very early.

Cubit. In *The Reprobate*, Bonsor's bribe-taking and humorously impolite butler.

Cuddon, Mrs. In *What Maisie Knew*, one of Beale Farange's mistresses.

Cumnor, John. In "The Aspern Papers," the narrator's British editor friend, who also admires Jeffrey Aspern's works.

Curd, Susan. In *The Awkward Age*, Mrs. Brookenham's maid.

Curtis, Ariana Randolph (née Wormeley) (1833–1922) and **Daniel Sargent Curtis** (1825–1908). Daniel Curtis came from a wealthy Boston family. He was a cousin of the father of John Singer Sargent.* Curtis's stepmother was Laura Greenough Curtis; hence Curtis was involved with the international Greenough family.* Curtis's wife Ariana was the daughter of a British admiral. They had a son named Ralph Wormeley Curtis (1854–1922). The couple together wrote a play called *The Coming Woman* . . . (1868). In the late 1860s, Daniel Curtis was jailed for hitting an apparently discourteous judge on a Boston train; after serving three months, he vowed to leave the United States permanently—and he did just that. In 1878 the expatriated Curtises settled in Venice, renting (1881) and then buying (1885) a large part of the Palazzo Barbaro on the Grand Canal there; they knew many of the Americans passing through or living in the region.

Their son, for example, escorted Isabella Stewart Gardner* through the Venetian museums in 1884. On occasion she rented the Curtis palazzo rooms (in August 1890, again in July–October 1892), entertaining James there in 1892. James knew the entire Curtis circle, including Mrs. Curtis's sister Katherine Prescott Wormeley,* who translated works by Honoré de Balzac* and other French authors. James often wrote to Mrs. Curtis (among others) to gossip about members of the American colony and their guests. The Curtises' rare Venetian garden may have inspired James when he described Juliana Bordereau's garden in "The Aspern Papers." According to a Notebook entry written in the Palazzo Barbaro (1 May 1899), James received from Mrs. Curtis the idea for his short story "The Tree of Knowledge," which sprang from a Greenough family anecdote. In a letter to Sir Edmund Wilson Gosse* ([18 Oct 1901]), James comprehensively calls the Palazzo Barbaro the "noblest of human habitations" and their occupants "the rare & racy Curtises." James may have had both Daniel Curtis and Edward Lee Childe* in mind when he depicted old Probert in *The Reverberator*. Ralph Curtis attended Harvard, returned to Europe (1881), married a rich widow, settled in Monte Carlo, and painted indifferently. He may be the model for the painter in "The Verdict," a 1908 short story by Edith Newbold Jones Wharton.*

Curtis, George William (1824–1892). American man of letters. Born in Providence, Rhode Island, he resided for a while at Brook Farm, traveled in and wrote about the Middle East, and then became a crusading editor, lecturer, and reform-organization official. He edited *Harper's Weekly* (from 1863 until his death), joined the staff of *Harper's New Monthly Magazine* (1853), and wrote "Easy Chair" editorials for it (from 1859 until his death). His best works include *Nile Notes of a Howadji* (1851, travel sketches), *Potiphar Papers* (1853, satirical sketches), *Prue and I* (1856, fantasy sketches), and *Trumps* (1861, sociopolitical novel). Charles Eliot Norton* edited his *Orations and Addresses* (3 vols., 1893–1894). Curtis defended James's book on Nathaniel Hawthorne* when it was adversely reviewed in the United States. James knew Curtis, and in letters to Norton and his sister Grace Norton* often sends him his best wishes.

Cutter, Mamie. In "Mrs. Medwin," Scott Homer's half-sister, who supports herself by getting people into British social parties.

Cynthia. In "A Landscape Painter," Captain Quarterman's old black maid.

D _____

Dadd, Miss. In "The Beldonald Holbein," Louisa Brash's deceased predecessor as Lady Beldonald's companion.

Daintry, Florimond. In "A New England Winter," the dilettante painter who takes a vacation from studying art in Paris to visit his mother in Boston.

Daintry, Lucretia. In "A New England Winter," the sister of Florimond Daintry's father. She rightly judges her nephew to be shallow and pretentious.

Daintry, Susan. In "A New England Winter," Florimond's mother, who foolishly wants Rachel Torrance to visit Boston to make her son's stay there more pleasant.

Daisy Miller: A Comedy. Dramatized version of James's celebrated 1878 short story "Daisy Miller: A Study." The play was privately printed at James's expense in 1882 to protect its copyright.

Daisy Miller: A Comedy in Three Acts. Dramatized version of James's 1878 story, privately printed as *Daisy Miller: A Comedy* in 1882; reprinted in the *Atlantic Monthly* (Apr–Jun 1883), and in Boston by Osgood, 1883. (Characters: Louisa Costello, Alice Durant, Eugenio, Miss Featherstone, Cavaliere Giacomo Giovanelli, Madame de Katkoff, Annie P. "Daisy" Miller, Ezra B. Miller, Mrs. Ezra B. Miller, Randolph Miller, Charles Reverdy, Mrs. Walker, Frederick Forsyth Winterbourne.) The first act takes place in the terrace and garden of a hotel in Vevey, Switzerland; the second and third acts, in Rome (first along the Pincian promenade, then in a Roman hotel public room with a balcony). Being blackmailed by the Miller family courier Eugenio, an attractive Russian widow named Madame de Katkoff continues to flirt with expatriated American Frederick Winterbourne to the annoyance of his aunt Mrs. Louisa Costello, who has come to Switzerland to introduce her young relative Alice Durant to her nephew, long resident in Geneva. The two American women are accompanied by Charles Reverdy, who loves Alice. Winterbourne is delighted but puzzled by Daisy Miller, who also arrives at Vevey with her rich mother and her little brother Randolph. Daisy talks Winterbourne into indiscreetly but harmlessly escorting her to the Castle of Chillon. Later in Rome, Daisy scandalizes the American colony (including Mrs. Walker, the consul's wife) by promenading unescorted with Giacomo Giovanelli. After many comings and goings, during which Eugenio forces Madame de Katkoff to play up to Winterbourne, now also here along with the other Americans, so that Giovanelli can have freer access to Daisy, Daisy contracts a fever because of going with Giovanelli to the Coliseum late one night. Madame de Katkoff reveals the truth to Winterbourne. He rescues the convalescent Daisy, who had been rashly taken by Giovanelli into the streets during the Roman carnival, and declares his love to her. Reverdy and Alice will also marry back home in America. Both Mrs. Walker and Mrs. Costello seem agreeable. Daisy's mother never appears on stage. Eugenio will find Giovanelli another heiress.

"Daisy Miller: A Study." Short story (23,100 words), published in the *Cornhill Magazine* (Jun–Jul 1878); reprinted in New York by Harper, 1878, and in London by Macmillan, as part of *Daisy Miller: A Study, An International Episode, Four Meetings*, 1879; revised and reprinted in *The Novels and Tales of Henry James*, Volume XVIII, 1909. (Characters: Mrs. Costello, Dr. Davis, Eugenio, Miss Featherstone, Giovanelli, Annie P. "Daisy" Miller, Mr. and Mrs. Ezra B. Miller, Randolph Miller, Mrs. Sanders, Mrs. Walker, Frederick Forsyth Winterbourne.) At Vevey, Switzerland, about 1875, Frederick Winterbourne sees pretty, thin-voiced, free-and-easy Daisy Miller, who is accompanied from America by her dull mother and bratty little brother Randolph. Their courier is Eugenio. In spite of his aunt Mrs. Costello's criticism of the gauche Millers, Winterbourne takes Daisy by boat over to the Château de Chillon and agrees to meet her next winter in Rome, where, at the home of an American friend named Mrs. Walker, he sees the girl again. He walks with her to meet her new Italian acquaintance Giovanelli, whom Mrs. Walker on the street beseeches the unmarried girl to discontinue being seen with in public. When innocent Daisy laughs and declines, Winterbourne sides with the proper Mrs. Walker, who later cruelly snubs the girl at a party the older woman gives. In annoyance, Daisy rejects Winterbourne's advice to leave Giovanelli alone. Imperceptive Mrs. Miller tells Winterbourne that she thinks her daughter and the Italian are engaged. The two stroll inside the miasmal Coliseum late one night—to Winterbourne's horror. Daisy becomes mortally ill, sends Winterbourne word that she fondly remembers their time on the lake at Vevey and that she was never engaged, and then dies. When at her grave Giovanelli tells Winterbourne that Miss Miller was the most innocent of girls, the Europeanized American has a long moment of self-doubt. This controversial story was James's first great success and remains his most famous short work. When it was rejected by *Lippincott's Magazine* in Philadelphia because it insulted American girls, James let Sir Leslie Stephen* publish it in his English *Cornhill Magazine* but was dilatory in protecting his American reprint rights. The story was promptly pirated twice; one such cheap edition sold 20,000 copies in short order. James later wrote to William Dean Howells* (17 Jun [1879]), "I have made $200 by the whole American career of D.M." James's sources for "Daisy Miller" include gossip about an easygoing American girl in Rome and also *Paul Méré* by Victor Cherbuliez.* This 1864 novel, mentioned in "Daisy Miller" by name, has a closely parallel plot: The action in each work of fiction starts in Switzerland and concludes in Italy; the free-and-easy heroine of each is slandered and otherwise hurt because she goes on unsupervised dates; and each has a weak "hero." James wrote from London to his brother William (23 Jul [1878]) that "Daisy Miller" "has been much noticed in the papers," further, that "the thing is sufficiently subtle, yet people appear to have comprehended it. It has given me a capital start here." He immediately wrote "An International Episode" as a contrasting companion piece. James broke a rule of his by writing a celebrated letter, to Eliza Lynn Linton* (Aug 1880), to explain what his story meant: Daisy was innocent, wounded, undefiant, unaggressive, sentimental, and nonflirtatious; and her story is "a little tragedy." James dramatized the work in 1882; the play was rejected, was privately printed (1882), and was serialized (as *Daisy Miller: A Comedy*) and also published (as *Daisy Miller: A Comedy in Three Acts*) the next year. In the preface to Volume XVIII of *The Novels and Tales of Henry James*, James explains that the Philadelphia editor saw "Daisy Miller" both as "an outrage on American girlhood" and as of a "disfavour[ed]" *nouvelle* length. He calls his heroine "scant and superficially vulgar," of a sort seen later in Venice with a friend, who accordingly accused James of depicting "awful young women" as graceful and pathetic. James counters by saying that he meant Daisy to be "pure poetry" and nothing else. The appeal of the story lies in Daisy's nature and her motivation, and also in Winterbourne's hesitation. Later printings of the story sometimes dropped the subtitle "A Study." In his long essay on Alphonse Daudet* (*Century Magazine*, Aug 1883), James implicitly defined "study" as a writing which is restrictive and observant and which involves truth without being literal. "Daisy Miller" may reflect James's admiration of "Asia," an early story (1858) by his friend Ivan Sergeyevich Turgenev.* In it, a cocky but hesitant Russian on holiday in Germany meets a strange girl called Asia, who combines shyness and forwardness; she could love him but for his indecisiveness, and so departs.

Daisy Miller: A Study, An International Episode, Four Meetings. Collection of three short stories published in London by Macmillan, 1879.

Dallow, George. In *The Tragic Muse*, Julia Sherringham Dallow's deceased husband.

Dallow, Julia Sherringham. In *The Tragic Muse*, George Dallow's widow and Peter Sherringham's sister. She loves Nicholas Dormer but will marry him only if he quits painting and enters politics.

Daly, John Augustin (1838–1899). Realistic playwright and theater manager, born in North Carolina and reared in New York City. He directed amateur theatrical performances in New York and was also a drama critic for newspapers there (1859–1869). He also opened and refurbished theaters in New York (1869–1879). Daly wrote or adapted about ninety plays, including *Leah the Forsaken* (1862), *Under the Gaslight* (1867), *Divorce* (1871), and *Horizon* (1871). After 1879 he did only adaptations and managerial work. He opened a theater in London in 1893. His progressive company, which included Maude Adams, Fanny Davenport, John Drew, Ada C. Rehan,* and Otis Skinner, offered popular, edited versions of comedies by William Shakespeare* and adaptations of German and French plays. Daly attended the opening performance of James's play *The American* in London, on 26 September 1891. At the request of his friend Ada Rehan, James offered his play *Disengaged* to Daly and his London company in October 1892. After reading, liking, and accepting the play, Daly demanded so many revisions and, according to letters by James, rehearsed it so badly that the author angrily withdrew it from further consideration in December 1893. In a letter to William James (29 Dec 1893), James calls Daly ''an utter cad.''

Damant, Sir Ralph, Bart. In *The Album*, a distant relative of Bedford, owner of Courtlands. When Sir Ralph lies about another relative, named Mark Moorsom Bernal, Bedford wills the estate to Sir Ralph and dies. Women then pursue him. To avoid Lady Basset, he gives the estate to Mark.

Damerel, Mrs. In ''The Great Condition,'' an American widow. She loves Bertram Braddle but marries Henry Chilver. Braddle wrongly suspects her past and loses; Chilver does not and wins.

Dandelard, M. and Mme. In *The American*, a brutal wife-beating Frenchman and his long-suffering wife. An Italian, she entered French society through marriage. Christopher Newman sympathizes with her, but to no avail.

Dane, George. In ''The Great Good Place,'' the terribly oppressed writer who dreams of spirit-restoring rest at a ''great good place.''

Dangerfield, Mrs. In ''Pandora,'' a shipboard companion of Count Otto Vogelstein. She lectures him on American social customs.

"Daniel Deronda: A Conversation." A critical essay, published in the *Atlantic Monthly* (Dec 1876); reprinted in *Partial Portraits*, 1888. Written in dialogue form, it concerns the novel *Daniel Deronda* (1876) by George Eliot. (Characters: Constantius, Fido, Pulcheria, Theodora.)

D'Annunzio, Gabriele (1863–1938). Important Italian poet, dramatist, fiction writer, and political essayist, and a combat pilot. He was born in Pescara and was educated in Florence and Rome. James published a long essay on D'Annunzio (*Quarterly Review*, Apr 1904; reprinted in *Notes on Novelists*, 1914), in which he comments on the Italian's novels to the earlier date: *Il Piacere* (1889), *L'Innocente* (1892), *Il Trionfo della morte* (1894), *Le Vergini delle Rocce* (1895), and *Il Fuoco* (1900). He begins with praise of D'Annunzio's quick artistic maturity, authentic artistry, and "amplitude of portrayal" in the novels. He compares certain translations, preferring G. Hérelle's 1899 *Le Triomphe de la morte* to others. (James evidently read at least some of D'Annunzio's works in the original.) The essence of James's critical commentary is this: "[T]he author's three sharpest signs are . . . first his rare notation of states of excited sensibility; second his splendid visual sense, the quick generosity of his response . . . to the beauty of places and things; third his ample and exquisite style, his . . . active employment of language as a means of communication and representation." James expands on these comments at length, summarizing plots and offering generous quotations. He calls *Il Trionfo* and *Il Fuoco* "the amplest and richest of our author's histories," but he treats more fully *Le Vergini* ("this exquisite composition"). He compares D'Annunzio, for his handling of "miseries and ecstasies," to Émile Zola* himself. But then he adversely criticizes D'Annunzio, the "total beauty" of whose works "fails to march with their beauty of parts." There is an "incessant *leak*," somehow, as of gas in a garden. D'Annunzio, says James, assigns too great a value to mere "zoological sociability" (i.e., sex), which without "congruity with the rest of life" becomes "sterilising passion." James closes by praising D'Annunzio's "fine images" and then offers a memorable one of his own, saying that the Italian novelist's shutting sexual passion from other activities gives it "no more dignity than . . . the boots and shoes that we see, in the corridors of promiscuous hotels, standing, often in double pairs, at the doors of rooms. Detached . . . these . . . objects present . . . no importance. What the participants do with their agitation . . . is the stuff of poetry, and it is never really interesting save when something finely contributive in themselves makes it so." Of this startling image of shoes Sir Max Beerbohm* made his best caricature of his wide-eyed friend James. James's library contained four books by D'Annunzio.

Darcy. In "An Animated Conversation," an observant, astute, optimistic American critic in London.

Darmesteter, Mary. The married name of a woman (later Mary Duclaux) whom James first met when she was Agnes Mary Frances Robinson.*

"Darmstadt" (1873 title, "An Ex-Grand-Ducal Capital"). Travel essay, published in the *Nation* (9 Oct 1873); reprinted in *Transatlantic Sketches*, 1875. In it, James discusses Darmstadt, a petty duchy until "the serpent" Bismarck "smoothly" swallowed it in 1866. In the sleepy town square, James notes a "heroic bronze" statue of Darmstadt's Grand-Duke Louis the First ("small potentate"), a few "droshkies," "sober" government buildings, loafers, and soldiers. He walks past "crooked" streets, "odorous" gutters, and their unpicturesque pools. The Schloss is ugly but picturesque: "solemn" façades, courts and dark archways, "queer . . . bell-tower," "a pile of . . . windows, roofs, and chimneys," pleasant moat, and spike-helmeted soldiers. He visits its musty library and unimpressive picture gallery with "acres . . . of mouldering brushwork," including some "dishonest" landscapes. James says that "German art rarely seems to me a happy adventure." But ecstasy comes when he stands before a "lovely Virgin holding her child," painted by Hans Holbein the younger* in Prince Karl's residence.

Darwin, Charles Robert (1809–1882). Eminent British naturalist, whose momentous discoveries and theories on evolution are expounded in *Zoology on the Voyage of the Beagle* (1840), *On the Origin of Species by Means of Natural Selection* (1859), *The Variation of Animals and Plants under Domestication* (1868), *The Descent of Man* (1871), and elsewhere. Through Charles Eliot Norton,* James met Darwin in Kent, outside London, in March 1869. Darwin was survived by two daughters and five sons. Four of his sons—George, Francis, Leonard, and Horace Darwin—were distinguished scientists. The fifth (and oldest), William Darwin, James knew socially, as well as that man's wife Sara (Sally) Sedgwick Darwin, the sister of Norton's wife. James often wrote to his family and to Grace Norton* about Sara and William Darwin, both before and after their marriage, and usually in disparagement. For one harsh example, he wrote to his brother William (28 Jan [1878]) that "Sara seems utterly unchanged by matrimony—neither exhilarated nor depressed: very sweet, soft, gentle and without initiative. . . . She has a densely English husband. . . . Darwin is a gentle, kindly, reasonable, liberal, bald-headed, dull-eyed, British-featured, sandy-haired little *insulaire* . . . " James often accepted overnight hospitality at the Darwins' home. He wrote to "dear Sally" as late as 1910.

Dashwood, Basil. In *The Tragic Muse*, an actor who provides an entrée for Miriam Rooth into London theatrical circles and later marries her.

Dashwood, Mrs. Basil. In *The Tragic Muse*, the married name of Miriam Rooth.

Daudet, Alphonse (1840–1897). French novelist, short-story writer, and autobiographer. He was born in Nîmes, had an unhappy childhood, was an usher at a school in Alais, and lived with his older brother, the historian and novelist Ernest Daudet, in Paris. Alphonse Daudet then began to enjoy a somewhat too bohemian youth, wrote poetry and plays, became Duc Charles-Auguste de Morny's secretary (until 1865), published short stories, collected as *Lettres de mon moulin* (1866) and *Contes du Lundi* (1873), and much later his autobiography, entitled *Trente ans de Paris* (1887). Happily marrying the writer Julie Allard (1847–1940) in 1867, Daudet began to publish fiction of an impressionistic, naturalistic turn, including *Le Petit Chose* (1868), *Les Aventures prodigieuses de Tartarin de Tarascon* (1872), *Fromont jeune et Risler aîné* (1874), *Robert Helmont* (1874), *Jack* (1876), *Le Nabab* (1877), *Les Rois en exil* (1879), *Numa Roumestan* (1881), *L'Evangéliste* (1883), *Sapho* (1884), *Tartarin sur les Alpes* (1885), *L'Immortel* (1888), and *Port Tarascon* (1890). Daudet knew Gustave Flaubert* and members of his *cénacle*, including Edmond de Goncourt,* who died in Daudet's home. The Daudets had three children (Léon, Lucien, and Edmée), of whom the politician novelist Léon Daudet (1867–1942) was the most unusual. This young man married a granddaughter of Victor-Marie Hugo,* divorced her, became a violently neo-royalist and anti-Semitic journalist of fearful invective, was in politics briefly, sued a man to try to prove his son Philippe Daudet's presumed suicide was murder, was fined and imprisoned, was freed by a royalist trick, and escaped to Belgium. James met Alphonse Daudet (avowedly anti-Semitic, like his son later) at Flaubert's Paris apartment in January 1876 and at first did not especially like him. In a letter to his mother (24 Jan [1876]), James calls the whole group "a queer lot, and intellectually very remote from my own sympathies." He wrote to his sister Alice (22 Feb [1876]) that it sickened him to hear Ivan Sergeyevich Turgenev* praising Daudet's *Jack* at a Flaubert gathering. In a letter to his friend Thomas Sergeant Perry* (2 May 1876), James describes Daudet as "a little fellow . . . with a refined and picturesque head, of a Jewish type. . . . A brilliant talker and *raconteur*. A Bohemian. An extreme imitator of [Charles] Dickens[*]—but a *froid*, without D.'s real exuberance." He adds that he much prefers Gustave Droz* to Daudet. James translated Daudet's fine eulogy on Ivan Turgenev (as "Tourguénieff in Paris: Reminiscences by Daudet," *Century Magazine*, Nov 1883). When James revisited Paris in 1884, he was able through his friend Theodore E. Child* to call upon the Daudets at their Rue de Bellechasse home in February and thus start a lifelong friendship of great joy to both literary men. (Child described the meeting in a May 1884 *Atlantic Monthly* essay.) Back in London, James wrote to Child (8 Mar [1884]) about the "divine" Daudet. Late in 1885 James, again in Paris, missed Daudet, who was absent through a dreadful sickness. (By 1878 the consequences of his bohemian youth had caught up with him when third-stage syphilis attacked him. By 1885 he had locomotor ataxia; within five years, he was taking chloral daily.) In 1889 James translates—"for pure and copious lucre [£350]," as he wrote to Grace Norton* (22 Sep [1889])—Daudet's *Port Tarascon*, going to Paris to do so. James was furious that in the serial publication of his quick translation (though not in the later book version) a seemingly anti-Catholic chapter (the fifth) was omitted. In March and April 1893 James was again in Paris, where he dined several times with Daudet and may possibly have met Marcel Proust* at the Daudets' home. Later that year James wrote to Grace Norton (20 Aug [1893]) that Daudet was "pathetic, . . . incurable." All the same, the life-loving man wrote to James that he and his wife, their three grown children, and even Victor Hugo's grandson Georges Hugo and his wife, all planned to visit England for three weeks in May 1895. Daudet asked James to make arrangements. James obtained hotel accommodations, escorted the group to Oxford University and Windsor, took Daudet to Box Hill, Surrey, to meet similarly paralytic George Meredith,* and hosted a large dinner party for Daudet at the Reform Club. One side effect of the sociable invasion was James's deepened awareness of his dislike of Daudet's son Léon, whom he recalled in a much later letter to Sir Edmund Wilson Gosse* (25 Jun 1915) as "perversely base & publicly pernicious," "the cleverest idiot & the most poisonous talent imaginable," and who he went on to predict might "swing." A happier result of the visit was Daudet's touching letter to James immediately upon his return to Paris saying, in effect, that Daudet had long admired James's talent but now hoped for his total friendship. Daudet's disease caused kidney trouble, which in turn caused James to pun in a letter to Gosse ([28 Apr 1895]) about the Frenchman's fear of "the flow of something more than either soul or champagne at dinner." Several years later, James declined to cross the English Channel to attend Daudet's December funeral, but to his widow he wrote a magnificent letter in French, of which language Daudet had long admired James's mastery. James frequently wrote about Daudet's literary production. His earliest such notice was a review (*Galaxy*, Aug 1875) of Daudet's *Fromont jeune et Risler aîné*, which the young reviewer finds "labored and cold." He adds that its depiction of the heroine's descent to hell is not different enough from Flaubert's earlier handling of the theme. Acknowledging that Daudet does present "pretty episodes," James charges the novelist with going astray while trying to follow Charles Dickens.* James reviewed (*Atlantic Monthly*, Jun 1882) Alphonse Daudet's brother Ernest Daudet's 1882 *Mon Frère et moi: Souvenir d'enfance et jeunesse*, calling it a work of courageous emotion, no reticence, taste, but too much puffing. Authors should live in their writings, not in their autobiographies or biographies. James summarizes Daudet's early life, calls the man a charming storyteller, best in short fiction and the novel *Les Rois en exil* (with its "light, warm, frank Provençal element"). Daudet is observant, feeling, painterly, satirical. He pleases at the expense of truth (à la Charles Dickens, contra Émile Zola*). Daudet's Parisian works are "false" when too imaginative. Some of his heroines are not "solid" (see *Fromont jeune et Risler aîné*). *Jack* has too much pathos. *Le Nabab* has a fine "gallery of portraits." Daudet excellently portrays real-life personages in his fiction. Where Zola is a deep observer, Daudet—"the happiest novelist of our day"—notes "the immediate, the expressive, the actual." James then published a long essay on Daudet (*Century Magazine*, Aug 1883; reprinted in *Partial Portraits*, 1888), in which he partly repeats himself. Daudet, "a pictorial artist," is now "at the head of his profession." James admires his *Lettres de mon moulin* ("perfect vignettes"), *Les Rois en exil* (which is "simple," has much "of the beautiful"), and especially *Numa Roumestan* ("a masterpiece" and "so happy a work" in spite of certain Zola strictures). *Jack, Le Nabab* (which shows off its author's "gymnastics of observation"), and *L'Evangéliste* have some unfelt characters. Daudet's works reveal his temperament, versatility, perceptions, and "*modernité*," but also his relative lack of concern with the moral world and with abstractions. Among Flaubert's dry, hard circle, Daudet alone is beautifully soft, with a Southern heart to go with his Northern mind. Unlike English and American writers, he is self-revelatory. He now possesses Paris, and readers not Parisianized cannot appreciate him fully. *Le Nabab* and *Les Rois en exil* have individualized characters, including some sketched protestingly from real life. Daudet observes better than he invents, and then he transmutes the observed into feeling humor. *Les Aventures prodigieuses de Tartarin de Tarascon* is high-spirited satire of the Provençal foible of preferring the imaginary to the real and then making it real. *Le Petit Chose* has Dickensian touches. *Fromont jeune et Risler aîné* is a "study" of life in the Marais quarter of seventeenth-century Paris, here depicted feelingly. *Jack*, which James summarizes at some length, has a well-drawn selfish mother and a bullying lover but overuses pathos. Here James briefly discusses literary criticism by Charles Dudley Warner,* which is "just" in condemning "the abuse of pathos" but incorrect in saying that a novel should "entertain." James feels that it should represent life, enlarge our experience. *L'Evangéliste*, too recently published for James to consider in detail, betrays Daudet's lack of knowledge of the coldly religious personality; therefore, its Madame Autheman is not a bigot but "simply a dusky effigy." Finally, James concedes that Daudet has few ideas but adds that one likes Daudet and that makes him "important." When James translated Daudet's *Port Tarascon: The Last Adventures of the Illustrious Tartarin*, he published his preface to it separately (*Harper's New Monthly Magazine*, Jun 1890) and then with the book (New York, Harper, 1891; London, Sampson Low, 1891). James recommends that all readers begin with the first two books, since they plus *Port Tarascon* form a consistent artistic unit. The picturesque hero from his touched-up Provençal town, which contrasts with cold, gray Northern climes, is " 'Don Quixote in the skin of Sancho Panza.' " Tartarin's intentions plus his mistakes equal the unsimplifiably antagonistic ambiguity of life. He and we want glory plus self-preservation. The resulting compromises are grotesque but inevitable. At the end, Tartarin is betrayed by his compromises. The moral is that if life lays traps for us, art provides us firm ground. Finally, nine days after Daudet died, James published a moving eulogy (*Literature*, 25 Dec 1897), in which he praised his friend as the last of Flaubert's now-antique group save Zola. In his productive years Daudet squeezed his talent dry, beat out all his gold, planted his entire garden. He exhausted his Midi for picture and point of view. He was vivid, warm, observant, touching. Unlike Flaubert, who attacked his canvas with a twenty-foot brush, Daudet stayed close to it and his readers. He was agitated, nervous; he caught talk in his net of style; he jumped from bit to bit, that is, was episodic; he evoked detail (see his "unsurpassable" eulogy of Edmond de Goncourt). James likes Daudet best among novelists without a high order of moral imagination, which he shows to a degree in *Sapho*. But he regularly lets us commiserate and laugh without pointing the moral. He turned finally to pity, melancholy, pessimism—but never bitterly. James sums up his Daudet with one word—"warmth." In a letter to Gosse (28 Aug [1896]), James privately called Daudet's eulogy of Goncourt "a little miracle of art." Late in his life, James enjoyed discussing Daudet, and Flaubert as well, with his Rye neighbor Sir Sydney Philip Waterlow.* Entries in his Notebooks make it clear that James the fiction writer was inspired by several specific works by Daudet. In one (8 Apr 1883) he records a letter he wrote to his publisher about *The Bostonians*, in which he says, "Daudet's *Évangéliste* has given me the idea of this thing." Another entry (19 Jun 1884) shows that James's 1888 short story "The Liar" derives in part from Daudet's *Numa Roumestan*. Yet another (5 Jan 1888) suggests that Daudet's *Trente ans de Paris* contributed to "The Lesson of the Master." James's library contained nineteen books by Daudet, in addition to one by his wife, eight by his son Léon, and one by his son Lucien.

Daumier, Honoré (1808–1879). Marseilles-born caricaturist and painter. He began his career by making plates for music publishers and pictures for advertisements, then he joined the staff of the newly established journal *La Caricature*, for which in 1832 he drew an offensive cartoon of Louis Philippe that landed him in jail for six months. Daumier then began his long association with the *Charivari*, drawing caricatures satirizing bourgeois follies, political corruption, governmental incompetence, and pseudo-classicism in the arts. He produced almost four thousand lithographs. In his serious paintings of biblical and literary scenes, Daumier prefigured naturalism. In 1878 a Paris exhibition was held to show his extraordinary range, by which time, Daumier had been blind for many years. James wrote an essay on Daumier ("Daumier, Caricaturist," *Century Magazine*, Jan 1890; reprinted as "Honoré Daumier" in *Picture and Text*, 1893), in which he places the man in a context of caricaturists including George Cruickshank, George Du Maurier,* Paul Gavarni, and John Leech. The "essence of the[ir] art . . . is to be historical"; they varyingly use "[i]rony, scepticism, pessimism," and they fasten on human weaknesses. Recently James had seen "superannuated piles" of copies of innumerable 1830–1855 Daumier lithographs in an old Parisian shop, had spent hours looking at them, had bought some, and had returned later to immerse himself anew. James reviews Daumier's life, on the basis of varied biographical and catalogue material. He says that Daumier shows "intensity of force" but is "too simple" to rank with Gavarni. Yet his simplicity enables him to single out the "hauntingly characteristic" in given targets for satire, especially Louis Adolphe Thiers, often imaged as "a clever owl." Daumier also drew cartoons, each with "a few masterly strokes," of swindlers and political bosses. Many once-eminent people are preserved only in these pictures. In truth, all art "preserves, . . . consecrates, . . . raises from the dead." Even though Daumier overemphasizes "the old and ugly" and leaves out "youth and beauty," happy children, and people with good manners, we agree that he is predominant—because he is "so peculiarly serious." Further, "the absolute bourgeois hems him in," and he reproduces it because "he is a bourgeois himself, without poetic ironies, to whom a big cracked mirror has been given." James identifies some of his favorite Daumier efforts. More recent caricaturists may have "more cunning," but he has "an impressive depth."

"Daumier, Caricaturist." Original title (1890) of "Honoré Daumier" in *Picture and Text*, 1893.

Davenant, Lady. In "A London Life," Laura Wing's pragmatic confidante. She is the companion of Lionel Berrington's expropriated mother. According to a Notebook entry (20 Jun 1887), she is modeled after Mrs. Duncan Stewart,* the mother of Christina Stewart Rogerson,* with whom Sir Charles Wentworth Dilke* was involved in the 1880s.

Davenant, Lord. In *The Tragic Muse*, an embassy official back in Mrs. Rooth's youth.

David. In "A Problem," Emma's husband. According to Magawisca's prophecy, their child dies and they remarry (each other).

David. In "Guest's Confession," the narrator. He is Edgar Musgrave's stepbrother, and he falls in love with Laura Guest.

Davidoff. In "The Siege of London," an ambassador invited by the Demesnes to their estate.

Davis, Rebecca Harding (née Blaine) (1831–1910). Philadelphia novelist and mother of Richard Harding Davis.* She started her career by writing a realistic account of a typical iron-mill town, then branched into fiction long and short concerning poverty and war, favoring blacks, and criticizing political corruption and lobbying. James reviewed (*Nation*, 21 Nov 1867) her *Waiting for the Verdict* (1868). He flippantly summarizes its dual plot: One young Northern heroine of humble background meets reformable Southern hero; another heroine, from South, meets weird old Northern surgeon, in whose veins "run . . . a few drops of negro blood." Mrs. Davis's purpose, inartistically achieved, is "to contrast . . . distinctively Northern and Southern modes of life and of feeling." The writer has "cultured strength" but strains for "realistic effects" marred by "lachrymose sentimentalism." James closes by fulminating against tearjerkers in general. Next he reviewed (*Nation*, 22 Oct 1868) Mrs. Davis's *Dallas Galbraith* (1868), calling it more natural and truthful but then digressing to rebuke vapid literary critics, even citing Harriet Beecher Stowe* as an example. He ridicules the tangled plot of *Dallas Galbraith*, which features "false" and "unreal" characters, especially an innocent, selfless youth imprisoned for forgery committed by a villain who combines unmixable traits, but also including "a coarse caricature," "a vulgar effigy" of a villainess. Mrs. Davis is earnest and sentimental, but not intellectually exciting. Art is too important to be so trickily treated.

Davis, Richard Harding (1864–1916). Widely popular American journalist, foreign reporter (of six wars), and melodramatic novelist and playwright. He was the son of Rebecca Harding Davis.* In one year he covered the Czar's coronation, the millennial celebration in Budapest, Queen Victoria's Jubilee, and several other events—all of which he wrote up in *A Year from a Reporter's Note-Book* (1898). In "American Letter" (16 Apr 1898), James sarcastically comments on this work as Davis's response to "our growing world-hunger" for "alert, familiar journalism," adding that Davis "gobbles up with the grace of a sword-swallower the showiest events of a remarkably showy year." James comments that the Jubilee "can scarcely have been better than his [Davis's] account of it."

Davis, Dr. In "Daisy Miller," the Miller family physician back home in Schenectady.

Dawes, Miss. In "The Story of a Year," a Ford family neighbor.

Dawling. In "Glasses," Geoffrey's father, who works in the Treasury.

Dawling, Geoffrey. In "Glasses," the unflappable admirer of Flora Saunt who marries her when she goes blind.

Dawling, The Misses. In "Glasses," Geoffrey Dawling's four sisters, who reside in Bournemouth.

Dawson. In "A Landscape Painter," a Chowderville storekeeper.

"A Day of Days." Short story (8,600 words), published in the *Galaxy* (15 Jun 1866); reprinted in *Stories Revived*, 1885. (Characters: Becky, Laura Benton, Thomas Ludlow, Adela and Herbert Moore, Rev. Mr. Weatherby Pynsent.) Adela Moore is living with her brother Herbert, a scientist, near Slowfield. Thomas Ludlow calls at Moore's house to try, without success, to see Herbert before going to Europe to study. He and Adela take a wistful walk and then part later in the afternoon. This story is James's earliest treatment of the theme of "what might have been," later handled more subtly in, for example, "The Aspern Papers" and "The Beast in the Jungle."

Day. In "Pandora," Pandora's weak-willed brother, age nineteen.

Day, Miss. In "Pandora," Pandora's young sister.

Day, Mr. and Mrs. P. W. In "Pandora," Pandora's sleepy parents from Utica. Pandora treats them considerately.

Day, Pandora. In "Pandora," a self-made American girl. She impresses Otto Vogelstein aboard ship and later in Washington, D.C. She will marry D. F. Bellamy, whom she wheedles the president of the United States into appointing minister to Holland.

The Days of a Year. A nature diary by a woman named M. D. Ashley Dodd,* published in London by Elkin Mathews, in 1907. When it was republished in London by Herbert Jenkins, in 1912, it included an "appreciation" in the form of a letter by James (30 Sep 1907).

Deacon, Edward Parker (1844–1901). American whom James knew slightly in London but did not admire. Parker killed his wife's lover in Cannes, France, and was imprisoned for a time. According to Notebook entries (28 Feb 1892, 15 Jun 1901), James planned a short story inspired by Parker's initial domestic mess but left only a June 1893 fragment, which he tentatively called "E. P. D. Subject."

Dean. In "The Bench of Desolation," the crooked partner of Drury, Nan Drury's father.

Deane, Drayton. In "The Figure in the Carpet," the third-rate critic who marries Gwendolyn Corvick after her husband George's death. Deane can tell the narrator nothing of any "figure" in Vereker's works.

Deane, Gwendolyn Erme Corvick. In "The Figure in the Carpet," the later name of Gwendolyn Erme Corvick.

"The Death of the Lion." Short story (13,400 words), published in the *Yellow Book* (Apr 1894); reprinted in *Terminations*, 1895; revised and reprinted in *The Novels and Tales of Henry James*, Volume XV, 1909. (Characters: Miss Braby, Lord Crouchley, Mr. and Mrs. Deedy, Lord Dorimont, Dora Forbes, Fanny Hurter, Mrs. Milsom, Lady Augusta Minch, Morrow, Mr. and Mrs. Neil Paraday, Pinhorn, Rumble, Guy Walsingham, Mr. and Mrs. Weeks Wimbush.)

Pinhorn, an editor, sends the narrator to interview novelist Neil Paraday, but the essay which results is rejected as too impersonal. The narrator begins to feel that likable old Paraday is going to be hurt by publicity. Morrow of *The Empire* magazine enters, and the narrator keeps the novelist's latest fine novel from him. So Morrow writes a chatty essay on the lion's home life. Londoner Mrs. Weeks Wimbush continues the lionizing process, showing off old Paraday at her country estate at Prestidge alongside novelists Guy Walsingham (a woman) and Dora Forbes (a man). Paraday is amused, professes to feel helpless but really contributes to his plight, grows sick, and soon dies, even as Lady Augusta Minch and Lord Dorimont deny knowing the whereabouts of Paraday's unpublished manuscript, circulating on loan between them. The narrator takes up with Fanny Hurter, whom he persuaded earlier not to bother Paraday for an autograph; together they will seek the missing literary treasure. A long Notebook entry (3 Feb 1894) sketches the plot of ''The Death of the Lion,'' which had the lead position of the first issue of the controversial *Yellow Book*. The story was longer than it needed to be because editor Henry Harland* offered James the inducement of much space. James must have seen himself as lionizable; so the story has an autobiographical touch, although totally without self-pity and although James would never have submitted to social exploitation the way Paraday foolishly does. In a letter to William James and his wife (28 May 1894), James self-deprecatingly boasts that ''The Death of the Lion'' ''appears to have had, for a thing of mine, an unusual success''; he goes on to complain of ''the horrid . . . company'' the story keeps in the *Yellow Book*. In the preface to Volume XV of *The Novels and Tales of Henry James*, James expresses delight at being permitted by Harland to write expansively, calling ''the beautiful and blest *nouvelle*'' ''— for length and breadth—our ideal.'' Furthermore, he suggests that he need not identify any specific source for the plot concerning his Neil Paraday because he has ''again and again closely noted in the social air all the elements of such a drama.'' The satiric point of ''The Death of the Lion'' is that famous authors are less read than sought for chic party value. The story is saved from being sad not only by its pervasive ironic and comic tone, but also by its unique ending: Two young people marry and pursue an impossible dream, symbolized by a sought-for but never-to-be-found literary treasure.

''The Deathbed Notes of Henry James.'' James's last attempts at dictation (original title: ''Henry James's Last Dictation''), published in the *Times Literary Supplement* (2 May 1968), and reprinted in the *Atlantic Monthly* (June 1968). The notes reveal mental confusion, verbal mastery, rich imagery, memories of places, recollections of war and history reading, and the physical appearance of Bonapartes; they include letters (one as from Napoleon) concerning the decoration of Parisian palaces.

Deborah. In "De Grey, A Romance," Mrs. De Grey's servant.

Deborah, Miss. In "The Ghostly Rental," the local gossip who tells the narrator part of Captain Diamond's story.

Decamps, Alexandre-Gabriel (1803–1860). French painter who traveled in Italy and then the Middle East (1827–1828), after which he exploited Oriental subjects. Along with Ferdinand Victor Eugène Delacroix,* he helped develop Orientalism in French art. In his review of *Contemporary French Painters* (1868) by Philip Gilbert Hamerton,* James criticizes Decamps's paintings for showing a "fund of reality," but also weakness and an absence of cleverness. In "Art" (*Atlantic Monthly*, Jan 1872), he describes some Decamps efforts as honest but "a little blank and thin" and "ambiguous." In "The Bethnal Green Museum" (1873), he says that Decamps is the occasion of enjoyment but not praise, but then he does praise the movement in a certain Eastern scene. James oddly notes that Decamps treats simple and complex subjects identically.

Dedrick, Maud-Evelyn. In "Maud-Evelyn," the Dedricks' deceased daughter.

Dedrick, Mr. and Mrs. In "Maud-Evelyn," deceased Maud-Evelyn's chronically grieving parents. They, along with Marmaduke, gradually build up an imaginary life in which he becomes their son-in-law, although in actuality he never saw the girl.

Deedy, Mr. and Mrs. In "The Death of the Lion," the deceased owner editor of a periodical, and his widow. The periodical is taken over by Pinhorn.

Deepmere, Lord. In *The American*, the insipid, unattractive young Irishman who is Madame de Bellegarde's cousin and who is unsuccessfully interested in her daughter Claire de Cintré. After the death of Claire's brother Valentin de Bellegarde, Christopher Newman sees Deepmere and Noémie Nioche together in London. In *The American: A Comedy in Four Acts*, Deepmere is English, gives Madame de Bellegarde an inventory of his land holdings, and is thereafter preferred by her as a son-in-law, but he kills her son Valentin de Bellegarde in a duel (over Bellegarde family etiquette and also over Noémie Nioche), is wounded himself, and does not reappear. In the rewritten fourth act, Deepmere does reappear, helps Claire to leave her convent (before taking vows) and thus to see Newman again, is happy when Valentin recovers after surgery, and also makes up to Noémie.

Deerfield Summer School. A symposium held in 1889 at Deerfield, Massachusetts. Invited to attend for the purpose of discussing novel writing, James declined by a courteous letter, which was read to the group and then published (New York *Tribune*, 4 Aug 1889). In it, James objected gently to the conference theme—"the materialism of our present tendencies"—and complained that there was too much talk and too little important writing. He then urged the students to see life, be free, write from unique points of view, and thus make novels "multifarious and illustrative."

De Forest, John William (1826–1906). American novelist and Civil War veteran. Before the war he traveled in the South; after the war he served as a Freedmen's Bureau official in South Carolina. He was a versatile writer, concerning himself with historical fiction, mystery novels, political satire, and travel fiction. His most famous novel, *Miss Ravenel's Conversion from Secession to Loyalty* (1867), was the first competent fictional account of the Civil War from a realistic point of view. De Forest's other works include *Witching Times* (1857), *Seacliff* (1859), *Overland* (1871), *Kate Beaumont* (1872), *The Wetherell Affair* (1873), *Honest John Vane* (1875), *Playing the Mischief* (1875), *Irene the Missionary* (1879), *The Bloody Chasm* (1881), and *A Lover's Revolt* (1898). His war letters and essays were published in 1946 and 1948. James reviewed (*Nation*, 31 Dec 1874) *Honest John Vane*, quickly objecting to the "turbid" style of its satire, which is about "unclean and unscrupulous" political lobbyists. James regards De Forest as possessed of "more energy than delicacy," and he savagely summarizes the central, " 'self-made' " villain's progress from simple to corrupt. The book is undramatic and flat, and it features grotesquely sketched minor characters. Its political "aroma" is deliberately "vulgar." James wonders why such a book should ever have been written.

"De Grey, A Romance." Short story (13,000 words), published in the *Atlantic Monthly* (Jul 1868). (Characters: Margaret Aldis, Deborah, Blanche Ferrars, Mary Fortescue, Antonietta Gambini, George De Grey, Mrs. George De Grey, John De Grey, Paul De Grey, Stephen De Grey, Father Herbert, Miss L—, Lucretia Lefevre, Magdalen Scrope, Henrietta Spencer, Isabel Stirling.) Widow Mrs. George De Grey is comforted near New York by Father Herbert and her paid companion Margaret Aldis. Mrs. De Grey's son Paul returns from Europe, sad because his estranged fiancée died there. Falling in love with Miss Aldis, Paul is warned by the priest that male De Greys have all vampirized their true loves. Margaret bravely determines to respond to the young man anyway. Drained by her, he sickens and dies in an accident, and she goes insane. This is James's first "sacred fount" story, which he handled a little better in "Longstaff's Marriage" and far better—if more tediously—in *The Sacred Fount*. The plot may be foolish; but the eldrich atmosphere, which is old worldly despite the nominal American setting, has the ring of psychological romantic truth à la Nathaniel Hawthorne.*

De Grey, George. In "De Grey, A Romance," Paul De Grey's ancestor. According to the family curse, he loved and hence caused the death of Antoniette Gambini. Another George De Grey caused Mary Fortescue to die. Another George was Paul's father, who died after a year of marriage.

De Grey, John. In "De Grey, A Romance," Paul's ancestor who caused Henrietta Spencer's death. Another John De Grey caused Blanche Ferrars's death.

De Grey, Mrs. George. In "De Grey, A Romance," Paul's mother. She was spared the family curse because her husband did not love her.

De Grey, Paul. In "De Grey, A Romance," Paul's ancestor who caused Lucretia Lefevre's death.

De Grey, Paul. In "De Grey, A Romance," another of Paul's ancestors. This one caused Magdalene Scrope's death.

De Grey, Paul. In "De Grey, A Romance," the present scion of the De Grey family. His estranged fiancée died in Italy. Next, he falls in love with Margaret Aldis, who braves the family curse; but then her Paul dies.

De Grey, Stephen. In "De Grey, A Romance," Paul's ancestor who caused Isabel Stirling's death.

Delacroix, Ferdinand Victor Eugène (1798–1863). Exuberantly romantic French painter, lithographer, and building decorator, he was inspired by religion, history, myths, contemporary political events, and Moroccan life and scenes. He read the classics until he was seventeen, then he turned to art. Admiring several English painters, Delacroix studied in London (1825) and then began quickly creating masterpieces (1827–1832); toured Morocco in the company of a French diplomat (1832); and returned to paint many murals of historical events, and biblical and mythological scenes. He decorated the central ceiling of the Galerie d'Apollon (1851). His works point both to impressionism and on to *fin-de-siècle* depression. Charles Baudelaire,* who almost alone in their day understood Delacroix's gloom, wrote insightfully about him (1868). Delacroix's paintings are too numerous to list, but his two most famous are undoubtedly *Dante and Virgil in Hell* (1822) and *Liberty Leading the People* (1830). In reviewing *Contemporary French Painters* (1868) by Philip Gilbert Hamerton,* James deplores the skimpy treatment therein of Delacroix and calls him "the most interesting of French painters." But in "Art" (Jan 1872), he opines that Delacroix combines charming strength with irritating weakness; furthermore, he offers "singular optical effects" in a certain Arab campfire scene, which though "forcible and true" is incorrectly drawn. In "Parisian Topics" (19 Feb 1876), James praises Delacroix's *Death of Sardanapalus* and his *Entombment of Christ*. The former has unsolved difficulties but "indicates the dawning of a great imagination"; the latter also reveals profound imagination and "extraordinary harmony of color" and "really inexpressible beauty" as well. James reviewed at great length (*International Review*, Apr 1880) the *Lettres d'Eugène Delacroix (1815 à 1863)*, edited by Philippe Burty (1878). He begins by calling Delacroix "most eminent,'' deplores the fact that critics sometimes make more money writing about him than the artist himself did, encourages the public to enjoy pictures by trusting "personal impressions," and consults "my memory of his works" with pleasure. Delacroix saw "earthly harmonies" and executed well but, more importantly, reflected morally, in a melancholy way, and responded to "the ideal." James finds his letters of interest but disappointing (less charming and bright than those of Henri Regnault,* for example). James criticizes Delacroix for being provincially Parisian but offers praise of his "best Eastern subjects." He agrees with the statement by editor Burty, whom he commends highly, that art and friendship were Delacroix's " 'mainstay,' " quotes many passages from the letters showing the artist's friendship with men, and stresses the importance of his short stay in England. Delacroix liked British paintings—especially those of Richard Parkes Bonington,* John Constable, and Sir Thomas Lawrence—but disliked London. James sympathizes with the artist's lifelong humiliation at the hands of reactionary critics. His occasionally not working was "equivalent to a sickness"; yet he enjoyed being lazy at the Nohant home of his friend George Sand,* associating with Frédéric Chopin and watching peasants dancing there, and was glad " 'chatterbox' " Honoré de Balzac* did not put in an expected appearance. James expresses sorrow that Delacroix bothered to feel wounded by the critics, even late in his career (to 1859); but he adds that in France "criticism is not only a profession, it is a power." James concludes: Delacroix combined disparate elements—imagination, contemplation, energy and delicacy, "a masculine and a feminine element." He was noble. James's library contained two books by Delacroix.

Delamere, Mrs. In *The Tragic Muse*, Miriam Rooth's friend who is unique in being able to tell the young actress something.

Delancey. In *The Princess Casamassima*, an anarchistic hairdresser. When he accuses Hyacinth Robinson of cowardice, the young man answers him oratorically.

Delaroche, Paul (1797–1859). Paris-born and popular painter of smooth, academic, realistic scenes out of history (mainly French and English). His best-known work is the poignant *Children of Edward [IV]* (which James describes at length in *A Small Boy and Others*). In his review of *Contemporary French Painters* (1868) by Philip Gilbert Hamerton,* James gently rebukes the critic for spending too much time on easy painters such as Delaroche while slighting more challenging ones. In "The Bethnal Green Museum" (1873), James calls Delaroche "fatally cold," even though "[h]e was the idol of our youth." He arranges cleverly, but he is flat and vulgar in execution.

Delavoy, John. In "John Delavoy," the recently dead author whose sister the narrator pleases by writing an interpretive essay on him, rather than a chatty one.

Delavoy, Miss. In "John Delavoy," the sister of John Delavoy. The narrator pleases her by writing sensibly about her dead brother.

Demesne, Lady. In "The Siege of London," Sir Arthur Demesne's suspicious mother.

Demesne, Lady Nancy. In "The Siege of London," Nancy Grenville Beck Headway's later designation.

Demesne, Sir Arthur. In "The Siege of London," the aristocratic Britisher of Longlands who wants to marry Nancy Headway. He is suspicious of her past but marries her anyway.

Demesne, Sir Baldwin. In "The Siege of London," Sir Arthur Demesne's deceased father.

Denbigh, Mrs. In "The Story of a Masterpiece," a distant relative of Stephen Baxter.

Dence, Sir Digby. In *The Awkward Age*, Gustavus Vanderbank's superior in government.

Dencombe. In "The Middle Years," the dying novelist who is befriended by Dr. Hugh, wants a second change, but finally has none.

Densher, Merton. In *The Wings of the Dove*, the British journalist, son of a deceased chaplain and a deceased copyist, who loves Kate Croy. The two plan for him to encourage rich, dying Milly Theale to marry him and then at her death to bequeath a large sum of money to him. Ultimately, he is willing to wed Kate without accepting the money, but she will accept him only with the money. Ford Madox Hueffer* incorrectly theorized that he was James's model for Merton Densher. A better candidate might be William Morton Fullerton.* Both Fullerton and Densher were sensual, well-traveled journalists, and Fullerton's middle name (by which he was known) is close to Densher's first name. Fullerton, however, was both more talented and less admirable than Densher.

Dent-Douglas, Captain. In *The Awkward Age*, a man who wishes to elope with Lady Fanny Cashmore.

Desmond, Mr. and Mrs. In "A Bundle of Letters," friends of Evelyn Vane.

Despard, Colonel. In "The Given Case," the philandering husband of Kate. He returns.

Despard, Kate. In "The Given Case," the object of Barton Reeve's affections, but her husband returns.

Devenish, Lord. In *Guy Domville*, the immoral aristocrat who is Maria Brasier Domville's lover and the father of her daughter Mary Brasier. Mrs. Domville will marry him and pay off his debts if he can get Guy Domville to wed her daughter (or any other woman) to thus continue the Domville line. After showing Guy the high life of London rakes, Lord Devenish fails, also fails to get Guy to marry Mrs. Peverel, but remains unabashed.

De Vere Gardens. At 34 De Vere Gardens, off Kensington Road, in London, James had a flat from 1886 to 1898. According to a present-day official London City Council blue-and-white wall marker on the building, "Henry James / 1843–1916 / Writer / lived here / 1886–1902," at what was then No. 13 De Vere Mansions. It is now Hale House, a seven-story building of twenty-two flats (some selling for more than £300,000 each) and a caretaker flat. (Across the street, at 29 De Vere Gardens, is the present Browning House, where Robert Browning lived from 1887 to 1889.) In March 1886, James took a twenty-one-year lease on a spacious fourth-floor flat. Kensington Gardens were near, and James could take a hefty walk through Hyde Park to the Piccadilly region. (For an excellent photograph of the De Vere Gardens mansion, see *The Complete Plays of Henry James*, ed. Leon Edel, opp. p. 64.)

Devereux, Guy. In "The Papers," the young man who, it is reported, will not marry Miranda Beadel-Muffet.

Diamond, Captain. In "The Ghostly Rental," the widowed, demented man who cursed his daughter and now accepts rent from her "ghost."

Diamond, Miss. In "The Ghostly Rental," Diamond's daughter, supposedly cursed to death. Later she provides rent money for the crazed man.

"The Diary of a Man of Fifty." Short story (11,900 words), published in *Harper's New Monthly Magazine* (Jul 1879) and in *Macmillan's Magazine* (Jul 1879); reprinted in *The Madonna of the Future*, 1879. (Characters: Count Camerino, Lady H—, Count Salvi, Countess Bianca Salvi, Countess Bianca Salvi-Scarabelli, Count Scarabelli, Signorina Scarabelli, Edmund Stanmer.) The diarist, a retired British general, records in 1874 his return to Florence after twenty-seven years. While asking about Countess Salvi, he meets young Edmund Stanmer. It seems that the diarist loved Countess Bianca Salvi, whose husband had been killed in a duel by Count Camerino; after the puzzled diarist left her, she wed Camerino for security. Now Stanmer loves her widowed daughter, Countess Bianca Salvi-Scarabelli. The diarist tries to warn Stanmer about this new Bianca, but to no avail. Later in London the two men meet again, and the young man says that the old man was mistaken about his Bianca—at which the diarist begins to wonder. He interestingly sees his youthful self in young Stanmer; so this tale has a fascinating alter-ego plot linked to the what-might-have-been theme. James seems to be saying here: Plunge into life. It is of interest that in his *Notebooks* (12 Dec 1878) James jotted down the original idea ("It has often occurred to me," he begins) which resulted in the story, but then the end of the entry is merely to the effect that the older man will warn the younger one "and open his eyes."

The Diary of a Man of Fifty and A Bundle of Letters. Two short stories, published in New York by Harper, 1880.

Dicey, Albert Venn (1835–1922). British jurist, essayist, and journalist, educated at Balliol College, Oxford. He taught law at Oxford and opposed home rule in Ireland. His main work is *Introduction to the Study of the Law of the Constitution* (1885). His brother was Edward James Stephen Dicey.* In 1873 James was distressed that the *Nation* published Albert Dicey's review of *Middlemarch* by George Eliot* after giving him the assignment. A few years later, as he wrote to his father (13 Feb [1877]), James met "excellent little Dicey" and "his ugly but equally excellent wife" through Viscount James Bryce.* Soon thereafter he complained snobbishly to his sister Alice (17 Feb [1878]) that both Diceys were "decidedly too ugly, useful informationish, grotesque-Oxfordish, poor-dinnerish . . . not to make one feel that one can do better."

Dicey, Edward James Stephen (1832–1911). British editor and journalist, whose brother was Albert Venn Dicey.* Edward Dicey's wife was the sister of the wife of Auguste Laugel.* Edward Dicey, educated at Trinity College, Cambridge, visited the United States during the Civil War and wrote favoring the Union side. He edited the London *Observer* (1870–1889) and wrote *England and Egypt* (1884), *Bulgaria, the Peasant State* (1895), and *The Egypt of the Future* (1907). James met Mrs. Edward Dicey at an 1877 dinner and was subsequently a guest at three Dicey dinners.

Dickens, Charles (1812–1870). Beloved, powerful, and influential Victorian novelist, whose childhood was blighted by family poverty and who therefore received little formal education. He became a skillful shorthand reporter of House of Commons debates and soon made a hit with *Sketches by Boz* (1836–1837), followed by *The Posthumous Papers of the Pickwick Club* (1836–1837). Dickens then combined editing, foreign travel, and writing which proved both popular and controversial. He toured the United States twice (1842, 1867–1868); lived in Italy, Switzerland, and France; and published steadily, often in serial form. He founded, edited, and contributed to *Household Words* (1850–1859) and then to *All the Year Round* (1859–). The following are among his best works: *Oliver Twist* (1837–1839), *Nicholas Nickleby* (1838–1839), *American Notes* (1842), *A Christmas Carol* (1843), *Martin Chuzzlewit* (1843–1844), *David Copperfield* (1849–1850), *Bleak House* (1852–1853), *Hard Times* (1854), *A Tale of Two Cities* (1859), and *Great Expectations* (1860–1861). *Little Dorrit* (1857) and *Our Mutual Friend* (1865) show a decline in powers; *The Mystery of Edwin Drood* (1870) remains a teasing fragment. Dickens married in 1836, fathered ten children, separated from his wife in 1856, and may have associated romantically with the actress Ellen Ternan. As a small boy, James wept aloud over an oral reading of the first installment of *David Copperfield*; he also attended stage productions based on Dickens's stories and evidently read Dickens with relish throughout his adolescence. Some of his father's publicly expressed dislike of Dickens's anti-Americanism must have remained, however, because James wrote only one review of Dickens and no essays on him. He adversely noticed (*Nation*, 21 Dec 1865) *Our Mutual Friend*, calling it Dickens's "poorest" and a revelation of authorial "exhaustion." It seems produced, not "seen, known, or felt." Its only merit is its occasional humor. Its characters are "grotesque creatures"; Jenny Wren is typical of "hunchbacks, imbeciles, and precocious children who have carried on the sentimental business in all Mr. Dickens's novels." His villains too are unnatural, with no connection to reality. *Our Mutual Friend* has a triangular plot which could have made "a very good story" if the three principals were characters rather than "simply figures." What we have are "vulgar" scenes "weak[ly]" conceived. Dickens is observant and funny but not philosophical; he does not generalize about mankind. James saw Dickens briefly at the home of Charles Eliot Norton* during the popular novelist's 1867 tour. In London, in March 1869, James at dinner with the Nortons met Dickens's unmarried daughter Kate. In his review (*Galaxy*, Feb 1877) of the letters of Honoré de Balzac,* James tardily praises Dickens, equating him with Balzac in terms of practicality, vigor, personality, egotism, and materialism; "they have had no rivals but each other and [William] Shakespeare[*]." When James wrote his critical study of Nathaniel Hawthorne* (1879), the publishers were so pleased that they asked him to prepare a study of Dickens for the same series (edited by Viscount John Morley*), but James declined. In later critical pieces, James often referred casually to Dickens; for example, in "London" (31 Jul 1897) he contrasts the authoritative treatment of lower middle-class characters by George Gissing* and their "prodigiously droll" handling by Dickens. According to his Pocket Diaries, James visited Dickens's daughter Kate, who was then Mrs. Perugini, in London, in 1913 and again in 1914, to talk with her about her father. James's autobiographical volumes are dotted with references to Dickens, indicating a long-standing familiarity with the author; for example, in *Notes of a Son and Brother*, James says that "it had been laid upon young persons of our generation to feel Dickens, down to the soles of our shoes,'' and then proceeds to picture him in vivid detail when they were together at the Nortons' dinner in November 1867. James's library contained three books by Dickens.

Dilke, Sir Charles Wentworth (1843–1911). Student at Trinity College, Cambridge, then powerful member of Parliament for Chelsea (1868–1886). Dilke was an enlightened imperialist, an extreme radical (favoring better conditions for workers), and an expert on military, naval, and foreign affairs. In 1885 he was named correspondent in a celebrated, unsuccessfully prosecuted divorce case, during which the name of Christina Stewart Rogerson,* wife of James Rogerson, was dragged in. In his defense, it was alleged that Dilke had been engaged the previous year to art critic Emilia Pattison, the recently widowed wife of the scholar Mark Pattison. Later in 1885 he and Mrs. Pattison were married; she became Dilke's second wife. But his effectiveness in politics was permanently diminished. He published widely, on military matters, colonial questions, and travel. In 1877 James met Dilke at a London dinner party. A year later James mentioned in a letter to his father (29 May [1878]) that he had been elected to the Reform Club, partly owing to Dilke, who was " 'struck' by my French essays.'' The two continued to meet socially. James also knew both Mrs. Rogerson and her mother Mrs. Duncan Stewart*, as well as Emilia Pattison (before she was widowed). A letter in 1885 from James to Grace Norton* (23 Aug [1885]) buzzes with gossip concerning the divorce case and mentions Mrs. Pattison, whom James had met at Oxford, in 1869, and described at that time in a letter to his brother William (26 Apr [1869]) as "very young (about 28) very pretty, very clever, very charming and very conscious of it all,'' and at the time married to "dessicated old scholar'' Mark Pattison (reputed model of Casaubon in *Middlemarch* by George Eliot*). Pattison died in 1884. James goes on in his letter to Grace Norton to hint at "another London Lady whom I won't name.'' She was Christina Rogerson. Toward the end of this letter, James adds naughtily that Dilke's "long, double liaison with Mrs. Pattison and the other lady . . . make[s] it a duty of honour to marry *both* (!!) when they should become free . . . '' In a letter to his brother William (9 Mar [1886]), James, obviously following the unsavory divorce trial with relish, describes Dilke as having "behaved . . . with strange pusillanimity and want of judgment and taste.'' After Dilke married Mrs. Pattison, Mrs. Rogerson's husband died, and the widow remarried; that husband was killed in the Boer War in 1899. Some of Dilke's better traits may have contributed to James's characterization of Lord Warburton in *The Portrait of a Lady*.

Disengaged. Three-act play (tentative titles, *Mrs. Jasper* and *Mrs. Jasper's Way*), published in *Theatricals: Two Comedies: Tenants* [and] *Disengaged*, in 1894. (Characters: Lady Amy Brisket, Sir Montagu Brisket, Charles Coverley, Mrs. Jasper, Captain Llewellyn Prime, Mr. and Mrs. Spicer, Mr. and Mrs. Stoner, Percy Trafford, Blandina Wigmore, Flora Wigmore.) On the Brisket

Place lawn, forty miles outside London and near some medieval ruins, complex social action occurs, involving host, hostess, and guests. Sir Montagu Brisket's sister Flora Wigmore wants to compromise Llewellyn Prime, a Guards captain, into proposing to her daughter Blandina. This plan a young widow Mrs. Jasper advances, with the help of Charles Coverley and his friend Percy Trafford, who flirts with Lady Amy. Blandina and Prime are encouraged to pose for a harmless photograph and then to go inspect the ruins unchaperoned, until dusk falls. Prime is made to feel obligated to propose, and he is accepted by Blandina and her mother. Next morning, inside Brisket Place, there is much coming and going: Sir Montagu wants Trafford to get out; Coverley (who now deplores the Blandina-Prime engagement and who to please Mrs. Jasper urges Trafford to leave) wants Mrs. Jasper (who also regrets the engagement); and Amy (tempted to visit Trafford in London) thinks Sir Montagu loves Mrs. Jasper (who despite Flora's opposition will disengage Prime and also seeks to assure the Briskets of their mutual love). So Mrs. Jasper meets Prime and walks off chatting with him. The two begin to fall in love. Next day Mrs. Jasper in her London drawing room presides over many entrances and exits. Prime comes in, the two express their love, and he hides in her den, as Trafford comes in, is rebuffed, asks about Amy, sees Coverley come in also, and leaves. Mrs. Jasper makes Coverley, who loves her and to whom she says Trafford will wed Blandina, go get Trafford. Prime emerges and embraces Mrs. Jasper. Sir Montagu enters, sees the couple, and leaves when not offered lunch. Amy enters, seeks her husband, learns that Mrs. Jasper never loved him, that Trafford has visited Mrs. Jasper here, and that Mrs. Jasper wants Prime. So Amy says they can find Blandina another husband. When Trafford returns, Amy tells him to marry Blandina; he admits that the girl is charming. Sir Montagu returns, and Trafford explains that he wants Blandina, who with her mother now enters. Trafford proposes and is accepted. Coverley reappears and reels at the news that Mrs. Jasper will wed Prime. James based this play on his own short story "The Solution." In 1891 the actress Ada C. Rehan* told James in London that theatrical manager John Augustin Daly* would like James to write a play for them. In August 1892 James gave *Disengaged* (then a draft called *Mrs. Jasper*) to her for Daly, who liked it but wanted revisions. James tried to comply; however, after much disagreement and annoyance on both sides, James in December 1893 ordered Daly to return his play, which was produced by other groups very briefly in New York (1902, 1909).

Disraeli, Benjamin (1804–1881). Important prime minister of England (1868, 1874–1880). He became the first Earl of Beaconsfield in 1876, enjoyed the intimate friendship of Queen Victoria, and was a novelist. James wittily reviewed (*Atlantic Monthly*, Aug 1870) *Lothair* (1870), the sixth of Disraeli's seven novels. He begins by criticizing previous reviewers for relating *Lothair* to its author's politics instead of judging it as merely an "amusing" entertainment, in which Disraeli shows a certain "small cleverness" but no "honest wisdom." James tells us everything about Lothair, the rich young Scottish hero, and his three admirers (one "a good Protestant," another "a keen Papist," and the third a married "Italian patriot"). James is not much concerned with the plot, however, nor in the possible "ruling idea" of *Lothair*—"the secret encroachments of the Romish Church"—but rather in the antidote to "dreary realism" which its romantic "elegance and opulence and splendor" provide. Such romanticism is spoiled, however, by the desire in Disraeli to present an "aristocratic world" which he "infantine[ly]" overvalues. In a private letter to Mrs. John Rollin Tilton (3 Apr [1878]), James calls Disraeli "the tawdry old Jew who is at the head of this great old British Empire." More publicly, in "The Reassembling of Parliament" (1879), James calls him "a charlatan of genius at the head of affairs." To William Dean Howells* (5 Dec [1880]), James defines Disraeli's 1880 novel *Endymion* as "contemptibly bad."

Dodd, M. D. Ashley (?–?). British authoress, whose works include *The Days of a Year* (1907) and *Verses of the Country* (1909). When Miss Dodd sent James a copy of *The Days of a Year*, he thanked her in a gracious letter (30 Sep 1907) that he permitted her to use as an "appreciation" in her "Foreword" to a reissue of the book, in London by Herbert Jenkins, in 1913. In his letter, James praises her work as "charming." He notes that she has obviously long observed and loved nature; envies her "knowledge, . . . feeling and . . . opportunities" with regard to nature; and senses that her love of "our south-country England, so mild and so rich," suffuses every scene, near and far, which she describes.

Dodd, Herbert. In "The Bench of Desolation," the man who, when he broke his engagement to loyal Kate Cookham, had to pay her a sum for breach of promise. He married Nan Drury, and they had two daughters. Then all three females died, and now Dodd renews his friendship with Kate.

Dodd, Major. In "Osborne's Revenge," Maria Dodd's cousin. He tells Philip Osborne that Henrietta Congreve did not cause Robert Graham to commit suicide.

Dodd, Maria. In "Osborne's Revenge," the woman who believes the false story that Henrietta Congreve caused Robert Graham's suicide.

Dodd, Nan Drury. In "The Bench of Desolation," Herbert's wife. The couple had two daughters; subsequently, all three females died.

Dodd, The Misses. In "The Bench of Desolation," the two early-dying daughters of Herbert and Nan Dodd.

Doe, Charles H. (?–?). American novelist, whose *Buffets* (1875) James reviewed (*Nation*, 13 Jan 76), calling it "wholesome to insipidity—unsophisticated to puerility." It was designed as an American novel, he adds, devoid of backwoodsmen and dialect but "savor[ing] of the soil." The book, with an uninventive plot of "primitive simplicity," concerns New York in Revolutionary War times. The book includes poor characterization, but it is agreeably written save when "severely humorous." James adds that Doe seems capable of better work.

Dole, Charles F. (1845–1927). Well-educated American clergyman, editor, and author of several idealistic theological books, including *The Coming People* (1897), which James in "American Letter" (21 May 1898) touches on, mainly to remark that the optimism expressed in it betrays ignorance of "the passions and perversities of men." Dole seems to exhort readers "already so good that they scarce need to be better."

Dolman, Miss. In "In the Cage," a recipient of telegrams from Lady Bradeen and Philip Everard.

Dolphin, Agnes Littlemore. In "The Siege of London," Reggie Dolphin's wife and George Littlemore's sister. At Lady Demesne's request, she unsuccessfully beseeches George to define Nancy Headway as not respectable.

Dolphin, Reggie. In "The Siege of London," George Littlemore's brother-in-law.

Domville. In *Guy Domville*, Maria Brasier Domville's husband and Guy Domville's cousin, deceased for ten years now.

Domville. In *Guy Domville*, Maria Brasier Domville's deceased son by her husband Domville, also deceased.

Domville, Guy. In *Guy Domville*, a young man from western England studying for the priesthood who is briefly sidetracked (and even rendered a bit rakish in London) by the prospect of inheriting Domville holdings, marrying Mary Brasier, and being the sole continuator of the family line. When he learns that Mary loves George Round, he helps the two elope, then even gives up the idea of proposing to the widowed Mrs. Peverel (whose son George he has tutored), and decides to become a priest after all. Guy is the cousin of the deceased Brasier, Mary's supposed father. In the stage production, Guy Domville was played by Sir George Alexander.*

Domville, Maria Brasier. In *Guy Domville*, an immoral London dowager and the mother of Mary Brasier by Lord Devenish. She is the widow of Brasier, Mary's supposed father. Maria promises to marry her lover Devenish and pay off his debts if he will get Mary to wed Guy (which Devenish fails to do) or to get Guy to marry anyone else in order to continue the Domville family line, which Devenish also fails to do.

Domville, Mrs. In *Guy Domville*, Guy Domville's pure mother, now deceased.

Domville of Gaye. In *Guy Domville*, Guy Domville's cousin, whose death in a riding accident means that Guy is the last of the Domvilles, since Domville of Gaye had only illegitimate children.

Donner, Beach. In *The Awkward Age*, Carrie's husband.

Donner, Carrie. In *The Awkward Age*, Beach Donner's shy, pretty wife and Tishy Grendon's sister.

Donovan, Mrs. In "The Chaperon," an Irish woman whose offer to help Rose Tramore socially the girl rejects, because of the woman's willingness to help Rose's mother only later.

Dora. In "Osborne's Revenge," the name mentioned as not that of Philip Osborne's wife.

Doré, Paul Gustave (1832–1883). Strasbourg-born French book illustrator, religious and historical painter, and minor sculptor. His spectacular illustrations (beginning in the 1850s) for the Bible and for works by Honoré de Balzac,* Miguel de Cervantes Saavedra, Dante Alighieri, Jean de La Fontaine, Charles Perrault, and François Rabelais are justly famous. In Paris, early in 1876, James was a fellow guest with the equally bored Doré at a musical party given by Michelle Pauline Garçía Viardot,* the companion of Ivan Sergeyevich Turgenev.* James's early memories of Doré's melodramatic artwork inspired graphic imagery in a few of his early tales and travel essays.

Doria, Prince. In "Adina," a nobleman said to be staying at an Albano villa, near Rome.

Dorimont, Lord. In "The Death of the Lion," a nobleman who helps Lady Augusta Minch lose Neil Paraday's last manuscript.

Dormer, Bridget (Biddy). In *The Tragic Muse*, the sister of Percival, Nicholas, and Grace. Biddy loves Peter Sherringham.

Dormer, Grace. In *The Tragic Muse*, the sister of Percival, Nicholas, and Bridget.

Dormer, Lady Agnes. In *The Tragic Muse*, Sir Nicholas Dormer's widow; the mother of Percival, Nicholas, Grace, and Bridget Dormer; and Julia Sherringham Dallow's cousin. She is sad because Nick prefers painting to politics.

Dormer, Nicholas (Nick). In *The Tragic Muse*, the hero of the novel. He is the son of Lady Agnes Dormer and her deceased husband Sir Nicholas; the brother of Percival, Grace, and Bridget. Nick's preference for painting over politics upsets his mother and causes Julia Sherringham Dallow to cancel their engagement. He is a close friend of Gabriel Nash and Miriam Rooth, whose portrait he paints.

Dormer, Percival (Percy). In *The Tragic Muse*, the disappointing brother of Nicholas, Grace, and Bridget.

Dormer, Sir Nicholas. In *The Tragic Muse*, Lady Agnes Dormer's deceased husband; the father of Percival, Nicholas, Grace, and Bridget.

Dorriforth. In "After the Play," the fellow playgoer in London with Amicia, Auberon, and Florentia. Dorriforth deplores the present condition of the British stage, dislikes massive stage effects because they eclipse good acting, criticizes the materialism and poor taste of audiences, and recommends more authoritative criticism, plays representative of British life, and more conveniently located theaters.

Dorrington, Lord and Lady. In "The Pupil," the Moreen family's casual friends, whose son Lord Verschoyle proposes to neither Amy nor Paula Moreen.

Dosson, Fidelia (Delia). In *The Reverberator*, Francie's loyal older sister.

Dosson, Francina (Francie). In *The Reverberator*, Whitney Dosson's younger daughter and Gaston Probert's fiancée. When she innocently tells George Flack much of the Probert family gossip and he prints it in his *Reverberator*, she is in real trouble.

Dosson, Whitney. In *The Reverberator*, the unflappable, rich American, who is the father of Fidelia and Francina.

Doubleday. In *The Reprobate*, Paul's father, who rescued the lad from Nina in Paris and died shortly thereafter.

Doubleday. In *The Reprobate*, the second Mrs. Doubleday's son, who died in infancy.

Doubleday, Paul. In *The Reprobate*, the domineering widow Mrs. Doubleday's downtrodden stepson, age about thirty. Ten years earlier, he innocently went to Paris with Nina (who calls him Dudley and Dud), now Mrs. Freshville, and has been made by his stepmother and coguardian Bonsor to feel guilty ever since. He decides to rebel, lectures his mother on love, and accepts and returns Blanche Amber's offer of affection.

Doubleday, Mrs. In *The Reprobate*, Paul Doubleday's mother, once indelicate and now deceased.

Doubleday, Mrs. In *The Reprobate*, Paul Doubleday's stepmother, who with coguardian Bonsor has long domineered the young man. She is pursued by hypocritical Captain Chanter, is worried by Mrs. Freshville's appearance, and at the end accepts Chanter.

Doudan, Ximénès (1800–1872). Born in Douai, this Frenchman of letters was a teacher, became "précepteur" of a son of Madame de Staël, and served in a few government positions. He published articles in the *Revue française* in 1838, which were collected as part of his later *Mélanges et lettres* (4 vols., 1876–1877). James reviewed these volumes in "Parisian Topics" (New York *Tribune*, 1 Jul 1876, and *Nation*, 24 Jan 1878) as they appeared in pairs. He begins the first review by calling good letters entertaining to read and Doudan's, exquisite and charming. (James notes that too many letters nowadays are like telegrams and postcards.) Doudan has little gossip, pitches his humor in "the minor key," and makes good comments on Jean-Jacques Rousseau, Saint Augustine, the 1848 Roman Revolution, Joseph Ernest Renan,* aging, and heroism. In a letter to his brother William (22 Jun [1876]), James reports that he is not sending to their sister Alice Doudan's *Mélanges et lettres*, in two volumes, because "they are so heavy and on the whole not worth it, in spite of my praise [in the *Tribune*] of them." In the second review, James says that Doudan's final volumes are excellent and show increasing "melancholy and latent depression," but present no really new picture of the author, who continued to observe, converse, depict his social milieu, and remain conservative. James delights in quoting from his subject's "running commentary," which shows his one passion—for literature, including British fiction. Doudan loved Italy, favored a preventive war against Germany in 1866, disliked the coming of " 'demagogy,' " and wrote sadly from Paris during the siege and the Commune. James's library contained one book by Doudan.

Douglas. In "The Turn of the Screw," the man who prepares Griffin's house-guests for the Christmas season reading of the governess's narrative. He is now dead. A major critical question: Is he Miles grown up?

Douves, Blanche de. In *The Reverberator*, Raoul de Douves's kleptomaniacal sister.

Douves, Jeanne Probert de (Jane). In *The Reverberator*, Raoul de Douves's wife and Gaston Probert's sister.

Douves, M. de. In *The Reverberator*, Raoul de Douves's embarrassed father.

Douves, Raoul de. In *The Reverberator*, Jeanne de Douves's husband and hence Gaston Probert's brother-in-law.

Dovedale, Lady. In "The Siege of London," Reggie Dolphin's casual friend.

Dovedale, Lord. In "The Marriages," a nobleman who is to marry Mrs. Churchley.

Doyne, Ashton. In "The Real Right Thing," the distinguished, deceased author whose spectral presence dissuades George Withermore from writing Doyne's biography.

Doyne, Mrs. Ashton. In "The Real Right Thing," the widow who wants George Withermore to be her husband's biographer.

Drack, Mrs. David E. In "Julia Bride," the elephantine widow who is the object of Pitman's desires. She generously admires Julia Bride's beauty.

Drake. In "In the Cage," Lord Rye's former butler, and now Lady Bradeen's butler. He will marry Mrs. Jordan.

"The Drama." Theater essay, attributed to James and published in the *Atlantic Monthly* (Dec 1874). The critic opines that drama in America is weak and often vulgar and that audiences are not discriminating. So it is pleasant to see *The School for Scandal* (by Richard Brinsley Sheridan, 1777) well performed in Boston. Though "meagre" and now even "threadbare," this drama is unique "for real intellectual effort, the literary atmosphere and the tone of society." It was well mounted, as to "chairs and tables," last year in London; but the present Boston show, "on the whole, is better." Then, however, after dilating on "the poverty of the English stage," if this comedy of coarse types and low morality is the best, the critic returns to the Boston show, criticizes the scenery, and praises the first-act minuet.

Draper, Ruth (1884–1956). New York–born monologist and monodramatist. She began her astounding career by giving, in private homes and for charity, monologues of people she knew or knew of. From 1910 into 1913, she averaged an engagement every week or two, near New York. She began performing for distinguished London hostesses in June 1913, occasionally before royalty. Henry Adams,* having met her in Washington, D.C., in 1911, befriended her in Paris in 1913. (She later called him "Uncle Henry.") Using only sketches she had written, she became an international success. She was magically adept at modulating her voice, features, and gestures. James met her at this time and enjoyed accompanying her to various places in London, even to his Athenaeum Club. She consulted him as to whether she should pursue a dramatic or a writing career, and she recalled later that he had informed her she had woven a beautiful Persian carpet and should stand on it. In December 1913 James sent her "Monologue" (his composition), hoped that she could use it in performance, and was disappointed when she declined with thanks—on the grounds that she wrote all of her own material. ("Monologue" was published as part of "Three Unpublished Letters and A Monologue by Henry James," *London Mercury* September 1922, and as "The Presentation at Court," *Vanity Fair* December 1922.) John Singer Sargent* made three portrait drawings of her. Miss Draper, an extraordinary genius whose later career was spectacular, always remained modest, charming, vivid, generous, and humane. In 1933 she published her translation of *Icaro*, the 1930 verse drama by Lauro de Bosis, whom she had met in Rome in 1928 (when she was age forty-three and he was twenty-six) and with whom she shared the one great love of her life. De Bosis was a brilliant young poet, scientist, scholar, and translator, who gave his life in 1931 opposing Italian fascism. In 1938 Ruth Draper's older sister Dorothea married Henry James's brother William's son Henry. Dorothea became a widow in 1948, and two years later gave Lamb House* to the National Trust.

Draper, Maggie. In "Madame de Mauves," Mr. and Mrs. Draper's young daughter.

Draper, Mr. and Mrs. In "Madame de Mauves," a Wall Street man and his wife. Maggie is their little daughter. Mrs. Draper is Longmore's friend and introduces the timid young man to Madame de Mauves.

Draper, Mr. and Mrs. In "Georgina's Reasons," names seen by Agnes Theory in a Roman hotel book.

Draper, Mrs. In "The Point of View," the recipient of a letter from Miss Sturdy.

Dreuil, Comte and Comtesse de. In *The Sacred Fount*, an aristocratic couple. She is Gilbert Long's casual, American-born friend.

Dreyfus, Alfred (1859–1935). Alsace-born French army officer of Jewish extraction. When Alsace was annexed by Germany in 1871, Dreyfus moved with his prosperous family to France. After fifteen years of military service, during which he rose to the rank of captain, he became the subject of the Dreyfus Affair, beginning in 1894. Charged with selling military secrets to the Germans, he was tried by court martial, convicted on evidence not made public, and sentenced to life imprisonment on Devil's Island off French Guiana. In 1897 Major M. C. F. Walsin-Esterhazy was charged with communicating with the Germans via documents in handwriting resembling Dreyfus's, but he was acquitted in 1898. Émile Zola* in "J'accuse" (13 January 1898) called the French authorities conspirators and Esterhazy a traitor. The Dreyfus Affair pitted anti-Semitic monarchical and Catholic forces against socialist, Republican Dreyfusards. A French army officer admitted forging documents to implicate Dreyfus, then committed suicide (1898). Dreyfus was court-martialed again (1899) and was found guilty once more, but he accepted an immediate presidential pardon. Revelation of more forgeries led to a third court martial (1904–1906), which found him innocent. After a civil trial, he was readmitted to the army and promoted to major. When Zola's remains were being reburied in the Pantheon (4 June 1908), an anti-Semitic fanatic shot at and wounded Dreyfus, who later served in World War I. James, who was a pro-Dreyfusard (as was his friend Urbain Mengin*) and followed the Dreyfus Affair with intense interest, wrote to Zola to praise his courage; he was hard put to write to his anti-Dreyfusard, anti-Semitic friend Paul Bourget* tactfully on the subject (26 Sep [1898], 23 Dec 1898), but he confessed by letter to Elizabeth Cameron* (15 Oct 1898), "I eat and drink, I sleep and dream Dreyfus. The papers are too shockingly interesting." More frankly, while he was Bourget's villa guest at Hyères, in southern France, James wrote to his brother William (2 Apr 1899) that the affair was helping to make France "a country *en décadence*." Typical is James's statement to William and his wife Alice (9 Aug [1899]) that the affair created "almost intolerable suspense" in the newspapers. In his 1899 essay "The Present Literary Situation in France," James criticizes "the anti-revisionist and anti-Semitic" position of Jules Lemaître.*

Droz, Gustave (1832–1895). Born in Paris into a family of artists of Swiss extraction, this son of sculptor Jean Antoine Droz was a painter and then, more importantly, a writer. After attending l'École des Beaux Arts and successfully exhibiting, Droz wrote romantic, psychological studies, including *Monsieur, Madame et Bébé* (1866), *Entre nous* (1867), *Le Cahier bleu de Mlle Cibot* (1868), *Autour d'une source* (1869), *Un Paquet de lettres* (1870), *Babolain* (1872), *Une Femme génante* (1875), *Les Étangs* (1875), and *Tristesses et sourires* (1884). James reviewed (*Atlantic Monthly*, Aug 1871) *Around a Spring*, the 1871 translation of *Autour d'une source*. He begins by praising both it and *Mademoiselle Cibot* as "the best and ripest fruits" of recent French literature, which since the end of the Franco-Prussian War has been less pretentious.

Monsieur, Madame et Bébé and *Entre nous* James calls "amusing," and their author "the wittiest of humorists," perceptive of social failures, but not philosophical. *Mademoiselle Cibot* is better, in fact, "among the very best fictions of recent years" and full of "sensuous detail." The "ingenious" plot of *Around a Spring*, which shows a growth of power, James then summarizes so as to show sympathy for its tragic hero, the tempted curé. James concludes that Droz is a fine humorist, analyst, and moralist. But then James reviewed (*Nation*, 23 Sep 1875) *Les Étangs*, beginning with the remark that Droz, once "brilliant," is now "in . . . eclipse." *Les Étangs* is better than "the inconceivable" *Une Femme génante* through having no story at all, being instead a collection of letters evidently put "in a slender fictitious setting." From Paris in 1876 James twice wrote his to friend Thomas Sergeant Perry* (3 Feb, 2 May [1876]) that the *cénacle* of Gustave Flaubert* did not like Droz but that James much preferred Droz to Alphonse Daudet.* Later he came to adore Daudet. James's library contained one book by Droz.

Drury. In "The Bench of Desolation," Herbert Dodd's father-in-law, whose partner's defection impoverishes him.

Drury, Nan. In "The Bench of Desolation," the maiden name of Nan Drury Dodd.

Dubois, Paul (1829–1905). French sculptor and painter. He turned from law to art at the age of twenty-six, progressed fast, and studied in Italy (1859–1863). He first exhibited at the Paris Salon in 1860. As a sculptor, he produced tomb figures and busts; as a painter, about seventy portraits, among other works. In an untitled note on the 1876 Salon (*Nation*, 22 Jun 1876), James comments that no exhibit is exceptional but that two Dubois statues—*Charity* and *Military Courage*—are noteworthy and yet "lack just that supreme element of ease and independence which makes the work that is rarest in quality." (The two statues James saw became part of Dubois's major work, his *Tomb of General [Louis de] Lamoricière* at Nantes).

Duclaux, Mary. The married name of a woman (earlier Mary Darmesteter) whom James first met when she was Agnes Mary Frances Robinson.*

Duff-Gordon, Lucie (née Austin), Lady (1821–1869). English writer, born into a liberal family which lived in Germany and France when she was young. She knew George Meredith,* John Stuart Mill, and William Makepeace Thackeray,* among other notables. Though a wife (from 1840) and mother, she went abroad alone to try to ward off tuberculosis. She lived in Egypt (from 1862), where she died early. She published translations from German and French, *Letters from the Cape* (1862–1863), and *Letters from Egypt, 1863–65* (1865). *Last Letters from Egypt* appeared posthumously (1875), with a memoir by her daughter

Janet Anne Ross,* who was also a writer and whom James met in Florence in 1887. James wrote a laudatory review (*Nation*, 17 Jun 1875) on *Letters from Egypt, etc.* (1875), which includes Lady Duff-Gordon's Capetown letters, last letters, and a memoir by her daughter, "written [James notes] . . . with charming simplicity and in the best taste." James says that we read travel books to learn not only about places but also their authors. Our authoress here is observant, genial, sympathetic, witty, and above all intelligent; her style is "happy, easy, natural" and vivid. In fact, her letters "rank among the most delightful in our language." James quotes at some length to prove that, until the end, Lady Duff-Gordon admirably remained "amused and interested," even though she was lonely. She loved the land. She was charitable and civilized, made an admirer of her dragoman Omar, conversed with Egyptian wise men, and yet could write beautifully of "the small details of her daily life." Her letters from South Africa are best when she writes about the "Dutch settlements . . . inland." James ventures to predict that *Letters from Egypt* will become a classic.

Duggit, Mr. and Mrs. In *The Other House*, the play, guests in the house of Kate Beever, who tells Jean Martle to send them away when Julia Bream becomes sicker in the other house.

Dumas, Alexandre *fils* (1824–1895). French poet, playwright, and novelist. The natural son of Alexandre Dumas *père* (1803–1870), he became an even more famous author. The son's novels include *La Dame aux camélias* (1848; adapted by Dumas as a play in 1852), *Diane de Lys* (1851, adapted by Dumas as a play in 1853), *Tristan le Roux* (1849), *Henri de Navarre* (1850), *La Dame aux perles* (1854), and *L'Affaire Clémenceau: Mémoire de l'accusé* (1866). His plays include *Le Demi-Monde* (1855), *La Question d'Argent* (1857), *Le Fils naturel* (1858), *Un Père prodigue* (1859), *L'Ami des femmes* (1864), *Les Idées de Madame Aubray* (1867), *Monsieur Alphonse* (1873), *L'Étrangère* (1876), *La Princess de Bagdad* (1881), *Denise* (1885), and *Francillon* (1887). In Paris in 1856 young James was not allowed to attend a performance of *La Dame aux camélias*, although several of his older girl cousins were enviably permitted to do so. A decade later, he reviewed (*Nation*, 11 Oct 1866) Dumas's *L'Affaire Clémenceau*. He praises its point of view, that of an indicted wife murderer, who presents his evidence without "prudery" or "bravado" to his reader as though to a lawyer. It seems that Pierre Clémenceau, after a sad childhood, shows signs of artistic talent, is successfully encouraged by a master sculptor, meets a Polish adventuress and her beautiful young daughter Iza. The two women travel to St. Petersburg and Warsaw for a while, and then Pierre has occasion to aid Iza in Paris. They marry, but she quickly becomes unfaithful. He retreats to Rome but cannot forget the idea of revenge; he returns to Iza, now a foreigner's impudent mistress, and stabs her to death. Although James admires its strong, Honoré de Balzac*-like touches, he regards the novel as inartistically depressing. "Life is dispiriting, art . . . [should be] inspiring," he concludes. Still, in an age of "universal literary laxity," it is bracing to read a novel so well executed. In "Dumas and Goethe" (*Nation*, 30 Oct 1873), James reviews an 1873 French translation of *Faust* by Johann Wolfgang van Goethe* but spends most of his space discussing Dumas, who provided the introduction. First, James assails the French provincial attitude toward foreign-language study. If certain French leaders had known German just before 1870, France might not have lost Alsace and Lorraine. Then he criticizes Dumas for imposing his notions of morality on Goethe, even to the extent of suggesting a heavenly conclusion for the second part of *Faust*. Dumas feels that Goethe lacked both imagination and morality, became a dirty old man, and left the world little good writing, especially when compared to Romance-language writers. James feels that Dumas "is ludicrously perverted by national prejudice," that it is irrelevant to consider a writer's life when criticizing his works, and that Goethe appeals to one's soul more than Dumas does. In "Parisian Affairs" (1876), James summarizes the plot of *L'Étrangère*, reports that it stars Sarah Bernhardt* and Benoît Constant Coquelin,* and notes that it has been "pronounced indifferent by some people, and shockingly bad by others." In "Parisian Life" (5 Feb 1876), James praises Dumas's rewriting of Pierre Newsky's 1876 play *Les Danicheff* for adding "smartness." (In "The London Theatres," 1877 James called *Les Danicheff* "extremely picturesque and effective.") But in "Parisian Topics" (1 Apr 1876), James deplores Dumas's recent election to the French Academy, noting that the theme of "the 'unfortunate' woman" is his only theme. In 1877 James saw (again) Dumas's *Le Demi-Monde* at the Théâtre Français and was irritated by the dramatic situation depicted in it of a hypocritical ex-lover's denunciation of the fallen heroine. Yet in "Occasional Paris" (1878) he called *Le Demi-Monde* "on the whole, in form, the first comedy of our day," adding, however, that British audiences would not like it. Reversing its unchivalrous formula a few years later, James in "The Siege of London" presents a knowledgeable young man's refusal to gossip about the heroine while she is trying to snare young Desmesne (whose name faintly echoes the word "demimonde"). Next, when in 1891 James received a letter from William Archer,* who was an early translator of Henrik Johan Ibsen* into English and who had written in part to praise Ibsen's *Hedda Gabler* over Dumas's *Francillon*, James replied (5 Jun [Jul 1891]) to agree: "Yes, *Hedda* as against *Francillon*. . . . Dumas *fils* is no great god of mine—*phraseur*, intensely prosaic I find him—with all his hundred clevernesses." Finally, just after Dumas died, James wrote a long essay on him, entitled "Dumas the Younger." Surprisingly, it was rejected by the editor of the *Century Magazine* because it touched on the topic of seduction. James promptly published it elsewhere (Boston *Herald* and New York *Herald*, both 23 Feb 1896; reprinted as "On the Death of Dumas the Younger" in *New Review*, Mar 1896; and as "Dumas the Younger" in *Notes on Novelists*, 1914). In it, James says that his "own world . . . [has] become historical" because of Dumas's death. He has often seen *La Dame aux camélias* (though irritated by parts of it) with different leading actresses in the title role. He knows that Dumas remained a force in France, though not in America apart from this play. James comments on the inadaptability into English of a Dumas play, says Dumas happily never failed, and notes that his natural father gave him "momentum" (though the two differed in imagination and morality). Dumas was saturated with a sense of Paris during its move out of "full-grown romanticism," hence could become "the great casuist of the theatre" and "a professional moralist." James then notes that Americans and the British, "confounding" his object with his subject, wrongly regard Dumas as immoral (and even think he smells "of bad company"). His plays show what happens when people "insufficient[ly] control . . . their passions," mainly "the passion that unites and divides the sexes." Next, James touches on play after play: *Diane de Lys* is "a pretty story" but "long-winded"; *Le Demi-Monde* starts Dumas's "argumentative series" and has a subject which "strongly expands from within"; *Le Père prodigue* is almost uniquely comic for Dumas; *Denise* has a "singularly fine" conclusion; vivid *Francillon*, a highly "adequate" form. In conclusion, James says that Dumas provided drama in his time with "the ground of general method"; what was "blooming" in Dumas is now "grizzled" in Ibsen; Dumas dramatizes will power; he uses wit, ability to pierce falsities, and an instinct for the dramatic. Perhaps he overstresses the immediate, is too earnest and dry (like a policeman or an umpire); but he has manly force. The plot of *Roderick Hudson* is similar in many respects to that of *L'Affaire Clémenceau*. The plot of *The American* is even closer to that of *L'Étrangère*; in addition, the first name of Noémie Clarkson in Dumas's play provides the first name of Noémie Nioche in James's novel. Indirect influence by Dumas on James is suggested by this comment in the latter's letter to his brother William James (1 May [1878]): "I have thoroughly mastered Dumas, [Guillaume Victor Émile] Augier[*] and [Victorien] Sardou[*]." Having his 1896 essay on Dumas rejected by the editor of the *Century Magazine* inspired James to write his 1898 short story "John Delavoy" about another prudish editor. James's library contained three books by Dumas *fils* and, in addition, four by his father Alexandre Dumas *père*.

Du Maurier, George (1834–1896). Versatile Paris-born and -educated artist, caricaturist, humorous writer, and novelist. He was a schoolboy in Paris, an analytical chemist briefly in England, and then an art student in the Latin Quarter of Paris, Belgium, and the Netherlands. In spite of chronic eye trouble, he drew satirical cartoons for *Punch* (from 1860), joining its staff four years later. He also illustrated books and shorter writings of others (including the two serial versions of James's *Washington Square*) and later his own three novels—*Peter Ibbetson* (1892), *Trilby* (1894), and *The Martian* (1897). Du Maurier and his delightful wife had two sons and three daughters. One son, Major Guy Du Maurier, was a soldier playwright. The other, Sir Gerald Du Maurier, was a popular actor manager. One of Gerald's daughters was Daphne Du Maurier, the novelist. James, first meeting George Du Maurier and his wife at a dinner given in London by Charles Hamilton Aïdé* in 1877, commented in a letter home (20

May [1877]) that his new acquaintance was "a delightful little fellow" and his wife "tall [and] handsome . . . like his picture-women." James, who had long admired Du Maurier's *Punch* cartoons, quickly developed a close friendship with the man. He often went to the Du Maurier home in Hampstead (then in suburban London), shared long walks with him there and elsewhere, wrote to him from New York (to lament that the witty illustrator was not there to depict the city) and from Venice (to invite the Du Mauriers to come and share the sunsets there), entertained him often (once to meet Guy de Maupassant,* later to meet Jean Jules Jusserand,* and still later to meet Alphonse Daudet*), visited the ailing James Russell Lowell* at Whitby with him, and commented on Du Maurier in many letters to others. In a letter to Elizabeth Boott* (11 Dec [1883]), for example, James called the artist "singularly intelligent and sympathetic and satisfactory." James was the devoted godfather of the Du Maurier children, one of whom, the actor Gerald, was considered for the part of Hugh Crimble in James's play *The Outcry*. In one Notebook entry (25 Mar 1889), James remarks that Du Maurier had told him the plot for a story, unsuccessfully offered it to him, and then turned it himself into the immensely popular *Trilby*. Two years later James records in another Notebook entry (22 Feb 1891) another Du Maurier idea, which this time he seized upon and which became "The Real Thing." Du Maurier attended the opening performance of James's play *The American* in London, on 26 September 1891. In 1894 James published "The Coxon Fund," in which a bench assumes importance as the place where the central character sits, meditates, and talks: When James later commissioned Alvin Langdon Coburn* to provide a photograph to illustrate Volume XV of *The Novels and Tales of Henry James*, 1909, in which "The Coxon Fund" was to appear, he had the young man take a picture of a bench in Hampstead Heath where James and Du Maurier had sat and memorably talked. Du Maurier attended the disastrous first performance of James's *Guy Domville*, in London, on 5 January 1895. In a letter to their mutual friend Sir Edmund Wilson Gosse* (27 Aug [1895]), James says that "the deafening roar of sordid gold flowing in to him [Du Maurier] from . . . *Trilby*" makes James "feel . . . an even worse failure than usual." On several occasions James published comments on Du Maurier. James begins his "Daumier and London Society" (*Century Magazine* May 1883; reprinted as "George du Maurier" in *Partial Portraits*, 1883) by recollecting the pleasure of reading *Punch* in New York in 1850–1855 and being transported to London by it. Reality in England now reminds him of old drawings in *Punch*, which provides many Americans their only notions of English life. *Punch* humor may be "innocent," but it is also "not coarse" like that of certain "French comic papers." James comments on old *Punch* illustrations by both John Leech and Charles Keene, then turns to Du Maurier, who seems "hard upon the French" and pro-English. Still, he has "Gallic . . . gifts"—taste, grace, refinement. Detailing Du Maurier's early life, James then praises his eloquent, "sportive" *Punch* work and also his illustrations for books by William Makepeace Thackeray* and Elizabeth Cleghorn Gaskell.* Contrasting Du Maurier and other caricaturists (French as well as English), James concludes that "[n]o one has rendered like du Maurier the ridiculous little people who crop up in the interstices of . . . huge and complicated London." His use of black and white, rather than color, produces "an effect of atmosphere." James especially likes Du Maurier's duffers, beach scenes, children, and "amiable" women. He depicts "social, as distinguished from popular life." His people posture, think, pretend, glare. He triumphantly limns representative foreigners, young and old, contrasting them well with their British counterparts. James concludes by discussing a few of Du Maurier's recurrent "queer" British characters and their influence on manners on both sides of the Atlantic Ocean. In 1884 James published *Notes . . . on a Collection of Drawings by Mr. George du Maurier*, as part of an announcement of an exhibition to be held at the Fine Art Society, Bond Street, London. In "Our Artists in Europe" (1889; reprinted as "Black and White" in *Picture and Text*, 1893), James includes a complimentary section on the "brilliant" Du Maurier, saying that we accept as truth "his types, his categories, his conclusions, his sympathies and his ironies," with respect to things British. But does he elongate the human frame too much? Is he now too elegant? Does he ignore "the short and shabby"? Perhaps, but James closes by praising this "striking and edifying" creator of "a general satiric picture of the social life of his time and country." Next, James published an essay entitled "George du Maurier" (*Harper's Weekly*, 14 Apr 1894), in which he expresses puzzlement at the caricaturist turning novelist "in the afternoon of [his] existence." Although novels are a different medium, Du Maurier did not worry but simply wrote, and successfully. But it is sad because now other illustrators will turn to writing as well. Love of beauty motivates all of Du Maurier's work and protects the man. His *Peter Ibbetson* sweetly depicts a dream world of "inevitable beauty," where everything is "young [and] . . . long [of] leg." As the story unfolds, even pains are more lovely than sad, as the hero "measure[s] the mystery of love." In *Trilby*, which is rich with rosy charm, even "the dirty, wicked people have the grace of satyrs in a frieze." Du Maurier shows Paris through his three English characters' eyes so well that we renounce our Paris to see theirs. However, the heroine is so attractive that we become "uneasy for her." (James hinted that he knew the climax of *Trilby*, even as it was being serialized.) Finally, James produced a long, loving tribute to his deceased friend entitled "George du Maurier" (*Harper's New Monthly Magazine*, Sep 1897). After an introduction in which James remembers their friendship from far back, Du Maurier's conversational ability, and his uncritical and unearnest liveliness, he offers a five-part, rambling elegy. First, he vaguely recalls dinners together, Du Maurier's *Punch* work, and details of his childhood and his love of tall women, children, and animals. Second, he discusses his friend's amiability, patience, reverence for privacy, pursuit of beauty, praise of colleagues, and keen powers of observation (despite his eye trouble). Third, James recalls Du Maurier's personal qualities, his love of music and musicians, his delight in "deeply detectable Whitby" and its coastal scenery, and his lecture platform problems and successes (the financial gain inspiring in James "a desperate dream of emulation''). Fourth, James suggests that Du Maurier's novels coalesce into one artistic unit, concerning beauty, reality, and the sadness which shadows youth; in them, text and illustration ''melt'' together. And fifth, James reports that Du Maurier had many never-told stories in his head, that his senses shocked his nerves, that publicity violated him at last, and that though desperately ill he still enjoyed the London passing parade and worked meticulously on *The Martian*. James concludes that Du Maurier's life was complete, secure, and rounded, and that his work is too. James's library contained two books by Du Maurier.

Duncan, Isadora (1878–1927). San Francisco–born dancer who early in her meteoric career became the rage of European capitals. James and Andrew Lang* in March 1900 were among a group sponsoring a London recital by Duncan. Her later years were marred by a series of dreadful tragedies. Her autobiography, *My Life*, was published in 1927.

Dundene, Alice. In ''The Special Type,'' the innocent correspondent in the divorce action of Frank Brivet. When the narrator paints Brivet's portrait, Alice claims it.

Dunderton, Lord. In ''Fordham Castle,'' Mattie Magaw's fiancé.

Dunn, Mrs. In ''Flickerbridge,'' a Londoner whose portrait Frank Granger paints.

Dunning, William Archibald (1857–1922). Professor at Columbia University, and writer on historical subjects and political theory. Among his half-dozen or so books is *Essays on the Civil War and Reconstruction and Related Topics* (1898), which James in ''American Letter'' (23 Apr 1898) calls ''admirable'' for its ''high lucidity.'' Dunning expertly discusses ''constitutional, legal, doctrinal'' aspects of life during and just after the Civil War, especially problems connected with weakened states' rights.

Dunoyer, Mlle. In *The Tragic Muse*, a Théâtre Français actress whom Miriam Rooth and Peter Sherringham observe and meet.

Durand. In *The Reverberator* and *The Tragic Muse*, a Paris café owner.

Durant, Alice. In *Daisy Miller: A Comedy in Three Acts*, the rather sharp-tongued but evidently attractive American girl accompanying Mrs. Costello and her escort Charles Reverdy to Europe. She calls Mrs. Costello Cousin Louisa. In the complex finale in Rome, Alice accepts Charles Reverdy's proposal of marriage. Daisy Miller labels Alice as Frederick Winterbourne's cousin.

Duveneck, Elizabeth Boott. The married name of James's old and dear friend Elizabeth Boott.*

Duveneck, Frank (1848–1919). Kentucky-born American painter, etcher, and sculptor. He studied art in Munich (from 1870), established a school there in 1878, moved it to Italy a year later, and etched a series of Venetian scenes (1880–1885). On the death of his wife Elizabeth Boott Duveneck in 1888, he sculpted a memorial for her grave in Florence, and soon thereafter returned to Cincinnati mainly to teach. In a note (*Nation*, 3 Jun 1875), James hints that Boston perhaps prematurely regards "very young" Duveneck as a "man of genius," but then he praises three of his "rigidly natural" portraits among five in a show there. Duveneck has declined an invitation from that city and intends instead (wisely, in James's view) to study further in Europe. In "On Some Pictures Lately Exhibited" (July 1875) James, repeating much from his June 3 review, reports that certain Bostonians are calling Duveneck "an American [Diego de Silva y] Velasquez[*]," grants that he has taken "giant strides" since his Munich schooling, and finds several of his portraits of "an extraordinary interest" because of their "reality and directness." In a kind of postscript, James adds (ominously, as it turned out) that "we shall take it hard if he fails to do something of the first degree of importance." In a later untitled note (*Nation*, 9 Sep 1875), he continues to laud Duveneck: Some of his new portraits are striking, rich, solid, consummate, magnificent, one (of a certain female subject) having "pulpy, blood-tinted, carnal substance in the cheeks and brow . . . of which a . . . master . . . might be proud." Duveneck painted a fine portrait of James's father Henry James, Sr., about 1880. Curiously, James's close friend Elizabeth Boott took art lessons from Duveneck in Munich and then in Florence, where she had long lived with her rich, widowed father Francis Boott* and where James met Duveneck in March 1880. In a letter to Charles Eliot Norton* (31 Mar [1880]), he described the artist as "much the most highly-developed phenomenon in the way of a painter that the U.S.A. has given birth to. His work is remarkably strong and brilliant." James limned the man in a more personal way to Catherine Walsh,* his aunt (3 May 1880); "an excellent fellow . . . [though] terribly earthy and unlicked." To his mother (16 Mar 1881) James described Frank and Elizabeth as gossiped about and their possible marriage "strange," given the painter's "roughness" and lack of intellectual attainments. When James learned that the two were married (1886), he wrote to his friend Henrietta Reubell* (11 Mar [1886]) that the painter "is illiterate, ignorant, and not a gentleman (though an excellent fellow, kindly, simple etc.)." James wrote to his parents (26 Dec [1886]) to report the birth of the Duvenecks' son; he added that although Duveneck "is a good frank fellow" James cannot converse two minutes with him; he will be a social burden to his wife, and his father-in-law's acceptance of the situation not only is "pathetic and heroic" but also is a subject fit for an Ivan Sergeyevich Turgenev* tale. When Lizzie died of pneumonia (March 1888) in Paris and was buried in Florence, James wrote to her father, asking that his condolences be transmitted to her husband. James subsequently followed the artist's career. In 1890 he expressed regret, in a letter to Francis Boott, Lizzie's father (11 Jan 1890), that Duveneck had contributed nothing to a certain Paris exhibition James had just visited. He asked Boott by letter from Ramsgate (14 Jul [1890]) to thank Duveneck for the photographs sent of "the magnificent [bronze] monument" made for Lizzie's grave. Late in his life, James was critical, in a letter to his niece Margaret James (1 Dec 1915), of Duveneck's ultimately disappointing career: "His only good work was done in his very few first years, nearly fifty of these ago—at least the long interval since has always looked like a deadly desert."

Dyer, Miss. In *Tenants*, Mildred Stanmore's companion, who is hired by Sir Frederick Byng, flirts with villainous Captain Lurcher, but is unceremoniously dropped toward the end.

Dyott, Mrs. In "The Story in It," Maud Blessingbourne's hostess and the object of Colonel Voyt's affections.

E

"E. P. D. Subject." An abortive tale for which James wrote Notebook entries (28 Feb 1882, 15 Jun 1901) and a fragment evidently in June 1893. E. P. D. stands for Edward Parker Deacon,* whose domestic mess triggered a Jamesian plot idea: foolish husband, bored wife, and her lover; divorce, new marriages, and maturing children.

Earle, Maria Theresa (Mrs. C. W. Earle) (1836–1925). British writer on gardening, vegetarianism, cooking, horticulture, flower arranging, and travel. Her *Pot-Pourri from a Surrey Garden* (1897) was incredibly popular, and later volumes in her *Pot-Pourri* series (1899, 1903, 1914) were popular as well. She also published *Memoirs and Memories* (1911). In a Notebook entry (13 Jul 1891), James credits "a word of Mrs. Earle's" for the idea resulting in his short story "The Chaperon." His Pocket Diaries indicate that he retained his friendship with Mrs. Earle as late as 1913 and 1914.

"The Early Meeting of Parliament." Political letter, published in the *Nation* (26 Dec 1878). Noting that war in Afghanistan has begun, James reports that Queen Victoria has called an extraordinary meeting of Parliament to discuss the situation. William Ewart Gladstone,* head of the Liberal opposition party, charges that Prime Minister Lord Beaconsfield (Benjamin Disraeli*) sent a truculent military embassy to Afghanistan, which is ruled by Shir Ali, the Amir, to demand the impossible, as an excuse for war, in order to counter Russian advances and thus protect India. James is critical of Beaconsfield for inconsistency and critical of Gladstone for having earlier led weakly, but he concludes that the British public would rather be patriotic than critical at the moment.

Edenbrook, Lord. In *Guy Domville*, Mrs. Peverel's uncle, whose chaplain recommended Guy Domville as a tutor for her son George Peverel.

Edgeworth, Maria (1767–1849). British novelist; she was born in Oxfordshire but lived with her eccentric inventor father in Ireland from 1782 until his death in 1817. Her best work is undoubtedly *Castle Rackrent* (1800). In his review of *Selected Essays* by Abraham Hayward,* James especially praises the essay concerning Maria Edgeworth, which reveals the peculiar relations she had with her father, that "terrible monitor." James describes her as a fine storyteller, with humor and powers of observation but little imagination.

Edison, Thomas Alva (1847–1931). Ohio-born railroad newsboy, telegraphist, and scientist whose well-known inventions are too well known and numerous to list here. Returning from the United States in 1911, James met Edison aboard ship, described him to his sister-in-law Alice James (6 Aug [1911]) as "great bland simple deaf street-boy-faced."

Edward VII (1841–1910). Oldest son of Queen Victoria, the Prince of Wales and, upon his mother's death, the king of England (1901–1910). He knew James's high-society friend Mary Morton Sands.* In October 1891, Edward, then the Prince of Wales, attended a performance of James's play *The American*. In a letter to Clara Woolson Benedict,* sister of Constance Fenimore Woolson,* and Clara's daughter Clare Benedict (22 Jan 1901), James calls Edward "an arch-vulgarian," goes on to gossip about his private life, and predicts that "vulgarity and frivolity" will mark his reign. Of Ariana Randolph Curtis* (3 Feb 1901) James asks, "[C]an the Sovereign change his spots, especially when they have been so big?" To Oliver Wendell Holmes, Jr.* (20 Feb 1901), James reports that the new king's nickname is "Edward . . . the Caresser." The death of Edward VII, in May 1910, required official mourning, which closed the theaters and contributed to the nonproduction of James's play *The Outcry*. In 1916 James was a recipient of the Order of Merit, which order Edward VII had instituted.

Edward, Lady. In "Mrs. Medwin," a fashionable lady who Mamie Cutter says has approved of Mrs. Medwin.

Edward, Lord. In "The Siege of London," a guest along with Mrs. Headway at the Demesne estate.

Edwards, Annie (?–1896). Prolific, popular British novelist. James reviewed (*Nation*, 13 Jan 1876) her *Leah: A Woman of Fashion* (1875), reporting that the authoress can cleverly describe disagreeable things—here, various kinds of "compromised and compromising" British ne'er-do-wells on the Continent. It is hard to analyze this British woman novelist's flirting with the subject of the "depths of depravity," including improprieties in women. She is pusillanimous but does present one well-drawn rake. The "slender . . . apology" of a plot "is simple to baldness"; yet it has improbabilities, for example, the transformation of vicious Leah herself. Furthermore, the book is irritatingly composed entirely in the present tense.

Egbert, Lady. In "The Lesson of the Master," a woman about whom Mrs. Henry St. George gossips.

Egbert, Lord. In *The Tragic Muse*, a snob whom Charles Carteret seems to want Nicholas Dormer to emulate.

Eggleston, George Cary (1839–1911). American lawyer, reporter, and editor. He was born in Indiana, studied law in Richmond, Virginia, enlisted in the Confederate cavalry during the Civil War, and after 1870 lived in New York. James in "American Letter" (7 May 1898) mentions Eggleston's *Southern Soldier Stories* (1898) as an "anecdotical [*sic*]" account of "military memories" which makes the nonveteran critic "groan" because the author does "so little with them."

Egidio. In "The Tree of Knowledge," Morgan Mallow's Italian servant.

Eléonore. In "Mrs. Temperly," the Marquise de Brives's friend who admires Maria Temperly.

Eliot, George (1819–1880). Important Victorian novelist. Eliot, whose real name was Mary Ann Evans, was born in Warwickshire, where her father was a land agent. She studied German, Italian, music, and rationalistic biblical history; then she traveled and became an assistant editor of the *Westminster Review* in London (1851). There she met a number of important writers of the day, including Thomas Carlyle,* Harriet Martineau, Herbert Spencer,* and George Henry Lewes,* an English editor, literary critic, and popularizer of philosophy, physiology, and psychology. In 1854 Lewes and Mary Ann Evans entered into a common-law marriage which lasted until his death in 1878. George Eliot first used her pen name in *Blackwood's Magazine* in 1857, and soon she began to produce highly significant fiction, including *Scenes from Clerical Life* (1858), the popular *Adam Bede* (1859), *The Mill on the Floss* (1860, partly autobiographical), and *Silas Marner* (1861). A trip to Italy resulted in her significant, money-making historical novel *Romola* (1863). Then came *Felix Holt, the Radical* (1866), after which Eliot published some poetry (notably *The Spanish Gypsy: A Poem* [1868] and *The Legend of Jubal, and Other Poems* [1874]). Finally, she wrote her masterpieces *Middlemarch* (1872) and the pro-Semitic *Daniel Deronda* (1876). Two years after Lewes's death she married John Walter Cross,* a New York banker who was twenty years her junior and who later wrote her biography, but she died a few months after the marriage. James, who read Eliot from his earliest years, reviewed her *Felix Holt* a bit brashly in 1866 (*Nation*, 16 Aug 1866). He regards its plot as "artificial," even "rusty" and "vulgar," its conclusions "signally weak," its style "lingering, slow-moving, expanding," and its minor characters too numerous. The result is that Eliot makes a "meager . . . whole" out of admittedly "vigorous parts." All the same, James contends, it is an accomplished piece of work, as were *Adam Bede* and *Romola* earlier. *Felix Holt* builds on "microscopic observation"; displays humanity, humor, and morality; "is . . . the fruit of a great deal of culture, experience, and resignation"; and sympathetically depicts country life in the English Midlands thirty years ago. Though not a masterpiece, it continues the tradition of Maria Edgeworth* and Jane Austen,* but in addition shows "a certain masculine comprehensiveness which they lack." Still, Eliot only annotates whereas Charles Reade,* for example, makes bold "guesses." She exemplifies "the feminine mind" here by her "unbroken current of feeling and . . . expression." In "The Novels of George Eliot" (*Atlantic Monthly*, Oct 1866), James asserts that it is the critic's "first duty" to discern his subject author's method, "literary convictions," and "ruling theory." Eliot explains hers in *Adam Bede*: She feels less for the "few sublimely beautiful" than for the "work-worn" multitudes. In her *Scenes of Clerical Life* she regularly concerns herself with "ignorant and obscure . . . parishioners" in the English region she calls Loamshire. Her affections and optimism lighten her pictures of "gross misery" into "broad felicity." James offers many examples. Her characters are generally respectable because their consciences overcome their passions. *Adam Bede* is a leap forward from *Scenes of Clerical Life*, but *Silas Marner* "is more nearly a masterpiece" than anything else by Eliot. It is balanced, presents "low life" well, and has the colors, lights, and shadows of "the Dutch masters whom she emulates." James quotes and summarizes at length, in obvious approval of character depiction through loving use of dialect. He notes the oddity that titular heroes and heroines in Eliot's works have minor roles and cites as proof Tito Melema in *Romola* and Hetty Sorrel in *Adam Bede*. The latter novel should have ended with the girl's execution; Eliot could then have followed, à la Honoré de Balzac,* with a sequel featuring surviving characters. James dislikes Mrs. Poyser ("*too* epigrammatic; her wisdom smells of the lamp") and Adam himself ("too good . . . and stiff-backed"). Dinah Morris has "many of the warm colors of life" but becomes too cool after her "religious conversion." James "accept[s]" Hetty heartily, as Eliot's "most successful" female portrait. Arthur Donnithorne, less well managed, is "superficial." But in *Adam Bede* Eliot draws "attitudes of feeling" better than "movements of feeling." She offers "original" touches, humor, satire, and serious philosophy, but not drama. *Felix Holt* is admirably detailed but "without character as a composition." Its minor characters do "reflect . . . life," for example, Mrs. Denner, whom James quotes and admires. *The Mill on the Floss*, among the four English novels, seems to have the "most dramatic continuity." Maggie Tulliver is Eliot's best female character after Hetty, just as Tom Tulliver is her best male after Tito. Yet Maggie is a far better person than her brother Tom. James finds the Dodson family handled as well as though by Balzac. But James judges the ending of *The Mill on the Floss* to be defective: The flood is not foreshadowed. *Romola* is executed on a grand scale: Savonarola is big; Tito's career is full. Yet the novel is more "a work of morals" than "a work of art." The drama drags. The setting is too big. But James forgives much in *Romola* "for the sake of its general feeling and its elevated morality." Using Tito as an example, Eliot presents her steadfast belief that deeds determine character. Her novel here is essentially prosaic, since Eliot lacks imagination. But she has more imagination than Anthony Trollope,* though less than Charlotte Brontë. (See Brontë sisters*.) James offers this conclusion: Eliot is conservative both morally and artistically. She offers us consciences challenged in old ways rather than new, and her novelistic closures are aesthetically "irritating." In an 1867 review of historical novelist Anne E. Manning,* James comments that as a picture of fifteenth-century life *Romola* "is quite worthless." He reviewed (*Nation*, 2 Jul 1868) *The Spanish Gypsy*, beginning with the statement that the author produces little, is patient, and is one of England's "best . . . writers." She is also a worthy poet though not a great one. (Yet her novels have sentences with "a certain poetic light, a poetic ring.") *The Spanish Gypsy*, which Eliot wrote before visiting Spain (then rewrote after doing so), is not centrally poetic; it is intellectual (like her novels) rather than sensuous and experienced, well wrought but not warm. Eliot is the reverse of that "born poet" Elizabeth Barrett Browning,* who is, however, tasteless, tactless, and with "faults of detail . . . unceasing." James summarizes the "story" of *The Spanish Gypsy*, which is "thrilling and touching," in a "dramatic form, with . . . narrative interlude." Cast in the fifteenth century, it has three main characters: a vivid hero named Don Silva; Fedalma, the "heretical" heroine; and Zarca, a militant gypsy leader (her forceful father). The intense plot pivots when the hero turns traitor and joins the proscribed gypsies. Typically, Eliot includes minor characters who have "true human accents," even while they are handled psychologically and morally. James especially likes Juan, whose lyrics provide a contrast to the intense action but do seem forced. James feels that Eliot has made her central characters too modern, as in *Romola*. Still, the work has polish, reflection, and "moral vision." Curiously, James again reviewed (*North American Review*, Oct 1868) *The Spanish Gypsy*, this time at great length. He begins by noting that when an author successful in one form tries another, enemies happily anticipate failure. Here we have Eliot, England's best prose stylist, now turning to poetry. *The Spanish Gypsy* is "much more of a poem than was to be expected." However, the first reviews of *The Spanish Gypsy* are more favorable than later ones. At first, readers were surprised to see any poetry from Eliot, in whom, however, by now the novelist has again absorbed the poet. As for her present work, it is notable for "rhetorical energy and elegance," perhaps too much "richness," since she sometimes overdoes it. James quotes much, not only to illustrate Eliot's use of vivid epigrams but also to show beauty spoiled by overstatement. He also praises her humor and descriptive powers, but he complains that Eliot criticizes her characters instead of creating them. He turns to "the story" of the narrative poem. Perhaps it was originally planned to present the conflict of "nature and culture," of "education and the instinct of the race." But, as it turned out, we have a "conflict of love and duty," thus a moral tale, which is hurt by Eliot's providing her heroine with a conscience but which is saved by making the work a romance—a "compromise with reality"—rather than a piece of realism. *The Spanish Gypsy* deals with the picturesque, the ideal; it is not a "transcript of actual or possible fact." In real life, for example, Fedalma would have kept her lover. Here, she is too "lofty" and lacks feminine "warmth," "petulance," and "graceful irrationality." James says that he likes to compliment a given plot by "imagining it otherwise constructed." A prose *Spanish Gypsy* might be "in a diction more nervous and heated" and with a different ending. James considers the four main characters. Fedalma might give in to love, marriage, regret, and then what? She might die as a tragic figure, neither gypsy nor Christian. Zarca is just right, as is: a plain romance figure, poised, noble, and eloquent. Don Silva is central: the agonizing, complex, passive recipient of fate's buffets. His best scene is his "lonely vigil," which occurs after he pledges to aid Zarca and in which Eliot powerfully reveals "the mingled dignity and pliancy of her style." James likes Juan best: He is inactive but eloquent, aloof, observant, alert to note and comment. James concludes that *The Spanish Gypsy* is not unified, not genuine. It is "a vast mural design in [varied] mosaic-work." It shows "effort," has "intellectual tension," but it lacks "passion." Its illumination is "artificial." Its partly fine background is "mechanical." Its characters are understood but are partly "factitious." The ending is beautiful but "untrue." The book is a "study of character" and "a noble literary performance," in short, "a romance written by . . . a thinker." Next, James reviewed (*Galaxy*, Mar 1873) *Middlemarch*, beginning negatively by calling it too descriptive and undramatic, less "moulded" into something balanced and more resembling a "chain of episodes," detailed but lacking wholeness. Its author's mind is "contemplative and analytic"; so we have here the "discursive and expansive." James grows complimentary, especially in praising the heroine Dorothea Brooke—"a genuine creation," whereas Eliot's earlier females are "less unfolded blossoms." Dorothea is a spiritually sweet being and should be placed more centrally, so that Mary Garth's love would get less attention. Also, we care less about Fred Vincy than Eliot evidently wants us to; his "tribulations" and "egotism" are presented in "irritating" detail. Dorothea's husband Casaubon is "an arid plant," and Eliot treats the two with more refinement than breadth, thus expanding a disappointment into a tragedy. After Casaubon's death, Dorothea ponders the question of marrying Will Ladislaw somewhat "factitious[ly]," while Will's characterization becomes an "eminent failure." Lydgate, "the real hero of the story," is presented as "strenuous, generous, fallible, and altogether human." His marriage and Dorothea's are broadly contrasted. Eliot splendidly analyzes Vincy's sister Rosamond, Lydgate's "gracefully vicious" wife, that "mulish domestic flower," whose flirting strikes James as "a discordant note'' in the novel. He goes on to praise Eliot's minor characters; they comprise "a large group . . . begotten of the super-abundance of the author's creative instinct." He especially likes Casaubon, calling him "unwholesomely, helplessly sinister," but he finds Bulstrode "too diffusely treated." Still, all of them are part of a "bravely rounded . . . little world." James begins his conclusion: Eliot's imagination is illuminated by generalizing thought, which makes her better even than Henry Fielding, because more philosophical, though at the cost of "simplicity." Her style becomes "obscure," at times scientific. But with *Middlemarch* she has taken the "old-fashioned English novel" to its limits; it almost becomes history. James reviewed (*North American Review*, Oct 1874) *The Legend of Jubal, and Other Poems*, beginning with the statement that Eliot's poetry, which is not so good as her prose, must be judged on its merits and not those of her prose. Her poetry is characteristic of her intellect and shows her versatility. James identifies the contents of the present volume, calls it a combination of "spontaneity of thought and excessive reflectiveness of expression," and finds its ideas more valuable than its "rigid" form. He discusses specific poems: One satirizes vegetarianism; another nicely shows brother-sister relations; still another, the artist's creed. One presents a generous woman of the sort we revere Eliot's novels for giving us. The title poem presents a musician who is productive but unappreciated; yet he dies knowing that his works have been assimilated by humanity. James closes with the wish that Eliot would not pervert to cleverness and scepticism what he calls her "passionate faith," which if expressed could result in great achievements. Curiously, James reviewed (*Nation*, 24 Feb 1876) the first serial installment of *Daniel Deronda*. Generally not liking this form of fiction, here he registers anticipation. The opening makes us wonder whether the heroine, Gwendolyn Harleth, will be more like Dorothea or Rosamond, of *Middlemarch*. We already sense aspects of the mysterious and the universal. Next, James published "Daniel Deronda: A Conversation" (*Atlantic Monthly*, Dec 1876, reprinted in *Partial Portraits*, 1888). In this piece, largely in the form of dialogue, James presents his partly contradictory opinions concerning Eliot. The three speakers are Theodora, who admires Eliot rather simplistically; Pulcheria, who is critical and somewhat more profound; and Theodora's friend Constantius, who as a well-read reviewer and neophyte novelist is closest to James himself and who mediates between the extremes of the other two. Idealistic, tearful Theodora dislikes French novels (George Sand,* for example, "is impure"; Balzac "gets down on all fours"); is opposed to mere aestheticism; prefers spirit to form; and has "a hopeless passion" for the titular hero of *Daniel Deronda* while admiring the Jewish patriarch Mordecai and the youthful heroine Gwendolyn Harleth in it. Pulcheria is more inclined to grin than weep while reading Eliot (she calls *Romola* "a kind of literary tortoise," says that too many Eliot characters drown, criticizes many of her fictive spouses as "disagreeable"); is more learned though with a touch of anti-Semitism; reveals her admiration of Austen, Balzac, Prosper Mérimée,* Nathaniel Hawthorne,* Ivan Sergeyevich Turgenev,* and William Makepeace Thackeray*; expresses her dislike of didacticism in fiction; says that Eliot overanalyzes her characters; and finds the hero of *Daniel Deronda* priggish and the heroine too light for tragedy. She likens the whole novel to oddly reflecting "uneven ponds" rather than a river with a flowing current. Constantius admires Eliot, who is always enjoyable; but the pronounces *Daniel Deronda* her "weakest" novel (much inferior, for example, to *Middlemarch*); dislikes her idealizing of Jewish characters ("the Jewish burden of the story tended to weary me," being "at bottom cold"); voices his preference for "liquid" George Sand to "solid" George Eliot; and calls the latter's style "sometimes too loose . . . [and] a little baggy." In all of this, Constantius agrees with Pulcheria, but then he sides with Theodora because the main ingredient in the novel is the heroine's evolving maturity through suffering: Her "whole history is vividly told." He agrees with Theodora that Eliot's "secondary people"—"born of the *overflow* of observation" and "spring[ing] from a much-peopled mind"—help to create a lifelike drama. But Constantius is sad that ever since *Felix Holt* Eliot has seemed pressured by the times to avoid spontaneity and feeling, and has instead cultivated skeptical criticism. James briefly reviewed (*Nation*, 25 Apr 1878) two short stories by Eliot which were reprinted in Blackwood's cheap 1878 edition of her *Works*. Regarding Eliot as "the great novelist who has written the fewest short stories," he pronounces "Brother Jacob," about a criminal exposed because of his retarded brother's craving for candy, more successful than "The Lifted Veil," which concerns a clairvoyant whose wicked wife's exposure is due to a macabre medical experiment. Eliot displays cleverness here, if too much epigrammatism, and also a mind seldom "found at play." Finally, James reviewed (*Atlantic Monthly*, May 1885; reprinted in *Partial Portraits*, 1888) Cross's 1885 biography of his deceased wife George Eliot. It is not a secret-revealing work; her journals and letters do not explain her novels. She had talent and knowledge, but she shaped her works mysteriously. Cross follows an admirable plan: He presents her unexceptional words with a minimum of marginalia. James reviews the main contours of Eliot's early life: religious upbringing, early avoidance of novels, study of German, association with Lewes, editorial work, and productive "sequestration." James offers this summary: "Her deep, strenuous, much-considering mind, of which the leading mark is the capacity for . . . luminous brooding, fed upon the idea of her irregularity with an intensity which . . . only her magnificent intellectual activity and Lewes's brilliancy and ingenuity kept from being morbid." James criticizes Eliot for too much reflection, too little spontaneity. He regards her "beneficent intimacy" with Lewes as an "example of good." The rest of James's review is mainly commentary on Eliot's works: *Scenes from Clerical Life* made success possible; *Adam Bede* proved to her that she was great; her stated dislike of Balzac's "hateful" *Père Goriot* reveals that she regarded fiction as best when it is "moralised fable" (for example, *Middlemarch*); her later works show imagination but little artistic sense; and gradually reflection (because of Lewes) crowded out perception. Her foreign journals lack descriptions of "spectacle" and "art." Thus, *Romola*, though her finest work, has fatal defects: It is bloodlessly erudite, too "Germanic." Eliot shows ability, steady labor, and avoidance of vulgar society. To guests, her home in the Priőry (1863–1880) resembled "a literary temple," with Lewes a businesslike guardian reducing "the friction of living" for her. But Alphonse Daudet* was right when he warned writers that too much reading can screen them from valuable direct experience. Without Lewes, Eliot's writings might have been "more familiarly and casually human." Still, though her letters display a "gray . . . tone" (if also "moral elevation"), Eliot was "one of the noblest, most beautiful minds of our time." Women today can see her as proof that limitations to their progress are few. George Eliot was a major influence on James from his earliest mature years; once he had met her personally, his letters, especially those he sent home to his family, were dotted with references to her. Beginning in the 1860s, he read her new works as soon as they appeared. He called upon her in 1869, taken there by Grace Norton,* and wrote to his father the next day (10 May [1869]) that he was "impressed, interested and pleased," although he added a grotesque description of the "magnificently ugly" features of "this great horse-faced blue-stocking." James adds that his visit was cut short because one of Lewes's sons had an attack of spinal pain. To Grace Norton (5 May 1873) James comments that *Middlemarch*, "with all its faults, is . . . a truly immense performance." James's private opinions of *Daniel Deronda*, expressed in letters home, are confusing: "It was disappointing, . . . [b]ut I enjoyed it more than anything of hers . . . I have ever read" (to Alice James [22 Feb (1876)]; and it is "a great failure compared with her other books" (to William James [22 Jun (1876)]). In April 1878 James lunched in London with John Cross; Lewes was present also and invited James to his home again. James went later the same month where he met Lewes's friend Herbert Spencer.* Shortly before Lewes's death, James made another pilgrimage to the home of Eliot, who let both James and his fellow guest, a Mrs. Greville, know this time that they were not especially welcome; in addition, the host and hostess returned unread James's *The Europeans*, which Mrs. Greville had loaned them and the authorship of which they were unaware. When Eliot died, James called upon Cross; he let James sit in her "empty chair" and praised her "amazing" memory and "exemption from the sense of fatigue" (as James wrote to Alice [30 Jan 1881]). George Eliot greatly influenced James's fiction, especially because of her moral seriousness and emotional restraint. More specifically, his *Watch and Ward* may owe something to *Silas Marner*. His first novel with the bigness of an Eliot canvas is *The Portrait of a Lady*, the tragically married heroine of which parallels situations in *Middlemarch* and *Daniel Deronda*; Isabel's husband Gilbert Osmond certainly resembles Casaubon of *Middlemarch*, while Ralph Touchett may resemble Philip Wakem of *The Mill on the Floss*. The heroine of *The Bostonians* may be likened to Dinah Morris, the redheaded orator in *Adam Bede*. Finally, in "The Art of Fiction" James praises Eliot for her depiction of maturing children; so his handling of Maisie Farange in *What Maisie Knew* may echo several of her young girls. Other, usually more minor influences have also been noted by the critics, who rightly see Eliot as a major influence on James, whose autobiographical volumes are replete with references to her. For two examples, in *Notes of a Son and Brother* he reports that his cousin Mary Temple* admired Eliot and asked James to give the novelist her love; and in *The Middle Years* he recalls in detail his visits to Eliot and her husband, especially dwelling on her appearance, her conversation, and their returning *The Europeans* to his escort Mrs. Greville. James's library contained nine books by George Eliot, as well as two by George Henry Lewes.

Elizabeth, Lady. In *The Tragic Muse*, a friend of Charles Carteret.

Elliot, Francis Minto (née Dickinson) (1820–1898). British writer of fiction, sketches, and art criticism (this last under the pen names Florentia and Florentine). Born in Reading, she married John Edward Geils (1838) and later (1863) became the wife of the Rev. Mr. Gilbert Elliot, dean of Bristol. She lived much in Rome and died in Siena. Among Mrs. Elliot's eleven books are *Diary of an Idle Woman in Italy* (1871), other "Idle Woman" *Diary* books (*in Sicily* [1883], *Spain* [1884], and *Constantinople* [1892]), *Old Court Life in France* (1873), and fiction, including *The Italians: A Novel* (1875). James reviewed (*Nation*, 12 Aug 1875) *The Italians*, beginning with the opinion that it is as disappointing as the "flippant and untrustworthy" *Diary of an Idle Woman in Italy*. Mrs. Elliot knows provincial Italian life superficially and might have used grassy Lucca as a background better than she does in her novel, which features a man of "new mobility" falling in love with an old marchesa's drooping niece. He rescues her from a fire, after which the villain, an improbable aristocratic communist, "drops . . . into utter darkness." James finds the theme of "exaggerated family pride" undeveloped, the marchesa insufficiently "studied," and "Italian levity" wrongly scorned here.

Elliott, Gertrude. The name of the actress wife of Sir Johnston Forbes-Robertson.*

Elliott, Maud Howe (1854–1948). Boston-born daughter of Samuel Gridley Howe and Julia Ward Howe,* and a writer in her own right. She was privately educated and traveled extensively in Europe. She became a journalist in the mid-1870s. She married the Scottish painter John Elliott (1887), and they lived in Chicago, Italy, and elsewhere. John Elliott died in 1925. Mrs. Elliott published fiction, travel writing (some concerning Newport, Rhode Island), and biographies (of her mother, her husband, and her cousin Francis Marion Crawford*). James knew the Elliots, and he met Hendrik Christian Andersen* in Elliott's studio in Rome in 1899. By letter (27 Jul 1899) he asked Andersen to tell "the Elliotts . . . I have a very affectionate memory of them." In her book on Crawford, Mrs. Elliott reports that his half-sister Margaret Terry Chanler told her that Crawford had pinpointed the spot in *What Maisie Knew* where James began to dictate, and alleges that James "admitted it."

Elliott, Sarah Barnwell (1848–1928). Georgia-born writer whose family was greatly hurt by the Civil War. An experienced novelist from the late 1870s, she began in the 1890s to write about poor whites in Tennessee. Her best work is *The Durket Sperret* (1898), which James discusses in "American Letter" (9 Jul 1898). He spends too much time worrying over its being written in dialect: "[T]he ignoble jargon of the population she depicts" simply "lacerate[s the] ear." Elliott has talent but lapses as well. She does not adequately treat her *donnée*: a young backwoods maid in a university professor's home.

Ellis. In *Pyramus and Thisbe*, Stephen Young's unseen friend, whose loud talk bothers Catherine West.

Embarrassments. Collection of four short stories, published in London by Heinemann, 1896, and in New York by Macmillan, 1896: "The Figure in the Carpet," "Glasses," "The Next Time," and "The Way It Came."

Emerson, Ralph Waldo (1803–1882). Highly significant transcendental essayist, poet, and friend of New England and other literati. Born in Boston, he was the son of a Unitarian pastor who died when the boy was only eight years old. He graduated from Harvard College (1821), taught school for a while, studied at the Harvard Divinity School (1825), was intermittently sickly, became the junior pastor in Boston's Second Church, and married Ellen Tucker (1829). She died in 1831 at the age of nineteen. Emerson resigned his church position and went abroad (1832–1833), where he met Walter Savage Landor, John Stuart Mill, Samuel Taylor Coleridge, William Wordsworth, and Thomas Carlyle,* among others. Once he returned to Boston, he preached irregularly and began a successful career as a lecturer. He soon inherited his deceased wife's estate (1834, 1837; total about $23,000). He married Lydia Jackson (1835) and participated in the Transcendental Club (1836–1843) with numerous other intellectual leaders, including Bronson Alcott, Orestes Brownson, Margaret Fuller, and Henry David Thoreau. He published *Nature* (1836) and had a son, Waldo (1836–1842). At Harvard he delivered two influential lectures, "The American Scholar" (1837) and "The Divinity School Address" (1838). His daughter Ellen was born (1839). He helped Fuller publish the transcendental magazine *The Dial* (1840–1844). His controversial *Essays* (1841) helped establish his international renown. His daughter Edith was born (1841) and then his son Edward was born and *Essays: Second Series* was published (1844). He bought a lot by Walden Pond, on which he let Thoreau (his live-in handyman starting in 1841) squat. *Poems* (146). He took his second trip abroad (1847–1848), this time meeting Frédéric Chopin, Charles Dickens,* Alfred, Lord Tennyson,* and Alexis de Tocqueville, among others, and seeing his beloved Carlyle again. *Nature, Addresses, and Lectures* (1849); *Representative Men* (1850). Emerson, who had discontinued preaching in 1838, was especially successful lecturing from 1850 through 1867. He helped establish the Concord Academy (1855), which James's younger brothers Garth and Robertson attended in 1860 and 1861. Emerson published *English Traits* (1856), met President Abraham Lincoln (1862), and was elected to membership in the American Academy of Arts and Sciences (1864). *May-Day and Other Poems* (1867), *Society and Solitude* (1870). In 1872, when his house burned, friends, mainly James Russell Lowell,* financed its extensive repair and Emerson's third foreign tour (1872–1873), during which he met Robert Browning* and Ivan Sergeyevich Turgenev,* among others. He published *Letters and Social Aims* (1875) and soon after lapsed into gentle senility. Henry James, Sr., heard Emerson lecture in 1842 in New York, wrote to him, welcomed him to his home, came to know him well in New York and Concord, and admired and was stimulated by much in his philosophy, but eventually regarded him as untheological, passive, ignorant of evil, and disorganized. He once called Emerson a "man without a handle." Through him, Henry James, Sr., met several transcendentalists, including Alcott, William Ellery Channing,* Fuller, Thoreau, and also Carlyle. Emerson wrote to congratulate the Jameses on the birth of Henry, Jr., calling him "the new friend." It was to Emerson that Henry James, Sr. wrote (summer 1849) expressing his desire that his sons should have the rootless, "sensuous education" which Europe could provide better than America could. Young Henry James heard Emerson read a poem in Boston when the Emancipation Proclamation was celebrated there in 1863. James was pleased but a little alarmed when he learned that his father read aloud to and loaned Emerson his 1869–1870 European travel letters. In the fall of 1870 James visited Emerson for a few days—"pleasant, but with slender profit," he wrote superciliously to Grace Norton* (26 Sep [1870]). In November 1872 he escorted Emerson and his daughter Ellen through the Louvre in Paris but was privately critical of the benign philosopher's passive aesthetic responses. Returning from Egypt, Emerson and his daughter borrowed Vatican passes from James in Rome in March 1873. Back in the United States, when his mother died in 1882, James attended Emerson's April funeral in Concord. (Incidentally, William James spoke in Concord on the hundredth anniversary of Emerson's birth, in May 1903.) Henry James reviewed (*Century Magazine*, Jun 1883) *The Correspondence of Thomas Carlyle and Ralph Waldo Emerson, 1834–1872*, edited by Charles Eliot Norton* (2 vols., 1883). James begins by remarking that Emerson and Carlyle had "a beautiful and distinguished friendship," but that many of their concerns are now remote. James regularly praises "the great Scotch humorist" at the expense of the somewhat aloof Emerson, and he details the beginning of their friendship, the frequency and purpose of the letters, and Emerson's aid to Carlyle through being his American agent. Emerson sent Alcott and Fuller to Carlyle's Cheyne Walk home in London. Carlyle praised "The American Scholar" and later *English Traits*, although he criticized much in transcendentalism. In general, Emerson was optimistic, saw too little evil, was Puritan and fine, was serene, listened well, saw men as "disembodied spirits," was quaint and pale in writing, was gently comic, and enjoyed his subjects. On the other hand, Carlyle was pessimistic, was too aware of evil, was Spartan and crudely Germanic, was irritating, listened badly, considered men's clothes too much, wrote like an avalanche, was smokily tragic, and hated and was not inspired by his subjects. But the two men were brothers. James reviewed (*Macmillan's Magazine*, Dec 1887; reprinted as "Emerson" in *Partial Portraits*, 1888) James Elliot Cabot's *A Memoir of Ralph Waldo Emerson* (2 vols., 1887), calling it a balanced study of a colorless life, of a man too quietly literary. Furthermore, the discreet book lacks sufficient treatment of Emerson's social ambiance (including his aunt, Mary Moody Emerson—"grim intellectual virgin and daughter of a hundred ministers") and accompanying pictorial effects. Emerson's once-"profane" opinions now seem "droll . . . " Unlike Wordsworth and Johann Wolfgang von Goethe,* Emerson never found the literary form he sought. Regarding it as delightful that Yankee audiences trooped through the cold to hear Emerson read his lectures, James repeatedly stresses here the thinness of New England culture, and he regards Emerson as a kind of fifty-year martyr, but without "cause . . . [or] persecutors." He castigates Emerson for coldness in his treatment of Fuller, who seemed "to bore him," and even in the death of a brother. " . . . [T]here was no familiarity in him, no personal avidity." Being "altogether passionless," he was familiar only with words and books. But books were not meat for him to feed on, only wine to sip. Like his beloved Michel Eyquem de Montaigne, he is allusive, with "a tincture of books" merely. He often uses words vaguely, for example, "scholar." He "never . . . mastered the art of composition—of continuous expression." Thoreau became Emerson's scholar "in the concrete." As for the transcendentalists, Emerson tasted their works but did not drink, "least of all to become intoxicated," and called them " 'bands of competing minstrels.' " James opines that they were "in a society too sparse for a synthesis" and were themselves only "a kind of Puritan carnival." James mentions Emerson's initial admiration of and later criticism of Daniel Webster because of the Fugitive Slave Law of 1850; Emerson also held a wrongheaded opinion of the novels of Nathaniel Hawthorne.* After reminiscing on Emerson at the Louvre and the Vatican, on his funeral, and on his "irresistible" voice and unfailing courtesy, James concludes that he will wear well and that he speaks to the soul with authority, purity, and often with "an exquisite eloquence," but that he never "achieved a style." In "American Letter" (26 Mar 1898 and another for 11 Jun 1898), James praises *Emerson and Other Essays* (1898) by John Jay Chapman* for containing the best work ever written on Emerson. James's library contained six works of Emerson, including the Carlyle-Emerson correspondence.

Emma. In "A Problem," David's wife. According to Magawisca's prophecy and that of others, their child dies and they remarry (each other).

Emma. In *Still Waters*, Mrs. Meredith's unmarried sister, age twenty, who is passively loved by Horace but loves superficial Felix.

Emma, Lady. In "Maud-Evelyn," the narrator, whose mother, Lavinia, rejected Marmaduke.

Emmet family. James had several blood relatives who, as well as their in-laws and children, were named Emmet. Available information, which occasionally seems confusing, is based on James's Notebook entries, his letters, and annotations by editors thereof. Two of the sisters of James's favorite cousin Mary Temple* married brothers named Emmet. The sisters were Katherine ("Kitty") Temple and Ellen ("Elly") James Temple. Kitty married Richard Stockton Emmet. Elly married Christopher Temple Emmet. The children of Kitty and Richard Emmet included a son William ("Willy") Temple Emmet and a daughter Elizabeth Emmet (both of whom James saw in London in 1895) as well, evidently, as a son named Grenville Temple Emmet (whom, with his bride, James entertained at Lamb House* in 1905). Elly and Christopher Emmet evidently had four daughters, Mary ("Minny") Temple Emmet (later Mrs. Archibald Russell Peabody, and the mother of a son), Ellen Gertrude ("Bay") Emmet (later Mrs. William Blanchard Rand), Rosina Hubley Emmet, and Edith Leslie Emmet. Christopher Emmet died in 1884, and his widow Elly subsequently married George Hunter. In 1897 James often visited Elly (then Mrs. Hunter, with a son named George Grenville Hunter by her second husband), in Harrow and Dunwich, England. In letters to his brother William, James mentioned Bay Emmet's "really very great talent," Paris enhanced, as a painter (7 Aug 1897), and he predicted that "success will be eventually . . . within her grasp" (2 Apr 1899). James squired Rosina Emmet and Leslie Emmet around Paris early in 1899. Bay journeyed from Paris to Lamb House in 1900 to paint James's portrait. By 1904 Bay was Mrs. Rand, and the couple resided in Connecticut. In 1910 Bay called upon James when he was sick in New York. In 1911 James, still in the United States, visited Elly Hunter, Bay, Leslie, and Rosina in Connecticut, and Bay (at least) also in New York City. In 1911 James had tea with William Temple Emmet, the son of Kitty and Richard Emmet, in New York. In 1914 James lunched with George Grenville Hunter in London. Another cousin of James's was Jane Emmet, later the wife of painter Wilfred von Glehn (who changed his last name to De Glehn in 1914). James saw them frequently in London in 1912, 1913, and 1914. Trouble developed when James wrote in *Notes of a Son and Brother* about Minny in ways that distressed Elly, who evidently complained to William James's widow Alice. When Alice informed James, he replied (29 Mar 1814), "I haven't felt I could communicate with Elly directly about the matter at all—over such depths of illiteracy as surround her. . . ." Mention is also made of Eleanor Temple Emmet (Mrs. John Willard Lapsley [related to Gaillard Thomas Lapsley*]) and of her daughters Eleanor Lapsley and Elizabeth Lapsley.

"England at War: An Essay." Essay published as part of *England at War: An Essay: The Question of the Mind* (London: Central Committee for National Patriotic Organisations, 1915). James's essay was later republished as "The Mind of England at War."

En Province. Original title of *A Little Tour in France*, when published in the *Atlantic Monthly* (Jul–Nov 1883, Feb, Apr, May 1884).

"An English Easter." Travel essay, published in *Lippincott's Magazine* (Jul 1877); reprinted in *Portraits of Places*, 1883, and in *English Hours*, 1905. James explains that Londoners with time and money leave town during Easter (many going to Paris) since the season at home features "rawness and atmospheric acridity." Passion Week is "ascetic," often rainy too. James describes walking from Piccadilly through parks to packed Westminster Abbey (with an "odour . . . not that of incense"). The crowds seem degraded, and James comments on "the shabbier English types" he has noted, including street mourners and protesters. So he goes to Rochester, for its castle and quaint shops, then to Canterbury, with its "ivy-muffled . . . castle," architecturally jumbled cathedral, memories of Thomas à Becket (a guide shows the pavement where his blood fell) and the Black Prince and Geoffrey Chaucer, "mouldy" cloister, and quadrangle.

English Hours. Loose collection of sixteen travel essays, with ninety-two illustrations by Joseph Pennell*; published in London by Heinemann, 1905, and in Boston and New York by Houghton, Mifflin, 1905. The essays are as follows: 1. "London," 2. "Browning in Westminster Abbey," 3. "Chester," 4. "Lichfield and Warwick," 5. "North Devon," 6. "Wells and Salisbury," 7. "An English Easter," 8. "London at Midsummer," 9. "Two Excursions," 10. "In Warwickshire," 11. "Abbeys and Castles," 12. "English Vignettes," 13. "An English New Year," 14. "An English Winter Watering-Place," 15. "Winchelsea, Rye, and 'Denis Duval,' " and 16. "Old Suffolk." Essays 15 and 16 appear here for the first time in book form. The rest appeared in book form earlier. The essays describe cities and towns, landscapes, cathedrals, architecture, and paintings; they often connect with James's reading of fiction, history, and guidebooks. They are both descriptive and analytical.

"An English New Year." Travel essay, published (as "The New Year in England") in the *Nation* (23 Jan 1879); reprinted (as "An English New Year") in *Portraits of Places*, 1883, and in *English Hours*, 1905. In London the winter has been viciously cold and business depressed, but the people seem active and stable, while "the gigantic poor-relief system" helps the distressed. James calls current labor strikes a "recreation," but he adds that newspaper accounts of Yorkshire and Lancashire poverty inspire some to charity. To avoid foggy, slushy London, James went north to a country "home . . . overflow[ing] with hospitality and good cheer." He describes its library, tea at six, and fireplaces, but also his helping his hostess distribute toys to 150 Dickensian workhouse children in "a large frigid refectory."

"English Vignettes." Travel essay, published in *Lippincott's Magazine* (Apr 1879, with illustrations which James called vile); reprinted in *Portraits of Places*, 1883, and in *English Hours*, 1905. The subjects of these brief sketches are six in number: Monmouthshire in April (six or so hours from London by fast train, hill called the Skirrid, ancient church, spacious country houses with gardens and turf and Scotch firs); the Isle of Wight (spoiled by "detestable little railway," ugly embankments and tunnels, cockneyfied town of Ventnor but "delicious" Bonchurch near it, and Shanklin on pretty coast); "untidy and prosaic" Portsmouth (lacking in local color but with entertaining harbor); Chichester ("respectable" cathedral with "delicate" spire and "three-sided cloister," fifteenth-century "market-cross"); Cambridge (stately, rich, and hospitable, with tangled charms—courts, porticoes, gardens, huge trees, and King's College chapel, "the most beautiful . . . in England"); and Cambridgeshire (flat meadows, horsy breezes, partridge shooting, Newmarket, and beyond it Bury St. Edmunds).

"An English Winter Watering-Place." Travel essay, published in the *Nation* (3 Apr 1879); reprinted in *Portraits of Places*, 1883, and in *English Hours*, 1905. Hastings is a miniature London on the sea and with adjacent St. Leonards presents miles of "united sea-front." James contrasts the place to gayer Brighton. Was his Hastings inn "mellow" or only "musty"? In truth, it displayed "venerable decency." The whole "middle-class" watering place had "the element of gentility" so lacking elsewhere: bath chairs, shops and stalls, circulating libraries, pier, Parade, bands. Nothing was "crude."

Epictetus (c. 60–?). Greek Stoic philosopher, probably from Phrygia. A slave freed by his master, he was taught in Rome and was later expelled to Epirus by the tyrannical Emperor Domitian in 90. His teachings are preserved only in his pupil Flavius Arrianus's works. Epictetus teaches that only our will is ours, and that we can neither anticipate nor control events. James reviewed (*North American Review*, Apr 1866) Thomas Wentworth Higginson's adapted translation of *The Works of Epictetus* (1865), calling it bookish but Epictetus of permanent relevance. James sums up the stoical position: "Virtue consists in a state of moral satisfaction with those things which reason tells us are in our power, and in a sublime independence of those things which are not in our power." Calling such virtue as "brutal" as the cruel age which produced it, James criticizes stoicism as blind to progress and responsibility, Epictetus uninquisitive and unimaginative, and his "reason" mere faith. But the Stoic does argue that retribution operates in this world.

Erckmann, Émile (1822–1899). French coauthor, as Erckmann-Chatrian,* with Alexandre Chatrian.*

Erckmann-Chatrian. Joint pen name of two French authors, Émile Erckmann* and Alexandre Chatrian.* They collaborated from 1847 until 1889 on several successful but not distinguished novels and plays, mainly depicting the horrors of war and imperialism and the goodness of democracy and the Alsatian countryside. In "The Minor French Novelists" (*Galaxy*, Feb 1876) James comments on their *L'Ami Fritz* (1864), *L'Histoire d'un conscrit de 1813* (1864), *Le Blocus* (1867), and *Les Confidences d'un joueur de clarinette* (1865)—works, he says, by "genius of the purest water," giving as they do a "sense of the decent, wholesome, human side of reality." In "MM. Erckmann-Chatrian's 'Ami Fritz' " (*Nation*, 4 Jan 1877), James discusses the furor caused by the 1876 stage performance of *L'Ami Fritz*. He calls the play "very pretty" and the novel on which it is based "a real masterpiece—a savoury idyll, a succulent pastoral." Summarizing its plot in detail, he concludes that it is "a very pretty cabinet picture." In "The Théâtre Français" (Apr 1877), however, James calls the novel "delightful" but the play based on it not "worthy of the first French stage." James's library included three Erckmann-Chatrian books.

Eric, Lord. In *What Maisie Knew*, one of Ida Farange's many lovers.

Erme, Gwendolyn. In "The Figure in the Carpet," George Corvick's fiancée, then wife, then widow. She later marries Drayton Deane and dies without revealing the details of the figure—if she ever knew them.

Erme, Mrs. In "The Figure in the Carpet," Gwendolyn's mother, who dies.

Ermine, Lizzie. In "The Impressions of a Cousin," the matchmaker who tries to pair up Eunice and Caliph.

Ermine, William. In "The Impressions of a Cousin," Lizzie's husband; he is in New York.

Ernesto. In "At Isella," the Signora's lover.

Erskine, Mrs. Thomas. Novelist whose *Wyncote* (1875) James reviewed (*Nation*, 23 Sep 1875), calling it a "*pretty* story"—the compact history of an old house—and also "simple and shrewd," with a "neat . . . style" and varied characters.

Essays in London and Elsewhere. Collection of eleven essays on writers, criticism in general, and travel, published in London by Osgood, McIlvaine, 1893, and in New York by Harper, 1893.

Esther. In "Adina," the narrator's aunt in Boston.

"Etretat." Paris letter, published as "A French Watering Place" in the New York *Tribune* (26 Aug 1876), reprinted in *Portraits of Places*, 1883. James mentions pretty and dreary "bathing stations" along the Normandy and Picardy coast, then praises Etretat for its scenery and the French for their varied activity there: sunbathing, diving, swimming, and the Casino at night.

Eugene, Mrs. In "The Modern Warning," a New York society friend of Agatha Grice, Lady Chasemore.

"Eugene Pickering." Short story (17,300 words), published in the *Atlantic Monthly* (Oct–Nov 1874); reprinted in *A Passionate Pilgrim*, 1875. (Characters: Anastasia Blumenthal, Blumenthal, Niedermeyer, Adelina Patti, Eugene Pickering, Pickering, Isabel Vernor, Vernor.) Suddenly fatherless, sheltered Eugene Pickering leaves America for Homburg, Germany, where he meets the narrator, a former friend, and then falls for a sleazy widow named Anastasia Blumenthal, age thirty-eight. She accepts and then cruelly rejects his proposal of marriage. All this time, young Pickering has been engaged to Isabel Vernor through an arrangement made by his father. Her father writes to the young man from a Middle Eastern business locale to release him from the engagement. Eugene wanders aimlessly to Smyrna, whence he writes the narrator that he has met Isabel and finds her charming. James wrote to William Dean Howells,* *Atlantic Monthly* editor, from Italy (9 Jan 1874), to offer "Eugene Pickering," adding that William James calls it " 'quite brilliant,' " and explaining that since he needs money he must place his fiction in more magazines than just the *Atlantic*, which, however, "shall have the best things I do." Howells accepted "Eugene Pickering" and much else by James. A French translation of it was published in 1876. This slight story has an absurd plot, as well as a German setting, for little apparent reason. Why Smyrna? The ruthless nature of Madame Blumenthal, who has written a novel on marriage, may be modeled partly on George Sand.*

Eugenio. In "Daisy Miller," the Miller family courier in Europe. He disapproves of Daisy Miller's innocent but gauche behavior. In *Daisy Miller: A Comedy in Three Acts*, he is identified as an Italian-Swiss from Lugano and he becomes the villain. He tries to blackmail Madame de Katkoff to flirt with Frederick Winterbourne so that Giacomo Giovanelli can snare rich Daisy Miller and pay Eugenio a reward of 50,000 francs.

Eugenio. In *The Wings of the Dove*, Milly Theale's smoothly competent Venetian guide and servant.

Eunice. In "The Impressions of a Cousin," Catherine Condit's cousin, who is Adrian Frank's fiancée. His half-brother Caliph unscrupulously handles her financial matters.

"Europe" (1899 title, " 'Europe' "; 1909 title, "Europe"). Short story (7,200 words), published in *Scribner's Magazine* (Jun 1899); reprinted in *The Soft Side*, 1900; revised and reprinted in *The Novels and Tales of Henry James*, Volume XVI, 1909. (Characters: Mr. and Mrs. Hathaway, Jane Rimmle, Maria Rimmle, Rebecca Rimmle, Mr. and Mrs. Rimmle.) After traveling in Europe, the narrator visits an ancient Boston widow named Mrs. Rimmle and her aging daughters, bright Becky, attractive Jane, and reserved Maria. Two daughters hope to see Europe while the third cares for the mother, but the old woman gets sick whenever plans are close to materializing. Finally the Hathaways take Jane to Europe, where—so says Maria—she is too happy ever to return. When the narrator next sees old Mrs. Rimmle, she says that Jane has died abroad (not so) and that Becky (now sick and lying down) is going next. Maria says not yet. When he last visits, Mrs. Rimmle tells the narrator that Becky has gone to Europe—which Maria hints is a euphemism for Becky's death. According to Notebook entries (27 Feb 1895, 7 May 1898), "Europe" is based on the attitude of the real-life widow, age ninety-five, of Boston clergyman historian John Gorham Palfrey, whose aging daughters could go nowhere because of their selfish old mother. The widow's selfishness had been described to James by her niece, his friend Lady Edith Playfair, wife of Baron Lyon Playfair.* An earlier Notebook entry (27 Jul 1890) reveals that James had already been thinking of the idea in general. In the preface to Volume XVI of *The Novels and Tales of Henry James*, he summarizes his source but without giving any family names, then he reminds his readers that his creative task was to "Dramatise!" the "obscure . . . tragedy" by "transfus[ing]" it into the "exiguous" compass of a "very short story."

" 'Europe.' " 1899 title of "Europe."

"A European Summer." The general title (occasional alternate title, "A Summer in Europe") of a series of seven 1872 and 1873 travel essays, which are individually entitled 1. "Chester," 2. "Lichfield and Warwick," 3. "North Devon," 4. "Wells and Salisbury," 5. "Swiss Notes," 6. "From Chambéry to Milan," and 7. "From Venice to Strassburg [sic]."

The Europeans. Short novel (59,700 words), published in the *Atlantic Monthly* (Jul–Oct 1878); revised and reprinted in London by Macmillan, 1878, and in Boston by Houghton, Osgood, 1878. (Characters: Lizzie Acton, Robert Acton, Mrs. Acton, Prince Adolf of Silberstadt-Schreckenstein, Augustine, Azarina, Rev. Mr. Brand, Broderip, Rev. Mr. Gilman, Mrs. Morgan, Baroness Eugenia-Camilla-Delores Young Münster of Silberstadt-Schreckenstein, Charlotte Wentworth, Clifford Wentworth, Gertrude Wentworth, William Wentworth, Mrs.

Catherine Whiteside, Adolphus and Catherine Young, Felix Young.) Artistic, likable Felix Young and his attractive but devious sister Baroness Eugenia Münster, Prince Adolph's morganatic wife, come from Germany to Boston to visit their well-to-do Wentworth cousins in the country. Felix soon meets William Wentworth, the stiff, half-brother of his deceased mother, and the Wentworth children—Gertrude, loved by the Rev. Mr. Brand; Charlotte; and Clifford, youthfully gauche and a little alcoholic. Soon both Felix and Eugenia call on the hospitable Wentworths. They loan Eugenia a cottage nearby, and they introduce her to their cool cousin, Robert Acton, who is attracted to Eugenia, and to Acton's gentle old mother. Eugenia hints that she might soon legally dissolve her German marriage. Felix learns from Gertrude that she will not wed Brand and thereupon suggests matching up Brand and Charlotte. Eugenia makes Clifford more suave but also embarrasses him. Acton might propose to Eugenia but for catching her in a fib. Charlotte asks her dour daddy, who sees life as duty not opportunity, to let Gertrude and Felix marry. Eugenia is soon to depart again. At the end, Felix marries Gertrude; Brand, Charlotte; Clifford, Lizzie (Acton's sister); and Acton (after his mother's death), a nice young woman. In a letter to William Dean Howells* (30 Mar [1877]), James touches on the "evaporated marriage" which ends *The American*; he says that although "the tragedies in life . . . arrest my attention," he will write a happy short novel for a change; he then briefly discusses the plot of what became *The Europeans*. James argues by letter with his brother William (14 Nov [1878]) about *The Europeans* but then wrongly concedes that it is " 'thin,' and empty." To his mother he prematurely writes (14 May [1879]) that *Confidence* "will be . . . much better than *The Europeans*." This novel is a small companion piece to *The American*, since in it we have Europeanized Americans returning from the Old World to the New World, specifically well-delineated New England. The best features of this charming work are probity-stiffened old Wentworth, who looks as if he were enduring "martyrdom, not by fire, but by freezing," and Felix Young, whose European sophistication cannot dampen the latent, up-bubbling New World freshness. The conclusion has displeased some critics for seeming to be superficial, mathematical, and uncommitted tonally and philosophically.

Evans, Amy. In "The Velvet Glove," the pseudonym of the writer who unsuccessfully tries to get John Berridge to write a puffing preface for *The Velvet Glove*, her trashy novel.

Evans, Charlotte. In "Travelling Companions," a young lady traveling in Italy with her father. She and Brook, the narrator, having met in Milan and then Venice, travel unescorted to Padua, only to miss the last train. Thinking that he is prompted only by honor to propose marriage to her, she declines (temporarily).

Evans, Mark. In "Travelling Companions," Charlotte Evans's widowed father. When he must visit a sick friend in Milan, his daughter and Brook are almost compromised, but the father accepts their explanation and later dies.

Evans, Marian (Mary Ann). The real name of George Eliot.*

Everard, Captain Count Philip. In "In the Cage," the strange sender of telegrams through the unnamed girl "in the cage." She helps him once by remembering the contents of a wire. He is to marry Lady Bradeen.

Everett, Marian. In "The Story of a Masterpiece," the fiancée of John Lennox and the subject of a portrait painted by Stephen Baxter.

Evers, Blanche. In *Confidence*, Angela Vivian's friend who marries Gordon Wright and is escorted a good deal by Captain Augustus Lovelock.

"An Ex-Grand-Ducal Capital." The 1873 title of "Darmstadt."

F

"The Faces." 1900 title of "The Two Faces."

Faguet, Émile (1847–1916). French literary critic. He was a student in Paris, a teacher in La Rochelle and Bordeaux, a professor at the Sorbonne, and a member of the French Academy (from 1900). He was the drama critic of the *Soleil* and the literary critic of the *Revue Bleue* and the *Journal des Débats* (succeeding Jules Lemaître* there). Faguet wrote several literary and political studies and monographs on Honoré de Balzac,* Gustave Flaubert,* Jean-Jacques Rousseau, Voltaire, and Émile Zola,* among others. In his 1899 essay "The Present Literary Situation in France," James confesses that he earlier regarded Faguet "as . . . perceptibly common" and is therefore happy to praise his 1899 study of Flaubert as "extraordinarily able"—if "almost too exhaustive." In his introduction to an edition of *Madame Bovary* (1902, revised 1914), James begins by repeating this praise and asserting that Faguet's work on Flaubert "is really in its kind a model." James reviewed Faguet's fine 1913 monograph on Balzac (*Times Literary Supplement*, 19 Jun 1913; reprinted in *Living Age*, 9 Aug 1913, and in *Notes on Novelists*, 1914). James uses his assignment as a reviewer to discuss Balzac more than he does Faguet. When he agrees with Faguet, James goes on to discriminate. He agrees, for example, that Balzac was vulgar and also that he displays more quantity than quality. James includes Faguet in his list of Balzac's best critics, but he also calls him "the dryest." James took this review for the *Times Literary Supplement* seriously, writing to the editor Bruce Richmond (23 May 1913) that he wanted "to make . . . [it] the best possible."

"Famous Novelist Describes Deeds of U.S. Motor Corps." Title of the 1915 shortened reprint of "The American Volunteer Motor-Ambulance Corps in France."

Fancourt, General. In "The Lesson of the Master," Marian's father and a friend of Henry St. George and his wife.

Fancourt, Marian. In "The Lesson of the Master," the object of the incipient affections of Paul Overt, until, that is, he is advised only to write by Henry St. George, who, when his own wife dies, marries Marian.

Fane, Greville. In "Greville Fane," the pen name of Mrs. Stormer, who writes potboilers to support both her daughter Lady Ethel Luard and her son Leolin Stormer.

Fanny. In *Guy Domville*, Mrs. Peverel's servant at Porches. She likes and respects Frank Humber. Lord Devenish flirts with her.

Farange, Beale. In *What Maisie Knew*, Maisie's philandering father. After he and her mother Ida are divorced, he marries the girl's governess, Miss Overmore. Later he consorts with Mrs. Cuddon and others.

Farange, Ida. In *What Maisie Knew*, Maisie's philandering mother. After she and her husband Beale are divorced, she marries Sir Claude. Continuing to neglect her daughter, she then consorts with Perriam, Lord Eric, and Tischbein, among other lovers.

Farange, Maisie. In *What Maisie Knew*, the poignantly presented little daughter of Ida and Beale Farange, who early in the narrative get a divorce. Maisie admires her governess Miss Overmore and Sir Claude; she learns moral consciousness from Mrs. Wix, her most recent governess.

Farange, Mrs. Beale. In *What Maisie Knew*, Miss Overmore's married name.

Fargo, Professor. In "Professor Fargo," a New England medium who entices his partner Colonel Gifford's daughter to go away with him.

Farrinder, Mr. and Mrs. Amariah. In *The Bostonians*, a Boston couple. She is Miss Birdseye's militant feminist friend.

Featherstone, Miss. In "Daisy Miller" and *Daisy Miller: A Comedy in Three Acts*, an English lady who wonders why Daisy Miller's brother Randolph has no teacher.

Fedder, Dr. Sidney. In "Lady Barbarina," a serious friend of Dr. Jackson Lemon, who marries Lady Barbarina Clement.

Felicia, Lady. In *The Portrait of a Lady*, a person mentioned as possibly Lord Warburton's fiancée.

Felix. In *Still Waters*, the handsome but superficial artist, age thirty-two, who harmlessly pursues Miss Walsingham, is loved by Emma, and is encouraged by passive Horace to propose to Emma.

Fenton, George. In *Watch and Ward*, the cousin of Nora Lambert; he tries to compromise her in order to blackmail her guardian Roger Lawrence.

Ferrars, Blanche. In "De Grey, A Romance," a woman loved and hence destroyed by John De Grey in accordance with the De Grey family curse.

Feuillet, Octave (1821–1890). French dramatist and novelist, born in Saint-Lô and schooled for a diplomatic career. He became a writer instead, however, much to the annoyance of his father, who was irascible, sick, and demanding. Feuillet started writing as a collaborator of Alexandre Dumas *père* and was a great favorite among the aristocracy of the Second Empire, especially for his romantic society novels. Among Feuillet's novels are *Bellah* (1852), *La Petite comtesse* (1857), *Dalila* (1857), *Le Roman d'un jeune homme pauvre* (1858), *Histoire de Sibylle* (1862), *Monsieur de Camors* (1867), *Julia de Trécoeur* (1872), *Un Mariage dans le monde* (1875), *Les Amours de Philippe* (1877), *Le Journal d'une femme* (1877), *Histoire d'une Parisienne* (1881), and *La Morte* (1886). The Empress Eugénie actually played a role on stage in his comedy *Les Portraits de la Marquise* (1882, written earlier). Among his other plays are *Le Pour et le contre* (1853), *Montjoie* (1863), *Le Sphinx* (1874), and *Chamillac* (1886). James reviewed *Camors; or, Life Under the New Empire* (the 1868 translation of *Monsieur de Camors*), *Un Mariage dans le monde*, and *Les Amours de Philippe* (*Nation*, 30 Jul 1868, 13 Jan 1876, 15 Nov 1877). He begins his first review by praising Feuillet's fifteen-year development and his later introduction of real-life situations in place of formerly artificial and conventional ones. Then he analyzes the main characters in *Camors*: a rich, debased father and his son, both brilliant but of "moral penury"; contrasting heroines—all combined by an author who is here "superficial . . . but . . . charming" into a novel which is "neat, compact, and . . . dramatic." James begins his review of *Un Mariage dans le monde* with his truism that a typical French novel is tidier and more shapely than a "clever" British one; the latter typically is "clever" only in parts. Feuillet presents his spicy *entrées* in "symmetrical shape," is regularly commendable, and never falls below his own fine level—unlike some of his contemporaries. Here Feuillet may be a bit "elegant and superfine," but he is at his best when writing once again about "conjugal aberrations." As for the popular *Les Amours de Philippe*, James notes its "interesting fable": When cousins find their marriage arranged for them (Feuillet married his cousin), the hero feels obliged to seek a mistress. But she is "a monster of corruption," who tries to trap the hero's "magnanimous" cousin, who proves lovable after all. James calls Philippe's amours "not very pretty . . . [but] very prettily told." The plot of James's "Eugene Pickering" (1874) is slightly similar. In a Notebook entry (30 Aug 1893) concerning lengths of fictional pieces, James reminds himself that "Feuillet is . . . , with all his flimsiness, singularly wise as to length." James's library contained three books by Feuillet.

"A Few Other Roman Neighbourhoods." Travel essay, published in *Italian Hours*, 1909. James calls it a postscript, by a *"mature* visitor," to five essays on Rome republished in *Italian Hours*. Rome gave him his "first unpremeditated rapture," and the city remains a paradise not lost to new generations. He had missed "conventional 'wild' " Subiaco earlier; therefore, he motored with friends to it recently, on a splendid June day, via "animated and even crowded" Tivoli, showing "pictorial felicity," and the Villa d'Este, with its tributes to style, either "wonderful or dreadful," suspended in time. James next describes a June drive to Ostia, with castle walls and "massive . . . tower[s]" along the way, and to Fiumincino, "the handy Gravesend or Coney Island of Rome." All elements there, including stacks of bicycles, combined in "the golden light" over "the darkening land" into a "perfect 'composition.' " The party returned by St. Peter's rear, which from that direction displays architectural waste, "pomp for pomp's sake." James was traveling with a sculptor; so they visited a small foundry nearby, "rickety" and redolent of old-time " 'art-life.' " A candlelit dinner near "the great obelisked Square" provided a final recall of the romantic Rome of James's youth.

Fido. In "Daniel Deronda: A Conversation," Pulcheria's lap-dog.

Field, Henriette (née Deluzy-Desportes) (1813–1875). French-born governess in the Parisian household of Duc Charles de Praslyn and his wife Altarice. After six years of service, Henriette was suddenly discharged by the countess in 1847. The duke sought a letter of recommendation for her from his wife, who denied it; he stabbed his wife to death and a week later committed suicide by taking poison. Henriette was arrested but later released, migrated to New York City, married Henry Field in New York in 1851, had an exhibition of her paintings at the National Academy of Design, and published one book, *Home Sketches in France, and Other Papers* (1875), which James briefly reviewed (*Nation*, 10 Jun 1875). He says that Mrs. Field had "much social eminence" and offered fine manners and conversation where they were not in evidence before. Her papers are "slight" though "agreeable." He is sad that her French letters are given here in translation. In a letter to Edith Newbold Jones Wharton* (26 Jul 1909), James recalls that he saw "Mrs. Deluzy Field" once, when she visited his mother: She was "a very expressive and demonstrative white-puffed person, impressing *les miens* as . . . most insinuating and dazzling. . . . She was a méridionale Protestant . . . , I think—and that worked badly for her relations with the

Duchess, etc.'' James then recalls that ''when we were *tout-jeunes* in Paris'' they walked past the murder site, the *''dead* closed Hotel P.'' Nathaniel Hawthorne* knew Field's father and brother, of Stockbridge, Massachusetts, and may have had the Praslyn murder in mind as background for *The Marble Faun*.

Fielder, Graham (Gray). In *The Ivory Tower*, the nephew of Frank B. Betterman, who wills him enormous wealth. Fielder is friendly with Rosanna Gaw and Horton Vint.

Fields, Annie Adams (1834–1915). American author, gracious hostess, and the wife of the publisher James Thomas Fields,* whom she married in 1854. Her literary salon at 148 Charles Street, Boston, was justly famous. She and her husband knew many important American authors, including Nathaniel Hawthorne,* Oliver Wendell Holmes, Julia Ward Howe,* Sarah Orne Jewett,* James Russell Lowell,* Harriet Beecher Stowe,* and John Greenleaf Whittier; they also knew Charles Dickens,* Sir Leslie Stephen,* William Makepeace Thackeray,* Walter Savage Landor, and Anthony Trollope,* among other foreign writers. Annie Fields traveled widely with her husband, after whose death in 1881 she continued to be a distinguished hostess in Boston. Among her many books are a biography of her husband (1881) and works on Whittier (1893), Stowe (1897), and Jewett (1911). James knew both Annie Fields and her husband. The drawing room of their Charles Street home may have been the model for that of Olive Chancellor in *The Bostonians*. James wrote about the Fieldses in a 1915 essay entitled ''Mr. and Mrs. James T. Fields.'' When Annie Fields commended James for his 1892 essay on the recently deceased Lowell, James replied (26 Jan 1892) not only that her note was ''the only echo of any kind that I can perceive it to have evoked,'' but also that one must ''testify'' when a friend dies. In September 1898 Mrs. Fields, then widowed and accompanied by Jewett, visited James at Lamb House.* He praised Miss Jewett's fiction, escorted them to nearby Winchelsea and Hastings, and was sorry that the pair could not be his overnight guests. Some years later (2 Jan 1910), he sadly wrote to Mrs. Fields, who was editing Jewett's letters, that he had ''preserved'' none that she had written to him. In *Notes of a Son and Brother*, James fondly remembers ''the delightful Fields salon.''

Fields, James Thomas (1817–1881). American publisher, businessman, author, and versatile lecturer. Born in Portsmouth, New Hampshire, and bookish as a child, he clerked in a Boston bookstore as a teenager, and soon became a partner in Ticknor, Reed & Fields (after 1854, Ticknor & Fields). He was a splendid friend of many authors, including Charles Dickens,* Nathaniel Hawthorne,* Oliver Wendell Holmes, Julia Ward Howe,* Walter Savage Landor, James Russell Lowell,* Sir Leslie Stephen,* Harriet Beecher Stowe,* William Makepeace Thackeray,* Anthony Trollope,* and John Greenleaf Whittier. Fields visited Europe on four occasions from the late 1840s to the late 1860s. In 1854

Annie Adams became his wife, Annie Adams Fields.* James Fields was a member of the Saturday Club. He edited the *Atlantic Monthly* (1861–1871). His most valuable book is *Yesterdays with Authors* (1872); he also wrote studies on Hawthorne (1876), whom he published, and Dickens (1876). James knew both Fields and his wife, and he wrote about them in a 1915 essay entitled "Mr. and Mrs. James T. Fields." Back in 1866 William Dean Howells,* when asked, advised Fields, then editing the *Atlantic*, to accept any story by young James. In addition to much short fiction by James, Fields accepted his first novel, *Watch and Ward*, for serial publication. To Howells, James wrote (25 Jan 1902) that his pet fox terrier's face happily resembled Fields'.

"The Figure in the Carpet." Short story (13,900 words), published in *Cosmopolis* (Jan–Feb 1896); reprinted in *Embarrassments*, 1896; revised and reprinted in *The Novels and Tales of Henry James*, Volume XV, 1909. (Characters: George Corvick, Drayton Deane, Gwendolyn Erme, Mrs. Erme, Lady Jane, Miss Poyle, Mr. and Mrs. Hugh Vereker.) Critic George Corvick gives the critic-narrator the job of reviewing Hugh Vereker's new novel. Later, the narrator meets Vereker at a party, and the novelist apologizes for a remark, overheard by the narrator, that his review contained only the usual twaddle. Vereker continues by saying that no critic has discovered the figure in the carpet of his oeuvre. The narrator rereads Vereker, fails to detect any figure, tells Corvick, and later learns from that man that he has discovered the secret, which, however, he will confide only to Gwendolyn Erme, his fiancé, and then only after their marriage. But on their honeymoon, Corvick is killed in a dogcart accident. Gwendolyn says she has the secret but will not tell the curious narrator; she marries an inferior critic named Drayton Deane. Death strikes again: Vereker dies of fever in Rome; his widow then dies; and Gwendolyn dies giving birth to Deane's second child. When the narrator quizzes Deane about the reputed figure in the carpet of Vereker's works, that imperceptive critic denies having any knowledge of it. In a long Notebook entry (24 Oct 1895) James sketched the situation for "The Figure in the Carpet": "the author of certain books . . . hold[s] . . . that his writings contain a very beautiful and valuable, very interesting and remunerative *secret*, or latent intention, for those who read them with a right intelligence—who see *into* them, as it were—bring to the perusal of them a certain perceptive sense"; further, James outlined his plot in detail. Confiding more thoughts to his Notebook later (4 Nov 1895), James advised himself to write ten chapters totaling 11,000 words. Ultimately the story ran to eleven chapters totaling 13,900 words. In the preface to Volume XV of *The Novels and Tales of Henry James*, James refuses to provide personal evidence about how "this anecdote" corresponds to his observation of society's attitude toward literature, but instead the calls his tale "a significant fable" illustrating an "odd numbness of the general sensibility," even a "marked collective mistrust of anything like close analytic appreciation." The puzzling fable, which is at times serious, but at other times fantastic and darkly comic, has especially intrigued and divided critics who love ambiguity. What is the figure in the carpet? Whose business is it to explicate the figure? Is there any figure? Can looking for an alleged figure in an author's works spoil casual reading of them? Is this story autobiographical? If so, do James's celebrated prefaces reveal or conceal master figures in the huge carpet of his writings?

Filer. In *The Bostonians*, an agent hired by Olive Chancellor to promote Verena Tarrant's lectures.

Filomena. In *Roderick Hudson*, Mme. Grandoni's washerwoman.

Filon, Pierre Marie Augustin (1841–1916). Son of the French historian Charles Auguste Désiré Filon. Augustin Filon was the tutor of the prince imperial in England (1867) and later became a literary critic. In letters to friends, James calls Filon's work "remarkably interesting and able" (to Grace Norton* [20 Aug (1893)]), and "charming" (to Robert Louis Stevenson* [21 Oct (1893)]). In a Notebook entry (27 Feb 1895) he adds that, though "intelligent," Filon is "always slightly vulgar." In his 1898 essay on Prosper Mérimée,* James notes "the two admirable volumes lately published" about him by Filon. James's library contained two books by Filon.

Finch, Dora. In *The American*, an American whom Christopher Newman sees at a party.

Finch, Dr. In *The Wings of the Dove*, a New York physician consulted by Milly Theale.

Findlater, Jane Helen (1866–1946), **and Mary Williamina** (1865–1964). Scottish sisters, who wrote popular fiction separately and together, and also with Kate Douglas Wiggin. Mary Findlater, born in Perthshire and educated at home, wrote *Over the Hills* (1897), *Betty Musgrave* (1899), *The Rose of Joy* (1903), *A Blind Bird's Nest* (1907), and more. Jane Findlater, born in Edinburgh and also educated at home, wrote *The Green Groves of Balgowrie* (1896), *Rachel* (1899), *The Story of a Mother* (1902), *Stones from a Glass House* (1904), *Seven Scots Stories* (1912), and more. Together they wrote *Crossriggs* (1908), *Penny Monypenny* (1911), *Beneath the Visiting Moon* (1923), and *Seen and Heard before and after 1914* (1916, reminiscences), and other works. With Wiggin, they wrote *The Affair at the Inn* (1904), *The Ladder to the Stars* (1906), *Robinetta* (1913), and more. The Findlaters visited the United States (January–April 1905), where they were befriended in Boston by William James and his wife Alice, Thomas Wentworth Storrow Higginson,* Charles Eliot Norton,* and others. In New York they met William Dean Howells,* the wife and daughter of George Washburn Smalley,* and others, including Henry James. William James, his wife, and his daughter Margaret visited the Findlaters at their home near Torquay. According to his Pocket Diaries, James maintained a sociable friendship in London with the Findlaters into 1915. William James's widow Alice maintained contact with the Findlaters after James's death. James's library contained one book by Jane Helen Findlater.

The Finer Grain. Collection of five short stories (the last to be published in book form in James's lifetime), published in New York by Scribners, 1910, and in London by Methuen, 1910: "The Velvet Glove," "Mora Montravers," "A Round of Visits," "Crapy Cornelia," and "The Bench of Desolation." In a dust-jacket blurb, James explains that in each story a vividly aware central character is involved in circumstances the importance of which lies in the "victim's or victor's sensibility." Each tale becomes "a moral drama," in which the hero "exhibits the finer grain of accessibility . . . to moving experience."

Finucane, Lord. In *The American*, he is mentioned as Lord Deepmere's grandfather.

Firmin, Mrs. In *The Spoils of Poynton*, a woman Owen Gereth talks to after a dinner party.

Firminger, Charlotte (Lottie). In "Lord Beaupré," Guy Firminger's cousin. The two marry despite his love for Mary Gosselin.

Firminger, Guy. In "Lord Beaupré," the man whom several family deaths convert into Lord Beaupré.

Firminger, Major Frank. In "Lord Beaupré," Guy Firminger's uncle and Charlotte's father.

Firminger, Mrs. Frank. In "Lord Beaupré," Charlotte's mother.

Firminger, The Misses. In "Lord Beaupré," Charlotte's three sisters.

Fiske, John (1842–1901). Connecticut-born lecturer, philosopher, historian, and professor. After he graduated from Harvard (1863), he was a lawyer, became a librarian at Harvard, took to the lecture circuit (from 1879) to explain evolution and to popularize and extend its philosophical and sociological implications, and taught history at Washington University, St. Louis (from 1884). Fiske published many books, not only on Darwinism, science, positivism, and religion, but also on American government and history. William James knew Fiske but opposed his brand of determinism, calling it on occasion pernicious and immoral. In 1872 James evidently attended his "long course . . . on Positivism" in Boston, reporting as much to Charles Eliot Norton* (4 Feb 1872). In 1873, first from Switzerland, James wrote to William Dean Howells* (22 Jun [1873]) to express pleasure that Fiske would soon be coming abroad, and second from Italy, he wrote to his father (22 Dec 1873) to say that he and his brother William might see Fiske in Florence. In June 1879 James dined with Ivan Sergeyevich Turgenev* at his London club and was able to include Fiske, who was thrilled. James's library contained two books by Fiske.

Fitzgibbon, Lady Laura. In "The Modern Warning," Sir Rufus Chasemore's Irish grandmother.

Flack, George B. In *The Reverberator*, the American journalist who violates Francina Dosson's confidence, invades the privacy of Probert family members, and publishes gossip about them revealed to him by Francina.

Flandrin, Jean Hippolyte (1809–1864). French painter, who was born in Lyon, studied under Jean Auguste Dominique Ingres in Paris (from 1829), then went to Rome (1832–1838), where he was influenced by fifteenth-century masters. Flandrin returned to France, and soon he became the most respected religious muralist and church decorator of his epoch. He painted a notable portrait (1863) of Napoleon III. Many of his works are now regarded as pure, simple, and sentimental. James reviewed an 1875 biography of Flandrin by Henrietta Louisa Lear.*

Flaubert, Gustave (1821–1880). One of the most famous French novelists and a founder of modern literature because of his realism, objectivity, prenaturalistic use of "shocking" subject matter, handling of point of view, and stylistic polish. Born and educated in Rouen, Flaubert went to the University of Paris to study law, but he failed his examinations and preferred to write. Subsidized by his father, who was a distinguished surgeon, Flaubert cultivated literary associates, later lived with his mother (widowed in 1846) and his sister in Rouen, traveled extensively in the Near East and North Africa (1849–1851), and made brief forays to Paris. He established a relationship with Louise Colet (to 1855). His *Madame Bovary* created a sensation when it was published in 1857; it caused its author to be unsuccessfully sued by the government for immorality (the same judge, at the same time, fined Charles Baudelaire* and suppressed his *Les Fleurs du mal*), and it helped create the French school of objective realism. After *Madame Bovary*, Flaubert published *Salammbô* (1862), *L'Education sentimentale* (1869), *Le Candidat* (1874, a play which quickly failed), *La Tentation de Saint Antoine* (1874), and *Trois contes* (1877—"Un Coeur Simple," "Le Légende de Saint Julien l'Hospitalier, and "Hérodias"). His *Bouvard et Pécuchet* appeared posthumously (1881), as did a total of thirteen volumes of his letters to leading French writers of his epoch, including his friend George Sand.* Flaubert suffered from a kind of epilepsy. He was devastated by the Franco-Purssian War and almost ruined himself financially late in life helping the bankrupt husband of his niece Caroline Hamard Commanville (later Mme. Franklin-Grout). James met Flaubert in Paris through their mutual friend Ivan Sergeyevich Turgenev* and wrote to his father (20 Dec 1875) a full description of the "great,

stout, handsome, simple, kindly, elderly fellow." By May, James had seen
Flaubert several times, once for an hour of conversation alone, after which he
bumped into Émile Zola* coming in just as James was leaving. In a long Notebook entry (25 Nov 1881), James recalls those times of a few years back and
includes the comment that Flaubert had "a powerful, serious, melancholy,
manly, deeply corrupted, yet not corrupting, nature." James wrote reviews of
Flaubert publications, a major essay on him, and minor comments concerning
his production as well. He reviewed *Le Tentation de Saint Antoine* (*Nation*, 4
Jun 1874), beginning with an expression of surprise that Flaubert did not treat
temptation in modern terms. James dislikes the form of the work—a long monologue interrupted by depictions of visions which are too much like photographs—and calls it "a ponderous failure." He opines that Flaubert has outlived
his genius. This novel lacks purpose; its hero's comments on his visions are
"meagre and desultory," and its author offers no "spiritual analysis." In short,
Saint Antoine is an example of the decadence of modern French literature. Next,
in his oddly entitled "The Minor French Novelists" (*Galaxy*, Feb 1876), James
reports that Honoré de Balzac* influenced Flaubert, who in turn influenced Zola.
James judges *Madame Bovary* to be Flaubert's "masterpiece," and he adds that
although it is called immoral it is "the pearl of 'Sunday reading' " since its
author is a moralist. Like all good novelists, Flaubert renders the real, which
includes the disagreeable. James discusses "naturally depraved" Emma Bovary's
tragic story, which provokes sympathy. He also analyzes the characters around
the heroine: Bovary, "poor fellow"; Homais, "inimitably rendered"; and the
club-footed ostler, whose surgery is "most repulsive." Is this novel great or
cynical? James slights *L'Education sentimentale* ("studied," "dreary") and
Salammbô ("not . . . easy . . . or . . . agreeable," although it displays "historical
imagination"). James reviewed *Correspondence de Gustave Flaubert*, Qua-
trième Série (1893) (*Macmillan's Magazine*, Mar 1893; reprinted in *Essays in
London and Elsewhere*, 1893). He notes that, whereas Balzac's letters are all
business, Flaubert's concern little but art, almost never the man himself. "Sedentary, cloistered, passionate, cynical, tormented in his love of magnificent
expression, of subjects remote and arduous, with an unattainable ideal," Flaubert
selected details from life but considered his feelings unrelated. And now here
comes his niece, Mme. Commanville, to expose them through his correspondence. After *Madame Bovary, Salammbô*, and the short story "Saint Julien l'Hospitalier"—all "firm masterpieces"—his later works are only "splendid and . . .
curious." After such fine early writings, why are his letters querulous rather
than serene? Should he not regard himself as a success, since in his maturity he
achieved the dreams of his youth by perfecting works planned then? Why are
these letters bitter? Why does he resign himself to bitterness so ungraciously?
Why hoot so often at "the imbecility of the world"? He gripes constantly in
his letters, especially to women, and especially to his good-humored friend Sand.
Flaubert took life as one does "a violent toothache." Although he liked William
Shakespeare,* Turgenev, and Victor-Marie Hugo* (among a few others), he

railed against many others, notably Balzac and Alfred de Musset.* He felt that prose is not only better but also more difficult to compose than poetry. Some of his letters to acquaintances reveal ugly little "tit-for-tat . . . dramas." In his literary works, he creates an "air of pure aesthetics," which makes them "hard as stone" and "cold as death." But we should "cherish him as a perfect example": He sought beauty through his "dry Benedictine years," was a pearl diver groping for "the priceless word," and also accomplished anguished research; he saw beauty as essentially verbal, hated clichés, felt that fine language could produce thought, and employed "visible" imagery. James concludes by querying the many paradoxes of Flaubert's active but unhappy life, and his strong but intolerant nature. James attended the lecture by his friend Paul Bourget* on Flaubert at Oxford University, on 23 June 1897, and wrote up his impressions, in "London" (21 Aug 1897), of the "poetic justice . . . in the introduction of Flaubert to a scene . . . so little to have been by himself ever apprehended or estimated." Finally, James wrote a long introduction to an edition of *Madame Bovary* (1902; reprinted in *Notes on Novelists*, 1914), using the 1899 book on Flaubert by Émile Faguet* as a sounding board but also adding insights from the point of view of an English-speaking fellow craftsman. He details his subject's timorous life and stresses his difficulties, which we can learn from. His *cénacle*, over which he presided in his "colloquial dressing-gown," James subjectively describes. The man was "huge," "diffident," "florid too and resonant," and courteous to young James. But you have to go more than halfway to meet the ensconced French. Flaubert combines the real and the romantic. *Madame Bovary* though a masterpiece is not its author's most imaginative work. It expresses his idiosyncrasies, irritations, and awareness of the dangers of romanticizing. (Not so his *Salammbô*, *L'Education sentimentale*, and *Saint Antoine*.) Emma Bovary is tragic because her real, sordid village does not provide her with the rare. James pauses to recall his first captivated reading of this perfect novel, which "both excites and defies judgment." Even its vulgar elements have fine form and hence beauty. James digresses to *L'Education sentimentale*, an "epic of the usual" and without lift, whose hero he does not like. It is a curiosity, especially from Flaubert, a "novelist's novelist." But some writers are interesting by virtue of their failures. Mme. Arnoux, the heroine, beautiful, vague, immaculate, and renunciatory, is seen only through the hero's eyes. Their "platonic purity" is a "false note." As for *Bouvard et Pécuchet*, it never should have been "embarked on" at all. Still, in our mean literary age, Flaubert is a fine example of conscience and sacrifice; and James can now write partly because of his costly pioneering. Whereas Flaubert is aware of "the requirements of form," women novelists (for example, Jane Austen*) simply are not. Style for him lets "beauty, interest and distinction" emerge. James discusses Flaubert's legendary search for the "one right sentence" and then its association with the other elements of style—all composing into "a shapely crystal box." Flaubert both liked his oddly chosen exotic subjects and hated his "bourgeois themes." Although he ignored many "sides of life," he achieved his goals, like a faithful homesteader on his faraway tract. James asserts that "we know nothing except by style"; only "those who know" about life (and not everyone does) truly judge Flaubert's "complete and beautiful . . . production." The man rendered and felt, not the reverse; he "adored a hard surface," included "rhythm and harmony," and hence produced little. Surely we do not wish that he, like "loose and liquid" Sand, whose style came easily, had written more but at the same time less well. Look at Alexandre Dumas *père*, who was hugely productive but without a speck of style. Finally, *Madame Bovary* is a rare and growing classic because its drama moves to its climax—all of which readers, one after another, are discovering. Late in his life, James enjoyed discussing Flaubert's unbuttoned morality with his Rye neighbor, Sir Sydney Philip Waterlow.* James's library contained three individual books by Flaubert, as well as his *Oeuvres complètes*.

Fleming, George. Pseudonym of Julia Constance Fletcher.*

Fleming, Lady Augusta. In "A Bundle of Letters," the Brighton recipient of a letter from Evelyn Vane.

Fletcher, Horace (1849–1919). American nutritionist. After an active business career, Fletcher did research on nutrition (from 1895), and he lectured and published *Glutton or Epicure* (1899, retitled *The New Glutton or Epicure* [1903]) to popularize his "fletcherizing" technique of overmastication. Fletcher also published other books, not only on nutrition but also on trap shooting, charity work, and popular psychology. James ruinously fletcherized for years (beginning in 1904), called Fletcher "divine" in a letter to Edith Newbold Jones Wharton* (8 Nov 1905), gave copies of Fletcher's book on chewing to Rye neighbors, and fortunately quit the fad in 1910. In a letter to James Jackson Putnam,* one of his helpful physicians (4 Jan 1912), James wrote of "the Fletcherized starvation which was the *fons et origo* of all my woes and which had so nearly done me to death." James's library contained one book by Fletcher.

Fletcher, Julia Constance (1858–1938). Sentimental fiction writer, playwright, and translator (pseudonym: George Fleming). She was born in Brazil to an American father, who was a missionary to South America and later to Italy, and a Swiss mother, whose second husband was Eugene Benson,* an American landscape painter in Rome and Venice. Constance Fletcher lived not only in Rome and Venice, but finally also in London. Her novels include *Kismet: A Nile Novel* (1877, extremely popular), *Mirage* (1878), *The Head of Medusa* (1880), *Vestigia* (1882), *Andromeda* (1885), *The Truth about Clement Ker* (1889), and *For Plain Women Only* (1896). Her plays include *Mrs. Lessingham* (1894) and *The Canary* (1899). James met Benson in Rome in 1873 and therefore also knew Constance Fletcher, through whom he learned details of the death of their friend Constance Fenimore Woolson* in Venice in 1894. In December 1906 James wrote to Constance Fletcher to ask her to show his photographer friend Alvin Langdon Coburn* certain Venetian sights. James reviewed (*Nation*, 7 Jun 1877) *Kismet*, immediately noting that, despite the name George Fleming on the title page, it was written by a woman. He pronounces the book "clever and graceful," but he says that there is too much description and dialogue for its plot. He ridicules the love story and castigates the heroine for her conduct, which results in "no struggle and no drama." James reviewed (*Nation*, 7 Mar 1878) *Mirage*, judging it to be better than *Kismet* but displaying the same faults. Again he ridicules the plot, which features a woman who loves a man who loves her but thinks she loves another man. James deplores the presence here of "the aesthetic young man" as too common a feature in American fiction. All the same, he calls *Mirage* fresh, witty, and better than 99 percent of the works "emitted by . . . [other] English fiction-mongers." It is thought that Eugene Benson may have been a model for Sam Singleton in *Roderick Hudson*. Fletcher's Venetian garden surely inspired James's description of Juliana Bordereau's rare garden in "The Aspern Papers." Heavyset Constance Fletcher may have been a model for huge, kind Rosanna Gaw in *The Ivory Tower*. (It was rumored that Constance once got stuck in James's Lamb House* bathtub.) James's library contained a book of short stories by George Fleming.

"Flickerbridge." Short story (7,400 words), published in *Scribner's Magazine* (Feb 1902); reprinted in *The Better Sort*, 1903; revised and reprinted in *The Novels and Tales of Henry James*, Volume XVIII, 1909. (Characters: Mrs. Bracken, Mrs. Dunn, Frank Granger, Adlaide Wenham, Adelaide Wenham, Dr. and Mrs. Wenham, Mrs. Wenham.) Frank Granger, an American artist, goes to London to paint Mrs. Bracken's portrait and gets the flu. He receives a letter from Addie Wenham, his pushy, successful journalist fiancée (or *is* she his fiancée?), suggesting Flickerbridge as a place for him to recuperate. Flickerbridge is a northern English village, in which a quaint estate is owned by a distant relative of hers also named Adelaide Wenham. Frank goes, rests, and reconsiders his "engagement." He is so charmed by the remote old estate and its shy owner that he grows fearful that his Addie will visit, write about it breezily, and thus ruin its fragility. Learning that the journalist is indeed on her way there, which news pleases old Miss Wenham, Franks says that he does not consider himself engaged and abruptly decamps. James reveals in a Notebook entry (19 Feb 1899) that his source for "Flickerbridge" was a passage in *Tales of New England* by Sarah Orne Jewett.* (The specific story was "A Lost Lover," and the collection was published in 1879.) In it a young girl, visiting a cousin, is impressed by the older woman's absence of chatter. James immediately planned to have a lawyer or journalist visit a previously unseen old cousin, then so fear for her "old-fashionedness" that he tries to keep his pushy fiancée, a writer, from meeting and exploiting the cousin—but fails, and with adverse results. In "Flickerbridge," James makes the young man a painter, and the older Addie the younger Addie's cousin. In the preface to Volume XVIII of *The Novels and Tales of Henry James*, James evasively says that he cannot recall the inspiration for "Flickerbridge," which he defines as a "highly-finished little anecdote." Then he lectures on its lesson, which is the danger of publicizing beautiful regions. It may be noted that although Flickerbridge is in northern England, its remoteness and untouched charm may have been suggested to James by his beloved Rye, and even his Lamb House* there. The story concerns James's hatred of journalistic publicity. A source for the tale may lie as far back as *Days Near Rome* by Augustus John Cuthbert Hare,* in a review of which in 1875 James humorously deplores the fact that this skillfully composed travel book may inspire tourists to flock to formerly out-of-the-way, picturesque nooks and thus vulgarize them. To the end, James deplored the exploitation of the ancient; in a letter to Antonio Fernando de Navarro* (12 Dec 1912), he criticized architect Edwin Landseer Lutyens for his restoration of old houses, adding that "[t]here is nothing left for *me* personally to like but the little mouldy nooks that Country Life [a magazine for which Navarro wrote] is too proud to notice and everyone else (including the photographers) too rich to touch with their fingers of gold."

Flora. In *The Tragic Muse*, a friend of Charles Carteret.

Flora. In "The Turn of the Screw," Miles's sister, age eight, and a niece of the governess's absent employer. She is perhaps victimized by the spirit of Miss Jessel.

Flora, Lady. In *The Portrait of a Lady*, mentioned as perhaps Lord Warburton's fiancée.

Florentia. In "After the Play," the fellow playgoer in London with Amicia, Auberon, and Dorriforth, whom she invites home for tea. Florentia attends plays as an escape, and she enjoyed a recent, evidently crude *Merry Wives of Windsor* production.

"Florentine Architecture." Travel essay, published as one of the eight-part "Florentine Notes" in the *Independent* (18 Jun 1874); reprinted in *Transatlantic Sketches*, 1875, and in *Italian Hours*, 1909.

"A Florentine Garden." Travel sketch, published as one of the eight-part "Florentine Notes" in the *Independent* (14 May 1874); reprinted in *Transatlantic Sketches*, 1875, and in *Italian Hours*, 1909.

"Florentine Notes." The title of each of three travel essays, published in the *Independent* (23, 30 Apr, 21 May 1874); reprinted as parts of an eight-part essay also entitled "Florentine Notes" in *Transatlantic Sketches*, 1875, and in *Italian Hours*, 1909.

"Florentine Notes." Eight travel essays, reprinted in *Transatlantic Sketches*, 1875, and in *Italian Hours*, 1909. They first appeared in the *Independent* as "Florentine Notes" (23 Apr 1874), "Florentine Notes" (30 Apr 1874), "A Florentine Garden" (14 May 1874), "Florentine Notes" (21 May 1874), "Old Italian Art" (11 Jun 1874), "Florentine Architecture" (18 Jun 1874), "An Italian Convent" (2 Jul 1874), and "The Churches of Florence" (9 Jul 1874). I. James describes a Florentine carnival, which had vigor but was not brilliant—in fact, was "cheap." Carnivals in Rome and Venice are better but worse than the New England reader of travel books imagines. II. James describes the Vincigliata castle, near Fiesole; it was restored by a rich British dilettante into something "ingenious," "grim," and "amusingly counterfeit," where violence relieved boredom. III. James notes that the Pitti Palace is "splendid rather than interesting," and he concludes that painter after painter there represents "the very flower of the sumptuous, the courtly, the grand-ducal." Naming several artists and their works, he seems initially critical. (Sometimes the traveler's mood causes mainly "crabbed notes.") He goes on to praise much but concludes that Tuscan artists saw sharp edges whereas Venetian artists "felt . . . indissoluble unity." (Hence James prefers a certain painting by Paolo Veronese* at the Pitti). IV. A visit to the convent of San Marco, decorated by Fra Angelico. James takes his time, even "sat out the sermon." He sees again the "dramatic" *Last Supper* of Domenico Ghirlandaio, who seems modern, realistic. Avoiding dour Beato Angelico, James crosses the square to the Academy to admire Sandro Botticelli, who is "rarity and distinction incarnate," and whose *Coronation of the Virgin* is "supremely beautiful." (Here James praises comments by Walter Horatio Pater* on Botticelli.) V. James likes "old Florentine domestic architecture," which is dignified, secure, and costly. He describes the windows, shields, roofs, and spaciousness of typical residences. James says that the Corsini Palace has interior views rivaling the charm of a landscape and is redolent of the spicy past. VI. Now the Carthusian Monastery, beyond Florence's Roman Gate. First one encounters tenements, crippled beggars, and old monks. But then James views the church, oratories, "bad pictures," chapels, a bishop's tomb with its "cunningest" Francesco di San Gallo monument, cloister and garden, and vantage points of loggias. VII. One notices fewer churches in Florence than in Rome, but "the best of the Florentine temples" are more dignified. In Florence, James likes the Annunziata, especially for its bronze statue and street views, and the "blooming" Duomo; he also admires the light interior of Santa Croce, deplores its coarse statue of absent Dante, and admires most of all Santa Maria Novella because of its fresco work (by Ghirlandaio) and choir. VIII. Finally, the "charming" Boboli Gardens, a "private preserve . . . in the heart of a city." Everything bad is excluded save traffic hum. We see here swept paths, trimmed scrubs, "mildewed sculpture," dry fountains, cypresses, "mossy marble steps," the amphitheatre, and "shady vistas." The Medici, reduced now to "a faint sigh in the breeze," have left an ineffaceable "stain of experience" on the region unlike anything in America.

Floyd-Taylor. In "Glasses," Fanny's husband.

Floyd-Taylor, Fanny. In "Glasses," a friend of Flora Saunt.

Flynn, Mrs. In "The Marriages," the housekeeper at the Chart family's estate in Brinton.

Foat, Ada T. P. In *The Bostonians*, a supposedly distinguished Boston feminist speaker. The name of Cora V. L. Hatch, a New Yorker whom James heard lecture on life after death, may have inspired him to name Ada T. P. Foat as he did.

Folliott, Mrs. In "A Round of Visits," a self-centered friend of Mark Monteith. The two both lost money at the hands of Phil Bloodgood.

Forbes, Dora. In "The Death of a Lion," a popular, bushy-browed, moustached novelist's pen name.

Forbes-Robertson, Sir Johnston (1853–1937). London-born actor, member of important British theatrical companies, manager, and producer. He acted opposite Mary Antoinette Anderson* and Mrs. Patrick Campbell,* and he starred in plays by William Shakespeare,* George Bernard Shaw,* Maurice Maeterlinck,* and others. He married the American actress Gertrude Elliott in 1900. He toured in the United States, and he retired in 1915. James knew both Forbes-Robertson and his wife. In 1907 Forbes-Robertson asked James to convert "Covering End" into a play for him. James explained that the story had originally been the one-act play *Summersoft*, and he agreed to rewrite it in three acts, which he did later in that year, retitling it *The High Bid*. In a letter from Edinburgh to Edith Newbold Jones Wharton* (23 Mar 1908), James praises Gertrude Elliott's dramatic qualities—"gallantry, capacity, and *vaillance*"—as Mrs. Gracedew opposite Forbes-Robertson as Captain Yule. Less than a year later, however, James griped to his brother William (26 Feb 1909) that Forbes-Robertson and his wife, having given five London matinee performances, had "hung up, but not abandoned" *The High Bid* in order to take an "insufferable 'vulgar' play" on spring tour. The play in question was Jerome K. Jerome's phenomenal hit *The Passing of the Third Floor Back* (1908). Forbes-Robertson accepted, modified, and produced *The Conqueror* (1905), a play by James's friend Millicent Fanny St. Claire-Erskine, Duchess of Sutherland.*

Ford, Ford Madox (1873–1939). English writer, who changed his name from Ford Madox Hueffer.*

Ford, Paul Leicester (1865–1902). American bibliographer, historian, editor, and popular novelist. Deformed by a spinal injury, he became a precocious, voracious reader. Among his almost innumerable works is his first novel, *The Honorable Peter Sterling, and What People Thought of Him* (1894). Ford was murdered by his brother, who then committed suicide, because of a dispute over family finances. In "American Letter" (7 May 1898), James states that the enormous sales success of *The Honorable Peter Sterling* keeps one from saying more than merely that the work is both formless and tasteless.

Ford, Lieutenant John (Jack). In "The Story of a Year," Elizabeth Crowe's fiancée. Mortally wounded during the Civil War, he is brought home to Glenham to die.

Ford, Mrs. In "The Story of a Year," John Ford's mother, who distrusts his fiancée Elizabeth Crowe, with good reason.

"Fordham Castle." Short story (7,800 words), published in *Harper's Magazine* (Dec 1904); revised and reprinted in *The Novels and Tales of Henry James*, Volume XVI, 1909. (Characters: Lord Dunderton, Mattie Magaw, Mr. and Mrs. Magaw, Mme. Massin, Abel F. Taker, and Sue Taker.) American Abel F. Taker gets mail in a Geneva pension from his wife Sue, who has planted him there under the name C. P. Addard while she is making her solitary way in British society under an assumed and prettier name also. To the pension comes Mrs. Vanderplank, who, it soon appears, is really Mrs. Magaw. Her daughter Mattie has abandoned her and has changed her name, too, and she is making her way alone in society as well. Taker receives a letter from his wife, now in Fordham Castle, England, at about the time Mrs. Magaw gets one from her daughter telling about helpful Mrs. Sherrington Reeves. Taker knows that Mrs. Reeves is really Sue. Next, Mattie writes of her engagement to Lord Dunderton, adding that Mrs. Reeves says Mrs. Magaw can now safely resurface. Taker miserably tells Mrs. Magaw that, while Lord Dunderton must be so in love with the daughter that the plain mother may now safely be introduced, he will never be recalled. Putting Mrs. Magaw on the train and feeling dead, he tells her that he will become Fordham Castle's ghost. An early Notebook entry (5 Feb 1892) suggests the general topic of this depressing story: "the immense typical theme of the *manless* American woman, in Europe. . . . The total suppression of the husband." In a later entry (11 May 1898), James credits his friend Gaillard Thomas Lapsley* with the following related idea: "the American phenomenon of the social suppression of the parents." Subsequent entries (15 Feb, 5 Oct 1899) reveal that James had difficulty deciding on family relationships, point of view, and length of story, the inclusion of the abused husband as well as the abused mother, the exclusion of the son to parallel the daughter, and the use of at least 50 percent more words, before he finished the story we have. In the preface to Volume XVIII of *The Novels and Tales of Henry James*, he ramblingly relates "Fordham

Castle'' to his frequent use of the international theme, explains that he hoped to create variety here by concentrating on parents instead of ''an eternity of mere international young ladies.'' and praises the story's ''compactness.'' Its mathematical symmetry cannot, however, disguise the brutality plotted in it concerning the mistreatment of allegedly gauche husbands and allegedly out-of-fashion parents.

Foreign Parts. The title for *Transatlantic Sketches* as published in 1883 in the Christian Bernhard Tauchnitz* *Collection of British Authors*. Some sketches from the original edition were revised; others, omitted.

Fortescue, Mary. In ''De Grey, A Romance,'' a woman loved and destroyed by George De Grey.

''The Founding of the 'Nation': Recollections of the 'Fairies' That Attended Its Birth.'' Short essay, published in *Nation* (8 Jul 1915). In it, James remembers that fifty years ago Charles Eliot Norton* told him of the founding of ''the most promising scion of the newspaper stock as that stock had rooted itself in American soil,'' and led him to its first editor, Edwin Lawrence Godkin,* whose friendship James calls ''one of the best of my life.'' That half century must now be regarded as ''the Age of the Mistake'' because World War I makes it seem so romantic and innocent. Asked by Godkin to be a contributor, James sent many book reviews from Boston (1867–1868), more from New York (1875), and then from Paris and London (1876–1878). Thus Norton and Godkin were ''favoring fairies'' at the cradle of James's career.

''Four Meetings.'' Short story (11,400 words), published in *Scribner's Monthly* (Nov 1877); republished in *Daisy Miller: A Study*, 1879; revised and reprinted in *The Novels and Tales of Henry James*, Volume XVI, 1909. (Characters: Alcibiade, Latouche, Mrs. Latouche, Mixter, Caroline Spencer.) The perhaps well-intentioned but assuredly supercilious narrator first meets schoolteacher Caroline Spencer at the New England home of his traveling partner Latouche's mother. He talks about Europe, and Miss Spencer says that she is saving up to go there herself. Three years later they meet a second time, in Le Havre. Her first glimpse of France delights her, but the narrator grows alarmed when she reports that her art student cousin is here to welcome her. When the two men are introduced, alarm turns to suspicion. Hours later, at their third meeting, Miss Spencer tells the narrator that she has given the cousin all of her savings—to aid him and his Provençal countess ''wife''—and is returning to America at once. The anguished narrator, who can do nothing, calls five years later on now-dead Latouche's mother, and he drops in on Miss Spencer for their fourth meeting: The ''countess,'' in reality a shabby creature from Paris, has come to live with, domineer, and be served by her dead ''husband's'' cousin. A simple tale, of four meetings between narrator and heroine. Yet critical questions arise:

What motivates the narrator? Why is Miss Spencer so callow? Does she come to know the best of Europe, in the form of a mountainous bogus countess, who, since the teacher cannot get to Europe, comes to her? The title "Four Meetings," may well have been suggested to James by the title "Three Meetings," an 1851 story by Ivan Sergeyevich Turgenev.*

Foy, Cecelia (Cissy). In *The Ivory Tower*, the Bradhams' friend. She may have had a liaison with Northover in Europe. Now she has supposedly set her cap for his stepson Graham Fielder.

France, Anatole (pen name of Jacques Anatole François Thibault, 1844–1924). French author, whose main works include *Le Crime de Sylvestre Bonnard* (1881), *Thäis* (1890), *L'Étui de nacre* (1892), *L'Orme du mail* (1897), *L'Île des pingouins* (1908), *La Vie de Jeanne d'Arc* (1908), *Les Dieux ont soif* (1912), and *Le Révolte des anges* (1914). In letters to Robert Louis Stevenson* (30 Oct 1891, 17 Feb 1893), James calls France "exquisite" and "a real master"; in the second letter, he labels *L'Étui de nacre* "charming." In "London" (5 Jun 1897), James says that France's *L'Orme du mail* is "as spicily sweet as a clove pink." Here and there in "The Present Literary Situation in France," James touches favorably again on France. In a letter to Sir Edmund Wilson Gosse* (19 Nov 1912), he praises France's romantic biography of Joan of Arc as "sinuously, yet oh so wisely, right!" James's library contained eleven books by France.

"France." War essay, published as part of *The Book of France in Aid of the French Parliamentary Committee's Fund for the Relief of the Invaded Departments*, published in London by Macmillan and Co., 1915; reprinted in *Within the Rim and Other Essays: 1914–15*, 1919. James starts by praising France as uniquely important "to the educated spirit of man." We English, he adds, have "the good fortune . . . of . . . being neighboured by a native genius so different from our own." France enables us to make comparisons, helps us to leave our insularity, and now—"menaced and overdarkened"—inspires in us the "noble passion" of generosity. France represents the best in the mind and the senses. We must not let "our Enemy" render us passive, while civilization depends so greatly on "erect, . . . incalculable, immortal France."

François. In *The Ambassadors*, a Parisian waiter for Lambert Strether and Mr. Waymarsh.

Frank, Adrian. In "The Impressions of a Cousin," Caliph's half-brother. When Caliph impoverishes Frank's fiancée Eunice, Frank makes restitution to please her cousin Catherine Condit.

Frankle, Bill. In "The Bench of Desolation," Kate Cookham's whilom friend, of whom Herbert Dodd was jealous.

Franks. In *Watch and Ward*, a junkman in business with George Fenton.

Freddy. In "The Impressions of a Cousin," a man Lizzie Ermine wants Eunice to marry.

Frederic, Harold (1856–1898). American novelist, short-story writer, and journalist. He was born in Utica, New York, was a reporter and editor there and in Albany, and then became the London correspondent for the New York *Times*. In addition to romantic, fantasy, and war fiction, Frederic published two important naturalistic novels, *Seth's Brother's Wife* (1887) and *The Damnation of Theron Ware* (1896). In London, Frederic had both a wife and a mistress, and children by each woman. He knew slightly but thought little of James, who, however, when Frederic died of a stroke, wrote to Cora Crane, the so-called wife of Stephen Crane,* to offer money and sympathy for Frederic's children. James read Frederic's posthumously published novel *The Market Place* (1899) and told Cora Crane that it showed what its author could have done if he had had a different lifestyle.

Freeman, Mary Eleanor Wilkins (1852–1930). Massachusetts-born fiction writer. She attended Mount Holyoke (1870–1871), wrote extensively as Mary E. Wilkins, married Dr. Charles M. Freeman rather late in life (1902), and lived thereafter in New Jersey, publishing as Mary E. Wilkins Freeman. Of her hundreds of short stories, most of the best are contained in *A Humble Romance* (1887) and in *A New England Nun* (1891). She wrote less significantly in the genres of the novel and drama. In "American Letter" (9 Apr 1898), James praises American local colorists, including "Miss Mary Wilkins," and says that if she should depart for Europe he would recommend her extradition. In another "American Letter" (9 Jul 1898), he calls her "admirable," expresses "enthusiastic admiration" for her early work (in which she excellently handles "the dry realities of rustic New England"), and comments that in *Silence and Other Stories* (1898) she wisely avoids "the dangerous desert of the 'long' story." More candidly, in a letter to William Dean Howells* (25 Jan 1902), James labels her "impossible" when she grows expansive; in a letter to Sarah Butler Wister* (21 Dec 1902), he deplores her "sentimentality."

Freer, Mr. and Mrs. Dexter. In "Lady Barbarina," a rich American couple who enjoy watching the passing parade of mounted British society in Hyde Park.

French, Basil. In "Julia Bride," a young man who likes Julia Bride but is kept from proposing marriage to her because of stories concerning her.

French Poets and Novelists. Collection of twelve critical essays and reviews, all previously published; revised and reprinted in London by Macmillan, 1878, and in Leipzig by Christian Bernhard Tauchnitz,* 1883. The essays are "Alfred de Musset[*]," "Théophile Gautier[*]," "Charles Baudelaire[*]," "Honoré de Balzac[*]," "Balzac's Letters," "George Sand[*]," "Charles Bernard and Gustave Flaubert[*]" (part of "The Minor French Novelists"), "Ivan [Sergeyevich] Turgénieff[*]," "The Two Ampères" (concerning André-Marie Ampère* and his son Jean-Jacques Ampère), "Madame [Eléanor de Jean de Manville] de Sabran[*]," "Mérimée's Letters," and "The Théâtre Français."

"A French Watering Place." Paris letter (1876), reprinted as "Etretat" in *Portraits of Places*, 1883.

Freshville, Mrs. In *The Reprobate*, the former Nina, who is both Paul Doubleday's whilom girlfriend, who went to Paris with him ten years earlier to sing, and the former close friend of Captain Chanter. Her appearance as the widow Mrs. Freshville at Hampton Court embarrasses not only Paul, who likes Blanche Amber, but also Chanter, who is pursuing Paul's stepmother Mrs. Doubleday. Mrs. Freshville ultimately goes after Pitt Brunt.

Frewen, Moreton (1853–1924). British economist, member of Parliament from West Cork, and adventurer. He was the husband of Clara Jerome Frewen (an aunt of Sir Winston Churchill*), an admirer of the American West, and an investor in cattle there. Frewen rented Brede Place, his big, cold, fourteenth-century manor house in Rye, to Stephen Crane* and his "wife" Cora. They were to pay £40 per year and continue restoration; but they never bothered to pay. James knew Frewen and his wife socially, received news of Crane from them, and at one point helped Frewen find the widow of Augustus Saint-Gaudens,* in a laudable but vain effort on Frewen's part to obtain a copy of the sculptor's statue created for the grave of the wife of Henry Adams.* James also knew the Frewens' daughter Clare Consuelo Frewen Sheridan, who became a sculptress, painter, writer, and traveler, and her gallant husband Wilfred Sheridan, who was killed in France in World War I.

Frezzolini, Madame. In *The American*, a celebrated singer whom Christopher Newman hopes to hire to sing at a party he would like to give in Madame Emmeline de Bellegarde's honor.

"The Friends of the Friends" (1896 title, "The Way It Came"; 1909 title, "The Friends of the Friends"). Short story (9,700 words), published in the *Chap Book* (1 May 1896), and in *Chapman's Magazine of Fiction* (May 1896, edited by James's friend Oswald John Frederick Crawfurd*); reprinted in *Embarrassments*, 1896; revised and reprinted in *The Novels and Tales of Henry James*, Volume XVII, 1909. (Characters: none named). Among a dead woman's papers is a story of two unnamed friends. A woman saw her father's spirit just before learning of his death. A man similarly saw his mother's spirit just before her death. Years later, the woman narrator is trying to introduce the man, now her fiancé, and the woman, now an estranged wife. But before the meeting can occur, the woman says that her husband has died. Now the narrator declines to permit her fiancé to meet the widow. Sad because of unfounded jealousy, the narrator goes to explain to the widow, who, however, died the night before. When the narrator reports this shocking fact to her fiancé, he denies the story, saying that the widow was in his room staring at him the night before. The narrator suspects another ghost, thinks that her fiancé is continuing to see it, grows suspicious and breaks off her engagement to him. He jokingly admits seeing the ghost, then retracts the statement; but the two people never marry. When the man dies, the narrator theorizes that he committed suicide to be with the other woman's spirit. In a Notebook entry (5 Feb 1895), James asks himself: "What is there in the idea of *Too late*—of some friendship or passion or bond— some affection long desired and waited for, that is formed too late?—I mean too late in life altogether." This general idea James later (21 Dec 1895) made more specifically the start of "The Friends of the Friends": "The idea for . . . a scrap of a fantasy, of 2 persons who have constantly heard of each other. . . . They have never met. . . . At last it has been arranged . . . by some 3rd person, the friend of each. . . . But before the event one of them dies . . . then comes . . . to the survivor . . . " In one more entry (10 Jan 1896), James frets with many additional details, some of which he discarded. For example, narrator and lover "go . . . on with their engagement" in the *Notebooks* but not in the finished tale. In the preface to Volume XVII of *The Novels and Tales of Henry James*, James rightly calls the original title of this story "colourless." Many critics ignore the story; others are intrigued because its obsessed, deluded female narrator may be a rehearsal for the governess in "The Turn of the Screw." "The Friends of the Friends" is quite unlike "Sir Edmund Orme," in which a ghost helps foster marriage. "The Friends of the Friends" may well contain James's most unfath- omable plot, down there with *The Sacred Fount*.

Fritz. In "In the Cage," a name mentioned on a telegram processed by the girl "in the cage."

Frohman, Charles (1860–1915). Ohio-born theater manager. While a teenager, he worked for New York newspapers. In 1877 he entered the theater business. For a while, he and his brother Daniel Frohman* managed the Madison Square Theater. In 1890 Charles Frohman organized his own stock company, showed brilliance in developing and managing talent, and syndicated to control other theaters. In 1897 he began to present plays in London. James wrote *The Outcry* for Frohman, but the death of King Edward VII* in 1910 caused the closing of the London theaters and ended his season. James was within his legal rights to keep Frohman's considerable advance and forfeit. In 1915 Frohman went down with the *Lusitania*.

Frohman, Daniel (1851–1940). American theatrical manager, for a time associated with his brother Charles Frohman.* In 1882 James rewrote "Daisy Miller: A Study" as a play for the Madison Square Theater at the request of Daniel Frohman, but he rejected it, on the grounds that it contained too much literary dialogue.

"From a Roman Note-Book." Travel essay, published in the *Galaxy* (Nov 1873); reprinted in *Transatlantic Sketches*, 1875, and in *Italian Hours*, 1909. In it, James ramblingly reports his impressions of Rome from 28 December 1872 through 17 May 1873. At first, the city is dark and empty, but two days later he is relishing the Colonna gardens. On January 2 he is impressed by the mortality-tainted air of the glorious Protestant cemetery, then he discusses Italian marble. On January 4, 16, 21, and 30, he records sundry drives, walks, and sunbaths. The January 26 entry concerns the Villa Medici, "the most enchanting place in Rome." On February 12 he finds the Villa Albani too formal but under magnificent light and with inspiring Casino marbles. On March 9 he visits the Vatican with "R[alph]. W[aldo]. E[merson].[*]"; the place, though padded, is full of treasures which define our notion of beauty. In April James attends a play by Carlo Goldoni, which he "could but half follow"; at another theater, he sees Princess Margaret in the audience. On April 27 he finds the Villa Ludovisi "blissfully *right*" and "consecrated to style." May 17 is devoted to St. John Lateran, with its attendant summery ivy and grass. To Italy he bids farewell with a "sharp pang" but promises to return. Throughout, James is observant, and certain scenes remind him of literary treatments thereof, for example, by Robert Browning* and Stendhal.*

"From Chambéry to Milan." Travel essay, published in the *Nation* (21 Nov 1872), as Part VI of "A European Summer"; revised and reprinted in *Transatlantic Sketches*, 1875, and in *Italian Hours*, 1909. James comments that it might be nice to enter Italy by whizzing like a bullet through the eight-mile Mont Cenis Tunnel. But he starts at shabby Chambéry, redolent of the past: [Jean-Jacques] Rousseau's house, shades of Madame [Louise Eléonore] de Warens, and an air of perversity and poverty hardly hidden by literary legends. Next, he visits the futuristic tunnel, a perfect shortcut at the pyramidal mountain's base, and then Turin on an August afternoon. Everything here stirs dormant memories of Italy seen some time ago. The architecture of Turin is meager, but the Turin gallery has fine works by Paolo Veronese* and even better ones by Anthony Van Dyke (especially his painting of Charles I's dimpled family). Milan is experienced, reserved, Germanized. It has a curious, rich cathedral: tall, massive, with painted ceiling, and chapel of St. Charles Borromeus (all clay and gems, all pastoral and ironic). James climbs to the duomo roof for a view of level Lombardy, then he pays his respects to the *Cenacolo* by Leonardo* da Vinci (now sadly defaced, the moral being that art too is mortal), the Brera, and the Ambrosian Library. Finally, James visits romantic Lake Como, with its waterside hotels and villas—all with scenery like a lavish opera.

"From Lake George to Burlington." Travel essay, published in the *Nation* (1 Sep 1870). James reports that he enjoyed a steamer ride up the lake, with varied sights: clouds, mountains, forests, bays, islands. On landing, he went on to Ticonderoga, past an ugly village to a park-like woodland to the "simple ruins of the grass-grown fort" by "noble, free, and open" Lake Champlain. A sail past simple shores and fine hills took him to "supremely beautiful" Burlington, in which he strolled past "solid . . . homes" to the university, "embowered in scholastic shade." Beyond were "distant mountains."

"From Normandy to the Pyrenees." Travel essay, published in *Galaxy* (Jan 1877); reprinted in *Portraits of Places*, 1883. As winter approaches, James can remember a perfect August morning on the Normandy coast: grassy cliff at Etretat, downs toward Dieppe, wind-twisted oaks, ten-mile walk to Fécamp for breakfast and Sunday races. Another memory: breakfast at St. Louin (which has "porphoritic" cliffs) served at the inn by pretty Ernestine, who collects trinkets and writings by customers (including celebrities). James contrasts French and American behavior, with respect to vacations, women, meals, furniture, bedrooms, beach etiquette, chaperoning, and marriage arrangements. Next he recalls a central French valley; he mentions *patois*, rustic scenes, buildings, talkative peasants, the neighborhood curé ("the pearl of the local priesthood"), and a town nearby with a street wonderfully named Les Belles Manières. Finally, down to Biarritz ("decidedly below its reputation"), with its casino (of "second-rate picturesqueness"). James admired the good-looking Basques. At last, he drove via St. Jean de Luz to "lively" San Sebastian, in Spain: "elegant" new quarter, old section with Jesuit church and "interior redolent of Spanish Catholicism" (including bejeweled "effigy" of the Virgin with "fringed eyelids and . . . hand to be kissed"), bullfight ("a disgusting thing"), and "bright-colored southern crowd."

"From Venice to Strasburg" (1873 title, "From Venice to Strasburg"). Travel essay, published in the *Nation* (6 Mar 1873), as Part VII of "A European Summer"; reprinted in *Transatlantic Sketches*, 1875, and (as "Venice: An Early Impression") in *Italian Hours*, 1909.

"From Venice to Strassburg." The 1873 title of "From Venice to Strasburg."

Fromentin, Eugène (1820–1876). A French painter and writer, he is most famous for being an early painter of Algerian scenes and inhabitants. His first phase is somewhat mechanical; his second, bland; his third, more vivid. He wrote one novel, entitled *Dominique* (1862); travel books, including *Un Eté dans la Sahara* (1857); and art studies, the best being in a series called *Les*

Maîtres d'Autrefois (1876). James reviewed (*Nation*, 13 Jul 1876) the Peter Paul Rubens* and Rembrandt Harmensz van Rijn* segments of the *Maîtres* series by Fromentin. James begins by calling Fromentin's *Dominique* "exquisite and perfect" but regards the present volume as more "curious" than "valuable." Fromentin is too subtle, and his technical comments would be better in a manual or a studio record book. James flatly confesses to a "mistrust of literary criticism of works of plastic art." Perhaps paintings should be simply enjoyed. Still, Fromentin, who is "just and delicate," is less excessive than John Ruskin,* with his "attribution of various incongruous and arbitrary intentions to the artist." Fromentin takes Rubens "too seriously"; James regards him as "coarse," vulgar, shallow, and careless, though energetic and also fine in managing colors and composition. James praises his *St. George*, in Antwerp. Fromentin discusses several minor painters well, especially the "enchanting" Jacob Ruysdael, but he is rather pointless on Rembrandt. Fromentin calls *The Night Watch* strange and adds that Rembrandt reveals the unknown. With both statements James disagrees, contending that Rembrandt reveals the homely known by rare execution. Still, Fromentin is acute, delicate, and charming. James's library contained two books by Fromentin.

Froome, Mrs. In *The Sacred Fount*, a woman expected to arrive later at Newmarch with Lord Lutley.

Frost. In *Tenants*, Sir Frederick Byng's servant, who serves tea to Eleanor Vibert.

Frothingham, Miss. In "A London Life," Lady Davenant's maid.

Froude, James Anthony (1818–1894). British historian, educated at Oriel College, Oxford, and specializing in the Tudor period. His major historical work is his *History of England from the Fall of Wolsey to the Defeat of the Spanish Armada* (12 vols., 1856–1870) and a series of volumes called *Short Studies on Great Subjects* (1867–1882). Froude was one of the literary executors of his friend and colleague Thomas Carlyle.* He published Carlyle's unauthorized *Reminiscences* (1881), a revealing biography of Carlyle (4 vols., 1882–1884), and an edition of Jane Carlyle's letters (1883). Froude supported himself by writing novels and essays, as well as his more important works, until he became regius professor of modern history at Oxford, beginning in 1892. His major work is attractive today because of its descriptions and narrative style; nevertheless, it is disfigured by Protestant bias, careless use of source material, and indifference to the socioeconomic forces producing historical change. James reviewed (*Nation*, 31 Oct 1867) an 1868 volume of *Short Studies on Great Subjects*, calling it not valuable. The historical pieces are superficial; the religious, sentimental. James prefers Froude's *History of England*, which has "spirit, . . . execution, . . . tone, . . . pictorial style." Froude is shaky when he generalizes that the world is moral but is wise to study historical figures in context. He is childish in his treatment of Mary Stuart, and not only childish and vague on Martin Luther but also prejudiced in his favor. Froude is better on the dissolution of the monasteries under Henry VIII, whom, however, he praises too highly. Best is Froude's "pure narrative" treatment of Elizabethan adventurers. During his busy social season in London, during the winter of 1876–1877, James met Froude at the home of hospitable George Washburn Smalley.* James generally deplored Froude's treatment of Carlyle and his wife Jane. In a letter to Lady Rosebery, wife of Archibald Philip Primrose, Earl of Rosebery* (16 Jun [1883]), James wrote that "we thirst for the blood of J.A. Froude," but that Jane Carlyle, though "rather squalid," is "great . . . for saying things well." In a letter to Carlyle editor Charles Eliot Norton* (6 Dec [1886]), James calls Froude "unspeakable" for his work on Carlyle.

Frush, Amy. In "The Third Person," the second cousin of older Susan Frush. Amy is an amateur writer who smuggles a book into England to appease Cuthbert Frush's ghost.

Frush, Cuthbert. In "The Third Person," an ancestor of Amy and Susan Frush, who was hanged for smuggling. His ghost haunts the Frush home at Marr until Amy appeases it by an act of smuggling of her own.

Frush, Mrs. In "The Third Person," the widowed aunt of Amy Frush and Susan Frush, who together inherit property at Marr from the old lady when she dies.

Frush, Susan. In "The Third Person," the second cousin of younger Amy Frush. Susan is an amateur watercolorist.

Fullerton, William Morton (1865–1952). Connecticut-born man of letters and one of James's most intimate friends. The son of a Congregational minister, Morton Fullerton grew up in Waltham, Massachusetts, in an indulgent family, became a journalist and literary editor in Boston, then freelanced in London. He was on the staff of the London *Times* (1890–1911). He soon met James, who quickly admired his personality and versatility and became his loyal friend. Fullerton also began to move in homosexual circles which included Oscar Wilde,* Ronald Sutherland (Lord Gower), and some of their friends. By early 1893 Fullerton was transferred to the *Times* bureau in Paris (until 1907). Vacationing in Paris in April 1893, James saw Fullerton socially a few times. Fullerton reported the infamous case (1894–1899) of Captain Alfred Dreyfus* with skill and daring. Fullerton's activities as a heterosexual included relationships with Margaret Alice Lili Brooke* (the Ranee of Sarawak, whom James knew well), with a married neighbor in Paris named Henrietta Mirecourt, perhaps with the celebrated Blanche Roosevelt* (at one time, the mistress of Guy de

Maupassant*), and certainly with a singer named Victoria Camille "Ixo" Chabert, whom he married in 1903. The couple had a daughter (very soon) and a divorce in a year. In 1905 Fullerton had another affair, with his cousin Katharine Fullerton, earlier mistakenly thought to be his sister, and he became engaged to her in 1907. In 1907 Fullerton through James met Edith Newbold Jones Wharton* in England, visited her (armed with a letter from James) and her unstable husband at their home in Lenox, Massachusetts, and saw her again in Paris (while her husband was elsewhere in France and soon sick). She was distressed that the man known as "M.F." in her 1908 diary was not more responsive. In truth, in November 1907, Fullerton had informed James that he was being pressured by Henrietta Mirecourt, who first wanted marriage, then rifled Fullerton's desk while he was away, found letters revealing his promiscuous bisexual activities, and was trying to blackmail him. James's letters to Fullerton about the whole affair contain words of advice, love, and flattery: "[T]here was always a muffled unenlightened ache for my affection in my not knowing" (14 Nov 1907); "I think . . . of your averted *reality* . . . as a . . . waste . . . of something—ah, so tender!—in *me* that was . . . yearningly ready for you" (14 Nov 1907); "throw yourself outside of the damned circle . . . on your work, on your genius, on your art, on your knowledge" (19 Nov 1907); Mirecourt is "a mad, vindictive, obscene old woman" who will be "'chucked out,' with refusal to touch or look at her calumnious wares," and "if you really *break* with her . . . you will find yourself free" (26 Nov 1907); "[a]s for R.G. [Gower], he is very ancient history" (26 Nov 1907); and "I . . . depend on your fortitude . . . [and] am with you, in the intensity of my imagination and my affection. . . . *Je vous embrasse bien*" (29 Nov 1907). Incredibly, Fullerton sent his cousin, Katharine Fullerton, James's letters. Early in 1908 Fullerton became Wharton's discreet, intermittent lover (until 1910). Wharton found him sophisticated, idealistic, and sensual. She never destroyed her 1908 diary about him, and he never destroyed her letters to him. He extricated himself from Mirecourt's clutches, with the help of James and Wharton, in the summer of 1909. From New York, James wrote to Howard Overing Sturgis* (18 Oct 1910) that "Fullerton had broken off his twenty years' Paris connection with the *Times* and is having a great journalistic and periodical *acceuil* here (he will gain, as to the employment of his great talent, immensely by the change)." James wrote to Wharton (25 Oct 1911) that Fullerton's English edition of *Gil Blas* "is nice—but not up to his best mark." And James was sad to share the news with Wharton (24 Mar 1915) that "W. M. F. hasn't done well in America and is coming back on that collapse." During World War I, Fullerton was an officer on the general staff of the American Expeditionary Force (1917–1918). He later joined the *Figaro* staff in Paris. He wrote several books, some in English and others in French; they include *In Cairo* (1891), *Patriotism and Science: Some Studies in Historic Psychology* (1893), *Terres Françaises: Boulogne, Franche-Comté, Narbonnaise* (1905), *Problems of Power: A Study of International Politics from Sadowa to Kirk-Kilissé* (1913), *Hesitations, the American Crisis and the War* (1916), *Au Seuil de la Provençe: Le Rhône Cévenol*

(1923), and several studies of U.S.–French political relations. Fullerton was a cousin of James's first bibliographer, Le Roy Phillips.* James's library contained two books by Fullerton.

"The Future of the Novel." Critical essay, published in *The International Library of Famous Literature* . . . (London: The Standard, 1899). James says that the novel from small beginnings is now flooding us and is being taken in by the "abysmally absorbent" public mind. But its present-day readers are mostly single women and schoolboys, plus some others with poor taste who like to live vicariously by viewing "elastic" prose pictures. Literature in general has recently been "vulgaris[ed]" for the "irreflective and uncritical." The future will offer us so many novels that we must either dump most of them overboard or be content merely to read inept reviews of them. All the same, the novel has a future, if it simply holds our attention by avoiding "superficiality . . . or . . . timidity." The quality of any novel will depend on "the society that produces it," and it is better if that society has an "acute, . . . mature" critical faculty and does not merely seek money and amusement. Free and fruitful novels will be soul-satisfying if they address mature readers, not "the 'young.' " In future, the novel ought to handle neglected subjects more frankly, stay in advance "of its farthest follower," and, for example, "treat . . . the great relation between men and women, the constant world-renewal," and the new freedom of women. It should try for variety and vividness, be penetrating but balanced. James mentions Charles Dickens,* Henry Fielding, Samuel Richardson, Sir Walter Scott,* and Robert Louis Stevenson.*

G

"Gabrielle de Bergerac." Short story (22,300 words), published in the *Atlantic Monthly* (Jul–Sep 1869). (Characters: Gabrielle de Bergerac, Baron de Bergerac, Baron and Baroness de Bergerac, Chevalier de Bergerac, Marie de Chalais, Marquis de Chalais, Pierre Coquelin, Mme. Coquelin, Marquis de Rochambeau, de Sorbières, Abbé Tiblaud, Vicomte Gaston de Treuil.) Pierre Coquelin tutors Chevalier de Bergerac, age nine, and falls in love with the boy's aunt Gabrielle de Bergerac, who is being courted by Vicomte Gaston de Treuil. Gabrielle's brother, the head of the family, favors Gaston but foolishly causes the elopement by Pierre and Gabrielle by accusing her of improper conduct with the honorable but passionately devoted Pierre. The loving pair are guillotined with other Girondists during the French Revolution. This historical romance à la Sir Walter Scott,* the style of which also shows the pervasive influence of George Sand,* is thoroughly charming. It is a pity that James never wrote more works in the same genre. Pierre and Gabrielle opt to live life with brief intensity. Like Hyacinth Robinson later, they balance fatally between sociopolitical excesses on both sides of an untenable position. James derived the name Coquelin from that of a teenaged schoolboy friend of his named Benoît Constant Coquelin* in Boulogne-sur-Mer; later the same Coquelin took the title role in Edmond Rostand's 1897 heroic comedy *Cyrano de Bergerac*.

Gainsborough, Thomas (1727–1788). Distinguished English painter. At age fourteen, he left Suffolk to study etching and painting in London. He returned home, married, painted landscapes and portraits (always preferring the former), established a studio at Bath (1759), and succeeded as a sought-after portraitist in the world of fashion and money. He opened a studio in London (1774), received numerous royal and other significant commissions, became one of the original Royal Academy members (1768), and continued to be popular and successful. Gainsborough was influenced more by nature than by earlier painters, although he emulated the Dutch to a degree in his landscapes. In "The Bethnal Green Museum" (1873), James praises Gainsborough's *Miss Boothby* as "rich with the morality of . . . English nurseries." But in "The Old Masters at Burlington House" (1877), James deplores an exhibition of too many unimpressive Gainsboroughs, "mere pot-boilers," with "streaky umbrage" in the background. He does praise a few portraits, especially one of composer Johann Fischer and one family group. In "The Old Masters at Burlington House" (31 Jan 1878), James complains again that there is a great difference between a fine Gainsborough and a so-so one, and he adds that, although the master was "too prolific," he never painted faces poorly. In "The Winter Exhibitions in London" (1879), James concludes thus: "It is hard sometimes to resist the impression that Gainsborough is an overrated painter, the number of his failures is so large and their quality is so very poor. His sketchiness and his want to science transcend the limits of the allowable."

Galopin, Cécile. In "The Point of View," the daughter of M. le Pasteur and Mme. Galopin.

Galopin, M. le Pasteur and Mme. In "The Pension Beaurepas," a Geneva minister and his wife; they are Cécile Galopin's parents. He is to show Mrs. Church and her daughter Aurora certain Reformation documents. Mrs. Church is impressed by Mme. Galopin, but Aurora Church is not. In "The Point of View," Mrs. Church writes to Mme. Galopin about Cécile's engagement.

Galsworthy, John (1867–1933). Distinguished, conservative British novelist and playwright, educated at Harrow and then at Oxford University. His most enduring work is a series of novels assembled as *The Forsyte Saga* (1906–1922). In 1909 a group was formed to offer a repertory season at the Duke of York's Theatre in London. James was approached and hoped that his play *The Outcry* would be performed there. Galsworthy wrote *Justice* (1910) as part of the plan. James met Galsworthy, perhaps at this time. In August 1909, James sent Galsworthy an eloquent letter in support of several playwrights' protest against the licensing of plays by the Lord Chamberlain. Galsworthy read James's letter during hearings before a parliamentary committee. No changes in drama licensing laws were made at this time. James Brand Pinker* was Galsworthy's agent, as well as James's. James's library contained one book by Galsworthy.

Gambini, Antonietta. In "De Grey, A Romance," a woman loved and hence destroyed by George De Grey.

Gannett, William Channing (1840–1923). Unitarian minister, theological writer, and editor. He was the son of a respected minister, writer, and editor. William Gannett graduated from Harvard (1860), worked among freed slaves late in the Civil War in South Carolina and Georgia, studied abroad, then returned to graduate from Harvard Divinity School (1868). He became a minister, moved about, and later preached in Rochester, New York (1889–1908). In addition to many radically anticreedal, mystical works, Gannett wrote critical essays, books for children, poems, and hymns. His most popular books were *Blessed Be Drudgery* (1886) and *The Faith That Makes Faithful* (1887). James reviewed (*Nation*, 1 Apr 1875) Gannett's book about his father, entitled *Ezra Stiles Gannett, Unitarian Minister in Boston, 1824–1871* (1875), calling it a "vivacious" biography of a "monotonous and colorless" mind. Why irreverently make a "shrinking personality" the subject for a "high-colored 'story' "? The author's manner is "unwholeness." James says that the best part of the book is the background history of New England Unitarianism in it. James calls Ezra Gannett practical, simple, pious, conservative, and morbidly conscientious—and wise not to publish his "painfully dry" sermons.

Gardner, Isabella Stewart (1840–1924). Wealthy and intelligent art patron, art collector, and social leader, born at 20 University Place, in New York City, near where James was born, into a rich family, on whose Long Island farm she vacationed. She went to a girls' school in Paris, visited Italy with her father (1857), married John Lowell Gardner, a school chum's wealthy brother (1860), and settled in Boston. The couple had a son, who died in his late twenties. Mrs. Jack, as she was called, was a graceful, beautiful hostess, publicity seeking and daring, and she was abetted by her tolerant, adoring husband. By 1867 she was interested in the arts. She studied art history under Charles Eliot Norton* of Harvard, painted, traveled extensively (in Europe, the Middle East, and Japan), collected European and Oriental art objects, sponsored concerts in her home, supported celebrated musicians, and took the advice of such artists and art experts as John Singer Sargent,* James Abbott McNeill Whistler* (both of whom did portraits of her), and Bernard Berenson* to augment her private collection—largely Italian, Spanish, Flemish, English pre-Raphaelite, and American masterpieces. When her beloved husband suddenly died in December 1898, his will revealed that the two had been planning a Boston museum, which, starting in January 1899, became an Italianate palace called Fenway Court and opened with much fanfare on New Year's Day 1903. Mrs. Gardner continued to entertain. She traveled to Europe a final time in 1906 but purchased widely until 1921; she suffered a paralytic stroke and died in Boston. Isabella Stewart Gardner knew innumerable establishment figures of wit, charm, and importance, including Henry Adams* and his wife Marian Adams,* Paul Bourget* and his wife, Johannes Brahms, Francis Marion Crawford* (who almost accompanied the Gardners to Japan in 1883), Julia Ward Howe* and her husband, Nellie Melba, Ignacy Paderewski, William Wetmore Story* and his family, John L. Sullivan,

Edith Newbold Jones Wharton,* Anders Zorn, and James. Mrs. Jack probably first met James through the Nortons but surely knew him by 1879. Thereafter, they were often together socially in London and then in Paris. James visited her in Cambridge after his mother's death (1882) and read her his dramatized version of "Daisy Miller"; gossiped by letter to William Dean Howells* of her flirtation with Crawford; welcomed her and her husband in London (summer 1884) after their fabulous tour of the Far East; was entertained by them two summers later when they were again in London; accepted their invitation to spend three weeks (July 1892) as their guest in a Venetian palazzo rented from their friends Ariana Randolph Curtis* and her husband Daniel Sargent Curtis*; wrote Mrs. Jack to ask her to entertain Bourget and his wife during their 1893 American tour; sent her a beautiful letter of sympathy when her husband died; entertained her overnight at Lamb's House* (November 1899); saw an aging Mrs. Jack in London (early 1907); and met with her a final time (1911) during his stay in New England following the death of his brother William. James admired Isabella Stewart Gardner immensely, was perhaps envious of her wealth and consequent mobility, and judged her to be innocent and unduly sympathetic. He paid a kind of florid and usually welcome epistolary court to her, and she saved almost a hundred letters from him in her private desk, where they still are, at Fenway Court. Some of the lithe, flexible charm of Isabel Archer, heroine of *The Portrait of a Lady*, may be owing to lovely, generous, naive Mrs. Jack. The art-collecting zeal of Adela Gereth in James's *The Spoils of Poynton* and that of Adam Verver in *The Golden Bowl* resemble that of Mrs. Gardner, who in 1899 purchased a pair of portraits by Hans Holbein the younger,* one of which (that of *Lady Butts*) helped to inspire James's story "The Beldonald Holbein." Furthermore, James described the gorgeous pearls of his heroine Milly Theale in *The Wings of the Dove* exactly as Mrs. Jack wore hers. And both she and his heroine Comtesse Marie de Vionnet in *The Ambassadors* reminded James of the Cleopatra of William Shakespeare,* with her infinite variety.

Garfield, James Abram (1831–1881). Twentieth president of the United States. James's devotion to his native land during his long expatriation may be judged by his request in a letter to his mother (28 Nov [1880]) for a photograph of Garfield, whose face, in due time in a letter to his sister Alice (30 Jan 1881), James praised as "pleasant and manly."

Garland, Hamlin (1860–1940). Wisconsin-born farm lad, who also worked in Iowa and South Dakota, then made a literary pilgrimage to Boston where he met William Dean Howells,* who encouraged him to write about oppressive Midwestern farm life. In turn, Garland encouraged Stephen Crane* at the outset of his career. Garland's best stories are collected in *Main-Travelled Roads* (1891). Thereafter Garland espoused idealistic causes, such as the Single Tax, political reform, Populism, and a literary style he called veritism, a combination of local color realism, individualism, and democratic romanticism. After hardheaded works, such as *Crumbling Idols* (1894) and *Rose of Dutcher's Coolly* (1895), Garland turned soft, writing thin, pro-Indian fiction and long-winded autobiography. During his tour of the United States in 1904–1905, James dined as a guest of George Brinton McClellan Harvey,* president of Harper and Brothers, publishers, in New York (8 December 1904); Garland, along with Elizabeth Jordan,* Booth Tarkington,* and Mark Twain,* was among some thirty guests. In Chicago later that winter, James was Garland's guest at dinner, during which he met Chicago artists and writers, including Henry Blake Fuller. James invited Garland to stay overnight with him at Lamb House,* in Rye (June 1906); the two discussed expatriation in ways which the younger, lesser writer later remembered inaccurately. In "American Letter" (9 Apr 1898), James, while praising American writers for confining themselves to what is "most local," offers Garland as "a case of saturation so precious as to have almost the value of genius." But James seems to damn him for being "the soaked sponge of Wisconsin." James does not mention any specific titles by Garland.

Garland, Mary. In *Roderick Hudson,* Roderick Hudson's beloved until Christina Light appears. Rowland Mallet hopelessly loves Miss Garland later.

Garlick. In *The Awkward Age*, Agnesina's literature teacher.

Garnyer, Eustace. In "Master Eustace," the spoiled natural son of Mrs. Henry Garnyer and Cope. When the lad learns the identity of his father, he tries to kill himself.

Garnyer, Henry. In "Master Eustace," Eustice Garnyer's supposed father, whom the lad idolizes.

Garnyer, Mrs. Henry. In "Master Eustace," Eustace Garnyer's indulgent mother. She later marries Cope, who was Eustace's real father.

Gaskell, Elizabeth Cleghorn (née Stevenson) (1810–1865). Popular English novelist, born in what is now Cheyne Walk, Chelsea. Her father William Stevenson was a minister, a treasury worker in London, and a writer. Upon her mother's death in 1810, Elizabeth was reared by an aunt, was schooled at Stratford-on-Avon, and then lived with colorful relatives. In 1832 she married a Manchester Unitarian minister. Mrs. Gaskell published an anonymous piece on the town of Stratford-on-Avon in 1840 and her first novel (also anonymous), *Mary Barton*, eight years later. The novel was a phenomenal success, although some conservative reviewers objected to her harsh treatment in it of Manchester manufacturers. She soon met Thomas Carlyle,* Charles Dickens,* and William Makepeace Thackeray,* among other notable writers. Dickens encouraged her to publish in *Household Words*, starting in 1850 at its inception. She also published in the *Cornhill Magazine*. After several shorter works, she published her second novel, *Ruth* (1853), and an assemblage of country-town sketches, *Cranford* (1853). Then came the significant *North and South* (1855), combining humor, better structure, and deeper sociopolitical philosophy. In 1850 Mrs. Gaskell met Charlotte Brontë (see Brontë sisters), whose biography she published in 1857. When she visited Rome that same year, she met William Wetmore Story.* She was hurt by harassing criticism and correspondence concerning her book on Brontë, which was inaccurate but through no fault of her own. She developed many friendships in England (for example, with Lord Houghton*), America, and France. *Sylvia's Lovers* (1863) concerns the evils of impressment. *Cousin Phillis* was published in 1865; then followed the incomplete *Wives and Daughters: A Novel* (1866). George Eliot* and George Sand,* among others, praised Elizabeth Gaskell's work. James reviewed (*Nation*, 22 Feb 1866) her *Wives and Daughters*, prefacing his remarks with the statement that *Cranford* will "become a classic." He likes *Wives and Daughters* tremendously and predicts continued popularity for it. Mrs. Gaskell draws us by a tissue of light touches into a story with real scenes and real people. Though not intellectual, she has a genius for feeling and character. Her Brontë biography showed "want of judgment and of critical power." Some would call *Wives and Daughters* so long that it becomes dull, but the details of Molly Gibson's "homely *bourgeois* life" and Cynthia Kirkpatrick's delightful "sayings and doings and looks" are fun to follow, if impossible to summarize. James finds Mrs. Gaskell's male characters "less successful." But he ends by praising the "everyday style" of this novel. James's library contained one book by Gaskell.

Gautier, Théophile (1811–1872). Precocious and then versatile French man of letters. First he studied painting and older French literature; then he became a protégé of Victor-Marie Hugo* and the leader of a flamboyant, romantic, "arts for art's sake" clique and school. Finally he was a fertile feuilletonist, poet, art and literary critic, editor, fiction writer, and travel writer. He worshipped precise diction, technique, and form; he cared nothing for philosophical or humanitarian content. His daughter Judith, a poet and novelist, married Pierre Loti.* Gautier's many important works include volumes of poetry (for example, *Poésies* [1830], *Albertus* [1832], and *Émaux et camées* [1856 and later]); novels (*Mademoiselle de Maupin* [1835] and *Le Capitaine Fracasse* [1863]); travel and descriptive writing (*Voyage en Espagne* [1843], *Constantinople* [1854], *Voyage en Russie* [1866], and *Tableaux de siège: Paris 1870–1871* [1871]); and criticism (*Les Grotesques* [1844], *L'Histoire de l'art dramatique en France* [6 vols., 1858–1859], and *Histoire du Romantisme . . .* [1872, 1874]). James wrote to his father from Paris (11 Apr [1876]) that he heard Gustave Flaubert,* in his Paris apartment, both remark that Gautier was the greatest French poet after Hugo and then beautifully recite his "Les Portraits ovales." James reviewed several works by Gautier, one review becoming an essay; James also reviewed what he regarded as a poor book about Gautier. First, James reviewed (*Nation*, 25 Jan 1872)

Gautier's *Tableaux de siège*, calling its descriptions picturesque, light, and visual. He says that it is as hard to quote Gautier well as it would be to cut off a piece of a Titian* canvas "for a specimen of his color." He praises Gautier's ability to depict sad animals during the siege and notes his "sensuous serenity." He criticizes his subject's absence of thought and his "moral levity." Next, James published (*North American Review*, Apr 1873) a review of *Théâtre de Théophile Gautier: Mystères, comédies, et ballets* (1872). (The review was later reprinted as "Théophile Gautier" in *French Poets and Novelists*, 1878). James calls Gautier a typical French poet because of his limitations and gifts. He shows spontaneity and temper, works well within his range, and is clear where Robert Browning* is mixed. Gautier is pagan, this-worldly, and stylish; he has "visual discrimination" and is lightly Rabelaisian. He was so little "a man of thought" that we laugh at the pretentious preface to his *Mademoiselle de Maupin*, which novel is his "one disagreeable performance" and a work by which he is wrongly remembered. His poem "L'Art" uniquely shows his "intellectual belief." In it we read "Tout passe.—L'Art robuste / Seul a l'éternité." While sensuously conservative, Gautier is democratically observant. In *Émaux et camées*, in spite of their images swallowing up their ideas, "every poem is a masterpiece." But his best poetry is in his prose. His travel books give the look of countries, never discuss their institutions. Gautier is "the prince of *ciceroni*," as solid an observer as any German academic "bristling with critical premises." Each of Gautier's books has its tone and unity. He found nature entertaining and could even describe ugliness strikingly. In his *Tableaux de siège* he resembles a nightingale warbling after a storm. His best fiction is *Le Capitaine Fracasse*—"this delightful work," this "model of picturesque romances"—which is pictorial but not dramatic. It has humor, relish, jocosity. Reading it is "an affair of the senses." Its theme is "brotherly sympathy with the social position of the comedian." It is one of the finest "works of imagination produced in our day." Gautier observes people as a barber or a tailor does; concerned with surfaces, he describes the human body with French frankness. Some have found him too genial to be a good critic, but his annual Salon reports "form, probably, the best history . . . of modern French art." In *L'Histoire de l'art dramatique en France*, Gautier reviews "jokes extinct and plots defunct," offering in the process "good-natured" judgments in an easy tone. To conclude here, James notes Gautier's "consistent levity," his "circumscribed" professional progress, his absence of the tiniest "spiritual spark," and his enviable "robustness of vision." In one essay (*North American Review*, Oct 1874), James both criticizes Ernest Feydau's *Théophile Gautier, souvenirs intimes* (1874) and praises Gautier's *Histoire du Romantisme* (1874). After repeating his standard praise of Gautier's imagery and visual effects, James calls Feydau's attempt to establish the author as thinker and scholar a "cruel service." He decries unattractive Feydau's aspiration to play "a miniature Boswell" to his supposed friend Gautier; he praises Gautier's *Mademoiselle de Maupin* as a "monument to juvenile salubrity" and his essays on art as "exquisite and penetrating." Feydau stresses the laboriousness of Gautier's career and the absence of leisure in it. Yet his writing always has a "chiselled quality." Like

Honoré de Balzac* and George Sand,* Gautier was wrongly denied admission to the French Academy. James calls Gautier's *Histoire du Romantisme* "hardly more than a string of picturesque anecdotes and reminiscences of the author's early comrades, reinforced by . . . obituary notices of the veterans in the grand army," then closes by discussing the fact that in any "important intellectual movement" minor writers often must fail in order to help major writers succeed. James reviewed (*Nation*, 12 Nov 1874) *A Winter in Russia*, an 1874 translation of Gautier's *Voyage en Russie*, but begins by saying that dull books should never be translated and certain good ones cannot be, since, although their matter can be rendered, their manner cannot be. He praises the fine verbal fantasies in Gautier's book on Russia, calls it charming and unified but "not one of his best," since it is not so "full and compact" as those on Spain and Italy. Still, it is "a verbal symphony on the theme *frost*," full of the simple happiness of looking and enjoying. Finally, James reviewed (*Nation*, 15 Jul 1875) *Constantinople*, an 1875 translation of Gautier's 1854 "masterpiece" on the Turkish city. James pronounces the translation "inexcusable," since what we have is "an abbreviated and mutilated edition of the original," and he offers extensive proof. He ends by again praising Gautier's "vividness," "incisiveness," "gaiety," "vivacity of . . . phrase," and fine imagery. James's library contained nine books by Gautier.

Gaw, Abel. In *The Ivory Tower*, Rosanna Gaw's fatally sick father, the former business associate of Frank B. Betterman and the friend of Graham Fielder.

Gaw, Rosanna. In *The Ivory Tower*, Abel Gaw's enormous but charming daughter. She is Graham Fielder's friend.

Gay, Walter (1856–1937). Massachusetts-born expatriate American painter. A flower-painting specialist in Boston (1873–1876), he went to Paris to study art (1876), visited Spain, and soon began to paint figures in eighteenth-century garb (à la Jean-Louis-Ernest Meissonier*). By 1884, he had become more serious and began to depict harsh Breton peasant life; finally, he turned to vigorous, popular portrayals of interiors full of fancy rococo furniture but devoid of people. He exhibited in Paris, Boston, and Philadelphia, and he sold widely. He and his fellow Catholic wife Matilda, who, not only as the daughter of a distinguished New York lawyer but also as a York socialite, had long known Edith Newbold Jones Wharton,* maintained a hospitable residence in Paris and a chateau near Fontainebleau. Having superb taste, Gay gradually amassed a fine art collection. He, his wife, and Wharton performed commendable refugee-relief work during World War I. *Memoirs of Walter Gay* appeared in 1930. James knew both Gays and occasionally wrote about them to Wharton.

Geddes, David. In "The Bench of Desolation," Herbert Dodd's uncle.

Gedge, Isabel. In "The Birthplace," Morris Gedge's wife, who fears that his critical honesty will cause him to lose his Birthplace job.

Gedge, Morris. In "The Birthplace," the scholarly lecturer at The Birthplace who converts himself into a successful barker there.

Gelsomina. In *The Awkward Age*, Agnesina's old nurse.

Gemini, Count. In *The Portrait of a Lady*, Amy Gemini's brutal husband. He does not appear.

Gemini, Countess Amy Osmond. In *The Portrait of a Lady*, Gilbert Osmond's promiscuous sister. She tells his wife Isabel that Pansy Osmond is the daughter of Gilbert and Madame Merle.

Geoffrin, Marie-Thérèse Rodet (1699–1777). Curiously influential French hostess, who was born and always lived in Paris, was married in 1713 to a rich manufacturer and military officer, and was widowed in 1750. Beginning in 1748 she regularly offered a weekly dinner for artists and another for literary men. She affected the pose of an aging coquette and generously mothered numerous guests. She was politically liberal and theologically moral. In 1766 she visited King Stanislas of Poland, one of her many friends of long standing, in his Warsaw palace. James reviewed (*Galaxy*, Apr 1876) *Correspondence inédite du Roi Stanislas Auguste Poniatowski et de Mme. Geoffrin (1764–1777)* (1875), praising its editorial apparatus. He was intrigued by Madame Geoffrin's mysterious influence, inexplicable despite her ambition, tact, and good sense; her discriminating judgment of people; her "excellent counsel"; and her wise opinions. Her mediocre intellectual talents, James adds, should make us revise our notion of eighteenth-century " 'culture.' " He sketches her life, stressing her friendship, which started in 1753, with Poniatowski, who called her "maman" and whose varied career in Paris, St. Petersburg, and Warsaw James also summarizes. He describes their letters as affectionate at first but acrimonious on her part later, since she could be "violent" and "perverse." James concludes that Stanislas had too little force to remain a king for long.

"Georgina's Reasons." Short story (23,700 words), published in the New York *Sun* (20, 27 Jul, 3 Aug 1884); reprinted in *Stories Revived*, 1885. (Characters: Amanda, Captain Raymond Benyon, Benyon, Bessie, Mr. and Mrs. Draper, Mr. and Mrs. Gressie, Harriet, Henry Platt, Mrs. Portico, Cora Roy, Georgina Gressie Benyon Roy, William Roy, Roy, Kate Theory, Mildred Theory, Agnes Roy Theory, Percival Theory, Mr. and Mrs. Vanderdecken.) Swearing him to silence until she releases him from the formal vow, Georgina Gressie secretly weds American naval officer Raymond Benyon, then she soon goes with her friend Mrs. Portico to Genoa, where she gives birth to Benyon's child and pays an Italian to take the boy. Just before dying, Mrs. Portico writes to Benyon about the circumstances, but he fails in his attempts to trace the lad. In Naples later, Benyon falls in love with Kate Theory, whose sister-in-law Agnes informs him that Georgina has bigamously married William Roy, a relative of Agnes. Benyon confronts Georgina in New York: She callously admits all, defies him, and even introduces him to her other husband. Since Benyon will not break his solemn word, he can only wait. This sensational story is valuable mainly because it proves that James could write simply for money: He wrote to Thomas Bailey Aldrich* (13 Feb [1884]) that the New York *Sun* had lured him with a *"prix d'or . . . en mille."* James wrote to John Milton Hay* (24 Dec [1886]) that the plot for his "ugly narrative" came from his friend Frances Anne Kemble,* who had heard it from her brother-in-law Edward Sartoris, who had heard it from his daughter-in-law Nelly Grant Sartoris, the gossipy daughter of Ulysses Simpson Grant.* A Notebook entry (26 Mar 1884) confirms James's real-life source and outlines the plot of the resulting fiction, in which, however, the hero is not an army officer in the Far West, as Mrs. Kemble had related, but a naval officer, who can hence get to Italy. The names Mildred Theory, Kate Theory, and Roy are close to Mary (Minny) Temple,* Milly Theale, and Kate Croy; also, Minny, Mildred, and Milly all share(d) similar fatal sicknesses.

Geraldine, Miss. In "The Liar," the tipsy model who visits the studio of Oliver Lyon while he is painting Colonel Clement Capadose's portrait. The colonel says that her real name is Harriet Pearson. She is also known as Miss Grenadine.

Gereth, Adela. In *The Spoils of Poynton*, the widowed collector of the spoils and Owen Gereth's mother. She urges Fleda Vetch to marry her son. In her memoirs, Lady Ottoline Violet Anne Morrell* says that her mother-in-law Mrs. Frederic Morrell was James's model for Mrs. Gereth, whose art-collecting zeal may owe something to that of James's friend Isabella Stewart Gardner.*

Gereth, Colonel. In *The Spoils of Poynton*, Adela Gereth's brother-in-law.

Gereth, Owen. In *The Spoils of Poynton*, the stolid but likable owner of Poynton and its spoils. He is engaged to Mona Brigstock but comes to regard Fleda Vetch more highly. Fleda urges him to be honorable in his relationship with Mona.

Gérôme, Jean Léon (1824–1904). French painter, who studied in Paris beginning in 1841 with Paul Delaroche,* with whom he later went to Italy (1844–1845). Gérôme won Salon prizes (1847, 1848) and then traveled—for example, to Turkey in 1854 and to Egypt in 1857. His exhibition in the 1857 Salon included popular depictions of Eastern scenes. He is now best known for *The Cock Fight, Turkish Prisoner, Turkish Butcher, Prayer, The Slave Market,* and

The Harem out Driving. He also painted anecdotal historical scenes (including *Louis XIV and Molière* and *Death of Marshal Ney*. He was also a successful sculptor and worker in ivory, metals, and gems. In his 1868 review of *Contemporary French Painters* by Philip Gilbert Hamerton,* James compares Gérôme's "heartlessness" in art to that of Gustave Flaubert* in literature. In "Art" (Feb 1872), James describes Gérôme's *Cock Fight* in detail, then concludes that it is a combination of a "horrid little game," "brassy nudity," and "sensible carnality" which gives no pleasure to the viewer, partly because of "the artist's sentimental sterility." In "Parisian Sketches" (1876), James calls the works of Jean-Louis-Ernest Meissonier* "dry and cold" but positively blooming and teeming when compared with some by Gérôme. In "Parisian Topics" (1 Apr 1876), James deplores the purchase by Alexander Turney Stewart* of Gérôme's *Chariot Race*, which he calls powerfully violent and of high technical finish, but crude in coloration. In "Art in Paris" (1876) James, with a sigh, notes that at a certain exhibition Gérôme "is, as usual, conspicuous for his cleverness." In his 1880 review of the letters of Ferdinand Victor Eugène Delacroix,* James notes that "Gérôme gives us most skilfully the surface of Eastern life," whereas "Delacroix gives us its substance."

"The Ghostly Rental." Short story (12,600 words), published in *Scribner's Monthly* (Sep 1876). (Characters: Belinda, Miss Deborah, Captain Diamond, Miss Diamond.) One day the narrator, a student at Harvard Divinity School, sees Captain Diamond bow in front of a strange house, enter, and then come out again—with money. A local gossip named Miss Deborah reluctantly tells the narrator that Diamond supposedly cursed his daughter to death because some man said he was her husband. This action now haunts Diamond, with whom the narrator becomes friendly. One day he sees Diamond emerge from the old house again with his quarterly payment. Diamond turns sick, and the narrator goes to collect—and notes that the ghost is a real woman, Diamond's daughter. It seems that when cursed she went away, never married, and posed as her own ghost not only to get back at her father but also because she cannot hope for forgiveness. Suddenly she sees the ghost of her father, and she drops her light. The narrator rushes to Diamond and learns that he is dead. The house burns. James wrote to his father (11 Apr [1876]) that the "pretensions" of this story and of "Crawford's Consistency" "are small." "The Ghostly Rental" is James's weakest ghost story, the only value of it may lie in what the rather weak-minded narrator learns: Abstract studies must be tempered by observation of reality.

Giacosa, Cavaliere Giuseppe (Giuseppino). In *Roderick Hudson*, Christina Light's natural father and now the rather beaten-down attendant in Italy of her mother Mrs. Light.

Gibbon, Edward (1737–1794). English historian. He was educated at Magdalen College, Oxford; he studied in Lausanne, Switzerland, where he reconverted from Roman Catholicism to Protestantism; and he returned to England in 1758. While vacationing in Italy in 1764, he decided to write *The Decline and Fall of the Roman Empire*, which he began in England but finished (because of the religious controversy occasioned by the first three volumes) in Lausanne (6 vols., 1776–1788). His *Memoirs* were issued posthumously (1796, enlarged and reprinted later); when a new and better edition appeared in 1896, James in "London" (6 Feb 1897) calls the autobiographical work "a flaming novelty" since it has been "at last disengaged from the weight of a hundred years of editorial ineptitude"; in "London" (27 Mar 1897), James adds that this new edition is "delicious and incomparable." James's library contained two books by Gibbon.

Gibson, John (1790–1866). British sculptor, who went to Rome and was befriended by Antonio Canova. Gibson succeeded quickly and attracted rich patrons. He executed a Queen Victoria group for Parliament and a Sir Robert Peel statue for Westminster Abbey, but his best work is in basso-rilievo. In 1836 he was elected to the Royal Academy, to which he left all of his property and work. In an untitled note (*Nation*, 15 Mar 1877), James praises the executors of the estate of Gibson, "who . . . may claim the not very exalted honor of being the first of English sculptors," for finally following the terms of his will and making possible a permanent exhibit in London of "the various marbles and models" he gave to the Academy. James mentions Gibson's notoriety as a tinter of marble and reviews the present collection, which he finds "not . . . interesting but . . . respectable," betraying too much Greek classical and too little Italian Renaissance influence.

Gide, André (1869–1951). Influential, controversial, versatile French man of letters. He wrote novels (*L'Immoraliste* [1902], *La Symphonie pastorale* [1919], *Les Faux-monnayeurs* [1926]); short stories; plays; poetry (*Les Nourritures terrestres* [1897]); criticism; travel books, dealing with the Congo and the Soviet Union; an autobiography (1920); journals; letters; and translations of works by Joseph Conrad* and Walt Whitman,* among others. Early in his life and late in James's, the two men met on New Year's Eve 1912, at a dinner given by Sir Edmund Wilson Gosse.*

Gifford, Colonel. In "Professor Fargo," Miss Gifford's father and Professor Fargo's mathematician partner.

Gifford, Miss. In "Professor Fargo," Colonel Gifford's deaf-mute daughter, who leaves her father to go with Professor Fargo.

Gilbert. In "The Story of a Masterpiece," John Lennox's artist friend.

Gilder, Richard Watson (1844–1909). New Jersey-born editor and minor poet. He was assistant editor of *Scribner's Monthly* (1870–1881), then, when it became the *Century Magazine*, editor (1881–1909). Gilder published sixteen books of poetry (including *The New Day* [1875]) and biographies of Abraham Lincoln (1909) and Grover Cleveland (1910). His letters were issued posthumously (1916). Since James published several times in *Scribner's Monthly* and even more often in its successor, the *Century*, he had much professional correspondence with Gilder. His wife Helena De Kay Gilder was a lifelong friend, since James may have met her (along with her sister Katherine De Kay Bronson*) as early as the old Newport, Rhode Island days. James was a guest in 1883 at the Gilders' summer home at Marion, Massachusetts. (James soon reworked Marion into the little resort town of Marmion in *The Bostonians*.) James did not especially respect Gilder, to whom he rightly complained by letter (1 Feb [1884]) about his dividing "Lady Barbarina" as he did: "I am sorry you are to publish it as *three* [parts]; the interest is not calculated for that." James wrote to Charles Eliot Norton* (15 Nov 1893) to protest that his edition of the letters of James Russell Lowell* slighted Lowell's relations with great British minds, adding that "I care comparatively so little for the play of his mind in contact, say, with R. W. Gilder." When Mrs. Gilder was in London in 1900, James called on her and encountered Mark Twain* there. Three decades after Gilder serialized *The Bostonians* in 1885–1886, James still smarted at its lack of popularity, writing to Sir Edmund Wilson Gosse* (25 Aug 1915) that "the thing was no success whatever on publication in the Century . . . , and the late R. W. Gilder, of that periodical, wrote me at the time that they had never published anything that appeared so little to interest their readers." Gilder declined to publish *Maggie: A Girl of the Streets* by Stephen Crane,* when he submitted it to the *Century*.

Gilman, Rev. Mr. In *The Europeans*, the minister of the congregation that included the Wentworths.

Gimingham. In "Louisa Pallant," the man who finally marries Linda Pallant.

Giovanelli, Cavaliere Giacomo. In "Daisy Miller," Daisy Miller's suave little Roman escort, who is willing to accompany the girl anywhere, even to the miasmal Colosseum at night. After her death, he tells Frederick Winterbourne that she was amiable and innocent. In *Daisy Miller: A Comedy in Three Acts*, Eugenio tries unsuccessfully to blackmail Madame de Katkoff to flirt with Winterbourne so that Giovanelli will have more freedom to go after Daisy, who ultimately chooses Winterbourne instead.

Girardin, Émile de (1806–1881). French publicist, born in Paris, the natural son of a general. After 1830 he became a violent journalist, founded *La Presse* and *La Liberté*, bought *Le Petit Journal*, killed a man in a duel, and was a member of the Chamber of Deputies. He published books on journalism, politics, and government censorship, many of which grew out of his newspaper columns. James reviewed (New York *Tribune*, 4 Mar 1876) *Grandeur ou déclin de la France* (1876) by Girardin, calling the author good-tempered and freedom-loving, and adding that France had need of more such men. Girardin was opposed to the current arms buildup, and instead hoped to see his country's "commercial and industrial" advancement. James closes by derisively quoting Bonapartists to whom Girardin objects in his book.

Girolamo, Padre. In "Adina," Angelo Beati's priest uncle at Lariccia.

Gissing, George (1857–1903). Yorkshire-born novelist, short-story writer, travel writer, and literary critic, who began as a talented classical student in Manchester but was expelled for alleged petty theft. He then lived in poverty in the United States (1876–1877), returned to England, married but soon separated (his wife later died), traveled intermittently to Italy and Greece (1888–1890), married again but soon resumed solitary travel for his health (1897–1898), then entered into a common-law marriage in France, where he lived for a time. Turning from idealist to realist in 1888, Gissing thereafter concerned himself with working-class life, the outcast thinker in opposition to pretentious society, the effects of a diminution of religious faith on conduct, and Victorian feminism. Of his twenty-two novels (the first was published in 1880), the most important are *New Grub Street* (1891), *Born in Exile* (1892), *In the Year of Jubilee* (1894), and *The Whirlpool* (1897). His best travel work is *By the Ionian Sea: Notes of a Ramble in Southern Italy* (1901). His curious book *The Private Papers of Henry Ryecroft* (1903) is an imaginary but partly autobiographical protagonist's journal of criticism and meditation. James tried to like Gissing and his work, but he found his lifestyle, especially with women, abhorrent and his writing unfocused and sloppy. In "London" (31 Jul 1897; reprinted in *Notes on Novelists*, 1914), James mentions his "enjoyment" occasioned by a reading of *New Grub Street*, even though "[t]he whole business of distribution and composition . . . [in it seems] cast to the winds." *The Whirlpool* he calls a work of "saturation" valuably concerning the lower middle class, "a region vast and unexplored," since novelists (apart from Charles Dickens*) present few characters in between thieves and peers. *The Whirlpool* suffers from poor form ("composition, . . . foreshortening, . . . the proportion and relation of parts"), weak handling of time, and too much dialogue. James prefers *In the Year of Jubilee*. He closes by praising Gissing for "frankness and straightness of . . . feeling" and his "strongest deepest sense of common humanity, of the general struggle and the general grey grim comedy." In June 1901, Herbert George Wells* presented Gissing to James at Lamb House,* where the two visitors were overnight guests. Wells tended Gissing when he was dying in the French Pyrenees and immediately thereafter began to help Gissing's two sons, writing to Sir Edmund Wilson Gosse* about them and asking him to tell James. Late in his life, James gossiped with his Rye neighbor Sir Sydney Philip Waterlow* about Gissing. James regarded him as physically unprepossessing, his style as ugly but graphically descriptive of the lower-middle classes, and *Grub Street* as his best work. James's library contained three books by Gissing.

Giuseppino. In "At Isella," the Signora's brother. Her lover drew Giuseppino's death sketch.

"The Given Case." Short story (9,400 words), published in *Collier's Weekly* (31 Dec 1898); reprinted in *The Soft Side*, 1900. (Characters: Colonel and Kate Despard, John Grove-Stewart, Mrs. Gorton, Margaret Hamer, Philip Mackern, Lady Orville, Barton Reeve, Amy Warden.) Barton Reeve loves the absent cad Colonel Despard's wife Kate, and he appeals to her friend Margaret Hamer to tell her so. Margaret agrees to try. At a country estate Philip Mackern, who loves Margaret and feels led on, asks Kate to praise him to her and to urge her to break her engagement to long-absent John Grove-Stewart. Margaret depresses Barton by telling him of Kate's loyalty to her husband. Barton tells Margaret that she would be generous if she were in Kate's position. Kate dismisses Barton and tells Philip that Margaret's one chance is to marry Grove-Stewart, now returning from India. Kate is oddly annoyed when her wandering husband returns to her; yet, deciding to abandon Barton, she righteously criticizes Margaret for not being loyal to her fiancé. Barton goes back to Kate. She says that her husband is home and that she will not see Barton again, but she also says that she loves him. Philip appeals again to Margaret, who feels responsible for leading him on and therefore will not act like Kate: She accepts Philip even though she knows that Grove-Stewart will never understand. In his *Notebooks* (10 Feb 1899), James explains that the idea for this story came from a conversation he had with George Meredith.* However, an earlier entry (13 May 1894) discusses its plot situation in general terms. The symmetrical plot of "The Given Case," which may be diagrammed as short-circuited love lines, is hard to follow and is not worth the effort to do so. This story was the first by James that his agent James Brand Pinker* sold for him.

Gladstone, William Ewart (1809–1898). Liberal British statesman, born in Liverpool and educated at Oxford University. He served often as prime minister (1868–1874, 1880–1885, 1886, 1892–1894) and also wrote several books on politics and literature. James proudly wrote to his brother William (29 Mar 1877) that he had dined the day before with Gladstone, Lord Houghton,* Alfred, Lord Tennyson,* "and half a dozen other men of " 'high culture.' " This dinner helped qualify James to write "The Early Meeting of Parliament," which appeared in 1878 and discusses Gladstone. James rhetorically asked his brother

William (21 Apr [1884]), "Did I tell you . . . that I spent at Easter nearly three days at the Durdans (Rosebery's) with Gladstone . . . ?" He adds, "Gladstone's mind doesn't interest me much . . ." (Archibald Philip Primrose, Earl of Rosebery* became prime minister in the 1890s.) James wrote to Edwin Lawrence Godkin* (3 Mar 1885) to predict inaccurately that Gladstone's "bewilder[ment]" in the face of Russian and Soudan complications means the "pitiful end of a great career." A year later, to Grace Norton* (9 May [1885]), he called Gladstone "an incurable shirker and dodger"; worse, again to Grace Norton (9 Dec [1885]), he called Gladstone "a dreary incubus." In 1888 James spent a few days around Easter at Rosebery's country home, with the Gladstones as fellow guests. In October 1886, James again was Rosebery's guest, this time enjoying the conversation of Sir Edward Walter Hamilton,* formerly Gladstone's private secretary. James and Hamilton became good friends. James wrote to Henry Adams* (28 Feb [1883]) that Gladstone's "favourite reading" a while back had been *Democracy* (Adams's anonymously published 1880 novel).

Glanvil, Mr. and Mrs. Maurice. In "The Wheel of Time," Lady Greyswood's third son and his Russian wife. In his youth, he fails to like ugly Fanny Knocker. Twenty years later Fanny's son fails to like Maurice's plain little daughter Vera, whose mother died in giving birth to her.

Glanvila Vera. In "The Wheel of Time," Maurice's plain little daughter, who fails to attract Fanny Knocker's handsome son Arthur Tregent.

"Glasses." Short story (17,300 words), published in the *Atlantic Monthly* (Feb 1896); reprinted in *Embarrassments*, 1896. (Characters: Betty, Lady and Lord Considine, Geoffrey Dawling, the Misses Dawling, Floyd-Taylor, Fanny Floyd-Taylor, Lord Iffield, Mrs. Meldrum, Flora Louise Saunt, Bertie Hammond Synge, Mr. and Mrs. Hammond Synge.) At Folkestone the painter narrator meets bespectacled old Mrs. Meldrum, who presents Flora Saunt. The girl needs glasses, but she refuses to wear them because they would disfigure her radiantly beautiful face. Geoffrey Dawling falls in love with the narrator's portrait of Flora, then with Flora herself; but she prefers Lord Iffield, who, however, disengages himself from her because of her defective eyes—soon encased in glasses. The vain girl next fails to capture a rich Italian. Returning from America, the narrator sees her, still radiant, at the London opera. She smiles at him—but is blind. Her husband Dawling now enters. In a Notebook entry (26 Jun 1895), James works out several details of the plot of "Glasses," which he says he could not entitle "The Spectacles" (perhaps because Edgar Allan Poe had used the title in 1844?). The idea for "Glasses" came to James when he saw a pretty girl wearing glasses on a London bus. He evidently promised Horace Elisha Scudder,* editor of the *Atlantic*, to hold this story to 10,000 words or so, but it ultimately ran to 17,300 words. In a letter to Scudder (4 Oct 1885), he explains its length as owing to his "great and invincible . . . instinct of completeness and of seeing things in all their relations," and he invites Scudder to return the story if he must—"in spite of its high merit!" It is difficult to decide whether James is more critical of such idiotic marriage-market victims as Flora, Dawling, and

Iffield, or more sympathetic with silly Flora, whose only recommendation is spectacular surface beauty. James offers a beautiful figure of speech concerning the death of the narrator's mother: "that high tide had ebbed."

Gloriani and Mme. Gloriani. In *Roderick Hudson*, the brilliant Roman sculptor and his wife. He admires Roderick Hudson's work but wonders about his stability. In *The Ambassadors*, in Gloriani's Paris garden, Chadwick Newsome introduces Lambert Strether to Marie de Vionnet. In "The Velvet Glove," in Gloriani's Paris salon, John Berridge meets Amy Evans. Mme. Gloriani is mentioned only in *Roderick Hudson* and *The Ambassadors*. William Wetmore Story* has been nominated as a possible model for Gloriani; but the choice seems unlikely since Gloriani is an able sculptor and a thrilling conversationalist whereas, in James's view, Story was neither.

Gobain, Prosper. In "A Bundle of Letters," the recipient of a letter from Léon Verdier.

Gobineau, Joseph Arthur, Comte de (1816–1882). French diplomat and writer, born near Paris, the son of a military officer. Gobineau worked briefly for Alexis de Tocqueville in 1848. Diplomatic assignments took Gobineau to Switzerland, Germany, and then Persia, which he studied lovingly (1854–1858). Later he went to Canada, Greece, Brazil, and Sweden, from which last post he retired unwillingly to Rome. In addition to fiction, drama, and poetry, he wrote on a great variety of topics, including history, politics, philosophy, and ethnology. James reviewed (*Nation*, 7 Dec 1876) Gobineau's *Nouvelles Asiatiques* (1876), a collection of six tales, pronouncing them "fascinating" because of their substance, rather than the usual "porcelain"-hard French form. James avers that Gobineau, whom he calls "a rich and serious mind" and a "philosophic observer," has produced the best Oriental fiction since *The Arabian Nights* and James Justinian Morier's *Hajji Baba*. Gobineau's stories combine to reveal Asian immorality and prevarication, but also bravery, romantic temper, goodness, honesty, patriotism, and other virtues. James says that Gobineau "has tried to reproduce . . . the local color of the Oriental mind and soul"; then he defines the personalities of Gobineau's various characters (mostly Oriental, some European, but never French), and praises his skillful use of the Oriental point of view. Of the tales, James especially likes "The Story of Gamber-Ali" and "The War of the Turcomans," both of which he calls "genuine masterpieces" and both of which he discusses in detail.

Godkin, Edwin Lawrence (1831–1902). American editor and author, born in Ireland of British forebears. His father was a dissenting minister and journalist. Godkin was educated in Armagh, Leeds, Belfast, and London. Interested in law, journalism, politics, and history, he joined a London publishing house, wrote a book on Hungary, became a reporter in the Crimea, lectured on military topics, moved to New York as a lawyer, traveled in and wrote about the South, and married in Connecticut in 1859. In 1865 he founded and became the first editor of the *Nation*, a fine weekly devoted to post–Civil War culture and politics. In 1881 Godkin started a long association with the New York *Evening Post*; two years later he became its editor (until 1900). He was influential, courageous, democratic, and patriotic. His wife died in 1875, two years after their daughter did; Godkin married again in 1884. His second wife was the former Katherine Sands (whom James came to know well and whose sister-in-law was his close friend Mary Morton Sands*). In 1901 Godkin paid a final visit to England, where he died and was buried in Northamptonshire. His friends included Viscount James Bryce,* James Russell Lowell,* Charles Eliot Norton,* William James, and Henry James, who published more than two hundred book reviews, art and theater notices, and travel essays in the *Nation*. In a letter to Grace Norton* (26 Sep [1870]), James praised Godkin's editorial treatment of the Franco-Prussian War. A decade later, he conveyed to his father (15 Feb [1880]) his delight in Godkin's laudatory letter concerning James's book on Nathaniel Hawthorne.* Still later James wrote to Lady Rosebery, wife of Archibald Philip Primrose, Earl of Rosebery* (16 Jun [1883]), to describe Godkin as "our first . . . journalist . . . " and to ask her to aid Godkin's son Lawrence socially. But in 1885 both James and his brother William were outraged by an unfriendly review in the *Nation* of their father's *Literary Remains* (1884), and it took Godkin's apologetic disclaimer to smooth matters over. James entertained Godkin at De Vere Gardens,* London, for some weeks in the summer of 1889. Furthermore, he generously loaned Godkin and his wife his De Vere Gardens residence during Queen Victoria's Jubilee, in August 1897. In "American Letter" (25 Jun 1898), James reviewed Godkin's *Unforeseen Tendencies of Democracy* (1898), praising comments therein on the American nominating system in party politics, various political reforms, "the figure of the [political] boss," and the decline of legislative power, and concluding that the book is "a work of art." At terrible inconvenience, James helped bury the remains of Godkin's second wife in remote Northamptonshire, in 1907, beside her husband. In *Notes of a Son and Brother*, James reminisces about his relationship with Godkin, calling it "one of the longest and happiest friendships of my life." The semicentennial number of the *Nation* (8 July 1915) contains several laudatory essays, including one by James, "The Founding of the 'Nation,' " in which he repeats his praise of Godkin, calling their friendship a "cherish[ed] . . . relation, one of the best of my life." James's library contained three books by Godkin.

Goethe, Johann Wolfgang von (1749–1832). Exemplary German man of letters, whose titanic and varied works include his dramas *Götz von Berlichingen* (1773) and *Egmont* (1788), his novels *The Sorrows of Young Werther* (1774, 1787) and *Wilhelm Meister's Apprenticeship and Travels* (1796), his two-part dramatic poem *Faust* (1808, 1832), the four autobiographical volumes of *Aus meinem Leben: Dichtung und Wahrheit* (1811–1833), other dramatic and fictional work, and poetry (including "Der Erlkönig" [1782]). James reviewed (*North American Review*, Jul 1865) the 1865 translation by Thomas Carlyle* of Goethe's *Wilhelm Meisters Lehrjahre* (1796), calling it an edifying, plotless, humorless, just novel which dawns on the reader phenomenally. It features a hero who seeks happiness through self-harmony. Its three female characters represent coquetry, sentiment, and practicality. As readers we infer from Wilhelm's experiences and learn about "moral economy." In a review (*Nation*, 30 Oct 1873) of a French translation of *Faust*, with an introduction by Alexandre Dumas *fils*,* James criticizes Dumas's prudish ignorance of Goethe's greatness; praises "the swelling, straining volume" of *Faust*, which appeals to one's soul and one's delight in reverie; and extols his "poetic faculty," which enabled Goethe to draw "mysterious music" from facts. In "The Acting in Mr. Irving's *Faust*" (*Century Magazine*, Dec 1887), James calls *Faust* "one of the greatest productions of the human mind." Elsewhere he sees Goethe as an ideal which only George Sand* approaches. It is possible that Goethe's powerful "Der Erlkönig" influenced "The Turn of the Screw." James's library contained three works by Goethe.

The Golden Bowl. Novel (192,200 words), published in New York by Scribner, 1904, and in London by Methuen, 1905; revised and reprinted in *The Novels and Tales of Henry James*, Volumes XXIII, XXIV, 1909. (Characters: Prince Amerigo, Principino, Fanny and Colonel Robert Assingham, Mrs. Betterman, Blint, Miss Bogle, Bradshaw, Dr. Brady, Sir John Brinder, Calderoni, Lord and Lady Castledean, Crichton, Guterman-Seuss, Dotty and Kitty Lutch, Miss Maddock, Father Mitchell, Mrs. Noble, Don Ottavio, Mr. and Mrs. Rance, Charlotte Stant, Adam Verver, Maggie Verver.) Prince Amerigo is engaged to Maggie Verver (a Roman Catholic) in London. When he visits their friend Fanny Assingham, he learns that his former mistress, Charlotte Stant, will attend the wedding. Charlotte and the prince decide not to buy a gilt bowl as a present for Maggie because it is probably cracked. A couple of years pass. Maggie has a baby boy (called the Principino), laments that her rich but widowed Catholic father, Adam Verver, a collector of art objects, is lonely, and persuades him to invite Charlotte to his British estate, called Fawns. She comes, drives off his harpy-like guests, and soon agrees to marry him. Though happy to give his daughter a sense that he is no longer lonely, Adam soon seems to prefer Maggie's company, which results in his wife Charlotte's being thrown into her former lover's company again. This turn of events terrifies Mrs. Assingham, who frequently discusses the ramifications of the situation with her patient husband Colonel Bob. One rainy London day, the prince and his Charlotte confide in each other that their spouses prefer each other to them, and they embrace tenderly and closely. Later the two attend a glittering party at an estate called Matcham. Feeling more and more confident, they stay on and later visit Gloucester together, even rejecting distressed Fanny's urgent request to return to London on the train with her. Maggie begins to feel neglected, gives a party, suggests that the prince take her seemingly docile father away for a trip. She is surprised when the prince says that Charlotte should make such a proposal. When Adam visits her sick Principino, Maggie asks him to go somewhere with her husband; Adam, however, says he would prefer that both couples spend time together at Fawns. Tormented Maggie feels relieved when Fanny—lying—denies any reason to be suspicious. But one day Maggie happens into the curiosity shop where the golden bowl is, buys it for her father, and is aghast when the remorseful shopkeeper comes to her to explain that it is flawed, adding details leading Maggie to conclude that the prince and Charlotte went shopping together just before his wedding. Maggie tells all of this to Fanny, who denies Maggie's interpretation, throws the bowl to the floor, and breaks it into three pieces. The prince enters, hears Maggie's commentary, and wonders what Adam may know. Next, Maggie at Fawns feels a touch of pity for her husband, who—she tells Fanny—has been lying to avoid discussing matters with Charlotte. When this domineering woman demands to know whether Maggie is silently accusing her of anything, Maggie serenely lies by saying no and senses that she is now closer to the prince, who has also lied to Maggie's rival. Soon Adam tenderly informs his daughter that he and Charlotte will move to American City, where he has started a museum, if doing so will improve the situation. Father and daughter wordlessly validate the supremacy of their mutual regard over all other affections. Later, at the close of a huge party at Fawns, Charlotte pursues Maggie into the garden and says that she is taking Adam away because Maggie has failed in her opposition to their marriage. Self-sacrificial Maggie seems to admit to such a failed effort. Passively staying in London, the prince approaches Maggie for an embrace but is told to wait. Adam and Charlotte enter for farewell tea. Charlotte appears regal. Adam knows the situation and voices a gentle goodbye. Prince Amerigo returns, seeing only his wife. James's earliest Notebook entry (28 Nov 1892) relating directly to this novel, originally thought of as a short story, concerns an unstable quartet: a widowed father, a sole daughter, her European fiancé, and the father's new young bride, whom his daughter's husband loves. A later Notebook entry (14 Feb 1895) indicates that James had planned out his quartet's actions into a short international novel. He cancelled the idea of an observer, instead making Prince Amerigo the central consciousness for the first volume and Maggie the contrapuntal consciousness for the second, of what evolved into a long novel. James might have called it *The Marriages* (*Notebooks*, 21 Dec 1895) except that he had already used that title for an 1891 short story. The present title most likely comes from Ecclesiastes 12:6: "Or ever the silver cord be loosed, or the golden bowl be broken . . . '' (But William Blake wrote in "The Book of Thel": "Can wisdom be kept in a silver rod, / Or love in a golden bowl.'') James wrote to his agent James Brand Pinker* (20 May 1904) about his ongoing novel: "I began it, some thirteen months ago. . . . I can work only in my own way . . . and am producing the best book . . . that I have ever done.'' It was published while James was touring the United States; he wrote to Sir Edmund Wilson Gosse* from Florida (16 Feb 1905) that it "has 'done' much less ill here than anything I have ever produced.'' (The book went into a fourth printing during James's tour.) When his brother William wrote to express his dissatisfaction with it, James boldly struck back (23 Nov 1905): "I mean . . . to produce some uncanny . . . thing, in fiction, that will gratify you . . . but let me say . . . that I shall be greatly humiliated if you *do* like it." But he wrote to Mary Augusta Ward* (25 Sep 1906) that he would never read *The Golden Bowl* if another novelist had written it because "it's too long and the subject is pumped *too* dry." Yet when James wrote to Fanny Prothero, the wife of Sir George Walter Prothero* (14 Sep 1913), to send her two lists (one easier and one more difficult) of five of his best novels, *The Golden Bowl* was the only title on both lists. Edith Newbold Jones Wharton* relates an amusing incident in her autobiography *A Backward Glance*: When she asked James why he had suspended his four main *Golden Bowl* characters in a vacuum, he replied, "My dear, I didn't know I had." Of the three major phase novels, some critics prefer *The Ambassadors* for form and *The Wings of the Dove* for poignancy, but most praise *The Golden Bowl* for stylistic richness and magisterial artistry. It is radiant and harmonious, with a captivatingly ambivalent titular symbol, six wonderfully developed and interrelated central characters, rhetorically challenging dialogue, rich imagery, and an endlessly intriguing theme still echoing beyond the final chapter. What is this novel about? Love and loss. Love surviving passion. International relations. Selfishness and selflessness. Great wealth and its effects. Revenge forsworn. It seems unlikely that, if he had been younger when *The Golden Bowl* was published, James could have taken the Anglo-American novel beyond any more stylistic frontiers. Literary sources include *Middlemarch* (1872) by George Eliot,* and *Cosmopolis* (1893) and *A Tragic Idyl* (1896) by Paul Bourget.* Real-life sources include the respective family situations of James's friend Francis Boott,* his daughter Elizabeth Boott* Duveneck, and her husband Frank Duveneck*; James's friend William Wetmore Story,* his daughter Edith, and her husband the Marchese Simone de Peruzzi de Medici; and Dr. Robert William Hooper and his daughter Marian Adams,* the wife of Henry Adams.*

Goldie, Augusta (Gussy). In "The Solution," Blanche Goldie's youngest daughter.

Goldie, Blanche. In "The Solution," deceased Lord Bolitho's daughter, now a widow in Rome with three daughters.

Goldie, Mr. and Mrs. In "The Aspern Papers," supposedly high-society former friends of the Bordereaus.

Goldie, Rosina (Rosy). In "The Solution," Blanche Goldie's oldest daughter.

Goldie, Veronica. In "The Solution," Blanche Goldie's second of three daughters. She almost snares Henry Wilmerding.

Goldsmith, Oliver (1730–1774). Irish-born poet, playwright, and novelist, who graduated from Trinity College, Dublin (1749), studied medicine at Edinburgh and Leyden, wandered about Europe (1755–1756), and then worked in London as a physician and hack writer. He began to publish in 1758. Among his best-known works are *The Citizen of the World* (1762), *The Vicar of Wakefield* (1766, novel), *The Good-Natured Man* (1768, comedy), *A History of England* (1771), *She Stoops to Conquer* (1773, comedy), *The History of Greece* (1774), and the poems "The Traveler" (1764) and "The Deserted Village" (1770). Goldsmith met Samuel Johnson in 1761, became an original member of his club, and was both ridiculed and liked by fellow members. In a review (*Nation*, 13 Jun 1878) of *Olivia*, a dramatic adaptation of incidents from *The Vicar of Wakefield*, James calls Goldsmith's novel a "delicate and humorous masterpiece, whose charm is almost wholly in the exquisite narrative style." Years later, James wrote an introduction to a new edition of *The Vicar of Wakefield*, published in New York by Century, 1900. In it he says that the plot of the novel "fails . . . to account for its great position and its remarkable career." The book has "incomparable amenity" and "little else." Its "happiest strokes" come mostly in the first quarter. The "infantine" remainder has mere "lovability." Olivia and Sophia are undifferentiated characters; the seducer, undramatic; Burchell, "nebulous"; and the overall tragedy, weak. But the novel's "exquisite" touches are immune to criticism, like faint spinet music or dead rose leaves. The vicar provides "the tone" and echoes Goldsmith's own frank sweetness and easy speech; and the Irish author is avenged by his "classic" on those Britishers who laughed at him.

Goncourt, Edmond de (1822–1896) **and Jules de Goncourt** (1830–1870). Literary brothers, the older born in Nancy and the younger in Paris. In collaboration, they wrote novels, historical studies (of the eighteenth century), art criticism (concerning eighteenth-century French and Japanese art), and morbidly sensitive journals. Their novels are *Soeur Philomène* (1861), *Renée Mauperin* (1864), *Germinie Lacerteux* (1865), *Manette Salomon* (1865), and *Madame Gervaisais* (1869). Edmond wrote *La Fille Elisa* (1877) alone. Edmond left most of his fortune to establish a Goncourt Academy to award prizes for meritorious prose books. James, who discusses all of the works just named, met Edmond de Goncourt at the Paris apartment of Gustave Flaubert* in December 1875 and described him in a letter to his father (20 Dec [1875]) as *"type de gentilhomme français."* In a letter to William Dean Howells* (24 Jan [1876]), he called Goncourt "the best of them" among Flaubert's "little *coterie* of . . . young realists in fiction," but he added that Goncourt was boasting of an episode in his ongoing writing cast in "[a] whore-house *de province*." Theodore E. Child* took his friend James, when the latter was visiting in Paris in February 1884, to call on the surviving Goncourt brother at the old home of the coauthors. In time, James began to dislike Goncourt, and he even wrote to Grace Norton* (20 Aug [1893]) that during a recent visit to Paris he "was spared the sight of Goncourt." In "The Minor French Novelists" (*Galaxy*, Feb 1876), James briefly considers the Goncourt brothers' novels, which show "a high relish for psychological research" and "are a magazine of curious facts," but in which time seems to stop at about 1730 and space at the borders of Paris. The brothers show observational ability, taste, and style, but they stress "the crudities and maladies of life" too much. James summarizes *Renée Mauperin* ("their most agreeable" novel) and touches on *Soeur Philomène* ("a masterpiece" of stylistic and visual effects but "morbid"). He concludes that the Goncourts display "perverted ingenuity and wasted power." James reviewed (*Nation*, 10 May 1877) Edmond de Goncourt's *La Fille Elisa* unsympathetically, calling it an audacious but amateurish emulation of *L'Assommoir* by Émile Zola.* The author is serious, not frivolous, but "intolerably unclean." More important is James's review (*Fortnightly Review*, Oct 1888; reprinted in *Essays in London and Elsewhere*, 1893), of the Goncourt brothers' three-volume *Journal*, which he calls uncomfortable in style, pictorially verbose, pretentious, and embarrassing in its vulgar frankness. The surviving brother should have burned it. Keeping it for publication was a kind of suicide, since in it are wrathful, detestable comments on such associates as Charles Augustin Sainte-Beuve,* Princess Matilde Bonaparte, Paul Gavarni, Théophile Gautier,* Flaubert, Paul de Saint-Victor, and Thérèse Païva. The brothers were loyal to their profession of writing and show artistic consciousness here; but they are also narrow, airtight, resentful, rancorous, joyless, annoyed, and disgusted. They spied on colleagues to expose them in their journal. Too painterly in style, they disliked what they saw and unselectively described it. James touches on their *Madame Gervaisais*, which, unlike Flaubert's works, cannot be read aloud and which also is the mere "exhibition of a palette." James's library contained eight works by the Goncourt brothers and their *Oeuvres historiques, romans, etc.* (1876–1882) as well.

Goodenough, Miss. In *The Ivory Tower*, one of Frank B. Betterman's nurses.

Goodwood, Caspar. In *The Portrait of a Lady*, a wealthy American textile industrialist and Isabel Archer's indefatigable, perennially unsuccessful suitor. He does memorably kiss her in the final chapter.

Gorham, Mrs. In *The Other House*, the novel, Effie Bream's redoubtable nurse. In *The Other House*, the play, Tony Bream comforts her after Effie is murdered.

Gorton, Mrs. In "The Given Case," Margaret Hamer's sister and the hostess visited by Barton Reeve, who seeks her help.

Gosse, Sir Edmund Wilson (1849–1928). Versatile man of letters, British Museum staff member (1867–1875), translator for the Board of Trade (1875–1904), lecturer on English literature at Cambridge University (1885–1890), and librarian of the House of Lords (1904–1914). He was born in London, the only son of naturalist Philip Henry Gosse. Soon after the death of Gosse's mother in

1856, the family moved to Devon. Gosse's 1871 visit to Norway began his lifelong interest in Henrik Johan Ibsen,* reviews of whom by Gosse beginning in 1872 first acquainted British readers with the Norwegian poet and dramatist. In 1875 Gosse married Ellen (Nellie) Epps. A year later, the couple established a quarter-century residence at 29 Delamere Terrace, near Regent's Park, London; in 1901, they moved to 17 Hanover Terrace. In both residences, they held sociable Sundays "at home." They had two daughters and one son. The son, Philip, became a physician and an authority on piracy. In 1907 Gosse's wife inherited £46,000 from an uncle who had made a fortune in cocoa. Edmund Gosse was indefatigable and influential. He wrote poetry (*Madrigals, Songs and Sonnets* [coauthored, 1870], *On Viol and Flute* [1873], *King Erik* [1875], *New Poems* [1879], *Firdausi in Exile and Other Poems* [1885], *In Russet and Silver* [1894], *Hypolympia or the Gods in the Island: An Ironic Fantasy* [1901], *The Autumn Garden* [1909], *Collected Poems* [1911], and *Poems* [1926]); drama (*The Unknown Lover* [1878]); criticism and biography (*Studies in the Literature of Northern Europe* [1879—revised as *Northern Studies* (1890)], *Gray* [1882], *Seventeenth Century Studies* [1833], *From Shakespeare[*] to Pope* [1885], *Raleigh* [1886], *Life of William Congreve* [1888], *A History of Eighteenth-Century Literature (1660–1780* [1889], *Life of Philip Henry Gosse F.R.S.* [1890], *Gossip in a Library* [1891], *Questions at Issue* [1893], *The Jacobean Poets* [1894], *Critical Kit-Kats* [1896], *A Short History of Modern English Literature* [1898], *The Life and Letters of John Donne* [2 vols., 1899], *English Literature: An Illustrated Record* [coauthored, 4 vols., 1903], *Jeremy Taylor* [1904], *French Profiles* [1904], *Coventry Patmore* [1905], *Sir Thomas Browne* [1905], *Ibsen* [1907], *Portraits and Sketches* [1912], *Two Pioneers of Romanticism: Joseph and Thomas Warton* [1915], *Inter Arma* [1916], *The Life of Algernon Charles Swinburne[*]* [1917], *Some Diversions of a Man of Letters* [1919], *Books on the Table* [1921], *Aspects and Impressions* [1922—includes an essay on James], *More Books on the Table* [1923], *Silhouettes* [1925], and *Leaves and Fruit* [1927]); novels (*The Unequal Yoke* [1886] and *The Secret of Narcisse* [1892]); translations (Ibsen's *Hedda Gabler* [1891] and *The Master Builder* [with William Archer,* 1893]); editions (Thomas Gray, 4 vols. [1884], and Henry Fielding, 12 vols. [1898], and literary supplements to the London *Daily Mail* [1906–1907]); autobiography (*Father and Son* [published anonymously, 1907] and *Two Visits to Denmark, 1872, 1874* [1911]); and history (*A History of the Library of the House of Lords* [1908]). Gosse met James in the summer of 1879 at a luncheon in London with Andrew Lang* and Robert Louis Stevenson.* James and Gosse became close friends, especially after James's return from America in 1883. James attended many Gosse Sundays "at home" and Christmas dinners there, gave copies of his books to Gosse and received many of Gosse's in return, commented critically on them, sympathized with Gosse's family problems, advised Gosse when he traveled (especially to France and Italy), discussed his own family and professional and health problems, gossiped with him about literary friends, agonized with him when World War I started, and often entertained him at Lamb House.* According to a Notebook entry (26 Mar 1884), Gosse gave James the idea for "The Author of Beltraffio." When James hosted his 1886 Greenwich luncheon for Guy de Maupassant,* Gosse was a guest, along with George Du Maurier* and Count Joseph-Napoléon Primoli.* Gosse attended the first performance of James's *Guy Domville*, in London, on 5 January 1895. In 1910 Edith Newbold Jones Wharton* sought to recommend James for the Nobel Prize, and she enlisted Gosse and William Dean Howells* in her unsuccessful effort. (The prize in 1911 went to Maurice Maeterlinck* instead.) In 1912, Gosse invited James on behalf of the Royal Society for Literature to present a lecture on Robert Browning* on the centenary of the poet's birth; James gave the speech, with Gosse presiding. Also in 1912 Gosse vouched for James when he sought his Carlyle Mansions* flat; a year later he was one of the sponsors of the John Singer Sargent* portrait of James. When James applied for naturalization as a British citizen in 1915, Gosse was one of four distinguished sponsors—along with Herbert Henry Asquith,* James Brand Pinker* and Sir George Walter Prothero.* Almost four hundred letters from James to Gosse, including a few to Nellie Gosse, are extant, and they are among his finest and most intimate. In letter after letter, James offers praise and encouragement. When John Churton Collins in the *Quarterly Review* (October 1886) savagely criticized Gosse's *From Shakespeare to Pope*, James applauded his friend's temperate rejoinder to the jealous reviewer: "You have been graceful without being evasive, sportive without being flippant, & effective without being violent" (22 Oct 1886). James calls Gosse's *A History of Eighteenth-Century Literature* "essentially entertaining & occupying" (29 Jan [1889]); describes Gosse's biography of his father as "admirable skilful delightful" (24 Feb [1891]); judges his *The Jacobean Poets* to be "charming, beguiling, . . . without a dull sentence" (2 Mar 1894); praises Gosse's preface to his edition of Fielding "noble," with "great vividness & interest," though not sufficiently "critical" (14 Sep 1898); calls *Hypolympia* "merry & mocking" ([26 Oct 1901]), and "full of wit & wisdom, . . . style & . . . fragrances" ([31 Oct 1901]); describes his *Jeremy Taylor* as "beautifully & cunningly done" ([12 Apr 1904]); regards reading *Two Visits to Denmark* as like "reading . . . charming old letters" (26 Oct 1911); says that Gosse's *Dictionary of National Biography* entry on Swinburne "bristles with items and authenticities even as a tight little cushion with individual pins," though lacking "conclusive estimate or appraisement" (10 Oct 1912); and regards *Portraits and Sketches* as "so-vividly interesting" (19 Nov 1912). James and Gosse confided in one another concerning the homosexuality of John Addington Symonds* and Oscar Wilde,* both of whom Gosse knew well. After James's death, Sir Max Beerbohm* recommended Gosse to edit a selection of the novelist's letters, but Pinker, James's agent, had told William James's widow that James did not wish Gosse to be the editor, and Percy Lubbock* was chosen instead. James's library contained twenty-six books by Gosse.

Gosselin, Hugh. In "Lord Beaupré," Mary Gosselin's brother and Bolton-Brown's friend.

Gosselin, Mary. In "Lord Beaupré," the young woman who loved Lord Beaupré while he was untitled Guy Firminger. Reluctantly allowing the false rumor to be started that they are engaged, she later marries her brother's friend Bolton-Brown.

Gosselin, Mrs. In "Lord Beaupré," Hugh and Mary's mother. She foolishly starts the rumor that Mary and Lord Beaupré are engaged to protect him from title-seeking ladies.

Gostrey, Maria. In *The Ambassadors*, Lambert Strether's knowledgeable American expatriate confidante. They meet in Chester and are often together later in Paris, where she has a beautiful little apartment. She was once Marie de Vionnet's schoolmate. She grows fond of Strether, but he enigmatically declines her tender advances.

Got, François Jules Edmond (1822–1901). Brilliant French actor, especially in comic roles. He was a prize-winning Conservatoire student, served briefly in the cavalry, and then made his début at the Comédie Française (1844), thus starting a long career ending in 1895. He wrote two opera libretti and kept a journal (2 vols., 1910). James's theater essays are replete with references to Got, from 1872 to 1901, and always in praise. For example, in "The Théâtre Français" (1877), he calls Got "the first of living actors." More personally, in a letter to his brother William (13 Feb [1870]), James comments on a certain performance and says that "Got . . . spoiled me."

Gotch. In *The Outcry*, the novel, and *The Outcry*, the play, Lady Amy Sandgate's butler in her London home.

Gotch, Mrs. In "The Patagonia," a *Patagonia* gossip who contributes to Grace Mavis's fatal misery.

Gougenheim, Professor. In *The Bostonians*, a Talmudic scholar invited to a New York party as a drawing card.

Goupil. In "The Story of a Masterpiece," Stephen Baxter's portrait framer.

Grace, Lady. In *The Outcry*, the novel, and *The Outcry*, the play, Lord Theign's lovely daughter and Lady Kitty Imber's younger sister (age twenty-five). Grace loves Hugh Crimble and supports him in his efforts to keep her father from selling his art treasures.

Gracedew, Mrs. In "Covering End," the young American widow whose sympathy and money rescue Captain Marmaduke Clement Yule—and the mortgage on Covering End, his country house—and thus pave the way for him to be free of Cora Prodmore, who loves Hall Pegg. In *Summersoft*, Mrs. Gracedew rescues Yule and his house, here called Summersoft, and thus enables Cora Prodmore to marry Buddle. In *The High Bid*, Mrs. Gracedew, a widow for four years, buys Covering from Prodmore, and thus both saves its owner Yule and enables Cora Prodmore and Hall Pegg to marry. Yule and Mrs. Gracedew will then wed. In the stage production of *The High Bid*, Mrs. Gracedew's part was played by Gertrude Elliott, the wife of Sir Johnston Forbes-Robertson.*

Gracie. In *The Bostonians*, Henry Burrage, Jr.'s friend and fellow Harvard Law School student.

Graham, Robert. In "Osborne's Revenge," a man for whose suicide his friend Philip Osborne at first wrongly blames Henrietta Congreve.

"The Grand Canal." Travel essay, published in *Scribner's Magazine* (Nov 1892); reprinted in *The Great Streets of the World* (New York: Scribner, 1892), and in *Italian Hours*, 1909. James suggests that life along Venice's Grand Canal, which is almost a street, is superficial now that the place has become a kind of tomb where we properly collect memorabilia. The Piazza San Marco has polyglot tourists; the (Santa Maria della) Salute, like a fine, robed lady, awaits photographers. Beyond both are the city's mouth and an array of catalogued buildings: the Longhena, with its great Jacopo Robusti Tintoretto,* whose *Marriage of Cana* is elsewhere (in the Salute); the well-preserved Palazzo Foscari; the Academy; the Montecuculi; and other decadent, weathered little palaces, many with shops, along the water promenade. Some residences have ghostly quiet and many views—of barges, gondoliers, spectacles, varied people (including religious pilgrims and exiled monarchs), and surprising little gardens. James comments on more places, including the delicate Palazzo Dario and the pretentious Sansovino—was it once his post office?—the coarse Pesaro, and the Mocenigo palaces (in one of which George Gordon, Lord Byron* lived and wrote). James expresses disappointment in the Rialto Bridge, with insects, fishmongers, and motorboats nearby. He closes by discussing the windowed Ca' d'Oro, the restored Museo Civico, the Jewish areas near Canareggio, and minor pompous, ambiguous places at the canal's end.

Grandoni, Mme. In *Roderick Hudson*, Christina Light's close friend. She tells Rowland Mallet about Christina. In *The Princess Casamassima*, she accompanies Christina, now the princess, to England but finally leaves her.

Granger. In "The Pupil," a rich American who proposes to neither Amy nor Paula Moreen.

Granger, Frank. In "Flickerbridge," an American portrait painter and young Adelaide Wenham's fiancé. He visits the Flickerbridge estate owned by Addie's old cousin Adelaide Wenham.

Grant, Ulysses Simpson (1822–1885). Resolute Union Army general during the Civil War; later, mediocre eighteenth president of the United States. For his nephew's publishing company, Mark Twain* outbid the *Century Magazine*, then edited by Richard Watson Gilder,* to obtain Grant's *Personal Memoirs* (2 vols., 1885–1886). Soon after Grant died, James journeyed from Dover to Westminster Abbey, in London, to attend a memorial service for him. In "American Letter" (16 Apr 1898), James comments on Grant's letters to E. B. Washburne, a political associate. They were published as *General Grant's Letters to a Friend, 1861–1880* (1897). James, who liked Grant's "strong and simple Autobiography," finds these letters "as hard and dry as sand-paper," austere, and careless as to spelling and grammar. They do have "the tone" of an old portrait or an awkward piece of furniture. James knew Grant's daughter Nelly Grant and several of her in-laws. She entered the interesting Sartoris family* by marrying Algernon Sartoris (the son of Edward Sartoris and Adelaide Sartoris, the sister of Frances Anne Kemble*). In a letter to his sister Alice (19 May [1879]), James describes Nelly Sartoris at a social gathering: She "sits speechless . . . understanding neither head nor tail of . . . high discourse. . . . She is as sweet and amiable (and almost as pretty) as she is uncultivated." According to a Notebook entry (26 Mar 1884), Nelly's gossip was the indirect source of James's story "Georgina's Reasons." In a letter to Grace Norton* ([c. 4 Jan 1888]), he says that he regards it as "touching and tragic" to see Nelly, "the daughter of . . . a great victorious warrior," in British society "with three . . . handsome but . . . common youngsters," and herself "illiterate, lovely, painted, pathetic and separated from a drunken idiot of a husband." In "New York and the Hudson: A Spring Impression," in *The American Scene*, James records his favorable impression of Grant's tomb. James's library contained one book by Grant.

Grantham, May. In "The Two Faces," Lord Gwyther's former mistress who vengefully overdresses his wife Lady Valda. Mrs. Grantham's face then seems hard to observant Shirley Sutton.

Grantham, Mrs. In *The Other House*, Julia Bream's stepmother, once married also to Rose Armiger's uncle.

Grant-Jackson. In "The Birthplace," the spokesman for The Birthplace company. He hires Morris Gedge as a barker, warns him, and then gives him a raise in pay.

Granville-Barker, Harley Granville (1877–1946). Charming, exceptionally able actor, playwright, theater manager, director, and producer. He was born in London, as Harley Granville Barker. While still a teenager, he became an actor (until about 1910) and writer. He appeared in plays by William Shakespeare* (from 1895), and later acted in support of the famous Mrs. Patrick Campbell.* Early in his career, Granville-Barker wrote *The Weather-Hen* (1899, coauthored) and *The Marrying of Ann Leete* (1901). In 1903 he and William Archer* sought to found a national theater; a year later, Granville-Barker became comanager (with J. E. Vedrenne) of the unrivaled Court Theatre in London (to 1907) and soon produced there and elsewhere plays by Henrik Johan Ibsen,* Elizabeth Robins,* George Bernard Shaw* (whose recognition he thus hastened), John Galsworthy,* and others, as well as his own drama *The Voysey Inheritance* (1905). In 1906 Granville-Barker married the beautiful and considerate actress Lillah McCarthy. In 1910 he managed the Duke of York's Theatre. His later works include *Prunella* (1906, coauthored with Laurence Housman), *Waste* (1907, banned by the censors, revised in 1936), *The Madras House* (1910, revised 1925), and *Vote My Ballot* (1917). During World War I, he combined professional work in England and the United States, Red Cross and safe military duties in France and England, and adultery with and marriage (in 1918) to wealthy Helen Huntington, who bought what she wanted and thus ruined her husband— he was her third—by discouraging his theater work. (She made him hyphenate his original name, and she hated his friend Shaw.) After World War I, Helen translated Spanish plays, and Granville-Barker tidied the results. He produced a play by Maurice Maeterlinck* in 1920. Granville-Barker published *The Exemplary Theatre* (1922); Helen and her husband moved to France; and he wrote *Prefaces to Shakespeare* (1934) and other drama criticism. Their final years were sad. In January 1908, Granville-Barker read the script of James's play *The Saloon* but evidently did not like it. In 1909, James showed Granville-Barker his dramatic version of *The Other House*. In the same year, James also had reason to hope that Granville-Barker would help persuade Charles Frohman* to produce his play *The Outcry*; Granville-Barker visited Lamb House* in April to discuss the possibility. A Pocket Diary note (1 Oct 1912) records James's opinion of Granville-Barker's production of Shakespeare's *A Winter's Tale*: "incredibly stupid and hideous." In 1914 Granville-Barker tried in vain to persuade James to ask the Moscow Art Theatre to produce *The Outcry*.

Gravener, George. In "The Coxon Fund," a Clockborough parliamentarian who loves Ruth Anvoy but breaks away from her when she awards Frank Saltram the Coxon Fund. After some family deaths, Gravener becomes Lord Maddock.

Gray, John Chipman (1839–1915). American lawyer and educator, born in Brighton, Massachusetts, the grandson of a wealthy shipowner. Gray graduated from Harvard (1859) and Harvard Law School (1861). After service in the Union Army (1862–1865) during the Civil War, he began a successful law practice in

Boston. He lectured in the Harvard Law School intermittently (1869–1873), then in distinguished professorships there (1875–1913); ultimately, he became dean. Gray cofounded the *American Law Review* (1886) and edited it for years. Gray married in 1873, and became the father of a son and a daughter. He published widely, mainly on property law; he was an officer in several companies, institutions, societies, and professional organizations; and he was a close and valued friend of Boston writers too numerous to name. Gray was one of several war veterans attracted to Mary Temple* in the summer of 1865 and undoubtedly later. In a letter from England to his brother William (8 Mar 1870), James asks for news of Gray: "Do you often see him and how does he wear?" A couple of years later (22 Sep [1872]), he wonders whether William has "sounded the mysteries of J. Gray's *morale*." When James visited Harvard during his extended 1904–1905 visit to the United States, he saw Dean Gray from a distance in the law school library but oddly did not walk over to speak. He describes the incident in *The American Scene* (without naming Gray). When James was writing *Notes of a Son and Brother*, he felt the need of certain letters which Mary Temple had written to Gray just after the Civil War. He evidently enlisted the help of his brother William's widow Alice. At any rate, Gray, then sick, or his wife released them. Calling Gray only "an admirable friend," James in *Notes of a Son and Brother* quotes extensively from Mary's letters. After sending Gray a copy of the book, he wrote to Alice (29 Mar 1914): "I can't help rather wondering how he feels about what I have done in that connection—yet can't doubt, on the whole, that he feels justified of his trust."

"The Great Condition." Short story (14,500 words), published in the *Anglo-Saxon Review* (Jun 1899); reprinted in *The Soft Side*, 1900. (Characters: Bertram Braddle, Henry Chilver, Mrs. Damerel.) Bertram Braddle has to leave Liverpool, and he thus seems to be neglecting Mrs. Damerel, one of his fellow passengers from America. So Henry Chilver, his friend and another passenger, volunteers to keep her company instead of proceeding straight to London. Henry recalls his so-so vacation in America and also how Mrs. Damerel, that attractive American widow on the ship returning, became friendly with Bertram very quickly. Henry dutifully escorts the woman on to London and then to Brighton, as promised, but then he finds himself falling in love with her himself. Later Bertram returns, explains that he loves Mrs. Damerel but mentions a fear of something strange in her background. Henry tells him to propose anyway and to hope that the woman will explain matters. Bertram fears that she would accept him but explain nothing. And so it happens. Soon Bertram tells Henry that she did tardily admit to something vaguely untoward in her background but vowed to tell him nothing specific until they had been married for six months. This is her "condition." Bertram hedges and even returns to America (and Hawaii) to investigate his fiancée's past life. Meanwhile, Henry calls on Mrs. Damerel and learns that she regards herself as entirely free, and he proposes to her within a week. They marry. Bertram finds nothing scandalous, returns to England, and gets her to admit confidentially—he promises to say nothing to Henry—that there never was anything improper in her past. She adds that Henry never queries her about her background and considers himself rather noble for his restraint. A long Notebook entry (10 Feb 1899) confides that "George Meredith[*] the other day . . . threw out an allusion . . . that suggested a small subject—5000 words." James sketches the plot and writes out a good bit of dialogue. The story as published is almost three times 5,000 words and concentrates not on all three characters, as in the notes, but simply the wise woman and her catalytic "condition." The two main points of this minor story are that lovers should be trusting, and that instead of measuring time abstractly one should enjoy life in real time.

"The Great Good Place." Short story (9,200 words), published in *Scribner's Magazine* (Jan 1900); reprinted in *The Soft Side*, 1900; revised and reprinted in *The Novels and Tales of Henry James*, Volume XVI, 1909. (Characters: Brown, George Dane, Lady Mullet.) George Dane, a busy writer, is oppressed one fine morning after a long, rainy night of unfinished work. He has a sense of varied duties: writing, social obligations, and an imminent breakfast guest, who now enters. Suddenly Dane awakens to a new environment, where all is at peace. He hears pleasant bells and slow footfalls about him; a Brother is seated on a nearby bench. Dane tells him about the young breakfast guest who volunteered to handle all his work for him while he indulgently and gratefully leaned back on the sofa. Three weeks seem now to pass at this good place with many comrades. Dane finds his soul again, but then he and the Brother notice rain outside the "hotel" and discuss the inevitability of his returning. He is refreshed, ready. Then his servant awakens him, and he observes that his young guest has indeed tidied up all of his work for him. In a Notebook entry (12 May 1892) dealing with the germ of his short story "The Middle Years," James suggests that his aging novelist (Dencombe in the story) enjoys "[a] deep sleep in which he dreams he *has* had his respite. Then his waking, to find that what he had dreamed of is only what he has *done*." This uniquely utopian Jamesian story, which repays the most careful reading, links with "Is There a Life after Death?", James's unique 1910 essay on immortality. Precisely what the great good place is may be left to individual readers to define. Is it heaven, nirvana, a Catholic retreat house, dreamland, a spa, a resort, a motel? Is it to be permanent, costly?

Green, John Richard (1837–1883). English historian, born in Oxford and educated there. He was ordained, became a librarian, contracted tuberculosis, read and wrote much, and died young. His publications include the popular *Short History of the English People* (1874, expanded to 4 vols., 1877–1880), *The Making of England* (1882), and *The Conquest of England* (1883). Sir Leslie Stephen* edited Green's letters (1901). The titular hero of *Robert Elsmere* by Mary Augusta Ward* may be based on Green. His wife Alice Stopford Green (1847–1929) was an Irish historian, whose main works are *Town Life in the 15th Century* (1894), *The Making of Ireland and Its Undoing* (1908), and *A History* *of the Irish State to 1914* (1925). James knew both Greens slightly. In a letter to his father (29 May [1878]), he unkindly called the sick Green "Alice's little worm of an historian," adding that "Mrs. Green . . . is, however, charming." James wrote to Mrs. Green when her husband died, avoided her when both were vacationing in Dover (1889), but, according to his Pocket Diaries, met socially with her in London in the early 1910s. James's library included nine books by John Richard Green and two by his wife.

Green, Susan. In "The Point of View," a celebrated American authoress mentioned in a letter by Gustave Lejaune.

Green-Erin, Duke of. In "An International Episode," a Britisher entertained by the Butterworths in America.

Greenough family. A Boston family, rich because of the business acumen of David Greenough, who made a fortune in building construction and real estate and who became the patriarch of an eventually far-flung international cultural family. He had nine children. His son John Greenough (1801–1852) was born in Boston, left Harvard to study art in London (1824), and became adept in portrait and landscape painting. He returned to Boston (1844–1850), then went back to Europe, and died in Paris. David's son Horatio (1805–1852) graduated from Harvard (1825), was a friend of Ralph Waldo Emerson,* and became a pioneer, expatriate, neoclassical American sculptor. He went to Italy to study (1825–1826) and subsequently did studio work in Florence (1828–1851). His leading statues are a huge *George Washington* and *The Rescue*, both located in Washington, D.C. The degree of his influence on modern functionalism is still a subject of debate. For a time, Horatio Greenough used the pseudonym Horace Bender. His Boston-born wife, Louise Gore Greenough (1812–1892), died in Florence and left her Villa Belvedere (near there) to Henry Huntington. David's son Henry Greenough (1807–1883) went to Florence in the 1830s and became a painter, architect, and author. About 1832 he married Frances Boott, the sister of Francis Boott.* Henry and his wife lived in Florence, Venice, Trieste, Bagni di Lucca, and Rome. He wrote poetry and published a novel entitled *Ernest Carroll, or an Artist's Life in Italy* (1858). David's son Richard Saltonstall Greenough (1819–1904) was born in Jamaica Plains, Massachusetts, went to Boston Latin School, started a career in business, but soon displayed such talent in art that two of his commercially successful brothers sent him (1837) to join Horatio in Italy. Richard studied in Florence for a while (1840), married Sara Dana Loring (1827–1885) of Boston (1846), and lived and worked permanently (from 1848) in Europe. In the 1870s and 1880s, he, his wife, and their son Gordon Greenough (a painter) resided in Paris. Richard had studios in Paris, Florence, and Rome; he produced portrait busts and ideal groups, always meticulous but sometimes lifeless. His wife published fiction: *Lilian* (1863), a novel showing the influence of *The Marble Faun* by Nathaniel Hawthorne,* and *Ar-*

abesques (1872, illustrated by her son Gordon), a collection of short stories. Sara died in Austria; Richard, much later, in Rome. John Singer Sargent* did a portrait of Richard. David's daughter Ellen Greenough married a Huntington, whose family owned Villa Castelani at Bellosguardo; she lived in Florence as a widow (from 1871) and died there (1893). Her son Henry Huntington (1848–1926) became the American vice-consul there. One of Ellen's daughters was Laura Huntington Wagnière, who married into a family of Swiss bankers who later privately published her memoirs, *From Dawn to Dusk* (1929?). David's daughter Laura Greenough Curtis was the stepmother of Daniel Sargent Curtis,* who was hence Laura Wagnière's cousin; Laura Curtis died in Paris (1878). Sargent's *Venetian Interior* shows Daniel Curtis and his wife Ariana Randolph Curtis,* and their son Ralph. David's daughter Louisa Greenough visited Florence, returned there in the 1870s, bought Villa Belvedere al Saracino, which was on Bellosguardo, in part of which Boott and his daughter Elizabeth Boott* resided; this villa was adjacent to Villa Brichieri-Colombi (in which Horatio Greenough lived for a while and in which James and also Constance Fenimore Woolson* rented widely separated rooms for a short while in 1887). James knew many of these expatriated Greenoughs. He met with Ellen Huntington and her children in Switzerland in the summer of 1869. (In subsequent years, he was a guest at the Huntington villa at Bellosguardo.) Later in 1869 (and again in 1873) James met Horatio Greenough's widow in Florence. James often called on his close friends Boott and his daughter Elizabeth Boott at Bellosguardo, in the 1870s. To the end of his life, James was friendly with Laura Wagnière. According to a Notebook entry written in Venice (1 May 1899), James learned from Ariana Curtis that Gordon Greenough had told his mother that his father was a poor artist. This incident became the basis for James's story ''The Tree of Knowledge.''

Greenstreet, Mr. and Mrs. Abraham. In *The Bostonians*, Verena Tarrant's maternal grandparents.

Gregorini. In ''Mrs. Temperly,'' a woman singer at a Paris party given by Maria Temperly.

Gregory, Lady Isabella Augusta Persse (1852–1932). Irish playwright, theatrical producer and director, translator, critic, biographer, and cofounder (with William Butler Yeats) of the Abbey Theatre, in Dublin, in 1899. James knew her over the years. In a Notebook entry (23 Jan 1894), he records a clever idea from her for a story he never wrote. In 1903 he met Lady Gregory's nephew Dudley Jocelyn Persse,* whom he began to like inordinately. In 1912 James attended a London exhibition of work by Lady Gregory's artist son Robert (killed in World War I, in Italy, in 1918). Robert Gregory was her only child.

Gregory, Dr. In "A Most Extraordinary Case," a good local physician recommended to Colonel Ferdinand Mason by Maria Mason.

Grenadine, Miss. In "The Liar," according to Colonel Clement Capadose, Miss Grenadine is a pseudonym of Harriet Pearson, the tipsy model who at Oliver Lyon's studio calls herself Miss Geraldine.

Grendon, Harry and Tishy. In *The Awkward Age*, a married couple. She is Carrie Donner's sister, who frequently entertains Nanda Brookenham.

Gresham, Mr. and Mrs. In *The Tragic Muse*, a married couple. He is absent. She is Julia Dallow's secretary.

Gressie, Mr. and Mrs. In "Georgina's Reasons," Georgina Gressie Benyon Roy's parents.

Greville, Charles Cavendish Fulke (1794–1865). British diarist, once a page of George III, who was educated at Eton and Christ Church, Oxford, and was clerk to the privy council (1821–1859) under George IV, William IV, and Victoria. His extensive private journals made posthumous fame when published in 1875, 1885, and 1887. James reviewed (*Nation*, 28 Jan 1875) *A Journal of the Reigns of King George IV. and King William IV.* (1875) with great relish, praising the author as a frank but never scurrilous "amateur annalist," an observant note taker with an " 'inside view' of public people and affairs" and "an uncompromising instinct of truth." James treasures the man's cutting, unflattering, ungossipy style. He notes "an undercurrent of melancholy, because Greville was fearful that no reform could stabilize " 'the rotten . . . society' " of his epoch. James singles out several of Greville's "brilliant portraits," especially those of George IV (despicable), the Duke of Wellington (great soldier but political incompetent), and Washington Irving* (too blunt for fine society). James closes by characterizing Greville as dry but dignified. James's library contained one book by Greville.

"Greville Fane." Short story (6,500 words), published in the *Illustrated London News* (17, 24 Sep 1892); reprinted in *The Real Thing and Other Tales*, 1893; revised and reprinted in *The Novels and Tales of Henry James*, Volume XVI, 1909. (Characters: Greville Fane, Sir Baldwin Luard, Lady Ethel Stormer Luard, Mr. and Mrs. Leolin Stormer.) When potboiler novelist Greville Fane (real name, Mrs. Stormer) dies, the journalist narrator privately reviews her life. Her daughter Lady Ethel Luard is a cold social climber. Her son Leolin Stormer sponged off his busy mother during his school years, and then later while he idled and professed to be gaining experience for never-written novels. Ethel married Sir Baldwin Luard, and her mother paid for everything—only to be informed that she could not live with the newlyweds. Once they have published the mother's posthumous writings, son and daughter quarrel over the profits. Leolin, marrying an old woman, still talks about the writing he will do—once he conquers problems of form. In a brief Notebook entry (22 Jan 1879), James jots down the notion that Anthony Trollope* thought "a boy might be brought up to be a novelist as to any other trade" and further that Anne Thackeray (Lady Anne Isabella Ritchie*) told him "she and her husband meant to bring up their little daughter in that way." James then sketches the notion of a lady novelist trying to make her son into one; then, in a later note (27 Feb 1889), James comments again on "the figure of a weary battered labourer in the field of fiction attempting to carry out this project with a child [i.e., training one to be a writer] and meeting . . . discomfiture." The sources of this story must also include the hordes of "scribbling females" (for one example, Ouida*) of whom both Nathaniel Hawthorne* and later James disapproved, and perhaps such fast-scribbling male equivalents as Francis Marion Crawford,* whose prolixity was at the expense of art, in James's view. In the preface to Volume XVI of *The Novels and Tales of Henry James*, James praises "Greville Fane" as "a minor miracle of foreshortening." Even as he deplored hasty, artistic superfertility, James could humanely sympathize with Mrs. Stormer's family plight.

Grey, Violet. In "Nona Vincent," an actress whose portrayal of the title rôle of Allan Wayworth's play entitled *Nona Vincent* Mrs. Alsager's example improves. Wayworth and Miss Grey later get married.

Greyswood, Lord. In "The Wheel of Time," Lady Greyswood's oldest son, formerly named Chumleigh.

Greyswood, Lord and Lady. In "The Wheel of Time," Maurice Glanvil's parents. He dies. She cannot persuade her son to like plain Fanny Knocker.

Grice, Agatha. In "The Modern Warning," an American who loves and marries Sir Rufus Chasemore but is driven to suicide because of the ill feeling between her husband and her brother Macarthy Grice.

Grice, Macarthy. In "The Modern Warning," Agatha's brother. He and her husband Sir Rufus Chasemore get along so badly that she commits suicide.

Grice, Mrs. In "The Modern Warning," Macarthy and Agatha Grice's mother, and Sir Rufus Chasemore's mother-in-law. She dies.

Griffin. In *The Princess Casamassima*, a London shoemaker radical. He associates with Paul Muniment and other anarchists.

Griffin. In "The Turn of the Screw," the host to whose Christmas guests Douglas reads the governess's manuscript.

Griffin, Mrs. In *The Other House*, the play, Rose Armiger's aunt and Julia Bream's bad stepmother. The woman's visit to Julia after she has given birth to Effie does not improve the new mother's health.

Grigsby, Emilie Busbey (1880?–1964). Beautiful Kentucky-born "ward" of Charles Tyson Yerkes, the millionaire American art collector. He deeded her a Park Avenue residence in 1898 (and died in her presence in New York, in 1905). Miss Grigsby also had homes in West Drayton, Middlesex, and Mayfair, London, and she was widely known as an Edwardian hostess. She boasted of crashing the coronation of George V in Westminster Abbey (July 1911). She held a public auction of her art and literary collections in New York (January 1912). Before and during World War I, she entertained a variety of soldiers, sculptors, and writers, supposedly including William Butler Yeats and Rupert Brooke.* When George Meredith* met her, she said that he said he had finally seen the heroine of his novel *The Ordeal of Richard Feverel*. Miss Grigsby met James at a London dinner in 1903, pursued him, had tea with him, asked him whether she resembled Milly Theale in *The Wings of the Dove*, and then dishonestly revealed that she was the original Milly to reporters who then hinted that the novelist and the beauty were engaged. James wrote to William James (6 May 1904) to scotch the rumor, and he called the incident an example of silliness "in this nightmare-world of insane *bavardage*." Miss Grigsby was in the United States when World War II began but returned to England late during the war. She died in London.

Grimm, Herman (1828–1901). German art critic, professor, and novelist. William James knew him in Germany and in 1867 published a review of one of his novels. In 1873, James introduced himself to Grimm and his wife in Perugia, Italy, and in a letter to William ([27 May 1873]) described Mrs. Grimm as frank and sweet, but expressed surprise that she did not speak French.

Grindon, Goodwood. In *The Tragic Muse*, a rich, young industrialist whom Lady Agnes Dormer knows but in whom her daughter Bridget Dormer is not interested. He is then won by Lady Muriel Macpherson.

Grose, Mrs. In "The Turn of the Screw," the seemingly simple, evidently illiterate, perhaps well-meaning Bly housekeeper in whom the governess confides.

Grosjoyeux, M. de. In *The American*, one of Valentin de Bellegarde's seconds in his duel with Stanislas Kapp.

Grospré, M. de. In *The Reverberator*, a friend of Suzanne de Brécourt.

"The Grosvenor Gallery and the Royal Academy." Art review, published in the *Nation* (31 May 1877). James says that the grand opening of the Grosvenor Gallery in London is "the most interesting thing that the season of 1877 has brought forward,'' with its two hundred or so paintings making a finer show than the larger one at the Royal Academy. He touches on several artists represented at the Grosvenor: Ferdinand Heilbuth (''his specialty . . . [is] cardinals and *monsignori* on the terraces of Roman gardens''), James Tissot (his *"tours de force* . . . most[ly] . . . are highly successful, but . . . not agreeable''), George Frederick Watts,* William Holman Hunt,* James Abbott McNeill Whistler,* and Sir Edward Burne-Jones.* James leaves little space to report the Royal Academy exhibition—he strolls through the rooms smelling ''aesthetic Philistinism'' and ''front-parlor aesthetics,'' but he briefly praises Lord Frederick Leighton,* Edward Longsden Long's *Egyptian Feast,* Sir John Everett Millais,* and George Henry Boughton.*

Grove-Stewart, John. In ''The Given Case,'' Margaret Hamer's nominal fiancé. He has been in India for a long time.

Grugan. In *The Princess Casamassima,* a fellow bookbinder with Hyacinth Robinson.

Gualdo, Luigi (1847–1898). Italian novelist and short-story writer of works including *Un matrimonio eccentrico* (1879, translated into English as *A Strange Marriage* [1881]), *La gran rivale . . .* (1880), and *Decadenza* (1893). According to a Notebook entry (7 May 1898), James learned through Paul Bourget* and his wife about a plot by Gualdo concerning ''the child *retournée.''* James comments to the effect that his story ''The Tone of Time'' also owes something to Gualdo. He developed Gualdo's general idea into ''Maud-Evelyn'' and began ''Hugh Merrow,'' which also evidently resembles Gualdo's idea.

Guérin, Eugénie de (1805–1848). Mystical French diarist, letter writer, and sister of Maurice de Guérin.* James reviewed (*Nation,* 14 Dec 1865) the 1865 English translation of her 1861 *Journal,* calling her a modest, humble genius, and her 1834–1840 journal (really letters to her brother Maurice and after his death words ''inscribed to his departed soul'') worthy of comparison to Madame de Sévigné's writings—for their taste, tact, familiar tone, and limited imaginativeness. James sincerely admires Mlle. de Guérin's quiet, strong piety. James also reviewed (*Nation,* 13 Sep 1866) her *Letters,* published in 1866. He calls them sweet, perfect, uniform, and simple, and their authoress ''a mediaeval saint'' for her display of ''unction, intensity, and orthodoxy.'' She read little, had no will power, and illustrates pure feeling without ideas. Her comments on her brother's death have, James concludes, ''a most painful beauty.''

Guérin, Maurice de (1810–1839). French poet and brother of Eugénie de Guérin.* Born in Languedoc, he studied for a religious career, then taught and free-lanced in Parisian poverty, married money, but died less than a year later. He wrote poetry, but his prose is more poetic in its expression of a pagan love of nature. James reviewed (*Nation*, 7 Mar 1867) the 1867 translation of Guérin's *Journal*, which had been published in 1861. He admires the translation for displaying essential "fidelity, sympathy, and intelligence," and he calls Guérin "an incomparable writer." After sketching the lethargic, self-deprecating man's melancholy life, James praises his journal for its "exquisite" style and also comments favorably on his prose poem "The Centaur."

Guest, John. In "Guest's Confession," Laura Guest's father and Edgar Musgrave's confessed swindler.

Guest, Laura. In "Guest's Confession," John Guest's daughter, Clara Beck's friend, and the object of the narrator David's affections.

"Guest's Confession." Short story (21,700 words), published in the *Atlantic Monthly* (Oct–Nov 1872). (Characters: Clara Beck, Crawford, David, John Guest, Laura Guest, Hale, Edgar Musgrave, Stevens, Stoddard.) At church in a watering spot called L—, narrator David meets Laura Guest, goes on to welcome his hypochondriacal stepbrother Edgar Musgrave at the railroad station, and learns that Edgar has been swindled out of $20,000 by John Guest. Edgar forces Guest to write a confession, which is witnessed by David, who later realizes that Laura is the swindler's daughter. He falls in love with her. At about this time, Crawford, a silver millionaire from the West, enters the scene and starts courting Laura's companion Clara Beck. Guest then saddens Laura by writing to her about his financial plight. When he returns to L— and finds his enemy Musgrave's stepbrother David with his daughter, Guest orders the young fellow to leave. But David obtains as his legacy, from the dying Musgrave, Guest's confession, with which he forces the man to permit Laura to accept him. A few critics have tried to rescue this early story, which most readers rightly regard as dull and unpleasant.

Gulp, Miss. In "The Point of View," Gwendolyn and Charlotte Antrobus's teacher.

Gunton. In "Miss Gunton of Poughkeepsie," Lily Gunton's wealthy Poughkeepsie grandfather.

Gunton, Lily. In "Miss Gunton of Poughkeepsie," the Poughkeepsie girl who repudiates her engagement to the Roman prince and plans to wed Adam P. Bransby.

Gurney, Ephraim Whitman (1829–1886). Head of the History Department and dean of the faculty at Harvard, an editor of the *North American Review* before Henry Adams,* and later Adams's brother-in-law. Gurney married Ellen Hooper; Adams, her sister Marian Hooper. Gurney died prematurely of pernicious anemia. James knew Gurney casually and wrote to Thomas Sergeant Perry* (15 Aug [1867]) that the man "seems retiring, diffident and inaccessible." Later, to Charles Eliot Norton* (4 Feb 1872), he wrote that Gurney seems "almost oppressed and silenced and saddened by perfect comfort and happiness." But in 1876 Gurney (with his wife) saw James in Paris and London, helped him socially, and seemed more friendly. The three again socialized in London several years later. In *Notes of a Son and Brother*, James reminisces tenderly about both Gurneys, saying that Gurney was the "trusted judge of all judgments" and that his "exquisite" wife had "infallible taste."

Gushmore. In *The Tragic Muse*, Basil Dashwood's friend, who is a play rewriter.

Guterman-Seuss. In *The Golden Bowl*, the Jewish dealer in Brighton who sells Adam Verver some Oriental tiles. The man has eleven children.

Guy, Mrs. In "Paste," the vulgar, manipulative woman who recognizes Charlotte Prime's supposedly paste pearls as genuine and valuable. James surely named her the way he did as a jocose tribute to his friend Guy de Maupassant,* whose stories "Les Bijoux" and "La Parure" inspired James's "Paste."

Guy Domville. Three-act play (original title, *The Hero*), privately printed in London by Miles, 1894, and published in Philadelphia and New York by J. B. Lippincott Company, 1949, in *The Complete Plays of Henry James*, ed. Leon Edel. (Characters: Mary Brasier, Lord Edenbrook, Lord Devenish, Guy Domville, Maria Brasier Domville, Domville of Gaye, Domville, Mrs. Domville, Domville, Fanny, Frank Humber, Father Murray, Peter, Mrs. Peverel, George Peverel, George Porter Round, Father White.) Frank Humber has ridden over to nearby Porches to propose again to its owner the widow Mrs. Peverel, whose little boy George (Geordie) is tutored by Guy Domville. Lord Devenish has come from London to give Guy some news from Maria Domville, the patriarch of the Domville family and the mother of Mary Brasier, whom Devenish wants Guy to marry: His distant cousin Domville of Gaye has just died without legitimate issue. Guy and Frank were Catholic school chums in France together and are still close friends. Guy is about to become a priest, but he grows uncertain when Devenish tells him it is his duty to marry and have a son to carry on the family name. When Mrs. Peverel rejects Frank, he suspects she loves Guy, who may now be available to her. Three months later, at Mrs. Domville's villa at Richmond, Lieutenant George Round (back from three months at sea) secretly calls on Mary Brasier. The two love each other, but Mary has been blandished by Devenish into accepting Guy, to whom Devenish has shown high-society life and who now seems willing to do his duty to his family. When the wedding of Guy and Mary, scheduled for this evening, will have occurred, Mrs. Domville will consent to wed Devenish and pay off his debts. But Round and Guy now meet (and participate in a drinking scene which James later deleted); when Round reveals that he has just learned Devenish is really Mary's father, Guy helps them elope. Once Devenish and Mary's mother know the truth, he lightly says they can use Guy's love for Mrs. Peverel to familial advantage. Next day Frank visits Mrs. Peverel in her parlor, and they discuss Guy's wedding. Bursting in, Devenish separately tells Mrs. Peverel and Frank that the ceremony has been cancelled and that Guy loves Mrs. Peverel and is coming to woo her. Guy enters, reminisces with Frank about their old days, learns that Mrs. Peverel rejected Frank (thus freeing Guy to approach her), sees Mrs. Peverel alone, tells her that he does not relish the selfish world, sees Devenish's special gloves, and guesses that the man came to undermine Frank's chance with Mrs. Peverel. Guy is sad to be causing others pain. He tells Mrs. Peverel that he will enter the Church; he criticizes zealous Devenish and his world; and he commends Mrs. Peverel and Frank to one another's love. James's plot may owe something to that of *A Foregone Conclusion*, the 1875 novel by William Dean Howells,* which James reviewed and in which an Italian priest loves an American woman. In his *Notebooks* (4 Aug 1892), James jotted down an idea concerning a Venetian monk taken out of the Church by his family to produce an heir. James wrote *Guy Domville* for the popular London actor manager Sir George Alexander.* Rehearsals began in December 1894, and the play opened in London, on 5 January 1895 (with Alexander in the title role and Marion Terry, the sister of Dame Ellen Terry,* playing Mrs. Peverel), to a sparkling audience which included the following friends of James: William Archer,* Arnold Bennett, Sir Edward Burne-Jones,* Francis Marion Crawford,* George Du Maurier,* Sir Edmund Wilson Gosse,* Lord Frederick Leighton,* Francis Davis Millet,* Elizabeth Robins,* Mary Morton Sands,* John Singer Sargent,* George Bernard Shaw,* Mary Augusta Ward,* George Frederick Watts,* and Herbert George Wells.* James was nervous, and he attended *An Ideal Husband* by Oscar Wilde,* at a theater nearby. At the close of his own play, James put in an appearance on stage, only to be booed by a rowdy part of the audience for reasons still not clear. The play had rhythmic lines of considerable subtlety, but its second act was too long (and in it Guy turns too rakish too fast, while Frank Humber and Mrs. Peverel are absent), and some of the actors and actresses were badly costumed and acted poorly. *Guy Domville* ran only five weeks, earned James less than £300, and cost Alexander's company more than £1,800. James was chagrined but immediately returned with great resolution of the writing of more fiction. The drinking scene in *Guy Domville* may owe something to a similar one in *L'Aventurière* by Guillaume Victor Émile Augier,* a scene James had praised in 1877 in "The Théâtre Français." James permitted passages from *Guy Domville* to be published in *The Drama Birthday Book* (London: MacQueen, 1895), prepared by Percy S. Phillips, and in *The George Alexander Birthday Book* (London: Lane, 1903).

Gwendolyn. In "Paste," Charlotte Prime's pupil.

Gwyther, Lady Valda. In "The Two Faces," Countess Kremnitz's daughter and Lord Gwyther's wife. She becomes May Grantham's overdressed victim. Valda's pathetic, innocent face then seems appealing to observant Shirley Sutton.

Gwyther, Lord. In "The Two Faces," May Grantham's former lover who has married Valda. When he daringly asks Mrs. Grantham to dress his wife for her British début, the woman seeks revenge.

Gyp. Pen name of the Comtesse Martel de Janville, Sibylle Gabrielle Marie Antoinette (de Riquetti de Mirabeau) (1849–1932), a French writer whose novels were popular in the 1880s and 1890s. In his preface to Volume IX of *The Novels and Tales of Henry James*, 1908, James praises the dialogue novels of Gyp, who, he says, "had long struck me as mistress, in her levity, of one of the happiest of forms." James's *The Awkward Age* owes much to her example. His library contained four of her works.

H

H—. In "The Madonna of the Future," the narrator, who is friendly with Theobald and Mrs. Coventry.

H—, Lady. In "The Diary of a Man of Fifty," the London hostess at whose home the narrator sees Edmund Stanmer after the latter's marriage.

Hack, Mrs. In "The Chaperon," Rose Tramore's former governess.

Haddon. In "In the Cage," a name mentioned in one of Lady Bradeen's telegrams.

Haggard, Sir Henry Rider (1856–1925). British novelist whose government service in South Africa gave him the background for several romantic novels, the most successful of which were *The Witch's Head* (1885), *King Solomon's Mines* (1885), and *She* (1887). Haggard also wrote on questions of lands and colonial settlement. In a letter to Robert Louis Stevenson* (2 Aug [1886]), James said that "unspeakable" Haggard's popularity moved him "to a holy indignation." In a later letter (17 Feb 1893), James deplored Stevenson's "toleration" of Haggard. Between these comments, James in his long 1888 essay on Guy de Maupassant* alludes in an aside to Haggard's glossing over of "African carnage."

Hague, Acton. In "The Altar of the Dead," a recently deceased public figure who wronged both George Stransom and his unnamed woman companion. Her forgiveness of Hague finally inspires Stransom.

Hale. In "Guest's Confession," Edgar Musgrave's lawyer. He is a partner in the law firm of Stoddard and Hale.

Hamer, Magaret. In "The Given Case," Mrs. Gorton's sister. Barton Reeve's appeal to Margaret makes her realize the force of her lover Philip Mackern's affection.

Hamerton, Philip Gilbert (1834–1894). Distinguished English writer, mostly on painters and their works, but also on various art techniques, travel, vacationing, higher education and language study, psychology, national characteristics, and animals. He helped found (1869) and was editor (1869–1894) of *The Portfolio*. He married a Frenchwoman and lived much of the time in France. James reviewed (*North American Review*, Apr 1868) Hamerton's *Contemporary French Painters: An Essay* (1868), beginning with the opinion that French art critics have been better than British ones. As a group, art critics both aid and antagonize, but the public is often "stupid" and hence needs "enlightenment." James mentions John Ruskin* and a few other British art critics, then he praises several French critics, especially Gustave Planche.* Noting that writers tolerate criticism better than painters do, James turns to Hamerton. His book treats twenty painters, all of whom James comments on, stressing Jacques-Louis David, Jean Auguste Dominique Ingres (Hamerton seems unfair to Ingres), Théodore Géricault, Ferdinand Victor Eugène Delacroix* (Hamerton thinks less of him than does James, who calls him "the most interesting of French painters"), Alexandre-Paul Protais (whose military painting James relishes), Rosa Bonheur, Constant Troyon (Hamerton usefully discusses "*tonality*"), Alexandre-Gabriel Decamps* (Hamerton has too little on him), and Jean Léon Gérôme* ("stinted"—James compares this painter's "*heartlessness*" to that of Gustave Flaubert* in literature). James, who parenthetically praises Hamerton's *Painter's Camp in the Highlands, and Thoughts about Art* (1862—Hamerton began his career as a painter), does not hesitate to offer himself as a competent art critic (in this first art-book review), and he questions both Hamerton's inclusions (for example, Horace Vernet) and his exclusions (for example, Thomas Couture and Denis Auguste Marie Raffet). James also reviewed (*Nation*, 3 Feb 1876) Hamerton's *Round My House: Notes of Rural Life in France in Peace and War* (1876), calling its title "trivial" but liking its personal, never egotistical contents: rural life in an unnamed provincial town (James guesses it to be Autun, in Burgundy), neighbors' activities, French thrift and orderliness, class consciousness, servants, women as fashionable or domestic, men in clubs, "matrimonial morals," peasants and the clergy, and Prussians and Giuseppe Garibaldi's soldiers nearby. Joseph Pennell* illustrated Hamerton's *A Summer Voyage on the River Saône* (1897).

Hamilton, Sir Edward Walter (1847–1908). Son of a bishop who knew William Ewart Gladstone,* prime minister of England. Young Hamilton was educated at Eton and Oxford, entered treasury work, and became Gladstone's private secretary (1873–1874, 1880–1885). He did financial rather than administrative work, was an amateur musician, and remained unmarried. In 1886 at the lavish country home of Archibald Philip Primrose, Earl of Rosebery* (later prime minister himself), James met Hamilton, according to whose diary James stated that the person he would most like to see from the epoch of 1760–1830 was George Gordon, Lord Byron.*

Hamilton. In *A Change of Heart*, an unseen guest at Margaret Thorne's birthday party.

Hapgood, Norman (1868–1937). Chicago lawyer, distinguished editor, reformer, drama critic, and author. James in "American Letter" (21 May 1898) welcomes Hapgood's *Literary Statesmen and Others: Essays on Men Seen from a Distance* (1897) as evidence of much-needed criticism, which, however, is more promising than accomplished, since the author, though "informed and urbane," seems to be still "feeling for his perceptions."

Hardman. In "Lady Barbarina," the lawyer of Lord Philip Canterville and his daughter Lady Barbarina. Hardman arranges dowry terms before she marries Dr. Jackson Lemon.

Hardy, Thomas (1840–1928). Distinguished Dorsetshire-born novelist, poet, and dramatist. After a brief career as an architect in London, Hardy returned to his first love, which was writing. He published a short story in 1865, was advised by George Meredith* in 1869 to accentuate plot, and met with success two years later. Hardy presents man's constant struggle against an indifferent universe in a series of novels, which he classified as follows: novels of character and environment, including *Far from the Madding Crowd* (1874), *The Return of the Native* (1878), *The Mayor of Casterbridge* (1886), *Tess of the D'Urbervilles* (1891), and *Jude the Obscure* (1896); romances and fantasies, including *A Pair of Blue Eyes* (1873); and novels of ingenuity, including *The Hand of Ethelberta* (1876). Hardy also published many books of lyrics, a vast epic-drama, *The Dynasts* (1904, 1906, 1908), and a minor Arthurian play. James unfavorably reviewed (*Nation*, 24 Dec 1874) *Far from the Madding Crowd*, beginning with a comparison between its style and that of George Eliot,* particularly with regard to rustic dialogue, and commenting that Hardy uses Eliot's "trick of seeming to humor . . . queer people and look down at them from the heights of analytic omniscience." But he is only clever, with little substance and much "shadow." Humorously suggesting that tales should be limited for a while to fifty pages and novels to two hundred, James regards *Far from the Madding Crowd* as too long for its simple plot, padded with description, diffuse, and out of shape; its author should abide by Aristotelian unities, and with characters and episodes reduced in quantity. He does commend Hardy for his ability to depict meadows, lanes, harvests, and sheep; but he voices dislike of flirtatious, "artificial" Bathsheba Everdene, a heroine of the sort invented by Charles Reade,* whom Hardy imitates here. James was critical of Hardy in letters to Robert Louis Stevenson*: in one (19 Mar 1892), he reports that *Tess of the d'Urbervilles* by "good little Thomas Hardy . . . is chock-full of faults and falsity and yet has a singular beauty and charm"; in another (17 Feb 1893), he comments on "the abomination of the language" and the treatment of " 'sexuality' " in the same novel. James and Hardy had occasional social contact, but Hardy expressed initial dislike of James's vague gaze and ponderous conversation. He was also put off by the allegedly small subject of James's *The Reverberator*. He did, however, read James's book on Nathaniel Hawthorne* with evident pleasure and care. Later, in his literary notebook, he records praise of *The Wings of the Dove* for its "extraordinarily complicated texture of subtle thoughts and minute sensations"; by 1903, he regarded James as the best living novelist, but one to be read only a little at a time. When James received the Order of Merit shortly before his death, Hardy sent him a gracious letter of congratulation and praise. In her two-volume life of Hardy (1928, 1930), his second wife, Florence Emily (née Dugdale) Hardy, said that her husband called James the Polonius of novelists. James's library contained three books by Hardy.

Hare, Augustus John Cuthbert (1834–1903). Popular English traveler and writer of guidebooks to several European countries and cities, including *Days near Rome* (1875), *Cities of Northern and Central Italy* (3 vols., 1876), and *Walks in London* (1878). He also published *Memorials of a Quiet Life* in three volumes (1872–1876) and a six-volume autobiography (1896–1900). James begins a review (*Nation*, 1 Apr 1875) of *Days near Rome* by praising Hare's earlier *Walks in Rome* (1871). In both works, the author combines quotations from other writers with a minimum of his own description, at which he is "agreeable" if "not brilliant." He offers passages from many Latin poets, especially that "most quotable of the ancients," Horace, and from modern "historians and antiquarians," including Ferdinand Gregorovius, whose descriptions illustrate "the deplorable German habit of transforming . . . the definite into the vague." Sadly, Hare's fine book may be responsible for ruining the Abruzzi and the Volscian hills, among many other picturesque nooks, by attracting herds of careless tourists to them. James reviewed (*Nation*, 10 May 1876) Hare's *Cities of Northern and Central Italy*, calling it better than "dry and meagre" Murray and Bädeker guidebooks but less "entertaining" than either *Walks in Rome* or *Days Near Rome*, even though Hare used the same formula of much quotation and little commentary. James mentions the geographical region each volume describes; he voices his pleasure that Hare again tells us about places "rarely visited" but wishes that such "lurking-places of the picturesque" were stressed even more, and Venice and Florence less. This "thorough" work is "an eloquent reminder of the inexhaustible charm and interest of Italy, and of her unequalled claims . . . as the richest museum in the world.'' Hare's introduction praises the ''beauty of detail'' in Italian architecture but wrongly adds that ''fine [Italian] scenery is rare.'' Hare admires ''the Italian character'' and rightly criticizes the rudeness of tourists, but he is ''childish'' to ''sneer'' at the political procedures that have unified Italy. Finally, James reviewed (*Nation*, 20 Jun 1878) *Walks in London*, which is ''entertaining'' but lacks the color of the earlier *Walks in Rome*. Although Hare knows London ''minutely'' and is observant, his ''descriptive powers are . . . meagre'' in *Walks in London*, which seems to be ''perfunctory and done-to-order.'' Still, the work will prove valuable for American tourists, especially since it ''divides . . . walks into districts'': Charing Cross, the Tower, Westminster Abbey, the City, and so on. London's ''daily press and jostle'' discourage ''contemplation,'' except, as Hare notes, on Sundays, during which one can observe ''curious and interesting detail . . . amid the general duskiness and ugliness.'' James comments on various London churches, especially post–1666 ones, and he praises St. Bartholomew the Great, Westminster Abbey, and St. Paul's; then he disagrees with Hare's high opinions of such now-razed Strand palaces as Northumberland House and Temple Bar. James is glad that London, the ''swarthy metropolitan Dulcinea[,] is at last . . . beautifying herself.'' James approves of Hare's use of the word ''frightful'' to describe West End modernizing, then concludes quickly that the present volumes on London, ''the most interesting city in the world,'' are ''full and agreeable.'' James's library contained two books by Hare.

Harland, Henry (1861–1905). Son of a Pennsylvania lawyer, born in New York, graduated from City College there (1880), attended Harvard Divinity School briefly, and then traveled to Rome and Paris (1882–1883). After becoming a law clerk in New York City, he married a musician (1884) and two years later determined to devote his life to writing. Under the pen name of Sidney Luska, he wrote four melodramatic novels based on the lives of German Jews he knew. He was influenced both by the conservative poet and businessman Edmund Clarence Stedman* and by the progressive William Dean Howells,* and accordingly he always confused romance and realism. Harland and his wife went to Paris in 1889 and a year later to London, where they established an informal salon. Harland soon came under the helpful influence of Sir Edmund Wilson Gosse.* Harland cotranslated *Fantasia* (1890) by Matilde Serao* under his own name, and he wrote five more novels, also under his own name, which were still autobiographical and sensational. With his *Mademoiselle Miss* (1893) came his first realistic stories in European settings. As an editor of the Bodley Head (cofounded with John Lane in 1887), he met Aubrey Vincent Beardsley.* The two, with the aid of Arthur Waugh (critic and editor) and Lane, established the *Yellow Book* (1894–1897). Harland was a superb editor, seeking out and rewarding fine contributors. He also wrote stories for the magazine. Collections of his short fiction are found in *Gray Roses* (1895) and *Comedies and Errors*

(1898). His novel *The Cardinal's Box* (1900) was immensely popular. Harland coauthored with his friend Hubert Montague Crackanthorpe* a farce entitled *The Light Sovereign: A Farcical Comedy in Three Acts* (posthumously published in 1917). Crackanthorpe dedicated his *Sentimental Studies and a Set of Village Tales* to Harland in 1895. Harland met James about 1890 probably through Gosse, introduced James to Beardsley, and recruited James to publish in their *Yellow Book*. James was pleased that Harland did not restrict the length of his contributions but soon disliked aspects of the controversial journal. James called Harland "your . . . acute . . . young friend" and "a very clever fellow" in a letter to Howells (17 May [1890]). Later he acidly wrote to Gosse ([1 May 1893]) that the "literary longings" of Harland, with whom he had just chatted in Paris, exceeded his "*faculty*." To William James and his wife, James cockily described Harland as "worshipful" (28 May 1894). It is true that Harland, whose 144 Cromwell Road home was near James's De Vere Gardens* address in London, esteemed James highly, calling him "the supreme prince of short story writers" in an 1897 essay "Concerning the Short Story." Perhaps feeling obliged to reciprocate, James published a flattering review (*Fortnightly Review*, Apr 1898) of Harland's *Comedies and Errors*. Even so, James begins with the generalization that an author is best when he writes about products of his own native soil, and then he avers that Harland is detached in *Comedies and Errors*, sounding no "native note." He does reveal an American sense of Europe. James calls the work Harland's most mature book, in his own well-developed short-story form, which form in general is both "delightful and difficult." It is hard to combine sharpness of incident and foreshortening of complexity, the latter of which Harland manages well. He gives us little plot, unpursued characters, and much suggestiveness—for example, "duration of time," "the lost . . . chance," and "the feeling of the American for . . . Europe." Does Harland go "astray . . . in the very wealth of his memories and the excess . . . of his wit"? May he soon "stop . . . and . . . dig" deeply and become an artistic "citizen of the world." After Harland had endured a painful death from tuberculosis, James wrote to his widow that her husband had lived abundantly, had not missed life. James reports to Gosse (22 Dec 1905), "I have most difficultly written to the poor little woman," and he contrasts himself as an expatriate with Harland, a "*dis-patriate*." James's library contained two books by Harland.

Harriet. In "Georgina's Reasons," Agnes Roy Theory's aunt. Agnes sends gifts to her.

Harris, Frank (1854–1931). Galway-born author, who immigrated to the United States in 1870, where he engaged in varied occupations, and became an American citizen. He went to London, where he became an editor, and was friendly with Sir Max Beerbohm,* George Bernard Shaw,* and Oscar Wilde,* among other writers. He returned to the United States for a time, was pro-German during World War I, and subsequently moved to France. Harris wrote several significant books, but is now remembered mainly for a notorious biography of Wilde (2 vols., 1916) and a sleazy autobiography (3 vols., 1923–1927). James disliked what he had heard of Harris and replied thus to a query from Theodore E. Child* (27 Mar [1888]): "I know Frank Harris not at all—to speak of. He is a queer brutal young adventurer who was once an hotel-waiter . . . in America and has lately married a very rich young woman . . . ''

Harrison, James Albert (1848–1911). Mississippi-born philologist, etymologist, professor, and editor. He studied at the University of Virginia and then (1868–1870) in Europe. Next came a distinguished academic career, at Virginia (from 1895). He pioneered Old-English studies in America and also wrote on black-American English. He vacationed often in Europe, and he amused himself by writing impressionistic travel sketches. His major achievement was a fine edition of the works of Edgar Allan Poe* (17 vols., 1902). James reviewed (*Nation*, 10 Jun 1875) *A Group of Poets and Their Haunts* (1875) by Harrison, railing at once against its high-pitched Southern style and adding that it has more words than substance. Harrison troubled to go to literary haunts but made little of it all, settling instead for the picturesque at any cost. Quoting dreadful examples, James especially deplores the "bad" essay on George Gordon, Lord Byron.* He concludes that Harrison does not support a "redundancy of precept" regarding certain writers with any "grains of example" but does have "a literary gift which ought to be turned to better account."

Harry. In "The Impressions of a Cousin," a man Lizzie Ermine wants Eunice to marry.

Harte, Bret (1836–1902). American local color fiction writer, born in Albany. He went to California in 1854 and soon began a literary career, dazzling at first but then faltering badly. He contributed poems and short fiction to the *Golden Era* and the *Californian* and to the *Overland Monthly*, which he edited (1868–1870). He returned in triumph to New York (1871–1878), where he continued to write, often for the *Atlantic Monthly*, until he went abroad as American consul in Prussia (1878–1880) and then in Scotland (1880–1885). Subsequently, he fizzled as a hack writer in London, rather imitating his former fresh work, until his death. His best titles are "The Luck of Roaring Camp" (1868), "The Outcasts of Poker Flat" (1869), "Tennessee's Partner" (1869), and "The Heathen Chinee" (1870). He was a friend of Mark Twain,* who turned against him in disgust, and John Milton Hay,* who remained loyal in spite of Harte's unworthy conduct. James met Harte at the home of William Dean Howells* and his wife, in Boston, in 1871. In "American Letter" (30 Apr 1898), James comments that Harte has made himself the head of a school of Western writers but wonders wryly what Harte himself has learned in this school. James does not think much of Harte's *Tales of Trail and Town* (1898).

Harvey, George Brinton McClellan (1864–1928). Highly successful editor and political journalist, born in Vermont. Rich by fortunate investments, he bought and edited the *North American Review* (1899–1926), refinanced and was president of Harper and Brothers, publishers (1900–1915), and edited *Harper's Weekly* (1901–1913). He was active in national politics behind the scenes, and he was ambassador to England (1921–1923). He wrote *Women* (1908), *The Power of Tolerance, and Other Speeches* (1911), and a biography of Henry Clay Frick (1928). Through publishing in the *North American Review* and through Harpers, James had professional contacts with Harvey, who also handled both William Dean Howells* and Mark Twain.* When James began his 1904–1905 American tour, the travel book resulting from which was to be published by Harvey, it was to his New Jersey "villa" at Deal Beach that James was immediately taken (September 1904). He wrote up his drive along the Jersey shore in the first chapter of *The American Scene*. When Harvey planned a lavish literary dinner for his illustrious visitor, James by letter (21 Oct 1904) begged him not to give it: "[S]uch an occasion would have for me . . . unmitigated terrors and torments." Harvey hosted it anyway for James, at the Metropolitan Club in New York on 8 December 1904, with thirty guests, including Hamlin Garland,* George Washburn Smalley,* Booth Tarkington,* and Mark Twain.

Harvey, Sir (Henry) Paul (1869–1948). Diplomat, scholar, and editor. Paul Harvey was educated at New College, Oxford, and then became private secretary to the Marquess of Lansdowne (secretary of state for war, 1895–1900), then delegate to conferences on Greek finance (1903) and Macedonian finance (1905), financial advisor to the Egyptian government (1907–1912, 1919–1920), and expert in important British governmental positions during World War I. He compiled *The Oxford Companion to English Literature* (1932) and *The Oxford Companion to Classical Literature* (1937), and he worked assiduously on *The Oxford Companion to French Literature* (completed by Janet E. Haseltine, 1959) until his death. Harvey was the natural son of Edward de Triqueti, the brother of Blanche de Triqueti Childe, and, when orphaned, he was adopted by her and her husband Edward Lee Childe,* with the result that much of his youth was spent in France. In 1876 James met Harvey at the Childes' summer home in Varennes, France, and in a letter to his mother (24 Aug [1876]) described the boy as "a lovely infant of about six years," with delightful eyelashes, and "a source of much delectation to me." James admired Harvey in later years, socialized with him, and wrote to him affectionately.

Harvey, Mrs. In "Broken Wings," unsuccessful painter Stuart Straith's unsuccessful writer friend.

Hatch, C. P. In *The American*, one of Christopher Newman's minor American friends in Paris.

Hatch, Dr. In *The Ivory Tower*, Frank B. Betterman's physician, along with Dr. Root.

Hathaway, Mr. and Mrs. In "Europe," the couple who take Jane Rimmle to Europe.

Hauff. In "Master Eustace," Eustace Garnyer's tutor.

Haven, Gilbert (1821–1880). Massachusetts-born teacher, fiery preacher, abolitionist, and Civil War chaplain (1861), editor, and Methodist Episcopal bishop. He endangered himself in Georgia because of his pro-black sermons and activities there. He visited Mexico (1873) on a church mission and later, for the same purpose, went to Liberia (1876), where he contracted malaria. His many publications are usually journalistic in nature and concern practical theology and politics. Reviewing (*Nation*, 8 Jul 1875) Haven's *Our Next-Door Neighbor: A Winter in Mexico* (1875), James says that Haven takes us on "an interesting journey but . . . is an insufferable travelling-companion." Haven's comments on the mission are "crude . . . scribbling," too long, and often on irrelevant topics, and are presented in a "bigoted, flippant, conceited" tone. Haven is observant and is aware of the beauty of Mexican landscapes, but he is complacent and totally ignorant of "Mexican society and manners" and offers an "ill-made book" here.

Hawley, Jack. In "The Real Thing," the painter narrator's highly critical but unproductive artist friend.

Hawthorne, Julian (1846–1934). The son of Nathaniel Hawthorne* and Sophia Peabody Hawthorne. He lived with his parents in Liverpool and Italy, then attended the Sanborn School in Concord, Massachusetts, with James's younger brothers. He went to Harvard (1863–1867), where he was a fine athlete but left without a degree. Having studied in Germany, he became a civil engineer (1870); after working on the New York docks for a year, he began a writing career. He moved to London (1874–1882) and became a critic, journalist, and story writer. He returned to America, where he was a feature writer, war correspondent, a literary and sports editor for many newspapers, and a contributor to numerous magazines. He wrote poems, stories, and more than fifty books, including novels, biographies of his parents and their associates (1884, 1903), and his memoirs. He was a colorful personality and was a close friend of politicians, literary figures, and artists of his era, including Ralph Waldo Emerson* and his circle, Charles Dickens,* Herman Melville, James Abbott McNeill Whistler,* and Dame Ellen Terry.* Hawthorne was tried in New York City (1912–1913) for fraudulently enticing the public to invest in a worthless Canadian gold mine; he was convicted (1913), sentenced to one year, and served time in the Atlanta penitentiary. Married twice, he had, by his first wife, seven children. James met

Hawthorne when the latter and James's younger brothers Garth and Bob were pupils together at the Sanborn School. Once Hawthorne had established a British residence, he and James met again, as fellow guests in distinguished homes, including that of Lord Houghton.* James reviewed three of Julian Hawthorne's books. He reviewed (*Atlantic Monthly*, Dec 1874) *Idolatry: A Romance* (1874), beginning with remarks about the likelihood that the son of a genius will be criticized harshly for his own accomplishments. James then calls Hawthorne's first novel, *Bressant* (1873), "valueless," even though he likes its subject, "the conflict between the love in which the spirit, and the love in which sense is uppermost." But the work has "faults of taste and execution." And now here comes *Idolatry*, with the same "arabesques and grotesques of thought" with which Hawthorne's imaginative father loved to play. But this novel has a "strange," not wholly comprehensible plot, and its "fairy-tale" quality is neither entertaining nor meaningful. James simply does not know what the allegory of this work means. "Who is the idol and who is the idolizer?" he asks. Still, Hawthorne has talent and imagination, and he writes with "vigor and energy." Next James reviewed (*Nation*, 30 Mar 1876) Hawthorne's *Saxon Studies* (1876). Again, the author is vigorous, but he is immature and has adopted the wrong tone. He is "acrimonious" and "unwholesome," shows his aversion to Dresden, and says that his Saxons "are . . . ignoble and abominable." Needing to provide examples, unobservant Hawthorne instead discusses indoor German ventilation and the harshness of German women's work, never "the theatre, literature, the press, the arts" in Germany. Further, his humor is "acrid and stingy." The book must be regarded as "trivial and . . . puerile." Finally, James reviewed (*Nation*, 21 Jun 1877) *Garth* (1877), calling this novel "sophomorical." Though it does not show Nathaniel Hawthorne's "profundity or delicacy," it does have his "symbolisms and fanciful analogies." James discusses its tangled plot— about a house built upon a bloody wrong expiated by its "future inhabitants." James analyzes Garth Urmson, the titular hero of *Garth*, who is a curious combination of scowling brutality and artistic aspirations, then his "wicked uncle," and a few other stereotypical characters. Trying to end with a compliment, James notes Hawthorne's powerful imagination. In spite of these adverse reviews, James in 1878 wrote to Hawthorne for permission to visit him in Hastings, England, where later the two walked along the beach and discussed James's projected book on Nathaniel Hawthorne, which Julian later said James was reluctant to write. At this time, James wrote to his brother William (4 Mar [1879]) that Julian Hawthorne," though "personally attractive and likeable," was not "cultivated or in any way illuminated." Next, James wrote to his father (11 Jan 1880) that Hawthorne's recent *Spectator* review of *Confidence* is "characteristically wrong-headed and crude." In October 1886 Hawthorne published gossipy items from an informal interview which he had had with James Russell Lowell* (about British royalty, politics, and writers). Not only was Lowell embarrassed, but James was outraged at what he called in his *Notebooks* (17 Nov 1887) a "beastly and blackguardly betrayal." Still, James and Hawthorne socialized once again, when James visited California in 1905. The two were basically uncongenial; one was a romancer and the other, a realist. James may have used Hawthorne as a model for George P. Flack, the opportunistic journalist in *The Reverberator*.

Hawthorne, Nathaniel (1804–1864). Famous American novelist and short-story writer, born in Salem, Massachusetts. His mother was widowed when Hawthorne was only four years old. Hawthorne had a lonely childhood, read a great deal, and attended Bowdoin College in Maine (1821–1825) with classmates Franklin Pierce and Henry Wadsworth Longfellow.* After graduation, Hawthorne spent about a dozen years in seclusion in his mother's home, where he wrote allegorical and historical pieces much concerned with the Puritanism of old New England. Hawthorne also did some editing, worked (1839–1841) in the Boston custom house, lived (1841) at Brook Farm (an experimental transcendental and socialistic commune near Boston), and then in 1842 married Sophia Peabody, sister of Elizabeth Palmer Peabody,* editor and friend of Ralph Waldo Emerson,* Henry David Thoreau, and other transcendentalists. The Hawthornes had three children, including Julian Hawthorne,* the novelist and journalist, and Rose Hawthorne, not only the wife of George Parsons Lathrop* but also later Mother Alphonsa, the founder of a Catholic sisterhood to care for victims of incurable cancer. After employment in the Salem custom house (1846–1849), Nathaniel Hawthorne enjoyed a burst of fictional production, partly written in the Berkshires near his friend and neighbor Herman Melville. Next Hawthorne, who had written the campaign biography of President Pierce (1852), took his family to Liverpool, England, where he served as U.S. consul (1853–1857). After two years in Italy, the Hawthornes went home again to Concord (1860), where Hawthorne spent his last years in much anguish because of the Civil War and also his failing literary powers. Hawthorne's novels are *Fanshawe* (1828), *The Scarlet Letter* (1850), *The House of the Seven Gables* (1851), *The Blithedale Romance* (1852), and *The Marble Faun* (1860). His short-story collections are *Twice-Told Tales* (1837, 1842), *Mosses from an Old Manse* (1846), and *The Snow-Image and Other Twice-Told Tales* (1851). His various notebooks and also several fictional fragments were posthumously published. In long fiction and short—regularly employing ambiguity, pessimistic irony, gothic allegory, and romantic symbolism—Hawthorne was concerned with the spiritual magnificence, intolerance, and decadence of historical New England. Along with Edgar Allan Poe* and Melville, both of whom appreciated his genius, Hawthorne added unique qualities to the American short story. Rather eerily, James began to publish fiction the year Hawthorne died. The two never met, but James knew Julian Hawthorne, first in Concord, later in England, and finally in California. James patronizingly reviewed (*Nation*, 14 Mar 1872) the posthumous *Passages from the French and Italian Note-Books of Nathaniel Hawthorne* (1872), half objecting at the outset to the violation of their reclusive author's privacy and adding his belief that the notebooks "throw but little light on his [Hawthorne's] personal feelings, and even less on his genius.'' They do show that Hawthorne, while seeming leisurely, was all the while feeding his magical writing talent. James prefers Hawthorne's English notebooks to his Italian ones. Hawthorne remained too ''detached . . . from Continental life.'' Even Paris ''said but little to him.'' His entries show that he was not ''either a melancholy or a morbid genius.'' Although he was generally a poor judge of Italian art, he occasionally ''surprise[s] you by some extremely happy 'hit.' '' James likes best the minuteness and vividness with which Hawthorne etches his trips from Rome to Florence and back. James suggests that Hawthorne was exposed to ''European influences'' too ''late in life.'' James's major work on Hawthorne was his initially controversial, now highly regarded *Hawthorne*, for the English Men of Letters series, edited by Viscount John Morley* and published in London by Macmillan, 1879. The study is divided into seven chapters: ''Early Years,'' ''Early Manhood,'' ''Early Writings,'' ''Brook Farm and Concord,'' ''The Three American Novels,'' ''England and Italy,'' and ''Last Years.'' From the outset, James not only explicitly demeans both the cultural milieu of Hawthorne's New England and Hawthorne's nonrealistic romances, but also implicitly suggests that James himself is doing and will continue to do better because of his European advantages and the advent of literary realism. James says that he will write an essay on, rather than a biography of, an author concerning whom information is limited (he cites the 1876 book by George Parsons Lathrop on his father-in-law Hawthorne) and whose life was ''simple . . . '' Yet his subject ''is the most valuable example of the American genius.'' Hawthorne proves the ''valuable moral . . . that the flower of art blooms only where the soil is deep, that it takes a great deal of history to produce a little literature, that it needs a complex social machinery to set a writer in motion.'' His pages emit ''[t]he cold, bright air of New England.'' James sketches Hawthorne's life, stressing his witch-hunting great-great-grandfather Judge John Hathorne, calling Salem ''quiet[,] provincial,'' and defining Bowdoin College as ''honorable, but not . . . impressive.'' His first dozen years after college had ''a . . . peculiar dreariness.'' His early notebooks show ''shyness,'' but no ''gloom'' or intellectual perplexity (or even any special ''development''). They do record much trivial observation by our ''romancer.'' James has fun writing about Hawthorne's editorial work for various magazines, some of which was marred by ''frightful'' woodcuts. Even after *Twice-Told Tales* brought him ''recognition,'' Hawthorne lacked money. Furthermore, *The Scarlet Letter* earned him mainly ''fame,'' and continued ''indolence'' prevented his thereafter becoming ''an abundant producer.'' His ''diaries'' show his constricted ambiance and imply what was missing: ''No State, in the European sense of the word, and indeed barely a specific national name. No sovereign, no court, no personal loyalty, no aristocracy, no church, no clergy, no army, no diplomatic service, no country gentlemen, no palaces, no castles, nor manors, nor old country-houses, nor parsonages, nor thatched cottages nor ivied ruins; no cathedrals, nor abbeys, nor little Norman churches; no great Universities nor public schools—no Oxford, nor Eton, nor Harrow; no literature, no novels, no museums, no pictures, no political society, no sporting class—no Epsom nor Ascot!'' The notebooks do suggest that Hawthorne read much, but they betray a ''not too cultivated . . . style.'' The man ''relish[ed] . . . the commoner stuff of human nature,'' showing this in minor fictional characters (for example, Uncle Venner in *The House of the Seven Gables*). James almost envies Hawthorne's first readers because of the freshness and newness of ''these delicate, dusky flowers in the blossomless garden of American journalism.'' James classes the early works as allegory and fantasy, New English history, and sketches of actualities. He quotes from ''Young Goodman Brown'' (later calling it ''magnificent'') but avoids discussing any allegory—''quite one of the lighter exercises of the imagination''—suggested by it. He then brings in Poe, mainly to define his critical ''judgments'' as ''pretentious, spiteful, vulgar.'' James calls Hawthorne's historical tales ''admirable.'' He next discusses the '' 'thralldom' '' of Hawthorne's unfortunate Boston custom-house work and then his brief time at Brook Farm, that ''little industrial and intellectual association.'' Hawthorne was motivated to join by economic rather than transcendental considerations, but a good result was *The Blithedale Romance*, whose narrator (Miles Coverdale) may be compared to Hawthorne and whose vivid character of Zenobia (based on Margaret Fuller) is superb. In a detailed aside, James calls transcendentalism a unique product of New England soil ''gently raked and refreshed by an imported culture.'' Once he married, Hawthorne moved to Concord, which James calls an ''ancient village'' redolent of the American Revolution. One Concord neighbor was Henry David Thoreau—''worse than provincial . . . parochial''—who James says displays a ''genius'' in *Walden*, if ''a slim and crooked one.'' Thoreau ''was Emerson's independent moral man made flesh.'' Then James notes that Hawthorne, who ''catlike . . . [could] see . . . in the dark,'' better judged that ''spiritual sun-worshipper'' Ralph Waldo Emerson. Turning to Hawthorne's three ''American novels,'' James calls the custom-house ''prologue'' of *The Scarlet Letter* ''delightful'' and ''perfect.'' He quotes the enthusiasm of James Thomas Fields,* Hawthorne's publisher, with regard to the novel, then suggests that its ''consistently gloomy'' tone derived from the ''somber mood'' induced by the author's circumstances, but then adds that it is ''the finest piece of imaginative writing yet put forth in the country.'' It is not a love story, but a story of torment and a villain's ''infernally ingenious'' plan for ''satisfaction.'' The novel ''is full of the moral presence of . . . Puritanism.'' James laments the lack of realism and the presence of too much ''superficial symbolism'' in *The Scarlet Letter*, and he compares it rather unfavorably to the 1822 novel *Adam Blair* by John Gibson Lockhart,* also about an adulterous minister. Still, *The Scarlet Letter* is ''original and complete,'' hence beautiful and harmonious, and of ''inexhaustible charm and mystery.'' By comparison, Hawthorne's later works have ''a touch of mannerism.'' Hawthorne moved to Lenox, Massachusetts, in the Berkshires, and there wrote *The House of the Seven Gables*, ''a rich, delightful, imaginative work''; ''not so rounded and complete as *The Scarlet Letter*,'' it has ''a greater richness and density of detail.'' Though set in almost "contemporary American life," it is not realistic. The "facts" of its plot, which James presents, exist for their "symbolic . . . application." He calls Hepzibah Pyncheon "a masterly picture . . . rather than a dramatic exhibition." Her brother Clifford Pyncheon is "more remarkable . . . though . . . not so vividly depicted." James praises Hawthorne for his "charming . . . manner" in offering Phoebe Pyncheon but adds that he "bestowed most pains" on that "full-blown . . . Pharisee," Judge Pyncheon. James opines that Holgrave seems mainly a "national type" and that Hawthorne ought to have "match[ed]" this "strenuous radical" with "a lusty conservative." But he wanted not to contrast old and new societies, rather to show "the shrinkage and extinction of a family." After pausing to recall his delight when as a boy he read Hawthorne's books for children, James then turns to *The Blithedale Romance*, written in West Newton, Massachusetts. The book is "charming," comparatively light, bright, and lively, though its ending is "tragical." The "spectator" narrator, a bit of a cynical skeptic, contrasts splendidly with the reformer, "barbarous[,] fanatic" Hollingsworth. But picturesque Zenobia is "[t]he finest thing" in the book and the closest its author ever came to creating a "complete . . . *person*," one both gifted and weak. Priscilla is handled "exquisite[ly]." James wittily discusses Hawthorne's biography of Pierce, then underlines the contrast between Hawthorne's "village life" and his European adventures which Pierce's election made possible. James patronizingly opines that we should not mistake "the simplicity of inexperience" revealed in Hawthorne's non-American notebooks for any long-lasting youth in their author. From his English jottings came *Our Old Home* (1863), which James says Hawthorne rightly judged to be "decidedly . . . light" though written with an admirable touch and presenting a land foreign to its author with charm and affection—which is more than many travelers (several of whom James names) can say in defense of their books on America. James discusses Hawthorne's "mistrust and suspicion" of foreign society and his typical American "self-conscious[ness]," but then he quotes many enjoyable descriptive passages. He turns to Hawthorne's time in Italy, full of "perfunctory" sight-seeing, old-fashioned responses, grievous discomforts, and finally "weariness." Out of it all came *The Marble Faun*, weaker than the American novels because it was cast in "a country which he [Hawthorne] knew only superficially." Though "a charming romance with intrinsic [structural] weaknesses," *The Marble Faun* concentrates efficiently on its four main characters. Donatello remains "rather vague and impalpable." The contrast between the two women is fine, but James deplores "the element of the unreal" in the novel and its faulty "art of narration." Toward the end of *Hawthorne*, James discusses Hawthorne's insistence on stating his constant admiration of Franklin Pierce and then Hawthorne's essay occasioned by his visit to Washington, D.C., during the Civil War—written with "delicate, sportive feeling," "consummate grace," "just appreciable irony," and sensible tolerance. James regards the posthumous fragment *Septimius Felton* (1872) as slight, weak, and "moonshiny," but he likes the beginning of the fragment *The Dolliver Romance* (1876). Finally he summarizes Hawthorne's last months and concludes that the man "was a beautiful, natural, original genius," whose life was "pure" and "simple" and whose works mix "the spontaneity of imagination with a haunting care for moral problems." As for American criticism of his monograph, James wrote to Thomas Sergeant Perry* (22 Feb [1880]) thus: "The hubbub produced by my poor little *Hawthorne* is most ridiculous. . . . The vulgarity, ignorance, rabid vanity and general idiocy . . . is truly incredible." When William Dean Howells* included adverse comments in his review of the study, James replied (31 Jan [1880]) that his "little book was a tolerably deliberate and meditated performance," and added, "I should be prepared to do battle for most of the convictions expressed"—and then briefly did just that. To Charles Eliot Norton* (31 Mar [1880]), James wrote that "the poor little *Hawthorne*" has created "a very big tempest in a very small tea-pot." (Incidentally, the publishers, who did not pay James for American profits, were pleased enough with his *Hawthorne* to ask him, without success, to write a book on Charles Dickens* for the same series.) On two other occasions, James specifically wrote on Hawthorne. He published an essay on Hawthorne for Volume XII of the *Library of the World's Best Literature Ancient and Modern* (New York: Peale and Hill, 1897), edited by Charles Dudley Warner.* It begins with a summary of Hawthorne's life and production and the remark that his inspiration was mainly "the latent romance of New England." Hawthorne treated the darker side of Puritanism. For him things became symbols, stories parables, and appearances covers. James classifies Hawthorne's works and now calls *The Scarlet Letter* "an ineffaceable image in the portrait gallery . . . of literature." He calls attention to its triangle plot, "bathed in . . . moonshiny light, and . . . neglecting the usual sources of emotion." He finds the relations between the two men "faintly . . . figured"; the two females, though partly inactive, are responsible for "vivify[ing] the work." James says that *The House of the Seven Gables* is almost "a novel of manners" and has much varied charm. The ghostly house has ghostly occupants, with "sorrows and atonements." The story idea regarding heredity may be "a trifle thin and a trifle obvious," but Hawthorne's "art . . . is exquisite," and the Judge is especially solid. As for *The Blithedale Romance*, its mild satire is valuable because it was inspired by a real socialistic experiment. James discusses Coverdale ("fitful" and lazy, like his creator when at Brook Farm), and then Hollingsworth and Zenobia (both admirably imaged). The realistic guidebook element in *The Marble Faun* is at odds with its "mystical and mythical" elements. Miriam's villainous model is portrayed with too much "obscurity." Being humanized by a crime makes Donatello a type. James likes Hilda, especially when she is at the confessional. He comments on *Our Old Home*, calling it a "mixture of sensibility and reluctance," since England both "delight[ed]" him and "rubbed him . . . the wrong way." Hawthorne, old in his early years, turned youthful later; but he was always aloof. He sensed human abysses oftener than he sounded and reported on them; he "dipp[ed] . . . into the moral world without being . . . a moralist." He was a bright, kind cynic. Finally, on 10 June 1904 from Rye James wrote a letter (published in *The Proceedings in Com-*

memoration of the One Hundredth Anniversary of the Birth of Nathaniel Hawthorne, Salem: Essex Institute, 1904 [1905]) declining to participate in the Salem celebration of the centenary of Hawthorne's birth but using the occasion to praise the novelist once more. James says that from a distance he endorses the ceremony with enthusiasm and almost with envy. He can see Hawthorne as a youth in Salem, walking now "familiar streets" and slowly rendering himself worthy of this "recognition." He related himself to his environment romantically. His leading works sound "the real as distinguished from the artificial romantic note," best in *The House of the Seven Gables*. *The Blithedale Romance* displays "artistic economy," making the real "rich and strange" by tonal devices. Hawthorne has become a classic, since time has accorded his finest writings "final value," because of their great influence. Amid journalistic trumpets, he is a still-heard violin, because he developed his feeling and his form from within. In *Notes of a Son and Brother*, James recalls his childhood and indeed lifelong love of the writings of Hawthorne, whose death, he says, "made me positively and loyally cry." Hawthorne's influence on James is enormous. Although he deplored Hawthorne's romanticism, provinciality, New England joylessness, timidity in Italy, and pervasive skepticism, James derived from this major American influence some of his own psychological seriousness, respect for the sanctity of the individual, dislike of materialism, and use of several character and action types— for example, aloof observer, domineering father, "fall" in garden, and portrait explication. Thus, Rowland Mallet in *Roderick Hudson* and the narrator of *The Sacred Fount* may derive in part from Coverdale in Hawthorne's *The Blithedale Romance*, James's "The Story of a Masterpiece" from Hawthorne's "The Prophetic Pictures," elements in James's *The Europeans* and *The Bostonians* from Hawthorne's various depictions of the old New England mind, and James's allegorical "Benvolio" from Hawthorne in general. Many other examples could be offered. James's library contained four books by Hawthorne.

Hay, John Milton (1838–1905). Indiana-born statesman, journalist, poet, travel and short-story writer, novelist, and biographer. He graduated from Brown University (M.A., 1858), studied law in Illinois, met and campaigned for Abraham Lincoln, was his assistant private secretary (under his private secretary John George Nicolay) in the White House (1861–1865), and was sent with the rank of major on sensitive missions with the Union Army (1864–1865). After the Civil War, Hay served in important diplomatic posts in Paris (1865–1867), Vienna (1867–1868), and Madrid (1869–1870). He did editorial work with Horace Greeley and Whitelaw Reid* on the New York *Tribune* (1870–1875, 1881). In 1874 Hay married Clara Stone, daughter of a wealthy railroad magnate in Cleveland, resided there a few years (1875–1879), then moved to Washington, D.C., living in a mansion adjoining that of Henry Adams* and his wife. Hay served President Rutherford B. Hayes as assistant secretary of state (1879–1881), President William McKinley as ambassador to England (1897–1898, during which time he was valuably assisted by James's friend Henry White*) and as secretary of state (1898–1901), and President Theodore Roosevelt* as secretary of state (1901–1905). Hay formulated the Open Door Policy in China (1900) and negotiated the first Panama Canal treaties (1900–1903). Hay's varied literary writings include *Pike County Ballads* (1871), *Castilian Days* (1871, travel essays), *The Bread-Winners* (1884, anonymous antilabor novel), *Poems* (1890), and *Abraham Lincoln: A History* (with Nicolay, 10 vols., 1890). He and Nicolay also edited Lincoln's works (2 vols., 1894; 12 vols., 1905). Posthumous publications include Hay's addresses (1906) and letters (1908 and later). Hay's closest literary friends were Adams, William Dean Howells,* Clarence King,* George Washburn Smalley,* Mark Twain,* Constance Fenimore Woolson,* and James. Hay also socialized with many Britishers whom James knew, for one example among many, Sir John Forbes Clark* of Tillypronie, Scotland. James met Hay early in 1875, perhaps through Howells, shortly before James was about to return to Europe and sought an assignment as Paris literary correspondent for the *Tribune*. Hay frequently vacationed abroad and often saw James in England. Hay and his wife gave lavish parties in London, at which James was always a welcome guest. James, Hay, and Howells attended a big September 1882 banquet for American writers in London given by Boston publisher James Ripley Osgood.* James and Hay went separately over to France; after James had concluded his research for *A Little Tour in France*, they met again in Paris in November. Woolson wrote to James the following May that Hay had told her he admired James and his writings but that James plainly cared neither for him nor for his writings. In truth, James had written Howells earlier (27 Nov [1882]) to praise Hay; however, he also saw that, although Hay had talent, he was too rich, sporadically lazy, and self-deprecating. James wrote to Richard Watson Gilder* (1 Feb [1884]) that "the *Breadwinners* (which I have received but not yet read— I mean to) is spoken of with London assurance as J. Hay's." (Gilder accepted, and evidently censored, Hay's novel for serial publication in the *Century* [August 1883 through January 1884] before it appeared as a book.) James and Hay corresponded on the occasion of the death of Woolson, whose January 1894 burial in Rome Hay handled. When Hay was ambassador to England, James saw him more frequently. When Hay and Adams invited James to join their party on a Nile River trip (for early 1898), he was pleased but declined. In January 1905, James, while in the United States on the tour which resulted in *The American Scene*, had dinner at the White House with President Roosevelt, Hay, and many others. Although James in later years admired Hay as a statesman, he did not think highly of most of Hay's literary works. He disliked the anonymous novel *The Bread-Winners* and lumped it with other contemporary bestsellers which struck him as meretricious, writing to Thomas Sergeant Perry* (6 Mar [1884]) thus: "[W]hen I look to the land you live in, I find 'To Leeward' [by Francis Marion Crawford*] in its 12th edition, the *Breadwinners* (the cleverness of which I don't contest) making a revolution, & the journals earnestly discussing *Newport* [by George Parsons Lathrop*]. Je suis bien seul! It's a filthy world." Did James know that Hay was the author of *The Bread-Winners*? James wrote to his sister Alice (3 May [1884]): "Have you read the 'Breadwinners,' which I am sure is his?" In 1890 he wrote to say that he would be happy to have a copy of Hay's poems but evidently failed to comment on them. He called Hay's *Lincoln* epical with its gallery of democratic pictures; still he managed to complain that it does not provide specific battle dates. After Hay's death, James graciously wrote to his widow (24 Dec 1905) that Hay to him was "a very admirable & special friend & appreciator, an exquisite & faithful critic, who had been so from far back."

Haycock, Lord and Lady. In *The Portrait of a Lady*, Lord Warburton's brother-in-law and sister.

Hayes, Mr. and Mrs. B. D. In "The Birthplace," a rich, attractive American couple who visit The Birthplace twice and note changes in the quality of Morris Gedge's lectures there. The two offer moral support to Gedge when he is worried.

Hayward, Abraham (1801–1884). Learned British barrister (from1832,) founder (1828) and editor (1828–1844) of *Law Magazine*, and miscellaneous writer— for example, on the art of dining, handwriting as evidence, the Crimean War, aspects of law (property, criminal, and marriage), whist, and travel. He also translated from the German, edited much eighteenth-century and early nineteenth-century English literary material, wrote biographical and critical essays, was a minor poet, and maintained a notable correspondence. James favorably reviewed (*Nation*, 26 Dec 1878) Hayward's *Selected Essays* (2 vols., 1878), expressing not only the wish that the author were better known but also pleasure that selections from his five previous volumes of essays are available here. James reports that Hayward, a fine London "talker and . . . *raconteur*," has a "fund of anecdote and illustration" gathered from a lifetime of important friendships. His essays contain old-fashioned, "wholesome" criticism of writers, politicians, "great British families," and "English and French manners and morals." James especially praises the chapters on Sydney Smith, Samuel Rogers, Maria Edgeworth,* and Hippolyte Taine.*

Headway. In "The Siege of London," Nancy's most recent husband.

Headway, Nancy Grenville Beck. In "The Siege of London," the oft-wed American who is the object of Sir Arthur Demesne's affections and his mother's suspicions. Nancy marries Sir Arthur.

Heidenmauer, Herman. In "Collaboration," a German musical composer. He and his writer friend Félix Vendemer collaborate on an opera.

Heinemann, William (1863–1910). Surrey-born British publisher of fiction, drama, and translations. After studying music in England and Germany, he worked for an English publisher. He later founded his own firm (1890) and soon began to publish such writers as Sir Max Beerbohm,* Joseph Conrad,* Rudyard Kipling,* Sir Arthur Wing Pinero,* Robert Louis Stevenson,* and Herbert George Wells,* as well as James. Sir Edmund Wilson Gosse* edited Heinemann's International Library of translations of works in several European languages. Heinemann commissioned translations of Feodor Dostoevski, Henrik Johan Ibsen,* Count Leo Nikolayevich Tolstoy,* and Ivan Sergeyevich Turgenev*; he also published the famous Loeb Classical Library. Heinemann was responsible for the first London publication of many books by James. Charles Wolcott Balestier* was Heinemann's young American business partner, and the two founded an inexpensive "English Library" (of books by British and American authors) in competition on the Continent with Christian Bernhard Tauchnitz.* When Balestier died in Dresden, Germany, in 1891, Heinemann's family handled the funeral arrangements, and James and Heinemann went together from London to attend. James and Heinemann, among a few others, attended the marriage of Kipling and Balestier's sister in 1892. By 1894 James and Heinemann were sharing a growing enthusiasm for Ibsen, especially acute in Heinemann's case since the publisher was in love with the Ibsen devotee Elizabeth Robins.* In 1900 James disputed with Heinemann over his right to have James Brand Pinker* as his literary agent. James's library contained two books by Heinemann.

Helps, Sir Arthur (1813–1875). Voluminous writer, born in Surrey, and educated at Eton and Trinity College, Cambridge. He became a privy-council clerk in London, and he was employed in the 1860s by Queen Victoria as a personal editor for both her writings and those of Prince Albert. Helps was also a dramatist, historian, novelist, and memoirist, whose works were published in thirty-eight volumes (1835–1884). In an amusing letter from London to his father (10 May [1869]), James explains how he did not "thrust . . . myself into my finery and travel . . . faraway to Kensington" to grin at Helps, his father's friend and now a guest of Charles Eliot Norton.* Some time later, James did comment on Helps's *Social Pressure* (1875) in a brief, neutral review (*Nation*, 18 Mar 1875), calling it "not very deep, but . . . very clear and very sound" and mentioning that it treats with dramatic humor such topics as governmental efficiency and paternalism, the right size of cities, and the ethics of ridicule, publicity, and reminiscence. In *Notes of a Son and Brother*, James quotes from an 1856 letter from his father to Ralph Waldo Emerson* to the effect that Helps is "an amiable kindly little man with friendly offers," who has a "vast" imagination but "narrow" sympathy.

Henley, William Ernest (1849–1903). British poet, critic, playwright, and editor. Tuberculosis caused him to have a foot amputated. While in an Edinburgh hospital (1874), he sent poems to the *Cornhill Magazine*. They were accepted by Sir Leslie Stephen,* the editor, who with Robert Louis Stevenson* visited Henley. He moved to London (1877) to start a career notable for his editing of the *National Observer* and the *New Review*. This work helped Joseph Conrad,* Rudyard Kipling,* and Herbert George Wells,* among others. Henley is remembered for several vigorous poems (often oddly metered), including "Invictus." His criticism is contained in *Views and Reviews* (1890). James knew Henley professionally; by letter, they exchanged opinions concerning various writers. In his diary, Arthur Christopher Benson* records that James regarded Henley as rude, loud, and unrestrained. James's library contained two books by Henley.

Henning, Millicent. In *The Princess Casamassima*, Hyacinth Robinson's sensual, undependable girlfriend, who finally prefers Captain Godfrey Sholto.

Henning, Mrs. In *The Princess Casamassima*, Millicent Henning's deceased mother. Hyacinth Robinson as a child knew her in the neighborhood.

"Henry James Writes of Refugees in England." Early (1915) title of "Refugees in Chelsea" (1919).

The Henry James Year Book (Boston: Badger, 1911). A charming book of selections from James's writings, managed by Evelyn Garnaut Smalley, the daughter of James's friend George Washburn Smalley.* The quotations, from two to thirty lines or so each, are dated for every day of the year; in addition, a quotation introduces each month. The selections are mostly from James's fiction but also include some passages from his critical and travel writings. In a tiny preface, Evelyn Smalley says that it was harder to omit than to make choices, and she thanks James for his aid. He provided an introductory letter (16 June 1910) to vouchsafe his "earnest approval" of Miss Smalley's plan and to praise her "gracious labour" as "friendly and discriminating." William Dean Howells* added a long note to the public commending the whole effort.

"Henry James's First Interview." Interview, which James granted to Preston Lockwood but wrote almost entirely himself. It was published in the New York *Times Magazine* (21 Mar 1915, with the subtitle "Noted Critic and Novelist Breaks His Rule of Years to Tell of the Good Work of the American Ambulance Corps"). James begins by stating his intention to resist the help of any "suggestive young gentleman with a notebook," then adds that he has agreed to the interview only because it will help American college men doing duty as ambulance drivers in France. He supports them because he is chairman of the American Volunteer Ambulance Corps, a position he holds only because he is the oldest American who is here and who is interested in the corps, the activities of which should strengthen Anglo-American ties. He comments on the Allied soldiers' motives: helping others, repelling the Germans, and seeking adventure. He rejoices in seeing "the character of this decent and dauntless [British] people,'' as it is revealed in wartime. James pauses, then says that the war is so hideous that it "has used up words," until they resemble worn-out automobile tires. When he is asked about his current literary endeavors, James simply appeals for donations to "our" corps. Lockwood comments on James's appearance, manner of speaking, and punctuation (including dashes).

"Henry James's Last Dictation." Dictation by James in December 1915, while on his deathbed; it was published in the *Times Literary Supplement* (2 May 1968, ed. Leon Edel), and reprinted (as "The Deathbed Notes of Henry James") in the *Atlantic Monthly* (Jun 1968).

Herbert, Father. In "De Grey, A Romance," Mrs. George De Grey's English-born confessor.

Hérédia, José Maria de (1842–1905). Cuban-born French poet, translator, editor, and librarian. Of Spanish-Creole and French descent, he was schooled in France, and, in the late 1860s, he joined the Parnassian poets. His flawless, shimmering sonnets are collected in *Les Trophées* (1893). He was elected to the French Academy (1894). James wrote to Robert Louis Stevenson* (8 Jun 1893) to praise Hérédia's sonnets: "[T]hey are to me of a beauty so noble and a perfection so rare."

The Hero. Original title of *Guy Domville*.

Hewlett, Maurice Henry (1861–1923). Prolific and popular British writer of poetry, essays, and historical novels (best when cast in medieval and Renaissance times). He was a friend of Sir Edmund Wilson Gosse,* in a letter to whom (1 Jan 1900) James praises Hewlett's *Little Novels of Italy* (1899) as "of so brilliant a cleverness & so much more developed a one than his former book [*The Forest Lovers*, 1898]." But James goes on to object to contemporary "cheap romanticism," presumably including Hewlett's, which does not "reflect . . . the life *we* live."

Hicks. In "My Friend Bingham," Lucy Hicks's sickly son, whom George Bingham accidentally kills.

Hicks, Lucy. In "My Friend Bingham," the widowed mother of the boy whom George Bingham accidentally kills. The two later marry.

Higginson, Thomas Wentworth Storrow (1823–1911). Cambridge-born, Harvard-educated clergyman, Union officer during the Civil War, author (often of biographies), reformer, editor, and friend of the New England literati. In 1866 James reviewed *The Works of Epictetus*[*] as edited by Higginson. In "American Letter" (11 Jun 1898), James touches on Higginson's autobiography, entitled

Cheerful Yesterdays (1898), praising it because it "marshal[s] his ghosts with a friendliness, a familiarity, that are documentary for the historian or the critic."

The High Bid. Three-act play, published in Philadelphia and New York by J. B. Lippincott Company, 1949, in *The Complete Plays of Henry James*, ed. Leon Edel. (Characters: Chivers, Mrs. Gracedew, Jane, Hall Pegg, Cora Prodmore, Prodmore, Dame Dorothy Yule, John Anthony Yule, Captain Marmaduke Clement Yule.) Chivers has admitted Mrs. Gracedew (now noisily upstairs) to Covering, the country house Clement Yule has just inherited. Cora Prodmore and Hall Pegg enter, both agitated. He leaves just before Cora's father enters. Prodmore tells the embarrassed girl to make Yule propose and Prodmore will burn the Yule mortgage he holds. Cora leaves as Yule enters, and Prodmore lectures him on his radical political opinions, encourages him to become a conservative leader in this region and marry, and says Cora awaits his inspection. Mrs. Gracedew bursts in, praising the house, meets Yule, and turns into a tour guide for some awestruck visitors. She tells everyone, including the pleased Prodmore, that the place is worth £50,000. When Yule tells Mrs. Gracedew that he can save Covering by treating with Prodmore, she urges him on and defends the past for preserving beauty. Saying that as a radical he feels for the houseless many, he goes upstairs to Prodmore. Cora slips in, tells Mrs. Gracedew that Prodmore wants her to marry Yule, who can thus retrieve his house, then leaves. Yule enters, says that he has closed with Prodmore, and returns to Prodmore. Cora comes back and tells Mrs. Gracedew that she will not marry Yule since she loves Pegg. Mrs. Gracedew promises to help. She fences with Prodmore regarding Yule, urges Prodmore to be gentle with Cora and Pegg, and agrees to buy Covering for £50,000. But he insists upon £70,000, then leaves. Mrs. Gracedew tells Yule that she has disburdened him; he can be her tenant, while she will have as repayment her image of the lovely old house. Yule praises her uniquely, and offers her his hand and life. To more tourists they present each other as husband and wife. When Dame Ellen Terry* asked James to write her a play, he did so and sent her *Summersoft* in 1895. She paid him £100 against future royalties but never produced the play. He asked for it back in 1898 and turned it into the short story "Covering End." When the actor Sir Johnston Forbes-Robertson* asked James in 1899 to write a play for him, James declined. When the actor renewed his plea in 1907, James agreed, turned "Covering End" into *The High Bid*, and sent it to Forbes-Robertson in November 1907. After minor changes, it went into rehearsal, in February 1908, and it enjoyed a fine run in Edinburgh, beginning on 26 March 1908, with Mrs. W. K. Clifford,* Dudley Jocelyn Persse,* James Brand Pinker,* and Lady Pollock (wife of Sir Frederick Pollock*), among others, sitting with James on opening night. When Terry, who happened to be performing in Edinburgh herself, in *Captain Brass-bound's Conversion* by George Bernard Shaw,* looked into James's play and saw that it closely resembled *Summersoft*, she notified Forbes-Robertson that he was performing a play she owned. Pinker explained to her that she had no contract, and the matter was dropped. James wrote to Sir Edmund Wilson Gosse* (6 Apr 1908) that the play in Edinburgh was " 'successfully' produced—so successfully as to diffuse for the evening a really quite large & genial glow. It has all the air of being a very clear & charming little victory." But since he was presenting a new smash hit in London, Forbes-Robertson delayed taking *The High Bid* to London as well; later, all he could manage were a few matinee performances, in February 1909, with the cooperation of theater manager Sir Herbert Beerbohm Tree.* These were well reviewed (for example, by Sir Max Beerbohm*).

Highmore, Dr. Cecil. In "The Next Time," Jane Stannace Highmore's husband, a former British army surgeon.

Highmore, Jane Stannace. In "The Next Time," a popular novelist. She is unsuccessful novelist Ralph Limbert's wife Maud Stannace Limbert's sister.

Hilary. In *The Portrait of a Lady*, Daniel Tracy Touchett's lawyer, who prepares the papers for Touchett's bequest to Isabel Archer.

Hill, Frank Harrison (1830–1910). Editor of the London *Daily News* and after 1886 writer for the *World* (to 1906). In 1877, James met Hill and Jane Dalzell (née Finlay) Hill, his physically ugly, but charming, bright journalistic wife, and soon he wrote to William Dean Howells* (30 Mar [1877]) that the couple were "among the cleverest people I have met here." They became lifelong friends. In 1878 Hill was a sponsor for James's election to the Reform Club. Next year, James wrote a lengthy letter (21 Mar [1879]) to Mrs. Hill to defend his short story "An International Episode," which in a *Daily News* review she had criticized. When his play *Guy Domville* was booed in January 1895, Mrs. Hill immediately sent James a letter offering welcome moral support.

Hill, Rosamond (1825–1902) **and Florence** (?–?). A pair of travel- and reform-writing sisters. James reviewed (*Nation*, 6 Jan 1876) their *What We Saw in Australia*, calling it "an excellent book of its kind"—a correctly, agreeably composed narrative of "useful information"—by two pleasant and observant women who visited relatives in Australia in 1873. The book has lively descriptions, but it is "clogged with small particulars" and is "a trifle dry." Australia in it seems "a duller and more mechanical form of our own Western civilization." On the other hand, the book offers valuable information on "public works and internal administration" and also on prisons.

Hillebrand, Karl (1829–1884). German journalist and historian, who after revolutionary activities fled to Paris (where he was Heinrich Heine's secretary a short while) and then to Florence, where he remained and later died. As a critic of European literature, he wrote in German, French, and English. He collected many of his essays in *Zeiten, Völker und Menschen* (7 vols., 1874–1885). Through Francis Boott,* James met Hillebrand upon first visiting Italy in 1869–1870 and was impressed by his command of French. In Italy again, in 1873, James renewed their friendship; but within a few months, he felt obliged to write to his brother William (3 May [1874]) that Hillebrand "is an unmistakable snob."

Hirsch, Dr. Julius. In "A Bundle of Letters," the scientist to whom Dr. Rudolph Staub writes a pro-German letter.

Hodge, D. Jackson. In *The Reverberator*, a name on luggage in a Parisian hotel.

Hoffendahl, Diedrich. In *The Princess Casamassima*, the shadowy European anarchist who, through Paul Muniment, gives Hyacinth Robinson his assassination orders.

Hofmann, Caroline. In "A Most Extraordinary Case," Maria Mason's niece and the object of Colonel Ferdinand Mason's affections. The colonel dies upon learning that she is engaged to Dr. Horace Knight.

Holbein, Hans, the younger (1497–1543). German painter, born in Augsberg, who accompanied his father, also a painter, to Basel, Switzerland, in 1515; he may have been sponsored by Erasmus. Holbein executed letters for books, signs, and table pictures, and portraits. He worked a while in Lucerne, but returned to Basel; he may have studied in Italy. He developed superb ability as a draughtsman, a realistic painter, a richly religious artist, and a versatile portraitist. He went to England, where he executed many portraits (notably of Sir Thomas More), some of which are now lost. After much work in Basel again, he returned to England, became a painter in the court of King Henry VIII, and also worked in other notable circles. Holbein died during the plague in London. His later work now graces the finest museums in the Western world. Greatly admiring Holbein, James discusses him in much detail in "A Northward Journey" (1874; retitled "The Splügen," 1875). In Basel at the time, James calls Holbein that "superb genius." He lingers over several of Holbein's "firm, compact" works, including "the famous profile of Erasmus." He concludes that Holbein preferred "verity" to beauty, and "had . . . an ideal of beauty of execution, of manipulation, of touch." In a note on John Singleton Copley* (*Nation*, 9 Sep 1875), James repeats his belief that Holbein was a "supreme genius." In "The Winter Exhibitions in London" (1879) he says that "[t]here is surely no one like Holbein for telling us how our forefathers of the early sixteenth century *looked*." His short story "The Beldonald Holbein" owes much to the fact that James admired the homely realism of many of Holbein's finest portraits, including that of *Lady Butts*, which James's art-collecting friend Isabella Stewart Gardner* bought in 1899. In 1909, when James was first projecting *The Outcry* (the play which became the novel of the same name in 1911), concerning the perennial attempts of American millionaires to grab British art treasures, Holbein's *Duchess of Milan*, owned by the Duke of Norfolk, was saved from a foreign purchaser only at the last minute.

Holland, George. In "Osborne's Revenge," the object of Henrietta Congreve's affections. At one time, the girl preferred him to Robert Graham.

Holmes, Oliver Wendell, Jr. (1841–1935). Son of the distinguished and versatile American physician, medical writer, novelist, poet, biographer, and essayist. Holmes, Jr., was a Boston-born and Harvard-educated American jurist, who served with distinction in the Union Army during the Civil War. Admitted to the bar in 1867, he practiced in Boston, taught at Harvard, served on the Supreme Court of Massachusetts, and then was appointed by Theodore Roosevelt* an associate justice of the U.S. Supreme Court (1902–1932). He wrote *The Common Law* (1881). His grand correspondence with Sir Frederick Pollock* was published (2 vols., 1941; James is occasionally mentioned). William James knew Holmes at Harvard. Early in August 1865, Henry James vacationed with his cousin Mary Temple,* Holmes, another Civil War veteran John Chipman Gray,* and a few others in the White Mountains, and he felt that the military tales told there put him in the rich American shade. Although James and Holmes often saw each other in future years—for example, James was a fellow passenger across the Atlantic with Holmes and his bride in September 1874—temperamental and attitudinal differences cooled their affection. For example, Holmes in letters to Pollock says that to understand James and his brother William one must keep in mind their Irish blood; he regards James as narrow, and he criticizes him for writing too often about Americans in Europe. He links James and Marcel Proust,* unfavorably, as a pair who discuss everything at too great a length.

"Homburg Reformed." Travel essay, published in the *Nation* (28 Aug 1873); reprinted in *Transatlantic Sketches*, 1875. In it, James explains that many romantics lament the end of gambling in Homburg. The Kursaal gaming rooms are chandeliered and gilded still, but silent now. Mother Nature outside seems to say that a woodsy walk is better than betting inside. James describes the city's position among the hills, the streets and stores, shopgirls, lodgings, and entertainment at the changed Kursaal: a reading room, music, food, garden, and crowd watching. Americans are especially keen at noting "national idiosyncrasies": English ladies are grim; Germans drink, smoke, know music, are ponderous, brainy, and militant; the French lightly love pleasure; the Italians smile and voice vowels uniquely well. James mentions Homburg's springs of medicinal waters, forests beyond, and peasants like woodcut and fairy-tale figures.

Homer, Scott. In "Mrs. Medwin," Mamie Cutter's bright, poor, sponging half-brother, whose shady past intrigues Lady Wantridge.

Hope, Miranda. In "A Bundle of Letters," a naive but enthusiastic girl who writes effusive letters home to Bangor, Maine, from the Pension Beaurepas about Paris and the people there. Her boyfriend at home is William Platt.

Hope, Mrs. Abraham C. In "A Bundle of Letters," the mother, in Bangor, Maine, of Miranda Hope, who writes letters home from Paris.

Hope, Mrs. Warren. In "The Abasement of the Northmores," Warren's wife, then his widow. She furnishes Lord Northmore's widow with some letters from Warren to Lord Northmore, whose old love letters to Mrs. Hope before her marriage she secretly prefers. Mrs. Hope prepares a private selection of her own husband's letters for later publication.

Hope, Sir Matthew. In *The Portrait of a Lady*, Daniel Tracy Touchett's physician during his final illness. In *The Tragic Muse*, Charles Carteret's physician during his final illness.

Hope, Warren. In "The Abasement of the Northmores," a sick man who dies after attending his more successful friend Lord John Northmore's funeral.

Hoppin, William Jones (1813–1895). Diplomat and writer, born in Providence, Rhode Island. He was educated at Yale, attended and graduated from Middlebury (1832), then obtained a Harvard law degree (1835). He became a playwright, editor, and author of essays on art. He was appointed secretary of legation in London (1876–1886), serving part of the time under James Russell Lowell.* While in London, Hoppin kept a journal (12 vols., unpublished) concerning British society and related matters. He had three talented brothers: Augustus (illustrator and author), Thomas (architect and sculptor), and Washington (physician). Ehrman Syme Nadal* was Hoppin's assistant secretary. James knew both Hoppin and Nadal.

Hoppus. In *The Tragic Muse*, a political writer whom Nick Dormer and Julia Dallow mention.

Horace. In *Still Waters*, the ugly but sensitive little man, age twenty-nine, who passively loves Emma but, seeing that she adores Felix, urges that superficial man to declare himself.

Horner, Margaret. In "My Friend Bingham," Lucy Hicks's second cousin. Lucy lives with her for a time.

Horridge, Mrs. In "A Passionate Pilgrim," Richard Searle's housekeeper at Lockley.

Hotchkin. In *The Princess Casamassima*, Hyacinth Robinson's fellow book-binder at Crookenden's shop.

Houghton, Lord (Richard Monkton Milnes) (1809–1885). English politician, friend of Victorian writers, patron, host, and man of letters. He graduated from Trinity College, Cambridge (M.A., 1831), where he knew Alfred, Lord Tennyson* (whom he much later helped to obtain a government pension) and William Makepeace Thackeray,* among others. He later became a lifelong friend of Thomas Carlyle.* After traveling abroad, he entered London society (1835) and became a splendid host. Milnes was an initially conservative member of Parliament (1837–1863), was elevated to the peerage (1863, as Baron Houghton of Great Houghton), and in the House of Lords espoused the cause of the Oxford Movement. In France in 1840, he met Alexis de Tocqueville. Beginning in the late 1840s, Milnes became more liberal and pro-reform. He helped modify copyright laws. In 1853 he and others formed a society of bibliophiles (some of their collected books were of erotica). Through the 1860s and 1870s, Lord Houghton was much occupied in attending meetings, speaking, traveling officially, writing, and editorial work. In 1875 he visited Canada and the United States, where he met Ralph Waldo Emerson,* Henry Wadsworth Longfellow,* and James Russell Lowell,* among others. In the 1880s he was an especially kind host of illustrious friends and acquaintances. Houghton is described as broadly amiable, always generous, amusing rather than profound, dilettantish, graceful, and, on occasion, coarse. He published on John Keats (1848), popularized Emerson in England, aided Algernon Charles Swinburne,* and was a loyal friend of such visiting Americans as Henry Adams,* Charles Eliot Norton,* William Wetmore Story* (who did a bust of him), and James. As early as 1869, James declined an opportunity, through Norton, to meet Houghton and "see his collection of [William] Blakes" (letter to William James, 19 Mar [1869]); but he breakfasted at Houghton's home in February 1877 through intermediaries Adams and Sarah Butler Wister.* Soon thereafter, James was able to write to Adams (5 May 1877): "Lord Houghton has been my guide, philosopher and friend—he has breakfasted me, dined me, conversationed me, absolutely caressed me. He has been really most kind and paternal, and I have seen, under his wing, a great variety of interesting and remarkable people." A few weeks later, James wrote to his father and sister (20 May [1877]) that at a recent Houghton dinner "the rooms swarmed with famous grandees" (including Anthony Trollope*). Over the years, James met or renewed acquaintance at Lord and Lady Houghton's home such people as Charles Hamilton Aïdé,* William Black,* Augustus John Cuthbert Hare,* Rhoda Broughton,* William Ewart Gladstone,* Heinrich Schliemann, and Tennyson. James was at one point able in return to introduce some of his friends (for example, Gustave Flaubert* and Ivan Sergeyevich Turgenev,* and their Paris-based confrères) to Houghton. James amusingly wrote to his sister Alice (31 Dec [1878]) of being Houghton's snowy New Year's house guest in the country, with his own private room, and having his letter writing interrupted by the entrance of his host, who took a snoring snooze in a handy armchair: "He is a very odd old fellow—extremely fidgety and eccentric; but full of sociable and friendly instincts, and with a strong streak of humanity and democratic feeling." After Houghton's death, James wrote to Grace Norton* (23 Aug [1885]): "I liked him (in spite of some of his little objectionableness), and he was always kind to me. A great deal of the past disappears with him." In *The Middle Years*, James fondly calls Lord Houghton "my supremely kind old friend."

Houses, mansions, and other imagined places in James's fiction and plays. Beauclere (*The Tragic Muse*), Beaurepas ("The Pension Beaurepas"), Beccles (*The Awkward Age*), Beechingham (*Tenants*), Blankley ("The Wheel of Time"), Bleet ("Paste"), Bly ("The Turn of the Screw"), Bounds (*The Other House*), Branches ("An International Episode"), Bridges ("The Figure in the Carpet"), Brinton ("The Marriages"), Burbeck ("The Two Faces"), Carrara ("The Tree of Knowledge"), Catchmore ("Mrs. Medwin"), Clere (*Tenants*), Covering (*The High Bid*), Covering End ("Covering End"), Crescentini (*The Portrait of a Lady*), Dedborough (*The Outcry*), Eastmead (*The Other House*), Fawns (*The Golden Bowl*), Flickerbridge ("Flickerbridge"), Gardencourt (*The Portrait of a Lady*), Harsh (*The Tragic Muse*), Kingscote ("A Bundle of Letters"), Lackley ("A Passionate Pilgrim"), Leporelli (*The Wings of the Dove*), Lockleigh (*The Portrait of a Lady*), Lomax (*The Princess Casamassima*), Longlands ("The Siege of London"), Marr ("The Third Person"), Matcham (*The Wings of the Dove, The Golden Bowl*), Medley (*The Princess Casamassima*), Mellows ("A London Life"), Mertle (*The Awkward Age*), Mundham ("Broken Wings"), Newmarch (*The Sacred Fount*), Pandolfini (*Roderick Hudson*), Paramore ("Owen Wingrave"), Pickenham ("The Given Case"), Plash ("A London Life"), Porches (*Guy Domville*), Poynton (*The Spoils of Poynton*), Prestidge ("The Death of the Lion"), Ricks (*The Spoils of Poynton*), Roccanera (*The Portrait of a Lady*), Severals (*The Tragic Muse*), Stayes ("The Liar"), Summersoft ("The Lesson of the Master," *Summersoft*), Tranton ("Sir Edmund Orme"), Waterbath (*The Spoils of Poynton*), Weatherend ("The Beast in the Jungle"), and Wilverley (*The Other House*).

Howe, Julia Ward (1819–1910). American editor, poetess, leader in the causes of women's suffrage and international peace, lecturer, biographer, sociologist, and autobiographer. She was the wife of humanitarian Samuel Gridley Howe, the mother of metallurgist Henry Marion Howe and writers Laura Richards and Maud Howe Elliott,* the sister-in-law of sculptor Thomas Crawford,* and the aunt of novelist Francis Marion Crawford.* James reviewed (*North American Review*, Apr 1867) her *Later Lyrics* (1866), calling them often too grand, vague, general, and lax, but also sometimes passionate and animated. James liked her 1862 poem "The Battle Hymn of the Republic," up to its incongruous ending. In London in 1877, James was a thoughtful host to Mrs. Howe, escorting her, for example, to an architecturally attractive old hospital. In a Notebook entry (16 May 1899), he records Maude Elliott's revelation to him in Rome that her mother in her late seventies looked like a "picturesque, striking, lovely old (wrinkled and *marked*) [Hans] Holbein [the younger*]," and hence had "artists raving" to paint her. This situation became the germ of James's story "The Beldonald Holbein," with Julia Ward Howe becoming the model for Louisa Brash. In *Notes of a Son and Brother*, James recalls meeting the Howes in the environs of Newport, Rhode Island, and being impressed by "the eminent, the militant Phil-Hellene, Dr. S.G. of the honoured name," and by his wife, "the most attuned of interlocutors, most urbane of disputants, most insidious of wits, even before her gathered fame as Julia Ward and the established fortune of her elegant Battle-Hymn."

Howells, William Dean (1837–1920). Significant American novelist, short-story writer, travel writer, dramatist, poet, autobiographer, editor, and friend and mentor of innumerable literary figures in his epoch. Born in Martin's Ferry, Ohio, Howells began his association with words as a hardworking, nine-year-old typesetter in his peripatetic, Swedenborgian printer and publisher father's printing office. Howells wrote for the *Ohio State Journal* in Columbus (1856–1861), published some minor poetry and essays, studied literature and several languages on his own, and in 1860 wrote the campaign biography of Abraham Lincoln, who when elected sent him to Venice, Italy, as consul (1861–1865). Just before he went abroad, Howells took a literary pilgrimage in the summer of 1860 to the East, where he met Ralph Waldo Emerson,* James Thomas Fields* and his wife Annie Adams Fields,* Nathaniel Hawthorne* and his young son Julian Hawthorne,* Oliver Wendell Holmes, Sr., James Russell Lowell,* Henry David Thoreau, George Ticknor, and Walt Whitman.* Howells was married in Paris (1862) to Elinor Mead (the cousin of future President Rutherford B. Hayes, whose campaign biography Howells wrote in 1876). The Howellses had three children. While in Italy, Howells wrote two books of travel, became fluent in Italian, and studied Italian literature (including Carlo Goldoni's plays), later publishing important critical works on the subject. He returned home and became an influential editor, first with the *Nation* in New York, under Edwin Lawrence Godkin* (1865–66); then with the *Atlantic Monthly* in Boston, as assistant to Fields (1866–1871) and then as editor (1871–1881). In the 1880s, declining various professorships, he associated with the *Century Magazine* and *Harper's Magazine*, his writings (including reviews of Henry James and Ivan Sergeyevich Turgenev,* among many others) helping the cause of realism, and became more concerned with morality. In 1888 he and his family moved to New York, where a year later his chronically sick daughter died. A New York transit-workers' strike, the Haymarket Riot in Chicago, and his study of Count Leo Nikolayevich Tolstoy* and Henry George (among other writers) combined to turn Howells toward socialism, anti-imperialism, and progressive editorializing (with the *Cosmopolitan*, among other journals). He became the first president of the American Academy of Arts and Letters (1908–1920). He traveled frequently in the 1890s, often with his invalid wife, who died in 1910. Howells's best novels are *Their Wedding Journey* (1871), *A Chance Acquaintance* (1873), *A Foregone Conclusion* (1874), *The Lady of the Aroostook* (1879), *The Undiscovered Country* (1880), *Dr. Breen's Practice* (1881), *A Modern Instance* (1882), *The Rise of Silas Lapham* (1885), *Indian Summer* (1886), *The Minister's Charge* (1886), *April Hopes* (1887), *Annie Kilburn* (1888), *A Hazard of New Fortunes* (1890), *The Shadow of a Dream* (1890), *The World of Chance* (1893), *A Traveler from Altruria* (1894), *The Landlord at Lion's Head* (1897), *The Story of a Play* (1898), *Their Silver Wedding Journey* (1899), *The Son of Royal Langbrith* (1904), *Through the Eye of the Needle* (1907), and *The Leatherwood God* (1916). His best travel books are *Venetian Life* (1866), *Italian Journeys* (1867), *Suburban Sketches* (1870), *Tuscan Cities* (1885, illustrated by Joseph Pennell*), *Niagara Revisited* (1884), *Certain Delightful English Towns* (1906), *Seven English Cities* (1909), and *Familiar Spanish Travels* (1913). His best books of criticism are *Criticism and Fiction* (1891), *My Literary Passions* (1895), *Literary Friends and Acquaintance* (1900), *Heroines of Fiction* (1901), *Literature and Life* (1902), and *My Mark Twain*[*] (1910). Howells advocated a brand of realism now considered timid: He wrote at first mainly for unmarried young women, he said, then for his own children, and in a celebrated letter (18 March 1882) once informed John Milton Hay* that there would be ''no palpitating divans in my stories.'' But he also bravely concerned himself with frontier democracy, social snobbery, spiritualism, feminism, commercial ethics, false charity, the problems of industrialism, social reform, crime, miscegenation, the artistic life, imperialism, and supernaturalism. His closest literary friends were James (whom he regarded as the greatest contemporary American novelist), Mark Twain, and John Hay. He encouraged Hjalmar H. Boyesen, Stephen Crane,* Henry Blake Fuller, Hamlin Garland,* Robert Herrick, and Frank Norris, among many others. Howells first met James in Cambridge, Massachusetts, in the summer of 1866, accepted some of his early short fiction for publication in the *Atlantic*, discussed fictional techniques with him, and encouraged (and learned from) him by means of informal debates, later by transatlantic letters, and always by skillful reviews (from 1875 through 1903) of James's fiction long and short. (In Cambridge, Howells also met and came to admire both Henry James, Sr., who in many ways resembled his own father, and William James.) Howells especially liked James's ''Gabrielle de Bergerac,'' which first appeared in the *Atlantic* and which the author once read aloud to the editor's delighted family. Since Howells liked ordinary characters, clarity, and overt drama in fiction, he preferred James's earlier, somewhat more melodramatic works and had trouble with the products of his later phases because of their detailed analysis, obscurity, unhappy endings, and absence of closure. He was always kinder to James than James was to him. James wrote reviews of works by Howells, a long essay on him, and also an appreciative public letter to him. James reviewed (*North American Review*, Jan 1868) Howells's *Italian Journeys*, calling the author charming, observant, truthful, never cynical. James says that Howells is a humorous, sentimental moralist (with "a healthy conscience"), who adds fresh touches to history and tradition. His book is entertaining rather than informative. Praising Italy for "represent[ing] the *maximum* of man's creative force," James says that Howells treats this land of beauty, pleasure, suffering, and an influential Church with "natural pathos and humor." Never criticizing the Italian character, Howells writes about "common roadside figures . . . and . . . the manners and morals of the populace." He does not generalize but remains pleasant, sure, and "light," like Hawthorne, but with an eye more on the seen world. James admires Howells's refined style and says that his delightful observations add to our joy of life. James reviewed (*Independent*, 8 Jan 1874) Howells's *Poems* (1873), calling his "verse . . . as natural and unforced as his prose." James likes their musical pathos, adds that Howells prefers form to feeling, and notes that he combines an Old World reading (admiring, for example, Heinrich Heine) with New World scenery and "impulse." James especially likes Howells's well-managed hexameters, then praises specific poems as graceful and delicate, with touching imagery and exquisite diction. One poem he notes is not melancholy, but instead is "tolerant of melancholy." James reviewed (*North American Review*, Jan 1875) *A Foregone Conclusion*, beginning with the note that Howells's earlier novel *A Chance Acquaintance* was "a charming book," "a peculiarly happy hit." This new effort is another fine story, which riskily returns to the same Venetian scene, but which successfully appeals both to "simply-judging" readers and to those seeking "lurking artfulness." James too thoroughly summarizes the plot in "rapid outline": Handsome, "caged" Italian priest falls in love with "fascinating," "brooding" American girl. James likes the vividly presented principal characters, especially the daughter and mother; he adds that Howells "is one of the few writers who hold a key to feminine logic and detect a method in feminine madness." Perhaps the mother is too talkative. Many readers will object to the conclusion, which involves a harsh change of scene from romantic Venice to realistically sketched America. But *A Foregone Conclusion* is "a singularly perfect production." James, somewhat strangely, reviewed this same novel again (*Nation*, 7 Jan 1875), this time regarding its heroine as a well-sketched American type—the product of "our institutions and our climate" with "a lovely face and an irritable moral consciousness." She makes "a very harmonious companion" to Kitty Ellison of Howells's *A Chance Acquaintance*. Again, James spoils the plot for readers by explaining who dies and who marries, and where. He says that the climax "is related with masterly force and warmth." He praises Howells for avoiding "bread-and-butter and commonplace" realism by the device of poetic heroines rather than by the usual device of "golden hair and promiscuous felony." But James again protests against the last twenty pages or so, with its ending on American soil. Nonetheless, Howells is an admirable American talent, in his use of details, nice shades, and pale coloration, his aggrandizing of small elements, his instinct for "style and shape"—Thomas Bailey Aldrich,* Bret Harte,* Henry Wadsworth Longfellow,* and James Russell Lowell* have it too—and his "great charm," if with it "limited authority." American novels are better, because of balance, polish, flavor, grace, humor, and delicacy, than the current ponderous, shapeless, padded British ones. James then published a general essay entitled "William Dean Howells" (*Harper's Weekly*, 19 Jun 1886—perhaps as a thank-you reply to Howells's laudatory 1882 *Century* essay entitled "Henry James, Jr.") in which he touches on Howells's early life, praises his "delightful" *Venetian Life* and "whimsical" *Italian Journeys*, both with their "mingled freshness and irony," and adverts to Howells's poetry. Now the versatile author is in a new phase, with editorial work in Boston and his "perfect" *Suburban Sketches*. Howells understands "the American character" uniquely well. It was fortunate that he started writing fiction later than most authors do. Why did he fancy that he was weak in dialogue? He certainly is observant and painterly. The American scenes he notes are not so much "rich" or "fair" as "positive." He writes copiously but always freshly, always "enlarg[ing] . . . his scope." An anti-romancer, Howells treats what is common, immediate, familiar, vulgar. He loves what is real, natural, colloquial, moderate, optimistic, domestic, democratic. In this he resembles Émile Zola,* but without the naturalist's "lapses" or "audacities." Howells's American canvases are neither "dazzling" nor "patriotic"; instead, he truthfully represents aspects of American social desolation. His Americans are usually "good," and in a country which is "innocent." His female characters are "of the best" but not "in the sense of being the best to live with." James praises both *The Minister's Charge*, even now appearing serially, and *The Rise of Silas Lapham*; he then rebukes Howells gently for expressing the opinion that style is becoming less important in fiction, further, for stressing dialogue at the expense of "narrative and pictorial matter." Suggesting that Howells follow the example of Alphonse Daudet,* James closes by predicting that Howells will produce well in the future. In "American Letter" (9 Jul 1898), James calls *The Story of a Play* by Howells a "short and charming novel." He likes its treatment of a woman in theater work, but he concludes that the book does "not cut into the subject so deep" as it might have done. In "The Manners of American Women" (1907), James says that Howells's fiction valuably shows that "fellowship" generated by crisis substitutes for old-fashioned manners in America now. In 1910, Howells was happy to join in the efforts of Edith Newbold Jones Wharton* to recommend James for the Nobel Prize, which, however, was awarded in 1911 to Maurice Maeterlinck.* Finally, James wrote an open letter (*North American Review*, Apr 1912) to be read "straight *at*" Howells during his seventy-fifth birthday banquet in New York. In it, James tenderly (if fulsomely) recalls that Howells as editor encouraged, advised, accepted, and paid James for his early work. He suggests that Howells has been a great garden in which new writers are helped while cultivating their individual patches. In addition, he produced innumerable "beautifully finished" works of his own—great "studies of American life"—while James only "practise[d] meaner economies." He goes on and on with his praise, citing specific novels and lauding them for their documentation of our "social climate." Critics have begun to track elements of his method as James Fenimore Cooper's Leatherstocking follows Indians in the forest. James recalls that Hippolyte Taine* once defined Howells as "a precious painter and a sovereign witness." In *Notes of a Son and Brother*, James calls Howells "my distinguished friend of a virtual lifetime"; in *The Middle Years*, he regards him as an "insidious disturber and fertiliser of that state [of innocence] in me." Privately, however, James was often critical of Howells. In personal letters to family members, professional colleagues, and friends, James frequently criticized Howells for careless style and structure, uninteresting characters, substantive timidity, and critical support of such shapeless writings as those of Walt Whitman and Leo Tolstoy. In a letter to Charles Eliot Norton* (16 Jan 1871), James said that "the face of nature and civilization in this our country is to a certain point a very sufficient literary field. But it will yield its secrets only to a really *grasping* imagination. This I think Howells lacks." In a second letter to Norton (9 Aug 1871), James added that Howells "has little intellectual curiosity, so here he stands with his admirable organ of style, like a poor man holding a diamond wondering how he can wear it." In a letter from London to Grace Norton* (9 Dec [1885]), James writes querulously, "Everyone here admires extremely the truth and power of 'Silas Lapham,' including myself. But what hideousness of life! They don't revile Howells when he does America, . . . and why do they revile me? The 'Bostonians' is sugar-cake, compared with it." James privately regarded Howells's *Suburban Sketches* as superficial, being visually realistic, rather than psychologically or sociologically so. He feared that Howells was too well-off to understand the impoverished thoroughly. James greatly enjoyed *A Modern Instance*, which he compared to *Romola* by George Eliot,* and he uniquely relished *The Landlord at Lion's Head*; on the other hand, he thought *A Hazard of New Fortunes* ignored too many segments of the New York population. In his published letters and criticism, James mentions more than forty works, long and short, by Howells. For his part, Howells, too long unsure of himself, was always impressed by James's command of French and his consequent understanding of avant-garde French fictional techniques, and perhaps also felt that James had been both right and more daring to expatriate himself instead of staying home to fight for American values not always worth defending. In any event, Howells increased James's readership by his published praise, especially in his 1875 *Atlantic Monthly* review of *A Passionate Pilgrim and Other Tales*, as well as in his 1882 *Century* essay. In the latter, Howells singled out James as a fine psychologist and humorist. The essay compared James to the detriment of British novelists so much that it cost Howells dearly when he went abroad the same year. In 1911 Howells allowed a laudatory letter by him to be included in *The Henry James Year Book* (1911), arranged by Evelyn Garnaut Smalley, the daughter of George Washburn Smalley.* As Howells lay on his deathbed, he was writing a reminiscence of his friend Henry James. According to a Notebook entry by James (31 Oct 1895), a remark which Howells made in Paris "Live all you can: it's a mistake not to . . . "—and which Jonathan Sturges* relayed to James—was the start of *The Ambassadors*. Another Notebook entry (9 Aug 1900) reports that Howells, with a "suggestion of an 'international ghost story,' " started James's thinking about what became *The Sense of the Past*, left incomplete at his death. James's library contained fifty-three books by Howells.

Hudson, Roderick. In *Roderick Hudson*, the talented but unstable American sculptor discovered and then befriended by Rowland Mallet. Mary Garland passively loves Hudson, whose love for Christina Light in Rome, however, upsets and ultimately ruins him. He may be a suicide. Hudson may have been partly modeled on the personality and career of Thomas Crawford,* the American sculptor in Rome.

Hudson, Sarah. In *Roderick Hudson*, Roderick Hudson's gentle but ineffectual widowed mother. Rowland Mallet invites her, together with Mary Garland, to visit her son in Rome.

Hudson, Stephen. In *Roderick Hudson*, Roderick Hudson's older brother, who died during the Civil War.

Hueffer, Ford Madox (1873–1939). English writer (full name: Joseph Leopold Ford Hermann Madox Hueffer), born in England of German descent. His father was a German music critic and librettist, and his maternal grandfather was Ford Madox Brown* the pre-Raphaelite painter, whose biography Hueffer wrote (and whose work James reviewed). Hueffer was married in 1894; he and his wife Elsie had two daughters. The Hueffer family lived in Winchelsea, near Rye. Hueffer was the founder (1908) and first editor of the *English Review* (in which James published four late short stories), as well as an editor of the *Transatlantic Review*. As both a writer and an editor, Hueffer associated with James's agent James Brand Pinker.* For a long while (1908–1914), Hueffer, who had left his wife in 1909, and Violet Hunt,* whom James had known from her childhood, were lovers. All of this nonplussed James. Hueffer changed his name to Ford Madox Ford after World War I and lived for a while in the United States where he gained much popularity. One of his later close friends was Ezra Pound. He was a prolific writer, first of popular historical novels, then of three books with his friend Joseph Conrad* (in 1901, 1903, 1924), and also of important novels: *The Good Soldier* (1915), *Some Do Not* (1924), *No More Parades* (1925), *A Man Could Stand Up* (1926), and *The Last Post* (1928). In addition, Hueffer published poetry, critical studies (including a book on James), and autobiographical volumes. Mrs. W. K. Clifford* provided Ford with a letter of introduction to James in the summer of 1896; Ford wrote, and James replied courteously; thus the two men met in Rye. Both James and Herbert George Wells* deplored the fact that Conrad and Hueffer were ever collaborators. In 1900 James wrote to Hueffer (23 May 1900) to thank him for the gift of his *Poems for Pictures*

(1900), which James praises as including "little rustic lays" that are "terribly natural and true and 'right.' " But it was not until 1901 that the two men met again. In due time, James and Hueffer associated together with several of their literary neighbors, including Conrad, Stephen Crane,* and Wells. A year later James wrote to Hueffer (9 Sep 1902) to thank him for commenting on *The Wings of the Dove* and thus trying to probe "the mystery of one's craft." Hueffer incorrectly theorized that he was James's model for Merton Densher in this novel. According to the diary of his secretary Mary Weld,* James once actually leaped over a dike to avoid Hueffer and his chronic, pushy flattery. To keep from being innocently embroiled in divorce proceedings threatened in 1909 by Hueffer's wife, James wrote to Violet Hunt (2 Nov 1909) telling her not to revisit Lamb House*; he then explained his neutral position in a careful letter to Hueffer (8 Nov 1909). Hueffer and Violet went to Germany and tried, unsuccessfully, to obtain a divorce which would hold up in England. By 1912 James was socializing again with the curious couple. When Hueffer's book *Henry James* appeared (1913), James wrote to William Roughead* (29 Jan 1914) that he planned to "cultivate the exquisite art of ignorance" concerning it. He evidently never read the book. Hueffer's autobiographical *Return to Yesterday* (1931) reminisces about James, often inaccurately. Several of Hueffer's novels show a Jamesian influence, especially *A Call: The Tale of Two Passions* (1910), which even has two characters named Brigstock and Stackpole in it. James's library included one book by Hueffer.

Hugh, Dr. In "The Middle Years," the well-read physician who abandons his main patient, a wealthy, sick countess, to comfort and flatter dying novelist Dencombe.

"Hugh Merrow." Incomplete short story (2,400 words), published as a fragment in the New York *Times Magazine* (26 Oct 1986); reprinted in New York by Oxford University Press, 1987, in *The Complete Notebooks of Henry James*, ed. Leon Edel and Lyall H. Powers. (Characters: Captain and Mrs. Archdean, Reggie Blyth, Hugh Merrow.) Impressed by a vividly alive portrait of little Reggie Blyth, painted by Hugh Merrow and now at the Academy in London, Captain and Mrs. Archdean call upon the bachelor artist at his studio and hesitantly reveal that they would like him to paint a portrait of the child they have never had and can never have. The child is to be represented as about eight years old. The "father" would like the child to resemble "his" mother; the "mother" would like the child to resemble "her" father. The lonely couple will give the artist's creative imagination free play. Hugh, though initially hesitant, finishes by entering enthusiastically into their conception. According to a Notebook entry (7 May 1898), James got the idea for this story in 1895 from Paul Bourget* and his wife, who told him of a similar subject, concerning a child, by Luigi Gualdo.* James later returned to the Gualdo idea, now outlining his plot in his *Notebooks* (11 Sep 1900): A couple asks a painter to create a portrait of their imaginary child, since they can never have a real one. James never finished this story, probably because it too much resembles "Maud-Evelyn," "The Tone of Time," and even "The Real Thing."

Hugo, Victor-Marie (1802–1885). Towering French poet, dramatist, and novelist, born in Besançon to an army officer and his wife, who was later unfaithful to him. While young, Hugo traveled much with his parents, and then precociously started his illustrious, versatile career with poetry and a government pension. He soon began to lead the French romantic literary movement. His play *Hernani* (1830) caused much classicist-romanticist controversy. *Notre-Dame de Paris* (1831) was his first great novel. After becoming a peer of France and then a member of the Constituent Assembly, Hugo was banished by Napoleon III. He resided first in Jersey and then in Guernsey, for a total of eighteen years (to 1870). Hugo then returned to become a member of the National Assembly at Bordeaux, but after the Commune he resigned and escaped to Belgium, then Luxemburg. His private life was marred by irregularities and tragedy. His other leading works include the following: poetry collections (*Odes et ballades* [1828], *Orientales* [1829], *Les Feuilles d'automne* [1831], *Les Chants du crépuscule* [1835], *Les Voix intérieures* [1837], *Les Rayons et les ombres* [1840], and *La Légende des siècles* [1859, 1877, 1883]); plays (*Cromwell* [1827, with a pro-romanticism preface], *Le Roi s'amuse* [1832], *Lucrezia Borgia* [1833], *Marie Tudor* [1833], and *Ruy Blas* [1838]); and novels (*Les Misérables* [10 vols., 1862], *Les Travailleurs de la mer* [1866], *L'Homme qui rit* [1869], and *Quatre-vingt-treize* [1873]). Early in his career, James hilariously reviewed (*Nation*, 12 Apr 1866) Hugo's *Les Travailleurs de la mer*, mainly summarizing its plot in climax-spoiling detail. He calls the villain "a mass of incongruities," says that the minor characters "are . . . described with a minuteness very disproportionate to any part they play in the story," regards the dialogue as full of "rockets and bonfires," notes that when the hero Gilliatt struggles against sea and sea monster "never was nature so effectually ousted from its place," and labels the entire romantic novel "the work of a decline." Next, James reviewed (*Nation*, 9 Apr 1874) *Ninety-Three*, finding in it "Hugo . . . himself again with a vengeance" and "escorted between the sublime and the ridiculous as resolutely as his own most epic heroes." James prefers fiction which shows "brevity," "conciseness," "elegance," and "perfection of form," none of which stylistic virtues does he find here. Hugo likes "the huge and the horrible," both of which he finds in the French Revolution, but he provides only a "meagre" plot. He does make "Revolutionary Paris . . . palpable to our senses." James sarcastically summarizes the action, but then praises the characterization of Michelle Fléchard and the scene presenting her three babies in the castle fire. James viciously concludes: "[T]he leading idea" in this novel seems to be that "the horrible—the horrible in crime and suffering and folly, in blood and fire and tears—is the delightful subject for the embroidery of fiction." Still, Hugo has style and imagination. In his 1875 essay on Adelaide Ristori,* James offers the insight that the climax of Hugo's *Lucrezia Borgia* "grazes the ludicrous"; then in his 1875 review of *Queen Mary* by Alfred, Lord Tennyson,* James calls Hugo's *Marie Tudor* "consummately unpleasant," adding that it has "little to do with nature and nothing with either history or morality." In "Parisian Topics" (19 Feb 1876), James ridicules Hugo's recent speech to the communal delegates, saying that it reveals only "a genius for pure verbosity," quoting examples at length, and concluding that its "transcendent fatuity" is yet another instance of "national vanity" in France. Finally, James reviewed (*Nation*, 3 May 1877) the two 1877 volumes of *La Légende des siècles*. The poems here display many faults, no humor, and pedantic research, but also much "imaginative power." James likes Hugo's poetizing on "pictorial subjects" ("L'Aigle de casque") and children ("Petit Paul"), but he dislikes Hugo's fixation on "the bloodiest chapters" in Parisian history. James never met Hugo, although he entertained the renowned writer's grandson, who with his wife was part of the Alphonse Daudet* party visiting London and James in 1895. When Hugo died in 1885, James wrote to his friend Theodore E. Child* (30 May [1885]) that the elaborately feted Frenchman was both "great and absurd."

Humber, Frank. In *Guy Domville*, Guy Domville's close friend from their Catholic school days in France. Humber, a neighbor of the widowed Mrs. Peverel, proposes to her, and when Guy decides to join the Church is accepted.

Hume-Walker, Captain. In "Owen Wingrave," the dead British soldier brother of Mrs. Julian. He was once engaged to Jane Wingrave. In *The Saloon*, he is mentioned as having been killed on the Afghan border.

Hunt, Violet (1862–1942). British fiction writer, biographer, and journalist. The daughter of pre-Raphaelite landscape painter Alfred William Hunt and novelist Margaret Raine Hunt, Isobel Violet Hunt grew up in a circle of artists, including Sir Edward Burne-Jones,* William Holman Hunt,* William Morris,* and Dante Gabriel Rossetti.* After abandoning art studies, Violet Hunt became a *Pall Mall Gazette* columnist, an advocate of women's rights, a daring Chelsea hostess, and a novelist. She was also the possessive, indiscreet lover first of Oswald John Frederick Crawfurd* (1892–1898) and then of Ford Madox Hueffer* (about 1908–1914). She wrote a novel called *Sooner or Later* (1904) based on her Crawfurd affair. In her autobiography, she calls Hueffer, Joseph Leopold. Her literary friends also included Joseph Conrad,* Douglas Goldring, W. H. Hudson, David Herbert Lawrence,* Ezra Pound, W. Somerset Maugham, and Oscar Wilde.* Her novels began with *The Maiden's Progress: A Novel in Dialogue* (1894) and soon included, among other early ones, *Unkist, Unkind!* (1897), *The Human Interest* (1899), *White Rose of Weary Leaf* (1908), and *The Wife of Altamont* (1910), with more later. Her short-story collections include *Tales of the Uneasy* (1910) and *More Tales of the Uneasy* (1925). She wrote a biography of Rossetti's wife (1932) and an autobiographical volume covering the years from 1908 to 1915 and entitled *I Have This to Say: The Story of My Flurried Years* (1926). James first met Violet Hunt when she was a child. He admired her early racy fiction and specifically praised *The Human Interest*, with typical reservations about its style. She first visited Lamb House* in the summer of 1903. She alleges in her diary that in 1907 she shocked James by frankly discussing her love affair with Crawfurd, but she frequently returned to Lamb House until, in November 1909, Hueffer told James that he was hoping to get a divorce and marry Violet. James instantly wrote to her (2 Nov 1909) that the news "compels me to regard all agreeable and unembarrassed communication between us as impossible." She protested, but he stood firm for a while. She and Hueffer went to Germany, obtained a bogus divorce, and were publicly embarrassed when it was held invalid in a British court (1912). By this time, however, James was her (and Hueffer's) friend again.

Hunt, William Holman (1827–1910). London-born artist. By the age of sixteen he was an independent artist. In art school Holman Hunt met his lifelong friend Sir John Everett Millais.* The two men, with their friend Dante Gabriel Rossetti,* founded the Pre-Raphaelite Brotherhood (1848–1849). Hunt's literary and religious paintings were popular from the late 1840s. John Ruskin* praised them. But sales were slow in the early 1850s, and Hunt thought of quitting his profession. Then he scored successes, enabling him to travel in 1854 to the Holy Land. His painting *The Scapegoat* was exhibited in 1856. He did a portrait of Rossetti. In later years, Hunt remained faithful to pre-Raphaelite principles when others of the movement did not. He published *Pre-Raphaelitism and the Pre-Raphaelite Brotherhood* in 1905. In a few of his art notices, James mentions Hunt but hardly in praise. For example, he twice comments in 1877 on Hunt's *After-Glow in Egypt*: First, he says that it "is a puzzle, so much of beautiful work does it contain, and yet so little of easy and natural charm" ("The Grosvenor Gallery and the Royal Academy," 31 May 1877); second, he notes the "beauty of workmanship" in it but also its "singular want of inspiration" ("The Picture Season in London," Aug 1877). James calls a later portrait by Hunt "garish" and the "perfection of hideousness" ("London Pictures and London Plays," *Atlantic Monthly*, Aug 1882). James met Holman Hunt and his wife in 1879 or 1880. With the two of them, he attended the funeral of the painter Sir Edward Burne-Jones* in 1898. James admired Hunt's wife more than he did Hunt, whose conversation, according to Sir Edward Howard Marsh,* James once "likened to a trickle of tepid water from a tap one is unable to turn off." In *A Small Boy and Others*, James recalls being terrified by Hunt's *Scapegoat* in London in 1858 because it was "so charged with the awful."

Hunt, William Morris (1824–1879). Vermont-born painter who studied in Paris and introduced Barbizon-style landscape painting to America after his return in 1855. He established studios in Newport, Rhode Island, and in Boston. Many of his paintings were lost in the 1872 Boston fire. He published *Talks about Art* in 1878. He drowned the following year. In 1860–1861, William James studied art in Hunt's studio, as did John La Farge.* Henry James tagged along to sample a few classes. In "Art" (Feb 1872), James regards the Boston exhibition he is reviewing as not containing Hunt's most representative works, some of which he identifies. Furthermore, he deplores Hunt's recent tendency "toward coarseness" and recklessness, but he does express general admiration for a few of his smaller canvases. James mentions Hunt several times in his autobiographical volumes. For example, in *A Small Boy and Others*, he calls Hunt "the New Englander of genius, the 'Boston painter' whose authority was greatest during the thirty years from 1857 or so"; in *Notes of a Son and Brother*, he says that Hunt "was distinguished and accomplished, charming and kind."

Hunter, Sir William Wilson (1840–1900). British civil servant, statistician, author, and editor. He was born in Glasgow, educated there, and later in Paris and Bonn, and learned Sanskrit in the process. Going to India in the Civil Service in 1862, he studied Indian dialects, did statistical work in Bengal, was a governmental council member and an education and finance commissioner, but, most important, he supervised the 128-volume statistical survey of the Indian Empire (1869–1881, later condensed). Among other works, he wrote *A Brief History of the Indian Peoples* (1880, later revised). He served briefly as vice chancellor of the University of Calcutta (1886). After he retired near Oxford in 1887, he supervised the series entitled *Rulers of India*, for which he wrote two volumes. In "London" (27 Mar 1897), James calls Hunter's early work, *Annals of Rural Bengal* (1868), "almost classic," then he recommends *The Thackerays of India* (1897) by Hunter "to readers whose feeling for Thackeray is still a living sentiment." James commends Hunter for his "light and competent hand."

Huntington family. An expatriated American family related by marriage to the Greenough family.*

Hurter, Fanny. In "The Death of the Lion," an American girl whom the critic narrator persuades to respect Neil Paraday's privacy. She later marries the narrator, and the two plan to seek Paraday's missing manuscript together.

Hutchby. In *The Tragic Muse*, a political organizer mentioned by Nick Dormer and Julia Dallow.

Huxley, Thomas Henry (1825–1895). Illustrious British biologist and, in time, head of a distinguished family of scientists and writers. After service in the navy, he was a professor of natural history and medicine; he advocated the theories of Charles Robert Darwin*; and he published widely. James met Huxley in 1877 during a dinner party at the home of George Washburn Smalley.* In a letter to his brother William (29 Mar [1877]), James described Huxley as "a very genial, comfortable being." In 1889 James caused his brother William to meet Leonard Huxley, T. H. Huxley's editor and author son and later the father of novelist and critic Aldous Huxley. In 1894 T. H. Huxley sent James his complete works, which occasioned a graciously turned letter of acknowledgment (27 Oct 1894).

Huysmans, Joris-Karl (real name, Charles-Marie Georges) (1848–1907). French novelist whose forebears included Dutch artists. He published a few realistic novels, then antimaterialistic and decadent ones. Huysmans patterned Des Esseintes in *À Rebours* (1884) partly after both Robert, Count de Montesquiou-Fezensac* and Gustave Moreau.* In a letter to Sir Edmund Wilson Gosse* ([3 Sep 1892]), James complains that Huysmans's *Soeurs Vatard* (1879) "is *not* my ideal." Later (9 Aug [1895]), he adds that Huysmans's *En Route* (1895) "is strange & vile & perverse, but of an extraordinary *facture* & an interesting sincerity."

I

Ibsen, Henrik Johan (1828–1906). Norwegian playwright and poet, born in Skien into the family of a merchant who failed. After working as a druggist's assistant in the small village of Grimstad, being a student in Oslo, and doing editorial work there (to 1851), Ibsen became a theater director and dramatist in Bergen (to 1857) and then Oslo (to 1862). Disliking the Norwegian political stance during the Dano-German war, he expatriated himself, first to Italy (to 1868) and then to Germany (until 1891), then he returned to Oslo. After writing minor dramas, he became successful with such romantic historical plays as *The Warriors at Helgoland* (1858) and the bitter dramatic poems *Brand* (1866) and *Peer Gynt* (1867). His early satirical social dramas, including *Love's Comedy* (1862), led to a sequence of brilliant, famous, and influential sociopsychological plays, including *The Pillars of Society* (1877), *A Doll's House* (1879), *Ghosts* (1881), *An Enemy of the People* (1884), *The Wild Duck* (1884), *Rosmersholm* (1886), *The Lady from the Sea* (1888), *Hedda Gabler* (1890), *The Master Builder* (1892), *Little Eyolf* (1894), *John Gabriel Borkman* (1896), and *When We Dead Awaken* (1899). Typically, Ibsen, lonely and detached from literary currents, dramatizes the plight of the individual who fights social conventions (including marital ones) and the inimical, impersonal state. He also shows, in a mystical Christian way, that tragedy results from denial of love. James learned of Ibsen through his friend Sir Edmund Wilson Gosse,* who helped popularize the playwright in England and to whom James wrote (29 Jan 1889), "I have perused your very interesting account of Ibsen. . . . You must tell me more . . . " But it took James a long time to appreciate Ibsen. Later in 1889 he may have seen a few Ibsen plays, one of which featured Elizabeth Robins,* whom he certainly saw in *A Doll's House*, met in January 1891, and saw again in *Hedda Gabler* in April 1891. In a letter to Robert Louis Stevenson* (18 Feb 1891), he called

Hedda Gabler Ibsen's "queerest." In a letter to Gosse (28 Apr [1891?]) he says that Gosse makes Ibsen "a richer phenomenon than he is," adding that certain named works by the dramatist seem "a grey mediocrity." But in his essay "On the Occasion of *Hedda Gabler*" (*New Review*, Jun 1891; reprinted as part of "Henrik Ibsen," in *Essays in London and Elsewhere*, 1893), he calls Ibsen "a barometer of the intellectual weather" and a guide "in the thickening fog of life," then finds the artistry of his plays arousing a range of emotions "from frantic enjoyment to ineffable disgust," but all "exclusively moral." The plays should be seen, not simply read. He concentrates on the unglamorously "suburban" *Hedda Gabler*, which on stage is "vivid and curious," owes more to form than to subject, and lacks humor, imagination, and style, though it is possessed of spirit and manner. Ibsen's characters are "inexpressive," limited, not prone to play or to be romantic, and when sarcastic "nearer to tears than to laughter." The playwright dourly squeezes us to make us pay attention, shows us "ugly interior[s]" and clothes, and presents conditions and psychological states, rather than actions. Thus, Hedda Gabler, "an exasperated woman," is immediately shown to be "ripe for her catastrophe," with no presentation of "preliminary stages": "[I]f we ask for antecedents and explanations we must simply find them in her character." It is foolish to "quarrel . . . with an artist over his subject." Though "wicked, diseased, disagreeable," Hedda "is human" and "acts on others." *The Pillars of Society* has such a "complexity of moral cross-references" that the audience is required "to see too many things at once." Ibsen is not "pleasant enough nor light enough nor casual enough" ever to be popular, but he will "be adored by the [acting] 'profession,' " which will be grateful for the challenge to present "our plastic humanity." James indicates familiarity with eleven Ibsen works in this essay, which William Archer,* drama critic and early Ibsen translator, praised highly in a letter to James. The actress Robins read Ibsen's brand-new play *The Master Builder* to James in November 1892. In his "Ibsen's New Play" (*Pall Mall Gazette*, 17 Feb 1893; also reprinted as part of "Henrik Ibsen," in *Essays in London and Elsewhere*), James briefly reviews a production of *The Master Builder*, translated by Gosse and Archer, and starring Robins. Here James calls Ibsen "the battered Norseman," and his new play a "mystic missile" which may weave an "irritating spell" but certainly "gives us the sense of life." What does this play, with "material so solid and so fresh," inspire in us? Imagination, sense of technique, moral judgment? James contrasts Hilda Wangel, its heroine, with Hedda earlier, concluding that Hilda is "a Hedda stimulating, fully beneficent in intention; in short 'reversed.' " *The Master Builder* is yet another challenge and an opportunity for actors and actresses. In his *Notebooks* (21 Dec 1896), James thanks a reading "in proof" of *John Gabriel Borkman* for enabling him to see that "the *scenic* method is . . . my *only* salvation" in completing *What Maisie Knew*. In "London" (23 Jan 1897), James voices a preference for reading plays by William Shakespeare* but for attending those by Ibsen. He adds that Ibsen's *Little Eyolf* spellbinds the audience within minutes: One simply "surrender[s] . . . the imagination to his microcosm." In "London" (6 Feb 1897), James calls Ibsen "a provincial of provincials" and a "sturdy old symbolist," praises him for writing *John Gabriel Borkman* at age seventy, and says the play offers a "dry . . . view of life" but has "intensity" and "mastery of form." Late in his life, James discussed Ibsen with his Rye neighbor Sir Sydney Philip Waterlow,* who later wrote that James could not understand how Ibsen could write so well so early in life, given the absence of literary influences during his cramped youth. Tight structure (including elimination of preliminary exposition by the technique of retrospection), moral accountability, and a movement from realism toward symbolism in James's major phase fiction may be attributed in considerable part to his admiration of Ibsen's works. Both *The Spoils of Poynton* and *The Other House* use an Ibsen-like retrospective technique. Further, in the latter, the characterization of violent Rose Armiger may owe much to certain Ibsen heroines, including Rebecca West in *Rosmersholm*, Hedda Gabler, and Hilda Wangel. Society in *The Awkward Age*, just as in Ibsen, is shown, though more wittily and lightly, to be corrupt and decadent. In both that novel and *The Outcry*, events are presented scenically. Many character echoes from *Rosmersholm* may be detected in *The Ambassadors*: Lambert Strether resembles John Rosmer; Madame de Vionnet, Rebecca West; and Mrs. Abel Newsome, Beata Kroll Rosmer. At the outset, Maggie Verver in *The Golden Bowl* has a touch of childishness resembling that of Nora Helmer in *A Doll's House*. James's library contained six books by Ibsen, comprising ten of his plays.

Iffield, Lord. In "Glasses," Lord and Lady Considine's son. He would be happy to marry Flora Saunt except for her blindness.

Imber, Lady Kitty. In *The Outcry*, the novel, and *The Outcry*, the play, Lord Theign's older daughter and Lady Grace's sister. Kitty has amassed gambling debts which her father considers paying by raising money through the sale of some of his art treasures.

"The Impressions of a Cousin." Long short story (27,300 words), published in the *Century Magazine* (Nov–Dec 1883); reprinted in *Tales of Three Cities*, 1884. (Characters: Caliph, Catherine Condit, Lizzie Ermine, William Ermine, Eunice, Adrian Frank, Freddy, Harry, Latrobe, Letitia, Willie Woodley.) The narrator is a painter named Catherine Condit. She visits New York cousin Eunice, whose financial matters are handled by a dishonest man named Caliph. His half-brother Adrian Frank courts Eunice but quickly falls in love with the narrator. Matchmaker Mrs. Ermine wants Eunice and Caliph to get married. When the narrator discovers Caliph's swindling and tells Eunice, that infatuated girl gets her to promise not to expose him. Still, the narrator drops hints to Frank, who because of his love covers the financial losses. In anguish, Eunice sends her cousin (the narrator) away. Thinking that the girl must now be cured, the narrator tauntingly tells Caliph that Eunice once would have loved him. Caliph then begins to attract the girl again, with the result that the narrator promises poor Frank that she will marry him if Eunice—now rich again—marries Caliph. The idea for this curious story came from what James admitted in two Notebook entries (17 Jan 1881, 30 May 1881) was a rather unreal incident appearing in a book about Madame de Sévigné by Lady Anne Isabella Ritchie.* James wisely alters the original idea that the victimized French girl would enter a convent. The name Caliph may come from *The Arabian Nights*, one of James's favorite books. As developed, James's uninspired story of deception is weakened by an implicitly happy ending in the offing. James's use of the first-person singular point of view, a technique he deplored, is problematic here.

"In Belgium." Travel essay, published in the *Nation* (3 Sep 1874); reprinted in *Transatlantic Sketches*, 1875. James begins by remembering aspects of Holland, which one should visit after Belgium for maximum effect: canals, trees, paths, brick walls, tulip gardens, ponds with goldfish and swans, gray clouds, and blue sky. He was introduced to Belgium at the simple, solemn, vast Antwerp cathedral, with devout Catholic worshippers and unveiled paintings by Peter Paul Rubens* ("monstrous flowers of art"). James visits the Antwerp Museum and is displeased by the works of Rubens there, despite the learned comments by Émile Montégut.* On to Brussels, which is solid, extensive, "less elegant than . . . Paris . . . but . . . more picturesque." He likes the Hôtel de Ville, its belfry, the St. Gudule cathedral, the high Parc, the bright Place Royale. He enjoys some Dutch school "gems" in the museum. Then Ghent, with "one of the [great] pictures of the world," *The Adoration of the Lamb* by Hubert and Jan Van Eyck, "too perfect for praise." James also likes "the precious [Hans] Memlings" at "drowsy little" Bruges.

"In Holland." Travel essay, published in the *Nation* (27 Aug 1873); reprinted in *Transatlantic Sketches*, 1875. James opens with praise of Rhine scenes, including crags, vineyards, and cloisters, along his watery route into Holland, which is familiar to him in advance because of "the undiluted accuracy of Dutch painters." Admirable things here are small, are pitched in "the minor key," and make visitors more reasonable and kind. Prosaic Amsterdam has canals, thin trees, scrubbed bricks, and Venetian elements combined into the reverse of poetic Venice (because of "a different view of life"). James wonders why he finds The Hague so much "to my taste." Halfway between "the bustling and the stagnant," it is Dutch enough to be comfortable, English and French enough to be cosmopolitan. But since his main goal is to see the art in Holland, James finds and admires Paul Potter's *Bull* and then works by Ruysdael [Jacob or Solomon?]. Ruysdael "gives me the largest sum of tranquil pleasure of any painter in the school." James disputes the tradition which exalts Rembrandt* Harmensz van Rijn as an artist of ideas.

"In Scotland." Travel essay, published in the *Nation* (10, 24 Oct 1878). James calls Edinburgh "a livelier place than London" in September, in fact, "a highly convenient play-ground for English idlers" right now. Some come up to hunt and fish. Their hunting dogs are "beautiful [and] silken-eared." Other tourists come for the scenery and the excellent inns. James observes "operatic" Princes Street, the awkward but complimentary monument to Sir Walter Scott,* and jumbled Calton Hill. He commends Scotsmen for being proud of their fine history, literature, landscapes, and democracy, and for their frank awareness of "national shortcomings." He turns to the topic of the British passion for sports, specifically, here, shooting deer and grouse. The gorgeous moors and hills of Scotland appear now to be divided into "playgrounds for English millionaires." The tourists also dance Highland reels in handy Scotish ballrooms. James finds local color aplenty: native sports, bagpipes, "grim Presbyterian" kirk services, and "most agreeable" picnics on Frenchified castle lawns.

"In the Cage." Long short story (32,800 words), published in London by Duckworth, 1898, and in Chicago and New York by Stone, 1898; revised and reprinted in *The Novels and Tales of Henry James*, Volume XI, 1908. (Characters: Lady Bradeen, Lord Bradeen, Mrs. Bubb, Buckton, Burfield, Mr. and Mrs. Buttons, Dr. Buzzard, Cissy, Cocker, Cooper, Miss Dolman, Drake, Captain Count Philip Everard, Fritz, Haddon, Mrs. Jordan, Ladle, Mason, Marguerite, Mary, Montenero, Mudge, Lady Agnes Orme, Lord Rye, Savoy, Simpkin, Thrupp, Lady Ventnor.) An unnamed girl works in the post-and-telegraph cage of Cocker's store. Her fiancé, a gruff but decent man named Mudge, asks her to leave this employment in Mayfair, move to Chalk Farm, and live with her mother to save money until their marriage. She refuses because she loves her work since it enables her to fantasize concerning her rich customers' lives. One such person is beautiful Lady Bradeen; another, glittering Captain Count Philip Everard. The caged girl also declines the invitation to come to work with her friend Mrs. Jordan, who arranges flowers for fancy parties. The girl helps astonished Lady Bradeen change a telegram for the better; she also locates Everard's home, sits with him in Hyde Park, cries, and tells the too solicitous man that she will gladly remain in her cage to be of help to him. During a brief vacation at Bournemouth with her mother and Mudge, she is upset by the news that her fiancé has been given a sufficient raise to permit their marriage. She insists that she must stay in Cocker's cage to help Everard, now embroiled in a bad love affair. One day that handsome man enters Cocker's seeking a certain wire sent earlier by Lady Bradeen and dangerously intercepted. The girl quotes its message from memory: All is well, since Lady Bradeen chanced to dispatch the wrong contents. Everard is both relieved and grateful. Later the girl sees Mrs. Jordan, who is going to marry Drake, Lady Bradeen's new butler. Through this connection the girl learns that Lady Bradeen is going to marry Everard, who compromised her while her husband was alive. Lady Bradeen stole something to save Everard and hence has him in her power.

Deciding now to wed Mudge, the girl ponders recent strange events in which she vicariously participated. James may have been partly inspired to write "In the Cage" by an episode in *Il Romanzo della fanciulla*, which was first entitled *Telegrafi dello stato* (1895), by Matilde Serao.* In his 1901 essay on Serao, James praises her "exhibition . . . of grinding girl-life in the big telegraph office" in that work. The main charm of "In the Cage," which was the first fiction James dictated to a secretary (William MacAlpine*), is the unnamed female telegraphist's incredible imaginative and inferential powers. He shows considerable ingenuity in restricting the reader's view to that of the telegraphist. His neat title is both literal and figurative; furthermore, "the cage" may be taken as a metaphor for most quietly desperate people's plight in this harsh world.

"In Warwickshire." Travel essay, published in the *Galaxy* (Nov 1877); reprinted in *Portraits of Places*, 1883, and in *English Hours*, 1905. The best way for a stranger to learn about England is to pass two weeks in "mellow, conservative" Warwickshire, "the core and centre of the English world." At Kenilworth, James visits "the quaintish village" and "the solid red castle," and he observes cottages, meadows, and sheep, and also a festival some miles away on "[t]he cushiony lawn" of a rectory (with tennis, dancing, Norman-windowed church, yard, and cemetery). He rhapsodizes on the appeal and goodness of " 'nice' " English girls. He goes to Warwick (castle, hospital), Coventry (charitable places, school), Charlecote park (of "venerable verdure"), Stratford-upon-Avon (with marvelous "old English houses," the tomb of William Shakespeare,* the Avon River, meadows, and "poetic . . . sheep"). Warwickshire is George Eliot* country, too, and James associates some of her works with the region. James travels on, in search of three fine but unpublicized country residences: Broughton Castle (steeped in Cromwellian history), Compton Wyniates ("ivy-smothered," empty), and Wroxton Abbey (occupied, "full of . . . splendid detail").

Income. James's income during his adult years came from family allowances, periodical and book publication, play royalties, lecturing, and inheritance. His literary income, exclusive therefore of income from family property, has been carefully estimated from 1864, when he published his first short story and first review, through 1915, the year of his fatal strokes. Broken down into decades and partial decades, this income is as follows in dollars (pounds have been converted at £1 = $4.85): 1860s, $2,147; 1870s, $20,186; 1880s, $50,187; 1890s, $36,788; 1900s, $49,041; and 1910s, $23,057. The total is $182,106, or $3,502 per year for fifty-two years. James's three worst years were 1864 ($12), 1870 ($265), and 1869 ($350). His three best years were 1905 ($9,520), 1888 ($8,698), and 1884 ($7,604). To figure equivalents in purchasing power a century and more later, one should multiply by seven to ten, or so. When James's father died in 1882, he left an estate worth $95,000. According to his will, Alice James was to receive an adequate income for life; William James,

Henry James, and Robertson James were to divide the estate; their brother Garth Wilkinson James was to receive nothing, since he had been given not only his inheritance earlier but also an additional sum upon declaring bankruptcy. James, who had been named executor of the father's will, persuaded the parties concerned to give Wilky a trust fund, dissuaded William from claiming more because he was a family man, and made over the income from his own share to Alice. After her death in 1892, James received property worth about $20,000 from her $80,000 estate. Accordingly, from 1893 to 1906, his unearned income was substantial; after the latter date, once his brother William's astute son Henry James III had begun to manage some of the James family holdings, the novelist's unearned income was even higher. During his tour of the United States in 1904–1905, James lectured several times for between $200 to $400 per performance.

Inglefield, Earl of. In *The Princess Casamassima*, Lady Aurora Langrish's father.

Ingram, Elizabeth. In "Crawford's Consistency," Peter and Sabrina Ingram's daughter. First they force her to give up Crawford; then smallpox blasts her beauty.

Ingram, Peter and Sabrina. In "Crawford's Consistency," Elizabeth's socially ambitious parents.

"International Copyright." Letter (15 Nov 1887), to the Executive Committee, American Copyright League (*Critic* 10 Dec 1887); reprinted in *What American Authors Think about International Copyright* (New York: The American Copyright League, 1888). James expresses regret at being unable to attend a late November London conference of the American Copyright League, applauds its efforts, comments on the generosity of British copyright laws toward foreign authors living in England, and hopes that America, usually very "liberal," will also extend reciprocity once it understands that it would not be financially harmful and would be culturally advantageous to do so.

"An International Episode." Long short story (29,300 words), published in the *Cornhill Magazine* (Dec 1878–Jan 1879); reprinted in New York by Harper, 1879; reprinted in *Daisy Miller: A Study . . .* , in London by Macmillan, 1879; revised and reprinted in *The Novels and Tales of Henry James*, Volume XIV, 1908. (Characters: Bessie Alden, Duke and Duchess of Bayswater, Percy Beaumont, Lady Beatrice Bellevue, Marquis of Blackborough, Mlle. Boquet, Mr. and Mrs. Butterworth, Duke of Green-Erin, Lady Julia, Lord Lambeth, Captain Littledale, Countess of Pimlico, J. L. Westgate, Kitty Alden Westgate, Willie Woodley.) In August 1874, New York businessman J. L. Westgate kindly arranges for two British visitors, Percy Beaumont and his younger cousin Lord Lambeth, to be hospitably welcomed by Westgate's wife Kitty and her unmarried sister Bessie Alden at the Westgate's lush summer residence at Newport, Rhode Island. Lambeth is entranced by Bessie, but when she innocently asks Beaumont about Lambeth's British rank and future, he warns Lambeth's mother, who summons the young man home by a subterfuge. The following spring Kitty and Bessie vacation in England, where through their traveling American friend Willie Woodley they see Lambeth again. Kitty warns her sister that she may appear to be pursuing Lambeth, who indeed is growing so attentive that he says he wants both American women to visit Branches, the country estate of his aristocratic family. Kitty abruptly asks Bessie whether she is in love with Lambeth. When the girl says no, Kitty suggests that they scare Lambeth's proud family by making them think so. Bessie turns silent. Beaumont warns Lambeth that his family will not accept Miss Alden; still, Lambeth persuades his mother (the Duchess of Bayswater) and his sister (the Countess of Pimlico) to call upon the Americans at their London hotel. Talk is cool: The British ladies are apprehensive, aloof; Kitty is aware that the pair hope the Americans will not visit Branches; Bessie professes to regard the callers as charming if reserved. Lambeth tells Beaumont that he would not like to propose to Miss Alden only to be rejected; yet all of that is evidently just what happens on the day following the momentous visit of his mother and sister. Bessie, apparently resenting nothing, writes to decline the invitation to Branches. Lambeth is sorrowful. Kitty is distressed to think that the British ladies will wrongly conclude that they scared off the American women. As he said in a letter to his brother William (23 Jul [1878]), James regarded "An International Episode" as "a counterpart to *D.M.* ["Daisy Miller"]." In a letter from London to Grace Norton* (4 Jan [1879]), James expresses disgust: "[M]y little 'International Episode' has given offence to various people . . . here. . . . So long as one serves up Americans for their entertainment it is all right— but hands off the sacred natives!" He voices more criticism of the British in a letter to his mother (18 Jan [1879]): "It is an entirely new sensation for . . . people here . . . to be . . ., *ironized* or satirized, from the American point of view." James may have challenged himself to write "An International Episode" when in his 1878 review of "Tender Recollections of Irene Macgillicuddy," by Laurence Oliphant,* he urged American writers to respond to Oliphant's fiction, which satirizes the eagerness of New York girls to snare titled Britishers. "An International Episode," though an excessively long tale, is nicely balanced, with three chapters in America and then three in England. It brilliantly evokes American settings. English readers regularly find James's portrayal of their countrymen a demeaning caricature; American readers too quickly applaud his depiction of hospitable Americans. In real life, Lambeth could hardly be so superficial. (In a letter to the wife of Frank Harrison Hill* [21 Mar 1879]), James agrees that he had Lambeth say "I say" too much.) And in real life Bessie not only would have turned on her meddling, rudely chattering sister, but also probably would have found more to love in Lambeth. One of the finest parts of the story is the well-staged conversation of the four women, toward the close.

Irving, Sir Henry (1838–1905). English actor, manager, and director (born John Henry Brodribb). After clerking for London merchants for a time, he tried acting, made his debut in 1856, and thereafter took five hundred parts in a decade of provincial stock-company touring. Then he enjoyed success in London from 1866 to 1867, acting with Dame Ellen Terry* among other notables. Irving achieved long-running successes in 1870 and 1871. Through the 1870s, he scored triumphs in several controversial Shakespearean performances (notably as Hamlet and Shylock). In 1878 he took over the Lyceum as manager and became a force in the British theater until the turn of the century. He and his Lyceum company visited the United States and Canada eight times. He was innovative, for example, with regard to lighting. The first actor ever to be knighted, in 1895, he was versatile, mannered, and influential. In an untitled note (*Nation*, 25 Nov 1875), James calls Irving's recent performance as Macbeth "the acting of a very superior amateur" who if younger ought to go to a drama school. His physical attributes are "meagre"; his declamation, "flat." But he is good at portraying terror. More tersely and candidly, in a letter to his parents (9 Nov [1875]), James called Irving "clever, but by no means a genius." In "The Parisian Stage" (1876), James digresses to opine that "Irving [in *Macbeth*] . . . is so meagre in the essentials and so redundant in the (relatively) superfluous." In "The London Theatres" (1877), James is most critical: Irving's Macbeth and Richard III cause James to "fall . . . among the sceptics"; Irving displays "aberrations"; his voice is unsuitable for declamation; and he wrongly thinks he need be "simply picturesque." In two letters home in 1878 (to William [2 Jan (1878)] and to his father [25 Mar (1878)]), James criticizes Irving harshly. But, later that year in an untitled note (*Nation*, 13 Jun 1878), he praises as "probably his most satisfactory creation" Irving's performance in the title role of Dion Boucicault's 1855 adaptation of Casimir Delavigne's *Louis XI* (1832). In "The London Theatres" (1881), James says that Irving's poor performance in his revival of *The Corsican Brothers* gives "a fiendish satisfaction" to his severe critics. In "London Pictures and London Plays" (1882), James says that attendance at a French-type training school in Irving's youth might have "suppressed some of his extraordinary peculiarities," then he ridicules his recent *Romeo and Juliet*, co-starring Terry. The publication by William Archer* of *Henry Irving, Actor and Manager: A Critical Study* (1883), which was antagonistic toward Irving, only reinforced James's opinions. In "The Acting of Mr. Irving's *Faust*" (*Century Magazine*, Dec 1887), James brands William Gorman Wills's adaptation of the dramatic poem by Johann Wolfgang von Goethe* "meagre, . . . common, . . . trivial." James goes on to complain that the theatrical "accessories," the "traps and panoramas, processions and coloured lights," of Irving's production are "a more important part of the business than the action." Further, his acting resembles "that of the star of a Christmas burlesque,—without breadth, without depth, with little tittering effects of low comedy." Terry, Sir George Alexander,* and others also perform ignorantly. James observes in "Mr. Henry Irving's Production of *Cymbeline*" (*Harper's Weekly*, 21 Nov 1896) that Shakespeare's play here being "a florid fairy-tale," Irving wisely makes Terry picturesque and the action a "merry . . . game," all showing off "his great art of visible composition." And in "London" (23 Jan 1897), James sees fit to praise Irving's ability, commenting that in a recent production of Shakespeare's *Richard III* the actor "plays on the chord of the sinister-sardonic, flowered over as vividly as may be with the elegant-grotesque."

Irving, Washington (1783–1859). New York–born professional man of letters. Influenced by eighteenth- and nineteenth-century British writers, he developed an engaging American prose style. Irving spent much of his life in Europe (1804–1806, 1815–1832, 1842–1846), mostly in England, but also in Spain (1826–1829, and 1842–1846 as ambassador there). His fiancée died in 1809, and the writer never married. In 1834 he bought an old Dutch house which he named Sunnyside, on the Hudson River. Among his many important literary friends abroad may be named Sir Walter Scott.* Irving's works include *A History of New York* (1809), *The Sketch-Book* (1819–1820), *Bracebridge Hall* (1822), *Tales of a Traveller* (1824), *A Chronicle of Granada* (1829), *The Alhambra* (1832), *A Tour of the Prairies* (1835), and biographies of Christopher Columbus (1828), Captain Benjamin Louis Eulalie de Bonneville (1837), Oliver Goldsmith* (1849), Mahomet (1850), and George Washington (1855–1859). Irving is best loved now for his satirical *History of New York* and for several sparkling short stories, notably "Rip Van Winkle" and "The Legend of Sleepy Hollow." In *A Small Boy and Others*, James recalls that, as a boy of seven with his father, he met Irving on a boat going from New York to Fort Hamilton. The two adults discussed the recent drowning of Margaret Fuller. In "New York and the Hudson: A Spring Impression," in *The American Scene*, James tells how visiting "ensconced and embowered" Sunnyside evokes memories of "the wonder of Rip Van Winkle." He hopes that "the Sleepy Hollow of the author's charming imagination was . . . off somewhere in the hills," away from automobiles on the Albany highway. James takes note of Irving's "original modest house," with its study, library, prints, and scenery—all coalescing into "easy elements" and a "fund of reminiscence and material" for Irving, but also, for us, "the last faint echo of a felicity forever gone." James's library contained seven volumes by Irving.

"Is There a Life after Death?" Essay, published in *Harper's Bazaar* (Jan, Feb 1910); reprinted as part of *In after Days: Some Thoughts on the Future Life* (New York and London: Harper, 1910), which book contains essays by Thomas Wentworth Storrow Higginson,* Julia Ward Howe,* and William Dean Howells,* among others. James says that the question of life after death becomes more interesting as we grow older. Some people long for "extinction"; others, for an expansion of consciousness. Our desire as to the future depends on what life has done to us thus far. Should "dull people," who have wasted their opportunities, be given still more chances? It is grim that science ignores the soul while we see physical decay all about. We are reduced to wondering about "renewal" of personality, which sadly, however, keeps contracting from former magnificence, prompting us to recognize "the absoluteness of death." The dead (even the strongest, even the youngest) are disconnected from us, and we from them; they throw no light on the problem and are indifferent, and so is nature. Faith and hope resist, but we conclude that "the laboratory-brain . . . [is] really all." James says that for a long time life alone busied him and death was remote. But now the universe tells him that it could do without his consciousness. If James's, then that of others too. Still, the question of death remained unsettled. Curiously, as he concluded more certainly that his consciousness was finite, he lived more in it, and the world seemed more exclusively interesting. He enjoyed his consciousness ever more amply, and found ever more exciting the possibilities of relating the self to the universe: "[E]ven should one cease to be in love with life it would be difficult . . . not to be in love with living." Such is "the consecrated 'interest' of consciousness." Each artist should wish to carry consciousness "in[to] the ineffable" and thus have a "share" in it. James wishes to mature his consciousness forever, and he hopes that "our prime originator" will not lead him on, like a teased dog, only to deny him. Surely we are not immersed "in the fountain of being" and allowed to "scent . . . universal sources," only to be "disconnect[ed]." The material world prepares us for "heaven," as a wooden frame with wheels guards an infant while it is being taught to walk. James " 'like[s]' to think" all this, and he yearns so steadily that "belief . . . [becomes] irrelevant" and he "acts from desire." If he desires, he cannot do less; nor could he do more, if he believed. He feels that he is doing something for his own "prospect . . . of immortality" and thus "reach[es] beyond the laboratory-brain."

"An Italian Convent." Travel essay, published in the *Independent* (2 Jul 1874); reprinted as one of the eight-part "Florentine Notes" in *Transatlantic Sketches*, 1875, and in *Italian Hours*, 1909.

Italian Hours. Loose collection of twenty-two travel essays, with thirty-two illustrations by Joseph Pennell*; published by Heinemann in London, 1909, and by Houghton Mifflin in Boston and New York, 1909. The essays, often with new titles, are as follows: 1. "Venice," 2. "The Grand Canal," 3. "Venice: An Early Impression" (former title, "From Venice to Strasburg"), 4. "Two Old Houses and Three Young Women," 5. "Casa Alvisi" (former title, "The Late Mrs. Arthur Bronson[*]"), 6. "From Chambéry to Milan," 7. "The Old Saint-Gothard" (former title, "The St. Gothard"), 8. "Italy Revisited," 9. "A Roman Holiday," 10. "Roman Rides," 11. "Roman Neighbourhoods," 12. "The After-Season in Rome," 13. "From a Roman Note-Book," 14. "A Few Other Roman Neighbourhoods," 15. "A Chain of Cities," 16. "Siena Early and Late" (former title of part 1, "Siena"), 17. "The Autumn in Florence," 18. "Florentine Notes," 19. "Tuscan Cities," 20. "Other Tuscan Cities," 21.

"Ravenna," and 22. "The Saint's Afternoon and Others" (former title of parts 1–5, "The Saint's Afternoon"). Essays 14, 16 (part 2), 20, and 22 (parts 6 and 7) were written for *Italian Hours*. Essays 4 and 5 appear here for the first time in book form. The rest appeared in book form earlier. In a letter to Sir Edmund Wilson Gosse* (11 Nov 1909), James curiously calls the Heinemann edition of *Italian Hours* "a lumpish . . . piece of catchpenny bookmaking."

"Italy Revisited." Travel essay, published in *Atlantic Monthly* (Apr 1878); reprinted as part of "Italy Revisited," in *Italian Hours*, 1909.

"Italy Revisited." Travel essay (originally two 1878 essays, "Italy Revisited" and "Recent Florence"), reprinted as a unit in *Portraits of Places*, 1883, and in *Italian Hours*, 1909. James waits in enchanting, autumnal Paris until after the October 14 elections (in 1877) to take "the odious and the charming" train through "ill-regulated" Italian customs offices and on to Turin, where he roams its noble porticoes and ponders the grand history of Italy and its "modern crudity." James laughs at the symbolism of a Tuscan shrine to the Madonna lighted by Pennsylvania kerosene. He goes on to tangled, sketchable Genoa and his enormous hotel there, planted amid clattering streets full of toiling, deprived people, who are, however, undepressed and smiling. Beyond are palaces on "very proper streets." James talks with an operatic-looking young Communist who longs for a French-style revolution in Italy. Spezia is fleet headquarters, and beyond are a plaque to George Gordon, Lord Byron* and an October boatride for James to Lerici, redolent of passionate Percy Bysshe Shelley.* Then James visits quiet, tinted Florence, with its sunny Arno, sallow houses, terraces, and villas—some full of "peace and ease," others sadly for rent to *forestieri*. James criticizes the "irritation" of John Ruskin* at the contrast of Italy's artistic past and its "wreck[ed]" present, as expressed in his *Mornings in Florence*, a recent rereading of which almost spoils James's enjoyment. James then went on to Santa Maria Novella with a friend, who mostly ignored Ruskin. Florence is full of brilliant art: the Uffizi, the Pitti Palace, the Academy, and the Bargello. James especially likes Andrea del Sarto (although he is not first-rate) and lists other favorites. The train via the cathedral town of Orvieto to Rome is now more efficient but sadly avoids Assisi, Perugia, and other fine old Italian cities. In a footnote, James cites *Notes of Travel and Study in Italy*, the first important book by his close friend Charles Eliot Norton.*

The Ivory Tower. Fragmentary novel (66,800 words), published posthumously in London by Collins, 1917, and in New York by Scribner, 1917. (Characters: Frank B. Betterman, Davey Bradham, Gussy Bradham, Crick, Graham Fielder, Cecelia Foy, Abel Gaw, Rosanna Gaw, Miss Goodenough, Dr. Hatch, Miss Mumby, Mrs. Fielder Northover, Northover, Dr. Root, Roulet, Miss Ruddle, Minnie Undle, Horton Vint.) At Newport, Rhode Island, Rosanna Gaw visits the estate of rich, dying Frank B. Betterman, her rich, sick, old father Abel Gaw's estranged former partner. She talks with her friend Gussy's husband Davey Bradham, about the anticipated arrival of Betterman's nephew Graham Fielder. Rosanna once knew Graham in Europe. Cissy Foy, also in Newport, is supposed to be after Graham now. Horton Vint, who once proposed to Rosanna, is there too. Cissy says that Graham loves Rosanna. Old Gaw grows worse when he hears that old Betterman is growing better. Graham Fielder, immensely cultured, reports to his uncle, who likes him and plans to leave him a fortune. When Graham then sees Rosanna, she gives him a letter in a little ivory tower. It is from her father, who has suddenly died. Cissy tells Horton not only that Graham and Rosanna are now probably engaged but also that she would like to steal Graham. Betterman dies. Graham and Horton meet and discuss their past, the two rich men's deaths, and Graham's possible inheritance. Telling Horton that he needs a trusted friend to handle the details of his new life, Graham shows him the unopened letter from Gaw, which he fears may lessen his high opinion of his uncle, Betterman. Yet he must not burn it because it could contain important information about Rosanna. Some weeks pass, and Graham is now thinking of past mistakes and his present inability to adjust to his prospects, when Davey Bradham arrives and evidently persuades him of his future responsibilities. The roots of this incomplete novel go far back. According to an early Notebook entry (25 Nov 1881), James thought of fictionalizing what he knew of the life of his friend Katherine ("Katrina") De Kay Bronson*—"but the milieu was too American," he adds. Decades later, he wrote to William Dean Howells* (31 Dec 1908) to report that he had "broken ground on an American novel," which would have to be *The Ivory Tower* (or something else of which no record remains). A Notebook entry a few days later (10 Feb 1909) records James's "divine and beautiful" thrill at "fingering a little what I call the . . . Katrina B. subject." In December 1909 and January 1910, James dictated material which was variously entitled "The 'K.B.' Case" and "Mrs. Max," and which has been preserved as extensive sketches with tentative lists of character names and much plotting (as well as some autobiographical data). Next, in summer 1914, James dictated to his secretary Theodora Bosanquet* what amounts to almost two hundred pages of typescript developing the "K.B. Case" into what he then called *The Ivory Tower*. James planned it to be a novel of ten books, each featuring a different character, thus having a form somewhat resembling that of *The Awkward Age*. Ironically, this projected fictional exposé of the corruption of vast and dark American wealth was secretly subsidized by rich Edith Newbold Jones Wharton,* who in 1912 connived with Charles Scribner, her publisher and James's, to pay James $8,000 (out of her own earnings) as an alleged advance against what *The Ivory Tower* would gain him. James, though a bit suspicious, was highly gratified. But when World War I broke out, James found it impossible to continue to depict a contemporary scene; he turned to his fantasy *The Sense of the Past* but left both novels in fragmentary form at his death. If completed,

The Ivory Tower might have been a ruthless, naturalistic demonstration—couched in James's most orotund prose—that wealth has blighted not only American men and women but Europeanized Americans as well, and America itself; for in the work, James shows his beloved old Newport now vulgarized. In 1918, *The Ivory Tower* was added as Volume XXV to *The Novels and Tales of Henry James*.

J

Jackson, Helen Maria Hunt (née Fisk) (1830–1885). Popular novelist, poet, and philanthropist, born in Amherst, Massachusetts, where her father taught Latin, Greek, and philosophy. She was a neighbor, schoolmate, and friend of Emily Dickinson, and in 1852 she married Edward Bissell Hunt, an engineer and army officer. The two moved about, until he was killed in a submarine accident in 1863. She also lost both of their sons. She moved to Newport, Rhode Island, where she met Thomas Wentworth Storrow Higginson,* who encouraged her to write. She began with poetry; one of her poems was published in the *Nation* in 1865. She wrote hundreds of essays and reviews, resided abroad and wrote travel pieces (1868–1870), and moved about in the Far West for health reasons (1872–1874). She married financier William Sharpless Jackson in Colorado in 1875 and began to publish novels, beginning with *Mercy Philbrick's Choice* (1876). After research in New York, she published *A Century of Dishonor* (1881), criticizing governmental mistreatment of American Indians. Two years later, commissioned by the government to investigate abuses of Indians in California, she published another indictment, which was largely ignored. So she wrote *Ramona* (1884), a fictional treatment of the same subject. This romantic novel, the only work for which Jackson is now famous, has proved to be incredibly popular only because of the tragic romance of Ramona and Alessandro in it. James adversely reviewed (*Nation*, 21 Dec 1876) the anonymously published *Mercy Philbrick's Choice*, ridiculing the authoress—he guesses that the writer is a woman—for taking "the pathetic view . . . of things in general." He does not like the young widowed poetess heroine Mercy, her nice old sick mother, the hero (of "slender virility"), or his "scold" of an invalid mother. These four persons "are hopelessly disagreeable." James also dislikes the "barbarous dialect of the 'American humor' family" spoken by Mercy's mother. When the hero finds a bag of gold that does not belong to him, his behavior turns "shabby." The authoress's handling of high-principled Mercy's consequent "choice" results in "a Sunday tract" tone. In the same review, James contrasts this feeble but pure American novel with the allegedly offensive sensational novel *Joan* (also 1876) by Rhoda Broughton.*

James, Alice (1848–1892). Henry James's sister. She was born in New York City and was sickly all her life. Her physical and nervous maladies are heartbreaking to review. She naturally accompanied the family to Europe during their 1855–1858 stay in France and Switzerland. From 1858 to 1859 they were in America again, at Newport, Rhode Island. In 1859 the family returned to Switzerland, where Alice was tutored; in 1860, they were back in Newport, where she attended school. In 1864 Alice moved with her parents to Boston. In the winter of 1866–1867, she was treated by a psychotherapist for neurasthenia, and in 1868 she suffered a nervous breakdown accompanied by hysteria. In 1872 she was well enough to travel with Henry James and Catherine Walsh*—their Aunt Kate—for five months in Europe. The following year, during which she met Katharine Peabody Loring,* and into the next, Alice seemed to be better and she could travel a little alone. But in 1878 she grew worse; by then, she had threatened suicide. Her father, however, gave her permission to do so, and she accordingly felt better. In 1879 and 1880, she and Loring took camping trips together in the Adirondacks and northern New England. In the summer of 1881, Loring accompanied Alice to Europe. Her mother's death in January 1882 seemed to improve Alice, who was now needed by her father. His death eleven months later, however, resulted in a relapse. After medical treatment near Boston and then in New York (1883–1884), Alice went with Loring to live in England (from late 1884). She tried Bournemouth and Leamington, and then London, to be near James's De Vere Gardens* residence. She was treated by James's friend Dr. William Wilberforce Baldwin* and by others. Alice eventually died in London of breast cancer. She had been teased and shouted down by her more brilliant brothers. William James treated her pseudo-amorously in their adolescence and then patronizingly once he became a medical expert. Henry was a devoted brother, who wrote to her tenderly, introduced her to his friends in England when possible, found lodgings for her and Loring in England, vacationed with her in England and also visited her, and even made over the income of his patrimony to her for life. Alice wrote letters, a commonplace book, and a journal (1889–1892) so frank that James destroyed his copy when the work was privately printed in 1894 by Loring, to whom Alice had willed $20,000. James did not know that Alice had kept such a thorough diary and he rightly feared that his frank gossip, duly recorded in it, would cause embarrassment. It was made available for general publication in 1934, badly edited by Anna Robeson Burr, when the manuscript was released by Robertson James's daughter Mary James Vaux (who sought thus to pay tribute to her father and her uncle Garth Wilkinson James). It was republished in 1964, edited by Leon Edel. Alice James should be remembered as an egocentric, observant invalid with fierce willpower and a talent for verbal expression, loyal to her family (especially for its Irish background), with a morbid fixation on death—mainly her own.

James, Alice Howe (née Gibbens) (1849–1922). Wife of James's brother William James; hence James's sister-in-law (and his favorite one). Henry James enjoyed a fine relationship with her, as well as with her children. When her husband died, James spent months in America with her trying to be of comfort. In a letter to Sir Edmund Wilson Gosse* (13 Jun 1910) he calls her "my blest sister-in-law." When he was mortally stricken in December 1915, Alice James crossed the wintry Atlantic Ocean in wartime to care for him until he died. She dispersed his marvelous library. She smuggled his cremated ashes home for burial in Cambridge, Massachusetts. Her dislike of Edith Newbold Jones Wharton* caused her to prefer Percy Lubbock* as the editor of James's letters.

James, Caroline Eames (née Cary) (Carrie). Wife of James's brother Garth Wilkinson James; hence James's sister-in-law.

James, Catharine (née Barber) (1782–1859). The third and last wife of James's grandfather William James; hence James's paternal grandmother. Her parents came from County Longford, Ireland. She bore her husband ten children, eight of whom survived. In *A Small Boy and Others*, James fondly reminisces about his grandmother's hospitality and reading habits in her Albany, New York, home during her later years.

James, Elizabeth (née Tillman) (?–1797). The first wife of Henry James's grandfather William James. She bore him twin sons and died in childbirth. She was of German extraction.

James, Garth Wilkinson (Wilkie, Wilky) (1845–83). Henry James's younger brother, who was born in New York City and was educated in various European schools, along with his brothers William, Henry, and Robertson; also in Newport, Rhode Island; and—with Robertson, part of the time—at the Sanborn School, Concord, Massachusetts, from 1860 to 1862. Wilky enlisted in the Union Army, in September 1862, during the Civil War; he transferred as an officer to the 54th Massachusetts Regiment, a black-soldier unit commanded by Colonel Robert Gould Shaw. Wilky was severely wounded in his side and a foot during the July 1863 charge against Fort Wagner, near Charleston, South Carolina. After recuperating at home with his parents, he rejoined his regiment in January 1864 but soon had to return home again, until December. In February 1865 he fell from his horse, injured himself, and reinjured his foot. He became aide-de-camp to General Quincy Adams Gillmore, was promoted to captain in March, and was mustered out in August at Hilton Head, South Carolina. In February 1866 Wilky bought several thousand acres of Florida land, as an investment with or for his father in a venture to raise cotton with freed black labor. Some of this time, Robertson, who was by then also a discharged Union Army veteran, worked with him. After a little success but much discouragement, Wilky abandoned the project early in 1871 and joined Bob that fall in Milwaukee, where Wilky worked intermittently and unsuccessfully for some years on the railroad, in an ironworks factory, and for the Internal Revenue Service; he later declared bankruptcy. In 1872 he married Caroline (Carrie) Eames Cary, the daughter of a rich Milwaukee businessman. Remaining in Milwaukee, the couple had two children (Joseph, born 1874; Alice, 1875). After his father's death in 1882, Wilky was embittered by being disinherited because of the disastrous Florida investment. Henry James, their father's executor, redivided the estate to include Wilky, who died in 1883, of heart trouble and Bright's disease.

James, Henry, Sr. (1811–1882). Son of rich Presbyterian William James of Albany, husband of Mary Robertson (née Walsh) James, and father of William, Henry, Garth Wilkinson, Robertson, and Alice James. Henry James, Sr., was badly burned at the age of thirteen (and lost a leg two years later as a consequence), became an alcoholic for a while (drinking for relief from prolonged pain), rebelled against family orthodoxy, turned studious, and graduated from Union College, in Schenectady, New York, in 1830. In 1832, Henry James, Sr., went to court and succeeded in breaking his displeased father's will to obtain what he considered his just patrimony. He studied at the Princeton Theological Seminary, in Princeton, New Jersey. Influenced by Swedenborgian thought and also Fourierism (through his friend Parke Godwin), he gradually developed his own brand of religious mysticism. He knew a number of writers of his time, including Albert Brisbane, William Cullen Bryant, Thomas Carlyle,* Ralph Waldo Emerson,* Horace Greeley, George Ripley, and William Makepeace Thackeray.* Henry James, Sr., wrote extensively (1846–1879) on Christianity, morality, and social change. After restlessly moving his family about during the children's early years, he settled with his dutiful wife and their sick daughter Alice in Newport, Rhode Island (1860), then in Boston (1864), and finally in nearby Cambridge (1866), where he died. His son William James edited *The Literary Remains of the Late Henry James* (1884). The degree of his influence on his other famous son, Henry James, Jr., is still an open question. When James received his copy of *Literary Remains*, he wrote to William (2 Jan 1885) as follows: "It comes over me as I read them . . . how intensely original and personal his whole system was, and how indispensable it is that those who go in for religion should take some heed of it. I can't enter into it (much) myself. . . . But I can enjoy greatly the spirit, the feeling and the manner of the whole thing . . . and feel . . . that poor Father . . . was . . . a great writer." Immediately after his father's death, James wrote to his publishers ordering the removal of "Jr." from the title page of his works. Henry James, Sr., had four brothers (Augustus James [1807–1866], John Barber James [1816–1856], Edward James [1818–1856], and Howard James [1828–1887]); three sisters (Jeannette [Janet]

James Barker [1814–1842, of the Barker family*], Catherine Margaret James Temple [1820–1854], and Ellen King James Van Buren [1823–1849]; and twin half-brothers (Robert James [1797–1821] and William James [1797–1868]). Aunt Janet died giving birth to Augustus James Barker (of the Barker family), James's cousin Gus, who was killed in 1863 in action during the Civil War. The other two sisters married thus: Catherine married Robert Emmet Temple of the Temple family*; Ellen married Smith Thompson Van Buren of the Van Buren family.* Late in his life, James wrote to his interested friend Howard Overing Sturgis* (12 or 13 May 1913) to explain many genealogical details, beginning thus: "[H]ow can I do anything toward clearing up those pale antediluvian spectres . . . ?" James's first two autobiographical volumes, A Small Boy and Others and Notes of a Son and Brother, have scattered references to many of his aunts and uncles.

James, Mary (née Holton). Wife of James's brother Robertson James; hence James's sister-in-law.

James, Mary (née Walsh) (1810–1882). Wife of Henry James, Sr., mother of William, Henry, Garth Wilkinson, Robertson, and Alice James, and sister of Catherine Walsh.* James's mother was strong, practical, efficient, and exacting, necessarily so, given her husband's nature. While Henry James, Sr., wrote, conferred with fellow scholars, supervised the children's moral and intellectual development, and was concerned with the material and spiritual future, Mary James handled the household activities, servants, schooling, and travel details; watched over finances; and was occupied with the present. She offered praise and sympathy to her children. She worried when William was sick and uncertain, and she was happy when he married. Henry was always her favorite, and she missed him dreadfully when he decided in 1875 to live abroad. She suffered when Wilky was wounded in the Civil War, and when he was brought home to her she nursed him devotedly. The misguided Florida venture of both Wilky and Bob depressed her. She did not admire Wilky's wife and was saddened by his bankruptcy. She worried over Bob's marriage and family, and during her final year she was obliged to mother that rebellious son, who was home again. For nearly two decades, Alice was mostly a homebound invalid, to whom at death Mary James willed her personal estate. James wrote faithfully to his mother, returned from London to visit her during her final illness, and a few days after her death recorded this in his Notebooks (9 Feb 1882): "She was our life, she was the house, she was the keystone of the arch. She held us all together, and without her we are scattered reeds. She was patience, she was wisdom, she was exquisite maternity. Her sweetness, her mildness, her great natural beneficence were unspeakable. . . . I can reflect, with perfect gladness, that her work was done—her long patience had done its utmost. . . . I can think with a kind of holy joy of her being lifted now above all our pains and anxieties. Her death has given me a passionate belief in certain transcendent things—the immanence of being as nobly created as hers—the immortality of such a virtue as that—the reunion of spirits in better conditions that these.'' James's autobiographical volumes *A Small Boy and Others* and *Notes of a Son and Brother* are full of detailed and affectionate comments about his mother.

James, Mary Ann (née Connolly) (?–1800). The second wife of Henry James's grandfather William James. She bore her husband one child and died in childbirth. Of Irish extraction, she was an Irish Catholic.

James, Robertson (Bob, Rob) (1846–1910). James's youngest brother, who was born in Albany, New York, and was educated in various European schools along with his brothers William, Henry, and Garth Wilkinson, and also—with Wilky—at the Sanborn School in Concord, Massachusetts from 1860 to 1861. After staying at home, idle and irritable, for more than a year, Bob enlisted in the Union Army in May 1863, helped quell the Boston draft riots that spring, transferred as an officer to the 55th Massachusetts Regiment, a black-soldier unit, saw combat duty in South Carolina and Florida in 1863 and 1864, suffered from dysentery and severe sunstroke, was later promoted to captain, and was mustered out in July 1865. Some months later he began to work unhappily for a railroad in Iowa. He appealed unsuccessfully to his parents to be allowed to study architecture in Boston—Bob had a decided artistic talent—and then joined Wilky in his Florida cotton-raising venture in the summer of 1866. He quit late the following year and returned to his railroad position. Later transferring to Milwaukee partly to be with Wilky, Bob married (1872) Mary Holton, the daughter of a well-to-do Milwaukee pioneer. Moving about in the immediate area, Bob worked for the railroad, as a newspaperman, and for his rich and disliked father-in-law, farmed, studied Emanual Swedenborg, wrote a few melancholy pieces, and began to suffer from alcoholism. He and his wife had two children (Edward "Ned" Holton James, born 1873; Mary James, 1875). Bob separated from his Wisconsin family from time to time, when he would live in Cambridge, Massachusetts, with William James and his wife Alice, and with his sister Alice, studying art, committing himself to asylums for alcoholism, and traveling erratically—to the Azores, Portugal, and London (to visit Henry). Bob went back to his family from time to time, but he could never establish stability in his marriage again. From 1885 he resided in Concord, where his wife and children also moved, though not to remain with him. After a stay (1898–1903) in a sanitorium near Buffalo, Bob returned to Concord, where he died alone. James willed gifts to various nephews and nieces but excluded Bob's son Ned, because he had once written a pamphlet critical of George V.

James, Susan (née McCartney) (1746–1824). The wife of William James of the townland of Curkish, Bailieborough, County Cavan, Ireland, and the mother of the William James who migrated to Albany, New York. Hence she was Henry James's great-grandmother.

James, William (1736–1822). The father of the William James who migrated to Albany, New York. He was thus Henry James's great-grandfather. This elder William James was a Presbyterian and a farmer in the townland of Curkish, Bailieborough, in County Cavan. His oldest son, Robert James, remained at home and helped his father with the farming. His youngest son, John James, died in 1831—perhaps lost at sea. In spite of discouragement by the British authorities, William James tried to educate himself. When his son William migrated to Albany, New York, he knew the Westminster Catechism and rudiments of Latin. The elder William's grave, and that of his wife Susan, both marked by large flat stones, are located in the weed-grown old cemetery behind the Anglican (Church of Ireland) church in Bailieborough. A church window of stained glass, called the St. Luke window, honors eight Jameses, beginning with the elder William and Susan.

James, William (1771–1832). The father of Henry James, Sr., and hence Henry James's grandfather. Born on the farm of his father William James in the townland of Curkish, Bailieborough, in county Cavan, Ireland, he migrated to Albany, New York, in 1789. William's first wife, Elizabeth Tillman James, died in childbirth in 1797. His second wife, Mary Ann Connolly James, also died in childbirth. In 1803 he married his third wife, Catharine Barber James of County Longford, Ireland, and by her had ten children, eight of whom survived, including Henry James, Sr. William became a successful businessman in Albany and also in Utica, Syracuse, and New York City—in salt, tobacco, transportation, and real estate ventures. He bitterly criticized his wayward, noncommercial son Henry's anti-Presbyterian religious position. When William James died, his estate of $3,000,000 rivaled those of John Jacob Astor and Stephen Van Rensselaer. His son Henry went to court, broke his father's will, and claimed his inheritance.

James, William (1842–1910). Henry James's favorite brother, the distinguished psychologist, philosopher, and spokesman for pragmatism. He was born in New York, was a school and tutored student (often with Henry James) in America (1852–1855 in New York, 1858–1859 at Newport, Rhode Island) and in Europe (1855–1858 in France and England and 1859–1860 Germany and Switzerland). He studied painting under William Morris Hunt* at Newport from 1860 to 1861. Finally, he studied at the Lawrence Scientific School, Harvard from 1861 to 1864, after which he became a student at Harvard Medical School. At this time, he discussed philosophical problems with fellow members in the Metaphysical Club, including Charles Sanders Peirce* (who later helped him conceptualize pragmatism) and Oliver Wendell Holmes, Jr.* (a lifelong friend). William James interrupted his medical studies to go as an assistant to the naturalist Louis Agassiz on a zoological expedition to Brazil from 1865 to 1866, after which—again with an interruption caused by sickness, to go to Germany from 1867 to 1868 to study science and philosophy—he obtained his medical degree in 1869. Personal depression and hypochondria long followed (1869–1872), alleviated only to a

degree by a self-willed, resolute declaration of moral freedom (1870). He began
to teach at Harvard, first physiology (1872), then anatomy as well (1873), then
psychology physiologically grounded (1875), and finally philosophy spiritually
oriented (1879). His teaching was interrupted by poor health and travel to Italy
(1873–1874). In 1878 he married Alice Howe Gibbens, a Boston schoolteacher.
The happy couple had five children: Henry (Harry) James, born 1879; William
(Billy) James, 1882; Herman James [1884–1885]; Margaret Mary (Peggy) James,
1887; and Alexander Robertson (Alec) James, 1890. The Jameses purchased a
summer residence in Chocorua, New Hampshire (1886). James taught intermittently (until 1907) and slowly composed his monumental classic *The Principles of Psychology* (2 vols., 1890; abridged as *Text-Book of Psychology*, 1892).
He often traveled to England and to the Continent (1892–1893, 1899–1901,
1901–1902, 1905, 1908–1909, 1910) to lecture and to confer with other leading
intellectuals of the time, as well as for health purposes. He edited his father's
works *The Literary Remains of the Late Henry James* (1884). Through the 1880s
and 1890s, James associated with members of the Society for Psychical Research,
including Frederic William Henry Myers.* James went on lecture tours in America in 1896 and again in 1898. In 1898 he injured his heart by hiking too
strenuously. His intellectual tolerance and liberalism manifested themselves in
his opposition to the Spanish-American War; he favored the defense of Alfred
Dreyfus*; and he took a stand against those who would limit the activities of
Christian Scientists and spiritualists. His 1901–1902 lectures at the University
of Edinburgh were published as *The Varieties of Religious Experience: A Study
in Human Nature* (1902). His book *Pragmatism* (1907) stimulated not only
followers (including John Dewey in the United States and scholars in England
and China as well) but also opponents (in Germany and Italy), to whom James
replied in piecemeal essays collected as *The Meaning of Truth: A Sequel to
"Pragmatism"* (1909). His 1908–1909 lectures at Oxford resulted in *A Plur-
alistic Universe . . .* (1909). His other important writings include the following:
The Will to Believe, and Other Essays in Popular Philosophy (1897), *Human
Immortality: Two Supposed Objections to the Doctrine* (1898), *Talks to Teachers
on Psychology: and to Students on Some of Life's Ideals* (1899), *Memories and
Studies* (1911, edited by Henry James [William James's son], with a section on
Myers), *Some Problems of Philosophy: A Beginning to an Introduction to Philosophy* (1911), *Essays in Radical Empiricism* (1912), *Selected Papers in Philosophy* (1917), *Collected Essays and Reviews* (1920), and *The Letters of William
James* (2 vols., 1920). In his writings, William James attempts to relate tough-
and tender-minded natures, the rational and the empirical way, and theory and
practice. His writing style vividly moves through these levels. To him, ideas no
matter in what realm of thought (theological, philosophical, scientific, political,
or interpersonal) are significant only when put into action. He argues (in opposition to his friend John Fiske*) that the will is assertable, relating to Darwinian
spontaneity, and further, that belief can create truth if one's nature wills it. He
shows how truth evolves as experience alters temperament: We organize con-

fusion and the organic universe by such experience. Survival after death he feels is unprovable, but he reasons that the existence of God is proved by manifold religious experiences, especially when people are troubled. His thought has influenced not only modern philosophy (especially existentialism and phenomenology), but also literature (especially stream-of-consciousness writings). The subject of the sibling rivalry of William and Henry James is complex. William was older, initially more articulate and always more direct, pro-American, and seemingly more successful; he also became a husband and a father. Henry was younger, more passive, verbally ambiguous and often tentative, pro-European, and less immediately successful; he remained celibate. It has been theorized that Henry's motives for expatriation may have included a desire to get away from his older brother. William repeatedly criticized his brother's fiction (notably *Roderick Hudson*, *The Bostonian*, and *The Golden Bowl*), perhaps often with the best intentions, whereas Henry regularly praised his brother's work. Renewed close associations of the two, especially in their middle years, may have triggered psychosomatic illnesses in each (notably in Italy, 1873, and in London, 1880); when they were apart, each seemed to be more productive. William was angry when their father named Henry executor of his will (1882). Henry was elected on the second ballot (February 1905) to membership in the Academy of Arts and Letters (a part of the National Institute of Arts and Letters, of which both brothers had been members since 1898); but William was elected only on the fourth ballot (May 1905) and declined. His rationalization (privately written [17 June 1905] to Robert Underwood Johnson,* the Academy secretary) included the puzzling assertion that one James—that is, his younger brother, who was also more shallow and vain—was enough for the Academy. When William wrote to Henry in puzzlement over *The Golden Bowl* (William regularly preferred Henry's literary and travel essays) and urged him to write something more pleasing, Henry replied (23 Nov 1905) that he would "greatly be humiliated" to learn that William liked anything he wrote. An example of William's comprehensive dislike of Henry's style is contained in a letter (4 May 1907): "You know how opposed your whole 'third manner' of execution is to the literary ideals which animate my crude . . . breast, mine being to say a thing in one sentence as straight and explicit as it can be made, and then to drop it forever; yours being to avoid naming it straight, but by dint of breathing and sighing all round and round it, to arouse in the reader who may have had a similar perception already . . . the illusion of a solid object, made . . . wholly out of impalpable materials, air, and the prismatic interferences of light, ingeniously focused by mirrors upon empty space. But you *do* it, that's the queerness!" Henry's kind comments in letters to William on his writings are revealing: William's introduction to their father's *Literary Remains* is "admirable, perfect" (2 Jan 1885); *The Principles of Psychology* is "your mighty and magnificent book" (6 Feb [1891]); and *Pragmatism* cast a "spell . . . I simply sank down, under it, into . . . depths of submission and assimilation. . . . Then I was lost in the wonder of the extent to which all my life I have . . . unconsciously pragmatised. You are immensely and universally *right* . . . '' (17 Oct 1907). Henry was a fine host at Lamb House* to William, his wife Alice, and later their children (especially Billy, who honeymooned there, and Peggy). When both brothers were sick in 1910, they traveled to Germany with William's wife Alice to recuperate; Henry was with William at Chocorua when William died. Henry James wrote as follows about his deceased brother to Sir Edmund Wilson Gosse* (10 Sep 1910): ''He was not only my dearest of Brothers but my best & wisest of friends—& his beautiful genius & noble intellect & character were really, I felt, at their high consummation. However, of this unutterable pang I can't pretend to talk—I only feel stricken & old & ended.'' The hero of James's autobiography, especially in its early parts, was his brother William. James willed his property to William's widow Alice (and thereafter to her children); thus Harry gained Lamb House and Peggy his insurance. There were remembrances to other nephews and nieces, but specifically excluded was Robertson James's son Edward James. James's library contained three books by his brother William.

Jane. In ''Osborne's Revenge,'' Anna Wilkes's maid.

Jane. In *Summersoft*, a tourist in a group visiting Summersoft. In *The High Bid*, a tourist in a group visiting Covering.

Jane, Duchess. In *The Awkward Age*, Edward Brookenham's cousin from Naples. She is Agnesina's aunt and Mrs. Brookenham's friend.

Jane, Lady. In ''The Lesson of the Master,'' a woman gossiped about by Mrs. Henry St. George.

Jane, Lady. In ''The Figure in the Carpet,'' the hostess at whose home the critic narrator meets Hugh Vereker.

Jasper, Mrs. In *Disengaged*, an unhappy but self-assured young London widow who knows Lady Amy and Sir Montagu Brisket, is admired by Charles Coverley and Percy Trafford, encourages Coverley to increase the pressure on Captain Llewellyn Prime to propose to Blandina Wigmore then regrets doing so, meets and begins to love Prime herself, helps to undo his unhappy engagement, and accepts him herself.

Jaume, Mme. de. In *The Spoils of Poynton*, an ugly but witty friend of Mrs. Adela Gereth.

Jay, Captain Bertram. In ''The Chaperon,'' the loyal friend of Rose Tramore. They finally get married.

Jay, Rose Tramore. In "The Chaperon," Rose Tramore's married name.

Jenkin, Henrietta Camilla (née Jackson) (1807?–1885). British novelist whose best work was perhaps *Who Breaks, Pays* (1861) and whose *Within an Ace* James (1875) reviewed (*Nation*, 23 Sep 1875). He calls it an "incongruous tale," the plot of which—an Edinburgh gentleman adopts a girl whom a French count marries and takes home—he summarizes, only thereafter to confess that he does not know the vivacious authoress's "purpose, moral or dramatic."

Jerdan, William (1782–1869). Genial, self-made editor, fiction writer, poet, translator, and patron of emerging authors. After clerking in London and then Edinburgh, he returned to London, became a reporter and editor, visited France, and then edited the *Literary Gazette* (1817–1850), soon making it an important journal. Jerdan helped to found many societies, edited the memoirs of celebrities, suffered grievous financial reverses through the dishonesty of others, and was pensioned in 1853. He published a wide-ranging autobiography (4 vols., 1852–1853) and also *Men I Have Known* (1866). James reviewed (*Nation*, 1 Apr 1875) *Personal Reminiscences of Moore and Jerdan* (1875), selected and edited by Richard Henry Stoddard.* James likes the *Memoirs* of Thomas Moore* but defines Jerdan, though an "estimable personage," as the author of "lucubrations" devoid of "moral or intellectual purposes." He also struck James as a "dull and colorless" storyteller.

Jeremie, Mrs. In "The Patagonia," a friend of Mrs. Peck and Grace Mavis.

"Jersey Villas." 1892 title of "Sir Dominick Ferrand."

Jesmond, Grace. In *The Album*, Bedford's amanuensis for five years at Courtlands. The daughter of a deceased vicar, she has financially aided her sister's troubled family. When dishonest Sir Ralph Damant inherits the estate, Grace threatens to expose him by using Mark Moorsom Bernal's album of sketches as damaging evidence. Sir Ralph gives the estate to Mark, and Mark and Grace will wed. Grace also aids Teddy Ashdown and Maud Vanneck.

Jessel, Miss. In "The Turn of the Screw," the former governess of Miles and Flora at Bly. It is her ghost that the governess narrator sees or thinks she sees.

Jessop. In *A Change of Heart*, an unseen guest, along with his two sisters, at Margaret Thorne's birthday party.

Jessop, The Misses. In *A Change of Heart*, Jessop's two sisters, who are also unseen guests at Margaret Thorne's birthday party.

Jewett, Sarah Orne (1849–1909). Maine local color fiction writer, born and raised in South Berwick. She learned about Maine folks while accompanying her physician father on his country house calls. Inspired by the regional work of Harriet Beecher Stowe,* Jewett published a story in the *Atlantic Monthly* when she was only twenty and used it as a start toward sketches assembled in *Deephaven* (1877). Friendship with Annie Adams Fields* drew her to the literary circles of Boston, where she soon met Thomas Bailey Aldrich,* William Dean Howells,* and James Russell Lowell,* among others. A carriage accident in 1901 so injured her spine that she could neither fully recover nor effectively write again. Jewett's best stories are included in *A White Heron and Other Stories* (1886), *Tales of New England* (1890), and especially *The Country of the Pointed Firs* (1896). Her novels are *A Country Doctor* (1884), *A Marsh Island* (1885), and *The Tory Lover* (1901). Annie Fields edited Jewett's letters in 1911. Jewett's technique derives in part from her reading of Honoré de Balzac,* Gustave Flaubert,* Émile Zola,* and James. Annie Fields noted in her diary that, when she and Sarah Orne Jewett visited James at Rye (September 1898), he praised the young writer's works for being elegant, exact, true, and "not . . . overdone." In a famous letter to Jewett (5 Oct 1901), James acknowledged her gift of *A Tory Lover* (her one historical romance, of a genre for which she had no talent), soon ended his sweet talk—calling such "the mere twaddle of graciousness"—blasted her for her "misguided" and " 'cheap' " effort to depict consciousnesses in a bygone time, and advised her to "[g]o back to the dear country of the *Pointed Firs*." More harshly, in a letter to Howells (25 Jan 1902), James lamented that *A Tory Lover* "was a thing to make the angels weep"; to Sarah Butler Wister* (21 Dec 1902), he complained of Jewett's "sentimentality." Toward the end of his 1904–1905 tour of the United States, James, while visiting Howells at Kittery Point, Maine, saw Jewett a final time. When Annie Fields asked him to send her whatever Jewett letters he had, James replied (2 Jan 1910) that he had received a few but had saved none. According to a Notebook entry (19 Feb 1899), James was reading Jewett's *Tales of New England* when he had the idea for "Flickerbridge"; the specific story which inspired him was "A Lost Lover." James's library included two books by Jewett.

Jex, Mrs. In "Maud-Evelyn," the medium used by the Dedricks to communicate with their daughter Maud-Evelyn. Marmaduke avoids her.

John, Lord. In *The Outcry*, the novel, and *The Outcry*, the play, the materialistic friend (age thirty-five or thirty-six) of Lord Theign, whose younger daughter Lady Grace he admires. If she consents to marry him, his mother will cancel the gambling debts which Grace's sister Lady Kitty Imber owes the older woman.

"John Delavoy." Short story (12,900 words), published in the *Cosmopolis Magazine* (Jan–Feb 1898); reprinted in *John Delavoy* in London by Macmillan, 1897; reprinted in *The Soft Side*, 1900. (Characters: Beston, John Delavoy, Miss

Delavoy, Windon, Lord Yarracome.) The critic narrator sees Miss Delavoy at the theater. She is the sister of the late John Delavoy, a novelist. She is with Beston, the crass editor of the *Cynosure*, to whom the narrator has just sent an essay on Delavoy's works. Beston tells the critic that he wants a chattier essay. When he introduces the critic to Miss Delavoy, Beston is startled by her praise of the essay. Against her orders, Beston publishes a reproduction of a unique portrait of her brother without the essay and thus loses Miss Delavoy to the sensitive critic. A Notebook entry (13 Feb 1896) reads as follows: "R. U. Johnson's letter to me the other day, returning my little paper on Dumas as shocking to their prudery, strikes me as yielding the germ of a lovely little ironic, satiric tale." It seems that Robert Underwood Johnson,* who was editor of the *Century Magazine* and who had previously accepted material from James, had asked him for an essay on Alexandre Dumas *fils*,* only to reject it because it too frankly discussed sexual attitudes. (James immediately published the essay elsewhere.) In his same Notebook entry, James sketches the bare plot for his "satiric tale," with three characters: a dead author's daughter and two rival writers, one a good critic who fails, the other a journalist who writes "superficial gossip and twaddle" and succeeds. James made obvious changes when writing "John Delavoy," but he hammers home the central point that editors often prefer marketable chit-chat to anything profound.

Johnson, Robert Underwood (1853–1937). American editor, author, traveler, and conservationist, born in Washington, D.C. After college in Indiana, he clerked in Chicago for Charles Scribner's Sons, publishers, then in 1873 joined the firm in New York. He did editorial work for *Scribner's Monthly* (which in 1881 became the *Century Magazine*). He was associate editor of the *Century* under Richard Watson Gilder* (1881–1909), then editor-in-chief (to 1913). He coedited several Civil War volumes and persuaded Ulysses Simpson Grant* to write four essays for the *Century* (1884–1885), which formed the nucleus of his book-length memoirs. In the early 1890s, Johnson worked to reform the copyright laws. As secretary of the National Institute of Arts and Letters, in 1904 he helped organize its American Academy of Arts and Letters, served as its permanent secretary, and wrote to James and his brother William in connection with their election thereto. Long perceived by his professional associates as ultraconservative in editorial policy, Johnson resigned from the *Century* in 1913. After yeoman war-relief work, he became ambassador to Italy (1919–1921). He originated the Keats-Shelley memorial in Rome. Johnson published many volumes of poetry over the years. As *Century* editor, he handled much of James's material. When he rejected James's 1896 essay on Alexandre Dumas *fils** for discussing sexual attitudes too frankly, James not only placed it elsewhere but also wrote "John Delavoy" to satirize prudish editors like Johnson who prefer gossip to substance. When James was elected to the Academy, in February 1905, but his brother William James was not elected until May, William sent an angry letter to Johnson (17 Jun 1905), in which he declined, was evasive, and added (perhaps humorously) that his "younger and shallower and vainer brother" sufficiently represented the James family. In *Remembered Yesterdays*, his long 1923 autobiography, Johnson discusses William and Henry James on only one page, simply in connection with the Academy.

Johnson. In "A Bundle of Letters," the standard pseudonym of the Battledown family governesses.

Johnson. In "The Abasement of the Northmores," a person whom Lady Northmore asks for the return of letters from her late husband.

"The Jolly Corner." Short story (12,700 words), published in the *English Review* (Dec 1908); revised and reprinted in *The Novels and Tales of Henry James*, Volume XVII, 1909. (Characters: Spencer Brydon, Mrs. Muldoon, Alice Staverton.) After more than thirty years abroad, Spencer Brydon returns to New York to supervise the razing of family property he has inherited on a jolly downtown corner. He begins to hear ghosts from his past in the house. He wonders what he might have been like had he not expatriated himself as a young man. Sensing his incipient business acumen, he discusses it with Alice Staverton, a companion from the old days, and begins to stalk his alter ego. While she dreams of his other nature, he prowls the fourth floor on the jolly corner, grows terrified, descends, sees his ravaged other being staring at him from the foyer, faints, and revives with his head in rescuer Alice's lap. Uneasy because of her dream, the woman had come around noon to check on him. They talk and embrace. It seems more likely that this story grew out of James's own memories than out of his reading. First, James as a young teenager visited the Galerie d'Apollon, in the Louvre, was impressed by its sense of triumphant artistic power, and later dreamed of turning the tables on a would-be attacker at his door by pursuing him through halls resembling those of the Louvre gallery. Second, James after his 1904–1905 visit to the United States began to wonder anew what his personality might have been had he stayed home in his native Manhattan and developed commercial acumen there. "The Jolly Corner" concerns Spencer Brydon's similar wonder about himself and also the pursuit of his alter ego turning into flight from it. Brydon's patient Alice is named after James's sister Alice and also his favorite sister-in-law (William James's wife Alice). In the preface to Volume XVII of *The Novels and Tales of Henry James*, James says that emotions evoked in fiction, not events detailed in it, excite, amuse, and thrill the reader; and he cites as one proof "The Jolly Corner," which has no "pirates or detectives." In a sketch in his *Notebooks* (Nov 1814) for a continuation of *The Sense of the Past* (set aside in 1900), James regrets his "filching" from it a certain theme, that of the effect of one's alter ego on others, for use in "The Jolly Corner."

Jones, Amanda T. (1834–1914). American poetess and autobiographer whose *Poems* (1867) James reviewed (*North American Review*, Apr 1867). He calls her writing patriotic, bellicose, somewhat erudite, verbose, rhetorical, and earnest rather than lyrical. She is diffuse if at times spirited. Her imagery is sensational.

Jones, Henry Arthur (1851–1929). English playwright who helped make modern drama more realistic and naturalistic. Jones quit school before his teens, became a traveling salesman (until 1879), and then turned to writing. His early plays, *It's Only round the Corner* (1878) and *Hearts of Oak* (1879), were produced in the provinces. He then coauthored *The Silver King* (1882), a successful melodrama which was produced in London. Considered shocking in their time were *The Triumph of the Philistines* (1895, poking fun at prudes) and *Michael and His Lost Angel* (1896, featuring an adulterous minister). Jones's well-constructed comedies *The Case of Rebellious Susan* (1894) and *The Liars* (1897) show high-society sophistication. His best plays follow Henrik Johan Ibsen* in theory and practice, as do his critical lectures and publications, including *The Renascence of the English Drama, 1883–94* (1895) and *The Theatre of Ideas* (1915). In "London" (24 Apr 1897), James grants Jones his subject in *The Physician* (1897)—the ridiculous infatuation of a "great doctor" for "a young lady" patient—but deplores his inept presentation of that subject. The play is "less . . . a work without a subject than . . . a subject without a work." James, who knew Jones slightly, did not appreciate his style and was jealous of his success; James describes Jones's popular hit *The Dancing Girl* (1891) in one letter to his brother William (12 Feb [1891]) as "the clumsiest trash of a play" and estimates royalties in the thousands of pounds; in a later letter to William (24 Mar [1894]), he refers to his rival as "the interposing and idiotic Jones."

Jones, Mary Cadwalader Rawle (1850–1935). Wife of Frederick Rhinelander Jones, who was the brother of Edith Newbold Jones Wharton.* Mary Jones and Edith Wharton were close friends and remained so even after the Joneses were divorced. Through Wharton, James came to know "Mary Cadwal" well, had important friends in common with her, socialized with her in England, was entertained by her in New York City during his last visits to the United States (1904–1905, 1910–1911), and wrote some of his most charming, chatty letters to her. In one of his last letters, he wrote to Wharton (19 Aug 1914) to describe Mrs. Jones as "admirably here—interesting and vivid and helpful to the last degree." James also knew her daughter Beatrix Jones (later Mrs. Max Farrand).

Jones. In *A Change of Heart*, an unseen guest at Margaret Thorne's birthday party.

Jones, Dr. In "A Light Man," Frederick Sloane's physician.

Jordan, Elizabeth (1867–1947). Milwaukee-born editor, fiction writer, and playwright. She was a reporter on the Chicago *Tribune* (1888–1890), a reporter editor with the New York *World* (1890–1900), an editor of *Harper's Bazaar* (1900–1913), and a literary adviser of Harper & Brothers, publishers (1913–1918). She was also a drama critic for *America*. Her first book, *Tales of the City Room* (1898), was followed by more than thirty novels, a play (*Lady from Oklahoma* [1911]), and romantic and detective stories. She wrote and lectured on woman suffrage. Her autobiography, *Three Rousing Cheers*, was published in 1938. Working with George Brinton McClellan Harvey* of Harper, Jordan helped to persuade James, whom she admired, to lecture during his 1904–1905 tour of the United States. She obtained his essays "The Speech of American Women" and "The Manners of American Women" for *Harper's Bazar* (1907, 1908) and recruited his participation in the *Harper's Bazar* round-robin novel *The Whole Family* (1908; James contributed "The Married Son").

Jordan, Mrs. In "In the Cage," a clergyman's widow who supports herself by arranging flowers in rich people's homes. She is going to marry Drake, Lady Bradeen's new butler.

Josephine. In "A Tragedy of Error," Hortense Bernier's maid.

Josling, Agatha. In "Longstaff's Marriage," Diana Belfield's friend. She acts as go-between for Diana and Reginald Longstaff.

Joubert, Joseph (1754–1824). French literary critic, moralist, and associate of René Chateaubriand, who in 1838 edited selections from what became Joubert's *Pensées, essais, maximes et correspondance* (1842). James reviewed (*Nation*, 27 Jun 1878) the 1878 translation entitled *Pensées of Joubert*. He begins by regarding the opinion of Joubert held by Matthew Arnold* as too flattering, adds that English is "a very unepigrammatic tongue" compared to French, and concludes that Joubert is less serious than Blaise Pascal though more so than François La Rochefoucauld. Joubert is often "more fanciful than substantial," but he does provide some "happy hits," especially on literary subjects.

Joukowsky, Paul (c.1849–?). Son of Vasili Andreyevich Zhukovsky. James, who knew Paul Zhukovsky,* spelled his last name "Joukowsky."

Julia. In "A Problem," David's friend. She helps David and his wife to become reconciled.

Julia, Lady. In "An International Episode," mentioned as Lord Lambeth's unmarried sister.

Julia, Lady. In *The Awkward Age*, Mrs. Brookenham's deceased mother and the former object of Longdon's unrequited but unforgotten affections.

"Julia Bride." Short story (13,300 words), published in *Harper's Magazine* (Mar–Apr 1908); revised and reprinted in *The Novels and Tales of Henry James*, Volume XVII, 1909; reprinted as *Julia Bride* in New York and London by Harper, 1909. (Characters: Julia Bride, Murray Brush, Connery, Mrs. Bride Pitman Connery, Mrs. David E. Drack, Basil French, Mary Lindeck, Mrs. George Maule, the Misses Maule, Pitman.) Young and pretty Julia Bride has already been engaged six times (and she has kept all six rings). She now rather likes prim, bright Basil French, says goodbye to him at a museum, and prepares to meet odd, decent Mr. Pitman, her often divorced mother's second ex-husband. Julia wants him to lie about her mother to help Julia get ahead with French. But instead, Pitman persuades her to tell the truth concerning her mother to help him get ahead with big, bland Mrs. David E. Drack, whose hesitancy is owing to gossip about his divorce. So to her own disadvantage, Julia vilifies her mother in conversation with massively appreciative Mrs. Drack. Then the girl meets Murray Brush, one of her rather coarse former fiancés. She still loves him, but he is not free to say much to help her since he is now engaged to proper Mary Lindeck. At the end, Julia seems pretty hopeless. In the preface to Volume XVII of *The Novels and Tales of Henry James*, James says that his basic theme in "Julia Bride" is the fun American girls have in "repeatedly . . . contract[ing] for the fond preliminaries of marriage." But his challenge was dramatically to analyze the effect of multiple engagements on a "young lady's consciousness." Doing so could lead him profitably to a study of divorce and remarriage. His recipe for such a "broth" would be a mother's freedom and "a daughter's inimitable career of licence." But James's bowl was too small for all his "admirable rich 'stock.' " So he foreshortens his heroine Julia admirably, even while he depicts her life in "full fusion with other lives" around her, as he did not do in the case of Daisy Miller, for example. Early in his career, James complained in "Daisy Miller" about American girls' lack of freedom. Now, at the end of his career, he shows in "Julia Bride" what happens when such girls are too free and easy.

Julian, Kate. In "Owen Wingrave," widowed Mrs. Julian's daughter. Owen Wingrave loves her, but she taunts him. In *The Saloon*, Mrs. Julian's daughter (age twenty), schooled briefly in France, and nominally engaged to Owen Wingrave until they dispute over the military life. When he defies the family ghost, she confesses her love to him and apologizes, but he dies.

Julian, Mrs. In "Owen Wingrave," a soldier's widow, Kate Julian's mother, and the sister of Captain Hume-Walker. He was once engaged to Jane Wingrave, with whom she now lives. In *The Saloon*, Mrs. Julian (age fifty) is from a military family and has been in the Wingrave home for five years. She deplores Owen Wingrave's impractical defiance of his family.

Jusserand, Jean Jules (1855–1932). Brilliant French scholar and diplomat. Lyon- and Paris-educated, he entered the Foreign Office in 1876 and was *conseiller* of the French Embassy in London (1887–1890), during which time he saw much of Robert Browning,* George Du Maurier,* Sir Edmund Wilson Gosse,* W. E. H. Lecky, Sir Leslie Stephen,* Hippolyte Taine* and his wife, Mary Augusta Ward* and her husband, and James, with whom he often dined, attended plays, and supped at Hampstead with Du Maurier. Shortly after meeting him, James described Jules Jusserand in a letter to Grace Norton* ([c. 4 Jan 1888]) as "a remarkably intelligent and pleasant little Frenchman," an opinion he never altered. After brief duty in Copenhagen, Jusserand became French Ambassador to the United States (1902–1925), where he served under five American presidents, lived graciously in Washington, D.C., and knew Henry Adams,* John Milton Hay,* and other important American men of letters. During his 1904–1905 tour of the United States, James was Jusserand's guest of honor at a French Embassy dinner in Washington (January 1905). In a letter to Gosse (16 Feb 1905), James mentions seeing "wondrous blooming, aspiring little Jusserand" there. Jusserand was instrumental in involving America in World War I. He wrote on English literature and history, William Shakespeare* in France, historiography, diplomacy, and sports. A popular critical study of his was *Le Roman au temps de Shakespeare* (1887; translated in 1890 by Elizabeth Lee*). In his autobiography, entitled *What Me Befell* (1933), Jusserand expressed his admiration of James's sense of humor, sarcasm, and style in personal letters, which he quoted and treasured. Late in his life, James gossiped with his Rye neighbor Sir Sydney Philip Waterlow* about Jusserand; James felt that Jusserand's interest in English literature was politically self-serving. James's library contained six books by Jusserand.

Justine, Sister. In *The Portrait of a Lady*, one of Pansy Osmond's convent teachers.

K

"The 'K. B.' Case." An early title for what was to become *The Ivory Tower*. Another tentative title for it was "Mrs. Max." "K. B." stands for James's friend Katherine De Kay Bronson.*

Kapp, Stanislas. In *The American*, the Strasbourg brewer's burly son who kills Valentin de Bellegarde in a duel caused by Noémie Nioche.

Katkoff, Madame de. In *Daisy Miller: A Comedy in Three Acts*, a Russian widow, perhaps about age thirty-eight, who owns a villa just outside Geneva, Switzerland, and has evidently been the object of Frederick Winterbourne's affections there and in Dresden. She is now being blackmailed by Eugenio, the Miller family courier, to flirt with Winterbourne in Rome to enable Eugenio's coconspirator Cavaliere Giacomo Giovanelli to be freer to snare the rich Daisy Miller. When Madame de Katkoff meets the innocent Daisy, she encourages Winterbourne to propose to the girl.

Keddie, Henrietta (1827–1914). British author who wrote under the pen name Sarah Tytler.*

Keith, Isabel Morton. In *Watch and Ward*, as Miss Morton, she is the cool object of Roger Lawrence's affections. As widowed Mrs. Keith, she befriends his ward Nora Lambert.

Keith, Mrs. In *Watch and Ward*, Isabel Keith's mother-in-law.

Kemble, Frances Anne (Fanny) (1809–1893). A daughter of Charles Kemble, whose parents Roger and Sarah Ward Kemble formed a British acting company, in which their children acted. Charles acted at Drury Lane and Covent Garden, the latter of which he also managed. One of his sisters was Sarah Siddons. Educated in Bath, Boulogne, and Paris, Fanny first acted for her father's group at Covent Garden (playing Juliet in *Romeo and Juliet* by William Shakespeare* more than a hundred times), toured the United States (1832–1834), and in Philadelphia unhappily married Pierce Butler in 1834. She left him for England the next year, after which he successfully sued for divorce (1849). She offered dramatic readings in England and America, lived in the United States intermittently (1849–1877), often summered in Switzerland, and finally resided in London. She was also a minor playwright, novelist, and poet. James first met Fanny Kemble and her daughter Sarah Butler Wister,* mother of Owen Wister,* in Rome (December 1872); he soon saw much of the older woman at parties given there by such expatriate Americans as William Wetmore Story* and Luther Terry.* In January 1875 James stayed at Kemble's New York home and heard the aging lady intone Pedro Calderon de la Barca in translation. Early in 1877, while *The American* was appearing serially, Kemble told James that she feared he would have his hero and heroine marry. By summer James could write to William James (28 Jun [1877]), when Kemble left for Switzerland, "I miss her as we had become very good friends." James spent Christmas Eve with her at her daughter Mrs. Wister's Stratford-upon-Avon home. He reviewed her popular 1878 *Record of a Girlhood* (*Nation*, 12 Dec 1878), saying that it should be longer, since it is a charming account of a remarkable personality. He likes many aspects of its vivid style and humor. He notes that although Kemble was a triumphant actress, she was socially and mentally independent of the theater, and was no Bohemian. Her letters show intellectual curiosity. He wonders whether actors and actresses who are happy with the stage have inferior minds. James criticizes the poor editing of Kemble's book. To his sister Alice, James wrote (26 Mar [1879]) that "Mrs. Kemble . . . is . . . a head and shoulders . . . above everyone else in London, and her conversation is strong meat." As Kemble aged, she socialized less, but James continued to see her, admire her, and praise her in his letters. Though hobbled by the gout, he attended her funeral and wrote a touching letter to Mrs. Wister the same day (20 Jan 1893). He quickly penned a memorial essay about Frances Anne Kemble (*Temple Bar*, Apr 1893; reprinted in *Essays in London and Elsewhere*, 1893). It discusses her mixture "of contrasts and opposites," her public and private nature, her marvelous gift for reminiscence, and her attitudes toward London and Paris. Sincere and generous, she had dramatic facial features; she wrote much when her high and low spirits moved her and then was indifferent to those books. James intermittently waxes personal, remembering that he saw her on a country road outside New York on horseback; later (while still a boy), he saw her on stage in London, heard her read memorably from Shakespeare, attended the theater with her, rode in her carriage afterwards, responded to her criticism of bad theatrical performances and her hatred of prigs and pedants, and listened spellbound to her direct and open-minded conversation. She spoke French as well as she did English, disliked the intermingling of the two languages, and avoided slang. She had two passions: Shakespeare and the Alps. James analyzes her challenging nature. She was all one—genuine talk, acting, and writing. She was never diplomatic, ambitious, or vain. Sadness underlay all of her other traits. James comments favorably on her writings, especially admiring the fact that she wrote her first novel at the age of eighty. James touches on her unhappy marriage and on her criticism and defense of America. James first knew her well in Rome; he was saddened to see her in her last years, in London, unable to return to her beloved Alps. But then she was "anecdotic" about personalities from her past, had loyal friends and servants, and finally welcomed death: She had "such arrogance of imagination" that she was contemptuous of life's limitations. Fanny Kemble had a serious character and was immensely gifted. It is of interest that she imparted to James ideas for several of his fictional works. According to one Notebook entry (21 Feb 1879), she outlined a domestic situation which resulted in *Washington Square*. A later entry (26 Mar 1884) summarizes another story told to James by Kemble; the outcome was "Georgina's Reasons." Next (5 Jan, 11 Mar 1888) is jotted down "Mrs. Kemble's anecdote," which suggested "The Patagonia." Finally (28 Feb 1889) James notes "an anecdote told me by Mrs. Kemble," which resulted in "The Solution." Upon her death, Fanny Kemble willed James a clock, with an accompanying poem. James also knew Fanny's sister, the opera singer Adelaide Sartoris, of the Sartoris family.* James's library contained six books by Frances Kemble.

Kenyon, Lady. In "Brooksmith," a member of Oliver Offord's social circle.

Keyes, Edith Archer. In *The Portrait of a Lady*, one of Isabel Archer's sisters.

Keynes, Sir Geoffrey Langdon (1887–1982). Brilliant, versatile surgeon, military officer, and scholar. He was also the brother of the distinguished economist John Maynard Keynes. During his Cambridge days, Geoffrey Keynes was a friend of Rupert Brooke,* Sir Edward Howard Marsh,* and Sir Sydney Philip Waterlow,* among others. Keynes served in both World War I and World War II, in the latter as a Royal Air Force vice marshal. He was a medical school professor; he published articles in medical journals; and he was also a prolific bibliographer, editor, biographer, and autobiographer (*The Gates of Memory: No Life Is Too Long* [1981]). He edited the poetry of Rupert Brooke (1946, 1970), compiled a bibliography of Brooke's works (1954), and edited his letters (1968). While they were undergraduates together, Keynes, Theodore Bartholomew, and Charles Sayle invited James in 1908 to visit them. In a series of witty letters, James delayed and then accepted; he was charmingly entertained 11–14 June 1909, during which time he memorably met Brooke. Decades later, Keynes wrote up the episode in *Henry James in Cambridge* (1967).

King, Charles (1844–1933). Army officer, educator, and writer. He graduated from the U.S. Military Academy at West Point in 1866, campaigned in the West against the Indians, was wounded, taught at West Point, was a daring general in the Spanish-American War, and saw duty in World War I. His military career spanned seventy-six years. He was the author of several military works, notably *Famous and Decisive Battles of the World* (1885), and a few novels, including *The General's Double* (1897), which James in "American Letter" (28 May 1898) calls "more sustaining" than most current military fiction. But even it is not "particularly nutritive" since it is a "medley" without an exact subject and has a hero and a heroine we cannot "really get intelligently near."

King, Clarence (1842–1901). American geologist, administrator, writer, and witty conversationalist. He was educated in science at Yale (B.S., 1862), took a horseback trip across the United States, and worked in Nevada and California mines for three years. Then he supervised an official survey of the Cordilleran ranges from eastern Colorado to California, which resulted in a seven-volume *Report of the Geological Exploration of the Fortieth Parallel* (1870–1880), now considered a classic in its field. Next he was in charge of the U.S. Geological Survey (1878–1881), after which he became a mining engineer. His most important writings are his popular *Mountaineering in the Sierra Nevada* (1872, serialized in the *Atlantic Monthly* in 1871) and the 1886 short story "Helmet of Mambrino." His *Memoirs* appeared posthumously (1904). Among his personal friends were Henry Adams,* John Milton Hay,* William Dean Howells,* John La Farge,* and James, who admired his mountaineering narrative and lauds its author in an 1871 review of *Hours of Exercise in the Alps* by John Tyndall.* By September 1882 James had met King, who was temporarily residing in London across the street from his Bolton Street apartment. Two months later, in France on research for *A Little Tour in France*, James chanced to meet Hay and King in Paris. In letters to Isabella Stewart Gardner* (12 Nov [1882]), Howells (27 Nov [1882]), Hay (5 Dec [1882], 5 Feb [1883]), and Marian Adams* (28 Feb [1883]), James variously describes King as "a delightful creature," "a charmer," "as genial as ever, though talking a little too much for one's nerves, perhaps," "a kind of fairy-godmother," and "a truly festive nature." In a more private letter, to his sister Alice (3 May [1884]), James hints at a darker side of King, whom he calls "queer, incomplete, unsatisfactory," and whom he criticizes for preferring London "publicans, barmaids, and other sinners" to persons who might advance him professionally. When news reached James that King had been hospitalized for nervous prostration and mental illness (1893–1894), he wrote to Hay (28 Jan 1894) that he "was infinitely shocked." King later contracted tuberculosis. James's library contained one book by King.

King, William Lyon Mackenzie (1874–1950). Distinguished Canadian statesman. He was a parliamentarian, minister of labor, and prime minister. James met young King in Rye, at a tea given in Rye, in September 1912, by Margaret Prothero, the wife of Sir George Walter Prothero.*

King. In "The Story of a Masterpiece," an admirer in Europe of Marian Everett.

Kinglake, Alexander William (1809–1891). English historian and travel writer. He was educated at Eton and Trinity College, Cambridge, and he was friendly with Alfred, Lord Tennyson* and William Makepeace Thackeray.* Kinglake is best remembered for his classic *Eothen* (1844) and a history of the Crimean War (8 vols., 1863–1887). James first met him in 1877 at a dinner at the home of George Washburn Smalley.*

Kingsbury, Mr. and Mrs. In *The Tragic Muse*, Nick Dormer's political opponent and that man's attractive wife. Julia Dallow and Nick discuss the two.

Kingsley, Charles (1819–1875). British clergyman, novelist, religious essayist, and minor poet. He was the older brother of Henry Kingsley.* Born in Devonshire to a vicar father, Charles Kingsley moved with his family to London, attended King's College there, then Magdalene College, Cambridge. In 1844 he became a lifelong rector at Eversley, in Hampshire. He began to write essays on Christian socialism under the influence of Thomas Carlyle.* Then he began to write novels. His *Yeast* (1848, revised 1851) was unfairly criticized. *Alton Locke* (1850) was accepted more readily. Kingsley vacationed in Germany in 1851, then published *Hypatia* (1853), *Westward Ho!* (1855), and *Two Years Ago* (1857). He was named a queen's chaplain in 1859, then became a genial but undistinguished history professor at Cambridge (1860–1869). His controversy with John Henry Newman led to the latter's *Apologia pro Vita Sua* (1864). In poor health, Kingsley toured France briefly (1864) with James Anthony Froude,* published *Hereward the Wake* (1866), then visited the West Indies (1869–1870), which he described in *At Last* (1870). Taking up his duties as canon of Chester in 1870, he taught geology and botany there, and inclined toward Darwinism. In 1874 he went to America, partly to lecture and partly because of his worsening health; he returned home and soon died. His wife, though sickly, survived him by sixteen years. In a review of Henry Kingsley's novel *The Hillyars and the Burtons*, James downgrades Charles Kingsley as an optimistic novelist cheapening historically valid notions of nobility of character. James reviewed (*Nation*, 25 Jan 1866) *Hereward*, summarizing its plot and noting that it shows how tradition leads to history, which leads to the fiction of Kingsley, who is a poet, storyteller, and preacher here praising adventuresome, dutiful, magnanimous courage. His notion of intelligence is muscle aiding morality. Weak as a philosopher, he is strong as a chronicler, a typically fine English raconteur showing imagination and sympathy. James heard Kingsley preach at Chester and wrote to his father (29 May [1872]) that the cathedral scene was pleasant but that "poor Kingsley is in the pulpit a decidedly weak brother, . . . flat and . . . boyish." James is similarly critical in his travel essay "Chester"; Canon Kingsley's sermon, from his "splendid canopied and pinnacled pulpit of gothic stonework," did not match the "almost gorgeous ecclesiastical march" preceding it. When Kingsley died,

James penned a memorial (*Nation*, 28 Jan 1875) which notes that the man had exhausted his limited genius and outlived his fame. His later works reveal foibles, not virtues. He had too many unwarmed irons in the fire. The historian in him spoiled the novelist. His Cambridge years were not notable. His sermons, praising sporting and "English pluck," are inadequate. Everything by him will be forgotten except some songs, and two or three novels, especially his splendid *Westward Ho!* When his widow issued *Charles Kingsley: His Letters and Memories of His Life* (1877), James in a review (*Nation*, 25 Jan 1877) criticizes its great length and the inclusion of solicited letters praising the subject, who was such a harried country parson and such a passionate sportsman and naturalist, that it is a wonder he wrote any novels. James calls Kingsley a kind of genius, with a vigorous temperament but a simple intellect, almost a cartoon of John Bull. He comments on Kingsley's non-Tractarian opinions, his love of nature, his part in "the Chartist agitation," his shallow radicalism, and finally his "fits" of sentimental activity. James's library contained one book by Charles Kingsley.

Kingsley, Henry (1830–1876). British writer, born in Northamptonshire, educated at King's College, London, and Worcester College, Oxford. He was the younger brother of Charles Kingsley.* Henry Kingsley worked and wandered in Australia (1853–1858), then returned to England and began to write novels, including *Geoffrey Hamlin* (1859) and *The Hillyars and the Burtons: A Story of Two Families* (1865), both about Australia. His work as an editor in Edinburgh was interrupted by the Franco-Prussian War, which he reported while attached to the German army. Kingsley resumed writing in London but died prematurely of tongue cancer. James reviewed (*Nation*, 6 Jul 1865) *The Hillyars and the Burtons* but in doing so spends too many words downgrading Charles Kingsley. Henry Kingsley, "a reduced copy of his brother," incompetently presents in his novel a girl's "conflict between love and duty." The work has too many characters, as though the author is afraid to be alone with his readers, and too many details concerning Australia, which Charles Reade* treats better without ever having been there. Kingsley diminishes nobility (by having it concern only duty and respect) and makes it wrongly seem exclusively British. Muscular Christianity is reduced to "a spurious nobleness." The only real hero in the novel is the villain, who displays "spirit."

Kington-Oliphant, Thomas Laurence (1831–1902). British historian, biographer, and scholar of linguistics. In addition to works on the thirteenth-century Roman emperor Frederick II, and on Old and Middle English, he published *The Duke and the Scholar, and Other Essays* (1875), James's review (*Nation*, 30 Sep 1875) of which is wholly laudatory. The Duc de Luynes, Honoré d'Albert (1802–1867), was a rich scholar and patron of scholars, including J. L. A. Huillard-Bréholles. The duke, who opposed Italian unity, was a Legitimist, admired the English, and was an expert on history, archaeology, and linguistics;

Huillard-Bréholles was a learned editor. Kington-Oliphant here offers a translation of Huillard-Bréholles's biography of the duke, a sketch of Huillard-Bréholles's life, a translation of a thirteenth-century Parmesan friar's "entertaining" and picturesque autobiography, and comments on the effects of the War of the Roses on British aristocracy.

Kipling, Rudyard (1865–1936). English novelist, short-story writer, and poet, born in Bombay, India. His father was a British artist who taught in Bombay, who was a school administrator and museum curator in Lahore, and whose wife's sister married Sir Edward Burne-Jones.* Young Rudyard Kipling was sent to England for schooling (1871–1882), during which time he was unhappy and mistreated. He returned to India and became a hardworking reporter in Lahore (1882–1887), then an editor in Allahabad (1887–1889). Even before this time, he was writing poems and stories which were soon collected in book form. He published six short railway library books, including *Soldiers Three* (1888, starring the immortal Terence Mulvaney) and *The Phantom 'Rickshaw* (1888). These early works show Kipling's cynical humor, gruesomeness, and love of the occult and the vulgar and his slick, jumpy, captivating style. After traveling in the Orient and America (1889), Kipling was greeted by an appreciative England, where through Andrew Lang* he quickly met Sir Walter Besant,* Sir Edmund Wilson Gosse,* Thomas Hardy,* and James. Kipling also became acquainted with George Meredith* and William Ernest Henley,* among other notable men of letters. Kipling engaged Alexander Pollack Watt* as his literary agent. (Together they fought the literary pirates, but to little avail.) Kipling also began a professional and personal relationship with Charles Wolcott Balestier* (1890) and through him met his domineering, moody sister Caroline, whom Kipling married in 1892. The couple lived in Brattleboro, Vermont, Carrie's home town (1892–1896); then, after a violent argument with his wife's brother Beatty Balestier, who was an alcoholic conniver but was liked in the region, Kipling returned with his wife to England. His novels include *The Light That Failed* (1890), *The Naulahka* (1892, written with Wolcott Balestier), *Captains Courageous* (1897), and *Kim* (1901). Kipling wrote much else, including *Mine Own People* (1891), the *Jungle Books* (1894, 1895), *The Seven Seas* (1896), the phenomenal poem "Recessional" (1897), *Stalky and Co.* (1899), and *Something of Myself* (1937, an unrevealing autobiography). He received the Nobel Prize for literature in 1907. In his later years, he theorized that the white man's burden (i.e., imperialism) was to hold the forces of darkness in India and elsewhere at bay; he espoused love of country and legal authority, admiration of good training, and delight in efficient machinery; and he distrusted thoughtless democratic processes. Kipling was unusual in appealing to readers worldwide with varying degrees of sophistication. James gave the bride away at Kipling's sparsely attended wedding (Gosse, William Heinemann,* and the groom's cousin Ambrose Poynter were the only other adult male guests) in influenza-ravaged London. James never especially liked Kipling's wife Carrie. In a letter to his brother

William (6 Feb 1892), he called her "a hard, devoted, capable, characterless little person, whom I don't in the least understand his marrying," but he added that Kipling was "the most complete man of genius . . . I have ever known." Nonetheless, James always remained of two minds concerning the man. He called Kipling "the infant monster" and a "little black demon" in letters to their friend Robert Louis Stevenson* (12 Jan, 30 Oct 1891), and in the earlier letter he criticized *The Light That Failed* as "wanting in composition and in narrative and . . . art." To the American publication of Kipling's short-story collection entitled *Mine Own People* (1891), James provided a spirited introduction. The essay was reprinted as an introduction to *Soldiers Three . . .* (Leipzig: Heinemann and Balestier, 1891), and as "Mr. Kipling's Early Stories" in *Views and Reviews*, 1908. In it, James praises the author's "freshness" and his dual appeal to challenge-liking critics and the "simple," even "vulgar" masses. He adds that Kipling quickly established his unique point of view concerning India, warfare, women, and primitive "low life"; and he succeeds in combining the artist and the amateur, to offer an "active, disinterested sense of the real." James expresses his delight in certain stories, in which India is painted with "vividness and drollery" based on "knowledge . . . and . . . invention," and which display both lyricism and patriotism. James divides the stories into "tales of native life," "Anglo-Indian episode[s]," and—best—yarns of common soldiers. He admits to a "perverse and whimsical" delight in reading Kipling, who knows how to use the "admirable, flexible form" of the short story, with its episodic "specimen and . . . illustration." James predicts that Kipling "will be [even] more active" later. In his 1901 essay "Edmond Rostand," James suggests that both Rostand and Kipling are popular because each patriotically trumpets "the note of the militant and triumphant race." In a letter to Kipling himself (30 Oct 1901), James calls *Kim* "magnificent." In letters not to Kipling, James expressed varying opinions concerning the man. He wrote to his brother William (10 Aug 1894) that he had been with Kipling and his wife overnight and that Kipling recited samples of his poetry, some "quite magnificent" "but all violent"; he recalls Kipling's 1894 *Jungle Book* as "thrilling, but so bloody." To Jonathan Sturges* ([5 Nov 1896]), James defines Kipling as "one of the very few first *talents* of the time." But in a letter to Grace Norton* a year later (25 Dec 1897), he sketches Kipling's professional devolution thus: "[H]e has come steadily from the less simple in subject to the more simple,—from the Anglo-Indians to the natives, from the natives to the Tommies, from the Tommies to the quadrupeds, and from the quadrupeds to the fish, and from the fish to the engines and the screws." It was to Gosse that James was habitually the most frank: He says that their friend Kipling combines "talent" and "brutality," but he adds that "the talent has sometimes failed" in *The Light That Failed* (6 Aug 1889 [1891]); he reports that he read the first *Jungle Book* "with extreme admiration," but that it "sets his [Kipling's] limit" and that he does not like all the violence (25 Jun 1894); and finally he mentions that *The Seven Seas* has "hellish cunning" ([8? Nov 1896]). The Kiplings and James of Lamb House* frequently entertained each other, the former alternately amusing and exasperating the latter with their expensive automobile in Sussex. In his autobiography, Kipling mentions James only once, to note that James attended his wedding. James's library contained twenty-eight books by Kipling.

Knight, Cornelia (1758–1837). British bluestocking novelist, historian, translator, poet, memoirist, and court lady. Early in life she lived abroad, including in Italy, and was a friend of Lord Nelson's Lady Hamilton; she became a companion of Princess Charlotte Augusta, the daughter of King George IV; and she died in Paris. Her major work is the *Autobiography of Miss Cornelia Knight, Lady Companion to the Princess Charlotte of Wales, with Extracts from Her Journal and Anecdote Book* (2 vols., 1861, including parts of her sixty-year diary, now missing). James reviewed (*Nation*, 24 Jun 1875) *Personal Reminiscences of Cornelia Knight and Thomas Raikes*, selected and edited by Richard Henry Stoddard* (1875). James begins by saying that although he dislikes being spoon-fed by books of extracts, Stoddard has performed usefully here: The editor chooses and skips for the lazy reader, and he offers us a broth of author gossip which requires no chewing. Knight was livelier than her companion; she has a "dry" style here but offers good anecdotes and clever touches "of portraiture."

Knight, Dr. Horace. In "A Most Extraordinary Case," Colonel Ferdinand Mason's casual army friend. Mason has a fatal relapse upon learning that Knight and Caroline Hoffmann have become engaged.

Knight, Mrs. In "A Most Extraordinary Case," a person with whom Caroline Hofmann stays at one point. She is probably Dr. Knight's mother.

Knocker. In "The Wheel of Time," General Knocker's brother, who dies.

Knocker. In "The Wheel of Time," either of General Knocker's sons.

Knocker, Fanny. In "The Wheel of Time," the maiden name of Fanny Knocker Tregent.

Knocker, General Blake. In "The Wheel of Time," Fanny Knocker's father.

Knocker, Jane. In "The Wheel of Time," Fanny Knocker's mother.

Knocker, Miss. In "The Wheel of Time," General Knocker's sister. She cares for the Knocker children in Heidelberg.

Kremnitz, Countess. In "The Two Faces," Lady Valda Gwyther's mother.

L

L., A. In "A Light Man," Maximus Austin's former girlfriend.

L.—, Miss. In "De Grey, A Romance," a girl whose engagement to Paul De Grey is broken. She later dies in Naples.

L—, Mr. and Mrs. In "Travelling Companions," the American consul in Venice and his wife.

Ladle. In "In the Cage," the name of a furnished apartment.

"Lady Barbarina" (1884 title, "Lady Barberina"; 1908 title, "Lady Barbarina"). Long short story (35,600 words), published in the *Century Magazine* (May–Jul 1884); reprinted in *Tales of Three Cities*, 1884; revised and reprinted in *The Novels and Tales of Henry James*, Volume XIV, 1908. (Characters; Lady Lucretia Beauchemin, Lord Beauchemin, Lord Philip and Lady Canterville, Mrs. Chew, Lady Agnes Clement, Dr. Sidney Feeder, Mr. and Mrs. Dexter Freer, Hardman, Lady Barbarina Clement Lemon, Dr. Jackson Lemon, Mary Lemon, Miss Lemon, Herman Longstraw, Sir Henry and Lady Marmaduke, Mr. and Mrs. Trumpington, Mrs. Vanderdecker.) In spite of being warned by a good friend that he will be sorry, Jackson Lemon, an American physician, falls in love with proud, cold Lady Barbarina, one of London-based Lord and Lady Canterville's dozen or so children. The parents permit marriage only after the rich doctor signs a generous marriage contract. Six months later, the couple are in New York, where Lady Barbarina's nubile sister Agnes meets Herman Longstraw, a parasite from the Far West. When those two elope to California, "Barb" is ordered home for an accounting. The upshot is that Barb, her demeaned husband, and their daughter begin a permanent residence in London, where Agnes and Longstraw are now in great demand socially. In two Notebook entries (8 Apr, 17 May 1883), James explains that here he is going to reverse his usual plot of American girl marrying British aristocrat, then he sketches tentative lines of action. Reversed also will be the usual movement from America to England, such as may be found in "An International Episode." James wrote to his London publisher Sir Frederick Orridge Macmillan* (19 Apr 1883) about three planned tales: "One of these is to be another international episode . . . —an earl's daughter who marries a New Yorker and comes to live in 39th St!" According to the second Notebook entry, James originally planned to provide his doctor with a "vulgar" brother and Lady Barbarina's sister with "a handsome minister of N.Y." to marry, but he conflated these two projected characters into one Longstraw, who is vulgar and handsome (though no minister). In the preface to Volume XIV of *The Novels and Tales of Henry James*, James indulges in much general theorizing about "the small comedies and tragedies of the international" community, then he says that he was "prompted" by observing that all "bridal migrations were eastward" to "put it [the reverse] to the imaginative test." Next, he confesses that for "Lady Barbarina" he saw the heroine as simple and the hero as requiring all the artistic touches. Beneath the glittering prose of the tale is little more than a marriage market closely resembling a horse fair, with long-legged products paraded before well-dressed buyers. The "vulgar" American cowboy, who provides character balance and contrast when he woos Lady Barb's sister, subtly reinforces the animal imagery (which James also uses in his prefatory remarks about the story). In a letter to James (8 December 1884), Robert Louis Stevenson* extravagantly praised James's brilliant opening Hyde Park scene for its "intangible precision."

"Lady Barberina." 1884 title of "Lady Barbarina."

La Farge, John (1835–1910). Brilliant New York-born Roman Catholic painter (of murals, landscapes, flowers, and figure pieces), stained-glass designer, and author. He was the son of a French-born naval hero who became rich in American shipping, banking, and real estate. Young La Farge was precocious in languages and reading, took valuable art lessons at an early age from his maternal grandfather (a miniaturist), graduated from Mount St. Mary's College in Emmitsburg, Maryland (1853), and studied law. Then he listened to his father's encouragement and pursued art studies in France, Germany, the Low Countries, and England (1856–1858) before he returned to law reading in America. Soon he studied art under William Morris Hunt* in Newport, Rhode Island (1858). In 1860 La Farge married Margaret Mason Perry; they had nine children. In 1866 La Farge began to suffer from some malady from which he never fully recovered. Beginning in 1866 he painted preimpressionistic landscapes. He was invited by Henry Hobson Richardson to do the Boston Trinity Church murals in 1876, and soon he followed them with murals in New York (including his 1887 masterpiece, *The Ascension*, in the Church of the Ascension) and at Bowdoin College. He did a panel in the New York residence of Whitelaw Reid.* He began to experiment with stained glass (with special success in Quincy, Massachusetts). He is credited with reviving the art in the United States, and he received the French Legion of Honor (Paris, 1889) for his work, especially in opaline glass. One of his closest friends was Henry Adams,* who regarded La Farge's mind as uniquely complex, and with whom he traveled extensively (1886, to Japan; 1890–1891, to Hawaii, Samoa—where they visited James's friend Robert Louis Stevenson*—Tahiti, Fiji, Australia, and Ceylon). Such travels yielded fine oil paintings and watercolors. La Farge's lectures at the Metropolitan Museum in New York in 1893 were published as *Considerations on Painting* (1895). In addition, he wrote *An Artist's Letters from Japan* (1897), a survey of the Fenway Court collection of Isabella Stewart Gardner* in Boston (1904), and *Reminiscences of the South Seas* (1912). James met La Farge at Newport in 1858, and the two became close friends. La Farge did not laugh at James's amateurish efforts at painting in Hunt's studio, saying instead that James had "a painter's eye." More to the point, La Farge encouraged his younger friend to read French literature, including the *Revue des Deux Mondes*, Honoré de Balzac,* and Prosper Mérimée* (even to translate Mérimée's "La Vénus d'Ille"). (La Farge's sensitive portrait of James at the age of nineteen is one of the best early likenesses of James. La Farge also did a portrait of Garth Wilkinson James as a youth.) At about this time, James also met Thomas Sergeant Perry,* who became another close friend and whose sister Margaret became La Farge's wife. On more than one occasion in 1869, James wrote to La Farge from Europe to come over and join him in rhapsodic travel. In "Art" (January 1872), James says that the most important of several paintings by Americans at an 1872 exhibition in Boston was a "remarkable" seascape by La Farge. In "On Some Pictures Lately Exhibited" (1875), James offers general praise of La Farge, whose pictures are always a challenge to the imagination and the culture of the critic, but whose *Psyche and Cupid* seems "over-wrought." When La Farge and Adams visited Stevenson in Samoa, James wrote to Stevenson (18 Feb 1891) that La Farge "is one of the two or three men now living whom . . . I have known longest since before the age of puberty. He was very remarkable then—but of late years I've seen less of him and I don't know what he has become. However, he never can have become commonplace—he is a strange and complicated product." In a letter to Sir John Forbes Clark* (13 Dec [1891]), James describes La Farge as "one of the most extraordinary and agreeable of men, a remarkable combination of France and America." La Farge provided an eerie illustration for James's "The Turn of the Screw" as it originally appeared in *Collier's Weekly*. During his 1904–1905 tour in the United States, James saw La Farge in Washington, D.C. In *The American Scene* (1907), James extravagantly praises La Farge's *Ascension* as "noble." On La Farge's death, James wrote to his daughter Margaret (15 Nov 1910) to recall his friend's "wondrous intelligence and rare and distinguished personality." James added that La Farge was "one of the very small number of *truly* extraordinary men whom I've known. He was that rare thing, a *figure*—which innumerable eminent and endowed men . . . haven't been.'' In *Notes of a Son and Brother*, James reminisces about his ''Franco-American'' friend La Farge: his refinement, worldliness, intelligence, artistic appearance, Catholicism, knowledge of the works of Robert Browning* and French literature, and landscapes, and especially their walks together. (In 1956 John La Farge's priest son John LaFarge, S. J., in his autobiography entitled *The Manner Is Ordinary*, recorded the following information concerning James: William and Henry James introduced John La Farge to Margaret Perry. She believed that she was the only woman whom James ever deeply loved. She, her son John, and her daughter Margaret in the summer of 1903 visited James for two weeks in Lamb House.* Young John LaFarge's brother Oliver helped arrange for James's 1905 California trip. James last wrote to Mrs. La Farge on 21 August 1914, sending her a copy of his *Notes of a Son and Brother*.) James may have gently spoofed aspects of his friend La Farge when he characterized Locksley, the painter in ''A Landscape Painter.''

Lagardie, Horace de (?–?). Possibly a pseudonym. Lagardie published a magazine essay in 1877 entitled ''French Novels and French Life,'' which James reviewed (*Nation*, 29 Mar 1877). Lagardie says that French novels do not accurately portray French life, whereas English novels do depict English life well. James, who had long agreed, points out the inaccuracy of certain French fictive stereotypes. Lagardie notes that French writers, who are often ''shabby, Bohemian,'' cannot know French society. James says that British novelists (for example, governesses) do, and he adds that young French girls do not read novels whereas young British girls do.

''Lake George.'' Travel essay, published in the *Nation* (25 Aug 1870). James so enjoys travel that even the train ride is pleasant from Saratoga to Glen's Falls, which is ''pretty'' but of ''elements so meagre.'' The drive on to Lake George is through romantic scenery. The town of Caldwell, on the lake, has a pretentious hotel with a fine piazza and a superb view of the forest-framed lake. James promptly compares it to Lake Como as to trees, light, tones, and human background. He tries one of the plank roads leading away from the lake. A little farmhouse along his path thrills him: ''[S]cattered accessories'' in the presence of ''spontaneous nature'' create a ''potent'' little picture. He walks on, trying to study and remember innumerable picturesque details this side of the everchanging mountains. Uniquely moved, he looks and looks. Later he takes a boat out onto the cool waters of Lake George. In early evening, the mountains lose their ''aerial charm . . . but . . . gain a formal grandeur.'' At night he sees picturesquely overdressed women on the dance floor, but he also senses in the band music the strains of German militarism.

Lamb. In *The Album*, dying Bedford's solicitor at Courtlands.

Lambert, Mr. and Mrs. In *Watch and Ward*, Nora's parents. Mrs. Lambert, who was poverty stricken, is now deceased. Mr. Lambert commits suicide when his daughter Nora is little.

Lambert, Nora. In *Watch and Ward*, Roger Lawrence's ward, perhaps loved by the Rev. Mr. Hubert Lawrence, certainly almost compromised by George Fenton, and ultimately wooed and won by the patient Roger.

Lambeth, Lord. In "A International Episode," the son of the Duke and Duchess of Bayswater. He meets Bessie Alden in America and comes to care for her fondly, but he loses her in England because of pride and prejudice.

Lamb House, West Street, Rye, East Sussex, TN31 7ES. James's happy home (and main residence) south of London, on the Channel coast just northeast of famed Hastings, from 1898 to 1916. James had long hoped for a house of his own and envied people richer than he (including popular novelists) for being able to live opulently. When Henry Adams* and his wife, for example, leased a house near St. James's Park, London, James describes the Adams quarters in a letter written from his Bolton Street flat to his mother (2 Feb [1880]) as "such a house as I hope to have here some day, when I shall entertain my family." In 1897 James felt able to lease Lamb House for twenty-one years, for £70 a year. In 1899 he bought the freehold for £2,000. Edward Prioleau Warren,* the distinguished architect, helped James select the place and in 1899 supervised repairs after a fire there. Lamb House, completed in 1723 of now time-gentled red brick, was named after James Lamb, an early owner, who was often mayor of Rye early in the eighteenth century. Facing the front door, of beautiful Georgian design, is an attractive staircase with twisted balusters. The right-hand room is a waiting room, now called the Henry James Room and also the Telephone Room; on the left, a parlor, now called the Morning Room, opens by French doors onto a spacious, red-walled garden. Also from the parlor is a dining room, with other French doors to the garden. Beneath the stairway is a door leading to the kitchen, which was originally of earlier construction (Elizabethan at least). Upstairs are four bedrooms and a bathroom. One paneled bedroom is called the King's Room, because for four nights in January 1726 George I slept there. It looks onto the cobbled street in front. Another bedroom, called the Green Room, doubled as a second reading room and study for James, especially in winter. On the third floor are four small bedrooms. A main attraction for James was a detached little building called the Garden House, later the Garden Room (with an adjacent greenhouse), which he used as a writing room and his primary study. *The Awkward Age* was the first novel James wrote at Lamb House. (On 18 August 1940, a bomb from a German aircraft, evidently aimed at a British radar installation nearby, destroyed this detached room, and with it part of James's library.) At this home, which James remodeled to some extent, and in this town, which he adored, James was a productive writer, a host to distinguished guests and many relatives, and a proud and loyal citizen. To help with the chores at Lamb House, James employed several servants, including a cook, a manservant (Burgess Noakes*), two maids, and a gardener. Visitors included Charles Hamilton Aïdé,* Hendrik Christian Andersen,* Sir Max Beerbohm,* Rupert Brooke,* Stephen Crane,* William Morton Fullerton,* George Gissing,* Sir Edmund Wilson Gosse,* Harley Granville Granville-Barker,* Ford Madox Hueffer,* Violet Hunt,* Rudyard Kipling,* the wife and two children of John La Farge,* Jonathan Sturges,* Alfred Sutro* and his wife Esther, Sir Hugh Seymour Walpole,* Herbert George Wells,* Mary Augusta Ward,* and Edith Newbold Jones Wharton* (who often brought her automobile). Relatives who visited included William James, his wife Alice, and often their children. James gave his younger nephew William the use of his home for the young man's long English honeymoon. James treasured his country home in Rye. In a letter ([18? Oct 1900]), he advised Gosse (unsuccessfully) to keep his own country house: "*It is everything* to have one—a refuge out of London. . . . I find this asylum . . . of unspeakable worth to me." From Florida he wrote to Gosse (16 Feb 1905) of yearning for "the . . . peace of Lamb House." Late in 1914 James grew too infirm to continue living at Lamb House and moved back to London. He willed Lamb House to his nephew Henry James, who rented it to an American widow and then to an American painter. The latter relinquished his lease to Edward Frederic Benson,* who shared the house with his brother Arthur Christopher Benson.* Both men wrote happily there. After A. C. Benson died in 1925, E. F. Benson leased Lamb House until his death in 1940. Two years after the death of James's nephew in 1948, Lamb House—empty through the war years and later—was given by his widow to the British National Trust for Places of Historic Interest or Natural Beauty. The most distinguished recent resident of Lamb House has been H. Montgomery Hyde (author of the informative *Henry James at Home*, 1969). For a photograph of Lamb House, taken by Alvin Langdon Coburn* in 1906, see the frontispiece to Volume IX of *The Novels and Tales of Henry James* (1908).

Lambinet, Émile Charles (1816–1878). Popular Versailles-born and Paris-trained landscape painter of the preimpressionistic, Barbizon school. He went to Algeria in 1845, then to England and Holland. He received the cross of the Legion of Honor in 1867. In "From Normandy to the Pyrenees" James likens a valley in central France to a Lambinet landscape—"in silvery lights and vivid greens." In *The Ambassadors* Lambert Strether compares a certain French countryside to a Lambinet. In *A Small Boy and Others* James mentions Lambinet as an indirect influence on William Morris Hunt,* under whom William James studied painting briefly.

"A Landscape Painter." Short story (13,200 words), published in the *Atlantic Monthly* (Feb 1866); republished in *Stories Revised*, 1885. (Characters: Alfred Bannister, Miss Blankenberg, Cynthia, Dawson, Josephine Leary, Locksley,

Prendergast, Miriam Quarterman, Captain Richard Quarterman.) Locksley, a rich young painter, has been jilted, and he retires to Chowderville, where he rents rooms with retired sea-captain Richard Quarterman. His daughter Miriam is a teacher and seems rather naive. Locksley pretends that he is poor, and the two fall in love. When he becomes sick, she sneaks a look into his diary and learns that he is rich. She determines to marry him and soon succeeds. On their honeymoon, she tells him what she did and says that his money made her love him all the more. Two abiding Jamesian elements already at work in this early, slight tale are appearance vs. reality in incipient lovers' play, and charming dialogue. Some aspects of this story may comprise a gentle spoof of James's close friend John La Farge.*

Lang, Andrew (1844–1912). Witty, ranging, and facile Scottish scholar, novelist, poet, biographer, historian (of Scotland and of English literature), writer of historical mysteries, translator of Homer, folklorist, and avid collector of fairy tales. He was educated at St. Andrew and at Balliol College, Oxford. From 1875 he resided in London. With Frederic William Henry Myers* in 1882, Lang was one of the founders of the Society for Psychical Research. He wrote 150 books and edited or contributed to 150 others. James met him in December 1876, shortly after taking up residence in London. James soon wrote to his friend Thomas Sergeant Perry* (18 Apr 1877) a judgment of Lang which he never modified: "His great gift is an extraordinary facility." James added in a letter to Robert Louis Stevenson* (31 Jul [1888]) that Lang "uses his beautiful thin facility to write everything down to the lowest level of Philistine twaddle." Still, James was happy to let Lang introduce him to many of his literary friends, for example, John Addington Symonds* in 1877 and Rudyard Kipling* in 1889. In a letter to their friend Sir Edmund Wilson Gosse* (19 Nov 1912), James twits Gosse for indicating recently deceased Lang's many faults in his *Portraits and Sketches* (1912). James goes on to charge Lang with a "puerile imagination and . . . fourth-rate opinion[s]," even "Scotch provincialism"—all this in spite of great talent. It may be said that, whereas Lang liked literature best when it was romantic and fanciful, James preferred it to make realistic cultural statements. Lang was widely regarded as a vain talker. James's library contained twenty-three books by Lang.

Langrish, Lady Aurora. In *The Princess Casamassima*, an aristocratic liberal friendly to Hyacinth Robinson, Paul and Rosy Muniment, and the princess.

Lansing. In "Pandora," a man whom D. F. Bellamy sends to help the Day family through the New York customs.

Lappington, Lady. In *The Outcry*, the novel, and *The Outcry*, the play, a British aristocrat who sells Breckenridge Bender a Longhi painting.

Lapsley, Gaillard Thomas (1871–1949). Distinguished constitutional historian, who graduated from Harvard (1893), did graduate work there in medieval English history, taught there and in California, then moved to England, where he lectured at Trinity College, Cambridge (1904), and became a tutor there (1919–1929). In 1931 he was appointed a don there in medieval history. He came to know well Arthur Christopher Benson,* Percy Lubbock,* Howard Overing Sturgis,* and especially Edith Newbold Jones Wharton,* among several other friends of James. Wharton frequently mentions him in her autobiography, *A Backward Glance* (1934), and finally named him her literary executor. Lapsley wrote *The County Palatine of Durham: A Study in Constitutional History* (1899), *Origin of Property in Land* (1903), and *Crown, Community, Parliament in the Later Middle Ages: Studies in English Constitutional History* (1951); he helped Wharton with a selection of poems published as *Eternal Passion in English Poetry* (1939); and he annotated works by Thomas Babington Macaulay and Frederic William Maitland.* Lapsley met James in 1897 by way of a letter of introduction from Isabella Stewart Gardner,* and the two often socialized thereafter, sometimes at Lamb House.* Some of James's most tender, affectionate letters are addressed to Lapsley, who, according to a Notebook entry (11 May 1898), gave him the idea for "Fordham Castle."

"The Last of the Valerii." Short story (11,100 words), published in the *Atlantic Monthly* (Jan 1874); republished in *A Passionate Pilgrim, and Other Tales*, 1875, and in *Stories Revived*, 1885. (Characters: Count Marco Valerio, Countess Martha Valerio.) The painter narrator is the godfather of Martha, an American married to Count Marco Valerio of Rome. He begins to worship a statue of Juno recently exhumed from his villa grounds. When he goes too far in his paganism, Martha breaks the clutch of the past on him by reburying his Juno and offering him present-day reality instead. James wrote to William Dean Howells* from Florence (9 Jun 1874) to thank him for praising "The Last of the Valerii," which, he adds, "reads agreeably enough though I suppose that to many readers, it will seem rather idle." The story, which is indeed slight, derives from *La Vénus d'Ille* (1837) by Prosper Mérimée* and *The Marble Faun* (1860) by Nathaniel Hawthorne,* though with their grisliness smoothed over.

Lathrop, George Parsons (1851–1898). American travel writer, poet, novelist, librettist, associate editor of the *Atlantic Monthly* (1875–1877), brother of painter Francis Augustus Lathrop (who was an associate of John La Farge*), and husband of Rose Hawthorne, hence son-in-law of Nathaniel Hawthorne* (whose critical biography he published in 1876, and whose works he edited in 1883). James knew Lathrop slightly; he regarded his study of Hawthorne as a "singularly foolish pretentious little volume" but useful "for dates and facts," according to a letter to Thomas Sergeant Perry* (14 Sep 1879).

Latimer, Miss. In "Osborne's Revenge," an amateur actress overshadowed by Henrietta Congreve in a private theatrical.

Latouche. In "Four Meetings," the narrator's traveling companion. The two visit Latouche's mother in New England. Latouche's later death in the Levant occasions another visit by the narrator to the woman's New England home.

Latouche, John. Pen name of Oswald John Frederick Crawfurd.*

Latouche, Mrs. In "Four Meetings," the mother of the narrator's traveling companion. While visiting in her New England hometown, the narrator meets Caroline Spencer for the first and fourth times.

Latrobe. In "The Impressions of a Cousin," a guest at one of Eunice's dinner parties.

Laugel, Auguste (1830–1914). Versatile French mining engineer, writer, and political correspondent to the *Nation*, which was edited by James's close friend Edwin Lawrence Godkin.* Laugel's books concern various European countries, British politics (and political leaders), the United States (including the Civil War), history, art (including music), and science (including acoustics). James met Laugel and his wife at the Parisian apartment of Gustave Flaubert,* in December 1875, soon thereafter writing to his father (29 Dec [1875]) that the man "is not (to me) particularly *simpatico (au contraire)*. He has a deadly melancholy tone and manner which depress and distance one." James later dined at the Laugels', who tried to help him socially when he was first in Paris. James reviewed two books by Laugel. His *Italie, Sicile, Bohème: Notes de Voyage* (1872) James praises (*Nation*, 27 Feb 1873) for avoiding the diffuse and the trivial and for providing fine descriptions of Naples, St. Peter's in Rome, and Bohemian battlefields (of the Seven Weeks' War). And James reports (*Nation*, 18 Oct 1877) that Laugel's *La France Politique et Sociale* (1877) covers the French race, nation, characteristics, monarchy, aristocracy, and Reformation. James regards the future of France, which he calls here "the most brilliant nation in the world," to be less grim than does Laugel, who says that his country's "chief hope" lies "in the army." James's library contained two books by Laugel.

Lavinia. In "Maud-Evelyn," Lady Emma's former governess's daughter, who rejected Marmaduke.

Lawrence, David Herbert (1885–1930). Versatile and prolific Nottinghamshire-born fiction writer, poet, travel writer, and critic. Ford Madox Hueffer* first encouraged Lawrence, whose best works include *The White Peacock* (1911), *Sons and Lovers* (1913), *The Rainbow* (1915), *Twilight in Italy* (1916), *Women in Love* (1921), *Psychoanalysis and the Unconscious* (1921), *Studies in Classic*

American Literature (1923), *Lady Chatterley's Lover* (1928), and a 1928 collection of poems. James, who came upon Lawrence's pioneering work too late in life, replied wearily to Sir Hugh Seymour Walpole* (21 Aug 1913) to ask, "Who is D. H. Lawrence, who, you think, would interest me? Send him and his book [*Sons and Lovers*] along. . . . Inoculate me . . . so far as I can be inoculated. I always *try* to let anything of the kind take." A few months later, in "The New Novel," he lists several recent novels, including *Sons and Lovers*, but adds unprophetically that "Lawrence . . . hang[s] in the dusty rear." When he gets back to Lawrence, James does admit that he does "fairly smell of the real."

Lawrence, Mrs. In *Watch and Ward*, Roger Lawrence's mother, who died while her son had scarlet fever at college.

Lawrence, Rev. Mr. Hubert. In *Watch and Ward*, Roger Lawrence's eccentric cousin, who temporarily attracts Nora Lambert.

Lawrence, Roger. In *Watch and Ward*, a young man who is rejected by Isabel Morton. He then adopts orphaned Nora Lambert and rears her to become his wife.

Lawson, John A. (?–?). Travel writer. In his review (*Nation*, 24 Jun 1875) of Lawson's *Wanderings in the Interior of New Guinea* (1875), James reports that the book has evidently been exposed as a "curious literary fraud," with some vagueness, but that it also displays credible narration. He explains that Lawson apparently did intrepidly explore the interior of New Guinea from early 1872 to February 1873 but then faked his discovery of a mountain nearly 33,000 feet in elevation. James notes that Lawson thus ranks with Baron Karl Friedrich Münchausen and the Arthur Gordon Pym of Edgar Allan Poe.*

Lazarus, Emma (1849–1887). New York–born Jewish poet, dramatist, essayist, and champion of the oppressed. She twice visited Europe (1883, 1885–1886). Her best verse is contained in *Songs of a Semite* (1882), and her famous sonnet is placed on the pedestal of the Statue of Liberty. James, who had met Lazarus in New York early in 1883, wrote her a little later from Boston (9 May [1883]) to provide her with professional contacts for use when she would be in London.

Lear, Henrietta Louisa (née Farrer) (1824–1896). British author of short fiction, books of instruction for children, and biographies of saints, church leaders, and artists. She also published poetry and was an editor of hymn books. She married the Rev. Mr. Francis Lear in 1859, used the pen name H. L. Sidney Lear, and was widowed in 1867. She then lived in Salisbury (from 1871), writing approximately fifty books in all. James reviewed (*Nation*, 26 Aug 1875) her *A Christian Painter of the Nineteenth Century: Being the Life of Hyppolite* [*sic*]

Flandrin (1875), praising its "taste and sympathy" but disliking its "goody" tone. He recommends the mild and earnest murals of Jean Hippolyte Flandrin* at St. Germain-des-Prés in Paris and, though not especially liking modern religious paintings, applauds the artist's "sincerity and naturalness." James also admires his letters, from which Lear quotes, for their "peculiar homeliness" and "childlike simplicity." James summarizes Flandrin's life: miserable Lyons apprenticeship, work in Paris under Jean Auguste Dominique Ingres, *prix de Rome* and study there, successful return to France, partial blindness, and death later in Rome.

Leary, Josephine. In "A Landscape Painter," a young woman who has jilted Locksley at the outset.

Leavenworth. In *Roderick Hudson*, a pretentious patron of Roderick Hudson in Rome. When Hudson insults him, he takes up with Augusta Blanchard.

Leblond, Abbé. In *Watch and Ward*, Isabel Morton Keith's Roman confessor.

Lechmere. In "Owen Wingrave," an obedient young pupil, along with Owen Wingrave, under the military coach Spencer Coyle. In *The Saloon*, he becomes Bobby Lechmere, age twenty-five, quiet and rather impressed by Kate Julian's appearance.

Ledoux. In *The American*, a second at Valentin de Bellegarde's duel with Stanislas Kapp.

Lee, Elizabeth (fl. 1890–1918). British translator, biographer, and editor. Her most noteworthy works are *Ouida: A Memoir* (1914) and *Wives of the Prime Ministers, 1844–1906* (1918). In 1890 she published her translation (entitled *The English Novel in the Time of Shakespeare*) of *Le Roman au temps de Shakespeare* (1887), by Jean Jules Jusserand.* In 1913 she unsuccessfully appealed to James for information about Ouida.*

Lee, Sir Sidney (1859–1926). London-born scholar and editor. A brilliant student of William Shakespeare* at Balliol College, Oxford, he graduated in 1882. He was assistant editor of the *Dictionary of National Biography* in 1883, under Sir Leslie Stephen,* and became editor in 1891. Lee wrote many entries himself, including one which he expanded into a book-length biography of Shakespeare (1898). His other works include *Shakespeare and the Modern Stage* (1906) and *The French Renaissance in England* (1910). He was appointed professor of English at the University of London in 1913. James knew Lee casually and wrote a preface in 1907 to *The Tempest* for an edition of Shakespeare prepared by Lee. James's friend Sir Edmund Wilson Gosse* wrote the Algernon Charles Swinburne* entry for the *Dictionary of National Biography Supplement, 1901–*

1911 (1912), about which Lee, who edited the volume, wrote to James appreciatively.

Lee, Vernon (1856–1935). Pen name of Violet Paget.*

Lee-Hamilton, Eugene Jacob (1845–1907). Half-brother of Violet Paget.* He was privately tutored, mostly on the Continent, won a scholarship to Oriel College, Oxford, left without a degree, and entered the British diplomatic service. In 1871 he developed a curious case of possibly self-induced partial paralysis, which confined him to bed and chair for twenty years—spent mostly at his sister's villa near Florence, Italy. Lee-Hamilton got better in 1894, vacationed in the United States, where he visited his sister's friend Edith Newbold Jones Wharton*, married in 1898, and died a few years later. By this time he and his sister were long estranged. According to a Notebook entry by James in Florence (12 Jan 1887), Lee-Hamilton "told me a curious thing of . . . Byron's *ci-devant* mistress" (see George Gordon, Lord Byron), which resulted in "The Aspern Papers." In letters to Grace Norton,* James describes Lee-Hamilton as Paget's "paralysed step-brother (from the legs down) formerly in diplomacy," then praises both siblings as "the best people for talk" in Florence (25 Jan [1887]); but from Venice James harshly adds that Lee-Hamilton is "a grotesque, deformed, invalidical, *posing* little old mother" (27 Feb [1887]).

Lefevre, Lucretia. In "De Grey, A Romance," a woman loved and hence destroyed by Paul De Grey, an ancestor of the present Paul.

Leighton, Lord Frederick (1830–1896). Popular and once-prestigious English painter and sculptor, who spent his childhood and early youth abroad; studied in Florence, Paris, and Frankfurt; knew Robert Browning* (whose tomb he later designed) and William Makepeace Thackeray*, visited London in 1858, meeting several pre-Raphaelites at the time; and settled there in 1860. He gained renown when Queen Victoria purchased a painting of his in 1855. Later opposing pre-Raphaelite romantic realism, he painted mainly classical and sacred subjects. He was elected to the Royal Academy in 1868 and later served as its president in 1878. He was an excellent draughtsman. He illustrated an edition of *Romola* by George Eliot.* In 1879 James dined with the sister of Leighton, whom, in two letters to Grace Norton* (8 Jun [1879], c. 4 Jan [1888]), he describes as "the pleasantest (for simple pleasantness) man in London" and "the urbane, the curly, the agreeably artificial." In December 1883, James enjoyed attending a Royal Society function chaired by Leighton, who years later was present at the first performance of James's *Guy Domville*, on 5 January 1895. About to go to Leighton's highly public funeral, James wrote to Sir Edmund Wilson Gosse* (2 Feb 1896) concerning the artist: "I had never known a man so long & so little," adding, however, "I much admired him;—he was very fine." James reported the funeral in "London" (20 Feb 1897). In several art notices James touched on Leighton and his work, usually in an unenthusiastic manner. For example, in an untitled note (*Nation*, 6 Jun 1878), James opines that "in Mr. Leighton's plasticism there is something vague and conciliatory." Four years later ("London Pictures and London Plays" [August 1882]), he calls the subject of Leighton's *Phryne at Eleusis* "tall, long-legged, dun-coloured" and the painting "brilliantly superficial," its texture having "the glaze . . . of a prune-box." Earlier, he did seem to like Leighton's statue *Young Man Struggling with a Python*: He praises it for showing "a surprising amount of beauty and truth" ("The Grosvenor Gallery and the Royal Academy" [31 May 1877]) and calls it "a wonderfully clever piece of sculpture for a painter," even "a noble and beautiful work" ("The Picture Season in London" [August 1877]). According to Notebook entries (27 Jul, 3 Aug 1891), James acidly modeled Lord Mellifont of "The Private Life" after Leighton.

Lejaune, Gustave. In "The Point of View," a member of the French Academy. He is critical of things American in a letter home. Aurora Church admires him.

Lemaître, Jules (1853–1914). Influential French professor, literary critic, and writer of plays, fiction, poetry, and nationalist political essays. He was elected to the French Academy in 1896. James, who thought little of the versatile man, wrote to Grace Norton* (20 Aug [1893]) as follows: "Jules Lemaître is going down and down, and perishing . . . of the monstrosity of his agility." James later pays him brief attention in his 1899 essay "The Present Literary Situation in France," in which he regards Lemaître as passé and deplores his "anti-revisionist and anti-Semitic" comments on Alfred Dreyfus.* James's library contained one book by Lemaître.

Lemoinne, John (1815–1892). English-born French journalist and critic, long on the staff of *Journal des Débats*. In 1876 Auguste Laugel* introduced him to James, who wrote to his mother from Paris (24 Jan [1876]) that Lemoinne "is a dwarfish man with a glittering eye." James wrote more publicly in "Parisian Topics" (New York *Tribune*, 1 Apr 1876) that Lemoinne's election to the French Academy was a mistake, since, although he was "clever" and wrote well, his political criticism is "dry and sterile," and his work in general displays a "peculiarly insidious hatred of England." Lemoinne has "erected futility into a system and raised flimsiness to a fine art." James concludes by stating that the Academy, whose members are often "dull, dreary, insipid" and whose writings are often "unreadable," has now become virtually meaningless.

Lemon, Dr. Jackson. In "Lady Barbarina," a rich New York physician. He marries Lady Barbarina Clement, cannot persuade her to reside permanently in America with him, and therefore feels obliged miserably to return to London with her.

Lemon, Lady Barbarina Clement. In "Lady Barbarina," a daughter of Lord Philip and Lady Canterville. Lady "Barb" marries Dr. Jackson Lemon, moves with him to New York City, hates the place, and returns to London. She has many siblings, including Lady Agnes Clement.

Lemon, Mary. In "Lady Barbarina," Dr. Jackson Lemon's mother.

Lemon, Miss. In "Lady Barbarina," the baby daughter of Dr. and Mrs. Jackson Lemon.

Lendon, Urania. In *The Tragic Muse*, Charles Carteret's sister.

Lennox, John. In "The Story of a Masterpiece," Marian Everett's fiancé. He slashes the portrait of her painted by Stephen Baxter but then marries her.

Leonardo da Vinci (1452–1519). Uniquely gifted Italian artist, scientist, and philosopher. His *Mona Lisa* and *The Last Supper* are among the art treasures of the world, but they represent only a part of his accomplishment. James wrote little about Leonardo in a direct manner, but his *Mona Lisa*, especially as described by Walter Horatio Pater,* was a shadowy influence on James from 1869 on. In his 1872 "From Chambéry to Milan," he laments the condition of "the Cenacolo" (*The Last Supper*): "The picture needs not another scar or stain, now, to be the saddest work of art in the world; and battered, defaced, ruined as it is, it remains one of the greatest. We may really compare its anguish of decay to the slow conscious ebb of life in a human organism. The production of the prodigy was a breath from the infinite, and the painter's conception not immeasurably less than the scheme, say, of his own mortal constitution." James then wonders if Leonardo deliberately painted into it an aesthetic lesson on the mortality of art as well as of artists. In his 1878 review "The Old Masters at Burlington House," James mentions "a series of deeply-interesting heads by Leonardo da Vinci," with no elaboration. In *A Small Boy and Others*, he calls the *Mona Lisa* "Leonardo's almost unholy dame with the folded hands."

"The Lesson of the Master." Short story (23,600 words), published in the *Universal Review* (16 Jul, 15 Aug 1888); reprinted in *The Lesson of the Master*, 1892; revised and reprinted in *The Novels and Tales of Henry James*, Volume XV, 1909. (Characters: Lady Egbert, Marian Fancourt, General Fancourt, Lady Jane, Lord Masham, Mulliner, Paul Overt, Mrs. Overt, Mr. and Mrs. Henry St. George, Lord and Lady Watermouth.) At a lovely British country estate called Summersoft, young Paul Overt meets his ideal, the master novelist Henry St. George, his wife, General Fancourt, and his pretty daughter. St. George almost bitterly tells the ambitious Paul to stay single and write a second novel. He explains that a wife is a hindrance rather than an inspiration. In London, Paul falls in love with Miss Fancourt but, remembering St. George's advice, proceeds alone to Switzerland, and completes his second work. Marian informs him that Mrs. St. George has died. Back in London, he learns from General Fancourt that Marian and St. George are engaged. Paul accuses the older man of duplicity, but the "master" defends himself by saying that he will never write anything solid again whereas Paul will achieve greatness. According to a Notebook entry (5 Jan 1888), James was chatting with his friend Theodore E. Child* the night before about the adverse effects of marriage on both the quality and the quantity of a writer's work. James at once decided to contrast "an elder artist or writer, who has been ruined (in his own sight) by his marriage and its forcing him to produce promiscuously and cheaply"—and "a younger confrère whom he sees on the brink of the same disaster and whom he endeavours to save, to rescue, by some bold act of interference." In the preface to Volume XV of *The Novels and Tales of Henry James*, James says coyly, "I can't tell you . . . who it is I 'aimed at' in the story of Henry St. George . . . and wouldn't name his exemplar publicly even were I able." It is intriguing that the master novelist's first name is Henry. Perhaps Paul Overt's first name was inspired by that of Henry's young novelist friend Paul Bourget,* whose marriage James deplored. The story is full of irony and, even better, ambiguity. Are Mrs. St. George and Miss Fancourt good or baneful influences? Is Henry St. George sincere, especially in his advice? In the company of James Russell Lowell,* James in June 1886 visited the country house called Osterley, in Middlesex near Heston; it became the model for Summersoft both in this short story and later in his play *Summersoft*, which he converted into the short story "Covering End."

The Lesson of the Master, 1892. Collection of six short stories published in London and New York by Macmillan, 1892: "The Lesson of the Master," "The Marriages," "The Pupil," "Brooksmith," "The Solution," and "Sir Edmund Orme."

Letitia. In "The Impressions of a Cousin," Eunice's mother.

Leverett, Louis. In "A Bundle of Letters," a fatuous American who writes from Paris to his friend Harvard Tremont in Boston about Aurora Church and her mother, Miranda Hope, Evelyn Vane, and things French. In "The Point of View," he writes from Boston to Tremont in Paris about dull America. He now likes Aurora even more.

Lewes, George Henry (1817–1878). English philosopher, literary critic, biographer (of Johann Wolfgang von Goethe,* 1855), editor, and novelist. He and George Eliot,* whom he met in 1851 and traveled to Germany with in 1854, lived together as husband and wife until his death. Through his association with Eliot, James often came into fortunate contact with Lewes, who, for example, introduced him early in 1878 to Herbert Spencer.* James's library contained two books by Lewes.

Lewis, Sir George (1833–1911). Able British solicitor. James in the 1880s dined occasionally at the home of Lewis and his wife Lady Elizabeth. According to his Pocket Diaries, James retained his friendship with Lewis (and then his widow) into 1915.

Lewis, Mrs. In *A Change of Heart*, an unseen guest at Margaret Thorne's birthday party.

"The Liar." Short story (19,600 words), published in the *Century Magazine* (May–Jun 1888); reprinted in *A London Life*, 1889; revised and reprinted in *The Novels and Tales of Henry James*, Volume XII, 1908. (Characters: Mr. and Mrs. Arthur Ashmore, Sir David Ashmore, Amy Capadose, Colonel Clement Capadose, Everina Brant Capadose, Dean Capadose, General Capadose, Oliver Lyon, Harriet Pearson [Miss Geraldine?, Miss Grenadine?], Grand Duke of Silberstadt-Schreckenstein.) Artist Oliver Lyon goes to the Ashmore estate to paint a portrait of Sir David, the aged father of his host. Lyon observes among fellow guests Colonel Clement Capadose, a confounded liar now married to Everina Brant, whom Lyon once loved and lost. While sitting for his portrait, Sir David describes Capadose's addiction to fibbing; the painter begins to wonder what refined Everina's attitude can be concerning a prevaricating partner. Next Lyon paints Amy, the Capadoses' daughter, and then "the liar" himself, during one of whose sittings a young woman enters Lyon's studio supposedly seeking work as a model. The colonel spins a story about her. Lyon returns to his studio secretly at one time and chances to spy unseen on the Capadoses in wrath over the finished portrait, which seems to reveal the lying colonel's inner qualities. Lyon then sees the colonel when alone slash the work savagely. Later Capadose suggests to Lyon that the unemployed model must have destroyed it. Worse, to the painter's anguish, Everina lies too, saying that she greatly admired the portrait. In a Notebook entry (19 Jun 1884), James sketches the idea for a story about a sensitive woman who has to fib to back up her perennially prevaricating husband's unusually "big lie," and who then "hates him." James then adds "(*Numa Roumestan.*)" More publicly, in the preface to Volume XII of *The Novels and Tales of Henry James*, James recalls that at a London dinner, "long ago" he met a "most unbridled colloquial romancer" and immediately watched the liar's "serene" wife's face for telltale signs. The main source must surely be *Numa Roumestan*, the 1881 novel by James's friend Alphonse Daudet*; it features a fluent liar and his concerned wife. A minor source may be "The Prophetic Pictures," the 1837 story by Nathaniel Hawthorne* in which portraits reveal hidden inner traits. James renders his story more subtle than his sketch of it by having the wife, far from ever hating her husband, continue to love him, and by emphasizing the painter's selfish desire to test both the liar and his wife. It is characteristic of James to leave his readers wondering; in this case, they are invited to wonder who the real truth-bender is—Capadose, Everina, or the painter himself, whose name sounds exactly like "lyin'." As for the name

Capadose, after James had used it, he received a letter from one Anton Capadose requesting an explanation of James's source. James replied (13 Oct 1896) to plead innocence; to praise the name Capadose as "striking," "picturesque and rare," "individualizing and not ungraceful"; and to explain how "[f]iction-mongers collect proper names, surnames, etc." from all sorts of places.

"Lichfield and Warwick." Travel essay, published in the *Nation* (25 Jul 1872), as Part II of "A European Summer"; reprinted in *Transatlantic Sketches*, 1875, and in *English Hours*, 1905. While one is at Oxford, where James now is, it seems strange to write of anything but "this scholastic paradise"; but he also wants to describe both Lichfield and Warwick. Lichfield is unique: sleepy marketplace, "rich" cathedral "oddly placed" on its hill, fine close, three spires, "noble . . . vista," grand choir window, and many walks outside, including to Haddon Hall and to Chatsworth. Warwick, in the Warwickshire of William Shakespeare*: "great spectacle of the castle" not "sequestered . . . in acres of park," towers of "ponderous antiquity," and the nearby Avon resembling "a lordly moat." James opines that the old pictures in the castle (especially those by Anthony Vandyke) belong there and not "crowded into public collections."

Light, Christina. In *Roderick Hudson* and *The Princess Casamassima*, the maiden name of the Princess Casamassima.

Light, Mrs. (née Savage). In *Roderick Hudson*, the widow of a former American consul at an Italian port city on the Adriatic. She is Christina's unprincipled, socially ambitious mother. Christina's natural father is Cavaliere Giuseppe Giacosa.

"A Light Man." Short story (11,500 words), published in the *Galaxy* (Jul 1869); revised and reprinted in *Stories by American Authors*, New York: Scribner, 1884. (Characters: Maximus Austin, Mrs. Austin, Brooks, Dr. Jones, A. L. Theodore Lisle, Miss Meredith, Mrs. Parker, Miss Parker, Robert, Frederick Sloane.) Maximus Austin, a worthless adventurer just back from Europe, starts a journal in New York. His ingenuous friend Theodore Lisle invites him by letter to the estate of rich, dying, foolish Frederick Sloane, at D—. The two young men begin to compete for his money. Sloane prefers Max and one day asks him to fetch his will, which Max finds Theodore anxiously reading. They note that it is made out in Theodore's favor. Max tells him that Sloane wants it destroyed; Theodore, in remorse, burns it. The old man dies without writing a new will, and his fortune goes to a niece. Max accordingly determines to pursue her. James had a high opinion of this weak story. He wrote to his mother (24 Mar 1873) that it "showed most distinct ability." He liked the technical challenge of having an unreliable narrator, in this case his diarist Max, aim to tell something about himself but reveal a different nature to the reader. As for substance, "A

388

Light Man'' is an unpleasant story: Max has been hurt by Europe, Theodore is shallow because of America, and Sloane mixes paganism and naiveté.

Lilienthal, Miss. In *Watch and Ward*, Nora Lambert's German piano-duet partner.

Limbert. In "The Next Time," any of the three children of Maud and Ralph Limbert.

Limbert, Maud Stannace. In "The Next Time," Ralph Limbert's pretty wife and the sister of Jane Stannace Highmore.

Limbert, Ralph (Ray). In "The Next Time," and unpopular, brilliant novelist who cannot write money-making trash, although he tries. He is popular novelist Jane Stannace Highmore's brother-in-law.

Lincoln, Robert Todd (1843–1926). Son of President Abraham Lincoln. A lawyer, he served on the staff of General Ulysses Simpson Grant* toward the end of the Civil War, was secretary of war (1881–1885) under presidents James Abram Garfield* and Chester A. Arthur,* and was ambassador to England (1889–1893) under President Benjamin Harrison. Robert Lincoln attended the opening performance of James's play *The American*, on 26 September 1891.

Lindeck, Mary. In "Julia Bride," Murray Brush's fiancée.

Lindsay, Lady Caroline Blanche Elizabeth (?–?). Member of the Rothschild family.* While at dinner parties given by Lady Lindsay, James engaged in conversation that gave him ideas for two works of fiction. According to one Notebook entry (18 May 1892), a fellow guest's talk inspired him to write "The Wheel of Time." According to two other Notebook entries (24 Dec 1893, 13 May 1895), a different fellow guest's talk inspired him to write *The Spoils of Poynton*.

Linton, Eliza Lynn (1822–1898). Youngest child of a British preacher and his wife. She lived in London and then in Paris; she became a journalist, was married in 1858, and was separated in 1867. Her twenty-five or so books include romantic novels and a collection of pioneering essays on women and their rights. Her anonymously published 1869 *Saturday Review* article entitled "The Girl of the Period" (of which she revealed her authorship in 1883) was very popular. When Lynn Linton wrote to James asking him to explain the heroine of "Daisy Miller," his magnificent reply (Aug 1880) attests to his heroine's innocence. A Notebook entry (18 Mar 1889) indicates that James knew Mrs. Linton socially.

Lisette. In *What Maisie Knew*, Maisie Farange's French doll. Maisie treats it the way adults treat her, that is, as a thing to patronize and puzzle.

Lisle, Theodore. In "A Light Man," rich, dying Frederick Sloane's naive companion and Maximus Austin's friend. Sloane knew Lisle's now deceased father.

Littledale, Captain. In "An International Episode," a Britisher whom J. L. Westgate once treated hospitably in New York.

Littlefield, Mr. and Mrs. In "The Story of a Year," a Leatherborough couple in whose home Elizabeth Crowe meets Robert Bruce.

Littlemore, George. In "The Siege of London," a rich American widower, who is Agnes Littlemore Dolphin's brother and Rupert Waterville's friend. Littlemore dispassionately watches Nancy Headway's siege of Sir Arthur Demesne.

Littlemore, Miss. In "The Siege of London," George Littlemore's baby daughter.

"A Little Tour in France." Original title of travel essay (*Atlantic Monthly*, Jan 1878) retitled "Rheims and Laon: A Little Tour," in *Portraits of Places*, 1883.

A Little Tour in France. Travel essays, published as *En Province* (*Atlantic Monthly*, Jul–Nov 1883, Feb, Apr, May 1884); revised and published as *A Little Tour in France* in Boston by James R. Osgood, 1884. A second edition (published in Boston and New York by Houghton, Mifflin, 1900) was illustrated by Joseph Pennell.* To correct a commonly held notion that France is only Paris, and Paris is divine, James tours for six weeks (starting mid-September 1882) from Touraine southwest through Provence, then north along the swollen Rhone River to Burgundy. The result is a curious, forty-chapter book of impressions, combining keen observation, much knowledge of French history and culture (especially literature and architecture), decorous subjectivity, and a light tone blending humor, easy irony, urbanity, and bookishness (including quotations not only from famous French writers, but also from standard guidebooks and even pamphlets purchased locally). James suffered much discomfort (crowded trains, dull hotels, and dreary museums) in search of out-of-way places, items, and views. Everywhere, he prefers picturesque ruins to careless restorations. Touraine is a garden of contented citizens, in their land of Honoré de Balzac, René Descartes, and François Rabelais. Its Loire is historically important. James observes the inns of Tours, the Rue Royale, the Palais de Justice, and evidence of both the French Revolution and more recent German militarism. He describes the pleasing cathedral, with scarred front, "stately" interior, flying buttresses, quiet cloister, turret, and gallery Church of Saint Martin, with towers, "garish" shrine, "exquisite" convent, uniquely "delicate" arcade. Church of Saint Julian: low, strong tower, vast interior. Houses in Tours, surburban Plessis-les-Tours, with smelly remnants of castle; and Marmoutier with partly restored abbey, talkative nun for guide, and seven-sleepers' legend. James recommends a stop at Blois, with its fresh waterfront complexion and historic brown elsewhere, elaborate château, "frigid" Gaston d'Orléans mansion, Louis II wing (sadly restored), Francis I wing ("the most joyous utterance of the French Renaissance"), and pottery studio nearby. Next, "touching" Chambord: huge park, "tidy" inns, Francis I château with "stupid" towers and complicated roof and dull later history; Cheverny "in the haunted dusk" nearby. Amboise, with "battlements and terraces" along the Loire, and "defaced" castle, partly modernized into small rooms, but fine for sunny stroll and full of bloody history. Then along the river to Chaumont, to sneak a useless look at its closed château. James describes Chinon, unseen by him save in photographs. On to Chenonceaux, the castle of which is "one of the most romantic in France" and "the architectural gem of Touraine." Azay-le-Rideau: dirty inn, "admirable château" (near "denuded" *parc*) rosily described in a recent guidebook. Langeais has castle important in history and literature, but is "simple . . . and most severe"; the trip to it (by train) and back (by *carriole*) was picturesque. Loches: "one of the greatest impressions . . . in central France," despite rainy train ride to its "strange . . . collegial church," tomb of Charles VII's mistress Agnes Sorel, keep, dungeons, gateways, crooked streets, and views. Bourges: talkative eaters and silent businessmen on the way, starlit and daylight views of cathedral, esplanade where a ceremony of military discipline drew a brutally curious crowd; the houses of Jacques Coeur, tragic merchant in Joan of Arc's time, and of Jacques Cujas, law scholar and teacher. Slow train for hill-perched Le Mans: famous but untidy houses, cathedral (carefully described with guidebook aid) redolent of history, and fine French enunciation. Angers: a "sell" because "vulgarly modernized" for unsentimental tourists; further, one can see graceless Château d'Angers in fifteen minutes, and waterfront is colorless. Nantes: "spacious, rather regular city" but neither "fresh nor . . . venerable," with gray quays, provincial museum of "touching" items, castle with "interesting" interior details, some "fine old houses," cathedral without choir but with "two noble sepulchral monuments," and history of revolutionary horrors. Then south to "dear little" La Rochelle: an "original mixture of brightness and dulness," with rampart, fortifications, shore, and small port; James sought evidence of the 1628 siege. Poitiers: "considerable hill," towers and roofs and chimneys, "two or three curious old churches" (especially twelfth-century Notre Dame la Grande), ancient Palais de Justice, and charming public garden with vistas into history. Angoulême; hill tunnel, cathedral, and people reminiscent of Balzac. On to "big, rich, handsome, imposing" Bordeaux for three days: "the best wine in the world," "vast curving quays," big bridges over "tawny river," and Grand-Théâtre. On through "a land teeming with corn and wine" to *méridional* Toulouse, oddly "both animated and dull,'' with tone not pictorial but historical, with Languedoc accent; James observed Floral Games at Capitol, museum with Roman objects and modern French pictures, monastery, Saint-Sernin (the "noblest" church in Toulouse), picturesque walks, and evidence of past floods. Felicitous Carcassonne: two detached towns there (one old and ghostly, one new and toylike), appealing citizens, citadel, city walls with strata of historical evidence (which James goes into, forward from A.D. 436 and Visigoths), and photograph salesmen. Narbonne ("sordid and overheated") on market day: wine dealers, dust, scarce accommodations, greasy breakfasters next morning; hôtel de ville (with "not . . . imposing" museum) and cathedral (with attached fortress). Montpellier: Hôtel Nevet ("le plus vaste du midi" and model of its provincial type), salubrious climate, "gem"-like Musée Fabre, locales mentioned by Stendhal* (whose travel writing James praises), glorious Peyrou terrace. Next, on the way to Nîmes: the Roman Pont du Gard, a "great structure" in a romantic setting (near which, by accident, was hospitable little château); and Aigues-Mortes, from the distance a "towered and embattled mass" reminding one of "the background of early Flemish pictures," drowsy canal, melancholy seaview, inactive town. Nîmes is "a town of three or four fine features": varied Roman ruins, garden fountain ("prettiest thing in the world"), views into "brilliant spaces of . . . air," Maison Carrée ("delicate little building," "little toy-temple")—and in addition bullfights (that "Iberian vice"). Sleepy Tarascon "beside the Rhone": with severe château converted into district prison, bridge to picturesque Beaucaire, and demolished castle and air of peace. Pagan Arles: "two shabby old inns" on "ill-proportioned" public square, mean streets, distracting *dame de comptoir*, "delightful" Saint Trophimus church, town museum opposite (really "a desecrated church" with old sarcophagi and some distinctly Roman pieces), ruined Roman arena with silenced voices. Nearby hill town of Les Baux: "enchanting spot," "pearl of picturesqueness"; along the entertaining and yet reposeful way was the dilapidated eleventh-century Montmajour abbey, after which ruins, school, church, and castle of storied little old Les Baux. Avignon at last: torrential rain, "little *musée*" (dignified by fragments of Roman glass), papal palace, and tough soldiers billeted in the cold therein. Villeneuve-lès-Avignon: "lonely . . . outworks," "half depopulated" town, Benedictine abbey (doing duty as church, monastery, and fortress, with distinct outside but jumbled interior), "crumbling enceinte," and moonlit Rhône. Flood-endangered Vaucluse: reluctant pilgrimage to Petrarch's "cockneyfied" shrine, ugly water-powered paper and wool mills. Orange: flooded desolation along the way, then two superb monuments (second-century A.D. Roman arch, perfect but for restoration, and Roman theater, "impressive," "stupendous fragment"). Then uncomfortable train ride (one of many, easily forgotten, during this tour) to Lyons and then Macon: "chronic numbness" in the air, "meagre" house of Alphonse de Lamartine's birth. Bourg-en-Bresse next crisp morning: "dairy-feeding plains," suburban Brou church (with historical connections and well-wrought tombs), and late breakfast of "eggs . . . so good." Finally, James stopped at Beaune (with "tidy" hospital and "melancholy" town museum) on his way to disappointing Dijon, the termination of his "little tour": "narrow and crooked," with "tortuous vistas," cistern he did not go to see, palace (stiff but not grand, with "rich" museum and gigantic banquet hall), and old park ("dear old place") with bench for lingering. From Paris a few days after he had completed his tour, James wrote to Isabella Stewart Gardner* (12 Nov [1882]) that during "six weeks of . . . wandering about the provinces . . . I spent a fortnight on the banks of the Loire, examining the old châteaux of that region . . . and . . . pushed my way farther and saw a hundred more castles and ruins, as well as cathedrals, old walled towns, Roman remains and curiosities of every sort." James concludes happily: "I have seen more of France than I had ever seen before, and on the whole liked it better."

Livingstone, David (1813–1873). The famous Scottish missionary and explorer in Africa. After working in a cotton mill until the age of twenty-four, Livingstone studied in Glasgow and London. He went for the first time to Africa in 1841, returned later, and then went north from Cape Town through west Central Africa and back (1852–1856). He wrote *Missionary Travels* (1857), was consul at Quelimane (1852–1856), commanded more exploratory expeditions, and then published *The Zambesi and Its Tributaries* (1865) to expose the Portuguese slave trade and foster Christian and commercial settlements. Backed by the Royal Geographical Society, he sought the Nile River sources and Central African watersheds (1866). After further, more dangerous exploring, he was rescued at Ujiji (1871) by Henry M. Stanley. Livingstone later died in Ilala and was buried at Westminster Abbey. James reviewed (*Nation*, 11 Mar 1875) *The Last Journals of David Livingstone in Central Africa, from 1866 to His Death, Continued by a Narrative of His Last Moments and Suffering, etc.*, by Horace Waller (1875). James calls the work interesting and praises Waller for laboriously deciphering Livingstone's scrawls, but he wishes the results had been condensed. He lauds Livingstone's missionary patience and resolve, as well as his powers of observation, and he contrasts Livingstone with Sir Samuel White Baker* and summarizes his activities and suffering. Livingstone wanted to find historical evidence pertaining to Moses and also to heal "the 'open sore' " of slavery. James calls him one of the greatest of travelers. Verney Lovett Cameron,* whose *Across Africa* (1877) James also reviewed, sought Livingstone beginning in 1872 but on the way to Lake Tanganyika learned of his death.

Lloyd, Arthur. In "The Romance of Certain Old Clothes," Perdita Willoughby's British-born husband in America. Upon her death, he marries her sister Viola Willoughby.

Lloyd, Miss. In "The Romance of Certain Old Clothes," the baby daughter of Arthur and Perdita Lloyd.

Lloyd, Perdita Willoughby. In "The Romance of Certain Old Clothes," Arthur's first wife. She dies in childbirth.

Lloyd, Viola Willoughby. In "The Romance of Certain Old Clothes," Perdita's sister. When Perdita dies, Viola marries her widowed brother-in-law Arthur. She then becomes fatally jealous of dead but hauntingly present Perdita's wedding clothes.

Locket. In "Sir Dominick Ferrand," the *Promiscuous Review* editor for whom Peter Baron refuses to write an essay using Sir Dominick Ferrand's personal papers.

Lockhart, John Gibson (1794–1854). Scottish novelist, biographer, editor, and contributor to *Blackwood's Magazine*. He married Charlotte Scott, the daughter of Sir Walter Scott,* whose biography he published (7 vols., 1837–1838). Lockhart's four novels include *Adam Blair* (1822), which James praised when he compared it in detail to *The Scarlet Letter* in his 1879 book on Nathaniel Hawthorne.* James's library contained one book by Lockhart.

Locksley. In "A Landscape Painter," a rich landscape painter. He is jilted by Josephine Leary and later marries Miriam Quarterman, whose reading of his secret diary causes confusion—at least momentarily. In his treatment of Locksley, James may be in part gently spoofing his artist friend John La Farge.*

Lockwood, Preston (?–?). Journalist who interviewed James in 1915 and wrote up the results in "Henry James's First Interview."

Loder. In "Nona Vincent," dramatist Allan Wayworth's manager.

Lodge family. Prominent Boston family of politicians and writers. Henry Cabot Lodge (1850–1924) was a Harvard graduate (and later a graduate student under Henry Adams* at Harvard, editor of the *North American Review*, conservative congressman and senator, opponent of the League of Nations, and author. Of the children of Lodge and his wife Anna Cabot Mills (née Davis) Lodge, their oldest son, George Cabot "Bay" Lodge (1873–1909), was a poet, dramatist, and soldier. The James family knew several Lodges, both in Massachusetts and in London. In a letter from London to his brother William (10 Sep 1886), James gossips thus: "Mrs. [Anna] Lodge has been here and innumerable other Americans—a swarm of locusts. Mrs. L. was delightful—but . . . her sister and brother-in-law, with whom she was, have no discoverable *raison d'être*." To Frances Rollins Morse, an old family friend, James wrote (7 Jun 1897), "I cannot swallow Senator [Henry] Cabot [Lodge] . . . but I much liked his clever and civilized, and withal modest and manly, young son [Bay]"—with whom James had dined at the residence of John Milton Hay,* then ambassador to England. In January

1905, while in Washington, D.C. during his 1904–1905 tour of the United States, James let Senator Lodge show him the Senate in session and also host him at lunch. James's library contained one book by Henry Cabot Lodge.

"London." Travel essay, published in the *Century Magazine* (Dec 1888); reprinted in *Essays in London and Elsewhere*, 1893, and in *English Hours*, 1905. James recalls his first mature impression of London, "the murky modern Babylon": black houses, gin shops, tortuous ride to "horrible" but friendly hotel in Trafalgar Square, walks to the Strand and Charing Cross, homesickness in more permanent lodgings near humming Piccadilly. He responded to the appeal of "the dreadful, delightful city" ("the capital of the human race"): privacy in and loyalty to the city, its vitality, the wonderful language, varied society, the "brown, dim, rich" tone, parks ("the drawing-rooms and clubs of the poor"), and the Westminster region (which "evokes as many associations of misery as of empire"). London is mistress and ogress, hurting reputations but forming character, and flirting with a thousand types. One sees in London so many varied items that it totals "wholes," not a whole: windows in the fog, the British Museum, club libraries, excursions outside the city to "the loveliest scenery," fascinating railway stations, the Thames (London's "busiest suburb" and "by far the prettiest"),"the personal energy of the people." James cannot give details of the carnival-like "multitudinous life" of London in late spring and midsummer, when varieties of people "flock to London," which is ever rich and good-humored.

"London." Each in a series of nine miscellaneous critical notes, published in *Harper's Weekly* (23 Jan; 6, 20 Feb; 27 Mar; 24 Apr; 5, 26 Jun; 31 Jul; and 21 Aug 1897), in which James discusses current British publications, plays, and art exhibitions. In notes published 23 January he touches on Sir Henry Irving* in *King Richard III* by William Shakespeare,* Elizabeth Robins* in *Little Eyolf* by Henrik Johan Ibsen,* Ibsen's *John Gabriel Borkman*, a production of Shakespeare's *As You Like It*, and paintings by George Frederick Watts* and Lord Frederick Leighton.* Notes published 6 February (partly reprinted as "London Notes, January, 1897" in *Notes on Novelists*, 1914) begin with the comment that the more theaters we have the less we read plays, with the exception of Ibsen, whose *John Gabriel Borkman* William Archer* has just translated. Mentioning *Forty-One Years in India* by Lord Frederick Sleigh Roberts,* James then turns to *Evan Harrington*, now part of a definitive edition of George Meredith* which is comparable to the ongoing volumes of the definitive edition of Robert Louis Stevenson* (edited by Sir Sidney Colvin*). Next, James treats *Story of Aline* by Lady Alice Ridley* and *Charlotte Brontë and Her Circle* by Clement King Shorter.* Notes for 20 February concern *The Life and Letters of Frederick Walker* by John George Marks,* and paintings by Frederick Leighton and Ford Madox Brown.* In notes for 27 March James discusses or touches on three works concerning India: *Forty-One Years in India* by Roberts (again), *The Thack-*

erays in India by Sir William Wilson Hunter,* and *On the Face of the Waters* by Flora Annie Steel.* He then mentions a new edition of the *Memoirs* of Edward Gibbon,* "The Idea of Comedy" by Meredith, and a production by Robins* of José Echegeray's play *Mariana*. Notes for 24 April, inspired by the 1897 *Fortnightly Review* article by Archer* entitled "The Blight on the Drama," include a discussion of a poor play (*Nelson's Enchantress*) based on the story of Horatio Nelson and Lady Hamilton, *The Physician* by Henry Arthur Jones,* and *The Second Mrs. Tanqueray* and *The Princess and the Butterfly* by Sir Arthur Wing Pinero.* Notes for 5 June combine comments on exhibitions of many paintings—by Sir John Everett Millais,* Leighton, Edwin Austin Abbey,* John Singer Sargent,* and a few other artists—with a brief look at *L'Orme du Mail* by Anatole France.* Notes for 26 June (partly reprinted as "London Notes, June, 1897" in *Notes on Novelists*, 1914) touch on Queen Victoria's Jubilee, but mainly review gallery showings of works by James Abbott McNeill Whistler,* Sargent, and Watts, together with mention of James's theory that "great painters . . . have often painted the small celebrities, and the small painters the great ones" (for an example of the latter, Joseph Severn's picture of John Keats). In notes for 31 July (reprinted as "London Notes, July, 1897" in *Notes on Novelists*, 1914), James begins by describing his pleasure in reading novels (doing so "muffles the ache of the actual"), then turns to works by George Gissing* and Pierre Loti.* In notes for 21 August (reprinted as "London Notes, August, 1897" in *Notes on Novelists*, 1914) James again touches on the Jubilee, but mainly discusses the Oxford lecture by Paul Bourget* on Gustave Flaubert* and pays homage to Margaret Oliphant,* recently deceased.

"London at Midsummer." Travel essay, published in *Lippincott's Magazine* (Nov 1877); reprinted in *Portraits of Places*, 1883, and in *English Hours*, 1905. London in August is rather empty but not impossible. The weather, food, and sedentary pleasures are acceptable. The "sheep-polluted" parks have rough sleepers. James goes out to Greenwich and mentions the activities and topics it evokes: fine dinners there (one of which he recalls fondly), strolls in the park, the dark Thames traffic, the observatory, the hospital, Blackheath Common, Woolwich's artillery barracks and grogshops, and "British valour."

"London in the Dead Season." Travel essay, published in the *Nation* (26 Sep 1878), Calling himself an "adoptive cockney," James notes that London, usually a noisy city, is rather quiet in September, which is "decidedly agreeable." Enjoyment can now become "subjective." But there are losses: Clubs are given over to housecleaning, journals in their reading rooms become "dull," and personal grievances get aired therein. James reports a disastrous collision on the Thames between a crowded little steamer and a large collier; and then, he describes his Sunday excursion to "dreadful" Gravesend to study the manners of the "coarse and dusky" British mob there.

"A London Life." Long short story (40,700 words), published in *Scribner's Magazine* (Jun–Sep 1888); republished in *A London Life*, 1889; revised and reprinted in *The Novels and Tales of Henry James*, Volume X, 1908. (Characters: Miss Bald [or Bold]; Lord Bamborough; Ferdy Berrington; Geordie Berrington; Lionel Berrington; Selina Wing Berrington; Mrs. Berrington; Booker; Mr. and Mrs. Collingwood; Captain Charley Crispin; Lady Davenant; Miss Frothingham; Motcomb; Lady Ringrose; The Babe, Fanny, and Katie Schooling; Smallshaw; Miss Steet; Lady Watermouth; Wendover; Laura Wing.) Laura Wing, a penniless American, is visiting her sister Selina Berrington, who does not get along well with her wealthy husband Lionel in London. Laura, who gossips too freely with Lady Davenant, Lionel's widowed, expropriated mother's friend, is sympathetic toward Lionel when he complains that Selina has gone to Paris with a lover named Charley Crispin. Lionel plans to divorce Selina and asks Laura not to speak against him. When Selina returns, Laura queries her about Crispin and doubts Selina's solemn protestations of innocence. Selina argues that her husband is corrupt and that his threats therefore are in vain. Through Selina, Laura meets a nice, boring American named Wendover. Lady Davenant opines that he will do as Laura's husband. Laura visits St. Paul's with Wendover and then the Sloane Museum, where Selina, who said she was going to call on a sick friend out of town, is rendezvousing with the bearded Crispin. Later, Selina criticizes Laura for going unescorted with Wendover, calls her a hypocrite, and rationalizes that since she herself is married to a cad she is free to roam. Lady Davenant advises Laura to leave Selina and hope to wed the increasingly interested Wendover. At the opera one night, Selina leaves Laura and Wendover unattended, hoping thus to compromise the girl. Laura frantically tries to force his hand before he has time to infer Selina's motives, but he remains simply gallant. Laura turns feverish at the home of Lady Davenant, who explains the situation to the puzzled Wendover. When Lionel tells Laura that Selina is off to Brussels with Crispin, the bewildered girl spurns Wendover's belated proposal, goes over to her sister, gets nowhere there, and sets sail for relatives in Virginia, to which Wendover evidently will proceed. In a long Notebook entry (20 Jun 1887), James explains that the plot of this unpleasant story (which is too long for its purpose) came partly from an incident Paul Bourget* had detailed to him in Venice in 1887. A girl was so shamed by her mother's supposed lovers that she sought escape by blurting out a proposal of marriage to a nice young man, was rebuffed by gallant vagueness, and killed herself. In his long Notebook sketch, James names as Lady Davenant the character who becomes Selina and rejects the device of heroine suicide since he had "used it the other day in the *Two Countries* [later retitled 'The Modern Warning']." Many details from the Notebook sketch underwent changes during composition: The man Laura hoped would rescue her was to be a British foreign office clerk, the old lady (now named Lady Davenant) who befriends Laura was to tell her the young man really wants to propose, and that same old lady was personally to persuade him to do so— only to be rejected. James also notes that the old lady is to be modeled on Mrs.

Duncan Stewart,* his friend and also the mother of his friend Christina Stewart Rogerson.* In the preface to Volume X of *The Novels and Tales of Henry James*, James confesses that Laura, Selina, and Wendover need not have been American at all; he fondly recalls writing the story in "an old Venetian palace . . . with a pompous Tiepolo ceiling and walls of ancient pale-green damask"; and he apologizes for the Lady Davenant–Wendover "interview" on the grounds that his central intelligence (Laura) was not a witness to it. James's story depicts a steamy social scene like those of *What Maisie Knew* and *The Awkward Age*. The ending is unsatisfactorily open-ended. Poor Laura is as frantic as Louisa Chantry in "The Visits" and deserves our pity, not criticism. She lived in a sad time for unmarried girls; on the other hand, her sister Selina is undoubtedly an out-and-out adulteress, of whose conduct James did not approve.

A London Life. Collection of four short stories, published in London and New York by Macmillan, 1889: "A London Life," "The Patagonia," "The Liar," and "Mrs. Temperly."

"London Notes . . . " Any of four critical essays, with each title including a date, reprinted (sometimes only in part) in *Notes on Novelists with Some Other Notes*, 1914, from four of James's 1897 *Harper's Weekly* columns entitled "London."

"London Pictures and London Plays." Art and theater review, published in the *Atlantic Monthly* (Aug 1882). Noting that English painting tells him more about the English than about painting, James mentions many items in the current Academy and Grosvenor exhibitions—by established artists such as Lawrence Alma Tadema, George Henry Boughton,* Sir Edward Burne-Jones,* William Holman Hunt,* Lord Frederick Leighton,* Sir John Everett Millais,* George Frederick Watts,* and James Abbott McNeill Whistler,* and also by less important painters. James does not hesitate to be critical: One artist seems to paint by merely "breath[ing] . . . on the canvas"; another's work is the "perfection of hideousness." James seems not to be pleased often. He makes a transition to the theater in London by suggesting that one finds much Philistinism in both drama and art exhibitions. But the acting is improving and may soon rival that of the French. He discusses Sir Henry Irving* and Dame Ellen Terry* in their "dull" *Romeo and Juliet*. He notes that many plays in London suffer from excessive set decorations. Finally he writes about a well-acted British version of *Odette*, by Victorien Sardou,* and about *The Squire*, by Sir Arthur Wing Pinero.*

"London Sights." Art review, published in the *Nation* (16 Dec 1875). James expresses the fear that the "treasures of florid architecture" of the new Albert Memorial will quickly be blackened by London smoke. He goes on to describe the pretentious memorial: colossal, with "second-rate" marble statuary symbolizing the continents, other symbolic groups, "an immense frieze" depicting famous artists, and a "flamboyant" canopy—all of the workmanship exceeding the designers' taste. Next, an exhibition of "crudely colored" Paul Gustave Doré* paintings, which James brands as more commercial than artistic. Best as a designer, Doré covers much canvas with "turbid and meaningless color," and he makes a lot of money doing so. James concludes that "Doré has cheapened himself."

"The London Theatres." Theater essay, published in the *Galaxy* (May 1877). James says that a foreigner coming to England can learn much about its civilization by attending its theaters. Plays in London today are usually short-lived adaptations from the French. Eighteenth-century English drama was conventional; today's is "irresponsible." James brings a "Parisianized . . . fancy" to wintry London, which needs a drama critic like Francisque Sarcey* to comment on its poor theater, prudish people, restaurants inconducive to conversation, pastry shops, and the buying of tickets. In England, playgoing is "a social luxury"; in France, "an artistic necessity." English audiences are "less Bohemian, less *blasé*, more *naïf*, and more respectful." James also contrasts the physical appearance and manners of British and French playgoers. Next he comments critically on Sir Henry Irving,* whose success he cannot understand. The best acting in London is at the Prince of Wales theater ("pretty") and in the Court. James discusses an English adaptation of *Nos Intimes* by Victorien Sardou* and a Tom Taylor* revival, starring Dame Ellen Terry.* He closes by commenting that in England broad comedy and high tragedy are performed in a businesslike manner, but serious and sentimental comedy, as well as comedies of manners, are handled amateurishly. He lacks space to comment on either a wretched adaptation of *Les Danicheff* by Alexandre Dumas *fils** or current offerings at any other London theaters.

"The London Theatres." Theater essay, published in the *Nation* (12 Jun 1879). James notes that the British theater, which is bad, is now the object of popular attention. It is probably good for the world but bad for art and literature that vulgar democracy is advancing. The British leisure class through boredom takes up the theater. Drama schools, such as flourish in France (in part, to polish "beautiful utterance"), are absent in England. James implies that Sir Henry Irving* and Dame Ellen Terry* would be better for having had such schooling. The best London theaters are the Court and the Prince of Wales. James names a couple of exceptional actors there. At present, British writing for the stage is thin, and adaptations of French plays are too righteous, without "literary savor," and formless.

"The London Theatres." Theater essay, published in *Scribner's Monthly* (Jan 1881). James does not call this essay "The English Stage" because there is no "collective organism" with "collective vitality" to be called the English stage, as there are in France and Germany, to be so designated. During the last century, the British had Drury Lane and Covent Garden, but writing and theater production have changed. Still, expensive playgoing is fashionable in London now. Young actors are amateurish. Play quality is poor (except for William Shakespeare,* often "rendered inadequately" by companies mainly purveying non-Shakespearean "vulgarity"). Adaptations are "pale." The air in the playhouses is better than in France. Audiences are calmer too. Scenery is clever. Next James considers Sir Henry Irving* (in detail and for the most part adversely) and Dame Ellen Terry* (again critically). James complains that there is too much touching (even kissing) on the stage in England. Next James ramblingly discusses many topics: a theater featuring revivals of classical comedies; the fate of fine theaters when they change hands; "the poverty of the[ir] repertory"; several actresses (either "delightful" or "lugubrious"); memories of fine acting "in the 'good old' days"; more actresses (including one he praises, Geneviève Ward, who has "a finish, an intelligence, a style, an understanding of what she is about"); and many actors (including two depicting old men well, one whose costumes are "an unduly large part of his success," and another who performed well in an Émile Zola* adaptation). In a postscript dated November 1880, James notes that in the last three months the English stage displays even more "destitution," its best shows being a "hackneyed and preposterous" revival (by Irving) of *The Corsican Brothers* and a certain adaptation having "the intellectual substance of a nursery-rhyme." A splendid recent performer has been Helena Modjeska.*

Loney, Allen D. (?–1915). Retired, well-to-do New York businessman and American Ambulance Corps supporter in the early days of World War I. Loney went down on the *Lusitania* on 7 May 1915 with his wife. Their daughter Virginia Bruce Loney, age fifteen, with them on the voyage, was a strong swimmer and survived (she later became Mrs. Abbott). Loney was the subject of James's "Allen D. Loney—In Memoriam" (New York *Times*, 12 Sep 1915, under the headline "A Tribute by Henry James; In Memory of Allen D. Loney, Who Perished on the Lusitania"). James offers "a few words . . . official and personal" about Loney—husband, father, and sportsman—who was a "signally gallant friend of our American Volunteer Ambulance Corps." While the *Lusitania* was sinking, he aided two women but then was himself lost.

Long, Gilbert. In *The Sacred Fount*, the observant narrator's handsome, notably more suave friend. He is perhaps the tapper of May Server's "sacred fount."

Long, Mrs. In "The Modern Warning," a New York high-society friend of Agatha Grice, who became Lady Chasemore.

Longdon. In *The Awkward Age*, the well-to-do, aging observer of Mrs. Edward Brookenham's social circle. He was a friend of her lovely, now deceased mother,

Lady Julia. Distressed by modern society, he wants to rescue Mrs. Brook's daughter Fernanda by adopting her.

Longfellow, Henry Wadsworth (1807–1882). Enormously popular, steadily productive poet, born in Portland, Maine. He graduated from Bowdoin College (1825) along with his classmate Nathaniel Hawthorne.* Longfellow studied languages abroad (1826–1829), taught at Bowdoin (1829–1835) and then at Harvard University (1836–1854), but he published so successfully that after 1854 he devoted himself fully to writing. His first wife died in 1835; after his second wife also died, in 1861, Longfellow for solace translated Dante's *Divine Comedy* (published 1867) with the aid of his close friends James Russell Lowell* and Charles Eliot Norton.* Longfellow is best known for metrically fine, romantic poetry, without much profundity. James met Longfellow casually and wrote about one such encounter thus to Norton (4 Feb 1872): "With Longfellow I lately spent a pleasant evening and found him bland and mildly anecdotal." At least two letters from James to Longfellow (undated but from the mid–1870s) have survived. In the mid-1880s James was pursued by Blanche Roosevelt,* who had vacationed with Longfellow and his family at Nahant (1880, 1881, and 1882), and she subsequently wrote *The Home Life of Henry W. Longfellow . . .* (1882) about her observations. In his biography of William Wetmore Story,* James includes several trivial comments about Longfellow, whom Story knew well. But James also notes that "complete and established, attuned and settled, Mr. Longfellow . . . was perhaps interesting for nothing so much as . . . for the way in which his 'European' culture and his native kept house together." Then James asks wickedly, "Did he owe the large, quiet, pleasant, easy solution at which he had arrived . . . to his having worked up his American consciousness to that mystic point . . . at which it could feel nothing but continuity and congruity with his European?"

Longmore. In "Madame de Mauves," Countess Euphemia Cleve de Mauves's curious American admirer.

Longstaff, Reginald. In "Longstaff's Marriage," the man who when supposedly dying proposes to Diana Belfield. Her refusal spurs him to recovery. Later, when Diana is sick, she proposes to him. He accepts and marries her, and then she dies to prove her tender love.

"Longstaff's Marriage." Short story (11,100 words), published in *Scribner's Monthly* (Aug 1878); reprinted in *The Madonna of the Future and Other Tales*, 1879. (Characters: Diana Belfield, Mrs. Belfield, Agatha Josling, Reginald Longstaff.) Diana Belfield is traveling with her companion Agatha Josling. At Nice they meet sick Reginald Longstaff, who on his supposed deathbed proposes to Diana. Her pitiless refusal so stimulates his pride that he recovers. Later, sick herself in Rome, Diana proposes to Longstaff, who accepts her, and they are married. Although he sincerely loves her, she deliberately dies; thus, she feels, can she most tenderly show him her love. In a letter to his brother William (4 Mar [1879]), James rightly calls this vampiric, tables-turned story "a poor affair." It is grim and perverse. Every reader should guess at the outset that a heroine named Diana Belfield will remain too virginal for words.

Longstraw, Herman. In "Lady Barbarina," a cowboy who marries Lady Agnes Clement, Lady Barbarina's sister. He then sponges off Lady Barb's husband Dr. Jackson Lemon.

Longstraw, Lady Agnes Clement. In "Lady Barbarina," the married name of Lady Agnes Clement.

"The Long Wards." War essay, published as part of *The Book of the Homeless* (New York: Scribner, 1916), edited by Edith Newbold Jones Wharton*; reprinted in *Within the Rim and Other Essays: 1914–15*, 1919. James begins by recalling that in the summer of 1861 he saw wounded soldiers returned to New England from Civil War combat. New Germany has "let loose upon the world" destruction on a greater scale. Where were all the soldiers between then and now? America lacked them. Europe now has plenty. The world now seems to be all military schools and hospitals. The average British " 'Tommy' " awaits mutilation with "jolly fatalism." For months now James has visited "tides" of wounded soldiers in long, "tunnel"-like hospital wards. He wants to complain or curse for them, so amiably do they seem to accept reality. James feels numbed "beyond all thought and pity"; however, he concludes thus: If these wounded are "strong and sound," surely the "tended and fostered and cultivated" ought to advance "Culture" greatly.

Longueville, Bernard. In *Confidence*, scientific Gordon Wright's rather artistic friend. Wright asks Longueville to pass judgment on Angela Vivian. He criticizes her to Wright but later marries her himself.

"Lord Beaupré" (1892 title,"Lord Beauprey"; 1893 title, "Lord Beaupré"). Short story (20,600 words), published in *Macmillan's Magazine* (Apr–Jun 1892); reprinted in *The Private Life*, 1893. (Characters: Maud Ashbury, Mrs. Ashbury, Lord Beaupré, Beaupré, Bolton-Brown, Mrs. Bolton-Brown, The Misses Bolton-Brown, Charlotte Firminger, Major Frank Firminger, Mrs. Frank Firminger, Guy Firminger, The Misses Firminger, Hugh Gosselin, Mary Gosselin, Mrs. Gosselin, Raddle, Raddle, Mrs. Raddle, Lady Bessie and Lord Whiteroy.) Guy Firminger is much beset by husband-hunters. He so informs Mrs. Ashbury, her daughter Maud, Mrs. Gosselin, and her daughter Mary. Later he jests to the Gosselins that they should all pretend he and Mary are engaged, to stop pursuit of him. A few years later, three family deaths have elevated Guy to the title of Lord Beaupré. Mrs. Gosselin boldly announces that he is engaged to her daughter

Mary to prevent him from marrying either Maud Ashbury or his cousin Charlotte Firminger, both of whom are circling about him eagerly. Sadly, Miss Gosselin has long loved Guy, now a lord, but she is disgusted by his obtuse delight that the ruse is working. Meanwhile, Bolton-Brown, a rich New York friend of her brother Hugh, loves Mary but is put off by the announcement of her engagement to Guy. Hugh tells Bolton-Brown the truth. Mary's relations with Guy are so strained by now that, before he can suggest that they make their professed engagement a reality, she asks him to break it off so that she may marry Bolton-Brown—which happens. Mary's mother tells Hugh that Mary may not like America, will probably return to England to find Guy wed to Charlotte (whom he does marry), and will then dangerously sympathize with him. Hugh counters by telling his mother that she sees too much. In a Notebook entry (5 Feb 1892), James mentions a little "*idée de comédie*": rich *parti* avoids "formidable assault of . . . mothers . . . and . . .*filles à marier*" by making engagement "compact" with girl who really loves him, who then has "real chance to marry" elsewhere, who, hoping *parti* will pop question, only distresses him by asking release, and who therefore marries suitor. James dropped his plans for an ending of tardy awareness and frustration, has the *parti* remain ignorant, and complicates the action by having the heroine's mother a conscious schemer and by creating a brother for the heroine. The resulting overly long story is rendered incredible by the hateful meddling of sad Mary's pseudo-perceptive mother and the improbability of the actions she generates.

"Lord Beauprey." 1892 title of "Lord Beaupré."

Loring, Katharine Peabody (1849–1943). Alice James's close friend and companion. Miss Loring came from a fine New England family. Vigorous and independent, she was at one time the head of the history department at the Society to Encourage Studies at Home (founded in Boston in 1873). She numbered Julia Ward Howe* among her many friends. John Singer Sargent* did a watercolor of her, together with her sister Louise Loring Putnam, in 1917. (The original was destroyed by fire in 1969, but a photograph survives.) Loring went blind late in life. She and Alice first met in 1873, became better acquainted when Alice taught history with her, and together took a few extended trips, which included camping out in the Adirondacks and in northern New England (1879, 1880). The two vacationed in Scotland and England together (summer 1881), at which time James met Loring. When Henry James, Sr., died late in 1882, Loring cared for Alice in her family's home in Beverly, north of Boston, well into 1883. In 1883 James lectured on the subject of touring in Provence before the Saturday Club, which Loring had founded earlier in Boston (1871). In the fall of 1884 Loring vacationed in Europe, returned to Boston, and then helped Alice voyage to England, where the two lived together much of the time (in Bournemouth, Leamington, and London, near James's De Vere Gardens* residence) for several years. Alice wrote tersely to her aunt, Catherine Walsh*

(31 Jan 1885): "Harry [Henry James] & Kath. being my only anchorage." James was appreciative of Loring's help, since it freed him from having to be with his demanding (if appreciative) sister for protracted periods of time. In a letter to Edwin Lawrence Godkin* (20 Sep [1889]), James wrote of "Katharine Loring, my sister's great friend." In a letter to Isabella Stewart Gardner* (29 May [1891]), he called Loring "the very foundation of our Universe." And in a letter to his brother William (31 Jul [1891]), he wrote: "As for Katharine,— abysses of gratitude only can respond to her name." Loring took letter and diary dictation from Alice, hypnotized her by hand movements (at William James's suggestion) to alleviate her severe pains, and was with her when she died in 1892. James wrote to his brother William (5 Mar 1892), just before Alice's death, of "the heroic, the colossal Katharine." Loring transported the cremated ashes home to Cambridge, Massachusetts. Alice willed her faithful companion $20,000. Loring published Alice's diary in four private copies, in 1894, in the firm belief that her friend wished it to be done. The diary shocked James, who wrote to his brother William and his wife Alice (25 May [1894]) to express "regret that K. P. Loring hadn't sunk a few names—put initials—I mean in view of the danger of accidents, some catastrophe of publicity." According to a Pocket Diary entry (12 Jun 1914), James lunched in London in 1914 with Katharine Loring and her sister. Katharine Loring was not related to Frank Loring, the Boston publisher who pirated James's short story "A Bundle of Letters." The intimate relationship of Olive Chancellor and Verena Tarrant in *The Bostonians* may owe something to the close friendship of Katharine Loring and James's sister Alice.

Loti, Pierre (1850–1923). Pen name of a French author (né Julien Viaud) and naval officer (captain 1906, on reserve 1910, recalled 1914–1918). Much of his sea duty was off Turkey, Japan, Senegal, and Tonkin. Because of his melancholy aloofness, his comrades nicknamed him after *le loti*, a shy Indian flower. In 1883 Loti was suspended briefly from the navy following his revelation of certain government scandals. In 1891 he was elected to membership in the French Academy. Much of his writing is half fictional, half autobiographical. His many works include *Aziyadé* (1876), *Rarahu* (1880, retitled *Le Mariage de Loti*, 1882), *Le Roman d'un Spahi* (1881), *Mon frère Yves* (1883), *Pêcheur d'Islande* (1886), *Propos d'exil* (1887), *Madame Chrysanthème* (1887), *Japoneries d'Automne* (1889), *Au Maroc* (1890), *Le Livre de la pitié et de la mort* (1891), *Fantôme d'orient* (1892), *Matelot* (1893), *Jérusalem* (1895), *Ramuntcho* (1897), *Les Derniers jours de Pékin* (1902), *L'Inde (sans les Anglais)* (1903), *Un Pèlerin d'Angkor* (1912), and *Journal intime, 1878–1881* (1925). Judith Gautier (1850–1917), the daughter of Théophile Gautier,* and a poet and novelist herself, married Loti in 1913. In February 1884 James met Pierre Loti in Paris, at the home of their friend Alphonse Daudet.* James admired Loti's exotic style, melancholy tone, and pictorial effects. In "Pierre Loti" (*Fortnightly Review*, May 1888), James calls Loti a "remarkable genius," connects his works to other French writings which also celebrate "the life . . . of the senses" (though not of the soul—exceptions being George Sand* and Octave Feuillet*), and commends the French language for "expressing shades and variations of the visible." James develops the image of Loti as "a mere sponge for sensations," and he praises (with ample quotations) his depiction of the sea (in sport and in victory). James likes the "unsurpassable little vignettes" of *Madame Chrysanthème* although the book "is comparatively a failure" because in it Loti does not take the Japanese seriously. He labels a few short pieces from *Propos d'exil* "admirable" and "valuable" and the whole collection "a chaplet of pearls," but he comes close to criticizing Loti for his "egotistic-erotic" exploits, revealed most intimately in the "complacent animalism" of *Aziyadé* and *Rarahu*, the latter of which displays "precocity of depravity." After all, affection should not be equated with "the loves of the quadrupeds." James regards *Mon frère Yves*, though too long and lacking in composition, and especially *Pêcheur d'Islande* as the finest of Loti's nine novels. James praises the author's handling in it of "the hard Breton country" and adds that the meagre plot, which he summarizes in detail, is given "freshness and meaning." In a Notebook entry (8 Apr 1893), James calls Loti's genius "exquisite" even in *Matelot*, which he regards as "shrunken and limited"; then he copies out a passage from it, for its "indefinable charm." Later, he wrote to Edmund Wilson Gosse* twice about *Matelot*; first, to say that it is "a mere empty *pleurnicherie* in reality but strangely charming for its exquisite manner" (20 Apr [1893]); and second, to praise its "strange *eloquence of suggestion and rhythm*" (1 May 1893). In "London" (31 Jul 1897), James calls *Ramuntcho* "a literary impression of the most exquisite order," adding that he loves Loti even when bad more than other writers when good. James provided an introduction to Loti's 1898 *Impressions* (Westminster, Constable, 1898), confessing that he simply surrenders to the charm and value of his friend's autobiographical, impressionistic writings—of the faraway, the unreserved, the amorous. James accepts the erotic here, to enjoy the rest. True, Loti—like other modern French authors—exhaustively describes the private for his public. He neither reflects nor composes, but simply loves the ocean, his feelings, and Brittany. He is both a success and a model to be avoided. We cannot analyze him. His work evokes our pity. His characters feel, have joys, are stricken. We grow "fond of his lovers." He is indifferent to big plots. His record of impressions is like the "tremor of the fiddlestring." His pictures are happily melancholy, and his exotic ones are so good that we should prefer them to realities— especially Morocco, Japan, and Jerusalem—which inspired them. *Au Maroc* "expresses him at his best"; here he so drinks up impressions that he leaves the place dry. In his two essays on Pierre Loti, James cites two dozen Loti titles. James's library contained twenty-six books by Loti.

Lottie. In "A Round of Visits," Newton Winch's sister-in-law.

"Louisa Pallant." Short story (14,000 words), published in *Harper's New Monthly Magazine* (Feb 1888); reprinted in *The Aspern Papers*; 1888, revised and reprinted in *The Novels and Tales of Henry James*, Volume XIII, 1908. (Characters: Gimingham, Henry Pallant, Linda Pallant, Louisa Pallant, Archie Parker, Charlotte Parker, Miss Parker.) In Homburg, the narrator happens to meet widowed Louisa Pallant, who once jilted him. With her is her beautiful but mercenary daughter Linda. Archie Parker, the narrator's callow nephew, age twenty, now joins the group. When Louisa concludes that Linda wants to seize rich Archie, she takes the girl away. But Linda writes to Archie from Italy, and the two men follow to Baveno. To assuage her conscience, perhaps still troubled by her treatment of the narrator, who may be gullible, Louisa tells Archie things about Linda so damaging that he does not propose. According to a Notebook entry (12 Jan 1887), James originally mapped out a slightly different plot, in which the older man was suspicious of Linda and warned her mother to take her away. By altering plans and having Louisa perhaps uniquely aware of her daughter's true nature, James intensified his effect. Soon after the story was published, James replied (10 Mar 1888) to his friend Laura Huntington Wagnière, a member of the Greenough family,* who had written to him to express curiosity as to what Linda could have told Archie to scare him off: "I have no light on what she said. . . . I am as ignorant as you and yet not as supposing!" He also suggested some tentative answers. In the preface to Volume XIII of *The Novels and Tales of Henry James*, James notes only that he wrote "Louisa Pallant" in colorful, noisy Florence, in February 1887.

Louÿs, Pierre (1870–1925). Ghent-born French fiction writer and poet. While in his teens, he began to associate with Parnassians and Symbolists, and he founded *La Conque*, a review in which Maurice Maeterlinck* and Algernon Charles Swinburne* published, but which soon collapsed. *Chansons de Bilitis* (1894) are prose poems (about Sapphic lewdness) by Louÿs; his decadent, erotic novels are *Aphrodite: Moeurs antiques* (1896, about ancient Alexandria) and *La Femme et le Pantin* (1898), neither of which James liked (according to James's friends).

Lovelock, Captain Augustus. In *Confidence*, Blanche Evers's British escort both before and after her marriage to Gordon Wright.

Lovick, Mr. and Mrs. Edmund. In *The Tragic Muse*, diplomat Peter Sherringham's colleague and his wife. She is the sister of Basil Dashwood, who marries Miriam Rooth, whom Peter Sherringham loves.

Lowder, Maud Manningham. In *The Wings of the Dove*, Kate Croy's aunt and Susan Shepherd Stringham's longtime friend. Through Susan, Maud meets Milly Theale and entertains her in London.

Lowe, Elena (?–?). An enigmatic young woman, whose father was Francis Lowe (of Boston) and whom James saw socially in Italy in 1873. She intrigued him greatly, and he gossiped about her in a few letters, especially when she married a Britisher in Venice in 1874. She may have been a model for Christina Light, heroine of both *Roderick Hudson* and *The Princess Casamassima*.

Lowell, James Russell (1819–1891). Important nineteenth-century American poet, essayist, critic, diplomat, lecturer, editor, linguist, and professor. He was born in the Lowell family home called Elmwood, in Cambridge, Massachusetts. His father was a Boston minister. Lowell went to Harvard College (1834–1838), then to Harvard Law School for a law degree (1840). He became an abolitionist. He published a book of verse (1841), then his popular *Poems* (1843). He broke into the field of literary criticism with *Conversations on Some of the Old Poets* (1844). He married in 1844, moved briefly to Philadelphia with his wife, and joined reform movements, writing antislavery essays (1845–1848). He met Edgar Allan Poe* in 1845. His first daughter was born in 1845 but died in 1847; a second daughter was born in 1847. He published his satirical *Fables for Critics* (1848) and *The Biglow Papers*, first series (1848). A third daughter was born in 1849 but died in 1850; his only son was born in 1850 but died in 1852. He and his family went to Europe (1851–1852). His wife died in 1853. Lowell published critical work on several British poets. Preparing to teach languages and literature by going abroad again (1855–1856), Lowell succeeded Henry Wadsworth Longfellow* at Harvard (1856–1872). He became the first editor of the *Atlantic Monthly* (1857–1861), and he married a second time in 1857. He coedited the *North American Review* (1863–1872, first with Charles Eliot Norton,* 1863–1868; then with Ephraim Whitman Gurney,* 1868–1870; finally with Henry Adams,* 1870–1872). Lowell assembled some of his literary essays in *Fireside Travels* (1864, dedicated to William Wetmore Story*). Lowell continued *The Biglow Papers*, with the second series (1866). He published more popular poetry, including "Ode Recited at the Harvard Commemoration" (1865), "The Cathedral" (1869, dedicated to James Thomas Fields*), and "[Louis] Agassiz" (1874). *Among My Books*, first series (1870) was followed by *My Study Windows* (1871). He revisited Europe (1872–1874), spending several months in Paris, often with James. Lowell accepted a reappointment to Harvard (1874–1877). Then he began a distinguished diplomatic career, first as American minister to Spain (1877–1880) and later as minister to Great Britain (1880–1885). James was excited in the summer of 1877 by the news that Lowell had requested that James be appointed secretary of legation in Madrid under him, but the request was denied. Lowell acted as godfather to Virginia Stephen, whose father Sir Leslie Stephen* he knew and who later became Virginia Woolf.* Lowell's second wife was periodically sick and insane in England, where she died in 1885. Summering in England year after year in the later 1880s, Lowell published *Democracy and Other Addresses* (1886), *Heartsease and Rue* (1888), and political essays; he then supervised an edition of his writings (10 vols., 1890). He was the second president of the Modern Language Association of America (1887–1891). After Lowell's death, Norton edited his friend's letters

(1893). James wrote an appreciative essay on Lowell (*Atlantic Monthly*, Jan 1892; reprinted in *Essays in London and Elsewhere*, 1893) which begins with the idea that the death of a friend enables us to "cut the silhouette . . . out of the confusion of life, we save and fix the outline." James will be the soft friend, not the cold critic, in this reminiscence of an essential "man of letters." James recalls attending Lowell's lectures on British literature and Old French at Harvard (in 1862–1863), walking with him in Paris ("he knew his Paris") in the winter of 1872–1873 and in Florence the following winter (he loved to hear Tuscan Italian spoken), an August 1877 dinner with him in London (in a Park Street hotel now sanctified by memories), associating with him repeatedly during the late 1880s in London and at Whitby in Yorkshire, the latter a picturesque vacation area lovingly recalled. James takes occasion to image London as a fat, unwieldy lady who demands to be fed from "the consecrated ladle," which "implement" she places "in Mr. Lowell's hands with a confidence so immediate as to be truly touching—a confidence that speaks for the eventual amalgamation of the Anglo-Saxon race in a way that no casual friction can obliterate." Between poignant reminiscences and clever asides, James praises his friend dispassionately. Lowell carried his literary style into diplomacy, politics, dinner speeches, letters, and droll, whimsical conversation. He so loved his native land, especially New England, that "he could play with his patriotism and make it various." James praises *The Biglow Papers* (for fine dialect), the Harvard "Commemoration Ode" ("the truest expression of his poetic nature"), "Agassiz" (which "takes its place with the few great elegies in our language, gives a hand to 'Lycidas' [by John Milton] and to "Thyrsis' [by Matthew Arnold*]"), certain public addresses (in which "he seems in mystical communication with the richest sources of English prose"), and especially his critical essays. When James reads such prose, he muses, "I seem to hear the door close softly behind me and to find in the shaded lamplight the conditions most in harmony with the sentient soul of man. I see an apartment brown and book-lined, which is the place in the world most convertible into other places. The turning of the leaves, the crackling of the fire, are the only things that break its stillness—the stillness in which mild miracles are wrought. These are the miracles of evocation, of re-surrection, of transmission, of insight, of history, of poetry. It may be a little room, but it is a great space; it may be a deep solitude, but it is a mighty concert." James also touches here and there on Lowell's "patent" patriotism, his love of the English language, his pacificism, his unique style—"an inde-feasible part of him"—his loyalty—"he would have done anything for his friends"—and his boyish hospitality. James closes by saying that Lowell had his troubles, but he stood tall for optimism and beauty. He displayed strength, wisdom, and gladness. James published an essay on Lowell for Volume XVI of the *Library of the World's Best Literature Ancient and Modern* (New York: Peale and Hill, 1897), ed. Charles Dudley Warner.* In it, partly going over old ground, James calls Lowell a versatile man of letters, "most saturated with literature and most directed to criticism." From an exemplary New England family, and with a dignified Puritan consciousness, he is best studied as a product of "race and place." James contrasts Lowell with Ralph Waldo Emerson,* Nathaniel Hawthorne,* Washington Irving,* Henry Wadsworth Longfellow, and Edgar Allan Poe; then he opines that in *The Biglow Papers* Lowell struck his most identifiable note, since in them he enlarged American humor. His political liberalism kept him from dryness and dilettantism; perhaps for too long he both taught "the promiscuous and preoccupied young" and also edited, although the *North American Review* contains his best criticism—criticism being, incidentally, "the most postponed and complicated of the arts." His literary life prepared Lowell for diplomacy. He was a superb occasional speaker, displaying both "breadth and wit." James praises the "Commemoration Ode" uniquely and then tries not to lament the absence of any Lowell *magnum opus*. He closes by extolling Lowell's voice, conscience, and wit. Sponsored by Lowell in June 1886, James visited Osterley Park, in Middlesex near Heston. They were guests there of Margaret, Countess of Jersey, and her husband, the owner. James later used the country house as a model for Summersoft, the mansion in both his short story "The Lesson of the Master" and his play *Summersoft*. James's autobiographical volumes *A Small Boy and Others* and *Notes of a Son and Brother* contain brief references to Lowell, and *The Middle Years* has an extended report on the two friends as fellow luncheon guests at the home of Alfred, Lord Tennyson* and his wife. James's library contained two books by Lowell and his collected edition as well.

Luard, Lady Ethel Stormer. In "Greville Fane," novelist Greville Fane's useless, selfish daughter. She is Leolin Stormer's brother and Sir Baldwin Luard's wife.

Luard, Sir Baldwin. In "Greville Fane," Lady Ethel Stormer Luard's husband.

Lubbock, Percy (1879–1965). London-born author and editor. He was educated at Eton (in the house of Arthur Christopher Benson*) and at King's College, Cambridge (to 1901). From the early 1900s Lubbock associated with the finest writers. He traveled and studied in Italy and Germany (to 1904), worked for the Board of Education and was a literary reviewer (to 1906), became the Pepys librarian at Magdalene College, Cambridge (to 1908), then resigned to read and write. During World War I, Lubbock did Red Cross work in France, Egypt, and London. He married Lady Sybil Cuffe (also a writer) in 1926, and the couple lived in Italy (Fiesole and Lerici). He spent the World War II years in Switzerland and was widowed in 1943. In his final years he was nearly blind. His books indicate his versatility: *The Craft of Fiction* (1921, on technical aspects of the novel, mainly as crafted by Gustave Flaubert,* William Makepeace Thackeray,* Count Leo Nikolayevich Tolstoy,* and James, and drawing heavily on the prefaces James wrote for *The Novels and Tales of Henry James*); *Earlham* (1922, the biography of a house in Norwich); *Shades of Eton* (1929, school reminiscences); *Roman Pictures* (1923, travel sketches and social comedy); *The Region Cloud* (1925, a novel, with a character perhaps based partly on James); and *Portrait of Edith* [Newbold Jones] *Wharton*[*] (1947). Lubbock published much else, including studies of Elizabeth Barrett Browning* (1906), Samuel Pepys (1909), George Calderon (1921), and Mary Cholmondeley* (1928); contributions to the London *Times Literary Supplement* (1908–1914); and his selections from Benson's gigantic diary (1926). Late in his life, James met Lubbock, who was his guest at Lamb House* as early as the summer of 1901. In a *Times Literary Supplement* Lubbock puffed James, who was pleased and at once wrote to Mary Augusta Ward* (11 Jul 1909) that Lubbock is a ''gentle and thoroughly literary and finely critical young man.'' More objectively, in a letter to Sir Edmund Wilson Gosse* (28 Jul 1909), James praises the essay as ''really intelligent & superior; a difficult thing very ably done.'' Lubbock was in the audience for James's 1912 lecture on Robert Browning.* James and Lubbock had many mutual friends and acquaintances, including Benson, Theodora Bosanquet,* Gosse, Gaillard Thomas Lapsley,* John Singer Sargent,* Howard Overing Sturgis,* and Wharton. After James's death, his family selected Lubbock rather than Wharton to edit his letters. (William James's widow Alice was particularly opposed to letting Wharton have a hand in the work.) Lubbock issued his choice of letters, made under difficult circumstances (2 vols., 1920). In addition, he prepared for 1917 publication the three books James had left in fragmentary form: *The Ivory Tower*, *The Sense of the Past*, and *The Middle Years*. Finally, Lubbock also assembled *The Novels and Stories of Henry James*, published in London by Macmillan, thirty-five volumes, 1921–1923.

Luce, Mr. and Mrs. In *The Portrait of a Lady*, Lydia Touchett's friends in Paris.

Ludlow, Edmund and Lilian Archer. In *The Portrait of a Lady*, Isabel Archer's brother-in-law and Isabel's sister.

Ludlow, John. In *Washington Square*, an unsuccessful suitor of Catherine Sloper.

Ludlow, Thomas (Tom). In ''A Day of Days,'' a New York scientist who stops to see his friend Herbert Moore but talks briefly with his sister Adela Moore instead.

Luke. In ''The Turn of the Screw,'' a servant at the estate of Bly. Did he mail Miles's letter?

Lumley, Laura. In *The Tragic Muse*, a woman who rents a London house to Mrs. Rooth and her daughter Miriam.

Luna, Adelina Chancellor. In *The Bostonians*, Olive Chancellor's older sister, who is widowed and sensual, and who is unrequitedly attracted to Basil Ransom.

Luna, Newton. In *The Bostonians*, Adelina Luna's young son, who Olive Chancellor thinks is spoiled.

Lurcher, Captain. In *Tenants*, Claude Vibert's unpaid tutor who tries unsuccessfully to blackmail Claude's mother Eleanor Vibert. He also flirts selfishly with Miss Dyer.

Lusignan, Duchesse de. In *The American*, a Parisian hostess whom Claire de Cintré does not visit.

Lutch, Dotty and Kitty. In *The Golden Bowl*, sisters who are parasites on Adam Verver until Charlotte Stant drives them out of Fawns, his estate.

Lutley, Lord John and Lady. In *The Sacred Fount*, guests at Newmarch. The narrator decides that Lady Lutley is not Gilbert Long's "sacred fount." Lord Lutley is to arrive later with Mrs. Froome.

Luttrel, Major Robert. In "Poor Richard," Gertrude Whittaker's dishonest suitor, foiled when Richard Maule tells Gertrude that both men lied to Captain Edmund Severn. Luttrel becomes a general during the Civil War and later marries Miss Van Winkle.

Lynch. In *A Monologue by Henry James*, the American legation secretary in London. He calls on Cora Tuff at her hotel, and she orders him to get her a court presentation.

Lyon, Oliver. In "The Liar," Everina Brant Capadose's old-time admirer. He paints a revealing portrait of her husband Colonel Clement Capadose to try to trap her into admitting that her husband is a liar.

M

Macalister. In *Washington Square*, an unsuccessful suitor of Catherine Sloper.

MacAlpine, William (?–?). Scottish shorthand stenographer-typist whom James employed and James dictated to, beginning in February 1897. The two bicycled together. When Annie Adams Fields* met MacAlpine in 1898, she noted in her diary that he was reverent and appreciative toward James. MacAlpine was succeeded by Mary Weld,* early in 1901, and then by Theodora Bosanquet,* late in 1907.

MacCarthy, Justin (1830–1912). Irish editor, historian, biographer, novelist, and pro–Home Rule parliamentarian (1879–1900). His novels include *Dear Lady Disdain* (1875) and *Miss Misanthrope* (1878). James met MacCarthy in 1880 and wrote to Thomas Sergeant Perry* (22 Feb [1880]) that he "is better than his novels, and a great journalist." McCarthy published *Reminiscences* (2 vols., 1899), in which he praises James's conversational talents.

MacCarthy, Sir Charles Otto Desmond (1877–1952). Plymouth-born literary and dramatic critic, biographer, and editor. He was educated at Eton and then at Trinity College, Cambridge. He became a successful free-lance critic, and he collected his drama reviews in *The Court Theatre 1904–1907* (1907). Next, MacCarthy began to edit and write columns for periodical publications. He did significant work with the *New Statesman* (1913–1952), where he succeeded Sir Edmund Wilson Gosse* as senior literary critic (from 1928). MacCarthy's best work may be found in *Portraits* (1931) and *Shaw* (1951). Beginning in 1901 James knew MacCarthy casually, socialized with him at Cambridge (June 1909), and eagerly followed his Red Cross ambulance work in France (1914–1915).

Among his acquaintances whom James also knew were Herbert Henry Asquith,* Joseph Conrad,* George Meredith,* John Ruskin,* Sir Leslie Stephen,* George Macaulay Trevelyan (of the Trevelyan family*), and Sir Sydney Philip Waterlow.* MacCarthy helped Trevelyan when he was preparing a book on Meredith. MacCarthy was rejected as the editor of James's letters, in favor of Percy Lubbock.*

McClellan, George Brinton (1826–1885). American Army officer, who served as a general during the Civil War, was defeated by Abraham Lincoln for the presidency in 1864, and was later governor of New Jersey (1878–1881). James called upon McClellan and his family in Florence, Italy, early in 1887, to discuss the flap over his naive daughter Mary Marcy McClellan's indiscreet letter to the New York *World* which proved embarrassing to Venetian society. James used the incident as background for his short novel *The Reverberator*.

McClure, Samuel Sidney (1857–1949). Dynamic editorial, publishing, and commercial genius. Born in Ireland, he immigrated as a youth to the United States, where he later established America's first newspaper syndicate (1884) and then founded *McClure's Magazine* (1893–1929), which became famous for publishing work by muckrakers (notably Ida M. Tarbell* and Lincoln Steffens). In 1914 McClure published *My Autobiography* (which was actually written by Willa Cather*), in which he says that James personally questioned him about Robert Louis Stevenson,* a valued portrait of whose wife he gave James in 1888. In the course of his work, McClure made professional contact, sometimes without success, with the following persons also known by James: Sir Walter Besant,* Sir Sidney Colvin,* Stephen Crane,* Hamlin Garland,* Richard Watson Gilder,* Sir Edmund Wilson Gosse,* Julia Ward Howe,* William Dean Howells,* Rudyard Kipling,* Andrew Lang,* George Meredith,* Ouida,* Theodore Roosevelt,* Booth Tarkington,* Alfred, Lord Tennyson,* and Mark Twain.*

Macgeorge. In *The Tragic Muse*, a politician who is mentioned by Julia Dallow but who bores her friend Nick Dormer.

McIlvaine, Clarence W. (c. 1864–1912). Princeton-educated employee of Harper and Brothers. He created their popular Odd Number Series. When James Ripley Osgood* started his publishing house independent of the Harpers in London, he secured McIlvaine as his partner (1891–1892), but then soon died. Osgood, McIlvaine & Co. was then absorbed by the American Harper company, and McIlvaine became vice president of its London branch. From the 1890s, James socialized with McIlvaine and his wife.

Mackenzie, Sir Edward Montague Compton (1883–1972). Son of Edward Compton,* producer of and actor in James's play *The American*. Compton Mackenzie's mother, the actress Virginia Bateman Compton, also appeared in it when it was performed in Southport, outside Liverpool. A Scottish nationalist, Mackenzie helped to found the Scottish National Party. He wrote a hundred books, including novels, essays, children's stories, and autobiographical volumes. His later works did not fulfill the promise of his early successes. James admired Mackenzie's first novel, *Carnival* (1912), and the first volume of *Sinister Street* (1913). The second volume of *Sinister Street* (1914) disappointed him. In a letter to Sir Hugh Seymour Walpole* (21 Nov 1914), James says that by the next day he will have seen Mackenzie only twice, then adds that the second volume of *Sinister Street* "is half a deadly failure and half an extraordinary exhibition of talent." James wrote about Mackenzie, among other young novelists, in his 1914 essay "The New Novel." James's several letters to Mackenzie evidently made their friend Walpole jealous. James's library contained two books by Mackenzie.

Mackenzie, George. In "The Story of a Year," a man Elizabeth Crowe facetiously tells John Ford she might be in love with.

Mackern, Philip. In "The Given Case," a man who loves Margaret Hamer, whose awareness that Barton Reeve loves Kate Despard makes her responsive to Phil.

Mackintosh. In *The Outcry*, the novel, and *The Outcry*, the play, the London art dealer with whom Lord Theign places his Mantovano* painting.

Mackintosh, Dr. In "The Author of Beltraffio," dying Dolcino Ambient's attending physician. He is dismissed by Beatrice, the boy's mother.

Maclane, Ella. In *Confidence*, Bernard Longueville's and Blanche Evers's friend from Baltimore. While touring in Europe, she wants to see Baden-Baden.

Maclane, Mrs. and Mrs. In *Confidence*, Ella Maclane's parents.

Macmillan, Sir Frederick Orridge (1851–1936). Son and nephew of the cofounders of Macmillan and Company (1843), which sold and published books. The firm gained impetus in 1855 by issuing *Westward Ho!* by Charles Kingsley,* founded *Macmillan's Magazine* (1859–1907), and published Lewis Carroll, Francis Marion Crawford,* John Richard Green,* Thomas Henry Huxley,* Alfred, Lord Tennyson,* and James, among other notables. First, young Macmillan was trained by the family, educated at Cambridge, and then assigned for five years to the New York branch of the firm. He married Georgiana Warrin of Long Island (1874), returned to London (1876) as a company partner, and was instrumental in developing its international organization. In 1890 the New York branch became a separate commercial entity. In 1893 Frederick Macmillan supervised the conversion of the firm to one of limited liability and became its president. In 1911 he played a key role in reforming the copyright law. Back in 1877 James offered his *French Poets and Novelists* to the Macmillan company, which wisely published it despite an adverse critique of it by their literary adviser Viscount John Morley.* Thus started James's long, generally pleasant association with Macmillan, who, for example, offered James valuable advice regarding the American publication of *The Bostonians* when James Ripley Osgood* went bankrupt in May 1885. James occasionally haggled over royalties with Frederick Macmillan, once memorably, in connection with *The Tragic Muse*. When James was offered seemingly demeaning (but commercially defensible) terms for book rights, he wrote to "dear Macmillan" (28 Mar 1890), "I . . . desire to get a larger sum [than a £70 advance], and have determined to take what steps I can in this direction. These steps . . . will carry me away from you. . . . Farewell then . . . " Macmillan offered a compromise, paid a larger advance, and lost money. James knew Macmillan and his wife well socially.

Macpherson, Lady Muriel. In *The Tragic Muse*, the young woman who captures Goodwood Grindon, in whom Bridget Dormer is not interested.

Macready, William Charles (1793–1873). Famous English tragedian, who acted, mostly in plays by William Shakespeare,* in London, Paris, and America. While managing Covent Garden, he produced *Strafford* by Robert Browning,* among other plays. James reviewed (*Nation*, 29 Apr 1875) *Macready's Reminiscences, and Selections from His Diaries and Letters* (1875), calling the book "copious and confidential." Young playgoers will regret never having seen this interesting actor, who was, however, "cold." James points out that Macready disliked acting and once considered moving his large family to Massachusetts. He was religious, was thought to be arrogant by his fellows, criticized his own inadequate performances and praised his own brilliance, and includes accounts of famous associates. James concludes that, although Macready's style may have been unnatural, even"pompous," by modern standards, it is likely that the stage of his time excelled that of more recent times.

"Madame de Mauves." Long short story (29,600 words), published in the *Galaxy* (Feb–Mar 1874); reprinted in *A Passionate Pilgrim, and Other Tales*, 1875; revised and reprinted in *The Novels and Tales of Henry James*, Volume XIII, 1908. (Characters: Butterworth, Mme. Marie de Mauves Clairin, Clairin, Chalumeau, Claudine, Mrs. Cleve, Maggie Draper, Mrs. Draper, Longmore, Countess Euphemia Cleve de Mauves, Count Richard de Mauves, Mme. de Mauves, Webster.) Mrs. Draper introduces her fellow American friend Longmore outside Paris to Euphemia Cleve de Mauves, the decent, sweet, sad American wife of Comte Richard de Mauves, who is older, fat, and faithlessly pagan, and who even urges Longmore to get closer to Mme. de Mauves. Longmore pities her but resists, until he sees evidence in a Parisian cafe of Richard's infidelity; then he rushes back to Euphemia to declare his love—but diffidently. His restraint moves her a bit, even while her immoral, widowed sister-in-law Mme. Clairin's encouragement baffles him. Sight of an artist and his amorous girl friend at a forest inn, togther with a disturbing dream about the Mauves couple, creates envy in the restrained Longmore, who two years later in America learns from Mme. Clairin (through Mrs. Draper) that Mauves, repentant but then unsuccessful in asking his wife's forgiveness, has committed suicide. Longmore thinks of returning to Europe but has not yet done so. This story is puzzling because it is told in part through Longmore's consciousness and also because the heroine remains enigmatic. Like Isabel Archer of *The Portrait of a Lady*, she is not aroused sexually; yet she is admirably pure, and her husband is evil. Still, when he repents, her outrage is too icy. Further, when she is free, Longmore does not rush to her. In the preface to Volume XIII of *The Novels and Tales of Henry James*, James says that he cannot recall the "origin" of "Madame de Mauves," but that he fondly remembers writing the story at an inn in Bad Homburg, in the summer of 1873, when his imagination was "visited by the gentle Euphemia." James has his hero *manqué* wonder whether "it was better to cultivate an art . . . [or] a passion"; James's career was his own personal answer.

"Mme. de Mauves." 1874 title of "Madame de Mauves," 1875.

"Madame Ristori." Theater essay, published in the *Nation* (18 Mar 1875), in which James highly praises the actress Adelaide Ristori.*

Maddalena. In *Roderick Hudson*, Sarah Hudson's maid in Florence.

Maddock, Lady. In "The Coxon Fund," George Gravener's sister-in-law.

Maddock, Lord. In "The Coxon Fund," George Gravener's brother. When he and then his son die, Gravener becomes Lord Maddock.

Maddock, Lord. In "The Coxon Fund," George Gravener's nephew. When he and his father die, Gravener becomes Lord Maddock.

Maddock, Lord George. In "The Coxon Fund," the later title of George Gravener.

Maddock, Miss. In *The Golden Bowl*, Adam Verver's Irish neighbor, who lives near Fawns, his estate.

"The Madonna of the Future." Short story (14,200 words), published in the *Atlantic Monthly* (Mar 1873); reprinted in *A Passionate Pilgrim, and Other Tales*, 1875; revised and reprinted in *The Novels and Tales of Henry James*, Volume XIII, 1908. (Characters: Mrs. Coventry, H—, Serafina, Theobald.) In Florence the narrator, H—, meets a painter named Theobald, who is chided by Mrs. Coventry, an American hostess, for his unproductivity. Theobald tells the narrator that he is slowly creating a masterpiece of a madonna, and then he introduces him to his model, the faded Serafina. H— abruptly calls the woman old, which pronouncement so stuns Theobald that he becomes mortally sick. Before the painter dies, H— visits him in his ragged room and sees that the madonna canvas is not only old but also blank. A literary source for this story is *Le chef d'oeuvre inconnu* (1831) by Honoré de Balzac,* in which a young man judges an eccentric old painter's extravagantly guarded work to be nothing but daubs and crazy lines. It is a mistake to regard James's redaction to be autobiographical, because, although James professed to fear his own occasional artistic inactivity, he always knew that he was steadily productive. For satiric balance, James at the end of "The Madonna of the Future" brings in an artist who is a meretricious commercial success with his statuettes of cats and monkeys in obscene poses. James wrote to his father (1 Feb [1873]) on learning that William Dean Howells,* editor of the *Atlantic Monthly*, had objected to the cats-and-monkeys episode; James says that Howells's "standard of propriety" means "a bad look out ahead for imaginative writing."

The Madonna of the Future and Other Tales, 1879. Collection of six short stories published in London by Macmillan in two volumes, 1879: "The Madonna of the Future," "Longstaff's Marriage," "Madame de Mauves," "Eugene Pickering," "The Diary of a Man of Fifty," and "Benvolio."

Maeterlinck, Maurice (1862–1949). Belgian dramatist, poet, essayist, and translator, who lived in Paris (from 1896), was influenced by the French symbolists, and in 1911 received the Nobel Prize for literature (for which James had been recommended by Edith Newbold Jones Wharton,* William Dean Howells,* and Sir Edmund Wilson Gosse,* among others). Maeterlinck's most famous play is *Pelléas et Mélisande* (1892), which in 1902 his friend Claude Debussy adapted for a successful opera. In December 1909 James attended a London performance of Maeterlinck's play *The Blue Bird* (1909) with the wife of Alfred Sutro* and the playwright's wife Georgette Le Blanc Maeterlinck; through Sutro, James met Maeterlinck afterwards. In a letter to Wharton (13 Dec 1909), James reported that he "vulgarly liked" Georgette and that Maeterlinck struck him as "shy and sympathetic." Maeterlinck later remembered James's spoken French as marvelous.

Magaw, Mattie. In "Fordham Castle," Mrs. Magaw's daughter, who uses the pseudonym Miss Vanderplank to help her catch Lord Dunderton.

Magaw, Mr. and Mrs. In "Fordham Castle," a married couple, the husband perhaps being deceased. The woman is forced by her daughter Mattie to leave England and receive her mail under the name Mrs. Vanderplank.

Magawisca. In "A Problem," an Indian woman who predicts that David and Emma will have a daughter who will then die.

Maisonrouge, Mme. de. In "A Bundle of Letters," the proprietress of the Pension Maisonrouge in Paris. She caters to Americans and Britishers. She is Léon Verdier's cousin.

Maitland, Frederic William (1850–1906). Cambridge University professor of civil law (from 1888) and distinguished legal historian. He and James's friend Sir Frederick Pollock* wrote *The History of English Law before the Time of Edward I* (2 vols., 1895). James knew Maitland socially. Thoby Stephen, the son of James's close friend Sir Leslie Stephen,* asked James in 1904 to provide Maitland, who was preparing the official biography of Leslie Stephen, with personal letters from his father; but James was in the United States and could not comply. *The Life and Letters of Leslie Stephen* was published in 1906, with none of his letters to James. In a letter to Sir Edmund Wilson Gosse* (18 Nov 1906), James calls the biography "excellent & interesting—even . . . rather charming," adding that he had been negligent in failing to send Maitland a few letters from Stephen which he possessed. In a letter to Lady Anne Isabella Ritchie* (21 Dec 1906), James went further in praise, calling the Stephen biography "a thing of Beauty . . . handsomely and feelingly done." James's library had a copy of it.

Major, Mrs. In *The Princess Casamassima*, Paul and Rosy Muniment's London landlady.

Mallet, Mr. and Mrs. Jonas. In *Roderick Hudson*, mentioned as Rowland's deceased parents. The father was an austere, puritannical businessman; the mother, the daughter of a retired sea captain named Rowland.

Mallet, Rowland. In *Roderick Hudson*, sculptor Roderick Hudson's wealthy sponsor in Rome. He speaks severely to Christina Light there, invites Hudson's mother and his fiancée Mary Garland over to Italy, and later secretly (and hopelessly) admires Mary.

Mallow, Lancelot (Lance). In "The Tree of Knowledge," Morgan Mallow's son, who paints badly and also discovers that his father is an untalented, pretentious sculptor. The character of Lance Mallow is partly based on Gordon Greenough, a member of the Greenough family.*

Mallow, Mr. And Mrs. Morgan. In "The Tree of Knowledge," Lancelot's parents. Morgan is an inoffensively pretentious and untalented sculptor at Carrara Lodge, in London. His loyal wife unsinfully loves Peter Brench. The character of Morgan Mallow is partly based on Richard Saltonstall Greenough, of the Greenough family.*

Manger, Algie. In *The Awkward Age*, Harold Brookenham's friend and the tutor of Baron Schack (Schmack?). Algie is evidently Booby Manger's brother.

Manger, Booby. In *The Awkward Age*, Harold Brookenham's friend and a rich American girl's fiancé. He is evidently Algie Manger's brother.

Manger, Mr. and Mrs. In *The Awkward Age*, friends of Harold Brookenham, and evidently the parents of Algie and Booby.

Mangler, Bessie, Fanny, and Maggie. In "The Chaperon," Lady Maresfield's daughters and Guy's sisters. They are also Charlotte Mangler Vaughan-Vesey's sisters.

Mangler, Guy. In "The Chaperon," Lady Maresfield's son, and the brother of Bessie, Fanny, and Maggie Mangler, and Charlotte Mangler Vaughan-Vesey. Rose Tramore will not encourage Guy because he refuses to support her ostracized mother socially.

"The Manners of American Women." Essay, published in *Harper's Bazar* (Apr–Jul 1907). James recently observed four young schoolgirls and a conductor on a train going south out of Boston. The girls were obstreperously noisy; the conductor, curt and nudgy. James blames modern American women for not setting them all a better example of manners. Mothers and aunts now allow illbred youngsters to "descant" egocentrically, inconsiderately, uncivilly. Traveling more widely, James concluded that all "amenities . . . [have been] dispensed with," and successfully, too, because there have been no "ferocious reprisals" for rudeness. James bewildered hotel workers by thanking them. Perhaps women do not thank them. James deplores the "incoherent and indiscriminate spooning" by women when eating, after which they "combat digestive drowsiness" by reading vulgar newspapers with screaming headlines. He recalls watching a big Illinois family on a train out of Chicago chew gum while discussing a performance of Richard Wagner's *Parsifal* they had just enjoyed. He loathes the tasteless billboards which deface "the breast of nature" along our highways. Can Americans with European manners hope to set an example of " 'finer' forms"? Jingoists will counter that Americans make money best and that foreigners want to come over. Returning to his complaint that American "maidens" outtalk their mothers, James says that he would recommend "discipline" except that all values are now "muddled" because the young do not "recognize . . . authority" or any "accomplishment" superior to their own. James recalls how miffed the pretty daughter of a distinguished American artist was when he, not she, received social invitations in Europe. She said she had expected to be pampered. James touches on American attitudes toward servants and divorce. Ignoring American women who are civil and those who are ignorant, James discusses those who seek a new civility. They are humane, helpful, and neighborly, but they are without manners. (New England short stories and fiction by William Dean Howells* show us as much.) Poverty-generated "fellowship" is the substitute. But loss of manners now will cost later. James admonishes American women to do more. American men have ceased to set an example or to "correct" their wives, who are now "queens." James closes by depicting such "queens," shut out from the commercial world, as free, successful, rich, rarely embarrassed, self-centered, gushy, and conscienceless. They are in limbo, outside knowledge and modesty, and hence "doomed."

Manning, Anne E. (1807–1879). British historical novelist. Her *Maiden and Married Life of Mary Powell* (1849) is told from the point of view of John Milton's first wife; *Deborah's Diary* (1859), from that of Milton's daughter; and *The Household of Sir Thomas More* (1851), from that of More's daughter. James reviewed (*Nation*, 15 Aug 1867) Manning's *Sir Thomas More* and with it her *Jacques Bonneval; or, The Days of the Dragonnades* (1867), but he spends most of his space theorizing on historical novels in general. He calls Manning fecund, informed, and skillful; then he says that histories are "long and dull," memoirs are too full of "local color," and historical novels, which fall between, are of two types: those with historical personages and those with imaginary figures against a backdrop of real events. Historical novels are more numerous now than they were thirty years ago, but we now lack a Sir Walter Scott* to combine their two types. Imaginative novelists should be better grounded in historical reality. Charles Reade* and William Makepeace Thackeray* are; George Eliot* is not.

Manning, Miss. In *The Other House*, the novel, and *The Other House*, the play, Kate Beever's businesslike parlormaid.

Mantovano, Rinaldo (fl. c. 1530–1540). Italian painter who was born in Mantua and studied there under Giulio Romano before 1546. Mantovano is represented by one picture in Sant'Agnese at Mantua and two pictures in the National Gallery, London. When James gave the name Mantovano to a painter in *The Outcry*, both the novel and the play, he thought that he was making it up.

Mantovano. In *The Outcry*, the novel, and *The Outcry*, the play, the painter of a work which Lord Theign owns, which is thought to be by Moretto, and which Breckenridge Bender wants to buy, especially when it is authenticated by Caselli as a Mantovano. Although James believed that he had invented the name Mantovano for his fictitious painter, there was a real Rinaldo Mantovano.* When a correspondent named Robert C. Witt so informed him, James replied to him in a pseudo-abject explanatory letter (27 Nov 1912).

Marbot, Jean Baptiste Antoine Marcelin, Baron de (1782–1854). General under Napoleon, with a distinguished military career, spanning Prussia, Russia, the Peninsular War, "the Hundred Days," Waterloo, the exile, Antwerp, and Algeria. He became a member of the Chamber of Peers and retired in 1848. According to a Notebook entry (26 Mar 1892), James was reading Général de Marbot's *Mémoires* (3 vols., 1891) when he conceived the idea of writing "Owen Wingrave." James's library contained a copy of Marbot's memoirs.

Marchant, Lady. In *The Princess Casamassima*, a neighbor at nearby Broome of the Princess Casamassima at Medley, where the woman visits with her daughters.

Marchant, The Misses. In *The Princess Casamassima*, the three daughters of Lady Marchant of Broome.

Marcher, John. In "The Beast in the Jungle," May Bartram's friend. He indifferently works for the British government, has a small patrimony, is an undedicated gardener and reader, entertains unmemorably, holds himself aloof from life, attends the opera with May too often, fails to respond to her gently proffered love, and after her death realizes that he is the one man in all the world to whom nothing has ever happened.

Marden, Charlotte (Chartie). In "Sir Edmund Orme," an attractive young woman whose acceptance of the narrator exorcizes the ghost of Sir Edmund Orme, who in life was rejected by Charlotte's now widowed mother.

Marden, Major. In "Sir Edmund Orme," the deceased husband of Mrs. Marden and the father of Charlotte. His marriage caused Sir Edmund Orme, who also loved the future Mrs. Marden, to commit suicide.

Marden, Mrs. In "Sir Edmund Orme," Charlotte's mother. When she married Major Marden instead of Sir Edmund Orme, the latter committed suicide and later haunted her. Her daughter Charlotte Marden's acceptance of the narrator exorcizes his ghost.

Maresfield, Lady. In "The Chaperon," rich Mrs. Bray's sister and the mother of Bessie, Fanny, Guy, and Maggie Mangler and of Charlotte Mangler Vaughan-Vesey. Lady Maresfield unsuccessfully urges Rose Tramore to accept her son Guy.

Margaret, Lady. In "The Siege of London," Nancy Grenville Beck Headway's fellow guest at Longlands, the Demesne estate.

Marguerite. In "In the Cage," a name mentioned in a Lady Bradeen telegram.

Marie. In *A Monologue by Henry James*, Cora Tuff's French maid.

Marignac, Gaston de. In *The American: A Comedy in Four Acts*, Valentin de Bellegarde's courteous second in his fatal duel with Lord Deepmere. Marignac helps Christopher Newman stop Claire de Cintré, Valentin's sister, from leaving Fleurières for the convent.

Marignac, Mme. de. In *The Reverberator*, a deceased friend of Gaston Probert's father. She was Mme. Léonie de Villepreux's mother.

Mark, Lord. In *The Wings of the Dove*, a friend of Maud Manningham Lowder, who wants her niece Kate Croy to marry him. But he loves Milly Theale, who declines his advances. In frustration he informs her of Kate's liaison with Merton Densher, who professes to love sick Milly.

Marks, John George. Biographer, whose *Life and Letters of Frederick Walker* (1896) James reviewed in "London" (20 Feb 1897). Frederick Walker,* a painter and illustrator (of books by William Makepeace Thackeray,* for example), was Marks's brother-in-law. James enjoyed the book on Walker but mostly for sentimental reasons: He reports that the subject was an "exquisite genius" in the genre of the " 'story picture,' " was charming, wrote letters combining "roughness and sweetness," and influenced George Du Maurier.* James's library contained a copy of this book by Marks.

Marmaduke. In "Maud-Evelyn," a strange fellow rejected by Lavinia. With the Dedricks' help, he comes to believe that he was their long-dead daughter Maud-Evelyn's bereaved husband.

Marmaduke, Sir Henry and Lady. In "Lady Barbarina," an aristocratic British couple. She introduces Dr. Jackson Lemon to Lady Barbarina Clement's sister Lady Beauchemin.

"The Marriages." Short story (12,000 words), published in the *Atlantic Monthly* (Aug 1891); reprinted in *The Lesson of the Master*, 1892; revised and reprinted in *The Novels and Tales of Henry James*, Volume XVIII, 1909. (Characters: Adela Chart, Basil Chart, Beatrice Chart, Godfrey Chart, Mrs. Godfrey Chart, Muriel Chart, Colonel Chart, Mrs. Churchley, Lord Dovedale, Mrs. Flynn, Mr. and Mrs. Millward, Lady Molesley, Nutkins.) Adela is afraid that her beloved father Colonel Chart, a widower, will remarry. So she goes to his florid fiancée, the rich and mannish widow Mrs. Churchley, and reports something so atrocious about her father that the woman postpones the wedding. Adela's brother Godfrey Chart, age twenty, studying for his foreign service examinations, becomes mysteriously infuriated, telling the girl that he is in trouble and that Mrs. Churchley was going to help him. Still, he passes the exams. Next, at the Chart country house Adela is suddenly visited by Godfrey's secret wife, a middle-aged hag who soon extorts money from Colonel Chart to disappear and not spoil Godfrey's career. It is apparent that the young man was counting on Mrs. Churchley's aid. Adela goes to the widow and tells her the truth, but she explains that she never countenanced the girl's horrible stories, wanted her father to send the girl away, and permanently broke with him when he sided with his daughter. Now Adela must make it up to her lonely father. James's original idea, recorded in a Notebook entry (12 Jan 1887), called for Colonel Chart to repent of his engagement and connive with his daughter in her lying—the specific (perhaps sexual) nature of which a writer more modern than James would have relished detailing. Later James expressed regret (*Notebooks*, 21 Dec 1895) that he had not reserved the title *The Marriages* for the fiction which became *The Golden Bowl*. In the preface to Volume XVIII of *The Novels and Tales of Henry James*, he registers great sympathy for "the possible pangs of filial piety" felt by a daughter whose widowed father supplants "the lost mother."

"The Married Son," Part VII (10,600 words, by James, 1908), of *The Whole Family: A Novel by Twelve Authors* (New York and London: Harper, 1908). (Characters added by James: Mr. and Mrs. Ronald Chataway.) (Earlier in the novel, an editor interviews Cyrus Talbert about the engagement of his daughter Peggy Talbert to her college friend Harry Goward. Harry was once interested in Aunt Elizabeth, but she was less interested than certain family members think. One of them follows her to New York because of her supposed elopement with the village doctor.) James continues the story: Charles Edward Talbert, "the married son," is contrasted with his canny brother-in-law Tom Price and suggests that Peggy's undesirable engagement can be terminated if Tom and his wife Lorraine will take the girl abroad. Charles would prefer to study art in Europe rather than continue working in his father's glass factory. (Later in the novel, Peggy's psychology professor, Stillman Dane, turns up, wins, and weds Peggy. Therefore, instead of three, four go over to Europe.) James was recruited for this curious round-robin project by Elizabeth Jordan.*

Marsh, Sir Edward Howard (1872–1953). Charming British writer, editor of poetry anthologies, translator, society wit, and friend of poets and authors, including James. Marsh was also a government official. He knew Prime Minister Herbert Henry Asquith* and Winston Churchill,* as well as William Holman Hunt,* Sir Geoffrey Langdon Keynes,* and Logan Pearsall Smith,* among other writers and artists of note. The long-standing friendship of James and "Eddie"

Marsh was deepened through their both knowing Rupert Brooke,* a biography of whom Marsh later published (1918). Marsh successfully appealed to Asquith in December 1915 to support the movement for James's being awarded the Order of Merit. Marsh includes memories of James in his book of reminiscences entitled *A Number of People* (1939). James's library contained an anthology edited by Marsh.

Marsh, Mr. and Mrs. In *The Other House*, guests of Kate Beever.

Marshal, Mortimer. In "The Papers," an inept playwright who likes Maud Blandy and seeks publicity through her fellow journalist Howard Bight.

Martin, Theodore (1816–1909). Edinburgh-born and -educated poet, essayist, versatile translator, and biographer. He was a solicitor in Scotland and then a parliamentary agent in London, married an actress, and wrote on dramatic subjects for magazines. At Queen Victoria's request, he wrote *The Life of His Royal Highness the Prince Consort* (1875–1880) in five volumes, the first three of which James reviewed (*Nation*, 4 Mar, 3 May 1877; 6 Jun 1878). He praises Martin's first volume, which takes Prince Albert's life to 1848, for being "fair and . . . flattering," "courtly without being fulsome," and for depicting well a subject who "adorn[ed] a brilliant position" without being brilliant himself. James discusses Albert's fine qualities and his service, his respect for Baron [Christian Friedrich] Stockmar, and his marriage—"a classic example of virtuous conjugal fidelity." James deplores the prose style of both Queen Victoria and her prince, and concludes that this first volume "is charged with an oppressive mediocrity." The second volume is too long in its recital of Albert's domestic activities. This "official life" is too big a frame for its little portrait. Many details are irrelevant; Stockmar now has a "dry, dogmatic manner," and the Queen's journals have "the same subdued complexion as . . . hitherto." The third volume was to have ended the series, but it gets bogged down in "anti-Russian" pleadings because of the Crimean War. Martin had access to too much official correspondence, which often shows Albert to be amiable and intelligent, but passive. True, when he was bolstering Turkey, he displayed a "warmth of tone." He was a valiant "scapegoat." This third volume also has much disagreeable material on the royal couple's overly friendly relations with the Emperor of France, in connection with the Alliance.

Martin, Mrs. In "Poor Richard," Captain Edmund Severn's sister, whom Gertrude Whittaker considers visiting to get news of Severn.

Martinet. In "The Sweetheart of M. Briseux," the owner of the studio which Pierre Briseux invades to complete Harold Staines's poor portrait.

Martle. In *The Other House*, the novel, Jean Martle's father and Kate Beever's second cousin. He is an invalid at Brighton. In *The Other House*, the play, Jean has recently been with her father at Brighton.

Martle, Jean. In *The Other House*, the novel, a friend of Kate Beever, who wants her son Paul to marry Jean. She comes to love Anthony Bream and, after Rose Armiger murders Tony's little daughter Effie, will probably marry him. In *The Other House*, the play, a house guest (age eighteen at the outset) of Kate Beever, whom Jean calls Cousin Kate. After Effie's death, Rose predicts that Tony and Jean will marry—and sooner than they think at first.

Mary. In "In the Cage," the recipient of a Captain Count Philip Everard telegram.

Masham, Lord. In "The Lesson of the Master," a guest at the luncheon given by Mr. and Mrs. St. George during which he sits next to Marian Fancourt.

Mason, Alice (1838?–?). The maiden name (which she later resumed) of the wife (very briefly) of Senator Charles Sumner. James met her through Sarah Butler Wister* in Rome, early in 1873, while she was there with friends awaiting a divorce. James took horseback rides with her, was impressed by her beauty and grace, and praised her in letters back home. James saw her again and again, through the years, in Paris and London. In a letter from Paris to his brother William (14 Mar [1876]), he names the German diplomat who in Washington, D.C., supposedly broke up the Sumner marriage. Mrs. Mason, as James later called her in several gossipy letters, knew many people familiar to him, including Henry Adams,* Ralph Waldo Emerson,* and John Singer Sargent.*

Mason. In "In the Cage," a name mentioned in a Lady Bradeen telegram.

Mason, Augustus and Maria. In "A Most Extraordinary Case," Colonel Ferdinand Mason's presumably deceased uncle and his kind wife. She tries unsuccessfully to nurse the colonel back to health.

Mason, Colonel Ferdinand. In "A Most Extraordinary Case," the convalescent Civil War veteran who grows worse and dies upon learning that Caroline Hofmann is to marry Dr. Horace Knight. Mason is unsuccessfully nursed by Mrs. Maria Mason.

Massin, Mme. In "Fordham Castle," the proprietress of a Swiss pension to which the wife of Abel F. Taker has sent him.

Masson, David (1822–1907). Scottish editor, historian, essayist, biographer, and professor of English literature in London. His best-known work is his *Life of Milton in Connexion with the History of His Own Time* (6 vols., 1859–1880). James reviewed (*Nation*, 18 Feb 1875) Masson's *Three Devils: Luther's, Milton's, and Goethe's; With Other Essays* (1874), branding the author at the outset interesting, but also vulgar and lacking in power. He summarizes and comments on Masson's discussion of Luther's devil (real), Milton's (exalted, poetic), and Goethe's (exquisite). James commends Masson's "handsome portrait" of young Milton, whom James calls a priggish, austere genius. James then responds in general terms to comments by Masson on William Wordsworth, John Dryden, and William Shakespeare,* and on scientific progress and contemporary cleverness.

"Master Eustace." Short story (10,700 words), published in the *Galaxy* (Nov 1871); reprinted in *Stories Revived*, 1885. (Characters: Cope, Eustace Garnyer, Henry Garnyer, and Mrs. Henry Garnyer.) Pampered Eustace Garnyer is reared by his widowed mother with the help of the narrator, a governess-companion. The lad goes to Europe at the age of seventeen at the urging of businessman Cope of India who, in the boy's absence, returns and marries Mrs. Garnyer. Eustace comes back home and raises such a howl that Cope must explain: He, not the idolized Mr. Garnyer, is the lad's father. Although Eustace must be restrained from committing suicide, his mother dies anyway of shock and a broken heart. This early, ugly story is a psychological case history of a spoiled kid, with Hamlet-Gertrude and Oedipus overtones.

Masters, Miss. In "A Most Extraordinary Case," a guest at a dance at the home of Edith Stapleton. Sick Colonel Ferdinand Mason rashly attended.

"Maud Blandy." Tentative title of "The Papers."

"Maud-Evelyn." Short story (10,200 words), published in the *Atlantic Monthly* (Apr 1900); reprinted in *The Soft Side*, 1900. (Characters: Maud-Evelyn Dedrick, Mr. and Mrs. Dedrick, Lady Emma, Mrs. Jex, Marmaduke.) The narrator Lady Emma recalls both Lavinia's rejection of Marmaduke long ago and also later circumstances in his life. Marmaduke hoped to work for his uncle in England after completing a tour in Switzerland, but while he was still there he met Mr. and Mrs. Dedrick, and he continued his travels with them. Back in England, he explained matters to both Lady Emma and Lavinia. It seems that after their daughter Maud-Evelyn's death at age fourteen, the Dedricks went to mediums to communicate with her spirit. Later they adopted Marmaduke, who gradually began to imagine with the parents a past life they all shared. The Dedricks included Maud-Evelyn in their fantasy: They began to believe that she was older than she really was when she died—that, in fact, she was married to Marmaduke. From time to time, Lavinia saw him and began to accept the fantasy. Then the

Dedricks died and left everything to their "son-in-law," who died three years later, tended by curiously sympathetic Lavinia. Marmaduke leaves his inherited effects to her, and Lady Emma plans to see them soon. According to several Notebook entries (22 Sep 1895, 7 May 1898, 11 Sep 1900, 12 Jun 1901), the source of this morbid tale of decorous necrophilia and "what might have been" was a story idea by Italian fiction writer Luigi Gualdo.* It was mentioned to James (*Notebooks*, 22 Sep 1895) by Paul Bourget* and his wife. James was also well aware of the Provençal "foible" of preferring the imagined to the real and then believing that the imagined has happened. In his 1883 essay on Alphonse Daudet,* James comments on this "foible" as dramatized in Daudet's *Tartarin de Tarascon* (1872). "Maud-Evelyn" is fascinating but absurd. James abandoned a short story to be called "Hugh Merrow" because it too closely resembled both "Maud-Evelyn" and "The Tone of Time."

Maule, Fanny. In "Poor Richard," Richard Maule's sister, who is now married and living with her husband in California.

Maule, Mrs. George. In "Julia Bride," a woman described by Julia Bride to Pitman as hating her and her mother, since Mrs. Maule wants any one of her four daughters to marry Basil French, whom Julia likes.

Maule, Richard. In "Poor Richard," the unstable young man who loves his rural neighbor Gertrude Whittaker. During the Civil War, he and Major Robert Luttrel lie to her about Captain Edmund Severn, whom she loves. When Severn is killed, Richard becomes despondent, resumes his habit of drinking, recovers to a degree, warns Gertrude about Luttrel, and leaves the region.

Maule, The Misses. In "Julia Bride," Mrs. George Maule's four daughters.

Maupassant, Guy de (1850–1893). Greatest French short-story writer, born near Dieppe to a Paris stockbroker and his wife, both with Norman family backgrounds. Disliking his father, who often lived apart from the family, young Maupassant grew up in a château near Le Havre. He became a student (finally studying law in Paris), and served in the Army during the Franco-Prussian War. He then tried to write plays, became a government clerk, was a protégé of Gustave Flaubert,* through whom he met Émile Zola* and Edmond de Goncourt,* and in 1880 published "Boule de Suif" (his first and one of the greatest of his three hundred or so stories). He became a prolific, well-paid free-lance writer; traveled to Corsica, Algeria, and later England; published *Un Vie* (1883), the first of his seven novels; wrote three travel books; contracted syphilis; suffered from eye trouble, migraine headaches, overuse of a variety of drugs, and finally locomotor paralysis; had hallucinations; and tried to commit suicide a year before he died in a Passy insane asylum. Zola delivered an eloquent tribute to Maupassant on the occasion of his funeral. Jacques-Émile Blanche* wrote a *roman* *à clef* entitled *Aymeris* (1922) about Maupassant's circle of decadent friends. It is hard to list the best *contes* of Guy de Maupassant, but surely "La Maison Tellier" (1881), "Les Bijoux" (1883), "La Ficelle" (1883), "Mademoiselle Fifi" (1883), "Miss Harriet" (1884), "La Parure" (1884), "Les Soeurs Rondoli" (1884), "L'Héritage" (1884), and "Monsieur Parent" (1885) should be included. Maupassant's novels include *Bel-Ami* (1885), *Mont-Oriol* (1887), and *Pierre et Jean* (1888). James first met Maupassant, then unpublished, at the Parisian home of Flaubert. In May 1877 they saw each other there again. When, in August 1886, Maupassant visited England, James not only arranged a dinner at Greenwich for him—along with George du Maurier,* Sir Edmund Wilson Gosse,* and Maupassant's friend Count Joseph-Napoléon Primoli*—but also spent some days with him at Waddesdon, a Rothschild family* château near Aylesbury. While Maupassant was in England, James met Blanche Roosevelt,* one of the French writer's many *amours plus élégants*, who escorted her lover around London and then to Oxford, which she said Paul Bourget* had urged Maupassant to visit. Anecdotes abound concerning James's response to Maupassant's ruinous sensuality. James long remembered an obscene yarn which Maupassant had told him at a Flaubert Sunday afternoon in 1875 or 1876 about two or three men (one of whom may have been Algernon Charles Swinburne*) and a pet monkey which caused fatal jealousy. James wrote to Robert Louis Stevenson* (30 Oct 1891) that Maupassant was dying of "the fruit of fabulous habits, I am told. . . . I shall miss him." James wrote two essays on Maupassant. The first essay, "Guy de Maupassant" (*Fortnightly Review*, Mar 1888; reprinted in *Partial Portraits*, 1888), has become a classic. James begins it by noting that Maupassant is a "soft" commentator on fiction but that his fiction has "an essential hardness." He is right when noting the necessary uniqueness of each fiction writer's viewpoint on reality and "truth." We must accept Maupassant's premises, since the man writes from a strength granted by distinct gifts. Life appeals to him almost exclusively through the senses, especially that of smell and of quick vision. He is aware of the dominance of sex. Maupassant is "a lion in the path," and he must be judged not by what he leaves out but by what he puts in. He does not analyze but confines himself to viewing the passing parade. Since each method, however, has bits of other methods in it, we expect some consideration of motives and are sad to note that "the sexual impulse . . . is . . . the wire that moves almost all M. de Maupassant's puppets." Although the French language has been worn by "three centuries of literature," Maupassant has enough faith in it to be patient. He uses forceful, firm, "masculine" language. His short stories are characteristic and original. Although Nathaniel Hawthorne,* Edgar Allan Poe,* and Bret Harte* are eminent in America in the genre, Maupassant has the advantage of "a tradition of indecency" and the "obscene" to build on. He stares at the "shabby, sordid" and squeezes until it "grimaces or . . . bleeds"—all to "droll" or "horrible" effects. Maupassant sees life as an ugliness relieved by the comical; but mostly "the comedy [is] of misery, of avidity, of ignorance, helplessness, and grossness." His short stories mainly concern Norman peasants, Parisian shopkeepers, and characters who are "fantastic, . . . whimsical, . . . weird, . . . supernatural, as well as the unexpurgated." He uses dialect well, especially in "La Maison Tellier." Citing examples, James theorizes that Maupassant handles misery and heroism with tenderness, and he avoids bestiality. But look at his omissions: sports, an awareness of decorum, the need for action, respect, sincerity, childhood. We see little pleasantness, less optimism. English writers show what we should pity rather than hate life. Look at Maupassant's "Monsieur Parent" (about ugliness) and "L'Héritage" (about ineptitude). Maupassant's female characters are detestable, sensual, mendacious. As for his novels, their negatives often make them "less complete." *Un Vie* is an "interesting experiment" and *Pierre et Jean* is "faultless." But *Bel-Ami*, though energetic enough to bribe us into liking it, relies on the "physiological" to explain all: Is every man a cad? every woman a harlot? *Mont-Oriol* seems "full of queerness"; in it, picture is more important than idea. *Un Vie* James sees as made dreary by omissions and formlessness. We need more verisimilitude, as in English fiction. It seems that if Maupassant does not treat "libertinage" he must turn only to "unmitigated suffering." *Pierre et Jean* is "masterly," its author's "best" novel. Pierre is neither helpless nor beastly, but responsible. Neither central character is cultivated, because making them so would give the novel too much beauty, and Maupassant must "belittle." Still, he is that lion in the path, to be reckoned with. Sadly, he leaves out "the whole reflective part of his men and women," and they show (except for Pierre) no "capacity for [disciplined] conduct." Maupassant is "at once so licentious and so impeccable," but fiction writers can follow and act as other examples. James's second essay on Maupassant is shorter (*Harper's Weekly*, 19 Oct 1889); reprinted as an introduction to *The Odd Number* (New York: Harper, 1889), a selection of thirteen Maupassant tales. It begins with comments about the difficulties English-speaking readers have with French authors and foreign scenes. Maupassant troubles but challenges foreign critics; James braves the difficulty in order to recommend him. We must leave him alone or accept him on his own terms. James discusses Maupassant in connection with Flaubert. Maupassant is aware of mortality, with its "beguilements and . . . woes." His style is unique: "concise and direct," vivid and colorful. His sensory perceptions are striking. He has droll, "cruel humor." "La Ficelle" "is a pure gem." Maupassant wrote so copiously that much is spotty and limited. It is encouraging that his most recent novels have "shades of feeling and delicacies of experience" not seen in his earlier work. James's short story "Paste" both parallels Maupassant's "Les Bijoux" and reverses the situation of his more famous "La Parure." In his various critical works, James cites about thirty-five of Maupassant's titles. Over and over, when in Notebook entries James happens to discuss fictional brevity, he mentions Maupassant. James's library contained fourteen books by Maupassant.

Mauves, Count Richard de. In"Madame de Mauves," Madame Euphemia Cleve de Mauves's philandering husband and Mme. Marie de Mauves Clairin's brother. When he repents but then fails to win his wife's forgiveness, he commits suicide.

Mauves, Countess Euphemia Cleve de. In "Madame de Mauves," Count Richard de Mauves's American wife and the object of Longmore's timid affections.

Mauves, Mme. de In "Madame de Mauves," the grandmother of Count Richard de Mauves and Mme. Marie de Mauves Clairin. She is puzzled by Euphemia Cleve, who later becomes Richard's wife.

Mavis, Grace (Gracie). In "The Patagonia," David Porterfield's fiancée. She is the object of so much gossip aboard the *Patagonia* because of selfish Jasper Nettlepoint's flirtatious ways that she commits suicide by jumping overboard.

Mavis, Mr. and Mrs. In "The Patagonia," Grace Mavis's parents. Her father is sickly. Her mother is Mrs. Nettlepoint's friend.

Max. In "The Siege of London," Mrs. Nancy Grenville Beck Headway's courier.

Mayfair. A weekly journal, established 2 January 1877 in London and running to 14 February 1880, which, along with *Truth*,* another weekly journal, established 4 January 1877 in London, James lightly ridicules in an untitled note (*Nation*, 1 Feb 1877). He exposes both as frivolous, gossipy, and "personal," but he adds that they are "more 'gentlemanly' " than their American counterparts. He ambivalently predicts that both *Mayfair* and *Truth* "will achieve the success . . . they deserve."

Mazade, Charles de (1821–1893). French writer and journalist for *Revue de Paris* and *Revue des Deux Mondes*. James reviewed (*Nation*, 30 Dec 1875) Mazade's 1875 *Revue des Deux Mondes* article on French literature and the Empire. The two agree that few meritorious authors flourished between 1848 and 1870. James ventures to nominate Joseph Ernest Renan* and Hippolyte Taine*; regards the Empire's so-called moral writers as dull, Napoleon III "hollow," and other writings "unclean"; but asks whether any government can help or harm literature. James reviewed (*Lippincott's Magazine*, Dec 1877) Mazade's 1877 *The Life of Count Cavour*, calling the work "interesting" and the subject a drama of formal parts. Magnetic Camillo Benso Cavour combined talent and use of circumstance, prudence and boldness, moderation and liberalism. He used Napoleon III and England realistically, and he planned beyond his own death.

James feels that Mazade slights both Giuseppe Mazzini and Giuseppe Garibaldi. James's library included one book by Mazade.

Meadows, Minnie. In "The Next Time," a humorist whose popular works contrast with Ralph Limbert's serious writing.

Medwin, Mrs. In "Mrs. Medwin," a woman who pays Mamie Cutter to obtain an introduction for herself into British society.

Meissonier, Jean-Louis-Ernest (1815–1891). Nearsighted French painter noted both for handling minute detail and for failing at epic effects. He began as an illustrator of books, after which he exhibited detailed, old-fashioned genre paintings (often of military life), beginning at the Salon in 1834. Perhaps his best big works are the documentary *Napoleon III at Solferino*, which records the Italian adventure he went with the army on, and *Campaign in France, 1814*. In "Art" (Jan 1872) James confesses that he could never become fond of paintings by Meissonier. Next, in "The Bethnal Green Museum" (1873) he laments their "elaborate immobility." In "Parisian Sketches" (1876) he calls the man "that prince of miniaturists," defines his *Battle of Friedland* (also called simply *1807*) as "a thing of parts rather than an interesting whole," and ridicules the perfect little soldiers for not being "place[d] . . . in any complex relation." James is also critical of the high price paid for it by Alexander Turney Stewart.* In "Art and Letters in Paris" (1876), James notes that "a couple of small but superlative Meissoniers," which he describes carefully, are for sale at a Paris art market; he concludes that he admires but does not care for Meissonier.

Meldrum, Mrs. In "Glasses," a bespectacled friend who introduces the painter narrator to Flora Louise Saunt.

Mellifont, Lord and Lady. In "The Private Life," a pleasant couple. He is an affably fluent man who is literally nothing without an audience. His personality is said to have been based on that of James's friend Lord Frederick Leighton,* a fashionable painter. Lady Mellifont seems to know that her husband is windily empty.

Mengin, Urbain (1869–1955). French critic and poet. His books include *L'Italie des romantiques* (1902, stressing George Gordon, Lord Byron,* John Keats, and Percy Bysshe Shelley,* in addition to several French writers), *Benozzo Gozzoli* (1909), and *Les Deux Lippi* (1932). Through Paul Bourget,* Mengin enjoyed the hospitality of James beginning in 1887 in England, where he taught and tutored French and studied English. James introduced Mengin to his friend Millicent Fanny St. Claire-Erskine, Duchess of Sutherland,* who employed Mengin to tutor her in Italian and to tutor her son in French. Beginning in the early 1890s, James wrote to Mengin several times (and in three languages) about literature, languages, and the younger man's work, especially on the English romantics. Mengin split with Bourget during the Dreyfus Affair because of the latter's anti-Semitic attitude toward Alfred Dreyfus.*

Meredith, George (1828–1909). English novelist, poet, and literary adviser. He was a schoolboy in Germany (until age sixteen), turned from law work in London to journalism there, and soon published contributions to periodicals. He met several pre-Raphaelites and also Charles Algernon Swinburne,* with whom he lived for a time. Meredith was a valued reader and adviser for a London publisher for thirty-five years. As such, he encouraged William Black,* Thomas Hardy,* and George Gissing.* Meredith's first wife, a strange woman, deserted him in 1858 and died three years later; his second died in 1884. Some of his best poetry is found in *Modern Love and Poems of the English Roadside* (1862). His novels include *The Ordeal of Richard Feverel* (1859), *Evan Harrington* (1861), *Emilia in England* (1864, renamed *Sandra Belloni*, 1886), *Rhoda Fleming* (1865), *Vittoria* (1867, a sequel to *Emilia in England*), *The Adventures of Harry Richmond* (1871, its sequel is *Beauchamp's Career*, 1876, the author's favorite among his novels), *The Egoist* (1879), *The Tragic Comedians* (1880), *Diana of the Crossways* (1885, uniquely popular), *One of Our Conquerors* (1891), and *Lord Ormont and His Aminta* (1894). From 1892 Meredith was paralyzed. As a teenager James read Meredith's fiction in serial publication, for example, in *Once a Week* in 1860. He preferred the style of Ivan Sergeyevich Turgenev,* who, according to a letter James wrote to William Ernest Henley* (28 Aug [1878]), "is most absolutely opposite to—the *un*realists—the *literary* story-tellers," such as Meredith. Later in 1878 James met Meredith at a dinner party and described him in a letter to his sister [31 Dec 1878]) as "a singular but decidedly brilliant fellow, full of talk, paradoxes, affectations, etc.; but interesting and witty." To Grace Norton* James wrote (c. 4 Jan [1888]) of Meredith, "I don't adore him, but I scoff still less, for he is brilliantly intelligent and the wreck of a prodigious wit. He is much the wittiest Englishman . . . that I have ever known." Meredith attended the opening performance of James's play *The American* in London, on 26 September 1891. Somewhat harshly, James wrote to Sir Edmund Wilson Gosse* (22 Aug [1894]) that he could read Meredith's *Lord Ormont* only "ten insufferable and unprofitable pages" at a time because of its prolix "obscurities and alembications," adding later (8 Sep [1894]) that the work is "infamous." All the same, James wrote to Alphonse Daudet* (22 Apr [1895]) that Meredith is "nôtre vieux romancier glorieux," and a month later, he arranged for a dramatic meeting between Daudet and Meredith at the latter's home at Dorking, in Surrey. In "London" (6 Feb 1897), James uses the publication of new volumes in "the beautiful, the stately 'definitive' edition of George Meredith" (ultimately 39 vols., 1896–1912) as an excuse for discussing the general subject of definitive editions of major authors. Then in "London" (27 Mar 1897), he defines as "dazzling" Meredith's 1877 lecture on "The Idea of Comedy." Late in his life, James often wrote to Gosse about Meredith. When the dead novelist's son W. M. Meredith edited *The Letters of George Meredith* (2 vols., 1912), James wrote (10 Oct 1912) that the letters "emanat[e] . . . something so admirable and . . . so baffled and so tragic," adding, however, that the job of editing is "mean . . . and poor." Later (11 Oct 1912) James, still troubled by Meredith's letters, notes "their rather marked non-illustration of his intellectual worth": their "aesthetic range . . . [is] meagre and short." James reports that he did not send the editor the few "charming and kind" notes he had received from Meredith, "preferr[ing] . . . to keep [them] unventilated." Next (13 Oct 1912) James criticizes Meredith for handling the French language poorly, for his uncritical opinion of Daudet's works, and for his evident ignorance of Honoré de Balzac.* Finally, James says (15 Oct 1912) that Meredith was "not an *entire* mind"; the stylistic side was less developed than the "moral" and the "manly." Late in his life, James talked with his Rye neighbor Sir Sydney Philip Waterlow* about Meredith, expressing admiration for his personal stoicism. In one Notebook entry (10 Feb 1899), James records a plot situation which Meredith mentioned and which resulted in "The Great Condition." In an even earlier Notebook entry (16 Mar 1894), James begins to tease himself with another idea from Meredith, about sexual prowess, which proved too hot for James to handle. Both writers admired ambiguity, analysis, and feminine sensitivity and both scorned British crudeness; however, Meredith had a more Celtic love of Mother Nature and of human passion. James's friend the playwright Alfred Sutro* adapted Meredith's *The Egoist* to the stage (1929). James's library contained fourteen books by Meredith and one edition of his works.

Meredith, Miss. In "A Light Man," rich Frederick Sloane's niece who, in the absence of a will, receives his money at his death.

Meredith, Mrs. In *Still Waters*, Emma's sister, unseen because she is sick. Horace goes to the village for medicine for her.

Mérimée, Prosper (1803–1870). Versatile French fiction writer, dramatist, essayist, linguist, translator, historian, and archaeologist, who was also a government official, courtier, and diplomat. He was born in Paris; his father was a painter and his mother was partly English. He studied law, tried public service, and quickly succeeded as a writer—combining romantic themes and classical control. In Spain in 1831 Mérimée met the Countess of Montijo, the mother of the future Empress Eugénie (wife of Napoleon III), later one of his closest friends at court. He was elected to the French Academy in 1844. His temperament was strange: cynical, aloof, sarcastic, dry, loyal. His main writings are fictional, historical, and epistolary. His leading works include *Chronique de Charles IX* (1829), "Matteo Falcone" (1829), "Tamango" (1829), "La Vénus d'Ille" (1837), *Colomba* (1841), *Carmen* (1845), "Lokis" (1869), "La Chambre bleue" (1872), *Les Dernières Nouvelles* (1873), and collections of letters to "*inconnues*" (to Jenny Dacquin, published in 1874, and to Countess Lise Przezdziecka, published in 1875). In 1860 or so John La Farge* suggested that James read some Mérimée. James did, and even sent his translations of two tales ("Tamango" and "La Vénus d'Ille") to a publisher, with no success. James wrote from London (27 Nov [1880]) to chide his brother William for having "bullied" him to condense in his early fiction à la Mérimée. James reviewed (*Nation*, 12 Feb 1874) Mérimée's *Dernières Nouvelles*, calling them "chiselled and polished little fictions" and their author "limited but perfect." He even says that Victor-Marie Hugo* and George Sand* should have followed, respectively, Mérimée's "sobriety" and "conciseness." Mérimée has such "pregnant brevity" that his tales are rereadable. Typically they are romantic and picturesque, have bloody and naughty action, and no sentiment. Their brutal subjects are expressed cynically. James especially likes "La Vénus d'Ille" and "Lokis." He reviewed (*Independent*, 9 Apr 1874; reprinted in *French Poets and Novelists*, 1878) Mérimée's *Lettres à une Inconnue* (Jenny Dacquin), much liking their "easy, full-flavoured, flexible prose." Then James voices his famous early opinion concerning Mérimée's dozen best tales that it should be "a capital offence in a young story-teller to put pen to paper without having read them and digested them." Before turning to the letters proper, James notes that in his fiction Mérimée suppresses emotion to present his action saliently—action concerning adultery, murder, and catastrophe. James is intrigued by Mérimée's writing letters to "an unknown" for more than thirty years. James indicates the letter writer's homely, unloving frankness here by ample quotations. Should we be compassionate toward the lady? Was she prudish, as Mérimée says, or merely modest? Should she have published his letters? Any tenderness which he expressed toward her disappeared in time, "but by absorption . . . not by evaporation." The second volume is less personal, more worldly, more cynical, with "mingled brevity and laxity." James concludes that Hippolyte Taine* was right in saying that Mérimée so feared being duped that he became a dupe of his own mistrust. In old age he grew contemptuous, and he liked only sunshine and good food. These letters are personal and racy, limited but palpably individual. James more briefly reviewed (*Nation*, 27 Jan 1876) Mérimée's *Lettres à une autre Inconnue* (Countess Przezdziecka), calling them reticent and not valuable. He quotes to show the vapidity of their court gossip. James informs Connecticut author Louise Chandler Moulton in a letter (20 Oct [1876]) that "the two best volumes of tales by Mérimée are *Colomba* and *Carmen*." In a letter to Grace Norton* (29 Oct [1883]), James comments that Mérimée "was a cynic of cynics, . . . and I haven't any particular pity for him in his old age." Years later, James published an essay entitled "Prosper Mérimée" (*Literature*, 23 Jul 1898), mainly to note the appearance of two books on Mérimée by Pierre Marie Augustin Filon.* Now downgrading Mérimée a bit, James calls him immortal but not infinite, in fact, "superficial," "[l]imited and hard" (though also "complete"). James subjectively records his youthful thrill upon first encountering "La Vénus d'Ille," adds that he tried to translate two of Mérimée's early tales, and says that some of Mérimée's work achieves "masterpiece" status by virtue of selection and concision. Naming some favorites, James concludes that Mérimée wrote best but did not become best. What about his soul? His letters reveal him to be worldly, idiosyncratic, coarse, even priggish. His English was flawless, and he knew the highest ladies at court; but perhaps his fine writing owed something to his having more leisure than, say, Honoré de Balzac* and Théophile Gautier.* James's library contained three books by Mérimée.

Merle, Serena. In *The Portrait of a Lady*, a Swiss merchant's widow and the former mistress of Gilbert Osmond, by whom she had Pansy Osmond. She is Lydia Touchett's friend and Isabel Archer's victimizer.

Merriman, Arthur and Joanna. In "A New England Winter," a New England couple who are the parents of six children. Joanna is Florimond Daintry's sister.

Merriman, Miss. In *The Awkward Age*, Agnesina's governess.

Merrow, Hugh. In "Hugh Merrow," the unmarried, lonely painter to whom Captain and Mrs. Archdean successfully appeal in London for a portrait of the child they never had and never can have.

Mesh, Donald and Pauline. In "A New England Winter," a New England couple. Donald is related to Rachel Torrance. Pauline is Lucretia Daintry's friend. When Florimond Dainty appears to be falling for Mrs. Mesh, his mother urges him to return to Paris.

Meynell, Alice Christiana Gertrude (née Thompson) (1847–1922). Prolific English poetess, religious essayist, biographer (of John Ruskin,* 1900), anthologist, and editor (with her husband Wilfrid Meynell). She resided in Italy in her early life, then published poetry (from 1893) and much else, twice putting selections of her essays into book form (1914, 1921). In "London" (6 Feb 1897), James praises her book *The Children* (1896) for displaying her "sense of subject," "singular acuteness" of observation, and lace maker's "concision."

Meyrau, Vicomte Louis de. In "A Tragedy of Error," Hortense Bernier's lover, who is erroneously murdered instead of her husband Charles Bernier.

Michael. In "A Most Extraordinary Case," Colonel Ferdinand Mason's servant.

Michael. In *Still Waters*, Mrs. Meredith's servant, who is probably an alcoholic.

Middlemas, Dr. and Mrs. In "A Most Extraordinary Case," Colonel Ferdinand Mason's New York physician and his wife. Through Mrs. Middlemas, Maria Mason learned of Mason's sickness.

Middleton, Mrs. In *Watch and Ward*, a would-be matchmaker who brings Roger Lawrence and Miss Sands together.

"The Middle Years." Short story (7,500 words), published in *Scribner's Magazine* (May 1893); reprinted in *Terminations*, 1895; revised and reprinted in *The Novels and Tales of Henry James*, Volume XVI, 1909. (Characters: Dencombe, Dr. Hugh, Miss Vernham.) Novelist Dencombe, widowed and now childless, is convalescing at Bournemouth from a serious illness. While he is sitting near the water and fingering the text of his latest book, which is entitled *The Middle Years*, Dr. Hugh suddenly leaves two women companions to come over and discuss the book. Dencombe becomes confused and faints. By the time he revives, Dr. Hugh has recognized him as the author and comforts him professionally. The novelist learns that Dr. Hugh is traveling with a sick, rich countess and her companion Miss Vernham; soon, however, he starts paying attention only to Dencombe, whose work he reveres (without, perhaps, quite understanding it). Miss Vernham brutally demands that the novelist stop monopolizing the physician, who could thus lose a bequest from his patient. A few days later, Dencombe has a dreadful relapse; he is attended by Dr. Hugh, who cheerfully tells him that the countess died and left him nothing. In a short Notebook entry (12 May 1892), James records the idea for this story, which, as worked out, has obvious autobiographical undercurrents. In the preface to Volume XVI of *The Novels and Tales of Henry James*, James registers his pleasure at successfully "keep[ing] compression rich" in "The Middle Years," which he adds is an example of "the concise anecdote." The moral of this perfect little story is not only that *ars [est] longa, vita brevis*, but that life is often too short even to give an artist, or anyone else, any second chance. Also that, as James has Dencombe triumphantly say, "We work in the dark—we do what we can—we give what we have." Furthermore, a lonely person achieves success if he or she has made someone care. It is charming that in several printings of this story, including the one in *The Novels and Tales of Henry James*, the tale begins with a numbered part I, followed, like Dencombe's career, with no part II. Eerily, the autobiographical volume which death prevented James from completing is entitled *The Middle Years*.

The Middle Years. Third (incomplete) volume of James's projected autobiography, published in *Scribner's Magazine* (Oct, Nov 1917); reprinted in London by Collins, 1917, and in New York by Scribner, 1917. (The first and second volumes are *A Small Boy and Others*, 1913, and *Notes of a Son and Brother*, 1914.) *The Middle Years* comprises seven chapters. 1. In March 1869 James, feeling young, landed at Liverpool and began to know impressions, revelations, recognitions, and meanings, in short, to renew his "vision of Europe." London, after his nine-year absence, was full of "images . . . of . . . saved intensity." He rented rooms in Half-Moon Street and soon began his "penetration of the London scene." 2. Helped at first by a fine landlord, James soon began to regard "mid-Victorian London" as "unaccommodating," "imperturbable," "overgrown," but "sincere." 3. He felt happily "disconnected" from America, but bright Londoners asked him, at breakfast and at other times, embarrassing questions about American current events. Further, he talked with embarrassingly profound fellow guests of Charles Eliot Norton* and his wife, then in London. The city's "very stones" began to offer him "sermons" and to "chatter" at James. 4. He recalls the "local colour" of many a Dickensian "eating-house," rows of cabs along Piccadilly, the theaters, the art galleries—he saw Algernon Charles Swinburne* at one of them—and museums. James haunted them "with a sense of duty and of excitement." He inspected courts, castles, heaths, commons, towers, and churches. Later he visited "socially sinister Dickens" regions near the Thames. 5. From many a remembered "social contact" enjoyed at this time, James selects George Eliot,* whom he met through the Nortons in April 1869. He recalls her books, her appearance, her conversation about a trip to France, and her husband George Lewes's injured son. James connects his going for a doctor to treat the youth with his own reading of later Eliot novels. This in turn reminds him of other visits to Eliot (in 1878), one of which he describes in detail, ending with the report that she hurriedly returned to Mrs. Greville, his escort from Surrey, the "declined" loan of a novel [*The Europeans*] he had written: She had not known it was his. 6. Mrs. Greville also took James (in 1878) to Aldworth to see Alfred, Lord Tennyson,* whom James recalls also encountering in London, and whom he generally found in person "not Tennysonian" (not "fine," not "fastidious," indeed, not intellectually "experience[d]"); James was a luncheon guest once with James Russell Lowell* at the Tennysons. James was disappointed in Tennyson's dull (if bardic) reading aloud of "Locksley Hall" to him at Aldworth and contrasts it with some animated (but not bardic) readings by Robert Browning.* 7. James recalls a London dinner given by Mrs. Greville and graced by a Victorian painter, Lady [Louise] Waterford, who possessed "genius as well as . . . beauty." This leads "the fond analyst" to theorize that old persons from his past "triumphed over time" better than do young persons from his present. Today we are mainly "a vast monotonous mob," and few of us are "touched . . . with the elder grace." James felt these conclusions to be validated when he attended a charity exhibition of some of Lady Waterford's work and later when he visited a beautiful Northumberland house belonging to her husband's family.

Midmore, Molly. In *The Sense of the Past*, the conservative fiancée of the eighteenth-century Ralph Pendrel. When the present Ralph Pendrel meets her, he prefers her more modern sister Nancy.

Midmore, Mrs. In *The Sense of the Past*, Ralph Pendrel's London tenant. She is the mother of Molly, Nancy, and Peregrine Midmore.

Midmore, Nancy (Nan). In *The Sense of the Past*, conservative Molly Midmore's more modern sister. Though engaged to Molly, Ralph Pendrel prefers Nancy.

Midmore, Peregrine (Perry). In *The Sense of the Past*, Molly and Nancy Midmore's rather thick brother.

Miles. In "The Turn of the Screw," the precocious nephew, age ten, of the governess's employer. Miles is Flora's brother. He is perhaps victimized by Peter Quint's spirit.

Millais, Sir John Everett (1829–1896). English painter, illustrator, and watercolorist. With William Holman Hunt* and Dante Gabriel Rossetti,* he established the Pre-Raphaelite Brotherhood (1848–1849). John Ruskin,* whose ex-wife Millais later married (in 1855, after her nullity decree), helped to popularize his work. After 1860 Millais broke from the Pre-Raphaelites. He became a high-society portraitist, numbering Thomas Carlyle* and Sir Henry Irving* among his subjects. He illustrated some of the novels by Anthony Trollope* and worked for *Once a Week* and other magazines. James comments in gallery reviews on Millais's work, but rarely in detail or in unqualified praise. In various notes to the *Nation*, James touches on Millais thus: "this strangely unequal painter . . . [of] imperfectly great powers" (23 May 1878); even though he is "the strongest genius present" in any exhibition in which his works appear, he "coquets" in an effort to be "amusing or . . . edifying," while a certain landscape of his has "some admirable painting, but with a curiously motionless and photographic quality" (6 Jun 1878); his 1879 portrait of William Ewart Gladstone* "is a brilliant success" (29 May 1879). In "London" (5 Jun 1897), James says that telling the story of Millais's career—fine youth, weak maturity—would have challenged Robert Browning.* More comprehensively elsewhere, James notes that "Millais . . . continues to be one of the most accomplished and most disappointing of painters" ("London Pictures and London Plays," 1882). In 1877, James did write about Millais's "indefeasible manliness" ("The Picture Season in London").

Miller, Annie P. (Daisy). In "Daisy Miller," an innocent, socially simple, naturally flirtatious American girl abroad with her uncomprehending mother and her noisy little brother Randolph. She intrigues stiff Frederick Forsyth Winterbourne first in Switzerland, where they visit the Château de Chillon, and then in Rome. When her Italian friend Giovanelli escorts her to the Colosseum long after dark, Daisy catches a fever. Poignantly, she sends word to Winterbourne that she was never engaged to Giovanelli and shortly thereafter dies. In *Daisy Miller: A Comedy in Three Acts*, Daisy is more shallow, flirts with both Winterbourne and Cavaliere Giacomo Giovanelli, is almost victimized by the Miller family courier Eugenio, recovers from her fever, goes into the streets (while still convalescing) during the carnival, is rescued by Winterbourne, and, once Madame de Katkoff has told Winterbourne that Daisy loves him, is proposed to by him and accepts him.

Miller, Mr. and Mrs. Ezra B. In "Daisy Miller," the rich parents of Daisy and Randolph Miller. While Ezra Miller stays home in Schenectady making money, his wife travels uncomprehendingly with their children in Europe. She competently nurses her daughter during her fatal sickness in Rome. In *Daisy Miller: A Comedy in Three Acts*, Mrs. Miller is even more simple; she never appears on stage. Once she learns that her daughter is recovering from the ill effects of going (while convalescing from her fever) into the streets during the Roman carnival, she goes back to bed.

Miller, Randolph. In "Daisy Miller," Daisy Miller's wild little brother, age nine, who prefers America to Europe, eats sugar, stays up too late, and is otherwise undisciplined. In *Daisy Miller: A Comedy in Three Acts*, Randolph adds a desire for cigars to his yen for candy, rides piggyback on Charles Reverdy, and frightens the adults by disappearing into the Roman streets at one point.

Millet, Francis Davis (1846–1912). Massachusetts-born painter, illustrator, and writer. He was a drummer boy during the Civil War, graduated from Harvard College (1869), and studied art in Antwerp (beginning 1871). During the Russo-Turkish War (1877–1878) he was a correspondent for London and New York newspapers. Millet had a studio at Broadway, in Worcestershire (shared by Edwin Austin Abbey* and John Singer Sargent,* among several other colleagues). During the Spanish-American War (1898–1899) he went to the Philippines as a correspondent for London and New York journals; later he undertook a government mission to Japan (1900). In 1912 Millet was lost on the *Titanic*. Among his books are *The Danube* (1891), *Capillary Crime and Other Stories* (1892), and *Expedition to the Philippines* (1899). While visiting Broadway in 1886, James met Millet and some of his fellow artists, whom he describes in a letter to his brother William (10 Sept 1886) as composing "a very pleasant and harmonious little artistic community," adding that Mrs. Millet was "charming." He wrote to William later that Millet "has ended up by painting very well indeed (he didn't at all at first) as a consequence of mere hard Yankee 'faculty' " (1 Oct 1887). James came to know Millet and his wife Lily very well. In "Our Artists in Europe" (1889; reprinted as "Black and White" in *Picture and Text*, 1893), James says that Millet was responsible for converting Broadway into the artists' haven it became: "[I]ts sweetness was wasted until he began to distil and bottle it." James praises Millet's versatility: The man created "striking sketches" of Russo-Turkish War soldiers and Oriental scenes as well as later *Harper's Magazine* black-and-white illustrations; in addition, he was a distinguished war correspondent ("[h]e has made pictures without words and words without pictures"), and he is a "clever" ghost-story writer. Millet attended the first performance of James's *Guy Domville*, on 5 January 1895. When Millet drowned, James wrote Lily a tender letter (18 Apr 1912), in which he offered his "participation."

Millington, Mr. and Mrs. In *The Princess Casamassima*, Broome neighbors of the Princess Casamassima.

Mills, Lady. In *The Wings of the Dove*, a guest at Milly Theale's party in Venice.

Millward, Mr. and Mrs. In "The Marriages," the host and hostess at whose home Colonel Chart and Mrs. Churchley have met.

Milsom, Mrs. In "The Death of the Lion," Fanny Hurter's sister.

Minch, Lady Augusta. In "The Death of the Lion," this lady and Lord Dorimont lose Neil Paraday's priceless last manuscript between them.

"The Mind of England at War." Title of a short essay (originally called "England at War: An Essay") by James in praise of England in wartime. It appeared as part of *England at War: An Essay: The Question of the Mind* (London: Central Committee for National Patriotic Organisations, 1915); reprinted in the New York *Sun* (18 Jun 1915) and the Philadelphia *Ledger* (18 Jun 1915).

Mirandola. In *The Bostonians*, a refugee whom Miss Birdseye once aided in Boston.

"Miss Gunton of Poughkeepsie." Short story (5,000 words), published in the *Cornhill Magazine* (May 1900), and in the New York *Truth Magazine* (May–Jun 1900); revised and reprinted in *The Novels and Tales of Henry James*, Volume XVI, 1909. (Characters: Adam P. Bransby, Mrs. Bransby, the Misses Bransby, Brine, Mrs. Brine, Lady Champer, Donna Claudia, Lily Gunton, Gunton). Lady Champer sympathizes with the prince, a crass Italian scion, on learning that rich, indulged Lily Gunton of Poughkeepsie seems to be toying with him. Although Lily admires Old-World tradition, she still wants the prince's mother to deviate from custom and write first to invite her into the family. Meanwhile, still encouraging the prince, Miss Gunton travels, from Rome to Paris to London, and finally to New York. The prince tells Lady Champer that his mother will probably write the demanded letter but will surely hate him afterward. Sure enough, the letter soon arrives. By this time, Lily has decided to refuse the invitation, and she becomes engaged instead to Adam P. Bransby, with whose family she returned home from London. The prince now learns that her grandfather has just died and has left her a fortune. The expected money was probably quite an attraction, but the prince tells Lady Champer that he really loved the girl, that his mother is disgraced socially, and that Miss Gunton most likely wanted mainly to humble a European family. According to a Notebook entry (27 Feb 1895), the idea for this story of different standards, stubborn pride, and the generation gap occurred to James when he heard about an incident of precisely the opposite

action: A rich American girl (actually the daughter of James's friend Katherine
De Kay Bronson*) wrote to her prospective Italian mother-in-law first.

"Mr. Henry James on England." Wartime letter by James to the editor of the
Observer (18 Apr 1915).

Mitchell, Father. In *The Golden Bowl*, Maggie Verver's unconsulted Roman
Catholic priest at the estate of Fawns.

Mitchett (Mitchy). In *The Awkward Age*, a wealthy member of Mrs. Brookenham's social circle. He loves Fernanda Brookenham, is rejected by her, and
marries Agnesina.

Mitton. In *The Tragic Muse*. Charles Carteret's lawyer. He arranges Carteret's
will to exclude Nick Dormer.

Mixter. In "The Four Meetings," the dull pupil of the "countess," who gives
him dilatory French lessons while sponging off Caroline Spencer.

Moddle. In *What Maisie Knew*, the nurse whom Beale Farange hired for his
daughter Maisie.

"The Modern Warning" (1888 title in magazine, "Two Countries"; 1888 title
in book, "The Modern Warning"). Short story (24,100 words), published in
Harper's New Monthly Magazine (Jun 1888); reprinted in *The Aspern Papers*,
1888. (Characters: Lady Bolitho, Sir Rufus Chasemore, Mrs. Eugene, Lady
Laura Fitzgibbon, Agatha Grice [Lady Chasemore], Macarthy Grice, Mrs. Grice,
Mrs. Long, Mrs. Redwood, Mrs. Ripley.) Mrs. Grice, with her daughter Agatha,
greets the arrival of her son Macarthy (Agatha's brother) near Lake Como. He
quickly removes uncomplaining Agatha from her suitor, a conservative Britisher
named Sir Rufus Chasemore. Six years later, when the pair has been married
for two years and Agatha's mother has been dead three, the Chasemores pay
New York a visit. While Agatha remains with her anti-British brother Macarthy,
Sir Rufus travels to see the United States. When she discovers that Rufus is
writing a book, to be called *The Modern Warning*, critical of American democracy, she persuades him to abandon it but then relents because she thinks that
his acquiescence is too generous. Later, just as Macarthy arrives at the Chasemore
door in London for a visit, servants scream the announcement that Agatha has
committed suicide. Sir Rufus blames Macarthy, whom he says his wife always
feared; in turn, Macarthy blames Sir Rufus for his critical British ways. This
improbably melodramatic yarn, as James reveals in a Notebook entry (9 Jul
1884), was initially inspired by his reading of *The Great Republic* (1884), an
anti-American book by Sir Lepel Henry Griffin, who was more astute in his

writings on India and Afghanistan. To counterbalance British Sir Rufus's anti-Americanism, James brings in American Macarthy Grice's Anglophobia.

Modern Women, and What Is Said of Them. An 1868, book-length reprint of anonymous articles in the *Saturday Review*. James reviewed the work (*Nation*, 22 Oct 1868) and called it trivial and vulgar, an irrational indictment of the marriage market and of women's concern with fashions. James would prefer to link women's follies to those of men. If women seem unfortunate, men should wonder if their own behavior is a cause.

Modjeska, Helena (1841–1909). Cracow-born actress. She made her debut in Poland in 1861, married in 1876, and moved to South Carolina. She performed in San Francisco in 1877 and later in New York and London. Seeing her on stage in London, James called her "charming and touching" and "exquisite" ("The London Theatres," 1881), furthermore, a "high-priestess" of the theater "with a great deal of art; with grace, with force, with intelligence, with a certain personal distinction" ("London Pictures and London Plays," 1882). Modjeska was interested in playing Claire de Cintré in James's *The American*, but she was not chosen. James wrote to her late in 1891 to suggest that she might prefer instead to perform in his *Tenants*; she read the script but declined.

Mohun, Lady. In *Guy Domville*, a London aristocrat who plays cards with Lord Devenish and Guy Domville.

Molesley, Lady. In "The Marriages," once Adela Chart's deceased mother's friend.

Molinari, Gustave de (1819–1912). Belgian political economist and journalist in Paris. He edited the *Journal des Débats* and the *Journal des Économistes*. James amusedly reviewed (*Nation*, 22 Feb 1877) Molinari's *Lettres sur les États-Unis et le Canada* (1876), noting that they are both entertaining and informative. He found it heartening that for a change a French commentator liked American things. James mentions Molinari's impressions of American scenery, cities, manners, politics, and culture. Molinari found French-Canada "uninstructed and . . . provincial." James finds his subject's political judgment naive.

Molyneux, Mildred. In *The Portrait of a Lady*, Lord Warburton's younger sister, who likes Isabel Archer.

Molyneux, Miss. In *The Portrait of a Lady*, another of Lord Warburton's sisters, who also likes Isabel Archer.

Monarch, Major and Mrs. In "The Real Thing," the painter narrator's amateur models, who prove too stiff and ineffectual, in fact too "real."

Monod, Auguste (1851–?). French man of letters, who translated James's "Paste" in 1909 and "The Siege of London" in 1912. James wrote to Monod several times on the subject of translation in general; in one letter (7 Sep 1913), he noted that it "is an effort—though a most flattering one!—to *tear* the hapless flesh, and in fact to get rid of so much of it that the living thing bleeds and faints away!"

A Monologue by Henry James. Short dramatic monologue James wrote in 1913 for Ruth Draper.* Declined with thanks, it was published as part of "Three Unpublished Letters and a Monologue by Henry James," London *Mercury* (September 1922), and as "The Presentation at Court" in *Vanity Fair* (December 1922). (Characters: Sir Robin Adair, Lynch, Marie, Alvin Tuff, Cora Tuff.) Cora Tuff, a rich American traveling through Europe, regally orders Lynch, the American legation secretary who calls on her at her London hotel, to get her a presentation at court—and quickly. She does not want her husband, who is back in New York making money, to come over to join her, that is, until his presence becomes a court requirement. Then she shows her adaptability by saying that will be nice. James met Draper, the American monologuist in 1913, was impressed by her ability, and sent an unsolicited monologue to her in December. She was grateful but never used it, since, as she explained, she recited only her own work.

Montaut, Guy de. In "The Solution," a French attaché in Rome. He and the narrator, as a joke, persuade callow Henry Wilmerding that he has compromised Veronica Goldie by walking in the woods unescorted with her.

Montbron, M. de. In *The Ambassadors*, the suitable young man selected to be Jeanne de Vionnet's husband by Comtesse Marie de Vionnet and Chad Newsome.

Monte-Carlo. Tentative title for a play which James planned to write based on his short story "The Chaperon." He completed only notes and part of a rough scenario.

Montégut, Émile (1825–1895). French literary critic and journalist. His translations include works by Thomas Babington Macaulay, William Shakespeare,* and Ralph Waldo Emerson.* In "In Belgium" (1873), James calls Montégut "acute," but he disputes his opinion that Peter Paul Rubens* was the world's greatest painter and that Rubens was thoughtful and dramatic. James reviewed (*Nation*, 23 Jul 1874) Montégut's *Souvenirs de Bourgogne* (1874), beginning with a summary of the author's accomplishments. He defines "pessimistic" Montégut as having a "peculiar . . . literary temperament" with a prolix and bookish but pleasantly "autumnal" style. His word pictures of Burgundian landscapes and monuments are ingeniously reflective. James early in 1876, first at the home of Auguste Laugel* and his wife and later in the salon of Louise

Adélaïde d'Eckmühl, Marquise de Blocqueville,* met Montégut, who was her pensioner, and described him in a letter to his sister Alice James from Paris (22 Feb [1876]) as "a little black man, with an abnormally shaped head and a crooked face," adding that he was "intense," humorless, shallow, and complacent. In a later letter (11 Apr [1876]), James reported to his father that he continued socially to meet Montégut, "whom I don't like so well as his writing." James in his *Hawthorne* repeatedly criticizes Montégut as "[a] very clever French critic, whose fancy is often more lively than his observation is deep," for wrongly calling Hawthorne a pessimistic romancer in a 1860 *Revue des Deux Mondes* essay. James's library contained one book by Montégut.

Monteith, Mark P. In "A Round of Visits," embezzler Phil Bloodgood's victim. He visits Florence Ash and Newton Winch.

Montenero. In "In the Cage," a name mentioned in a Lady Bradeen telegram.

Montesquiou-Fezensac, Robert, Comte de (1855–1921). Precious, bizarre, hyperrefined French homosexual poet, novelist, biographer, and memoirist. Joris-Karl Huysmans* used him (along with Gustave Moreau*) as a partial model for Des Esseintes in *À Rebours* (1884). James met Montesquiou by way of a letter of introduction from their mutual friend John Singer Sargent,* and he introduced him to James Abbott McNeill Whistler* in London in July 1885.

Montgomery, Mrs. In *Washington Square*, Morris Townsend's sister and the widowed mother of five children. Dr. Austin Sloper forces her to speak critically of her brother.

Montravers, Mora. In "Mora Montravers," the daughter of the half-sister of Jane Traffle, Mora's foster mother now. The girl marries Walter Puddick simply to gain some of Jane's money for him, whereupon she divorces him for a relationship with Sir Bruce Bagley.

Montravers, Mr. and Mrs. Malcolm In "Mora Montravers," Mora's deceased parents. Mrs. Montravers was Jane Traffle's half-sister.

Moore, Thomas (1779–1852). Dublin-born and -educated national lyricist of Ireland, musician, novelist, biographer, editor, and historian. He traveled in America, satirized the prince regent (1813), and wrote popular Oriental verse tales in a collection called *Lalla Rookh* (1817) and much else later, including a life of Richard Brinsley Sheridan (1825) and another of his close friend George Gordon, Lord Byron* (1830) and his *Memoirs* (8 vols., 1853–1856). James reviewed (*Nation*, 1 Apr 1875) *Personal Reminiscences of Moore and Jerdan*, selected and edited in 1875 by Richard Henry Stoddard.* James begins by lamenting the need in these busy times for books of extracts but commends

Stoddard for his "useful work" here. Moore's *Memoirs*, though "diffuse," contain "half the best anecdotes in the language." James rejoices that Moore commemorated literary conversations of such people as Byron (full of "unamiable folly"), Samuel Taylor Coleridge, Sir Walter Scott* (full of "genial good sense"), and Sydney Smith; and he summarizes Moore's researches into "Sheridan's smart sayings and loose doings."

Moore, Adela. In "A Day of Days," Herbert Moore's sister. When scientist Thomas Ludlow tries to visit Herbert but meets only Adela instead, the two poignantly attract one another—but only briefly.

Moore, Herbert. In "A Day of Days," Adela Moore's scientist brother whom Thomas Ludlow tries to visit but without success.

"Mora Montravers." Short story (21,800 words), published in the *English Review* (Aug–Sep 1909); reprinted in *The Finer Grain* 1910. (Characters: Sir Bruce Bagley, Mr. and Mrs. Malcolm Montravers, Mora Montravers, Walter Puddick, Jane and Sidney Traffle.) Jane Traffle's deceased half-sister's daughter Mora Montravers has been living with diffident Jane and her sensitive husband Sidney. The young woman, age twenty-one, now leaves them to join an arty group including painter Walter Puddick. She begins to lodge, probably innocently, in his studio. To protect her reputation, prim Jane offers Mora £450 per year if she will marry Puddick. The two do wed, so Jane must pay. Mora immediately leaves her husband. Traffle wistfully admires jaunty Mora and her independence. He returns from a chance encounter with her at an art gallery to learn that Puddick, a decent enough young fellow, had just charmed Jane into honorably continuing the annual stipend—which Mora made over to him before taking up with Sir Bruce Bagley. This plot is a subtle refinement on a piece of gossip James heard from George Ashburner (of the Ashburner family*) and recorded in his *Notebooks* (22 Aug 1901). It seems that a man living with the niece of "Sir J. S." feared that he would lose control of her if the two got married. The resulting refinement by James, with stress on the frustrated uncle and the prissy aunt, was the last short story he ever wrote.

Moreau, Gustave (1826–1898). Paris-born innovative and symbolist painter, the son of an architect. He was most famous for depicting religious and mythological subjects with perverse, erotic, and decadent twists. Often his pictures are more interesting for narrative content than for pictorial elements. His female figures often combine charm and cruelty. In the 1853 Salon he exhibited *Scene from the Song of Songs* and *Death of Darius*. His most famous works include *Oedipus and the Sphinx*, *Orpheus*, *Hercules and the Hydra of Lernos*, *Salomé Dancing before Herod*, *Galatea*, *Hesiod and the Muse*, and *Jupiter and Semele*. He illustrated La Fontaine's *Fables* in 1886. Moreau became reclusive for a time (1880–1888), especially after his mother's death in 1884, but then he began to teach influentially. He left a number of paintings incomplete. Joris-Karl Huysmans* admired his watercolors and patterned the character Des Esseintes in À Rebours (1884) partly after him. James confesses in "Art in Paris" (5 Jun 1876) to being puzzled by Moreau's Hercules and Salomé, calling them "rare and curious," but too far "into the domain of the arbitrary and the fantastic." Still, in a note a few weeks later (Nation, 29 Jun 1876), James surrenders to Moreau's spell despite the poor drawing and strange coloring of Hercules, and he compares the effect of Salomé, which he describes in detail, to that of "Kubla Khan" by Samuel Taylor Coleridge—"a strange dream made visible." Further, in "Parisian Topics" (1 Jul 1876), James confesses that the two Moreau paintings "have greatly improved on acquaintance," are even "if not of first-class power at least of first-class subtlety."

Moreen, Amy and Paula. In "The Pupil," Morgan Moreen's sisters, who cannot attract suitors.

Moreen, Morgan. In "The Pupil," tutor Pemberton's precocious pupil. The boy adversely judges his embarrassing parents, likes Pemberton a lot, and later dies of a heart attack.

Moreen, Mr. and Mrs. In "The Pupil," the wandering, meretricious parents of Amy, Morgan, Paula, and Ulick. The mother thinks that Pemberton is trying to steal Morgan's affections. The father takes the boy's death "like a man of the world."

Moreen, Ulick. In "The Pupil," Morgan's older brother, a toady who takes the boy's death "like a man of the world."

Morgan, Mrs. In The Europeans, a bold woman of whom William Wentworth is reminded by news of Baroness Eugenia Münster's morganatic marriage.

Morley, John, Viscount (1838–1923). Lancashire-born statesman, political historian, biographer, literary critic, and editor. Educated at Lincoln College, Oxford, he became a vigorous, liberal journalist in London (from 1859), occupied several important staff and editorial positions (on the Literary Gazette, Saturday Review, Fortnightly Review, Macmillan's Magazine, and Pall Mall Gazette, to 1883), was a member of Parliament (1883–1895, 1896–1908), and held vital cabinet posts (concerning Ireland and India, for example, to 1910). He published books on Edmund Burke, Richard Cobden, Oliver Cromwell, Ralph Waldo Emerson,* William Ewart Gladstone,* Jean-Jacques Rousseau, and Voltaire, among others. Morley edited the English Men of Letters series (from 1878). He published his Recollections (2 vols., 1917). In a letter to Charles Eliot Norton* (16 Jan 1871), James comments on an essay on George Gordon, Lord Byron* by Morley as "red-radical and intemperate," though having "great tone" and "admirable style" and showing "critical genius." In a letter to his brother William (29 Mar 1877), James comments that Morley was recently a fellow guest at a Lord Houghton* breakfast. In a letter to his sister Alice (17 Feb [1878]), James explains that Cobden's daughter told him she had "prepared all the materials for her father's biography" and had given them to Morley, with whom she "seems rather in love." By 1879 James could describe Morley in a letter to Thomas Sergeant Perry* (14 Sep 1879) as "a charming fellow—still a young man . . . and rather shy." James did not know that "charming" Morley had earlier urged Sir Frederick Orridge Macmillan* to reject James's *French Poets and Novelists* since its chapters were, in his wrong-headed opinion, "mediocre . . . honest scribble work and no more." Macmillan published it anyway (in 1878), and a year later James's *Hawthorne* as well, as part of the English Men of Letters series which Morley was editing. James included Morley among his guests at a dinner party for Alphonse Daudet,* in London in 1895. To Edward Lee Childe,* James wrote (19 Jan 1904) to praise Morley's three-volume biography of Gladstone: "formidable, but rich, and . . . very well done; a type of frank, exhaustive, intimate biography, such as has been often well produced here, but much less in France." Still, Morley's blindness to James's professional virtues remained to the end: When, in 1915, Herbert Henry Asquith* proposed James for the Order of Merit, Morley unsuccessfully opposed the idea on the grounds that James's fiction merely dramatized the activities of the idle rich. James's library contained eight books by Morley.

Morrell, Lady Ottoline Violet Anne (Cavendish-Bentinck) (1873–1938). Famous literary hostess, in London and at Garsington Manor (near Oxford), fine conversationalist, and skillful amateur photographer of the illustrious, including T. S. Eliot, André Gide,* Thomas Hardy,* Aldous Huxley, David Herbert Lawrence,* Lytton Strachey, Herbert George Wells,* Virginia Woolf,* William Butler Yeats, and James, who met her late in his life. Ottoline had an unconventional youth, combining evangelical religion, poetry, music, and travel— including travel to Italy, where she fell briefly in love with Axel Martin Fredrik Munthe.* She married Philip Morrell, a liberal Oxonian who became a parliamentarian. Their pacifism caused them problems during World War I. In 1928 they left Garsington for London again. Lady Ottoline was a close friend of Ethel Sands, the daughter of James's much-admired friend Mary Sands.* Her posthumously published reminiscences are *Ottoline: The Early Memoirs of Lady Ottoline Morrell* (1963), in which she comments about James's talk, dreams, gout, and uncanny eyes. In these memoirs, she says that her mother-in-law, Mrs. Frederic Morrell, was the model of Adela Gereth, in *The Spoils of Poynton.* James, who relished her hospitality at least into 1914 (according to his Pocket Diaries), poked fun at her oddly flowing dresses and, according to Lord David Cecil, compared her to a heraldic gryphon or dragon.

Morris, William (1834–1896). Oxford-educated English poet, translator, editor, versatile artist (in architecture, anticommercial interior decorating, and printing), and socialist. Among his friends at Exeter College was Sir Edward Burne-Jones.* Morris helped found the short-lived *Oxford and Cambridge Magazine* (1856) and through it met Dante Gabriel Rossetti.* He published *The Defence of Guenevere* (1858), and a year later married Jane Burden, his model (and that of other pre-Raphaelites), settling in London until they moved (1871) to Kelmscott Manor in the upper Thames Valley thirty miles from Oxford. In 1861 he started a firm of church and house decorators (becoming the sole owner in 1875) which literally reformed Victorian taste. In 1884 he helped establish the Socialist League but quit it when anarchistic elements became dominant. The crowning achievement of his Kelmscott Press, founded in 1890, was the *Kelmscott Chaucer* (1896). Among Morris's many literary works are *The Life and Death of Jason* (1867), *The Earthly Paradise* (1868–1870), translations of Virgil's *Aeneid* (1875) and Homer's *Odyssey* (1887), the epic *Sigurd the Volsung* (1876, influenced by his two trips to Iceland in 1871 and 1873), *Poems by the Way* (1891), and the utopian *A Dream of John Bull* (1888) and *News from Nowhere* (1891). James reviewed (*North American Review*, Oct 1867) Morris's *The Life and Death of Jason* (1867), pronouncing it a beautiful "work of imagination," welcome in this age of facile poetry. James notes that the poet fortunately resembles Geoffrey Chaucer more than he does Algernon Charles Swinburne,* then he quotes Morris's "quaint" prefatory argument, the prose of which resembles Anglo-Saxon. Despite its length, *Jason* is crisp and quick, showing ingenuity and imagination, a "sense of . . . proportion," and "romantic dignity" when handling such mythological properties as flying rams and dragon's teeth. James admires the heroism of the Argonauts, the short episodes, the songs, and wise, brave Medea. The versification is harmonized; the vocabulary, abundant. Soon thereafer, James reviewed (*North American Review*, Jul 1868) *The Earthly Paradise* (1868), calling it another big and meritorious work and admirable escapist reading about a past we still cling to. Here are some old Norse mariners who find a Western paradise, then sit around and listen to versified tales from Greek mythology which differ widely though not as to merit. Morris's graceful, easy, and vital style is neither primitive nor modern; instead, it recalls that of Chaucer. Almost simultaneously, James reviewed *The Earthly Paradise* again (*Nation*, 9 Jul 1868), now extravagantly averring that reading "these perfect tales," "linked . . . loosely . . . by a narrative prologue," is "as pleasant a thing as the heart of man can desire." But any account of a search for an earthly paradise must inevitably be tragic. James likes the balance here between Greek and "broadly . . . Gothic" redactions. He concentrates on and prefers the Greek, especially the stories about Atalanta, Cupid and Psyche, and—best of all—Pygmalion. After touching on the non-Greek tales in the series, James concludes with high praise of Morris for his style and artistic health. During his first adult trip abroad, James was introduced by Charles Eliot Norton* to the Morrises at their Bloomsbury home, and he wrote at length to his sister Alice (10 Mar [1869]) about Morris ("delicate sensitive genius''), his art work (''superb and beautiful''), and his wife (''an apparition of fearful and wonderful intensity''). James ran into Mrs. Morris a few years later, in Italy, and wrote this time to Frances Anne Kemble* (24 Mar 1881) to describe her as ''strange, pale, livid, gaunt, silent'' and to demean her husband as ''the poet and paper-maker.'' In response to a reading of J. W. Mackail's 1899 biography of Morris, James wrote to Norton (24 Nov 1899) that Morris struck him as ''a boisterous, boyish, British man of action and practical faculty . . . floundering and romping and roaring through the arts . . . [like] a bull through a chinashop.'' James's library contained one work by Morris.

Morrish. In ''Sir Dominick Ferrand,'' a music publisher who buys the song written by Mrs. Ryves and Peter Baron.

Morrow. In ''The Death of the Lion,'' a journal syndicate representative whose articles provide Neil Paraday with publcity that proves to be fatal.

Morton, Isabel. In *Watch and Ward*, the maiden name of Isabel Morton Keith.*

Morton, Miss. In *Watch and Ward*, the Mortons' little daughter.

Morton, Mr. and Mrs. In *Watch and Ward*, Isabel Morton's brother and sister-in-law. Roger Lawrence visits Isabel at their home.

Moseley, Eliza P. In *The Bostonians*, an abolitionist still known in Boston feminist circles. Basil Ransom says, supposedly in jest, that she caused the Civil War. James probably had in mind Abraham Lincoln's comment on Harriet Beecher Stowe.*

''A Most Extraordinary Case.'' Short story (15,200 words), published in the *Atlantic Monthly* (Apr 1868); reprinted in *Stories Revived*, 1885. (Characters: William Bowles, Mrs. Bradshaw, Dr. Gregory, Caroline Hofmann, Dr. Horace Knight, Mrs. Knight, Augustus and Maria Mason, Colonel Ferdinand Mason, Miss Masters, Michael, Dr. and Mrs. Middlemas, Edith Stapleton, George Stapleton, Stapleton, Thomas.) Sick Union Army Colonel Ferdinand Mason is taken from a New York hotel by his aunt Maria Mason to her home up the Hudson River, where he convalesces and falls in love with her niece Caroline Hofmann. Caroline, however, becomes engaged to Dr. Horace Knight, who by chance is an army acquaintance of Mason. The news forces premature gaiety on Mason, who, weakened by a relapse following a drive with Miss Hofmann, suddenly dies, leaving a sum of money to the physician. This is the last of James's three Civil War stories; the others are ''The Story of a Year'' and ''Poor Richard.'' Here Colonel Mason prefigures common later fictive types in James, including Ralph Touchett (*The Portrait of a Lady*), barred from love by sickness, and Milly Theale (*The Wings of the Dove*), barred by sickness and other circumstances. Poignantly handled, Mason's debilitation may be related to James's "obscure hurt" at the outset of the Civil War.

Mostyn, Mrs. In "Nona Vincent," Mrs. Alsager's casual, ignorant acquaintance.

Motcomb. In "A London Life," a man who saw Selina Wing Berrington with Lady Ringrose in Paris, or so says Lionel Berrington.

Motley, John Lothrop (1814–1877). Massachusetts-born historian, novelist, and diplomat. He graduated from Harvard (1831), studied in Germany (where he knew Bismarck), returned to Boston (1834) to study law, married (1837), and anonymously published two novels: *Morton's Hope* (1839) and *Merry Mount, a Romance of the Massachusetts Colony* (1849). He was secretary of legation at St. Petersburg briefly in 1841, contributed essays to the *North American Review*, then spent a decade in the United States, Germany, Belgium, and the Netherlands doing research, after which he published *The Rise of the Dutch Republic* (3 vols., 1856), *The History of the United Netherlands* (4 vols., 1860, 1867), and *The Life and Death of John Barneveld* (2 vols., 1874). These works were interrupted by Motley's diplomatic duties as minister first to Austria (1861–1867) and then to Great Britain (1869–1870). Motley spent his last years in England. During his hectic winter social season of 1876–1877, James met Motley at a big banquet given by George Washburn Smalley* and his wife in London. In a Notebook reminiscence (25 Nov 1881), James records this comment: "Poor Motley, who died a few months later, and on whom I had no claim of *any* kind, sent me an invitation to the Athenaeum, which was renewed for several months, and which proved an unspeakable blessing. When once one starts in the London world . . . *cela va de soi*." In an 1875 review of recent fiction, James quotes a silly line from *Leah: A Woman of Fashion* by Annie Edwards* and sarcastically calls it "almost as serious as reading Motley . . . and so much more exciting." James criticizes Anthony Trollope* in his 1883 essay on Trollope for violating a credible narrative point of view, adding that his doing so is the same as though "Motley were to drop the historic mask and intimate that . . . the Duke of Alva [was] an invention."

Moyle, Pat. In "The Next Time," a political correspondent whose writing competes with Ralph Limbert's literary efforts in a journal.

"Mr. and Mrs. James T. Fields" (*Atlantic Monthly*, Jul 1915). A delightful reminiscence in which James defines Annie Adams Fields,* wife and then widow of publisher James Thomas Fields,* as a faithful link to the treasured past. She had a beautiful face, smile, and voice. James recalls his half-dozen years of residence in now-legendary Boston. Fields was "stately" and "brilliant." An important publisher, he was the close friend of Ralph Waldo Emerson,* Nathaniel

Hawthorne,* Oliver Wendell Holmes (especially vivacious and liberal), Julia Ward Howe,* Henry Wadsworth Longfellow,* James Russell Lowell,* Francis Parkman,* and John Greenleaf Whittier, among others. James describes the Fieldses' Charles Street residence as a veritable "waterside museum" of literary treasures, which Charles Dickens* and William Makepeace Thackeray* visited. Fields fostered the *Atlantic Monthly*, which was ably edited by William Dean Howells* (who first cultivated "[t]he new American novel") and which serialized works by many of the above-named authors. James recalls that being encouraged to write happy serial endings evoked his "perversity." He remembers such distinguished guests at the Fieldses' home as impresario Charles Fechter, singer Christine Nielson, Harriet Beecher Stowe,* and Anthony Trollope.* In widowhood, the ever-optimistic Mrs. Fields became "the literary and social executor . . . of a hundred ghosts." Once she visited James's residence in Sussex, England, bringing with her Sarah Orne Jewett,* whom James compares to Hawthorne, praises for her "truthful rendering," and called upon once in Maine.

Mrs. Gracedew. Original title of *Summersoft*.

Mrs. Jasper. Tentative title of *Disengaged*.

Mrs. Jasper's Way. Tentative title of *Disengaged*.

"Mrs. Max." Early title of what was to become *The Ivory Tower*. Another tentative title for it was "The 'K.B.' Case."

"Mrs. Medwin." Short story (8,100 words), published in *Punch* (28 Aug–18 Sep 1901); revised and reprinted in *The Novels and Tales of Henry James*, Volume XVIII, 1909. (Characters: Lady Bellhouse, Lord Considine, Mamie Cutter, Lady Edward, Scott Homer, Mrs. Medwin, Mrs. Pouncer, Mrs. Short Stokes, Lady Wantridge.) Mamie Cutter argues with her attractive sponge of a half-brother Scott Homer until he tells her he can help in her odd job of getting fallen persons back into British society. Mrs. Medwin, a would-be socialite out of favor, learns from Mamie that Lady Wantridge may approve of her readmittance. Mamie explains her embarrassment at again being bothered by her half-brother. After the two women leave, Scott returns and takes a nap in the drawing room. Later Mamie is aghast to learn that Lady Wantridge has been there and has seen Scott, who correctly evaluates the formidable woman. Just as he predicts, next morning Lady Wantridge comes back and refuses to sanction Mrs. Medwin's return to proper society, but she shows some sympathy and offers to pay the fee due Mamie, who can thus be free of the woman. But then Scott enters and talks familiarly with both Mamie and Lady Wantridge. Once the lady is gone, Mamie has a sudden inspiration: Scott's offensiveness and evil past intrigue the lady, who is manifestly smitten. Mamie follows this revelation by saying that Scott will attend Lady Wantridge's upcoming party at Catchmore as a "feature" only if Mrs. Medwin is also invited. Soon the lady capitulates, and Mrs. Medwin sends Mamie a check from Catchmore. James got his idea from some gossip, touched on in several Notebook entries (7 May 1898; 15, 16 Feb, 16 May 1899), about real-life high-society Britishers; he added an international note by making Mamie and Scott Americans, and in due time he wrote what he rightly called "a little cynical comedy" (*Notebooks*, 15 Feb 1899).

"Mrs. Temperly" (1887 title, "Cousin Maria"; 1889 title, "Mrs. Temperly"). Short story (12,300 words), published in *Harper's Weekly* (6, 13, 20 Aug 1887); reprinted in *A London Life*, 1889. (Characters: Raymond Bestwick, Mlle. Bourde, Marquise de Brives, Eléonore, Gregorini, Mr. and Mrs. Parminter, Dora Temperly, Effie Temperly, Maria Temperly, Tishy Temperly, Susan Winkle.) When artist Raymond Bestwick asks his cousin Maria Temperly in New York if he may marry her daughter Dora, age seventeen, Maria explains that she, Dora, and the girl's younger sisters Effie and Tishy are off to Paris— presumably to find the daughters rich husbands. Following the family five years later, Bestwick observes that Dora is mutely loyal to her mother: Her sisters must wed well before she will be permitted to marry below their high aim. Dora is self-sacrificial, since Tishy remains of stunted growth. Bestwick's probation continues. This is a minor tale about a common character type in James—the meddling parent.

Mrs. Vibert. Tentative title of *Tenants*.

Mudge. In "In the Cage," the unnamed "caged" girl's somewhat thick but well-intentioned fiancé.

Muldoon, Mrs. In "The Jolly Corner," the Irish cleaning woman at Spencer Brydon's "jolly corner" property.

Mullet, Lady. In "The Great Good Place," a woman eager to meet busy George Dane.

Mulliner. In "The Lesson of the Master," an editor who sits next to Marian Fancourt during the luncheon at the home of Mr. and Mrs. Henry St. George.

Mulock, Dinah Maria. The maiden name of Dinah Maria Mulock Craik.*

Mulville, Adelaide and Kent. In "The Coxon Fund," a couple who help but are basely treated by Frank Saltram.

Mumby, Miss. In *The Ivory Tower*, one of Frank B. Betterman's nurses.

Munden, Mrs. In "The Beldonald Holbein," the painter narrator's friend and Lady Beldonald's sister-in-law.

Muniment, Mr. and Mrs. In *The Princess Casamassima*, the deceased parents of Paul and Rosy Muniment. The father was a coal miner and an inventor. The mother was a washerwoman.

Muniment, Paul. In *The Princess Casamassima*, a tough-minded anarchist and a friend of Hyacinth Robinson, whom he abandons, and the Princess Casamassima, whom he tolerates for her usefulness. Paul is Rosy's brother.

Muniment, Rosy. In *The Princess Casamassima*, Paul Muniment's brave invalid sister. She is a friend of Lady Aurora Langrish, Hyacinth Robinson, and the Princess Casamassima. Rosy is based partly on James's sister Alice.

Munson. In "Travelling Companions," Mark Evans's friend whose sickness in Milan obliges Evans to leave his daughter Charlotte Evans and the narrator Brooke compromisingly alone in Venice.

Munster. In *The Reverberator*, Whitney Dosson's former partner.

Münster, Baroness Eugenia-Camilla-Delores Young. In *The Europeans*, William Wentworth's half-sister's daughter. She is Felix Young's sister and the morganatic wife of Prince Adolf of Silberstadt-Schreckenstein. She superficially charms Robert Acton but finally fails to lure him because she is somewhat unprincipled.

Munster, Mr. and Mrs. In *The Ambassadors*, friends of Maria Gostrey, who was with them at Liverpool upon Lambert Strether's arrival there.

Munthe, Axel Martin Fredrik (1857–1949). Swedish physician, psychiatrist, fabulous host, and author. He studied in Paris under Jean-Martin Charcot. He knew and perhaps envied William Wilberforce Baldwin,* a rival physician who had also expatriated himself to Italy. James's friend Lady Ottoline Violet Anne Morrell* claimed that she had fallen in love with Munthe during her youthful travels. James met Munthe on an Italian train in the spring of 1899, and, while visiting Francis Marion Crawford* in Sorrento that June, he took a side trip to Capri for an overnight stay at San Michele, Munthe's villa, which James described in "The Saint's Afternoon," a 1901 essay reprinted (as "The Saint's Afternoon and Others") in *Italian Hours*. According to a Pocket Diary entry, James and Munthe met again in London in August 1915. Munthe's popular book *The Story of San Michele* (1929) concerns his experiences as a successful high-society doctor in Paris and Rome and also his retirement on Capri. Munthe mentions James, saying that he called San Michele "the most beautiful place in the world" and thanking the novelist for encouraging him in 1915 to write about it as a relief from insomnia. James's library contained one book by Munthe.

Murfree, Mary Noailles (1850–1922). Popular Tennessee-born writer of fiction, under the pen name Charles Egbert Craddock. A childhood fever left her lame and partly paralyzed. Well-educated, she read widely and vacationed in the Cumberland Mountains. Among her many, sometimes carelessly composed novels is one in dialect entitled *The Juggler* (1897). In "American Letter" (9 Jul 1898) James calls *The Juggler* inferior to another book in dialect, *The Durket Sperret* by Sarah Barnwell Elliott.* James dislikes both "the strange overgrowth" of conscientiously reported dialect in *The Juggler* and also "the representation of . . . particular manners" perhaps necessarily attendant.

Murillo, Bartolomé Esteban (1617–1682). Spanish painter, born in Seville. After brief training in art, he became a dexterous painter of religious pictures for quick money on the street. In 1642 he went to Madrid, was aided by Diego de Silva y Velasquez* for two years, then returned to Seville and convent painting (in a cold style), married a wealthy woman (1648), created many fine religious paintings (in a warmer style), then in the late 1660s turned to his final style (vapory). In 1660 he founded the Academy of Seville. He fell from a painting scaffold in Cadiz in 1681 and never recovered from the injuries he sustained. Murillo's works may be divided into depictions of legendary and religious figures, and pictures of street children. In "The Bethnal Green Museum" (1873), James complains that the praises of popular painters such as Murillo "have been sung in every possible key"; he proceeds to note "his ease, his grace, his dusky harmonies, his beggars and saints, his agreeable Spanish savour" but adds that "[h]is drawing . . . is . . . loose, and his intentions . . . vague." In "Art" (1874) James describes in detail Murillo's *Virgin of the Swaddling Clothes*: It is "full of . . . mild, mellow harmony"; the master never forced his talent, "is . . . sincerely tender," hence "seems . . . a better Catholic in painting than any other artist subsequent to the fourteenth century."

Murray, Father. In *Guy Domville*, Guy Domville's Bristol priest and mentor who patiently waits for Guy to return to the Catholic Church.

Murray, Miss. In *Watch and Ward*, Nora Lambert's piano teacher.

Musgrave, Edgar. In "Guest's Confession," the narrator David's step-brother, whom John Guest swindled.

Musset, Alfred de (1810–1857). French poet and dramatist, born in Paris to well-to-do parents. He was an excellent student (though only a temporary one in law and in medicine), wrote poetry at an early age, and for a time was a protégé of Victor-Marie Hugo.* His first play failed on the stage; so he wrote more plays simply to be read. All have since been performed well. He and George Sand* indulged in a wild love affair (1833–1834), mostly in Venice. Thereafter Musset led a somewhat self-indulgent, dissipated, and lazy life in

Paris. He was elected to the French Academy in 1852. His main works include poetry ("Rolla" [1833], *Poésies nouvelles* [1852]); plays (*Lorenzaccio* [1834], *On ne badine pas avec l'amour* [1834]); a novel (*La Confession d'un enfant du siècle* [1836], about Sand); and short-story collections (*Nouvelles* [1840], *Contes* [1854]). A short while after James, at the urging of his friend John La Farge,* translated two stories by Prosper Mérimée,* in 1860 or 1861, he translated Musset's *Lorenzaccio*. James wrote to his father from Paris (11 Apr [1876]) that Gustave Flaubert* had told him he regarded Musset as a poet to be much below Victor Hugo and Théophile Gautier.* All his life, James deplored the notoriety which Sand and Musset, and their biographers, gave to their love affair, feeling that literary biography should not include such intimacies. James obligingly reviewed (*Atlantic Monthly*, Sep 1870) the 1870 translations by his friend Sarah Butler Wister* in *Selections from the Prose and Poetry of Alfred de Musset*, quoting much but saying little. Later he published (in *Galaxy*, Jun 1877; reprinted in *French Poets and Novelists*, 1878) a substantial review of both Paul de Musset's *Biographie de Alfred de Musset* (1877) and Paul Lindau's *Alfred de Musset* (1877, in German). He says that Paul de Musset (1804–1880), being the poet's brother, was not the ideal biographer, but should be allowed both to prettify and to be reticent; further, that Lindau, as is typical of a German, is thorough but often dreary. James begins with negatives: We have too few letters from Musset, who was too inactive, had a small horizon, and passed up good opportunities. Though like Percy Bysshe Shelley* in sensitivity, Musset lacked Shelley's "energy and curiosity." James sums up his subject's life, objects to the "displeasing . . . publicity" given to his affair with Sand and hints that Lindau's treatment of it is scandalous, but he goes on to review in detail the affair and the books that it generated. He jocosely suggests that Sand's *Elle et Lui* (1859) is fairer than Paul de Musset's *Lui et Elle* (1860). Adding that Lindau seems too sure that Venice ruined Musset, James notes that in his first five post-Italian years Musset produced fine verse, charming fiction, and original dramas. But then he "out-lived himself." It was well that Paul "is mindful . . . to glide, not to press" on his brother's last fifteen years. As for Alfred de Musset's poetry, it is often of the first order, but it deals with youthful passion and not with nature or big issues. Lindau is right to stress this fact. James compares Musset to George Gordon, Lord Byron* and contrasts him with Gautier. Did Musset write with seeming amateurishness to put critics off guard? James highly praises Musset's "Lettre à Lamartine," "Nuit d'Août," "Nuit de Mai" (with its famous symbol of poet as pelican), "Rolla," and "À la Malibran"—all poems of the 1830s. Musset is a poet of one idea, which is that love is best in this "miserable world." James slights Musset's plays: They are neither well structured nor realistic; they are best when lyrical and sentimental, and they show some of the "lightness and freedom" of certain plays by William Shakespeare.* James admires *Lorenzaccio* for its vigor. He also slights Musset's short stories but says that two or three are "masterpieces"; their light touch requires help from the reader's imagination. James concludes that Musset's varied and wasteful life is compressed into a very "little art." James's library included two books by Musset.

Myers, Frederic William Henry (1843–1901). English essayist, poet, and researcher in psychical experiences. He was brilliant at Trinity College, Cambridge, as a student and then as a teacher. Thereafter, he became a government school inspector. He married in 1881 and lived on at Cambridge. His *Essays, Classical and Modern* (2 vols., 1883) contains a fine essay on Virgil. Long interested in hypnotism and spiritualism, he, Andrew Lang,* and a few others founded the Society for Psychical Research in 1882, one result of which was his *Phantasms of the Living* (2 vols., 1886). He was obsessed with a hope for immortality and a desire to prove it scientifically. He concluded that spirits exist and that the soul survives physical death. His most important work is *Human Personality and Its Survival after Death* (2 vols., 1903). In this work, he reasons that if there is a spiritual world it should be manifest and be governed by scientific laws, that one's knowable personality is only part of a larger self obscured to a degree by one's body, that Buddhism may provide more corroboration of these hypotheses than Christianity, and that we may not only unite with God but also continue to grow spiritually. Myers influenced William James, who came to know him well and who has a section on him in his *Memories and Studies* (1911). Henry James also knew Myers as early as 1879, describing him then in a letter to Thomas Sergeant Perry* (14 Sep 1879) as "a very pleasant, gushing, aesthetic Briton, but not powerful." In the fall of 1890, James was induced to read a paper written by his brother William on trance phenomena to the Society for Psychical Research in London. James wrote to Myers (7 Oct [1890]) to mention "my complete detachment from my brother's labour and pursuits, my *outsideness*, as it were, to the S.P.R."; nevertheless, he read the paper, later writing to William (7 Nov 1890) that he did so before "a full house—and Myers was rayonnant." On two occasions, James evasively wrote to Myers to avoid explicating two of his stories: In the first such letter (13 Nov 1894), he mainly says that "Georgina's Reasons" was "one of the worst [stories] I was ever guilty of"; in the second such letter (9 Dec 1898), he blatantly calls "The Turn of the Screw" "essentially a pot-boiler and a *jeu d'esprit*." According to his Pocket Diaries, James socialized with Myers's widow into the 1910s. James's library contained two books by Myers.

Myers, Philip Van Ness (1846–1937). Economist, historian, writer, and educator. He was born in Tribes Hill, New York, graduated from Williams (1871), and while still a student there went on an expedition to South America. He then traveled and studied for two years in Europe and Asia. He studied law and economics at Yale University (1873–1874). He published *Remains of Lost Empires: Sketches of the Ruins of Palmyra, Nineveh, Babylon, and Persepolis* (1875). In later life he was a college professor and administrator, and he wrote several history textbooks. James reviewed (*Nation*, 28 Jan 1875) his *Remains* *of Lost Empires*, calling it a "handsome" book but "a disappointing record of an extremely interesting journey." Myers can neither observe nor describe well, and he employs a "pietistic" style. Summarizing Myers's journey from Damascus to the Vale of Cashmere, James clearly envies the author his opportunities and deplores his "tame" account of places seen too hurriedly.

"My Friend Bingham." Short story (8,100 words), published in the *Atlantic Monthly* (Mar 1867). (Characters: George Bingham, Rev. Mr. Bland, Charles, Lucy Hicks, Hicks, Margaret Horner.) The narrator Charles has a rich friend named George Bingham. While the two men are vacationing at B——, Bingham goes hunting on the beach and accidentally shoots and kills widowed Lucy Hicks's little son. The men do what they can for the grief-stricken mother, and Bingham even remains in the little town when Charles returns to his work in the city. Margaret Horner, a relative with whom Lucy is living, is outraged to see that she receives Bingham and hence turns her out. Lucy goes to the city with Bingham and sets up lodgings there. Six months pass. Lucy and Bingham get married; she becomes a devoted wife, he a somewhat complacent husband. This melodramatic early tale has little to recommend it but a few delicate touches. In a letter to his sister Alice (3 Feb [1867]), James rightly calls it "[a] slight romance."

N

Nadal, Ehrman Syme (1843–1922). Born in Lewisburg, West Virginia, this son of a prominent clergyman and educator attended Columbia and Yale, graduating from the latter in 1864. He served as second secretary, partly under James Russell Lowell* (ambassador) and William Jones Hoppin* (first secretary), of the American legation in London (1870–71, 1877–1884) and published *Impressions of London Social Life, with Other Papers Suggested by an English Residence* (1875) as a result of his earlier tour of duty. This book he followed with *Essays at Home and Elsewhere* (1882). Once back in America, he became a journalist and later published *Zweibak; or, Notes of a Professional Exile* (1887) and *A Virginia Village* (1922). James met Nadal at a Fourth of July legation ceremony in 1877, and the two became acquaintances. In a letter to his sister Alice (26 Feb [1879]) James called Nadal "a most amiable nature but the feeblest and vaguest mind" and in addition "a wonderful specimen of American innocence." James reviewed (*Nation*, 7 Oct 1875) Nadal's *Impressions of London Social Life*, beginning with the notion that reading about vast London's society may help Americans develop a society of their own. He calls Nadal entertaining, gentlemanly, and discreet, but also vague and light. He is glad that Nadal admires British women but deplores the weakness of his generalizations, especially concerning conversation and habits of dress. Why did he not simply offer a variety of anecdotes "arranged under heads"? James ends by admiring Nadal's picturesque descriptions of churches and gardens. James saw Nadal as late as 1911, according to an entry in his Pocket Diary. In a 1920 essay, Nadal recalls his friendship with James, and he comments on James's deportment, conversational ability, powers of observation (particularly of women), expatriation, love of London, ambition (in society and diplomacy), and miscellaneous opinions. Some of Nadal's traits may have gone into the characterization of Rupert Waterville in James's "The Siege of London."

Nash, Gabriel. In *The Tragic Muse*, the well-educated, idle, decadently aesthetic, plump, and wonderfully loquacious friend of Nick Dormer and Miriam Rooth. He may be partly patterned on Oscar Wilde* and also on James's friend Herbert James Pratt.*

The National Gallery, London. In an untitled note (*Nation,* 25 Jan 1877), James praises newly opened rooms of the National Gallery in London, compares them to aspects of the Louvre in Paris, and mentions a few "rehung" favorites of his.

Naturalization of Henry James. In 1915 James sought to become a naturalized British citizen because, as he explained in a letter ([25] July 1815) to his sponsors—Herbert Henry Asquith,* Sir Edmund Wilson Gosse,* James Brand Pinker,* and Sir George Walter Prothero*— he had lived and worked in England for forty years, was fond of and sympathized with its people, had friendships and interests in England, owned property there, and wished "to throw his moral weight & personal allegiance . . . into the scale" during World War I. He took the oath on 26 July 1915 and then received his Certificate of Naturalization. On that same day, he wrote to Gosse again to say that he could now call himself "Civis Britannicus" but that he felt no different. Two days later the London *Times* (28 Jul 1815) printed a statement from James explaining that he had petitioned for citizenship because of his long residence in England, sympathy with the English, friendships and interests in England, and the moral support his allegiance in wartime might provide.

Navarro, Antonio Fernando de (1860–1932). Versatile Italian-English Papal Privy chamberlain, engineer, and man of letters, whose father had Basque blood. Navarro and the actress Mary Antoinette Anderson* were married in 1890 in England. They lived in Broadway, Worcestershire. Navarro published poetry in Portuguese and essays associated with the magazine *Country Life,* collected in *Causeries on English Pewter* (1911) and *Offerings to Friends* (1931). He also wrote *France Afflicted: France Serene* (1920), about France during World War I and its aftermath. James was a friend of both Navarros. When Navarro asked for an opinion on a fictional fantasy he had written, James answered "dear Tony" (15 Jun 1898) with embarrassing tenderness but also with firm criticism of its slightness, innocence, vagueness, old-hat form and style, and absence of verisimilitude. In February 1899, the fact that James stayed up late to write to Navarro enabled him to detect a fire in Lamb House*; he and a servant put it out, and then he returned to his verbose letter to add a verbose message of gratitude. When Navarro wrote to James to complain of depression, James replied (1 Nov 1905) with tenderness and advice (from one "cosmopolite" expatriate to another) to "get . . . out of yourself," "to invent" and "force open" any "door of exit" out of self-"immersion." In a later letter (12 Dec 1912), James, though sick, elaborately praises as "lucid sheets" an essay on a country estate which Navarro was asked by *Country Life* editors to write about.

Nencioni, Enrico (1836–1896). Florence-born Italian poet, literary critic, and translator. His books include *Poesie* (1880), *Medaglioni* (1883), *Saggi critici di letteratura Inglese* (1897), *Saggi critici di letteratura Italiana* (1898, with a preface by Gabriele D'Annunzio*), *Studi di letterature straniere* (1897–1898), *Nuovi saggi critici di letterature straniere . . .* (1909), and *Impressioni e ricordanze* (1923). Nencioni translated works by Robert Browning,* Algernon Charles Swinburne,* Alfred, Lord Tennyson,* and James, who through Violet Paget* met him in Florence in February 1887.

Nettlepoint, Jasper. In "The Patagonia," the flirtatious Bostonian whose conduct toward Grace Mavis aboard the *Patagonia* is partly responsible for her suicide. Their mothers are friends.

Nettlepoint, Mrs. In "The Patagonia," Jasper's mother and Mrs. Mavis's friend.

"New England: An Autumn Impression." Travel essay, published in the *North American Review* (Apr–Jun 1905); reprinted in *The American Scene*, 1907.

"A New England Winter." Short story (21,400 words), published in the *Century Magazine* (Aug–Sep 84); reprinted in *Tales of Three Cities*, 1884. (Characters: Beatrice, Florimond Daintry, Lucretia Daintry, Susan Daintry, Arthur and Joanna Merriman, Donald and Pauline Mesh, Rosalie, Rachel Torrance, Mrs. Torrance.) Untalented Florimond Daintry is about to return from art study in Paris to visit his widowed mother Susan Daintry briefly in Boston. Susan asks her sister-in-law Lucretia Daintry to invite Rachel Torrance to visit them from Brooklyn, to brighten and perhaps even prolong her son's vacation. Lucretia declines but gets Pauline Mesh to visit; Rachel is related to Pauline's husband. Florimond arrives and soon visits his Aunt Lucretia, who quickly regards him as affected, and urges him to call on Mrs. Mesh and thus meet her guest Miss Torrance. Lucretia hopes Rachel will attract and then jilt the cocky fellow, but when he pays his call, he bores Rachel and yet dangerously intrigues Mrs. Mesh. Florimond's sad mother is relieved to lure the artist away and embark on a Parisian vacation herself, with him in tow. James records the germ of this story in a Notebook entry (18 Jan 1881): Mother invites young female relative to visit her, hopes thus to get son to delay return to Europe; son likes girl, but girl is too bright, sees through plan, departs; he follows, and "mother, as a just retribution, loses his society almost altogether"; son returns to Europe and marries; "mother is left lamenting." Obviously James made changes in what might have become a story "too harsh," as he also notes, and even dark and tragic. James wrote to Richard Watson Gilder,* editor of the *Century* (1 Feb [1884]), that this story "is all about Boston; where it probably (though most *lacteal* in its satire) won't be liked." More accurately, he wrote to William Dean Howells* (21 Feb 1884) that "It is not very good—on the contrary." The best feature of "A New England Winter" is James's observant, local color depiction of greater Boston.

Newman, Christopher. In *The American*, the rich American Civil War veteran and successful businessman, who comes to Paris to find culture and a brilliant wife. His friend Tom Tristram's wife Lizzie introduces him to widowed Comtesse Claire de Cintré. In spite of her brother Comte Valentin de Bellegarde's support, Newman's desire to marry her is finally thwarted by Claire's mother Emmeline de Bellegarde and that woman's son Urbain de Bellegarde, who resist pressure brought on by an incriminating letter Newman obtains from the woman's servant Catherine Bread. In *The American: A Comedy in Four Acts*, Newman is accepted by Madame de Bellegarde and Urbain until they prefer Lord Deepmere, who, however, kills Valentin in a duel, caused by Noémie Nioche, in the garden of a Parisian house Newman has bought. When Newman magnanimously surrenders Mrs. Bread's letter to Urbain at the request of Claire, she accepts him. In the rewritten fourth act (which occurs in Newman's house, as does the third act), Nóemie asks Deepmere to have Claire come from her convent (before taking vows) to see Valentin (and Newman), Valentin recovers after surgery, and Newman (somehow independent of Mrs. Bread's letter, which provides the evidence) learns that Claire's mother caused the death not only of Claire's father but also of her husband Comte de Cintré. When Newman gives the letter to Urbain, Claire accepts the American. In the stage productions, Newman was played by Edward Compton.*

"The New Novel" (revision, in *Notes on Novelists*, 1914, of "The Younger Generation," *Times Literary Supplement* 19 Mar, 2 Apr 1914). James suggests that the contemporary English novel should be subjected to careful criticism because it is at flood stage now and out of control. We stop short of calling it stupid, but it is certainly devoid of "force and suggestion," since it has been demoralized and is loose, copious, too thorough. James names Arnold Bennett, Gilbert Cannan,* Joseph Conrad,* John Galsworthy,* Maurice Hewlett, David Herbert Lawrence,* Sir Edward Montague Compton Mackenzie,* Sir Hugh Seymour Walpole,* and Herbert George Wells*; then he takes up several of them, in no discernible order. All have changed our sensibilities. Wells and Bennett use the method of saturation and documentation. These new writers dislike sentiment and romance, whereas James still greatly admires Jane Austen,* Charles Dickens,* and William Makepeace Thackeray.* Bennett treats a theme as one squeezes an orange, thoroughly. But what should be made of the juice? It is not enough to be told that an author reveals complete knowledge of his subject. *The Old Wives' Tale* (1908) by Bennett is a big, detailed canvas, even a rubble of "dump[ed building] . . . material," but with no final, meaningful ideas. Bennett's characters exist only to show us a "slice of life." Occasionally they are real, even charming. Wells has taken "all knowledge for his province," expressing much and implying more, but merely dumps it on us as from a high, open window. For example, the awkwardly sequenced love relationship in *Marriage* is ineffectively presented. Cannan's *Round the Corner* (1913) has an "enormous inauspicious amount" of material, and it "go[es] *on and on*" about the domestic life of "an amiable clergyman" in an ugly, Liverpool-like British city. We are given experiences but no impressions because values are not "wrought and shaped." Walpole's novel *The Duchess of Wrexe* (1914) offers juice from a "remarkably sweet" orange, but his only method seems to be to squeeze and squeeze. His theme is youth—passionate, curious, sincere, frank. His slice of life is buttered thick, but we want our slices more carefully selected and "illustrational of the loaf." A good novel cries out to be read again. Now for Conrad, who shows us "a beautiful and generous mind at play," and *Chance* (1914), which James says reveals a unique method involving difficulties deliberately set in order to be overcome, especially with regard to point of view. James praises Conrad's "reciter" and his "infinite sources of reference," but he wishes that the fictive predicament had been "invoked" rather than "presented." James briefly praises the "scientifically satiric" novel *The Custom of the Country* (1913) by Edith Newbold Jones Wharton* for integrating dialogue well. Wharton is an example not of saturation but of extract, and she uses imagery splendidly. Now, is Mackenzie saturation or extract? His *Sinister Street* (1913, 1914) has ornamental, beadlike episodes nicely threaded into lovingly expressed form. Its youthful hero's actions are valuable if only for their "mere recovered intensity." The heroine of Mackenzie's *Carnival* (1912) is too frail to carry the experiences detailed in it. She is a mere "slice *of* a slice." If James had more space, he would continue to show that the new novel has not had enough "criticism to reckon with" yet.

"New Novels." Reviews, published in the *Nation* (23 Sep 1875), of works by Gustave Droz,* Mrs. Thomas Erskine,* Henrietta Camilla Jenkin,* Margaret Oliphant,* Anne Isabella Thackeray (later Lady Anne Ritchie*), André Theuriet,* and Lucy Bethia Walford.*

"Newport." Travel essay, published in the *Nation* (15 Sep 1870); reprinted in *Portraits of Places*, 1883. A "splendid, stupid stream" of visitors still comes to Newport, the beauties of which continue to resist corruption uniquely well. What is Newport's appeal to idle pleasure seekers? Not its few drives and walks, not its limited scenery, but its perfection of simplicity. Many people come here, especially women, simply because others do. Women in America are social leaders. (They are not in England. They are on the Continent but seem sneaky about it.) Women in America are "free and unsophisticated," modest but not shy. Men in Newport like this. James contrasts Saratoga (difficult, common, with hotels, democratic, unsentimental) and Newport (easy, public, with villas and cottages, "lordly," sentimental). Newport seems European (though without the "vice" of Baden-Baden, for example), full of leisure, uncommercial, hence "picturesque." James confesses that he knows Newport too well to write about it well. He ticks off details of the region: sea, Point, harbor, cliffs, trees, town, houses, streets and drives, and walks. The whole area has a low-toned painterly charm, with both "fineness" and "roughness," and of varied colors. Newport combines "society . . . [and] solitude" and thus promotes both "manners and fancies."

Newsome, Chadwick (Chad). In *The Ambassadors*, Mrs. Newsome's son, Sarah Newsome Pocock's brother, Jim Pocock's brother-in-law, Mamie Pocock's nominal fiancé, and Comtesse Marie de Vionnet's lover. Chad, as he is always called, rather puts his case into Lambert Strether's ambassadorial hands.

Newsome, Mrs. Abel. In *The Ambassadors*, the awesome, never-seen widowed mother of Chad Newsome and Sarah Newsome Pocock. Mrs. Newsome will marry Lambert Strether only if he succeeds as her ambassador to rescue Chad from a Parisian femme fatale. James may have been inspired to make Mrs. Newsome an absent but influential character because of his admiration of the use of this device by Victorien Sardou* in his play *La Famille Benoîton*, and by Henrik Johan Ibsen* (who was influenced by Sardou) in his play *Rosmersholm*.

"The New Year in England." Original title of a 1879 travel essay reprinted in 1883 and 1905 as "An English New Year."

"New York and the Hudson: A Spring Impression." Travel essay, published in the *North American Review* (Dec 1905); reprinted in *The American Scene*, 1907.

The New York Edition. The popular designation of *The Novels and Tales of Henry James* (26 vols., New York: Scribner, 1907–1909, 1918).

"New York Revisited." Travel essay, published in *Harper's Magazine* (Feb, Mar, May 1906); reprinted in *The American Scene*, 1907.

"New York: Social Notes. I." Travel essay, published in the *North American Review* (Jan 1906) and in the *Fortnightly Review* (Feb 1906); reprinted in *The American Scene*, 1907.

"New York: Social Notes. II." Travel essay, published in the *North American Review* (Feb 1906); reprinted in *The American Scene*, 1907.

"The Next Time." Short story (15,100 words), published in the *Yellow Book* (Jul 1895); reprinted in *Embarrassments*, 1896; revised and reprinted in *The Novels and Tales of Henry James*, Volume XV, 1909. (Characters: Bousefield, Dr. Cecil Highmore, Jane Stannace Highmore, Maud Stannace Limbert, Ralph Limbert, Limbert, Minnie Meadows, Pat Moyle, Mr. and Mrs. Stannace.) Popular Jane Highmore asks the critic narrator to publish a favorable review of her latest trashy novel. She is the sister of Maud Stannace Limbert, whom the narrator used to love until she married Ralph Limbert, a brilliant but commercially unsucessful novelist. Ray, as he is called, once lost a job as a London correspondent for writing a profound rather than a chatty review of the narrator's first book of criticism. The lost job meant a delay in Ray's marrying Maud; now his household includes Maud, three babies, and a mother-in-law. Ray writes superb but unselling fiction; he even gets and loses a good editorial position because his own fiction in the fine journal is simply too subtle for his readership. So Ray writes a novel which he hopes will be crude enough to become a financial success. Not so: It too is artistically superb. Going to Egypt for his failing health, Ray tries for money again but can produce only yet another masterpiece. He had to write as he did, and so did shallow Mrs. Highmore. According to a Notebook entry (26 Jan 1895), the impetus for this clever story was purely autobiographical: In the entry, James begins by discussing the plot and then recalls that some twenty years ago he wrote to Whitelaw Reid* (30 Aug 1876), then publisher of the New York *Tribune*, to answer editorial criticism that the letters which became his *Parisian Sketches* were not newsy and gossipy enough. James resigned the post, and in a closing flourish added: "I am honestly afraid that they are the poorest I can do, especially for the money!" Four days after his play *Guy Domville* had its disastrous opening in competition with popular items such as *An Ideal Husband* by Oscar Wilde* at a theater nearby, James wrote to his brother William (9 Jan 1895) in brave rationalization: "[Y]ou can't make a sow's ear out of a silk purse." James uses the identical ear-purse image in "The Next Time." So Ray Limbert, the nonselling literary genius, is clearly based on James. And who inspired his popular, meretricious Jane Highmore? In his *Notebooks* (4 Jun 1895), while continuing his plot sketch for "The Next Time," James names Mary Elizabeth Braddon,* authoress of eighty popular novels (whose *Lady Audley's Secret* [1862] and *Aurora Floyd* [1865] James reviewed); other nominees might include Francis Marion Crawford* and John Milton Hay* (whose initials are the same as Jane Highmore's). In the preface to Volume XV of *The Novels and Tales of Henry James*, James circuitously declares that the moral of "The Next Time" is that the public ought to support "sincere" writers better than it does.

"Niagara." Travel essay, published in the *Nation* (12, 19 Oct 1871); reprinted in *Portraits of Places*, 1883. The quiet sail from Toronto on Lake Ontario was a "hush" before Niagara's anticipated "uproar," the approach to which up Niagara River is picturesque. Its "cliffs . . . form a *vomitorium*." But first the hotel and cheap shops. James wishes that we could isolate the Falls like an art object, instead of abusing its environs. James finds the Falls "perfect," "enshrined in . . . surging incense." His detailed description makes a dramatic picture of "the most beautiful object in the world": Horseshoe, Goat Island, American Fall, white mist, and tired river downstream; also "vendors." James raves about line, green, wall of water, cliff, rainbow, fluidity, proportion. New York State should buy Goat Island to prevent its being commercialized. He laments with the billows of the rapids as they dive shrieking to their doom below. Four miles downriver he sees the rest: elevator, cliffs, verdure, whirlpool. groping waters.

Niblett. In "Crawford's Consistency," an old patient who gossips with the physician narrator about Crawford's bad luck.

Niedermeyer. In "Eugene Pickering," the narrator's gossipy Austrian friend, who reveals Anastasia Blumenthal's background.

Nineteenth Century. A British monthly journal, the first issue of which James favorably reviewed in a note (*Nation*, 22 Mar 1877). He fears that its contents may be generally "too heavy . . . to catch the fancy of a luxurious generation," praises its Matthew Arnold* piece on Viscount Falkland, and offers details of the baseless lawsuit brought against the editor of *Nineteenth Century* for leaving an inferior journal which he had previously edited well.

Ninetta. In "Adina," Angelo Beati's former girlfriend.

Nioche. In *The American*, Noémie Nioche's downtrodden father. He tutors Christopher Newman in French and criticizes his daughter, but ultimately he knuckles under to her as she climbs socially. In *The American: A Comedy in Four Acts*, Nioche is an interpreter at a hotel in Paris, where Christopher Newman first stayed. He introduced Newman to Noémie at the Louvre before the action commences. In the rewritten fourth act, Nioche helps slightly in Valentin de Bellegarde's recovery.

Nioche, Noémie. In *The American,* a heartless, mercenary copyist whom Christopher Newman meets at the Louvre. He buys some of her copies of paintings. Her father Nioche tutors Newman in French. Newman introduces her to Valentin de Bellegarde, who becomes intrigued with her and dies in a duel with Stanislas Kapp because of an argument over her. The Nioches later go to England, where Newman sees her in Lord Deepmere's company. In *The American: A Comedy in Four Acts*, Noémie has met Valentin independent of Newman before the first act, which takes place in the Nioche home. She later annoys Valentin's mother and brother by hanging some of her copies in Newman's Parisian house. She praises the absent Newman to Claire de Cintré. In the rewritten fourth act (in which Valentin recovers after surgery), Noémie solicits Deepmere's help in bringing Claire back to Newman, and she accepts Deepmere's attentions thereafter. The name Noémie comes from the name of the heroine, Noémie Clarkson, of *L'Étrangère*, the 1876 play by Alexandre Dumas *fils*.*

Noakes, Burgess (1887–1980). James's small, faithful servant, beginning at Lamb House* in 1901, first as houseboy and later as butler and valet. James took him to the United States, as his servant, in 1910–1911. Noakes became bantamweight boxing champion of Sussex. He entered the British army, in 1914, and during his short service at the front James wrote fatherly letters to him, and sent him food and foot ointment. In 1915 Noakes was wounded by shrapnel, partially deafened for life, and put on unpaid leave. He returned to serve James in London until the latter's death. In various letters, James called Noakes babyish, gnomelike, and Lilliputian, but he valued him immeasurably. He left Noakes £100 in his will.

Noble, Mrs. In *The Golden Bowl*, the nurse of the Principino, the son of Prince Amerigo and his wife Maggie Verver.

Noel, Martha. In *A Change of Heart*, a young lady, now age twenty-three, who was obliged to become Jane Thorne's paid companion after Charles Pepperel stole her patrimony. Robert Staveley persuades her not to expose Pepperel, but instead to let Jane's insultingly haughty daughter Margaret have the fortune-hunter and to accept Staveley herself.

"Nona Vincent." Short story (11,600 words), published in the *English Illustrated Magazine* (Feb–Mar 1892); reprinted in *The Real Thing and Other Tales*, 1893. (Characters: Alsager, Mrs. Alsager, Mr. and Mrs. Beaumont, Violet Grey, Loder, Mrs. Mostyn, Nona Vincent, Allan Wayworth, Mr. and Mrs. Wayworth, the Misses Wayworth.) Aided in London by wealthy Mrs. Alsager, Allan Wayworth puts his play on stage, with Violet Grey in the title rôle. Both women love Allan, but Mrs. Alsager is married. Violet proves to be an ineffective actress during the first performance, although the play is well received generally. Napping the next afternoon, Allan has a dream in which Nona Vincent appears in her own nature, not that of either the actress Violet or the inspirational Mrs. Alsager. The dream woman tells him, "I live." That night Violet acts perfectly and then at supper tells Allan that Mrs. Alsager visited her late in the afternoon and by her example inspired the girl to alter her performance to accord with Allan's conception. Mrs. Alsager returns to Torquay to visit a sick friend; Allan marries Violet. This rather unconvincing story, weakened by a hasty close, derives from James's efforts in the early 1890s to make himself into a playwright. Mrs. Alsager may be partly based on James's friend Lady Florence Eveleen Eleanore Bell.*

Nordhoff, Charles (1830–1901). Born in Prussia but brought by his father to the United States at the age of four, Nordhoff worked in a printing office briefly, went to sea (1844–1853), and then gained employment with newspapers (1853–1857). He became a successful journalist (1857–90) with several New York magazines and newspapers. His work as managing editor of the New York *Post* brought him into contact with William Cullen Bryant. Nordhoff published several books on the merchant service and commercial fishing, political and labor problems in connection with the Civil War and Reconstruction, and California and the Hawaiian Islands. James reviewed (*Nation*, 14 Jan 1875) Nordhoff's book entitled *The Communistic Societies of the United States, from Personal Visit and Observation* (1875), admiring its solid research and "lucid . . . exposition." Taking an economic, not a sentimental approach, in an effort to decide whether communal living is preferable to trade unionism, Nordhoff studied eight distinct communities, some with numerous subdivisions, from Maine to Oregon and south to Kentucky. James wittily comments on his detailed reports concerning religion, leadership, work habits, finances, asceticism (including considerable celibacy), family life, and negative culture in these communities; he concludes that "morally and socially" a typical group "strikes us as simply hideous" since it aims at "the complete effacement of privacy in life and thought."

Norris, William Edward (1847–1925). Eton-educated English lawyer (from 1874) who, encouraged by Sir Leslie Stephen,* turned novelist—with *Heaps of Money* (1877). Thereafter, he published steadily until the year of his death. James visited him at his Devonshire home in 1894, writing to their friend Sir Edmund Wilson Gosse* (22 Aug [1894]) about "the urbanity of my host and the peerless beauty of Torquay." Norris attended the disastrous first performance of *Guy Domville*, in London, on 5 January 1895, and immediately offered James much-needed moral support. James was grateful, writing to Norris (10 Jan 1895), "I shall never forget your kind, tenderly embarrassed face when you came in to see me." James socialized with Norris steadily to 1915 (according to his Pocket Diaries) and regularly wrote him sweet and informative Christmas letters. James's library contained four books by Norris, whose friendship, however, more than his writing James appears to have valued.

"North Devon." Travel essay, published in the *Nation* (8 Aug 1872, as Part III of "A Summer in Europe"); reprinted in *Transatlantic Sketches*, 1875, and in *English Hours*, 1905. Devon is "the perfection of the rural picturesque" in England, with its rich soil, delicate flowers, green vistas, lanes, and thatched cottages–all a relief from inspecting cathedrals. After Exeter, with its Norman towers, James went by coach through "bosky . . . combes" to Ilfracombe, all "ease and convenience": a path to the cliffs full of lights and shades, solitude up there, then "almost uproarious" conversation at the hotel dinner table; next, Lynton on the cliffside and Lynmouth by the beach. On to Porlock, in "pastoral

... Somerset," where James half-expected to see Sir Roger de Coverley walk in.

Northmore, Lady. In "The Abasement of the Northmores," Lord Northmore's widow.

Northmore, Lord John. In "The Abasement of the Northmores," the presumably illustrious, recently deceased statesman whose family Mrs. Warren Hope decides not to abase. His published letters are evidently fatuous.

Northover. In *The Ivory Tower*, a deceased Britisher, who was Graham Fielder's mother's second husband.

Northover, Mrs. Fielder. In *The Ivory Tower*, Frank B. Betterman's half-sister and Graham Fielder's mother.

"A Northward Journey." The 1874 title of "The Splügen."

Norton, Charles Eliot (1827–1908). American professor of art history (Harvard, 1873–1898), scholar, critic, editor (of the *North American Review*, 1864–1868, with James Russell Lowell*), cofounder (with Edwin Lawrence Godkin* and others) of the *Nation* (1865), and translator. Norton was an influential, conservative figure in the Boston intellectual community, and he knew most of the leading American and European writers in the late nineteenth century. He was the son of Andrews Norton, a distinguished, well-to-do, anti-Emersonian biblical scholar. Norton grew up in Shady Hill, the family mansion near Harvard Yard, and enjoyed vacations at the family summer home in Newport, Rhode Island. Norton had three sisters, Louisa Norton (later Mrs. William S. Bullard), Jane Norton, and Grace Norton.* Norton graduated from Harvard (1846), worked for an import firm in Boston (to 1849), and alternated business and travel abroad (to 1857, with his sisters Jane and Grace). In 1862 he married Susan Ridley Sedgwick. She had three sisters and one brother, Arthur George Sedgwick*; the four siblings had been cared for by Anne and Grace Ashburner, who were their maternal aunts and also members of the Ashburner family.* Norton and his wife had three children; she died in Germany in 1872, after which Norton began his long and distinguished career as a professor of the history of fine art, especially as it relates to general culture, social evolution, and traditional morality. In addition to innumerable articles and reviews, Norton wrote many books, including *Considerations on Some Recent Social Theories* (1853), *Notes of Travel and Study in Italy* (1859), *Historical Studies of Church Building in the Middle Ages: Venice, Siena, Florence* (1880), and *Henry Wadsworth Longfellow[*]: A Sketch of His Life . . .* (1907). He translated Dante Alighieri's *Divine Comedy* (1891–1892). He edited many works, including letters by Anne Bradstreet (1897), Thomas Carlyle* (1883–1891), George William Curtis* (1893–1894),

John Donne, 1895, Ralph Waldo Emerson* (1883, 1886), Lowell (1894), and John Ruskin* (1904). Norton's letters were published in 1913. As editor of the *North American Review*, Norton welcomed work by such young authors as Henry Adams,* Godkin, and William Dean Howells,* as well as James. A list of Norton's professional and personal friends and acquaintances would be almost endless but should here include at least the following whom James also knew (sometimes because Norton had first introduced him to them): Adams, Matthew Arnold,* Robert Browning,* Sir Edward Burne-Jones,* Carlyle, Curtis, Charles Robert Darwin,* Charles Dickens,* Emerson, James Anthony Froude,* Isabella Stewart Gardner,* Godkin, Oliver Wendell Holmes, Jr.,* Howells, Rudyard Kipling,* Henry Wadsworth Longfellow,* Lowell, William Morris,* Francis Parkman,* Dante Gabriel Rossetti,* Ruskin, Sir Leslie Stephen,* and Edith Newbold Jones Wharton.* (James was able to reciprocate later, giving, for example, Sir Edmund Wilson Gosse* a letter of introduction of Norton in 1885. He also entertained Norton and one of his daughters at Lamb House* in 1900.) James valued his long friendship with Norton for three main reasons: Norton accepted some of his early writings for publication, he introduced him to important men of letters, and he acted as a conservative aesthetic ideal (and sounding board) in later years. James first came to know Norton after he had submitted his first review, that of a book by Nassau William Senior,* to the *North American Review*. It was soon accepted (as were other reviews), and James called on the editor at Shady Hill, in December 1864. One of Norton's wife Susan's sisters, Sara Sedgwick, whom James soon met, married William Darwin, the son of Charles Darwin. Norton's wife's brother, Arthur George Sedgwick,* became an editor, and James knew him also. At the start of his first adult trip through Europe, James in March 1869 called on Norton and Susan, and his sisters Grace and Jane, all in London at that time. The Nortons advised and guided him; through them, he quickly met Darwin, Rossetti, and Ruskin, and indirectly other distinguished persons as well. In 1873 Norton thrilled James by relaying praise of him from Ruskin. Over the years, James wrote revealing, witty, and complimentary letters to Norton. In one (16 Jan 1871) he says that "the face of nature and civilization in this our country is . . . a very sufficient literary field . . . [b]ut . . . will yield its secrets only to a really grasping imagination." And he goes on: "To write a series of good little tales I deem ample work for a lifetime." In another letter (4 Feb 1872), he comments thus: "It's a complex fate, being an American, and one of the responsibilities it entails is fighting against a superstitious valuation of Europe." James praises (6 Dec [1886]) Norton's edition of Carlyle's letters: "You seem to me a most perfect and ideal editor." He commends (4 Jul [1892]) Norton's translation of Dante's *Purgatorio*: "Great glory is yours—for making something else come out of America than railway-smashes and young ladies for lords." But as for Norton's edition of selected letters by Lowell, James expresses (15 Nov 1893) the wish that some might have been omitted, to avoid repetition. As the years advanced, Norton grew discontented with James's fiction and was even puzzled and repulsed by some of it. James wrote to Gosse (27 Oct 1904) about the joke, which was current after Norton completed his translation of Dante's *Commedia*, that his three daughters were called Paradiso, Purgatorio, and (the "very plain" one) Inferno. Shortly after Norton's death, James published "An American Art-Scholar: Charles Eliot Norton" (*Burlington Magazine,* Jan 1909; reprinted in *Notes on Novelists with some Other Notes*, 1914). In this essay, James recalls that Norton accepted some of his earliest pieces for the *North American Review* and provided an example for him of the civilized, cultured New England man of letters— especially when surrounded by "spoils" from Europe in his "hereditary home" in Cambridge. He disliked both dilettantism and vulgarity. He was urbane and straight as a lecturer, inculcated ideals, led "an esthetic crusade." He could "plead for style," but "for substance" still more. James especially praises Norton's work on Dante and medieval cathedrals, and his letters. In "The American Volunteer Motor-Ambulance Corps in France" (1914), James praises Norton's son Richard Norton for his work in organizing an American ambulance corps in France during World War I. James's *Notes of a Son and Brother* is full of references to Norton, his wife, and his sisters: James reminisces about their hospitable home, recalls seeing Dickens there, quotes letters from his father to Norton and his sister Jane, and expresses gratitude to Norton for his extensive and varied help to James as neophyte writer and resident in England. James's library contained two books by Norton.

Norton, Grace (1834–1926). One of Charles Eliot Norton's three sisters; the others were Louisa Norton Bullard and Jane Norton. Grace Norton, who lived in Cambridge, Massachusetts, was one of James's closest friends and was the recipient of scores of his best letters. One (28 July [1883]) ranks among the finest personal letters he ever wrote; in it, he responds to Miss Norton's sense of estrangement: "Before the sufferings of others I am always utterly powerless. . . . You are not isolated in such states of feeling as this. . . . I have a terrible sense that you give all and receive nothing. . . . I am determined not to speak to you except with the voice of stoicism. I don't know *why* we live—the gift of life comes to us from I don't know what source or for what purpose; but I believe we can go on living for the reason that . . . life is the most valuable thing we know anything about and it is therefore presumptively a great mistake to surrender it while there is any yet left in the cup. In other words consciousness is an illimitable power. . . . We all live together, and those of us who love and know, live so most. We help each other . . . we lighten the effort of others, we contribute to the sum of success, make it possible for others to live. . . . [Y]ou are passing through a darkness . . . but it is only a darkness it is not an end, or *the* end. Don't think, don't feel . . . don't do anything but *wait*. . . . You will do all sorts of things yet, and I will help you." James was happy to see Miss Norton in Boston, in September 1910 and again in July 1911, during his 1910–1911 visit to the United States. One terse little Pocket Diary entry (27 Jul 1911) notes "Dear Grace I probably . . . saw for the last time!"

Notes of a Son and Brother. Second volume of James's projected autobiography, published in New York by Scribner, 1914, and in London by Macmillan, 1914. (The first and third volumes are *A Small Boy and Others*, 1913, and *The Middle Years*, 1917.) *Notes of a Son and Brother* comprises thirteen chapters, usually long ones. 1. The James children were put into various Swiss schools again in 1859: James briefly studied pre-engineering in Zurich, then French, Latin, and German literature more happily at the Academy in Geneva. Successful William, relaxing from scientific classes, once took James to a students' beer "carouse . . . in the Vaud back-country" and occasionally sent him letters with clever pencil drawings. James remembers certain Anglo-Saxon friends and neighbors, and off-duty reading of Victorian fiction. 2. Next, James and Wilky attended school in Bonn, Germany (beginning summer 1860), and James sought to unify "life and knowledge" (by reading *Once a Week*, sent by his father, by reading German classics, and by early morning walks) as though he were an author. Airlessly rooming with a grinning German professor's family, James felt caged, liked the German woods and the Rhine but found everything else "ugly," envied Wilky his sociability with other youths (all "gothic") in the house, thinks about Bob (left behind in the Geneva school, enjoying a visit to Italy, learning to paint). William rented quarters from a Bonn tutor, and he and James once saw Adelaide Ristori* at the theater, which moves James to quote from his father's description of her and then from one of William's letters about their Bonn work and fun. 3. When William said that he wanted to be an artist, his father encouraged him but he wanted him also to be—spiritually, widely—apart from any mere doing. Late in 1860 James reluctantly abandoned what "the glittering régime" of France included (marquise glimpsed on Cologne-to-Paris train, Louvre, Palais Royal, American cousins even), so that William could study painting under Frenchified William Morris Hunt* in Newport, Rhode Island. The master's pupils also included John La Farge* (and James himself, briefly). 4. Life for the James family in Newport was detached and leisurely, as it had been in Europe. When asked, James's nonworking father told the boys to say he was a student. James "devoutly" read the *Revue des Deux Mondes* and associated with Europeanized cousins, including Mary Temple,* who became a "shining apparition" in his life. He revered sketches William did of their cousins Augustus (Gus) Barker (of the Barker family*) and Katherine Temple (of the Temple family*), and lovingly remembers "Franco-American" La Farge as artist, reader, and friend. 5. William's abruptly quitting art school pleased his impractical father, who saw every "experiment" and change as growth. He also saw no point in the older sons going to college or entering business. James liked being "in" but not "of" New England. He recalls his cousins William James Temple and Gus Barker (both killed in the Civil War). His bright, witty brother William, who seemed to James and their father a college graduate already, entered the Harvard Scientific School (fall 1861); from his letters home (into 1863), attesting to his "vivacities and varieties of intellectual and moral reaction," and to his "animation and spontaneity of expression," James quotes in detail, about his "initiation" into higher education, then "further impressions." James comments on Wilky and Bob (in Franklin Sanborn's school in nearby Concord), and on professors and studies and friends and relatives, including another cousin, "richly erratic" Robert Temple (W. J. Temple's older brother), who studied in Scotland, humorously criticized America, became a Roman Catholic, and returned home. 6. James discusses his father at length: his patience, his regular writing, his "insuperable gaiety," his tolerant wife, his conversations (mainly with intelligent William), his personal religious philosophy (which did not "touch . . . me . . . directly," since it was not social or material), and the "narrow[ing]" influence (from 1844) of Swedenborgianism on the man. James also quotes several letters (1842–1869) from his father to Ralph Waldo Emerson* (in one of which he called Emerson a "man without a *handle*") about spiritual depression, mutual friends (including Thomas Carlyle,* Charles Sumner, Nathaniel Hawthorne,* Henry Wadsworth Longfellow,* and William Ellery Channing*), travel plans, English friends Emerson recommended, dislike of mere literary folk, and desire for a sensuous European education for his four sons, self-criticism, and Londoners met (including Sir Arthur Helps*). James touches on his father's "wild" youth, his patient acceptance of both his leg injury and his absence of "public recognition," his friendship with London physician J. J. Garth Wilkinson,* and Emerson's opinion of James's father and of his visit to the Jameses' New York home. James admires his father's "belief . . . in the imminence of a transformation-scene in human affairs." 7. James discusses his family's rich, witty, traveling friends William Tappan and his wife Caroline Sturgis Tappan, James's visit to Sanborn's experimental, coeducational Concord school (a place more for "pastime" than education), and his father's optimistic comments on the place. As a youth James always had faith in the synthesizing vision of his father, who often wrote Caroline Tappan curious letters (quoted here), once about Wilky's being wounded at Fort Wagner, in July 1863. James recalls his anguish, and that of relatives of other soldiers wounded and dead, at that time. 8. James quotes more of his father's letters, to indicate his spirit and writing style: to Annie Adams Fields,* wife of publisher James Thomas Fields*; to Charles Eliot Norton* (at whose home James met Charles Dickens*) and his family; to his son Henry himself at various times (about William's teaching at Harvard, about the father's own youthful visit to Ireland and England, about friends and celebrities, about recent publications); etc. 9. James reports [a bit inaccurately] on his activities from 1861 to 1863: Harvard Law School; his back injury, "a horrid even if an obscure hurt," which happened while he was helping to put out a fire in Newport and which he made worse by ignoring the advice of "a great surgeon" in Boston to try "supine 'rest' "; details à la Honoré de Balzac* about his Cambridge boardinghouse; his visit to a Union army hospital in Rhode Island (his "sole vision of the American soldier in his multitude"); and learning of the Gettysburg Address "in an almost ignobly safe [Newport] stillness." 10. James discusses more "Cambridge impressions": Professor Francis James Child,* folklorist and patriot; "diverg[ing]" and "straggling" from William, an unremitting "genius," and his kind of friends; several students (a couple of the "sickly New England type," another from New Jersey, others related to or knowing important people); James's talk in moot court, which drifted into "collapse and cessation"; writing and sending off fiction, attending morning law school lectures (without understanding them), reading Charles Augustin Sainte-Beuve,* observing professors and fellow students in their provincial villagelike setting; escaping to the Boston theater; and two contrasting students, a New York fop with monocle and terrier and "G.A.J." [George Abbot James] with splendid vitality. 11. James explains that he strings "apparently dispersed and disordered parts upon a fine silver thread" to present "[t]he personal history of an imagination," namely his. He therefore now presents free recollections: visiting Wilky outside Boston during "the War," all sociable among "sunburnt young" fellow soldiers soon tragically to lead black troops; missing the later "military metamorphosis and contemporary initiation" of still-younger Bob (later to suffer a sunstroke in Florida); and aspects of Bob's military and later career (including his "spoken overflow," which was like William's animated writing, and his idleness). James envies the "privileged" soldier's sensations and even his active younger brothers' post-War cotton-farming failures in Florida; he quotes from their wartime letters, less for their contents than for his unique responses. 12. Early in 1864 the James family moved to Ashburton Place, Boston, and James's literary career began, with a $14 royalty check and an acceptance by Charles Eliot Norton,* the new editor of the *North American Review*, of his youthful critical pieces. At the same time, James thinks of victorious Ulysses Simpson Grant,* defeated Robert E. Lee, murdered Abraham Lincoln, and Nathaniel Hawthorne,* whose death made him "loyally cry." He thinks of letter-writing William, on a scientific expedition in Brazil with Professor Louis Agassiz, and of his own 1865 visits to Bostonians, Newport, and New York. At Newport, James sat to portraitist La Farge and saw Julia Ward Howe* and Thomas Sergeant Perry.* James recalls his association with the *Nation*, beginning in the summer of 1865, and its editor Edwin Lawrence Godkin.* James remembers the end of the war and "the monster tide" of returning soldiers ("bronzed, mature faces and even more . . . bronzed matured characters") who had known "unprecedented history" had seen and felt things and—again—the "classic woe" of Lincoln's death (and having Andrew Johnson "inflic[ted]" on the nation). While hearing from his brothers, James read but mainly wrote much ("production, such as it was, floundered on," since "difficulty and slowness of composition were clearly by this time not in the least appointed to blight me"); even while he felt ashamed that his short stories competed in his mind with national history in the making, they were precious to him for fusing his "direct and indirect experience," and they were encouraged by William Dean Howells* (back from Venice and editing the *Atlantic Monthly*). In 1866 James summered at Swampscott, Massachusetts, and sympathized with the French at Sadowa [Königgrätz] in their struggle against the Prussians; his parents moved to Cambridge; and William began to study medicine at Harvard and in Boston. In 1867 and 1868 William studied in Germany (part of the time with Perry), vacationed near Lake Geneva, and wrote letters home about his impressions. 13. James writes in detail about his "delightful young cousin" Mary Temple*, known as Minny. He quotes from her charming and brave letters both to James ("essentially not love-letters") and also to another man (John Chipman Gray*), about sleighing, dancing, handsome escorts, reading, great admiration of "Willy James," the visit of "Harry" before his 1869–1870 trip to Europe, fatal symptoms of tuberculosis, and her response to Philadelphia sermons by Phillips Brooks. James recalls the Albany scene of "orphaned young cousins" guarded by an "erect great-aunt" who looked like George Washington. He admires Minny's unique "sense for verity of character and play of life in others," being "the heroine" of friendly outings, her "sincerity and . . . wonder," and that "lightness all her own." He goes on and on, about his last hour with Minny, in Pelham, New York, and their plan to meet "romantically" in Rome, her desire that he give George Eliot* her love, his meeting in London with "five . . . distinguished persons" (George Eliot, John Ruskin,* William Morris,* Charles Robert Darwin,* and Dante Gabriel Rossetti*), Minny's awareness of Europe through her Boston and Newport friendship with Francis Boott* and his daughter Elizabeth Boott,* Minny's response to her two sisters' marriages to men of the Emmet family,* her aborted plan to voyage to California for her worsening health, her joy in music, her attitude toward Christ's example and her desire to please God by listening to both her heart and her head, and her doctors' prognoses. James closes by reporting that "all illusion failed," that he determined to wrap her ghost "in the beauty and dignity of art," and that Minny Temple's death marked the end of his own youth.

Notes on Novelists with Some Other Notes. Collection of eighteen critical essays, all previously published; reprinted, some revised, in London by Dent, 1914, and in New York by Scribner, 1914. The essays have the following titles (each with a year date, sometimes inaccurate, and omitted here): "Robert Louis Stevenson"; "Émile Zola"; "Gustave Flaubert"; "Honoré de Balzac" (two in number, one an introduction to a translation, the other originally entitled "Balzac"); "George Sand" (three in number, two originally entitled "She and He: Recent Documents," and "George Sand: The New Life," the third a review); "Gabrielle D'Annunzio"; "Matilde Serao"; "The New Novel" (original title, "The Younger Generation"); "Dumas the Younger" (original title of one printing, "On the Death of Dumas the Younger"); "The Novel in 'The Ring and the Book' " by Robert Browning; "An American Art-Scholar: Charles Eliot Norton"; and "London Notes" (four in number, two reprinted only in part, original title, "London"). (All of these authors are discussed under their own names.)

"Notes on the Theatres." Theater essay, published in *Nation* (11 Mar 1875). Current offerings by New York theaters do not tell us about American civilization; instead, they too often reflect foreign dramatic standards and also merely entertain high-paying, unthinking audiences. Irish types appear in Dion Boucicault's *Shau-*

graun (1874). *The Two Orphans* is an adaptation of an 1874 French play. A home-grown effort, *Women of the Day*, is popular but "ghastly, monstrous," and it should be hissed off the stage. James praises the leading man in a revival of *Henry V* by William Shakespeare* but ridicules the efforts at scenic verisimilitude.

"The Novel in 'The Ring and the Book.' " Critical essay on *The Ring and the Book* by Robert Browning,* in *Transactions of the Royal Society of Literature* (2nd series, 31: 4, 1912; reprinted in *Browning's Centenary*, 1912; revised and reprinted in *Quarterly Review* (Jul 12); reprinted in *Living Age* (24 Aug 1912), and in *Notes on Novelists*, 1914.

"Novelist Writes of Refugees in England." Early (1915) title of "Refugees in Chelsea" (1919).

The Novels and Stories of Henry James (35 vols., London: Macmillan, 1921–1923). This large publication, edited by Percy Lubbock,* purports to include all the fiction James published in book form. It includes 113 novels and stories. It excludes the following twenty-three, for various reasons: "Adina," "At Isella," "Covering End," "Crawford's Consistency," "De Grey, A Romance," "Gabrielle de Bergerac," "The Ghostly Rental," "Guest's Confession," "Hugh Merrow," *The Ivory Tower*, "The Married Son," "My Friend Bingham," "Osborne's Revenge," *The Other House, The Outcry*, "A Problem," "Professor Fargo," *The Sense of the Past*, "The Story of a Masterpiece," "The Story of a Year," "The Sweetheart of M. Briseux," "A Tragedy of Error," and "Travelling Companions."

The Novels and Tales of Henry James (26 vols., New York: Scribner, 1907–1909, 1918), often known as "The New York Edition." The sumptuously beautiful, justly famous edition of a selection by James of the sixty-seven novels and short stories which he most wished to preserve. Entitled *The Novels and Tales of Henry James*, it was published in 1907, 1908, and 1909 by Charles Scribner's Sons, in twenty-four volumes. In 1918 two posthumous volumes were added. James wrote eighteen prefaces for this edition, one for each of the nine novels selected, and one for each of the nine volumes of short novels and short stories selected. Each of James's original twenty-four volumes has a frontispiece; they were made from photographs by Alvin Langdon Coburn,* with whom James worked closely and extensively advised. The contents of the volumes are as follows: Volume I, *Roderick Hudson*; II, *The American*; III and IV, *The Portrait of a Lady*; V and VI, *The Princess Casamassima*; VII and VIII, *The Tragic Muse*; IX, *The Awkward Age*; X, *The Spoils of Poynton*, "A London Life," and "The Chaperon"; XI, *What Maisie Knew*, "In the Cage," and "The Pupil"; XII, "The Aspern Papers," "The Turn of the Screw," "The Liar," and "The Two Faces"; XIII, *The Reverberator*, "Madame de Mauves," "A Passionate

Pilgrim,'' ''The Madonna of the Future,'' and ''Louisa Pallant''; XIV, ''Lady Barbarina,'' ''The Siege of London,'' ''An International Episode,'' ''The Pension Beaurepas,'' ''A Bundle of Letters,'' and ''The Point of View''; XV, ''The Lesson of the Master,'' ''The Death of the Lion,'' ''The Next Time,'' ''The Figure in the Carpet,'' and ''The Coxon Fund''; XVI, ''The Author of Beltraffio,'' ''The Middle Years,'' ''Greville Fane,'' ''Broken Wings,'' ''The Tree of Knowledge,'' ''The Abasement of the Northmores,'' ''The Great Good Place,'' ''Four Meetings,'' ''Paste,'' ''Europe,'' ''Miss Gunton of Poughkeepsie,'' and ''Fordham Castle''; XVII, ''The Altar of the Dead,'' ''The Beast in the Jungle,'' ''The Birthplace,'' ''The Private Life,'' ''Owen Wingrave,'' ''The Friends of the Friends,'' ''Sir Edmund Orme,'' ''The Real Right Thing,'' ''The Jolly Corner,'' and ''Julia Bride''; XVIII, ''Daisy Miller,'' ''Pandora,'' ''The Patagonia,'' ''The Marriages,'' ''The Real Thing,'' ''Brooksmith,'' ''The Beldonald Holbein,'' ''The Story in It,'' ''Flickerbridge,'' and ''Mrs. Medwin''; XIX and XX, *The Wings of the Dove;* XXI and XXII, *The Ambassadors*; XXIII and XXIV, *The Golden Bowl*; XXV, *The Ivory Tower*; and XXVI, *The Sense of the Past*. There is uncertainty as to the reasoning behind James's choice and grouping of titles. He may have wished to create his own kind of human comedy à la Honoré de Balzac.* He may have wished to stress the international quality of his best work, at the expense of certain American-based fiction (notably *The Bostonians*). He certainly grouped many short stories thematically. His prefaces discuss the myriad sources of his inspiration for individual works, autobiographical or at least subjective elements, creative difficulties, critical challenges, and personal delights. These prefaces were later separately republished as *The Art of the Novel* in New York by Scribner, 1934, edited by Richard P. Blackmur. Blackmur's detailed introduction discusses James's complex prefatory themes: the relationship of art and other elements, looseness, pleas for appreciation, amusement, the indirect approach, dramatic scene, central intelligences, the international theme, the theme of the literary life, types of characters, the supernatural, romanticism, time, geographical representation, compositional centers, puzzlement, fools, revisions, illustrations, the nouvelle, appearances, development and continuity, structure, improvisations, anecdotes, irony, foreshortening, first-person narratives, *ficelles*, etc. Taken together, the eighteen prefaces provide astounding, even unique personal critical commentary by a literary genius on his own production. James would have included more titles, undoubtedly *The Bostonians* among them, but for the quickly demonstrated unpopularity of the entire project. In fact, poor sales of the edition made him suicidally melancholy for some time. He confided in Sir Edmund Wilson Gosse* ([29 Dec 1908]) that ''The Edition has been a weary grind (such a mass of obscure & unmeasurable labour . . .).'' He added much later (25 Aug 1915) that royalties in 1915 were £25 in London and only a little more in America. At this time, he reported that although he had ''intimately & interestingly revised his 'earlier things,' '' the edition was never accorded ''the least intelligent critical justice.''

Nugent. In *The Tragic Muse,* the name of a family whose members, though not seen, are often associated with Nugent Castle.

Nutkins. In "The Marriages," the gardener at Brinton, the Chart family's country estate. Adela Chart's mother taught him.

O

___

Obert, Ford. In *The Sacred Fount,* a painter who is tolerant of his friend the narrator.

"Occasional Paris." Travel essay (original title, "Paris Revisited," *Galaxy,* Jan 1878); reprinted in *Portraits of Places,* 1883. James discusses the dangers of generalizing about races if one is a homeless cosmopolite. He has lived more than a year now among the likable English in London but during a recent visit to Paris (an utterly different city) has resisted making comparisons. Instead, he notes everything afresh: windows, the 1878 Exhibition buildings ("a mighty mass"), the new Avenue de l'Opéra ("quite on the imperial system" but destroying the "ancient individuality" of old streets), and various local color items new to "honest Anglo-Saxon" vacationers on first arriving. James mentions soldiers, French officials, porters, undignified but "expressive" French faces, girls formerly called "grisettes," "neat-waisted" female shop attendants, men with "a Bohemian, empirical look," Boulevard meals (served by friendly waiters), cabarets, and theaters. James concludes by going into detail about the play *Le Demi-Monde* by Alexandre Dumas *fils.**

Offord, Oliver. In "Brooksmith," the recently deceased master of Brooksmith, who is therefore unemployed now.

"Old Italian Art." Travel essay, published in the *Independent* (11 Jun 1874); reprinted as one of the eight-part "Florentine Notes" in *Transatlantic Sketches,* 1875, and in *Italian Hours,* 1909.

"The Old Masters at Burlington House." Art review, published in *Nation* (1 Feb 1877). James commends generous art owners for loaning their possessions for Royal Academy exhibitions during foggy winters in London. He specifies many works he has thus seen—by Sir Joshua Reynolds,* Thomas Gainsborough,* George Romney,* Sir Henry Raeburn, Sir David Wilkie, foreign portraitists, early Tuscan pictures, a few landscapes, a superb Franz Hals, and a big Peter Paul Rubens* ("interesting on a first glance; but it proves on a longer inspection to be rather inexpensively 'got up' ").

"The Old Masters at Burlington House." Art review, published in *Nation* (31 Jan 1878). The present Royal Academy offerings are thinner than the ones last year. James therefore stresses those representing the Norwich School, for example, paintings by John Crome (whose landscapes are "charming" but mainly have "historic or social" value) and his followers. James also mentions some works by Joseph Mallord William Turner,* George Romney,* Rembrandt Harmensz van Rijn,* and other Dutch painters; John de Capella is noteworthy. The Thomas Gainsborough* examples here are only "fairish."

"The Old Saint-Gothard" (1874 title, "An Autumn Journey"; 1875 title, "The St. Gothard"). Travel essay, published in the *Galaxy* (Apr 1874); reprinted in *Transatlantic Sketches*, 1875, and in *Italian Hours*, 1909. James is in choked Berne, late in the tourist season (September 1873.) A wave of comfort-seeking Anglo-Saxons is leaving also. By comparison, Lucerne (September) is almost empty. James has a quiet hotel room with an operatic balcony looking out at mountain crags, massed clouds, and scattered light. Walking to the Saint-Gothard coach office for a ticket, he contrasts a quaint old bridge and luxurious new one, spanning the Reuss, then loafs about, reading a New York newspaper. In Milan (October) James recalls his predawn lake-steamer ride to catch his pleasant coach at Flüelen, where he joyfully ate acrid peaches and delighted in the genuine fun of travel. On toward Bellinzona. The coach conductor, beside whom James sat, talked resignedly about the coming of the tunnel—they call it progress—which will put him out of work. James was in awe of the nature-humbling, beauty-ruining conduits channeling water to run the tunnel-piercing machinery. Then the Grisons and Andermatt, for dinner—with an Irish lady and a Holbeinesque Briton. Up to cool Hospenthal and down zigzaggingly to Faido and twilit Airolo. Bellinzona gleamed in the late moonlight. The next day's progress was through an ineffable region of lakes, slopes, masses, trees, vineyards, and tawdry shrines—all in the yellow light of magic Italy. Earlier and again at the frontier custom house, James helped a timid seamstress passenger, whose employer had gone ahead to Cadenabbia. Then Como.

"Old Suffolk." Travel essay, published in *Harper's Weekly* (25 Sep 1897); reprinted in *English Hours*, 1905. James knew of Suffolk through *David Copperfield*, by Charles Dickens,* before he ever saw the region. Now Yarmouth seems "cockneyfied"; but "desolate, exquisite Dunwich" is not disappointing in that way: cliff-perched, ruined church and tower, straight tide, diked land, "sweet . . . commons." James mentions writers who have extolled the old region. Dunwich admonishes one "to be pleased"—by Wesselton (lemonade, park, walls, hedges), Priory, hill cottages, sea-gnawed acres, coast-guard station, and everything composing into little rural, coastal pictures which epitomize England itself.

The Old Things. The 1896 title of *The Spoils of Poynton*.

Olimpia. In "The Aspern Papers," Juliana Bordereau's red-haired maid.

Oliphant, Laurence (1829–1888). British diplomat, traveler, author, and mystic. He was born in Capetown, traveled with his parents, and was irregularly educated. He became secretary to his father in Ceylon, then secretary to Lord Elgin in Washington, D.C. (1854), administrator in Quebec (1854), and war correspondent in the Crimea (1855). He became Lord Elgin's secretary in China and Japan (1857–1859), then first secretary of legation in Japan (1861), where he was seriously wounded. Back in England, he started a journal called *The Owl* (in 1864) and later joined the Chautauqua commune in New York state (in 1867), donating all his money to it. He was a correspondent during the Franco-Prussian War (1870–1871), later lived in Palestine (beginning in 1882), and at last died in Twickenham. He published numerous books, starting in 1852, on politics, religion, sociology, travel, and war, and also some fiction, including "The Tender Recollections of Irene Macguillicuddy" (in *Blackwood's Magazine*, 1878). James reviewed (*Nation*, 30 May 1878) the American reprint of the tale, which satirizes New York manners, especially those of "marriageable maidens in . . . 'hooking' a member of the English aristocracy." James grants that Oliphant knows "the mysteries of Fifth Avenue" but says that he does not use that knowledge skillfully. Further, he disposes of his heroine arbitrarily. James calls for "native talent" to write American "society stories," depicting American types, and including local color touches. He took his own advice and a few months later published "An International Episode," a tale replete with local color, concerning a marriageable American girl and a British lord. James's library contained one book by Oliphant.

Oliphant, Margaret (née Wilson) (1828–1897). Prolific Scottish novelist, historian, biographer, letter writer, and autobiographer. She wrote more than 120 books, many of which were best-sellers. In 1852 she married an artist and moved with him to Italy, but he soon died there of tuberculosis. She returned to England, where she continued to write assiduously to support her three children (all of whom then predeceased her). Her best works include *Adam Graeme* (1852), *Salem Chapel* (1863), *Miss Marjoribanks* (1866), *A Beleaguered City* (1880), and *Autobiography* (1899). James reviewed (*Nation*, 23 Sep 1875) her novel

Whiteladies (1875). He praises its high quality, which he adds comes as a surprise considering that the woman publishes six novels a year. He summarizes the meandering plot, which involves a false heir in the time of Henry VII and a farfetched "imbroglio of nationalities." He opines that Mrs. Oliphant seems "clever" but that she should let her ideas "ripen" more. In "London" (21 Aug 1897; reprinted in *Notes on Novelists*, 1914), James expresses sorrow at her recent death and comments on the volume of her work and its success. Her "fecundity" was owing to her "rare original equipment, . . . courage, health and brain," Scottish background, organizational powers, understanding of life, "capacity for labour," reading background, powers of observation, and sense of humor. Her ability to improvise resulted in a "reckless rustle over depths and difficulties." James commends her handling of "Scotch talk." Touching on her recently published novel *Kirsteen: The Story of a Scotch Family Seventy Years Ago* (1890), he notes that it is lively but baffling, boldly clever but hardly artistic. According to the diary of Arthur Christopher Benson,* James said of Mrs. Oliphant in 1900 that he "had not read a *line* that the poor woman had written for years . . . [T]he poor soul had a simply *feminine* conception of literature: such slipshod, imperfect, halting, faltering, peeping, down-at-heel work . . . " James's library contained two books by Mrs. Oliphant.

"On Some Pictures Lately Exhibited." Art review, published in *Galaxy* (July 1875). James recognizes the shortcomings of art criticism but still favors it. Painters dislike art critics who are "literary"; yet they need each other, and, further, some painters are "erudite" while some art critics are "picturesque." The best art critics today are in Paris. These prefatory remarks out of the way, James comments on items in current New York exhibits. He mentions many artists, usually in brief, witty derogation. But he pauses over items by Winslow Homer (perhaps "[t]he most striking"; "simple, and . . . ugly; but there is nevertheless something one likes about him"), John La Farge,* Frank Duveneck,* Thomas Moran ("the rocks were most delectable . . . in his picture of certain geological eccentricities in Utah"), and George Henry Boughton.*

"On the Death of Dumas the Younger." Critical essay, on Alexandre Dumas *fils** (*New Review*, Mar 1896).

Orme, Lady Agnes. In "In the Cage," a name mentioned in a Lady Bradeen telegram.

Orme, Sir Edmund. In "Sir Edmund Orme," the rejected suitor of the woman who later became Mrs. Marden. After he committed suicide by taking poison, his ghost haunted her daughter Charlotte until she accepted her suitor, the narrator.

Oronte. In "The Real Thing," the impoverished Italian who becomes not only the painter narrator's model but his valet as well.

Orr, Alexandra Leighton (1828–1903). British writer who (under the name Mrs. Sutherland Orr) published *A Handbook to the Works of Robert Browning* [*] (1885, 7th ed., 1896) and *Life and Letters of Robert Browning* (1891). She was the sister of Lord Frederick Leighton.* James availed himself of Mrs. Orr's hospitality from the late 1870s. In a letter to Grace Norton* (8 June [1879]), he describes his hostess facetiously as "a very nice woman who writes . . . against the 'emancipation' of women (sensible creature) . . . " A year later in a letter to his mother (11 Sep [1880]), he adds that Mrs. Orr "is a genuinely serious woman." James's library contained one book by Mrs. Orr.

Orville, Lady. In "The Given Case," the Pickenham hostess who was embarrassed because Kate Despard did not bring her lover Barton Reeve along.

Osborne, Philip. In "Osborne's Revenge," Robert Graham's friend. When Graham commits suicide, Osborne wrongly blames Henrietta Congreve.

"Osborne's Revenge." Short story (15,300 words), published in the *Galaxy* (Jul 1868). (Characters: Mrs. Carpenter, Henrietta Congreve, Maria Dodd, Major Dodd, Robert Graham, George Holland, Jane, Miss Latimer, Philip Osborne, Rev. Mr. Stone, Angelica Thompson, Anna Wilkes, Tom Wilkes.) Jilted by Henrietta Congreve of Newport, Robert Graham kills himself. His friend Philip Osborne plans revenge until he learns that Henrietta was innocent of any wrongdoing. This weak early story is of value mainly for preaching that reality is more complex than subjectively distorted appearances.

Osbourne, Lloyd (1868–1947). Son of Fanny Van de Grift Osbourne and Samuel Osbourne. When his mother later married Robert Louis Stevenson*, Lloyd Osbourne became Stevenson's stepson. Born in San Francisco, he was tutored in England, France, and Switzerland; then he studied civil engineering at the University of Edinburgh. He accompanied Stevenson (1887–1894) and became American vice consul-general in Samoa (ending in 1897). Showing skill in devising plots, he coauthored three novels with Stevenson (*The Wrong Box* [1889], *The Wrecker* [1892], and *The Ebb Tide* [1894]). Later he wrote *Memories of Vailima* (1902, with his sister Isobel Strong) and *An Intimate Portrait of R.L.S.* (1925), among other works. His best work is probably *Infatuation* (1908). Through the Stevensons, James knew Osbourne, whom he often befriended and also commended in letters to Stevenson, once for example (17 Feb 1893), calling him "the lusty and literary Lloyd." James's library contained one book by Osbourne.

Osgood, James Ripley (1836–1892). Maine-born, precocious, Bowdoin-educated, controversial, rheumatic Boston and London publisher. After clerking for and then joining the firm of Ticknor & Fields (1855–1869), he established his own companies: James R. Osgood & Co. (1871–1878); Houghton, Osgood & Co. (1878–1880); and James R. Osgood again (1880–1885). Always better at courting authors (among them Bret Harte,* Mark Twain,* and James) than in handling the commercial aspects of publishing, he went bankrupt in May 1885. He worked for Harper and Brothers later that year, became their agent in London (1886–1890), and finally, with Clarence W. McIlvaine,* established Osgood, McIlvaine & Co. there (1891–92). Their biggest coup was publishing *Tess of the D'Urbervilles* by Thomas Hardy.* Osgood died in London. James knew Osgood both in Boston and in London since the publisher had issued the American editions of James's first four books and a few later ones. When he persuaded James to let him publish *Watch and Ward* in book form (1878), James wrote from London to his father, who was handling business details for him with Osgood (19 Apr [1878]), that releasing the weak novel as a book "seemed . . . a good way of turning an honest penny." While in London on a business trip, Osgood gave a typically extravagant dinner party at the Continental Hotel, in September 1882, for his American writers, along with other friends there. Guests included John Milton Hay,* William Dean Howells,* Charles Dudley Warner,* and James. It was easy for James to bargain well with the generous Osgood for high royalties, for example, $5,000 for the book rights to *The Bostonians*, but just before paying, Osgood went bankrupt. Obtaining legal advice from Sir Frederick Orridge Macmillan,* James dickered at once with Ticknor and Company, which succeeded Osgood.

Osler, Sir William (1849–1919). Ontario-born physician, educated at Trinity College, Toronto, and McGill University, Montreal. He then studied medicine in England, Germany, and Austria. After teaching in Canada and the United States (1874–1905), Osler became a professor of medicine at Oxford (1905–1919). He published, lectured, and edited in his field, and he is credited with advancing theories about psychosomatic medicine. In London, in March 1910, James consulted Dr. Osler, who had examined James's brother William earlier. The physician examined James thoroughly, found no maladies, and advised walks and a more varied life.

Osmond, Gilbert. In *The Portrait of a Lady*, the refined but uncreative and psychologically cruel former lover of Serena Merle, the father of Pansy, the brother of Countess Amy Osmond Gemini, and then (at Madame Merle's suggestion) the husband of Isabel Archer. When James depicted the domineering Osmond and his subservient daughter Pansy, he may have been influenced by his observation of his friends Francis Boott* and his daughter Elizabeth Boott.*

Osmond, Isabel Archer. In *The Portrait of a Lady*, Isabel Archer's married name.

Osmond, Mrs. In *The Portrait of a Lady*, Gilbert Osmond and Amy Osmond Gemini's deceased mother. She was "The American Corinne," a pretentious writer.

Osmond, Pansy. In *The Portrait of a Lady*, the sweet, pallid, passive, convent-educated daughter of Gilbert Osmond and his mistress Serena Merle. She greatly respects her stepmother Isabel and hopelessly loves Edward Rosier. Her sub-servience to her father may have been suggested to James by his observation of his friends Elizabeth Boott* and her father Francis Boott.*

Oswald. In "An Animated Conversation," an American painter who lives in Paris with his wife Camilla. He is critical of British novels because they are shallow.

The Other House. Short novel (70,500 words), published in the *Illustrated London News* (4 Jul–26 Sep 1896); reprinted in London by Heinemann, 1896, and in New York by Macmillan, 1896. (Characters: Rose Armiger, Kate Beever, Paul Beever, Anthony Bream, Julia Grantham Bream, Effie Bream, Paul Bream, Mrs. Gorham, Mrs. Grantham, Miss Manning, Mrs. and Mrs. Marsh, Jean Martle, Martle, Dr. and Mrs. Robert Ramage, Dennis Vidal, Walker.) Widowed Mrs. Beever, whose estate, called Wilverley, is near the other house, called Bounds, goes over there with her guest Jean Martle for lunch. But Julia Bream, mistress at Bounds, has just given birth to Effie, is sick, and is being attended by Dr. Ramage. Mrs. Beever stays to chat with Rose Armiger, Julia's former school friend. Julia exacts a promise from her husband Tony not to remarry should she die and Effie live. Rose's fiancé Dennis Vidal appears. He is on his way to China on a long business trip, but he cannot get Rose to marry him yet. Four years pass: Julia is dead, Rose loves Tony, Vidal is returning, Tony loves Jean, and Mrs. Beever is upset because she wants Jean for her son Paul. When Tony visits Wilverley, Jean goes to the other house for little Effie. Urged by Rose, Tony advises Jean to marry Paul, but the girl turns pensive. Disappointed, Mrs. Beever accuses Tony of loving Jean. Rose says that she is loyal to Effie and suspicious of Jean. When Vidal enters, Rose first apologizes to him in front of Tony but then privately tells Vidal to be wary of Jean with Effie. Rose sees Jean's joy at the knowledge of Vidal's engagement to Rose and now knows that Jean loves Tony. Rose argues with Jean, takes Effie back toward the other house, but drowns the child. Out of much confusion comes all this: Loyal Dr. Ramage will report that Effie had a fatal disease, Tony must stop feeling obliged to shield anyone, Jean must foreswear revenge, Rose rejects the still-willing young Paul, and Vidal will claim Rose, who accepts Vidal. The first Notebook entry (26 Dec 1893) concerning the idea which became *The Other House* suggests that it might make either a tale or a play. James then sketches the plot in detail. A few weeks later, according to his *Notebooks* (23 Jan 1894), he still did not know whether the plot would be better in dramatic or fictional form, further, that "a story of from 80,000 to 100,000 words . . . would greatly resemble a play." Then he planned a three-act play, seemingly inspired by some Henrik Johan Ibsen* dramas and by his friend the Ibsen actress Elizabeth Robins.* Next, he submitted to no avail at least a scenario of what he tentatively entitled *The Promise* to his friend Edward Compton,* a theater manager, for consideration. Then James rewrote the perhaps inchoate play into what he hoped would be a thrilling serial novel for Clement King Shorter,* editor of the *Illustrated London News*. Once terms were agreed upon, the rewriting was exceptionally rapid: In a letter to Shorter (24 Feb 1896), James promised "a story energetically designed to meet your requirement of a 'love-story' — and to let you have it at the time . . . you mention." Two days later he wrote to Shorter again, promising "to be thrilling, and my material is such that I think I shall succeed." James wrote to Sir Edmund Wilson Gosse* ([6 Oct 1896]) that the novel version is "a little thrifty pot-boiling turning-to-acct. of the scheme of a chucked-away 3 act play— an old relinquished scenario turned into a little story on exactly the same scenic lines"; he immediately added, "I am doing much better things [now]." Finally, in 1908 and 1909, James rewrote the play-turned novel back into a play, but it was never produced. James liked the form of the novel *The Other House*. In a late Notebook entry (4 Jan 1910), he advises himself to pattern an early scene of his projected novel *The Ivory Tower* "after the manner in which the first Book is a Prologue in *The Other House*. Oh, blest *Other House*, which gives me thus . . . a divine little light to walk by." All the same, *The Other House* is one of James's weakest novels. It is incredible that Rose Armiger should commit murder, rationalize, and escape—even if only to a sad marriage.

The Other House. Play (tentative title, *The Promise*), in a prologue and three acts, published in Philadelphia and New York by Lippincott, 1949, in *The Complete Plays of Henry James*, ed Leon Edel. (Characters: Rose Armiger, Kate Beever, Paul Beever, Black, Mr. and Mrs. Duggit, Anthony Bream, Effie Bream, Julia Bream, Mrs. Gorham, Mrs. Griffin, Jean Martle, Martle, Dr. Robert Ramage, Dennis Vidal.) Rose Armiger is a guest at Bounds, the home of Anthony Bream and his wife Julia (Rose's friend from school days), who has just given birth to Effie and who is quite weak. Jean Martle is a guest at Eastmead, the house of Kate Beever (a domineering widow and Jean's distant relative) nearby and connected by a bridge over a river to Bounds, near the town of Wilverley. Dr. Ramage attends Julia, who is sick and makes her husband promise not to remarry, should she die—during, that is, the life of their Effie. Julia has a vicious stepmother, whose visit has upset Julia, who does not want her daughter to suffer under a bad stepmother. Meanwhile, Dennis Vidal, Rose's fiancé, has returned from a venture in China. He visits and asks for a wedding date but is rebuffed. Next: June, four years later, at Mrs. Beever's house. (Julia has died.) Kate encourages her son Paul (now out of Oxford and in love with Rose, here as Kate's house guest) to marry Jean (also Kate's guest). Vidal returns from abroad to check on Effie's health, because he still wants Rose. But she loves Tony, who (at her request) urges Jean to accept Paul. She refuses him, however, since she loves Tony (though without hope). Warning Tony to guard Effie, Rose for her earlier behavior apologizes to Vidal in front of Tony, who invites him to stay at Bounds, then leaves for business in town. Rose tells Vidal she does not love Tony, offers herself to Vidal (who, baffled, leaves when Jean enters), and tells Jean she is engaged to Vidal and is sorry Jean rejected Paul because now that girl will still hope Effie dies. Rose then takes the child to the other house. Jean tells Paul that Rose is engaged to Vidal and has taken Effie home. Jean praises Paul, then leaves to bid the child goodnight. While Paul and his mother are talking, Tony returns from town, says his house is devoid of guests and Effie and learns from Paul that Jean says Rose took the child. Rose returns, accepts congratulations from Tony and Paul, lies that Jean took Effie, and bids Tony farewell since she is off to China with Vidal. Dr. Ramage rushes in: Effie has been drowned. When Rose wonders where Jean is and all suspect the girl, Tony confesses he did it. By evening, Paul has brought in the body, and Vidal comes to see Mrs. Beever, says he left Tony, Rose, and Jean together, and asks to see Rose alone. She asks him to confirm her engagement statement. He tells her he saw her at the bridge carrying Effie. She says Jean killed the child to gain Tony. Dr. Ramage talks alone with Vidal, says Jean is sick, and accepts the statement from Vidal that he and Rose are engaged. Ramage will certify Effie died of sickness, adds that Tony confessed to murder to shield Jean. Knowing Rose murdered because of passion, Vidal and Tony will lie to save both Rose and Jean. The latter enters, is near hysteria because she let Rose take Effie away, would like to crucify Rose, who, however, will hate thinking her act freed Tony and Jean. Tony leaves to comfort Gorham, Effie's weeping nurse. Rose tells brooding Paul to take comfort in knowing that she failed, predicts that Tony and Jean will marry—and sooner than they think. Paul offers to aid Rose in any way he can, but then he sees Vidal summon her brusquely away. James recorded in his Notebooks (26 Dec 1893, 23 Jan 1894) the idea for this play, showed a scenario of it in three acts to the actor and manager Edward Compton* a year or so later, then shelved it. James converted it into a short novel, entitled *The Other House* and published in 1896. In 1908 he prepared a new scenario, and in 1909, this play, which a London producer gave him £90 for against royalties, but it was never produced.

"Other Tuscan Cities." Travel essay, published in *Italian Hours*, 1909. The other cities (some already treated in earlier essays) are "charming Pisa," smiling Lucca, "high-seated" Volterra, "dirty" Montepulciano, "small stewing" Torrita, Perugia, and "strange" San Gimignano. James now sees Pisa as "the small sweet scrap of a place of ancient glory," anemic because of old wars against Florence. He used to write daily in a Pisa inn-room and then enjoy "contemplative perambulations,'' café ices, and nearby student chatter in perfect Tuscan Italian. He also liked the sights along the Lung' Arno, with its ''river-fronting palace[s], '' including one where George Gordon, Lord Byron* and Leigh Hunt stayed in 1822. James returned to Lucca, the happiest ''brown-and-gold Tuscan city'' ever, this time viewing its Bagni sitting there in ''perfect felicity'' and paying homage to Matteo Civitale's sane Duomo sculpture. James also drove dustily through the countryside and wished he could ''live back'' into a simpler past. His treatment of Volterra is ''impressionism unashamed'': massive gates, zigzag roads, volcanic hills, thin air, islands in the nearby sea. Why James went to Montepulciano, except for the wine, he does not know; or to Torrita, which lacked decent food. Then on to hospitable (but changed) Perugia. Then San Gimignano, now ''cracked and battered,'' ''cleaned out,'' ''maimed,'' its many towers like a ''heroic skeleton'' emerging from the dust. Its Santa Fina is a ''domestic treasure'' but an ''ill-set gem'' as well. James delighted in the drive back to Siena ''through the darkening land that was like a dense fragrant garden,'' with its singing ''young countryfolk.''

Ottavio. In *The Golden Bowl*, Prince Amerigo's Roman cousin.

Ouida. Pen name of Marie Louise de la Ramée (1839–1908). Popular, eccentric English novelist, whose father was French and whose mother was English. Ouida wrote many fashionable society romances, once regarded as spicy, and is best known now for her *Under Two Flags* (1867) and *A Dog of Flanders* (1872). She lived in Florence, Italy (from 1874), wrote about Italian peasants, and died in poverty. James sarcastically begins a review (*Nation*, 1 July 1875) of Ouida's *Signa: A Story* (1875) by saying that the authoress, ''a charlatan,'' used to write ''unmitigated nonsense'' but here writes ''nonsense very sensibly mitigated.'' He ridicules the characters in *Signa*, and also its style, plot, local color touches, and allusions: but he acknowledges ''a certain power of dramatic conception and effective portraiture,'' adding that its ''poetry'' and ''coloring'' create ''a sort of gaslight illusion.'' In a review of *Cities in Northern and Central Italy* by Augustus John Cuthbert Hare,* James deplores the writer's bothering to quote Ouida's ''spurious rhapsodies'' about things Italian. James's one Notebook entry (27 Feb 1889) about Ouida is derogatory: His novelist Mrs. Stormer (pen name Greville Fane) in ''Greville Fane'' is to have ''a penchant to license à la Ouida.'' In July 1907, James may have met Ouida at the London home of Sir Edmund Wilson Gosse* and his wife. When Ouida's biographer Elizabeth Lee* appealed to James for assistance, he replied (10 Feb 1913) that he had seen Ouida in Florence only a few times, had received a few ''short, very sprawling notes'' from her which were ''abusive of . . . harmless persons'' and which he had not kept, and regards her as of ''tarnished lustre.'' She was able, however, to perceive ''the beauty . . . of Italy'' but might best be treated by a biographer as a ''pathetic *grotesque*.'' Lee published *Ouida: A Memoir* in 1914.

"Our Artists in Europe." The 1889 title of the art essay retitled "Black and White" in 1893.

The Outcry. Short novel (56,400 words), published in London by Methuen, 1911, and in New York by Scribner, 1911. (Characters: Banks, Bardi, Breckenridge Bender, Hugh Crimble, Gotch, Lady Grace, Lady Kitty Imber, Lord John, Lady Lappington, Mackintosh, Mantovano, Pappendick, Mrs. and Mrs. Penniman, Lady Amy Sandgate, Lord Theign, Duchess of Waterbridge.) Widowed Lord Theign has many art treasures at Dedborough Place, and also two daughters—widowed Lady Kitty Imber and lovely young Lady Grace. Now, Lord John wants to marry Grace, whose sister Kitty owes John's mother, a duchess, thousands of pounds in gambling debts. To rescue Kitty, Theign must both persuade Grace to marry John and also promise her a big inheritance. The Duchess would then be willing to cancel Kitty's debt. So Theign invites Breckenridge Bender, a rich, avid art collector from America, to come bid on his *Duchess of Waterbridge* by Joshua Reynolds.* Theign's close friend Lady Sandgate owns a portrait by Sir Thomas Lawrence of her great-grandmother, which Bender covets. A young art critic named Hugh Crimble, whom Grace prefers to John, accepts her invitation to evaluate the Dedborough art collection, which includes a supposed Moretto. Bender spurns this painting, when it is offered in place of the Reynolds, until he gets wind of Crimble's theory that it is really a rare, unsuspected Mantovano. A family argument ensues: Theign might sell the painting; Grace wants him to be loyal to England and keep it; John wants Grace; and Grace sides with Crimble, whom she urges to authenticate the alleged Mantovano. When the newspapers raise a patriotic outcry, Bender is simply delighted. Grace, out of favor with her mettlesome daddy, meets Hugh at Lady Sandgate's London home. He reports that an art authority named Pappendick denies that the so-called Moretto is really a Mantovano. The outcry causes Theign not only to dislike the idea of selling his painting out of England but also to suspect John of being mercenary. Visiting Lady Sandgate and armed with his checkbook, Bender fails to meet Theign, who has just left for Kitty's. Later Bender is making out a check for Lady Sandgate's Lawrence when Theign returns with a premature but accurate report: He is giving his Moretto to the National Gallery, for which the prince is coming to commend his munificent patriotism. Hugh arrives with superior art authority Bardi's statement that the Moretto is really a Mantovano. All depart except Theign and Lady Sandgate. He spies Bender's check, tears it up, and challenges its would-be recipient to match his generosity by donating her Lawrence to the Gallery. Her agreeing to do so unites the two. This novel, the last which James was to complete, began in 1909 as his last play. He was inspired in part by the uproar caused when foreign money nearly took *The Duchess of Milan* by Hans Holbein the younger* out of England. James turned his play into a novel, during his last visit to the United States, in less than a year; it was published in 1911 and surprised its author by selling well. In a dust-jacket prospectus written in 1911 for his novel, James suggests that British inheritors of precious works of art should be "jealous" rather than "lax guardians." James thought that he had made up the name Mantovano, only to learn from an appreciative reader in November 1912 that there really was a painter of that name—Rinaldo Mantovano* of Mantua, Italy. A critical mini-outcry can be raised over James's theme here. How should American money be spent? James's friend Isabella Stewart Gardner*—that is, "Mrs. Jack," the friend and advisee of art-critic Bernard Berenson*—used her millions to raid Europe and fill her beautiful Fenway Court in Boston with art treasures (including a pair of portraits by Hans Holbein the younger*). James's fictive Mrs. Gracedew purchased Covering End and thus saved Captain Clement Yule ("Covering End"). And James's millionaire Adam Verver seems to be a responsible art collector (*The Golden Bowl*).

The Outcry. Three-act play, published in Philadelphia and New York by Lippincott, 1949, in *The Complete Plays of Henry James*, ed. Leon Edel. (Characters: Banks, Breckenridge Bender, Caselli, Hugh Crimble, Gotch, Lady Grace, Lady Kitty Imber, Lord John, Lady Lappington, Mackintosh, Mantovano, Pappendick, Lady Amy Sandgate, Lord Theign, Duchess of Waterbridge.) To Lord Theign's Dedborough Park mansion, laden with fine paintings, come three men. They are Breckenridge Bender, American art purchaser; Hugh Crimble, art scholar who likes Theign's daughter Lady Grace; and Lord John, Grace's suitor to whose mother Grace's widowed sister Lady Kitty Imber owes gambling debts. Hugh sees a supposed Moretto painting, believes it to be by Mantovano, and will ask an expert (Pappendick of Brussels) his opinion; but he then annoys Theign by expressing the hope the painting will never be sold. Bender wants a Joshua Reynolds* painting owned by Theign but becomes excited about a possible Mantovano. He also wants a Thomas Lawrence painting owned by Lady Amy Sandgate, Theign's friend. John persuades Theign to support his proposal of marriage to Grace, and he suggests that he sell some art treasures and give Grace a dowry; if so, John's mother will not only cancel Kitty's debt to her but also settle a sum on her son. Hugh and Grace, who rejects John, oppose these plans and resolve to work together, thus angering Theign. In her London drawing room three weeks later, Lady Sandgate greets the principals, who come and go: Grace and Hugh, whom whe likes and who report that the newspapers are raising an outcry against rumors of art sales to foreigners; Bender, who wants but cannot have Lady Sandgate's Lawrence; John, who is inactive; and Theign, who is indifferent to the outcry, and who will not sell Bender his Reynolds but offers him the supposed Mantovano. Theign argues with Grace, who offers to give up Hugh if her father promises not to sell the picture. But then Hugh returns with news: Pappendick says the Moretto is not a Mantovano. Hugh requests a second expert opinion (that of Caselli, of Milan). Alone with Grace, Theign now agrees to retain the picture if she will not see Hugh again; but this time she refuses. Two weeks later, again in Amy's drawing room, people come and go. Grace and Hugh meet to explain matters and exchange vows of love. Theign returns from Easter abroad, tells John he is indifferent to the outcry but resents both being the center of a controversy over a possibly fraudulent artistic attribution and also Bender's excessive offer of £100,000 if the painting is a Mantovano. Bender relishes the publicity, which now includes the public exhibition of the controversial painting. John is so eager that Theign accuses him of working on Bender's behalf for a commission, says he would rather donate the painting to the government, and orders John to go stop the exhibition. Theign goes to see Kitty in her house nearby. Bender, alone with Amy, starts to discuss her Lawrence when John returns to announce the prince went to the exhibition, wants it to continue, and will see Theign here at Amy's. John goes for Theign. Hugh returns to report that Caselli defines the painting as a Mantovano and will professionally praise Hugh. Bender is thus interrupted while writing a check for Amy and goes off to consult Caselli. Theign returns, sees the check, writes Bender a letter which Hugh (now with Grace beside him) will deliver. Alone with Amy, Theign explains that John told the prince that Theign will donate the picture, tears up her incomplete check from Bender, persuades her to donate her Lawrence, and proposes to her with a kiss of her hand. John announces the arrival of the prince. In 1909 American producer Charles Frohman* asked James to write a play to be included in a big repertory season, which would also feature works by Sir James Matthew Barrie,* Harley Granville Granville-Barker,* John Galsworthy,* John Masefield, W. Somerset Maugham, and George Bernard Shaw.* This group was crying out against British censorship of the theater. Although James joined this outcry as well, his play *The Outcry*, which he finished late in 1909 and revised early in 1910, overtly concerns another outcry—the one raised against American millionaires looting Europe of art treasures. British theaters were closed when King Edward VII* died on 6 May 1910, and Frohman cancelled production plans and paid James a £200 forfeit. James then turned his play into the novel *The Outcry*. In 1914 Granville-Barker tried in vain to induce James to seek a production of *The Outcry* by the Moscow Art Theatre.

Outreau, Paul. In "The Beldonald Holbein," the narrator's French painter friend who sees Holbeinesque qualities in Louisa Brash's ugly face.

d'Outreville, Duchess. In *The American*, a French aristocrat whom Christopher Newman meets at the Bellegarde party in his honor. He later decides not to tell her about the Bellegarde family scandal.

d'Outreville, Mme. In *The Reverberator*, Suzanne de Brécourt's friend.

Overmore, Miss. In *What Maisie Knew*, the attractive woman whom Beale Farange first hires as his daughter Maisie's nurse, then marries, and later ignores. Miss Overmore then becomes Beale's ex-wife Ida Farange's second husband's mistress.

Overt, Mrs. In "The Lesson of the Master," Paul Overt's recently deceased invalid mother.

Overt, Paul. In "The Lesson of the Master," the young novelist who takes the experienced novelist Henry St. George's advice to continue writing instead of weakening his talent by marrying Marian Fancourt, whom St. George, when later widowed, marries puzzlingly. James may have given Overt the first name Paul because of his friendship with Paul Bourget.*

"Owen Wingrave." Short story (12,600 words), published in the *Graphic* (28 Nov 1892); reprinted in *The Private Life* (London), 1893, and in *The Wheel of Time*, 1893; revised and reprinted in *The Novels and Tales of Henry James*, Volume XVII, 1909. (Characters: Mr. and Mrs. Spencer Coyle, Captain Hume-Walker, Kate Julian, Mrs. Julian, Lechmere, Jane Wingrave, Owen Wingrave, Sir Philip Wingrave, Philip Wingrave, Colonel Wingrave, Wingrave.) Owen Wingrave tells his preparatory school superintendent Spencer Coyle that he will not follow the Wingrave family wishes and train any longer for a military career. Coyle reminds the young man of his family background: Owen's grandfather Sir Philip Wingrave was an illustrious soldier and is now a tough old man of eighty; Owen's father was killed by Afghans; and Owen has an imbecilic older brother (Philip) and an unmarried aunt (Jane Wingrave), whose companion (Mrs. Julian) is the sister of Captain Hume-Walker, once engaged to Jane but broken with and sent to a soldier's death in India. Then Coyle confers with Jane and meets Mrs. Julian's impertinent, silly daughter Kate, who loves Owen, but doubts and taunts him. Owen goes home when ordered, but the massed family cannot force him to alter his pacifist decision. A week later Coyle and his wife, the latter sympathetic to young Owen, attend an overnight party at Paramore, the Wingraves' country estate. Kate will not believe that Owen is brave enough to spend a night in a room haunted by the ghost of his great-great-grandfather, who in anger struck and accidentally killed his son there long ago. Owen insists that he spent last night there and does so again. At dawn he is found dead in the haunted room. James got the idea for this story, he says in a Notebook entry (26 Mar 1892), while reading *Memoirs of His Life and Campaigns* (1891) by Jean Baptiste Antoine Marcelin, Baron de Marbot,* one of Napoleon's most articulate generals. A personality like that of Marbot—an almost supernaturally forceful military spirit—should confront a descendant who, though hating ugly and bloody war, proves himself to be brave and honorable as well. According to a later Notebook entry (8 May 1892), James thought of casting the ghostly action in an English country house during Napoleon's time. In 1907 and 1908, James converted the story into a one-act play, entitled *The Saloon*. George Bernard Shaw* read it in manuscript and wrote to James early in 1909 that he would have preferred to have the hero conquer the ghost. James replied at considerable length (20 Jan 1909) to defend his play but also to deprecate his short story as "an obscure pot-boiler." After unavoidable delays, the play finally opened in London, on 17 January 1911. In the preface to Volume XVII of *The Novels and Tales of Henry James*, James explains that storytellers who keep notebooks find that their notes "sometimes explicitly mention, sometimes indirectly reveal, and sometimes wholly dissimulate . . . clues" as to story sources. Then he muses about seeing a young man—tall, thin, grave—seated in Kensington Gardens reading a book. There was his Owen, "by . . . magic."

The Oxford-Cambridge Boat Race. In a brief report (*Nation*, 12 Apr 1877), James wonders why he paid a sovereign to stand on Barnes Bridge, on 24 March 1877, to observe the annual four-mile boat race between the "powerful" Oxford crew and the "plucky" Cambridge crew. Should he "laugh or . . . feel very solemn" while "witness[ing] twenty minutes' boyish sport on the part of a few young gentlemen engaged in book-learning at college"? But then the boats shot under the bridge "like great, white, water-skimming birds, with eight-feathered wings," and James enjoys describing in detail their dead-heat finish.

P

Packard, General. In *The American*, an unimportant friend of Christopher Newman's in Paris.

Page, Walter Hines (1855–1918). American journalist, editor, publisher, and diplomat. He was associate editor (1895–1898) and then editor (1898–1899) of the *Atlantic Monthly*. He founded *World's Work* (1900) and edited it for a time. Page was ambassador to England (1913–1918). His letters were published (3 vols., 1922–1925). James knew Page and his wife socially and through him may have met Franklin Delano Roosevelt,* in June 1914.

Paget, Violet (1856–1935). Versatile British woman of letters, whose pen name was Vernon Lee. She was born near Boulogne, France, of English parents. Her father was a distinguished diplomat. She became a precocious writer and lived (from 1871) mostly in her villa at Maiano, near Florence, Italy. Her paralyzed half-brother was Eugene Jacob Lee-Hamilton,* a poet. The two lived uneasily together until their estrangement. Her varied books, about forty in number, include *Studies of the Eighteenth Century in Italy* (1880, praised by Robert Browning* and Walter Horatio Pater*), *Belcaro: Being Essays on Sundry Aesthetical Questions* (1881), *Euphorion: Being Studies of the Antique and the Medieval in the Renaissance* (1884), *Miss Brown* (3 vols., 1884, a novel), *Limbo, and Other Essays* (1897), *Hauntings: Fantastic Stories* (1890), *Vanitas: Polite Stories* (1892, including "Lady Tal"), *Genius Loci: Notes on Places* (1899), *Ariadne in Mantua: A Romance in Five Acts* (1903), *Pope Jacynth, and Other Fantastic Tales* (1905), *Gospels of Anarchy* (1908), *The Sentimental Traveler: Notes on Places* (1908), *Vital Lies: Studies on Some Varieties of Recent Obscurantism* (1912, essays), *Satan the Waster: A Philosophical Trilogy* (1920),

The Handling of Words and Other Studies in Literary Psychology (1923, including an analysis of James's style), and *Music and Its Lovers* (1932). James began to socialize with Violet Paget in London in 1884, through Mary Augusta Ward* and Agnes Mary Frances Robinson.* (Paget, who evidently had lesbian tendencies, deplored Mary Robinson's marriage to James Darmesteter). James encouraged Paget more than he realized and was therefore surprised when she dedicated *Miss Brown* to him. He thanked her by letter (21 Oct [1884]), said that he was unworthy, and praised her earlier book *Euphorion* as ''a prodigious young performance, so full of intellectual power, knowledge, brilliance, the idea of being *comme chez vous* at the dizziest heights of the Idea.'' But to Thomas Sergeant Perry* he wrote (12 Dec [1884]) that *Miss Brown* is ''very bad . . . and . . . painfully disagreeable in tone.'' To Grace Norton* (24 Jan [1885]) he was more frank and detailed: *Belcaro* and *Euphorion* were ''imperfect but . . . able and interesting books,'' whereas *Miss Brown* ''is a rather serious mistake . . . with an awful want of taste and of tact . . . yet . . . interesting . . . if . . . unsavoury . . . ''After a delay, James wrote to Paget (10 May [1885]) to call *Miss Brown* ''an imperfect, but a very interesting book,'' but then proceeded to mention its flaws in style and form. When he called on her in Italy a few years later, he thought even less of her, now describing her in a letter to Grace Norton (25 Jan [1887]) as ''clever, tactless and tasteless (intellectually),'' though adept as a conversationalist. To Sarah Butler Wister* (27 Feb [1887]) he admits that Paget, ''though very ugly, disputatious and awkwardly situated *comme famille*[,] . . . possesses the only mind I could discover in the place [Florence] . . . '' He stresses her intellect in a letter to Sir Edmund Wilson Gosse* (24 Apr [1887]): ''She has one of the best minds I know—almost worthy to be French.'' In a letter to Paget (27 Apr 1890), James lauds ''the bold, aggressive speculative fancy'' displayed in *Hauntings* and loves her evocation therein ''of the air of Italian things.'' When Paget spoofed James through her depiction of him as a character named Jervase Marion in ''Lady Tal,'' James wrote to William Morton Fullerton* (16 Jan [1893]), ''I don't *care* to care.'' But he did care, for he wrote to his brother William a few days later (20 Jan [1893]) that in *Vanitas* ''tiger-cat'' Paget ''directed a kind of satire of a flagrant and markedly 'saucy' kind at me (!!)—exactly the sort of thing she has repeatedly done to others . . . and [a] particularly impudent and blackguardly sort of thing to do to a friend and one who has treated her with such particular consideration as I have.'' Although James asked his brother not to betray this confidence, William dispatched a critical letter to Paget, who apologized. (William James reverted to dislike again when Paget adversely reviewed his 1897 book *The Will to Believe*, in the *Fortnightly*.) After 1893 James cooled his friendship with Paget; it had been a relationship shared with many notables, including Bernard Berenson,* Paul Bourget,* Margaret Alice Lili Brooke,* Katherine De Kay Bronson,* Mrs. W. K. Clifford,* Ariana Randolph Curtis* and Daniel Sargent Curtis,* Anatole France,* Ouida,* Pater, John Singer Sargent* (to whom she had loaned her paint box when he was a child, and who sketched and painted her), and Herbert George Wells.* James's library contained sixteen books by Paget.

Pakenham family. Anglo-Irish military family of some distinction. Through a letter of introduction from Sarah Butler Wister,* James in 1877 became a frequent guest at functions in the London home of Elizabeth Staples Clark Pakenham, a belle from New York and the wife of General Thomas Henry Pakenham, who was a distant in-law of the Duke of Wellington. In a letter to his brother William (28 Feb [1877]), James described Mrs. Pakenham as "a very nice woman with a very nice husband." James also happily spent some time around Christmas 1880 as a guest of the Pakenhams at the general's Government House headquarters in Plymouth. James enjoyed a lavish military dinner there but felt outranked afterward. The Pakenhams had two sons, who later entered the army. His Pocket Diaries indicate that James continued his friendship with the Pakenhams into the 1910s.

Palgrave, Francis Turner (1824–1897). English educator, anthologist, poet, and critic. Trained at Balliol College, Oxford, he became an education administrator, taught at Oxford, and published some poetry and literary criticism, but he is best remembered for his anthology *The Golden Treasury of English Songs and Lyrics* (1861; 2d series, 1897). In 1877 James met Palgrave at a London dinner party. A month later Palgrave called on James, who in a letter to his brother William (28 Feb [1877]) pronounces the man "not *sympathique*, but apparently well intentioned." In a letter to Henry Adams* (5 May 1877), James indicates that, although he did not like Palgrave at first, "each time we have met I thought better of him," and says that "[h]e pitches into people too promiscuously" only because he is an exuberant conversationalist. In a letter to his father (25 Mar [1878]), James does some pitching-into himself, calling Mrs. Palgrave "the most unattractive form of the *Anglaise*." Palgrave's volubility and his wife's silence intrigued James, who in a Notebook entry (23 May 1901) records an idea for a story (never written) about an "overwhelming and inconsiderate . . . chatterbox" who discovers after his wife has died that her conversation was admired by others; James adds a sufficient identification: "Think . . . of F.T.P."

Pallant, Henry. In "Louisa Pallant," mentioned as the deceased husband of Louisa and therefore Linda's father.

Pallant, Linda. In "Louisa Pallant," Henry and Louisa Pallant's daughter. Her selfish ambition to marry Archie Parker is thwarted by her mother's tardy honesty. Linda later marries Gimingham.

Pallant, Louisa. In "Louisa Pallant," Linda Pallant's mother, who warns Archie Parker about her cold, socially ambitious daughter since her own conscience troubles her for having jilted Parker's uncle, the narrator, long ago. Or does Louisa want her daughter to make a richer catch?

"Pandora." Short story (18,500 words), published in the New York *Sun* (1, 8 June 1884); republished in *The Author of Beltraffio*, 1885, and in *Stories Revived*, 1885; revised and reprinted in *The Novels and Tales of Henry James*, Volume XVIII, 1909. (Characters: D. F. Bellamy, Alfred Bonnycastle, Mrs. Alfred Bonnycastle, Mrs. Dangerfield, Pandora Day, Mrs. and Mrs. P. W. Day, Day, Miss Day, Lansing, Mrs. Runkle, Commodore Steuben, Mrs. Steuben, Count Otto Vogelstein.) Aboard ship from Germany to Southhampton to New York, Count Otto Vogelstein observes an American family named Day. He talks to Pandora, the older daughter; but he is warned by Mrs. Dangerfield against the Days' vulgarity, and he is prejudiced anyway against pushy American girls by a recent reading of "Daisy Miller." So he fears he will not like his assignment at the Washington, D.C., German legation. Eighteen months later, Vogelstein again sees Pandora Day, this time at fashionable Mrs. and Mrs. Alfred Bonnycastle's party attended by the president. Vogelstein watches Pandora hit up the president for a foreign assignment for her friend D. F. Bellamy of Utica. Through Mrs. Steuben, Pandora's Washington society sponsor, the count renews acquaintance with the irrepressible girl at a Mount Vernon picnic. She recalls his offish shipboard conduct and cools his present ardor in other ways as well. It is later announced that Bellamy will be minister to Holland and that he and Miss Day are to be married. According to a Notebook entry (2 Jan 1884), James planned to "do the 'self-made girl' . . . in a way to make her a rival to D[aisy] M[iller]." We can watch James's mind at work: He wants "the concision of *Four Meetings*, with the success of *Daisy M.*" Then, "It must take place in New York. Perhaps indeed Washington would do." Then, "[t]his would give me a chance to *do* Washington . . . I might even *do* Henry Adams and his wife." Then, "The hero might be a foreign secretary of legation—German—inquiring and conscientious." Then, "show the contrast between the humble social background of the heroine, and the position which she . . . is making." James mentions ideas concerning the hero and heroine in New York, then Washington, the president, the heroine's helpless family, and the planned story length, which, as usual, he exceeds. James placed this story and "Georgina's Reasons" in the New York *Sun* simply for high pay. In the preface to Volume XXVIII of *The Novels and Tales of Henry James*, he describes Pandora Day as an example of "the 'self-made,' or at least self-making, girl," at one time "quaint or fresh or . . . exclusively native to any one tract of Anglo-Saxon soil," but not so any longer. He implies that his treatment of downtown New York City in "Pandora" is skimpy owing to his inexperience there. A neat touch in the story comes when Vogelstein is seen aboard ship, on his way to America, uneasily reading "Daisy Miller," whose heroine is a kind of psychological twin of Pandora, who so puzzles the earnest count. The Bonnycastles are indeed patterned after Henry Adams* and his wife Marian Adams,* whom James visited in January 1882 and in whose home he met President Chester A. Arthur.* The fictive Bonnycastle party, where Vogelstein sees Pandora again, may be dated April 1881; therefore, the president was James Abram Garfield.* But James deliberately blurs time lines and presidential facial features so that the casual reader may wonder whether Garfield or Arthur, or even Rutherford B. Hayes, was the guest. Washington non-culture is scathingly depicted.

"The Papers." Long short story (tentative title, "Maud Blandy"; 35,000 words), published in *The Better Sort*, 1903. (Characters: Sir A. B. C. Beadel-Muffet, Lady Beadel-Muffet, Miranda Beadel-Muffet, the Misses Beadel-Muffet, Beatrice Beaumont, Howard Bight, Maud Blandy, Mrs. Chorner, Guy Devereux, Mortimer Marshal, Lord and Lady Wispers.) Maud Blandy and her suitor Howard Bight, both of whom are reporters, discuss publicity-hound Sir A. B. C. Beadel-Muffet, K.C.B., M.P., a "distinguished" nonentity whom Bight says he has driven into hiding and perhaps suicide. It seems that Beadel-Muffet's fiancée Mrs. Chorner professes to hate publicity and is distressed by seeing his name in the tabloids. Meanwhile, Miss Blandy's friend Mortimer Marshal, a weak playwright, wants publicity. So Bight suggests that to kid him they create news about Beadel-Muffet, whose suicide in Frankfort is later announced. Both Bight and Maud are upset. But he continues to twit Marshal, with whom Maud begins to sympathize. Then it is announced that Beadel-Muffet is alive and well: His "suicide" merely created more publicity for him. Having valuable notes from interviewing Mrs. Chorner, Maud is glad she did not write them up for publication, since doing so might have hurt the woman's chances with Beadel-Muffet. Bight promised to produce Beadel-Muffet after his disappearance and before his "suicide" and Maud promised to marry Bight if he could do so. But the man's return baffles clever Bight, who decides to quit journalism, to the delight of Maud, who has been further disillusioned by Mrs. Chorner's suppressed but tardily revealed desire for publicity of her own. Given his desire to present contrasting characters, it is not surprising that James began "The Papers," according to a Notebook entry (19 Oct 1901), with the notion of a "little antithesis" between a journalist who sadly fails to get answers from the great and one to whom the illustrious scream for attention in ugly ways. He went on to contrast not merely Maud and Howard, but Beadel-Muffet and Marshal as well. The villain of this prolix piece, as it is in *The Reverberator*, is sensational journalism itself. Perhaps James remembered with discomfort his own attempts to send chatty columns, now published as *Parisian Sketches*, from Paris to the New York *Tribune* in 1875–1876.

Pappendick. In *The Outcry*, the novel, a Brussels art critic, less able than Bardi of Milan, who asserts that Lord Theign's painting supposedly by Moretto is really by Mantovano. In *The Outcry*, the play, Pappendick, based in Brussels, is overruled by an art critic from Milan named Caselli.

Paraday, Mr. and Mrs. Neil. In "The Death of the Lion," the distinguished novelist and his estranged wife. His suddenly being lionized is the indirect cause of his death.

Pardon, Matthias. In *The Bostonians*, a pushy Boston journalist, just under age thirty, who would like to marry Verena Tarrant and exploit her talents as a speaker to his advantage.

"Paris As It Is." Paris letter, published in the New York *Tribune* (25 Dec 1875); reprinted in *Parisian Sketches*, 1957. James discusses an exhibition of the late Louis Barye's statues of "wild beasts, in attitudes more or less ferocious"; James praises their realistic depiction of natural cruelty. He comments on Jean-Baptiste Carpeaux, another recently deceased sculptor, whose sensational group statue *La Danse*, in the new (1875) Paris Opera house, caused "mingled admiration and perplexity" because the figures are perpetually smiling and "their poor, lean, individualized bodies are pitifully real." He lists the artistic embellishments in the renovated Odéon Theater foyer and praises the aged actress Pauline Virginie Déjazet, who had just died.

"Parisian Affairs." Paris letter, published in the New York *Tribune* (25 Mar 1876); reprinted in *Parisian Sketches*, 1957. James discusses the political consequences of a Republican majority (led by Léon Gambetta) over the defeated Bonapartists (led by Louis Buffet) in the Assembly. Next, James criticizes *L'Étrangère*, the new play by Alexandre Dumas *fils*,* starring Sarah Bernhardt* and Benoît Constant Coquelin*). Next, James demeans a masked ball held in the new Opera (with the orchestra conducted by Johann Strauss) as featuring "laborious gambols of the rabble."

"Parisian Festivity." Paris letter, published in the New York *Tribune* (13 May 1876); reprinted in *Parisian Sketches*, 1957. James humorously describes the advent of cartoonable British tourists in Paris now that the religious holidays are over. He touches on the "fantastic and picturesque horsemanship" at the Concours Hippique but deplores all military implications. Next, an exhibition of impressionist paintings, which James calls "decidedly interesting " but which does not reveal any "first-rate talent." Then he calls Auguste Mermet's new opera, *Jeanne d'Arc*, "hopelessly dull and tame" but confesses that "musical things are fathomless mysteries" to him anyway. Finally, brief comments on *Chroniques Parisiennes* and *Cahiers de Sainte-Beuve*, by Charles Augustin Sainte-Beuve,* and *Son Excellence Eugène Rougon* by Émile Zola.*

"Parisian Life." Paris letter, published in the New York *Tribune* (5 Feb 1876); reprinted in *Parisian Sketches*, 1957. James says that one should avoid discussing French politics if possible, but that it is almost the only current topic. The French tend to group persons delimitingly. Louis Buffet, an influential political leader, agitates and goads. James offers a plot summary of *Les Danicheff*, a "fanciful" new play (by "Pierre Newsky," and considerably rewritten by Alexandre Dumas *fils*) at the Odéon Theater. James praises that "consummate artist" Ernesto

Rossi's Romeo in a "scandalously mutilated" Italian version of *Romeo and Juliet* by William Shakespeare.*

"Parisian Sketches." Paris letter, published in the New York *Tribune* (22 Jan 1876); reprinted in *Parisian Sketches*, 1957. James discusses the sale to Alexander Turney Stewart* of the painting by Jean-Louis-Ernest Meissonier* entitled *The Battle of Friedland* (also called *1807*). James describes the display of wealth, energy, and joy in Paris during the Christmas season. He loves the sights along the Seine, especially Notre Dame, and higher, to St. Étienne du Mont and St. Geneviève.

Parisian Sketches. James's twenty letters from Paris to the New York *Tribune* (11 Dec 1875–26 Aug 1876); reprinted in New York by New York University Press, 1957, as *Parisian Sketches*, ed. Leon Edel and Ilse Dusoir Lind. The letters, with dates of newspaper publication, are as follows: 1. "Paris Revisited" (11 Dec 1875); 2. "Paris As It Is" (25 Dec 1875); 3. "Versailles As It Is" (8 Jan 1876); 4. "Parisian Sketches" (22 Jan 1876); 5. "The Parisian Stage" (29 Jan 1876); 6. "Parisian Life" (5 Feb 1876); 7. "Parisian Topics" (19 Feb 1876); 8. "Paris in Election Time" (4 Mar 1876); 9. "Parisian Affairs" (25 Mar 1876); 10. "Parisian Topics" (1 Apr 1876); 11. "Art and Letters in Paris" (22 Apr 1876); 12. "Chartres Portrayed" (29 Apr 1876); 13. "Parisian Festivity" (13 May 1876); 14. "Art in France" (27 May 1876); 15. "Art in Paris" (5 Jun 1876); 16. "Parisian Topics" (17 Jun 1876); 17. "Parisian Topics" (1 Jul 1876); 18. "George Sand" (22 Jul 1876); 19. "Summer in France" (12 Aug 1876); and 20. "A French Watering Place" (26 Aug 1876). In *Portraits of Places*, 1883, "Chartres Portrayed" was reprinted as "Chartres," "Summer in France" as "Rouen," and "A French Watering Place" as "Etretat." Nine other letters were partly reprinted in New Brunswick, New Jersey, 1948, by Rutgers University Press, in *The Scenic Art: Notes on Acting & the Drama: 1872–1901*, ed. Alan Wade; and in London by Rupert Hart-Davis, 1956, in *The Painter's Eye*, ed. John L. Sweeney. In 1875 James decided to leave the United States and live abroad, specifically (at first) in Paris; so he wrote to his friend John Milton Hay,* then an editorial writer for the New York *Tribune* under its general editor Whitelaw Reid,* to offer to send back letters for pay. He was hired at $20 per letter, went to Paris and in due course sent nineteen letters, and then asked for $30 per letter. Reid replied to complain gently that James's writing was suitable for magazines, but that to fit into the *Tribune* they should be more journalistic, more newsy; he then suggested that James submit shorter and more frequent letters, for $20 per letter, as before. James, who had already dispatched what became the final letter, wrote to Reid (30 Aug 1876) to resign, saying that his letters "are the poorest I can do, especially for the money!" Reid was right. James's Parisian letters do not offer chatty gossip but instead analytical, critical, reflective comments on plays, paintings, politics, and writers, and painterly impressions of scenic locales. James wrote inaccurately to his father (16 Sept

[1876]) that "Whitelaw Reid . . . stopped off my letters . . . practically . . . by demanding that they should be of a flimsier sort. I thought . . . they had been flimsy
enough. I am a little sorry to stop, but much glad. I can use the material more
remuneratively otherwise." James was right too.

"The Parisian Stage." Theater essay, published in the *Nation* (9 Jan 1873);
reprinted in *Transatlantic Sketches*, 1875. James says that the theater is important
to the French and adds much about "French ideas, manners, and philosophy."
Going to the Théâtre Français makes one "an ardent Gallomaniac." He ecstat-
ically recalls seeing both Molière's *Mariage Forcé* ("strong ale") and *Il ne faut
jurer de rien* by Alfred de Musset* ("fine sherry") performed there to perfection.
James discuss plots and quality of acting (by Benoît Constant Coquelin,* Aimée
Olympe Desclée, and François Jules Edmond Got*) and notes that French audiences also interest him. Dramatists rework old material to amuse or moralize
(too often on adultery). James closes with praise of a recent splendid production
of Pierre de Corneille's *Le Cid*.

"The Parisian Stage." Paris letter, published in the New York *Tribune* (29
Jan 1876); reprinted in *Parisian Sketches*, 1957. Calling the theater more than
"a mere amusement," indeed "an institution connected . . . with literature, art,
and society," James reports on contemporary Parisian plays, actors, and actresses, all seeming weaker than those of the past. He notes that current examples
of the *opéra bouffe* are not "vulgar or trivial or indecent," simply "unhis-
trionic." Ernesto Rossi as Macbeth was "decidedly bungling." Victorien Sardou* used his "well-tested recipe" to concoct a fine "pudding," his new play
Ferréol, and Gustave Hippolyte Worm's acting in it is satisfyingly realistic.
James comments on a few other stage offerings and the acting therein.

"Parisian Topics." Paris letter, published in the New York *Tribune* (19 Feb
1876); reprinted in *Parisian Sketches*, 1957. James ridicules the recent address
by Victor-Marie Hugo* to the communal delegates as yet another instance of
"national conceit" in France. We ought to be allowed to "enjoy . . . the various
succulent fruits of French civilization" without having to prostrate ourselves
before France. James discusses the oddity of Frenchmen crowding together to
hear a poetry reading to raise money for a statue honoring Alphonse de Lamartine.
James discusses *conférences*, that is, public lectures in Paris, usually unattractive
except when Francisque Sarcey* performs. James concludes by complimenting
a posthumous exhibition of paintings by Isidore Pils and two paintings by Ferdinand Victor Eugène Delacroix.*

"Parisian Topics." Paris letter, published in the New York *Tribune* (1 Apr
1876); reprinted in *Parisian Sketches*, 1957. Noting the reception at the French
Academy of John Lemoinne,* James criticizes that journalist bitterly. Then he
comments on the purchase by Alexander Turney Stewart* of a painting by Jean

Léon Gérôme* called *Chariot Race*, which has all kinds of Roman detail but also crude coloring. Next, an "exhilarating," eight-act show at the Théâtre Historique featuring Abraham Lincoln and Stonewall Jackson, with a "tangled web" of a plot which James "cannot begin to unweave," although he then humorously tries to do just that. Finally, he ridicules the new anti-German book by Victor Tissot* entitled *Les Prussiens en Allemagne*.

"Parisian Topics." Paris letter, published in the New York *Tribune* (17 Jun 1876); reprinted in *Parisian Sketches*, 1957. James begins with a review of *Dialogues et Fragments Philosophiques* by Joseph Ernest Renan.* Then he turns to the funeral of controversial historian Jules Michelet, whose widow successfully contested with her Cannes in-laws for his reinterment in Paris; James includes commentary on a recent essay on Michelet. Next he details the career of actress Jeanne Arnould-Plessy, whose "extraordinary perfection" he lauds and who is now retiring. Then he discusses an exhibition of paintings refused by the Salon and showing elsewhere. Finally, he says a few words about a show of architectural drawings (for a generally unwanted, lavish 1878 Exhibition)—all "so much darkness visible" to James.

"Parisian Topics." Paris letter, published in the New York *Tribune* (1 Jul 1876); reprinted in *Parisian Sketches*, 1957. First James reviews the recently published letters of the late Ximénès Doudan.* Then he touches on several topics: an anti-Catholic university bill, the season of Italian music now concluding (he calls the *Requiem* of Giuseppe Verdi "a feast of vocalism"), recent sculpture and painting (he likes the "fantastic" work of Gustave Moreau* better now), and the recent death of George Sand.*

"Paris in Election Time." Paris letter, published in the New York *Tribune* (4 Mar 1876); reprinted in *Parisian Sketches*, 1957. James reports on recent French Senate and imminent French Assembly elections, politician Léon Gambetta's anticlericalism with respect to French university education, politician Louis Buffet's appearance and reputation, *Grandeur ou Déclin de la France* by Émile de Girardin,* and the ability of recently deceased actor Frédéric Lemaître (compared to that of more modern actors).

"Paris Revisited." Paris letter, published in the New York *Tribune* (11 Dec 1875); reprinted in *Parisian Sketches*, 1957. Only upon his returning to Paris does an American's "sense of Parisian things become . . . supremely acute." Then the city seems better or worse. The French know how to live. Americans abroad pay for delights, shop much (making Paris "a vast fancy bazaar"), have an American colony near the Grand Hotel, and can enjoy new plays (by Alexandre Dumas *fils** and Victorien Sardou,* for example) and the new Opera house ("perhaps a trifle disappointing"), and performances by established and popular actors (including Ernesto Rossi).

"Paris Revisited." Original title of "Occasional Paris."

Parker, Archie. In "Louisa Pallant," the narrator's nephew and predatory Linda Pallant's temporary object. Linda's conscience-stricken mother frustrates the girl's plan.

Parker, Charlotte. In "Louisa Pallant," the narrator's sister and Archie's mother.

Parker, Miss. In "A Light Man," Theodore Lisle's infant niece.

Parker, Miss. In "Louisa Pallant," Archie Parker's delicate little sister.

Parker, Mr. and Mrs. In "The Pension Beaurepas," a couple mentioned by Mrs. Ruck as having stayed at the Pension Beaurepas.

Parker, Mrs. In "A Light Man," Theodore Lisle's sister.

Parkman, Francis (1823–1893). Great nineteenth-century American narrative historian. He was the son of a Boston Unitarian minister, whose father bequeathed the future historian an inheritance. In the 1830s Parkman was in frail health and attended private schools. He went to Harvard (1840–1844), then law school there (1844–1846). By the time he had earned two degrees, he had already begun to vacation, for health and research, in New England, New York, Canada, Europe, Pennsylvania, Michigan, and Maryland. He then explored "the California and Oregon Trail" (April to October 1846). Back home, his eyes, nerves, and general health worsened. He serialized (1847) and then published in book form (1849) what was later called (1872) *The Oregon Trail*. He married in 1850. He and his wife had two daughters and one son. The son died in 1857; his wife, in 1858. Parkman published *The History of the Conspiracy of Pontiac* in 1851, the eighth title in order of events, but the first completed of his history of the French and Indian Wars. Other segments followed, often composed under trying physical conditions: *Pioneers of France in the New World* (1865, first title "chronologically"), *The Jesuits in North America in the Seventeenth Century* (1867, second title), *The Discovery of the Great West* (1869, later called *La Salle and the Discovery of the Great West,* third), *The Old Régime in Canada* (1874, fourth), *Count Frontenac and New France under Louis XIV* (1877, fifth), *Montcalm and Wolfe* (1884, seventh), and *A Half-Century of Conflict* (1892, sixth). The series was produced at a great cost in time, money, and physical resources: Parkman intermittently studied documents and sites in Canada (1856–1879); Europe (1858–1887); Washington, D.C., and Virginia (1865); Iowa, Illinois, Missouri, and Minnesota (1867); New York State (1876, 1878); and South Carolina and Florida (1885). He also published a novel and a book on roses, wrote letters, and kept journals. He avidly followed Civil War events and, in the 1870s, published articles on democracy and suffrage. His historical narratives concern French Huguenots opposing Spanish Catholics in Florida, Samuel de Champlain, Jesuit missionaries to the Indians, Sieur de La Salle, French feudal theocracy in Canada, Comte de Frontenac, Marquis de Montcalm vs. General James Wolfe, and Chief Pontiac. Parkman favored neither British democracy nor French monarchy, but rather conservative republicanism, or, better still, frontier individualism in an unspoiled land. James evidently knew Parkman well, since he wrote to the historian from the Reform Club, London (18 Jul [1881]), offering to help him there "again"; and wrote to him later, from Dover (24 Aug [1884]), to praise his *Wolfe and Montcalm*, recall his verandah and wisteria, and ask to be remembered to his sisters. James wrote on occasion to their friend Grace Norton* about the historian's health. James published reviews of two of Parkman's works. The first review (*Nation*, 6 Jun 1867) was of *The Jesuits in North America*, which he calls the "touching story," both "dramatic and instructive," of a heroic failure. He praises the Jesuits for their hope and endurance, and the historian for his use of French documents, for his frank discussion of Indian cruelty, squalor, and religious hypocrisy, and for his contrast of New England and French modes of colonizing. James says that the moral of the narrative here is that self-sacrifice works better for individuals than for communities. James's second review (*Nation*, 15 Oct 1874), of *The Old Régime in Canada*, begins with the statement that "Canadian history is . . . meagre in quantity," but that "Parkman has made it his own province" and has given it a "quality of . . . interest." James is intrigued by the story of Adam Daulac and his suicidal band aganst the Iroquois, mainly because it illustrates "early Canadian character"; James notes that Parkman uses courage as "the constant savor of . . . [his] subject." James adds that the historian possesses courage too, admires Parkman's "fairness" in handling Catholicism, and lauds his pictorial wizardry. James comments on the "almost comical history" of Louis XIV's "infant colony" in Canada. English self-reliance won over the French "passion for administration," but both sides displayed "stouter stuff than [we see] now." James finds the *coureur de bois* picturesque, Vicar-General Laval "an ascetic of the rigorous mediaeval pattern," female French immigrants "magnificently tough," and the "combination of celibate priests and nuns and . . . prolific citizens" "artificial and anomalous." James's library contained one book by Parkman.

Parminter, Miss. In "Mrs. Temperly," the piano-playing daughter of Mrs. Temperly's friends in Paris.

Parminter, Mrs. and Mrs. In "Mrs. Temperly," Mrs. Temperly's friends in Paris.

Parodi, Dominique Alexandre (1842–1901). French author of Italian extraction (naturalized 1881), best known for *Passions et Idées* (1865) and *Vaincus et Vainqueurs* (1898) and for four plays—*Ulm le Parracide* (1872), *Rome Vaincue* (1876), *La Reine Juana* (1893), and *Le Pape* (1899). In a note (*Nation*, 16 Nov 1876), James calls *Rome Vaincue*, seen at the Théâtre Français, "pompous and tedious," though rescued by the acting in it of Sarah Bernhardt.* The five-act verse tragedy, out of tune with the times, has "too much talk and too little action" but also has much feeling and "some very happy lines."

Parsons, Alfred (1847–1920). English painter (mostly of gardens and flowers), landscapist, illustrator (sometimes with Edwin Austin Abbey* and Francis Davis Millet*), and garden designer. One of Parsons' best works is *When Nature Painted All Things Gay*. Parsons was a member of the Royal Academy (from 1911) and president of the Royal Society of Painters in Water Colours (1914–1920). James met Parsons in 1883 and in a letter to Elizabeth Boott* (11 Dec [1883]) called him Abbey's *"fidus achates."* James wrote a preface to *Catalogue of a Collection of Drawings by Alfred Parsons*, London, 1891. The essay was reprinted as part of "Our Artists in Europe" (1889; reprinted as "Black and White" in *Picture and Text*, 1893). In it, James comprehensively notes that Parsons "knows everything that can be known about English fields and flowers," and he goes on to say that "the richest illustration of the English landscape . . . offered us today" is by Parsons, whose magazine illustrations, he adds, are especially appealing to Americans. James theorizes that Parsons has a "male vision" and a "French . . . manner." Parsons designed the sets for James's play *Guy Domville*, and he attended the first performance of that play in London, on 5 January 1895. In 1898 Parsons helped James plan garden improvements at Lamb House.* According to his Pocket Diaries, James cultivated his friendship with Parsons into the 1910s.

Partial Portraits. Collection of eleven critical essays, all previously published; reprinted in London and New York by Macmillan, 1888. The essays are "Emerson" (original title, "The Life of Emerson"); "The Life of George Eliot" (original title, "George Eliot's Life"); "Daniel Deronda: A Conversation"; "Anthony Trollope"; "Robert Louis Stevenson"; "Miss Woolson" (original title, "Miss Constance Fenimore Woolson"); "Alphonse Daudet"; "Guy de Maupassant"; "Ivan Turgénieff"; "George du Maurier" (original title, "Du Maurier and London Society"); and "The Art of Fiction" (original title of unauthorized publication, *Walter Besant: The Art of Fiction*). (All of the authors mentioned here are discussed under their own names.)

Pasquale. In "The Aspern Papers," the narrator's Venetian gondolier.

Pasquale. In *The Wings of the Dove*, Milly Theale's Venetian gondolier.

"A Passionate Pilgrim." Long short story (25,800 words), published in the *Atlantic Monthly* (Mar–Apr 71); revised and reprinted in *A Passionate Pilgrim, and Other Tales*, 1975; revised and reprinted in *The Siege of London* (Leipzig),

1884; reprinted in *Stories Revived,* 1885; revised and reprinted in *The Novels and Tales of Henry James*, Volume XIII, 1908. (Characters: Mme. Bosio, Mrs. Horridge, Rawson, Clement Searle, Cynthia Searle, Margaret Searle, Richard Searle, Miss Searle, Abijah Simmons, Tottenham). Arriving from Italy in London, the narrator meets American Clement Searle, sick and now sad that his lawyer cannot substantiate his claim to a Middleshire estate presently owned by Richard Searle, Clement's distant relative. While visiting the estate, Clement and the narrator first meet the strange Miss Searle, who supports Clement's claim; then they encounter her suspicious brother Richard, whose unpleasant anecdotes upset Clement. He and the narrator go to Oxford, when Clement, now dying, helps a down-and-out gentleman in his plans to go to America. Clement then sends for Miss Searle, who enters only to announce that her brother is dead—thrown from a horse. Clement dies: he is buried in England and is mourned for a while by Miss Searle. The impetus for this early, important story was a combination of James's personal love of England from his earliest years and his reading of such travel books as *Our Old Home* (1863) by Nathaniel Hawthorne.* Just as Mark Twain* created a literary type of American traveler in *The Innocents Abroad* (1869), so James gives us here an antithetical type in "A Passionate Pilgrim." He tells us in the preface to Volume XIII of *The Novels and Tales of Henry James* that this story is the first of his "sops instinctively thrown to the international Cerberus," that is, "the keeper of the international 'books.' "

A Passionate Pilgrim, and Other Tales, 1875. Collection of six short stories published in Boston by Osgood, 1875: "A Passionate Pilgrim," "The Last of the Valerii," "Eugene Pickering," "The Madonna of the Future," "The Romance of Certain Old Clothes," and "Madame de Mauves."

"Paste." Short story (5,900 words), published in *Frank Leslie's Popular Monthly* (Dec 1899); revised and reprinted in *The Novels and Tales of Henry James*, Volume XVI, 1909. (Characters: Blanche, Lady Bobby, Mrs. Guy, Gwendolyn, Arthur Prime, Charlotte Prime, Rev. Mr. Prime, Mrs. Prime.) Two weeks after Arthur Prime's country vicar father dies, that man's second wife also dies. She was a former actress (then Miss Bradshaw). In due time Arthur tells his cousin Charlotte Prime to select whatever piece of paste jewelry her stepmother left. Miss Prime chooses a string of pearls so heavy that they seem real. Arthur scoffs, wonders how an actress could get such pearls, and feels that the dead woman's reputation may have been insulted. Charlotte takes her pearls back to Bleet, where she is a governess. At a party there, she is helping dress guests for a tableau vivant when vulgar Mrs. Guy judges the "paste" pearls to be genuine. She even wears them at dinner and offers to purchase them. But Charlotte takes them back to Arthur, who still pretends that they are paste and later says that he smashed them to counter any slur on his family. Later, however, Charlotte notices that Mrs. Guy is wearing the same pearls at another party given by her employers. The woman rather sickens Charlotte by informing her that she bought the pearls from a dealer to whom Arthur had sold them. The first hint for this story comes in a Notebook entry (18 Nov 1894): "the way certain persons . . . are affected by an event . . . which reflects . . . on the . . . honour of their house"; then, in a later entry (4 Mar 1895), James considers having two persons react in opposite ways to news of the family scandal. In the preface to Volume XVI of *The Novels and Tales of Henry James*, James reveals the obvious, that in "Paste" he has openly transposed the plot of "La Parure," which is the admirable short story by Guy de Maupassant.* James goes on to explain that Maupassant's "false treasure supposed to be true and precious" became his own "real treasure supposed to be false and hollow." (Further, in his 1883 "Les Bijoux" Maupassant fictionalizes on real jewels thought to be paste.) James complicates his "Paste" by not telling us how the actress acquired her massive pearls and whether they were really bought by Mrs. Guy (incidentally named, no doubt, with Guy de Maupassant in mind).

"The Patagonia." Short story (21,300 words), published in the *English Illustrated Magazine*, Aug–Sep 1888); reprinted in *A London Life*, 1889; revised and reprinted in *The Novels and Tales of Henry James*, Volume XVIII, 1909. (Characters: Mrs. Allen, Mrs. Amber, Mrs. Gotch, Mrs. Jeremie, Jasper Nettlepoint, Mrs. Nettlepoint, Grace Mavis, Mrs. and Mrs. Mavis, Mrs. Peck, David Porterfield.) The narrator is about to sail on the *Patagonia* from Boston to Liverpool. First he calls on fellow passenger Mrs. Nettlepoint, at whose home he meets Grace Mavis. She is also sailing, to marry her fiancé of long standing, David Porterfield, who is studying architecture in Paris. Meeting Grace also is Mrs. Nettlepoint's rakish son Jasper, who on an impulse decides to become a passenger also. The voyage starts, and the narrator soon senses trouble: Mrs. Nettlepoint is too indulgent a mother; Mrs. Peck, a blatant gossip who says that Grace is flirting outrageously with Jasper. There is more gossip, which annoys even the captain. So the narrator warns, puzzles, and intimidates Jasper. Grace, now lonely and insulted, but proud still, commits suicide by quietly dropping overboard. In Liverpool harbor, the narrator faces the task of explaining matters to Porterfield. According to a Notebook entry (5 Jan 1888), this story was suggested to James (who was compassionate at once) by a similar real-life episode relayed to him by Frances Ann Kemble.* A later Notebook entry (11 Mar 1888) worries out specific plot details, and James beseeches the "spirit of Maupassant . . . [to] come to my aid!" He adds, "This may be a triumph of robust and vivid concision." Not so; the dismal story is too long. But its local color touches of activities aboard a Boston-to-Liverpool Cunarder are deft.

Pater, Walter Horatio (1839–1894). Sensitive, aloof, sometimes morbid English essayist and literary critic. He was educated at Queen's College, Oxford, then became a fellow at Brasenose College, Oxford, where he spent much of his uneventful life thereafter. He associated with many pre-Raphaelites and became an influential expert on Renaissance art and literature. Pater's works include *Studies in the History of the Renaissance* (1873, art criticism), *Marius the Epicurean* (1885, historical, philosophical quasi novel), *Imaginary Portraits* (1887, philosophical, partly fictional essays), and *Appreciations, with an Essay on Style* (1889). In 1879 James met Pater during a London dinner given by a hospitable Jewish family. After lightly ridiculing his hosts in a letter to his mother (18 Jan [1879]), James went on to add that Pater "is far from being as beautiful as his own prose." In "Florentine Notes" (1874), James praises Pater incidentally as "[a]n accomplished critic" for his *Studies in the History of the Renaissance*," especially for his comments on Sandro Botticelli therein. But it was Pater's renowned description of the *Mona Lisa* by Leonardo* da Vinci that haunted James for decades and indirectly influenced his comments not only on Italian art but also on certain enigmatic female characters in his fiction. When Pater died, James wrote to Sir Edmund Wilson Gosse* ([10 Aug 1894]) to cite "my non-communication with him [Pater] for so long" as a reason for not attending his funeral; then he adds this graceful comment about Pater's passing: "What is more delicate than the extinction of delicacy . . . ?" Later, however, James defined Pater to Gosse as "curiously negative & faintly-gray," calling him "the mask without the face," and "faint, pale, embarrassed, exquisite" ([13 Dec 1894]). Finally he wrote to Gosse that Pater's *Gaston de Latour* (1896, abandoned fiction) has a "faint, feeble sweetness" ([8?] Nov 1896). James's fiction frequently shows two subtle, often indirect influences from Pater: first, for the man's comments on Italian art; second, for his notion that a successful life is one devoted to aesthetic worship. James respected the first but resisted the second. James's library contained nine books by Pater.

"The Path of Duty." Short story (13,500 words), published in the *English Illustrated Magazine* (Dec 1884); reprinted in *The Author of Beltraffio*, 1885, and in *Stories Revived*, 1885. (Characters: Lady Emily Bernardstone, Joscelind Bernardstone, General Bernardstone, Lord Clanduffy, Ambrose Tester, Sir Edmund Tester, Francis Tester, Master and Miss Tester, Roland Tremayne, Lady Margaret Vandeleur, and Lord Vandeleur.) The narrator is an American woman. She says that her British friend Ambrose Tester loves Lady Vandeleur, whose husband is still alive. Sir Edmund wants his son Ambrose to marry; so the dutiful fellow proposes to Joscelind Bernardstone. Lord Vandeleur dies. The narrator will not encourage Ambrose to break his engagement, which crass London society hopes he will do. He marches to his wedding with a smile like that of a condemned prisoner. He fathers two children, and his own father dies happy. Ambrose and the widowed Lady Vandeleur are often thrown together socially. The world judges them to be virtuous, but the narrator regards them as superciliously smug about their conduct. Poor Joscelind cannot understand why she cannot please her husband. In a Notebook entry (29 Jan 1884), James records some gossip about the real-life Lord Stafford, who loved Lady Grosvenor, whose young husband was so healthy that Stafford yielded to family pressure and became engaged to Lord Rosslyn's daughter Miss Rosslyn. But before the wedding, Lord Grosvenor freed his wife by dying. James sketches out five possible plots based on this situation, including one he might adopt "If I were a Frenchman or a naturalist"—i.e., have Miss Rosslyn learn the truth, demand marriage to Lord Stafford anyway, enjoy his "wealth and splendour," and freely and quietly let him make Lady Grosvenor his mistress. But then James chose a sixth plot, to concentrate on Lord Stafford's "quandary" while keeping Miss Rosslyn, whom he marries, pathetically ignorant. A French naturalist might have made a better story than the resulting "Path of Duty," which is emotionally neutral and lacking in satirical bite.

Patten, Rev. Mr. In "The Third Person," the vicar of Marr, where Susan and Amy Frush inherit a house and now live.

Patti, Adelina (1843–1919). Operatic soprano, born in Madrid of Italian parents. In *A Small Boy and Others*, James mentions hearing "that rarest of infant phenomena, Adelina Patti," in New York (in 1851 or 1852). In *The American*, Patti is heard in Paris; in "Eugene Pickering," in Homburg; in "The Chaperon," in London.

Paul, Mrs. In *Watch and Ward,* Nora Lambert's dishonest New York hostess, who is in league with George Fenton.

Payn, James (1830–1898). British novelist, short-story writer, essayist, poet, and editor. He attended Eton, then Trinity College, Cambridge (1849–1854). He began to publish in 1852, soon contributed to *Household Words* and other periodicals, and became a "disciple" of Charles Dickens.* Payn married in 1854, had seven children, became editor of *Chambers's Journal* (1859–1874), and published the first of his forty-six novels in 1859. He worked with Sir Walter Besant* to improve authors' rights. He knew Sir Leslie Stephen* and succeeded him as editor of the *Cornhill Magazine* (1883–1896). Payn helped Arthur Conan Doyle get started. Payn wrote two autobiographical volumes (1884, 1894). His two most popular novels were *Lost Sir Massingberd: A Romance of Real Life* (1864) and *By Proxy* (1878). An exuberant personality, he is remembered now mainly for his sensational neo-Gothic Victorian fiction. James knew Payn slightly and wrote a brief memorial note on him in "The Late James Payn" (*Illustrated London News*, 9 Apr 1898). James remembers Payn not as a fellow writer but simply as "the most lovable of men," to whom "talk and hospitality and whist" were as important as the books he "liked . . . and produced." He was gentle, droll, witty, whimsical, and human. He had knowledge of and sympathy for an English "literary fashion" long past, going back to Dickens. James last saw him in severe physical discomfort but with a clear mind.

Peabody, Elizabeth Palmer (1804–1894). Boston educator, editor, reformer, feminist, and transcendentalist. She was the sister-in-law of Nathaniel Hawthorne* and Horace Mann. She also knew Ralph Waldo Emerson,* Margaret Fuller, and Henry David Thoreau, among other New England intellectuals. Her home and her bookshop were important meeting places of liberal men and women of letters. She started the first kindergarten in the United States in 1860. The James family casually knew Miss Peabody. James, visiting her in 1878 while she was vacationing on the Isle of Wight, called her in a letter to his brother William (1 May [1878]) "very nice, intelligent and charming." It is rather obvious that James used Miss Peabody as his model for Miss Birdseye, the brave, bumbling reformeress in *The Bostonians*. When William, among others, wrote to him that the first installment of the novel was raising much outrage in Boston circles, James protested too assiduously to be credible (14 Feb [1885]): "Miss Birdseye was evolved entirely from my moral consciousness"; he confessed, however, that he did recall her displaced spectacles when he limned his old lady. In a second letter to William (15 Feb [1885]), he suggested not only that Miss Peabody should be pleased but also that Miss Birdseye's "death . . . is the prettiest thing in the book."

Pearson, Harriet. In "The Liar," the real name, according to Colonel Clement Capadose, of the tipsy model who at Oliver Lyon's studio calls herself Miss Geraldine.

Peck, Mrs. In "The Patagonia," the main gossip aboard the *Patagonia*. She has four uncontrollable children. She is friendly with Mrs. Gotch and Mrs. Jeremie; all three contribute to Grace Mavis's suicidal misery.

Pegg, Hall. In "Covering End," the ultimately successful object of Cora Prodmore's affection, in spite of her father's objections to him. In *The High Bid*, the agitated object of Cora Prodmore's love. They will marry.

Peirce, Charles Sanders (1839–1914). Cambridge-born son of a Harvard mathematician and astronomer and the younger brother of another Harvard mathematician. After graduating from Harvard (1859) and the Lawrence Scientific School (1863), Charles Peirce became a mathematician, physicist, and logician. He worked for the United States coast survey; published (1878) on pragmatism, which he later called pragmaticism; and lectured widely but irregularly on logic and pragmatism (1880–1904). Peirce's contributions may be seen in his posthumous *Chance, Love, and Logic* (1923) and his collected papers (10 vols., 1931–1934). William James, who was much influenced by and sometimes clashed with Peirce, knew him better than did Henry James, who also knew him. James saw much of Peirce in Paris beginning in the fall of 1875, and reported home about him. To his father (18 Nov [1875]), James notes that "Charles Peirce, who is wintering here and who had heard of me from William

[,] . . . took me up very vigorously, made me dine with him . . . , and spend the evening at his rooms. . . . He seems quite a swell (at least from the point of view of that little house on the car-track where I last knew him)—has a secretary, etc.'' To his brother William (3 Dec [1875]), he describes Peirce's ''swinging pendulums at the Observatory'' and feeling snubbed by his Parisian counterparts. Later, when informed that his comments about Peirce were amusing, James replied objectively and perceptively (14 Mar [1876]): ''It was no intimacy, for during the last two months of his stay I saw almost nothing of him. He is a very good fellow, and one must appreciate his mental ability; but he has too little social talent, too little art of making himself agreeable. He had however a very lonely and dreary winter here. . . . I did what I could to give him society . . . '' In a more honest Notebook entry (25 Nov 1881), James recalls that ''I saw a good deal of Charles Peirce that winter [Paris, 1875–1876]—as to whom his being a man of genius reconciled me to much that was intolerable in him.''

Pemberton. In ''The Pupil,'' Morgan Moreen's tutor and friend.

Pemble, Mrs. and Mrs. In ''The Beast in the Jungle,'' casual friends of John Marcher but not of May Bartram.

Pendexter, Miss. In ''Poor Richard,'' Gertrude Whittaker's recently deceased father's relative, who is now Miss Whittaker's house companion.

Pendrel. In *The Sense of the Past*, Ralph Pendrel's recently deceased father.

Pendrel, Philip Augustus. In *The Sense of the Past*, Ralph Pendrel's cousin, who upon dying wills Ralph a London house.

Pendrel, Ralph. In *The Sense of the Past*, a New York historian refused by rich widow Aurora Coyne. He then goes to London to a house he has inherited there. In this house he meets in fantasy Molly Midmore, the fiancée of his eighteenth-century ancestor Ralph Pendrel, and he also meets her mother Mrs. Midmore, her brother Peregrine Midmore, and her sister Nancy Midmore.

Pennell, Joseph (1857–1926). Born in Philadelphia into a Welsh-Irish Quaker family, this brilliant artist was a moody, sickly, picture-drawing child. He showed promise in art school and took more lessons at the Pennsylvania Academy School. He established a studio and became a success (from about 1880). He published drawings in *Scribner's Monthly* (1881), met his text writer, Elizabeth Robins (1855–1936), and in 1884 married her. (She is not be confused with the actress Elizabeth Robins.*) After illustrating George Washington Cable's *The Grandissimes*, Pennel was commissioned to illustrate essays by William Dean Howells* on Italian cities. This work took Pennell and his wife to Italy; they proceeded to England and Ireland, on an extended honeymoon. Twelve books of their "holidays"—Pennell's pictures and Elizabeth's texts—were eventually published. Settling in London, they met Sir Edmund Wilson Gosse,* George Bernard Shaw,* Robert Louis Stevenson,* James Abbott McNeill Whistler,* and some aging pre-Raphaelites, among other notables, including James. Pennell enjoyed enormous success: exhibitions, works in leading magazines, commissions to illustrate books by Francis Marion Crawford,* John Milton Hay,* Howells, Washington Irving,* James, and others. Too outspoken to last as an art critic beyond 1888, Pennell purchased his own press (1892) to reproduce his own etchings; later, he studied innovative photoengraving processes and modern French lithographic techniques. Pennell and his wife published a biography of Whistler in 1908. Pennell traveled more, and he published illustrations of the Panama Canal, California and other western scenes. Philadelphia, Washington, D.C., and Greece. During World War I, he sketched British war plants and sickening scenes at Verdun, as propaganda. In the 1920s he taught art in New York even though the rawness and bad manners of that city appalled him. Overwork contributed to his death. In his will, he provided for the enrichment of Library of Congress pictorial holdings. Pennell's opinions on pre-Raphaelites, magazine illustrating, fin-de-siècle decadents such as Aubrey Vincent Beardsley,* skyscrapers, and Manhattan undoubtedly influenced James, whose 1888 essay "London," *A Little Tour in France* (2nd ed., 1900), *English Hours*, and *Italian Hours* Pennell illustrated. When asked for suggestions, James by letter urged Pennell (6 Jan [1888]) to illustrate his "London" essay "freely and fancifully," rather than "with neat, definite photographic 'views.' " Then he added, "But do your own London, and it will be sufficiently mine." According to his Pocket Diaries, James associated with the Pennells in London into the 1910s.

Penniman, Lavinia. In *Washington Square*, the sister of Dr. Austin Sloper and Elizabeth Almond. Mrs. Penniman is the widow of a recently deceased minister. She is also the ineffectual, romantic aunt of Dr. Sloper's daughter Catherine, and the would-be aid of Morris Townsend, Catherine's suitor.

Penniman, Mr. and Mrs. In *The Outcry*, unimportant society people.

Penniman, Rev. Mr. In *Washington Square*, Lavinia Penniman's recently deceased husband.

Pensil, Lady. In *The Portrait of a Lady*, Bob Bantling's sister, to whose estate Henrietta Stackpole finally gets an invitation.

"The Pension Beaurepas." Short story (20,000 words), published in the *Atlantic Monthly* (Apr 1879); reprinted in *Washington Square* (London), 1881, and *The Siege of London*, 1883; revised and reprinted in *The Novels and Tales of Henry James*, Volume XIV, 1908. (Characters: Mme. Beaurepas, Mlle. Beaurepas, Célestine, Mme. Chamousset, Aurora Church, Mrs. Church, M. le Pasteur and Mme. Galopin, Mrs. and Mrs. Parker, Pigeonneau, Sophy Ruck, Mr. and Mrs. Ruck.) The narrator, an American studying in Geneva, observes life in Mme. Beaurepas's pension. American lumberman Ruck's wife and daughter are domineering and go on lavish shopping sprees. Aurora Church talks of traveling cheaply through Europe with her anti-American mother. Miss Church begins to attract a Frenchman named Pigeonneau but tells the narrator she dislikes Europe. He resists Mrs. Church's suggestion that he accompany them to Chamouni even though he is interested in Aurora. At his bank, the narrator encounters Ruck and learns that the man is having financial reverses; the two then bump into the Ruck women on another buying binge. The narrator returns to the Pension Beaurepas to check out. In the preface to Volume XIV of *The Novels and Tales of Henry James*, James says that he recalls this story tenderly because it reflects ''a day that is dead,'' killed by ''the vast diluvian occidental presence in Europe,'' i.e., of American tourists. Incidents and characters in many of James's novels and stories derive indirectly from the fiction of Honoré de Balzac,* but in ''The Pension Beaurepas'' James has his bookish narrator explicitly refer in the first paragraph to boardinghouse life in Balzac's *Père Goriot*. The story is oppressive, with sweet Aurora's mother and both Ruck women simply horrible creatures. Yet James felt challenged enough by them to place all four females in ''The Point of View'' three years after ''The Pension Beaurepas.''

Pepperel, Charles. In *A Change of Heart*, a scoundrel, age thirty-six, who stole from Martha Noel and is now after Margaret Thorne's money. Margaret will not listen to Robert Staveley's warning.

Percival. In *The American*, Rev. Mr. Benjamin Babcock's art-loving friend.

Percy. In *The Tragic Muse*, Nick Dormer's uncle. (His full name is probably Percy Dormer.)

Percy, Florence. The pen name of Elizabeth Akers.*

Perriam. In *What Maisie Knew*, one of Ida Farange's many lovers.

Perry, Thomas Sergeant (1845–1928). Newport-born scholar, author, educator, and translator. He was a grandson on his father's side of Oliver Hazard Perry (the naval hero) and a grand-nephew of Matthew Calbraith Perry (a negotiator with Japan); and was a great-great-grandson on his mother's side of Benjamin Franklin. Perry graduated from Harvard College (1866), studied in Europe, taught French and German at Harvard (1868–1872), joined the editorial staff of the *North American Review* (1872–1877), and taught English at Harvard (1878–1882, ending with his dismissal by the president). He married Lilla Cabot (a painter) in Boston in 1874; the couple had three daughters. His publications include *The Life and Letters of Francis Lieber* (1882), *English Literature of the*

Eighteenth Century (1883), *From Opitz to Lessing (1885)*, *The Evolution of a Snob* (1887), *The History of Greek Literature* (1890), and *John Fiske*[*] (1906). He was a professor of English at the University of Keiogijiku in Japan (1898–1901). In his later years, Perry read and studied more (including Sanskrit and Russian) but wrote less. In 1929 Edwin Arlington Robinson, who knew Perry well, edited his letters. Perry's innumerable friends included Henry Adams,* James Thomas Fields,* Edwin Lawrence Godkin,* John Chipman Gray,* Oliver Wendell Holmes, Jr.,* William Dean Howells,* John La Farge,* Henry Wadsworth Longfellow,* James Russell Lowell,* Charles Eliot Norton,* John Addington Symonds,* Mary Temple,* Ivan Sergeyevich Turgenev,* Mark Twain,* Charles Dudley Warner,* Edith Newbold Jones Wharton,* and James (as well as James's brothers William and Wilky). Perry helped to popularize certain French novelists, Turgenev and other Russian novelists, and Edward FitzGerald's *Rubáiyát of Omar Khayyám*. He published criticism in support of modern realism, as opposed to both melodramatic romanticism and sordid naturalism. James first met bookworm Perry in the summer of 1858 at Newport, where the two were Latin-reading schoolmates together. When the James family returned to Europe in 1859–1860, James wrote revealing letters from Geneva and Bonn to his close Newport friend—whom he then and later addressed as Perry, Peri, Tom, Sargey, Sarge, T. S., Thomas, Tammas, Tommy, and Thomasino. James and Perry were friendly during their Harvard years together. James introduced Perry to Howells in 1869. After James first established himself in Europe, the two kept up a correspondence for years. James persuaded Turgenev to let Perry translate his *Virgin Soil* into English, which Perry did in 1877. In a letter to Perry (8 Jul [1883]), James commended his book on eighteenth-century English literature, adding, "I envy you much all you have read." But James wrote negatively in part about Perry to Symonds (22 Jan [Feb] 1884) to the effect that Perry, whom James had seen in Boston the year before, is "the most lettered American almost, and most unsuccessful writer I know." In 1886 a rift developed between James and Perry; James wrote to his brother William (1 Oct 1887) thus: "as to T. S. Perry, . . . I have neither seen nor heard anything whatever of him, and don't want to. He wrote me a most offensive and impertinent letter about a year ago— . . . that he disapproved of my living in London. It set the seal upon the conviction I have always privately had that he is a singularly poor creature." (The rift was probably occasioned by Perry's envy of James's money, energy, and critical success.) Still, when the Perrys vacationed in Europe, beginning in June 1887, they visited James later that year in London. During a long working vacation in Europe (1906–1908), the Perrys again saw him, for a week at Rye in 1906 and twice later in Paris. In 1910 James visited the Perrys at their summer home in New Hampshire. James's *Notes of a Son and Brother* has several references to Perry, "superexcellent and all-reading, all-engulfing friend of those days," at Newport in the late 1850s. He further notes that his brother William shared rooms with Perry when the two were students in Germany. When Percy Lubbock* was preparing his 1920 edition of James's letters, Perry refused to make them available but instead wrote Lubbock a long memorandum which describes his early Newport days with James and which Lubbock published toward the beginning of his edition. Perry's daughter Margaret Perry released the letters, by then badly damaged through neglect, to Virginia Harlow, who included them as an appendix to her 1950 biography of Perry.

Persse, Dudley Jocelyn (1873–1943). Fashionable dilettante in London, originally from Galway, Ireland. Jocelyn Persse was the nephew of Lady Isabella Augusta Persse Gregory* and a friend of the wife of Sir Sidney Colvin,* at whose London wedding luncheon, in July 1903, Persse was introduced to James. He quickly became one of James's most intimate young male friends. Within days James had welcomed Persse to his London club, then to Lamb House* for a weekend. The two attended theatrical and music-hall performances together. Persse proved the depth of his friendship for James by journeying nonstop from Algeria to Edinburgh to attend the opening night performance of James's play *The High Bid*, on 26 March 1908. When Persse was away vacationing, as he often was, and when James was in the United States (1904–1905, 1910–1911), the two corresponded. James closed one letter (18 Oct 1911) with the statement that "nothing else matters save that I am, dearest Joceln, yours all and always." At least seventy letters from James to this handsome, hedonistic, nonliterary, considerate, adored, and envied young man have survived. James's Pocket Diaries are dotted with notes of their dates in the 1910s. Sir Hugh Seymour Walpole,* who was perhaps jealous, believed that James was in love with Jocelyn. James remembered Persse with a gift of £100 in his will.

Peter. In *Guy Domville*, Mrs. Peverel's servant at Porches.

Petherton, Lord. In *The Awkward Age*, Mitchett's parasite and the lover of Duchess Jane of Naples.

Pets. James was fond of animals and over the years in England owned several dogs. They included Max, a dachshund; Nicholas (Nick), a wirehaired fox terrier; Peter; Tim; and Tosca, a dachshund.

Peverel, George. In *Guy Domville*, widowed Mrs. Peverel's little son, nicknamed Geordie, who is tutored by Guy Domville.

Peverel, Mrs. In *Guy Domville*, a West of England widow whose son George is tutored by Guy Domville. She owns the house called Porches. She prefers Guy to her neighbor Frank Humber, but when Guy definitely decides to become a Catholic priest and commends his friend Frank to her, she accepts him. She is Lord Edenbrook's niece.

"Philadelphia." Travel essay, published in the *North American Review* (Apr 1906), and in the *Fortnightly Review* (Apr 1906); reprinted in *The American Scene,* 1907.

Phillips, Claude (1846–1924). British art critic and later (1900–1911) keeper of the magnificent Wallace Collection, London. James knew him casually in the 1880s, sought his help in connection with photographic illustrations for *The Novels and Tales of Henry James,* and (according to his Pocket Diaries) continued to see Phillips socially, both in London and at Lamb House, into the 1910s.

Phillips, Le Roy (1870–?). Ohio-born editor, anthologist, compiler, bibliographer, publisher, and minor playright who lived in Boston. He was a cousin of William Morton Fullerton.* When Phillips wrote to James to ask for cooperation in compiling a bibliography of James's writings, James replied (8 Sep 1904) to object to "a mercilessly complete resuscitation" of his works, since there were many that he wished "to forget and keep buried." Phillips went ahead anyway and published a valuable bibliography, the first one of book length (1906, rev. ed. 1930). In addition, he edited James's *Views and Reviews* (Boston: Ball, 1908).

Pickering. In "Eugene Pickering, ingenuous Eugene Pickering's deceased father, who recommended Isabel Vernor to his son as a charming young girl.

Pickering, Eugene. In "Eugene Pickering," the narrator's ingenuous friend, who is briefly infatuated with Mme. Anastasia Blumenthal but who then really loves Isabel Vernor, recommended to him by his now deceased father.

Picture and Text. Collection of seven essays, all previously published; revised and reprinted in New York by Harper, 1893. The essays are "Black and White" (original title, "Our Artists in Europe"); "Edwin A. Abbey"; "Charles S. Reinhart"; "Alfred Parsons"; "John S. Sargent"; "Honoré Daumier" (original title, "Daumier, Caricaturist"); and "After the Play." (All of these artists are discussed under their own names.)

"The Picture Season in London." Art review, published in *Galaxy* (Aug 1877). James contrasts deliberately glittering Paris with London, which "pleases by accident"; discusses sandwich-boards in London advertising music and art shows; and mentions British leisure activity, which includes amateurish sketching and the purchase of fine pictures. Many are now on exhibit in Bond Street and Pall Mall. James touches on a number of art works, by J. J. J. Tissot (a *tour de force* modern manners painter), Ferdinand Heilbuth (whose works seem based on photographs), George Frederick Watts* ("the first portrait painter in England"), James Abbott McNeill Whistler,* William Holman Hunt,* Sir Edward Burne-Jones* ("a vast deal to enjoy"), Lord Frederick Leighton* (represented by "a wonderfully clever" statue), Sir John Everett Millais,* and others. James ridicules certain minor works: One ought to be hidden in a curtain; others reveal "violent imbecility of colour."

Pictures and Other Passages from Henry James. A book of quotations from James's works, authorized by James; published (shortly after his death) in London by Chatto & Windus, 1916, and in New York by Stokes, 1916.

Pigeonneau. In "The Pension Beaurepas," Aurora Church's Geneva admirer.

Pimlico, Countess of. In "An International Episode," the daughter of the Duke and Duchess of Bayswater, and thus Lord Lambeth's sister.

Pinero, Sir Arthur Wing (1855–1934). Prolific, London-born pre-modern dramatist. He was an actor in Edinburgh (1874–1876) and later in London, this time with the troupe of Sir Henry Irving.* Pinero then began to write plays. His smash hit *The Second Mrs. Tanqueray* (1893) was not only a "problem play" sympathetically treating a lady with a shady past in conflict with conventional society but also a vehicle starring the actor and manager Sir George Alexander,* whom James came to know well, and carrying the actress Mrs. Patrick Campbell* to fame and fortune. It had followed frivolous comedies by Pinero and now led to such sombre, "well-made" depictions of heroines as in *The Notorious Mrs. Ebbsmith* (1895), *Iris* (1901), *The Thunderbolt* (1908), and *Mid-Channel* (1909). Pinero's comedies include *The Money Spinner* (1880, his first such success), *Trelawny of the Wells* (1898), and *The Gay Lord Quex* (1899). In "London Pictures and London Plays" (1882), James reviewed Pinero's early serious play *The Squire* (1881), says that it "doesn't stand very straight," likes the sets and acting, and notes that the plot seemed to be borrowed from *Far from the Madding Crowd* by Thomas Hardy.* Much later, Pinero attended the opening performance of James's *The American*, on 26 September 1891. James attended the opening night of *The Second Mrs. Tanqueray*, on 27 May 1893, liked it, and wrote as much to Pinero, who replied to commend James for the innate comic qualities in his short story "The Chaperon." James tried to convert the story into a play, tentatively entitling it *Monte-Carlo*, but without success. In "London" (24 Apr 1897), James expresses dislike of a new production of *The Second Mrs. Tanqueray* and defines a presentation of *The Princess and the Butterfly* (1897) by Pinero merely as "a series of beautiful pictures" doubtless costly to construct. When James spoke at the Robert Browning* Centenary in 1912, he followed a long, vigorous lecture by Pinero on Browning and the theater. In a letter (12 May 1912) to Edith Newbold Jones Wharton,* James mentions the ceremony and says that "Pinero was by far the most salient feaature of it (simple, sensuous, passionate—that is artless, audible, incredible!)." James's library included two works by Pinero.

Pinhorn. In "The Death of the Lion," the critic narrator's editor.

Pinker, James Brand (1863–1922). James's literary and dramatic agent (after Alexander Pollack Watt*), beginning in 1898. Experience as a magazine editor (of *Pearson's Weekly*) stood Pinker in good stead. He became the exceptionally able agent for Arnold Bennett, Joseph Conrad,* Stephen Crane,* John Galsworthy,* George Gissing,* Ford Madox Hueffer,* Violet Hunt,* Sir Edward Montague Compton Mackenzie,* and Herbert George Wells,* among other writers James knew. Always looking for new talent, Pinker helped Elizabeth Robins* get her novel *The Convert* published (1907). He regularized James's copyrights, made business arrangements with publishers (including William Heinemann,* who objected to James's employing any agent), handled correspondence, and negotiated with Charles Scribner's Sons for the publication of *The Novels and Tales of Henry James*. Pinker was one of James's naturalization sponsors in 1915, along with Herbert Henry Asquith,* Sir Edmund Wilson Gosse,* and Sir George Walter Prothero.* James's letters to Pinker are a mine of biographical information. James was familiar enough with his agent to confide in him by letter (29 Aug 1900) that he regarded Stephen Crane's "widow" Cora as a swindler. In a letter to William James's wife Alice (1 Oct 1900), James describes Pinker as "excellently effective." According to his Pocket Diaries, in the 1910s James frequently consulted Pinker, who was also his Lamb House* guest. After James's death, Pinker was not dissuaded by William James's widow from seeking to publish *The Middle Years*, and he had a hand in securing Percy Lubbock,* rather than Gosse or Edith Newbold Jones Wharton,* as the editor of James's letters. Pinker contracted influenza on shipboard during one of his periodic business trips to New York and died of pneumonia in a hotel there. His older son Eric was in business with him at the time.

Pinks. In *The Tragic Muse*, a deceased politician discussed by members of the Dormer family.

Pinthorpe, Mary. In *The Awkward Age*, the Brookenhams' casual friend.

Pirated editions of James's works. *The American*, in 1877; "A Bundle of Letters," 1880; *Daisy Miller*, 1879.

Pitman. In "Julia Bride," one of Julia Bride's stepfathers. He loves widowed Mrs. David E. Drack, and Julia helps him advance his cause.

Pitman, Mrs. In "Julia Bride," An earlier name of Mrs. Connery.

Planche, Gustave (1808–1857). Antiromantic French art critic praised by James in his review of *Contemporary French Painters*, by Philip Gilbert Hamerton,* for clarifying "the French school of painters" and for encouraging spectators to become interested in their works.

Platt, Henry. In "Georgina's Reasons," Agnes Roy Theory's uncle.

Platt, William. In "A Bundle of Letters," the stay-at-home boyfriend of Miranda Hope, whose letters to her mother in Bangor, Maine, mention him.

Playfair, Baron Lyon (1818–1898). British chemist, sanitation reformer, civil-service commissioner, and parliamentarian (1868–1892). Beginning in the late 1870s, James was an occasional guest of the hospitable Playfairs. He especially relished the companionship of Lady Edith Russell Playfair, the baron's American wife. John Singer Sargent* painted her portrait. To Grace Norton* (4 Jan [1880]), James once wrote that Lady Playfair "is a very natural and uncorrupted little American, who likes her life here greatly, and would like it still better . . . if she had . . . more health and . . . money." He adds that her husband is "redfaced, but clever and canny." According to a Notebook entry (27 Feb 1895), Edith Playfair's account of her aged aunt's family situation provided the impetus for James's story "Europe." His Pocket Diaries indicate that James continued to socialize with Lady Playfair into the 1910s.

Plummeridge. In "The Point of View," Edward Antrobus's servant.

Pochintesta. In "The Aspern Papers," Juliana and Tina Bordereau's Venetian lawyer friend.

Pocock, Jim. In *The Ambassadors*, Mrs. Abel Newsome's daughter Sarah's coarse husband. He is Mamie Pocock's brother.

Pocock, Mamie. In *The Ambassadors*, Jim Pocock's charming sister and Chad Newsome's nominal fiancée. Lambert Strether would like to see her become more friendly with Little John Bilham in Paris.

Pocock, Sarah Newsome. In *The Ambassadors*, Mrs. Abel Newsome's daughter, Chad Newsome's sister, Jim Pocock's wife, and Mamie Pocock's sister-in-law. To give moral support to her mother, she ridicules Lambert Strether. Once in Paris as Strether's successor, she becomes extremely friendly with Waymarsh.

Poe, Edgar Allan (1809–1849). Distinguished, influential, erratic American poet, short-story writer, literary critic, and editor. When orphaned (1811), he was reared by John Allan, a Richmond, Virginia merchant. Poe attended the University of Virginia briefly (1826), served in the army (1827–1829) and was a cadet briefly at West Point (1830–1831), than he resumed a literary career, in Richmond, Philadelphia, New York, and Baltimore, where he married his youthful cousin in 1835 or 1836. They moved about. His wife died in New York in 1847; Poe died, in Baltimore, two years later, under mysterious circumstances. Poe is the author of many world-famous poems, including "The City in the

Sea," "To Helen," "Israfel," "The Raven," "Ulalume," and "Annabel Lee"; tales, including "Ligeia, " "The Fall of the House of Usher," "The Murders in the Rue Morgue," "The Purloined Letter," and "The Cask of Amontillado"; and critical pieces, including a review of *Twice-Told Tales* by Nathaniel Hawthorne* and "The Philosophy of Composition." James did not think highly of Poe. In his *Hawthorne* (1879), James, having occasion to comment on Poe and his literary criticism, calls him "a man of genius," whose "intelligence was frequently great." But his criticism, while "curious and interesting," contains judgments which are "pretentious, spiteful, vulgar," if sometimes sensible and discriminating, and once in a while with "a phrase of happy insight imbedded in a patch of the most fatuous pedantry." James is glad that Poe both praised Hawthorne and deplored his overuse of allegory, and he commends Poe for calling *The Pilgrim's Progress* by John Bunyan "ludicrously overrated." In the preface to Volume XVII of *The Novels and Tales of Henry James*, 1909, James castigates Poe's handling of "the horrific" in *The Narrative of Arthur Gordon Pym* (1838) because it remains unconnected to "the human consciousness that . . . amplifies and interprets."

Poets' Corner, Westminster Abbey, London. In June 1976 a floor tablet of dark gray stone with white lettering was placed in the Poets' Corner in honor of James. It reads thus: "Henry James / O.M. / Novelist / New York 1843 / London 1916." Near it are tablets honoring Dylan Thomas, George Eliot,* W. H. Auden, T. S. Eliot, Alfred, Lord Tennyson,* and Robert Browning,* among others.

"The Point of View." Short story (16,800 words), published in the *Century Magazine* (Dec 1882); reprinted in *The Siege of London*, 1883; revised and reprinted in *The Novels and Tales of Henry James*, Volume XIV, 1908. (Characters: Charlotte Antrobus, Edward Antrobus, Gwendolyn Antrobus, Susan Antrobus, Lord Bottomley, Adolfe Bouche, Aurora Church, Mrs. Church, Marcellus C. Cockerel, Mrs. Cooler, Mrs. Draper, Cécile Galopin, Mme. Galopin, Susan Green, Miss Gulp, Gustave Lejaune, Louis Leverett, Plummeridge, Sophy Ruck, Mr. and Mrs. Ruck, Miss Sturdy, Harvard Tremont, Louisa Whiteside.) Aurora Church is at sea, on her way home to America. She writes a letter about two fellow American passengers, pro-European Louis Leverett and pro-American Marcellus Cockerel. She also writes about Edward Antrobus, a British parliamentarian. Next, her mother Mrs. Church writes from New York to criticize America and to deplore Aurora's marriage prospects. Miss Sturdy then writes about vigorous, curious Antrobus, a guest in her brother's Newport home, and about changes in youthful America. Antrobus writes home from Boston concerning America's women, school system, and manners. Leverett writes of languishing in Boston but of liking Miss Church. Gustave Lejaune writes from Washington to Paris criticizing almost everything American but the women. From Washington, Cockerel writes to his sister in praise of everything American and in derogation of European institutions and manners; he adds that he liked Miss Aurora but that Europe had harmed her. Finally Aurora writes that since she is still unmarried she must go west with her mother in search of a husband. In a brief Notebook entry (16 Mar 1879), James says that he might describe a situation "in an alternation of letters, written from an aristocratic, and a democratic, point of view." This story does just that. In the preface to Volume XIV of *The Novels and Tales of Henry James*, James observes that he first saw Washington, "that interesting city," in 1881, visited it again in 1882, and had many impressions, but concluded to record in this story the "mysteriously and refreshingly different" impressions of others. Like "A Bundle of Letters," "The Point of View" is in epistolary form, and it picks up Louis Leverett and Harvard Tremont from the former story, as well as the Churches and the Rucks from "The Pension Beaurepas," also an earlier story. Like James's better story "An International Episode," "The Point of View" presents, though more sarcastically, American pride in America and prejudices against the British, and British pride in England and prejudices against America. Critics commenting on "The Point of View" often reveal their own national point of view.

Pollock, Sir Frederick (1845–1937). Member of a distinguished English legal family going back to the time of George III. Pollock was educated at Eton College, then Trinity College, Cambridge; he married Georgina Harriet Deffell in 1873; and he subsequently became a professor of jurisprudence at University College, London (1882) and Oxford University (1883–1903). Still later, he accepted important appointments, including that of Cinque ports admiralty-court judge in 1914. Pollock wrote legal textbooks now considered standard and was also an able editor. He was coauthor of *History of English Law before the Time of Edward I* (1895), with Frederic William Maitland.* Pollock was a mountaineer, fencer, modest versifier, and erudite amateur philosopher. The magnificent 1874–1932 correspondence of Pollock and his American friend and professional colleague Oliver Wendell Holmes, Jr.* was published (2 vols., 1941; James is occasionally mentioned in passing). In 1877 Lady Pollock invited James to lunch. He wrote to his brother William (12 Jan [1877]) that she was "an *admiress* of my literature (!)—tho' who she is I haven't an idea." He went anyway, and soon reported to his mother (31 Jan [1877]): "Lady P., an amiable, mildly pretentious woman, being addicted to *littérateurs* and theatrical people." In later years James associated (both in London and in the Rye region) with Pollock and his wife, their son Sir (Frederick) John Pollock* (and his theater friends), their daughter Alice Pollock Waterlow, and Sir Sydney Philip Waterlow* (Alice's husband until their divorce). In a letter from Rye to Mrs. W. K. Clifford* (17 Feb 1907), James reports lunching with the nearby Pollocks, then comments in a snide manner on both father and son: "Fred" is "graceful and sinuous and serpentine and overflowing," while "Jack," though a "charming and sympathetic youth," is probably "too much of a featherhead" to be able to practice law. Lady Pollock attended the opening performance of *The High Bid*, in Edinburgh, on 26 March 1908. From 1909 through 1913, James saw Princess Bariatinsky (stage name: Lydia Javorska, or Yavorska) in Henrik Johan Ibsen* and other roles, and also socialized with her, along with her husband Prince Bariatinsky and Jack Pollock. Jack later married the princess.

Pollock, Sir (Frederick) John (1878–1963). Son of Sir Frederick Pollock.* John (Jack) Pollock was educated at Eton College, at Trinity College, Cambridge, and briefly at Harvard Law School (1903–1904). He associated with theatrical people; wrote several short plays; translated material concerning Anatole France* and by Eugène Brieux; and wrote on such diverse subjects as British history, Paris, German militarism, Russian bolshevism, and world politics. Pollock published his memoirs, *Time's Chariot*, in 1950. A *Quarterly Review* essay by Pollock about his father's friendship with Oliver Wendell Holmes, Jr.* was included in the 1961 reprint of the correspondence of Frederick Pollock and Holmes (first published, 2 vols., 1941). James, through his association with Sir Frederick and Lady Pollock (beginning in the late 1870s), knew Jack from his childhood. In a letter to Mrs. W. K. Clifford* (17 Feb 1907), James calls Jack "charming and sympathetic," but harshly adds that he is probably "too much of a featherhead" to be able to practice law. All the same, Pollock, "featherhead"or not, kindly helped get James's play *The Saloon* produced in 1911. In 1920 Pollock married Princess Bariatinsky (stage name: Lydia Javorska, or Yavorska), whom from 1909 through 1913 James saw in Henrik Johan Ibsen* and other roles. She died in 1920.

"A Poor Play Well Acted." Theater essay, published in *Pall Mall Gazette* (24 Oct 1883), in which James first ridicules *Young Folks' Ways* by Frances Eliza Burnett,* calling it "inanimate," and then praises the actors and actresses who try to "vivif[y]" it.

"Poor Richard." Short story (22,300 words), published in the *Atlantic Monthly* (Jun–Aug 1867); reprinted in *Stories Revived*, 1885. (Characters: Miss Catching, Major Robert Luttrel, Mrs. Martin, Fanny Maule, Richard Maule, Miss Pendexter, Captain Edmund Severn, Miss Van Winkle, Gertrude Whittaker.) Richard Maule loves his rich rural neighbor Gertrude Whittaker, who likes the unstable, unpromising fellow well enough but loves Edmund Severn, a Union army captain. Richard and Major Robert Luttrel, the local recruiting officer, lie to Captain Severn at the end of his convalescent leave when they tell him that Miss Whittaker is not at home. The despondent man returns to combat duty and is later killed. Richard returns to drink and catches typhoid fever, leaving Luttrel to become Miss Whittaker's only suitor; but Richard recovers in time to warn the girl. Luttrel remains brash, advances to the rank of general, and later marries a wealthy Philadelphia woman. Gertrude would now accept Richard, but he is ashamed. He sells his farm, joins the army, and after the war plans to head west. Miss Whittaker travels abroad and resolves to stay single. The hero manqué of "Poor

Richard'' may have sad autobiographical overtones. James like Richard was a stay-at-home during the Civil War; he felt unworthy to court an admired young woman (in James's case, his beloved cousin Mary Temple*) in the presence of army officers; and he contracted typhoid. "Poor Richard" is one of James's three Civil War stories; the others are "The Story of a Year" and "A Most Extraordinary Case." "Poor Richard" reveals the young James trying to present challengingly unpleasant characters and dramatic scenes, but the result is unconvincing. Like *Fanshawe*, the early novel by Nathaniel Hawthorne,* this work is filled with portents of better things to come.

Porterfield, David. In "The Patagonia," an architecture student in Paris. He is Grace Mavis's fiancé until her suicide.

Portico, Mrs. In "Georgina's Reasons," pregnant Georgina Benyon's reluctant companion on a trip to Italy. After Georgina abandons her baby boy there, Mrs. Portico writes to Captain Raymond Benyon, the baby's father, and then she dies.

The Portrait of a Lady. Novel (at 217,300 words, James's longest fiction), published in *Macmillan's Magazine* (Oct 1880–Nov 1881), and in the *Atlantic Monthly* (Nov 1880–Dec 1881); revised and reprinted in London by Macmillan, 1881, and in Boston and New York by Houghton, Mifflin, 1882 [1881]; revised and reprinted in *The Novels and Tales of Henry James*, Volumes III, IV, 1908. (Characters: Isabel Archer, Archer, Bob Bantling, Bunchie, Sister Catherine, Annie Climber, Miss Climber, Lady Felicia, Flora, Countess Amy Osmond Gemini, Count Gemini, Caspar Goodwood, Lord and Lady Haycock, Hilary, Sir Matthew Hope, Sister Justine, Edith Archer Keyes, Mrs. and Mrs. Luce, Edmund and Lilian Archer Ludlow, Mme. Serena Merle, Mildred Molyneux, Miss Molyneux, Gilbert Osmond, Pansy Osmond, Lady Pensil, Edward Rosier, Mrs. and Mrs. Rossiter, Henrietta Stackpole, Daniel Tracy Touchett, Lidia Touchett, Ralph Touchett, Mrs. Varian, Lord Warburton.) Through the generosity of her aunt Lydia Touchett, Isabel Archer goes from Albany to London and visits her rich uncle Daniel Tracy Touchett's mellow estate at nearby Gardencourt. She also meets her cousin, sick, pleasant Ralph Touchett, and his robust friend Lord Warburton. Isabel declines Warburton's quick proposal of marriage. Next, after the death of Uncle Daniel provides the girl with great wealth (which Ralph urged his daddy to bestow), she travels to the Continent, where she is unfortunately introduced in Florence to an expatriate American dilettante named Gilbert Osmond. He is a close friend of Madame Serena Merle, whom Isabel first met at Gardencourt through Aunt Lydia. Isabel has rejected not only Lord Warburton's overtures but also repeated proposals from a rich American textile manufacturer named Caspar Goodwood, to the dismay of her traveling American journalist friend Henrietta Stackpole. But now, to Ralph's articulate disgust, Isabel accepts the hand of Osmond, who—we later learn—was encouraged to propose by Madame Merle, who detailed the girl's wealth and naiveté. The Osmonds settle in Rome. Times passes, during which Isabel loses an infant son but becomes more devoted to Osmond's gentle daughter Pansy, presumably the product of his first marriage. When sweet little Pansy, a convent-bred teenager, is sought in marriage by Ned Rosier, a shallow but sincere young American in Europe, Isabel, though numbed by her husband's increasing criticism of her, supports Rosier in spite of Warburton's turning up in Rome and appearing to be eager to marry Pansy—much to socially snobbish Osmond's delight. Ralph Touchett, now visiting in Rome, grows terribly sick and is accompanied home to England both by Goodwood, after one of his periodic negative audiences with Isabel, and also by the voluble Henrietta Stackpole. Later, Isabel learns from Aunt Lydia that Ralph is now dying at Gardencourt, and at once she determines to go and comfort him during his final hours. Choosing to blame Isabel for Warburton's decision not to propose to Pansy after all, Osmond selfishly voices his opposition to his wife's travel plans. Next, Isabel learns from her husband's licentious but friendly sister, Countess Amy Gemini, that Pansy is her brother Gilbert's daughter by Madame Merle. The two had an adulterous relationship for several years. Isabel silently confronts Madame Merle at Pansy's convent, then goes swiftly to England, and remains with her beloved Ralph at Gardencourt until the end. Goodwood encounters her there once more, beseeches her to leave Osmond, and passionately embraces and kisses her; but she resists and soon returns to the Eternal City. *The Portrait of a Lady* is perhaps James's most beloved novel. Before starting to write it, the author, then age thirty-seven, had published forty-three fictional pieces; but only "A Passionate Pilgrim," "Madame de Mauves," *Roderick Hudson, The American*, "Four Meetings," "Daisy Miller," and "An International Episode" pleased him much. Now he was determined to write something "big," as he wrote to his brother William (16 Dec 1879), and he did so. *The Portrait of a Lady* is twice as long as anything he had written previously. His real-life inspirations for it include his beloved cousin Mary Temple,* whose death in 1870 led him to promise to immortalize the lithe, witty girl's personality in some future fictional character. She partly becomes Isabel Archer. Further, in Europe James observed expatriate types like Gilbert and Pansy Osmond (for example, his friends Francis Boott* and his daughter Elizabeth Boott*), the Touchetts (Ralph may be partly a picture of invalid Robert Louis Stevenson* and even in part autobiographical), and Henrietta Stackpole (her first name is a feminized form of "Henry," and James too sent journalistic columns back to an American newspaper). Isabel's Albany background rings changes on James's own. As for literary sources, they are legion and include *Germaine* (1858) by Edmond About,* *Le Roman d'une honnête femme* (1866) by Victor Cherbuliez,* *Middlemarch* (1872) and *Daniel Deronda* (1876) by George Eliot,* *Far from the Madding Crowd* (1874) by Thomas Hardy,* *Indiana* (1832) by George Sand,* *The Duke's Children* (1880) by Anthony Trollope,* and so on. *The Portrait of a Lady* has a fairy-tale plot, with a Cinderella, a fairy godmother (plus a rich uncle), three suitors, a perverse villain, a sick lover, a young girl needing protection, her wooer, and the like.

As early as 1876 James thought about the contours of *The Portrait of a Lady*; in that year, he wrote to William Dean Howells* (24 Oct [1876]) of a long-range plan: "My novel is to be an *Americana*—the adventures in Europe of a female [Christopher] Newman [hero of *The American*]." He soon wrote to Howells again (2 Feb [1877]), this time about his "portrait of the character and recital of the adventures of a woman—a great swell, psychologically." In due time James was fretting in his *Notebooks* (18 Mar 1879) over several scenes, mainly the matter of revealing Pansy's true mother. In the preface to Volume III of *The Novels and Tales of Henry James*, James tells us inaccurately that he started *The Portrait of a Lady* in Florence in the spring of 1879 (actually it was 1880), and he continued work on it the next year in Venice, a city which was both distracting and "fertilising" to his mind. Even before completing the novel, he began serializing it on both sides of the Atlantic late in 1880, and thus earned about $5,000 (exclusive of book profits). James revised the work slightly for book publication. Years later, when he was revising early works for his *Novels and Tales*, he took special pains with *The Portrait of a Lady*; as he wrote Charles Scribner's Sons (12 Jun 1906), "what I have just been very attentively doing for the 'Portrait' must give it a new lease of such life as it may still generally aspire to." He rewrote the ambivalent final chapter of the novel with unique care. He may have had its problems in mind when he recorded in his *Notebooks* (after 18 Mar 1879) that "The *whole* of anything is never told; you can only take what groups together." In his preface he makes many critical points: Following the advice of his friend Ivan Sergeyevich Turgenev,* he began this fiction with a vision of central characters; sincerity and accuracy of presentation invalidate worry over whether a literary work is "moral" or not; the view of action from a given window in "[t]he house of fiction" provides "the 'literary form' "; *The Portrait of a Lady* is "the most proportioned of his productions after 'The Ambasadors' "; Henrietta Stackpole, like Maria Gostrey, is a "light *ficelle*"; and chapter 42, depicting his heroine's "meditative vigil . . . by her dying fire, far into the night, . . . is obviously the best thing in the book."

Portraits of Places. Collection of twenty travel essays, all previously published; reprinted, often much revised, in London by Macmillan, 1883. The essays are "Venice," "Italy Revisited" (originally two essays, "Italy Revisited" and "Recent Florence"); "Occasional Paris" (original title, "Paris Revisited"); "Rheims and Laon: A Little Tour" (original title, "A Little Tour in France"); "Chartres" (original title, "Chartres Portrayed"); "Rouen" (original title, "Summer in France"); "Etretat" (original title, "A French Watering Place"); "From Normandy to the Pyrenees"; "An English Easter"; "London at Midsummer"; "Two Excursions" (original title of longer essay, "Three Excursions"); "In Warwickshire"; "Abbeys and Castles"; "English Vignettes"; "An English New Year" (original title, "The New Year in England"); "An English Winter Watering-Place"; "Saratoga"; "Newport"; "Quebec"; and "Niagara."

Pouncer, Mrs. In "Mrs. Medwin," a lady of fashion who Mamie Cutter says has approved of Mrs. Medwin.

Poupin, M. and Mme. Eustace. In *The Princess Casamassima*, a French book-binder socialist in London and his fat, common-law wife. They are friendly with Anastasius Vetch and later with Hyacinth Robinson.

Poyle, Miss. In "The Figure in the Carpet," the woman to whom Hugh Vereker says the critic narrator's article on him is twaddle.

Prance, Dr. Mary J. In *The Bostonians*, a no-nonsense Boston physician. She is friendly with several feminists and attends Miss Birdseye during her fatal sickness.

Pratt, Herbert James (1841–1915). Harvard-trained physician, who knew William James in Cambridge and practiced medicine for a short time in Denver, Colorado. He then spent forty years traveling extensively. According to a Notebook entry (25 Nov 1881), James spent a month in Venice, in the spring of 1881, with Pratt, who spoke enticingly about Spain and the Middle East. James noted that "[h]e was a most singular, most interesting type, and I shall certainly put him into a novel. . . . A good deal might be done with Herbert Pratt." A few years later, James appears to have used Pratt as a partial model for his character Gabriel Nash of *The Tragic Muse*.

Prendergast. In "A Landscape Painter," a lawyer unsuccessfully interested in Miriam Quarterman.

Prescott, Harriet Elizabeth. Maiden name of Harriet Elizabeth Spofford.*

"The Present Literary Situation in France." Critical essay, published in the *North American Review* (Oct 1899). James begins what amounts to a rambling, out-of-breath survey by saying that as the nineteenth century draws to a close we should acknowledge our literary debt to France. Gone are the great old French writers, including Honoré de Balzac,* Gustave Flaubert,* Victor-Marie Hugo,* Joseph Ernest Renan,* Charles Augustin Sainte-Beuve,* George Sand,* and Hippolyte Taine.* Only Émile Zola* of that epoch remains alive, a solid presence almost "patriarch[al]" now, along with critic Jules Lemaître,* who is passé and whose anti-Semitism in connection with the trials of Alfred Dreyfus* James deplores. He then proceeds to comment on numerous contemporary writers. Anatole France* has a "complex . . . talent." Vincent Brunetière is an ungenial, "confused" editor. Paul Bourget* is a novelist of exciting ideas who "literally *inhabits* the consciousness," unlike Zola, whose "heroic system" of writing is more solid than any of his characters. The study of Flaubert by Émile Faguet* is "full and . . . intelligent," though perhaps inaccurate regarding the character of Emma Bovary, a "two-penny lady." Faguet's brief obituary lines on theatrical reporter Francisque Sarcey* are miraculously expressive. James mentions Vicomte Eugène Melchior de Vogüé* as another "eminent" drama critic. As for novelists, those now gone are better than several current ones, some of whom James identifies. Too often the latter group deals with "Paris only and ever" and with love triangles. Surely there is passion "other . . . than the sole sexual." We should return to Balzac.

The Presentation at Court. The title later given by Ruth Draper* in 1922 to a monologue, now called *A Monologue by Henry James*, which James had written for her in 1913 but which she never performed.

Prest, Mrs. In "The Aspern Papers," a woman in Venice who helps the narrator start his search for the Aspern papers. She is modeled in part on James's friend Katherine De Kay Bronson.*

Prévost, Marcel (1862–1941). Paris-born civil engineer (to 1890), then popular novelist and playwright. His sensational 1894 novel *Les Demi-Vierges*, which he dramatized the following year, concerns the effects of education and society on young Parisian girls. In 1909 Prévost was elected to the French Academy. In an 1894 letter to Sir Edmund Wilson Gosse* (22 Aug [1894]) reporting that Paul Bourget* was with Prévost in England, James calls *Les Demi-Vierges* a "fetid *étude* . . . clever and . . . common." James's library contained seven books by Prévost.

Prime, Arthur. In "Paste," Charlotte Prime's cousin. He pretends to believe that his deceased stepmother's valuable pearls are paste. He then lies about them and then sells them.

Prime, Captain Llewellyn. In *Disengaged*, a naive Guards captain led by Charles Coverley, Percy Trafford, and others to believe that he must propose to Blandina Wigmore because he posed for a photograph with her and then walked unchaperoned with her to some medieval ruins outside London. Repenting her part in the matter, Mrs. Jasper strives in London to "disengage" Prime; liking him more and more, she accepts his proposal.

Prime, Charlotte. In "Paste," Arthur Prime's cousin. She is a governess. She accepts his deceased stepmother's pearl necklace as a gift but then discovers it to be genuine, not paste.

Prime, Mrs. In "Paste," the former actress Miss Bradshaw, owner of the pearl necklace. She is now deceased.

Prime, Rev. Mr. In "Paste," Arthur's deceased father, and the husband of the actress owner of the pearl necklace.

Primoli, Count Joseph-Napoléon (1851–1927). Son of Charlotte Bonaparte, hence the grandson of Napoleon's brother Joseph Bonaparte. In August 1886 James was host at a dinner in Greenwich, England, mainly for Guy de Maupassant.* James also invited his friends Sir Edmund Wilson Gosse,* Jean-Jules Jusserand,* and George Du Maurier.* Maupassant brought along his traveling companion Count Joseph Primoli. In March 1894, when in Rome, James was a guest at a luncheon given by Primoli, who introduced him at that time to Matilde Serao.* Much later, in a letter of reminiscence to Gosse (21 Jan 1914), James described Primoli as "a very amiable & rather singular person." According to his Pocket Diaries, James retained his friendship with Primoli to his final years. At times, James referred to him as Giuseppe and Joseph.

Primrose, Archibald Philip. Original name of James's friend Lord Rosebery, who married into the Rothschild family.* (See Rosebery, Archibald Philip Primrose, Earl of.)

Prince, Morton Henry (1854–1929). Boston-born, Harvard-trained neurologist and psychologist. After studying in Vienna and Strassburg, Dr. Prince returned to the United States to specialize in neurology, abnormal psychology, and psychotherapeutics. He became a distinguished professor, scholar, and editor. He was a professional associate of Dr. James Jackson Putnam.* James consulted Dr. Prince in Boston, in 1911, and saw him again, informally, in London, in 1914.

The Princess Casamassima. Novel (197,800 words), published in the *Atlantic Monthly* (Sep 1885–Oct 1886); revised and reprinted in book form in London and New York by Macmillan, 1886; revised and reprinted in *The Novels and Tales of Henry James*, Volumes V, VI, 1908. (Characters: Assunta, Baskerville, Mrs. Bowerbank, Dr. Buffery, Mrs. and Mrs. Bunbury, Prince Gennaro Casamassima, Princess [Christina Light] Casamassima, Mrs. and Mrs. Chipperfield, Mr. and Mrs. Crookenden, the Misses Crookenden, Delancey, Mme. Grandoni, Griffin, Grugan, Millicent Henning, Mrs. Henning, Diedrich Hoffendahl, Hotchkin, Earl of Inglefield, Lady Aurora Langrish, Mrs. Major, Lady Marchant, the Misses Marchant, Mr. and Mrs. Millington, Paul Muniment, Rosy Muniment, Mrs. and Mrs. Muniment, M. and Mme. Eustace Poupin, Lord Frederick Purvis, Amanda Pynsent, Hyacinth Robinson, Roker, Mrs. Ruffler, Schinkel, Captain Godfrey Gerald Sholto, Mrs. and Mrs. Tripp, Anastasius Vetch, Florentine Vivier, Hyacinthe Vivier, Lady Eva and Lord Warmington, Lord Whiteroy Withers.) Amanda Pynsent, a lowly seamstress, has adopted Hyacinth Robinson, who is the delicate illegitimate son of a French adventuress and a British lord whom she stabbed to death. Pinnie, as Miss Pynsent is called, takes the lad to prison to visit his now dying mother, of whose identity he later reads in old newspapers. Years pass. Hyacinth works in a bookbindery. While visiting his friends the Poupins one day, he meets the revolutionary Paul Muniment; later he meets Paul's crippled sister Rosy and also philanthropic Lady Aurora Langrish. Lady Aurora pathetically likes the selfish Paul. Hyacinth has a coarse and fickle girlfriend, sexy Millicent Henning. One evening the two go to the theater, where Captain Sholto, remembering Hyacinth from a political argument in a café a while back, introduces him to the Princess Casamassima. Soon this radiantly beautiful enigma of a woman has met Paul, his sister Rosy, and Lady Aurora, and she is happy to be penetrating the lower social orders. But her husband the prince turns up and is displeased by the report given to him by her companion Madame Grandoni, who also advises Hyacinth to resist the unstable princess. But he cannot. At the same time, he suspects Millicent of gettng involved with Sholto. Hyacinth enjoys a visit to the princess at an estate named Medley which she rents; he stays on and on, even giving up his job at a bookbinder—to Madame Grandoni's distress. Now trusted by the professional anarchists, he tells the princess that he has promised to murder any nobleman fingered by revolutionary leader Diedrich Hoffendahl. When he finally returns to London, Hyacinth finds Pinnie at death's door, with neighbor Anastasius Vetch and Lady Aurora caring for her. Pinnie wills Hyacinth a small sum, sufficient for him to go see Paris and Venice. Those art centers alter the young man profoundly. He would now fight for old culture, but he will not seek to be released from his fatal vow. Back home, he works again but he is different, is suspicious of the princess, and tries to confide in Paul. The princess is unable to get Paul to have Hyacinth relieved of duty in the anarchist movement. When Prince Casamassima returns and observes his wife with Muniment, he cuts off her income at last. Hyacinth goes to the Poupins' home, where a fellow radical delivers the fatal orders. Hyacinth meets a final time with the princess but says nothing to her of his summons. Later Paul tells her that Hyacinth is trusted, since he now has his orders to shoot a nobleman. She wants to be given the assignment instead. Feeling that the princess, Paul, Millicent, and Lady Aurora are all drifting away from him, and unable either to commit murder or break his promise to do so, Hyacinth goes to his room and shoots himself through the heart. James was inspired to write this unusual novel, his closest approach to a naturalistic work, by his reading of Charles Dickens,* Émile Zola,* *Virgin Soil* (1876) by Iva Sergeyevich Turgenev,* prolabor novels by Victorian writers such as George Gissing* and Sir Walter Besant,* and contemporary accounts in the London *Times* of acts by saboteurs, assassins, revolutionists, anarchists, and nihilists. He was also eager to match his American political novel, *The Bostonians*, with a European one. In fact, before *The Bostonians* finished appearing serially, *The Princess Casamassima* started doing so. James wrote to his friend Thomas Sergeant Perry* one memorable day (12 Dec [1884]) that he had spent "all the morning at Millbank prison (horrible place) collecting notes for a fiction scene." He adds, "You see I am quite the Naturalist. Look out for the same—a year hence." Thus James was preparing for what became chapter 3 of *The Princess Casamassima*, in which Pinnie takes little Hyacinth to see his dying mother in prison. James was far into the writing of *The Princess Casamassima* when he penned the following significant Notebook entry (10 Aug 1885): "It is . . . necessary that at this point I should make the future evolution of *The Princess Casamassima* more clear to myself. I have never yet become engaged in a novel in which, after I had begun to write and send off my MS., the details had remained so vague. This is . . . owing to the fact that I have been . . . preoccupied with the . . . *Bostonians*. . . . The subject of the *Princess* is magnificent and if I can . . . give . . . my mind to it . . . the form will shape itself. . . . I have plunged in rather blindly, and got . . . many characters on my hands; but these will fall into their places if I . . . think it out. . . . The *Princess* will give me hard, continuous work for many months to come . . . '' In a letter to Grace Norton* (23 Aug [1885]), he defined the same novel as ''long-winded.'' In due time, he confessed in a letter to his brother William (10 Sep 1886) that composing *The Bostonians* and then *The Princess Casamassima*, ''especially the second, . . . quite exhausted me.'' James soon lamented in a letter to William Dean Howells* (2 Jan 1888) that poor sales of both of these big novels ''have reduced the desire, and the demand, for my productions to zero.'' In the preface to Volume V of *The Novels and Tales of Henry James*, James starts with a consideration of Hyacinth Robinson, who ''sprang up for me out of the London pavement,'' and who like James saw the great city's ''public show'' but unlike him lacked money. James determined to depict his hero as sensitive but not too sentient, surrounded by bewildering characters, and capable in only a limited way of seeing the ''pictorial whole'' about him. Only after these considerations were settled upon did James turn to matters of plot: His hero feels left out, and his jealousy becomes tragic only when he ''fall[s] in love with the beauty of the world.'' Next, James half apologizes for bringing Christina Light into a new fiction, then theorizes about reappearing fictional characters in general. Finally, he rationalizes that his vague treatment of the anarchistic underground is artistically defensible because society itself does not know, only guesses, suspects, and ignores ''what 'goes on' irreconcilably, subversively, beneath the vast smug surface.'' *The Princess Casamassima* is notable for background accuracy, naturalistic depiction of seamy settings, and the hero's dilemma: Hyacinth cannot accept Muniment's proposal to ''cut up the ceilings of Veronese into strips, so that every one might have a little piece.''

Principino. In *The Golden Bowl*, the infant son of Prince Amerigo and his wife Maggie Verver.

"The Private Life." Short story (12,800 words), published in the *Atlantic Monthly* (Apr 1892); reprinted in *The Private Life*, 1893; revised and republished in *The Novels and Tales of Henry James*, Volume XVII, 1909. (Characters: Blanche Adney, Vincent Adney, Chafer, Lord and Lady Mellifont, Lady Ringrose, Clarence Vawdrey.) Vacationing at a Swiss hotel is a friendly group of successful people. They include polished statesman Lord Mellifont and his wife, quiet writer Clare Vawdrey, actress Blanche Adney and her violinist husband Vincent Adney, and the narrator, an observant writer. After dinner Vawdrey is to read part of a new play designed for Blanche. When he cannot find the manuscript, Lord Mellifont bridges the gap with windy rhetoric. At evening's end, the narrator sees Blanche and Vawdrey on the terrace, and he goes as requested to Vawdrey's room to pick up the manuscript: He eerily sees Vawdrey's alternate identity at his desk writing. Next evening, the narrator talks about the matter with Blanche. The two conclude that Vawdrey has a dual personality; furthermore, they reason that Mellifont (with whom Blanche has taken Alpine walks) has no private identity, being instead nothing but a public impression. Blanche recalls that when she left Mellifont to return to the hotel he simply disappeared until her seeking him caused him to spring up again. Learning that Vawdrey is walking outside, Blanche enters his room and gratefully encounters his alter ego. Meanwhile the narrator approaches Mellifont's room to obtain his signature on a sketch; but when he meets embarrassed Lady Mellifont at the door, he senses that she wishes him not to expose her husband's vacuity. Blanche later tells the narrator that the ghostly Vawdrey will write her play. The start of this story may have been James's repeated observation, as early as the 1870s and recorded in *William Wetmore Story and His Friends*, that Robert Browning* had "a double identity," since "[t]he poet and the 'member of society' were, in a word, dissociated in him." Hence Clare Vawdrey. Then, typically, James cast about for a counterweight and found him in Lord Frederick Leighton,* who when all by himself was nothing. All of this is certain, because of this entry in James's Notebooks (27 Jul 1891): "*The Private Life* (. . . founded on the idea of F. L. and R. B.)." In the preface to Volume XVII of *The Novels and Tales of Henry James*, James makes it clear that his "rich proud genius" of a writer not only must be "*double*, constructed in two quite distinct and 'water-tight' compartments," but also must be "balance[d]" in the plot by a totally "public" figure for "contrast and antithesis." In this preface James names Browning but naturally not poor Leighton. Vawdrey is partly an autobiographical figure as well, since James must have regarded himself as simultaneously participating in public social activity and being privately inspired by it to his best fictive effects.

The Private Life . . . Collection of six stories published in London by Osgood, McIlvaine, 1893: "The Private Life," "The Wheel of Time," "Lord Beaupré," "The Visits," "Collaboration," and "Owen Wingrave." Also a collection of three short stories published in New York by Harpers, 1893: "The Private Life," "Lord Beaupré," and "The Visits."

Probert. In *The Reverberator*, Gaston Probert's deceased grandfather.

Probert. In *The Reverberator*, Gaston's father, who is shocked to learn that Francina Dosson, his son's fiancée, has revealed embarrassing Probert family secrets to American journalist George P. Flack. Old Probert may have traits combining those of James's friends Edward Lee Childe* and Daniel Sargent Curtis.*

Probert, Alphonse. In *The Reverberator*, Gaston's deceased brother.

Probert, Gaston. In *The Reverberator*, the brother of Suzanne de Brécourt, Marguerite de Cliché, and Jeanne Probert de Douves. He is Francina Dosson's fiancé.

Probert, Mme. In *The Reverberator*, Gaston Probert's deceased mother.

"A Problem." Short story (5,800 words), published in the *Galaxy* (Jun 1868). (Characters: Rev. Mr. Clark, David, Emma, Julia, Magawisca.) Newlyweds David and Emma are shaken when Magawisca, and old Indian woman, prophesizes that their first child will be a girl and will die. Their baby, a girl as predicted gets sick, but she recovers. Then the parents recall an earlier prediction—that they will marry twice. This estranges the couple. Later Emma writes to David that their little daughter has died. Attending her funeral, the two are reconciled and in a sense remarry under the minister's benedictory hand. This story ranks low among James's least effective writings.

Procter, Anne Benson Skepper (1798–1888). Wife and then widow (from 1874) of Barry Waller Procter,* In 1877 at a dinner party given by Hamilton Aïdé,* James sat beside Mrs. Procter and thus began a valuable friendship with a delightful old lady. In a letter to his father and his sister Alice (20 May [1877]), he describes Mrs. Procter as "a most shrewd, witty and juvenile old lady—a regular London diner-out. . . . She has known everyone." A year and a half later, again to Alice (31 Dec [1878]), James calls the lady "the ever-delightful Mrs. Procter, whose talk is most delectable—full of genuine *English* wit and wisdom, and reflecting . . . her immense experience of society." To Grace Norton* (4 Jan [1879]), he describes Mrs. Procter as "the best talker, in a certain way, I have met in England, " adding that "she has . . . known clever and eminent people." Her acquaintance with writers went back to all of the major English romantic poets and also included Thomas Carlyle,* Thomas Babington Macaulay, and Sydney Smith and contemporaries Robert Browning* and James Russell Lowell.* Late in her long life, James wrote of Mrs. Procter to Frances Anne Kemble* (20 May [1887]) to praise the old woman's "capacity for *caring*." In due time, James, accompanied by Browning, attended her funeral. Years after her death, James in a Notebook entry (28 Oct 1895) recalls a bright idea from Mrs. Procter for a short story which he did not manage to compose.

Procter, Barry Waller (1787–1874). Leeds-born conveyancer and barrister in London, then commissioner of lunacy (1832–1861). Using the pen name Barry Cornwall, he wrote a few books of poetry and one play. James knew his widow

Anne Benson Skepper Procter.* James's library contained one book by Barry Cornwall.

Prodmore. In "Covering End." the mortgage holder of Covering End, Captain Marmaduke Clement Yule's estate. Mrs. Gracedew buys him off to prevent his scheming to force his daughter Cora to entice Yule into marriage. In *Summersoft*, Mrs. Gracedew buys Summersoft from Prodmore and thereby helps his daughter Cora to achieve her desire, which is to marry Buddle. In *The High Bid*, Mrs. Gracedew buys off Prodmore so that Yule can keep Covering End, his estate, and so that Cora and Hall Pegg can get married.

Prodmore, Cora. In "Covering End," the daughter of the mortgage holder of Covering End, Captain Marmaduke Clement Yule's estate. She loves Hall Pegg and is befriended by Mrs. Gracedew. In *Summersoft*, Cora's father holds the mortgage to Summersoft, and Cora loves Buddle. Mrs. Gracedew deals with Mr. Prodmore and helps the young lovers. In *The High Bid*, the daughter, age twenty-two, of Prodmore, whom Mrs. Gracedew buys off, so that Cora and Hall Pegg can get married.

"Professor Fargo." Short story (15,200 words), published in the *Galaxy* (Aug 1874). (Characters: Professor Fargo, Colonel Gifford, Miss Gifford.) Since the narrator is delayed in P—, a grubby New England village, he attends the show of spiritualist Professor Fargo, mathematician Colonel Gifford, and the colonel's deaf-mute daughter who can quickly perform arithmetical calculations. Later in a squalid part of New York City the narrator sees the professor hypnotize Miss Gifford into leaving her father for him. Colonel Gifford then goes insane. This gruesome little sketch is important only for showing James's hatred of aspects of backwoods America. The professor's handling of the Gifford girl may prefigure Selah Tarrant's attempts to manipulate his daughter Verena in *The Bostonians*.

The Promise. Tentative title of the play *The Other House*.

Prothero, Sir George Walter (1848–1922). Son of a Westminster Abbey canon, Prothero was educated at Eton College, then King's College, Cambridge, and he pursued a teaching career in history (at Eton, Cambridge, and Edinburgh University [1894–1899]). Then he edited the *Quarterly Review* (1899–1922). He did Foreign Office work during World War I and peace conference work thereafter. He published and edited extensively. James knew well and admired not only Prothero but especially his wife Margaret (Fanny), who in addition to a London residence had a cottage in Rye. James's Pocket Diaries from 1909 through 1915 contain dozens of notes about social meetings with the Protheros, both in Rye and in London. After his Robert Browning* lecture, James was asked by Prothero for a revised copy, which he sent and which was published in the *Quarterly Review* (Jul 1912). Prothero was one of the sponsors of James when he requested and obtained his British naturalization papers in 1915, along with Herbert Henry Asquith,* Sir Edmund Wilson Gosse,* and James Brand Pinker.* In his last letter, one sent to his niece Margaret James in the second year of World War I (1 Dec 1915), James writes to praise the Protheros for their war work: "George Prothero is a haggard hero of labour and courage, and she as wonderful as ever in her indefatigability."

Proust, Marcel (1871–1922). Well-to-do, delicate, unusually gifted French essayist, translator (of John Ruskin*), and then aloof author of a series of novels comprehensively entitled *À la Recherche du Temps Perdu* (1913–1928). It is possible that James saw Proust at the home of Alphonse Daudet* in 1893. In 1914 he surely had news of Proust through the French dramatist Henri Bernstein. Although Bernstein promised to send James *Du Côté de Chez Swann* (1913), the first volume of Proust's ongoing series, it was Edith Newbold Jones Wharton* who did so. Walter Van Rensselaer Berry,* a friend of both Wharton and James, knew Proust well. In her autobiography *A Backward Glance* (1934), Wharton said that Proust's work had fascinated both James and her but that neither had ever met Proust. Proust's biographer reports that James wrote to Proust to praise his work, to rank him with Stendhal,* and to lament that both were ahead of their time.

Puddick, Walter. In "Mora Montravers," the painter whom Mora Montravers marries simply to gain her foster mother Jane Traffle's money for him. She then divorces him.

Pudney, Mr. and Mrs. In "The Coxon Fund," the host and hostess of Frank Saltram until he turns offensive.

Pulcheria. In "Daniel Deronda: A Conversation," the anti–George Eliot* reader, who is opposed by Theodora. Constantius mediates between the two.

"The Pupil." Short story (16,500 words), published in *Longman's Magazine* (Mar–Apr 1891); reprinted in *The Lesson of the Master*, 1892; revised and reprinted in *The Novels and Tales of Henry James*, Volume XI, 1908. (Characters: Mrs. Clancy, Lord and Lady Dorrington, Granger, Amy and Paula Moreen, Morgan Moreen, Ulick Moreen, Mr. and Mrs. Moreen, Pemberton, Lord Verschoyle, Zénobie.) Pemberton, an impoverished American ex-student from Oxford, hires on in Nice to tutor Morgan Moreen, the precocious but sickly son, age eleven, of a wandering, gypsy-like American family. He becomes attached to the boy but increasingly dislikes Mr. and Mrs. Moreen, their toadying older son Ulick, and their husband-seeking daughters Paula and Amy. A year passes. The group has moved to Switzerland, Florence, and Paris. Pemberton is unpaid but stays on through friendship with ashamed little Morgan. Pemberton finally demands and gets partial payment. Back in Nice, the pupil interrupts a lesson one day to advise Pemberton to quit the whole shabby family. Instead, however, the tutor refuses more pay and puts his relationship with the parents on a franker footing, even while feeling emotionally blackmailed for doing so. He fears that the boy will suffer should he leave. But Morgan says that such thinking is just what his parents are counting on and voices his preference for going away with his tutor. Pemberton counters by promising the boy that he will take any suitable paying job in the hope that he can later call Morgan to him. In Venice now, and noting a decline in the Moreen family fortunes, Pemberton accepts a tutoring position in England. Soon, however, he returns to Morgan (now fourteen) in Paris, upon receiving a telegram that the youth is sick. Finally, at the end of a long winter walk in the Parisian woods, the pair return and find the family being evicted from their hotel. The parents lugubriously agree that Pemberton can now take Morgan away. But as Pemberton hesitates, Morgan dies—of a heart attack. In the preface to Volume XI of *The Novels and Tales of Henry James*, James cites as his source some gossip told to him in Italy by "a friend . . . from a far country" who was "a doctor of medicine . . . in Florence" (actually, American Dr. William Wilberforce Baldwin,* whose many friends included expatriate members of the American literati). Dr. Baldwin's anecdote concerned an American family of "high but rather unauthenticated pretensions" whose "prowling precarious life" embarrassed their little boy. The lad was precocious and had a weak heart. In his preface, James goes on irrelevantly to express his hatred of what modern tourists, "unconscious Barbarians," have been doing to the Nice, Venice, Paris, and Florence "of old, of irrecoverable years." Incredibly, "The Pupil," which James called in a letter to Horace Elisha Scudder* (10 Nov [1890]) "a little masterpiece of compression," was rejected in November 1890 by that man, who was the newly appointed editor of the *Atlantic Monthly*. James sent his story elsewhere—to *Longman's*, which gratefully serialized one of the finest short stories ever written. Critical cruxes in "The Pupil" include the nature of the Moreen family, the ability and sincerity of Pemberton, the kind of intimacy obtaining between tutor and pupil, and the fatal climax.

Purvis, Lord Frederick. In *The Princess Casamassima*, Hyacinth Robinson's natural father. The mother, Florentine Vivier, murdered Purvis.

Putchin, Miss. In "The Birthplace," the retiring guide of The Birthplace. She brashly answers her successor Morris Gedge's preliminary questions about the place.

Putnam, James Jackson (1846–1918). Boston neurologist and student of Freudian psychology. He was much concerned with psychoneuroses. He was a professional associate of Morton Henry Prince.* During his 1910–1911 stay in the United States, James, who had known Dr. Putnam for decades because of the latter's friendship with William James, consulted him several times. From Lamb

House,* James wrote to Putnam (4 Jan 1912) a long, grateful, egocentric letter about symptoms and progress. James's problems were largely psychosomatic.

Pynsent, Amanda (Pinnie). In *The Princess Casamassima*, the devoted little seamstress guardian of Hyacinth Robinson. She is friendly with Anastasius Vetch; in her will, she leaves Hyacinth a small sum.

Pynsent, Rev. Mr. In "A Day of Days," Herbert and Adela Moore's friend.

Pyramus and Thisbe. One-act play, published in the *Galaxy* (Apr 1869). (Characters: Ellis, A. T., Catherine West, Stephen Young.) Catherine West, a young music teacher, and Stephen Young, a journalist, have adjacent rooms in a rooming house. She has been distracted by his smelly smoking and loud talks with a friend; he, by her piano playing. When flowers for her are delivered to him by mistake, he brings them to her; they voice their dislikes, but soon love encourages them to compromise.

Q _____

Quarterman, Captain Richard. In "A Landscape Painter," Miriam's father. He is a retired sea captain.

Quarterman, Miriam. In "A Landscape Painter," the young lady who marries rich painter diarist Locksley when he is on the rebound. She read his diary but explained coolly that the information in it concerning his wealth only made her like him the more.

"Quebec." Travel essay, published in the *Nation* (28 Sep, 5 Oct 1871); reprinted in *Portraits of Places*, 1883. After a monotonous ride to Quebec, James sees "the old world" appear like magic: shining river, "water-side *faubourg*," "rocky promontory," wall-belted town with "granite citadel," watercolor sky. Things here are not American: naively painted houses, courtesy, Ursuline convent, tin roofs, casement windows, quaint shops, "old market-women," and "garish" cathedral smelling "of the seventeenth century." The citadel is Protestant British. While taking in the view from there, James thinks of British militarism, and does so again on the "less inspiring" Plains of Abraham. Little houses in Quebec may look stale but have at least not been replaced by "horrible" brownstones. Gallic life here must be dull, especially in winter. Much gossip, little culture? There is more "vitality" among the pious "peasantry" out of town, where the landscape reminds James of Normandy and Brittany. He pronounces the Montmorency falls "fine." Near the prettily named village of Château-Richer he observes "sketchable" views. He would regret it if the area is ever Americanized.

"The Question of Our Speech." Lecture, published in *Appleton's Booklover's Magazine* (Aug 1905); republished in *The Question of Our Speech: The Lesson of Balzac: Two Lectures*, 1905. James says that "imparting . . . a coherent culture is a matter of communication and response" but that it is fallacious to think that Americans converse well. Their words run wild; they lack "a tone-standard." Good breeding, manners, and examples promote good speech. Vulgarity reduces speech to the level of animal sounds. Make civil utterance a habit through practice. Resist criticism from the "impudent." Observe "the forms and shades of our language," its "discriminated units of sound and sense." The importance of how we say something "is impossible to overstate." It is "evil" to utter "simple toneless noise," flatly, crudely, and "in the dark," as millions of Americans do. They "slobber . . . disconnected vowels," omit consonants, and add unneeded ones (examples, "Yeh-eh," "idea-r-of," "good ways-off"). James castigates the drawl ("dawg") and the untidy "e" ("vurry"). He calls the American voice, especially in women, "neglected" and therefore now "inferior." English was wrenched once it migrated to vast America because of social, political, educational, journalistic, and ethnic influences. James concentrates on the adverse influence of schools, newspapers ("roar[ing] . . . myriad-faced monster"), and aliens ("vast contingent . . . we make welcome"). Language, like matrimony, needs "conservative" restraints against change. You cannot look for guidance to permissive parents or irresponsible teachers. Emulate articulate "representatives of . . . decent tradition" until good speech "has become . . . second nature."

The Question of Our Speech: The Lesson of Balzac: Two Lectures. Collection of two lectures, published in Boston and New York by Houghton, Mifflin, 1905. The two lectures are "The Question of Our Speech" and "The Lesson of Balzac."

The Quest of the Holy Grail. An 1895 exhibition catalogue of certain paintings by Edwin Austin Abbey,* written by his wife. It is believed that James helped her.

Quilter, Roger (1877–1953). British composer of orchestral music, an operetta, and songs and settings of lyrics, for example, from Alfred, Lord Tennyson.* James socialized in London with Quilter (1912–1915).

Quint, Peter. In "The Turn of the Screw," the male ghost at Bly seen by the governess and perhaps by Miles. In life Quint may have been too intimate with Miss Jessel. It has been suggested that Quint physically resembles George Bernard Shaw* when he was young.

R

Raddle. In "Lord Beaupré," young Raddle's deceased glue manufacturing father.

Raddle. In "Lord Beaupré," a rich young man who does not marry Maud Ashbury, to her mother's distress.

Raddle, Mrs. In "Lord Beaupré," young Raddle's rather old wife.

Raffalovich, Marc André (1864–1934). Poet, novelist, editor, and author of books on homosexuality, including *L'Affaire d'Oscar Wilde* (1895), *L'Uranisme, inversion sexuelle congénitale: Observations et conseils* (1895), *Uranisme et unisexualité: étude sur différentes manifestations de l'instinct sexuel* (1896), and *Annuales de l'unisexualité* (1897). When Raffalovich, who was incredibly ugly, sent James his 1904 edition of *Last Letters of Aubrey Beardsley* in 1913, James acknowledged the gift in a gracious letter (7 Nov 1913). James wrote to Logan Pearsall Smith* (17 Nov 1913) that he had known Raffalovich slightly in London but had not seen him for years. James also wrote to Sir Edmund Wilson Gosse* (29 Jan 1894 [1914?]) that his memory of "R." was "dim & mythic." According to his Pocket Diaries, James lunched twice with Raffalovich later in 1914.

Raikes, Thomas (1777–1848). Eton graduate, observer of court officials, and diary-keeping dandy. He nominally helped his influential merchant father for a time, became a club man, traveled much abroad, and tried to recover his health at Bath (1846), but he died soon thereafter at Brighton. Tall and pock-marked, he was often caricatured as a London rake. In 1838 Raikes published an account of his 1829–1830 visit to St. Petersburg. His daughter published his correspondence (2 vols., 1861). His 1831–1847 journal was published in part (4 vols., 1856–1857) and includes notes on great men of the early nineteenth century in London and Paris. Richard Henry Stoddard* selected and edited *Personal Reminiscences of Cornelia Knight and Thomas Raikes* (1875), which James reviewed (*Nation*, 24 Jun 1875). Although James dislikes being spoon-fed extracts of reminiscences, he admits that Stoddard has skipped and chosen usefully here. Noting that Raikes is imperceptive and offers "thin gossip" mainly about "the Duke of Wellington, Talleyrand, and the Orleans family," James summarizes and quotes briefly.

Ramage, Dr. and Mrs. Robert. In *The Other House*, the novel, and *The Other House*, the play, friends of the Beever and Bream families. He treats Julia Bream after she gives birth to Effie but she dies. And he covers up Armiger's murder, four years later, of Effie Bream.

Ramée, Marie Louise de la (1839–1908). The real name of Ouida.*

Ramsey, Rutland. In "The Real Thing," presumably the hero of a volume by the tardily famous Philip Vincent which the painter narrator is commissioned to illustrate.

Rance, Mr. and Mrs. In *The Golden Bowl*, Adam Verver's friends. Rance is absent; his parasitic wife bothers Adam until Charlotte Stant drives her away from Fawns.

Randage. In *The Awkward Age*, the deceased possessor of dirty books. Mrs. Edward Brookenham and Mitchett discuss him.

Ranee of Sarawak. The official title of James's close friend Margaret Alice Lili Brooke.*

Ransom, Basil. In *The Bostonians*, a Confederate Army veteran from Mississippi, and a lawyer and writer. He works in New York, visits Boston, attracts widowed Adelina Chancellor Luna, outrages her unmarried sister Olive Chancellor, falls in love possessively with Verena Tarrant, and wins Verena away from the feminist movement.

Rasch, Cornelia. In "Crapy Cornelia," White-Mason's friend during their distant youth. Later they happily renew their acquaintance.

"Ravenna." Travel essay, published in the *Nation* (9 Jul 1874); reprinted in *Transatlantic Sketches*, 1875, and in *Italian Hours*, 1909. James writes his lines about "glowing" Ravenna in cold Switzerland. A week ago he went from warm Florence to a Bologna festa (a "medley of colour"), thence to "drowsy" Ravenna and a night walk there. The next morning he inspected "shabby" houses and old church mosaics (including San Apollinare Nuovo's "potent and positive Christ"). Ravenna reminds James of many writers, especially George Gordon, Lord Byron,* who lived two years and wrote "in this stagnant city," and Dante, who died there and fortunately needs no fine monument, having "built himself his temple of fame in verses more solid than Cyclopean blocks." On the way to the pine forest outside town, James mused in San Apollinare in Classe, Ravenna's best temple, impressive because it is lonely. From the "shadeless" forest's edge, he saw boats at sea.

Rawson. In "A Passionate Pilgrim," the fallen English gentleman whom the narrator and Clement Searle meet in Oxford.

Ray, Mr. and Mrs. In "A Bundle of Letters," a well-to-do New York couple vacationing in Paris. He is called home, and she stays on with their daughter Violet.

Ray, Violet. In "A Bundle of Letters," a New York businessman's conceited daughter staying in Paris with her mother. She writes letters to Agnes Rich critical of Miranda Hope, a fellow guest at Mme. Maisonrouge's pension.

Reade, Charles (1814–1884). English novelist and playwright. He graduated from Magdalen College, Oxford (1835), was admitted to the bar (1843) but did not practice law, and lived in London. After traveling abroad, he enjoyed success in the theater, and then published *It Is Never Too Late to Mend* (1856), a prison reform novel. His fiction, like that of Charles Dickens,* was popular and melodramatic. His best-known book, *The Cloister and the Hearth* (1861), is set in Renaissance Europe and features the unwed parents of the scholar Erasmus. His careful research and documentation make him a precursor of Émile Zola.* James's essays on other authors reveal in passing his appreciation of Reade. In a review of *The Hillyars and the Burtons* by Henry Kingsley,* James comments that Reade could depict Australia without having been there better than Kingsley could after being there. In his review of *Felix Holt* by George Eliot,* James calls Reade "the most readable of living English novelists . . . and . . . a distant kinsman of Shakespeare." In reviewing two novels by Anne E. Manning,* James praises *The Cloister and the Hearth* for its historical accuracy. His review of *Far from the Madding Crowd* by Thomas Hardy* closes with praise of Reade's virtual invention of a type of fictive heroine. In reviewing *Honest John Vane* by John William De Forest,* James links that author and Reade for criticizing public abuses with similar forcefulness. In "The London Theatres" (1881), James mentioned Reade's 1879 dramatic adaptation, entitled *Drink*, of *L'Assommoir* by Émile Zola.* James's library contained two books by Reade.

"The Real Right Thing." Short story (4,900 words), published in *Collier's Weekly* (16 Dec 1899); reprinted in *The Soft Side*, 1900; revised and reprinted in *The Novels and Tales of Henry James*, Volume XVII, 1909. (Characters: Ashton Doyne, Mrs. Ashton Doyne, George Withermore.) Author Ashton Doyne's widow offers eager journalist George Withermore the opportunity to write her husband's biography. Soon Withermore, happily working away in the dead man's study, senses that Doyne's ghost is helping him locate material. But then papers seem to be missing, and the ghost seems to be warning Withermore off. One evening he sees an immense dim presence urging him to quit. He tells Mrs. Doyne that he is discontinuing the project. Evidently she too sees the ghost in the study, for she gives up as well. According to a Notebook entry (7 May 1898), Augustine Birrell, an English essayist, educator, and chief secretary for Ireland, told James that when he began to consult the personal papers of British politician Sir Frank Lockwood, for the purpose of writing his biography, he began to feel that the man "might come in." The resulting ghost story is rather wispy, though in keeping with James's dislike of meddling biographers. In the preface to Volume XVII of *The Novels and Tales of Henry James*, James lists several stories and indicates that in them he has tried to avoid "waste . . . from the sense that in art economy is always beauty." "The Real Right Thing" avoids waste with a vengeance: It is James's shortest short story.

"The Real Thing." Short story (9,600 words), published in *Black and White* (16 Apr 1892); reprinted in *The Real Thing and Other Tales*, 1893; revised and reprinted in *The Novels and Tales of Henry James*, Volume XVIII, 1909. (Characters: Artemisia, Miss Churm, Jack Hawley, Major and Mrs. Monarch, Oronte, Rutland Ramsey, Claude Rivet, Philip Vincent.) The painter narrator agrees to hire Major and Mrs. Monarch as models. They are handsome, sociable, and destitute, but also—as it quickly becomes apparent—inflexible and cocky. So they cannot help him in his trial illustrations for a de luxe edition of tardily acclaimed Philip Vincent's writings. The narrator therefore relies more on Cockney model Miss Churm and later on a newcomer named Oronte, a lithe Italian immigrant to England. Their poses are eloquent, whereas the Monarchs, assuredly "the real thing," have a predictable, photographic sameness. The narrator, harshly warned to this effect by his critical painter friend Jack Hawley, reluctantly pays off the mutely appealing Monarchs but will always remember his poignant experience with them. According to a Notebook entry (22 Feb 1891), James got his idea for the Monarchs—a "faded, ruined pair . . . trying to find employment as models"—from his friend George Du Maurier,* author of three self-illustrated novels. (The note suggests that the painter narrator might be illustrating *Joseph Andrews* by Henry Fielding). In the preface to Volume XVIII of *The Novels and Tales of Henry James*, James gives Du Maurier public credit for the germ of "The Real Thing"; he adds that the aesthetic problem of the story—real thing vs. "make believe"—"struck me as exquisite, and out of a momentary fond consideration of it 'The Real Thing' sprang at a bound." The resulting story, one of James's neatest works, is important as poignant fiction, aesthetic parable, antiaristocratic satire, and sunken autobiography. The reversal of roles toward the end—the Monarchs serve Churm and Oronte—is a fine example of Jamesian chiasmus. Critical debate continues as to just what "the real thing" is. James notes that country-house living in England has given the Monarchs "pleasant intonations" but no intellectual sophistication. And the de luxe edition with illustrations of Philip Vincent, the novelist tardily prized in "the full light of a higher criticism," is surely a Jamesian prophecy, ultimately self-fulfilled.

The Real Thing and Other Tales. Collection of five short stories published in New York and London by Macmillan, 1893: "The Real Thing," "Sir Dominick Ferrand," "Nona Vincent," "The Chaperon," and "Greville Fane."

"The Reassembling of Parliament." Political letter, published in the *Nation* (20 Mar 1879), which James begins by calling the current session of Parliament vacuous. News from South Africa is deplorable. The Zulus under Cetewayo have slaughtered "slim and juvenile" British soldiers, all predictably brave, under Sir Bartle Frere, whom Liberal opponents in the House of Commons may cause to be censured. This war is not popular, as the one in Afghanistan has been. James is glad that he is a "disinterested stranger" in England, hence without "the obligation of party allegiance." He half hopes that England will suffer a setback, to be reminded thus of the cost of imperialism. If it is bent on dominating savages, it can expect hostilities.

"Recent Florence." Original title of travel essay (*Atlantic Monthly*, May 1878; reprinted as part of "Italy Revisited" in *Italian Hours*, 1909).

"Recent Novels." Reviews, published in the *Nation* (13 Jan 1876), of works by Frank Lee Benedict,* Charles H. Doe,* Annie Edwards,* Octave Feuillet,* Michel Lévy, and George Sand.*

"Recent Volumes of Poems." Reviews, published in the *North American Review* (Apr 1867), of works by Elizabeth Akers,* Elizabeth Rundle Charles,* Amanda T. Jones,* and Julia Ward Howe.*

Redwood, Mrs. In "The Modern Warning," a New York society friend of Agatha Grice, later Lady Chasemore.

Reeve, Barton. In "The Given Chase," Mrs. Kate Despard's lawyer-lover who appeals to Margaret Hamer for help.

Reeves, Mrs. Sherrington. In "Fordham Castle," the pseudonym of Sue Taker.

"Refugees in Chelsea." War essay, published as "Novelist Writes of Refugees in England," Boston *Sunday Herald Supplement* (17 Oct 1915), as "Henry James Writes of Refugees in England," *New York Times* (17 Oct 1915), and as "Refugees in Chelsea," *Times Literary Supplement* (23 Mar 1916); reprinted in *Within the Rim and Other Essays: 1914–15*, 1919. James calls the invasion of Belgium by Germany "the greatest public horror of our age, or of all the preceding." Belgian domestic life has been "dismembered, disembowelled, and shattered." But Belgian suffering has occasioned British "sympathy and . . . beneficence": Innumerable homeless refugees are now sheltered in London's Chelsea district. When "earlier Huns" poured into Rome, the Romans were "besotted." But the Belgians, exiled by "shamelessly cynical" latter-day Vandals, will preserve "their living tradition." James has studied their faces. The face of a mutilated Belgian soldier, now weaving socks, displays "courage and patience and . . . humility." A female Belgian victim's face is noble and sweet. James will write more later, but for now he will describe only what he saw and heard "in a tiny Sussex town [Rye]" that first September: From a refugee train came a mother carrying a child, and "her sobbing and sobbing cry was the voice itself of history." She cried not in anguish but because she was assured of protection.

Regnault, Henri (1843–1871). French genre and portrait painter, born in Paris. His father was a distinguished chemist and physicist. Regnault studied art, exhibited in 1864, won a prize two years later, studied Hispanic-Italian masters in Rome, traveled and studied in Spain, and painted in Tangiers. He never realized his ambition to see the East because he was killed during the Franco-Prussian War. James wrote to his brother William (22 Sep [1872]) to comment on a pair of Regnault's paintings: "They are very juvenile . . . but . . . make one feel that their author if he had lived and kept his promise, would have been the first of all modern painters. . . . He seems to have thought . . . in color." James wrote a touching review (*Nation*, 2 Jan 1873) of the *Correspondance de Henri Regnault* (1872), predicting that the young artist, dying so tragically and yet already so "complete," might well become a legend. James sums up not only Regnault's versatility (painter, musician, singer, horseman, gymnast, writer, traveler, friend, and fiancé) but also his work in Italy, Spain, and Africa. Regnault especially loved Michelangelo, Spanish gypsies, the Alhambra, and Diego de Silva y Velasquez.* Finding the letters of Henri Regnault delightful and charming, James says that death "could hardly have extinguished a life of greater promise." James in a note (*Nation*, 26 Oct 1876) describes the Regnault monument in the cloister of the École des Beaux Arts, Paris: two columns, pediment with pedestal and ugly bronze bust. The best feature is the graceful statue by Henri-Michel-Antoine Chapu of *La Jeunesse*, mourning at the pedestal.

Rehan, Ada C. (1860–1916). Actress born in Limerick, Ireland (as Ada Crehan), who migrated with her family to Brooklyn in 1865. She debuted early, performed in Philadelphia and New York, and from 1877 associated with John Augustin Daly,* notably in New York and later (starting in 1884) in London and on the Continent, until his death in 1899. She took more than two hundred parts in twenty-six years of acting. She was notable as Katherine in *The Taming of the Shrew* by William Shakespeare,* Roxane in *Cyrano de Bergerac* by Edmond Rostand,* and in Restoration comedy. She retired in 1905, and thereafter lived in New York and on the Cumberland coast of England. According to George Bernard Shaw,* her tempestuous, artificial, overemphasized (though charming) style made it hard for her to accommodate to later, more naturalistic drama. James met Miss Rehan in 1891, wrote to her (6 Jan 1892) to offer her his three-act play *Disengaged*, in which, he notes, "I saw you at every turn," and read it to her in August. Daly agreed to try to produce it; but after much unpleasantness, James withdrew it in December 1893. He wrote to Daly (11 Dec 1893) to complain of his treatment even while praising Miss Rehan's "great talent"; however, he wrote to William James and his wife (29 Dec 1893) to describe the actress's "singular artistic (and social!) baseness," "unmistakeable unintelligence," and even shame.

Reid, Whitelaw (1837–1912). Ohio-born Civil War correspondent (1861–1862), correspondent in Washington, D.C. (1862–1868), New York *Tribune* journalist (staff member, 1868; managing editor, 1869; editor, 1872–1905), and diplomat (minister to France, 1889–1892; Spanish-American War peace commissioner, 1898; and ambassador to Great Britain, 1905–1912). He published several books, on the Civil War, diplomacy, and education. On the recommendation of John Milton Hay,* one of his *Tribune* editorial writers, Reid hired James in 1875 to be his Paris correspondent. James wrote twenty letters for him (1875–1876), which became *Parisian Sketches*. When Reid suggested that he make the letters more journalistic and newsy, James quit, with this flourish in a letter to the editor (30 Aug 1876): "If my letters have been 'too good' I am honestly afraid that they are the poorest I can do, especially for the money! I had better, therefore, suspend them altogether." Much later, he recalled Reid's criticism when he was jotting down plot details in his *Notebooks* (26 Jan, 4 Jun 1895) for what became his short story "The Next Time."

Reinhart, Charles Stanley (1844–1896). Pittsburgh-born illustrator and genre painter, who after service in the Union Army during the Civil War studied art in Paris and Munich. He returned to the United States (1870), settled in New York, worked for Harper & Brothers (to 1877), went to Paris (1880–1891), traveled about Europe to find material, and illustrated books for several authors and publishers. He exhibited a few paintings with considerable success. James's "Cousin Maria" (later called "Mrs. Temperly"), "Louisa Pallant," and "Two Countries" (later called "The Modern Warning") were all illustrated in the late

1880s by Reinhart, about whom in 1890 James published a complimentary essay entitled "Charles S. Reinhart" (*Harper's Weekly*, 14 Jun 1890; reprinted in *Picture and Text*, 1893). He begins it by inveighing against "the machinery of publicity" but soon proceeds to "notice . . . with candor" the American art of black-and-white periodical illustration. The writer and the black-and-white "draughtsman" alike have a common purpose, which is to record "contemporary life." Reinhart is a quick sketcher who preserves the present scene for posterity. After much practice in Munich, he now has "facility and felicity." His book illustrations typically catch "character" via "the specific touch." James includes praise of Reinhart's landscape paintings and his poignant *Washed Ashore* (Paris Salon, 1887). If his paintings are big bank notes, his sketches in black and white are scattered coins of great value too.

Rembrandt Harmensz van Rijn (1606–1669). Magnificent Dutch painter and etcher, who was born in Leyden and lived in Amsterdam (from 1631), where he was a portrait painter and art teacher. He was married to wealthy Saskia van Uylenborch (from 1634 to 1642), had a son Titus (1641–1668), went bankrupt (1656), and thereafter lived in poverty and some seclusion. Rembrandt was a unique master painter of portraits, biblical and mythological scenes, landscapes, still life, and genre pictures. A list of his masterpieces would be too protracted for inclusion here. James in "The Bethnal Green Museum" (1873) praises several of Rembrandt's portraits as "very frank and simple" but feels that the artist "abuse[s] . . . *chiaroscuro*." In his travel sketch "In Holland" (1874), James curiously contends that Rembrandt "is not an intellectually suggestive painter"; furthermore, that, because he was only capriciously observant and hence does not display "verity," "he was really not, strictly speaking, a painter" at all. In his 1876 review of *Les Maîtres d'Autrefois* by Eugène Fromentin,* James makes a few casual remarks on Rembrandt, whom he calls "an alchemist" of "the known, the familiar, the common, the homely." In "The Old Masters at Burlington House" (1878), he praises Rembrandt's famous *Windmill* as "one of the artist's strongest landscapes," with colors showing "the painter's characteristic magic." He also singles out a 1635 self-portrait and the head of a Jewish rabbi—the latter "full of that profundity of life which we find in Rembrandt's greatest works."

Renan, Joseph Ernest (1823–1892). French man of letters, philologist, historian, Orientalist, and critical philosopher. Born at Tréguier, he was trained for the priesthood in Paris but broke away, and began a long career as an ascetic, idealist Semitic scholar and, after the 1848 Revolution, a gentle critic of democracy and much else. His works include *Averroès* (1852), *Études d'histoire religieuse* (1857), *De l'Origine du langage* (1858), *La Vie de Jésus* (1863), *Marc Aurèle et la fin du monde antique* (1880), *Souvenirs d'enfance et de jeunesse* (1883), and *L'Histoire du peuple d'Israël* (1887–91). James met Renan in Paris in 1875 and soon described him in a letter to his brother William (8 Feb [1876]) as "hideous and charming" and his dinner conversation as exquisite, urbane, fine, witty, "all quite without show-off." James delighted in Renan's successive belletristic volumes, especially for their style. In a note (*Nation*, 30 Dec 1875), he comments on Renan's eloquent letter from Ischia concerning his ten-day visit to Sicily. In a review of Hippolyte Taine* (New York *Tribune*, 8 Jan 1876), James called Taine "the most brilliant French writer," with one exception, namely, Renan. In "Art and Letters in Paris" (New York *Tribune*, 22 Apr 1876), James notes that the first installment of Renan's *Souvenirs d'enfance*, then appearing in the *Revue des Deux Mondes*, is "enchanting." In "Parisian Topics" (New York *Tribune*, 17 Jun 1876), James praises Renan as "the first of French writers," and he reviews his *Dialogues et fragments philosophiques* (1876) as intellectually fertile, if a little foppish and perfumy: Renan wonders about future sources of energy, the coming uselessness of artists and virtuous people, the possibility of space travel, and much else. James says that Renan's style is the best in France, now that Charles Augustin Saint-Beuve* is dead, adding that George Sand* employed, "after all (with all respect), a woman's style." In "George Sand" (New York *Tribune*, 22 Jul 1876), James gratuitously remarks that, although Renan comments on Sand, he has probably "not perused any very great number of Madame Sand's fictions." James's major work on Renan is his long review (*Atlantic Monthly*, Aug 1883) of *Souvenirs*, the fine style of which he compares favorably to that of Matthew Arnold* among the English. James comments on Renan's Breton ancestry; he is highly sympathetic when Renan discusses "the interruption of his clerical career"; and he admires his combination of modesty, generosity, self-appreciation, tact, and truthfulness. Translating a beautifully imagistic remembrance by Renan about his childhood in Brittany, James explicates the town of Is mentioned in the passage as representing Renan's education, "early faith," and former mental state—all "long since sunk deep into the sea of time." James also appreciates both Renan's pervasive dislike of democracy (called "Americanism") and his revealing prefaces, and he concludes by calling *Souvenirs* a bit pale and abstract concerning others, but Renan a "masterly narrator" of "his own spiritual history." Late in life, James wrote to Sir Edmund Wilson Gosse* (22 Feb 1908) that Renan was "one of [the] blessings of my youth, & idols of my prime & influences, generally, of my life." James's library contained twelve books by Renan.

Repplier, Agnes (1855–1950). Philadelphia-born essayist, biographer, scholar, and autobiographer. She introduced James when he lectured on Honoré de Balzac* at Bryn Mawr College on 19 January 1905. In a letter to Sir Edmund Wilson Gosse* (16 Feb 1905), James praises "her bravery & (almost) brilliancy."

The Reprobate. Three-act farce, published in *Theatricals: Second Series: The Album* [and] *The Reprobate*, 1894. (Characters: Blanche Amber, Bonsor, Pitt Brunt, Captain Chanter, Cubit, Paul Doubleday, Mrs. Doubleday, Mrs. Doubleday, Doubleday, Doubleday, Mrs. Freshville.) Into Bonsor's Hampton Court villa comes an unannounced stranger, Mrs. Freshville. She pumps Cubit the butler. She is Nina, Paul Doubleday's girlfriend, a singer who went with him to Paris years earlier. For the last decade his widowed stepmother Mrs. Doubleday, with bachelor Bonsor as coguardian, has kept repentant Paul locked away from life's temptations. Amid entrances and exits, we learn that Bonsor wants his niece Blanche Amber, back from Germany, to meet with and marry his friend Pitt Brunt, a pompous parliamentarian; and that Mrs. Doubleday is pursued by Captain Chanter, who also knew Mrs. Freshville as Nina. Blanche meets timid Paul, likes him, and dislikes how he is treated. Chanter sees Mrs. Freshville and silences her by promising a wedding ring. All exit for dinner except for Paul and Mrs. Freshville, who meet face to face. The next day, Chanter tells Bonsor he wants to marry Mrs. Doubleday, who will let him help care for Paul. Bonsor recommends Brunt to Blanche, who prefers to help Paul, whom Chanter bribes with a larger allowance. Blanche tells Paul he should be glad he once loved someone. Mrs. Freshville still likes Paul, wants Chanter, but knows he wants Mrs. Doubleday. Chanter tries to bribe Paul to lure away Mrs. Freshville, by offering him a cigar, brandy, cards, and an Émile Zola* novel. Chanter will try to locate an incriminating photograph of Paul and Nina, missing from Mrs. Freshville's handbag, and exchange it for incriminating love letters she has from him. Paul tells his stepmother he shocks Chanter by his new behavior, and he tells Cubit to mail her wedding announcements, even against Bonsor's wishes. Then Mrs. Freshville proposes to Paul, which relieves Chanter until Paul tells him he will not go to Paris again with her. Paul feels free but strangely moral. Twenty hours later, discussion in Bonsor's drawing room concerns Paul's disappearance. Chanter is in London looking for him. Returning with gifts, Paul says he had to get away a while but not with Nina. He demands his inheritance. Chanter returns to hear from Paul that Nina was not with him but that Chanter should let Blanche believe he was naughty so that she will find him more attractive. Mrs. Freshville enters, talks with Brunt, gives him Chanter's love letters written to Nina; Brunt can thus embarrass Mrs. Doubleday. But Brunt gives them to Blanche, thinking they are Paul's to Nina and hoping thus to win Blanche. Paul tells Chanter Mrs. Freshville is back. Chanter has not found the photograph to trade for the letters; so Mrs. Doubleday orders him to get some papers from her maid. Paul lectures his stepmother on the need to love and avoid griping. Her papers are not Chanter's letters but old instructions from her husband on how to treat Paul. Blanche produces the love letters, thinking they are Paul's to Nina. When Mrs. Freshville wonders where the photograph is, Paul persuades her to go rowing with Brunt, to the relief of Chanter, who accepts his letters. Bonsor can keep all these secrets. Blanche produces the photograph and accepts Paul, though innocent, as his stepmother embraces Chanter. The title *The Reprobate* comes from the fact that almost everyone labels misunderstood Paul thus. A source of the play may have been James's memory, recorded in *A Small Boy and Others*, of Helen Wykoff Perkins, his mother's cousin who dominated her brother Henry Wykoff, much as Mrs. Doubleday dominates her stepson Paul.

In a letter to Sir Edmund Wilson Gosse* (c. 10 Dec 1894), James describes *The Reprobate* as a better play than *The Album*. *The Reprobate* was not produced in James's lifetime.

The Return of the Native. A title which James said in 1904 he might have used for what became *The American Scene* but for the fact that Thomas Hardy* had published a novel by that name.

The Return of the Novelist. A title for *The American Scene* which James considered in 1904 but discarded.

Reubell, Henrietta (Etta) (c. 1839–1924). Paris resident whose father was French and whose mother was American. She was a hostess to artists and writers, including John Singer Sargent* and Oscar Wilde.* James met Miss Reubell in Paris, in April 1876, and at first was ambivalently impressed. In a letter to his brother William (25 Apr [1876]), he describes her as "ugly, but . . . frank, intelligent and agreeable," adding cockily that if he were in the market she had qualities which could make her a good wife for him. In the next decade he came to admire her greatly. In a letter to Elizabeth Boott* (7 Jan [1886]) he recommends "tall Etta" as having "much *cachet*." Lizzie and her father Francis Boott* were subsequently friendly to Etta. When Lizzie married Frank Duveneck,* James wrote to Etta (11 Mar [1886]) to express private alarm. Later, he urged Jonathan Sturges* to visit Miss Reubell, who, he says in a letter to Sturges (19 Oct 1893), "keeps a saloon for gifted infants." (Does he mean a Parisian day-care center or a sitting room for *artistes*?) In several Notebook entries (4 Aug 1892, 21 Dec 1895, 7 May 1898, 5 Oct 1899), James mulls over a clever idea from her for a short story which he never wrote. Proof of the closeness of their friendship is contained in two quite different letters he sent to her. In one ([12 Nov 1899]), James elaborately justifies aspects of his misunderstood novel *The Awkward Age*. In the other (15 Dec 1901), she is treated to gossip, some quite detailed, about no less than sixteen people. James wrote to her at least a hundred letters. Henrietta Reubell is a possible model for the willowy Miss Barrace of *The Ambassadors*.

The Reverberator. Short novel (53,000 words), published in *Macmillan's Magazine* (Feb–Apr 1888); reprinted in London and New York by Macmillan, 1888; revised and reprinted in *The Novels and Tales of Henry James*, Volume XIII, 1908. (Characters: Alphonse de Brécourt, Suzanne de Brécourt, Mme. de Brives, Carolus, Marquis Maxime de Cliché, Marguerite de Cliché, M. de Courageau, Blanche de Douves, Raoul de Douves, Jeanne Probert de Douves, M. de Douves, Fidelia Dosson, Francina Dosson, Whitney Dosson, Durand, George P. Flack, M. de Grospré, D. Jackson Hodge, Mme. de Marignac, Munster, Mme. d'Outreville, Alphonse Probert, Gaston Probert, Probert, Probert, Mme. Probert. Cora and Mr. and Mrs. D. S. and Samuel Rosenheim, Mlle. de Saintonge, R. P. Scudamore, Florine [or is her first name Dorine?] Topping, Lord and Lady

Trantum, Mme. Léonie de Villepreux, Charles Waterlow.) George P. Flack works in Paris for an American newspaper called *The Reverberator*. In a hotel he meets his American friends the Dossons: rich old Whitney Dosson, his plain daughter Fidelia, and her pretty sister Francina (Francie), whom he convinces to sit for a portrait by the American painter Charles Waterlow. In the studio one day is Gaston Probert, born in France but of an American family from Carolina. He quickly falls in love with Francie, to whom Flack unsuccessfully proposes. Gaston, ever more in love, introduces Francie to one of his Frenchified sisters. She is Suzanne de Brécourt, who dispproves of the girl and says that the Probert family will not accept her. But Gaston asks Mr. Dosson, who is receptive and calm. In time the Parisian Proberts meet the Dossons in their hotel, and Gaston's rigid father gradually accepts the idea of an international marriage. Gaston goes to look into family property in America at about the time Flack returns from America to Paris. He takes naive Francie for a drive, of which Marguerite de Cliché is violently critical. Suddenly *The Reverberator* publishes horrible but true stories about members of the Probert family. When Suzanne queries Francie, the girl admits innocently relaying to Flack family gossip which Gaston had told her. A noisy family scene follows: Francie cannot see the enormity of her violation of confidence, and Suzanne surprisingly defends her. When Gaston returns home, he initially seems outraged. Flack professes innocence of any wrongdoing. Francie tells Gaston that she will not put any blame on Flack. Waterlow advises Gaston to follow his heart. He does so, supports his fiancée's attitude, and will quietly accept predictable familial denunciation. The origin of this story was unusual. Late in 1886 General George Brinton McClellan,* his wife, and their daughter were in Venice; the daughter sent a naive, crude, ill-written letter of gossip about Venetian society to the New York *World*, which published it (14 November 1886). Making its way back to Venice, it caused a scandal. James, in Italy for many months beginning in December 1886, heard about the uproar, called on the McClellans in Florence, and wrote to his close friend Katherine De Kay Bronson* ([15 Jan 1887]) to report that Mrs. McClellan was confused and mortified, and that her daughter felt "distress and remorse." James hopes that Mrs. Bronson will help smooth the McClellans' path socially, if the family should return to Venice, but then adds this: "[W]hat a superfluous product is the smart, forward, over-encouraged . . . American girl!" James promises in a later letter to Mrs. Bronson (26 Jan [1887]) to "take no more interest in the McClellan episode—as the young lady strikes me as flippant and spoiled and deserving of any fate that may overtake her." He goes on: "I should like to write a story about the business, as a pendant to *Daisy Miller*, but I won't, to deepen the complication." Changing his mind, James records in his *Notebooks* (17 Nov 1887) details for a story based on the incident: "[P]retty and 'nice' American girl" writes gauche letter to New York *World* full of Venetian gossip; her unsuccessful American suitor has "no tradition of reserve or discretion— . . . simply . . . gross newspaper instinct"; and fiancé is "young Italian or Frenchman." Even as he mulls over his original conception, James decides on France as his setting and fixes on a Europeanized American family there ("an old *claquemuré* Legitimist circle"), through fear of spoiling matters as with the Bellegarde collection in *The American*. James goes on to consider a tragic ending. Some of the background of the Edward Lee Childe* family may have found its way into the story. The novel which resulted is notable for beneficial changes and additions, not least the Mark Twain*-like innocent-abroad old Whitney Dosson, and the surprising but credible happy ending. In the preface to Volume XIII of *The Novels and Tales of Henry James*, James calls *The Reverberator* "a *jeu d'esprit*" based on a specific anecdote which became an action with "parts all clinging together." He hints at his source, in a certain "grand old city of the south of Europe (neither . . . Rome nor . . . Florence)," where "a graceful amateur journalist had made use of her gathered material." Then he vilifies her newspaper as a "recording, slobbering sheet," typically loving to ventilate unsavory stories. The girl in question was innocent, "*unaware*"; her act was nothing; but its consequences were intriguing. On the other hand, youthful American "negatives" can become "lively positives and values."

Reverdy, Charles. In *Daisy Miller: A Comedy in Three Acts*, Mrs. Louisa Costello's traveling companion (from New York) in Switzerland and Italy. He follows her orders and gives Randolph Miller piggyback rides; but at the end he slips away with her relative Alice Durant and samples the Roman carnival with her, proposes to her, and is accepted.

Reynolds, Sir Joshua (1723–1792). Devonshire-born English painter, apprenticed at age seventeen to a London portraitist. Reynolds accompanied a British squadron commander into the Mediterranean area, stayed at Minorca, enjoyed two years in Rome (where he caught a cold which deafened him), and after seeing other Italian art centers returned to England in 1752. He established a studio in London, where in the late 1750s he became a preeminent portraitist and social celebrity. In 1764 he helped found the literary club made famous by Dr. Samuel Johnson and many others. Reynolds became the first president of the Royal Academy (1768). He spoke well at academy proceedings. In 1784 he was named the king's painter. His eyesight began to dim in 1789. He painted powerful male portraits, did touching studies of women and children, and wrote on artistic theory and other subjects. James, in his 1868 review of *Contemporary French Painters* by Philip Gilbert Hamerton,* praises Reynolds's art lectures as "the best" by any president of the Royal Academy. In "The Bethnal Green Museum" (1873), he commends Reynolds's *Nelly O'Brien* as "justly famous," and wonders whether one should admire the subject or the painting more. He goes on lovingly to describe the archly posed subject, then praises the artist's handling of "mild richness of colour," "watery English sunlight," and shadow. He contrasts Reynolds's poetic treatment of children (specifically in *Strawberry Girl*) and the historical treatment of them by Diego de Silva y Velasquez.* In "The Old Masters at Burlington House" (1877), James expresses disappointment at a showing of twenty-one Reynolds portraits ("they are not all of the first excellence"), but he does call *Doctor Burney* "capital."

"Rheims and Laon: A Little Tour." Travel essay (original title, "A Little Tour in France," *Atlantic Monthly* Jan 1878); reprinted in *Portraits of Places*, 1883. This October tour reminds James that much of interesting and dignified France lies outside Paris, "that huge pretentious caravansary": along the Marne valley (the autumn color seems American), past Meaux, through champagne country to Rheims. Its cathedral has "the beauty of soberness." The densely sculptured front deceives one as to its size. He remembers prints of the building seen in childhood, thinks of Joan of Arc and of many French kings in the "rather shabby" square, touches on the "glorious company" of carved figures, and praises the magnificent double buttresses and humorous gargoyles. He muses inside the cathedral (richly gloomy, all of a "large perfection," with "enchanting perspective") until a beadle motions him out merely because "[s]undry . . . old gentlemen in red capes" are moving into the choir. James is exasperated by such evidence of authority and ponders "the anti-catholic passion" it generates. He climbs to "the upper wilderness" of the roof: attics, chambers, abysses, balustrade, sculptured eagles with human legs. The city of Rheims, though "not . . . interesting," is prosperous and clean. An hour away is "ancient," "brownish" Laon, "full of history," resembling "a quaint woodcut" and representing "one of the most interesting chapters of the past." The view all about (especially the "sea-like plain") is fine, the cathedral "noble" and well positioned in its "picturesque" precinct, the old wall "charming," and the town full of colorful soldiers. James analyzes the sadness of young Frenchmen conscripted for five years' military service. He studies the "mediaeval architecture" of one town gate. Finally he describes his inn activities and a twenty-mile drive out to the "half-spectral" Château de Coucy in its "sleepy little borough." Then to Soissons, with old and new quarters, its cathedral displaying "natural elegance."

Rhodes, Albert (1840–?). American writer whose subjects were Middle Eastern travel and French social customs. His books include *Jerusalem As It Is* (1865), *The French at Home* (1875), and *Monsieur at Home* (1885). He later wrote in French. James reviewed (*Nation*, 5 Aug 1875) Rhodes's *The French at Home*, starting positively but ending negatively. The observant, diligent author has produced an amusing, light work which reports without moralizing and generalizes only after adducing examples. But he uses French phrases badly, mistranslates, and is "lax . . . in his economic statements." James adds that some of the illustrations Rhodes uses came from a book by James Jackson Jarves (1818–1888), who also borrowed illustrations without giving proper credit to his French sources but whose 1852 *Parisian Sights and French Principles* "anticipated" Rhodes's work.

Rich, Agnes. In "A Bundle of Letters," the recipient of a letter from Violet Ray.

"Richmond, Virginia." Travel essay, published in the *Fortnightly Review* (Nov 1906); reprinted as "Richmond" in *The American Scene*, 1907.

Ridley, Lady Alice (Davenport) (?–?). British authoress of at least five books (published 1896–1913). In "London" (6 Feb 1897), James says that her novel *The Story of Aline* (1896, 1897) has "a certain distinction of feeling," although its subject—"a passion returned"—is better than timid Mrs. Ridley's treatment of it.

Rignold, George (1839–1912). British actor. He began acting as a child, then performed in Bath and Bristol, and later appeared most successfully in London (from 1870), the United States, and Australia, where he resided from 1880. He produced Shakespearean plays in Sydney and retired in 1907. In a theater review (*Nation*, 27 May 1875), James says that he prefers Rignold's New York performance in *Henry V* over his recent Macbeth. Rignold is good in movement, not in declamation. Ridiculing Clara Morris's Lady Macbeth, James theorizes that Shakespearean realism is like porcelain; that of Rignold and Morris, like pudding. They baked their pudding but cracked the porcelain.

Rimmle. In "Europe," Jane, Maria, and Rebecca's late, well-traveled, windy father.

Rimmle, Jane. In "Europe," Maria and Rebecca Rimmle's sister. In spite of their mother's selfishness, she goes to Europe.

Rimmle, Maria. In "Europe," Jane and Rebecca Rimmle's sister. Because of their mother's selfishness, she does not go to Europe but instead supports Jane's journey there.

Rimmle, Mrs. In "Europe," Jane, Maria, and Rebecca's selfish, old, widowed mother. She feigns sickness to try to prevent her daughters from ever going to Europe.

Rimmle, Rebecca (Becky). In "Europe," Jane and Maria Rimmle's sister. Because of their mother's selfishness, she never goes to Europe. She later dies.

Ringrose, Lady. In "A London Life," Selina Wing Berrington's promiscuous traveling companion from London to Paris, according to Selina's unhappy husband Lionel's report.

Ringrose, Lady. In "The Private Life," a society lady gossiped about by Clarence Vawdry.

Ripley, Mrs. In "The Modern Warning," a New York society friend of Agatha Grice, later Lady Chasemore.

Ristori, Adelaide (1822–1906). Italian actress, born in Cividale del Friuli. She was a child performer, then a member of a Sardinian company and another at Parma, played in Turin, then rivaled Rachel in Paris (1855) as a tragedienne. She performed in Madrid (1857) and the United States (four times, beginning in 1866). She retired in 1885 and published *Studies and Memoirs* in 1888. Tommaso Salvini,* the Italian actor whom James saw and extolled, joined her company in 1847. James attended her New York performances, early in March 1875, and wrote to polyglot Elizabeth Boott* (8 Mar [1875]) in his own amusing Italian that the singer is now "vecchia e faticata, ma grand' artista, gran *stile*, e atmosfera Italiana." He then reviewed her in "Madame Ristori" (*Nation*, 18 Mar 1875), beginning with high praise: She is a "great foreign artist," now in "the final twilight . . . of her brilliant career." Her farewell repertory in America, a stop on her last world tour, includes pieces from *Mary Stuart* (by Johann Christoph Friedrich von Schiller) and *Medea* (by Ernest Legouvé). Americans may think she overacts; but being a member of "the most artistic race in the world," she has an instinctive feeling for the picturesque and hence exhibits "the grand style": presence, language, firmness, assurance, dignity. James likes her portrayal of Queen Elizabeth best. Medea is "a termagant." And he is critical of her "hideous" part in *Lucrezia Borgia* (by Victor-Marie Hugo,* 1833), seen recently: The "climax . . . grazes the ludicrous." In *A Small Boy and Others*, James comments on Ristori's "high and hard virtuosity."

Ritchie, Lady Anne Isabella (née Thackeray) (1837–1919). The other daughter of William Makepeace Thackeray,* and the sister of the first wife of Sir Leslie Stephen.* Anne Ritchie was a writer herself—of novels, short stories, biographies, essays, journals, and reminiscences. Her best works are *The Village on the Cliff* (1867) and *Old Kensington* (1873). In "New Novels" (1875), James reviewed her *Miss Angel* (1875), regarding it as "pretty" and charmingly phrased, but neither vivid nor coherent, and with "fatally unbusinesslike" descriptions and "pale and tame" historical characters. James met her briefly in London in 1877 just before her marriage to Richmond Ritchie (later a high official in India), and again in 1878, calling her then, in a letter to his sister Alice (17 Feb [1878]), foolish in talk, plain, but amiable. A month later he wrote to his father (25 Mar [1878]) that Lady Anne was good, gentle, and "exquisitely irrational." According to Notebook entries (22 Jan 1879, 27 Feb 1889), she gave James the idea for his story "Greville Fane"; other Notebook entries (17 Jan 1881, 30 May 1883) credit her for the idea for his story "Impressions of a Cousin." James wrote Lady Ritchie friendly letters through the years, at least as late as 1908, and, according to his Pocket Diaries, saw her socially in London in the 1910s.

Rivet, Claude. In "The Real Thing," the landscape painter who recommends that Major and Mrs. Monarch apply to his friend the painter-narrator as models.

Rivière, Henri Laurent (1827–1883). French naval officer, historian, fiction writer, and dramatist. He was murdered by pirates near Hanoi. James took the plot for his *Tenants* from Rivière's short story "Flavien: Scènes de la vie contemporaine."

Robert. In "A Light Man," Frederick Sloane's servant.

Roberts, Lord Frederick Sleigh (1832–1914). British military man and autobiographer, whose *Forty-One Years at Sea* (1897) James discusses in two notes entitled "London" (6 Feb, 27 Mar 1897). In the first note, James merely calls the work a "rich history." In the second, he comments on it in detail, saying that the book is written with "colorless clearness"; he wishes that the author's exciting Indian campaigns—"the march to Kandahar, . . . the taking of Delhi and the relief of Lucknow"—were offered with a more "living look."

Robertson. In "The Story of a Year," a partner in the firm of Bruce and Robertson.

Robineau, Mme. In *The American*, a hostess whom Claire de Cintré is to visit.

Robins, Elizabeth (1862–1952). Actress, author, and fighter for women's rights. She was born in Louisville, Kentucky, and grew up in Zanesville, Ohio. Her mother was committed to an insane asylum. Young Elizabeth left premedical studies at Vassar College to become a beautiful, charismatic actress; soon she began touring the Continent. She married an actor in Boston, but because she allegedly neglected him, he drowned himself in a suit of stage armor. His widow began to associate with women writers in Boston and then visited Norway. By the late 1880s she was in London, where she organized subscription performances of plays by Henrik Johan Ibsen,* whose plays she persuaded George Bernard Shaw,* William Archer,* and James to admire. Elizabeth Robins was the first actress in London to star as Hilda in *The Master Builder* and in the title role of *Hedda Gabler*. She later said that Ibsen converted her to the feminist cause. She met James in London, in January 1891, impressed him in her Ibsen roles, and won a contract to play Claire de Cintré in James's 1891 dramatic version of *The American* (replacing in the role Virginia Bateman Compton, wife of Edward Compton* and mother of Sir Edward Montague Compton Mackenzie*). The contract permitted her to act in avant-garde matinee plays. Through the early 1890s, James and Robins became close friends, often meeting and writing letters to share thoughts on the theater. She attended the first, disastrous performance of his *Guy Domville*, in London, on 5 January 1895. William Heinemann,* the British publisher and James's close friend, was evidently in love with the sensuous, manipulative actress in the early 1890s. James and his friend Lady Florence Eveleen Eleanore Bell* enjoyed observing and discussing Robins. James may have had her in mind for the role of bad-heroine Rose Armiger in his 1894 dramatic version of *The Other House* (unproduced). In the late 1890s Robins began writing and publishing novels (using the pen name C. E. Raimond). In "London" (23 Jan 1897), James reports testily that Robins, "in England, has rendered Ibsen all the pious service of a priestess of the altar." But in "London" (27 Mar 1897), James calls her performance in José Echegaray y Eizaguirre's *Mariana* (1892) a "singularly interesting presentation." (James and Robins had worked together to render a literal translation of the Spanish play more idiomatic.) In 1900 Robins went to Alaska to seek a brother who was missing there and then wrote a novel about the region. James, Robins, and Walter Van Rensselaer Berry* were fellow passengers from Boston to Liverpool, in July 1905. Robins began to propagandize for the feminist movement (mainly to call attention to the sexual exploitation of women and also to grant women the right to vote). She did so most notably with her profitable play *Votes for Women!* (1907), which Herbert George Wells* (whose personal life and betrayal of the feminist cause subsequently revolted her), Archer, and James helped her to rework, and which Harley Granville Granville-Barker* produced. Later in 1907 she turned *Votes for Women!* into a novel entitled *The Convert*. James's agent James Brand Pinker* aided in its publication, which was a financial success. It identifies many still-current feminist problems. She published essays on militant feminism and collected them in *Way Stations* (1913). She used her royalties to buy a home in Sussex, in which she helped neglected women. According to his Pocket Diaries, James socialized with Robins in London into the 1910s. After his death, Robins obtained his nephew Henry James's permission to publish a book of selections— *Theatre and Friendship: Some Henry James Letters* (1932)—from the 150 or so letters James wrote to her (1891–1911). Typically, the letters are friendly and superficial. Robins's running commentary is self-serving and occasionally fanciful. The best part of the book is her inclusion of fine letters from James to Florence Bell. (The actress Elizabeth Robins is not to be confused with the Elizabeth Robins who married Joseph Pennell.*)

Robinson, Agnes Mary Frances (1857–1944). Versatile English poet, fiction writer, biographer, literary critic, historian, sociologist, and translator, born in Leamington. She married James Darmesteter (1888) and then, some years after his death in 1894, married Pierre Émile Duclaux (1901). These men were both remarkable. Darmesteter was an Alsace-born French author, Oriental scholar, professor, and translator, whose works include *Études Iraniennes* (1883), *Lettres sur l'Inde* (1888), a translation of and commentary on the *Zend Avesta* (3 vols., 1892–1893), and studies of Afghan literature and songs. (His older brother was Arsène Darmesteter, Old French philologist and Sorbonne professor.) Pierre Émile Duclaux was a professor of biochemistry at the Sorbonne (from 1885) and director of the Pasteur Institute (from 1895). Mary Robinson, using the names Robinson, Darmesteter, and Duclaux, published *A Handful of Honey-suckles* (1878, poetry), *The Crowned Hippolytus* (1881, novel), *Emily Brontë* (1883), *La Vie de Ernest Renan* (1897), *Madame de Sévigné* (1914), *La Pensée de Robert Browning*[*] (1922), and other works. James first knew Mme. Duclaux as Miss Mary Robinson, as early as 1884, since he wrote to their mutual friend Violet Paget* about her then. Years later James wrote to Paget again (27 Apr 1890) that "Mme Darmesteter" was in England "at Easter, very much alive, very fresh and happy, apparently." James's library contained one book by Mary Darmesteter.

Robinson, Hyacinth. In *The Princess Casamassima*, Lord Frederick Purvis's and Florentine Vivier's illegitimate son. He lives with his foster mother Amanda Pynsent; likes Millicent Henning, Paul Muniment, and the Princess Casamassima; works for bookbinder Crookenden; and joins the international anarchist movement. When a trip to Paris and Venice, financed by Miss Pynsent's bequest, shows him what culture can be produced from admittedly unfair social conditions, he finds it impossible to fulfill his vow to be an assassin and so commits suicide.

Rochambeau, Marquis de. In "Gabrielle de Bergerac," a nobleman mentioned as providing troops to aid the American revolutionists.

Rochefidèle, Count and Countess de la. In *The American*, French nobility whom Christopher Newman meets at the party Mme. Emmeline de Bellegarde gives in his honor.

Rodenberg, Julius (1831–1914), German writer and editor, whose *England, Literary and Social, from a German Point of View* (1875), James reviewed (*Nation*, 16 Mar 1876). He calls the book, which concerns Kent, London, Jews in England, and much else, disappointing, not from a German point of view, bookish rather than observant, but "agreeable [in] style."

Roderick Hudson. Novel (133,100 words), published in the *Atlantic Monthly* (Jan–Dec 1875); revised and reprinted in Boston by Osgood, 1875, and in London by Macmillan, 1875; revised and reprinted in *The Novels and Tales of Henry James*, Volume I, 1907. (Characters: Assunta, Monsignor B—, Mme. Baldi, Bessie, Augusta Blanchard, Prince Gennaro Casamassima, Cecilia, Mary Garland, Cavaliere Giuseppe Giacosa, Gloriani and Mme. Gloriani, Mme. Grandoni, Roderick Hudson, Sarah Hudson, Stephen Hudson, Leavenworth, Christina Light, Mrs. Light, Mr. and Mrs. Jonas Mallet, Rowland Mallet, Maddalena, Sam Singleton, Schafgans, Barnaby Striker, Miss Striker, Rev. Mr. Whitefoot.) Before returning to Europe, rich Rowland Mallet visits his cousin Cecilia in Northampton, Massachusetts. She introduces him to Roderick Hudson, a talented sculptor living nearby. Mallet offers to finance the young man during a residence in Rome. Before leaving, Hudson introduces Mallet to his widowed mother

Sarah and his fiancée Mary Garland. Once in Rome, Hudson displays quick talent—even genius—but appalling egocentric instability as well. He goes to Baden-Baden and gambles there; back in his Roman studio, he insults a rich patron named Leavenworth, and—worst of all—he cannot resist the fatal beauty of Christina Light, whom stolid Mallet urges to stay away from Hudson. Then Christina's mercenary mother tells the girl that she is illegitimate and thus forces her to wed rich Neapolitan Prince Casamassima. Mallet takes the distraught sculptor, together with his mother and Miss Garland, by now brought over to Rome by Mallet, with him to Florence for a change of scene. Hudson's will to work has vanished. The little group goes on to Switzerland, where the sculptor is fatally discouraged first by seeing Christina, now the Princess Casamassima, with her husband at Interlaken, and second by learning from angry Mallet that he has long unselfishly adored Miss Garland himself from afar. Hudson wanders into an Alpine storm. Next morning Mallet, aided by a friendly American painter named Sam Singleton, finds the corpse of the sculptor, who fell or jumped to his death. James began writing *Roderick Hudson* in Florence in 1874, continued it in Baden-Baden, and finished it in New York after it had begun to appear serially. Several possible literary sources for *Roderick Hudson* include *Le Roman d'une honnête femme* (1866) by Victor Cherbuliez,* *L'Affaire de Clemenceau* (1866) by Alexandre Dumas *fils*,* *The Marble Faun* (1860) by Nathaniel Hawthorne,* and *The Initials* (1850) by Jemina Montgomery, Baroness von Tautphoeus.* Further, elements in the life of the expatriate American sculptor Thomas Crawford,* father of James's friend the popular novelist Francis Marion Crawford,* parallel many in Hudson's career. James preferred to forget his 1871 novel *Watch and Ward* and call *Roderick Hudson* his first novel instead. Even so, he then undervalued it. For example, in a letter to Robert Louis Stevenson* (5 Dec [1887]), he called it "a book of considerable good faith, but . . . of limited skill." He also criticized himself in the preface to Volume I of *The Novels and Tales of Henry James* for not developing Northampton better (although Ivan Sergeyevich Turgenev* called its treatment masterly), unacceptably having Hudson get engaged to Miss Garland only to depart for Rome, and collapsing the young sculptor into suicidal passivity too fast. James did like Mallet as a cool reflector of the action and Miss Light as its hot catalyst.

Rogerson, Christina Stewart (?–?). Daughter of Mrs. Duncan Stewart* and the wife of James Rogerson. Mrs. Rogerson was romantically linked to Sir Charles Wentworth Dilke,* who, after a divorce scandal in 1885, dropped her and married Emilia Pattison, widow of scholar Mark Pattison. Mrs. Rogerson, once her own husband had died, married G. W. Stevens; subsequently, that man was killed in the Boer War in 1899. James, who knew Mrs. Rogerson, as well as her mother, her husband, her lover, and Emilia Pattison, was a frequent guest at dinner parties given by Mrs. Rogerson beginning in 1877. He met a number of interesting people through these parties, for two examples among several, Sir Donald Mackenzie Wallace* and James Abbott McNeill Whistler.* In a letter to his brother William (28 Feb [1877]), he calls Mrs. Rogerson "a clever, liberal woman"; a year and a half later, in a letter to his sister Alice (15 Sep [1878]), he calls her "my hospitable, though somewhat irregular friend." A couple of years after that, he reports to his mother (31 Oct 1880) that "Mrs. R. has many domestic troubles. . . . Her husband is a fierce drunkard and muddles away the funds. Fortunately he doesn't show up much, in London." Then James adds, "But a truce to this cockney gossip!" Still, he gossiped further: In a letter to Grace Norton* (23 Aug [1885]), he includes a discussion of "the great 'Dilke Scandal'—no very edifying chapter of social history," mentions a few names, and hints at "another London lady whom I won't name." She was Christina Rogerson. He adds naughtily that Dilke's "long, double liaison with Mrs. Pattison and the other lady . . . make[s] it a duty of honour to marry *both* (!!) when they should become free." According to a Notebook entry (19 Jun 1884), Mrs. Rogerson gave James the idea for his short story "Brooksmith."

Roker. In *The Princess Casamassima*, a fellow bookbinder with Hyacinth Robinson in Crookenden's shop.

"A Roman Holiday." Travel essay, published in the *Atlantic Monthly* (Jul 1873); reprinted in *Transatlantic Sketches*, 1875; revised and reprinted in *Italian Hours*, 1909. Secularized Rome, after September 1870, no longer celebrates the Carnival properly. The pope and the king are not involved now, and Corso scenes are tame compared to pictures from the dreamy infancy of James, who therefore walks away. Americans at present regard costumed Italian families in a carnival parade as infantile. On to the mole-hill Capitol, with its charming Forum beyond, populated by customary "beggars, soldiers, monks and tourists"—and with the weedy steps of the Ara Coeli. The statue of Marcus Aurelius calls to mind the perfect description of it by Nathaniel Hawthorne* [in *The Marble Faun*]. Near the Arch of Titus, James enters a church, whose langorous young priest satirizes the Carnival humming away outside. The Colosseum, its interior like an Alpine valley. The battered Arch of Constantine. San Giovanni e Paolo, with sketchable *contadini* nearby. Theatrical St. John Lateran, interesting mainly because of its surroundings. Santa Croce in Gerusalemme (gone in 1909). Shapely, storied Santa Maggiore, "most delightful" and vividly colorful of a sunny afternoon. And then St. Peter's, ever sublime, with Michelangelo's "ineffable 'Pièta,' " with cadenced light, and with vastness dwarfing little people strolling inside. St. Peter's, since it is "one of the greatest of human achievements," helps us put away our doubts. James ends his holiday back on the Corso again, where he relished seeing a man lugubriously costumed as a starving scholar, and then fireworks—and then Lent.

"Roman Neighborhoods." The 1873 title of "Roman Neighbourhoods."

"Roman Neighbourhoods" (1873 title, "Roman Neighborhoods"). Travel essay, published in the *Atlantic Monthly* (Dec 1873); reprinted in *Transatlantic Sketches*, 1875; revised and reprinted in *Italian Hours*, 1909. Near the Alban

Mount, James finds that strolling outside L'Ariccia provides uniquely picturesque views. Note the crumbling black houses perched at chasms' flowered edges, the feudal, haunted Palazzo Chigi, a nearby domed but unfilled church, a Renaissance temple like a shell, and the Palazzo Cesarini. The woods feature contorted trees, including queer oaks, and are profuse with little flowers. Smiling ilex, vaporous olives, and twittering birds are also near. At twilight James enters a scary Capuchin convent, with tangled garden and view of nearby lake. And so from smelly Genzano toward Frascati along a tree-bordered road near the lake of "desperately queer" Nemi. James recalls debating with a friend who preferred New England villages to any in Europe. Past Rocca di Papa to Monte Cavo, to the delightful Palazzuola convent, with shaded garden and sweet-smiling monk. James goes on by train to Frascati, with its "ruined Vatican" perched high, to see the colorful March 25 Annunziata feast, a peasant fair at nearby Grotta Ferrata, and jovial crowds. Sipping wine, he looks across at Castel Gandolfo and at Marino above the trees, and he adversely judges the just-seen Domenichino frescoes—"effort detached from inspiration." Fine old Villa Aldobrandini. Immense Villa Mondragone's waterworks are splendid. The Casino of Mondragone figures, James adds, in *La Daniella* (1857) by George Sand.*

"Roman Rides." Travel essay, published in the *Atlantic Monthly* (Aug 1873); reprinted in *Transatlantic Sketches*, 1875; revised and reprinted in *Italian Hours*, 1909. James's first memorable ride on horseback was in winter, through Porta del Popolo and over the Tiber by the Ponte Molle, toward the mellow purple Campagna, and the sapphire and amber Sabine mountains, with everything "bright and yet . . . sad." Roman rides make city scenes a little smaller and encourage the "double life" of pastoral/cosmopolitan. A friend, comparing this duality to novel vs. newspaper, told James of his gallop with an admired lady past the Tor di Quinto Road to Veii, then back to a fine villa dinner. James praises an April ride during which he overtopped crumbling walls along outer city lanes, flaming poppies, and rococo gateways. The Campagna is a background for taverns, with beggars and acrid wine. City ramparts sport "portentous dates and signs," with blue sky and white dust too, all inviting the sketcher. James compares differing rides on the two sides of the Tiber, smooth beyond Porta San Giovanni and melancholy beyond Porta Cavalleggieri. But all gallops help landscape lines to merge pictorially, especially as spring steps near. Then larks and early flowers come. The sirocco relaxes one morbidly. James went with a friend to the Doria gallery to check the validity of two Claude Lorraine landscapes, but the reality is always more arcadian. He prefers to ride in the Villa Doria with its views, but to walk through the Villa Borghese with its "grassy arena" and clear-voiced schoolboys.

"The Romance of Certain Old Clothes." Short story (7,400 words), published in the *Atlantic Monthly* (Feb 1868); revised and reprinted in *A Passionate Pilgrim, and Other Tales*, 1875; reprinted in *Stories Revived*, 1885. (Characters: Arthur

Lloyd, Perdita Willoughby Lloyd, Miss Lloyd, Bernard Willoughby, Mrs. Bernard Willoughby, Mrs. Bernard Willoughby, Perdita Willoughby.) The story is set in the mid–1700s in provincial Massachusetts. Mrs. Willoughby's son Bernard brings a British friend named Arthur Lloyd home from Oxford University to Massachusetts. Lloyd marries Bernard's sister Perdita, making Viola, her older sister, jealous. Perdita dies giving birth to a daughter, whom Viola and her mother care for while Lloyd visits in England. On returning he marries Viola, who persuades him to give her the key of Perdita's chest of wedding clothes. Lloyd has sacredly promised to keep them locked away for his daughter. He later finds his wife dead in the attic, with claw-like wounds inflicted by ghostly hands. This ineffective early tale shows the influence of Nathaniel Hawthorne.*

Romney, George (1734–1802). Lancashire-born portrait and historical painter. After being an itinerant north-counties portrait sketcher, he left his wife and family for London in his late twenties. He became so popular that he rivaled Sir Joshua Reynolds,* studied in Italy (1773–1775), and returned to London and greater success. Ruined in body and mind in the late 1790s, Romney went back to his wife. Although he tried for grandiose series, he is best remembered for several portraits and for scenes in the lives of General James Wolfe, John Milton, and Sir Isaac Newton. James in "The Old Masters at Burlington House" (1877) calls Romney "strong, deep, mellow," then in "The Old Masters at Burlington House" (1878) praises a pair of Romney portraits of Lady Hamilton. But in "The Winter Exhibitions in London" (1879) he defines the Romneys then being shown as "products of a very primitive degree of skill."

Roosevelt, Blanche (1853–1898). Classically beautiful singer, writer, and fascinating personality, born in Sandusky, Ohio, and reared in LaCrosse, Wisconsin, from which state her father was the first U.S. senator. After several years in Europe doing literary work, she studied singing with Michelle Pauline García Viardot* (the companion of Ivan Sergeyevich Turgenev*), and in 1876 she became the first American-born woman to debut in Italian opera at Covent Garden, London. She also appeared in concerts in Italy, Holland, Belgium, and France. In Milan she married the Marchese d'Alligri, who soon thereafter kept his distance. She visited America again, vacationed with Henry Wadsworth Longfellow* and his family at Nahant, mounted an unsuccessful stage production of his *Masque of Pandora* (1875), and after performing in Gilbert and Sullivan shows in New York, returned to Europe in 1882. Victor-Marie Hugo* and Robert Browning* extravagantly praised her stunning beauty. She was one of the *amours plus élégants* of Guy de Maupassant,* in whose Étretat house she lodged for a time in 1884. She escorted Maupassant during his 1886 visit to London and then to Oxford, which his friend Paul Bourget* had urged him to see. In *The Woman's World*, edited by Oscar Wilde,* she published the first description in English (1889) of Maupassant, whose burial in Paris she attended (1893). Jacques-Émile

Blanche* wrote *Aymeris* (1922), a roman à clef about the group of rich, talented decadents, including Roosevelt, surrounding Maupassant. While in London, she was a correspondent for newspapers in Paris, Italy, and Chicago. It is possible that one of her amours was with William Morton Fullerton.* Her literary works include novels. One of them, an autobiographical novel, is called *Stage-Struck; or, She Would Be an Opera-Singer* (1884); another is *The Copper Queen: A Romance of Today and Yesterday* (1886), which Victorien Sardou* adapted for the stage. Roosevelt also wrote biographical sketches of Longfellow (1882), Paul Gustave Doré* (1884), Giuseppe Verdi (1887), Carmen Sylva, the literary queen of Roumania (1891), and Sardou (1892). Blanche Roosevelt was killed in a carriage accident at Monte Carlo. Her full name was Mrs. Blanche Roosevelt (née Tucker) Macchetta, the Marquesa d'Alligri. James met her while Maupassant was visiting in London and was happy to avoid her lionizing clutches. He wrote to Francis Boott* (15 Aug [1886]) "I have but just escaped from the jaws of Blanche Roosevelt, . . . who is now here married to a Milanese, trying to be literary and assaulting me (with compliments) on my productions."

Roosevelt, Franklin Delano (1882–1945). Thirty-second president of the United States (1933–1945). Through Walter Hines Page,* American ambassador to England, it is likely that James met Roosevelt, in June 1914, when Roosevelt was serving in London in his capacity as assistant secretary of the U.S. Navy (1913–1920).

Roosevelt, Theodore (1858–1919). Twenty-sixth president of the United States (1901–1909). He was born in New York City, graduated from Harvard (1880), where he knew Owen Wister,* studied law, entered state politics, ranched in the West (1884–1886), returned to politics, became assistant secretary of the U.S. Navy (1897–1898), and served with the Rough Riders (1898) during the Spanish-American War. Thereafter, his political career was meteoric: governor of New York (1899–1900), vice president of the United States (1901), and president. He received the Nobel Peace Prize (1906) for helping to end the Russo-Japanese War. Roosevelt remained active in his post-presidential years, in travel, hunting, and writing. James and Roosevelt first met in Boston, in January 1882. In an 1884 political speech Roosevelt said that James, of whose expatriation and alleged snobbishness he disapproved, was to regular writers as a pampered poodle was to regular dogs. James undoubtedly knew that Roosevelt disliked him. In "American Letter" (23 Apr 1898), James comments on Roosevelt's *American Ideals, and Other Essays, Social and Political* (1897), saying that Roosevelt "tighten[s] the screws of the national consciousness as they have never been tightened before." James notes that Americans prefer to practice patriotism instead of theorizing about it, calls Roosevelt confused when he tries to tell us how to be Americans and to express ourselves as such, and concludes that Roosevelt is better when he describes his exemplary experiences than when he tries immaturely to indoctrinate. James disliked Roosevelt's Philippine policy, called Roosevelt in a letter to his friend Jessie Allen (19 Sep 1901) "a dangerous and ominous Jingo," whom "I don't either like or trust." But during his 1904–1905 tour of the United States, James was a guest, early in January 1905, of his close friend and Roosevelt's secretary of state John Milton Hay,* and had a pleasant dinner at the Hays' mansion with the president as a fellow guest. A few days later James dined at the White House, at a party of a hundred or so guests, with James placed at Roosevelt's table of eight; sculptor Augustus Saint-Gaudens* was a fellow guest. James was impressed and wrote to several friends. To Mary Cadwalader Jones, sister-in-law of Edith Newbold Jones Wharton* (13 Jan 1905)—Roosevelt is "Theodore Rex," with "native intensity, veracity and *bonhomie*." To Jessie Allen (16 Jan 1905)—Roosevelt commands "extraordinary talk and . . . [an] overwhelming, but . . . attaching personality." To Wharton (16 Jan 1905)—Roosevelt is "a wonderful little machine . . . not . . . betraying the least creak." And to Sir Edmund Wilson Gosse* (16 Feb 1905)—Roosevelt is "extraordinary and rather personally-fascinating . . . [and] kind to me." In 1912 James disapproved of the ex-president for comments on England vis-à-vis Germany, now calling him in a letter to Philadelphia surgeon J. William White (14 Nov 1912) an "embodiment of . . . Noise."

Root, Dr. In *The Ivory Tower*, Frank B. Betterman's physician, with Dr. Hatch.

Rooth, Miriam. In *The Tragic Muse*, a talented Jewish actress, trained by Mme. Honorine Carré, loved vainly by Peter Sherringham, painted by Nick Dormer, and at last married by Basil Dashwood. She lives almost for the sole purpose of being a splendid actress. The success in London of James's friend the actress Mary Antoinette Anderson* (later the wife of Antonio Fernando de Navarro*) may have contributed to his portrayal of Miriam Rooth.

Rooth, Mrs. Rudolph. In *The Tragic Muse*, Miriam Rooth's aggressive, widowed mother. Her husband was Rudolph Roth. (Mrs. Rooth changed the spelling of her husband's last name.)

Roper, Captain. In "The Bench of Desolation," Kate Cookham's suitor. Kate snubs him to prove her loyalty to Herbert Dodd.

Rosalie. In "A New England Winter," Mrs. Donald Mesh's sister.

Rose-Agathe. In "Rose-Agathe," the hairdresser dummy mistaken by the narrator for the hairdresser's wife.

"Rose-Agathe" (1878 title, "Théodolinde"; 1885 title, "Rose-Agathe"). Short story (7,100 words), published in *Lippincott's Magazine* (May 1878); revised and reprinted in *Stories Revived*, 1885. (Characters: M. and Mme. Anatole, Clementine, Rose-Agathe, Sanguinetti.) Sanguinetti, a bric-a-brac collector, is late in arriving to dine with the narrator, because (as the narrator could see from his balcony) the man had been looking for a while into Anatole's hairdressing shop at a pretty head there. The narrator jokes with Sanguinetti, who says that he might pick up what he was admiring. The narrator thinks that the desired object is Mme. Anatole. But when Sanguinetti buys "Rose-Agathe," the pretty creature turns out to be Anatole's attractive dummy. A tonic little trifle.

Rosebery, Archibald Philip Primrose, Earl of (1847–1929). Distinguished British statesman, historian, biographer, and educator. He was born in London into the Primrose family of Scotland, was educated at Christ Church, Oxford, married fabulously wealthy Hannah de Rothschild (a member of the Rothschild family*) in 1878, entered government work (beginning 1881), visited Australia (1883–1884), was foreign secretary (1886, 1892–1894) under William Ewart Gladstone,* and then was liberal prime minister (1894–1895). He became imperialistic (with Herbert Henry Asquith,* in 1901) during the Boer War. He later held high administrative positions in universities (London, Glasgow, St. Andrews). He published significant books on Oliver Cromwell, Napoleon, Robert Peel, and William Pitt, as well as other works. Lord Rosebery was known for his brilliant oratory and his passion for horse racing. During World War I, one of his sons was killed in action (Palestine, 1917). In November 1880 James was invited to Mentmore, Rosebery's Bedfordshire estate, and James wrote to his mother (28 Nov [1880]) a graphic, witty account of sights and activities there: fellow guests John Bright and Sir John Everett Millais,* horses, "Rothschildish splendour," "Lady R." ("large, fat, ugly, good-natured, sensible and kind"), "Lord R." ("remarkably charming—'so *simpatico* and swell' "), the house (halls, galleries, colonnades, and chairs all reminiscent of Venice, and other "wonderful objects accumulated"), private bedrooms, and servants. James admired Rosebery in many ways (he has "youth, cleverness, a delightful face, a happy character, . . . tact and bonhomie"), but was concerned that the "Rothschild . . . millions [may both] distinguish and . . . demoralize him." Through the years, James was occasionally a guest again at Rosebery residences (at Mentmore and Waddesdon). During one such visit, in April 1884, James met Gladstone. In his private diary, Sir Edward Walter Hamilton* records that in October 1886 he and James were Rosebery's house guests, and that "[t]he society of men of letters like H. James is I believe the society which Rosebery . . . most enjoys." Rather ungenerously, James wrote to his brother William (1 Oct 1887) that he had just "spent a week with the Roseberys (to make up for not having been near them for a year, thank heaven!) but Mentmore is always a peculiar experience, half pleasant and half insupportable." James goes on to admit to a "scoffing shallowness on my part." James's library contained one book by Rosebery.

Rosenheim, Cora, Mr. and Mrs. D. S., and Samuel. In *The Reverberator*, names appearing on a banker's record in Paris.

Rosier, Edward (Ned). In *The Portrait of a Lady*, a friend of Isabel Archer's childhood. He falls in love with her stepdaughter Pansy Osmond, begs Isabel to help him, sells his collection of bibelots to impress Pansy's father Gilbert Osmond financially, but then is not encouraged.

Ross, Janet Anne (1842–1927). London-born writer, the daughter of Lady Lucie Duff-Gordon.* In 1860 she married Henry Ross, a banker in Egypt, where she became a London *Times* correspondent (1863–1867); the couple moved in 1867 to Italy, where she studied and published on Italian culture, among other subjects. She knew Lord Frederick Leighton,* George Meredith,* John Addington Symonds,* George Frederick Watts,* Virginia Woolf,* and other English artists and writers. Mrs. Ross appended a memoir to her mother's posthumous *Last Letters from Egypt* (1875). Mrs. Ross died in Florence, where James had met her in February 1887.

Ross, Robert B. (1869–1918). Canadian student at Cambridge University, a friend of Oscar Wilde (and later his literary executor), and also a friend of Sir Edmund Wilson Gosse* and James. When Ross sued Lord Alfred Douglas for slander, he lost and was ruined. Ross was aided by Gosse, to whom by letter (29 Jan 1894 [1914?]) James expressed sympathy for "poor tragic Bobby R." James also wrote to Sir Hugh Seymour Walpole* (21 Nov 1914) about Ross.

Rossetti, Dante Gabriel (1828–1882). London-born painter, illustrator, stained-glass designer, poet, and translator. He studied art under Ford Madox Brown.* Rossetti helped to found the Pre-Raphaelite Brotherhood (1848–1849), with William Holman Hunt,* Sir John Everett Millais,* and others. He knew and made disciples of William Morris* (whose wife Jane he often painted) and Sir Edward Burne-Jones.* Rossetti's work was praised and supported by John Ruskin.* Rossetti was briefly married (1860–1862) to a beautiful model, who died from tuberculosis. For a short while thereafter, he lived on Cheyne Walk, Chelsea, with fellow artists and writers, including Algernon Charles Swinburne* and also his brother William Michael Rossetti, who later married Ford Madox Brown's daughter. Rossetti's sister Christina Georgina Rossetti, a poetess and religious writer, modeled for D. G. Rossetti, Brown, Hunt, and Millais. In later life Rossetti became chronically depressed. Through Charles Eliot Norton,* James met Rossetti in 1869 at the artist's Chelsea home. James soon wrote to John La Farge* (20 Jun [1869]) that Rossetti "struck me as unattractive, poor man. I suppose he was horribly bored!—but his pictures, as I saw them in his rooms, I think decidedly strong . . . with lots of beauty and power." James mentions Rossetti several times in his art notices but without elaboration. James knew Ford Madox Hueffer,* whose grandfather was Ford Madox Brown and whose aunt married William Michael Rossetti. James also knew Violet Hunt,* whose parents were friends with most of the members of Rossetti's circle and who published a biography of D. G. Rossetti's wife (1932). Mark Ambient's sister Gwendolyn in "The Author of Beltraffio" is hardly praised when James compares her affected posturing to a figure in a Rossetti picture. James's library contained one book by Dante Gabriel Rossetti and one by William Michael Rossetti.

Rossiter, Mr. and Mrs. In *The Portrait of a Lady*, a couple mentioned as owning a New York house suitable for Isabel Archer to rent.

Rostand, Edmond (1868–1918). Marseilles-born playwright, the last great nineteenth-century romantic writer for the French stage, who triumphed even though literature at the time was dominated by Émile Zola* and naturalism. Rostand revived verse drama. His *Cyrano de Bergerac* (1897) remains one of the most popular plays ever written. His other works include *Les Romanesques* (1894), *La Princesse Lointaine* (1895, first showing the author's attitude toward love and renunciation), *La Samaritaine* (1897), *L'Aiglon* (1900, about Napoleon's son), *Chantecler* (1910, a satirical animal allegory), and *La Dernière Nuit de Don Juan* (1921). *La Princesse Lointaine* and *L'Aiglon* were both written for the actress Sarah Bernhardt.* Benoît Constant Coquelin* was Rostand's Cyrano. Rostand was elected to the French Academy at an early age (in 1902). He was a victim of the influenza epidemic at the close of World War I. In a letter to Antonio Fernando de Navarro* (29 Dec 1900), James, who had been reading *L'Aiglon*, calls "[t]he talent, the effect, the art, the mastery, the brilliancy . . . [in it] all prodigious." He adds that Rostand "has talent like an attack of smallpox—I mean it rages with as purple an intensity, and might almost (one vainly feels as one reads) be contagious." James's last theater essay was "Edmond Rostand" (*Cornhill Magazine*, Nov 1901, and the *Critic*, Nov 1901). James begins it by pondering "the mystery of popularity," wondering why "acclamation" and "distinction" (even "glory") are so often associated. He explains why Rostand and Rudyard Kipling* may be linked as public favorites: Each patriotically trumpets a "militant and triumphant race." *Cyrano de Bergerac* is "the fantastic, romantic, brilliantly whimsical expression of an ardent French consciousness." Even when its crackling verse is simplified in translation, it has a worldwide appeal because Rostand, somewhat like Robert Louis Stevenson,* is a romantic virtuoso. James notes that Rostand's romantic touch was present (though light) as early as in *Les Romanesques*, the "rococo world" of which flourishes in later plays. He images Rostand's execution of later ideas as daring tightrope acts: a distant lady and a princely pilgrim who have not met (*La Princesse Lointaine*), a "grand soul" to match a grand nose (*Cyrano de Bergerac*), a hero who must do nothing (*L'Aiglon*). James discusses the implications of Rostand's writing specifically for Bernhardt, possibly also for Coquelin, certainly with the "romantic or fantastic" in view. Next, he discusses *Cyrano de Bergerac*, the hero's historical model, his capering eloquence in wooing, handsome Christian's stupidity, the wondrous "atmosphere." Will any later romantic writer "go . . . [Rostand] 'one better'?" James wonders whether

Rostand can "keep it up" and recommends the example of *La Course du Flambeau*, a 1901 play by Paul Hervieu, who "come[s] out wherever life itself does." James's library contained two books by Rostand.

Roth, Mrs. Rudolph. In *The Tragic Muse*, the original name of Mrs. Rudolph Rooth.

Roth, Rudolph. In *The Tragic Muse*, Miriam Rooth's deceased father.

Rothschild family. Illustrious, far-flung Jewish family, of enormous influence on British and Continental finance, politics, and culture. The family was begun in eighteenth-century Frankfurt, Germany, by Mayer Anselm Bauer (1744–1812), whose sign was the red shield (Rothschild) and who financed allied sovereigns against Napoleon. He had ten children, including five sons, four of whom branched out into Vienna, London, Paris, and Naples. The third son, especially brilliant Nathan Mayer Rothschild (1777–1836), was the one who went via Manchester, England, to London (about 1805) where he soon demonstrated financial genius. He had seven children, including Mayer Amschel Rothschild (1818–1874), father of Hannah de Rothschild (1851–1890). She married Archibald Philip Primrose, Earl of Rosebery,* in 1878 (Benjamin Disraeli* gave the bride away), had four children, was hostess at Mentmore (built in 1851 by Mayer Rothschild, then stocked with fabulous objets d'art), at Waddesdon Manor (built in 1874–1881 by Ferdinand "Ferdy" James de Rothschild [1839–1898]), and elsewhere; she tragically died young. On four occasions at Mentmore between 1880 and 1886, James was a guest of the hospitable Roseberys and thus came to know several other members of the Rothschild family. His Rothschild friends, in addition to Hannah Rosebery, included the following: (1) Alice de Rothschild (1847–1922), Ferdinand de Rothschild's sister, a friend of Queen Victoria, and hostess at Waddesdon after Ferdinand's death; (2) Caroline Blanche Elizabeth Fitzroy (wife of Coutts Lindsay, hence Lady Lindsay), daughter of Hannah Rosebery's aunt Hannah Mayer de Rothschild Fitzroy (1815–1864); (3) Constance Rothschild Flower (1843–1931, wife of Cyril Flower, later Lord Battersea—hence Constance became Lady Battersea), daughter of Hannah's uncle Anthony "Billy" de Rothschild (1810–1876); (4) Ferdinand de Rothschild, son of Hannah's uncle, Lionel Rothschild (1808–1879), and his wife Charlotte Rothschild von Rothschild of Frankfurt (Ferdinand, Alice de Rothschild's brother, esteemed Rosebery, and was the man who bought and extended Waddesdon, visited by James, August 1885, and by several of his friends, including Paul Bourget,* Guy de Maupassant,* John Lothrop Motley,* and Mary Augusta Ward*); and (5) Lady Louise Montefiore de Rothschild (1821–1910), Lady Battersea's aged mother.

"Rouen." Paris letter, published as "Summer in France" (New York *Tribune*, 12 Aug 1876); reprinted in *Portraits of Places*, 1883. Summer being hot in Paris, James, after sampling boulevard cafés by the lava-like asphalt, tries a steamer down the Seine to Auteuil and also dinner in the Bois de Boulogne. Even better is Le Havre: inn, sea view, wine, and memories of his recent tour of Rouen. He is critical of urban renovation there, but the buildings are fine: cathedral, churches, Palais de Justice, quaint houses. James describes the cathedral: battered façade, Norman towers, side porches, choir and lady chapel, tombs of great artistry. He closes with a description of Rouen's English-looking St. Ouen church (a "consummate combination of lightness and majesty") and then a recommendation: Sail down the Seine from Rouen, for varied views.

Roughead, William (1870–1952). Learned Edinburgh-born and -educated jurist, admitted to the Society of Writers to her Majesty's Signet (1898). He published and edited many works dealing with crime (mostly murder) and criminal trials. In 1913, Roughead began to send James copies of his informative and urbane studies of murder trials (collected in *Twelve Scots Trials* [1913] and *The Trial of Mary Blandy* [1914]). His doing so opened a correspondence with the novelist, who ultimately wrote Roughead fourteen letters, met him, and lunched with him in London, in April 1915. James especially relished Roughead's account of Mary Blandy ("I devoured the tender Blandy in a single feast" [29 Jan 1914]; Mary Blandy had been hanged in 1752 for poisoning her father). James praises the witty criminologist for throwing a vivid "light on manners and conditions" of past Scottish times (5 Aug 1913), cannot "enter into . . . matters best when they are *very* archaic or remote from our familiarities" but likes to see "comparatively modern . . . *special* manners and morals . . . queerly disclosed" (9 Aug 1913), therefore urges Roughead to study "the dear old human and social murders and adulteries and forgeries in which we are so agreeably at home" (24 Aug 1913), and expresses regret that he "never . . . had the good fortune of a chance of talk with a great defender or arraigner of murderers," adding that he finds most interesting "what happens to such glorified persons [acquitted murderers] *afterwards*: Their escape is so much more interesting than their punishment" (6 Mar 1914). In several letters James tells Roughead about his dismay at the outbreak of World War I, noting once that in wartime "the smothered mind needs, absolutely, an occasional whiff of the outer, some *other*, air" (22 Jan 1915) of the sort his friend's writings provide. The two men shared an admiration for Robert Louis Stevenson* and a dislike of Andrew Lang.* After James's death, Roughead continued to produce books in his field, for one of which, *Bad Companions* (1930), their friend Sir Hugh Seymour Walpole* provided a forward. James's library contained three books by Roughead.

Roulet. In *The Ivory Tower*, Graham Fielder's and Horton Vint's traveling friend in Neuchatel years earlier.

Round, Lieutenant George Porter. In *Guy Domville*, the navy nephew of the deceased Brasier, Maria Brasier Domville's first husband. When Guy Domville discovers that Round and Mary love each other, he helps them elope.

"A Round of Visits." Short story (10,600 words), published in the *English Review* (Apr–May 1910); republished in *The Finer Grain*, 1910. (Characters: Bob Ash, Florence Ash, Phil Bloodgood, Mrs. Folliott, Lottie, Mark P. Monteith, Tim Slater, Newton Winch, Mrs. Newton Winch.) Swindled by an absconding cousin named Phil Bloodgood, Mark Monteith returns from Europe to wintry New York—and promptly catches cold. Recovering by Sunday, he meets Mrs. Folliott, who has also been cheated out of money by Bloodgood and is viciously resentful. Through her Mark meets the recently widowed sister-in-law of his old and unpleasant acquaintance Newton Winch. She asks Mark to visit Newton, now depressed and sick. But first Mark calls on Florence Ash, who tells him about her impossible husband. Beginning to feel fated to hear the woes of others, he reluctantly proceeds to Newton, only to find the man sensitive, even charming, now. He guesses at Mark's worry over Bloodgood. Mark defends the absent swindler, saying that he must be remorseful after betraying his friends. Newton is surprised, becomes agitated, and asks the restless Mark to sit down. Mark suspects that Newton does not want him to see something nearby, glances about, and notices a gun under a chair and rug-edge. Newton turns wild, confesses his need for sympathy too, and says he is another Phil Bloodgood—involved in larceny. He then thanks Mark for helping him through his time of waiting for the police, who now ring the doorbell. As Mark lets them in and is speaking briefly to them, they hear the shot which ends poor Newton's life. The police turn critical of Mark, who ruefully admits his partial responsibility. This short story was the last one James published. It had a long Notebook incubation. In the first entry (17 Feb 1894), James records his "notion of a young man . . . who has something—some secret sorrow, trouble, fault—to *tell* and can't find the *recipient*." A few months later (21 Apr 1894), he adds notes concerning the plight of a person in London with a burden and seeking "a confidant, a listening ear and answering heart," then adds plot ingredients later abandoned. Next (16 Feb 1899), he begins to think that the burdened man might be relieved upon hearing the story of some one else in "trouble so much greater than his own . . . that he sees the moral: the balm for his woe residing not in the sympathy of some *one* else, but . . . in giving it—the sympathy—*to* some one else." Long after James returned from his 1904–1905 visit to the United States, he took up his fable, switched its locale to New York, and gave it tragic overtones. In "A Round of Visits," the contrast between New York poverty cold outside and luxurious hothouse hotel heat inside is nightmarish. James's portrayal of the Pocahontas Hotel (i.e., the Waldorf-Astoria) is hellish. But the moral is divine: Sinned-against Mark finds sinner Newton not only in need of more comfort than Mark is but also more humanized—by sin (akin to Bloodgood's)—than Mark is by sorrow.

Rover, Fanny. In *The Tragic Muse*, a London actress whom Miriam Rooth likes.

Rowland, Captain. In *Roderick Hudson*, Rowland Mallet's deceased mother's retired sea captain husband, also deceased.

Roy. In "Georgina's Reasons," William and Georgina Roy's son.

Roy, Agnes. In "Georgina's Reasons," the maiden name of Agnes Roy Theory.

Roy, Cora. In "Georgina's Reasons," Agnes Roy Theory's deceased sister. She was William Roy's first wife.

Roy, Georgina Gressie Benyon. In "Georgina's Reasons," William Roy's bigamous wife. Earlier she is Captain Raymond Benyon's wife, swearing the honorable man to secrecy regarding the marriage. Then she abandons their infant son in Italy and coolly marries William Roy.

Roy, William. In "Georgina's Reasons," bigamous Georgina Gressie Benyon Roy's second husband.

"The Royal Academy and the Grosvenor Gallery." Art review, published in the *Nation* (29 May 1879). James covers the two leading exhibitions of the season. He mentions works by Lord Frederick Leighton,* Sir Edward Burne-Jones,* and a few less important artists. Throughout, James makes adverse remarks about the examples he singles out.

Rubens, Peter Paul (1577–1640). Flemish painter. He went to Paris (in 1622) to decorate the Luxembourg; then to Madrid as a diplomat (1628), where he met Diego de Silva y Velasquez* and painted several portraits of King Philip V, among other works; and then to London (1629). Rubens was prolific; he excelled in historical and biblical subjects, portraits, and landscapes, usually with exuberant coloring. James wrote to his brother William (13 May 1869), "I enjoy Rubens." He did not materially alter this restrained judgment in later years. In "Art: The Dutch and Flemish Pictures in New York" (1872), he is content to note "the opulent serenity of Rubens." In his travel essay "In Belgium" (1874), he pooh-poohs the opinion concerning Rubens expressed by Émile Montégut,* who regarded him as "not only one of the greatest of mere painters, but . . . the greatest genius who ever *thought*, brush in hand"; James prefers to regard Rubens as "the great painter of rosy brawn" without *finesse*. In "Parisian Topics" (19 Feb 1876), James regards a Ferdinand Victor Eugène Delacroix* painting as "like the work of a more delicate and more spiritual Rubens." In his 1876 review of *Les Maîtres d'Autrefois* by Eugène Fromentin,* James says that the author "takes Rubens too seriously by several shades" and brands the painter "coarse." And in "London Pictures and London Plays" (1882) he mentions—though in compliment—"the impudence of . . . Rubens's flesh and blood."

Ruck, Mr. and Mrs. In "The Pension Beaurepas," a couple traveling with their daughter Sophy in Europe. He is financially worried, while his wife and daughter spend extravagantly. They stop in Geneva. In "The Point of View," he is mentioned as now bankrupt, in a letter from their daughter's friend Aurora Church to Miss Whiteside.

Ruck, Sophy. In "The Pension Beaurepas," a spendthrift daughter traveling with her parents in Europe. They stop in Geneva. She is Aurora Church's casual friend. In "The Point of View," her father is mentioned as now bankrupt, in a letter from Aurora to Louisa Whiteside.

Ruddle, Miss. In *The Ivory Tower*, Frank B. Betterman's nurse, along with Miss Goodenough and Miss Mumby.

Rue de Luxembourg, Paris. When James moved from the United States to Paris for what he erroneously thought might well be permanently, he engaged rooms at 29 Rue de Luxembourg (November 1875–December 1876).

Ruffler, Mrs. In *The Princess Casamassima*, an actress in a play seen by Hyacinth Robinson and Millicent Henning.

Ruggieri. In *The Tragic Muse*, Miriam Rooth's friend, who, unlike others, could tell the actress something of use to her.

Rumble. In "The Death of the Lion," a painter popular in society.

Runkle, Mrs. In "Pandora," the sister-in-law, from Natchez, of the president of the United States.

Rushbrook. In "The Solution," the narrator's fiancée's deceased naval officer husband.

Rushbrook, Miss. In "The Solution," the narrator's widowed fiancée's young daughter.

Rushbrook, Mrs. In "The Solution," a naval officer's widow. She is the fiancée of the narrator, who asks her to aid Henry Wilmerding. She extricates Henry from his forced engagement with Veronica Goldie by marrying him herself.

Ruskin, John (1819–1900). London-born art critic and sociologist, the son of well-to-do, indulgent parents. Ruskin was educated at Christ Church, Oxford (to 1841), winning a poetry prize but also interrupting his studies by much travel.

Meeting the painter Joseph Mallord William Turner* in 1840, Ruskin decided to defend him against critics and to extol modern landscapists over earlier ones. *Modern Painters* (1843) was the immediate result; it was followed by four later volumes, innovative and in fine prose style, all with the same title (1846–1860). These later books concern aesthetics, landscape painting through history, specific landscape artists, architecture, and much else. Ruskin was unsatisfactorily married to Euphemia Gray in 1848; the marriage was annulled in 1854, and his ex-wife married the painter Sir John Everett Millais.* Meanwhile, Ruskin published *Seven Lamps of Architecture* (1849), about the aesthetics of noble Gothic architecture, and *Stones of Venice* (3 vols., 1851–1853), in praise of Gothicism and in criticism of Renaissance art. Ruskin offered treatises and lectures on art (including praise of the pre-Raphaelites), then about 1860 began to publish on economics, education, labor, poverty, philanthropy, and much else. His *Sesame and Lilies* (1865), *The Crown of Wild Olive* (1866), *Time and Tide* (1867), and *Fors Clavigera* (1871–1884) reflect these social interests. He was a professor of art, Oxford (1870–1879, 1883–1884); he published innumerable lectures; and he issued *Praeterita* (1885–1889), comprising incomplete parts of an autobiography. James in London, in March 1869, dined with Charles Eliot Norton* and his family, then went with them to hear a Ruskin lecture. A few days later he was a dinner guest with Norton and his family at the home of Ruskin, whom James called in a letter to his mother (20 Mar [1869]) "simple" and "weak" as to face, manner, talk, and mind; James adds that reality has "scared [him] back . . . into the world of unreason and illusion," where "he wanders . . . without . . . any light save the fitful flashes of his beautiful genius." In a letter to John La Farge* (20 Jun [1869]), James boasts that he dined at Ruskin's home, and that "R. was very amiable and shewed his Turners." Norton wrote to James (23 March 1873) that Ruskin greatly admired James's essay "From Venice to Strassburg [sic]" and expressed a wish that James might have been appointed to a Cambridge fine arts professorship instead of Sir Sidney Colvin.* James in "Roman Neighborhoods" (Dec 1873) and in "Italy Revisited" (1878) comments critically on Ruskin. In a review of Elizabeth Thompson* (26 Apr 1877), James counters Ruskin's admiration for one of her paintings, adding that "Mr. Ruskin's praise is sometimes as erratic as his blame." In a note (*Nation*, 18 Apr 1878), James reviews Ruskin's collection of drawings by Turner. In two more notes (*Nation*, 19 Dec 1878, 13 Feb 1879), James amusingly discusses the suit which James Abbott McNeill Whistler* brought against Ruskin for libeling his art work. Over many years, James evolved from subservience to Ruskin's judgments on Venetian painters, especially Titian* and Jacopo Robusti Tintoretto,* to independence from his imperfect mentor.

Russell, Addison Peale (1826–1912). Politician, educator, and author, born in Wilmington, Ohio. After a hardworking youth, he was apprenticed to a Zanesville printer, became an editor, and served his state as an elected and an appointed official, through 1868. Then he was able to follow a literary career. His works include two popular pairs of books: *Library Notes* (1875) and *Characteristics* (1884, a collection of essays); and *A Club of One* (1887) and *In a Club Corner* (1890). His best book is probably *Sub-Coelum: A Sky-Built Human World* (1895), a utopian protest against materialistic socialism. James reviewed (*Nation*, 6 Jan 1876) *Library Notes*, praising the author as "a voracious reader," but of the collecting not critical kind. Russell ranges from the classics to trivia and classifies his "extracts . . . under heads, in the Emersonian taste." James scores the man's lapses in taste but says that the result is "pleasant."

Rye, Lord. In "In the Cage," a client of Mrs. Jordan, who arranges flowers for a living.

Ryves, Mrs. In "Sir Dominick Ferrand," deceased Sir Dominick Ferrand's widowed illegitimate daughter, and the mother of young Sidney. She is a song-writer who collaborates with Peter Baron.

Ryves, Sidney. In "Sir Dominick Ferrand," widowed Mrs. Ryves's young son.

S

Sabran, Eléanor de Jean de Manville (1750–1827). French countess, courtesan, niece of the Bishop of Laon, and letter and journal writer. She was married to a naval officer named Sabran, who was fifty years her senior; she had children by him and, after his death, associated with and married, in 1797, the Chevalier de Boufflers. During his absences as colonial governor of Senegal, they exchanged many letters. James reviewed (*Galaxy*, Oct 1875; reprinted in *French Poets and Novelists*, 1878) *Correspondance Inédite de la Comtesse de Sabran et du Chevalier de Boufflers* (1875). James begins by praising 1720–1790 letters as superior in general to 1800–1875 letters. He notes that earlier writers had more leisure and wrote more, but did not pad. Cultivated men were then in the army, church, or government; women's lives were "less exacting." French society was constricted and hence more thoroughly written about. Though well researched, the eighteenth century still yields new literary treasures, including the Sabran-Boufflers correspondence. James details events in Madame de Sabran's dour early life, her meeting Boufflers, their intimacy, their travels, their separations, and her moods and solitary activities. Why should we like these letters? They are not historically valuable, they have little "psychological and dramatic interest," and they are not philosophical; instead, they are simply "charming" and "perfect." James sketches a fascinating picture of eighteenth-century life, which these letters elucidate.

The Sacred Fount. Short novel (71,300 words), published in New York by Scribners, 1901, and in London by Methuen, 1901. (Characters: Grace Brissenden, Guy Brissenden, Comte and Comtesse de Dreuil, Mrs. Froome, Gilbert Long, Lord John and Lady Lutley, Ford Obert, May Server.) On the train platform at Newmarch, near London, the narrator observes that Gilbert Long seems more suave and handsome, whereas Grace Brissenden, though ten years older than her husband Guy, seems younger. Mrs. Briss tells the narrator that Long has been made wiser through association with Lady John, who is coming to Newmarch with Guy on the next train. Before dinner, the narrator observes that Guy is almost unrecognizably older. Long rather angrily agrees. The narrator impresses his painter friend Ford Obert by theorizing that Mrs. Briss is growing younger by damagingly tapping her husband's "sacred fount." Next morning he theorizes that Lady John cannot be Long's source of vitality since she does not appear depleted. Doubting other possibilities, Mrs. Briss nominates May Server as Long's fount. The narrator seems shocked in case he has compromised May, but Mrs. Briss plans to find out more. The narrator leads May from her, and the two go to the estate picture gallery, where Long is heard discoursing intelligently about art to Obert. They all seek resemblances in life about them to the face and a mask of a man in a portrait. When Obert criticizes May, the narrator—feeling responsible now—defends the woman and is soon happy to hear him express the thought that she may be tapping someone else's source of vitality. But then Obert tires of seeking supposedly dried-up founts. When Mrs. Briss gossips about May as Long's likely fount, the narrator urges her to abandon the theory and even lets her abuse him a bit. He even suggests that May is perhaps after Briss because Mrs. Briss ignores him a good deal. But Mrs. Briss counters by wondering whether May uses Briss to keep people from thinking that she really wants Long. Nervously avoiding his friends by taking an afternoon stroll, the narrator happens to òbserve Lady John and Mrs. Briss, and starts to think that Lady John, loving Long, uses Briss as a screen. Long appears, and the narrator thinks he is using Lady John as a screen for his love of May. Next the narrator discusses May with Briss, who says he fears her but wants to help her avoid a breakdown. Alone again, the narrator happens upon May in the garden; she seems dessicated (because of Long) but lovable. When he talks suggestively about Briss, May falters and vaguely smiles. Briss comes up. At dinner the narrator hopes to stop theorizing but soon is imaginatively pairing up various guests some more. He assigns Long's improvement to May's depletion; Mrs. Briss's, to Briss's. Lady John tackles him and counters his comment about her freedom with Briss by accusing Mrs. Briss of being fast and loose with the narrator. As the two fence, they observe Mrs. Briss and Long in close conversation. The narrator also sees Obert chatting with eternally smiling May. A bit later Obert blurts out to the narrator that he is tired of his theories but is still intrigued. Obert praises May. Fatigued Briss reports that his wife wants to see the narrator. She informs him that May is not the source of Long's new radiance although she may appear to be so. The narrator is surprised until he concludes that Long asked Mrs. Briss to protect May thus. Mrs. Briss then denies any knowledge of Long's fount, criticizes the narrator's hypersensitivity, deplores talking with him so much, and adds that both she and Long now fear his intervention. Saying that she must feel peaceful now, the narrator asks her to help him destroy his imagination. She accuses him of being crazy on the whole subject of sacred founts. He asks her to explain when she first thought so, and she says it was when she began talking with Long and found him dull. In a flash the narrator sees two things: first, that this comment is a subterfuge to cover her own draining of poor Briss; and second, that Mrs. Briss and Long are wickedly shamming together to throw him off the track to the truth. When he asks about Lady John, Mrs. Briss explains that she chattered about that woman simply to try to be sympathetic toward his theory concerning founts. Finally, saying that she feels driven to the wall, she declares that she has proof from Briss that there is a woman in Long's life and that the woman is Lady John. The narrator is shocked: He did not want his fount theory to cause any humiliating exposures but only a scurrying to cover. She adds that Briss innocently enough took the train to Newmarch with Lady John but that the effect was to screen Long. The narrator wonders, in that case, why Mrs. Briss was annoyed when she observed Briss and May together; she denies any such anger, blames the narrator's infernal imagination yet again, and adds that horrid May tried to make love to Briss. This seems to be yet more disproof of the narrator's theory. Again Mrs. Briss calls the narrator crazy. He appears abashed and determines to leave Newmarch early in the morning. This is James's most controversial novel. To some critics, including William Dean Howells,* it holds the key to the Jamesian method. To other critics, it is a prolix lemon. Reading it upset many of James's friends, including Henry Adams* and John Milton Hay.* The immediate idea for the novel came from the following suggestion Stopford Augustus Brooke* gave James, as recorded in his *Notebooks* (17 Feb 1894): "The notion of the young man who marries an older woman and who has the effect on her of making her younger and still younger, while he himself becomes her age." James was immediately inspired to alter this pattern so as to include not only two couples but a transference of "cleverness and stupidity" as well. James let the idea rest for years; then he returned to it in a later Notebook entry (15 Feb 1899), adjuring himself not to "lose sight of the little *concetto* . . . of the young man who marries an old woman and becomes old while she becomes young. Keep my play on idea: the *liaison* that betrays itself by the *transfer* of qualities . . . from one to the other . . . " James wrote to Howells (11 Dec 1902) thus: "I would have 'chucked' *The Sacred Fount* at the fifteenth thousand word, if . . . I could have afforded to 'waste' 15,000, and if . . . I were not always ridden by a superstitious terror of not finishing . . . what I have begun. I am a coward about *dropping*, and the book in question . . . is . . . a monument to that superstition." The resulting fiction grew from a planned 10,000-word story to a novel seven times as long, and one which James described as "fantastic," "sustained," and "calculated to minister to curiosity," in a letter to his agent James Brand Pinker* (25 Jul 1900). Pinker's selling it to Charles Scribner's Sons started James's ultimately profitable relationship with that publishing firm. When it was issued in New York and then in London, it earned James $3,500 in advances alone. But once adverse reader responses began to reach him, he defined *The Sacred Fount* in letters as a "joke" (to Mary Augusta Humphry Ward,* 15 Mar 1901) and "chaff in the mouth" (to William Dean Howells, 11 Dec 1902). The fairy-tale plot has analogues worldwide, even including James's "De Grey, A Romance" and "Longstaff's Marriage." The trouble for readers begins with the narrator, who confusingly reports on ambivalent events (critics have called him demented, meddlesome, intelligent, clairvoyant), and continues with Mrs. Briss, whose motives remain unclear (critics have called her intelligent, tolerant, adulterous, evil). Criticism of this novel continues to mount and rivals commentary on "The Turn of the Screw."

St. Dunstans, Lady. In *The Tragic Muse*, Nick Dormer's deceased father's aged godmother.

Saint Dunstans, Lord Earl of. In *The American*, Mme. Emmeline de Bellegarde's deceased father.

Sainte-Beuve, Charles Augustin (1804–1869). French man of letters. Born in Boulogne, he studied medicine in Paris, but quit to devote himself to literature, first as a poet and novelist, then as an influential critic. He relates details of a given subject's physical, moral, and artistic life to that person's literary production; the result is distinguished aesthetic analysis. Especially notable are his studies of sixteenth-century French poets, Port-Royal figures, and major and minor writers figuring in Sainte-Beuve's famous *Lundis*—his innumerable Monday columns. Throughout his life, James greatly admired Sainte-Beuve's criticism, beginning in 1862–1863 (while in law school) to read his *Causeries du Lundi* (1849–1861) and *Nouveaux Lundis* (1861–1866). In an early review, of Edmond Schérer* (*Nation*, 12 Oct 1865), James called Sainte-Beuve "the first of living critics." James reviewed (*Nation*, 4 Jun 1868) the 1868 translation by H. W. Preston of Sainte-Beuve's *Portraits de femmes* (1864), saying that most of the women discussed are forgotten (except Jeanne Manon Roland, Madame de Sévigné, and Madame de Staël). James carps at aspects of the present translation and calls Miss Preston's feminist reading premature: Sainte-Beuve's women here were mostly salon ladies writing about lovers. In a review of Hippolyte Taine* (*Atlantic Monthly*, Apr 1872), James registers his preference for Sainte-Beuve over Taine, since the former is less "doctrinal" and avoids "dogmas, moulds, and formulas" better. James reviewed (*Nation*, 18 Feb 1875) Sainte-Beuve's *Premiers Lundis* (1874), calling his subject the world's "most acute critic." Although the present essays are early, unrevised pieces, they show that their author from the start had a firm tone, penetrating irony, and "wisdom." Here Sainte-Beuve praises two poets, Victor-Marie Hugo* and Alphonse de Lamartine, whom he later disliked. James notes that English readers will enjoy Sainte-Beuve's comments on Sir Walter Scott* and James Fenimore Cooper, although James calls his liking for Cooper a "mistake." James reviewed (*Nation*, 15 Apr 1875) *English Portraits* (1875), which are translated selections from *Causeries de Lundi*. James calls the translations good, but he says that the book is "a spurious . . . service to culture," since Sainte-Beuve was thoroughly French and his comments on writers using English are hardly authoritative. Sainte-Beuve writes here on Lord Chesterfield, William Cooper, Benjamin Franklin, Edward Gibbon,* and Alexander Pope—best on Franklin and Gibbon. James pauses to praise Sainte-Beuve reverently, for being a scholarly man of the world, with a hospitable, flexible intellect (though with a blind spot when it came to Honoré de Balzac*). James closes by quoting Sainte-Beuve's high opinion of Nicolas Boileau. In "Parisian Festivity" (1876), James defines two little books by Sainte-Beuve, *Chroniques Parisiennes* (1876) and *Cahiers de Sainte-Beuve* (1876), as "literary remains" and the result of "disagreeable and painful . . . posthumous rummaging." Finally, James brilliantly reviewed *Correspondance de C. A. Sainte-Beuve (1822–69)* (2 vols., 1878) for the *North American Review* (Jan 1880); the review was revised and reprinted in *American Literary Criticism* (New York: Longmans, Green, 1904). It begins with the assertion that the subject, a totally literary man, painted his own picture in his works, and so these volumes merely complete an already vivid portrait. James comments on the letters as "technical" and "professional," with personal and sociable asides slipped in; on Sainte-Beuve's mind and style ("rich and fine and flexible"); on his two passions ("scholarship and . . . life"); on his combination of the feminine ("tact," "penetration," "subtlety," "pliability," "rapidity of transition," "divinations," "sympathies and antipathies," "insinuation") and the masculine ("completeness," "sense," "reason," "moderation," "knowledge," "exactitude"); on his joy in doing literary battle (his "malice," reactive "feline scratch," faultfinding); and on his knowledge of "the moral physiognomy" of opponents. Sainte-Beuve aided "the cause of liberty," commented restlessly in order to characterize his subject, and was uncompromisingly sure of himself. Quoting marvelously here, James admires Sainte-Beuve's defining himself as critic in the broadest terms, praises him for advising younger writers (Charles Baudelaire,* Ernest Feydeau, Gustave Flaubert,* and Edmond de Goncourt* and his brother Jules de Goncourt*), and images the man as a scalpel-wielding surgeon seeking to "show the weak point of the breastplate—show the *seam*, as it were, between the talent and the soul." He especially likes his autobiographical touches. James images Sainte-Beuve's mind as a polished stone with "a hundred facets," hence with some "displeasing" angles. But Sainte-Beuve was "the very genius of observation, discretion and taste." In *Notes of a Son and Brother*, James recalls "the swim into my ken of Sainte-Beuve" while James was ostensibly studying law at Harvard. James's library contained twelve books by Sainte-Beuve.

Saint-Gaudens, Augustus (1848–1907). American sculptor, born in Dublin. His mother was Irish; his father, French. Saint-Gaudens was brought to the United States as an infant. After study in Paris and Rome, he established a successful studio in New York (1873–1885), then another in Cornish, New Hampshire (1885–1907). He was commissioned by John La Farge* to embellish a New York church. Between larger assignments, Saint-Gaudens executed medallion portraits of friends (including Robert Louis Stevenson*). Saint-Gaudens' most famous works include *Lincoln* (in Chicago), the *Shaw Memorial* (in Boston—this work took Saint-Gaudens twelve years to complete, and William James spoke at its 1897 dedication), *The Puritan* (in Springfield, Masssachusetts), *General Sherman* (in New York), and *Parnell* (in Dublin). His masterpiece may well be the memorial figure in Rock Creek Cemetery (Washington, D.C.) at the grave of the wife of Henry Adams.* When James dined at the White House, in January 1905, as the guest of President Theodore Roosevelt,* Saint-Gaudens sat at the same table. Also, while in Washington at this time, James visited the grave of Adams's wife and was intensely moved by Saint-Gaudens' memorial figure there. In *The American Scene*, James calls Saint-Gaudens' statue of Sherman in New York's Central Park "the best thing in the picture," showing as it does "an irresistible march into an enemy's territory . . . [by] the Destroyer"; but he does object to the ambiguous figure of peace which is part of the group. He praises Saint-Gaudens' "magnificent" *Lincoln* in Chicago. As for Boston, James describes Saint-Gaudens' tribute to Colonel Robert Gould Shaw and the Fifty-Fourth Massachusetts there as "noble and exquisite." In *Notes of a Son and Brother*, James praises the *Shaw* as the work of "a great sculptor" holding "the image aloft forever" of the colonel and the men he commanded, including James's brother Wilky.

St. George, Mr. and Mrs. Henry. In "The Lesson of the Master," the master novelist and his wife. She has allegedly diminished the quality of his work by forcing him to write too fast. At her death, he marries Marian Fancourt, whom the young novelist Paul Overt admires but whom St. George has advised him not to weaken his work by marrying. James may have given St. George the first name Henry because Paul Bourget* regarded James as his master.

"The St. Gothard." The 1875 title of "The Old Saint-Gothard."

Saintonge, Mlle. de. In *The Reverberator*, Suzanne de Brécourt's friend.

"The Saint's Afternoon." Travel essay, published in *The May Book* (London: Macmillan, 1901); reprinted as Parts I–V in "The Saint's Afternoon and Others," in *Italian Hours*, 1909.

"The Saint's Afternoon and Others." A seven-part travel sketch, published in *Italian Hours*, 1909; Parts I–V are "The Saint's Afternoon," while Parts VI and VII were added in 1909. At last, a new experience for the presumably seasoned traveler: In June, James visits the cliff home of a friend [Axel Martin Fredrik Munthe*] on "beautiful, horrible and haunted" Capri, an island now unfortunately invaded by German tourists and businessmen. First he notes "general bravery" and "robust odour" during St. Antony's procession in Anacapri.

Then he goes to the "temple of art and hospitality" of his generous host, to join three hundred other wine-bibbing guests. James takes in the view from the height: the Bay of Naples, Vesuvius, the other islands, Barbarossa's castle and Tiberius's villa nearby, and other shadows from antiquity. The host shows off relics and reproductions in his galleries, and James enjoys listening to the ardent copyists brought over from Naples and to local musicians. Politically feeble races contribute ravishing songs to us, but what are their prospects? (Oh, for our part, we have opened saloons in Manila.) Other afternoons James spent motoring from Rome into Naples by mountain and then back again by sea. Naples has an "emptier . . . face" than when first seen forty years earlier. Pompeii's "lengthening shadows" he saw again, "absolutely alone." And a Posilippo rock garden. He philosophizes on the automobile—"the chariot of fire," "the monster," but also "on occasion a purely beneficent creature." We can now see more but at the sacrifice of "some hard grain of difficulty . . . [which is] always a necessary part of the composition of pleasure." At any rate, two more days of driving (Baiae, Capua, Terracina, Gaeta, the Pontine Marshes, Velletri, Castelli Romani, and "tha darkening Campagna") reinforced his old conclusion: "Italy is really so much the most beautiful country in the world . . . that others must stand off and be hushed while she speaks." She fuses "human history and mortal passion." James poetizes on "the luxury of loving Italy."

Sales figures of some of James's books. The following incomplete but representative figures, usually estimates, are of sales in the United States and in England during James's lifetime, including the 1883 Macmillan Collective Edition (but not the New York Edition, listed separately below) and excluding pirated editions and translations: *The Ambassadors*, under 7,000 copies; *The Aspern Papers . . .*, over 4,500; *The Awkward Age*, 3,000; *The Bostonians*, under 6,000; *Confidence*, 10,000; *The Europeans*, just over 8,000; *Daisy Miller . . .*, under 30,000; *Embarrassments*, over 3,000; *The Golden Bowl*, 5,000; *Julia Bride* (as a book), 4,000; *The Lesson of the Master . . .*, under 3,000; *A London Life . . .*, 4,500; *The Other House*, under 5,000; *The Portrait of a Lady*, 13,500; *The Princess Casamassima*, almost 8,000; *The Real Thing and Other Tales*, 1,500; *The Reverberator*, 4,500; *Roderick Hudson*, 10,500; *The Sacred Fount*, probably under 6,000; *The Soft Side*, probably 6,000; *The Spoils of Poynton*, 4,000; *Tales of Three Cities*, 3,000; *The Tragic Muse*, 3,500; *The Two Magics*, under 4,000; *The Wings of the Dove*, 7,000. Some of these figures have been recently revised upward.

The Saloon. One-act play, published in Philadelphia and New York by Lippincott Company, 1949, in *The Complete Plays of Henry James*, ed. Leon Edel. (Characters: Mr. and Mrs. Spencer Coyle, Captain Hume-Walker, Kate Julian, Mrs. Julian, Bobby Lechmere, Jane Wingrave, Owen Wingrave, Mrs. Owen Wingrave, Owen Wingrave, Sir Philip Wingrave, Wingrave.) A few overnight guests, entering and leaving the saloon (i.e., salon) of the Wingrave estate, are upset one October evening by Owen Wingrave's decision to quit all preparations for a military career. His army coach Spencer Coyle is distressed, although he admires Owen's stalwart manner. Militant Mrs. Julian and her stiff daughter Kate, who is nominally engaged to Owen, are distraught. Especially disgusted is Owen's grandfather General Sir Philip Wingrave, who threatens to disown the cowardly scion. Mrs. Coyle, uneasy in the creepy house, admires Owen's conduct in the face of family wrath. Bobby Lechmere, Owen's fellow student, is neutral and retires to his bedroom near a ghost room, in which Owen explains a Wingrave long ago beat his grandson for refusing to go to a military school: The lad died, and his father reentered the death room never to emerge. Coyle is summoned to Sir Philip upstairs, sadly returns to tell Owen he is disinherited, and retires. The young man, alone with Kate, disputes with her. She cannot marry a coward, she says; he wonders if she saw their marriage as a means to security. He is for life and peace; she, for knightly courage. She calls soldiers heroes; he, brutes and slaves. She regards meeting the family ghost as a test of courage. Therefore Owen, in spite of her mounting fear, shouts defiance at the ghost, which, even as Kate tells Owen she likes and loves him and apologizes to him for her behavior, swoops through the darkness of blown-out candles at the gasping young man. Coyle returns, pronounces Owen dead, and praises him as a soldier. James based this play, written in December 1907 and touched up later, on his short story "Owen Wingrave." In 1908 he was invited, and agreed, to submit *The Saloon* to a stage society offering subscription performances of financially unpromising but worthy plays. In January 1909 *The Saloon* was rejected by the society's reader, George Bernard Shaw,* who exchanged letters with James on it. Socialist Shaw felt that the play unencouragingly dramatized the weight of the dead past and gave the victory to the wrong side; James defended his work as artistic and historically valid. *The Saloon* was performed as a curtain raiser in London in January 1911.

Saltram. In "The Coxon Fund," any of the four children of Frank Saltram and his wife.

Saltram, Mr. and Mrs. Frank. In "The Coxon Fund," a fluent but irresponsible genius and his long-suffering wife. They have four children. He is the guest of Adelaide and Kent Mulville and of Mr. and Mrs. Pudney. When he is awarded money from the Coxon Fund through Ruth Anvoy's generous honesty, he fails thereafter to produce. Frank Saltram's characteristics may be based on those of Samuel Taylor Coleridge.

Salvi, Count. In "The Diary of a Man of Fifty," Countess Bianca Salvi's husband and Countess Bianca Salvi-Scarabelli's father. Count Camerino killed him in a duel.

Salvi, Countess Bianca. In "The Diary of a Man of Fifty," Count Salvi's widow. The diarist narrator loved but distrusted her. Edmund Stanmer loves her widowed daughter Countess Bianca Salvi-Scarabelli. After her first husband's death, Countess Salvi married Count Camerino, who had killed Count Salvi in a duel.

Salvini, Tommaso (1829–1915). Milan-born son of an actor and an actress. He started as a child actor, then became a member (from 1847) of the company of Adelaide Ristori* in Rome. In 1849 he fought briefly for Italian independence. Salvini performed in England (including at Covent Garden, London, 1884), toured the United States five times (beginning in 1873 and including Boston in 1883), starred in many Italian plays, and appeared in Shakespearean roles (as early as 1856). Retired in 1890, Salvini published his autobiography in 1893, and he participated in Ristori's eightieth-birthday celebration in Rome in 1902. James saw Salvini in Boston and London, wrote to his sister Alice from London (29 Feb [1884]) that he preferred Salvini's Othello in Boston to the one in London ("toned . . . down and weakened"), but wrote a few days later to Theodore E. Child* (8 Mar [1884]) that Salvini "is the greatest of the great." James published two essays on Salvini. In "Tommaso Salvini" (*Atlantic Monthly*, Mar 1883), he begins by contrasting acting with and without elaborate stage settings, then praises Salvini's Boston "triumph" without any "aids to illusion." But he calls the procedure of having Salvini take roles from William Shakespeare* and recite the lines in Italian to English-speaking fellow actors "grotesque, unpardonable, abominable." And yet James glories in the actor's magnificent physical attributes, confidence, force, ease, intelligence, and Italian "imagination" and "intentions." His Othello is a thorough "picture of passion . . . beginning in noble repose and spending itself in black insanity," Acts IV and V being "the finest piece of tragic acting that I know." (James's description is electrifying.) James commends Salvini's "temperate and discreet" Macbeth, but deplores much else in the production. He extols Shakespeare's *King Lear* as "a great and terrible poem," suggests that it cannot be acted, then commends aspects of Salvini's performance. He uniquely congratulates Salvini, whose "acting is absolutely perfect" here, for his role ("exclusively his own") as Corrado in Paolo Giacometti's 1861 *La Morte Civile* (a "play . . . meagre and monotonous," but with a "situation [which] . . . is the perfection of tragedy"). He closes by first criticizing *The Gladiator* (1841) by Alexandre Soumet and Gabrielle Daltenheym, in which Salvini should never have appeared, and then by demeaning the "American stage" ("in . . . confusion") and "American taste" ("wanting in light"). James opens "A Study of Salvini" (*Pall Mall Gazette*, 27 Mar 1884) by lamenting "the great actor's" limited London repertory, with a "dingy and feeble" company. Audiences were wrongly indifferent to his "perfect . . . rendering" of Giacometti's Corrado, which rôle James analyzes at length, before turning to Salvini's Othello ("rich and overflowing"), and Macbeth and Lear (both "less deeply assimilated"). James calls *Il Gladiatore* "a desperately bad play." He closes by calling Salvini "a lesson and . . . a standard."

Salvi-Scarabelli, Countess Bianca. In "The Diary of a Man of Fifty," Countess Bianca Salvi's widowed daughter. Her marriage to Edmund Stanmer causes consternation and then doubt in the diarist narrator's mind.

Sand, George (1804–1876), the pseudonym of Mme. Amandine Lucile Aurore Dudevant (née Dupin), French novelist. She spent her childhood at Nohant ("that rustic chateau of Nohant, in the old province of Berry," to quote James), happily close to nature and peasants. She married Casimir Dudevant in 1822, but after giving birth to a son (Maurice) and a daughter (Solange) separated from him in 1831 because of his infidelity. She became intimate with Jules Sandeau,* with whom she collaborated on writings signed Jules Sand. Following an affair with Prosper Mérimée,* the next important man in her life was French poet Alfred de Musset,* with whom she went to Venice in 1833. They quarreled and parted a year later, partly because she had a new lover, Pietro Pagello. Then Sand formed a liaison in 1837 with Frédéric Chopin, Polish-born composer and pianist, whom, when he became sick, she took to Majorca for his health; they argued and separated in 1847. Back in Nohant, she established professional relationships with a number of brilliant men, including Franz Liszt, Honoré de Balzac,* and Ferdinand Victor Eugène Delacroix,* and she continued her fast, unremitting mode of writing. Her collected edition numbers 109 volumes, plus twenty autobiographical volumes. Her best works include *Indiana* (1832, the first novel she signed George Sand), *Valentine* (1832), *Lélia* (1833), *Jacques* (1834), *Léone Léoni* (1834), *Lettres d'un voyageur* (1834–1837), *Mauprat* (1837), *Spiridion* (1838), *Un Hiver à Majorque* (1841), *Consuelo* (1842–1843), *Teverino* (1845), *La Mare au Diable* (1846), *Lucrezia Floriani* (1846–1847), *L'Histoire de ma vie* (1854–1855), *La Daniella* (1857, which James mentions in his "Roman Neighbourhoods"), *Elle et lui* (1859), *L'Homme de neige* (1859), *Le Dernier amour* (1867), *Mademoiselle Merquem* (1867), and *Flamarande* (1875). Sand's first works dramatize her rebellion against marital constraints, particularly when they harm women; her second phase concerns politics and philosophy; her third phase is notable for rustic romances. In his review of Sand's *Mademoiselle Merquem* (*Nation*, 16 Jul 1868), James tells us that he first heard of Sand in detail when he read the "impertinen[t]" criticism of her *Spiridion* by William Makepeace Thackeray* in his *Paris Sketch-Book*. James started seriously reading Sand in 1860, when he became addicted to the *Revue des Deux Mondes*, to which she was then a contributing editor. Beginning in 1875 he associated with several French writers, including Gustave Flaubert* and Alphonse Daudet,* who knew and admired Sand professionally. James uniquely respected Ivan Sergeyevich Turgenev* in Paris at this time; not only Turgenev, who esteemed Sand's writing, but also Turgenev's mistress Michelle Pauline García Viardot* could regale James with stories of seeing Sand at Nohant. (Mme. Viardot was a model for Sand's heroine Consuelo in *Consuelo.*) James later diverged from Sand's artistic practice but always revered her independent artistic personality. He read new biographical and critical material (especially the biography by Mme. Wladimir Karénine, published in parts in 1899 and 1912) about Sand, whose region of Nohant he visited in 1907 with his friend Edith Newbold Jones Wharton.* He wrote reviews of and articles about "Madame Sand" and her works (from 1868 to 1914), referring in those works (and in his letters as well) to about fifty of her titles. His review of *Mademoiselle Merquem* contains praise of its "extraordinary facility in composition," with its "gush[ing]" narrative, which "lives and breathes." Disagreeing with the famous statement by Hippolyte Taine* that Sand was an idealist, James said he would call her instead an optimist. Next, James reviewed (*Nation*, 13 Jan 1876) *Flamarande*, calling its authoress "a wonderful improvisatrice," who in the "evening" of her career can still produce a smooth, softly told story. Case in point: *Flamarande*, which is not "argumentative," as Sand's earlier novels often are, but purely entertaining. In "Parisian Topics" (17 June 1876), while writing about Joseph Ernest Renan,* James gratuitously comments that Sand's style is only "after all (with all respect), a woman's style." James memorialized Sand's death in "Parisian Topics" (1 Jul 1876), describing the woman as "a singular mixture of quietude and turbulence," but her old age as "very tranquil and reasonable." Next, in "George Sand" (New York *Tribune*, 22 Jul 1876), he mentions her intimacies, praises her description of her "plain old country-house" at Nohant, discusses her moderate income in light of her incessant scribbling, mentions that he had seen a letter from her written shortly before her death (in which she boasted of her keen eyesight and spritely step), reports that her final deathbed words were *"Laissez verdure,"* and quotes Renan concerning her. Then James, though calling her "a decidedly superficial moralist" and criticizing her inability to distinguish between pure and impure love, praises her genius for improvisation ("she told stories as a nightingale sings"), her "ripe and flexible" style, and her varied interests and active sympathies. He closes by admitting that she was not a realist, since her novels are not exact or probable, have few "living figures," and produce little illusion. James reviewed her 1877 *Dernières Pages* (*Nation*, 25 Oct 1877), praising them for quality matching their quantity, and noting her unflagging wisdom and style to the end. His first long essay on Sand was published in the *Galaxy* (Jul 1877; reprinted in *French Poets and Novelists*, 1878). In it, commenting on her *Histoire*—"full of charming recollections and impressions," though "ill made"—James stresses the stellar portraits in it of her forebears, her absence of veracity, and her combination of familiarity and reticence. He notes that this enemy of the institution of marriage (she could never show "wifely submissiveness"), the established Church, and conservative politics may have been feminine in "the quality of her genius," but was certainly masculine in quantity, force, mass, energy, temperament, and character. From the start she shows style, and her "language has to the end an odour of the hawthorn and the wild honeysuckle." Her prefaces, which are beautiful self-

examinations, "commemorate the writer's extraordinary facility and spontaneity." She philosophized vaguely, was nobly curious but rebelliously agitated,
did not take life very seriously, wrote indefatigably, was left behind by the
advent of realism—in cheerful rejection of which she remained hopeful. She
distinguished too little between "virtuous" love and "vicious" love (to her, all
love is "divine" and "ennobling"), but she treated erotic passion better than
her English-writing counterparts. Love in Sand's early romances is too anxious
to prove "itself . . . some fine thing that it really is not"; the later romances
"have an indefinable falsity of tone." Sand's books are hard to reread: "They
are the easy writing which makes hard reading." (James wonders whether this
is because of her typically feminine "intellectual laxity.") She wrongly
"dresses" a human weakness "as a virtue." James calls Sand's *Valentine* harmonious and eloquent, *Léone Léoni* a masterpiece, *Lucrezia Floriani* argumentative, *Mauprat* solid and manly, and *André* and *La Mare au Diable* perfectly
formed. James's last three essays on Sand are "She and He: Recent Documents"
(*Yellow Book*, Jan 1897); "George Sand: The New Life" (*North American
Review*, Apr 1902), a review of Mme. Wladimir Karénine's biography of Sand
(to the year 1838), vols. 1 and 2 (1899); and a review of Karénine's vol. 3 a
dozen years later (*Quarterly Review*, Apr 1914). All three final essays were
reprinted in *Notes on Novelists*, 1914. The "She and He" essay contains James's
most curious commentary on Sand. It concerns mainly the relationship of experience (here, Sand's) and art (here, her *Elle et lui*, about her affair with Musset,
and her *Correspondance: 1812–1876*). In *Elle et lui* Sand converts "crude primary stuff" into a "slight" book for "commercial profit." James wonders
whether the public has a right to know about private lives, although it loves to
look at "soiled" linen. We must remember that information is not the same as
truth. Inquiries from "envenomed" critics cannot hurt the "granite" of art.
James laments that details of Sand's early life, with stress on Mérimée, Musset,
and others, must be recorded, because genius is "self-registering" even before
a "great snickering public." Sand and Musset lacked respect for each other,
which was hard on their love. Stylish *Elle et lui* has squalid *laideurs*. Sand was
essentially mannish save in her constant desire to prove herself right. She was
eager to grind men just as women have been "ground . . . in the volitional mill."
Her *Histoire* is delightful but not veracious. Her *Correspondance* presents her
composure and articulateness to advantage. By comparison, her novels begin to
seem "pale and faint." Precious though *Elle et lui* is, it is all feeling but with
persona not authoress as informant. In "George Sand: The New Life," James
notes that there are few great French biographies, because French discretion
overcomes enthusiasm; Mme. Karénine, Sand's present biographer, is therefore
predictably a foreigner. The work is in poor form and taste, prolix and repetitious,
expert but provincial (i.e., Russian). It also combines "psychological intelligence
and a lame esthetic." But it is "rich and full," and it makes good use of
unpublished documents. Sand was a "remarkable . . . creature"; her works, however, as the nineteenth century wanes, are fading because of their "want of

plastic intensity.'' Discussing Sand's fiercely strong forebears, James stresses her ''heredity.'' He notes that Sand seceded from a bad marriage, stumbled onto her literary genius, produced full-blown masterpieces at once, and converted ''amorous experience and . . . woe'' alike into fiction. Detailing the former, James calls her lovers ''nurslings'' and ''greasy males,'' and her affairs tragicomic. He says that ''her distinction and her vulgarity'' are irreconcilable. He extends Balzac's opinion of her as essentially masculine, and he concludes that at the end Sand was ''serene and superior'' and is an abiding example of ''monstrous vitality.'' The third volume (1912) of Mme. Karénine's biography of Sand, which James reviewed in 1914, takes this ''greatest of all women of letters'' to 1848. The book, though not of the first order, is patient and persistent. Use of materials just released by Sand's two great-granddaughters results in neither lucidity nor conclusions. (We must await vol. 4 to see Sand's ''placid'' phase.) Sand had her cake, ''to the last crumb,'' and shelved it too; she lived and produced energetically, had style, was gifted (if voteless), and took what she wanted. She annexed the male identity, enriched the masculine by emphasizing the feminine, and was virile, efficient, ranging. After touching on Sand, Musset, and Pagello in Venice, James discusses Chopin, ''the divine composer,'' in ''the hysteric pitch of [Sand's] family life,'' which included illegitimate relatives but more importantly her weak son Maurice, her ''wicked'' daughter Solange, and Solange's husband, sculptor Jean-Baptiste Auguste Clésinger. Sand converted this adversity into fiction. For example, she wrote lucid and harmonious *Lucrezia Floriani* at this time and later incorporated Solange's ''humiliating'' ''character and conduct'' into *Mademoiselle Merquem*. Feeling ''sympathy and admiration'' for Sand, James closes with a laudatory analysis of an April 1852 letter from mother to daughter—''the gem of her biographer's collection,'' ''a document of the highest psychological value and a practical summary of all the elements of the writer's genius.'' The letter shows ''moral authority'' and ''the rights of wisdom.'' In his review (*Galaxy*, Jun 1877) of two biographies of Alfred de Musset (one by his brother Paul and the other by Paul Lindau), James discusses Musset's love affair with Sand too much. James's early tales, notably ''A Tragedy of Error,'' ''Gabrielle de Bergerac,'' ''Travelling Companions,'' and ''Eugene Pickering,'' are indebted to Sand, especially with regard to passion, setting, tone, and heroine complexity. In ''Eugene Pickering,'' the character named Anastasia Blumenthal is patterned after Sand. *Watch and Ward* may owe its Roger-Nora situation to Sand's *Mare au Diable*. Hudson's death in *Roderick Hudson* may relate to Jacques's suicide in Sand's *Jacques*. Indiana and Sir Ralph (from Sand's *Indiana*) may have been in James's mind when he delineated Isabel Archer and her cousin Ralph Touchett (*The Portrait of a Lady*). Sand's treatment of the artist in conflict with society may have influenced James's similar depiction in *The Tragic Muse*. James seemed to share her well-recorded awareness that husbands can be brutal and marriages horrible. Finally, the formula of James's famous prefaces is almost identical to that of Sand, whose earlier mood-recalling, self-analytical prefaces to many of her works

James read with care. James's library contained twelve books by Sand and, in addition, Karénine's biography of her.

Sandeau, Jules (1811–1883). Romantic French novelist and playwright. He was intimate with George Sand* early in her career. James reviewed (*Nation*, 5 Feb 1874) Sandeau's novels *Jean de Thommeray* and *Le Colonel Evrard* (both in 1 vol., 1873). Although he says that Sandeau has a "slightly conscious style," James regards him as his favorite French novelist, now that Sand is quiescent. James summarizes the plot of *Jean de Thommeray* so as to show how the downhill dissipation of the hero is unrealistically, too sentimentally redeemed by patriotism during the Franco-Prussian War. James dismisses *Le Colonel Evrard* as charming in style "though . . . otherwise slight."

Sanders, Mrs. In "Daisy Miller," a woman mentioned as a possible teacher for Daisy Miller's little brother Randolph.

Sandgate, Lady Amy. In *The Outcry*, the novel, and *The Outcry*, the play, Lord Theign's close friend, a mature, modest, and pleasant woman. Breckenridge Bender tries without success to buy the painting by Thomas Lawrence of her great-grandmother, which portrait Lady Amy owns and eventually donates to the National Gallery. Theign will probably propose to her after the end of the action.

Sands, Mary Morton (née Hartpence) (1853–1896). Beautiful, nervous American woman in high London society. She knew important cultural, political, and social figures, including the Prince of Wales (later Edward VII*), William Ewart Gladstone,* Viscount John Morley,* members of the Rothschild family,* John Singer Sargent* (James introduced the two), and Henry White* and his wife, among many others. Mary Hartpence married Mahlon Sands in 1872. (His first wife died in India.) Late in 1883, James met Mary Sands and her husband, whose sister Katherine Sands married Edwin Lawrence Godkin* in 1884. James told Mary Sands in 1885 that the heroine of his "Madame de Mauves" was "a prevision" of her. James and Mrs. Sands were friends until her early death. They exchanged letters and gifts, and shared opinions on literary, social, and political matters. He offered sympathy when her husband was killed when thrown from his horse in Hyde Park (1888). She attended the first performance of *Guy Domville*, in London, on 5 January 1895. In a letter to Godkin (20 Sep [1889]), James calls Mrs. Sands "that gracious lady." In an 1894 letter, James humorously advises her to sit unhelpfully to Sargent so as to challenge the portraitist to his best efforts. She gave James a canary for Christmas in 1895. James attended her Hanover Square memorial service (28 July 1896), and he often wrote to her daughter Ethel Sands (1873–1962), a painter, about her. In a letter to his brother William and his wife Alice (4 Sep 1896), he recalls Mrs. Sands as "a pathetic, *ballottée* creature—with nothing small or mean and with a beauty that had once been of the greatest." In time James came to know Ethel Sands well and to regard her highly. They became Chelsea neighbors when she moved there in 1914. Among her friends were Arnold Bennett, Jacques-Émile Blanche,* André Gide,* Percy Lubbock,* Sir Charles Otto Desmond MacCarthy,* George Moore, Lady Ottoline Violet Anne Morrell,* Logan Pearsall Smith,* Howard Overing Sturgis,* Edith Newbold Jones Wharton,* Virginia Woolf,* and William Butler Yeats. She broadcast her memories of James on British radio (June 1956).

Sands, Miss. In *Watch and Ward*, a New York lady introduced to Roger Lawrence by would-be matchmaker Mrs. Middleton.

Sanguinetti. In "Rose-Agathe," the American-born collector of hairdresser dummies who picks up pretty Rose-Agathe in Paris.

Santayana, George (1863–1952). Cosmopolitan philosopher, man of letters, and professor, born in Madrid, of Spanish parents who had family connections in New England. He came to the United States in 1872, lived in Boston, and earned undergraduate and doctoral degrees at Harvard (1886, 1889), where he studied under William James and where he taught until 1912. Disliking America, Santayana expatriated himself to France, England, and Italy. He published widely and in many forms. His works were issued in fourteen volumes (1936–1937). As early as 1893, James who was reading Santayana's poetry, remarked in a letter to William Morton Fullerton* (4 Feb 1893) that "Santyana's [sic] sonnets [later included in *Sonnets and Other Verses* (1894)] are very delicate indeed and verge upon the exquisite—or *would*, if one didn't feel they were not *naïfs*—not somewhat painfully distilled." Later, James read Santayana's *Interpretations of Poetry and Religion* (1900), which William James had recommended and which in a letter to William (22 May 1900) James calls "an irresistible distraction." He also wrote to Gaillard Thomas Lapsley* (25 Dec 1913) that he "prize[d]" Santayana's "admirable mind and style." At the home of Logan Pearsall Smith,* James and Santayana were fellow luncheon guests in 1915. In *The Middle Span*, the second volume of his autobiography *Persons and Places* (3 vols., 1944, 1945, 1953), Santayana fondly recalls that "one interview," calls James "subtle and bland," and says that he preferred him to his brother William. James's library contained three books by Santayana.

Sarah. In "The Story of a Masterpiece," Stephen Baxter's beautiful fiancée.

"Saratoga." Travel essay, published in the *Nation* (11 Aug 1870); reprinted in *Portraits of Places*, 1883. Saratoga is different from what James imagined: It is not a "primitive Elysium" but has all "the complex machinery of a city of pleasure"—a Broadway full of shops and loafers, two "monster hotels," a casino, mineral springs, and groups of "dense, democratic, vulgar" people. The women exceed their men, both in quantity and in quality. The men are often "lean, sallow, angular," also smart, entertaining, narrowly experienced, and hard. The women, often ignorant but with unerring instincts, are tastefully if "excessively dressed"—but to do nothing. They are pathetic, and they ought to be in Europe sitting beside castles or in parks, and flirting. But at Saratoga, they often dance with each other. Here, some people dance while others sell horse-racing tickets, all in the same steamy building. The spirit of democracy extends even to the free-roaming children. Because of the bad roads, it is hard to walk out of town and into nature's "beautiful unsoftened freedom" of blackberries, pines, "murmur[ing] . . . air," and distant "blue . . . American hills." But one can get away to the two nearby lakes, for a tavern drink or a philosophically solitary skiff ride.

Sarcey, Francisque (1827–1899). Influential French journalist and drama critic. After teaching briefly, he turned to journalism, wrote for periodicals, including the *Figaro*, then concentrated on writing dramatic criticism (from 1859), notably feuilletons for *Le Temps* (from 1867). He made himself a dictator for decades in this genre. The public welcomed his narrow, increasingly conservative judgments on acting and stage effects: A satisfactory drama should have a tight plot, tight form, and tense conflict. His works include *Comédiens et comédiennes* (1878–1884) and *Quarante ans de théâtre* (1890); the latter is a selection of his dramatic feuilletons. In "Parisian Topics" (19 Feb 1876), James calls Sarcey a master at the informal academic lecture. In "The Théâtre Français" (1877) James commends the periodical publications of what became Sarcey's *Comédiens et comédiennes*, noting that reputations depend on this critic, who writes with "pictorial force." In 1889 James wrote to his brother William (28 Nov [1889]) from Paris that he had recently dined with Sarcey, among other named jingoistic Frenchmen. In "The Present Literary Situation in France" (1899), he remarks that Sarcey was for thirty years "a massive and genial figure" and yet was "little of a light" and displayed "vulgarity of judgment."

Sardou, Victorien (1831–1908). Popular Paris-born playwright. He was rescued from garret poverty and sickness by a benefactress whom he later married. Success came fast, and he soon was as popular as Guillaume Victor Émile Augier* and Alexandre Dumas *fils*.* Sardou was elected to the French Academy in 1878. He used the works of Augustin Eugène Scribe* as partial models for his well-made plays, which combine tight construction, lively plot, quick and easy dialogue, thin characterization, and theatrical effects. Among Sardou's seventy or so plays are works in these genres: comedy of manners (*Les Pattes de mouche* [1860], *Nos intimes* [1861], *La Famille Benoîton* [1865]); political comedy (*Rabagas* [1872]); satire (*Divorçons* [1880]); tragedy (*La Tosca* [1887]); and history play (*Madame Sans-Gêne* [1893], *Robespierre* [1902]). Sardou wrote plays for the brilliant French actresses Virginie Déjazet and Sarah Bernhardt,* including, for the latter, *Fédora* (1882) and *La Tosca* (later the basis for Giocomo Puccini's 1900 opera); he wrote *Robespierre* for Sir Henry Irving.* James knew innumerable Sardou plays well and comments briefly on several in early reviews. In "Paris Revisited" (1875), he calls Sardou a "supremely skillful contriver and arranger." In "The Parisian Stage" (1876), he praises Sardou's *Ferréol* (1875) as "[t]he most successful play of the winter . . . and . . . also the best." In "The London Theatres" (1877), he pronounces *Nos intimes* one of the playwright's "cleverest comedies," disagreeing when some call it immoral, and he adds that *Peril*, the 1876 English adaptation of *Nos intimes*, is immoral through being so "ill-made." In "London Pictures and London Plays" (1882), James discusses an English arrangement of Sardou's "ingenious comedy" *Odette* (1881), with fine sets and excellent acting; but he adds that *Odette* is not "the best [work by] . . . the author of the most successful pieces of our time," even though it "hangs neatly together." In a letter to Frances Anne Kemble* (24 Feb [1881]), James calls *Divorçons* "genuine comedy, without French morality." When James began to think of writing plays, he informed his brother William (1 May [1878]) that he had "thoroughly mastered Dumas, Augier and Sardou . . . and I know all they know," as though that might guarantee his success. In his 1893 notes to himself for converting his short story "The Chaperon" into a play, James comments on the importance of an absent character in Sardou's *La Famille Benoîton*. James used this device when he created the absent but influential Mrs. Newsome in *The Ambassadors*.

Sargent, John Singer (1856–1925). American bachelor painter, born in Florence, Italy. His father was an expatriate Philadelphia physician; his mother, a cultured musician who suffered from hypochondria. Sargent studied in an art academy in Florence and sketched as a boy in various parts of western Europe. As a formal art student in Paris, he made Diego de Silva y Velasquez* his ideal. He first visited the United States in 1876, partly to establish his American citizenship. He studied Velasquez in Madrid, went on to Morocco, and then to Haarlem to view paintings by Franz Hals. Sargent exhibited his controversial *Madame G* (of courtesan Madame Gautreau) in the 1884 Paris Salon; the ensuing scandal forced him to London, where, by the time of his *Carnation, Lily, Lily, Rose*, he achieved fame. Sargent was a stylish, elegant virtuoso with colors and light. He did problematic work for the Boston Public Library (1890–1910). He was at the height of his fame in the 1890s. He was made a member of the Royal Academy in 1894 and declined knighthood fifteen years later. Sargent painted portraits of Ruth Draper,* Isabella Stewart Gardner* (who purchased his famous *El Jaleo*), Henry Lee Higginson (which portrait James mentions in *The American Scene*), Coventry Patmore, Violet Paget* (who says she loaned him her paint box when he was a child), Edith Playfair (wife of Baron Lyon Playfair*), Theodore Roosevelt,* Mary Morton Sands,* Robert Louis Stevenson,* Margaret White (wife of diplomat Henry White*), Dame Ellen Terry,* and James, among many others. After about 1910 Sargent concentrated on huge murals and impressionistic watercolors, in some of which he went beyond Joseph Mallord William Turner* and Winslow Homer toward expressionism. James met Sargent in Paris, in February 1884, and was immediately struck by his intelligence, charm, and modesty. He wrote to Grace Norton* (23 Feb 1884) that the painter "has high talent, a charming nature, artistic and personal, and is civilized to his finger-tips." A few months later James wrote to Elizabeth Boott* (2 Jun 1884) from London, to which city he energetically helped induce Sargent to move, that "I like him extremely (he is more intelligent about artistic things than all the painters here rolled together) and in short we are excellent friends." Later James explained in a letter to Henrietta Reubell* (11 Mar [1886]) that "Paris taught him [Sargent] how to paint so well that she can't teach him better, and . . . he is . . . wise to apply all this acquired power here, where he can get such fine models and subjects. . . . Sargent seems . . . to *like* London, its social opportunities and great variety. . . . Why, therefore, should he be chained all his life to the school from which he has graduated?" In 1885 Sargent sent Robert, Comte de Montesquiou-Fezensac* to James, who introduced that odd man to James Abbott McNeill Whistler,* as promised. By 1886 Sargent was leasing space in the Worchestershire studio of Francis David Millet,* along with Edwin Austin Abbey,* both American artist friends of James whom Sargent sketched there. Letters at about this time and later indicate that James was following Sargent's social progress and his exhibitions of female portraits, only some of which James liked. In 1887 he wrote a major essay entitled "John S. Sargent" (*Harper's New Monthly Magazine*, Oct 1887; reprinted in *Picture and Text*, 1893). He begins by wondering whether Sargent is American, since he was born in Florence and studied in Paris, where he was hailed as an impressionist. He has often "commemorate[d] the fair faces of women." James praises two of Sargent's works, which are "emphatically . . . his finest": his portrait of a young woman (*Miss Burckhardt*) and his picture of *The Daughters of Edward D*[arley] *Boit*.* James describes both works lovingly, then adverts to the artist's earlier devotion to "the god of his idolatry," Velasquez. From his Spanish sojourn came Sargent's *El Jaleo*, which features a Spanish dancer and which James describes. He regards the depiction of the children victorious impressionism; that of the dancer, less so. But Sargent is so knowledgeable that he "does not fear emergencies" and experiments out of exuberance, even wastefully. James recalls several portraits, noting that so many of their subjects have been French that some of "the physiognomy of this nation . . . perhaps remains in the brush with which . . . he represents other types." Now for *Madame G* which "excited a kind of unreasoned scandal": It is a "superb picture, noble in conception and masterly in line." James calls attention to the intense femininity of Sargent's *Lady Playfair* and *Mrs. Henry White*. He is glad to note that adverse criticism of three 1886 Royal Academy canvases, which have an almost impertinent brilliance, clears the air so as to allow people their own "unborrowed impression." James closes with the hope that Sargent's future will bring more portraits. "There is no greater work of art than a great portrait," he concludes, and a portrait is best when it combines "quick perception" and "brooding reflection." Charles Waterlow, the impressionistic painter in James's 1888 novel *The Re-*

verberator, may be based on Sargent in part. Sargent attended the first performances of James's plays *The American*, in London, on 26 September 1891, and *Guy Domville*, in London, on 5 January 1895. James discusses Sargent in three miscellaneous "London" notes. In "London" (23 Jan 1897), he calls Sargent's Patmore portrait a "magnificent work"; in "London" (5 Jun 1897), he calls Sargent's *Mrs. Hammersley* "the very finest flower of a method all shimmering off into mystery"; but in "London" (26 Jun 1897), he calls Sargent's portrait of Ellen Terry as Lady Macbeth a "curiosit[y]." In 1912 Edith Newbold Jones Wharton* commissioned Sargent to do a charcoal drawing of James. In 1913 a number of James's friends (269, to be exact) subscribed to a fund, handled by Percy Lubbock,* to commission Sargent to paint what became his famous portrait of James. Sargent asked that the money raised for the portrait be assigned to sculptor Francis Derwent Wood* for a James bust (sat for, July 1913). During some of the nine required London sittings for Sargent, the portraitist encouraged friends of James, including Ruth Draper and Dudley Jocelyn Persse,* to come by and chat. James liked the resulting portrait (willed to the National Portrait Gallery, London), calling it in a letter to Rhoda Broughton* (25 Jun 1913) "a living breathing likeness and a masterpiece of painting." However, Jacques-Émile Blanche,* who had painted James's portrait in 1908, disliked Sargent's portrait of James, calling it (in his *Portraits of a Lifetime*) that of "a business man from the provinces." In May 1914, an unbalanced suffragette named Mary Wood used a meat cleaver to chop at the portrait, then on exhibition at the Royal Academy; later, she attempted to explain that she had done so to fight for women's freedom. Sargent successfully repaired the three gashes inflicted on the painting. James's *Notebooks* are dotted with brief comments on Sargent, his sisters Emily Sargent (James's Carlyle Mansions* neighbor) and Violet Sargent Ormond, and the latter's daughter Rose Marie Ormond Michel. James had Christmas dinner in 1914 with Emily and her brother.

Sartoris family. An English family, some of whose members James knew. They include Adelaide Kemble Sartoris, opera singer and sister of Frances Anne Kemble*; Adelaide's husband Edward Sartoris; their son Algernon Sartoris; and his wife Nelly Grant Sartoris, daughter of Ulysses Simpson Grant.* Lord Frederick Leighton* drew a picture of Adelaide Sartoris.

Saulges, M. de. In "A Tragedy of Error," Vicomte Louis de Meyrau's friend.

Saunt, Flora Louise. In "Glasses," the beautiful young woman whose approaching blindness (aggravated by vanity) causes Lord Iffield to decline marriage with her but enables faithful Geoffrey Dawling to win her hand.

Savage. In *Roderick Hudson*, a mild consular official and evidently Christina Light's father; long dead.

Savoy. In "In the Cage," a name mentioned in a Lady Bradeen telegram.

Scarabelli, Count. In "The Diary of a Man of Fifty," Countess Bianca Salvi's daughter Countess Bianca Salvi-Scarabelli's deceased husband.

Scarabelli, Countess Bianca. In "The Diary of a Man of Fifty," the short name of Bianca Salvi's daughter Bianca Salvi-Scarabelli.

Scarabelli, Signorina. In "The Diary of a Man of Fifty," Countess Salvi-Scarabelli's little daughter.

Schack (or Schmack), Baron. In *The Awkward Age*, Algie Manger's rich pupil.

Schafgans. In *Roderick Hudson*, a German painter in Rome. Mme. Grandoni knew him a long time ago.

Schérer, Edmond (1815–1889). French Protestant journalist and clergyman, professor in Geneva, and literary critic. James reviewed (*Nation*, 12 Oct 1865) Schérer's *Nouvelles études sur la littérature contemporaine* (1865), declaring that its eclectic author's steady theme is "the love of liberty." Schérer conforms to the notion of the "ideal critic" of Matthew Arnold.* James contrasts in detail "great" (general, philosophical) and "small" (particular, historical) critics, exemplified respectively by Johann Wolfgang von Goethe* and Charles Augustin Sainte-Beuve,* whom he regards as the greatest living critic, with Schérer next. James likes his morality and consequent melancholy. James is tempted to place Hippolyte Taine* above Schérer, except that the former is more a philosopher-historian than a critic. James barely mentions Schérer's essays here on Mme. de Sévigné and Mme. Roland. Later James reviewed (*Nation*, 6 Apr 1876) Schérer's *Études critiques de littérature* (1876), now stating that the French critic is disappointingly interested in politics, lacks imagination, and has lapses in taste. For example, he does not like William Makepeace Thackeray.* Schérer is fine, however, in rebuking Taine for his high opinion of George Gordon, Lord Byron.* James has explicit reservations about Schérer on John Milton; he admires his comments on Jacques Bossuet and Goethe, but he cannot accept his finding " 'charm' " in German literature, which has normally not "duped" the French.

Schinkel. In *The Princess Casamassima*, a cabinet-maker anarchist. He is the friend of Paul Muniment, Eustace Poupin, and Hyacinth Robinson.

Schmack. In *The Awkward Age*, a variant of the name Schack.

Scholastica. In "Benvolio," the learned object of part of Benvolio's affections.

Schooling, The Babe, Fanny, and Katie. In "A London Life," Wendover's friends. Some or all may be siblings. The Babe is a young male flirt. One Schooling is called Mrs. Schooling.

"The Science of Criticism," critical essay (*New Review*, May 1891; reprinted as "Criticism" in *Essays in London and Elsewhere*, 1893). James begins by complaining that there is too much review writing for periodicals. Magazines resemble mouths to be fed or railroad trains which must be fully loaded with passengers—even if only dummies—before they can move out of the station. Many reviews are vulgar, crude, and stupid, and good literature may be choked by their plenitude. James praises French reviewers for seeming less desperate, for being dignified, exquisite, and selective. Fine critical sense is "absolutely rare" and operates best when combined with "experience and perception." Critics can greatly help artists. The life of a good critic is "heroic, for it is immensely vicarious."

Scott, Sir Walter (1771–1832). Romantic novelist and poet, born in Edinburgh to middle-class, educated parents. In 1786 Scott was apprenticed to his lawyer father, intermittently studied art and law at Edinburgh University (to 1892), married (1897) and had four children (his daughter Charlotte married John Gibson Lockhart,* Scott's biographer), and published a collection of Scottish ballads (3 vols., 1802, 1803). He wrote popular poetry, including *The Lay of the Last Minstrel* (1805), *Marmion* (1808), and *The Lady of the Lake* (1810). Then came a stream of historical novels, beginning with *Waverley* (1814), continuing with others set in seventeenth- and eighteenth-century Scotland, and more branching into medieval times with *Ivanhoe* (1820) and *Quentin Durward* (1823), and the faraway with *The Talisman* (1825). Other popular titles include *The Antiquary* (1816), *Old Mortality* (1816), *Rob Roy* (1818), *The Bride of Lammermoor* (1819), and *Redgauntlet* (1824). Among many nonfictional prose works is a biography of Napoleon (1827). Scott became rich and lived well at Abbotsford (from 1812) until the collapse (1826) of the publishers with whom he was associated. He honorably assumed a debt of £120,000, wrote steadily to clear it to the penny, hurt his health in the process, sustained the first of several strokes in 1830, went briefly to Italy, and soon thereafter died. His best fiction combines accurate natural description, solid historical background, folklore, colloquial speech, and romantic characterization and action. He is the father of the melodramatic historical novel. Although James never published an essay devoted to Scott alone, he often mentions him and names specific works, knowledgeably, usually with respect, and implying that he is a measure of excellence. For one example among several, in his 1867 review of a work by Anne E. Manning,* James includes Scott among "[t]he great novelists." When devoting essays to Honoré de Balzac,* George Sand,* Ivan Sergeyevich Turgenev,* Émile Zola,* and lesser Continental writers, James often brings in Scott, always in compliment. In three of his prefaces to *The Novels and Tales of Henry James*, James mentions Scott, again in high praise; for example, in the preface to Volume V, he calls Scott and nine other world-class writers "fine painters of life." To be sure, in his first critical review, that of Nassau William Senior* in 1864, James agrees that Senior "correctly holds" that Scott has many defects; but he goes on to defend him, calling him a "great success" and likening him to "a strong and kindly elder brother" improvising yarns for us "at eventide." In one Notebook entry (26 Dec 1881), James more privately touches on "the badness" of *Red-gauntlet*, associating the work with "*l'enfance de l'art.*" It may be demonstrated that James got the phrase "virtuous attachment," used in *The Ambassadors*, from Scott's 1815 *Quarterly Review* essay on *Emma*, in which Scott praises Jane Austen* for depicting the human heart at the service of virtue. James's library contained three nonfictional books by Scott.

Scribe, Augustin Eugène (1791–1861). Paris-born author of several hundred suspenseful, "well-made" plays, mostly about bourgeois society praising realistic aspects of business and family life. He was elected to the French Academy in 1836. He influenced Guillaume Victor Émile Augier,* Alexandre Dumas *fils*,* and Victorien Sardou,* among others. Scribe became rich and treated his several collaborators generously. His best plays include *Le Verre d'eau* (1840), *Une Châine* (1841), *Adrienne Lecouvreur* (1849), and *Bataille des dames* (1851). He wrote many libretti for operas, notably *La Juive* (1835) and *Les Huguenots* (1836). James calls *Une Châine* a "clever comedy," in his essay "The Théâtre Français"; and *Batailles des Dames*, "a clever light comedy" which "belongs at this time of day to the dramatic scrap-bag," in his "The London Theatres" (1879). James's library contained one book by Scribe.

Scrope, Magdalen. In "De Grey, A Romance," a woman loved and hence destroyed by Paul De Grey, an ancestor of the present Paul De Grey.

Scrope, Sam. In "Adina," the scientist whose greed for Angelo Beati's Tiberian topaz causes him to lose his fiancée Adina Waddington to Beati.

Scudamore, R. P. In *The Reverberator*, a name on luggage in a Paris hotel.

Scudder, Horace Elisha (1838–1902). Boston-born teacher, author, and editor. He graduated from Williams (1858), taught school in New York for three years, then scored a success with his anonymously published *Seven Little People and Their Friends* (1862). He returned to Boston, edited *The Riverside Magazine for Young People* (1867–1870, to which Sarah Orne Jewett* contributed), and began to work in the editorial offices of Houghton, Mifflin (to 1890). Scudder followed Thomas Bailey Aldrich* as editor of the *Atlantic Monthly* (1890–1898). Scudder's many publications include a partly autobiographical study of his missionary brother David Coit Scudder (1864), *The Life and Letters of* [James] *Bayard Taylor*[*] (1884, with Taylor's widow), and a life of James Russell Lowell* (2 vols., 1901). In October 1890 James mailed "The Pupil" to Scudder, then the new editor of the *Atlantic Monthly*, only to have the story rejected, perhaps because of homosexual touches, but more likely because it depicts an American family embarrassing their little son. James answered in two letters, the second of which (4 Mar 1891) includes not only the statement that "I quite fail to see that you . . . treated me fairly," but also the news that *Longman's Magazine* had purchased the story and was publishing it at once. Scudder mended his ways, for during his editorial tenure at the *Atlantic Monthly*, he welcomed "The Marriages," "The Chaperon," "James Russell Lowell," "The Private Life," "Glasses," and *The Old Things* (later retitled *The Spoils of Poynton*). Although Houghton, Mifflin wanted James to write a biography of Lowell in 1902, he declined on the grounds that the 1894 edition of Lowell's letters by his friend Charles Eliot Norton* and the 1901 Scudder biography provided sufficient coverage.

Searle, Clement. In "A Passionate Pilgrim," the present-day Searles' Oxford ancestor.

Searle, Clement. In "A Passionate Pilgrim," an American who returns as "a passionate pilgrim" to England. He tries unsuccessfully to claim Lackley, the estate of his distant cousin Richard Searle. Searle later dies and is buried in England.

Searle, Cynthia. In "A Passionate Pilgrim," the present-day Searles' ancestor. Her younger sister Margaret eloped to Paris.

Searle, Margaret. In "A Passionate Pilgrim," the present-day Searles' ancestor. She left her older sister Cynthia and eloped to Paris with an impoverished violinist.

Searle, Miss. In "A Passionate Pilgrim," Richard Searle's sister.

Searle, Richard. In "A Passionate Pilgrim," the British owner of the estate called Lackley. He is a distant cousin of Clement Searle, the American "passionate pilgrim" who tries to claim Lackley.

Sedgwick, Arthur George (1844–1915). Lawyer, journalist, and editor. He was the son of Theodore Sedgwick, prominent author and diplomat, and of Sarah Ashburner Sedgwick (of the Ashburner family*), and he was the brother of Susan Sedgwick Norton, the wife of James's friend Charles Eliot Norton.* Arthur Sedgwick graduated from Harvard (1864), then entered the Union Army, and was captured by Confederate soldiers, imprisoned at Libby, and paroled as sick

(1864). He graduated from Harvard Law School (1866). Norton encouraged him to publish in the *Nation*, recently cofounded by Norton, Edwin Lawrence Godkin,* and others. Sedgwick was an intermittent member of the staff of the *Nation* (to 1905). He did other editorial work, wrote and also edited law treatises, practiced law in Boston (1868) and New York (1875–1881), and lectured on law. James knew Sedgwick and several members of his family, and occasionally wrote to him on professional matters. At first, he liked Sedgwick, calling him "a very pleasing fellow" in a letter to Thomas Sergeant Perry* (1 Dec 1866). But later in a letter to his brother William (24 Mar [1894]), he criticizes Sedgwick's "big-barrelled unloadedness" and wonders what could ever have made one think the man "promising—if one did." Still later, James saw Sedgwick at times in London. Finally, he wrote to Sedgwick's niece Elizabeth Gaskell Norton (6 Aug 1915) to comment enigmatically on the suicide of the troubled man, who had been badly injured in an automobile accident and developed pneumonia.

Sedley, Henry D. (1835–1899). Boston-born civil engineer, journalist, and novelist. His novels are *Dangerfield's Rest; or, Before the Storm, a Novel of American Life* (1864) and *Marian Rooke; or, The Quest for Fortune, a Tale of the Younger World* (1865). James reviewed (*Nation*, 22 Feb 1866) *Marian Rooke*, calling it "an average novel and a very bad book," and explaining that it is his duty as a critic to point out defects. We cannot easily conclude whether the author is a Yankee or a cockney. He is gratuitously anti-New England and eager to present American vulgarity, thus appealing by vulgar falsities to "the ignorant sympathy of foreign readers." His use of "local color becomes quite appalling." His handling of dialect is coarse and humorless. James details the plot: hero torn between allegiance to father's England and mother's America; Creole heroine torn between Louisiana father and slave mother; etc.

Seemüller, Anne Moncure (née Crane) (1838–1872). American novelist who died young after producing *Emily Chester* (1864), *Opportunity* (1867), and *Reginald Archer* (1871). James wrote a letter (15 Oct 1864) to Charles Eliot Norton,* whom he had not then met, asking permission to write "a notice" for the *North American Review*, which Norton edited, of Seemüller's *Emily Chester* on the ground that it had "gained sufficient . . . notoriety to justify a brief review." He then penned a long, sarcastic one, his fifth publication, for the journal (Jan 1865), calling the novel well-meaning, serious, dull, and worthless. He describes the familiar plot triangle in detail, concentrating on the supposedly perfect but really shadowy heroine, the analysis of whose motives he ridicules. James suggests that Miss Crane has produced an "immoral" book by wrongly theorizing in it that the finer a person is, the more he is "apt to be the slave of his instincts." Her heroine indulges in passion but "without . . . the excuse of loving well." She loathes, yearns, feels only sensations, knows "no deep sorrow," hence is irresponsible and becomes "profoundly vicious." James then reviewed (*Nation*, 5 Dec 1867) *Opportunity*, calling it better than *Emily Chester* because shorter. It, too, is "feeble" and without "the vital spark." He theorizes that a writer's second book is more important than the first. He sketches the plot of *Opportunity* and analyzes its modes of talk, listening, and loving, to show its silliness: "[N]othing comes of it." We have a sweet old couple, seemingly "created only to be destroyed," who leave "three orphans": contrasting brothers and an unrelated girl. Then in comes the "high-toned, free-thinking" heroine, who turns "pedantic and unnatural." Love relationships move toward "a very trivial and silly conclusion."

Senior, Nassau William (1790–1864). Versatile English author. He was educated at Eton and Magdalene College, Oxford, became a barrister in 1819, made his home at Hyde Park Gate (1827–1864), was professor of political economics at Oxford (1825–1830, 1847–1852), and was a member of governmental commissions. He wrote commission reports (on education, factory work and manufacturing, finance, poor laws, population and emigration, and trade), journals of his travels (to Egypt, France, Greece, Ireland, Italy, Malta, and Turkey), and memoirs of his conversations (with François Pierre Guillaume Guizot, Louis Adolphe Thiers, and Alexis de Tocqueville). James's first published review was of Senior's *Essays on Fiction* (1864). James sent it, unsolicited, with a courteous cover letter (30 Jul [1864]) to the editors of the *North American Review*; it was accepted and published (Oct 1864). He begins negatively: Since Senior's book concerns only five novelists, its title is poor; the essays, which are reprints from 1821 to 1857, resemble exhumed corpses "crumbling into nothing" when exposed to the air; "the judgments of intelligent half-critics" such as Senior appeal only to fatigued readers of fiction by reminding them of forgotten trivia. Although Senior discusses Sir Walter Scott,* Harriet Beecher Stowe,* Edward George Bulwer-Lytton, William Makepeace Thackeray,* and a certain "Colonel Senior," James considers only his comments on Scott. Senior notes Scott's manifest defects but still admires his novels, which were written both fast and well. James says that Scott "was the inventor of a new style," "was the first English storyteller," wrote "simply to amuse the reader," depicted the "frail" past "with . . . poetic reverence," and offered a "dazzling array of female[s]." Saying that "it is useless to dogmatize upon Scott," James closes by noting that Senior on Thackeray is "singularly pointless" and that the remarks on Stowe concern slavery not literature.

"The Sense of Newport." Travel essay, published in *Harper's Magazine* (Aug 1906); reprinted in *The American Scene*, 1907.

The Sense of the Past. Incomplete novel (71,800 words), published posthumously in London by Collins, Sons, 1917. It was also published in New York by Scribner, 1917, with part of the printing used as *The Novels and Tales of Henry James*, Volume XXVI, 1918. (Characters: Sir Cantopher Bland, Townsend Coyne, Aurora Coyne, Coyne, Molly Midmore, Nancy Midmore, Peregrine Midmore, Mrs. Midmore, Philip Augustus Pendrel, Ralph Pendrel.) Rich young Ralph Pendrel of New York has written a fine book on how to read history. It so pleased an English relative named Philip Augustus Pendrel that he wills Ralph an eighteenth-century London house. Ralph proposes to the rich widow Aurora Coyne, who has traveled much in Europe and should be delighted at his prospects now; but she rejects him, saying that she wants him to become intellectually great and that he should go and sample the Old World. She suspects that he will never willingly return to America. So Ralph goes to London and delights in the evocative spirit of everything there, especially his Mansfield Square house. Crossing its threshold is like stepping back in time. The tenant in his house is a distant kinswoman, Mrs. Midmore of Hampshire. Her temporary absence permits him to wander about inside. One night a wall portrait, of an ancestor also named Ralph Pendrel—young like himself, with averted face—turns in its frame: The face and figure are like Ralph's. The historical Ralph steps out of the frame, and the two commune. Ralph soon goes to the urbane American ambassador in London and tries to share his extraordinary secret—while the other Ralph is waiting in a cab outside. Ralph now appears to become his eighteenth-century alter ego. He returns to his mansion, where he meets Mrs. Midmore's older daughter, Molly, and then the mother, who is delighted that rich Ralph—Molly's fiancé—is safely back from America to meet them. Intuitively feeling his way in the past, Ralph meets Mrs. Midmore's surly son Peregrine, who reminds him that the family has a younger daughter also. She is Nancy, and Ralph quickly shows an interest in her which distresses the Midmores present. They speak now of Sir Cantopher, the man presumably interested in Nan. Ralph guesses that he must be Sir Cantopher Bland, who soon appears. They fence awhile. Ralph becomes annoyed that they all seem to want to use his wealth and presence. When Sir Cantopher and Mrs. Midmore leave, Perry hints at financial embarrassment, which Ralph generously offers to alleviate. Nan enters, having come daringly alone from Hampshire to see him. Their instantaneous emotional rapport, together with his continuing clairvoyance, bothers thick Perry. Ralph revels in Nan's fresh, direct, modern nature. The period of gestation of *The Sense of the Past* was long. Evidently Rudyard Kipling* suggested that publisher Frank Doubleday ask James to follow "The Turn of the Screw" with another ghost story, and James had written perhaps 30,000 words by 1900. Then William Dean Howells* urged him to do an international ghost story in about 50,000 words for some Chicago publishers. James replied (29 Jun 1900), "I brood . . . on your ingenious, your really inspired, suggestion that I shall give you a ghost, and that my ghost shall be 'international.' " He soon wrote Howells again (9 Aug 1900) to add not only that he had already started such a ghost story but that "I shall not be able to squeeze my subject into 50,000 words." As for real-life models of some of the characters, the ambassador resembles James's friend James Russell Lowell,* while Bland has traits reminiscent of James's friend Sir Hugh Seymour Walpole.* Howells gave up his association with the Chicago firm, and James turned to other matters. Not until World War I had started and made it impossible for him to work further on *The Ivory Tower*, a novel with a contemporary setting, did he return, late in 1914, to *The Sense of the Past*. In November he dictated to Theodora Bosanquet,* his secretary, a long statement of his plans for the work; from December to May 1915, he dictated pages of additional notes, which were printed with the novel in 1917.

Serafina. In "The Madonna of the Future," the unproductive painter Theobald's aging model.

Serao, Matilde (1856–1927). Greek-born Italian novelist and journalist, who lived in Naples (where she was a telegraph clerk for a time) and Rome, and married Eduardo Scarfoglio in 1885 and with him founded the short-lived *Il Corriere di Napoli* (1891). Her leading works are *Cuore infermo* (1881), *Fantasia* (1883), *Fior di passione* (1883), *Piccole anime* (1883), *La Conquista di Roma* (1885), *Ventre di Napoli* (1885), *Addio amore!* (1890), *Il Paese di Cuccagna* (1890–1891), *Castigo* (1893), *Gli Amanti* (1894), *Il Romanzo della fanciulla* (1895), *La Ballerina* (1899), *Storia di due anime* (1904), *Ella non rispose* (1914), and *Mors tua* (1926). In a letter to Grace Norton* (29 Mar 1894), James calls Serao, whom he met in Rome through Count Joseph-Napoléon Primoli,* "the she-Zola of Italy . . . [and] a wonderful little burly Balzac in petticoats—full of Neapolitan life and sound and familiarity." He wrote a long essay (*North American Review*, Mar 1901; reprinted in *Notes on Novelists*, 1914) concerning much of her fiction. He says that he started reading her "striking romantic work" about 1885. He deplores British and American novelists for their timid, "blight[ing]" conventionality, which is indeed seemingly "a conspiracy of silence" designed to preserve "the 'innocence' of literature." Women, now freer, are writing more frankly about sex, he adds. Serao is a Neapolitan journalist— a double advantage! Her works may lack form, but they surely have "remarkable spontaneity" and vividly depict Naples. Still, they do not quite fulfill her promise. Her specialty is passion, better expressed by the Italian word *passione*, which tends to "sponge . . . everything not itself." *Fantasia* is "all concentration and erotics," with a sacrificed " 'good' heroine" and a " 'bad' heroine" who faints upon seeing a prize bull at a cattle show! This and other scenes evoke Émile Zola* and Gustave Flaubert.* Serao is best when depicting deprived people, since her well-to-do characters unduly tempt her into fashion and society journalism. "Nella Lava," a story from *Il Romanzo della fanciulla*, is an example of "slice of life" naturalism. Too often, Venus in Serao's fiction, by taking up all the space, wrongly modifies truth and beauty, and leaves "dry desolation . . . behind her." Serao's lovers, lighted by a "flood of flaring gas . . . in her pages," have fury but lack affection, duration, friends, children. The effect of such fiction is comic, without either dignity or gaiety. So let taste and discretion guard against such "new . . . vulgarity." James closes by wistfully preferring

Jane Austen.* An episode from *Il Romanzo della fanciulla*, which was originally entitled *Telegrafi dello Stato*, may partly have inspired James's own "In the Cage," about a female telegraphist. James's library contained one book by Serao.

"The Servant." The first, tentative title for "Brooksmith."

Servants. James was accustomed to having servants from his earliest years. At various times during his long residence in England, he employed the following servants: Joan Anderson, cook and housekeeper; George Gammon, gardener and carpenter; Minnie Kidd, house-parlor maid; Burgess Noakes,* houseboy and then valet; Mrs. Paddington, cook and housekeeper; Alice Skinner, parlor maid; Mr. and Mrs. Smith, butler and cook (discharged for drinking to excess).

Server, May. In *The Sacred Fount*, the woman who may be Gilbert Long's "sacred fount."

Severn, Captain Edmund. In "Poor Richard," the Union Army officer who during the Civil War loves but fails to propose marriage to Gertrude Whittaker because of her wealth. He is killed in the war.

Seymour, Mrs. In *A Change of Heart*, an unseen ghost, as are her daughters, at Margaret Thorne's birthday party.

Seymour, The Misses. In *A Change of Heart*, unseen guests, as is their mother, at Margaret Thorne's birthday party.

Shakespeare, William (1564–1616). World-renowned English playwright and poet, born in Stratford-upon-Avon, educated in a grammar school there, and married in 1582; he left the area in 1585. He was in London beginning in 1586 and became associated with theaters, soon as an actor. He had begun writing plays by 1591, published two long poems few years later, also wrote sonnets (published 1609), and purchased a large house in Stratford in 1597. Meanwhile he was steadily producing brilliant histories, comedies, and tragedies, during the end of Queen Elizabeth I's reign and the beginning of James I's (1603). Evident personal gloom in Shakespeare's life at this time resulted in his monumental tragedies and then his final romances. Shakespeare settled back in Stratford about 1610. James revered Shakespeare all his life; he mentions his works in his *Notebooks*, letters, autobiographical writings, and criticism. He attended the theater before he was ten, recalls attending his first Shakespearean experience, *A Comedy of Errors* (he entitled his first short story "A Tragedy of Errors") about 1855, soon thereafter saw *Much Ado about Nothing*, *A Midsummer Night's Dream*, and *King Henry VIII*, read Charles and Mary Lamb's retelling of Shakespeare's plots, often visited Stratford, wrote of Warwickshire, during his later

years attended performances of Shakespeare's plays by the best actors and actresses in America and abroad, and read more of his works. James reviewed
eleven productions of Shakespeare (1873–1896). In "Tommaso Salvini" (1883),
James curiously protests that *King Lear*, "the most sublime, possibly, of all
dramatic poems," should not be acted. In "London" (23 Jan 1897), he expresses
a preference for reading Shakespeare's plays and for seeing those of Henrik
Johan Ibsen.* As for the Baconians, in a letter (5 Dec 1902) to his friend Manton
Marble, New York *World* editor, James says that "the plays and the sonnets
were never written but by . . . a Poet and Nothing Else, . . . who . . . could never
be a Bacon . . . into the bargain." When his friend Sir Sidney Lee* was editing
The Complete Works of Shakespeare, James wrote a preface to *The Tempest* for
Lee's Volume XVI (New York: Sproul, 1907). This long essay, which is complex
and obscure, but revealing, begins by noting that we do not have "conditions
of . . . birth" of Shakespeare's works, especially *The Tempest*, which resembles
an "unwinking and inscrutable . . . divinity in a temple." Brief, simple, and
elegant, it was first performed only three years or so before its mysterious author's
death. Shakespeare was then still young, having begun to write when "a monster
of precocity—which [James adds] all geniuses of the first order are not." After
The Tempest, could Shakespeare have lapsed into silence? Certainly not because
of any decline of artistic power. In *The Tempest* is his awareness of unique
creative "Expression." From whatever angle we approach this author, we never
do so with many facts about him. "The man . . . is . . . imprisoned in the artist,"
who "plunges" into his characters. Here James names a dozen of his favorites.
In Shakespeare we find a "conjunction" of "his charged inspiration and his
clarified experience," or, let us say, "his human curiosity and his aesthetic
passion." James "surrender[s]" to Shakespeare's unique "artistic consciousness," praises *The Tempest* for showing his mind and skill best, and then images
the Bard as "a divine musician" improvising alone at his instrument "in the
summer dusk." With him, expression was a "force," a "passion," "the greatest
ever laid upon man." He poured it like a glittering, clinking "treasure" on the
"great flat table" "of our poor world." Not life but expression was Shakespeare's "paste to be kneaded." He shows us how "style" and "manner" relate
to "meaning" and "motive." For Shakespeare, "Style . . . [was] the joy of life."
Each play has its tone, pushed to reveal character. "The 'story' in *The Tempest*
is a thing of naught." Any plot can provide us "a shipwreck and a coincidence."
James takes up some critics and their approaches. First he disagrees that "Pros-
pero's surrender of his magic" parallels Shakespeare's own. Would the Bard
"shut down the lid, from one day to another, on the most potent aptitude for
vivid reflection ever lodged in a human frame"? James expresses annoyance at
the notion that the plays and sonnets of "the Poet" tell us all we need to know
about "the Man." It must be that poet and man interpenetrate: "[W]e are here
in presence of the human character the most magnificently endowed, in all time,
with the sense of the life of man, and with the apparatus for recording it." So
we want to know how his gift affected him. His life may have been "mainly
inward," but his "spirit [was] in hungry quest." James images Shakespeare as

a man leaping out of his window into the street to pursue "experience and adventure." We watch but lose sight of him. He "slink[s] past" us. What could have become of his torrential energy after *The Tempest*? We seek the answer in "recorded circumstances which are . . . dim and few." We seek by indirections, since "we shall never touch the Man *directly* in the Artist." In the prefaces to *The Portrait of a Lady*, *The Princess Casamassima*, and *The Tragic Muse*, James notes that several characters in those novels owe something to aspects of Portia, Hamlet, and King Lear; these prefaces are, respectively, in *The Novels and Tales of Henry James*, Volumes III, V, and VII (all 1908). Deriving from Shakespeare are many characters, themes, and plot situations in James's fiction, most notably "The Birthplace," in which the birthplace though unspecified is clearly that of the man from Stratford. Furthermore, "Master Eustace" and *The Ivory Tower* may owe something to *Hamlet*; "Guest's Confession" may owe something to *The Merchant of Venice*; "The Papers," to *As You Like It*; "The Bench of Desolation," to *The Winter's Tale*; and *The Outcry*, to *King Lear*. James's library contained one book of Shakespeare's poems, another just of his sonnets, and two editions of his works.

Shaw, George Bernard (1853–1950). Versatile Dublin-born playwright, critic, economist, reformer, and novelist. He moved to London (1876), was unsuccessful for a while, evolved as a forceful public speaker and debater (1883–1895), wrote tracts and otherwise worked for the Fabian Society in London (1884–1911, associating early with William Morris,* among other socialists), composed five wretched novels (1879–1883), and turned to journalism (1885–1898), publishing criticism on art, drama, literature, and music. He praised the dramas of Henrik Johan Ibsen* and downgraded those of Sir Arthur Wing Pinero.* Shaw and the actress Dame Ellen Terry* exchanged more than three hundred letters (1896–1922). He sought to emancipate her from the professional restrictions of producer-actor Sir Henry Irving.* Shaw wrote many vapid love letters to the actress Mrs. Patrick Campbell.* He had started a play with William Archer in 1885, which he later reworked into *Widowers' Houses* (1892), with Ibsen as his inspiration. Shaw's *The Quintessence of Ibsenism* (1891, 1913) shows his understanding of and reverence for Ibsen. Shaw continued as a busy playwright, collecting seven efforts in *Plays Pleasant and Unpleasant* (1898, including *Mrs. Warren's Profession* and *Candida*, the latter written to star Ellen Terry), and continuing with one controversial play after another. His friend the producer Harley Granville Granville-Barker* was of great help, especially from 1904 to 1907; from 1918, Granville-Barker's second wife, the former Helen Huntington, who hated Shaw, kept the friends apart. Shaw's titles include *Arms and the Man* (1894, an international favorite), *The Devil's Disciple* (1897, a financial success), *Caesar and Cleopatra* (1900), *Man and Superman* (1903), *John Bull's Island* (1904), *Major Barbara* (1907), *Fanny's First Play* (1911, a long-running success), *Pygmalion* (1912, produced with great financial success by Sir Herbert Beerbohm Tree* in 1914), and *Androcles and the Lion* (1913).

Shaw became unpopular during World War I because of his pacifism, his attack on alleged official British hypocrisy, and a seemingly pro-German stance, as expressed in his pamphlet *Common Sense about the War* (1914). His *Heartbreak House* (1917) was followed by *Back to Methuselah* (1921), *Saint Joan* (1923), and more plays. Shaw attended the first performance of James's *Guy Domville*, in London, on 5 January 1895, liked its delicate dialogue, fine story, and touching climax, and reviewed the play favorably. But in January 1909 he rejected James's play *The Saloon* when it was submitted to a stage society for which he was a reader; he wrote to James that the work did not encourage the people to throw off the burden of the past and strive for social change. In the exchange of letters which followed, James defended his play as artistically and historically sound. James and Shaw were basically antithetical: James favored artistic shapeliness, fine psychology, and subtle dialogue; Shaw was impatient, polemical, and didactic. Both, however, wrote explanatory prefaces to their best works. During the war, James wrote to his agent James Brand Pinker* (6 Jan 1915) to brand Shaw's anti-British pamphlet a "huge . . . frivolity." It has been said that Peter Quint in "The Turn of the Screw" resembles Shaw as a young man. James's library contained one book of plays by Shaw.

"She and He: Recent Documents." Critical essay on George Sand* (*Yellow Book*, Jan 1897).

Shelley, Percy Bysshe (1792–1822). English romantic poet, born in Sussex to wealth. He attended University College, Oxford, until he was expelled for circulating his pamphlet on atheism. Shelley married Harriet Westbrook in 1811 and traveled; she drowned herself in 1816. He married Mary Wollstonecraft Godwin in 1816, and they visited George Gordon, Lord Byron* in Switzerland. From 1818 on, the Shelleys, sometimes with Mary's stepsister Mary Jane— Clare—Clairmont,* who became one of Byron's mistresses, lived in Italy. Shelley was drowned while sailing off Spezzia. His works include *Queen Mab* (1813), *Alastor* (1816), *The Revolt of Islam* (1818), *Prometheus Unbound* (1820), *The Cenci* (1820), wondrous lyrics, and *A Defence of Poetry* (1840). James never devoted an essay to Shelley but mentions him often. In a Notebook entry (12 Jan 1887), he records an incident in the later life of Shelley's sister-in-law, whom he names "Miss Claremont," which inspired him to write "The Aspern Papers." In his 1893 review of the correspondence of Gustave Flaubert,* James calls Shelley "a 'poets' poet.' " In his 1877 review of the biography of Alfred de Musset* by his brother Paul, James praises Shelley's "energy and curiosity" and inner toughness. In a letter to Urbain Mengin* (1 Jan 1903), he calls Shelley "one of the great poets of the world, of the rarest, highest effulgence, the very genius and incarnation of poetry . . . " In his 1912 address on Robert Browning,* James says that "Shelley . . . is a light and [Algernon Charles] Swinburne[*] . . . a sound; Browning alone . . . is a temperature."

Sherringham, Peter. In *The Tragic Muse*, Julia Sherringham Dallow's diplomat brother. He loves but fails to win actress Miriam Rooth and is loved hopelessly by Nick Dormer's sister Bridget Dormer.

Sholto, Captain Godfrey Gerald. In *The Princess Casamassima*, the Princess Casamassima's attendant. He introduces Hyacinth Robinson to the princess and also attracts Hyacinth's girlfriend Millicent Henning.

Shorter, Clement King (1857–1926). English literary critic, journalist, and editor. His first wife, Dublin-born Dora Sigerson Shorter (1866–1918), a poet and novelist, supported the Irish literary revival. After a trying childhood and early youth including odd jobs, night schools, and vacation study, Shorter became a gossip columnist in London (from 1888), then an editor (from 1891) of two illustrated periodical publications, the *Illustrated London News* and the *English Illustrated Magazine*. In 1893 he founded and edited the *Sketch* (for the *Illustrated London News*), then did other energetic editing, and then founded, edited, and wrote for the *Sphere* (1900–1926) and the *Tatler* (1903). Seven of his books concerned the Brontë sisters,* the most important publication of which was *Charlotte Brontë and Her Circle* (1896, reissued in 1914 as *The Brontës and Their Circle*). Shorter also wrote and edited much else, often exhibiting more rush than acumen. In 1896 Mrs. W. K. Clifford* encouraged Shorter to invite James to send him a love story for publication in the *Illustrated London News*. James dickered by letter ("the sum you name is less than that I am in the habit of receiving"—24 Feb 1896), resurrected *The Other House*, which had first been a dramatic scenario called *The Promise*, then agreed, for £300 (for British serial rights), "to endeavour to be thrilling" over thirteen installments (26 Feb 1896). James hated to keep at his writing chore through the summer, and he wrote first to Arthur Christopher Benson* to complain of "niggling at my little trade" (29 June 1896), and next to Sir Edmund Wilson Gosse* not only "of the fear of breaking down" but also having to feed "the devouring maw" of the *News* (28 Aug [1896]). In "London" (6 Feb 1897), James praises Shorter's *Charlotte Brontë and Her Circle* as "very interesting," although "the decisive word about the unhappy [Brontë] family . . . has still to be written." The letters by the Brontës which Shorter publishes show "how much their unhappiness was the making of their fame."

"The Siege of London." Long short story (32,000 words), published in the *Cornhill Magazine* (Jan–Feb 1883); reprinted in *The Siege of London*, 1883; revised and reprinted in *The Novels and Tales of Henry James*, Volume XIV, 1908. (Characters: Rev. Mr. and Mrs. April, Mrs. Bagshaw, Philadelphus Beck, Davidoff, Sir Arthur Desmesne, Sir Baldwin Desmesne, Lady Desmesne, Agnes Littlemore Dolphin, Reggie Dolphin, Lady Dovedale, Lord Edward, Nancy Grenville Beck Headway, Headway, George Littlemore, Miss Littlemore, Lady Margaret, Max, Rupert Waterville.) George Littlemore is a rich, bored widower.

While with fellow American Rupert Waterville at the Comédie Française, he spots a former acquaintance named Mrs. Nancy Grenville Beck Headway. This attractive, middle-aged, American widow is devotedly attended by Sir Arthur Desmesne. She asks Littlemore, who has a well-married sister in London, to help her get into British society. He declines but is amused by her determined assault, which is the result of a snub by New York society. Desmesne, though puzzled by Mrs. Headway, is attracted to her and introduces her to his widowed mother in Waterville's presence. Next season in London Waterville visits the Desmesne estate, called Longlands, where Mrs. Headway is also a guest. More successful by now, she accuses him of spying on her but then confides to him that Desmesne's mother is hateful. Lady Desmesne then requests information of Waterville but fails to elicit anything adverse about the American woman. Mrs. Headway warns Littlemore in London that Desmesne's mother is going to visit him to ask whether she is corrupt and begs him not to give her away. Next, his sister tells him that Lady Desmesne has written to her for information. Littlemore tells his sister that Mrs. Headway is not respectable but that he will say nothing to jeopardize her chance with Desmesne. He maintains this position with Waterville, who feels that Mrs. Headway is succeeding so well that she ought to be checked. In her presence, Littlemore refuses to say anything adverse to Desmesne. Next day she writes to him that she is engaged. Then his sister brings Lady Desmesne, to whom he says only that Nancy Headway is not respectable. But the marriage occurs anyway. Littlemore finally suspects that irate Waterville fell for her himself. Both in a Notebook entry (24 Nov 1892) and in the preface to Volume XIV of *The Novels and Tales of Henry James*, James says that this story calls to mind the situation of *Le Demi-Monde*, the 1855 play by Alexandre Dumas *fils*,* in which a man wonders whether to tell a man he esteems about the past of a woman he does not. As usual, James gives an old source a new turn.

The Siege of London. Collection of three short stories published in Boston by Osgood, 1883, and in Leipzig by Tauchnitz, 1884: "The Siege of London," "The Pension Beaurepas," and "The Point of View."

"Siena." First part (published in the *Atlantic Monthly*, Jun 1874; reprinted in *Transatlantic Sketches*, 1875) of what became "Siena Early and Late" (1909).

"Siena Early and Late." Two-part travel sketch, combining "Siena" (1874) with a new second part, all in *Italian Hours*, 1909. James begins the first part with a description of the famed Piazza by moonlight: horseshoe in shape, with palace and huge houses. James next enjoyed a week of daylight observing. He lived at the inn, walked the streets, and sat in the Piazza. The built-up hilltops reveal the grand manner of Siena's past, but the local colors are at present "peeling, . . . rotting." James describes "sinuous flagged" streets, animated conversations, midnight singing, coffee and ices, "great private palaces" (what part can they play in the city's present shrunken economy?), waiter gossip concerning the aristocracy (still fourteenth-century in outlook), market, artists of the Sienese school (Sodoma and Beccafumi "never efflorescing into a maximum"), and Cathedral (meagre architecturally, though "richly and variously scenic" with superb wood carvings like "frost-work"). The second part makes amends for the scantiness of the first part, amplified now after later visits to Siena. New inns are visible. James remembers the crude Palio. He now stresses Pinturicchio's pictorial Cathedral record of the restless career of Pope Pius II. He visits the Lizza, the fortified promontory, and beyond to the Monte Oliveto convent (a "vast, cold, empty shell" but with "strong and brave" cloister frescoes by Luca Signorelli and Sodoma which defy time).

Silberstadt-Schreckenstein, Grand Duke of. In "The Liar," the nobleman who took Oliver Lyon's portrait of Everina Brant Capadose, according to her liar of a husband.

Silberstadt-Schreckenstein, Prince Adolph of. In *The Europeans*. See Adolph of Silberstadt-Schreckenstein, Prince.

Simmons, Abijah. In "A Passionate Pilgrim," the present-day Clement Searle's lawyer.

Simpkin. In "In the Cage," the name of a furnished apartment.

Simpson. In "The Story of a Year," Mr. and Mrs. Littlefield's guest at a party also attended by Elizabeth Crowe.

Singleton, Sam. In *Roderick Hudson*, Roderick Hudson's and Rowland Mallet's ineffectual but plodding and likable American painter friend in Rome. Some of his characteristics may be based on those of Eugene Benson,* a painter James knew in Italy.

"Sir Dominick Ferrand" (1892 title, "Jersey Villas"; 1893 title, "Sir Dominick Ferrand"). Short story (20,200 words), published in the *Cosmopolitan Magazine* (Jul–Aug 1892); reprinted in *The Real Thing and Other Tales*, 1893. (Characters: Peter Baron, Mrs. Bundy, Sir Dominick Ferrand, Locket, Morrish, Sidney Ryves, Mrs. Ryves, Miss Teagle.) Peter Baron is an unsuccessful young writer whose material does not interest Locket, the editor of *The Promiscuous Review*. Baron buys an old desk; and when Sidney, the young son of his rooming-house neighbor widowed Mrs. Rvyes, is playing near it, he finds some secret papers, which prove to be damaging to the reputation of Sir Dominick Ferrand, a once-renowned public figure now dead. Mrs. Ryves is a music teacher, and she and Baron write a song together. She declines his proposal of marriage. When he shows the Ferrand letters to Locket, the sensation-seeking editor offers

£300 for them and also agrees to take some of the young man's fiction. But Baron decides that he has no right to besmirch the dead man's name and burns the letters. The moment he does so, Mrs. Ryves appears, almost occultly, reports that their song has been accepted for publication, and accepts his renewed proposal. First she must tell him a deep, dark family secret: She is Sir Dominick Ferrand's illegitimate daughter. This story, about biographers' impropriety, sprang almost full-blown from the recesses of James's being. In a Notebook entry (26 Mar 1892), James jotted down "[t]he idea of the *responsibility* of destruction—the destruction of papers, letters, records, etc., connected with the private and personal history of some great and honoured name and throwing some very different light on it from the light projected by the public career." James then seems to have made up the plot of this story as fast as he could add to the same entry.

"Sir Edmund Orme." Short story (10,700 words), published in *Black and White* (25 Nov 1891); reprinted in *The Lesson of the Master*, 1892; revised and reprinted in *The Novels and Tales of Henry James*, Volume XVII, 1909. (Characters: Captain Teddy Bostwick, Charlotte Marden, Major Marden, Mrs. Marden, Sir Edmund Orme.) The narrator meets widowed Mrs. Marden and her attractive daughter Charlotte at Brighton. As they talk, Mrs. Marden turns pale and later drops a cup of tea handed to her—evidently not even seeing it. At a nearby estate called Tranton the narrator, falling in love with Charlotte, sees a ghost sitting beside her in church. Mrs. Marden also sees it, but her daughter does not. The narrator proposes to Charlotte that evening—while the ghost looks on. When the aloof girl retires to ponder the proposal, her mother proceeds to tell the narrator that years ago Sir Edmund Orme loved her but she married another, upon which Orme poisoned himself. After her husband's death, Orme's ghost began to haunt her. Next day the discouraged narrator, bidding goodbye to Charlotte, sees the ghost again and feels that it is on his side. At Brighton again, three months later, the narrator sees Charlotte once more; but before they can talk much, they both see a darkened figure nearby. Is it the ghost? Charlotte quickly goes to her fainting mother inside. Next day the narrator is summoned by Mrs. Marden, who though now dying is happy to say that Charlotte wants to marry him. The ghost stands near the mother. Charlotte sees it and rushes into the narrator's embrace. The mother dies, and the ghost is never seen again. In a Notebook entry (22 Jan 1879), James records the idea which more than a decade later turned into his first representatively Jamesian ghost story: "A young girl . . . is followed . . . by a figure which other persons see. She is . . . unconscious of it—but there is a dread that she may cease to be so. . . . Her mother dies, and the narrator . . . discovers . . . that the figure is that of a young man whom she has jilted in her youth, and who . . . committed suicide." In the preface to Volume XVII of *The Novels and Tales of Henry James*, James says that he delights in the theme of "unconscious . . . *hauntedness*," then explains that "the penalty suffered by the mother" here because of "some hardness . . . of her own youth'' is to see her daughter, though for now ''in . . . blest ignorance,'' endangered by the ''forked lightning'' of ''a dark visitation.''

Sitwell, Frances (1839–1924). British society woman with whom James shared information about their esteemed friend Robert Louis Stevenson.* James was later a guest at her wedding ceremony, in June 1903, when she married Sir Sidney Colvin.*

Sixty American Opinions on the War. A book of quotations from eminent Americans concerning World War I, edited by Samuel Robertson Honey and James Fullarton Muirhead (London: Unwin, 1915). Contributors include John Burroughs,* John Jay Chapman,* Richard Harding Davis,* George Brinton McClellan Harvey,* William Dean Howells,* Robert Underwood Johnson,* Agnes Repplier,* Theodore Roosevelt,* and James. James permitted the inclusion of part of a letter in which he praises the ''moral position'' of ''grand old'' England for its present militant stand—all the more admirable considering its limited preparation time. He feels that the present moment is the finest hour in England's grand history.

Sketches and Studies in Local Colour. The tentative title for a collection of essays which James planned and about which he wrote to Sir Frederick Orridge Macmillan* (8 May [1883]). It was never published, but some of its contents may have been included in *Portraits of Places.*

Slater, Tim. In ''A Round of Visits,'' Newton Winch's business friend.

Sloane, Frederick. In ''A Light Man,'' a dying man whose wealth both Theodore Lisle and Maximus Austin want but fail to seize.

Sloper. In *Washington Square*, Dr. Austin Sloper's son, who died at the age of three.

Sloper, Catherine. In *Washington Square*, Dr. Austin Sloper's plain, firmminded, good daughter. She refuses to abide by his wishes concerning Morris Townsend, who is the materialistic object of her steady affections. The two do not marry.

Sloper, Catherine Harrington. In *Washington Square*, Catherine Sloper's deceased mother. She and her husband Dr. Austin Sloper married in 1820 and had a son who died at the age of three. Mrs. Sloper then died after five years of marriage, while giving birth to their daughter.

Sloper, Dr. Austin. In *Washington Square*, the autocratic father of Catherine Sloper. He disapproves of and rightly judges her grasping suitor Morris Townsend. Dr. Sloper is Lavinia Sloper Penniman's and Elizabeth Almond's brother.

A Small Boy and Others. The first volume of James's projected autobiography, published in New York by Scribner, 1913, and in London by Macmillan and Co., 1913. (The second and third volumes are *Notes of a Son and Brother*, 1914, and *The Middle Years*, 1917.) *A Small Boy and Others* comprises twenty-nine chapters. 1. James, "the brooding painter and fond analyst," starts the book as a memoir of his enviably older brother William, records early memories of numerous family members (including paternal grandmother and fatherless Temple cousins, of the Temple family*) in Albany, and early schooling in Albany and New York. 2. The James boys went to several New York schools, taught by "resolute" women (both American and "imported") and reflecting Europe. New York was a place of railroad construction and browsing animals, near which young James "dawdle[d] and gape[d]." 3. He recalls his early summers: Staten Island resort hotel, salt water, "social scene" there, French-speaking Swiss friend. 4. His mother introduced timid James to family dances in New York (at Washington Square and also in hotels), which remind him of "easy" manners encouraged during his youth and stories of "tipsy" elders. He touches on Charles Sumner and Winfield Scott. 5. The Mexican War makes James think of Robert Temple, his army captain uncle, then French war stories overheard, then his own infant vision of the Place Vendôme in Paris. He defines his family as sheltered, "provided for," but commercially ignorant. He names artists and authors they knew (including Washington Irving* but not Edgar Allan Poe*). 6. New York's Broadway meant Barnum's Museum, while Wall Street meant dental visits (with reading material before and ice cream after). James remembers his indulgent father—shopping with him in fruit stores, his travel stories, shared walks, visiting New York *Tribune* offices. 7. James mentions early reading (both enjoyed and forbidden); recalls a store where he smelled books redolent of England, about which his Aunt Kate (Catherine Walsh*) reminisced; and remembers being daguerreotyped by Matthew Brady in a buttoned jacket which William Makepeace Thackeray* himself admired. 8. Next, James remembers his father's visits to a Mrs. Cannon (near Fourth Street), who sold Eau de "Cullone" and hemmed handkerchiefs, then aspects of Union Square (refreshments), Fourteenth Street (stores), and Sixth Avenue (houses), workmen refurbishing the James residence nearby, and theater placards. 9. In much confused detail, James reminisces on "the old American stage," its offerings and performers (of William Shakespeare* on Chambers Street, a "Lyceum" up Broadway, "the Broadway," Charles Dickens* adaptations, Adelina Patti,* Tripler Hall, Niblo's, and other "temple[s] of the art"), and on family readings of *David Copperfield* by Dickens, sometimes in the presence of orphaned Wyckoff cousins from Albany. 10. James writes of relatives, including the curious Wyckoffs: dictatorial maternal great-aunt, her three children—Alexander (a plague victim),

Helen (and her "spectral spouse"), and "eccentric" Henry. 11. The aunt's ward Albert resembled an Honoré Daumier* cartoon. Helen distrusted her "simple," "blameless" brother Henry and deprived him of his funds [James used this situation as the basis of his play *The Reprobate*]. Eventually numerous female cousins sought Henry Wyckoff's inheritance. 12. James returns to Barnum's Museum and Broadway billboards seen on the way back home, all of which remind him of actress Emily Mestayer and a dramatization (was it absurd or tragic?) of *Uncle Tom's Cabin* by Harriet Beecher Stowe,* theater parties, and acrobats and clowns at Niblo's (somehow mixed in James's mind with European memories). 13. James felt "vague and small" at school compared to others; visited by slow train the military school of cousin Gus Barker (of the Barker family*), nearby Sing-Sing, and an Albany uncle and more cousins (living by the Hudson River); and witnessed a family "scene" there. 14. More about Albany cousins, their connection with business, and the Jameses' indifference to it; also the artistic cousins' interests in Europe. 15. James "broods . . . over" two unathletic schools on Broadway: the Institution Vergnès, with "bristling" M. Vergnès in charge, a noisy staff, and "small homesick Cubans and Mexicans" for fellow pupils; and the "cooler" school run by "genial" Richard Pulling Jenks, with classes in drawing (William learned well) and penmanship. 16. Next Forest's school in arithmetic and bookkeeping (at 14th Street and 6th Avenue, during the 1854–1855 winter), where it was hoped that James would "convert" boredom into virtue but avoid becoming a pedantic prig. His father continued to encourage his humanizing and socializing, but not his competing and being disciplined. He recalls the haughty responses of lads to his inability in mathematics and legerdemain, and he remembers "sticky waffles" purchased at recess. 17. A recent visit by James to New York awakened old memories: friends outside school, street meetings, church being built, embarrassingly eclectic church attendance, rides in rented carriages, Europeanized dancing school (complete with dashing master, fat-footed instructress, fiddlers, and costume balls), and opera academy. 18. James remembers more: goat pastures and florist shops, all gone now; neighborhood children (including some tough boys attending public school, some well-educated ones, some "slim and fair sisters" from Kentucky, whose parents brought two slaves who promptly fled); theatricals managed in friends' attics and parlors by brother William; and growing awareness of social and cultural distinctions. 19. William ably drew pictures and played with boys who cursed, while James stayed home, wrote dramas, and tried to represent the scenes with accompanying pictures (an easier task once the Jameses returned to art-filled Europe). In New York the Düsseldorf art school prevailed (cf. Emanuel Leutze's *Washington*, which James saw one "memorable . . . evening"), but there was Italian art work in the Jameses' parlor. 20. Friends and relatives (Kings, Masons, and members of the Temple family and the Tweedy family*) who knew Italy and Switzerland visited and wrote to the Jameses, thus keeping Europe alive in their yearnings. James can with "ease . . . re-capture" memories of such relatives and tangential "London aspects." Suddenly he recounts his family's move to Europe [July 1855]: Atlantic steamer, Liverpool, London hotel four-poster (sick abed with malarial fever), then Parisian rest, Lyons to Geneva (with Italian courier)—James, though still sick, began to "swig . . . the wine of perception" now. 21. Genial Wilky, the younger James brother, made friends at a boarding school near Geneva, which he attended with William while James was still sick. Later James enjoyed Swiss-style education (friendly teachers, "polyglot" pupils, arcadian tours), to be followed in October by a dash back to Lyons and Paris. 22. On to London: a Scottish tutor, and first a house near Berkeley Square (amid residences now demolished), then another one in St. John's Wood, where "gaping" James sensed echoes of Dickens; visits to London tourist spots (Tower, St. Paul's, Abbey, Madame Tussaud's); French conversations with a "longish procession" of Swiss and French governesses (some with "art and grace"); Hogarthian street scenes. 23. The James parents "formed" their children (now including Bob and Alice) in part by showing them British art, including pictures by pre-Raphaelites (for example, *The Scapegoat* by William Holman Hunt,* which scared James) and drama (for one example, among much else named, Charles Kean in Shakespeare's *Henry the Eighth*). 24. The following summer in a house in Paris, James had a new tutor, who lasted only a few months but under whom he translated Jean de La Fontaine "with . . . felicity." James compares one governess to Rebecca Sharp and recalls visiting her later in London; he describes the 1850s Paris in detail, concluding that "[i]t was not . . . then so beautiful as now" but that he loved Parisian street strolls, the family's "social aspect," and French food. 25. He and William "took long and beguiled walks" (Luxembourg, Champs-Elysées, streets and boulevards, shops for books and prints, vistas, cafés, Tuileries, Palais Royal, works by many named painters—who together "gathered . . . into a vast deafening chorus"—and the magnificent Louvre, especially its Galerie d'Apollon). All of this "Art" uniquely and permanently impressed James with a notion of "Style." 26. James (often with mother, aunt, and older brother) "fumbled" for "the aesthetic clue in general," by means of circuses, vaudevilles, theaters (many uncomfortable), actors and actresses (some old, even "osseus"). 27. James recalls his school at this time, the odd, indescribable Institution Fezandié. More "social . . . than . . . tuitional," it was run by a "sympathetic ex-Fourierist" (which pleased James's father) and had easy activities ("taking *dictées*," reading aloud, practicing his French "r," hearing dramatic recitations, picking up idioms unconsciously, enjoying déjeuners, and mingling with more serious pupils). 28. James rambles on about the school of M. and Mme. Fezandié (too many older students, including supercilious British ones, lessons in French pronunciation, the palpable influence of Honoré de Balzac). He recalls associating in Paris with various New York cousins (taking dawn walks past jewelry stores and playbills with some of them, attending a little one's baptism, memorializing another later killed in the Civil War). 29. James turns to "the vast little subject" of two stays at Boulogne-sur-Mer, where he was small, "ambulant," and observant: "spacious and pompous" rooms in spite of family economies (after the 1857 crash), James's recovery from typhus, more school (Collège Communal), mixed student body (including a pastry cook's son named Benoît Constant Coquelin*), Sunday visits to the *musée de province*, scenes positively out of William Makepeace Thackeray,* English library near the "sunny, breezy, bustling Port," Victorian visitors and native "sea-faring and fisher-folk" (especially "free-limbed" women). He recalls musing about history on rampart benches, visits at home by dull lady writers, "infatuated" escape to three-volume novels (which were advantageous to his "intelligence or . . . imagination"), and morning hours with a literature tutor (a "provincial . . . *cuistre*" but valuably redolent of "the vieux temps").

Smalley, George Washburn (1833–1916). Energetic, controversial, gracious, successful, often pompous Massachusetts-born writer and bibliophile. He graduated from Yale (1853), attended Harvard Law School, was admitted to the bar (1856), then became a combat-zone correspondent during the Civil War for the New York *Tribune*. He scooped all other reporters with a famous account of the Battle of Antietam (20 September 1862). Later he reported the Prussian-Austrian War (1866); he used the transatlantic cable to announce its end. Smalley organized the *Tribune* bureau in London, where he lived (on Hyde Park Square) with his wife (Phoebe Garnaut, whom he married in 1862 and who was the adopted daughter of Wendell Phillips) for many years, until their legal separation in 1898. He established a partnership between the *Tribune* and the London *Telegraph*. He was the *Tribune* representative in London (1867–1895), then the London *Times* correspondent in the United States (1895–1906). He remained anti-Confederate, was liberal until late in life, admired William Ewart Gladstone,* and criticized Benjamin Disraeli.* He was released by the *Times* shortly after his controversial coverage of the Portsmouth Peace Conference (1905) and spent his last ten years in England. Among his published works are *London Letters and Some Others* (1890), *Anglo-American Memories* (1911, 3nd series, 1912), and biographical studies. He was a voluminous correspondent. James met Smalley in Paris, was entertained by the hospitable Smalleys in London beginning in 1876, and enjoyed many dinners there in the company of the Smalleys' wide circle of friends, which included Robert Browning,* Theodore E. Child,* Roscoe Conkling,* James Anthony Froude,* John Milton Hay* (a long-time friend for whom Smalley acted as spokesman), Thomas Henry Huxley,* Alexander William Kinglake* (who praised Smalley extravagantly), James Russell Lowell* (whom Smalley knew intimately), and John Lothrop Motley.* James admired Smalley, calling him "divine, . . . very civil and friendly," and praising his *Tribune* work, in a letter to William James (25 Apr [1876]). In a letter to his mother (31 Jan [1877]), James called Smalley "a real benefactor." By 1880 Smalley was offering James advice on how to market his fiction. In letters to Grace Norton* (16 Jul [1886], 23 Jul 1887), James hints that Mrs. Smalley and Lowell were too fond of one another. James called on Smalley's favorite daughter, Evelyn Garnaut Smalley, when he was in New York in 1905. She planned

The Henry James Year Book (Boston: Badger, 1911). James's Pocket Diaries indicate that he maintained his friendship in London with Mrs. George Smalley into the 1910s.

Smallshaw. In "A London Life," Lionel Berrington's clever solicitor.

Smiles, Samuel (1812–1904). Scottish reformer, biographer, and historian. He was apprenticed to a physician, attended Edinburgh University, received his medical diploma in 1832, and became a lecturer and author on health problems. He edited a radical Leeds newspaper (1838–1842), and became a railroad administrator in Leeds (1845–1854) and then in London (1854–1866). He espoused reform causes in politics, labor, and education. He followed the success of his 1857 biography of George Stephenson, inventor and founder of railroads, with biographies of industrial leaders. He expanded his lectures on knowledge obtained under difficulties into his popular *Self-Help* (1859) and expanded his lectures on Huguenot problems into *The Huguenots: Their Settlements, Churches, and Industries in England and Ireland* (1867), another popular success. A paralytic stroke in 1871 did not stop Smiles from wide travel and steady writing. His incomplete autobiography was published posthumously (1905). James reviewed (*Nation*, 9 Jan 1868) Smiles's book on the Huguenots along with a novel entitled *The Huguenot Family in the English Village* by Sarah Tytler.* James begins by praising Smiles's *Self-Help* as "very good," but then, after disposing of Tytler's work, calls Smiles's history "a naked recital of facts and figures" with "no claim to originality." He summarizes in detail the events in France before the Revocation of the Edict of Nantes, and its consequences not only in France for the Huguenot sufferers, but also in Germany, Holland, and England for the emigrants thereto. He criticizes Smiles's hasty conclusion that the Huguenot departure from France "bequeathed to the country a total cessation of intellectual life and a long literary dearth."

Smith, Corinna (1876–?). Granddaughter of George P. Putnam and the daughter of George H. Putnam (publishers), and wife (from 1899) of Boston mural painter Joseph Lindon Smith (1863–1950). She was her father's hostess in London and later accompanied her husband as he painted archaeological treasures unearthed in the Middle East, the Orient, and Central America. Memories of her associations with such notables as Margot Asquith (wife of Herbert Henry Asquith*), Sir Edward Burne-Jones,* Annie Adams Fields,* John Milton Hay,* George Meredith,* Isabella Stewart Gardner,* Thomas Hardy,* Theodore Roosevelt,* John Singer Sargent,* and Mark Twain,* as well as James, fill her informative *Interesting People: Eighty Years with the Great and Near-Great* (1962), in which she describes hearing James read "The Turn of the Screw" aloud to her husband, Sargent, and her when they were overnight guests at Lamb House* in 1901. Through Sargent she and her husband had met James a few days earlier, and they saw him again in Italy, in 1906, and in London, in 1909.

Smith, George Barnett (1841–1909). Yorkshire-born writer. He became a reporter in London (from 1865), contributed to literary magazines, and developed into a sensitive critic. He wrote about Elizabeth Barrett Browning* so well that her husband Robert Browning* sought out his friendship. Smith wrote short lives of important authors and politicians, and was invalided, then pensioned, in Bournemouth (from 1889). Under the pen name Guy Roslyn, he published poetry and a biography of George Eliot.* James reviewed (*Nation*, 30 Dec 1875) Smith's *Poets and Novelists: A Series of Literary Studies* (1875), criticizing his wrong-headed generalizations concerning the narrative skill, satirical ability, and love scenes of William Makepeace Thackeray*; his inability to note both "merits and defects" in the works of Elizabeth Barrett Browning; his finding humor in Nathaniel Hawthorne*; his excessive praise of Emily Brontë (see Brontë sisters); and his eulogizing of Robert Buchanan. In short, James regards Smith as "scantily . . . equip[ped]" to be a critic.

Smith, Logan Pearsall (1865–1946). Erudite, humane, witty, bookish, celibate man of letters (best as an essayist and literary critic, weakest as a poet and fiction writer), and friend of the great. He was born in New Jersey into a rich family, attended Haverford (1881–1884), Harvard (1884–1885), the University of Berlin (1885–1886), and then the love of his life, Balliol College, Oxford (1888–1891). Smith went on to Paris and elsewhere on the Continent (to 1895), then resided in England for the remainder of his life. He became a British subject in 1913 and moved from Sussex to Chelsea the following year. His mother was an influential religious writer; his two sisters married Bertram Russell and Bernard Berenson.* Smith's list of friends is legion; it includes the following who also knew James: Herbert Henry Asquith,* Sir Max Beerbohm,* Julia Constance Fletcher,* Percy Lubbock,* Sir Edward Howard Marsh,* George Santayana* (to whom he introduced James in 1915), George Bernard Shaw,* Edith Newbold Jones Wharton,* and Virginia Woolf.* Smith's many works include the following: a collection of short stories (1895, which James gently told him he disliked); books on Sir Henry Wotton (1907), George Santayana (1920), William Shakespeare* (1933), and John Milton (1940); *The English Language* (1912); and his popular *Trivia* series (1917, 1921, 1933). Smith met James in 1888, often saw him socially, exchanged gossip with him happily, was often his host and visitor (into 1915), and missed him eloquently when he died. In his memoirs, *Unforgotten Years* (1939), and in his brilliantly styled letters, Smith often discusses James (one of his literary "deities"), his complex personality, conversation, letters, love of gossip, and works (especially *Terminations* and *The Golden Bowl*). James once forcefully told him that an artist must reconcile himself to loneliness. James's library contained two books by Smith.

Smyth, Dame Ethel Mary (1858–1944). Versatile, energetic British composer, conductor, violent feminist, and author. She studied music in Germany; after she returned to London (1888), many of her compositions were performed (from

1890). Her 1911 battle song "The March of the Women" proved immensely popular. She wrote several autobiographical volumes (1919, 1935, 1940) and other works, including a book for dog lovers. Smyth's close friends, apart from musical ones, included John Singer Sargent* (who did a drawing of Smyth in 1901), George Moore, Emmeline Pankhurst and her daughter Christabel, Violet Paget,* Virginia Woolf,* and James, who attended the 1902 Covent Garden première of her opera *Der Wald*. He also knew Smyth's beautiful sister Mary Smyth, who was two years older than Ethel. Mary became the wife of Charles Hunter (an army captain, rich by coal), aided Ethel financially and socially, was a ruinously lavish social success everywhere (including Boston, New York, Venice, and Egypt), and had an Epping Forest mansion (northeast of London) where she entertained James (and members of his family), as well as some of his friends (including Sir Max Beerbohm,* Ariana Randolph Curtis and Daniel Sargent Curtis,* and Edith Newbold Jones Wharton*). Mrs. Hunter was nicknamed "the Lion Hunter." James wrote to Wharton (13 Mar 1912) to criticize suffragette violence but to lament losing the society of "window-smashing women" such as Mary Hunter's sister Ethel Smyth, now in jail. His Pocket Diaries indicate that on into his last years (1909–1915) James and Mary Hunter remained friendly in and out of London, during automobile drives, and at tea, dinners, and the theater.

The Soft Side. Collection of twelve short stories published in London by Methuen, 1900, and in New York by Macmillan, 1900: "The Great Good Place," "Europe," "Paste," "The Real Right Thing," "The Great Condition," "The Tree of Knowledge," "The Abasement of the Northmores," "The Given Case," "John Delavoy," "The Third Person," "Maud-Evelyn," and "Miss Gunton of Poughkeepsie."

"The Solution." Short story (18,000 words), published in the *New Review* (Dec 1889–Feb 1890); reprinted in *The Lesson of the Master*, 1892. (Characters: Lord Bolitho, Augusta Goldie, Blanche Goldie, Rosina Goldie, Veronica Goldie, Guy de Montaut, Rushbrook, Mrs. Rushbrook, Miss Rushbrook, Henry Wilmerding.) Outside Rome, an American diplomat named Henry Wilmerding, a rich but callow Carolinian, goes for an innocent but unchaperoned stroll with Veronica Goldie into a secluded grove, after which he is made to feel by some practical jokers—including the diplomat narrator—that he has compromised the unmarried girl. Wilmerding then honorably proposes marriage to her and is accepted. The conscience-stricken narrator then asks his near-fiancée, the widow Mrs. Rushbrook, to aid. She does so: She persuades Wilmerding to buy off Veronica and she marries him herself. According to a Notebook entry (28 Feb 1889), this spicy story grew from some gossip told to James by Frances Anne Kemble*— "something that had taken place years ago—in the diplomatic body in Rome— I think—under her observation." As usual, James reverses action elements. In Mrs. Kemble's story, the "naïf," though uncaring, marries the girl. In 1891 or so, James returned to his story plot as the basis for a play *Disengaged* (first called *Mrs. Jasper*) submitted in response to a request by John Augustin Daly,* the dramatist and theater manager, who wished Ada C. Rehan,* the Irish-American comic actress, to star in it. But Daly had tardy reservations about the play and never produced it.

Sorbières, de. In "Gabrielle de Bergerac," Vicomte Gaston de Treuil's rich, dying uncle.

Southworth, Alvan S. (?–?). American travel writer and biographer. After a long trip on the Nile, through the Sudan, and into Central Africa, in part to study the slave trade, he published *Four Thousand Miles of African Travel: A Personal Record of a Journey up the Nile* (1875). He later wrote the *Life of Gen. Winfield S. Hancock* (1880). James reviewed (*Nation*, 2 Dec 1875) *Four Thousand Miles of African Travel*. He summarizes the details of Southworth's arduous trip, praises only his "graphic" description of "physical discomfort" in the Nubian Desert, and lightly criticizes his having "conceived large designs, which were defeated by circumstances." Thus, he never got to Mecca, nor did his pretending to want to buy an Abyssinian slave girl in Khartoum lead to anything.

"The Special Type." Short story (6,800 words), published in *Collier's Magazine* (16 Jun 1900); reprinted in *The Better Sort*, 1903. (Characters: Frank Brivet, Mrs. Frank Brivet, Rose Cavenham, Alice Dundene, Remson Sturch.) To provoke his wife into a divorce, Frank Brivet, the painter narrator's friend, treats Alice Dundene in public as his mistress. She loves him but loses out after the resulting divorce, because Brivet planned everything this way so as to marry beautiful, smug Rose Cavenham, whom the narrator once painted. Brivet's ex-wife then marries unpleasant Remson Sturch. As an indication of her approaching success, Mrs. Cavenham commissioned the narrator to do Brivet's portrait, which in time the narrator shows to long-suffering Alice, who when promised by grateful Brivet a present as payment for aiding him asks meekly for the portrait. She gets it, and it will partially recompense her for never being alone with the man she passively loved. Several Notebook entries are pertinent to this story: First, James records (21 Dec 1895) the information that William Kissam Vanderbilt, who was the older brother of James's friend George Washington Vanderbilt,* had hired a Parisian "*demi-mondaine* . . . to *s'afficher* with him in order to force his virago of a wife to divorce him." A couple of years later (7 May 1898), James lists " 'Vanderbilt' story" as still worth pursuing. During the following year (19 Feb 1899), he reminds himself "to cipher out a little further the 'Vanderbilt'. . . . There is probably something in it. . . . The *cocotte s'y prête*—from real affection for him: knowing the terms, etc." James's story took its own contours, with characteristic concentration on and refinement of "the *cocotte*" in question.

"The Speech of American Women." Essay, published in *Harper's Bazar* (Nov, Dec 1906, Jan, Feb 1907). American women are a success and are published as such. Their explanation is loose: They are an "encouraged" product of an unsettled democracy. Unlike women in Europe, American women are fearless, simple, without respect or discipline, immune, cocky, unembarrassed, serene, unaccountable, unpetitioned, and unpenalized. They do not have to speak like ladies. They "emit" sounds with less "consistency and harmony" than animals do because American schoolhouses and "culture-clubs" are presided over by women who do not speak charmingly. It is "hollow" for women to blame their men, who have indifferently set the standard, and whose noisy spheres are "the stock-exchange and the football-field." In America, women have "the authority" everywhere else. James says that European women take trouble to speak charmingly, but that American women's speech is loose and flat, "slipshod and slobbery," because Americans feel that it does not matter. James turns particular. While in Boston recently, he heard girls from a fashionable school (not from tenements, factories, or slums, mind you) shrieking, bawling, hooting, and howling at each other—in training to yell in polite society—and no authority rebuked them. They need Victorian governesses or French nuns. (In an aside, James observes that in America expensive boys' schools offer no training in speech, American advertising is blatant, and young people are indifferent to their elders.) New Yorkers used to speak worse than New Englanders, but now there is no difference. James was recently regarded as bossy and picky, first when he lectured some "luckless maids" on the difference between "do" and "due," etc., and then when he articulately defended good speech as interesting, tasteful, artistic, amusing, sensitive, moral, discriminating, and joyful. He got told both that American girls could say even more than they do and that they are internationally admired. His answer was that the fates have ironically locked such girls in a fools' paradise but that if they steal out he will tutor them.

Spencer, Herbert (1820–1903). Eminent and influential English evolutionary and ethical philosopher, sociologist, and psychologist. His leading works include *Social Statics* (1851), *Principles of Psychology* (1855; 2nd ed., 2 vols., 1872), *Education, Intellectual, Moral and Physical* (1861), *First Principles* (1862), *Principles of Biology* (2 vols., 1864, 1867), *Principles of Sociology* (3 vols., 1876, 1882, 1896), *Principles of Ethics* (2 vols., 1892, 1893), *Man versus the State* (1884), *Factors of Organic Evolution* (1886), and *Autobiography* (2 vols., 1904). Spencer knew Charles Robert Darwin,* George Eliot,* Thomas Henry Huxley,* George Henry Lewes,* and John Stuart Mill, among other distinguished thinkers of his day. James was happy to write to his father (13 Feb [1877]) from the library of the Athenaeum Club, London, that "[o]n the other side of the room sits Herbert Spencer, asleep in a chair (he always is, whenever I come in)." James's library contained four books by Spencer.

Spencer, Caroline. In "Four Meetings," a sweet, trusting, gullible New England schoolteacher. She saves up to go to Europe, but in Le Havre gives her money to her art student cousin and thus deprives herself of her European tour. Later she becomes an oppressed hostess of her dead cousin's "wife."

Spencer, Henrietta. In "De Grey, A Romance," a woman loved and hence destroyed by John De Grey.

Spicer, Mr. and Mrs. In *Disengaged*, guests of Lady Amy Brisket and Sir Montagu Brisket. The Spicers, as well as the Stoners, are served dinner late because of the confusion.

"The Splügen" (1874 title, "A Northward Journey"). Travel sketch, published in the *Independent* (20, 27 Aug 1874); reprinted in *Transatlantic Sketches*, 1875. Northern Italy is too hot this summer; so, after a visit to Milan's cathedral and another look at the fair Milanese women, James heads north. First, up to Monte Generoso near Lake Lugano, where all is "vast and silent and sublime." Then Lake Como, and a steamer to "raw little" Colico, where he waits for the Splügen coach. The trip starts by moonlight through "dusky valleys" and under "fantastic crags" and includes "the spectacle of an Alpine morning twilight," then fissures, cliffs, and "soft slopes" to Chur. This town has "a labyrinth of . . . quiet streets" and a sixth-century church, which James admires, especially its big sixteenth-century altar piece (an "almost uncomfortably lifelike" wood carving of the Nativity and the Magi) and some early Carlovingian documents. On to "prosaic and prosperous" Basel and several "firm, compact" works by Hans Holbein the younger.*

Spofford, Harriet Elizabeth (née Prescott) (1835–1921). Prolific short-story writer, poetess, novelist, critic, biographer, playwright, and essayist, born in Calais, Maine, into an old New England family. A school essay of hers attracted the attention of helpful Thomas Wentworth Storrow Higginson.* When her parents both became invalids, Miss Prescott began to write assiduously though still in her teens. She was quickly published in leading journals. In 1865 she married Richard S. Spofford, a lawyer in Newburyport, Massachusetts. Mrs. Spofford was widowed in 1888. Her many novels, beginning with *Sir Rohan's Ghost* (1860) and *Azarian: An Episode* (1864), are regularly superficial, verbose, sentimental, weakly romantic, and lacking in focus. James reviewed (*North American Review*, Jan 1865) *Azarian*, calling it "defiant . . . of wisdom and taste" and a typical example of the post-Tennyson "ideal descriptive style." He praises its subject, which he sketches, but complains that its "central element" is mere feeling and that only the outward appearance of its four main characters is described. Miss Prescott thus resembles a "little girl . . . [who] fingers her puppets to death," and her novel becomes "true to nothing." She has an "almost morbid love of the picturesque." She prides herself on her so-called "fine" but really "cheap . . . " style, her "fancy" (in truth, properly a garnish to the "dish of solid fiction"), her diction (which is affected), and her fluency (most "female writers . . . possess . . . in excess the fatal gift"). Miss Prescott should learn to blot out and redo, like a good painter. Although James says that he prefers the new "vulgar realism . . . leavened by a little old-fashioned idealism," he does "counsel" Miss Prescott to learn from Prosper Mérimée,* Honoré de Balzac,* Charles Reade,* and Anthony Trollope.* These authors are faithful to details of social reality only as as they relate to the action.

The Spoils of Poynton (tentative title, "The House Beautiful"; 1896 title, *The Old Things*; 1897 title, *The Spoils of Poynton*). Short novel (65,000 words), published in the *Atlantic Monthly* (Apr–Oct 1896); revised and reprinted in London by Heinemann, 1897, and in Boston and New York by Houghton, Mifflin, 1897; revised and reprinted in *The Novels and Tales of Henry James*, Volume X, 1908. (Characters: Mona Brigstock, Mrs. Brigstock, Mrs. Firmin, Adela Gereth, Owen Gereth, Colonel Gereth, Mme. de Jaume, Fleda Vetch, Maggie Vetch, Vetch.) The widow Adela Gereth tells sensitive Fleda Vetch that she is afraid her rather uncomprehending son Owen is falling for crass Mona Brigstock. With her mother, Mona visits Poynton, the Gereth home which is filled with wisely gathered art spoils of many sorts. Fleda reproaches Mrs. Gereth for appearing to offer Owen to her. The young man soon reports his engagement to Mona and their plan to take over legally expropriated Mrs. Gereth's Poynton. He asks Fleda to persuade his mother to vacate without making a scene. Taking the young woman with her as a guest, Mrs. Gereth moves to Ricks, the other family estate, and soon she thinks that something can be made of it. Fleda is so uncomfortable, since she is sympathetic to both imperious mother and oppressed son, that she returns to London, where her sister is being married. Fleda and Owen bump into each other; he goes shopping with her and buys her a pincushion for being kind to mummy. He seems to regard her too fondly to be a happily engaged young man. Returning to Ricks, Fleda notes with displeasure that Mrs. Gereth has furnished the place with Poynton's finest treasures. Owen comes in to report Mona's anger at the "theft." Fleda feels that she could wreck his engagement by merely urging her hostess to retain the spoils; however, respecting probity, she advises Owen to honor his pledged word. She even tries to deny to his mother her own increasing devotion to his cause. Owen finds Fleda at her father's London home, and when the two talk she honorably tells Owen that his mother is stalling to bluff Mona out of the engagement. Owen now prefers refined Fleda to sulking Mona. When Mrs. Brigstock calls on Fleda, she is so annoyed at finding Owen there that he defends the girl. Then he follows her to her sister's home and declares his love. After momentarily responding, Fleda insists that he remain an honorable fiancé until Mona breaks with him. Ten days pass. Then Mrs. Gereth tells Fleda that Mrs. Brigstock feels that her daughter has lost Owen. So Mrs. Gereth returns the spoils to Poynton. She admires Fleda but criticizes her overly sensitive scruples. Three days later Owen and massive Mona are reported to be married. They go abroad. Reconciled to Mrs. Gereth, Fleda receives a letter from Owen begging her to select any one fine treasure from the spoils to keep. She journeys to Poynton, only to find it burning to the ground. James wrote more in his *Notebooks* about what became *The Spoils of Poynton* than about any other fictional piece. The idea started (23 Dec 1893) with some sordid gossip—"a small and ugly matter"—relayed to him at a dinner party given by Lady Caroline Blanche Elizabeth Lindsay,* concerning a young Scot whose father's death gave him title to certain property and art treasures; the man married, but his mother wanted to keep the treasures, carted them off, and even tried to circumvent the law by declaring her son illegitimate. Planning a three-chapter short story (15 May 1895) but ending with a short novel, James altered his melodramatic source to stress Mrs. Gereth's love of art, the poignant confusion of Owen, and Fleda as central consciousness, in love with Owen (11 Aug, 15 Oct 1895; 13, 19 Feb 1896; 30 Mar 1896). Owen was originally named Albert; Fleda was Muriel Veetch. From the beginning, James had difficulty trying to control the length of this work. He wrote to Horace Elisha Scudder,* editor of the *Atlantic Monthly* (3 Sep 1895), " 'The House Beautiful' . . . absolutely declines to be contained in 15,000 words." In the preface to Volume X of *The Novels and Tales of Henry James*, James voices his famous dislike of being given more than the tiniest "germ of a 'story.' " "If one is given a hint at all designedly one is sure to be given too much." This is unfortunate, since whereas inclusion of too many facts produces confusion, art properly depends on "discrimination and selection"—all of which relates to the aesthetic moral of his short story "The Real Thing." As for *The Spoils of Poynton*, out of a quarrel between an "embroiled" mother and her son, James trusted his artistry to tease "the positive right truth" and to avoid "the so easy muddle of wrong truths." Two main problems have beset critics of this splendid novel: the nature of the spoils and Fleda's attitude toward Owen.

Spooner. In *Roderick Hudson*, Roderick Hudson's former employer. He is a law partner of Barnaby Striker in Northampton.

Spottiswoode, William (1825–1883). English mathematician and physicist of Scottish heritage. He pioneered in determinants and also experimented with surfaces, light, and electricity. James wrote a snobbish letter to his father (25 Mar [1878]) that he had recently "dined with the Spottiswoode's [sic]—deadly dull." James later declined other such invitations.

Stackpole, Henrietta. In *The Portrait of a Lady*, Isabel Archer's close American friend. She writes travel letters about Europe for American newspapers. After criticizing both Europe and men, she decides to marry Britisher Bob Bantling.

Staines. In "The Sweetheart of M. Briseux," Lucretia Staines's late husband, who died of overwork at age thirty-five.

Staines, Harold. In "The Sweetheart of M. Briseux," a mediocre painter. His fiancée, the narrator, gives him up to let Pierre Briseux use her as a model while he paints over Staines's poor portrait of her.

Staines, Lucretia. In "The Sweetheart of M. Briseux," Harold Staines's widowed mother, who is the informal guardian of his fiancée, the narrator.

Stamm, Lisa. In *Watch and Ward*, Mlle. Stamm's cloistered sister.

Stamm, Mlle. In *Watch and Ward*, Nora Lambert's German friend.

Stanmer, Edmund. In "The Diary of a Man of Fifty," the young man who loves and marries the widowed Countess Bianca Salvi-Scarabelli. This non-plusses the diarist narrator, who years earlier loved her widowed mother under similarly disturbing circumstances.

Stanmore. In *Tenants*, Sir Frederick Byng's closest friend, who, when dying two years earlier, had asked Sir Frederick to accept his daughter Mildred as ward. Sir Frederick did so.

Stanmore, Mildred. In *Tenants*, Sir Frederick Byng's ward, now age eighteen. She loves Sir Frederick's son Norman Byng, is briefly pursued by Claude Vibert because she will inherit £7,000 per annum in four years, but accepts Norman.

Stannace. In "The Next Time," Mrs. Stannace's father-in-law, a pallid writer.

Stannace, Mr. and Mrs. In "The Next Time," the parents of popular novelist Jane Stannace Highmore and unpopular novelist Ralph Limbert's wife Maud. Stannace published his father's pallid writing.

Stant, Charlotte. In *The Golden Bowl*, Maggie Verver's close friend, and the second wife of Maggie's widowed father Adam Verver. Charlotte is Maggie's husband Prince Amerigo's lover both before and after his (and then her) marriage. To win out in the end, Maggie must let Charlotte seem to be victorious.

Stapleton. In "A Most Extraordinary Case," Edith and George Stapleton's older brother.

Stapleton, Edith. In "A Most Extraordinary Case," a young woman who admires unknowing convalescent Colonel Ferdinand Mason, who after attending a party at her home has a relapse and dies.

Stapleton, George. In "A Most Extraordinary Case," the second son in the Stapleton family, which includes Edith. They have a brother.

Staub, Dr. Rudolph. In "A Bundle of Letters," the militantly pro-German guest at Mme. Maisonrouge's pension. He criticizes French, British, and American guests there in a letter to his scientific colleague Dr. Julius Hirsch.

Staveley, Robert. In *A Change of Heart*, Jane Thorne's nephew and hence her daughter Margaret's cousin. He is thirty-seven years old. He tries to warn Margaret that her suitor Charles Pepperel is a scoundrel who stole from Martha Noel earlier and is now after Margaret's money. Margaret declines to believe the truth. In disgust, Staveley asks Martha Noel not to provide proof but to accept him instead. She agrees.

Staverton, Alice. In "The Jolly Corner," a New Yorker who loves and will win Spencer Brydon when he returns to "the jolly corner," talks to her about his hidden personality, and stalks his alter ego there.

Stedman, Edmund Clarence (1833–1908). American businessman, Wall Street broker, essayist, critic, editor, and once popular poet. His *Poetical Works* (1873) collect his best efforts. When Stedman wrote James to praise his 1875 essay on Alfred, Lord Tennyson,* James replied (1 Sep [1875]) to thank him, to commend him as "one who speaks on poetic matters with authority," and to confess that poetry was pretty much "a mystery" to him.

Steel, Flora Annie (née Webster) (1847–1929). British novelist who married an official in the Indian Civil Service (1867) and moved with him to India (1868). She avidly studied social conditions there, favored emancipation and expanded education for women, and became an inspectress of girls' schools. She knew the father of Rudyard Kipling* there. She left India regretfully when her husband retired (1889) and returned for visits on two occasions (1894, 1897–1898). Her several books concerning Anglo-Indian life include an immensely popular fictionalized account of the 1857–1858 Sepoy Mutiny entitled *On the Face of the Waters* (1896), of which James in "London" (27 Mar 1897) confesses he has bitten only into the preface—a "tough . . . morsel." He objects to Mrs. Steel's telling us in it just where history ends and fiction begins in her novel. Fact and fancy are properly fused, James asserts, in the "crucible" of art. Mrs. Steel's autobiography, *The Garden of Fidelity*, appeared posthumously (1929).

Steet, Miss. In "A London Life," Ferdie and Geordie Berrington's governess.

Stendhal. The pen name of Marie-Henri Beyle (1783–1842). This versatile French writer was born in Grenoble, lived in Paris, and became French consul in Trieste and then Civitavecchia. He served in the French army and participated in the retreat from Moscow. Stendhal wrote several biographies, but he is most notable for his romantic novels *Le Rouge et le Noir* (1831) and *La Chartreuse de Parme* (1839). James adversely reviewed (*Nation*, 17 Sep 1874) Andrew

Archibald Paton's *Henry Beyle (otherwise Stendahl* [sic]*): A Critical and Biographical Study* (1874), calling the author not qualified and weak in judgment. James then launches into his own discussion of Stendhal, whom he likes because of his unsystematic, "instinctive method." Stendhal rejoiced in collecting examples of good and bad human passions. He wrote to his sister Pauline to help him do so (as Paton, James notes, shows). James comments on Stendhal's life, gross appearance, and traits; voices his admiration of *Le Charteuse de Parme* ("among the dozen finest novels we possess") but also his dislike of *Le Rouge et le Noir* (almost "unreadable"); and concludes that Stendhal's "subject is always Italy." James comments negatively, to the effect that Stendhal thought most people contemptible, and deserved the charge of being an "immoral" writer since his works often display "unredeemed corruption," and show him to be a "mixture of sentiment and cynicism." James's library contained one book by Stendhal and one collection of his works.

Stenterello. In *Roderick Hudson*, Christina Light's poodle, which habitually accompanies her. At one point Rowland Mallet impatiently raps it on its noisy muzzle.

Stephen, Sir Leslie (1832–1904). Brilliant London-born essayist, biographer, literary critic, philosopher, editor, and mountain climber. He was educated at Eton and King's College, London, then at Trinity College, Cambridge. He studied mathematics, took holy orders but later became an agnostic, visited the United States three times, and came to know Oliver Wendell Holmes, Jr.,* Charles Eliot Norton,* and James Russell Lowell* especially well. Stephen resided in London from 1864. In 1867 he married Harriet Marian Thackeray, the younger daughter of William Makepeace Thackeray* (and the sister of Lady Anne Isabella Ritchie*). From 1871 to 1882 Stephen edited the *Cornhill Magazine*, in which he recruited Sir Edmund Wilson Gosse,* Thomas Hardy,* Eliza Lynn Linton,* George Meredith,* Margaret Oliphant,* Robert Louis Stevenson,* and James to publish. (The *Cornhill* editor succeeding Stephen was James's friend James Payn.*) Stephen wrote widely, on many subjects, in essay and book form, notably *The History of English Thought in the Eighteenth Century* (2 vols., 1876), several monographs on authors for the English Men of Letters series, *The English Utilitarians* (3 vols., 1900), and *English Literature and Society in the Eighteenth Century* (1904). He edited *The Dictionary of National Biography* (1882–1891—Sir Sidney Lee* was an assistant editor from 1883) and contributed nearly four hundred entries to it himself. In 1901 he edited the letters of John Richard Green.* Stephen became deaf during his last eight years. A daughter by his second wife, Julia Jackson Duckworth (whom James admired), was Virginia Woolf* (whose godfather was Lowell). James met Stephen in 1868 in Boston during the latter's second visit to America. A year later James was aided socially and professionally in London by Stephen, whom he described in a letter to his sister Alice (10 Mar [1869]) as a "blessed man ... who came unsolicited and . . . invited me to dine with him . . . the next day.'' In his review (*Atlantic Monthly*, Nov 1871) of *Hours of Exercise in the Alps*, by John Tyndall,* James calls Stephen's *The Playground of Europe* (1871), a book of essays about his Alpine ascents, ''delightful'' and its author ''a very happy humorist.'' Once James established a permanent residence in London, beginning in 1876, he and Stephen deepened their friendship. James wrote to his brother William (28 Feb [1877]) that the death of his wife had rendered Stephen ''more inarticulate than ever.'' A year later James wrote to his sister Alice (17 Feb [1878]) that at Stephen's home he had met Mrs. Duckworth, who ''consented to become, matrimonially, the receptacle of his [Stephen's] ineffable and impossible taciturnity and dreariness.'' Three months later James wrote to his father (29 May [1878]), ''I don't see what he [Stephen] has done to merit so grandly fair a creature'' as his new wife. While Stephen was editor of the *Cornhill Magazine*, James published ''Daisy Miller: A Study,'' ''An International Episode,'' and *Washington Square* in it. In August 1894 James visited the Stephens in Cornwall and incidentally saw the locale of Virginia Woolf's much later novel *To the Lighthouse* (1927). James wrote Stephen a poignant letter (6 May 1895) when his second wife died. When Stephen was dying of cancer, James visited him (in 1903), and admired his humor and patience. James ultimately regarded Stephen as the finest Britisher he ever knew. James was in the United States, in September 1904, and was hence unable, when asked, to provide Frederic William Maitland* with letters from Stephen, whose biography the historian was then preparing. In an 1884 letter to Norton, Stephen called William James ''a clever fellow, but, I think, rather flighty.'' William James opposed Stephen's agnostic unity-of-truth theory by espousing relativism and pluralism and by pragmatically betting on belief. Stephen reviewed William James's *The Will to Believe* (1897) in the 1898 *Agnostic Annual*, saying that the author ''is trying . . . [to] twist . . . 'faith' out of moonshine.'' James's library contained five books by Stephen.

Steuben, Commodore. In ''Pandora,'' Mrs. Steuben's deceased Southern husband.

Steuben, Mrs. In ''Pandora,'' the Southern widow of Commodore Steuben, whose portrait she wears as a big pendant. In Washington, D.C., she discusses her protégée Pandora Day with Count Otto Vogelstein.

Stevens. In ''Guest's Confession,'' Edgar Musgrave's business associate. Musgrave mentions him to swindler John Guest.

Stevenson, Robert Louis (1850–1894). Distinguished Scottish writer. Born in Edinburgh, he studied engineering and then law at the university there, but then combined writing (soon encouraged by editors Sir Sidney Colvin* and Sir Leslie Stephen*) with travel, most happily to southern France, to improve his diseased lungs. His writings include *An Inland Voyage* (1878), *Travels with a Donkey*

(1879), *Virginibus Pueresque* (1881), *The New Arabian Nights* (1882), *The Silverado Squatters* (1883), *Treasure Island* (1883), *A Child's Garden of Verses* (1885), *Prince Otto* (1885), *The Strange Case of Dr. Jekyll and Mr. Hyde* (1886), *Kidnapped* (1886), *The Merry Men* (1887), *The Master of Ballantrae* (1889), *Father Damian* (1890), and *Vailima Letters* (1895). Helping Stevenson with some of his later works was his stepson, Lloyd Osbourne,* whom James knew and befriended. Stevenson's critical essay "A Humble Remonstrance" (1884) gently argues against James's theory of realism as expressed in his "The Art of Fiction" by suggesting that art can never compete with life, since life is illogical, jumpy, gripping, and infinite, whereas a work of art is by comparison neat, rational, and emasculate. In an effort to improve his health, Stevenson and his American-born wife Fanny—they had married in 1880—voyaged in the South Seas and then settled in Samoa, where he died four years later. In 1885 he and James met in Bournemouth, where the Stevensons lived (1884–1887) and where James had brought his invalid sister Alice for a vacation. The two writers became friends, and James was disconsolate when Stevenson left England in 1887 and especially when he died far from home. In "Robert Louis Stevenson" (*Century Magazine*, Apr 1888; reprinted in *Partial Portraits*, 1888), James comments that Stevenson is an ideal subject for an old-fashioned literary portrait rather than a new-style critical piece with "dig[s]." Struck by "the beauty . . . of this personage," who also has "character," James, continuing the analogy of essay and portrait, is glad to include his charming subject's "frippery." He deplores the implication in an 1885 essay on Stevenson by William Archer* that Stevenson's style is unfortunately more to the fore than his matter. So it is, but rightly so: Stevenson handles language as a Don Juan does beautiful women. Further, his "moral message" is that "it is a delight to read him," with his variety, love of form, "jauntiness" (which also "irritate[s]" Archer), and yet with it all a belief that "an expressive style [is] . . . only . . . a means." Stevenson loves youth, especially "the romance of boyhood," writes with sophistication about its naiveté, and seems to prefer it to a time of more mature passions. He loves heroism and glory, especially in gaudy costumes, and also likes "high-sounding names." Deploring marriage, he seems "to regard women as so many superfluous girls in a boy's game"; and though writing well of "childish life he takes no interest in the fireside." He sees marriage as a battle and a cause for "terrible renunciation." Turning biographer, James notes that Stevenson valuably grew up near Edinburgh Castle and Scottish lighthouses, is imbued with "the colour of Scotland," writes enthusiastically despite being an invalid, rarely mentions sickness, insists that we "leave death . . . out of our calculations," and is optimistic. His autobiographical works recommend life naturally; his fiction, reflectively. Endorsing Stevenson's theory that fiction must be free, James praises his "exquisite" story "The Will of the Mill" (1878) because it has "a dash of alternative mystery as to its meaning, . . . half inviting, half defying you to interpret." James also relishes *The Silverado Squatters* (with its "hundred humorous touches") and *Prince Otto* ("an experiment in style" and "perhaps the most literary of his works"). If Stevenson were physically stronger, he would perform literary tricks more frequently. In our journalistic age, he is right to pursue the romantic, "the extraordinary," to encourage us "to make believe" by waving the imaginative and the improbable before us, to prefer Alexandre Dumas [*père*] to Honoré de Balzac.* *Kidnapped* combines a Dumas "fable" and Balzacian "closeness of notation"; *Jekyll and Hyde* adds "psychology." James calls *The New Arabian Nights* "pure adventure in the setting of contemporary English life, and . . . in the placidly ingenuous tone of Scheherazade." In that collection, "The Suicide Club" represents "Mr. Stevenson's greatest success," with the scene brilliantly left to the reader to sketch in. James delights in the opening of *Treasure Island*, that " 'boy's book' "—full of chances and feelings, but with "a moral side"—which adults read as though over a boy's shoulder. John Silver is a picturesque, genial villain. The book has "humorous braveries and quaintnesses." Is *Jekyll and Hyde* philosophical or merely irresponsible? It concerns "the relation of the baser parts of man to his nobler"; but James likes its art, its concise form better than its idea. Its shuddery tone is that of "a foggy winter Sunday" afternoon when even the furniture looks wicked. James finds "the business of the powders" in the plot too "explicit and explanatory" as "machinery of . . . transformation." He leaves *Kidnapped*, Stevenson's "best book" thus far, to the last: It weakly includes the "boy's book" ingredient of a wicked uncle, but its last "five-sixths . . . stand by *Henry Esmond* [by William Makepeace Thackeray*] as a fictive autobiography in archaic form." James admires not merely the last-century and Scottish idioms but also the romantic episodes and the central characters David Balfour and Alan Breck, whose mountainside quarrel he praises as a stroke of genius and as proof of "what the novel can do at its best, and what nothing else can do so well." In "London" (6 Feb 1897), James compares Stevenson's definitive edition ("the massive monument") and that of George Meredith.* James reviewed (*North American Review*, Jan 1900; reprinted as "Robert Louis Stevenson" in *Notes on Novelists*, 1914) the edition by Sidney Colvin of *The Letters of Robert Louis Stevenson to His Family and Friends* (2 vols., 1899), beginning with affectionate praise of Stevenson as man and writer. Reading him is like meeting him. And now reading his letters is like continuing to live with someone we already know well. Stevenson had "matter and manner, substance and spirit," and "lived to the topmost pulse"; so he had much to report. James praises Colvin for the knowledge and judgment displayed in his introduction to the edition. James is happy that Stevenson "never covered his tracks," since it is charming to follow his life now. James comments on how the letters illuminate the writings, the activities, and especially the personal traits of this "incurable scribbler and . . . incurable invalid." He finds the letters from Samoa, Stevenson's "treasure island," the most revealing: They are often "in the terms . . . of the sports of childhood." James quotes from the letters at length, compares a certain page to writing by Pierre Loti,* and closes by saying that his friend "has passed ineffaceably into happy legend," important (unusual in literary annals) both for his writings and for himself. Just over forty letters between James and Stevenson (1884–1894) are extant and have been published. In them the two friends exchange delightful personal and professional commentary. When Stevenson died, James wrote to his widow Fanny Stevenson (26 Dec [1894]) to express his gratitude "[t]o have lived in the light of that splendid life, that beautiful, bountiful thing"; to say that he has "been sitting in darkness, but what is our darkness to the extinction of your magnificent light?"; and to remind himself of her "courage, and patience, and fortitude." James adds that Stevenson "has gone in time not to be old, early enough to be so generously young and late enough to have drunk deep of the cup." James also wrote to Sir Edmund Wilson Gosse* (17 Dec 1894) to lament "this ghastly extinction of the beloved R.L.S.," calling it "an absolute desolation." James declined to act as an executor of Stevenson's estate. In his critical pieces, James mentions almost forty of Stevenson's titles, and his library contained twenty-two works by Stevenson.

Stewart, Alexander Turney (1803–1876). American merchant and philanthropist. He was born near Belfast, migrated to New York City at age twenty-three, and developed a legacy from his grandfather into a phenomenally successful drygoods business and a world-renowned mercantile organization. He invested and built shrewdly, was a close friend of Ulysses Simpson Grant,* carried out magnificent charitable plans (including relief work during the Civil War and abroad), and amassed a notable art gallery in his mansion at Thirty-Fourth Street and Fifth Avenue. James mentions Stewart both in "Parisian Sketches" as the purchaser of *The Battle of Friedland* (also called *1807*) by Jean-Louis-Ernest Meissonier* and in "Parisian Topics" (1 Apr 1876) as the purchaser of *Chariot Race* by Jean Léon Gérôme.*

Stewart, Mrs. Duncan (1797–1884). Wife of a businesssman from Liverpool and mother of Christina Stewart Rogerson.* James knew both women. According to a Notebook entry (19 Jun 1884), he got the idea for his short story "Brooksmith" when Mrs. Rogerson told him about the unique sorrow of Mrs. Stewart's maid after the old woman's death. According to a later Notebook entry (20 Jun 1887), Mrs. Stewart was the model for Lady Davenant in James's short story "A London Life."

Still Waters. One-act play, published in the *Balloon Post* (12 Apr 1871, and reprinted in *The Dial of the Old South Clock* (8, 9 Dec 1879). (Characters: Emma, Felix, Horace, Mrs. Meredith, Michael, Miss Walsingham.) The scene is the piazza of a seaside cottage on an August Sunday. During many entrances and exits, "sensitive little Horace passively loves Emma but sees that she loves self-centered, tall Felix. So Horace tells Felix, encourages him to declare himself to her, and leaves, asking the bemused girl only for her annotated copy of a book of poetry.

Stirling, Isabel. In "De Grey, A Romance," a woman loved and hence destroyed by Stephen De Grey.

Stock-Stock, Mrs. In "The Aspern Papers," the supposedly high-society former friend of Juliana Bordereau and Tina Bordereau.

Stoddard, Elizabeth Drew (née Barstow) (1823–1902). Novelist and poetess, born in Mattapoisett, Massachusetts. Her father was a shipowning sea captain. She was an avid reader as a child. Her husband Richard Henry Stoddard* (with whom she coedited) first encouraged her to write. After success in periodicals with stories, poems, and sketches, she published three novels: *The Morgesons* (1862), *Two Men* (1865), and *Temple House* (1867). Her grim humor and harsh New England realism limited her appeal at first. However, both Nathaniel Hawthorne* and Sir Leslie Stephen* praised her highly. Her poetry is often morbid, in spite of her husband's opinion that her blank verse was the best ever written by an American woman. James savagely reviewed (*Studies in Bibliography*, 1867) *Two Men*, beginning with the statement that *The Morgesons* "was a thoroughly bad novel" and that *Two Men* "is practically but a repetition." It is "feebly conceived" but "violently written," crude, original but disordered, with characters partly natural but at times "violently unnatural." Mrs. Stoddard does have "an admirable command of language" when she describes nature. James says that she fails to present her characters adequately, offers too many deathbeds, is cheaply dramatic, and lets her imagination avoid the truth. He ridicules her treatment of plot and concludes that her readers have to do too much of her work for her while she irresponsibly "amuses herself" by writing "nonsense." In a letter to Sarah Butler Wister* (21 Dec 1902), James criticizes both *The Morgesons* and *Two Men* for their "ugly crudity."

Stoddard, Richard Henry (1825–1903). American poet, critic, and editor, and the husband of Elizabeth Drew Stoddard.* He was born in Massachusetts, endured a squalid youth in New York, became an iron molder, was self-educated, knew Edgar Allan Poe,* was helped by Nathaniel Hawthorne* to become a New York customs inspector, wrote reviews for newspapers and became a literary editor, and with his wife established a New York literary salon in which James Bayard Taylor* and Herman Melville, among others, were guests. James reviewed (*Nation*, 1 Apr, 24 Jun 1875) book-length snippets put together by Stoddard from the published reminiscences of Cornelia Knight,* William Jerdan,* Thomas Moore,* and Thomas Raikes.*

Stoddard. In "Guest's Confession," Edgar Musgrave's lawyer, a partner in the firm of Stoddard and Hale.

Stokes, Mrs. Short. In "Mrs. Medwin," a woman mentioned by Mamie Cutter as a person whom she got into society.

Stone, Rev. Mr. In "Osborne's Revenge," Henrietta Congreve's casual friend. He is a serious young minister.

Stoner, Mr. and Mrs. In *Disengaged*, guests of Lady Amy Brisket and Sir Montagu Brisket. The Stoners, as well as Mr. and Mrs. Spicer, are served dinner late because of the confusion.

Stories Revived. Collection of fourteen stories published in London by Macmillan, in three volumes, 1885: "The Author of Beltraffio," "Pandora," "The Path of Duty," "A Light Man," "A Day of Days," "Georgina's Reasons," "A Passionate Pilgrim," "A Landscape Painter," "Rose-Agathe," "Poor Richard," "The Last of the Valerii," "Master Eustace," "The Romance of Certain Old Clothes," and "A Most Extraordinary Case."

Stormer, Leolin. In "Greville Fane," novelist Greville Fane's pretentious, unproductive son and useless Lady Ethel Stormer Luard's brother. He thinks that he is preparing to be a writer.

Stormer, Mrs. In "Greville Fane," the real name of Greville Fane.

Stormer, Mrs. Leolin. In "Greville Fane," an old woman Leolin marries.

Story, William Wetmore (1819–1895). Salem-born son of the distinguished Massachusetts jurist and politician Joseph Story. William Story graduated from Harvard (1838) and then Harvard Law School (1840), married Emelyn Eldredge (1843), and then practiced law in Boston and wrote legal treatises (for example, on contracts and on personal property sales). At the same time, he was also developing an interest in literature and sculpture. He published *Poems* (1847), visited Italy briefly (1847, commissioned to execute a statue honoring his father, who had died in 1845), and began studying sculpture, painting, and music; he moved to Rome in 1856, where he devoted himself to sculpture and writing there. He became a friend of many English-speaking travelers to and residents in Italy, including Henry Adams* and his wife Marian Adams,* Robert Browning* and his wife Elizabeth Barrett Browning,* Nathaniel Hawthorne,* Harriet Hosmer, Walter Savage Landor, John Lothrop Motley,* and Charles Eliot Norton.* Story's best-known statues, *Libyan Sibyl* (1862), *Cleopatra* (1862; Hawthorne describes it in *The Marble Faun*), *Saul* (1863), *Medea* (1864), *Jerusalem in Her Desolation* (1873), and *Alcestis* (1874), all reveal not only smoothness but also plastic lifelessness. Additional volumes of poems by Story are *Poems* (1856, dedicated to James Russell Lowell,* who dedicated his *Fireside Travels* [1864] to Story), *Graffiti d' Italia* (1868), *He and She; or, A Poet's Portfolio* (1884), *Poems* (1885), and *A Poet's Portfolio: Later Readings* (1894). Most are imitative of Browning and Lowell, but are also sentimental and vapid. Story also wrote several books on Italy: *Roba di Roma* (1862, his best), *Vallombrosa*

(1881), *Fiammetta: A Summer Idyl* (1886), and *Excursions in Art and Letters* (1891). He also wrote plays, usually for private theatricals. In addition, he edited his father's letters (2 vols., 1851) and miscellaneous papers (1852). Story received several official honors and decorations. James met the Story family in Rome (they had a lavish, forty-room apartment in the Palazzo Barberini) in January 1873 and greatly enjoyed dinners there, as well as musical and dramatic entertainments. He met Matthew Arnold* there one evening. When James revisited Rome in December 1873, he again availed himself of Palazzo Barberini hospitality (this time taking his brother William along). In London in the summer of 1887, James dined with Story (on his way to Boston) and Lowell. In April 1880 (en route from Florence to Naples) and again in April 1894 (to see the grave of Constance Fenimore Woolson*), James called on the opulent Storys. But in truth James never respected Story except as a histrionic conversationalist. So, when after his death the Story family asked James to write the sculptor's biography, he was embarrassed and hedged. After all, in private letters James had written critically of the man: His studio statues resemble "an army of marble heroines . . . suggestive of . . . waxworks[,] . . . clever, but . . . almost fatally unsimple" (to Grace Norton,* 5 Mar 1873); "I have rarely seen such a case of *prosperous* pretention [sic] as Story" (to Norton, 31 Mar [1873]); and "poor W.W. in Rome sixteen months ago . . . was the ghost, only, of his old clownship," with his innumerable unwanted statues a "great unsettled population" (to Francis Boott,* 11 Oct [1895]). In addition, James depicted Mrs. Story as "fair, fat, and fifty" (to his mother, 26 Jan 1873). James reviewed (*Nation*, 25 Nov 1875) Story's *Nero: An Historical Play* (1875), saying that it is proof of the author's "versatility and facility." James says that if he had not known Story was a sculptor, he would have judged this play to be a painter's work. Although it is evident here that Story knows Roman narrative history (especially Tacitus and Suetonius), his *Nero* is a "goodly picture" rather than a drama. It is all horror, unrelieved by "complexity or development," moving on "no dramatic pivot"; it is simply "a rolling chronicle." After praising Story's characterization of "low-browed, inexorable, and insatiable" Agrippina (Nero's mother), James concludes that the diffuseness of Story's poetry dilutes his dramatic effects. In 1900, James used Story as the model of the ineffectual sculptor Morgan Mallow in his short story "The Tree of Knowledge." In all likelihood, James agreed to write *William Wetmore Story and His Friends* not only because the Story family pressed him hard but also for money to help pay for Lamb House*: He signed with the publisher William Blackwood in October 1897 for £250 down and another £100 if the biography should sell 7,000 copies. In a Notebook entry (16 May 1899), James suggests that the overarching subject of his biography of Story should be the contrast "of old Rome" and today. James wrote to William Dean Howells* (25 Jan 1902) to express regret at his promise to the Story family, because "there is no *subject*—there is nothing in the man to write about." To Sarah Butler Wister* he reported (21 Dec 1902) that "W.W.S. is . . . thinner than thin." To Millicent Fanny St. Claire-Erskine, Duchess of Sutherland,* he wrote (23 Dec 1903) that "Story was the dearest of men, but . . . his artistic and literary baggage were of the slightest and the materials for a biography *nil*." James knew the Storys' three children, Thomas Waldo Story (sculptor), Julian Russell Story (painter), and Edith Story (who married the Marquis Simone Peruzzi di Medici in 1876). He was sympathetic when in 1907 Edith Peruzzi's son Benido (Bindo) Peruzzi committed suicide. William Wetmore Story has been nominated as a model for Gloriani in James's *The Ambassadors*; the choice seems unlikely, however, since Gloriani is a great sculptor and a superb conversationalist, and James regarded Story as neither.

"The Story in It." Short story (6,400 words), published in the *Anglo-American Magazine* (Jan 1902); reprinted in *The Better Sort*, 1903; revised and reprinted in *The Novels and Tales of Henry James*, Volume XVIII, 1909. (Characters: Maud Blessingbourne, Mrs. Dyott, Colonel and Mrs. Voyt.) On a rainy day in her country home, Mrs. Dyott is entertaining a sweet young widow named Maud Blessingbourne. While her hostess writes some letters, Maud is reading a dull French novel until Colonel Voyt, a married man, arrives. Maud steps out of the room for a while, and Mrs. Dyott and the rather rakish colonel talk intimately of old times. When Maud returns, she and Voyt begin to chat about French novels. Routine though they are, Voyt says, he prefers them to evasive Anglo-American fiction. Maud counters with her theory that a completely moral and inactive woman can provide an interesting plot for a novel. Voyt critically browbeats her, but she remains serene in her happy fancy. When Voyt leaves, Mrs. Dyott extracts the suggestion that Maud silently loves him. After Maud's eventual departure, he returns to Mrs. Dyott (and appears to be her lover). The two discuss Maud's curiously tender position: They soon agree not only that Maud's theory concerning fiction gains plausibility by virtue of her own untold, unrewarded love but also that an author might make more money writing up their own passionate affair. James started this work with a Notebook entry (8 May 1898) about a cliché: "*L'honnête femme n'a pas de roman*. . . . [E]ither it's not a '*roman*,' or it's not *honnête*. When it becomes the thing it's guilty; when it doesn't become guilty it doesn't become the thing." In a later entry (15 Feb 1899), James sketches his contrary plot (which in time he changed somewhat): In the presence of woman of whom he is the "hidden" lover, married artist debates *honnête-femme* thesis with "young, 'innocent,' yearning woman" who "obscurely" loves him "with nothing coming out," etc. In a final entry (5 Oct 1899), James advises himself (incorrectly) that "5000 words are ample" for this story. In the preface to Volume XVIII of *The Novels and Tales of Henry James*, James strikes a blow in favor of women's liberation by explaining that the idea for this story came when he debated with a friend who believed that "ladies who respected themselves took particular care never to *have* adventures." The story proves that James could make subtle fiction out of mere states of mind.

"The Story of a Masterpiece." Short story (13,500 words), published in the *Galaxy* (Jan–Feb 1868). (Characters: Stephen Baxter, Mrs. Denbigh, Marian Everett, Gilbert, Goupil, King, John Lennox, Sarah, Frederic Young, Mrs. Young.) John Lennox, a rich, childless widower, meets Marian Everett in Newport. While she was traveling in Europe with Mrs. Denbigh, an invalid widow, she met a painter named Stephen Baxter, who fell in love with the unresponsive girl. They quarreled, and the relationship ended. She and Lennox are engaged to each other, when through a friend he meets Baxter, who is painting a work which reminds Lennox of Miss Everett. He commissions Baxter to paint his fiancée's portrait, but he dislikes the work when it is finished because it reveals the frivolity and cynicism of the original. Meeting Baxter's fiancée, Lennox concludes that his own is thoroughly hard. Nonetheless, he goes through with the marriage but permits himself the satisfaction of hacking up her portrait. "The Prophetic Pictures" (1837) by Nathaniel Hawthorne* may well have inspired this minor story, which in turn led James to his own later and better stories, "The Liar" and "The Tone of Time."

"The Story of a Year." Short story (15,000 words), published in the *Atlantic Monthly* (Mar 1865). (Characters: Jane Bruce, Robert Bruce, Dr. James Cooper, Miss Cooper, Elizabeth Crowe, Miss Dawes, Lieutenant John Ford, Mrs. Ford, Mr. and Mrs. Littlefield, George Mackenzie, Robertson, Simpson.) During the Civil War, Lieutenant John Ford becomes engaged to Elizabeth Crowe, informs his mother, who disapproves, and soon leaves for the South with the Union Army. At a nearby town Lizzie, growing restless and critical while living with Mrs. Ford, meets Robert Bruce. She begins to fall in love with him, but they learn that Ford has been severely wounded. His mother goes south to nurse him and then bring him home, where, dying, he releases confused Lizzie. This was James's first signed story. ("A Tragedy of Error" had appeared anonymously a year earlier.) It is one of James's three Civil War stories; the others are "Poor Richard" and "A Most Extraordinary Case." Since James saw no war as a soldier, he is being honest when he concentrates here, as he does later in *Notes of a Son and Brother*, on the effects of war on civilians. This crudely written tale has inspired a host of psychoanalytical interpretations.

Stowe, Harriet Beecher (1811–1896). Amazingly popular authoress, born in Litchfield, Connecticut, the daughter of a dour Calvinist minister. She received a traditional religious education and began mature reading and writing before she was a teenager. In 1834 she moved with her family to Cincinnati, where she became a teacher. Two years later she married Calvin Stowe, a biblical scholar and professor in the antislavery seminary of which her father was president. The first years of the Stowes, who eventually had seven children, were difficult, with little money and much sickness. When Stowe began teaching at Bowdoin, in Maine (1850), his wife espoused New England opposition to the Fugitive Slave Law. Mrs. Stowe's *Uncle Tom's Cabin, or Life among the Lowly*

was serialized (1851–1852) in a Washington, D.C., antislavery paper, was published in book form (1852), and became a controversial, phenomenal best-seller.
Mrs. Stowe was honored by humanitarians when she visited England. Next was
her *Dred: A Tale of the Great Dismal Swamp* (1856). She toured England twice
more, went to the Continent as well, and met notables, including the wife of
Lord Byron,* of whom she published sensational defenses (1869, 1870). Once
started, Mrs. Stowe became and remained a prolific writer, composing, among
other books, the following: *The Minister's Wooing* (1859), *Agnes of Sorrento*
(1862), *The Pearl of Orr's Island* (1862), *Oldtown Folks* (1869), *My Wife and
I* (1871), its sequel *We and Our Neighbors: Records of an Unfashionable Street*
(1875), and *Poganuc People* (1878). She wrote poetry and items about house-
keeping. Her collected works were published (16 vols., 1896). She was always
sincere and impassioned, but also inartistic, odd, and impractical. She lived in
Florida during some of her declining years, during which she became senile.
James reviewed (*Nation*, 22 Jul 1875) Stowe's *We and Our Neighbors*, which
is about the wife of a busy editor who brings a British guest home for dinner.
James criticizes the authoress's syntax, vague characterization, and vulgar dialogue. But in *A Small Boy and Others*, he says that *Uncle Tom's Cabin*, which
was perhaps his "first experiment in grown-up fiction," appealed to all kinds
of readers when it was first published, was "less a book than a state of vision,
of feeling and of consciousness," and told many people how they should "conduct . . . themselves."

Straith, Stuart. In "Broken Wings," an unsuccessful painter friend of the
unsuccessful writer Mrs. Harvey.

Stransom, George. In "The Altar of the Dead," the altar-keeping friend of
Mary Antrim, now dead. He reluctantly forgives the wrongdoing of recently
deceased Acton Hague and can then die content.

Strether. In *The Ambassadors*, Lewis Lambert Strether's son, who died at age
ten.

Strether, Lewis Lambert. In *The Ambassadors*, widowed Mrs. Abel Newsome's fiancé and her first ambassador to Paris to rescue her son Chad. Instead,
Strether becomes friendly with Maria Gostrey and Comtesse Marie de Vionnet,
and he learns to appreciate the beneficent effects of Paris on one's expanding
consciousness.

Strether, Mrs. Lewis Lambert. In *The Ambassadors*, the long-deceased wife
of Lewis Lambert Strether.

Strett, Sir Luke. In *The Wings of the Dove*, Milly Theale's impressive and considerate London physician, who advises the dying girl to live and love. He travels to Venice to attend her. He may be patterned partly after James's friend Dr. William Baldwin and Alice James's physician Sir Andrew Clark.

Striker, Barnaby. In *Roderick Hudson*, the Northampton lawyer of the firm of Striker and Spooner. He disapproves of his former employee Roderick Hudson's plan to study sculpture in Rome.

Striker, Miss. In *Roderick Hudson*, The daughter of Roderick Hudson's former employer Barnaby Striker.

Stringham, Susan Shepherd. In *The Wings of the Dove*, a Vermont-born writer. She is Milly Theale's faithful traveling companion in Europe and also an old-time friend of Mrs. Maud Manningham Lowder, to whom she introduces Milly in London.

"A Study of Salvini." Theater essay, published in *Pall Mall Gazette* (27 Mar 1884), about the Italian actor Tommaso Salvini.*

Sturch, Remson. In "The Special Type," an unpleasant man who marries Mrs. Frank Brivet after she divorces her husband Frank Brivet.

Sturdy, Miss. In "The Point of View," the sister of Edward Antrobus's Newport host. She writes to Mrs. Draper at Ouchy.

Sturges, Jonathan (1864–1911). Brave, bright, well-to-do writer, student of French literature, translator, friend of the illustrious (notably Mary Antoinette Anderson,* William Dean Howells,* Gaillard Thomas Lapsley,* Stuart Merrill, Antonio Fernando de Navarro,* John Singer Sargent,* George Washington Vanderbilt,* Francis Vielé-Griffin, Edith Newbold Jones Wharton,* Oscar Wilde,* and James Abbott McNeill Whistler*), dandy dresser, and victim of polio from childhood. He was born in Paris; at the time, his father was a Union Army purchasing agent in Europe. Young Sturges published the history of his 1885 Princeton class (1885) and studied in Germany and briefly at Columbia Law School, but then he became a journalist and creative writer. He was an early appreciator of Henrik Johan Ibsen,* sent travel letters to the New York *Times*, and published short stories in American magazines. By 1889 Sturges had expatriated himself to London. With James's help, he prepared a translation of thirteen short stories by Guy de Maupassant* (New York, 1889; London, 1891; for each publication, James's 1889 essay on Maupassant was reprinted as the introduction). Sturges also published *The First Supper and Other Episodes . . .* (London, 1893, a collection of five short stories). He spent much of his pain-wracked adult life in Paris, London, and Eastbourne, England, in hotels and nursing homes; late in life he became an alcoholic. James came to know him well in the 1890s, socialized with him when circumstances permitted, visited him faithfully during his severe sicknesses, and admired him enormously. James wrote to Sir Edmund Wilson Gosse* (30 Oct [1890?]) to say of "Little Brother Jonathan" that he "has his share of the national genius." In a Notebook entry (31 Oct 1895), James summarizes advice that Sturges said Howells had given to him eighteen months earlier, in Whistler's Parisian garden, to the effect that time had passed Howells by and that the young should live all they can while they still had time. This comment was the inspiration for *The Ambassadors*. In November 1895, Sturges unsuccessfully appealed to James to try to help Oscar Wilde, then in prison. Visiting James at Lamb House* as often as he could, Sturges stayed there once for two full months, until just after Christmas 1898. James wrote to his brother William's wife, Alice, (19 Dec 1898) of his guest that "save as making against pure intensity of concentration, he is altogether a boon." To Henrietta Reubell,* James wrote from Lamb House ([12 Nov 1899]) that "Jonathan Sturges lives, year in, year out, at Long's Hotel, Bond St. [London], and promises to come down here and see me, but never does. He knows hordes of people, every one extraordinarily likes him, and he has tea-parties for pretty ladies: one at a time. Alas, he is three quarters of the time ill; but his little spirit is colossal." In July 1909 James and Wharton visited Sturges at Eastbourne together. Shortly before the young man died there, James wrote Lapsley (1 Jan 1910) of the unique "compassion" he felt for "that tragic and terrible little figure." Little Bilham of *The Ambassadors* is passive, attractive to the ladies, and witty; so was Jonathan Sturges.

Sturgis, Howard Overing (1855–1920). London-born youngest son of Russell Sturgis* and his third wife. An older brother was Boston-born Julian Russell Sturgis (1848–1904), a novelist and the author of their father's biography. Howard Sturgis was a minor writer, a rich and generous host, and a witty personality. He was educated at Eton College and then at Cambridge University; thereafter, he returned home to care for his parents. When his father died in 1887, then his mother in 1888, he was left an immense inheritance. He grew depressed, visited the United States, where he met Edith Newbold Jones Wharton* (among other notables), returned to England in 1889, and bought a villa and estate called Queen's Acre (nicknamed "Qu'Acre") near Windsor Park. (Sturgis enjoyed crocheting and needlework there, lived there much of the time, and traveled abroad with a boyfriend named William Haynes [The Babe] Smith.) Sturgis wrote three novels: *Tim: A Story of School Life* (1891), *All That Was Possible: Being a Record of a Summer in the Life of Mrs. Sybil Crofts, Comedian* (1895), and *Belchamber* (1904). James, who had met the Sturgises socially in 1877, was their dinner guest on occasions beginning soon after that, and was often a guest at Qu'Acre, calling it in a letter to Arthur Christopher Benson* (13 Dec 1908) "the sybaritic sea." James, especially late in life, wrote often to Sturgis. For example, he invited the younger man to Lamb House* by letter (2 Feb 1900), explaining that he invariably wrote until luncheon, "but after that I am genial and diffuse. I can be with nobody more so than with you." Trouble came in connection with the ongoing composition of *Belchamber* by Sturgis, who sent James batches of proofs which James could not help criticizing. Although he praised the handling of the point of view, he disliked the inclusion of excessive high-society details and regarded the hero as ignobly passive and as learning nothing through defeat. James was aghast, however, when Sturgis replied that he wished to withdraw *Belchamber* from publication. James wrote to him (2 Dec 1903) not to do so since such an action would "bring my grey hairs, the few left me, in sorrow and shame to the grave," adding that the novel "will be the joy of thousands." Sturgis published it but then nothing more, and the legend grew (denied by his friend Percy Lubbock*) that James's criticism was the cause. The relationship of James and Sturgis was unprofessional but no less amiable thereafter. The two were guests at Wharton's home in Lenox, Massachusetts, when James was on his 1904–1905 tour of the United States. At one point, James confidentially wrote to Wharton (2 Apr [1906]) about "H[oward] S[turgis's] . . . strange drop into dullness." In the spring of 1907 James stayed with Edward Darley Boit* and his wife Mary Boit in their villa outside Florence, Italy, for a few days, "with poor dear Howard . . . and the Babe," as he wrote to Wharton (12 Aug 1907) once he got home again. In 1909–1912 James occasionally called upon Sturgis at Qu'Acre by courtesy of Wharton's automobile and chauffeur. Sturgis and Lubbock attended James's 1912 lecture on Robert Browning.* James favored Sturgis with a detailed letter (12 or 13 May 1913) answering questions about family members and friends named in his first autobiographical volume, *A Small Boy and Others*, which his friend had been reading. James's later Pocket Diary entries (1909–1915) indicate his continuing friendly association with Sturgis, who in one memo (25 Jul 1912) is called "inexhaustibly patient and kind." Lubbock attributed to James what may be the best comment describing various friends' relationship with Sturgis: "Our dear Howard is like a cake—a richly sugared cake—always on the table. We sit round him in a circle and help ourselves." James and Sturgis had in common numerous friends not already mentioned. James also knew Sturgis's older brother Julian.

Sturgis, Russell (1805–1887). Expatriate American banker in London and senior partner with Baring Brothers. He began his career as a Boston lawyer; he made a fortune by banking in the Philippines, returned to the United States in 1844, married a third time, found the cost of living in Boston too high, and moved to London. He had four sons, including Julian Russell Sturgis (1848–1904) and Howard Overing Sturgis,* both of whom were writers. Russell Sturgis became a senior partner in the banking firm of Baring Brothers in 1846, made another fortune, and retired in 1882. He knew many British men of letters, including William Makepeace Thackeray,* and many Americans traveling to and through London, including the father of Henry Adams,* Edward Darley Boit* and his wife Mary Boit, William Wetmore Story,* and also James. James met the Sturgises socially in 1877 and soon became a frequent dinner guest at their London home. He seems to have accepted their hospitality with reluctance, at least at first: He wrote to his father (25 Mar [1878]) that "[t]he Sturgis's [sic] is a materially brilliant, but not an interesting, *milieu*." A year later he wrote to his sister Alice (26 Mar [1879]) that "at the Sturgis's . . . the dinner will be superlative, but the play of intellect restricted." Then to his mother (7 Feb [1881]): "the Sturgis's . . . caress me very much." In his biography of Story, James writes courteously about "Mr and Mrs Russell Sturgis's . . . career, character, hospitality, general bounty and benignity." He came to know Howard Sturgis well. Daniel Tracy Touchett, Ralph Touchett's expatriate banker father in *The Portrait of a Lady*, may owe something to James's observation of banker Russell Sturgis. James's library contained one book by Russell Sturgis, as well as one by his son Julian Sturgis.

Sturtevant, Miss. In *Washington Square*, the young woman who marries John Ludlow after he is rejected by Catherine Sloper.

"The Suburbs of London." Travel essay, published in *Galaxy* (Dec 1877). James criticizes London's inner-city sights and also America's suburbs, but lavishes praise on London's suburbs, beginning with Kensington. After digressing to mention the attractive carriages and riders in Hyde Park and elsewhere, he describes Windsor Castle (Thames valley, trees, park, open terrace, "irregular magnificence" of the castle proper, treasures within) and Eton (college, "rosy" cricket players, shops, chapel, river and elms, and nearby Virginia Water—for lunch). Next "cocknified" but not "vulgarized" Hampton Court Palace (with second-rate art works in open apartments, "delightful" red main building, charming garden, "old" Bushey Park, pretty river nearby). The well-used Thames is "the great feature of suburban London." Everything is rural by the time you reach "most beautiful" Richmond ("happy" bridge, lovely park, inn providing fine views). Then Twickenham, Kew, and Sudbrook. James closes, however, with a complaint: Suburban inns generally offer "barbaric" evening meals.

"A Summer in Europe." The general title (occasional alternate title, "A European Summer") of a series of seven 1872 and 1873 travel sketches, which are individually entitled I. "Chester," II. "Lichfield and Warwick," III. "North Devon," IV. "Wells and Salisbury," V. "Swiss Notes," VI. "From Chambéry to Milan," and VII. "From Venice to Strassburg [sic]."

"Summer in France." Paris letter (1876), reprinted as "Rouen" in *Portraits of Places*, 1883.

Summersoft. One-act play (original title, *Mrs. Gracedew*), published in Philadelphia and New York by Lippincott, 1949, in *The Complete Plays of Henry James*, ed. Leon Edel. (Characters: Buddle, Chivers, Mrs. Gracedew, Jane, Cora Prodmore, Prodmore, Dame Dorothy Yule, John Anthony Yule, Captain

Marmaduke Clement Yule.) On a hot Saturday afternoon in August, Prodmore hopes to force impoverished, politically radical Captain Yule into turning conservative and marrying his daughter Cora Prodmore in return for canceling the mortgage Prodmore holds on Summersoft, Yule's beautiful country house. Cora is reluctantly visiting the place with her father when Mrs. Gracedew, a rich young American widow, enters during a tour of local sights. She loves the old place to the extent of acting as an impromptu tour guide to some gawking visitors, convinces the attractive Yule (who is immediately smitten by her lithe verve) that keeping such a treasure from the past is his religious duty, but is nonplussed when he says Cora is part of the cost. Learning from the desperate girl that she loves a nice man named Buddle, Mrs. Gracedew agrees to pay Prodmore his exorbitant price of £70,000 for Summersoft if he will free Cora. During what might have been their farewell, Mrs. Gracedew and Yule agree to get married and live there themselves. Years before and in the company of James Russell Lowell,* James visited a country house called Osterley House, near Heston, in Middlesex. It became the model of Summersoft in both "The Lesson of the Master" (in which Henry St. George owns an estate called Summersoft) and this sparkling little play, which James wrote in 1895 at the request of Dame Ellen Terry,* whose actress sister Marion Terry had played Mrs. Peverel in James's badly received *Guy Domville* earlier in 1895. Ellen Terry gave James £100 against future royalties but never produced the work; James retrieved it in 1898 and turned it into the short story "Covering End." In 1907 he rewrote it again, this time as the three-act play *The High Bid*.

Sutherland, Millicent Fanny St. Claire-Erskine, Duchess of (1867–1955). Oldest daughter of the Earl of Roslyn and, at age seventeen, the bride of a man who became the Duke of Sutherland. When her father died in 1892, she inherited a castle and a brilliant London house. She became a generous hostess. She sent her anonymous play called *The Conqueror* to Sir Johnston Forbes-Robertson,* who produced it in 1905. She wrote fiction and more plays, was widowed in 1913, remarried in 1914 and in 1919), did courageous work during World War I, moved to France, and died in Biarritz. James, who knew her socially, introduced her to his friend Urbain Mengin,* who became a language tutor for her and for one of her sons. James describes the Duchess of Sutherland in a letter to his brother William (7 Aug 1897) as "young, amiable and 'literary.' " James knew her well enough to write her a letter (23 Dec 1903) criticizing William Wetmore Story*—"his artistic and literary baggage were of the slightest"—in reply to her praise of his biography of the man; then James proceeded to tell her how to read *The Ambassadors* so as to bring out its "full charm."

Sutro, Alfred (1863–1933). London-born author and translator. He wrote more than forty plays (from 1900 to 1929), including farces, one-act playlets, and "duologues." He published some fiction, translated seven or so plays by his friend Maurice Maeterlinck,* adapted *The Egoist* by George Meredith* for the stage, and offered his reminiscences, including anecdotes about James, in *Celebrities and Simple Souls* (1933). Sutro's wife Esther Stella (née Isaacs) Sutro published a book on Nicolas Poussin and compiled a book of thoughts from Maeterlinck. James knew both Sutro and his wife socially, attended the theater with them, met Maeterlinck through them, and wrote Esther Sutro some especially charming letters. James's Pocket Diaries (1909–1915) are full of memos concerning social engagements with the Sutros.

Sutton, Shirley. In "The Two Faces," the passive observer who studies the hard face of Mrs. May Grantham and the frightened but pretty face of her victim, Lady Valda Gwyther.

"The Sweetheart of M. Briseux." Short story (12,000 words), published in the *Galaxy* (Jun 1873). (Characters: Pierre Briseux, Martinet, Harold Staines, Lucretia Staines, Staines.) While the narrator is visiting an art gallery in the French city of M—, he sees a woman looking at a portrait of which she was the original long ago. When asked about it, she tells the narrator how while she was unhappily engaged to an insensitive, ineffectual painter, named Harold Staines, the then-novice painter Pierre Briseux invaded the studio and began to paint brilliantly over Harold's mediocre portrait of her. Harold was so irate that she had to sacrifice her engagement so that Briseux could complete the work, which launched his illustrious career. It is possible that James was inspired to write this story by *Le Chef d'Oeuvre* (1831) by Honoré de Balzac.* The value of this story lies in the moral that art reveals truth, not vice versa, and that in it James hints that he prefers romantic to classical French painting.

Swetchine, Anne Sophie (née Soymanov) (1782–1857). Russian-French writer, born in Moscow, educated in St. Petersburg while her father held a diplomatic post there, happily married in 1799 to General Swetchine (twenty-five years her senior), and influenced by the illustrious Count Joseph de Maistre (anti-Napoleonic ambassador from the King of Sardinia to Russia) to become a Roman Catholic in 1815. A year later she moved to Paris, where she pursued religious studies, devoted herself to charities, and established a brilliant salon. Her books are *Life and Works* (1860), and *Letters* (1861, edited by Count Frédéric de Falloux). James reviewed (*North American Review*, Jul 1868) *Life and Letters of Madame Swetchine* (Boston, 1867). Saying that the work is not important to American readers, he sketches Mme. Swetchine's life, praises her research into Greek and Roman Catholicism, treats her conversion snidely ("perfume of mysticism," "insanity of piety"), and praises her salon. James suggests that "the juxtaposition" of her drawing room and her specially built chapel off it in her long-time Faubourg St. Germain residence "symbolizes very well the constitution of her mind."

Swinburne, Algernon Charles (1837–1909). Frail, peculiar, London-born Victorian poet and literary critic. While at Balliol College, Oxford, he associated with several pre-Raphaelites (including William Morris*) and helped to found a politically radical and theologically skeptical club. He left college in 1860 to avoid expulsion. In 1862 he reviewed Charles Baudelaire* and defended George Meredith* in *Spectator* articles, and a year later went to Paris, where he met James Abbott McNeill Whistler* and other painters. His talents in verse drama and poetry are well represented in *Atlanta in Calydon* (1865), *Chastelard: A Tragedy* (1866), three series of *Poems and Ballads* (1866 [called libidinous], 1878, 1889), *A Song of Italy* (1867), *Songs before Sunrise* (1871), *Bothwell* (1874), *Erechtheus* (1876), *Tristram of Lyonesse* (1882), and *Marino Faliero* (1885). He combined some early critical pieces into *Essays and Studies* (1874), and his criticism of William Blake (1868) and of William Shakespeare* (1880) is verbose but sound. At his best, Swinburne is exhilarating and illuminating; when less so, he trails into ornateness. James reviewed (*Nation*, 18 Jan 1866) Swinburne's *Chastelard*, calling it immature though on the promising subject of romantic Queen Mary of Scotland. Swinburne does not show whether he regards his heroine as martyr or criminal, and he fatally "substitute[s] color for design." James calls the scene before Chastelard's death a "compound of radical feebleness and superficial cleverness," and he regards the subplot as having a potential "flagrantly missed." Throughout, the hero "descants" while "the play languish[es]." Next, he reviewed (*Nation*, 29 Jul 1875) Swinburne's *Essays and Studies*; before starting, he comments irrelevantly on Swinburne's recent combination of "measureless praise and . . . furious denunciation" of Ralph Waldo Emerson.* He notes Swinburne's valuable "insight into the poetic mystery" as shown in his essays here on Victor-Marie Hugo* (who "is his divinity," is like "a thunder-storm at sea"), Matthew Arnold* (whose style differs much from Swinburne's), George Gordon, Lord Byron* (comments on whom "as a man . . . are consummately futile" here), and John Ford. James argues that Swinburne does not judge, interpret, or guide, but he is imaginative—indiscreetly so at times. When his "magnificent talk" pretends to probe morally, it is only "dabbling in . . . the picturesque." "As psychology it is . . . puerile." James reviewed (*Nation*, 11 Jan 1877) *Note of an English Republican on the Muscovite Crusade*, Swinburne's 1876 pamphlet, calling it "as hysterical and vociferous as usual," though on "a better text": it rightly though too "thunderous[ly]" attacks Thomas Carlyle,* lover of force and no defender of liberty, for praising the Russians over the Turks, when both are equally brutal. James wrote to Sir Edmund Wilson Gosse* (2 Oct [1890]) to complain of Swinburne's "awful prose manner," which, however, proceeds from "real . . . thought." For the *Dictionary of National Biography, 1901–1911* (1912), Gosse wrote the Swinburne entry, which James humorously praised. He wrote to Gosse (15 Oct 1912) that Swinburne was a "gifted being." In 1912 James and Gosse tried to remind each other by letter of details concerning a ribald story going back to the 1870s about Swinburne, some of his friends, Guy de Maupassant,* and a monkey. In *The Middle*

Years, James recalls his excitement at seeing Swinburne at a London art gallery in 1869 and noting that both admired a painting by Titian* at the same time. James's library contained twelve works by Swinburne.

"Swiss Notes." Travel essay, published in the *Nation* (19 Sep 1872), as Part V of "A European Summer"; reprinted in *Transatlantic Sketches*, 1875. James wonders why American tourists visit Switzerland when they have rough, mountainous scenery at home, and also why they overtip and rush when abroad. He prefers people, cathedrals, and palaces to Swiss mountains. Swiss village fountains present varied life. Geneva ("the Presbyterian mother-city"), though "strongly featured," lacks humor, architecture, art, and much else. The "cool-hued" Rhone gushes well. James resists saying much about various authors attracted to the region, but adds that hotels here are named after George Gordon, Lord Byron* and Edward Gibbon.* Throngs of tourists (including "terrible German" ones) pass by and are busy "rub[bing] off the precious primal bloom of the picturesque." James admires Vaudois chalets and also the "sweet sub-Alpine scenery" beyond Villeneuve more than he does over-visited Chillon. Colorful Berne has some interesting details (especially its street fountains), but it is mainly prosaic and angular, with bandy-legged arcades. A two-day, "consummately pictorial" drive takes James to Thusis, and once there he sees the Via Mala, which is charming.

Symonds, John Addington (1840–1893). Bristol-born Victorian literary historian, biographer, essayist, poet, and translator. He went to Harrow and Oxford, studied law to please his father, married Catherine North in 1864, turned to literature more intensely, suffered from tuberculosis, and settled in Davos Platz, Switzerland, to recuperate (with many trips to Italy). He and his wife had three daughters. (One, Dame Katharine Symonds Furse, rendered distinguished service as a nurse in France in World War I.) Symonds's most enduring work is *Renaissance in Italy* (7 vols., 1875–1886). He also published studies of Percy Bysshe Shelley* (1878), Ben Jonson (1886), Sir Philip Sidney (1886), Michelangelo (1893), and Walt Whitman* (1893, a pioneering effort). Symonds translated works by Michelangelo, Tommaso Campanella, and Benvenuto Cellini. Symonds also wrote autobiographical verse and two privately printed autobiographical volumes discussing his homosexuality (*A Problem in Greek Ethics* [1883] and *A Problem in Modern Ethics* [1891]). James and Symonds had many friends in common, including Margot Asquith (the wife of Herbert Henry Asquith*), Sir Sidney Colvin,* Sir Edmund Wilson Gosse,* Andrew Lang,* Axel Martin Fredrik Munthe* (who was at Symonds's deathbed in Rome), Sir Leslie Stephen,* Robert Louis Stevenson,* and Algernon Charles Swinburne.* Through Lang, James met Symonds in 1877 and wrote to his brother William (28 Feb [1877]) to describe him as "a mild, cultured man, with the Oxford perfume." James admired his work on the Italian Renaissance. In 1883 he sent Symonds a copy of his 1882 essay "Venice." Symonds replied to praise the work. According to a letter from James to Gosse later (16 Sep [1901]), Symonds called it "the best image of V. he had ever seen made." James replied (22 Feb 1884) to Symonds's letter to commend the man as "one of a small number of people who love it [Italy] as much as I do." In a Notebook entry (26 Mar 1884), James summarizes a report by Gosse that their pro-Italian friend Symonds's Calvinist wife disliked his writing. This was the start of "The Author of Beltraffio." James read Symonds's *A Problem in Modern Ethics* and called it, in a letter to Gosse (7 Jan 1893), "infinitely remarkable" but added that he "wish[ed] him [Symonds] more *humour*, it is really *the* saving salt. But [James added] the great reformers never have it—& he is the Gladstone of the affair." On hearing of Symonds's death in Rome, James wrote to Gosse (21 Apr 1893) and was oddly curious to learn "any circumstances about Symonds—or about his death that may be interesting." When the biography of Symonds by his close friend Horatio F. Brown appeared, James read it, as he wrote Gosse (27 Dec 1894), "with the liveliest—and almost painful—interest the 2 volumes on the extraordinary Symonds. They gave me an extraordinary impression of his 'gifts'—yet I don't know what keeps them from being tragic." In an elaborate letter to Ariana Randolph Curtis* (1 Mar 1895), James rejects the idea of writing anything about Symonds, calls "a whole side" of Symonds "strangely morbid and hysterical," hints that he could neither ignore Symonds's homosexuality nor "deal with it either ironically or explicitly," and concludes that Symonds's apparent "need" to write intimate autobiography seems "almost insane." In spite of praising James's essay on "Venice," Symonds once criticized his style as a "laborious beetle-flight." James's library contained twenty books by Symonds, as well as Brown's biography of Symonds.

Symons, Arthur (1865–1945). Welsh-born poet, critic, and translator. His critical works concern Elizabethan drama, English romantic poetry, and Robert Browning.* Symons translated the letters of Charles Baudelaire.* Although in a letter to Sir Edmund Wilson Gosse* (3 Apr 1900) James praises Symons's *The Symbolist Movement in Literature* (1899) as "intelligent & charming," he goes on to object comprehensively to any "English writing on French subjects."

Synge, Bertie Hammond. In "Glasses," Mr. and Mrs. Hammond Synge's son.

Synge, Mr. and Mrs. Hammond. In "Glasses," a couple who chaperon and bilk Flora Louise Saunt.

T

T., A. In *Pyramus and Thisbe*, Catherine West's female pupil, age ten, whose gift of flowers causes Stephen Young momentary jealousy.

Tacchini, Dr. In *The Wings of the Dove*, Milly Theale's Venetian physician. His name undoubtedly derives from that of Taccini, a friend of James's Italian-based American friend William Wilberforce Baldwin.* In July 1890, James, Baldwin, and Taccini took a four-day hike in Tuscany.

Taine, Hippolyte (1828–1893). French philosopher and art and literary critic. He contributed to distinguished literary journals, was an examiner at Saint Cyr, became professor of aesthetics and art history at École des Beaux-Arts (from 1864), and developed into a highly influential critic. He was elected to the French Academy in 1878, by which time he was added travel books to his critical production. He resigned from teaching in 1884 to do research on the French Revolution and its political consequences. Taine's leading works are *Essai sur les Fables de La Fontaine* (1853), *Voyage aux Pyrénées* (1855), *Histoire de la littérature Anglaise* (1865), *Philosophie de l'art* (1865), *Voyage en Italie* (1866), *Vie et opinions de Thomas Graindorge* (1867), *De l'Intelligence* (1870), *Notes sur l'Angleterre* (1872), and *Les origines de la France contemporaine* (3 vols., 1871–1894). Taine's most famous contribution to criticism was his theory that literature was the product of "la race, le milieu, le moment." James began to read and review Taine in the 1860s, and he wrote to Thomas Sergeant Perry* (20 Sep [1867]) that *Thomas Graindorge* was nicely descriptive but not profound. James reviewed (*Nation*, 7 May 1868) *Italy: Rome and Naples*, the 1868 translation of part of Taine's *Voyage en Italie*, calling Taine "the most powerful writer . . . of the day," but also "vehement, impetuous, uncompromising, arrogant—insolent, if you will.'' Though a professor, he is not dry and prudish, James adds. In between general comments on Taine's career and critical position, he quotes his imagistic description of Pisa, calls the author an unsentimental materialist, says that he bleakly sees man as a mere plant or a machine, and voices his special admiration of Taine when he depicts the beauties of Naples; James characterizes the whole work as ''a contribution to literature and history,'' not great morally or philosophically, and with ''many errors of judgment.'' James reviewed (*Nation*, 25 Jan 1872) *Notes sur l'Angleterre*, calling it methodical jottings (taken in England) for Taine's book on English literature— notes on conversations and observations. He criticizes British weather, but James praises it for its variety and picturesqueness. Taine compares England's ''material civilization'' to that of the Roman Empire. James sums up his author's dilations on British beauty, ''moral graces,'' lack of taste, gauche salon etiquette, education, language, and family life (so different from that of France), and the ''English mind.'' James concludes that Taine prefers facts to ideas, answers to doubts. Taine praises British poetry, stable politics, and sound religion, but prefers France for its wealth-distribution system, family life, and society. James drily notes that such ''French optimism has been pretty rudely tested through the whole course of French history.'' James reviewed (*Atlantic Monthly*, Apr 1872) the 1871 translation of Taine's *History of English Literature*. To begin with, James dislikes the overly literal, unidiomatic translation. He calls Taine's work, not a biographical or philological study, but a depiction of the psychology of the English people, an effort ''to discover in the strongest features of the strongest works the temper of the race and time.'' Thus, he feels, Taine ignores much. His theory of race, medium, and time rules out consideration of ''the supernatural'' and other elements helping to create other mixtures. Charles Augustin Sainte-Beuve* is a better critic, since he avoids ''dogmas, moulds, and formulas.'' Sainte-Beuve is empirical, provisional, whereas Taine is prematurely philosophical, sketches distorted portraits, draws quick conclusions. Taine is better when he offers casual impressions and lets his big theory become merely a patterned tapestry in the background. James praises his ''rich and vivid'' imagery and generally admires his energetic style. James addresses Taine on John Bunyan, John Milton, Jonathan Swift, George Gordon, Lord Byron,* William Wordsworth, William Makepeace Thackeray,* and Charles Dickens,* calling some critical comments just and suggestive, some ''defective,'' ''incomplete,'' and ''fallacious.'' James says at last that Taine's work here is ''not conclusive in the sense in which the author tenders it,'' since it fails ''[a]s a philosophical effort'' and applies its theory ''ineffective[ly]''; but it is ''vividly contributive'' as ''a great literary achievement.'' James wrote to his brother William (22 Sep [1872]) that he admired William's review of Taine's book on intelligence, which review he ''but imperfectly understood.'' He wrote to his friend Elizabeth Boott* (24 Jan [1874]) that Taine's book on English literature was wrongly regarded as ''something new under the sun.'' Next, James reviewed (*Nation*, 6 May 1875) the 1875 translation called *Notes on Paris. The Life and*

Opinions of Mr. Frederic-Thomas Graindorge, which he disliked intensely. James defines it as "a brilliant failure," since it is "grave" although it tries to be "light." He says that Taine here is trying to be a combination of Stendhal* and Théophile Gautier*—with their genius for describing city life and material objects, respectively. James notes that when Taine tries to discuss the American West he is ludicrous. James does admit that even though the character Graindorge is brutal and materialistic, Taine cannot help making him "write . . . admirably." In December 1875 or so, James missed by a week meeting Taine at one of the Sunday parties given by Gustave Flaubert.* In "Versailles As It Is" (8 Jan 1876) James includes a review of the first volume of Taine's *Les origines de la France contemporaine*, praising the book for its "literary quality," since it is "narration and exposition," not logic, metaphysics, thought, or scholarship. James relishes its vivid depictions of the ancien régime and Taine's anecdotal "indictment . . . of the social orders that the [French] Revolution swept away." He expects that in later volumes Taine will criticize what that revolution paved the way for. James reviewed (*Nation*, 27 Jul 1876) Taine's *Journal des débats* letter on George Sand,* just published. James quotes Taine extensively on Sand's background, challenging works, fictive world, and spontaneous style. In an untitled note (*Nation*, 6 Jun 1878), James pays Taine a supreme compliment by saying that when he goes to a British art exhibition he puts on "spectacles" provided by Taine's *Notes sur l'Angleterre*. On 18 May 1889, James finally met Taine, at a luncheon in London arranged by their friend Jean Jules Jusserand,* the French diplomat and literary critic. In a Notebook entry the next day, James describes Taine in highly complimentary terms, for his *"bonhomie*, mildness and geniality," charming conversation, and high opinion of Ivan Sergeyevich Turgenev.* James's library contained ten books by Taine.

Taker, Abel F. In "Fordham Castle," a man whose wife Sue has forced him to call himself C. P. Addard and to stay alone in Geneva while she, calling herself Mrs. Sherrington Reeves, climbs in English society. He meets Mrs. Magaw, similarly exiled by her daughter, whom "Mrs. Reeves" meets in England.

Taker, Sue. In "Fordham Castle," Abel F. Taker's wife. She forces him to stay in Geneva while she makes her way in British society as Mrs. Sherrington Reeves.

Tales of Three Cities. Collection of three short stories published in Boston by Osgood, 1884, and in London by Macmillan, 1884: "The Impressions of a Cousin," "Lady Barberina," and "A New England Winter." James's book title is an obvious variation of the title *A Tale of Two Cities*, the popular 1859 novel by Charles Dickens.*

Tarbell, Ida M. (1857–1944). Pennsylvania-born author, lecturer, and editor, who first gained fame as a muckraker for Samuel Sidney McClure.* Her most important work is *The History of the Standard Oil Company* (2 vols., 1904). It is likely that she visited James in Boston, in March 1911, while he was sitting for a portrait being painted by his brother William's son William.

Tarkington, Booth (1869–1946). Indiana novelist, whose works include *Monsieur Beaucaire* (1900), *Penrod* (1914), and *The Magnificent Ambersons* (1918). Tarkington was one of the thirty guests, along with Hamlin Garland,* Elizabeth Jordon,* and Mark Twain,* at the dinner given in James's honor by publisher George Brinton McClellan Harvey* in New York, 8 December 1904. Tarkington later helped to arrange the Indianapolis part (17 March 1905) of James's lecture tour.

Tarrant, Dr. and Mrs. Selah. In *The Bostonians*, Verena Tarrant's parents. He is a mesmerist-healer, whom Olive Chancellor bribes into releasing his daughter to her. Mrs. Tarrant is Mr. and Mrs. Abraham Greenstreet's passive daughter.

Tarrant, Verena. In *The Bostonians*, Dr. and Mrs. Selah Tarrant's feminist orator daughter, who becomes the protégée of Mrs. Amariah Farrinder and especially Olive Chancellor. She is loved by both Miss Chancellor and Basil Ransom. She leaves the feminist movement for Ransom and a married life probably not free of tears.

Tatton. In *The Awkward Age*, the Brookenhams' butler.

Tauchnitz, Christian Bernhard (1816–1895). Member of a distinguished German printing and publishing family. In 1837 he established his own firm in Leipzig, and four years later he began to publish the Tauchnitz *Collection of British and American Authors*. The books were inexpensive but of good quality; they resulted in royalties to the authors, but were not sold in England (to protect copyrights there). By 1908 there were more than four thousand titles. Tauchnitz republished sixteen of James's books between 1878 and 1912, including *Transatlantic Sketches* (retitled *Foreign Parts*, 1883). In "The Third Person" James has Amy Frush smuggle an illegal Tauchnitz volume into England to appease the ghost of an ancestor hanged for more serious smuggling.

Tautphoeus, Jemima Montgomery, Baroness von (1807–1893). Writer, born in County Donegal, Ireland, who married a Bavarian baron named Cajetan Joseph Frederick (1838), published four multivolume novels, was widowed in 1885, and died in Munich. Her novels are *The Initials* (3 vols., 1850), *Cyrilla* (3 vols.,

1853), *Quits* (3 vols., 1857), and *At Odds* (2 vols., 1863). James relished reading *The Initials* when he was a young boy (of perhaps twelve), since it appeared to be "grown-up," as he explains in *A Small Boy and Others*. In a letter to Elizabeth Jordan* (3 May 1907) he recalls his juvenile enthusiasm for *The Initials*, which he remembers as more connected to real life than his fairy-tale favorites. William Dean Howells* regarded Tautphoeus's *The Initials* as the first international novel, but James's novel *The American* has a better claim.

Taylor, James Bayard (1825–1878). Energetic traveler, author, diplomat, and translator, born in Kennett Square, Pennsylvania. Bayard Taylor was apprenticed to a printer, wrote poetry which editor Rufus Griswold praised, published a book of poems (1844), and made arrangements to send travel letters from Germany back to Horace Greeley and his New York *Tribune*, and to other publications. Two years abroad, from Scotland to Italy, resulted in his popular *Views Afoot* (1846). He then became a friendly bohemian editor in New York, a California gold-rush reporter, a husband back in Kennett Square, and a widower. Another two years of travel took him back to Europe, and on to the Middle East and the Far East, which he wrote and lectured about (1851–1855). Two more years of travel, mostly in Scandinavia and Russia, resulted in additional books. He remarried in 1857 and settled down on an eastern Pennsylvania farm, but he had become too cosmopolitan to relax. During the Civil War he was a correspondent and then a legation secretary in St. Petersburg. Once back on his farm, he published three mediocre novels (1863–1866) and wrote undistinguished verse. His acclaimed translation of Goethe's *Faust* (2 vols., 1870, 1871) was probably his greatest achievement. In his last years Taylor became a professor, an occasional poet, a dramatist, and finally a diplomatic appointee to Germany, but— burned out by intense overwork—he died after only a few months there. James harshly reviewed (*Harvard Library Bulletin*, Spring 1957) Taylor's *John Godfrey's Fortunes; Related by Himself; A Story of American Life* (1865), beginning with a sketch of the hero's activities: Godfrey leaves a Pennsylvania village to become a reporter in New York, moves into bohemian literary circles of the sort which Charles Dickens* and William Makepeace Thackeray* satirize better, and gets involved in a ridiculous love plot. Taylor fails to follow his hero's dissipation convincingly. James does not find here the ingredients essential to a good novel. Why do Americans so "misrepresent . . . " their countrymen in fiction? Taylor gives us "a domestic tragedy . . . tainted with the elements of farce." Spoiled by "defective execution" is a good idea [part of James's review is missing here], which is the maturing of a "friendless youth." As is frequently the case, here we have a poor novelist excelling in the presentation of his hero's childhood. This is easy because it is autobiographical. But Taylor tries for two stories here: that of the hero's character and that of the hero's account of it. But the hero incongruously is not what he says he is. Good luck to Taylor next time. James reviewed (*North American Review*, Jan 1875) Taylor's blank-verse play *The Prophet: A Tragedy* (1874), explaining at once that it has "Joe Smith [the prophet] and Brigham Young for . . . heroes." He avers that Taylor displays more pluck than ability here, having "changed the names of his personages, elaborated his plot, left certain details gracefully vague, and, for the most part, steered clear of local color." Taylor's prophet, renamed David Starr, James defines as "neither a fierce monomaniac nor a clever charlatan, but a mysterious mixture of the two." James ridicules the plot, calls the prophet's "pathetic" wife Rhoda "the best [character] in the drama," and quotes a long, dull passage which he says is "the best." James concludes that *The Prophet* is "a suggestive failure," lacking "style," "heat," and "atmosphere." In a letter of reminiscence to the wife of William Dean Howells* (24 Feb 1907), James unaccountably describes Taylor as "ichthyosaurus." In *The Middle Years*, James recalls meeting Taylor at the Howellses' home in the 1860s.

Taylor, Tom (1817–1880). English playwright, short-story writer, editor (of *Punch* [1874–1880]), biographer, lawyer, and government official. According to a letter to his sister Alice (10 Mar [1869]), James declined an invitation to meet Taylor and his wife in London. But in *A Small Boy and Others*, he does recall seeing in London, when he was a child, Taylor's 1855 play *Still Waters Run Deep*. Taylor's 1855 short story "Temptation" may have provided a long-sunken inspiration for "The Turn of the Screw."

Teagle, Miss. In "Sir Dominick Ferrand," little Sidney Ryves's governess.

Temperly, Dora. In "Mrs. Temperly," Maria Temperly's oldest daughter and Effie's and Tishy's sister. Dora is frustratedly in love with Raymond Bestwick.

Temperly, Effie. In "Mrs. Temperly," Maria Temperly's second daughter and the sister of Dora and Tishy.

Temperly, Maria. In "Mrs. Temperly," uncooperative Dora's socially ambitious mother. Maria is Raymond Bestwick's cousin; he loves Dora. Maria is also Effie's and Tishy's mother.

Temperly, Tishy. In "Mrs. Temperly," Maria Temperly's third daughter, who remains diminutive and therefore perhaps not marriageable. She is the sister of Dora and Effie.

Temple, Edith. In *The Tragic Muse*, Miriam Rooth's stage name at one time.

Temple, Mary (Minnie, Minny) (1845–1870). A member of the Temple family*, James's favorite cousin, and the subject of much loving commentary in his autobiographical volumes, especially *Notes of a Son and Brother*. When both of her parents died in 1854, Minny and her three sisters became the wards of Mary Temple Tweedy and Edmund Tweedy, of the Tweedy family.* James had met Minny earlier; but it was at Newport, Rhode Island, in 1865, that "she . . . renewed her appearance to our view, shone with vividest lustre, an essence that preserves her still, more than half a century from the date of her death, in a memory or two where many a relic once sacred has comparatively yielded to time." James vacationed in her company that summer in the White Mountains. She enjoyed reading, talking, drawing, dancing, and sleigh rides. She attracted Oliver Wendell Holmes, Jr.,* John Chipman Gray,* William James, and James himself (who kept his distance), among other young men. Before James left for Europe in 1869 he visited Minny, then sick in Pelham, New York. She often wrote to her "darling Harry." The two hoped to meet a few months later, in Rome. On 8 March 1870, the very day Minny died (of tuberculosis), James happened to write to his brother William, in part to complain about British women: "I revolt from their dreary deathly want of—what shall I call it?— Clover Hooper [later Marian Adams,* wife of Henry Adams*] has it—intellectual grace—Minny Temple has it—moral spontaneity." In a letter to his mother about Minny (26 Mar 1870), James remarks that "[i]t will count in old age, when we live more than now, in reflection, to have had such a figure in our youth." More than forty years later, in *Notes of a Son and Brother*, James solemnly notes that Minny's death marked "the end of our youth." James treated Miss Temple's personality in at least three works of fiction, the last two of them important. In "Poor Richard" the hapless hero is perhaps autobiographical through his being sketched as hopelessly in love with a heroine who is more attracted to Civil War soldiers. And in both *The Portrait of a Lady* and *The Wings of the Dove*, the heroines are made to resemble lithe, doomed Minny. But James wrote to Grace Norton* (28 Dec 1880) that Isabel Archer in the former novel is not an exact portrait of Minny because "[p]oor Minny was essentially *incomplete* and I have attempted to make my young woman more rounded, more finished."

Temple family. James's father's second sister Catherine Margaret James married Robert Emmet Temple, an officer in the American army. Their children, and hence James's cousins, were Robert (Bob) Temple, Jr., William James (Will) Temple (killed in the Civil War), Katherine (Kitty) Temple (who married Richard Stockton Emmet), Mary (Minnie, Minny) Temple,* Ellen (Elly) Temple (who married her sister Kitty's husband's brother Christopher Temple Emmet), and Henrietta Temple (who became Mrs. Leslie Pell-Clarke). Thus, the Temple family became connected through marriage with the Emmet family.* In 1854 Catherine and Robert Temple both died. Their six children became wards of their paternal aunt Mary Temple Tweedy (actually the daughter of Robert Temple by his first marriage and hence the stepdaughter of Catherine James Temple) and her husband Edmund Tweedy, members of the Tweedy family.* The Twee-dys lived in Newport, Rhode Island, and Pelham, New York. James often mentions these lively Temple relatives in his letters and in *A Small Boy and Others* and *Notes of a Son and Brother*. James attended a feminist lecture in

New York with Bob in 1863, and was much amused. In a letter to his brother William (28 Jan [1878]), James describes Henrietta's husband Leslie as "a very charming and attractive boy." James entertained the young couple in London later in 1878. In 1884–1885 Bob evidently appealed to James for money to help him get out of prison.

Tenants. Three-act play (tentatively entitled *Mrs. Vibert*), published in *Theatricals: Two Comedies: Tenants* [and] *Disengaged*, 1894. (Characters: Sir Frederick Byng, Norman Byng, Miss Dyer, Frost, Captain Lurcher, Mildred Stanmore, Stanmore, Claude Vibert, Eleanor Vibert, Vibert.) Widowed Sir Frederick Byng has retired to Beechingham, his Devonshire estate, which includes a nearby lodge called Clere. To keep his ward Mildred Stanmore secure from his son Norman—the two sincerely love each other—Sir Frederick forces him to leave on no notice for his civil service post in India until the girl becomes of age. Meanwhile, long-widowed Eleanor Vibert, Sir Frederick's former beloved and the mother of his natural son, Claude Vibert, rents the lodge for herself, Claude (who does not know about his real father), and his evil tutor Captain Lurcher. Four months later it is Christmas Eve. Lurcher has a hold over Mrs. Vibert, who wants to marry Sir Frederick and have Claude marry Mildred. But that girl, in spite of Sir Frederick's wishes, rejects him; furthermore, she criticizes to him the pushiness of his mother and his tutor, and rejoices at the sudden appearance of Norman, whom she has summoned home from India. Sir Frederick tells Norman instantly that he plans to marry Mrs. Vibert. The next afternoon, Lurcher encourages Claude to compete with Norman, who rebukes the young man, criticizes his mother's plan to marry Sir Frederick, and then tells him that he should never have permitted Claude to get close to Mildred. Threatening to expose Claude as a "bastard," Lurcher urges Mrs. Vibert first to force Sir Frederick to eject Norman and then make Claude win Mildred. Mrs. Vibert tries to smooth things over with Norman; but Claude enters, fancies his mother is being insulted, and tries to hit Norman. Mrs. Vibert tells the two that they are brothers! The upshot: Lurcher is ejected; Norman and Mildred will marry; Claude forgives and offers to care for his mother. She rejects plaintive Sir Frederick. But Mildred gives Mrs. Vibert a unifying family embrace. In a prefatory note, James says that the plot for *Tenants* was suggested by a short story by Henri Rivière.* The story is "Flavien: Scènes de la vie contemporaine" (1874), which features a retired officer, his son and his ward (who fall in love), the officer's former mistress and their son, and that young man's evil tutor. To his great disappointment, James's play was never produced.

Tennyson, Alfred, Lord (1809–1892). Important Victorian poet, born in Lincolnshire, the son of a rector. He was a member of "The Apostles" at Trinity College, Cambridge, which he left without a degree. After publishing *Poems, Chiefly Lyrical* (1830), he traveled on the Continent with his friend Arthur Henry Hallam. Tennyson's *Poems* (1832) were adversely reviewed. When Hallam died

(1833), Tennyson started *In Memoriam* and slowly composed what became *Poems* (2 vols., 1842, including "Locksley Hall"). *The Princess* (1847) concerns women's rights. In 1850 he published *In Memoriam*, married, and was named poet laureate. He lived much of the time on the Isle of Wight (from 1853) and slowly wrote *The Idylls of the King* (1859–1885). He established another residence, called Aldworth, near Haslemere (from 1868). Tennyson wrote several plays, notably *Queen Mary* (1875), *Harold* (1877), and *Becket* (1879). He continued to be productive, with, for example, *Ballads, and Other Poems* (1880), *Tiresias, and Other Poems* (1885), *Locksley Hall, Sixty Years After* (1886), and *Demeter, and Other Poems* (1889). James reviewed (*Galaxy*, Sep 1875) Tennyson's *Queen Mary* and at the outset registers awareness that the poet is not dramatic. *Queen Mary* has "hardly a trace of the Tennyson we know." Here he broods, is not impulsive, is "static"; however, he "represents repose and stillness and . . . fixedness . . . with a splendour that no [other] poet has surpassed." James compares Tennyson with other English poets, then recommends "simply enjoying" the "perfect picturesqueness" of, for example, the *Idylls* ("prig" though King Arthur is) and his imagery in general. By comparison, *Queen Mary* suffers: Its subject cannot be made to fit into the five-act form; instead, the play is shapelessly episodic, too rigidly follows history (whereas Victor-Marie Hugo* in his *Marie Tudor* is too inventive), is theologically simplistic, and is "deficient in [interesting] male characters." James praises some aspects of the play, including its "elevated spirit." James reviewed (*Nation*, 18 Jan 1877) *Harold*, and pronounces it "decidedly weak, decidedly colourless, and tame." It is not Tennysonian in form or quality. The author wrongly regards drama as "[a] succession of short scenes," lets his hero "falter and succumb," gives us a "didactic" heroine, brings in too many minor characters, and offers dialogue without many "sparks." James closes by quoting some well-turned phrases from *Harold*. (James republished these two reviews as "Tennyson's Drama" in *Views and Reviews*, 1908.) Through the hospitality of Lord Houghton,* James met and dined with Tennyson, among other celebrities, in 1877, and describes him in a letter to William James (29 Mar 1877) as a great drinker of port, as "swarthy and scraggy, . . . less handsome than his photos" but "with a face of genius," and as speaking "with a strange, rustic accent." He was "like a creature of some primordial English stock." James later wrote to Charles Eliot Norton* (17 Nov [1878]) that while visiting George Eliot* in Surrey he called on Tennyson for lunch: "[H]e took me up into his study and read aloud . . . 'Locksley Hall,' from beginning to end. James went on to opine that Tennyson "personally is less agreeable than his works." James preferred Robert Browning,* both as a poet and as a puzzling personality. James attended Tennyson's interment at Westminster Abbey. In *The Middle Years*, James describes meeting Tennyson ("the poet I had earliest known and best loved"), his being less "fine," less "fastidious" than he should have been, his "growl" of a voice, his being different from Browning, Tennyson's commending a short

story by James, and especially James's being a guest with James Russell Lowell*
at the Tennysons' home. James's library contained seven books by Tennyson.

Teresa (Teresita). In *Watch and Ward*, a Peruvian woman whom Roger Lawrence loves but only until Nora Lambert writes to him.

Terminations. Collection of four short stories published in London by Heinemann, 1895, and in New York by Harper, 1895: "The Death of the Lion,"
"The Coxon Fund," "The Middle Years," and "The Altar of the Dead."

Terry, Dame Ellen (1847–1928). Celebrated English actress, born into a provincial theatrical family in Coventry. She was a child actress in Charles Kean's
company from (1857 to 1859), made her adult debut in Bristol in 1862, played
in stock companies, and in 1864 married the famous painter George Frederick
Watts.* She was his model, and he painted her portrait, often idealized, several
times. (They separated after ten months of marriage, and were divorced in 1877.)
She began acting with Sir Henry Irving* in 1867. She lived with Edward Godwin,
architect and theatrical designer, beginning in 1868, and bore him two children.
When the novelist Charles Reade* induced her to return to the theater, she
became Irving's leading lady (1878–1902), in plays by William Shakespeare*
(John Singer Sargent* painted her as Lady Macbeth), traditional comedies, and
melodrama. She and Irving toured the United States eight times (1883–1901).
After discontinuing her association with him, she acted in plays by Henrik Johan
Ibsen* and George Bernard Shaw,* including ones the latter wrote with her in
mind. She and Shaw exchanged more than three hundred delightful letters (1896–
1922) in what has been called a "paper courtship" (published 1931). He had
long urged her to leave Irving, whom he regarded as too conservative for her
talents. She married three times, never with much stability. In 1908 she published
The Story of My Life (which does not mention James). In later years, she lectured
and also appeared in movies. Her home in Kent is now the Ellen Terry Memorial
Museum. In his drama notices, it took James a long time to begin praising
Terry's acting ability. In 1877 he described her as "picturesque . . . like a
preRaphaelitish drawing in a magazine . . . but . . . simply *not* an actress" ("The
London Theatres"). In 1878 he called her performance in the title role of W.
G. Wills's 1878 *Olivia* "amateurish," even though he liked her "pathetic, even
beautiful countenance" (*Nation*, 13 Jun 1878). In 1879 he observed that she has
"a certain amateurish, angular grace, a total want of what the French call *chic*,"
while her voice has a "monotonous husky thickness which is extremely touching,
though it . . . interferes with . . . many of her speeches" ("The London Theatres"). In 1881 he praised Terry for several specific roles (especially that of
Ophelia in Shakespeare's *Hamlet*), criticized her in others (notably that of Portia
in Shakespeare's *The Merchant of Venice*), and generalized that she "has too
much nature, and we should like a little more art" ("The London Theatres").
He objected to Irving's casting "the large, the long, the mature Miss Terry" as

Juliet to his Romeo ("London Pictures and London Plays," 1882). And he deplored her misunderstanding of Margaret's part in an Irving production of *Faust*, and with it her "strange amateurishness of form" ("The Acting in Mr. Irving's *Faust*," *Century*, Dec 1887). By 1896, however (perhaps partly because he was then dickering with Terry for her to produce one of his own plays), James favorably reviewed her performance in Shakespeare's *Cymbeline*: "naturally poetic, . . . delightful breadth and tenderness, delightful grace and youth" ("Mr. Henry Irving's Production of *Cymbeline*," *Harper's Weekly*, 21 Nov 1896). After James's play *Guy Domville* suffered its disastrous opening (5 January 1895), Terry (whose sister Marion Terry acted as Mrs. Peverel opposite George Alexander's Guy Domville) asked the author for a play. James wrote the one-act *Summersoft* for her in the summer of 1895, sent it to her, and accepted £100 in August 1895 against future royalties. When it was not produced, he retrieved it three years later, turned it into the short story "Covering End," and in 1907 turned it back into the *The High Bid*. Oddly, when this play opened in Edinburgh, on 26 March 1907, Terry was performing in Edinburgh in Shaw's *Captain Brassbound's Conversion*. She learned about James's play and protested that she held the rights to it but was informed by James's agent James Brand Pinker* that she had no contract. Later, James called Terry "perfidious" in a letter to his old friend Mrs. W. K. Clifford* (20 Oct 1907).

Terry, Louisa Crawford (née Ward) (1823–1897). The sister of Samuel Ward, Julia Ward Howe,* and Annie Ward Mailliard. Louisa Ward married Thomas Crawford* in Rome in 1844. One of their children was the novelist Francis Marion Crawford.* After Thomas Crawford's death, she married one of his best friends, the painter Luther Terry,* in 1861. The couple lived in Italy the remainder of their lives. One of their children was Margaret Terry (later Mrs. Winthrop Chanler). James met the Terrys in Italy in the 1870s. James wrote to his sister Alice from Rome (2 Nov 1877) that "[t]he poor Terrys of former fame are down in the world, having lost two thirds of their property." James also knew Sam Ward, Julia Ward Howe, and Margaret and Winthrop Chanler.

Terry, Luther (Eleutereo) (1813–1900). American portrait, genre, religious, and allegorical painter, long resident in Italy. He left his native Connecticut in 1833 to recover his health and to study art in Rome. He knew Thomas Crawford,* married his widow Louisa Ward Crawford* in 1861, and was regarded by Francis Marion Crawford,* her son, as a good stepfather. Terry worked in New York for a time (1879–1881) but then returned to Italy. James knew Terry, his wife, his stepchildren, and the Terrys' daughter Margaret Chanler and her husband Winthrop Chanler.

Tester, Ambrose. In "The Path of Duty," Lady Margaret Vandeleur's lover, who to please his father becomes engaged to Joscelind Bernardstone. But then Lady Margaret's husband dies. Ambrose and Joscelind marry, and have a son and a daughter.

Tester, Francis (Frank). In "The Path of Duty," Ambrose Tester's older brother, who drinks, gambles, and dies.

Tester, Master and Miss. In "The Path of Duty," Ambrose and Joscelind Tester's young children.

Tester, Sir Edmund. In "The Path of Duty," Ambrose Tester's father.

Thackeray, Anne Isabella. The maiden name of Lady Anne Isabella Ritchie.*

Thackeray, William Makepeace (1811–1863). Great, critically challenging Victorian novelist, born in Calcutta, India (where his father was a civil servant), and educated from 1817 in England at Chiswick and Charterhouse, then at Trinity College, Cambridge, which he left in 1830 without a degree. Thackeray traveled, studied law, wrote and sketched for a short-lived journal, went to Paris to study drawing, and married in 1836. He began to write successfully for several magazines (including *Fraser's* and, later, *Punch*). His first book was *The Paris Sketch-Book* (1840). He deepened his light style following the insanity, diagnosed in 1840, of his wife (who long outlived him). He turned out a stream of brilliant novels: *Barry Lyndon* (1844), *Vanity Fair* (1847–1848), *Pendennis* (1848–1850), *Henry Esmond* (1852), and *The Newcomes* (1853–1855). Thackeray continued to publish short pieces and began to lecture; a tour took him in 1852 to the United States, where he lectured on eighteenth-century British humorists. *The Virginians* (1857–1859) is a sequel to *Henry Esmond*. (All but *Henry Esmond* were first published serially.) Having retired from the staff of *Punch* in 1854, he became the first editor of the *Cornhill Magazine* (1860–1862). Notable among his later works are *Philip* (1861–1862) and the unfinished *Denis Duval* (1864). Always less popular than his contemporary Charles Dickens,* Thackeray portrayed British society more profoundly and realistically, and with more melancholy, satirical humor. Thackeray during his 1852 lecture tour in America called on James Thomas Fields* and his wife Annie Adams Fields* in Boston, and also on James's father in New York, where he met young James, admired his jacket with its brass buttons, and nicknamed him "Buttons" because of them. (James recalls this incident in *A Small Boy and Others*.) Thackeray visited the James family once more, this time in 1857 in Paris, where he teased little Alice because of her fancy dress. James's childhood reading of Thackeray turned his first mature London experiences into literary adventures. James knew Thackeray's oldest daughter Anne Isabella Thackeray (later Lady Anne Isabella Ritchie*), met her often socially, and wrote to her frequently. His criticism is dotted with passing references to Thackeray, and he published two pieces on him. He unfavorably reviewed (*Nation*, 9 Dec 1875) *Thackerayana: Notes and Anecdotes* (1875), regretting both that Thackeray's "exceedingly amateurish" drawings are published here and also that neither his biography nor his "delightful" letters have been. James complains that this "reprehensible and inartistic . . . book" merely teases one's desire for biographical data and calls it padded, but he is grateful that it includes some of Thackeray's college burlesques and "a great deal of gossip about Thackeray's personal and literary career." Finally, James wrote "Winchelsea, Rye, and 'Denis Duval' " (*Scribner's Magazine*, Jan 1901; reprinted in *English Hours*, 1905). Hoping to find that a "reperusal" of the novel would illuminate its locales, Winchelsea and Rye, James found instead that the towns shed light on the novel. James praises the narrator Duval's reminiscences about "his wondrous boy-life at Winchelsea and Rye" when the "Huguenot fugitives" landed there; then he describes the " 'Antient Towns' " in their sea setting. Did Thackeray find the subject or the setting for *Denis Duval* first? Touching on the habit of Sussex coastal smuggling, James then discusses the brilliance of Thackeray's combining his own eighteenth-century English background with his hero's nineteenth-century English background. Did the author know what his public wanted or only what it would take? Why does he avoid depicting, even the "haunted square of Winchelsea"? What was the subject of this literary fragment to have been? Thackeray never says. A novelist is like a fox hunter, the fox being his idea; here, "[t]he fox has quite got away." James returns to the notion that Winchelsea is "haunted," and he discusses its battle with the sea, its fragment of a church, and its square. He turns to Rye: its channel cliff, gardens and walls, cobbles, and river and harbor and their sketchers; then Hastings, ten miles west: its old gates (with an Italian-looking road leading out of one of them), its church (which feeds a sense of "obliterated history"), and its shabby houses and one intriguing cottage ("perched" near the east gate and owned by a famous actress [Dame Ellen Terry*]). James looks in vain for buildings frequented by Thackeray's Duval family and associates and would like to lock up the author until he points them out. Finally, James discusses the mellow, painterly view of Rye from "the pedestal of Winchelsea." The Rye church should have been a bit taller, as it would have been in France or Italy! At sunset, the town looks like "a huge floating boat," "a miniature Mont-Saint Michel"; in summer, its marsh "recall[s] . . . the Roman Campagna." Thackeray was often in mind when James wrote his fiction. Thus, Mme. Grandoni in *Roderick Hudson* says that Christina Light's mother resembles something out of a Thackeray novel. Further, *Roderick Hudson* repeats the dual theme of failing artist plus marriage market that James found in *The Newcomes*, which novel may have suggested to the author of *The American* certain scenes, techniques, plot elements, a satirical target, and Christopher Newman's victory in defeat. Plot ingredients in *The Portrait of a Lady* would appear to be borrowed from Thackeray and his contemporaries. Several of James's so-called bad heroines—and near heroines—from Christina Light and Serena Merle through Olive Chancellor to Kate Croy and Charlotte Stant, are as sympathetically treated as Thackeray's Becky Sharp (from *Vanity Fair*) and Beatrix Esmond. The complex relationship involving Lady Castlewood, her daughter Beatrix, and the hero in *Henry Esmond* may also have influenced James in depicting Comtesse Marie de Vionnet, her daughter Jeanne de Vionnet, and Chad Newsome of *The Ambas-*

sadors, in which novel Maria Gostrey is oddly said to look like Thackeray's Major Pendennis. James's library contained eighteen books by Thackeray.

Theale, Milly. In *The Wings of the Dove*, Susan Shepherd Stringham's rich, dying young companion from New York. She is a manipulated guest of Maud Manningham Lowder in London, and she becomes the victim of Kate Croy's machinations but, in the process, redeems Kate's fiancé Merton Densher. Milly's motivation is a matter of ongoing critical debate. In 1903 Emilie Busbey Grigsby* started the false rumor that she was the model for Milly Theale.

"The Théâtre Français." Theater essay, published in *Galaxy* (Apr 1877); reprinted in *French Poets and Novelists*, 1878. James begins (and later continues) with comments on Francisque Sarcey* and his *Comédiens et Comédiennes: La Comédie Française*. James says that the Théâtre Français rests on "accumulate[d]" traditions. Long performances there are "smooth and harmonious" with "graceful," well-costumed actresses and gentlemanly actors. He discusses other Parisian theaters: the Gymnase and the Palais Royal, both merely adequate; the Odéon and the Conservatoire Dramatique (each a "nursery" for the Français, which appropriates personnel from the lesser houses as it pleases). He notes that the Français sometimes is less than superb (especially in tragedy, which is excellent in England). He praises "the exquisite humour" of François Joseph Régnier's performance in *L'Aventurière* by Guillaume Victor Émile Augier*: A drinking scene Régnier played with Jean Baptiste Prosper Bressant remains "one of the most perfect things I have seen on the stage." Next James praises "*philosophic*" François Jules Edmond Got* as a uniquely fine actor, then provides a list of other meritorious performers, including Benoît Constant Coquelin* and Sarah Bernhardt.* James offers examples (mainly Molière's *Médecin Malgré Lui*) to show that Got's repertory belongs both "to reality and . . . to fantasy," then lauds the "incomparable" Coquelin. James turns to actor Louis Arsène Delaunay ("the popular favorite" now accused by some of mannerisms) and actress Marie Favart ("powerful rather than . . . interesting"). James concludes with notes on four more actresses discussed by Sarcey: Madelaine Brohan ("delightful" to see and hear but with "redundancy of contour"), Jeanne Arnould-Plessy ("brilliant" but "cold"), Bernhardt ("deserves a chapter for herself"), and Sophie Alexandrine Croizette ("a secondary . . . Bernhardt").

Theatricals: Second Series: The Album [and] *The Reprobate*. Collection of two unproduced plays published in London by Osgood, McIlvaine, 1894, and in New York by Harper, 1894. In a prefatory note to the book, James says that these plays, both plain little "domestic fairy-tale[s]," were written in response to a theater emergency. His theory clashed with the demands of managers and actors, and he had to practice "excision" and "selection."

Theatricals: Two Comedies: Tenants [and] ***Disengaged.*** Collection of two unproduced plays published in London by Osgood, McIlvaine, 1894, and in New
York by Harper, 1894. In a prefatory note to a book, James explains that these
plays were written as pure comedies to be acted by a particular company but
were never produced; hence, he is issuing them here in textually accurate forms.
He also mentions that the source of the plot of *Tenants* is a short story by Henri
Rivière.*

Theign, Lord. In *The Outcry*, the novel, and the *The Outcry*, the play, Lady
Kitty Imber's and Lady Grace's widowed father, and Lady Amy Sandgate's
close friend (age fifty-eight to sixty). Among many other paintings at his Dedborough estate (including a Joshua Reynolds portrait of his ancestor the Duchess
of Waterbridge), Theign owns the Mantovano* which Hugh Crimble reveres
and Breckenridge Bender wants to buy (among others). After Theign donates
the Mantovano to the National Gallery, it is likely that he and Lady Amy will
get married.

Theobald. In "The Madonna of the Future," the loquacious, sterile painter in
Florence. His Madonna, to be modeled by aging Serafina, remains "of the
future."

"Théodolinde." 1878 title of "Rose-Agathe."

Theodora. In "Daniel Deronda: A Conversation," the pro-George Eliot* reader,
who is opposed by Pulcheria. Constantius mediates between the two.

Theory, Agnes Roy. In "Georgina's Reasons," William Roy's sister, Percival
Theory's wife, and hence Mildred and Kate Theory's sister-in-law.

Theory, Kate. In "Georgina's Reasons," the younger sister of Percival and
Mildred Theory. Captain Raymond Benyon would like to divorce Georgina
Gressie Benyon Roy and marry Kate.

Theory, Mildred. In "Georgina's Reasons," the sick sister of Percival and
Kate Theory.

Theory, Percival. In "Georgina's Reasons," the brother of Mildred and Kate
Theory; he is Agnes Roy Theory's husband.

Theuriet, André (pen name of Claude Adhémar André, 1833–1907). Prolific
French novelist, short-story writer, and playwright. James reviewed (*Nation*, 23
Sep 1875) his *Le Mariage de Gérard* (1875). James begins by contrasting English
novels, which are addressed mainly to single young women, and French novels,

which "count them [such readers] out." He then notes that the heroine of Theuriet's present novel is dull; in fact, the whole book is "flat and pointless."

"The Third Person." Short story (11,900 words), published in *The Soft Side*, 1900. (Characters: Amy Frush, Cuthbert Frush, Susan Frush, Mrs. Frush, Rev. Mr. Patten.) Watercolorist Susan Frush and her younger second cousin Amy Frush, an amateur writer, inherit property from their aunt at Marr, in southern England. Going there, the two meet for the first time and discover that they like each other and want to live together in the home instead of selling it. They rummage in the basement and find a chest full of old papers which they ask the local vicar, the Rev. Mr. Patten, to decipher for them. That night, Susan sees the ghost of a man with his neck twisted to one side. Later, Rev. Patten tells them that according to the family papers their ancestor Cuthbert Frush was hanged. Next Amy reports seeing the neck-twisted ghost. Rev. Patten now adds that Cuthbert was hanged for the once necessary, even aristocratic crime of smuggling. When Susan sees the ghost again, Amy grows jealous and wants an experience with it also. The two are briefly suspicious of each other. Then Susan admits sending £20 to the government to ease the ghost's conscience. Saying that such a procedure is insufficient, Amy goes to France and smuggles a Christian Bernhard Tauchnitz* volume into England on her return. The ghost leaves in peace. The southern English setting of this slight ghost story owes much to James's love of Rye and Winchelsea.

Thomas. In "A Most Extraordinary Case," Maria Mason's phaeton driver.

Thompson, Elizabeth (née Southerden) (1844–1933). Popular British painter, who specialized in battle scenes, and author. Born in Lausanne, she studied art in London, Rome, and Florence and began to exhibit with great success in the 1870s. She married Colonel William Butler in 1877 and accompanied him to Egypt, South Africa, and elsewhere. She was patronized by Queen Victoria. She published *Letters from the Holy Land* (1903) and her autobiography (1923). James reviewed a London exhibition of three paintings by Elizabeth Thompson (*Nation*, 26 Apr 1877). He likes them better than advanced praise made him think he would, and he especially admires the modulation of color and "anecdotical" sincerity displayed in a Crimean War scene. He ventures to criticize the praise John Ruskin* accorded her painting of a Battle of Waterloo episode. James opines that, although she could never have observed battle scenes, she paints with "feminine subtlety" and without "feminine weakness or vagueness." He notes that French art critics would deplore her technique and verve, but adds that a French artist painting these same scenes might have mixed "less real sincerity" but with greater "*chic* of execution."

Thompson. In "The Abasement of the Northmores," a person whom Lady Northmore asks for letters from her late husband.

Thompson, Angelica. In "Osborne's Revenge," the fictitious name which Philip Osborne gives to a person whose photograph he has purchased to deceive Henrietta Congreve.

Thomson, John, F.R.G.S. (?–?). British traveler who between 1867 and 1895 wrote books (some illustrated with his own photographs) on Cambodia, China, Cyprus, Formosa, London, and Siam. He also published a book on techniques of photography, a translation of a book in French on photography, and a translation of a book on Spain. James reviewed (*Nation*, 22 Apr 1875) Thomson's *The Straits of Malaca, Indo-China, and China; or, Ten Years' Travels, Adventures, and Residence Abroad* (1875), which he praises as "entertaining" though "bulky." He quotes with relish Thomson's descriptions of a boat ride down the Yangtze River, a Bangkok magistrate holding court, the ruined Cambodian temple of Nakhon, and the tricks of a Chinese magician. James likes Thomson's "picture of life and manners in the commercial stations" of various Far-Eastern capitals now invaded by various Westerners, and he finds his account of penetrating the interior of Formosa "most interesting"; however, he is worried by his hints that China, a land of pauperism, filth, dense population, and efficient arsenals, may be growing xenophobic.

Thorne, Jane. In *A Change of Heart*, Margaret Thorne's sick mother and Robert Staveley's aunt, widowed for ten years. Martha Noel is her paid companion.

Thorne, Margaret. In *A Change of Heart*, Jane Thorne's haughty daughter and Robert Staveley's cousin. Margaret has just turned twenty-one years of age and has inherited a fortune. At her well-attended birthday party, Charles Pepperel appears, proposes, and is accepted in spite of Staveley's telling her that Pepperel once stole from Martha Noel, Jane's paid companion, and is now after Margaret's fortune.

"Three Excursions." Travel essay, published in the *Galaxy* (Sep 1877); reprinted in part as "Two Excursions" in *Portraits of Places*, 1883, and in *English Hours*, 1905. First, James describes Derby Day, "the great festival of the English people." He takes a four-horse coach from Piccadilly for a crowded but "pretty" drive to Epsom. All are prepared for " 'larks,' " especially stout women. The Epsom course resembles "the crater of a volcano without the mountain." The crowd is a "rich representation of human life off its guard." The race whizzes, "is anything but beautiful," is quickly over. Then comes the "demoralisation": milling crowds, lunch, varied entertainment, drunkenness—in short, "a huge Bohemian encampment." Then the carriage traffic back again. The event is an "unbuttoning of the public strait-jacket." Second, James visited Hatfield House, twenty miles outside London. This Jacobean mansion, owned by the Marquis of Salisbury, is "one of the most beautiful things the world possesses." Beyond an oak-filled park and "the most picturesque of stables" (once a chapel), one sees the "long red house," with square windows and "castellated top," shaped like a parallelogram with two wings. This "labyrinth of rooms" features beds, hangings, cabinets, "long gallery" above, "chapel . . . [with] cushioned niches," and banquet hall. James made contact here "with the protective virtues of the past." Third, James was happily invited to a commemoration at Oxford. He slept in a student's room near the quadrangle and clock tower. Then he had breakfast with American students, watched the conferring of honorary degrees in the Sheldonian Theatre, accompanied by noise from boisterous students, then observed tiresome "collegiate exercises." Afterward came a colorful procession of robed academics and "ladies in bright finery" to a luncheon offered in the dining hall of a graduate college. The rest of his time at Oxford was memorable too: gardens, lawns, trees, music, ices, observed flirtations, "quiet dinner," portraits and windows, "superior talk," and that unique air of Oxford "over all."

Thrupp. In "In the Cage," the name of a furnished apartment.

Tiblaud, Abbé. In "Gabrielle de Bergerac," a friend of the narrator's mother the Baroness de Bergerac. The narrator's father dislikes Tiblaud.

Tinayre, Marguerite Suzanne Marcelle Chastreau (1872–1948). French novelist and biographer. Her many frank, feminist novels include *Avant l'amour* (1897), *Maison du Péché* (1899), *La Vie amoureuse de François Barbazanges* (1904), *La Rebelle* (1905), and *L'Ennemi intime* (1931). By letter (8 Nov 1905), James queries Edith Newbold Jones Wharton* about *Avant l'amour* and calls its authoress "the amazing little Mme Tinayre"; in a later letter to Wharton (18 Dec 1905), he gossips about the effect of Tinayre, whom he punningly calls "attentuated," on rigidly righteous Mary Augusta Ward.*

Tintoretto, Jacopo Robusti (c. 1518–1594). Great and vigorous Italian painter of the Venetain school. He was influenced by Michelangelo (for design), Titian* (for color use), Schiavoni (for rapidity), and Paolo Veronese.* Tintoretto painted oils and frescoes of mythological, allegorical, historical, and biblical scenes of great power, often with fine light effects, poetic coloration, and movement in multiplaned counterpoint. " . . . Tintoretto is assuredly the greatest of painters"—so James wrote from Venice to his brother William (25 Sept [1869]). More temperately, he numbered Tintoretto among the "really great masters" in "Art" (*Atlantic Monthly*, Jan 1872). James commented on Tintoretto so tellingly in his travel essay "From Venice to Strassburg [*sic*]" (1873) that John Ruskin,* when he read it, wrote to Charles Eliot Norton* to commend the young author. James complimented Ferdinand Victor Eugène Delacroix* in his review of his letters by saying that the French painter reminded him of Titian through also being "a great colourist and a great composer." James's letters, particularly his early ones, contain several comments on Tintoretto. In the preface to Volume

VII of *The Novels and Tales of Henry James*, 1908, James notes that when he was contriving to unify two plots (political and theatrical) in *The Tragic Muse*, he remembered that Tintoretto could also combine separate actions into one picture.

Tischbein. In *What Maisie Knew*, one of Ida Farange's lovers.

Tissot, Victor (1845–1917). A French writer of many socioethnological travel books (some coauthored with Constant Améro), on Germany, Austria, Hungary, Switzerland, Russia, and several non-European regions. In "Parisian Topics" (New York *Tribune*, 1 Apr 1876), James tersely reviewed Tissot's *Les Prussians en Allemagne* (1876), saying that its "being placed under an interdict in Berlin" (presumably for its "Teutophobia") constitutes "the one presumption in favor of M. Tissot's veracity"! He adds that Frenchmen studying Germany should avoid Tissot's books. James reviewed (*Nation*, 17 May 1877) Tissot's *Voyage aux Pays Annexés* (1876), noting that Tissot, who is "consistently scurrilous and abusive," is popular with the French because of their ignorance and hatred of the Germans, whom Tissot regards as depraved, immoral, brutal, indecent, and base. James brands Tissot cheap and inaccurate, "ingenious but essentially vulgar."

Titian (c. 1477–1576). Great painter of the Venetian school, born in Pieve di Cadore. He was apprenticed to a Venetian painter and mosaicist, studied under Giovanni Bellini, and then worked with Giorgione. After painting in Padua about 1511, Titian returned to Venice to execute mythological and religious paintings in governmental buildings and churches. He also worked in Ferrara at this time and later, and soon he found himself famous. In the 1540s and early 1550s he went to Rome and Germany to execute portraits. He became court painter to royalty. When elected to the Florentine Academy in 1566, he was in splendid health and enjoyed much prosperity. He entertained well and was generous, but sometimes he had trouble collecting payments for the splendid work he had done. He continued painting until the plague killed him in his very late nineties. Titian painted landscapes (especially mountains) feelingly, was a competent draftsman, worked on several paintings at once, and used colors marvelously. "I admire Raphael; I enjoy Rubens; but I passionately love Titian"—so James wrote to his brother William (13 May 1869). James mentions Titian in a dozen art reviews, usually, however, only to note that other painters do not measure up to him. For example, in a note (*Nation*, 23 May 1878), James says that a certain painting "looks at first like . . . some richly-glowing Titian." In some of his novels and short stories, James has characters view and be influenced by Titians; in addition, references and allusions in his fiction to specific works by Titian add symbolic overtones.

Tolstoy, Leo Nikolayevich, Count (1828–1910). World-renowned Russian novelist, moral philosopher, and religious mystic. As a nobleman, he inherited large estates. After university study at Kazan (1844–1847) and army service (1851–1857), he traveled abroad, farmed at Yasnaya Polyana, emancipated his serfs, married (1862), and experienced a spiritual transformation (1876) leading to a creed of nonresistance to evil. His major works include *Childhood* (1852), *Sevastopol* (1855), *War and Peace* (1866), *Anna Karenina* (1877), *A Confession* (1884), "The Death of Ivan Ilyich" (1884), and *The Kreutzer Sonata* (1889). In a letter to Mary Augusta Ward (26 Jul 1899), James places Tolstoy among the greatest novelists. He criticizes Tolstoy for "promiscuous shiftings of standpoint and centre," but excuses such point-of-view violations on the grounds that Tolstoy aims to present "*quantity*" and "pile up" "complexity." James wrote to Sir Edmund Wilson Gosse* (14 May 1900) to decline an invitation to write an essay on Tolstoy, pleading that he knew only "his 2 or 3 great novels (& one or two Kreutzer Sonatas &c.;) . . . " In letters to Sir Hugh Seymour Walpole,* James says that "Tolstoi and D[ostoevsky] are fluid pudding, though not tasteless, because the amount of their own minds and souls in solution in the broth gives it savour and flavour, thanks to the strong, rank quality of their genius and experience" (19 May 1912); and later adds that Tolstoy "doesn't *do* to read over," labels *War and Peace* "interminable," and criticizes it for the ugly wastefulness of its "flopping looseness," "formless shape," and "denial of composition, selection and style" (21 Aug 1913). More publicly, in the preface to Volume VII of *The Novels and Tales of Henry James*, 1908, James calls Tolstoy's *War and Peace* and other such huge novels "large loose baggy monsters." James's library contained one book by Tolstoy.

"Tommaso Salvini." Theater essay, published in the *Atlantic Monthly* (Mar 1883), about the Italian actor Tommaso Salvini.*

"The Tone of Time." Short story (7,700 words), published in *Scribner's Magazine* (Nov 1900); reprinted in *The Better Sort*, 1903. (Characters: Mrs. Bridgenorth, Mary Juliana Tredick.) The painter narrator turns over to fellow artist Mary Tredick the commission for a portrait of a handsome, imaginary man. The order came to him from Mrs. Bridgenorth, and the painting must have the tone of about twenty years' time. Miss Tredick agrees. When the narrator, acting as intermediary, returns, sees the painting, and commends her for a brilliant depiction of an insolent, unsuffering man, Miss Tredick cries out that she painted it in hate, implying that she knew and was injured by the original. The narrator takes the portrait to Mrs. Bridgenorth, who recognizes the portrayed person: She also knew the original. She desperately wants the picture, but when Miss Tredick hears the details from the narrator, she suspects that Mrs. Bridgenorth is the woman for whom the original left her and whom he would have married but for his sudden death. She refuses to sell her work at any price. Both women later die, and the narrator—grown old—now owns the portrait. This story of impossible coincidence had a long gestation, as is recorded in James's *Notebooks*. According to one entry (22 Sep 1895), Minnie, the wife of his novelist friend Paul Bourget,* suggested to James the idea that someone imitating Bourget's work might, by accentuating the aspects "liked least" in it, make her disenchanted with his work in general. Several years later (7 May 1898), James turned to the plot again, this time linking it with an idea evidently from Italian novelist Luigi Gualdo* about a "woman who wants to have *been* married—to *have become* a widow." She has a painter paint a portrait of her imaginary, now-deceased husband. Then (16 Feb 1899) James sketched out the contours of what became "The Tone of Time," tentatively complicating everything by having the imaginary widow consult one painter, be referred to "his old friend and comrade," and even argue with the commissioned painter, who also knew the original of the portrait. Not only "The Tone of Time" but also James's "Maud-Evelyn" and "Hugh Merrow," which split off from the Gualdo inspiration, deal with the Jamesian theme of "what might have been." James abandoned "Hugh Merrow" because it too closely resembled both "The Tone of Time" and "Maud-Evelyn."

Toovey, Mrs. Blanche Bertha Nancy Vanderbank. In *The Awkward Age*, Gustavus Vanderbank's sister, called Nancy.

"The Top of the Tree." Tentative title of "The Velvet Glove."

Topping, Florine (Dorine?). In *The Reverberator*, a journalist who aids George B. Flack.

Torrance, Mrs. In "A New England Winter," Rachel Torrance's sick mother.

Torrance, Rachel. In "A New England Winter," a woman whom Pauline Mesh invites to Boston at Susan Daintry's indirect request to brighten her son Florimond Daintry's vacation. Miss Torrance correctly judges the young man to be shallow.

Tottenham. In "A Passionate Pilgrim," Richard Searle's Lackley butler.

Touchett, Daniel Tracy. In *The Portrait of a Lady*, a rich, retired, sick old American-born banker who worked in London and now lives at his nearby estate called Gardencourt. He is Lydia Touchett's semiseparated husband, Ralph Touchett's father, and Isabel Archer's uncle. At his death, he bequeaths Isabel a great sum of money. James may have patterned him in some ways after Russell Sturgis,* the expatriate banker father of Howard Overing Sturgis.*

Touchett, Lydia. In *The Portrait of a Lady*, Daniel Tracy Touchett's independent, crotchety, semiestranged wife, Ralph Touchett's mother, and Isabel Archer's aunt. She is Serena Merle's friend.

Touchett, Ralph. In *The Portrait of a Lady*, Daniel and Lydia Touchett's invalid son. He is Lord Warburton's firm friend and becomes his cousin Isabel Archer's hopelessly devoted admirer. He persuades his dying father to leave Isabel a great sum of money. His stated adverse opinion of Gilbert Osmond just before her marriage to him causes a rift between Ralph and Isabel. She is, nevertheless, at his deathbed.

Townsend, Arthur. In *Washington Square*, Morris Townsend's cousin. He is to wed Dr. Austin Sloper's niece Marian Almond.

Townsend, Morris. In *Washington Square*, loyal Catherine Sloper's self-centered, unsuccessful suitor, of whom her father, Dr. Austin Sloper, rightly but callously disapproves. Townsend marries elsewhere; much later, when widowed, he renews his plea to Catherine, but is denied.

Townsend, Mrs. Morris. In *Washington Square*, Morris Townsend's unhappy wife, who dies.

Traffle, Jane and Sidney. In "Mora Montravers," Mora Montravers's foster mother and her husband. She gives Walter Puddick a large sum of money to marry Mora. Sidney wistfully admires Mora's bohemianism.

Trafford, Percy. In *Disengaged*, a young British diplomat, soon to go to Copenhagen, who flirts irresponsibly with Lady Amy Brisket. He helps pressure Captain Llewellyn Prime into proposing to Blandina Wigmore, but is later convinced by Mrs. Jasper and others that he admires the girl himself and hence proposes to her, thus "disengaging" Prime.

"A Tragedy of Error." Short story (8,000 words), published in the *Continental Monthly* (Feb 1864). (Characters: Charles Bernier, Hortense Bernier, Mme. Bernier, Josephine, Vicomte Louis de Meyrau, M. de Saulges, Valentine.) Hortense Bernier loses her lover Vicomte Louis de Meyrau's support when she reveals that her crippled husband Charles is returning home to the French port city of H—. She accordingly hires a boatman to kill her husband. Through a mix-up, however, Louis is murderously drowned instead, and Charles limps back to her after all. This story was the first one James ever published, and he did so anonymously. It has little to recommend it besides competent handling of the scene and the surprise ending. In its love triangle, wrong killing, final scene, and tone, the story owes much to *Léone Léoni* (1834) by George Sand,* one of James's favorite authors.

The Tragic Muse. Novel (199,600 words), published in the *Atlantic Monthly* (Jan 1889–May 1890); revised and reprinted in Boston and New York by Houghton, Mifflin 1890, and in London by Macmillan, 1890; revised and reprinted in

The Novels and Tales of Henry James, volumes VII, VIII, 1908. (Characters: Mrs. Billinghurst, Lord Bottomley, Mme. Honorine Carré, Charles Carteret, Chayter, George Dallow, Julia Sherringham Dallow, Basil Dashwood, Lord Davenant, Mrs. Delamere, Lady Agnes Dormer, Bridget Dormer, Grace Dormer, Sir Nicholas Dormer, Nicholas Dormer, Percival Dormer, Mlle. Dunoyer, Durand, Lord Egbert, Mr. and Mrs. Gresham, Goodwood Grindon, Sir Matthew Hope, Hoppus, Hutchby, Mr. and Mrs. Kingsbury, Urania Lendon, Mr. and Mrs. Edmund Lovick, Laura Lumley, Macgeorge, Lady Muriel Macpherson, Mitton, Gabriel Nash, Nugent, Percy, Pinks, Miriam Rooth, Mrs. Rudolph Rooth, Rudolph Roth, Fanny Rover, Ruggieri, Lady St. Dunstans, Peter Sherringham, Edith Temple, Florence Tressilian, Gladys Vane, Maud Vavasour, Mlle. Voisin, Lady Whiteroy, Lady Windrush.) Nick Dormer's preference for painting over politics annoys his widowed mother Lady Agnes, his older sister Grace, and his fiancée, the widow Julia Dallow, whose diplomat brother Peter Sherringham becomes attracted in Paris to an actress named Miriam Rooth, to the sorrow of Nick's sweet young sister Biddy Dormer. If Nick runs for election in his county of Harsh, Julia will back him, and he will also undoubtedly inherit substantially from sonless old Charles Carteret. But Oxford friend Gabriel Nash encourages Nick to rebel for art. Nick wins his political office and proposes to the domineering Julia, but then they decide to wait. Carteret's advice and promises make Nick fear for his independence. Meanwhile, in Paris, Peter is torn between a career in diplomacy and love for Miriam, whose acting improves under Madame Honorine Carré's coaching. When Julia leaves Nick free in London to paint a while, talkative aesthete Nash abets but also upsets him. Miriam, in London seeking engagements through actor agent Basil Dashwood, comes to Nick for a sitting; he wonders if artistic success similar to hers would increase his own self-confidence. Julia returns to the studio, is angered to see Miriam (and Nash) there, offers Nick his release, and leaves for Paris, where she advises her brother Peter to marry Biddy. Instead, he rushes to London, is impressed by Miriam's ability, and is attracted to the young woman all the more, but he reconciles himself to final disappointment. Nick visits the dying Carteret, gently refuses his generosity, and subsequently loses £60,000—which enrages his selfish mother Lady Agnes. Nash windily theorizes to Peter that Nick and Miriam are unconsciously in love with each other. Peter asks for and receives a Central American assignment, which annoys Biddy's mother and sister. Time now passes. Nick plugs away at his painting without material progress, which causes him to feel responsible for serious family reverses. Miriam and then Nash discontinue their sittings for him, but Biddy reveals that Julia would like him to do her portrait. Miriam with Dashwood returns to London to play Juliet; Peter suddenly comes home and attends the drama, but he learns that Miriam and Dashwood are now married. Later Julia gives a party to announce Peter's betrothal to Biddy. Nick finishes Julia's portrait and successfully exhibits it. Will the two marry? According to a Notebook entry (19 June 1884), his friend Mary Augusta Ward* gave James the germ of *The Tragic Muse*, when she told him about an actress who is aided by her admirer but "soars away and is lost to him." (Mrs. Ward's first novel *Miss Bretherton* [1884], featuring an actress and her problems, is another major source.) James was concerned mainly with Miriam, since he wanted the novel to be "a study of a certain particular *nature d'actrice*," in whose being is situated what in the preface to Volume VII of *The Novels and Tales of Henry James* James called "the conflict between art and 'the world.' " His abiding awareness of this conflict is partly due to his perennial attachment to the writings of George Sand,* one of whose major fictive concerns is the clash of the working artist and society. By 1887, according to a letter (23 Jul 1887) to his friend Grace Norton,* James was starting *The Tragic Muse*, which soon grew bigger than he had planned. Curiously, his *Notebooks*, even as the early installments were appearing, record ideas for later installments which he modified in the writing. For example, in an undated note (c. late 1888), he planned to have Julia try to "seduce" and "bribe" Nick into becoming "a great statesman," which in the novel she does not do. In another note (2 Feb 1889), James wrote of his hope to make Nick's visit to Carteret and Peter's visit to the Comédie Française with Miriam into short, successive chapters, which in the novel they are not. When published, *The Tragic Muse* suffered poor sales. Frederick Macmillan reluctantly advanced James £250 for five years of sales, at the end of which time the novel had earned James only £80. William James liked it, and James replied with gratitude in a typically self-deprecating letter (23 Jul 1890): "I can only thank you tenderly for seeing so much good in the clumsy thing." In his preface, James reminisces about composing *The Tragic Muse* and discusses his technical problems: unremembered inspiration for it, London room and then Paris hotel in which he wrote it, difficulty in meeting serial deadlines, absence of initial reader response, desire to satirize those who are curious about all "things of the theatre . . . except the drama itself," challenge of blending art and politics; then stylistic problems of "structural centre," "counterplotting," foreshadowing, balancing of halves, "economic representation," touching busy (hence personally dull) artists into exciting characters, and "achieved unity and quality of tone." Critics have been concerned with the diagrammatically balanced central figures—male diplomat, actress; male painter, politically inclined widow—and also the length of the novel, as well as that disappearing oddity, Gabriel Nash, whose final silence may be positive or negative, symbolic or decadent.

Tramore, Edith. In "The Chaperon," Rose Tramore's selfish younger sister.

Tramore, Eric. In "The Chaperon," Rose Tramore's polo-playing older brother.

Tramore, Julia. In "The Chaperon," Rose Tramore's aunt through being the girl's deceased father's sister. The woman intends to will her money to Rose's sister Edith.

Tramore, Mr. and Mrs. Charles. In "The Chaperon," Rose Tramore's parents. He is deceased. He left an order in his will that Rose have nothing to do with her mother, who is socially ostracized, but Rose wins her mother a position in society again.

Tramore, Mrs. In "The Chaperon," the grandmother of Rose Tramore; Rose disregards the old woman's wishes and pressure.

Tramore, Rose. In "The Chaperon," widowed and ostracized Mrs. Charles Tramore's daughter, who through great determination wins her mother a position in society again. She spurns Guy Mangler and marries Captain Bertram Jay.

Transatlantic Sketches. Collection of twenty-five travel essays, published in Boston by Osgood, 1875; revised and in part reprinted in 1883 as *Foreign Parts* in the Christian Bernhard Tauchnitz* *Collection of British Authors*. The essays are as follows: 1. "Chester," 2. "Lichfield and Warwick," 3. "North Devon," 4. "Wells and Salisbury," 5. "Swiss Notes," 6. "From Chambéry to Milan," 7. "From Venice to Strasburg," 8. "The Parisian Stage," 9. "A Roman Holiday," 10. "Roman Rides," 11. "Roman Neighborhoods," 12. "The After-Season in Rome," 13. "From a Roman Note-Book," 14. "A Chain of Cities," 15. "The St. Gothard," 16. "Siena," 17. "The Autumn in Florence," 18. "Florentine Notes," 19. "Tuscan Cities," 20. "Ravenna," 21. "The Splügen," 22. "Homburg Reformed," 23. "Darmstadt," 24. "In Holland," 25. "In Belgium." All had been previously published serially (1872–1874), often with different titles. Several were later reprinted in *English Hours*, 1905, and (again sometimes with different titles) in *Italian Hours*, 1909.

Trantum, Lord and Lady. In *The Reverberator*, Suzanne de Brécourt's friends.

"Travelling Companions." Short story (16,800 words), published in the *Atlantic Monthly* (Nov–Dec 1870). (Characters: B—, Signora B—, Brooke, Charlotte Evans, Mark Evans, Mr. and Mrs. L—, Munson.) Brooke, the American narrator, while touring meets Mark Evans and his attractive daughter Charlotte in Milan. They meet again in Venice. When Evans returns to Milan to visit a sick friend, the young couple proceed to Padua and enjoyably talk so long that they miss their return train. Miss Evans feels embarrassed and perhaps even compromised, but her father accepts their explanation. Later Evans dies, and his daughter accepts Brooke's fervent, unforced proposal of marriage. This slight work is valuable for providing early evidence of what became James's lifelong adoration of Italian art, but it began as something partly bookish, since George Sand* and her Venetian experience are indirectly reflected here.

Travels. James was an inveterate traveler almost from his birth in New York City. From 1843 to 1845 he was in England and France with his parents and brother William James. From 1845 to 1855 the family was in New York City (where Garth Wilkinson James was born), Albany, New York (where Robertson James was born), and New York City again (where Alice James was born). From 1855 to 1858 the James family was in Liverpool, France, Switzerland, and London. In 1858 they were in Newport, Rhode Island. From 1859 to 1860 they were in Switzerland and Germany. From 1860 to 1869 James (sometimes with his parents) lived in Newport, Cambridge, Massachusetts, Boston, and New York. From 1869 to 1870 he traveled alone in England, France, Switzerland, and Italy. From 1870 to 1872 he was in Cambridge and New York, with a brief trip to Canada in 1871. From 1872 to 1874 he toured and stayed in England, France, Switzerland, Italy, Austria, Germany, and the Low Countries. In 1874 and 1875 he was again in Cambridge and New York. In 1875 he settled in Paris. In 1876 he traveled in southern France (dipping into Spain) and then moved to London. He established a permanent residence there until 1898, with innumerable visits and holidays in England outside the city (for example, to Bournemouth and Cornwall), and vacations (usually working ones) on the Continent, sometimes alone but often with friends. In 1877 he vacationed in Paris and Rome. In 1880 he stayed for a few months in Florence. In 1881 he passed through France and stayed a long while in Italy, especially Venice, then went briefly to Switzerland and Scotland; late in the year, he visited his parents in Massachusetts. In 1882 he returned to London, visited Ireland, toured central and southern France, then returned to the United States. In 1883 he returned to London. In 1884 he visited Paris for a month. In 1885 he went to Paris for the autumn. In 1886 and 1887 he stayed for some months in Florence and then in Venice. In 1888 he vacationed in Switzerland, Monte Carlo, Italy, and Paris. In 1889 he went to Paris briefly. In 1890 he toured in Italy and went briefly to Germany. In 1891 he vacationed in Ireland and late in the year attended a funeral in Dresden. In 1892 he vacationed in Italy and, briefly, in Switzerland and Paris. In 1893 he stayed a long while in Paris and went on, briefly, to Switzerland. In 1894 he went to Italy and, briefly, to Switzerland. In 1895 he vacationed briefly in Ireland. In 1898 he moved permanently to Rye, in Sussex. In 1899 he vacationed in France and Italy. In 1901 he engaged and occasionally used a room in a London club. In 1904 and 1905 he toured in the United States (New York, New Jersey, Massachusetts, Connecticut, Rhode Island, Pennsylvania, Washington, D.C., Virginia, North and South Carolina, Georgia, Florida, Missouri, Illinois, Indiana, California, Oregon, Washington, Maryland, and Maine). In 1905 he returned to Rye. In 1907 he vacationed by automobile in France and Italy. In 1908 he visited in Paris and went briefly to Scotland. In 1910 he traveled in Germany and Switzerland, then to the United States. In 1911 he returned to Rye but soon rented writing rooms in London. In 1913 he moved into a London apartment, where he died in 1916.

Tredick, Mary Juliana. In "The Tone of Time," the artist commissioned by Mrs. Bridgenorth to paint a supposedly imaginary portrait, which turns out to be that of a friend of both women.

Tree, Sir Herbert Beerbohm (1853–1917). London-born actor and theater manager. His half-brother was Sir Max Beerbohm.* Tree first acted in London in 1876, began to manage in 1887 (having notable successes with plays by Henrik Johan Ibsen,* Maurice Maeterlinck,* and Oscar Wilde*), staged elaborate revivals of plays by William Shakespeare* beginning in 1897, and founded a drama school in 1907. Tree gained wealth for George Bernard Shaw* by producing his *Pygmalion* in 1914. In a letter (1 Nov 1905), James reminds Antonio Fernando de Navarro* that they last met under "Tree's fantastic influence," that is, a Tree production in London. It was Tree who later made room on his London stage for matinee performances, in February 1909, of James's play *The High Bid*. In a Pocket Diary note (1 Jun 1912), James tersely calls Tree's *Othello* "awful, unspeakable."

"The Tree of Knowledge." Short story (5,400 words), published in *The Soft Side*, 1900; revised and reprinted in *The Novels and Tales of Henry James*, Volume XVI, 1909. (Characters: Peter Brench, Egidio, Lancelot Mallow, Mr. and Mrs. Morgan Mallow.) Decent Peter Brench is hopelessly in love with the pretty, rather vain, seemingly uncomprehending wife of Morgan Mallow, the slow, kind, unproductive sculptor of Carrara Lodge, which is located in a London suburb. The Mallows' son Lance reports that he wants to leave Cambridge to study painting in Paris. The Mallows josh Brench, who regularly dines with them on Sundays, for presuming to advise Lance not to study in France. But within a year young Lance returns and confesses that he is now aware that Brench's advice was based on his knowledge that the youth lacked talent; further, he sees that Brench feared he would also discover that his father had no talent either. Surprised that Lance learned so much so fast, Brench makes him promise not to tell his mother that Mallow is professionally worthless. Later, when Lance comes close to arguing with his complacent father about art and its demands on the artist to produce, Brench bribes the youth into silence. Then Lance tells Brench that he nearly had a scene with papa but that his mother later asked him to be quiet, as she had learned to be, out of love. This revelation astounds Brench, who always felt that Mrs. Mallow regarded her husband as a genius. At the Palazzo Barbaro, in Rome, James recorded in his *Notebooks* (1 May 1899) the source for this tersely developed tale: "Mrs. C" (Ariane Randolph Curtis*) told James that Gordon Greenough regarded his father's sculpture as miserable and grotesque, and so informed his mother. The sculptor in question was Richard Saltonstall Greenough, the brother of Horatio Greenough, the earliest American expatriate sculptor to go to Italy, specifically to Florence, which city is mentioned in James's note. A little later, in 1840, Richard also studied sculpture in Florence, and for many years thereafter had studios in Rome and

Paris. Richard Greenough's son Gordon was a painter who had a studio in Paris in the 1870s and 1880s. In a later Notebook entry (5 Oct 1899), James reminds himself not to "forget the . . . *Greenough* . . . idea" and to write it up "on the . . . Maupassant . . . system." "The Tree of Knowledge," one of James's shortest stories, has concision à la Guy de Maupassant.* In the preface to Volume XVI of *The Novels and Tales of Henry James*, James evasively calls the real-life son of the sculptor "a young artist long dead," without naming names. James knew several members of the international Greenough family* well. Another possible candidate for the model of the mediocre sculptor was William Wetmore Story,* whose hospitality in Rome James relished, but whose work he did not admire and whose biography he wrote with great reluctance.

Tregent, Arthur. In "The Wheel of Time," Fanny Tregent's handsome son, who cannot become interested in plain little Vera Glanvil.

Tregent, Fanny Knocker. In "The Wheel of Time," a woman who in her youth was so plain that she repelled Maurice Glanvil. Twenty years later, her son Arthur fails to like Vera, Maurice's plain little daughter.

Tremayne, Roland. In "The Path of Duty," the hero of an imaginary novel entitled *A Lawless Love*. The narrator says that Ambrose Tester resembles him.

Tremont, Harvard. In "A Bundle of Letters," the Boston recipient of a letter from Louis Leverett in Paris. In "The Point of View," Tremont in Paris receives another letter from Leverett, now discontentedly back home in Boston.

Tressilian, Florence (Florry). In *The Tragic Muse*, a London friend of Bridget Dormer.

Treuil, Vicomte Gaston de. In "Gabrielle de Bergerac," the aristocrat whom Baron de Bergerac wants his sister Gabrielle to marry. She marries Pierre Coquelin instead.

Trevelyan family. James knew the following members of the distinguished British Trevelyan family: Sir George Otto Trevelyan (1838–1928) and his wife Caroline Philips Trevelyan; his second son, Robert Calverley Trevelyan (1872–1951); and his third son George Macaulay Trevelyan (1876–1962) and his wife Janet Penrose (née Ward) Trevelyan (1879–1956). Sir George, the nephew of Thomas Babington Macaulay, was educated at Harrow and then Trinity College, Cambridge; he acted as his father's secretary in India, wrote several humorous and serious books on social and political aspects of Indian life, returned home and became a member of Parliament (beginning in 1865), wrote a biography of Macaulay (2 vols., 1876), and did important government work, partly under William Ewart Gladstone*. Among his other significant books is a history of the American Revolution (6 vols., 1899–1914). George Macaulay Trevelyan was also educated at Harrow and Trinity. He wrote three influential volumes on Giuseppe Garibaldi (1907, 1909, 1911), a book on the poetry and philosophy of George Meredith* (1906—Sir Charles Otto Desmond MacCarthy* helped him formulate his thoughts on Meredith), and studies of aspects of British history. Trevelyan was an ambulance worker in Italy in World War I, taught modern history at Cambridge University (from 1927), and continued in a distinguished career, full of variety and honors, for several more decades. He published an autobiography (1949). His wife Janet, the daughter of Mary Augusta Ward,* did important work in education and war-refugee care, and she published a few books on children's activities and on Italy, and a biography of her mother (1923); she was also a translator. In a letter to his brother William (4 Mar [1879]), James gossiped that George Otto Trevelyan had been falling out of favor "thanks to 'priggishness.' " A few weeks later, James reported to his sister Alice (26 Mar [1879]) that he was about to dine at the Trevelyans'. To Grace Norton* (7 Nov [1880]), James reported that Trevelyan's book *The Early History of Charles James Fox* (1880) was "both solid and brilliant." James was a guest for some days at Welcombe, the Trevelyans' mansion near Stratford-upon-Avon, in 1898; in a letter to William (20 Apr 1898), he describes the family as "extraordinarily rich and much-housed." Just before George Macaulay Trevelyan started on an academic lecture tour in the United States early in 1915 (his subject was Serbia, on which he later published a book), James entertained him (and Janet) at lunch. He immediately wrote to his nephew Henry James (2 Apr 1915) that the historian might appreciate some James family help in America and further that his books on Garibaldi are "admirable" even though their author, "of great ability and virtue, great general literary accomplishment," is also "perhaps of rather limited *grace*." James felt obliged to continue: The man "is really full of substance and knowledge and intelligence, though without great outward ornament." In a Pocket Diary note (7 May 1909), James indicates that when he visited his sick friend Jonathan Sturges* at Eastbourne, Robert Trevelyan was present. Late in his life, James and his Rye neighbor Sir Sydney Philip Waterlow* discussed G. M. Trevelyan, whom James then called narrow-minded and rigid. George Otto Trevelyan's oldest son, Sir Charles Philip Trevelyan (1870–1958), married Mary Katharine Bell, the daughter of James's friends Hugh Bell and Lady Florence Eveleen Eleanore Bell.* According to a Notebook entry (12 Jun 1901), George Otto Trevelyan's wife gave James the idea for "The Birthplace" while he was a guest at their mansion near Stratford. James's library contained two books by George Otto Trevelyan and three by his son George Macaulay Trevelyan.

Tripp, Mr. and Mrs. In *The Princess Casamassima*, the Princess Casamassima's Broome neighbors.

Tristram, Lizzie and Tom. In *The American*, an American expatriate couple living in Paris. Tom, Christopher Newman's long-unseen friend, is a light but likable idler. Lizzie arranges for Newman to meet Claire de Cintré, partly because he is eager but also partly out of curiosity. Tom is critical of Claire.

Trollope, Anthony (1815–1882). Durable London-born Victorian novelist. His father was an eccentric and financially careless barrister turned farmer. His mother, Frances Trollope (1780–1863), was a novelist, whose *Domestic Manners of the Americans* (1832) stirred up much resentment in the United States. His older brother was Thomas Adolphus Trollope,* also a writer. Anthony Trollope details his sad early years in his *Autobiography* (1883): strange father, interrupted day-boy schooling, escape by family from debts to Belgium, mother writing for money there, and job as postal clerk (starting in 1834). Advancing in the post office, he served in Ireland for most of the years from 1841 to 1859. Beginning with *The Macdermots of Ballycloran* (1847), Trollope turned out an incredible stream of writing, eventually by employing a mechanical and timed mode of morning production. In thirty-six years, he produced sixty-three works in 129 volumes. With *The Warden* (1855), the first of the Barsetshire series, he came into his own. His subsequent production may be divided into the Barsetshire chronicles (including *Barchester Towers* [1857], *The Small House at Allington* [1864], *The Last Chronicle of Barset* [1867]); political novels (for example, *Can You Forgive Her?* [1864], *Phineas Finn: The Irish Member* [1869], *The Eustace Diamonds* [1873], *The Duke's Children* [1880]); novels of social manners and conventions (*Orley Farm* [1862], *The Belton Estate* [1866], *The Vicar of Bullhampton* [1870], *Sir Harry Hotspur of Humblethwaite* [1871], *The American Senator* [1877]); social satires (*Miss Mackenzie* [1865], *The Way We Live Now* [1875]; Irish and Australian novels (*The McDermots, John Caldigate* [1879]); historical and romantic novels (*Nina Balatka* [1867], *Linda Tressel* [1868]); and miscellaneous works (including the analytical *He Knew He Was Right* [1869], fantastic and short fiction, and also travel and biographical writings). He retired from postal work in 1867, and both before and after that year traveled widely— to the West Indies, Egypt, the United States, Australia and New Zealand, and South Africa—but he continued to write to the end. Trollope wrote to entertain his readers, hence he uses humor and pathos. Forthright and dramatic, he seldom probes psychologically, often intrudes himself into his story, gives us a varied gallery of females, and reveals his faith in stoical Christianity and idealistic democracy. According to James's *Notes of a Son and Brother*, his family and friends had a long tradition of reading and discussing Trollope's fiction, in both its serial and book forms. When James decided in 1875 to live abroad permanently, he chanced to cross the Atlantic Ocean with Trollope as a fellow passenger and noted the following in a letter back home (1 Nov [1875]): "Anthony Trollope . . . wrote novels in his state room all the morning (he does it literally every morning of his life, no matter where he may be,) and played cards with Mrs. [Katherine De Kay] Bronson[*] all the evening. He has a gross and repulsive face and manner, but appears *bon enfant* when you talk with him. But he is the dullest Briton of them all." Two winter seasons later, James encountered Trollope socially, through the hospitality of Lord Houghton,* who invited the two to a club breakfast, where, according to a letter to his brother William (28 Feb [1877]), James "amid a little knot of Parliamentary swells conversed chiefly with Anthony Trollope—'all gobble and glare,' as he was described by someone who heard him make a speech." During later social occasions, however, James found Trollope to be more genial; after Trollope's death, James described his *Autobiography*, in a letter to Thomas Sergeant Perry* (25 Nov [1883]), as "one of the most curious and amazing books in all literature, for its density, block-ishness and general thickness and soddenness." By this time, James had published reviews of four novels by Trollope. His review of *Miss Mackenzie* (*Nation*, 13 Jul 1865) begins with a half-apology for being partial to his subject's works, the present one being "the history of the pecuniary embarrassments of the middle-aged spinster." He criticizes the story for lacking "passion" and "action." Trollope may be "true to common life" through his "accumulation of . . . circumstances," but his characters lack reality and "take life . . . *stupidly*." It may be "pernicious," to be sure, to paint the truth black; but Trollope here paints it merely pale. Realists are not expected to "contribute to the glory of human nature," but Trollope purposely "detract[s] from it." Wholly without imagination, he succeeds because he has mastered the "small manner," has a narrow "scale of emotion," and presents details like a photographer. James found *Can You Forgive Her?* no better, when he reviewed it (*Nation*, 28 Sep 1865). It has "very little story," lacks seriousness and humor alike, and flattens out all distinctions inherent in different "incidents of society." When Trollope does offer us Lady Glencora, his "one really poetic figure" here, he does not boldly follow up. James even wishes that Trollope had forced his troubled character George Vavasor to commit suicide instead of unsensationally dispatching him to America. Next James reviewed (*Nation*, 4 Jan 1866) *The Belton Estate*, in which, though it is "more readable than many of its predecessors," "we are not . . . introduced to very new ground." The book is short and has no subplot. The heroine has two suitors, worries, then chooses wisely. How to flesh out this "dramatic skeleton . . . "? The three principals travel, write letters, drink tea. The heroine may be "charming," and the better lover well drawn, but the whole novel is "as flat as a Dutch landscape" and resembles "a work written for children." James concludes that *The Belton Estate* is worse than dull; it is stupid. Trollope observes, but he fails to present either ideas or inferences. Finally, James reviewed (*Nation*, 18 Jun 1868) *Linda Tressel*, the style of which he calls flat, simple, ponderous, and verbose. But he likes it and its companion, *Nina Balatka*, since both are "rich with their own intrinsic merits," and though told in a "simple and uninspired . . . fashion" are "full of truthfulness and pathos." James finds the conclusion of Linda's narrative "touching and forcible"—all the more so for including neither "wit nor . . . poetry." But he cannot resist offering his opinion that Trollope was unaware of the tragic tone of his book and "builded better than he knew." In these reviews James occasionally compares Trollope to William Makepeace Thackeray* and once to Sir Walter Scott*—always to Trollope's disadvantage. By the time of Trollope's death, James had modified his judgment of Trollope and penned a long, appreciative essay on him (*Century Magazine*, Jul 1883; reprinted in *Partial Portraits*, 1888), in which he places him below Charles Dickens,* George Eliot,* and Thackeray but in "the same family," and calls him "strong, genial and abundant." James deplores his "fecundity," his mechanical method of composition, his unwillingness to treat literature as an art, and his concentration upon mere plot. Trollope appreciated the usual and the familiar, did not exaggerate like Dickens nor satirize like Thackeray nor philosophize like George Eliot, was a genius at perceiving "human varieties" (though without digging into motives), and preferred character (which is plot) to plot (which is not character). His stories are rarely suspenseful or complex, but are instead uncomposed, inartistic pictures. James cites *The Vicar of Bullhampton* as an example. Trollope's fictive love affairs show "his plain good sense and good taste." James notes that Trollope had lived and observed a good deal (for example, about the English clergy) before his writing career effectively commenced. James discusses *The Warden* at considerable length and calls it "delightful." On the other hand, he regards the author's habit of intruding himself into his make-believe world "suicidal" and "pernicious." Nor does James like the "fantastic names" Trollope gives some of his characters: as for Mr. Quiverful (of *The Warden* and *Barchester Towers*) and his fourteen children, James "can believe in the name and . . . in the children; but . . . cannot manage the combination." By the late 1860s, James quit trying to read every new work by Trollope because "his activity became a huge 'serial' " by then. James became selective, as when "in the vast fluidity" such "an organic particle detached itself" as *The Last Chronicle of Barset*, which he defines as one of Trollope's "most powerful things." But some of his other works (and James names may) "betray the dull, impersonal rumble of the millwheel." He calls Trollope's American depictions "always friendly," praises the man for retaining his "sturdy" (if "superficial") British middle-class commonsense while traveling, and contrasts him favorably with three French novelists (Alphonse Daudet,* Gustave Flaubert,* and Émile Zola*), who are stylish "votaries of art for art," exclusively "concentrated and sedentary." Trollope "tells us . . . more about life than the 'naturalists' in our sister republic." In his conclusion, James touches briefly on two or three dozen specific characters (often female) in Trollope; longs for space to evaluate his habit (à la Honoré de Balzac* and Thackeray) of "carrying certain actors from one story to another"; brands the political novels "distinctly dull"; and predicts that Anthony Trollope, who "wrote for the day" rather than "for posterity," will be put by "posterity . . . into its pocket." Since he deals not in "emotions of surprise" but in "emotions of recognition," he helps us to know ourselves, in our hearts. A few of James's fictional characters may derive characteristics from Trollope. For example, the Rev. Mr. Hubert Lawrence (*Watch and Ward*) is as egocentric and unpleasant as some of the Victorian writer's churchmen. Isabel Archer (*The Portrait of a Lady*) may owe something to Isabel Boncassen in Trollope's *The Duke's Children*. In general, however, although he admired Trollope in several ways, James avoided his example, since deep down he regarded him as inartistic and often pedestrian. According to an early Notebook entry (22 Jan 1879), Trollope's "theory that a boy might be brought up to be a novelist as to any other trade" helped prompt James to write "Greville Fane." James's library contained only one book by Anthony Trollope.

Trollope, Thomas Adolphus (1810–1892). Anthony Trollope's older brother, also a writer. He wrote for *Household Words*, which was edited by Charles Dickens,* lived in Florence, Italy (from 1843), was a generous host to visiting authors there, supported the Italian revolutionary movement, and wrote about Pope Pius IX, Catherine de Medici, and Florentine history, and also wrote several novels. James reviewed (*North American Review*, Jan 1865) Adolphus Trollope's *Lindisfarn Chase* (1864), harshly defining it as a good example of the popular "second-rate novel." To write such a book, one must observe the manners of his equals and inferiors and must emulate first-rate writers. The "recipe" of the author of *Lindisfarn Chase*: Have good taste, observe polite society, show no awareness of drama, stay general, lard your work with description, summarize antecedent action generously, and avoid "all analysis of character." James then criticizes the book for being a product of this formula, and in addition for regarding Paris as responsible for the heartlessness of its heroine. James met Adolphus Trollope's daughter Bici at a London dinner party in 1879 and wrote to Elizabeth Boott* (28 Jun [1879]) that she was "the most charming little creature I have ever seen in my life (except you). . . . I thought her adorable. . . . How could such a flower have blossomed on that coarse-grained Trollope stem?" James's library contained one book by Thomas Adolphus Trollope.

Trumpington, Mr. and Mrs. In "Lady Barbarina," the hosts at a London party attended by Dr. Jackson Lemon and Lady Barbarina Clement.

Truth. A London weekly journal, established on 4 January 1877 (and running to 1957), which James ridiculed, along with another London weekly, entitled *Mayfair.**

Tucker, Mrs. In *What Maisie Knew*, the real name of the woman Beale Farange introduces to his daughter Maisie as "the countess."

Tuff, Alvin. In *A Monologue by Henry James*, Cora Tuff's husband, who is in New York making money. She agrees to let him join her in London only because his being there will enable her to get a court presentation.

Tuff, Cora. In *A Monologue by Henry James*, a rich, egocentric, demanding, bland, charming American traveling in Europe while her husband Alvin makes money back in New York. She lets him come to London only because Lynch, the American legation secretary there, says her husband is required for a court presentation, which she orders Lynch to get for her.

Turgenev, Ivan Sergeyevich (1818–1883). Russian novelist, born far south of Moscow at Orel, to a womanizing father and his older, serf-owning tyrant of a wife. After studying in Moscow, St. Petersburg, and Berlin, Turgenev after working for the government became pro-Western. He incurred his mother's displeasure by falling in love with a French singer Michelle Pauline García Viardot,* who was married to a man twenty-one years older than she but whose entourage and even household Turgenev joined. In 1842 he sired an illegitimate daughter (by a servant of his mother), who was acknowledged, provided for, and reared in Mme. Viardot's home, but who later gave him trouble. (Incidentally, Pauline Viardot coached Blanche Roosevelt* in singing, in the 1870s.) His mother's death in 1850 enriched Turgenev. After trying poetry and drama, he turned to writing fiction and scored a success in 1852 with *A Sportsman's Sketches*. But that same year his laudatory obituary on Nikolai Gogol resulted in his brief exile at his family estate. Soon much fine fiction followed, notably *Rudin* (1856), *A Nest of the Landed Gentry* (1859), *First Love* (1860), *On the Eve* (1860), and *Fathers and Sons* (1862). Unjustly criticized by radicals, Turgenev went to Western Europe, mostly Paris, where he met Gustave Flaubert* and members of his literary circle. His later novels, including *Smoke* (1867), *A Lear of the Steppes* (1870), *Torrents of Spring* (1872), *Virgin Soil* (1877), and *Clara Milich* (1882) are often bitter. He was permanently saddened by the Russo-Turkish War. Turgenev last visited his homeland in 1880 and 1881; he died of spinal cancer in Bougival, near Paris. Turgenev, though much admired in Europe, was less popular in Russia, since he was thought to be too poetic, idealistic, and delicate. Even before meeting Turgenev, James wrote to Henry Wadsworth Longfellow* (late 1874) to report that a few of the popular Russian's short stories "are the best . . . ever written—to my knowledge." When James met Turgenev in Paris in November 1875, he was immediately struck by the tall Russian's magnificent appearance and gentle, hospitable nature. Through Turgenev he met Flaubert. James called on Turgenev, wrote to his parents about him, dined out with him, praised him to his friends in America, and played charades and attended musicals at the Viardots' residence with him. James wrote to William Dean Howells* (28 May [1876]) the following judgment concerning Flaubert's group: "Tourguéneff [*sic*] is worth the whole heap of them. . . . [H]e is the most lovable of men." After James moved from Paris to London in 1876, he wrote to his sister (13 Dec [1876]) that at their farewell Turgenev called him "*cher ami*." James obtained permission for his friend Thomas Sergeant Perry* to translate into English the French version of Turgenev's *Virgin Soil*. Although James fancied that Turgenev did not particularly like his writings, evidence is to the contrary. He especially praised the first chapters of James's *Roderick Hudson*. In addition, through Turgenev's friendship, James met and came to revere several émigré Russians in Paris, especially Princess Marie Ouroussov and Paul Zhukovski.* James was close enough to Turgenev in 1878 to offer Lord Houghton* a letter of introduction to the Russian. A year later, James entertained Turgenev (on the occasion of his receiving an honorary Oxford degree) at a Reform Club dinner in London, and he found him still sweet, intelligent, and witty. James wrote to his father from Paris (11 Oct [1879]) that he and Charles Hamilton Aïdé* had gone out together to see "the divine Turgénieff [*sic*]." During another French vacation, James again wrote to his father, this time from Marseilles (24 Feb 1881), that on his way to the Riviera he had seen Turgenev three times in Paris, laid up with the gout and still living with the Viardots—"a rather poor lot." The following year, while touring in preparation for *A Little Tour in France*, James again called upon his mortally sick friend. James considered him to be the principal professional influence on his life, and he long remembered not only the Russian's telling him that a novelist should start with character and let its subtleties invoke plot, but also that Turgenev definitively combined a genteel realism (not naturalism) and a jeopardized idealism. James published a rambling review (*North American Review*, Apr 1874; reprinted in *French Poets and Novelists*, 1878) of the 1873 German translations of *Torrents of Spring* and *A Lear of the Steppes*, calling their author the best novelist then alive. James praises his taking notes, varied characterization (even of "simpletons and weak-minded persons"), love of detail, handling of landscape, and "judicial . . . treatment of all his heroines." James places him in the company of Honoré de Balzac* and George Eliot* and recommends his exquisite, picturesque short stories. Turgenev has "a poet's quarrel" with his beautifully rendered native land. James contrasts Turgenev's *A Sportsman's Sketches*, which disinterestedly concerns Russian serfdom, and *Uncle Tom's Cabin* by Harriet Beecher Stowe.* *Rudin*, the hero of which is a moral failure, "like many of the author's heroes," starts with character but quickly develops "dramatic form." James says that he admires *Hélène* (i.e., *On the Eve*) for its realism and idealism, unity of tone, and fine women characters, especially Hélène herself, who combines will and charm. He summarizes the touching plot of *A Nest of the Landed Gentry* (called here both *A Nest of Noblemen* and *Lisa*), with its moral of growth through renunciation. James notes in Turgenev's "Russian young girls" the "Puritan angularity" of New England women: They all have will and can "resist, . . . wait, . . . attain." James notes that here, as elsewhere, Turgenev does not act as chorus but lets his fictive "situations speak for themselves." *Smoke* is a powerful novel but lacks sweetness. Its coquette, like her grand sisters in fiction, lacks credibility. *Fathers and Sons* dramatizes the undated, necessary battle of old vs. young, with both sides finally "assent[ing] to fate"—here, "fading tradition" vs. nihilistic denial. *Spring Torrents* shows Turgenev's recurrent "delight . . . in sadness"; it concerns the folly of youth, especially when charming young Sanin abandons sweet Gemma to consort with cruel, depraved Madame Polosoff. Next James discusses Turgenev's artistic writings in general (concerned with pictur-esque misery, gloom, irony, vanity, failure, melancholy, "hollow pretensions and vicious presumptions," and profligacy). Like Nathaniel Hawthorne,* he deals in "dusky subjects." James says that entertaining fiction better concerns "wooing and weddings . . . than death and burial." James generalizes on life's preponderance of wickedness, weakness, defiance, and unhappiness; but he adds that we should welcome experience, develop our will, and "seek to understand." Turgenev tries valiantly but "tend[s] . . . to the abuse of irony." (Four years after publishing this essay, James wrote to William Ernest Henley* [28 Aug (1878)] to confess that he could do a better job if he were to rewrite it.) James translated into prose (*Nation*, 5 Oct 1876) Turgenev's gory anti-British poem about croquet at Windsor, written to protest Queen Victoria's condoning Turkish atrocities during the Russo-Turkish War. James reviewed (*Nation*, 26 Apr 1877) the 1877 French translation of *Virgin Soil*, beginning with the indirect comment that Turgenev and George Eliot are the two most important living novelists. The recent war has hurt Russian artists; at work now are the anti-czarist revolution-aries, whom Turgenev's new novel treats in a "moral and psychological" way. Regarding various such nihilists in ironic Turgenev as combining "puerility and heroism," James offers a plot summary which stresses the pure hero Neshdanoff (contracted with "dusky, unlovely, but . . . fatally consistent" Markeloff) and the "original, . . . real" heroine Marianne. James praises Turgenev for his strong minor characters and his "[s]ubtle intentions." In 1883, shortly after Turgenev's death, James translated the essay by Alphonse Daudet* on the Russian for November publication in *Century Magazine*. At about this time, James wrote to Sir Edmund Wilson Gosse* (26 Dec [1883?]) to call his dead friend a uniquely "pure, beautiful, delightful mind." James's best essay on Turgenev (*Atlantic Monthly*, Jan 1884; reprinted in *Partial Portraits*, 1888) followed soon after the revered Russian's death. James contrasts the funeral comments of Joseph Ernest Renan* ("beautiful") and Edmond About* ("very clever"). James says that through Turgenev we have our meagre knowledge of the patient Russian people. He adored his native language. James wrote about him, met him in Paris, and found him adorable. The two often conversed at the home of Flaubert, who once amused Turgenev by branding him with an "epithet . . . good-naturedly opprob-rious" (soft pear). James found Turgenev versatile, free, indifferent to criticism, somewhat out of sympathy with James's own works, fluent in English and French, attracted to the writings of Charles Dickens* (who perhaps "merely diverted him") and George Sand* ("noble and sincere"), critical of much modern French literature (by "the grandsons of Balzac"), eloquent on the subject of literary taste, opposed to didacticism, attuned to life, and manly. James discusses Tur-genev's appearance, home, attitudes, writing habits, idiosyncrasies, Parisian ways, and friends. For his fiction, Turgenev began with "certain persons," never with plot; he said that his weakness was "want of 'architecture.' " His plots started inwardly, not outwardly like an arbitrary dance. James says that all of Turgenev's works have "richness and . . . sadness" with characters who are "particular, and yet . . . general." Flaubert appealed to sympathetic Turgenev but was unglowing. James concludes by recalling when he last saw Turgenev, very sick in Paris. The glorious, justice-loving man wrote to help Russia "struggle for a better state of things." James has a pair of revealing Notebook entries on Turgenev: First, James calls him the "most delightful and lovable of men" (25 Nov 1881); second, he records his pleasure in the technical comment by Hippolyte Taine* that Turgenev "perfectly cut the umbilical cord that bound the story to himself" (19 May 1889). Finally, James wrote an introductory essay on Turgenev for Volume XXV of the *Library of the World's Best Literature Ancient and Modern* (New York: Peale and Hill, 1897) ed. Charles Dudley Warner.* In it, James notes Turgenev's value to foreign readers, contrasts his friend with Count Leo Nikolayevich Tolstoy* ("elephantine"), reviews his life (stressing his responses to Baden-Baden and the Franco-Prussian War), comments on Turgenev in translation, and reviews Turgenev on character (his heroes fail through a collapse of will, while his heroines are "striking"), plot, and use of detail. James mentions many of Turgenev's works, likes *On the Eve* best, and says that his friend has created "the world of our finer consciousness." James's "Daisy Miller" may owe something to Turgenev's short story "Asia" (1858). James's library contained twenty-three books by Turgenev.

Turner, Joseph Mallord William (1775–1851). London-born landscape and seascape painter, watercolorist, sketcher, and engraver. His father was a barber; his mother died insane. Turner had a restricted childhood and was always a troubled person; he even had difficulty with the English language. From age thirteen he wanted to be an artist. He became a Royal Academy student in 1789 and worked for Sir Joshua Reynolds.* Turner first exhibited in 1790. A 1797 visit to the rugged Yorkshire countryside was catalytic. In 1802 he became an Academician and also went to the Continent. For the next two decades, he depicted historical and mythological subjects, often in imitation of Nicolas Poussin and in an attempt to outdo Claude Lorrain. Turner's visit to Italy (1819) inaugurated his middle phase (to the late 1830s), which is marked by colorful idealizations of scenery and also watercolors of Venetian sights. Next, to about 1845, Turner became more impressionistic, visionary, and oneiric. His work turned more light-struck and vivid in color. Toward the end, both his eyesight and his mental faculties deteriorated. John Ruskin* in *Modern Painters* (beginning in 1843) praised Turner in the face of initial adverse criticism. In "Art" (Jan 1872), James calls Turner, Jacopo Robusti Tintoretto,* and Ferdinand Victor Eugène Delacroix* "great brothers in art." In "The Bethnal Green Museum" (1873), James says that the Turner watercolors on exhibit represent "almost a full measure of his genius" and that "his rendering of space, light, and atmosphere" must be called "[m]agic." James images Turner's pigments as "dissolved in the unconscious fluid of a faculty more spontaneous even than thought— something closely akin to deep-welling spiritual emotion." In "The Old Masters of Burlington House'' (1878), James touches on Turner's ''unequalled art'' in depicting a certain condition of sky. In a note (*Nation*, 18 Apr 1878), James reviews a John Ruskin* collection of drawings by Turner, ''this mightiest of all painters of landscape.'' Indicating the groups into which the drawings fall, James especially likes the English series, as ''the richest and finest,'' and a certain ''splendid little 'Rouen' from the 'Rivers of France.' '' James lauds Turner's vision, feeling, and solid execution.

"The Turning Point of My Life." Note, dictated about 1900 or 1901, and published in *The Complete Notebooks of Henry James*, ed. Leon Edel and Lyall H. Powers (New York: Oxford University Press, 1987). When a friend [perhaps William Dean Howells*] tells him that each person's life has a vital turning point, James recalls that his own turning point probably came when he sent, while in law school at Harvard, his ''first literary nosegays'' to that friend, an editor, and soon felt that ''smiling Opportunity'' was standing before him.

"The Turn of the Screw." Long short story (39,600 words), published in *Collier's Weekly* (27 Jan–16 Apr 1898); revised and reprinted in *The Two Magics*, 1898; revised and reprinted in *The Novels and Tales of Henry James*, Volume XII, 1908. (Characters: Douglas, Flora, Griffin, Mrs. Grose, Miss Jessel, Luke, Miles, Peter Quint.) To Griffin's several Christmas season guests, Douglas reads the following story in manuscript. Shortly after arriving at the country estate of Bly, the narrator (known and respected by Douglas), a young (unnamed) governess who is to have complete charge of her absent (and admired) employer's orphaned nephew Miles and niece Flora, sees the ghost of rather peremptory Peter Quint, the dead valet of that employer, and then the ghost of ravaged beauty Miss Jessel, the governess's possibly immoral predecessor. Quint and Miss Jessel evidently were intimate with each other, and perhaps with beautiful little Miles and his sweet younger sister Flora as well. The governess becomes increasingly distraught in her eerie new environment, feeling that the children see the ghosts but pretend not to do so. Late one night, the governess is roused while reading; she finds Quint on the stairs, outfaces him, and returns to find Flora at the window. During another night, the governess awakens to see the little girl at the window again—this time Miles is out in the yard. After other incidents, the governess tells Mrs. Grose, the apparently sympathetic housekeeper in whom she confides much, that she now believes the ghosts are corrupting the children. To no immediate avail, Mrs. Grose suggests informing the governess's employer. Miles wants to get away to a new school, having been expelled from his former one for unstated reasons, but the governess stalls, preferring to have him stay at Bly where she can protect him from Quint and can also shield Flora from Miss Jessel. After writing a letter at last to her employer but then not mailing it at once, the governess closely questions Miles until he asks to be let alone. She and Mrs. Grose then seek Flora and find her by the nearby lake; the governess sees Miss Jessel again, and her pointing at the ghost drives the frightened Flora into the housekeeper's ample arms. Now Mrs. Grose is to take Flora to the girl's uncle. Alone with Miles, whom she suspects of stealing her unsent letter, the governess tries to save the boy by encouraging him to confess all his wickedness. Quint suddenly appears outside the window; the governess shields Miles from the apparition while the boy admits that he took the letter and also that he said improper things at school. The governess gloatingly tells Quint that he cannot have the penitent boy now. Miles strains apparently to see Quint and dies—dispossessed?—in his governess's embrace. This is the most controversial and challenging piece of fiction James ever wrote. It is also one of his most abidingly popular works. Critical problems concerning it will never be solved to everyone's satisfaction. The two main schools of critics are the apparitionists, that is, those who believe that the ghosts are real, and the non-apparitionists, that is, those who believe that the ghosts are figments of the governess's imagination. A smaller number of critics believe that James deliberately planted evidence to support arguments of both critical schools. Corollary critical problems stem from possible sources for the story; Douglas, his relationship with the governess, and his possible connection with Miles; the governess's attitude toward her unnamed Harley Street employer; his irresponsible conduct toward his nephew Miles and his niece Flora and what that conduct may symbolize; the timing of the ghosts' various appearances, the governess's activities just before those appearances, and the possible symbolic import of locales of those appearances; the ghosts' relationships with Miles and Flora and with each other; Mrs. Grose's attributes and the motives behind her conduct; the possibility that Bly has more living inhabitants than the governess is aware of; the part played by literary works in the story and also their analogical functions; the relationship between the story and the Victorian world out of which its actions spring; the governess and real-life cases involving illusions, hallucinations, and insanity; the whole question of innocence, experience, evil, possession, confession, and salvation as treated here; and—not least—the combination of helpfulness and obfuscation in James's own varied statements concerning his masterpiece. James called it a "bogey-tale" (in a letter to Louis Waldstein, an American physician, 21 Oct 1898), "*a jeu d'esprit*" (in a letter to Herbert George Wells,* 9 Dec 1898), "a shameless pot-boiler" (in a letter to Frederic William Henry Myers,* 19 Dec 1898), and "a fairy-tale pure and simple," "a piece of ingenuity . . . of cold artistic calculation, an *amusette* to catch those not easily caught (the 'fun' [he went on] of the capture of the merely witless being ever but small)" (in the preface to Volume XII of *The Novels and Tales of Henry James*). This marvelous work of fiction owes its origin, according to James's *Notebooks* (12 Jan 1895), to a ghost story relayed to the eager writer by Edward White Benson,* who was the Archbishop of Canterbury and the father of James's friends Arthur Christopher Benson* and Edward Frederic Benson.* It seems that some children, when their parents died, were left to the care of wicked servants in a country house. The servants corrupted the children, died, and returned as ghosts to invite the children to their destruction. James waited more than two years, then sought, in the autumn of 1897, to create a Christmas ghost tale but found his original idea growing to long-story length and therefore could not make his deadline; he published "The Turn of the Screw" in serial installments early in 1898. (This *Collier's Weekly* publication was eerily illustrated by James's friend John La Farge.*) James creates his unique sense of evil in "The Turn of the Screw" by using his now-famous formula, as presented in his preface: "Only make the reader's general vision of evil intense enough . . . and his own experience, his own imagination, his own sympathy . . . and horror . . . will supply him quite sufficiently with all the particulars. Make him *think* the evil, . . . and you are released from weak specifications." Critics have been ingenious in pointing out literary sources for "The Turn of the Screw." They include such obvious ones as *Amelia* (1751) by Henry Fielding, *The Mysteries of Udolpho* (1794) by Ann Radcliffe, and *Jane Eyre* (1847) by Charlotte Brontë (see Brontë sisters*); more debatable ones such as "Der Erlkönig" (1782) by Johann Wolfgang von Goethe* and certain case histories recorded by psychoanalyst Sigmund Freud; and especially "Temptation," an 1855 cliffhanger story by Tom Taylor,* which features a house in Harley Street, governesses, housekeepers, a victimized brother and sister, and characters named Peter Quin and Miles.

Turnover, Miss. In "A Bundle of Letters," the Vane family's new governess, mentioned in Evelyn Vane's letter to Lady Augusta Fleming.

"Tuscan Cities." Travel essay, published in the *Nation* (21 May 1874); reprinted in *Transatlantic Sketches*, 1875, and in *Italian Hours*, 1909. The cities are Leghorn, Pisa, Lucca, and Pistoia. Leghorn, although located in Tuscany, is hardly Tuscan; it resembles Liverpool—it has no worthwhile buildings or pictures but can boast some political statues, and it has "magnificent spaces." Pisa's Leaning Tower has been "vulgarised," and the city air is "a sedative." James's favorite small cathedral in all of Italy is Pisa's: It is "modest," "clean and compact," with a splendid mosaic Byzantine Christ and some Sodoma paintings in the choir. James turns to the Campo Santo, and he praises Orcagna's powerful paintings and Benozzo Gozzoli's charming (if peeling) ones within. Tranquil Pisa's buried past is larger than its present. Lucca has a rampart reminiscent of England, and also baths and churches. Its cathedral has "a wonderful inlaid front." James enjoyed lounging in medieval Pistoia's quiet streets more than inspecting its cathedral. He also liked the bright Luca Della Robbia frieze across the front of the town hospital.

Twain, Mark (1835–1910). Pen same of Samuel Langhorne Clemens, colorful, beloved, and puzzling Missouri-born American journalist, humorist, fiction writer, travel writer, satirist, lecturer, and friend of such notables, also known by James, as Thomas Bailey Aldrich,* William Wilberforce Baldwin,* Richard Watson Gilder,* Ulysses Simpson Grant,* Bret Harte,* George Brinton McClellan Harvey,* John Milton Hay,* William Dean Howells,* Robert Underwood Johnson,* James Ripley Osgood,* Whitelaw Reid,* Harriet Beecher Stowe,* and Charles Dudley Warner.* Mark Twain's books include *The Innocents Abroad* (1869), *Roughing It* (1872), *The Gilded Age* (1873, with Warner), *The Adventures of Tom Sawyer* (1876), *Life on the Mississippi* (1883), *The Prince and the Pauper* (1882), *Adventures of Huckleberry Finn* (1884), *A Connecticut Yankee in King Arthur's Court* (1889), *The Tragedy of Pudd'nhead Wilson* (1894), *Personal Recollections of Joan of Arc* (1896), *Christian Science* (1907), *The Mysterious Stranger* (1916), and *Letters from the Earth* (1963). Twain also wrote many short works of great power, significance, and popularity. Twain got into the publishing field by working with his nephew Charles L. Webster (among others); the two outbid the *Century Magazine* in 1884 for Grant's *Personal Memoirs*. James and Mark Twain were temperamentally and artistically antithetical; this, in spite of the fact that they were exact contemporaries and both wrote about childhood, family relationships, austere fathers and admirable women, travel, money and politics in post-Civil War America, and innocent Americans in Europe. In his 1875 review of a book by David Masson,* James takes a gratuitous swipe at Twain, remarking that "[i]n the day of Mark Twain there is no harm in being reminded that the absence of drollery may . . . be compensated by the presence of sublimity." All the same, there are numerous parallels between the behavior of Christopher Newman, James's American naif, and the innocent Americans in Twain's *The Innocents Abroad*. James met Mark Twain in London in May 1900. James wrote to his brother William's wife Alice (22 May 1900) that "M.T. looked as rosy as a babe," but he talked in a "muddled and confused" way about Sweden and a certain physician. (It was James who was confused, since he thought that when Mark Twain was talking about Dr. Kellgren, his Swedish physician, he was talking about the English scientist Lord Kelvin.) James saw Twain again in August 1904 at the New Jersey home of their publisher George Harvey. Finally, Twain was one of the thirty guests, along with Hamlin Garland,* Elizabeth Jordan,* and Booth Tarkington,* at the dinner party Harvey gave in James's honor in New York on 6 December 1904. In the preface to Volume XVIII of *The Novels and Tales of Henry James*, 1909, James expresses his fixed dislike of one of Twain's major artistic talents, the use of dialect in fiction. James calls it "bastard vernacular" and images it thus: "dialect with the literary rein loose on its agitated back and with its shambling power of traction . . . trusted for all such a magic might be worth." James and Twain never found much to talk about. Twain's comment on James, which he recorded in a letter to Howells (21 July 1885), is well known: "And as for the Bostonians [James's novel], I would rather be damned to John Bunyan's heaven than read that."

Tweedy family. Well-to-do American family, many of whose members were related or otherwise known to James and his family. The Tweedys were also linked to the Temple family* by a marriage. Catherine Margaret James, a sister of James's father, was the second wife of Robert Emmet Temple. They had six children, including Mary Temple* (Minny), James's most beloved cousin. When in 1854 both Margaret and Robert Temple died, the six children became the wards of Robert Temple's daughter Mary Temple Tweedy (by his first marriage) and her husband Edmund Tweedy. Edmund was one of the closest friends of James's father. The principal residence of the Tweedys was in Pelham, New York, but they also had a summer residence in Newport, Rhode Island. James was a frequent visitor at this vacation place in the 1860s, and an occasional one later. He regularly called Mrs. Tweedy "Aunt Mary." while traveling through Europe with his sister Alice and Catherine Walsh,* their Aunt Kate, James called on the Tweedys in Paris in mid–1872. A few months later, in Italy by himself, in 1872 and 1873, James often wrote home about the Tweedys, who by then had drifted on to Rome. He wrote of Edmund's sicknesses. He mentioned that Aunt Mary was concerned and sharp with others, but hospitable to him. He wrote about the arrival in Rome of Edmund's brother John, his wife, and their daughter, and how the girl caught typhus fever in Naples and moved with her family to Albano. James wrote that the Tweedys moved in May to Florence and that they were planning to meet soon with Edmund's wife Mary's sister Charlotte Temple Rose. Charlotte was Sir John Rose's wife and the aunt of Minny and James's other Temple cousins. In a letter to his father and sister (20 May [1877]), James notes that "Lady Rose is one of the easiest, agreeablest women I have seen in London." In April 1874, James, in Italy again, wrote home of Aunt Mary's annoyance at being stuck in Dresden, Germany, with her family. In November 1875, James wrote home that he had seen Charlotte and her lovely daughter, Mrs. Mary Clark, in London. Later, Aunt Mary evidently lived again in Newport, Rhode Island. In December 1883, James wrote to his friend Elizabeth Boott* to comment on Charlotte's recent death, evidently in Newport, and of Mary's sorrow therefor. Years later, when William James wrote about naming his last son, he said he was considering Francis, with Tweedy or Temple for a middle name; James replied in a long letter (12 Feb [1891]), one point of which is that he "hate[s]" the name Tweedy and further feels that the name Temple is dishonored. He recalled that "Aunt Mary's father was a *bastard* son of Sir John Temple, the 'founder' of the family in America." James went on to criticize Aunt Mary's family and the Roses in England in vituperative terms. He concluded thus: "I . . . think Alexander Robertson James a very good name." Curiously, William's son was given the name Francis Tweedy James anyway but later changed it to Alexander Robertson James. James often affectionately remembers Edmund and Mary Tweedy in *A Small Boy and Others* and *Notes of a Son and Brother*.

"Two Countries." 1888 title in magazine of "The Modern Warning."

"Two Excursions." A reprint, in *Portraits of Places*, 1883, and in *English Hours*, 1905, of the Derby and Oxford parts of the travel essay "Three Excursions" (*Galaxy*, Sep 1877), which also includes the Hatfield House part.

"The Two Faces" (1900 title, "The Faces"; 1903 title, "The Two Faces"). Short story (5,300 words), published in *Harper's Bazar* (11 Dec 1900); reprinted in *The Better Sort*, 1903; revised and reprinted in *The Novels and Tales of Henry James*, Volume XII, 1908. (Characters: Miss Banker, Bates, May Grantham, Lady Valda Gwyther, Lord Gwyther, Countess Kremnitz, Shirley Sutton.) Mr. Shirley Sutton observes May Grantham receive Lord Gwyther, her whilom lover, as he enters to report his marriage to Valda, the English-born daughter of a Britisher and a German countess. Gwyther asks Mrs. Grantham to lead his naive little wife through the English social labyrinth. Sutton later tells Mrs. Grantham that Gwyther has thus put her on her honor not to wreck the girl socially, for revenge. During an important gathering at operatically vast Burbeck soon thereafter, Sutton watches poor little Lady Gwyther enter: She is hideously, fatally overdressed by the vindictive Mrs. Grantham. But he also sees that Lady Gwyther's face is beautiful as well as pathetic, whereas Mrs. Grantham's face has hardened horribly. According to entries in James's *Notebooks* (7 May 1898, 16 Feb 1899), the idea for this story seems to have come from an event in April 1898 at the Riviera villa of Paul Bourget* and his wife Minnie. The resulting tale pleased James mainly because of its brevity.

The Two Magics. Collection of two long short stories published in London by Heinemann, 1898, and in New York by Macmillan, 1898: "The Turn of the Screw" and "Covering End." The magic in the first story is sinister; in the second, beneficent.

"Two Old Houses and Three Young Women." Travel essay, published in *Italian Hours*, 1909. Some old places, reluctant to renew acquaintance with tourists, give but do not give away. The aging of Venice has been fortunate: History is there, all about, especially at night and in winter. Arrival at a high old house by gondola can be stately. Inside often are gemmy old women and beribboned men. James recalls attending a betrothal ceremony once: The fiancée was of a royal Venetian house; her fiancé, a blushing young Austrian. Next James tells of being lost in Venice one day and being escorted by three aristocratic sisters to their low, little house—the Hotel Daniel where George Sand* had lived in 1834. It has a big *sala* and relic-filled rooms, redolent of memories and ennui. James remembers an evening on the Corsini palace terrace overlooking the Arno. Inside the solid structure were paintings summarizing Florence, once grand but now threatened by international tug-of-war "improvements."

Tyndall, John (1820–1893). Irish-born British physicist, professor, governmental adviser, and author. Inspired by Thomas Carlyle* and largely self-made, he became a colleague of Michael Faraday and Thomas Henry Huxley.* He wrote on heat, water, light, sound, electricity, magnetism, molecular physics, and glaciers, and he lectured in the United States in 1872 and 1873. James reviewed (*Atlantic Monthly*, Nov 1871) Tyndall's *Hours of Exercise in the Alps*

(1871), praising the unsentimental charm of its style. James wishes that literary writers could be as rigorous as this scientific writer is graceful. For Tyndall, noting "component facts" of his Alpine scenes only deepens their picturesqueness. James quotes examples of his "explanatory gaze," which make "our lighter descriptive arts somewhat inexpensive." Tyndall "gives the mind a higher lift" than John Ruskin* (who also wrote about the Alps), but he lacks the humor of Sir Leslie Stephen,* who has also written delightfully of summering in Switzerland. (James also mentions the mountaineering exploits of Clarence King.*) Tyndall strikes James as too earnest and a little egotistical, but admirable for his disciplined energy and his thoughts on dangerous audacity. Conquering the Alps makes not only other work but even solitude easier to manage. Tyndall's theme is nature's eloquence. James closes by warning, however, "that nature dwells within us as well as without, and that we have each of us a personal Alp to climb." In a letter to his sister Alice (19 May [1879]), James mentions seeing Tyndall at "a small feast" in a London club.

Tytler, Sarah (1827–1914). The pen name of Henrietta Keddie, a prolific British writer of novels, short stories, sociological studies, biographies, and art and music appreciation—much from a feminist point of view. James discusses her novel *The Huguenot Family in the English Village* (1867) in a review (*Nation*, 9 Jan 1868), which pays more attention to *The Huguenots: Their Settlements, Churches, and Industries in England and Ireland* by Samuel Smiles.* James says that Tytler's novel moralizes more than it romances, but also that she "is intensely sentimental," is pleasant and knowledgeable, has a "sense of the picturesque" and "an exuberant vocabulary, and includes a "vivid, . . . charming" grandmother character.

U

Undle, Minnie. In *The Ivory Tower*, Rosanna Gaw's friend.

The Uniform Tales of Henry James (14 vols., London: Secker, 1915–1920). This edition reprints fourteen fictional works, in a volume each. The titles are "The Turn of the Screw," "The Lesson of the Master," "The Aspern Papers," "Daisy Miller," "The Death of the Lion," "The Coxon Fund," *The Reverberator*, "The Beast in the Jungle," "The Altar of the Dead," "The Figure in the Carpet," "Glasses," "The Pupil," "The Jolly Corner," and "In the Cage." The texts are those in *The Novels and Tales of Henry James*, 1907–1909, except for "Glasses," which was not included in that edition and which James revised for the Secker edition.

Upjohn, Kitty. In *The American*, an American mentioned by Christopher Newman as one of his friends in Paris.

V

Valentine. In "A Tragedy of Error," Hortense Bernier's cook.

Valerio, Countess Martha. In "The Last of the Valerii," Count Marco's American wife. When he neglects her, she reburies the cause—an exhumed statue of Juno.

Valerio, Count Marco. In "The Last of the Valerii," an Italian who neglects his American wife Martha because of his temporary love of an exhumed statue of Juno.

Vallès, Jules (1832–1885). French author. He was a member of the *Figaro* staff, was in Paris during the 1870 siege, became a Commune member, founded *Le Cri du Peuple*, fought in the streets, and fled in exile to London, in 1871. His best work is the autobiographical novel *Jacques Vingtras: Le Bachelier* (1879). He added two volumes to it, thus composing a trilogy: *L'Enfant* (1881), *Le Bachelier*, and *L'Insurgé, 1871* (1886). Vallès published much else, including *La Rue à Londres* (1884), and, dying in Paris, left other items for posthumous release. James wrote to his father (11 Oct [1879]) that he had sent Alice James an "unread" copy of *Jacques Vingtras* because Ivan Sergeyevich Turgenev* recommended it; calling Vallès "the Communist," he added that on later looking into the work he found it "disagreeable" and therefore regretted sending it. James's library included one book by Vallès.

Van Buren family. James was related to several Van Burens, including Martin Van Buren (1782–1862), eighth president of the United States (1837–1841) and formerly a resident of Albany. James's father's youngest sister was Ellen King

James, the first wife of Smith Thompson Van Buren, President Van Buren's son. Ellen James Van Buren, the daughter of Ellen and Smith Van Buren, was thus James's cousin. In a letter to his mother (28 Jun [1877]), James dutifully reports from London that he called on a certain Mrs. Van Buren there but found only her two daughters at home—"two amiable little sprigs of Fishkill [south of Albany]." From Washington, D.C., James writes to his mother amusingly (22 Jan [1882]) that President Chester A. Arthur,* whom he met at a big dinner given by Senator James G. Blaine and who knew Smith Van Buren and also some Albany Jameses, insistently mistook him for the son of Henry James Sr.'s older brother William James. And James wrote to his mother from Bordeaux (16 Oct [1882]) to relay news that his brother William while in Venice saw "Mrs. Van Buren, the widow of the husband of one of our deceased aunts." In *A Small Boy and Others*, James says gleefully that "our uncle, our aunt's husband, was the son of Mr. Martin Van Buren, and . . . *he* was the President." After this autobiographical volume was published, James wrote to his interested friend Howard Overing Sturgis* (12 or 13 May 1913) to explain his family's Van Buren connection.

Vandeleur, Lady Margaret. In "The Path of Duty," Ambrose Tester's married mistress. When Tester becomes engaged to Joscelind Bernardstone to please his father, Lord Vandeleur dies.

Vandeleur, Lord. In "The Path of Duty," Ambrose Tester's mistress's husband, who, after Tester becomes engaged to Joscelind Bernardstone, dies.

Vanderbank, Gustavus (Van). In *The Awkward Age*, Longdon's friend, who loves but does not marry Fernanda Brookenham. He is a government employee.

Vanderbank, Mary and Miles. In *The Awkward Age*, Gustavus Vanderbank's deceased sister and brother.

Vanderbilt, George Washington (1862–1914). Youngest of the four sons of William Henry Vanderbilt (1821–1885), hence a grandson of fabulously wealthy Cornelius Vanderbilt (1794–1877). Privately tutored, well-traveled, and shy as a youth, George Vanderbilt became a multimillionaire agriculturalist, forestry pioneer, founder of a school of forestry, linguist, and public and university benefactor. He loved the western North Carolina mountains and began, in 1889, to acquire 130,000 acres just southwest of Asheville, where he built his fabulous country home called Biltmore at a cost of about $3,000,000 and started to live in it in the 1890s. Married in 1898, he had one daughter, Cornelia. James was a guest of the Vanderbilts at Biltmore for a few days in February 1905. While there, he felt sick, cold, lonely, and supercilious, and he wrote critical letters about the region ("this irretrievable niggery wilderness"—to his nephew Henry James [4 Feb 1905]), the mansion ("a gorgeous practical joke"—to Edith Newbold Jones Wharton* [8 Feb 1905]), and his host ("an imperfectly aesthetic young billionaire"—to Sir Edmund Wilson Gosse* [16 Feb 1905]). In *The American Scene* James more publicly defines Biltmore (without naming it) as "a castle of enchantment" and praises its owner for caring enough to place something attractive in Carolina's "dreary land." George Vanderbilt had three older brothers; the second oldest, William Kissam Vanderbilt (1849–1920), was in an unsavory divorce action in 1895 which, according to a Notebook entry (21 Dec 1895), inspired James to write "The Special Type." In subsequent notes to himself, he referred to the work as the Vanderbilt story.

Vanderdecken, Mr. and Mrs. In "Georgina's Reasons," names seen by Agnes Roy Theory in a Roman hotel book.

Vanderdecker, Mrs. In "Lady Barbarina," a woman who attends Lady Barbarina Clement Lemon's New York salon.

Vanderplank. In "Fordham Castle," the pseudonym of Mrs. Magaw and her daughter Mattie Magaw.

Vane, Adelaide, Fred, Georgina, Gus, Harold, and Mary. In "A Bundle of Letters," siblings of Evelyn Vane mentioned in her letter to Lady Augusta Fleming.

Vane, Evelyn. In "A Bundle of Letters," a vain British girl traveling on the Continent. She writes to Lady Augusta Fleming of Brighton to criticize the people at Mme. Maisonrouge's pension in Paris. In her letter, she mentions her parents Mr. and Mrs. Vane and her siblings Adelaide, Fred, Georgina, Gladys, Gus, Harold, and Mary.

Vane, Gladys. In *The Tragic Muse*, a stage name of Miriam Rooth at one time.

Vane, Mr. and Mrs. In "A Bundle of Letters," Evelyn Vane's parents, mentioned in her letter to Lady Augusta Fleming.

Vanneck, Maud. In *The Album*, a hanger-on at Courtlands, loved by Teddy Ashdown but initially aiming higher. At the end, when Grace Jesmond praises Teddy, Maud agrees to marry him.

Van Winkle, Miss. In "Poor Richard," a rich Philadelphian whom General Robert Luttrel marries.

Varian, Mrs. In *The Portrait of a Lady*, Isabel Archer's paternal aunt.

Vaughan-Vesey, Bob and Charlotte. In "The Chaperon," Lady Maresfield's son-in-law and daughter. The latter is the sister of Bessie, Maggie, young Fanny, and Guy Mangler.

Vavasour, Maud. In *The Tragic Muse*, the stage name of Miriam Rooth at one time.

Vawdrey, Clarence (Clare). In "The Private Life," a brilliant but socially inept writer, admired by actress Blance Adney. Vawdrey's dual nature is based on that of James's admired friend Robert Browning.*

Velasquez, Diego de Silva y (1599–1660). Famous Spanish painter. He was born in Seville, went to Madrid (1622), quickly became court painter (1623), then later quartermaster general of the king's household (from 1652). He painted historical scenes, genre pictures, portraits of royalty and courtiers and court functionaries, and religious and mythological works. In "Art: The Dutch and Flemish Pictures in New York" (1872), James calls a certain still life by Velasquez "a map of mighty Spanish pomegranates, grapes, and figs, blocked into shape by a masterly brush, upon that gloomy ground-tone which we associate with the Spanish genius in general." In "The Bethnal Green Museum" (1873), James contrasts Velasquez's children with those of Sir Joshua Reynolds*: the former are "of history"; the latter, "of poetry." In "Art" (1874) James extravagantly praises the sketch of a head by Velasquez: "It is impossible to imagine a greater *maestria* of brush." His canvases have "a noble gravity and solidity"; he is "one of the most powerful of painters." On a few occasions, James suggests that Frank Duveneck* is a kind of American Velasquez. More importantly, James comments a few times concerning the influence of the mighty example of Velasquez on the works of his friend John Singer Sargent.*

"The Velvet Glove." Short Story (10,600 words) (tentative title, "The Top of the Tree"; original title, "The 'Velvet Glove' "), published in the *English Review* (Mar 1909); republished in *The Finer Grain*, 1910. (Characters: John Berridge, Amy Evans, Gloriani and Mme. Gloriani.) In Gloriani's garden one April in Paris, novelist John Berridge meets a lord, whom he slowly recollects knowing when the fellow introduces him to a beautiful girl Berridge assuredly remembers having seen with the lord in Italy once. She turns out to be Amy Evans, authoress of trashy novels. She spoils everything, once she has enticed Berridge to her home, by beseeching him to write a preface for her latest junk work. *The Velvet Glove*. He refuses. When he kisses her gently and tells her that she is romance and should therefore not meddle in art—his field—she cries uncomprehendingly. This is a clever exemplum on the proper objectivity of art. James planned to call this story "The Top of the Tree" because he had been asked, without the permission of Edith Newbold Jones Wharton,* to write something favorable about her 1907 novel *The Fruit of the Tree*. The description of Amy Evans's automobile may derive from James's verbose responses to Wharton's celebrated "chariot of fire," but Amy's prose is nothing like hers. In a letter to Wharton (9 May 1909) James says that "The Velvet Glove" "*reeks* with you . . . and with *our* Paris."

Vendemer, Félix. In "Collaboration," the French poet friend of the German musician Herman Heidenmauer. Their collaborating on the libretto and score of an opera costs Félix his engagement with Paule de Brindes.

"Venice." Travel essay, published in the *Century Magazine* (Nov 1882); reprinted in *Portraits of Places*, 1883, and in *Italian Hours*, 1909. James notes that he cannot say much that is new about Venice, partly because of John Ruskin,* whom he praises but accuses of an occasional childish tone. Tourists in Venice often feel sated, confined; however, if they stay, the city charms them the way a sad, mysterious woman does. Tourists and tradesmen are converting the city into a noisy booth, and restorations have been generally botched. James suggests that St. Mark's may now be well depicted for its palpable loneliness and treasury of aged bits. Although he often enjoyed observing people from his Riva windows, he now remembers most fondly a certain enchanting little canal in the inner city. After mid-May, warmly glowing Venetian elements begin to "compose." James discusses gondoliers—their grace and awkwardness, silence and bawling. Carefully discriminating, he comments on several painters, some of their works, and the rightness of their locations: Jacopo Robusti Tintoretto* (uniquely at home here), Carpaccio and Bellini, Titian* and Paolo Veronese* (who can be profitably studied elsewhere). Notable are Tintoretto's uniquely human *Crucifixion* at the Scuola de San Rocco and Veronese's happy *Rape of Europa* at the Ducal Palace, so redolent of history. He mentions certain hours in the rosy Venetian June so pleasant as to be almost a pain to recall. He deplores recent changes in the now cockney Lido, adding that Burano and Chioggia are full of handsome, impolite fisherfolk, all prettily draped.

"Venice: An Early Impression" (1873 and 1875 title, "From Venice to Strassburg [*sic*]"; 1909 title, "Venice: An Early Impression"). Travel essay, published in the *Nation* (6 Mar 1873); revised and reprinted in *Transatlantic Sketches*, 1875; reprinted in *Italian Hours*, 1909. James entered Venice once, to renew sensations, and envied a certain American painter friend still there and still responding to sea breezes and surfaces bathed in magic light. Torcello is the best vantage point, with its ineffable grassy places, handsome beggar children, forlorn eleventh-century cathedral, and silence. James revisited the Ducal Palace, then San Cassano. Inspired Bellini, Paolo Veronese,* Giorgione, and Titian* paintings all strain together; but Jacopo Robusti Tintoretto* is a lone master, who harmonizes idealism and realism much like William Shakespeare.* Tintoretto's San Rocco masterpieces are frowning into decay; no wonder his Louvre self-portrait is so sad. James then stopped at Verona, where he saw a play in the amphitheatre, visited the Tombs of the Scaligers, and wandered through the manly city chapel and other impressive cathedrals.

Ventnor, Lady. In "In the Cage," a client of flower-arranger Mrs. Jordan.

Verdier, Léon. In "A Bundle of Letters," the cousin of Mme. Maisonrouge of the Pension Maisonrouge in Paris. He writes to Prosper Gobain about teaching French to Miranda Hope.

Vereker, Mr. and Mrs. Hugh. In "The Figure in the Carpet," a distinguished novelist and his wife. He says that there is a figure in the carpet of his works. This challenges the critic narrator and then his critic friend George Corvick. Vereker dies of fever in Rome. Soon thereafter, his wife also dies.

Verneuil, Marie. In *The Bostonians*, a militant feminist visited by Olive Chancellor and Verena Tarrant.

Vernham, Miss. In "The Middle Years," the sick countess's mercenary companion who upbraids sick Dencombe for distracting her friend Dr. Hugh from the countess, who is his rich patient.

Vernor. In "Eugene Pickering," Isabel Vernor's father, the beneficiary of Eugene Pickering's now deceased father.

Vernor, Isabel. In "Eugene Pickering," the object of the slow affections of Eugene Pickering, whose father recommended the girl to him.

Veronese, Paolo (1528–1588). Verona-born painter who succeeded Titian* as the Venetian-school master. James greatly admired Veronese. Many of his art notices are dotted with casual praise of several specific works; he especially revered Veronese's *Alexander* and his *Marriage at Cana*. An early letter by James to his brother William (25 Sep [1869]) is replete with commentary on several Italian painters, most notably Veronese; James especially likes "the perfect unity and placidity of his talent." In a note (*Nation*, 17 Jun 1875), James replies to a Boston newspaper correspondent who has recommended a mechanical system of enhancing one's appreciation of a certain Veronese painting. James says that the "only . . . rule of general application . . . for appreciating a picture . . . [is] to enjoy it." The pictorial effects in the Venetian section of *The Wings of the Dove* may owe something to Veronese's *Marriage at Cana*.

"Versailles As It Is." Paris letter, published in the New York *Tribune* (8 Jan 1876); reprinted in *Parisian Sketches*, 1957. James reports that senators are now being elected at Versailles, the "pompous architecture" of which he notes. The new Republic is like a baby that is weaned and should now be encouraged to toddle alone. He complains that it is hard for "a poor proser" properly to depict the park "terraces and avenues" outside, in the "soft, humid mildness" of the winter weather. He eyes the "old garden" sculpture ("kept in a trifle too good repair"), skaters on "some very sloppy ice" in fountain basins, and soldiers drilling nearby. Then he reviews in detail the first volume of *Les Origines de la France contemporaine* (1871–1894) by Hippolyte Taine.*

Verschoyle, Lord. In "The Pupil," Lord and Lady Dorrington's son, who does not propose to either Amy or Paula Moreen.

Verver, Adam. In *The Golden Bowl*, a rich American art collector in Europe. He is Maggie Verver's Roman Catholic widowed father, then Prince Amerigo's father-in-law. Largely to please his daughter, he marries her friend Charlotte Stant (the prince's mistress). After many difficulties, Adam and Charlotte permanently leave London for America.

Verver, Princess Maggie. In *The Golden Bowl*, rich Adam Verver's Catholic daughter, Prince Amerigo's wife, the Principino's mother, and the friend of Charlotte Stant and Fanny Assingham. To win her husband back to her and to save her father's image, Maggie lets Charlotte seem to be in charge.

"Very Modern Rome." Travel essay (*Harvard Library Bulletin*, Spring 1954). James explains the feelings he had upon returning to Rome [in November 1877]. The city seems "shabby": The Forum region is "prosaic," the Corso has "professional loungers," the Antonine column implies the "impermanence" of grandeur, the Pincian is an "exasperation," the Colosseum is "a lost cause." Still, the Villa Medici is "untouched by the reforming hand." James seeks out old friends to discuss matters. At the residence of a painter, a servant and her children are picturesque. In the streets again, James, surrendering to the charm of the Eternal City, concludes that its "mixture" of varied elements still weaves a spell. He concludes by mentioning American tourists, cabs, horseback rides in the Campagna, and a picnic by the beach near Ostia.

Vesey, Bob and Charlotte. In "The Chaperon," better known as Bob and Charlotte Vaughan-Vesey.

Vetch. In *The Spoils of Poynton*, Fleda and Maggie Vetch's unprepossessing father.

Vetch, Anastasius. In *The Princess Casamassima*, a loyal neighborhood friend of Amanda Pynsent and her ward Hyacinth Robinson.

Vetch, Fleda. In *The Spoils of Poynton*, a friend of Owen Gereth's mother Adela Gereth. Although Fleda falls in love with Owen, she so successfully urges him to be honorable toward his unpleasant fiancée Mona Brigstock that she loses him herself.

Vetch, Maggie. In *The Spoils of Poynton*, Fleda Vetch's sister, who marries a parson.

Viardot, Michelle Pauline Garcia (1821–1910). Actress and mezzo-soprano singer. She was the wife of Louis Viardot, who, twenty-one years her senior, was a Parisian journalist, friend of George Sand,* theater manager, and miscellaneous writer. Ivan Sergeyevich Turgenev* became infatuated with Mme. Viardot and attached himself to her household, where he was accepted and entertained but also demeaned and exploited financially. All of this so displeased his mother that she stopped his allowance, but when she died in 1850 Turgenev inherited her wealth. Mme. Viardot evidently did not regularly return his affection but did influence his work. James first met Turgenev, in November 1875, at the Viardots' hotel. He disliked Pauline Viardot and was maliciously critical of her, but he accepted her social invitations, beginning early in 1876, to parties and recitals for the sake of Turgenev's companionship. To his father (11 Apr [1876]), James describes the woman graphically: "She . . . is a most fascinating and interesting woman, as ugly as eyes in the sides of her head and an interminable upper lip can make her, and yet also very handsome or, at least, in the French sense, *très-belle*." He goes on: "Her musical parties are rigidly musical and . . . rigidly boresome, especially as she herself sings very little." Annoyed when Mme. Viardot criticized Turgenev after his death, James wrote to Alice James (28 Feb [1884]): "I am much horrified to learn that . . . Mme. Viardot complains of him—of his having impoverished them; whereas he ruined himself for her and her children."

Viaud, Julien. The real name of Pierre Loti.*

Vibert. In *Tenants*, the deceased husband of Eleanor Vibert. When dying estranged, he made the evil Captain Lurcher promise to work for her.

Vibert, Claude. In *Tenants*, the natural son of Sir Frederick Byng and Eleanor Vibert, and the unacknowledged half-brother of Norman Byng. Claude is unsuccessfully encouraged by his mother's blackmailer Captain Lurcher to pursue Mildred Stanmore. When the truth comes out, Claude embraces his mother and is accepted by the Byng family.

Vibert, Eleanor. In *Tenants*, the widowed mother of Claude Vibert by Sir Frederick Byng. Resisting at last her blackmailer Captain Lurcher's pressure, she tells Claude who his real father is and perhaps at the end will marry him.

Vidal, Dennis. In *The Other House*, the novel, Rose Armiger's commercial, hard, but reliable lover, rejected because of her love for Anthony Bream. After she murders Tony's daughter Effie, he helps her with her alibi and her escape. In *The Other House*, the play, Vidal (in his mid- and then late thirties) is rejected by Rose Armiger, goes back to China, then returns in time for her to pretend they are engaged. After the murder, he agrees to take her to China—but not into matrimony.

Views and Reviews. Collection of twelve critical essays and reviews, all previously published; reprinted in book form in Boston by Ball, 1908, with an introduction by Le Roy Philips.* The essays are "The Novels of George Eliot," "On a Drama of Robert Browning," "Swinburne's Essays," "The Poetry of William Morris" (originally two separate reviews), "Matthew Arnold's Essays," "Mr. Walt Whitman," "The Poetry of George Eliot" (originally two separate reviews), "The Limitations of Dickens," "Tennyson's Drama" (originally two separate reviews), "Contemporary Notes on Whistler vs. Ruskin," "A Note on John Burroughs," and "Mr. Kipling's Early Stories." (All of these authors and artists are discussed under their own names.)

Villari, Pasquale (1827–1917). Naples-born historian, professor, and politician. His several historical studies include books on Girolamo Savonarola and Niccolò Machiavelli. His wife translated his writings into English. James evidently met her in Italy. His library contained one book by Villari.

Villepreux, Mme. Léonie de. In *The Reverberator*, Mme. de Marignac's daughter. According to gossip, Gaston Probert's brother-in-law Marquis Maxime de Cliché takes tea with her.

Vincent, Nona. In "Nona Vincent," the titular heroine of Allan Wayworth's play. She appears to Wayworth in a dream.

Vincent, Philip. In "The Real Thing," the author whose de luxe edition the painter narrator hopes to illustrate. Details of his tardy fame, in the light of better critical standards, as well as the sumptuous illustrated edition, make it obvious that Philip Vincent is a prophetically autobiographical character.

Vinci, Leonardo da (1452–1519). Immortal artist Leonardo* da Vinci.

Vint, Horton (Haughty). In *The Ivory Tower*, Graham Fielder's friend. Fielder asks him to be his financial manager.

Vionnet, Comte de. In *The Ambassadors*, Comtesse Marie de Vionnet's absent, evidently brutish husband and Jeanne de Vionnet's father.

Vionnet, Comtesse Marie de. In *The Ambassadors*, absent Comte de Vionnet's wife (age thirty-eight), Jeanne's mother, Chad Newsome's charming mistress, and Lambert Strether's grateful, profound admirer.

Vionnet, Jeanne de. In *The Ambassadors*, Comtesse Marie de Vionnet's charming daughter, age eighteen, who—it is decided for her—is to marry M. de Montbron.

"The Visit." 1892 title of "The Visits."

"The Visits" (1892 title, "The Visit"; 1893 title, "The Visits"). Short story (6,000 words), published in *Black and White* (28 May 1892); reprinted in *The Private Life*, 1893. (Characters: Jack Brandon, Christopher Chantry, Helen Chantry, Louisa Chantry.) At a country home, the woman narrator meets Louisa Chantry, the nervous daughter of a former school friend. The narrator senses that something is amiss between Louisa and Jack Brandon, who are sitting nearby. Later, the narrator encounters the distraught girl in the garden. She cries hysterically in the woman's arms, then exacts a promise of silence. A few days later, the narrator visits the mother of Louisa, who is dying—of secret shame. It seems that she was sexually attracted to Jack and made improper advances, but she turned remorseful and reviled him irrationally, and now she is mortally ashamed. Her vow keeps the narrator from telling Louisa's parents the true account. This unnerving little story dramatizes the Victorian double standard.

Vivian, Angela. In *Confidence*, the object of Gordon Wright's affections. His friend Bernard Longueville adversely judges her but then marries her himself.

Vivian, Mrs. In *Confidence*, Angela Vivian's mother.

Vivier, Florentine. In *The Princess Casamassima*, Lord Frederick Purvis's mistress and then his murderess. They are the natural parents of Hyacinth Robinson, who visits her in prison.

Vivier, Hyacinthe. In *The Princess Casamassima*, Florentine Vivier's deceased father. He was a revolutionary, killed in Paris.

Vogelstein, Count Otto. In "Pandora," the German legation secretary in Washington. He admires but is puzzled by Pandora, a typical self-made American girl.

Vogüé, Vicomte Eugène Melchior de (1848–1910). French diplomat, novelist, and literary critic whose *le Roman russe* (1886) helped to popularize Ivan Sergeyevich Turgenev* and other Russian novelists in France and elsewhere. Vogüé opposed literary naturalism and scientism. He became a member of the French Academy in 1888. In March and April 1899, James was a guest with Vogüé and Urbain Mengin* in the villa of Paul Bourget,* at Hyères, on the French Riviera. In a letter to his brother William (2 Apr 1899), James calls Vogüé the "most brilliant of *commensaux*." But in "The Present Literary Situation in France" (1899), he defines Vogüé as "critically eminent" but not yet "having created a manner." James's library contained five books by Vogüé.

Voisin, Mlle. In *The Tragic Muse*, a Théâtre Français actress admired by Miriam Rooth and Peter Sherringham. She is based on the French actress Jeanne Julia Bartet [Regnault] (1854–1941) whom James admired.

Vose. In *Watch and Ward*, a butcher mentioned by Nora Lambert and Roger Lawrence.

Voyt, Colonel and Mrs. In "The Story in It," Mrs. Dyott's admirer and his absent wife. The rakish colonel is secretly and passively adored by Mrs. Dyott's guest, the young widow Mrs. Maud Blessingbourne.

W

Waddington, Adina. In "Adina," Sam Scrope's fiancée. Because of his greed for the Tiberian topaz, which Angelo Beati owns, Scrope loses Adina to Beati.

Waddington, Mrs. In "Adina," Adina Waddington's mother.

Wagnière family. A Swiss banking family into which Laura Huntington, of the Greenough family,* married.

Walford, Lucy Bethia (née Colquhoun) (1845–1915). Prolific Scottish novelist, short-story writer, and biographer, whose novel *Mr. Smith, a Part of His Life* (1874) James reviewed (*Nation*, 23 Sep 1875), calling its start "a very successful" imitation of Jane Austen.* But then it becomes tedious because every speck of conversation is recorded among "the marriageable young ladies" who are after Mr. Smith, "a rich old bachelor" visiting their village one winter. James spoils his review by giving away the climax of the novel, in all its "rather vulgar morality."

Walker, Frederick (1840–1875). British wood engraver, subject painter, and illustrator. His drawings were first published in *Once a Week* in 1860. The *Cornhill Magazine* carried his lively illustrations of fiction by William Makepeace Thackeray.* Walker died of tuberculosis. James often praised his character and work, especially in "London" (20 Feb 1897), when he reviewed Walker's biography by his brother-in-law John George Marks.*

Walker. In *The Other House*, Anthony Bream's servant.

Walker, Mrs. In "Daisy Miller," a prominent American woman in Rome. She entertains Daisy Miller, tries to prevent her from flirting with Cavaliere Giacomo Giovanelli, then criticizes her innocent if gauche behavior, and cruelly snubs her. In *Daisy Miller: A Comedy in Three Acts*, Mrs. Walker is the wife of the American consul in Rome (who lives near the Pincian promenade). She criticizes Daisy but, in the end, is gentle with the girl, who does not die.

Walkley, Arthur Bingham (1855–1926). English drama critic for the London *Star* (1888–1900) and the London *Times* (1900–1926), and the author of *Dramatic Criticism* (1903) and essays. James long enjoyed the critical pieces by Walkley, who in a 1913 review compared the early fiction of Marcel Proust* to aspects of James's *A Small Boy and Others*. In a letter to Brander Matthews (22 Aug 1914), James praises his "very accomplished friend" Walkley for his "free critical intelligence," "ripeness of . . . wit," "admirable, delightful pen," "keen . . . form," and ever-growing "beneficent authority." In the early 1920s, Edith Newbold Jones Wharton* called Walkley asinine for his dislike of Marcel Proust.

Wallace, Sir Donald Mackenzie (1841–1919). Scottish-born journalist, author, and editor. He was educated in Scotland, Germany, and Paris. Then he lived in Russia for six years (to 1875); was a foreign correspondent for the London *Times* in Russia, Germany, Turkey, and Egypt (to 1884); was secretary to two viceroys in India (1884–1889); was director of the foreign department of the *Times* (1891–1899); and was the editor of new volumes of the *Encyclopaedia Britannica* (1899–1902). He was the author of *Russian Village Communities* (1876), the very popular *Russia* (1877, rev. and enlarged ed., 1912), *Egypt and the Egyptian Question* (1883), and lesser works. James reviewed (*Nation*, 15 Mar 1877) *Russia*, which he called "excellent and interesting" and also pertinent given the current "delicate relations" between England and Russia. First, Wallace tells how he sampled Russian steamers and hotels, lived in secluded Russian villages, mastered the language, and studied local governments and religious practices. Then he shifts to a consideration of various topics: lazy and materialistic village priests, state-church relations, "Dissenters" and nonreligious progress, proprietors and peasants, communes as extended families, absence of pauperism, post–Crimean War spirit, and current Russian territorial ambitions. James regards Wallace's *Russia* as intelligent and important. In May 1877 James met Wallace at a London dinner party given by Christina Stewart Rogerson* and breakfasted with him several days later. The two men evidently did not become close friends.

Wallon, Henri Alexandre (1812–1904). French historian, Sorbonne professor, politician, and educational reformer. Among this prolific researcher's work should be included his popular *Jeanne d'Arc* (1860), the third edition of which (that of 1875) James reviewed (*Galaxy*, Aug 1875). James regards it as "the last word" on the subject (though too orthodox) and Joan of Arc as a Christ-like figure in an epic story. A military genius, she had definite ideas and "almost ... entertain[ingly] ... confound[ed]" all critics at her "travesty" of a trial. James theorizes that Joan's "voices" are evidence of a primordially urged personal will.

Walpole, Sir Hugh Seymour (1884–1941). New Zealand–born, New York- and Cambridge-educated English son of a peripatetic Scottish Episcopal clergyman. Hugh Walpole was a novelist, critic, and homosexual. Unable because of poor eyesight to join the army, he became a war correspondent and then served bravely with the Red Cross in Russia during World War I (1914–1916). This versatile, fecund, often superficial author's nearly forty novels may be divided into books about children (*Jeremy* [1919], etc.); provincial novels (*The Cathedral* [1922], etc.); tales of terror (*Portrait of a Man with Red Hair* [1925], *The Killer and the Slain* [1942], etc.); works based on his Russian experiences; and a multivolumed chronicle of British social history (*Rogue Herries* [1930], etc.). His early novels outside these categories include *The Wooden Horse* (1909), *Maradick at Forty* (1910), *Mr. Perrin and Mr. Traill* (1911), *Fortitude* (1913, with a character, a novelist named Henry Galleon, patterned after James), and *The Duchess of Wrexe* (1914). His *Roman Fountain* (1940) is partly autobiographical. Eager to launch a literary career, Walpole sent copies of his work to established authors, wrote to James (among others) in 1908, accepted his invitation to dinner in London, in February 1909, then often visited James at Lamb House.* In his diaries, letters, and published writings, Walpole lauds James to the skies. Some of their friends, including Arthur Christopher Benson,* Dudley Jocelyn Persse,* and certain associates of Oscar Wilde,* were less kindly disposed than James was toward Walpole, who was dazzled by his Master's intellectual complexity and personal kindness. Walpole was not put off by James's fierce professional criticism of his early fiction. James wrote to Benson (5 Jun 1909) of Walpole that "I feel for him the tenderest sympathy and an absolute affection"; but when Walpole sent James a copy of *Maradick at Forty*, he fired back a letter (13 May 1910) defining it as "irreflectively juvenile," illustrating "the abuse of voluminous dialogue," lacking "a plan of composition, alternation, distribution, structure," in fine, revealing "formless featherbediness." Worst of all, perhaps, James told Walpole that "you *can't*" present the main topic of *Maradick at Forty*, which is "the marital, sexual, bedroom relations of M. and his wife." Later, from New York, James wrote to Walpole (15 Apr 1911) to complain regarding *Mr. Perrin and Mr. Traill* that "I don't quite recognize the *centre of your subject*, that absolutely and indispensably fixed and constituted point from which one's ground must be surveyed and one's material wrought." To Walpole's report that his novel *Fortitude* was making money, James replied sourly (11 Apr 1913), "What an abashment to my little play of the lantern of criticism over its happy constitution! But I am familiar with that irony of fate (others' fate)." Most of James's sixty-odd letters to his "darling little Hugh" and "beloved boy" overflow with affection from a lonely old writer.

Walpole recommended new writers to James, among them, for example, David Herbert Lawrence* in 1913. James's Pocket Diaries from 1909 into June 1914 are peppered with notes of social engagements with Walpole, after which James took pride in Walpole's conduct during World War I. James remembered Walpole in his will with a gift of £100. Years after James's death, Walpole provided a foreword for *Bad Companions* (1930), by James's criminologist friend William Roughead.* Walpole dedicated his popular book *The Apple Trees: Four Reminiscences* (1932) to James, who is also the subject of one of the chapters. Hugh Crimble of *The Outcry* resembles Hugh Walpole in appearance, and Sir Cantopher Bland of *The Sense of the Past* may be patterned in part after Walpole. James's library contained five books by Walpole.

Walsh, Catherine (c. 1812–1889). Sister of James's mother Mary Walsh James and hence his Aunt Kate. She was married briefly to William H. Marshall, but she called herself Walsh, lived many years in the James household, and traveled with the James family. James admired her steadily and loyally and wrote to her faithfully; when he mentioned her in letters to his parents, his brother William, and his sister Alice, it was always with affection. James escorted Aunt Kate and Alice on a tour (May to October 1872) through England, France, Switzerland, Italy, Austria, and Germany; finally, he put them on a steamer at Liverpool and remained behind. Aunt Kate was a devoted nurse during the separate fatal illnesses of both of James's parents (1882). James was upset when in 1885 she joined the critical chorus and wrote to him that Miss Birdseye in his novel *The Bostonians* adversely reflected on Elizabeth Palmer Peabody.* Aunt Kate was friendly with Alice's companion Katharine Peabody Loring.* Upon receipt of William's description of their aunt's funeral, James replied in a poignant letter from London concerning the woman (22 Mar 1889).

Walsingham, Guy. In "The Death of the Lion," popular Miss Collop's pen name.

Walsingham, Miss. In *Still Waters*, a girl whom Felix sees on the beach.

Wantridge, Lady. In "Mrs. Medwin," a prominent British woman intrigued by Mamie Cutter's half-brother. She approves of Mrs. Medwin.

Warburton, Lord. In *The Portrait of a Lady*, a prominent, ruddy, British aristocrat whose proposal Isabel Archer quickly refuses. Later, he comes close to proposing to her stepdaughter Pansy Osmond. He has some sisters and is Ralph Touchett's close friend. Sir Charles Wentworth Dilke* may have contributed to the characterization of Warburton.

Ward, Mary Augusta (née Arnold) (1851–1920). The popular Victorian blue-stocking novelist, better known as Mrs. Humphry Ward. She was born in Tasmania, where her father, the brother of Matthew Arnold,* was teaching before his conversion to Roman Catholicism. The family then settled in Oxford, England, where young Mary grew up under the influence of many scholars. She married T. Humphry Ward, an Oxford don, in 1872; the couple moved to London in 1881, where her husband edited and she wrote for periodicals. She advocated many social changes but was an active antisuffragette. Mrs. Ward became a close friend of James, and the two visited each other on numerous occasions—notably in Rome and at Lamb House.* In their countless conversations, Mrs. Ward gave James several ideas for his fiction. She attended the first performance of his *Guy Domville*, in London, on 5 January 1895. Of her more than twenty didactic novels, several of which are romans à clef, her first one, *Miss Bretherton* (1884), which features an actress (based on Mary Antoinette Anderson*), may have influenced James's *The Tragic Muse*. The best-known of her novels is *Robert Elsmere* (1885), which espouses Christian social responsibility rather than undue concern for the miraculous. In a letter to Theodore E. Child* (27 Mar [1888]), James called *Robert Elsmere* "quite remarkable." He wrote an article about her (*English Illustrated Magazine*, Feb 1892; reprinted in *Essays in London and Elsewhere*, 1893), which in a letter to William Morton Fullerton* (4 Feb [1893]) he called "a civil perfunctory *payé* (with words between the lines) to escape the gracelessness of refusing when asked." The essay starts by noting the emerging importance of women novelists and by calling Mrs. Ward's *Robert Elsmere* "a momentous public event." He compares her book to an old-fashioned ship full of cargo, praises it for being moral and wise, and says that the public eagerly awaits her next "study." James wrote to Sir Edmund Wilson Gosse* (22 Aug 1895) that Mrs. Ward "is incorribly [*sic*] wise & good, & has a moral nature as [Adelina] Patti[*] has a voice . . . ; but, somehow I don't, especially when talking art & letters, *communicate* with her worth a damn. All the same she's a dear." James's Pocket Diaries reveal that the two writers retained social contact into 1915. In an amusing letter to Edith Newbold Jones Wharton* (18 Dec 1905), James gossips about Mrs. Ward's debate with Marguerite Suzanne Marcelle Chastreau Tinayre* over the latter's frank treatment of sex in her fiction. James knew Mrs. Ward's daughter Janet Ward, who married George Macaulay Trevelyan, of the distinguished Trevelyan family.* James's library contained twelve books by Mrs. Ward.

Warden, Amy. In "The Given Case," John Grove-Stewart's sister.

Warmington, Lady Eva and Lord. In *The Princess Casamassima*, Lady Aurora Langrish's sister and brother-in-law.

Warner, Charles Dudley (1829–1900). American writer and editor. He was born in Massachusetts, graduated from Hamilton (1851), was a Missouri railroad surveyor, and earned a law degree at the University of Pennsylvania (1858). After practicing in Chicago briefly, he moved to Hartford, Connecticut (1860), turned to writing, and issued many autobiographical, critical, and travel books. He and Mark Twain* coauthored *The Gilded Age* (1873), after which Warner published a trilogy of novels about the immorality of big money. He was an editor of the Hartford *Courant* (1867–1900), a contributing editor of *Harper's New Monthly Magazine* (1884–1898), and coeditor of *The Library of the World's Best Literature Ancient and Modern* (30 vols., 1896–1897). From Paris in 1876, James wrote to William Dean Howells* (4 Apr [1876]) that Warner had dropped in on him "from Munich—very amiable and diffusing into the Parisian air a sensible savor of Hartford." A week later, James amplified in a letter to his father (11 Apr [1876]) to the effect that Warner "is a very amiable and, in a mild way, intelligent personage." Years later, from London, James wrote to Howells (27 Nov [1882]), to criticize an essay by Warner thus: "Warner's article on England exposes him; . . . it seems to me crude, boyish and not well written— especially for an editor of Men of Letters." James and Warner, among others, were fellow guests at a lavish dinner given by publisher James Ripley Osgood* in London in September 1882. For Warner's popular *Library of the World's Best Literature*, James wrote essays on Nathaniel Hawthorne,* James Russell Lowell,* and Ivan Sergeyevich Turgenev.*

Warren, Edward Prioleau (1856–1937). Distinguished British architect, who studied under George Frederick Bodley (about whom he wrote a book). He was influenced by William Morris,* knew materials (including fabrics) well, specialized in restoration work (calling it "architectural dentistry"), and built and administered hospitals in Greece during World War I. Warren and his wife Margaret were long-time friends of James. Warren helped James find a house at Playden, Sussex, in the summer of 1896, and a year later he inspected nearby Lamb House* and pronounced it worthy. James took it on a long lease, in 1897, and two years later purchased it. Warren and his wife advised him how to furnish, alter, and improve it, in 1897 and 1898. When part of Lamb House was damaged by fire, James sent Warren a famous 72-word supplicating telegram (27 Feb 1899), part of which reads "will bless you mightily if you come." During his 1904–1905 tour of the United States, James wrote to Warren (19 Mar 1905) a perceptive letter about Chicago and urban blight. In another of the many letters James wrote to him, he extolled the architect as a tenderly admired, incomparable classic.

"Washington." Travel essay, published in the *North American Review* (May–Jun 1906); reprinted in *The American Scene*, 1907.

Washington Square. Short novel (62,200 words), published in the *Cornhill Magazine* (Jun–Nov 1880, illustrated by George Du Maurier*), and in *Harper's New Monthly Magazine* (Jul–Dec 1880); reprinted in New York by Harper, 1881 [1880] (with the same Du Maurier illustrations), and in London by Macmillan, 1881 (with "The Pension Beaurepas" and "A Bundle of Letters," 2 vols.). (Characters: Elizabeth Almond, Jefferson Almond, Marian Almond, John Ludlow, Macalister, Mrs. Montgomery, Lavinia Penniman, Rev. Mr. Penniman, Dr. Austin Sloper, Catherine Harrington Sloper, Catherine Sloper, Sloper, Miss Sturtevant, Arthur Townsend, Morris Townsend, Mrs. Morris Townsend.) Wealthy widower Dr. Austin Sloper lives in Washington Square, New York City, with his stolid daughter Catherine and his busybody widowed sister Lavinia Penniman. His other sister, Elizabeth Almond, gives a party, at which Catherine meets Morris Townsend, who sweeps her off her feet but whom Dr. Sloper distrusts. When Townsend calls on the enamoured girl, her father checks into the penniless, parasitic young fellow. Townsend proposes marriage to Catherine, and Sloper volubly disapproves. Meanwhile Lavinia Penniman espouses the couple's cause and bothers Catherine by meeting Townsend privately. Sloper enjoys testing his daughter; he takes her to Europe for six months, and he is angered in the Alps by her continued determination. Home again, she learns that Townsend wants her to placate papa to avoid being cut off penniless. She will not, nor could she; so the two quarrel, and Townsend leaves the city. Feeling that the couple may be only waiting, Sloper—though mocking and boastful— never feels secure. Seventeen years pass. Catherine declines to promise not to marry Townsend after her father's death. When that sad ogre dies soon thereafter, he leaves his daughter badly cared for financially. Through Mrs. Penniman, Townsend, now a fat and balding widower, sees Catherine again; but she refuses even to be his friend. James records in his *Notebooks* (21 Feb 1879) an elaborate chunk of gossip from his friend Frances Anne Kemble*: Her brother Henry, a handsome soldier, wooed simply for her expected money a rich Cambridge master's only daughter, Miss T., who loved him. Not only did the father "strongly (and justly)" disapprove, but Fanny also warned the girl about her "selfish" brother, who after ten years abroad returned and tried again with the help of another of his sisters (the disapproving master having died and left his daughter a fortune), but he was refused, although the unmarried heiress still loved only him. James seized on the plot, changed the locale, and in less than a year wrote to William Dean Howells* (31 Jan [1880]) that the *Cornhill Magazine*, which had published his sensational "Daisy Miller" in 1878, would soon start publishing his "poorish story in three numbers—a tale purely American." James always downgraded this fine, easily read novel, even though in it he brilliantly characterizes the two Slopers. To adverse comments on the book from Grace Norton,* James replied negatively (20 Sep 1880) thus: "I understand quite what you mean about the absence of local colour in *Washington Square*, a slender tale, of rather too narrow an interest. I don't . . . take much stock in it." When he was considering fiction for *The Novels and Tales of Henry James*, he rejected this work; as he wrote Robert Herrick (7 Aug 1905), ''I have tried to read over *Washington Square* and I *can't*, and fear it must go!''

Washington Square / The Pension Beaurepas / A Bundle of Letters. Collection of three works of fiction, published in London by Macmillan, in two volumes, 1881.

Watch and Ward. Short novel (56,200 words), published in the *Atlantic Monthly* (Aug–Dec 1871); revised and reprinted in Boston by Houghton, Osgood, 1878. (Characters: Amy, Lucinda Brown, Mrs. Chatterton, George Fenton, Franks, Isabel Morton Keith, Mrs. Keith, Nora Lambert, Mr. and Mrs. Lambert, Rev. Mr. Hubert Lawrence, Roger Lawrence, Mrs. Lawrence, Abbé Leblond, Miss Lilienthal, Mrs. Middleton, Mr. and Mrs. Morton, Miss Morton, Miss Murray, Mrs. Paul, Miss Sands, Lisa Stamm, Mlle. Stamm, Teresa, Vose, Princess X.) Roger Lawrence (about age thirty) is rejected again, presumably in Boston, by Isabel Morton. When he hears a stranger, to whom he had refused financial assistance, shoot himself in a hotel room, he adopts, in lonely remorse, the stranger's daughter, Nora Lambert, age twelve. He supervises her education and hopes to marry her himself in half a dozen years or so. He writes as much to Isabel, now Mrs. Keith, in Rome. While traveling in South America, Roger decides not to propose to a Peruvian beauty when his Nora writes to him from home that she likes him. Her formal education complete, the girl travels a while with her guardian, who later reluctantly lets her cousin, a worthless but attractive fellow named George Fenton, come calling. While visiting from New York, Parson Hubert Lawrence, Roger's younger cousin, advises Roger to woo and marry his ward quickly, but Roger lets Mrs. Keith take Nora to Rome for a year instead. Nora seems somewhat more attracted now to Hubert than to anyone else, but Roger stays loyal and resists the charms of lovely Miss Sands. He contracts a fever by sleeping in a damp room, and Nora, back from Europe, attends him in spite of her growing affection for Hubert, whom, however, the militant Mrs. Keith ejects by threatening to reveal his New York engagement. Roger, well again and encouraged by Mrs. Keith, proposes to Nora. He loves her sincerely, but she rejects him. Mrs. Keith tries to help by showing the girl a letter which Roger had written to her years earlier and in which he says he hopes to rear Nora as a perfect wife. This only bewilders the girl, and she makes her way to the opportunistic Fenton, now a junk dealer in New York. He hides her in his rooming house and tries to extort money from Roger, who has followed his ward. Nora forces the abashed Fenton to release her, and she proceeds to Hubert, finding him vainly posing for a picture. In addition, his fiancée enters. Nora leaves in embarrassment, sees Roger approaching, and is happy to return home with him. James wrote to Charles Eliot Norton* (9 Aug 1871) about *Watch and Ward*, saying that its ''subject is . . . slight'' and that its ''form will be its chief merit.'' Seven years passed before *Watch and Ward* appeared as a much-revised book. Shortly before its issuance, James wrote to his publisher James

Ripley Osgood (8 Sep [1877]) thus: "I have been half hearted about it" and added, with regard to the printer's sheets, "I have *riddled* them with alterations." He later called *Roderick Hudson*, not *Watch and Ward*, his first novel.

Waterbridge, Duchess of. In *The Outcry*, the novel, and *The Outcry*, the play, Lord Theign's ancestor and the subject of his Sir Joshua Reynolds* painting. Breckenridge Bender would like to buy it but fails to do so.

Waterlow, Charles. In *The Reverberator*, an American impressionistic painter at whose studio his friend Gaston Probert meets Francina Dosson. Waterlow's characterization owes something to James's friend John Singer Sargent.*

Waterlow, Sir Sydney Philip (1878–1944). British diplomat, educated at Eton College, then Trinity College, Cambridge, where he studied philosophy and classical literature, and where he knew Leonard Woolf (later the husband of Virginia Woolf*) and Sir Geoffrey Langdon Keynes,* among others. Later, he knew Sir Charles Otto Desmond MacCarthy* and David Herbert Lawrence.* Waterlow was fluent in German, French, and Italian, and later in Greek. He enjoyed a distinguished diplomatic career: He was a secretary at the Paris Peace Conference (1919), then a minister to Siam (1926–1928), to Ethiopia (1928–1929), to Bulgaria (1929–1933), and to Greece (1933–1939). He was the husband, until their divorce, of Alice Pollock, the daughter of James's friends Sir Frederick Pollock* and his wife; hence, the brother-in-law of Alice's brother Sir (Frederick) John Pollock,* James's theater friend. Through the Pollocks, James met Waterlow; when both men lived in Rye, they occasionally took walks together. They discussed many writers, including Alphonse Daudet,* Gustave Flaubert,* George Gissing,* Henrik Johan Ibsen,* Jean Jules Jusserand,* George Meredith,* George Macaulay Trevelyan of the Trevelyan family,* and Edith Newbold Jones Wharton.* Waterlow valuably recorded many of James's comments in a remarkable diary just before and a little after 1910. According to his Pocket Diaries (1913–1914), James socialized with Waterlow in London and Rye, after Waterlow's divorce.

Watermouth, Lady. In "A London Life," Selina Wing Berrington's sick friend.

Watermouth, Lord and Lady. In "The Lesson of the Master," the hosts at Summersoft, where young novelist Paul Overt meets master novelist Henry St. George.

Waterville, Rupert. In "The Siege of London," an American legation official in London. He is the friend of George Littlemore, who declines to gossip about Nancy Grenville Beck Headway.

Waterworth. In *Confidence*, the name of a family living in Europe and known by Mrs. Vivian and her daughter Angela Vivian.

Watt, Alexander Pollack (?–1914). Glasgow-born literary agent in London, recommended to James by his friend Sir Edmund Wilson Gosse* and retained by him for a few years, beginning in 1888. James then engaged Charles Wolcott Balestier* briefly and, after that young man's death, settled permanently on agent James Brand Pinker.*

Watts, George Frederick (1817–1904). London-born painter and sculptor, largely self-taught. He exhibited from 1837 and won a prize in 1843 which enabled him to visit Italy. Upon his return home, poor health caused chronic depression. Watts gained fame only in the 1880s. He had a brief marriage with Dame Ellen Terry* in 1864 and married again in 1886. His home near Guildford is now Watts Museum. In a few gallery reviews, James mentions Watts briefly, thus: [H]is "masterly" portrait of Sir Edward Burne-Jones* "has in an extraordinary degree that quality of transmuted reality distinctive of the highest portraiture" ("The Grosvenor Gallery and the Royal Academy," 1877); Watts "is the first portrait painter in England" ("The Picture Season in London," 1877); but "in the evening of his days he [Watts] has taken to allegory, and it must be declared that in this pursuit his zeal has decidedly outrun his discretion" (*Nation*, 23 May 1878). Watts attended the first London performances of James's plays *The American*, on 26 September 1891, and *Guy Domville*, on 5 January 1895. In "London" (23 Jan 1897), James expresses his preference for a few paintings by Watts, not his whole production. The man is "Victorian" but not in the currently common "invidious" sense. He paints feelingly, as a woman might. In "London" (26 Jun 1897), James notes that a considerable "space . . . separates his custom and habit from his few highest flights."

"The Way It Came." 1896 title of "The Friends of the Friends."

Waymarsh, Mr. and Mrs. In *The Ambassadors*, Lambert Strether's sour friend and his estranged wife. The two men go together from England to Paris, where Waymarsh gets rather too friendly with Sarah Newsome Pocock.

Wayworth, Allan. In "Nona Vincent," the young author of the play *Nona Vincent*. Mrs. Alsager advises him, and he later marries the actress Violet Grey.

Wayworth, Mr. and Mrs. In "Nona Vincent," Allan Wayworth's parents, who also have two daughters.

Wayworth, The Misses. In "Nona Vincent," Allan Wayworth's two sisters.

Webster. In "Madame de Mauves," the friend with whom Longmore, tarrying for timid love of Countess Euphemia Cleve de Mauves, does not tour the Low Countries.

Weld, Mary (?–1953). James's secretary after William MacAlpine* and before Theodora Bosanquet.* Miss Weld's father was an English judge (in India) and a classical scholar from Trinity College, Dublin. The young woman had studied at a ladies' college, in Berlin, and at a London secretarial school. James dictated his major phase novels to her (for example, *The Wings of the Dove* in 194 days of work). He was exceedingly considerate to her and once wrote her a charming letter (16 Feb 1913) encouraging her in her hobby of bookbinding. She kept a diary during her three and a half years with James (from May 1901). She wrote that typing for him was like accompanying a singer at the piano. She quit working for him to get married.

Wells, Herbert George (1866–1946). Versatile English novelist, historian, and sociologist. He came from the lower middle class (his father was a shopkeeper; his mother, a lady's maid). He was himself apprenticed to a pharmacist and then a draper; he graduated from a South Kensington normal school in science (1890), taught school (to 1893), and then became an ambitious man of letters. He wrote first-rate science fiction of a romantic, pioneering, prophetic sort; novels which are humorous character studies; and pessimistic, socialistic, dystopian, anarchistic, sociopolitical problem works. A partial list of this prolific man's writings would include *The Time Machine* (1895), *The Invisible Man* (1897), *The War of the Worlds* (1898), *Love and Mr. Lewisham* (1900), *The First Men in the Moon* (1901), *A Modern Utopia* (1905), *Kipps* (1905, which James especially admired), *Tono-Bungay* (1909), *The History of Mr. Polly* (1910), *The New Machiavelli* (1911), "The Contemporary Novel" (1911, opposing the notion of some critics, including James, that technique is more important than content in fiction), *Marriage* (1912), *Boon* (1915, offensively critical of James), *The Outline of History* (1920), *The Bulpington of Blup* (1932, based partly on Ford Madox Hueffer*), *Mr. Blettsworthy on Rampole Island* (1928), *An Experiment in Autobiography* (1934), *The Fate of Homo Sapiens* (1939), and *Complete Stories* (1966). Wells attended the first performance of James's *Guy Domville*, in London, on 5 January 1895, and he reviewed it, calling it well conceived and beautifully written, but criticizing the second act (and the acting of Sir George Alexander*). James met Wells in about 1898, at a time when James had turned magisterial but was not popularly successful, and when Wells was impudently on the rise. In 1900 Wells established a home at Sandgate, near Rye, where James was living at Lamb House.* The two, with other literary folk (including Joseph Conrad,* Stephen Crane,* Hueffer, and George Gissing*), met in the immediate region. Uniquely, James wrote to Wells (23 Sep 1902) that his novel

The First Men in the Moon had the effect of making him "sigh . . . to *collaborate* with you." (Nothing came of this quasi offer.) With sales successes, certainly by about 1905, Wells had grown out of any master-pupil relationship with James, who continued to praise his younger friend, though in terms which sometimes offended Wells when they did not amuse him. Sir Edmund Wilson Gosse* and James tried to persuade Wells to become a fellow of the Royal Society of Literature. When he declined on principle, James wrote to Gosse (20 Mar 1912) that Wells's "attitude is tiresome"; that fall, James went on to note (10 Oct 1912) that Wells's novel *Marriage* was hard, weak, loose, and without good "composition and expression." In response to James's essay "The Younger Generation" (reprinted as "The New Novel"), concerning formless modern writers, including Wells, the younger man, provoked by James's condescension, blasted back—with *Boon*, supposedly essays by a dead critic named George Boon. In part of *Boon*, Wells parodies James and he otherwise ridicules the bloodlessness of his hypermetaphorical stress on technique. James opened a brief but remarkable exchange of letters defending his view of art and terminating their abrasive friendship. First he wrote to Wells (6 Jul 1915) concerning *Boon*: "I have more or less mastered your appreciation of H.J., which I have found very curious and interesting . . . though it has naturally not filled me with a fond elation." He goes on to suggest that the loss of their former "common meeting-ground . . . is like the collapse of a bridge which made communication possible." Then he defends his view that technique is as important as content in fiction: "[T]he fictional form . . . opens such widely different windows of attention; . . . I like the window . . . to frame the play and the process!" James answers Wells's weak rejoinder that *Boon* was merely a wastebasket for old essays by ridiculing the figure of speech and defending his own critical theory (10 Jul 1915): " . . . I live, live intensely and am fed by life, and my value . . . is in my own kind of expression of that. . . . [T]he extension of life . . . is the novel's best gift. . . . I hold your distinction between a form that is (like) painting and a form that is (like) architecture for wholly null and void. There is no sense in which architecture is aesthetically 'for use' that doesn't leave any other art whatever exactly as much so; and so far from that of literature being irrelevant to the literary report upon life, . . . I regard it as relevant in a degree that leaves everything else behind." Then James ringingly concludes: "It is art that *makes* life, makes interest, makes importance, for our consideration and application of these things, and I know of no substitute whatever for the force and beauty of its process. . . . I wouldn't be Boon for the world . . . " James had seventeen of Wells's books in his library.

Wells, Lady. In *The Wings of the Dove*, Milly Theale's guest in Venice.

"Wells and Salisbury." Travel essay, published in the *Nation* (22 Aug 1872, as Part IV of "A Summer in Europe"); reprinted in *Transatlantic Sketches*, 1875, and in *English Hours*, 1905. Wells was quite a surprise to James. Its "minster-front . . . ranks among the first three or four in England." The façade is elegant; although it is partly mutilated, it is in the process of restoration. The cathedral is of a "charming" mouse-gray color. The interior has architectural interest but is too well lighted. Nearby are the precinct called the Vicars' Close ("adorably of another world and time"), the episcopal palace, and high-towered St. Cuthbert's church. Out of town is the Abbey of Glastonbury, its "ancient splendour" now in flowery ruins which have a "broken eloquence." Then Salisbury cathedral: "Perhaps the best-known typical church in the world" but seemingly "*banal*" to James now, with its "sweet perfection." Stonehenge is lonely and enigmatic, to be sure, but "hackneyed" too, with a beer party going on; it stands for "the pathless vaults beneath the house of history." Finally, James went back to Wilton House, a "delightful old residence" with marbles and Pembroke portraits.

Wendell, Barrett (1855–1921). Professor of English at Harvard (1880–1921). He was a cofounder of the Harvard *Lampoon*. He was a colleague of Charles Eliot Norton,* among many others at Harvard. Wendell knew Edith Newbold Jones Wharton,* her husband, and many of her friends. A list of his distinguished students would include Bernard Berenson* and William Morton Fullerton.* Wendell lectured at the Sorbonne in 1904 and 1905. His books are on world literature, France, American literary history, William Shakespeare,* and education. James met Wendell in London, in 1895, and wrote to his brother William (30 Sep 1895) that he was disappointed in the man's 1895 book on Shakespeare, which struck him as "critically very thin and even common." But James promised "to write him, with anguish, a mendacious letter of thanks." James socialized with Wendell again in London in June 1914.

Wendover. In "A London Life," the serious young American whom Laura Wing in London meets through her sister Selina Wing Berrington. He loves and is puzzled by Miss Wing but ultimately follows her to America.

Wenham, Adelaide. In "Flickerbridge," the odd, charming old owner of the estate of Flickerbridge. She is distantly related to Adelaide Wenham, Frank Granger's fiancée. Frank greatly admires the older Miss Wenham.

Wenham, Adelaide (Addie). In "Flickerbridge," a short-story and article writer, engaged to painter Frank Granger and distantly related to Adelaide Wenham of Flickerbridge. When she plans to exploit the older Miss Wenham's estate in an article, Frank breaks their engagement.

Wenham, Dr. and Mrs. In "Flickerbridge," Addie Wenham's father and stepmother. Addie's mother is deceased.

Wenham, Mrs. In "Flickerbridge," Addie Wenham's deceased mother.

Wentworth, Charlotte. In *The Europeans*, William Wentworth's daughter, and Gertrude and Clifford Wentworth's sister. She will marry the Rev. Mr. Brand.

Wentworth, Clifford. In *The Europeans*, William Wentworth's son, and Gertrude and Charlotte Wentworth's younger brother. He has a drinking problem.

Wentworth, Gertrude. In *The Europeans*, William Wentworth's daughter, and Charlotte and Clifford Wentworth's sister. Although her father wants her to marry the Rev. Mr. Brand, she falls in love with and is won by Felix Young.

Wentworth, William. In *The Europeans*, a rigidly honorable New Englander. He was the half-brother of Baroness Eugenia Münster's and Felix Young's mother. He is Gertrude, Charlotte, and Clifford Wentworth's father. In a letter to Francis Boott* (30 Oct [1878]), James admits that, "yes, Mr. Wentworth *was* a reminiscence of Mr. Frank Loring, whose frosty personality I had always in my mind in dealing with this figure." Loring was the Boston publisher who in 1880 pirated James's short story "A Bundle of Letters." He was no relation of Alice James's close friend Katharine Peabody Loring.*

West, Catherine. In *Pyramus and Thisbe*, a music teacher, age twenty-six, who dislikes her rooming-house neighbor Stephen Young's smelly smoking and loud conversation until the two meet and fall in love.

Westgate, J. L. In "An International Episode," the husband of Kitty Alden Westgate, who is Bessie Alden's sister. He is a rich New York businessman who befriends Lord Lambeth and Percy Beaumont when they visit America.

Westgate, Kitty Alden. In "An International Episode," J. L. Westgate's wife and Bessie Alden's older sister. She is more hospitable to Lord Lambeth and Percy Beaumont when they visit America than they are to Bessie and to Kitty when the two young women go to London.

Wharton, Edith Newbold Jones (1862–1937). Important American novelist, short-story writer, travel writer, critic, essayist, and minor poet. She was born into a rich, prominent Manhattan land-holding family, which had residences in New York and Newport, Rhode Island, and which also lived at times in Europe (1866–1872, 1880–1882). Edith read eclectically, began juvenile writing, and had some publishing success in the late 1870s. After the death of her father in 1882, she remained with her mother in New York and Newport. In 1883 she met Walter Van Rensselaer Berry,* but, in 1885, she married Edward Robbins (Teddy) Wharton (1850–1928), a Boston socialite, who, unstable and spoiled by his rich family, was twelve years older than she. At first, the couple lived and entertained in New York and Newport, but they also memorably cruised the Aegean Sea (1888) and spent some spring seasons in Italy. They bought an expensive Newport estate in 1893, where they entertained Paul Bourget* and his wife Minnie. Edith was intermittently nervous and melancholy (1894–1896, 1898, 1902), and she turned to writing in a more serious way as prescribed therapy; renewed European travel also proved beneficial. Teddy occasionally absented himself. In 1897 Berry was a house guest, and he helped Edith with *The Decoration of Houses* (1897, coauthored, which espoused anti-Victorian interior design). Teddy became neurasthenic (with the first of several breakdowns in 1902). He eventually proved to be unfaithful and, in addition, in 1909, embezzled $50,000 in trust funds belonging to Edith and began housing a mistress in Boston. In spite of having a lavish home, which she designed and called The Mount, in Lenox, Massachusetts (from 1902), she established rather solid residences in France (from 1907—she had long known Henry White,* the American ambassador to France, and his wife Margaret). She separated from her husband (intermittently in 1909, more formally in 1911), sold The Mount (1911), and obtained a divorce (1913, in Paris). She had already started two liaisons, one (perhaps not sexual) with Berry (1897–1927), the other (profoundly sexual) with William Morton Fullerton* (1908–1910). As for Berry, a unique influence in her life, he never married. He was a distinguished lawyer and a valued friend of the illustrious (including James); he read widely and enjoyed travel, was the first person to encourage Edith's writing (and helped with revisions), and let her act as his hostess. As for Fullerton (by then a Harvard graduate, indulged scion of a New England family, man of letters, husband, father, adulterer, and homosexual), Edith met him in Paris (April 1907). Armed with a letter from James, he called upon her at The Mount in October 1907, discussed writing (including James's) and so much else with her that she (with Teddy briefly) soon sought him out in Paris. In 1913 and 1914 Wharton traveled widely: in Luxembourg and Germany with Bernard Berenson,* in Africa with Percy Lubbock* and Gaillard Thomas Lapsley,* and in Italy, Spain, and Africa with Berry. She did war-relief work during World War I. In 1917 she traveled for some weeks in Morocco. In 1923 she returned for the only time since 1912 to the United States (for an honorary degree from Yale). In 1927 Berry died; a year later, her exhusband. Edith Wharton wrote forty-seven books, among them the early *The Greater Inclination* (1899, eight short stories), *The Valley of Decision* (1902, a historical novel somewhat like *Romola* by George Eliot*), *The House of Mirth* (1905, an instant best-seller; for the 1908 French translation, Bourget provided an introduction), *The Fruit of the Tree* (1907), and *Madame de Treymes* (1907, contrasting innocent American and complex French morality). Several of these works are grounded in character (especially feminine) and are concerned with form and eclectic moral values, hence revealing the influence of James, whose works she had long admired. *Ethan Frome* (1911, partly written earlier in French), though perhaps Wharton's most popular work, is less representative than *The Reef: A Novel* (1912, concentrated moral drama) and *The Custom of* *the Country* (1913, social satire). Wharton wrote factually about World War I and also based fiction on it (for example, *Fighting France, from Dunkerque to Belfort* [1915], *The Book of the Homeless* [1915], and *French Ways and Their Meaning* [1919], *The Marne* [1918], and *A Son at the Front* [1923]). After the war, she established two French residences (one just outside Paris, the other on the Riviera). She continued to write excellently; she received awards, traveled, enjoyed good sales (until the Great Depression), later made money from stage and film adaptations of her fiction, and suffered the loss of old friends. Perhaps her finest novel is *The Age of Innocence* (1920), again Jamesian with respect to point of view, formal symmetry, and ironic, insightful treatment of high society. Her *Old New York* (1924) contains four nouvelles, a form James revered. Again, like James, she wrote well in the realm of ghosts and hysteria (for example, *Tales of Men and Ghosts* [1910] and *Ghosts* [1937]); and, like him, she wrote sympathetically of children (notably in *Twilight Sleep* [1927] and *The Children* [1928]). She was also a skillful writer of travel books, for example, *Italian Villas and Their Gardens* (1904), *Italian Backgrounds* (1905), *A Motor-Flight through France* (1908, about a three-week automobile tour by both Whartons and James), and *In Morocco* (1920). Her handbook *The Writing of Fiction* (1923) reveals that she found uniquely exciting the fictive depiction of the dramatic conflict between a freedom-seeking individual and society's restrictive conventions (again like the conflict of many of James's caged characters). The long relationship of Wharton and James is fascinating. James and Wharton evidently first saw each other in the Parisian apartment of Edward Darley Boit* and his wife Mary Boit, in about 1887. At this time, Wharton was more eager for a friendship than was James. In 1899 she sent him "a fruit of literary toil," as James called it in a letter to their friend the wife of Paul Bourget ([8 Apr 1899]). In 1900 Wharton sent him one of her short stories and only half-appreciated his criticism of it: "[T]he . . . tale is a little *hard*. . . . But that's because you're so young, and . . . clever" (26 Oct 1900). In 1902 she welcomed his appreciation of *The Valley of Decision* but, even more, his advice, which was to "*Do New York!*" (17 Aug 1902). In December 1903 the two met in London. In 1904 Edith visited James in Rye and took him for a Sussex tour by automobile; later that year, she complained that reviewers called her an echo of James. In 1905 James visited her in New York and also at The Mount during his 1904–1905 tour of the United States; James also wrote her to praise *The House of Mirth*, which he was reading in serial form, for its "compact fulness, vivid picture and 'sustained interest' " (8 Feb 1905). On completing the novel, once he was back in Rye, he demurred: "[I]t is better written than composed" (8 Nov 1905). In March–April 1907, the Whartons and James toured France in Edith's automobile. Later that year an unscrupulous New York editor wrote to James that Mrs. Wharton wanted him to puff her novel *The Fruit of the Tree*; she denied it all; James thought of complying (for money) but then did not like the novel; later he used the incident as the basis of his short story "The Velvet Glove." In April 1908 he visited Edith in Paris, where she commissioned Jacques-Émile Blanche* to paint his portrait; in October James wrote to Edith (back in the United States) of his anguish concerning her marriage and her relationship with Fullerton—"I move in darkness; . . . I don't pretend to understand or imagine" (13 Oct 1908); still later in the year, back in England, she saw much of James. In 1909 she persuaded him to help her extricate Fullerton from the grip of an ex-mistress blackmailer. In 1910 Edith started a process to recommend James for the Nobel Prize, and she enlisted the help of Sir Edmund Wilson Gosse* and William Dean Howells* in her unsuccessful effort. (Maurice Maeterlinck* was awarded the 1911 prize.) Later in 1911 James was her guest at The Mount for a final time. Also in 1911 James wrote to her (25 Oct 1911) that "I exceedingly admire . . . *Ethan Frome*. A beautiful art and tone and truth—a beautiful artful Rightdownness, and yet effective cumulations. It's a 'gem'—and excites great admiration here." In 1912 she schemed with publisher Charles Scribner to pay James an advance of several thousand dollars from her earnings on his never-finished novel *The Ivory Tower*. Also in 1912 James wrote to Edith ([4], 9 Dec [1912]) to praise her novel *The Reef* extravagantly: "The beauty of it is that it is . . . a Drama and almost . . . of the psychologic Racinian unity, intensity and gracility." In 1913 she tried to raise a huge gift of money for James on his seventieth birthday, but he heard about the plan and stopped it. Early in 1914 Edith sent James *Du Côté de Chez Swann* by Marcel Proust.* Later that year, in "The Younger Generation" (retitled "The New Novel"), James praised Wharton's *Ethan Frome, The Valley of Decision*, and *The House of Mirth* because they display "artistic economy" instead of being novels of saturation; and he especially admired *The Custom of the Country* for being "almost scientifically satiric." Still later in 1914, after the war had started, Edith visited England, where she saw James at Rye and had trouble returning to Paris. In 1916 James contributed "The Long Wards," a war essay, to *The Book of the Homeless*, which Edith edited. In his later letters, James often referred humorously to Wharton as "The Angel of Devastation" and "The Firebird" because of her generosity, energy, imperiousness, and automobile. A full list of the dozens of their mutual friends would be too long to include here. After James's death, his family did not want Wharton to edit his letters (William's widow Alice was especially adamant) and chose Lubbock to do so instead. Perhaps Alice knew of Edith's long-standing resentment of James's devotion to William, of whose writings Edith was highly critical. Her fourteen-chapter autobiography *A Backward Glance* (1934) is a compendium of significant memories, with a whole chapter (the eighth) and many touches elsewhere devoted to James. She discusses their first meetings, his appearance, expatriation, conversation, "bubbling" sense of humor, ability to "chant" Emily Brontë (see Brontë sisters) and "croon" Walt Whitman,* overpowering intellect and "[s]implicity of heart," non-vain "sensitivity to criticism," love of family, preference for Boston over "hated" New York, friends, opinions of several works by Wharton, and mannerisms. At her own request, Edith Wharton was buried beside Walter Berry's ashes in a Versailles cemetery. James's library contained eleven books by Wharton.

What Maisie Knew. Novel (89,200 words), published in the *Chap Book* (15 Jan–1 Aug 1897), and (revised and abridged) in the *New Review* (Feb–Sep 1897; revised and published in Chicago and New York by Stone, 1897, and in London by Heinemann, 1897 [1898]; revised and reprinted in *The Novels and Tales of Henry James*, Volume XI, 1908. (Characters: Susan Ash, Sir Claude, Mrs. Cuddon, Lord Eric, Beale Farange, Ida Farange, Maisie Farange, Lisette, Moddle, Miss Overmore, Perriam, Tischbein, Mrs. Tucker, Clara Matilda Wix, Wix, and Mrs. Wix.) Since her parents, Beale and Ida Farange, are just being divorced, their little daughter Maisie begins to shuttle between them. After Beale marries Maisie's pretty nurse Miss Overmore, whom Ida hired (then replaced her with the ugly but moralistic Mrs. Wix), Ida marries Sir Claude. Maisie meets likable Claude while he is having a nice chat with Beale's wife, whom Ida soon senses Claude is falling for. Ida leaves Claude, Mrs. Wix, and Maisie, and she goes off with a series of lovers, including Perriam, Lord Eric, a certain captain, and Tischbein. Claude's seeing Beale's wife distresses Mrs. Wix, but little Maisie likes both of her foster parents and she is happy to bring them together. When she bumps into her father, he takes her to the apartment of his American "countess." He distresses his daughter by so much talk that she declines an invitation to accompany them to America. Then she feels guilty. Later, however, she learns that they lied about their plans. After Ida saddens Maisie by talking lugubriously of going off to South Africa, Claude takes the girl over to Boulogne, where Mrs. Wix soon joins them. Against that woman's advice and wishes, he returns to England and to Beale's wife, who is evidently now free. Maisie and Mrs. Wix debate the propriety of men paying women: Mrs. Wix reveals that Claude pays Beale's wife, but Maisie counters that he also pays Mrs. Wix! By the time Claude and Beale's wife return to them in Boulogne, Maisie has accepted Mrs. Wix's lecture on that pair's sinfulness. Claude returns to England, and Beale's wife behaves so considerately that Mrs. Wix is almost persuaded that she has morally improved. Beale's wife says that after their divorces she and Claude are going to get married and will keep Maisie. But Claude too swiftly returns to Beale's wife, which angers Mrs. Wix again. Claude asks Maisie if she will go to the south of France with Beale's wife and himself, but without Mrs. Wix. The poor little girl asks for time to ponder. When all four confront each other, Maisie learns that Claude and Beale's wife will assuredly make a unit and therefore determines to stay only with Mrs. Wix. What Maisie now knows is the moral sense. James wrote many Notebook entries, some quite elaborate, in connection with the inspiration for and the composition of this novel. First, he explains (12 Nov 1892) that he got his idea for it when he was a dinner guest in the home of Viscount James Bryce,* historian, diplomat, and law professor, whose wife's sister (or perhaps sister-in-law) told James about "[a] child . . . *divided* by its parents in consequence of their being divorced." He saw the possibilities of having each parent remarry and the child—a girl, he decided, in order to make the story different from "The Pupil"—relating to "these new parents." Later he recorded more thoughts (26 Aug 1893), tentatively named the divorced couple Hurter, and he gave up an earlier temptation to kill off his little girl's father. Next (22 Dec 1895) he began to outline the action substantially as it appears in the novel, with its point of view startlingly clear: "the consciousness, the dim, sweet, scared, wondering, clinging perception of the child." *What Maisie Knew* was the first novel that James dictated. It was originally intended for the *Yellow Book*, but, when it grew far beyond its originally planned length of 10,000 words, he sent in its place his 1897 essay on George Sand,* entitled "She and He: Recent Documents." In the preface to Volume XI of *The Novels and Tales of Henry James*, James discusses many technical problems he confronted in composing *What Maisie Knew*: "for a proper symmetry the second parent should marry too"; Maisie's "expanding consciousness" is "a register of impressions"; her being ignored by her parents produces both "a relation between . . . [her] step-parents . . . [and] a fresh system of misbehaviour"; James decided to present situations beyond Maisie's power "to interpret and appreciate" since "children have . . . more perceptions than . . . terms to translate them"; Maisie's "good faith" renders her parents, especially Ida, "concrete, immense and awful"; involving Maisie in adult unpleasantness can have clean artistic "value." Critical problems arise because of James's highly obscurantist style here. What does Maisie think of her parents? And their later lovers? Mrs. Wix may be grotesque, but how does she aid in Maisie's spiritual development? Is Maisie corrupted by the lessons life puts her through? What does she "know"? What will Maisie do after the novel's last page?

"The Wheel of Time." Short story (17,100 words), published in the *Cosmopolitan* (Dec 1892–Jan 1893); reprinted in *The Private Life . . .* (London), 1893, and in *The Wheel of Time . . .* (New York), 1893. (Characters: Mr. and Mrs. Crisford, Mr. and Mrs. Maurice Glanvil, Vera Glanvil, Lord and Lady Greyswood, Lord Greyswood, General Blake Knocker, Jane Knocker, Knocker, Miss Knocker, Arthur Tregent, Fanny Knocker Tregent.) Lady Greyswood fails to induce her third son, useless Maurice Glanvil, to pay more attention to plain Fanny Knocker. Twenty years later, Maurice, now a widower, returns to London with his daughter Vera. She is bright, but plain and diminutive as well. They meet Arthur Tregent, the handsome son of Fanny Knocker, who is now widowed Mrs. Tregent. Fanny agrees to ask her son to try to like Vera, but he simply cannot. Poor little Vera gets sick at Blankley, the Tregent summer estate, and later dies of a broken heart. Thus the wheel of time accords unintending Fanny a kind of revenge. James summarized in his *Notebooks* (18 May 1892) some chat at a dinner given by Lady Caroline Blanche Elizabeth Lindsay* the night before about an "ugly" woman snubbed in her youth but turning "handsome" later in life. Loving fictive symmetry, James quickly thought, first, of contrasting such a woman, who marries elsewhere, with the snubber's beautiful wife who turns plain, and, second, of providing the once-ugly woman with a handsome son and the snubber with an ugly daughter.

Whistler, James Abbott McNeill (1834–1903). American artist, born in Lowell, Massachusetts, but raised in Russia and England as well as in the United States. He attended West Point (1851–1854) but did not graduate; thereafter, he lived permanently abroad. First he went to Paris (1855), where he studied painting. He had studios there and in London; he was influenced by French impressionists and realists and by Japanese prints; and soon he published etchings (1858) and later he exhibited many controversial paintings, including portraits of his mother, Thomas Carlyle,* and others, and magnate F. R. Leyland's Peacock Room decorations (from the 1860s.). He nominally won a lawsuit against art critic John Ruskin* for the latter's adverse comments on his perspectiveless, colorless, undetailed, non-narrative work, but he was bankrupted by legal expenses in the process. Whistler was eccentric in dress, acidly witty in conversation, and fluent in articles and books, notably *The Gentle Art of Making Enemies* (1890) and his posthumously published *Journals* (1921). Before meeting Whistler, James commented adversely on some of his paintings, but, then, during his relentless dinings-out during the 1877–1878 London winter season, at a dinner party given by Christina Stewart Rogerson,* he met the fascinating painter, who soon invited him to breakfast at his Chelsea house. Softening a little, James still wrote to his father (19 Apr [1878]) that he preferred Whistler's food and fellow guests to his ''abominabl[e]'' art. When Whistler sued Ruskin, James wrote two untitled pieces on the subject for the *Nation* (19 Dec 1878, 13 Feb 1879; reprinted together as ''Contemporary Notes on Whistler vs. Ruskin,'' in *Views and Reviews*, 1908). In the first part, James summarizes the legal action, comments on defense testimony given by Sir Edward Burne-Jones,* favors ''liberty of criticism'' but calls Ruskin's words not decent and the man himself ''a general scold'' to whom Whistler, however, should have remained indifferent. In an aside, James calls Whistler's paintings ''eccentric and imperfect,'' although his etchings are ''altogether admirable.'' In the second part, James comments amusingly on Whistler's colloquial, French-spiced pamphlet (December 1878) concerning his lawsuit against Ruskin, whom he brands a mere ''penman.'' Whistler would like to suppress all art criticism, as an impertinent nuisance, and he reasons that Ruskin preaches about what he cannot perform. James voices his preference for French art notices over British ones and feels that Whistler here has a legitimate complaint. In fact, creative artists in all media ''have a standing, . . . just . . . quarrel with criticism.'' Yet, since the public is busy, criticism ''gratifies'' artists on occasion. On the other hand, while art is a necessity, criticism is only a luxury. In 1885 James entertained Whistler and the odd Robert, Comte de Montesquiou-Fezensac* at a Reform Club dinner. In 1891 he provided Whistler and his wife with tickets to his play *The American*. In 1895 Jonathan Sturges,* who was a friend of both James and Whistler, told the novelist about a now-famous remark made by William Dean Howells* in 1894 in the artist's Parisian garden, ending with the advice from Howells that one should live all one can, that it is a mistake not to do so. This little action in Whistler's garden became the germ for James's *The Ambassadors*. By letter (18 Feb [1897]), James thanked

Whistler for the gift of an evidently fine etching, which he later took with him to Lamb House.* In "London" (26 Jun 1897), he calls Whistler's painting of Sir Henry Irving* as Philip in *Queen Mary* by Alfred, Lord Tennyson* an "exquisite image" and "one of the finest of all distillations of the artistic intelligence." James's several published art notices in which Whistler is merely mentioned evolve from adverse to complimentary. In 1877 he calls Whistler's pictures unprofitable combinations of paint, canvas, and frames, and he says that they "belong to the closet, not to the world" and that they may well be only "good studio-jokes" ("The Grosvenor Gallery and the Royal Academy"); furthermore, "I frankly confess they do not amuse me" since they "have no relation whatever to life" ("The Picture Season in London"). In 1882 James does call the portrait of Whistler's mother a "noble . . . masterpiece" ("London Pictures and London Plays," Aug 1882). Finally in "London" (26 June 1897), he lauds Whistler thus: "Look . . . at his best . . . enough and hallucination sets in." Whistler's personality has a part in James's aesthete Gabriel Nash of *The Tragic Muse*. In 1908 James's illustrator Joseph Pennell* and his wife Elizabeth Robins Pennell published a biography of Whistler. James's library contained one book by Whistler, and the Pennell biography as well.

White, Father. In *Guy Domville*, a Catholic priest on whom Mrs. Domville and Lord Devenish feel they can count.

White, Henry (1850–1927). Baltimore-born American diplomat. He was privately educated in the United States and France, and he was adept in foreign languages. In 1879 he married Margaret Stuyvesant Rutherfurd, of New York City and Newport, Rhode Island. (They had a son and a daughter, who became a countess.) White was an important American legation officer in Vienna (1883–1884) and then in London (1884–1893, partly under James Russell Lowell,* and 1897–1905, partly under John Milton Hay*). White was then appointed ambassador to Italy (1905–1907), ambassador to France (1907–1909), and a member of the United States Peace Commission (1918). The Whites made their American home in Newport, Rhode Island, where Edith Newbold Jones Wharton* was an old friend of the entire, colorful Rutherfurd family. James knew and admired both Henry and Margaret White. In a letter to Elizabeth Boott* ([2 Jun] 1884), James calls the portrait of Margaret White by John Singer Sargent* a "splendid and delightful . . . masterpiece . . . of style and tone." In a letter to Grace Norton* (c. 4 Jan [1888]), James praises Mrs. White as "very handsome, young, rich, splendid, admired and successful, to a degree which leaves all competitors behind." Then he feels he must add, "She has never read a book in her life; but she is 'high up' all the same." Over the 1908 Christmas season, James wrote to her (29 Dec 1908) a pathetic letter of remembrance, praising her active life in Paris and calling himself "a *stopped* clock" by comparison.

Whitefoot, Rev. Mr. In *Roderick Hudson*, a New England minister who goes on the picnic attended by Roderick Hudson, Rowland Mallet, and Mary Garland, among others.

White-Mason. In "Crapy Cornelia," the middle-aged traveling American whose affection for Mrs. Worthingham dims when he renews his acquaintance with his old friend Cornelia Rasch.

Whiteroy, Lady. In *The Tragic Muse*, a hostess whose party Nicholas Dormer promises to attend but fails to do so.

Whiteroy, Lady Bessie and Lord. In "Lord Beaupré," an aristocratic couple. He is sociable. She is a clever woman who evidently likes Guy Firminger (Lord Beaupré) and therefore sponsors Mary Gosselin for him, but her plan fails.

Whiteroy, Lord. In "The Chaperon," a nobleman who loans his yacht to Bob Vaughan-Vesey.

Whiteside, Catherine. In *The Europeans*, the aunt of William Wentworth and the grandmother of Baroness Eugenia-Camilla-Delores Young Münster and Felix Young.

Whiteside, Louisa. In "The Point of View," the recipient of a letter from Aurora Church.

Whitman, Walt (1819–1892). One of the greatest American poets, born on Long Island into a family of ten children. He spent his childhood in Brooklyn and was educated there, worked in a printing office, taught school, was a newspaper editor, and read widely. He became interested in politics, published unimportant poems and stories, and edited the Democratic Brooklyn *Eagle* (1846–1848) until his Free-Soil tendencies resulted in his being fired. He worked in New Orleans briefly, returned to Brooklyn, turned from dandy to roughneck, absorbed German and Emersonian romantic philosophy, and published his bombshell, *Leaves of Grass* (1855), successively larger editions of which (in 1856, 1860, 1867, 1871, 1876, 1881–1882, 1882, 1888–1889, and 1891–1892) incorporated his later, magnificently evolving free-verse, musically rhythmic corpus. During the Civil War and after, Whitman was an unofficial army nurse in Washington, D.C. (1862–1865), and he held minor federal jobs (1862–1873). He also wrote and published controversial prose, not initially understood well but now regarded as vitally significant. Whitman had a paralytic stroke in 1873 and thereafter lived in Camden, New Jersey, except for brief out-of-state trips. James reviewed (*Nation*, 16 Nov 1865) Whitman's *Drum-Taps* (1865) adversely and without comprehending its prosodical virtuosity or liberal democratic contents. James snidely calls his task "a melancholy one," saying that good poetry required more than sympathy, admiration, and picturesqueness, that Whitman should have extracted more meaning from what he saw, and that he blows his own trumpet too much. James recognizes that the poet is celebrating our great armies and the fine city of New York, but he criticizes Whitman's "anomalous style," absence of melody, eccentricity, "medley of extravagances and commonplaces," and paucity of ideas. He adds (perhaps uneasily) that Whitman may well be original; still, he should let the public refine his "spurious poetry" so that he may become more than careless, inelegant, ignorant, rude, lugubrious, and grim. Later, James developed a more appreciative awareness of Whitman's genius, writing in "American Letter" (16 Apr, 7 May 1898) about his democratic appeal, the affectionate sincerity of his letters, and his humane patriotism, as revealed in his *Calamus* (1897), edited by Richard M. Bucke. In a letter to Manton Marble (10 Oct 1903), James expresses tardy regret at having written in 1865 as he did about *Drum-Taps*, blaming that review on "the gross impudence of youth." Edith Newbold Jones Wharton* recalls that late in his life James appreciatively read several of Whitman's poems aloud to her. James's library contained two books by Whitman.

Whitney, Adeline Dutton (née Train) (1824–1906). Author, born in Boston, and schooled in Latin and composition. She read widely, especially popular nineteenth-century women writers. She married Seth D. Whitney in 1843, lived in Milton, Massachusetts, reared four children, and began to write in her middle years. In the 1860s, Mrs. Whitney started publishing—among more serious work—what proved to be a number of popular novels about young people. The 1870s saw no significant change, and four of her books were collected in "The Real Folks Series." She remained an ultraconservative, prodomestic, antisuffrage writer, and she continued to publish until she turned eighty. James reviewed (*North American Review*, Oct 1865) her novel *The Gayworthys: A Story of Threads and Thrums* (1865), the unoriginal thesis of which is that "life is largely made up of broken threads, of plans arrested in their development, of hopes untimely crushed." James discusses the plot here, with its three pairs of lovers, and one particular episode too "radically defective" to merit comment. The trouble is that a character's "childhood and . . . manhood" cannot combine into one good love story. Mrs. Whitney shows cleverness, inventiveness, humor, and power—all sadly misused here to create something "vulgar and false."

Whittaker, Gertrude. In "Poor Richard," Richard Maule's rich rural neighbor. Richard loves her ineffectually. Captain Edmund Severn also loves her, to no avail. Richard prevents Major Robert Luttrel from winning her.

The Whole Family: A Novel by Twelve Authors. Composite novel, written by twelve authors and published in *Harper's Bazar* (Dec 1907–Nov 1908). The authors are William Dean Howells,* Mary Eleanor Wilkins Freeman,* Mary Heaton Vorse, Mary Stewart Cutting, Elizabeth Jordan,* John Kendrick Bangs,

Henry James, Elizabeth Stuart Phelps, Edith Wyatt, Mary R. Shipman Andrews, Alice Brown, and Henry Van Dyke. It is not revealed who wrote which chapters. Howells started the idea and suggested that *Bazar*-editor Elizabeth Jordan, whom James knew well, develop it. Howells had a subject for the plot: How an engagement or a marriage would affect and be affected by a whole family. He also wanted the heroine of the novel to go to a coeducational college. To please Miss Jordan (and earn $400), James wrote chapter seven, entitled "The Married Son." Some famous writers were asked to participate but declined, for example, Mark Twain.* Many, however, were eager to join in the fun. When the novel was serialized, the June 1908 episode was James's. The novel was then published in book form in New York by Harper in 1908.

Wigmore. In *A Change of Heart*, Margaret Thorne's lawyer for ten years. He is tired of protecting the haughty girl from fortune hunters.

Wigmore, Blandina. In *Disengaged*, Flora Wigmore's daughter and Sir Montagu Brisket's niece. The vapid, overly obedient girl accepts the forced proposal of Llewellyn Prime and then the better one of Percy Trafford, who finds her charming.

Wigmore, Flora. In *Disengaged*, Sir Montagu Brisket's sister and Blandina Wigmore's mother. The demanding, insensitive woman wants someone, anyone, to propose to her daughter.

Wilde, Oscar (1856–1900). Versatile Dublin-born man of letters. He was educated at Trinity College, Dublin, and then at Magdalen College, Oxford (1874–1878), where he was a brilliant student under John Ruskin,* among others; he was also slothful and was mistreated by fellow students. Wilde cultivated the image of an affected, witty, art-for-art's-sake dandy; he lectured in the United States in 1882; he married in 1884; and he wrote a stream of clever, popular works. His best plays are *Lady Windermere's Fan* (1892), *Salomé* (1893), *A Woman of No Importance* (1893), *An Ideal Husband* (1895), and *The Importance of Being Earnest* (1895). His finest fiction is the novel *The Picture of Dorian Gray* (1891). His nonfictional prose includes *The Soul of Man under Socialism* (1891) and *De Profundis* (1905). He also wrote poetry (collected and published in 1892). After Wilde was convicted of sodomy and jailed from 1895–1897, he went to the Continent friendless and in financial straits. He wrote under the pen name Sebastian Melmoth and died under mysterious circumstances in a Paris hotel. "The Ballad of Reading Gaol" (anonymously published in 1898) and his posthumous apologia *De Profundis* concern his tragic imprisonment and homosexuality. *Salomé* was produced in Paris in 1894 by Sarah Bernhardt.* James met Wilde in Washington, D.C., early in 1882 and was probably jealous of the social attention he was given there. In letters to Edwin Lawrence Godkin* (22 Jan 1882) and to Isabella Stewart Gardner* (23 Jan [1882]), he described Wilde as "an unclean beast" and "repulsive and fatuous." (Wilde, on the other hand, admired James and his art.) James was in the audience at *Lady Windermere's Fan*, which featured his friends Sir George Alexander* and Marion Terry, on opening night; he described the play in a letter to Mrs. Hugh Bell ([23 Feb 1892]) as "infantine . . . in subject and in form," but he did like the " 'cheeky' . . . dialogue." Much later, in a letter to Edith Newbold Jones Wharton* (25 Oct 1911), he labeled the same Wilde play "doddering rococo and . . . flat 'fizz.' " On the opening night of his own *Guy Domville*, James went to see *An Ideal Husband* and immediately realized, in a combination of jealousy and fear, that, as he wrote to his brother William (9 Jan 1895), since Wilde's work was considered a play and a success, "my thing is necessarily neither." Salt for James's wound came when *Guy Domville* closed and Wilde's *The Importance of Being Earnest* opened in the same theater. James and Wilde had mutual friends in Lady Florence Eveleen Eleanore Bell,* Paul Bourget,* Margaret Alice Lili Brooke,* Joseph William Comyns Carr,* Dame Ellen Terry,* William Morton Fullerton,* Sir Edmund Wilson Gosse,* George Moore, Violet Paget,* Marc André Raffalovich,* Henrietta Reubell,* Blanche Roosevelt,* John Singer Sargent,* and Jonathan Sturges,* among others. When Wilde was imprisoned for homosexual conduct, James almost instantly wrote to Gosse ([8 Apr 1895]) about the "hideously, atrociously dramatic & really interesting" case, with its "sickening horribility . . . [and] squalid gratuitousness." He added that Wilde had fallen from " 'brilliant' conspicuity." He added that Wilde "was never . . . interesting to me—but this hideous human misery has made him so." James declined to sign a petition for mitigation of sentence, once Wilde was jailed. Something of Wilde's background, plumpness, and wit may have gone into James's portrayal of Gabriel Nash in *The Tragic Muse*. James's library contained one book by Wilde.

Wilkes, Anna. In "Osborne's Revenge," Henrietta Congreve's invalid married sister.

Wilkes, Tom. In "Osborne's Revenge," Henrietta Congreve's little nephew, whom Philip Osborne rescues from drowning, thus meeting Miss Congreve.

Wilkins, Mary. Maiden name of Mary Eleanor Wilkins Freeman.* In more than one "American Letter" and in a Notebook entry, James cites her as Wilkins.

Wilkinson, James John Garth (1812–1880). London-born homoeopathic physician, poet, student of Icelandic and Scandinavian literature, and Swedenborgian scholar, translator, and proscience, prohistory interpreter. Wilkinson opposed both vaccination and vivisection. He knew Thomas Carlyle,* Charles Dickens,* James Anthony Froude,* and Alfred, Lord Tennyson,* among others whom James met in due time. Ralph Waldo Emerson* praised Wilkinson's writings. Carlyle introduced Henry James, Sr., to Wilkinson in London in 1843. Wilkinson became the most intelligent critic of the elder James's writings and was disturbed by his mystical, Gnostic tendencies. Henry James's younger brother Garth Wilkinson James was named after Wilkinson, who dedicated his *The Human Body and Its Connection with Man* (1851) to James's father. During his early years in London, James kept in touch with Wilkinson and his family, for his father's sake. In 1879 Wilkinson treated James for a headache; James wrote to his mother about the experience (8 Apr [1879]): "Dr. Wilkinson . . . rendered me . . . no assistance whatever—though he consented to accept a goodly fee." A year later James, having another headache, wrote to his mother (20 Jul [1880]) that he tried "a less metaphysical physician than poor old Wilkinson." James wrote to his mother (7 Feb [1881]) that he defined Wilkinson's solution for governing Ireland, which was "by the sword—by a reign of terror"—to be "all rubbish, as I think the rest of his opinions are." As a kind of summation, James wrote to Howard Overing Sturgis* (24 Aug 1912) that "Wilkinson was, in his early career, a very wonderful and splendid writer . . . though it all left him early . . . " James then quotes a passage from Wilkinson's *War, Cholera, and the Ministry of Health . . .* (1854).

William Wetmore Story and His Friends: From Letters, Diaries, and Recollections. James's biography of the once-esteemed expatriate-American sculptor and writer William Wetmore Story,* published in two volumes in Edinburgh and London by Blackwood, 1903. James met Story in Rome in 1873 and often enjoyed his hospitality there. Shortly after Story died in 1895, his family assembled his voluminous personal papers and persuaded James to use them as the basis for a biography. The result, in two volumes, was published in Edinburgh and London by Blackwood, in 1903, and in Boston by Houghton, Mifflin, also in 1903. James experienced trouble from the start since he regarded Story as a merry host, to be sure, but also as merely a rich dilettante. He converted what might have been a biography into a study of Story's artistic milieu, and he allowed generous selections of letters to and from Story to take over the text, with a minimum of his own commentary. Story's correspondents included Robert Browning* and his wife Elizabeth Barrett Browning,* James Russell Lowell,* Charles Eliot Norton,* and Charles Sumner. Story's net of friends was far wider; it included Henry Adams* and his wife Marion Adams,* Hans Christan Andersen, Matthew Arnold,* Isa Blagden, Francis Boott* and his daughter Elizabeth Boott,* Katherine De Kay Bronson,* the Crawfords (Thomas Crawford,* his widow Louisa Crawford Terry* and her second husband Luther Terry,* and Crawford's son Francis Marion Crawford*), Elizabeth Cleghorn Gaskell,* Nathaniel Hawthorne,* Harriet Hosmer, Lord Houghton,* Leigh Hunt, Alexander William Kinglake,* Walter Savage Landor, Henry Wadsworth Longfellow,* Robert Bulwer (Lord) Lytton, Margaret Fuller Ossoli, William Page, Theodore Parker, Charles C. Perkins, Adelaide Ristori,* Tommaso Salvini,* William Makepeace Thackeray* and his daughter Lady Anne Isabella Ritchie,* and Alexis de Tocqueville. Just before *William Wetmore Story* was published and then again after it was reviewed and commented on by friends, James explained his difficulties, as well as his formula for overcoming them, in a few letters: "[T]here is no *subject*.... There is nothing for me but to do a *tour de force*, or try—leave poor dear W.W.S. *out*, practically, and make a little volume on the old Roman, Americo-Roman, Hawthornesque and other bygone days . . . " (to William Dean Howells,* 25 Jan 1902); "I wanted to invest dear old Boston with a mellow, a golden glow—and . . . for those who know, like yourself, I only make it bleak—and weak!" (to Henry Adams, 19 Nov 1903); "I *had* to invent an attitude (of general evocation and discoursiveness) to fill out the form of a book at all" (to Anne Ritchie, 19 Nov 1903); and "the magic is but scantly mine—it is really that of the beloved old Italy, who always *will* consent to fling a glamour for you, whenever you speak her fair" (to Millicent Fanny St. Claire-Erskine, Duchess of Sutherland,* 23 Dec 1903). James divides his book into twelve chapters: Story's antecedents; his youthful Massachusetts years; his first years in Europe (Rome, Venice, and Berlin) and back in America (three chapters); his move into the Palazzo Barberini; his time in Siena and his friendship with Sumner; Story's *Cleopatra* and *Libyan Sibyl*; his time with English society; his poetry; his American commissions; and his last years, in Vallombrosa. Of least value, as James himself knew, are his comments on Story. The biography, however, is a significant document for two reasons: James tenderly evokes the Rome of the Anglo-American colony there in the late nineteenth century, and he extensively quotes fine, informative letters by persons more significant than their nearly forgotten recipient. James put it best in a tactful letter to Story's daughter-in-law Mrs. Waldo Story (6 Jan 1903): "I have looked at the picture, . . . given me by all your material, *as* a picture—the image . . . a little ghostly, of . . . a society practically extinct, with Mr. and Mrs. Story . . . the centre, the pretext.... The Book was not makeable . . . unless I used the letters of other people, and the letters . . . were useable . . . only so far as I could more or less evoke and present the other people."

Willoughby, Bernard. In "The Romance of Certain Old Clothes," Mrs. Bernard Willoughby's son, and Viola and Perdita Willoughby's brother. His friend Arthur Lloyd marries Perdita and later Viola.

Willoughby, Hugh Laussat (1864–1939). American author, whose *Across the Everglades: A Canoe Journey of Exploration* (1898) James touches on in "American Letter" (11 June 1898), calling it a "charming" account of an "ingenious trip." He confesses to finding any "veracious notes of exploration" fascinating and compares Willoughby's depiction of the "unknown" to effects by Edgar Allan Poe.*

Willoughby, Mrs. Bernard. In "The Romance of Certain Old Clothes," the widowed mother of Bernard, Viola, and Perdita Willoughby.

Willoughby, Mrs. Bernard. In "The Romance of Certain Old Clothes," Mrs. Bernard Willoughby's son's wife.

Willoughby, Perdita. In "The Romance of Certain Old Clothes," Bernard, Viola, and Perdita Willoughby's sister; she dies in infancy.

Willoughby, Perdita. In "The Romance of Certain Old Clothes," the maiden name of Perdita Willoughby Lloyd—the daughter of Mrs. Bernard Willoughby and the sister of Bernard and Viola Willoughby.

Willoughby, Viola. In "The Romance of Certain Old Clothes," the maiden name of Viola Willoughby Lloyd—the daughter of Mrs. Bernard Willoughby and the sister of Bernard and Perdita Willoughby.

Wilmerding, Henry. In "The Solution," a callow American secretary of legation in Rome. He is fooled into believing that he has compromised Veronica Goldie by walking with her unchaperoned in a secluded grove. He is saved from having to marry her by the widowed Mrs. Rushbrook, who marries him herself.

Wilson, Andrew (1831–1881). British traveler and writer. He was educated in Edinburgh and Tübingen, lived briefly in Italy, then became an editor, journalist, and traveler in India and China. Wilson returned to England in the late 1850s, the 1860s, and the early 1870s. He visited the United States during the Civil War. In addition to writings based on his wanderings, he published books on Charles George Gordon (1868) and Richard F. Burton (1886). His most popular book was *The Abode of Snow: Observations on a Tour from Tibet to the Indian Caucasus through the Upper Valleys of the Himalaya* (1875), which James reviewed (*Nation*, 11 Nov 1875), calling it a "superior specimen" of the effort, common today, to combine "traveling and scribbling." Wilson and his servants, some of whom thought him "most insane," went from Simla and Kashmir to "the border of pugnacious Afghanistan" and on to India and Chinese Tibet. He regularly chose arduous mountain routes (one up to 18,000 feet) for his health. His discussions of "adventures, . . . politics, . . . religion, [and] . . . ethnography" reveal his experience and ability.

Wimbush, Mr. and Mrs. Weeks. In "The Death of the Lion," a rich brewer and his wife. He owns the estate of Prestidge. She lionizes novelist Neil Paraday to death.

Winch, Newton. In "A Round of Visits," a larcenist. Mark P. Monteith visits him and so sympathizes with the probable feeling of Phil Bloodgood, who has swindled Monteith, that Winch goes ahead with his plan and commits suicide.

Winch, Mrs. Newton. In ''A Round of Visits,'' Winch's recently deceased wife. She was the sister of Lottie, whom Mark P. Monteith meets.

''Winchelsea, Rye, and 'Denis Duval.' '' Travel and critical essay, published in *Scribner's Magazine* (Jan 1901); reprinted in *English Hours*, 1905. The essay in large part discusses *Denis Duval* by William Makepeace Thackeray.*

Windon. In ''John Delavoy,'' a poor dramatist whose play the critic narrator and Miss Delavoy attend.

Windrush, Lady. In *The Tragic Muse*, Peter Sherringham and Julia Sherringham Dallow's mother.

Wing, Laura. In ''A London Life,'' Selina Wing Berrington's nervous, unmarried sister. While visiting Selina in London, Laura is befriended by Lady Davenant and falls in love with puzzled Wendover.

Wingrave. In ''Owen Wingrave,'' the son of Colonel Wingrave, who in anger struck and killed him. In *The Saloon*, the youngster was fatally beaten by his grandfather for declining to go to a military school.

Wingrave, Colonel. In ''Owen Wingrave,'' Owen Wingrave's great-great grandfather, who lived in George II's time. The colonel in anger fatally struck his own child. Next morning the colonel was found dead in the room, which since then has been regarded as haunted. His frightening portrait hangs over the stairs in the family estate. In *The Saloon*, it is merely said that a legendary Wingrave in a black periwig struck his allegedly cowardly grandson and caused his death. The older man soon thereafter reentered the death room, never to emerge.

Wingrave, Jane. In ''Owen Wingrave,'' Owen Wingrave's militant aunt, once engaged to Captain Hume-Walker. In *The Saloon*, she is described as tall and erect, and she would have married Hume-Walker but for his death. She takes care of her father General Sir Philip Wingrave.

Wingrave, Mrs. Owen. In ''Owen Wingrave,'' the mother of Philip and Owen Wingrave; she died in childbirth in India. In *The Saloon*, this deceased mother is said to have come from a traditional military family, too.

Wingrave, Owen. In ''Owen Wingrave,'' Owen Wingrave's father, who was killed in an Afghan raid. In *The Saloon*, he is said to have been killed on an Egyptian battlefield.

Wingrave, Owen. In "Owen Wingrave," a sensitive young man who in spite of family pressure (and the coaching of Spencer Coyle) gives up his plan to study under Spencer Coyle for a military school and a military career. Because of Kate Julian's taunts, he spends a night in a haunted room and dies there. In *The Saloon*, the young man speaks passionately for life and peace. He defies the Wingrave family ghost and Kate Julian apologizes to him. He dies confronting the family ghost.

Wingrave, Philip. In "Owen Wingrave," Owen Wingrave's imbecilic older brother.

Wingrave, Sir Philip. In "Owen Wingrave," Owen Wingrave's military grandfather who opposes the young man's pacifist inclinations. In *The Saloon*, in which he is called General Sir Philip Wingrave, K.C.B. (age eighty), he has Spencer Coyle report to Owen that he is disinherited.

The Wings of the Dove. Novel (172,100 words), published in New York by Scribner, 1902, and in Westminster by Constable, 1902; revised and reprinted in *The Novels and Tales of Henry James*, Volumes XIX, XX, 1909. (Characters: Lord and Lady Aldershaw, Dr. Buttrick, Bertie and Guy and Kitty and Maudie Condrip, Rev. Mr. Condrip, Marian Croy Condrip, the Misses Condrip, Kate Croy, Lionel Croy, Merton Densher, Eugenio, Dr. Finch, Maud Manningham Lowder, Lord Mark, Lady Mills, Pasquale, Sir Luke Strett, Susan Shepherd Stringham, Dr. Tacchini, Milly Theale, Lady Wells.) Lionel Croy agrees in London that his daughter Kate should appear to ignore him, go to her aunt Maud Lowder, and let that massive woman negotiate a fine marriage for her. Kate visits her widowed sister Marian Condrip, who urges her to drop Merton Densher, a London journalist soon going briefly to America, in favor of Lord Mark, Maud's choice. Rich but dying Milly Theale and her friend Susan Shepherd Stringham leave New York, where the girl happened to meet Densher, for Italy, Switzerland, and then London. Mrs. Stringham introduces Milly to her old school friend Mrs. Lowder, at whose home the girl becomes friendly with Kate and also attracts Lord Mark. Through Kate, Milly also meets Marian, who tells her of Densher's love for Kate. Milly says nothing about this, however, because Mrs. Lowder dislikes any mention of Densher. Nor does Kate speak of him. Lord Mark is intrigued by Milly's response when he notes her resemblance to a Bronzino portrait. Milly asks Kate to accompany her to the eminent physician Sir Luke Strett, who advises Milly to make the most of her remaining days. Densher returns to London. Milly is puzzled: She sees him at the National Gallery with Kate; then, at Kate's instigation, he calls upon and is attentive to Milly. We now learn that Kate hopes that Densher can marry the fatally ill Milly, inherit her money when she dies, and then defiantly wed Kate. On Sir Luke's advice, Milly goes to Venice for the winter, accompanied by Mrs. Stringham faithfully, Kate and her aunt briefly, and Densher hesitantly. To assure himself of Kate once their unsavory plan is consummated, he demands that she visit him privately in his room. She thus pledges herself to him. He then so charms Milly that she falls in love. However, Lord Mark, also in Venice now, has proposed to Milly and has been rejected; in bitter frustration—as Mrs. Stringham soon tells the tardily remorseful Densher—he informs Milly of Kate's permanent liaison with Densher, which Lord Mark somehow found out about. Back in London, Densher cannot bring himself to go and see Kate. He hears on Christmas Day, through Mrs. Lowder at Sir Luke's home, of Milly's death in Venice. He receives a letter written in Milly's hand and takes it unopened to Kate; ill at ease, they burn it, sensing that it contains an offer of money so that they can marry. Sure enough, in due course a letter comes to Densher from a New York law firm. He sends it unopened to Kate, who comes to him with it. He will marry her, he says, without the money but not with it; she will marry him, she says, but not without it. She now knows that he loves Milly's memory and wants no other love; like herself, he has been changed. James's *Notebooks* have several entries concerning the plot of *The Wings of the Dove*. In the first entry (3 Nov 1894), James pens detailed notes about a "young creature . . . preferably a woman" on life's threshold but suddenly terrified by news that she has "consumption, heart-disease, or whatever." James quickly expands a cast of characters to include a young man who "deeply pities her" but loves elsewhere, although his fiancée is poor and her family dislikes him. James is bothered by the "nastiness . . . of the man's 'having' a sick girl," but his character's fiancée agrees even to let him marry the dying girl for the money in it. A few days later (7 Nov 1894), James considers having his young man, tardily humanized, give his fiancée a choice—himself or the money—with the woman going for the latter! James soon returns to his basic idea (14 Feb 1895), "struck with all it contains. It is there, the story; . . . a thing . . . of great potential interest and beauty and of a strong, firm artistic *ossature*." In a later entry (21 Dec 1895), James calls the story La Mourante. As James thought, scribbled, and pondered, he began to create one of his finest heroines, Milly Theale, who is based partly on his long-dead cousin Mary Temple.* The title of this imagistically rich novel derives from Psalms 55:6: "And I said, Oh that I had wings like a dove! for then would I fly away, and be at rest." James also must have had in mind Hilda from *The Marble Faun* by Nathaniel Hawthorne,* since doves circle that pallid American heroine's high foreign abode. But wings not only carry one to safety but also shield others from harm. Critics of *The Wings of the Dove* have written much about such problems as point of view (Milly's is almost completely avoided); grand scenes thrown away (for example, Lord Mark's brutal revelation to the dying heroine); information simply withheld (what is the Bronzino painting to Milly? what disease is destroying her body? is it tuberculosis, chlorosis, inoperable cancer?); and gray areas in the leading characters' psyches (is Kate purely vicious? is Milly finally generous? how has Densher changed?). James, in the preface to Volume XIX of *The Novels and Tales of Henry James*, addresses most of these concerns. In it, he discusses the appeal of his sick heroine, sickness in fictive characters generally, freedom of movement owing to wealth, how trouble comes to his heroine, building a fiction from the edge and working toward the center, making "picture . . . and drama" aid each other although they are "jealous" of each other, a fear that the finale is rushed, distress that his revelatory centers shift and that the first volume is overprepared at the expense of the second, and his "instinct . . . for the *indirect* presentation of his main image."

Winkle, Susan. In "Mrs. Temperly," Maria Temperly's New York maid.

Winkworth, Miss. In *The Bostonians*, Henry Burrage, Jr.'s supposed fiancée.

Winterbourne, Frederick Forsyth. In "Daisy Miller," the Europeanized, Geneva-based American, age twenty-seven, whom Daisy Miller first meets in Vevey, Switzerland, where they visit the Château de Chillon together, and whom she later encounters in Rome. She is attracted to him; but his timidity in the face of her social gaucherie prevents his responding, thus quite indirectly causing her death by fever. He later experiences some self-doubt. In *Daisy Miller: A Comedy in Three Acts*, it is revealed that Winterbourne has been intimate with Madame de Katkoff in her villa just outside Geneva and also in Dresden, for some three years now. She defies the blackmailing attempts by Eugenio, the Miller family courier, and she successfully urges Winterbourne to propose marriage to Daisy, who recovers from her fever and accepts him.

"The Winter Exhibitions in London." Art review, published in the *Nation* (13 Feb 1879). James comments that the Burlington House exhibition, sponsored by the Royal Academy, which can borrow from more extensive holdings, overmatches the current Grosvenor Gallery show. But the academy this year presents portraits of inferior quality by Thomas Gainsborough,* George Romney,* and other English masters. Reserving his praise for the Dutch works shown, James generalizes that British society simply does not value art so intensely as Dutch society. He comments on rooms of drawings and miniatures, and he admires several splendid chalks of heads by Hans Holbein the younger*; he closes with a mere word on the watercolors shown at the Grosvenor Gallery.

Wispers, Lord and Lady. In "The Papers," Sir A. B. C. Beadel-Muffet's hosts.

Wister, Owen (1860–1938). Philadelphia-born lawyer, musician, and writer. He was the grandson of actress Frances Anne Kemble* and the son of Sarah Butler Wister,* both of whom James knew. Wister graduated from Harvard in 1882, then studied music in Paris, but returned home in 1883 for business and to improve his health. He vacationed in Wyoming (first in 1885), went to Harvard Law School (to 1888), and passed the Pennsylvania bar (1889). But he found that he had fallen in love with the American West, and he often returned. He published short stories, and collections thereof, set in the West (*Red Men and White* [1896], *Lin McLean* [1898], *The Jimmyjohn Boss, and Other Stories* [1900], *Members of the Family* [1911], and *When West Was West* [1928]). His novel *The Virginian* (1902) made him famous. It became the paradigm of most subsequent Western novels, with its reticent, chivalric hero; pliant heroine from the East; vivid setting; romantic adventure plot; local color and Western humor; and the gunfight between Good and Evil. Wister wrote other novels, books for children, and biographical studies of George Washington, Ulysses Simpson Grant,* and his close friend Theodore Roosevelt.* Wister's friends also included Henry Adams,* John Jay Chapman,* Oliver Wendell Holmes, Jr.,* William Dean Howells,* Frederic Remington, and Mark Twain.* Wister's journals and letters from 1885 to 1895 were published in 1958. In 1882, James met Wister, whom he had known when Wister was a lad, in England, and again later that year in France while James was preparing for his book *A Little Tour in France*. At that time, James was unimpressed by the young man, whom later, however, he recommended to Robert Louis Stevenson* by letter (18 Dec [1887]) as "brilliant and accomplished." In later years, James and Wister occasionally met and regularly corresponded. In 1896, in England, James offered the young author professional criticism, page by page, of *Red Men and White*. James prescribed more landscape description in later fiction. James read *The Virginian* and wrote to the author (7 Aug 1902) thus: The hero's "personal and moral complexion and evolution" are well exhibited; the hero should not have been shown to marry and prosper, but should have "perish[ed] in his flower and in some splendid noble way"; further, he should not be the subject of a second volume (he was not). During James's 1904–1905 tour of the United States, Wister showed his friend around Charleston, South Carolina (February 1905); without naming his guide, James comments on his knowledge of the area in *The American Scene*. In May 1914, after the death of his wife the previous August, Wister visited James in England. James's library contained three books by Wister.

Wister, Sarah Butler (1835–1908). Bright, much-traveled woman famous for being the daughter of the actress Frances Anne Kemble* and the mother of the novelist Owen Wister.* James met her in Rome late in 1872. Although he wrote to his mother at once (29 Dec [1872]) that he "mistrust[ed] her" slightly and that she was too "conscious," he attended several receptions at the Roman residence she and her husband enjoyed, met many people there (and also later through her), and went about Rome with her (sometimes on horseback). Soon he and Mrs. Wister became good friends, and she was the recipient over the years of many of his most informative letters. He stayed three days with her in Washington, D.C., early in 1882, in spite of his "impression that the lady takes life too tragically" (as he wrote to Grace Norton, 10 Jan [1882]). He was her guest again, in Philadelphia, in January 1905, during his 1904–1905 tour of the

United States. The personal attributes of Mrs. Rushbrook in James's "The Solution" owe much to Mrs. Wister.

Withermore, George. In "The Real Right Thing," the young man who tries to write deceased author Ashton Doyne's biography until Doyne's ghost convinces him to desist.

Withers. In *The Princess Casamassima*, the Princess Casamassima's servant at Medley.

"Within the Rim." War essay, published in *Fortnightly Review* (Aug 1917), *Living Age* (8 Sep 1917), and *Harper's Magazine* (Dec 1917); reprinted in *Within the Rim and Other Essays: 1914–15*, 1919. James compares and contrasts the advent of World War I ("vivid") with that of the American Civil War ("faded"). Old now, he was young then. Nevertheless, many elements are identical: the tension, the danger of a whole region collapsing, the thrill of crisis tasted, the anticipation of prolonged conflict, the suffering of the endangered side. Under beautiful skies, the horror of war, which James can imagine with "intensity . . . akin to pain," beyond the English Channel "rim" is all the more unspeakable. War makes it necessary for "ploughed-up" James to "re-identify" things near and dear to him. He is glad for the sea which defends his insular England and makes her different from "her tragic sisters," France and Belgium. James sees Germany as "the spiked helmet," under which France "all but bled to death in 1871." Now, once again, Germany is trying to squeeze "the variety and spontaneity" out of France between "hideous knuckly fingers." Private dismay in James combines with a desire to support war efforts. He does so by praising British tradition and by responding to the smiling, candid, virtuous people of this land, of which he is an "associated outsider." He closes thus: Insolent, deluded Germany cannot defeat the "unquenchable association" of England and America, alike in "race and tongue, temper and tradition."

Within the Rim and Other Essays: 1914–15. Collection of five war essays, published in London by Collins, 1919: "Within the Rim," "Refugees in Chelsea," "The American Volunteer Motor-Ambulance Corps in France," "France," and "The Long Wards."

Wix. In *What Maisie Knew*, Mrs. Wix's mysterious, long-deceased husband.

Wix, Clara Matilda. In *What Maisie Knew*, Mrs. Wix's deceased little daughter.

Wix, Mrs. In *What Maisie Knew*, Maisie Farange's dowdy, righteous governess, who is critical of Sir Claude and Beale Farange's wife, the former Miss Overmore.

Wolseley, Field-Marshal Viscount Garnet Joseph (1833–1913). British military hero and writer, and memoirist. Born in County Dublin, Ireland, he became an army officer in 1852, lost an eye in the Crimean War (1855—he observed and admired General Charles George Gordon there), fought in India and China, held an administrative post in Canada, and visited General Robert E. Lee (whom he admired) during the American Civil War. He worked in London to reform the British army in the early 1870s and late 1880s—interrupted by African duty, including at Ashanti, in Egypt, and at Khartoum (but too late to save General Gordon). Wolseley was commander in chief of the British Army from 1895 to 1899. He wrote *The Soldier's Pocket Book for Field Service* (1869), books on Marlborough (1894) and Napoleon (1895), and his autobiography, *The Story of a Soldier's Life* (2 vols., 1903). Wolseley married Louisa Erskine in 1867; they had a daughter named Frances. James wrote to his mother (6 Aug [1877]) about meeting Wolseley in 1877 during a visit to a Warwickshire country house and about becoming "quite 'thick' " with his "very charming wife." A few months later, he wrote to his brother William (28 Jan [1878]) about being a dinner guest at the Wolseleys' "beautiful old house in Portman Square [London]": "Sir Garnet is a very handsome, well-mannered and fascinating little man—with rosy dimples and an eye of steel: an excellent specimen of the *cultivated* British soldier." James was a guest of the Wolseleys at their Dublin castle in 1895, and, in a letter to William James and his wife (28 Mar 1895), he described the couple as "sweet, really angelic" but his six-day stay as "wasteful and expensive social idleness." Two days later he wrote to Theodora Sedgwick, the youngest sister of Grace Norton,* to describe Wolseley's colorful military entourage in much detail. Viscountess Wolseley helped James furnish Lamb House*; further, she and her distinguished husband visited James there in June 1900, causing a public sensation and making the novelist seem like a suddenly, doubly important Rye resident. James wrote to Wolseley (7 Dec 1903) to praise his autobiography as "a 'human document' of a fascinating order" and as "a beautiful, rich, *natural* book." James further calls himself "a poor worm of peace," but one who still finds "communicating . . . with the military temper and type" and "the brilliant man of action" to be "irresistible." More privately, James wrote to Sir Edmund Wilson Gosse* (27 Aug [1895]) that "the Wolseleys . . . are the best 'circus' one knows"; further (24 Nov 1909), that Wolseley's autobiography comprises "2 vast & artless volumes, a most gallant forlorn hope of a book." His Pocket Diaries indicate that James socialized with Wolseley's widow and daughter into 1915. His library contained two books by Wolseley.

Wood, Francis Derwent (1871–1926). English sculptor noted for his *Psyche* (1919), *William Pitt* (1920), and Machine Gun Corps memorial (1925), now located in Hyde Park, London. When John Singer Sargent* declined to accept pay for his 1913 portrait of James, the money collected was given to Wood for a bust of James, which was done in July 1913.

Woodley, Willie. In "An International Episode," an American in London. He escorts Kitty Alden Westgate and Bessie Alden, and he finds Lord Lambeth in Hyde Park.

Woodley, Willie. In "The Impressions of a Cousin," a guest at Eunice's dinner party.

Woolf, Virginia (1882–1914). Significant British author, whose novels *Jacob's Room* (1922), *Mrs. Dalloway* (1925), *To the Lighthouse* (1927), and *The Waves* (1931) are experimental compared to her several other books. Virginia (whose godfather was James Russell Lowell*) and Vanessa Stephen were the daughters of Sir Leslie Stephen* by his second wife; therefore, James saw much of them both, as well as their brothers, when they were young. While vacationing in Rye in 1907, the two sisters called upon James at Lamb House.* He never liked the pre-Bloomsbury group as it was developing, perhaps felt envious of their youthful energy, and was viciously critical of Vanessa's husband Clive Bell. In a letter to Mrs. W. K. Clifford* (17 Feb 1907), James called him "the quite dreadful-looking little stoop-shouldered, long-haired, third-rate Clive Bell," but he added that Virginia had, "by the way, grown quite elegantly and charmingly and almost 'smartly' handsome." In a letter to Sara Darwin (11 Sep 1907), the sister-in-law of Charles Eliot Norton,* James depicted the Stephen sisters in some detail, then added "And the hungry generations tread me down!" In 1912 Virginia married Leonard Woolf, a Cambridge University friend of James's friend Sir Sydney Philip Waterlow.* (Woolf met and commented on James.) In 1917 the Woolfs founded the influential Hogarth Press, which published, among much else, *Henry James at Work* by Theodora Bosanquet* (1924).

Woolson, Constance Fenimore (1840–1894). Novelist, writer of short stories and sketches, and poet, born in Claremont, New Hampshire, into a large family. Her father was a businessman, and her mother was a niece of James Fenimore Cooper. The family moved to Cleveland, from which she accompanied her father on trips through Ohio and into Wisconsin; the family also vacationed on Mackinac Island. After a solid schooling in New York City and then her father's death (1869), Miss Woolson began to write local color stories, culminating in the successful *Castle Nowhere: Lake Country Sketches* (1875). At about this time, she traveled with her mother (who died in 1879) and with Clara Woolson Benedict,* a widowed sister, along the Atlantic coast. Miss Woolson lived for a while in North and South Carolina and in Florida. Reconstruction era tales went into *Rodman the Keeper: Southern Sketches* (1880). She was encouraged by her friends John Milton Hay* and William Dean Howells* to travel. She lived in Europe from 1879 on, moving about restlessly—to England, France, Switzerland, Egypt, Italy, and Greece—but also residing for long periods of time in London and nearby (1883–1886, 1890–1893), also in Florence (1887–1889), and finally in Venice (1893–1894), where she died. Her novels are *Anne* (1883, her most popular book and therefore a financial winner), *For the Major* (1883, her best novel), *East Angels* (1886), *Jupiter Lights* (1889), and *Horace Chase* (1894). Armed with a letter of introduction from a cousin of James, Miss Woolson, who was lonely and partially deaf, sought to meet him in London late in 1879 but missed him. She settled for a time in southern France to write, but met, flattered, and was charmed by him the next spring in Florence, where he acted as her guide for a few weeks. She wrote about him often in letters home. James visited "Fenimore," as he called her, in Rome the following spring, and he occasionally saw her in London and nearby for several years, beginning late in 1883. For example, they visited Stonehenge together in September 1884, and also attended the London theater together now and then. Early in 1886, she left for Italy. Aided by James's friend Francis Boott,* Miss Woolson found temporary accommodations in Florence, and she took a year's lease (1887, renewed) in nearby Bellosguardo on the fourteen-room Villa Brichieri, part of which James sublet for December 1886. He returned from sickness in Venice to the villa where Miss Woolson then lived, from February to April 1887. In October 1888, the two met by arrangement in Geneva. In 1889 she returned to England, and they saw each other several times over the next few years. She attended the opening performance of James's play *The American*, in London, on 26 September 1891. In the summer of 1893 she returned to Italy, this time to Venice. She hoped that James would visit her in the spring, as he had promised, and further that they might collaborate on a play. But on 24 January 1894, she fell from her second-story palazzo window and died, possibly by suicide, while she was sick, feverish, and perhaps delirious. James prepared to go to Rome to the funeral (arranged by Hay) but, when he learned that the death might not have been accidental, he did not go. Instead, he wrote to Miss Woolson's sister Mrs. Benedict most courteously, offered to help her in Italy with the dead woman's effects, met and assisted Mrs. Benedict and her daughter Clare Benedict in Genoa late in March, met them again in Venice a few days later, and helped to ship home twenty-seven boxes of effects and also to dispose of the rest, including letters, during the next five weeks. James and Miss Woolson often corresponded, but evidently only four letters of hers are extant. These verbose letters are filled with flattery of James and gentle rebukes at his personal indifference to her. Shortly after her death, James wrote to Sir Edmund Wilson Gosse* (30 Jan [1894]) that it was "unspeakable," an "unmitigated . . . tragedy," and "an overwhelming, haunting horror." He wrote to other friends similarly agitated letters. James subsequently wrote to Mrs. Benedict many unctuous letters (and a few to her daughter as well), but his opinion of the older woman was not high. For example, he wrote, perhaps defensively, to Francis Boott (11 Oct [1895]) that she and her daughter "lately passed through London on their way back to the U.S.—very futile and foolish, poor things . . . Mrs. B. is very considerably mad. But . . . the little girl is gentleness incarnate." James wrote one essay on Miss Woolson (*Harper's Weekly*, 12 Feb 1887; reprinted in *Partial Portraits*, 1888), which is unusually kind. He starts with comments on women's literary advances, relating them to his subject's conservative, private stance. He has not read *Castle Nowhere*, but he admires "the strenuous studies of . . . life . . . in Florida, Georgia and the Carolinas" as presented in *Rodman the Keeper*; these are post–Civil War regions usually "so unrecorded, so unpainted and unsung." Familiar local color touches are accurate, but the effect is "dreariness." In *East Angels*, too, "sadness . . . is more striking than . . . high spirits." Miss Woolson writes of sacrifice, failure, suffering, renunciation, and various disappointments. James finds *Anne* the author's "least happily composed" effort and gently ridicules the handling of hurried marriages in it. He likes the subject of *For the Major*: An aging woman tries to appear young, not for her own sake, but for her husband's. Miss Woolson has the great talent of enlisting our sympathy for her female characters. She indulges in many references to the Episcopal church and to "family histories," is picturesque, and nicely evokes the sense of towns more ancient than real. *East Angels* is best for "evoking a local tone," especially that of "warm, rank . . . Florida." The book is "thoroughly worthy" though "not flawless." Miss Woolson watches life, waits, "to catch it in the fact," since she regards "the novel as a picture of the actual, of the characteristic." But *East Angels* has two defects: Her characters are too detached—"they have a certain shipwrecked air"—and their emotional complications concern love almost exclusively. She does, however, make the transcendent self-sacrifice of her heroine seem real and hence acceptable: Her "distinguished" heroine convincingly "look[s] at life from a high point of view." James commends three fine episodes: a certain New England woman's late bitterness, a strange forest search, and the dramatic farewell of two clashing characters. Miss Woolson's "patience and conscience" are a promise of more fine books. James's library contained seven books by Miss Woolson and, in addition, one book by her niece Clare Benedict, who became a minor writer.

Wormeley, Katherine Prescott (1830–1908). Author and translator. Born in Ipswich, England, she moved to the United States in the late 1840s. She spent more than forty years translating forty volumes of works by Honoré de Balzac* (1855–1896, interrupted by Sanitary Commission work during the Civil War) and also published a book on Balzac (1892). In addition, she translated works by other French writers, including Alphonse Daudet* and Charles Augustin Sainte-Beuve,* and she published *The Other Side of War* (1889). She was the older sister of Ariana Randolph Curtis,* hence the sister-in-law of Daniel Sargent Curtis.* Through the Curtises, long-time residents of Venice, James came to know Miss Wormeley, whom he frequently mentions in letters beginning in the late 1880s. She startled him when, in 1894, she revealed that she had heard of the publication of his sister Alice's "letters." He wrote to Miss Wormeley, then at home in New Hampshire, a beautiful letter (8 Feb 1900) about Balzac, Balzac papers, and her work on Balzac—"I find your zeal, your devotion, your thoroughness, your mastery of your subject beyond praise." During his 1904–1905 tour in the United States, James visited Miss Wormeley in New Hampshire, in September 1904.

Worthingham, Mrs. In "Crapy Cornelia," the rich, flashy woman for whom White-Mason cares less and less as he renews his acquaintance with Cornelia Rasch.

Wright, Gordon. In *Confidence*, the young American who asks his friend Bernard Longueville to pass judgment on Angela Vivian. Longueville criticizes her. Wright later marries Blanche Evers.

Wyckoff, Walter Augustus (1865–1908). American born in India, the son of a missionary. After being educated in America, he began to study the plight of unskilled laborers. He became a migrant worker, working from New England to California (1891–1893); then he lectured in sociology and published *The Workers: An Experiment in Reality—The East* (1897) and then *The West* (1898). In "American Letter" (23 Apr 1898), James declines to consider current fiction but instead notes that *The Workers* "has held me as under a spell," though without "a solitary ray" of any "magic" style.

Wynter, Andrew (1819–1876). Bristol-born physician, author, and editor, educated in London and at St. Andrew. Although he often wrote on general topics in the field of medicine, Wynter concentrated on discussing treatment of the insane. *The Borderlands of Insanity and Other Allied Papers* (1875) is his most important professional publication. He also collected various subjective papers on miscellaneous subjects into book form on several occasions. James reviewed (*Nation*, 1 Jul 1875) his *Fruits between the Leaves* (2 vols., 1875), which James regards as entertaining but trivial, and in a style "convenient for the lighter magazines." Wynter appears here to be "a walking encyclopaedia" stuffed with "secondary and tertiary facts" on such subjects as dogs, female convicts, toys, lifeboats, cats and rats, tunnels, food additives, garbage, infanticide, and jewels.

X, Princess. In *Watch and Ward*, a pleasant woman who gives a ball in Rome that Nora Lambert attends.

Y

Yarracome, Lord. In "John Delavoy," a member of the audience attending Windon's play. It is also seen by the critic narrator and Miss Delavoy.

Yonge, Charlotte Mary (1823–1901). Prolific British novelist and writer of stories for children. Her 160 or so books, mostly domestic or historical novels, served the Church of England and helped to popularize the Oxford Movement. *The Heir of Redclyffe* (1853) gained her fame and influence; and she followed it with *Heartsease* (1854), *The Daisy Chain* (1856—its sequel is *The Trial* [1864]), *The Dynevor Terrace* (1857), *The Young Stepmother* (1861), and *The Clever Woman of the Family* (1865), among many others. *The Prince and the Page* (1865), *The Dove in the Eagle's Nest* (1866), *The Caged Lion* (1870), and *Unknown to History* (1882) are examples of Yonge's romancing of history. James reviewed (*Nation*, 8 Apr 1875) both her *Life of John Coleridge Patteson, Missionary Bishop to the Melanesian Islands* (2 vols., 1875) and its abridgement, *The Story of a Fellow Soldier* (1875), by Francis Awdry.* (For the 1883 edition of this abridgement, Yonge provided a preface.) James praises Yonge's work, based on Patteson's letters, as "careful and intelligent," tasteful and discreet, though limited by its "conservative Anglicanism." He calls Patteson a hero "almost picturesque, . . . almost dramatic," whose life as a missionary in Auckland, New Zealand, and to the north, from 1855 until his martyrdom in 1871, is "complete and touching," almost that of a "saint of ecclesiastical legend." James reviews Patteson's life and praises his character and skill in languages, but wonders at the wisdom of his "converting unconscious barbarians into puzzled catechumens." Still, he was "a brilliant figure in the noble class of men . . . whose idea and effort have been a passionate personal example." James mentions Awdry's work only to note that it is "simply an abstract . . . for the use of children" and as such "a happy idea."

Young, Adolphus and Catherine. In *The Europeans*, they are named as the deceased parents of Baroness Eugenia Münster and Felix Young. The father was an American who had been born in Sicily. The mother was William Wentworth's headstrong half-sister.

Young, Felix. In *The Europeans*, the son of Catherine Young, William Wentworth's half-sister. Felix is Baroness Eugenia Münster's brother. He loves and wins the hand of Wentworth's daughter Gertrude.

Young, Frederic. In "The Story of a Masterpiece," an admirer of Marian Everett in Europe.

Young, Mrs. In "The Story of a Masterpiece," Frederic Young's handsome old mother.

Young, Stephen. In *Pyramus and Thisbe*, a journalist, age thirty-three, who dislikes his rooming-house neighbor Catherine West's loud piano-playing until the two meet and fall in love.

"The Younger Generation." Critical essay (*Times Literary Supplement*, 19 Mar, 2 Apr 1914); revised and reprinted as "The New Novel" in *Notes on Novelists*, 1914.

Yule, Captain Marmaduke Clement. In "Covering End," the owner of the estate called Covering End, mortgaged to Prodmore, who wants Yule to marry his daughter Cora. Yule is rescued by the American widow Mrs. Gracedew's money and sympathy. In *Summersoft*, Yule, called simply Captain Yule, is rescued, along with his country house, called Summersoft, from Prodmore's clutches by Mrs. Gracedew, whom he will marry. In *The High Bid*, the owner, called here Captain Marmaduke Clement Yule, of the estate called Covering, who is rescued from the Prodmores by the generosity of Mrs. Gracedew, whom he will marry. In the stage production of *The High Bid*, Sir Johnston Forbes-Robertson* played the part of Captain Yule.

Yule, Dame Dorothy. In "Covering End," *Summersoft*, and *The High Bid*, an ancestor of Captain Marmaduke Clement Yule. She was more than a hundred years old when she died.

Yule, John Anthony. In "Covering End," *Summersoft*, and *The High Bid*, an ancestor of Captain Marmaduke Clement Yule.

Z

Zénobie. In "The Pupil," Morgan Moreen's former governess, who was evidently cheated by his parents.

Zhukovsky, Paul (c. 1849–?). Pampered son of Vasili Andreyevich Zhukovsky (1783–1852). Vasili Zhukovsky was a distinguished Russian poet and translator, a tutor to Alexander II (from 1818), and a friend of Nikolai Gogol and Alexander Pushkin. Zhukovsky, whose wife was German and who knew Johann Wolfgang von Goethe,* died in Germany. Paul Zhukovsky was a minor painter, art devotee, and associate of homosexuals. James (who spelled the family name Joukowsky) met Paul Zhukovsky in Paris, in 1876, through Ivan Sergeyevich Turgenev.* James wrote home to William (25 Apr [1876]), to his mother (8 May [1876]), and to Alice (24 May [1876]): Zhukovsky has helped him to understand the Russian nature; he is gentle and perceptive, though not energetic; he has a Parisian studio and an apartment filled with art treasures; and he is affectionate. Through him, James met several titled, cultured Russians in Paris. But by autumn, James, still in Paris, wrote to his father (11 Nov [1876]) that the young émigré was "a lightweight and a perfect failure," though "a most *attachant* human creature." Still later, James sent letters home from Italy, in the spring of 1880, filled with criticism of Zhukovsky for associating with the international homosexuals surrounding Richard Wagner in Naples. To his father (30 Mar [1880]), he called the man "peculiar"; to his sister Alice, Zhukovsky "is the same impracticable and indeed ridiculous mixture of Nihilism and bric à brac as before." In a Notebook entry (25 Nov 1881), James privately cautioned himself about Zhukovsky thus: "*Non ragioniam di lui—ma guarda e passa.*" Subsequently, James lost touch with him.

Zola, Émile (1840–1902). Premier representative of French naturalism in fiction. Born in Paris of an Italian-Greek father (who died in 1847) and a French mother, and passing part of his childhood in Aix-en-Provence, Zola then worked for a Parisian publishing house, wrote some romantic fiction, and with *Thérèse Raquin* (1867) began his lifelong naturalistic phase. Four years later he published *La Fortune des Rougon*, the first of his prodigious, twenty-volume *Rougon-Macquart* series (with something like the sweep of the *Comédie Humaine* of Honoré de Balzac*) about a many-branched, Second Empire family, whose hereditary traits Zola examined with scientific detachment. The outstanding titles of the popular fictional cycle include *Le Ventre de Paris* (1873), *Son Excellence Eugène Rougon* (1876), *L'Assommoir* (1877, his masterpiece), *Une page d'amour* (1878), *Nana* (1880, very popular), *Au bonheur des dames* (1883), *La Joie de vivre* (1884), *Germinal* (1885), *La Terre* (1887), *La Bête humaine* (1890), *La Débâcle* (1892, popular), and finally *Le Docteur Pascal* (1893). Zola also wrote the trilogy entitled *Les Trois Villes* (*Lourdes* [1894], *Rome* [1896], and *Paris* [1898]), much other fiction (including *Fécondité* [1899], *Travail* [1901], and *Vérité* [1903]), and short stories), plays, and criticism. In 1870 he married; in 1888, he took a mistress by whom he had a daughter and then a son. Zola delivered an eloquent, comprehensive tribute at the funeral of his friend Guy de Maupassant* in 1893. "J'accuse," Zola's spirited defense (13 January 1898) of Alfred Dreyfus,* wrongly condemned by a dishonest French military court as a traitor in 1894, obliged Zola to seek refuge in England for almost a year; shortly after his return to his home in Paris, he was asphyxiated by carbon monoxide from a blocked chimney. Zola regarded personality as the outgrowth of physical traits, mostly heredity; virtues and vices as merely their products, and those of environment and chance; and novelists as, ideally, diagnosticians of fictive characters (as physicians are of their patients). Hence literary naturalism. James first met Zola late in 1875 at one of the Sunday afternoon get-togethers held by Gustave Flaubert* for literary folk, and he wrote to his father (20 Dec [1875]) that Zola was "a very common fellow." Soon thereafter James wrote to Thomas Sergeant Perry* (3 Feb [1876]) that Zola was "affreusement borne . . . [but] amusant . . . " When James sent his editor friend Theodore E. Child* a review of *Nana* for his *Parisian*, he wrote to Child (17 Feb [1880]) that the novel was "unutterably filthy." Soon, however, he revised his general opinion of Zola, writing to Perry (16 Feb 1881) that although he had faults "his merits are rare, valuable, extremely solid." In February 1884, James, again in Paris, saw more of Zola, and he wrote to William Dean Howells* (21 Feb 1884) that the literary friends around Alphonse Daudet,* of whom Zola was one, were intense, intelligent, and pessimistic, that they treated "unclean things," but that Zola's *La Joie de vivre* was "solid and serious." A year later James wrote to Child (13 May [1885]) that Zola's *Germinal* was "admirable," second only to his *L'Assommoir*. In 1890 James wrote to Howells (17 May [1890]) to define Howells as less big than Zola, but also less clumsy and more various. A little later James wrote to Sir Edmund Wilson Gosse* (11 Apr [1892]) about "great big dear dirty Zola.'' By 1893 James could write to his friend William Morton Fullerton* (14 Jul [1893]), ''I love my Zola.'' Late in the same year, James met Zola for a London luncheon, and soon thereafter wrote to Robert Louis Stevenson* (21 Oct [1893]) that nothing ever happened to the French novelist aside from his writing *Les Rougon-Macquart*, further, that he was ''very sane, common and inexperienced.'' In 1896 James wrote to Gosse ([25 July 1896]) that Zola's novel *''Rome* is of a *lourdeur.''* When in 1898 Zola was in mortal danger because of his defense of Dreyfus, James regarded him as courageous and honorable, and he wrote him a letter of praise which has evidently not survived. In ''Parisian Festivity'' (New York *Tribune*, 13 May 1876), James briefly reviewed Zola's *Son Excellence Eugène Rougon*, calling it clever but unclean. James reviewed (*Nation*, 30 May 1878) Zola's *Une page d'amour*, regarding its innocent but ''detestable'' little heroine pure enough but Zola's treatment of her lacking the vigor and stylistic brilliance found in *L'Assommoir*. James adverts to Zola's announcement, given here, of his *Rougon-Macquart* series, comparing him to Balzac in relation to the immensity of planning. James ridicules the plot of the present novel, and he says that Zola applies relentless realism to subjects ''ignorantly chosen and bathed in . . . low-class Parisian cockneyism.'' James reviewed (*Parisian*, 26 Feb 1880) *Nana* negatively, especially when compared to *L'Assommoir*. The naturalist in Zola would reason that enjoying a piece of literature is ''superficial, contemptible.'' James defines *Nana* as ''dull'' and compares it to other dull novels, but they are still amusing. In one respect, *Nana* is not so bad as *L'Assommoir*, which is ''pervaded by . . . [a] ferociously bad smell . . . like an emanation from an open drain.'' The opinion that *Nana* is ''indecent . . . Zola holds to mean nothing.'' But James asks, in outrage: ''On what authority does M. Zola represent nature to us as a combination of the cesspool and the house of prostitution?'' We should make novels—''the most human form of art''—clean not dirty vessels, to pour realism into. Sadly, in England and the United States few writers have Zola's ''system, . . . conviction, . . . plan'': Narrative art in English is ''feminine,'' its writers ''mainly . . . timid . . . women,'' its readers mostly ''unmarried young ladies,'' indeed, ''virgins and boys.'' This is bad for the novel. Hence, we must respect the Zola of *L'Assommoir*, which has ''power'' and ''the art of carrying a weight.'' *Nana* is dry and solemn. It should have some wit, which Zola thinks is ''an impertinence in a novel,'' but which ''would have operated . . . as a disinfectant.'' Its lack of humor makes it unreal. British writers by contrast have a better grasp of psychological and spiritual matters. The impudent character of Nana is brutal, with no conscience or soul, only ''devouring appetites.'' Zola here has given us a bad-tasting dish with no nourishment. In ''The London Theatres'' (1881), James praises the 1879 dramatic adaptation, entitled *Drink*, by Charles Reade,* of Zola's *L'Assommoir*. Finally, James wrote a long, rambling essay on Zola (*Atlantic Monthly*, Aug 1903; reprinted in *Notes on Novelists*, 1914), which begins with criticism of the modern taste for shapeless fiction. We got used to the grimly hardworking Zola, now dead, but rightly long praised for his *Rougon-Macquart* series, which is as great and courageous an achievement as anything in the sciences. He packed it like a ship receiving cargo. But Zola was inexperienced in life. When James met him in London, long before his exile following the Dreyfus trial, it was apparent that nothing in life had occurred to him but writing his cycle, in the course of which he evolved simply and artistically. His works have weight, not "fineness"; breadth and energy, not "penetration" or "taste." In fact, good taste and timidity would have ruined him. James recalls that Zola once told members of a literary circle that he was making a dictionary of filthy speech, as part of his research. James says that in a summary essay of this sort he should not stress one title over others, but he must say that the *Rougon-Macquart* volumes constitute Zola's very best, "swarm[ing]" with life, whereas some of the other novels betray "wasted energy." James recalls, almost with horror, the ever-patient Zola's telling him that he was going to write *Rome* after spending a few days in Genoa. Too often, Zola simply "got up" his subject, then wrote in his documentary style. Books like *Rome* are without taste, discretion, or "intellectual modesty." *Vérité* is a simplistic appeal to science, as are other Zola books; more offer "social pictures"; still others try for moral vision. Zola's experimental novel is too concerned with science, as if it can explain life, rather than the reverse. James names *L'Assommoir, Germinal*, and *La Débâcle* as the best illustrations of how Zola's subject and treatment can harmonize. In these novels, how could the sedentary, scientific writer get so near life? Here he is solid, never cheap; he deals with simple, shallow, common characters; and he makes their "malodorous" lives interesting, sometimes even "epic." James contrasts Zola and Balzac: Balzac was pursued by life; Zola stayed on his treadmill, pigeonholing and documenting. The Dreyfus affair should have made *Vérité*, his book inspired by it, franker; but it is "flat . . . and grey . . . " James closes with renewed praise of his favorite Zola novels and says that the man's "heartiness and grossness" have led him to a lasting distinction. James's library contained thirty-seven books by Zola.

APPENDIX A

FICTION

Titles of collections reprinting short stories are not included unless collection titles are new; posthumous reprints are not included.

NOVELS

The Ambassadors

The American

The Awkward Age

The Bostonians

The Golden Bowl

The Portrait of a Lady

The Princess Casamassima

Roderick Hudson

The Tragic Muse

What Maisie Knew

The Wings of the Dove

SHORT NOVELS

Confidence

The Europeans

The Ivory Tower

The Other House

The Outcry

The Reverberator

The Sacred Fount

The Sense of the Past

The Spoils of Poynton

Washington Square

Watch and Ward

LONG SHORT STORIES

"The Aspern Papers"

"Covering End"

"The Impressions of a Cousin"

"An International Episode"

"In the Cage"

"Lady Barbarina"

"A London Life"

"Madame de Mauves"

"The Papers"

"A Passionate Pilgrim"

"The Siege of London"
"The Turn of the Screw"

SHORT STORIES

"The Abasement of the Northmores"
"Adina"
"The Altar of the Dead"
"At Isella"
"The Author of Beltraffio"
"The Beast in the Jungle"
"The Beldonald Holbein"
"The Bench of Desolation"
"Benvolio"
"The Birthplace"
"Broken Wings"
"Brooksmith"
"A Bundle of Letters"
"The Chaperon"
"Collaboration"
"The Coxon Fund"
"Crapy Cornelia"
"Crawford's Consistency"
"Daisy Miller: A Study"
"A Day of Days"
"The Death of the Lion"
"De Grey, A Romance"
"The Diary of a Man of Fifty"
"Eugene Pickering"
"Europe"
"The Figure in the Carpet"
"Flickerbridge"
"Fordham Castle"
"Four Meetings"
"The Friends of the Friends"
"Gabrielle de Bergerac"
"Georgina's Reasons"
"The Ghostly Rental"

"The Given Case"
"Glasses"
"The Great Condition"
"The Great Good Place"
"Greville Fane"
"Guest's Confession"
"Hugh Merrow"
"John Delavoy"
"The Jolly Corner"
"Julia Bride"
"A Landscape Painter"
"The Last of the Valerii"
"The Lesson of the Master"
"The Liar"
"A Light Man"
"Longstaff's Marriage"
"Lord Beaupré"
"Louisa Pallant"
"The Madonna of the Future"
"The Marriages"
"The Married Son"
"Master Eustace"
"Maud-Evelyn"
"The Middle Years"
"Miss Gunton of Poughkeepsie"
"The Modern Warning"
"Mora Montravers"
"A Most Extraordinary Case"
"Mrs. Medwin"
"Mrs. Temperly"
"My Friend Bingham"
"A New England Winter"
"The Next Time"
"Nona Vincent"
"Osborne's Revenge"
"Owen Wingrave"
"Pandora"
"Paste"

"The Patagonia"

"The Path of Duty"

"The Pension Beaurepas"

"The Point of View"

"Poor Richard"

"The Private Life"

"A Problem"

"Professor Fargo"

"The Pupil"

"The Real Right Thing"

"The Real Thing"

"The Romance of Certain Old Clothes"

"Rose-Agathe"

"A Round of Visits"

"Sir Dominick Ferrand"

"Sir Edmund Orme"

"The Solution"

"The Special Type"

"The Story in It"

"The Story of a Masterpiece"

"The Story of a Year"

"The Sweetheart of M. Briseux"

"The Third Person"

"The Tone of Time"

"A Tragedy of Error"

"Travelling Companions"

"The Tree of Knowledge"

"The Two Faces"

"The Velvet Glove"

"The Visits"

"The Wheel of Time"

COLLECTIONS OF SHORT STORIES

The Better Sort

Embarrassments . . .

The Finer Grain

The Soft Side

Stories Revived

Tales of Three Cities

Terminations

The Two Magics

APPENDIX B

CRITICAL ESSAYS, CRITICAL BOOKS, THEATER ESSAYS AND NOTES, AND AUTOBIOGRAPHICAL VOLUMES

Only final titles are given here; James used some titles more than once; many titles are omitted here if treated under persons' names.

"After the Play"

"American Letter"

"An Animated Conversation"

"The Art of Fiction"

"The Comédie Française in London"

"Daniel Deronda: A Conversation"

"The Drama"

Essays in London and Elsewhere

"The Founding of the 'Nation' ": Recollections of the 'Fairies' That Attended Its Birth"

French Poets and Novelists

"The Future of the Novel"

Hawthorne

"London"

"London Pictures and London Plays"

"The London Theatres"

"Madame Ristori"

The Middle Years

"Mr. and Mrs. James T. Fields"

"The New Novel"

"New Novels"

Notes of a Son and Brother

Notes on Novelists with Some Other Notes

"Notes on the Theatres"

"The Novel in 'The Ring and the Book' "

"On the Death of Dumas the Younger"

"The Parisian Stage"

Partial Portraits

"A Poor Play Well Acted"

"The Present Literary Situation in France"

"Recent Novels"

"Recent Volumes of Poems"

"The Science of Criticism"

"She and He: Recent Documents"

A Small Boy and Others

"A Study of Salvini"

"The Théâtre Français"

"Tommaso Salvini"

"The Turning Point of My Life"
Views and Reviews
William Wetmore Story and His Friends
"Winchelsea, Rye, and 'Denis Duval' "

APPENDIX C

TRAVEL BOOKS AND ESSAYS

James used some titles more than once. Some titles are omitted here if treated under persons' names.

"Abbeys and Castles"

"The After-Season in Rome"

The American Scene

"Americans Abroad"

"The Autumn in Florence"

"Baltimore"

"Boston"

"Browning in Westminster Abbey"

"Casa Alvisi"

"A Chain of Cities"

"Chartres"

"Chester"

"The Churches of Florence"

"Darmstadt"

"An English Easter"

English Hours

"An English New Year"

"English Vignettes"

"An English Winter Watering-Place"

Essays in London and Elsewhere

"Etretat"

"A European Summer"

"A Few Other Roman Neighbourhoods"

"Florentine Architecture"

"A Florentine Garden"

"Florentine Notes"

"From a Roman Note-Book"

"From Chambéry to Milan"

"From Lake George to Burlington"

"From Normandy to the Pyrenees"

"From Venice to Strasburg"

"The Grand Canal"

"Homburg Reformed"

"In Belgium"

"In Holland"

"In Scotland"

"In Warwickshire"

"An Italian Convent"

Italian Hours

"Italy Revisited"

"Lake George"

"Lichfield and Warwick"

A Little Tour in France

"London"

"London at Midsummer"

"London in the Dead Season"

"New England: An Autumn Impression"

"Newport"

"New York and the Hudson: A Spring Impression"

"New York Revisited"

"New York Social Notes"

"Niagara"

"North Devon"

"Occasional Paris"

"Old Italian Art"

"The Old Saint-Gothard"

"Old Suffolk"

"Other Tuscan Cities"

"Paris As It Is"

"Paris Revisited"

"Parisian Affairs"

"Parisian Festivity"

"Parisian Life"

"Parisian Sketches"

Parisian Sketches

"Parisian Topics"

"Philadelphia"

Portraits of Places

"Quebec"

"Ravenna"

"Rheims and Laon: A Little Tour"

"Richmond, Virginia"

"A Roman Holiday"

"Roman Neighbourhoods"

"Roman Rides"

"Rouen"

"The Saint's Afternoon"

"Saratoga"

"The Sense of Newport"

"Siena"

"The Splügen"

"The Suburbs of London"

"A Summer in Europe"

"Summer in France"

"Swiss Notes"

"Three Excursions"

Transatlantic Sketches

"Tuscan Cities"

"Two Old Houses and Three Young Women"

"Venice"

"Venice: An Early Impression"

"Versailles As It Is"

"Very Modern Rome"

"Washington"

"Wells and Salisbury"

"Winchelsea, Rye, and 'Denis Duval' "

APPENDIX D

PLAYS

The Album

The American: A Comedy in Four Acts

A Change of Heart

Daisy Miller: A Comedy in Three Acts

Disengaged

Guy Domville

The High Bid

A Monologue by Henry James

The Other House

The Outcry

Pyramus and Thisbe

The Reprobate

The Saloon

Still Waters

Summersoft

Tenants

APPENDIX E

ART ESSAYS, REVIEWS, AND NOTICES

James used some titles more than once; reviews and essays by artist title, as well as unsigned notes and untitled notes, are not included; some titles are omitted here if they are treated under persons' names.

"An American Art-Scholar: Charles Eliot Norton"

"Art"

"Art and Letters in Paris"

"Art: Boston"

"Art in France"

"Art in Paris"

"Art: The Dutch and Flemish Pictures in New York"

"The Bethnal Green Museum"

"Black and White"

"The Grosvenor Gallery and the Royal Academy"

"London"

"London Pictures and London Plays"

"London Sights"

"The Old Masters at Burlington House"

"On Some Pictures Lately Exhibited"

Picture and Text

"The Picture Season in London"

"The Royal Academy and the Grosvenor Gallery"

"The Winter Exhibitions in London"

APPENDIX F

NONLITERARY ESSAYS AND NOTES

"The Afghan Difficulty"

"Allen D. Loney—In Memoriam"

"The American Volunteer Motor-Ambulance Corps in France"

"The Deathbed Notes of Henry James"

"The Early Meeting of Parliament"

"France"

"Henry James's First Interview"

"Henry James Writes of Refugees in England"

"International Copyright"

"Is There a Life after Death?"

"The Long Wards"

"The Manners of American Women"

"The Mind of England at War"

"Paris in Election Time"

"The Question of Our Speech"

"The Reassembling of Parliament"

"Refugees in Chelsea"

"The Speech of American Women"

"Within the Rim"

Within the Rim and Other Essays: 1914–15

APPENDIX G

WRITERS WHOM JAMES REVIEWED, COMMENTED ON, MENTIONED, OR WAS INFLUENCED BY

Most titles, secondary names, and initials have been omitted.

About, Edmond

Aikin, Lucy

Akers, Elizabeth

Alcott, Louisa May

Alger, William

Altsheler, Joseph

Ampère, André and Jean

Arnold, Matthew

Atherton, Gertrude

Augier, Émile

Austen, Jane

Awdry, Frances

Baker, Samuel

Balzac, Honoré de

Barrès, Maurice

Baudelaire, Charles

Baxley, Henry

Beardsley, Aubrey

Beerbohm, Max

Benedict, Frank

Bernard, Charles de

Besant, Walter

Black, William

Bornier, Henri de

Bourget, Paul

Braddon, Mary

Brontë, Anne, Charlotte, and Emily

Brooke, Rupert

Brooke, Stopford

Burnaby, Frederick

Burnett, Frances

Burroughs, John

Busch, Moritz

Butler, Nicholas Murray

Byron, Lord

Cameron, Vernon

Calvert, George

Cannan, Gilbert

Carlyle, Thomas

Cather, Willa

Chambers, Robert

Channing, William Ellery

Chapman, John Jay

Charles, Elizabeth

Cherbuliez, Victor

Chocarne, Bernard

Churchill, Winston

Cobb, Sanford

Colvin, Sidney

Conrad, Joseph

Cook, Dutton

Crackanthorpe, Herbert

Craik, Dinah

Crawford, Francis Marion

Crawfurd, Oswald

Cross, John

D'Annunzio, Gabriele

Daudet, Alphonse

Davis, Rebecca Harding

Davis, Richard Harding

De Forest, John

Dickens, Charles

Disraeli, Benjamin

Doe, Charles

Dole, Charles

Doudan, Ximénès

Droz, Gustave

Duff-Gordon, Lucie

Dumas, Alexandre *fils*

Du Maurier, George

Dunning, William

Earle, Maria

Edgeworth, Maria

Edwards, Annie

Eggleston, George

Eliot, George

Elliot, Frances

Elliott, Sarah

Epictetus

Erckmann-Chatrian

Erskine, Mrs. Thomas

Faguet, Émile

Feuillet, Octave

Filon, Pierre

Flaubert, Gustave

Fletcher, Constance

Ford, Paul Leicester

France, Anatole

Freeman, Mary E. Wilkins

Fromentin, Eugène

Froude, James Anthony

Galsworthy, John

Gannett, William

Garland, Hamlin

Gaskell, Elizabeth

Gautier, Théophile

Geoffrin, Marie-Thérèse

Gibbon, Edward

Girardin, Émile de

Gissing, George

Gladstone, William

Gobineau, Joseph

Goethe, Johann Wolfgang von

Goldsmith, Oliver

Goncourt, Edmond de

Goncourt, Jules de

Gosse, Edmund

Greville, Charles

Gualdo, Luigi

Guérin, Eugénie de

Guérin, Maurice de

Gyp

Haggard, H. Rider

Hamerton, Philip

Hapgood, Norman

Hardy, Thomas

Hare, Augustus

Harland, Henry

Harris, Frank

Harrison, James

Harte, Bret

Haven, Gilbert

Hawthorne, Julian

Hawthorne, Nathaniel

Hayward, Abraham

Helps, Arthur

Hérédia, José Maria de

Hewlett, Maurice Henry

Higginson, Thomas Wentworth

Howe, Julia Ward

Howells, William Dean

Hugo, Victor

Hunter, William

Huysman, Joris-Karl

Ibsen, Henrik

Irving, Washington

Jackson, Helen Hunt

Jenkin, Henrietta

Jerdan, William

Jewett, Sarah Orne

Jones, Amanda

Jones, Henry Arthur

Joubert, Joseph

Kemble, Frances

King, Charles

King, Clarence

Kingsley, Charles

Kingsley, Henry

Kington-Oliphant, Thomas

Kipling, Rudyard

Knight, Cornelia

Lagardie, Horace de

Lang, Andrew

Lathrop, George Parsons

Laugel, Auguste

Lawrence, D. H.

Lawson, John

Lear, Henrietta

Lemaître, Jules

Lemoinne, John

Livingstone, David

Lockhart, John

Loti, Pierre

Louÿs, Pierre

Lowell, James Russell

Lubbock, Percy

MacCarthy, Justin

Mackenzie, Compton

Maitland, Frederic

Manning, Anne

Marbot, Marcelin

Marks, John

Martin, Theodore

Masson, David

Maupassant, Guy de

Mazade, Charles de

Meredith, George

Mérimée, Prosper

Meynell, Alice

Molinari, Gustave de

Montégut, Émile

Moore, Thomas

Morley, John

Morris, William

Murfree, Mary

Musset, Alfred de

Myers, Philip

Nadal, Ehrman

Nordoff, Charles

Norton, Charles Eliot

Oliphant, Laurence

Oliphant, Margaret

Ouida

Paget, Violet

Parkman, Francis

Parodi, Dominique

Pater, Walter

Payn, James

Pinero, Arthur Wing

Planche, Gustave

Poe, Edgar Allan

Prévost, Marcel

Raikes, Thomas

Reade, Charles

Renan, Ernest

Rhodes, Albert

Ridley, Alice

Ritchie, Anne Thackeray

Rivière, Henri

Roberts, Frederick

Rodenberg, Julius

Rosebery, Lord

Rostand, Edmond

Ruskin, John

Russell, Addison

Sabran, Eléanor de

Sainte-Beuve, Charles Augustin

Sand, George

Sandeau, Jules

Santayana, George

Sarcey, Francisque

Sardou, Victorien

Schérer, Edmond

Scott, Sir Walter

Scribe, Eugène

Sedley, Henry

Seemüller, Anne

Senior, Nassau

Serao, Matilde

Shakespeare, William

Shaw, George Bernard

Shelley, Percy Bysshe

Smiles, Samuel

Smith, George

Smith, Logan Pearsall

Southworth, Alvan

Spofford, Harriet

Stedman, Edmund Clarence

Steel, Flora

Stendhal

Stephen, Leslie

Stevenson, Robert Louis

Stoddard, Elizabeth

Stoddard, Richard

Stowe, Harriet Beecher

Sturgis, Howard

Swetchine, Anne

Swinburne, Algernon Charles

Symonds, John Addington

Symons, Arthur

Taine, Hippolyte

Tautphoeus, Baroness von

Taylor, Bayard

Taylor, Tom

Tennyson, Alfred, Lord

Thackeray, William Makepeace

Theuriet, André

Thomson, John

Tinayre, Marguerite

Tissot, Victor

Tolstoy, Leo

Trollope, Anthony

Trollope, Thomas Adolphus

Turgenev, Ivan

Tyndall, John

Tytler, Sarah

Vallés, Jules

Walford, Lucy

Walkley, Arthur

Wallace, Donald

Wallon, Henri

Walpole, Hugh

Ward, Mrs. Humphry

Wells, H. G.

Wendell, Barrett

Wharton, Edith

Whitman, Walt

Whitney, Adeline

Willoughby, Hugh

Wilson, Andrew

Wister, Owen

Wolseley, Garnet Joseph

Woolson, Constance Fenimore

Wormeley, Katherine

Wyckoff, Walter

Wynter, Andrew

Yonge, Charlotte

Zola, Émile

APPENDIX H

ARTISTS, SCULPTORS, ARCHITECTS, AND PHOTOGRAPHERS MENTIONED BY JAMES

Most titles, secondary names, and initials have been omitted.

Abbey, Edwin
Blanche, Jacques-Émile
Bonington, Richard
Boughton, George
Brown, Ford Madox
Burne-Jones, Edward
Coburn, Alvin Langdon
Copley, John Singleton
Daumer, Honoré
Decamps, Alexandre-Gabriel
Delacroix, Eugène
Delaroche, Paul
Doré, Gustave
Dubois, Paul
Du Maurier, George
Duveneck, Frank
Field, Henriette Deluzy-Desportes
Flandrin, Hippolyte
Gainsborough, Thomas
Gérôme, Léon
Gibson, John

Holbein, Hans, the Younger
Hunt, William Holman
Hunt, William Morris
La Farge, John
Lambinet, Émile
Leighton, Frederick
Leonardo da Vinci
Mantovano, Rinaldo
Meissonier, Jean
Millais, John Everett
Millet, Francis
Moreau, Gustave
Murillo, Bartolomé Esteban
Parsons, Alfred
Pennell, Joseph
Regnault, Henri
Reinhart, Charles
Rembrandt
Reynolds, Joshua

Romney, George
Rossetti, Dante Gabriel
Rubens, Peter Paul
Saint-Gaudens, Augustus
Sargent, John Singer
Story, William Wetmore
Thompson, Elizabeth
Tintoretto

Titian
Turner, J. M. W.
Velasquez, Diego de Silva y
Veronese, Paolo
Walker, Frederick
Warren, Edward
Watts, George Frederick
Whistler, James Abbott McNeill
Wood, Derwent

ACTORS, ACTRESSES, THEATER MANAGERS, COMPOSERS, AND SINGERS MENTIONED BY JAMES

Most titles, secondary names, and initials have been omitted.

Alexander, George

Anderson, Mary

Barrett, Lawrence

Bernhardt, Sarah

Campbell, Mrs. Patrick

Compton, Edward

Coquelin, Benoît Constant

Daly, Augustin

Draper, Ruth

Forbes-Robertson, Johnston

Frohman, Charles

Got, François

Granville-Baker, Harley

Irving, Henry

Macready, William

Modjeska, Helena

Patti, Adelina

Quilter, Roger

Rehan, Ada

Rignold, George

Ristori, Adelaide

Robins, Elizabeth

Salvini, Tommaso

Terry, Ellen

Tree, Herbert

APPENDIX J

MISCELLANEOUS NAMES OF PERSONS AND OTHER ITEMS MENTIONED BY OR ASSOCIATED WITH JAMES

Bosanquet, Theodora
Clairmont, Clare
Crawford, Thomas
Deacon, Edward Parker
Dreyfus, Alfred
Duncan, Isadora
Fletcher, Horace
Foat, Ada T. P.
Lewis, George
Lockwood, Preston
Loney, Allen D.
MacAlpine, William
Mason, Alice
Mayfair
Nineteenth Century
Noakes, Burgess
Phillips, Le Roy
Stewart, Alexander Turney
Tauchnitz, Christian
Terry, Luther
Truth
Weld, Mary

APPENDIX K

ITEMS RELATING TO JAMES PERSONALLY

Autobiographical Volumes
  Notes of a Son and Brother
  A Small Boy and Others
  The Middle Years
Families James Knew
  Ashburner
  Barker
  Emmet
  Greenough
  Huntington
  Lodge
  Pakenham
  Rothschild
  Sartoris
  Temple
  Trevelyan
  Tweedy
  Van Buren
  Wagnière
Income from Writing

Naturalization
Pets
Pirated Editions
Presidents James Commented on
  Arthur, Chester A.
  Cleveland, Grover
  Garfield, James A.
  Grant, Ulysses S.
  Roosevelt, Franklin Delano
  Roosevelt, Theodore
Residences Abroad
  Bolton Street, London
  Carlyle Mansions, London
  De Vere Gardens, London
  Lamb House, Rye
  Rue de Luxembourg, Paris
Sales Figures
Servants
Travels

APPENDIX L

FRIENDS OF JAMES

Most titles, secondary names, and initials have been omitted; many of these persons are listed in other appendices; James also knew the spouses, relatives, and companions of many of these persons.

Abbey, Edwin

Adams, Henry

Adams, Marian

Aïdé, Charles

Alcott, Louisa May

Aldrich, Thomas Bailey

Andersen, Hendrik

Archer, William

Arthur, Chester A.

Asquith, Herbert

Baldwin, William

Balestier, Wolcott

Barbey d'Aurevilly, Jules-Amédée

Barrès, Maurice

Barrie, James M.

Bell, Florence

Benedict, Clara

Benson, Arthur Christopher

Benson, Edward Frederic

Benson, Edward White

Benson, Eugene

Berenson, Bernard

Berry, Walter

Blanche, Jacques-Émile

Bloqueville, Marquise de

Boit, Edward

Boott, Elizabeth

Boott, Francis

Bourget, Paul

Boutroux, Émile

Bronson, Katherine

Brooke, Margaret

Brooke, Rupert

Brooke, Stopford

Broughton, Rhoda

Browning, Elizabeth Barrett

Browning, Robert

Bryce, James

Buchan, John
Burne-Jones, Edward
Cameron, Elizabeth
Cameron, James
Child, Francis James
Child, Theodore
Childe, Edward
Church, Francis
Churchill, Winston Spencer
Clark, John
Clifford, Mrs. W. K.
Coburn, Alvin Langdon
Colvin, Sidney
Compton, Edward
Conkling, Roscoe
Conrad, Joseph
Coppée, François
Coquelin, Benoît Constant
Crane, Stephen
Crawford, Francis Marion
Cross, John
Curtis, Ariana and Daniel
Curtis, George William
Daly, Augustin
Darwin, Charles
Daudet, Alphonse
Dicey, Albert
Dicey, Edward
Dilke, Charles
Doré, Gustave
Draper, Ruth
Du Maurier, George
Duveneck, Frank
Edison, Thomas
Edward VII
Eliot, George
Elliott, Maud
Emerson, Ralph Waldo

Fields, Annie
Fields, James
Findlater, Jane and Mary
Fiske, John
Flaubert, Gustave
Fletcher, Constance
Frederic, Harold
Frewen, Moreton
Frohman, Charles
Froude, James Anthony
Fullerton, Morton
Galsworthy, John
Gardner, Isabella
Garland, Hamlin
Gay, Walter
Gide, André
Gilder, Richard Watson
Gissing, George
Godkin, Edwin
Goncourt, Edmond de
Gosse, Edmund
Grant, Ulysses S.
Gray, John Chipman
Green, Richard
Gregory, Lady Augusta
Grigsby, Emilie
Grimm, Herman
Gurney, Ephraim
Hamilton, Edward
Hardy, Thomas
Harland, Henry
Harte, Bret
Harvey, George
Harvey, Paul
Hawthorne, Julian
Hay, John
Heinemann, William
Helps, Arthur

Henley, W. E.
Hill, Frank
Hillebrand, Karl
Holmes, Oliver Wendell, Jr.
Hoppin, William
Houghton, Lord
Howe, Julia Ward
Howells, William Dean
Hueffer, Ford Madox
Hunt, Violet
Hunt, William Holman
Hunt, William Morris
Huxley, Thomas
Jewett, Sarah Orne
Johnson, Robert
Jones, Mary
Jordan, Elizabeth
Jusserand, Jules
Kemble, Frances
Keynes, Geoffrey
King, Clarence
King, Mackenzie
Kinglake, Alexander
Kipling, Rudyard
La Farge, John
Lang, Andrew
Lapsley, Gaillard
Lathrop, George Parsons
Laugel, Auguste
Lazarus, Emma
Lee, Elizabeth
Lee, Sidney
Lee-Hamilton, Eugene
Leighton, Frederick
Lemoinne, John
Lewes, George
Lincoln, Robert
Linton, Eliza

Longfellow, Henry Wadsworth
Loring, Katharine
Lowell, James Russell
Lubbock, Percy
MacCarthy, Desmond
MacCarthy, Justin
McClellan, George
McClure, S. S.
Mackenzie, Compton
Macmillan, Frederick
Maeterlinck, Maurice
Maitland, Frederic
Marsh, Edward
Maupassant, Guy de
Mengin, Urbain
Meredith, George
Millet, Francis
Monod, Auguste
Montégut, Émile
Montesquiou, Robert
Morley, John
Morrell, Ottoline
Morris, William
Motley, John Lothrop
Munthe, Axel
Myers, F. W. H.
Nadal, Ehrman Syme
Navarro, Antonio de
Nencioni, Enrico
Norris, William
Norton, Charles Eliot
Norton, Grace
Orr, Alexandra
Osbourne, Lloyd
Osgood, James
Osler, William
Ouida
Page, Walter Hines

Paget, Violet
Palgrave, Francis
Parkman, Francis
Parsons, Alfred
Pater, Walter
Payn, James
Peabody, Elizabeth
Peirce, Charles Sanders
Pennell, Joseph
Perry, Thomas Sergeant
Persse, Jocelyn
Phillips, Claude
Pinero, Arthur Wing
Pinker, James
Playfair, Lyon
Pollock, Frederick
Pollock, John
Pratt, Herbert
Primoli, Joseph
Prince, Morton
Procter, Anne
Prothero, George
Proust, Marcel
Putnam, James
Raffalovich, André
Rehan, Ada
Reid, Whitelaw
Renan, Ernest
Repplier, Agnes
Reubell, Henrietta
Ritchie, Anne Thackeray
Robins, Elizabeth
Robinson, Mary
Rogerson, Christina
Roosevelt, Blanche
Roosevelt, Franklin Delano
Roosevelt, Theodore
Ross, Janet

Ross, Robert
Rossetti, Dante Gabriel
Roughead, William
Ruskin, John
Sands, Mary
Santayana, George
Sarcey, Francisque
Sargent, John Singer
Scudder, Horace
Sedgwick, Arthur
Serao, Matilde
Shaw, George Bernard
Shorter, Clement
Sitwell, Frances
Smalley, George
Smith, Corinna
Smith, Logan Pearsall
Smyth, Ethel
Spencer, Herbert
Spottiswoode, William
Stedman, Edmund Clarence
Stephen, Leslie
Stevenson, Robert Louis
Stewart, Mrs. Duncan
Story, William Wetmore
Sturges, Jonathan
Sturgis, Howard
Sturgis, Russell
Sutherland, Duchess of
Sutro, Alfred
Symonds, John Addington
Taine, Hippolyte
Tarbell, Ida
Tarkington, Booth
Taylor, Bayard
Temple, Mary
Tennyson, Alfred, Lord
Terry, Ellen

Terry, Louisa

Thackeray, William Makepeace

Trollope, Anthony

Turgenev, Ivan

Twain, Mark

Tyndall, John

Vanderbilt, George

Viardot, Pauline

Villari, Pasquale

Vogüé, Eugène

Walkley, Arthur

Wallace, Donald

Walpole, Hugh

Walsh, Catherine

Ward, Mary Augusta

Warner, Charles Dudley

Warren, Edward

Waterlow, Sydney

Watt, A. P.

Wells, H. G.

Wendell, Barrett

Wharton, Edith

Whistler, James Abbott McNeill

White, Henry

Wilde, Oscar

Wilkinson, J. J. Garth

Wister, Owen

Wister, Sarah Butler

Wolseley, Garnet Joseph

Wood, Derwent

Woolf, Virginia

Woolson, Constance Fenimore

Wormeley, Katherine

Zhukovsky, Paul

Zola, Émile

BIBLIOGRAPHY

Adams, Henry. *The Selected Letters of Henry Adams*. Edited by Newton Arvin. New York: Farrar, Straus and Young, Inc., 1951.

Anderson, Mary. *A Few Memories*. New York: Harper, 1896.

Anesko, Michael. *"Friction with the Market": Henry James and the Profession of Authorship*. New York: Oxford University Press, 1986.

Annan, Noel Gilroy. *Leslie Stephen: His Thought and Character in Relation to His Time*. London: MacGibbon & Kee, 1951.

Baron, Wendy. *Miss Ethel Sands and Her Circle*. London: Owen, 1977.

Bass, Eben. "Henry James and the English Country House." *Markham Review* 2, ii (February 1970): 4–10.

Bassan, Maurice. *Hawthorne's Son: The Life and Literary Career of Julian Hawthorne*. Columbus: Ohio State University Press, 1970.

Beckson, Karl. *Henry Harland: His Life and Work*. London: The Eighteen Nineties Society, 1978.

Benedict, Clare, ed. *Five Generations (1785–1923)* . . . 3 vols., London: Ellis [1929–1930].

Berkove, Lawrence. "Henry James and Sir Walter Scott: A 'Virtuous Attachment'?" *Studies in Scottish Literature* 15 (1980): 43–52.

Birkenhead, Lord. *Rudyard Kipling*. New York: Random House, 1978.

Blanche, Jacques-Émile. *Portraits of a Lifetime: The Later Victorian Era / The Edwardian Pageant / 1870–1914*. Translated by Walter Clement. London: J. M. Dent and Sons Ltd., 1937.

Boase, Frederic. *Modern English Biography*. London: Cass & Co., Ltd., 1965.

Bosanquet, Theodora. *Henry James at Work*. London: Hogarth Press, 1924.

Bryan, Michael. *Bryan's Dictionary of Painters and Engravers*. 2 vols., 1816; rev. and enlarged ed., George C. Williamson, 5 vols., 1903–1904; 5 vols., Port Washington, N.Y.: Kennikat Press, 1964.

Cady, Edwin C. *Novels 1875–1886*. Edited by William Dean Howells. New York: The Library of America, 1982.

Cargill, Oscar. "The First International Novel." *PMLA* 73 (September 1958): 418–25.

———. *The Novels of Henry James*. New York: The Macmillan Company, 1961.

Cazamian, L[ouis]. *A History of French Literature*. Oxford: Clarendon Press, 1955.

Cecil, Lord David. "Introduction" to *Lady Ottoline's Album* . . . New York: Alfred A. Knopf, 1976.

Champlin, John Denison. *Cyclopedia of Painters and Paintings*. New York: Scribner, 1913.

Chanler, Mrs. Winthrop. *Autumn in the Valley*. Boston: Little, Brown, 1936.

Collis, Louise. *Impetuous Heart: The Story of Ethel Smyth*. London: William Kimber, 1984.

Colvert, James B. *Stephen Crane*. New York: Harcourt Brace Jovanovich, 1984.

Cowles, Virginia. *The Rothschilds: A Family of Fortune*. New York: Alfred A. Knopf, 1973.

Croft-Cook, Rupert. *Rudyard Kipling*. Denver: Alan Swallow, 1948.

Daugherty, Sarah B. *The Literary Criticism of Henry James*. Athens: Ohio University Press, 1981.

Davis, Richard. *The English Rothschilds*. Chapel Hill: University of North Carolina Press, 1983.

Delbanco, Nicholas. *Group Portrait: Joseph Conrad, Stephen Crane, Ford Madox Ford, Henry James, and H. G. Wells*. New York: William Morrow and Company, 1982.

Dictionary of American Biography: Authors Edition. Edited by Allen Johnson and Dumas Malone. 21 vols. New York: Charles Scribner's Sons, 1928.

Dictionary of National Biography. Edited by Sir Leslie Stephen and Sir Sidney Lee. 21 vols., plus supplements. London: Oxford University Press, 1921–1971.

Draper, Ruth. *The Letters of Ruth Draper: 1920–1956: A Self-Portrait of a Great Actress*. Edited by Neilla Warren. New York: Charles Scribner's Sons, 1979.

Edel, Leon. "Henry James and Sir Sydney Waterlow: The Unpublished Diary of a British Diplomat." *Times Literary Supplement*, 8 August 1968, pp. 844–45.

———. *Henry James: The Untried Years; Henry James: The Conquest of London; Henry James: The Middle Years; Henry James: The Treacherous Years; Henry James: The Master*. Philadelphia and New York: J. B. Lippincott, 1953–1972. Rev. ed., as *Henry James: A Life*. New York: Harper & Row, 1985.

———. "Introduction" to Henry James, *The Other House*. New Directions Book, n.p., n.d.

———. "Jonathan Sturges." *Princeton University Library Chronicle* 15 (Autumn 1953): 1–9.

———. "Walter Berry and the Novelists: Proust, James, and Edith Wharton." *Nineteenth-Century Fiction* 38 (March 1984): 514–28.

Edel, Leon, ed. *The Complete Plays of Henry James*. Philadelphia and New York: J. B. Lippincott Company, 1949.

———. Henry James, *The American Scene*. Bloomington and London: Indiana University Press, 1968.

Edel, Leon, and Dan H. Laurence, aided by James Rambeau. *A Bibliography of Henry James*, 3rd ed. New York: Oxford University Press, 1982.

Edel, Leon, and Ilse Dusoir Lind, eds. Henry James, *Parisian Sketches: Letters to the "New York Times" 1875–1876*. New York: New York University Press, 1957.

Edel, Leon, and Gordon N. Ray, eds. *Henry James and H. G. Wells* . . . London: Rupert Hart-Davis, 1958.

Edel, Leon, and Adeline R. Tintner, eds. *The Library of Henry James*. Ann Arbor, Mich.: UMI Research Press, 1987.

Edwards, Herbert. "Henry James and Ibsen." *American Literature* 24 (May 1952): 208–23.

Ellmann, Richard. *Oscar Wilde*. New York: Knopf, 1987.

Franc, Miriam Alice. *Ibsen in England*. Boston: The Four Seas Company, 1919.

Gale, Robert L. *John Hay*. Boston: Twayne Publishers, 1978.

———. "A Letter from F. Marion Crawford to Henry James." *Studi Americani* 4 (1958): 415–19.

———. *Plots and Characters in the Fiction of Henry James*. Hamden, Conn.: Archon, 1965.

———. "An Unpublished Letter from Henry James to F. M. Crawford." *Revue des Langues Vivantes* 42, ii (1976): 179–82.

Gard, Roger. "Appendix II: James's Sales." In *Henry James: The Critical Heritage*. Edited by Roger Gard. London: Routledge & Kegan Paul, 1968; New York: Barnes & Noble Inc., 1968.

Gettman, Royal A., ed. *George Gissing and H. G. Wells: Their Friendship and Correspondence*. Urbana: University of Illinois Press, 1961.

Gill, Richard. *Happy Rural Seat: The English Country House and the Literary Imagination*. New Haven and London: Yale University Press, 1972.

Goldring, Douglas. *South Lodge: Reminiscences of Violet Hunt, Ford Madox Ford and the English Review Circle*. London: Constable & Co. Ltd., 1943.

Grosskurth, Phyllis. *The Woeful Victorian: A Biography of John Addington Symonds*. New York: Holt, Rinehart and Winston, 1964.

Gunn, Peter. *Vernon Lee: Violet Paget, 1856–1935*. London: Oxford University Press, 1964.

Habegger, Alfred, ed. Henry James, *The Bostonians*. Indianapolis: Bobbs-Merrill Company, Inc., 1976.

Hardy, Thomas. *The Literary Notebooks of Thomas Hardy*. Edited by Lennart A. Björk. 2 vols. New York: New York University Press, 1985.

Harkness, Marjory Gane. "Introduction" to *Percy Lubbock Reader*. Freeport, Maine: The Bond Wheelwright Company, 1957.

Harlow, Virginia. *Thomas Sergeant Perry: A Biography and Letters to Perry from William, Henry, and Garth Wilkinson James*. Durham, N.C.: Duke University Press, 1950.

Harper, J. Henry. *The House of Harper: A Century of Publishing in Franklin Square*. New York and London: Harper, 1912.

Harris, Marie P. "Henry James, Lecturer." *American Literature* 23 (November 1951): 302–14.

Harrison, James. *Rudyard Kipling*. Boston: Twayne Publishers, 1982.

Hasler, Jörg. *Switzerland in the Life and Work of Henry James / The Clare Benedict Collection of Letters from Henry James*. Bern, Switzerland: Francke Verlag, 1966.

Hemmings, E. W. J. *The Life and Times of Émile Zola*. New York: Charles Scribner's Sons, 1977.

Howe, Irving, ed. Henry James, *The American Scene*. New York: Horizon Press, 1967.

Howe, Mark DeWolfe. *Justice Oliver Wendell Holmes . . .* 2 vols. Cambridge: Harvard University Press, 1957, 1963.

Hunt, Violet. *I Have This to Say: The Story of My Flurried Years.* New York: Boni and Liveright, 1926.

Hyde, H. Montgomery. *Henry James at Home.* London: Methuen & Co, 1969.

Hynes, Samuel. *The Edwardian Turn of Mind.* Princeton, N.J.: Princeton University Press, 1968.

James, Alice. *The Diary of Alice James.* Edited by Leon Edel. New York: Dodd, Mead & Company, Inc., 1964.

James, Henry. *The American Scene.* New York: Harper & Brothers, 1907.

————. *The Complete Notebooks of Henry James.* Edited by Leon Edel and Lyall H. Powers. New York and Oxford: Oxford University Press, 1987.

————. *The Complete Plays of Henry James.* Edited by Leon Edel. Philadelphia and New York: J. B. Lippincott, 1949.

————. *Henry James Letters.* 4 vols. Edited by Leon Edel. Cambridge: Harvard University Press, 1974–1984.

————. *Letters of Henry James to Walter Berry.* Paris: The Black Sun Press, 1928.

————. *Literary Criticism: Essays on Literature, American Writers, English Writers.* New York: The Library of America, 1984.

————. *Literary Criticism: French Writers, Other European Writers, The Prefaces to the New York Edition.* New York: The Library of America, 1984.

————. *The Notebooks of Henry James.* Edited by F. O. Matthiessen and Kenneth B. Murdock. New York: Oxford University Press, 1947.

————. *The Novels and Stories of Henry James.* 35 vols. Edited by Percy Lubbock. London: Macmillan, 1921–1923.

————. *The Novels and Tales of Henry James.* 26 vols. New York: Charles Scribner's Sons, 1907–1918.

————. *The Other House.* New York: Macmillan, 1896.

————. *The Outcry.* New York: Charles Scribner's Sons, 1911.

————. *Selected Letters.* Edited by Leon Edel. Cambridge: The Belknap Press of Harvard University Press, 1987.

————. *The Selected Letters of Henry James.* Edited by Leon Edel. New York: Farrar, Straus and Cudahy, 1955.

————. *The Two Magics: The Turn of the Screw: Covering End.* London: William Heinemann, 1898.

James, William. *The Letters of William James.* Edited by Henry James (son). 2 vols. Boston: The Atlantic Monthly Press, 1920.

Jersey, The Dowager Countess of. *Fifty-One Years of Victorian Life.* London: Murray, 1923.

John, Arthur. *The Best Years of the "Century": Richard Watson Gilder, "Scribner's Monthly," and the "Century Magazine," 1870–1909.* Urbana: University of Illinois Press, 1981.

Jones, Vivien. *James the Critic.* New York: St. Martin's Press, 1985.

Jusserand, Jean Jules. *What Me Befell: The Reminiscences of J. J. Jusserand.* Boston and New York: Houghton Mifflin Company, 1933.

Kaledin, Eugenia. *The Education of Mrs. Henry Adams.* Philadelphia: Temple University Press, 1981.

Kenney, Blair Gates. "The Two Isabels: A Study in Distortion." *Victorian Newsletter* 25 (1964): 15–17.

Keynes, Geoffrey. *Henry James at Cambridge*. Cambridge: W. Heffer & Sons Ltd., 1967.

Kimball, Jean. "A Classified Subject Index to Henry James's Critical Prefaces to the New York Edition (Collected in *The Art of the Novel*)." *Henry James Review* 6 (Winter 1985): 89–133.

Kirk, Clara M., and Rudolf Kirk. *William Dean Howells*. New York: Twayne Publishers, 1962.

Kotzin, Michael C. "*The American* and *The Newcomes*." *Études Anglaises* 30 (1977): 420–29.

Kraft, James. *The Early Tales of Henry James*. Carbondale and Edwardsville: Southern Illinois University Press, 1969.

LaFarge, John, S.J. *The Manner Is Ordinary*. New York: Harcourt, Brace and Company, 1954.

Langstaff, Eleanore De Selms. *Andrew Lang*. Boston: Twayne Publishers, 1978.

Le Clair, Robert C. *Young Henry James: 1843–1870*. New York: Bookman Associates, 1955.

Leslie, Anita. *Mr. Frewen of England: A Victorian Adventurer*. London: Hutchinson, 1966.

Lewis, R. W. B. *Edith Wharton: A Biography*. New York: Harper & Row, Publishers, 1975.

———. "The Jameses' Irish Roots." *New Republic* (6–13 January 1982): 30–37.

Long, Robert Emmet. *The Great Succession: Henry James and the Legacy of Hawthorne*. Pittsburgh: University of Pittsburgh Press, 1979.

Lubbock, Percy, ed. *The Letters of Henry James*. 2 vols. New York: Charles Scribner's Sons, 1920.

Lucas, E. V. *The Colvins and Their Friends*. New York: Charles Scribner's Sons, 1928.

Luttrell, Barbara. *The Prim Romantic: Biography of Ellis Cornelia Knight 1758–1837*. London: Chatto & Windus, 1965.

Lynn, Kenneth S. *William Dean Howells: An American Life*. New York: Harcourt Brace Jovanovich, 1971.

Lyon, Peter. *Success Story: The Life and Times of S. S. McClure*. New York: Charles Scribner's Sons, 1963.

Mackenzie, Eileen. *The Findlater Sisters: Literature and Friendship*. [London]: John Murray, 1964.

McMaster, R. D. " 'An Honorable Emulation of the Author of *The Newcomes*': James and Thackeray." *Nineteenth-Century Fiction* 32 (1978): 399–419.

Maher, Jane. *Biography of Broken Fortunes: Wilkie and Bob, Brothers of William, Henry, and Alice James*. Hamden, Conn.: Archon Books, 1986.

Maitland, Frederic William. *The Life and Letters of Leslie Stephen*. London: Duckworth & Co., 1906.

Marcus, Jane. "Introduction" to Elizabeth Robins, *The Convert* (1907). London: The Women's Press Limited, 1980.

Martin, W. R. " 'The Eye of Mr. Ruskin': James's Views on Venetian Artists." *Henry James Review* 5 (1984): 107–16.

Mathews, Joseph J. *George W. Smalley*. Chapel Hill: University of North Carolina Press, 1973.

Mercer, Caroline G., and Sarah D. Wangensteen. " 'Consumption, Heart-Disease, or Whatever': Chlorosis, a Heroine's Illness in *The Wings of the Dove*." *Journal of the History of Medicine and Allied Sciences* 40 (July 1985): 259–85.

Milicia, Joseph. "Henry James's Winter's Tale: 'The Bench of Desolation.' " *Studies in American Fiction* 6 (1978): 141–56.

Mix, Katherine Lyon. *A Study in Yellow: The Yellow Book and Its Contributors*. Lawrence: University of Kansas Press, 1960.

Mizener, Arthur. *The Saddest Story: A Biography of Ford Madox Ford*. New York: World Publishing Company, 1971.

Moore, Harry T. *Henry James*. New York: The Viking Press, 1974.

Moore, Rayburn S. *Constance F. Woolson*. New York: Twayne Publishers, 1963.

———. *Selected Letters of Henry James to Sir Edmund Gosse, 1882–1915*. Baton Rouge: Louisiana State University Press, 1988.

Moran, John C. *An F. Marion Crawford Companion*. Westport, Conn.: Greenwood Press, 1981.

Mordell, Albert. *Discovery of a Genius: William Dean Howells and Henry James*. New York: Twayne Publishers, 1961.

Morrell, Lady Ottoline. *Ottoline: The Early Memoirs of Lady Ottoline Morrell*. Edited by Robert Gathorne-Hardy. London: Faber and Faber, 1963.

Mossman, Robert E. "An Analytical Index of the Literary and Art Criticism of Henry James." Ph.D. diss., University of Pittsburgh, 1966.

Mott, Frank Luther. *A History of American Magazines: 1850–1865*. Cambridge: Harvard University Press, 1938.

———. *A History of American Magazines: 1865–1885*. Cambridge: Harvard University Press, 1938.

———. *A History of American Magazines: 1885–1905*. Cambridge: Harvard University Press, 1957.

Murray, Peter, and Linda Murray. *The Penguin Dictionary of Art and Artists*. 5th ed. Harmondsworth: Penguin Books Ltd., 1983.

Myers, Gerald E. *William James: His Life and Thought*. New Haven and London: Yale University Press, 1986.

Nadal, E[hrman] S[yme]. "Personal Recollections of Henry James." *Scribner's Magazine* 68 (July 1920): 89–97.

The National Cyclopaedia of American Biography . . . 62 vols. and supplementary vols. New York and later Clifton, N.J.: James T. White & Company, 1929–1984; Ann Arbor, Mich.: University Microfilms, 1967.

Navarro, Mary Anderson de. *A Few More Memories*. London: Hutchinson, 1936.

Nettels, Elsa. *James & Conrad*. Athens: University of Georgia Press, 1977.

Newsome, David. *On the Edge of Paradise: A. C. Benson: The Diarist*. Chicago: University of Chicago Press, 1980.

Ney, John. *Palm Beach: The Place, the People, Its Pleasures and Palaces*. Boston and Toronto: Little, Brown and Company, 1966.

Nowell-Smith, Simon, comp. *The Legend of the Master*. New York: Charles Scribner's Sons, 1948; rev. ed., Oxford and New York: Oxford University Press, 1985.

Ohsima, Jin. *A Unified Sensibility: A Study of Henry James' "The Ambassadors" and Its Scenario*. Tokyo: The Hokuseido Press, 1982.

Olson, Stanley. *John Singer Sargent: His Portrait*. New York: St. Martin's, 1986.

Page, Norman, ed. *Henry James: Interviews and Recollections*. New York: St. Martin's Press, 1984.

Painter, George D. *Proust: The Later Years*. Boston and Toronto: Little, Brown, 1965.

Payne, Darwin. *Owen Wister: Chronicler of the West, Gentleman of the East*. Dallas, Tex.: Southern Methodist University Press, 1985.

Payne, Robert. *The White Rajahs of Sarawak*. New York: Funk & Wagnalls Company, 1960.

Pearson, Hesketh. *The Marrying Americans*. New York: Coward McCann, 1961.

Pennell, Elizabeth Robins. *The Life and Letters of Joseph Pennell*. 2 vols. Boston: Little, Brown, 1929.

Pillement, Georges. "The Precursors of Impressionism." In *Phaedon Encyclopedia of Impressionism*. Edited by Maurice Sérullez. Oxford: Phaedon, 1978, pp. 29–62.

Putt, S. Gorley. *Henry James: A Reader's Guide*. Ithaca, N.Y.: Cornell University Press, 1966.

Raitt, A. W. *Prosper Mérimée*. London: Eyre & Spottiswoode, 1970.

Rothschild, Mrs. James R. *The Rothschilds at Waddesdon Manor*. London: Collins, 1979.

Roughead, William. *Tales of the Criminous: A Selection from the Works of William Roughead . . . Together with Fourteen Letters to the Author from Henry James*. Edited by W. N. Roughead. London: Cassell and Company Ltd., 1956.

Runciman, Steven. *The White Rajahs: A History of Sarawak from 1841 to 1946*. Cambridge: Cambridge University Press, 1960.

Russell, John. "Henry James and His Architect." *Architectural Review* 93 (March 1943): 69–72.

St John, Christopher. *Ethel Smyth: A Biography*. London: Longmans, Green and Co., 1959.

Scharnhorst, Gary. "Henry James and the Reverend William Rounseville Alger." *Henry James Review* 8 (Fall 1986): 71–75.

Selig, Robert L. *George Gissing*. Boston: Twayne Publishers, 1983.

Sérullez, Maurice, ed. *Phaedon Encyclopedia of Impressionism*. Oxford: Phaedon, 1978.

Singer, Armand E. *Paul Bourget*. Boston: Twayne Publishers, 1976.

Smith, Corinna Lindon. *Interesting People: Eighty Years with the Great and Near-Great*. Norman: University of Oklahoma Press, 1962.

Smith, Janet Adams. *Henry James and Robert Louis Stevenson . . .* London: Rupert Hart-Davis, 1948.

Smith, Logan Pearsall. *A Chime of Words: The Letters of Logan Pearsall Smith*. Edited by Edwin Trimble. New York: Ticknor & Fields, 1984.

———. *Unforgotten Years*. London: Constable and Co., 1938.

Soria, Regina. *Dictionary of Nineteenth-Century American Artists in Italy 1760–1914*. Rutherford, N.J.: Fairleigh Dickinson University Press, 1982.

Speed, Jno. Gilmer. "Theodore Child." *Harper's Weekly* 36 (19 November 1892): 1121.

Stafford, William T. "James Examines Shakespeare: Notes on the Nature of Genius." *PMLA* 73 (1958): 123–28.

———. *A Name, Title, and Place Index to the Critical Writings of Henry James*. Englewood, Colo.: Microcard Editions Books, 1975.

Stafford, William T., ed. *James's "Daisy Miller": The Story, the Play, the Critics*. New York: Scribners, 1963.

Steegmuller, Francis. *Maupassant: A Lion in the Path*. New York: Random House, 1949.

Strouse, Jean. *Alice James: A Biography*. Boston: Houghton Mifflin, 1980.

Sweeney, John L., ed. *The Painter's Eye: Notes and Essays on the Pictorial Arts by Henry James*. London: Rupert Hart-Davis, 1956.

Tebbel, John. *A History of Book Publishing in the United States*. Vol. 2, *The Expansion of an Industry 1865–1919*. New York and London: R. R. Bowker, 1975.

Tharp, Louise Hall. *Mrs. Jack: A Biography of Isabella Stewart Gardner*. Boston: Little, Brown and Company, 1965.

Thomson, Patricia. *George Sand and the Victorians: Her Influence and Reputation in Nineteenth-Century England*. New York: Columbia University Press, 1977.

"Three Unpublished Letters and a Monologue by Henry James." *London Mercury* 6 (September 1922): 492–501.

Thwaite, Ann. *Edmund Gosse: A Literary Landscape 1849–1928*. London: Secker & Warburg, 1984.

Tintner, Adeline R. *The Book World of Henry James: Appropriating the Classics*. Ann Arbor, Mich.: UMI Research Press, 1987.

———. "Henry James Writes His Own Blurbs." *AB Bookman's Weekly* (19 May 1980): 3873–76.

———. *The Museum World of Henry James*. Ann Arbor, Mich.: UMI Research Press, 1986.

Vanderbilt, Kermit. *Charles Eliot Norton: Apostle of Culture in a Democracy*. Cambridge: Harvard University Press, 1959.

Wade, Allan, ed. Henry James, *The Scenic Art: Notes on Acting & the Drama: 1872– 1901*. New Brunswick, N.J.: Rutgers University Press, 1948.

Wagenknecht, Edward. *Cavalcade of the American Novel*. New York: Henry Holt, 1952.

———. *Cavalcade of the English Novel*. New York: Henry Holt, 1943.

———. *The Novels of Henry James*. New York: Frederick Ungar Publishing Co., 1983.

———. *The Tales of Henry James*. New York: Frederick Ungar Publishing Co., 1984.

Watters, Tamie. "Introduction" to Rhoda Broughton, *Belinda* (1883). London: Virago Press, 1984.

Weinreb, Ben, and Christopher Hibbert, eds. *The London Encyclopedia*. 1983; Bethesda, Md.: Adler & Adler, 1986.

Wharton, Edith. *A Backward Glance*. New York: Appleton-Century, 1934.

———. "Edith Wharton Letters [to William Morton Fullerton, 1907–1915] Selected, Transcribed, and Annotated by Alan Gribbin." *The Library Chronicle of the University of Texas at Austin* n.s. 31 (1985): 21–71.

———. *The Letters of Edith Wharton*. Edited by R. W. B. Lewis and Nancy Lewis. New York: Scribners, 1988.

Wood, Christopher. *The Dictionary of Victorian Painters*. 2d ed. Woodbridge, Suffolk: Antique Collectors' Club, 1978.

Wood, James Playsted. *Magazines in the United States*. 2d ed. New York: The Ronald Press Company, 1956.

Wright, Nathalia. "Hawthorne and the Praslin Murder." *New England Quarterly* 15 (March 1942): 5–14.

———. "Henry James and the Greenough Data." *American Quarterly* 10 (Fall 1958): 338–43.

Yeazell, Ruth Bernard. *The Death and Letters of Alice James*. Berkeley: University of California Press, 1981.

In addition, the usual standard desk-reference books and invaluable encyclopedias, including the *Academic American*, the *American*, the *Britannica, Collier's, Enciclopedia Italiana, Larousse*, and the *World Book*; and biographical dictionaries such as *Webster's, Who's Who*, and *Who Was Who* publications; and obituaries in the New York *Times* and other standard big-city newspapers.

About the Author

ROBERT L. GALE is Professor Emeritus of American Literature at the University of Pittsburgh. He has written numerous articles, reviews, and books, including critical studies of Louis L'Amour, Henry James, Ernest Haycox, Charles Marion Russell, Luke Short, and John Hay.